Handbook of Bloodstain Pattern Analysis

The *Handbook of Bloodstain Pattern Analysis* captures the latest understanding of the science that supports bloodstain pattern analysis (BPA) and includes the results of numerous research studies using modern technologies not found in previously published books. It provides the BPA community with a modern, up-to-date reference and training manual to outline and validate the utility, repeatability, and reliability of BPA science.

BPA has recently been presented in the news media as an example of "junk" science used in a handful of cases involving wrongful convictions. However, the reality is that the primary issue for BPA in these wrongful convictions is not the science: it is the result of substandard *training* and the lack of experience of BPA analysts, prior to beginning casework and testifying in court as experts. As such, this book is written to serve as an essential study guide for analysts preparing to sit for the International Association for Identification (IAI) Bloodstain Pattern Analyst Certification exam. The contents of the book are guided by the ANSI/ASB *Standards for a Bloodstain Pattern Analysis Training Program*. Each chapter has been written by top experts conversant on the relevant BPA terminology, forensic science, physics, fluid dynamics, crime scene analysis, education/training, bias, and current relevant legal considerations for use of BPA in court.

Handbook of Bloodstain Pattern Analysis is the most up-to-date resource on BPA currently available, providing a definitive training manual for practitioners, and an essential reference for forensic pathologists, police investigators, crime scene investigators, attorneys, and students enrolled in forensic science university courses.

Handbook of Bloodstain Pattern Analysis

Edited by
Toby L. Wolson

CRC Press
Taylor & Francis Group
Boca Raton London New York

CRC Press is an imprint of the
Taylor & Francis Group, an **informa** business

Front cover image: Kelsey Lynch, Johnson County Sheriff's Office Criminalistics Laboratory

First edition published 2025
by CRC Press
2385 NW Executive Center Drive, Suite 320, Boca Raton FL 33431

and by CRC Press
4 Park Square, Milton Park, Abingdon, Oxon, OX14 4RN

CRC Press is an imprint of Taylor & Francis Group, LLC

Library of Congress Cataloging-in-Publication Data
Names: Wolson, Toby L., editor.
Title: Handbook of bloodstain pattern analysis / edited by Toby L. Wolson.
Description: First edition. | Boca Raton, FL : CRC Press, 2025. | Includes
bibliographical references and index.
Identifiers: LCCN 2024029591 (print) | LCCN 2024029592 (ebook) |
ISBN 9780367742072 (hardback) | ISBN 9780367757212 (paperback) |
ISBN 9781003163695 (ebook)
Subjects: LCSH: Bloodstains. | Forensic hematology. | Crime scene searches.
Classification: LCC HV8077.5.B56 H36 2025 (print) |
LCC HV8077.5.B56 (ebook) | DDC 363.25/62--dc23/eng/20240627
LC record available at https://lccn.loc.gov/2024029591
LC ebook record available at https://lccn.loc.gov/2024029592

ISBN: 978-0-367-74207-2 (hbk)
ISBN: 978-0-367-75721-2 (pbk)
ISBN: 978-1-003-16369-5 (ebk)

DOI: 10.4324/9781003163695

Typeset in Berling
by KnowledgeWorks Global Ltd.

Access the Instructor Support Material: www.routledge.com/9780367742072

CONTENTS

CONTRIBUTORS

Ravishka Arthur completed a Doctor of Philosophy (PhD) in Forensic Science at the University of Auckland, New Zealand. Ravishka's research involved the use of digital methods as part of the development of an automated method of bloodstain pattern characterization. Her work has demonstrated the immense potential that technology has for bringing greater objectivity to the bloodstain pattern discipline. Ravishka has interests in the fields of forensic science and medicine. She is currently pursuing a Bachelor of Medicine and Bachelor of Surgery (MBChB) at the University of Auckland and will graduate as a medical doctor at the end of 2024.

Dr. Silke M.C. Brodbeck, MD, graduated from medical school at the Goethe University in Frankfurt am Main, Germany, and wrote her doctoral thesis on gunshots in CAT scans. She is the head of the Blutspureninstitut and serves as an appointed and sworn expert for BPA and crime scene reconstruction in national and international cases. She is also a decisive expert for courts in the field of BPA. The Blutspureninstitut was the first European provider for continuous BPA training, starting in 2009 and it has trained many working in forensics from different countries. She is a lecturer in bloodstain pattern analysis at Brandenburg University of Technology and at the Hessian University for Police and Administration. Her written work includes two forensics books and numerous research articles in the field of BPA. She is a full member of the IABPA, the German Association of Criminalistics, and other professional organizations. Currently, she is the head of the scientific working group in the German Association of Criminalistics.

Fons Chafe received BA, BEd, BSc, and MEd degrees from Memorial University. He has worked as a crime scene investigator with a municipal police service and as an assistant professor in the Police and Investigations program at MacEwan University. He has been qualified as an expert witness in Canadian courts.

Martin Eversdijk began his career with the Dutch police and later joined the Forensic Department in the city of Amstelveen. He started a private forensic company named Loci Forensics B.V. along with his colleague René Gelderman, which provides training and consulting in BPA (basic, advance, chemical, and fabric) and has educated over 2000 forensic experts from 36 countries during weeklong courses, and has given expert testimony internationally. Martin is an internationally known lecturer and author of various articles and textbooks on the topic of bloodstain patterns. He was a member as well as an executive board member of Scientific Working Group on Bloodstain Pattern Analysis (SWGSTAIN) from 2003 until 2014. Martin is also a distinguished member and former vice-president of the IABPA.

Cristina Gonzalez received a BSc degree in Biochemistry from California State University, Los Angeles. She has worked as a criminalist in Southern California for over 30 years for the one of the largest law enforcement crime laboratories in the country. She previously worked at the Los Angeles County Medical Examiner-Coroner's Office. For over 25 years, she processed hundreds of crime scenes and was the laboratory's primary coordinator/trainer for crime scene (criminalists) investigators. Currently, she is a member of the Association for Crime Scene Reconstruction (ACSR) and a member of the IABPA.

Jeff Gurvis is an independent bloodstain pattern analyst from Chicago who has his roots at the Northern Illinois Police Crime Laboratory where he served as a latent print examiner, crime scene coordinator, and bloodstain pattern analyst. He has taught several basic and advanced bloodstain classes for the FBI and the National Forensic Academy at the University of Tennessee as well as in service classes for Baltimore PD, Illinois State Police, Washington DC Metro, among several others. He was a founding member of the SWGSTAIN and currently is the Chair of the ASB Bloodstain Consensus Body. Jeff also serves on the Board of Directors of the IAI and is also a member of the IABPA. He is also co-founder of Visionations, who developed CrimePad, a mobile-based criminal investigation and crime scene software solution.

Cecilia Hageman, PhD, LLB, LLM, is graduate of the Western Ontario University in London, Ontario, and York University (Osgoode Hall) in Toronto. She is an associate member of the Law Society of Ontario (Call to Bar in 1991). She was employed as a forensic biologist and manager at the Centre of Forensic Sciences (Ministry of the Solicitor General, Ontario) in Toronto for over 20 years and has been an expert witness in criminal proceedings in Ontario courts in the fields of body fluid identification, forensic DNA analysis, and BPA. Since 2013, she has been an associate teaching professor at Ontario Tech University in Oshawa, Ontario, and also a scientist at Wyndham Forensic Group, a private laboratory based in Guelph, Ontario.

Jonathan W. Hak, KC, PhD, is a barrister and solicitor who served as a crown prosecutor in Canada for over 30 years. He has extensive experience prosecuting serious and violent crime and leading and challenging expert evidence in the courtroom. He has successfully led expert BPA evidence in several murder prosecutions. Jonathan holds a Diploma in Criminal Justice from Mount Royal University, Canada; a BSc (with distinction) in Criminal Justice from California State University, USA; an LLB from the University of British Columbia, Canada; an LLM from the University of Cambridge; and a PhD in Law from Leiden University, the Netherlands. The focus of his recent PhD work is on the use of non-textual evidence in international criminal prosecutions. He is the author of *Image-Based Evidence in International Criminal Prosecutions: Charting a Path Forward* (Oxford University Press, 2024). Jonathan was appointed as Queen's Counsel in 2006 and lives in The Hague.

Rebecca Hooks has over 22 years of law enforcement experience with the Illinois State Police. She is a lieutenant colonel and serves as the chief of staff in the Illinois State Police, Office of the Director. She obtained a BSc degree in zoology and chemistry. After graduation, she worked as a forensic autopsy assistant for 15 years. To date, she has assisted in over 2000 forensic autopsies. She has obtained her Certified Crime Scene Investigator and Certified Bloodstain Pattern Analyst certifications through the IAI. She is on the American Academy of Forensic Sciences Standards Board Bloodstain Pattern Analysis Consensus Body and the Organization of Scientific Area Committees for Forensic Science Bloodstain Pattern Analysis Subcommittee. Her forensic science experience with the Illinois State Police encompasses the roles of crime scene investigator, quality assurance administrator, northern crime scene lieutenant, crime scene captain, and lieutenant of the division of forensic services.

Max M. Houck, Ph.D., FRSC, is an award-winning international expert in the forensic sciences with over 30 years of expertise in casework, research, management, and writing. His casework includes the Branch Davidian Investigation, the September 11 attacks on the Pentagon, the D.B. Cooper case, and the West Memphis Three, among hundreds of others, including his casework at the FBI Laboratory. He has managed tens of millions of dollars in grants and his committee work includes the White House, the National Academies of Science, the Royal Society, and Interpol. He is one of the most published professionals in his field and his work is among the top 2% of legal and forensic medicine researchers in the United States. He is editor-in-chief of Forensic Science

International: Synergy, the first gold open access and registered reports journal in the discipline. Dr. Houck is also editor-in-chief of the third edition of *The Encyclopedia of Forensic Sciences*. He is also an editorial board member of Nature Science Studies.

Mike Illes, PhD, is a retired professor of forensic science at Trent University. Prior to becoming an academic, he spent 24 years as a Canadian forensic science practitioner instructing on BPA in the United States, Switzerland, the Netherlands, Scotland, and for other Canadian Academic Institutions. Mike has taught undergraduate and graduate courses in BPA, crime scene investigations, new trends in forensic science, scientific methodology, and research design. In addition, he has worked with students, academic researchers, and practitioners on a variety of forensic research projects, from BPA to forensic epistemology. Dr. Illes is the lead author of the textbook *The Scientific Method in Forensic Science: A Canadian Handbook* and has published extensively on BPA.

Stuart H. James of James and Associates Forensic Consultants, Inc. in Fort Lauderdale, Florida, is a graduate from Hobart College in Geneva, New York, where he received a BA degree in biology and chemistry. He received his MT(ASCP) in Medical Technology from St. Mary's Hospital in Tucson, Arizona. A former Crime Laboratory supervisor in Binghamton, New York, he has been a private consultant since 1981. He has instructed in Forensic Science at the State University of New York and Broome Community College in Binghamton, New York. Stuart is a co-author of *Interpretation of Bloodstain Evidence at Crime Scenes* and has contributed to other forensic texts including *Introduction to Forensic Science, Practical Fire and Arson Investigation* and the *Practical Methodology of Forensic Photography*. Mr. James is a fellow in the AAFS, a distinguished member of the IABPA, and past historian as well as the past editor of the quarterly Journal of Bloodstain Pattern Analysis.

Mark Jermy, PhD, received his BSc (Hons) in Physics from the University of Birmingham, UK and his PhD from the University of Kent, UK. He worked for the UK Ministry of Defence and Cranfield University before moving to the University of Canterbury, New Zealand. He teaches fluid mechanics to engineering undergraduates. His research mostly concerns particles carried by fluids: blood spatter droplets, pathogen-carrying droplets exhaled by humans, silica particles in geothermal fluids, and fuel droplets in combustors. He has also worked on gas flows in the human upper airway and the aerodynamics of cyclists. Mark has provided expert testimony on biomechanics to the New Zealand courts in cases concerning blunt and sharp force trauma.

Natalia Kabaliuk, PhD, is a lecturer in thermo-fluid mechanics in the Department of Mechanical Engineering at the University of Canterbury, New Zealand. Dr. Kabaliuk holds applied physics BSc and MSc degrees from the National Aviation University, Ukraine. Her PhD in mechanical engineering from the University of Canterbury focused on the experimental and computational study of blood atomization mechanisms relevant to BPA. Dr Kabaliuk's current research is focused on fluid mechanics of bloodstain pattern formation and bloodstain pattern simulation and reconstruction in Augmented Reality (AR) for virtual crime scene analysis; the mechanics and mitigation of traumatic brain injuries in contact sport players and victims of abuse; and thermodynamics and heat transfer for vapor deposition processes and electronic equipment thermal management.

Jason Keller is a special agent with the Naval Criminal Investigative Service (NCIS) and is presently assigned as NCIS' forensic graphics specialist, wherein he provides subject matter expertise in 3D forensic reconstruction, 3D laser scanning, and photogrammetry. Previously, Jason served as a forensic consultant for NCIS' Office of Forensic Support, providing forensic expertise to NCIS field offices in the Northeast, Northwest, and Central United States as well as multiple offices in Europe and the Middle East. Jason has conducted research on the 3D documentation of clandestine graves and has published in the ACSR Journal. He is also a task group leader of the newly formed forensic metrology task group within the OSAC Crime Scene Investigation and Reconstruction Subcommittee and a member of the National Institute of Justice (NIJ) sponsored Terrestrial Laser Scanner (TLS) Working Group.

Terry Laber is a Forensic Consultant at Laber, Simser and Thomas Forensic Consulting. He is a graduate of the University of Wisconsin where he received a BS degree in math and chemistry. He conducts forensic training and provides forensic consulting in the areas of bloodstain pattern analysis and crime scene reconstruction. Terry has over 40 years of experience as a forensic laboratory scientist in the areas of DNA, BPA, and crime scene processing. He has several publications in the areas of serology, DNA, and BPA. Terry has taught over 30 40-hour BPA courses and coauthored *Experiments and Practical Exercises in Bloodstain Pattern Analysis*, which is a manual widely used in the teaching of BPA courses. He is a member of the IABPA and the IAI.

Holly Latham, CBPA, is an operations manager of the Kansas Bureau of Investigation and has been a forensic scientist since 1999. Her current duties include project management in latent prints, firearms, digital evidence, and BPA, as well as serving on her agency's crime scene response team. Additionally, she is the technical leader of her agency's bloodstain program, and that responsibility includes authoring the BPA training manual and SOPs. Holly is currently the Chair of the Bloodstain Pattern Analysis Subcommittee of the Organization of Scientific Area Committees (OSAC) under NIST. Holly is a member of the Bloodstain Certification Board for the IAI and serves on the Editorial Review Board for the Journal of Forensic Identification. Holly is both a certified bloodstain pattern analyst (CBPA), and a certified latent print examiner (CLPE).

Emma O. Lew, MD, graduated from the University of Saskatchewan, College of Medicine and did a one-year rotating internship in Vancouver, British Columbia where she began her pathology residency. One year in the Department of Forensic Medicine at the University of Leeds provided forensic pathology experience in England before she completed her residency in Saskatoon and worked at the Royal University Hospital. Forensic pathology motivated her to join the Miami-Dade County Medical Examiner Department where she started as a forensic pathology fellow and was successively promoted to staff associate medical examiner and deputy chief medical examiner before retiring as the chief medical examiner. During her 30-year career in Miami, she attended approximately 1400 death scenes, many of which had blood.

Eugene Liscio is a registered Professional Engineer in the Province of Ontario, Canada and is the owner of ai2-3D, a consulting company that specializes in 3D forensic documentation, analysis, and visualizations. He is also the developer of Recon-3D, a new iPhone 3D scanning app dedicated to forensics. Eugene has testified in court in both the United States and Canada, and in Europe, utilizing 3D technologies such as photogrammetry and laser scanning and has also provided interactive 3D crime scene reconstructions to aid the jury. He is the past-president of the International Association of Forensic and Security Metrology (IAFSM) and is an adjunct professor at Laurentian University and the University of Toronto, where he teaches a 3D forensic reconstruction and mapping course as part of the forensic sciences program. Eugene is actively engaged in research, publishing, and mentoring students focusing on 3D documentation and analysis techniques.

Andy Maloney has been involved in software since he wrote his first program in 1981 and has been a professional software developer since 1995 when he earned a bachelor of science with honors in computing and information science from Queen's University in Kingston, Canada. Professionally, Andy has worked in several fields including banking & insurance, derivatives trading, video game engines, disaster restoration management, cognitive modelling research, and forensics. He also contributes to many open-source software projects. He started working in the field of BPA in 2005 and is the creator of the HemoSpat BPA software, which was first released in 2006. In addition to attending and presenting at many IABPA and ACSR conferences over the years, Andy has conducted research and published several articles relating to BPA and crime scene reconstruction.

Stephen Michielsen, PhD, is a professor in the Centre for Materials Innovation and Future Fashion at the Royal Melbourne Institute of Technology (RMIT) University, Australia. He has been researching the interaction of liquids with textiles since 2004. He has lead workshops on the evolution of bloodstains on textiles and is a co-creator of the SWEAT (Single-pore Wicking and Evaporation Apparatus for Textiles) test, which mimics the sweating behavior of humans at physiological relevant rates. Dr. Michielsen received his PhD in chemistry from the University of Chicago followed by a post-doctoral appointment at Stanford University. He began his research in textiles at the DuPont company in the 1980s, spinning Teflon fibers and later in the mechanics and surface modification of fibrous materials. In 1995, he moved to the Georgia Institute of Technology (Georgia Tech) and in 2004, he joined North Carolina State University in the Wilson College of Textiles.

Jeremiah (Jeremy) Morris is a forensic scientist supervisor at the Johnson County Sheriff's Office Criminalistics Laboratory in Kansas and is the technical leader in BPA. He has been performing casework examinations since 2005 and is a court-qualified expert in BPA. He is a distinguished member of the IABPA and is a certified bloodstain pattern analyst through the IAI. He is a member of the Netherlands Register of Court Experts (NRGD) Advisory Committee of Standardization of Bloodstain Pattern Analysis and was previously a member of the Bloodstain Pattern Analysis Subcommittee in the Organization of Scientific Area Committees (OSAC) for Forensic Science as well as the SWGSTAIN. In OSAC and SWGSTAIN, he was assigned to the taxonomy and terminology task groups. Jeremy is a past editor of the Journal of Bloodstain Pattern Analysis.

Nikola Osborne has a PhD in psychology from the University of Otago, New Zealand, and a post-doc from the Department of Criminology, Law, and Society at the University of California Irvine. Niki specializes in understanding and improving human factors issues in forensic evidence interpretation and presentation. Her primary research focus has been on the role of contextual information and the potential for cognitive and contextual bias in BPA. From this research, she has developed practical methods to manage contextual information for BPA in the laboratory and at the crime scene. Niki is currently contracted to the National Institute of Standards and Technology (NIST) to provide managerial support to the NIST/NIJ Expert Working Group on Human Factors in Forensic DNA Interpretation and other NIST Forensic Science Program efforts.

Elizabeth Richards, PhD, is a special agent (SA) with the Air Force Office of Special Investigations (AFOSI). She earned a BSc degree in biology from Arizona State University, an MSc degree in entomology from the University of Hawaii, and a PhD in biology from Texas Tech University. Elizabeth served as a member of the NIST, Organization of Scientific Area Committees in Forensic Science (OSAC), Bloodstain Pattern Analysis Subcommittee from 2014 to 2020. She has been a member of the AAFS since 1996 and a fellow in the pathology/biology section since 2014. Elizabeth graduated from the highly acclaimed Federal Bureau of Investigations (FBI), National Academy (NA), Session #268 in 2017.

Susan Rinehart (ret.), MS, CBPA, was a criminalist III in the Los Angeles Police Department (LAPD), Forensic Science Division. Ms. Rinehart holds a BSc degree in chemistry from California State Polytechnic University, Pomona, and an MSc degree in criminalistics from California State University, Los Angeles. Between 2003 and 2015, she was an adjunct professor at the Los Angeles City College in the Criminal Justice Curriculum. She is a member of the IABPA, IABPA vice president for Region I, and a member of the AAFS. Ms. Rinehart received certification in BPA from the IAI in 2016 and was voted in as a member of the NIST Organization of Scientific Area Committees (OSAC) BPA Subcommittee in 2017. She is currently the vice chairperson for that subcommittee.

Sergeant Celestina Rossi serves at the Crime Laboratory of the Montgomery County Sheriff's Office in Conroe, Texas. With 28 years of law enforcement expertise, she holds a Master Peace Officer's License. Since her promotion into the crime laboratory in 2002, she has gained recognition as a court-qualified expert in various fields, including latent print examination, BPA, crime scene reconstruction, and shooting incident reconstruction. She is currently president at the Texas Division of the IAI. Furthermore, she has served as the president of both the Association of Crime Scene Reconstruction and the IABPA. In addition to these roles, she also takes on the responsibility of being the executive secretary for the BPA sub-committee of the NIST/OSAC.

Rosalyn Rough, BSc, MSc (Hons), is a graduate from Massey University and Auckland University, New Zealand. She is employed as a forensic senior scientist at ESR, New Zealand's primary provider of forensic services to the New Zealand Police. Ms. Rough has over 20 years of professional experience in crime scene examination, body fluid identification, and BPA. Since 2014, she has been involved in basic and advanced BPA training besides serving as the co-instructor of ESR's fluid dynamics of bloodstain formation course. Since 2018, Ms. Rough has also been involved in BPA research with a particular focus on quantitative analysis of bloodstain patterns.

Amy Santoro, MFS, CBPA, CSCSA, is a bloodstain pattern analyst in the Kansas City area. Amy began working as a forensic scientist as a bench analyst in forensic biology and transitioned into a career as a crime scene investigator. She later became the technical leader of the crime scene investigations unit of the Johnson County, Kansas Sheriff's Office Criminalistics Laboratory. She is currently the owner of Santoro Forensic Consulting, a consulting firm specializing in BPA, shooting incident reconstruction, and crime scene reconstruction. She is IAI certified as a bloodstain pattern analyst, senior crime scene analyst, and forensic photographer. She is an active member of the IABPA. She is currently a doctoral candidate seeking her PhD in forensic investigative sciences.

Edmund (Ted) Silenieks worked at Forensic Science SA in Adelaide, South Australia for close to 35 years and was the evidence recovery coordinator for the Biology Section at FSSA, retiring from that role in August 2019 to continue research, teaching and to undertake forensic consultancy. Ted has been actively involved in the BPA discipline within Australia and internationally for over 20 years. He was an active member of the Australian NIFS Scientific Working Group on BPA, developing policy, training benchmarks, and standards for BPA conducted in Australia and New Zealand. He has served as the vice president for Region VI (Oceanic-Asian Region) of the IABPA and is an invited affiliate member of the NIST Organization of Scientific Area Committees (OSAC) Bloodstain Pattern Analysis Subcommittee. The NIST is an agency of the US Department of Commerce.

LeeAnn Singley accepted a position as a forensic scientist in the Pennsylvania State Police (PSP) Crime Laboratory in 1987, and spent the majority of her career working in the serology section. During her employment, she served as a regional supervisor and as the statewide serology technical coordinator, where her responsibilities included the development of quality assurance and procedural manuals and the training of new hires. She retired to continue her forensic work as the owner of Grayson Singley Associates, LLC, providing consulting and education services in bloodstain pattern analysis (BPA). She was an inaugural appointee to the National Institute of Standards and Technology (NIST) Organization of Scientific Area Committees (OSAC) Bloodstain Pattern Analysis Subcommittee having also served as chair of the Quality Assurance Task Group. She is a former President of the IABPA and was bestowed the honor of distinguished member by the organization.

Steve Sklavounos received his bachelor's degree in marine biology from Jacksonville, and his master's degree in marine science from the University of Alaska – Fairbanks. He joined the Miami-Dade Police Department as a sworn police officer in 2007, and in 2010, he became a crime scene detective. As a crime scene detective, he processed over 1500 scenes, including homicides, robberies, mass shootings, and sexual batteries. His most high-profile case was as the lead crime scene detective for the Champlain Towers building collapse in Surfside, FL. He is a trained bloodstain pattern analyst and an FAA certified drone pilot. He teaches crime scene to academy students at the Miami-Dade Public Safety Training Institute and Research Center and co-teaches bloodstain pattern analysis workshops with Toby Wolson. He was promoted to sergeant in 2023.

Theresa Stotesbury, PhD, is an associate professor and early career researcher in forensic science at Ontario Tech University in Oshawa, Ontario, Canada. She completed her BSc honors in forensic science and a PhD in materials science at Trent University (Canada) and completed MSc in forensic science at the University of Auckland (New Zealand). She has (co)authored 42 peer-reviewed journal articles in the forensic, analytical, and materials sciences and has one patent. Her most recent works explore bloodstain degradation in efforts to develop time science deposition models, particularly as they are influenced by extreme environmental conditions. Theresa regularly collaborates with members of the BPA and other forensic communities, has held a previous appointment of Research Scientist at the Ontario Provincial Police, and is an associate editor of the Canadian Society of Forensic Science Journal.

Dr. Elisabeth Williams, PhD, FHEA, MRSNZ, is a senior lecturer in applied biomechanics in the Faculty of Science and Engineering at Swansea University in Wales, UK. Originally from New Zealand, Elisabeth has a background in forensic science, completing her PhD in the biomechanics of blunt weapon assault and BPA for crime scene reconstruction at the University of Auckland in 2013. Dr. Williams' current research interests lie in head impact biomechanics in contact sports, with a particular focus on female athletes and rugby union. Current projects include head impact biomechanics and associations with neck strength, menstrual cycle, injury reporting, and neurocognitive outcomes in female rugby players. She was the scientific lead in the development of an instrumented mouthguard and principal investigator of a 2020 Women's Rugby Union Global Survey project.

Brian Yamashita, PhD, received a BSc (Hons) degree from the University of Manitoba. He then attended graduate school at the University of Western Ontario in London, Ontario, where he received a PhD in chemistry. After stints as a postdoctoral fellow at Dalhousie University in Halifax, Nova Scotia, an instructor at the University of Victoria in Victoria, British Columbia, and a research associate with Atomic Energy of Canada, he was offered a position with the Royal Canadian Mounted Police (RCMP) in Ottawa, Ontario. Dr. Yamashita worked for almost 28 years as a research scientist for the RCMP, retiring in 2017. His duties there included conducting research, mentoring colleagues and students, providing training, troubleshooting problems in the field, and serving on various national and international scientific working groups and committees. Over the past 20 years, he has taught BPA courses in Canada, the Unites States, and Singapore to students from a total of 11 different countries.

ABOUT THE EDITOR

Credited to Sam Wolson

Toby L. Wolson, MS, ABC-MBT, and CBPA, has a Master of Science degree from Michigan State University. He retired after 33 years of service as a criminalist and supervisor in the Forensic Biology Section of the Miami-Dade Police Department Forensic Services Bureau. He has received forensic training in serology, DNA (RFLP, PM, HLA DQ-alpha and STR), and bloodstain pattern analysis (BPA). Mr. Wolson is certified as a molecular biology technical specialist by the American Board of Criminalistics (ABC) and as a bloodstain pattern analyst by the International Association for Identification (IAI). He has presented papers concerning his studies in forensic biology and BPA at meetings of the American Academy of Forensic Sciences (AAFS), the Southern Association of Forensic Scientists, the IAI, and the International Association of Bloodstain Pattern Analysts (IABPA). He is a distinguished member and a past president of the IABPA. Mr. Wolson is a member of the Organization of Scientific Area Committees (OSAC) Physics/Pattern Scientific Area Committee and was the Chair of the Bloodstain Pattern Analysis Subcommittee (BPASC) from October 1, 2014, to September 30, 2019, and as a regular member of the BPA SC beginning in October 2019. OSAC is an initiative of the National Institute of Standards and Technology (NIST) and the Department of Justice to strengthen forensic science in the United States. He is a member of the AAFS Academy Standards Board Bloodstain Pattern Analysis Consensus Body, the Chairperson of the IAI's Bloodstain Pattern Analysis Science and Practice Subcommittee, a member of the IAI's Bloodstain Pattern Analysis Certification Board, and is on the Editorial Board of the IAI's Journal of Forensic Identification. Mr. Wolson is a retired fellow in the AAFS and a member of the IAI. He has testified as an expert witness in the United States District Court for the Southern District of Florida, Circuit Court of the Sixth Judicial Circuit of Florida, Circuit Court of the Eleventh Judicial Circuit of Florida, Circuit Court of the Twelfth Judicial Circuit of Florida, Circuit Court of the Fifteenth Judicial Circuit of Florida, Circuit Court of the Sixteenth Judicial Circuit of Florida, Circuit Court of the Twentieth Judicial Circuit of Florida, Grand Jury of the Seventeenth Judicial Circuit of Florida, Circuit 18th Judicial Circuit Court of Shelby County (Alabama), Court of Common Pleas of Allegheny County (Pennsylvania), Court of Common Pleas of Cuyahoga County (Ohio), Grand Court, Georgetown, Cayman Islands, British West Indies (BWI), Superior Court of the United States Virgin Islands, St. Thomas, Unites States Virgin Islands, District Court, Clark County (Nevada), Circuit Court of Prince Georges County (Maryland), Montana 13th Judicial District Court, and Detroit Recorder's Court (Michigan). Mr. Wolson became involved in teaching in 1983 and has instructed in more than 200 workshops, seminars, and conferences.

In Memoriam: Dr Michael Taylor 1953–2020, In 1979, after obtaining his PhD in Chemistry from the University of Canterbury, New Zealand, Michael joined the New Zealand Department of Scientific and Industrial Research (DSIR). When DSIR was restructured, he continued his career under the banner of the Institute of Environmental Science and Research (ESR), from which he retired as a Science Leader in 2020 after 41 years of dedicated service.

Early in his career, Michael developed a keen interest in Bloodstain Pattern Analysis which quickly became a passion, and he began researching bloodstain mechanisms. His aim was always to strengthen the understanding of the fundamental mechanisms which create blood stains. He collaborated widely with bloodstain pattern analysts from around the globe, hailing from New Zealand, Australia, the United States of America, Canada, the United Kingdom, Singapore, France, and The Netherlands. Michael, together with his many collaborators, published widely and his papers and book chapters included topics such as the formation of drip, cast-off, gunshot, and expirated patterns, swipes and wipes and bloodstains on fabrics. He researched blood droplet flight, the reliability of bloodstain classification, contextual bias influences on bloodstain interpretation, methods for objective bloodstain classification, image processing, sequencing of stains and investigated blood substitutes for the use in research and training scenarios. He contributed frequently to the Australian and New Zealand Forensic Science Society, the International Association of Bloodstain Pattern Analysts, SWGSTAIN and the OSAC BPA Subcommittee. He supervised many students involved in Masters and PhD research projects. Michael remained an active and thoughtful mentor to many in the BPA community, both novice and experienced practitioners.

Michael, together with Bart Epstein and Terry Laber, pioneered the use of high-speed video analysis of bloodstain mechanisms and created a publicly available library of high-speed videos illustrating different bloodstain creation mechanisms in 2007. In 2010, Michael developed and initiated the world‘s first course on the fluid dynamics of bloodstain pattern formation, co-taught with Mark Jermy of the University of Canterbury, and later Rosalyn Rough of ESR.

Alongside his research work, Michael remained an active crime scene investigator, and developed a strong reputation for thorough and patient work. In 2002, he was asked to investigate a high-profile case in the Solomon Islands, where the New Zealand High Commissioner had been found dead in her home. Michael travelled and worked with New Zealand Police officers and after a careful investigation determined that the Commissioner’s death was an accident.

Besides his work, Michael loved sport and was a passionate supporter of the New Zealand national Rugby Union team, the All Blacks, and in his later years had received a signed jersey from the team. He was a keen field hockey player in his youth and remained a dedicated spectator throughout his life. He made a great contribution to basketball in New Zealand as manager of regional and national teams, and as a statistician.

Michael was awarded the IABPA Distinguished Member in 2015. Michael was an inspiration to many of the contributors to this book and to all those he worked with. His guidance and mentorship are sadly missed.

ACKNOWLEDGMENTS

Thank you to all the authors who contributed to this book and made it a reality. Without you, your time, effort, and encouragement, this book would have never happened. Thank you, Holly Latham, for teaching me fingerprint terminology and providing editorial review and comment on several articles. Thank you, Jeremy Morris, for contributing so many pictures for use in the visual reference appendix. Thank you, Mark Listewnik of CRC Press, for being so understanding every time a deadline was missed. Most importantly, thank you Julia Wolson for providing review and grammar support, and most of all, emotional support.

CHAPTER 1

HISTORICAL EVOLUTION OF BLOODSTAIN PATTERN ANALYSIS

Stuart H. James

It is of the highest importance to the field of Forensic Medicine to give the fullest attention to bloodstains found at the scene of a crime because they can throw light on a murder and provide an explanation for the Essential moments of an incident.

Eduard Piotrowski 1895

INTRODUCTION

The emergence of bloodstain pattern analysis (BPA) as a discipline in forensic science can trace its roots to the interest and research of scientists in Europe in the 19th century, notably Hans Gross and Eduard Piotrowski. Original research and experimentation on BPA was accomplished by the French scientist, Dr. Victor Balthazard in the early 20th century.

In the United States, the research by Dr. Paul Leland Kirk at the University of California, Berkeley was highlighted in 1955 with his submission of an affidavit based upon his analysis of bloodstain evidence in the case of the *State of Ohio v. Samuel Sheppard*. The further growth of interest in this discipline was recognized by the research and practical application of bloodstain pattern interpretation in teaching and casework by Herbert Leon MacDonell from Corning, New York.

Since the 1970s and early 1980s, the discipline of BPA has continued to evolve and is now generally accepted by the legal systems in the United States and abroad. Research and development of standards for scientific methodology and validation have made great strides over the past 37 years.

THE EARLY DAYS

In 1846, Enrico Bayard and Giovanni Duodo published *Manuale Pratico di Medicina Legale*. In Venice, Italy, they reported interesting considerations about the physical characteristics of dried blood with respect to the changes in color. The changes were dependent on the volume of blood, the size of the stain, and the surface texture (permeable or non-permeable). They also described the skeletonization of blood phenomenon, which depends, in their opinion, on the type of deposit surface and the inner quality of the substance itself. It is also interesting to read their statements concerning the shape of bloodstains; they believed that it depended upon the direction from which they originated. In their conclusion, the authors suggested the use of an artificial light as a method of searching for bloodstains because they are scarcely visible in daylight, especially on dark-colored surfaces; in fact, the use of a lamp makes them appearing "bright" to observation.[1]

DOI: 10.4324/9781003163695-1

Figure 1.1 Hans Gross (1847–1915).

Charles Meymott Tidy (1843–1892) was a physician who was also involved in medical jurisprudence in London, UK. In his texts entitled, *Legal Medicine* and *A Handy Book of Forensic Medicine and Toxicology* published in 1882, he emphasized the importance of determining the precise nature and exact position of various blood spots or stains found on garments or instruments. He concluded that the color of bloodstains depends on their age, thickness, moisture, temperature, and the kind of material upon which they have fallen.[2,3]

Hans Gross (1847–1915) was a judge and prosecutor in Styria, Austria. He introduced the concept of criminalistics (Figure 1.1). He was the author of *Handbuch für Untersuchungsrichter als System der Kriminalistik* (*Handbook for Examining Magistrate as a System for Criminalistics*) published in 1893, which was translated into English in 1907. A second edition was published in 1924. He wrote an entire chapter entitled "Traces of Blood" on the study of bloodstains at a crime scene. He described the concepts of directionality, angle of impact, and other general characteristics of bloodstains.[4]

Giuseppe Lapponi (1851–1906) was the personal physician of Pope Leo XIII and also involved in legal medicine in Italy (Figure 1.2). His work, *Compendio di Medicina Legale* published in 1894 in Rome, Italy, dedicated a chapter entitled "Segni per Ladeterminazione Fiscio-biologica Della Identità (Signs for the Physical and -Biological Determination of Identity)" to the study of bloodstains. He described the coagulative processes of blood when exposed to external agents. He also focused on the mechanism of the production of bloodstains from transfer with reference to plantar (footwear) imprints. Moreover, he also described the shape of bloodstains originated both from the cut of the arterial vessels and from the impact of drops obliquely on the surface. He considered the shape of bloodstains, originated by the impact of drops with an angle different from 90°, on non-smooth and absorbent tissues.[5]

Eduard Piotrowski (1864–1916) studied medicine at the Faculty of Medicine of the Jagiellonian University in Kraków, Poland. He later became an assistant at the Institute of Forensic Medicine in Kraków[6] (Figure 1.3). His work entitled *Ueber Entstehung, Form, Richtung und Ausbreitung der Blutspuren nach Heibwunden des Kopfes* (*Concerning the Origin, Shape, Direction and Distribution of Bloodstains Following Head Wounds Caused by Blows*) was published in Vienna in 1895 (Figure 1.4). This was the earliest known significant study in bloodstain pattern research. Through the efforts of Herbert Leon MacDonell, the work was translated into English in 1992. According to MacDonell, "No one preceded Piotrowski in designing meaningful scientific experiments to show blood

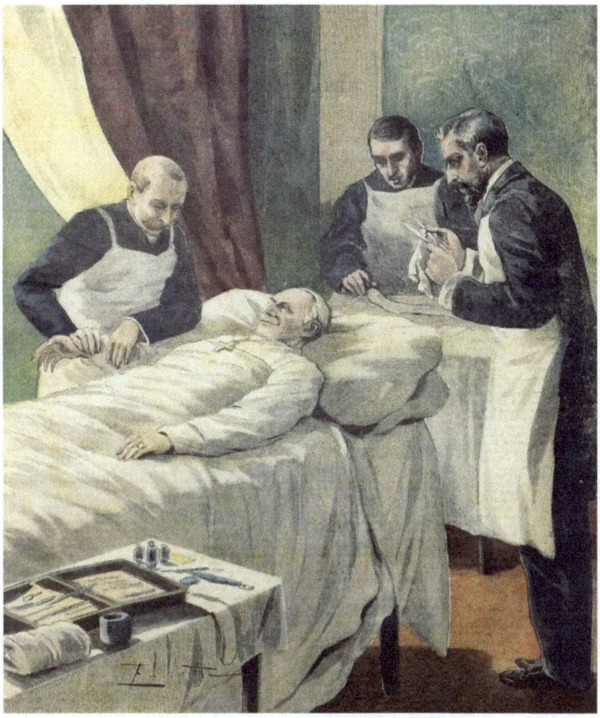

Figure 1.2 Giuseppe Lapponi (1851–1906) (left), physician of Pope Leo XIII 1899. (Courtesy of Gabriele Rotter, Italian State Police Regional Forensic Science Office, Reggio Calabria, Italy.)

Figure 1.3 Eduard Piotrowski (1864–1916). (Courtesy of Kacper Chromanski, University of Warsaw, Poland.)

Figure 1.4 The 1895 publication of Eduard Piotrowski, *Ueber Entstehung, Form, Richtung und Ausbreitung der Blutspuren nach Heibwunden des Kopfes (Concerning the Origin, Shape, Direction, and Distribution of Bloodstains Following Head Wounds Caused by Blows).*

dynamics with such imagination, methodology and thoroughness. He had an excellent knowledge of the scientific method and a good understanding of its practical application to bloodstain pattern interpretation."

Piotrowski described his experiments in detail and they were supplemented with 22 color plates. His experiments utilized pieces of blood-soaked cotton and rabbits as a more realistic source of blood that were struck in the head with a hammer, hatchet, and a stone from various directions. Impact spatters produced from repetitive blows were formed on targets that were vertical walls placed in front of and to the sides of the blows being struck to the object. He noted that the direction of the force of the blows dictated the location of the spatters as seen in Figure 1.5.[7,8]

John Glaister (1856–1932) was a forensic scientist and a police surgeon in Glasgow, Scotland (Figure 1.6). He compiled a chapter entitled "Bloodstains and the Examination of Blood" in the text, *Medical Jurisprudence, Toxicology and Public Health,* which was published in 1902. He described how the examination of bloodstains ought to be conducted. He defined the variety of stains that the examiner must expect to meet as (a) sprays, spurts, or jets, (b) smears of various forms, or (c) pools of blood. He described the relation of the direction of the spray of blood to the position and location of the wounded victim and stressed the importance of measurements and sketches. He also

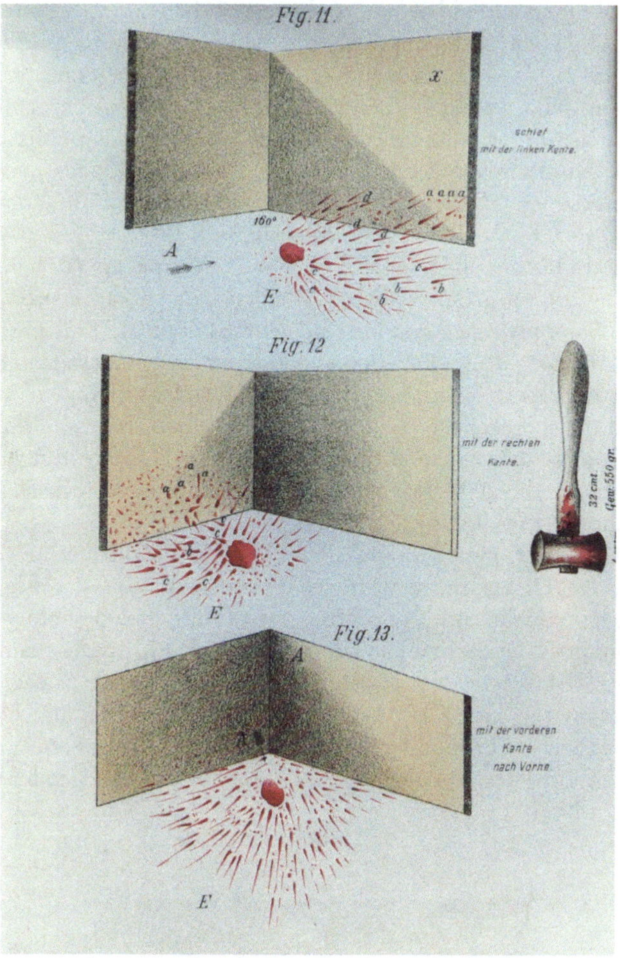

Figure 1.5 Color plate illustrated by Eduard Piotrowski demonstrating the direction of the spatters based upon the direction of force applied to the source of blood by a hammer.

Figure 1.6 John Glaister (1856–1932).

noted that the color of blood varied because of the age of the stain, the amount of blood composing it, and the nature and color of the material upon which it had been effused (disseminated).[9,10]

Albert Florence (1851–1927) was a French forensic scientist at the Forensic Medicine Laboratory of the Faculty of Lyon, who developed a system for the classification of bloodstains caused by dripping, spurting, splashing or, grazing contact. His research was published in an article "Les Taches de Sang au Laboratoire De Medicine Legale De Lyon (Bloodstains, Their Significance, Their Importance in Forensic Medicine)" in 1901. The article initially appeared in the journal, *Archives D' Anthropologie Criminelle de Criminologie* in 1901.[9,11]

Dr. Edward S. Wood (1846–1905) was a physician and professor of chemistry at the Harvard Medical School. He wrote an article entitled "Medico-Legal Examination of Bloodstains" that was published in the *Boston Medical and Surgical Journal* in 1901. This journal became the *New England Journal of Medicine* in 1928. Dr. Wood conducted a detailed study of bloodstain patterns, including excellent observations on the drying of blood and its change of color as a function of time. He also studied the shape of the stains of spattered blood that would sometimes show accurately the direction from which the blood came. In 1893, Dr. Wood testified in the celebrated trial of Lizzie Borden in New Bedford, Massachusetts, who was accused of the ax murders of her father and mother in reference to the clotting and drying times of blood.[9,12]

Dr. Paul Jeserich (1854–1927) was a forensic chemist in Berlin who developed the first microscope with a comparison bridge. He examined crime scenes and performed significant work in bloodstain analysis during the first decade of the 20th century. He recommended photography of the scene that would faithfully record little details that may supply a valuable link to the chain of custody later on.[13]

Ernst Ziemke (1867–1935) was a professor of forensic medicine at the Institute of Forensic Medicine, Kiel, Germany (Figure 1.7). He was the author of the chapter, "Die Untersuchung von Blutspuren (The Investigation of Blood and Traces of Blood)" in the book, *Gerichtsärztliche und Polizerärzliche Technik* (Forensic and Police Medical Technology) by Theodore Lochte published in Wiesbaden, Germany in 1914.

Figure 1.7 Ernst Ziemke (1867–1935).

Figure 1.8 Dr. Victor Balthazard (1872–1950). (Courtesy of Philippe Esperanca, Laboratoire d'Analyses, Criminalistiques Marseille, France.)

Ziemke recognized that it was erroneous to think that an offender must have been heavily bloodstained when severe wounds opened arteries in a victim. He offered some rules to determine the volume of blood required to produce bloodstained areas and also highly recommended that photographs be taken at a crime scene including a ruler or other scale of reference.[14,15,16,17]

Victor Balthazard (1872–1950) was a professor of forensic medicine at Sorbonne University in Paris, France and became the director of the Forensic Institute of Paris in 1923 (Figure 1.8). His specialties were internal pathology and forensic medicine. He conducted original research and experimentation in bloodstain trajectories and angles of impact.

He presented his paper entitled "Des Gouttes De Sang Projecte (Research on Blood Spatter)" at the 22nd Congress of Forensic Medicine in 1939. The paper was also published in 1939 and provided useful information related to BPA.

- Diameter of bloodstains in a horizontal plane linked to the dropping height of drip stains
- Number of spines linked to the dropping height of drip stains
- Shape of the drip stains on inclined planes
- Effects of target surface taking into account shape and texture
- Length-to-width ratio of a bloodstain was a function of its angle of impact (Figure 1.9)
- Point of origin of bloodstains utilizing the convergence of the axes of the stains and their angle of impact[18,19,20]

Dr. LeMoyne Snyder (1898–1989) was a former medicolegal director of the Michigan State Police. His book, *Homicide Investigation – Practical Information for Coroners, Police Officers and Other Investigators* was published in 1941, with later editions and reprints published through 1977. Chapter 4 of this book is entitled "The Examination of Bloodstains." He discussed the issue of the length of elapsed time since bloodshed by addressing the amount of coagulation, drying, and color changes associated with the aging of blood. He also described methods of preserving and collecting samples of blood for analysis.[21]

Paul Leland Kirk (1902–1970) was a professor of biochemistry and criminalistics at the University of California, Berkeley (Figure 1.10).

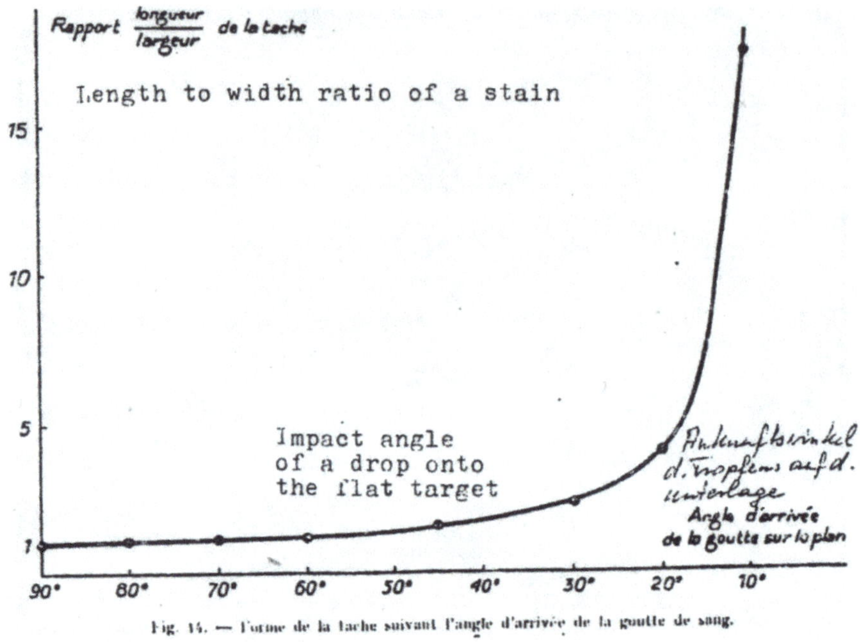

Figure 1.9 Graph from the work of Victor Balthazard, Des Gouttes De Sang Projecte (Research on Blood Spatter) demonstrating that the length-to-width ratio of a bloodstain was a function of its angle of impact.

Figure 1.10 Paul Leland Kirk (1902–1970).

His text, *Crime Investigation* was published in 1953 and contained practical information and theory on forensic science, including a chapter on bloodstain analysis. A second edition was published in 1974, which was edited by John I. Thornton, an associate professor of forensic science at the University of California, Berkeley, who worked directly under Dr. Kirk. The book presented 36 chapters on the principles and practice of criminalistics, including chapters on general testing of blood, individual factors of blood, identification of blood, and physical investigation of blood. This chapter described blood distribution patterns and investigation of blood in the field. He stated emphatically that "no other type of investigation of blood will yield so much useful information as an analysis of the blood distribution patterns."[22]

Dr. Kirk presented an affidavit regarding his findings based upon his examination of the bloodstain evidence to the Court of Common Pleas in the case of the *State of Ohio v. Samuel Sheppard* in 1955. Dr. Sheppard had been convicted of the beating death of his wife, Marilyn Sheppard, in December 1954. This was a significant milestone in the recognition of bloodstain evidence by the legal system. Dr. Kirk was able to demonstrate the relative position of the attacker and the victim at the time of administration of the fatal beating sustained by Dr. Sheppard's wife, Marilyn.[23] He testified in the second trial of Dr. Sheppard in 1966 on behalf of the defense for Attorney F. Lee Bailey.

THE MODERN DEVELOPMENT OF BLOODSTAIN PATTERN ANALYSIS (1969–2021)

Herbert Leon MacDonell (1928–2019) was a chemist at the Corning Glass Works in Corning, New York, and a friend of Paul Leland Kirk. He conducted bloodstain research in 1969 and 1970 at the request of Kirk. His research was supported by a grant from the then Law Enforcement Administration Assistance (LEAA) within the United States Department of Justice. He submitted a report to the LEAA that became the basis for the first edition of his book, *Flight Characteristics and Stain Patterns of Human Blood*.[24] The book written with the assistance of Lorraine Fiske Bialousz was published in 1971 by the United States Department of Justice and was available for his students at the Bloodstain Institute (Figure 1.11). In 1982, MacDonell expanded his original

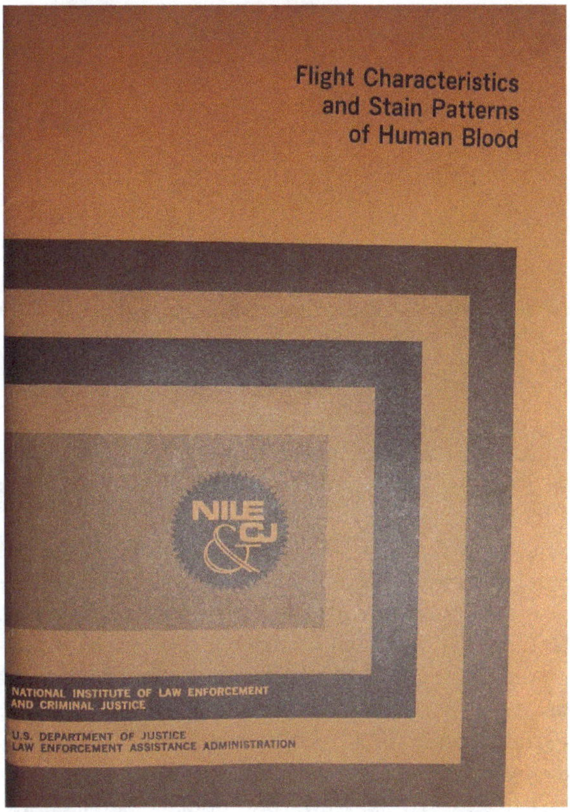

Figure 1.11 Copy of *Flight Characteristics and Stain Patterns of Human Blood* written by Herbert Leon MacDonell with the assistance of Lorraine Fiske Bialousz and published in 1971.

Figure 1.12 Copy of *Bloodstain Patterns – Second Revised Edition* written by Herbert Leon MacDonell and published in 2005.

book in a publication entitled *Bloodstain Pattern Interpretation*, with two revised editions of this book entitled *Bloodstain Patterns, Revised Edition* in 1997 and *Bloodstain Patterns, 2nd Revised Edition* in 2005 (Figure 1.12).[25]

MacDonell and Lorraine Fiske Bialousz published a manual entitled *Laboratory Manual on the Geometric Interpretation of Human Bloodstain Evidence* in 1973 (Figure 1.13).[26]

The manual was used in conjunction with their book by students in the first 40-hour course in bloodstain pattern interpretation they instructed during March 19–23, 1973 in Jackson, Mississippi. The course was sponsored by the Mississippi Law Enforcement Assistance and coordinated by the Extension of the University of Mississippi.[27] The book and laboratory manual were used for many years by students pursuing basic courses from his Bloodstain Institute situated in Corning, New York and throughout the United States and abroad. MacDonell and Paul E. Kish, a bloodstain pattern analyst from Corning, New York, updated the laboratory manual in the 1995 edition.

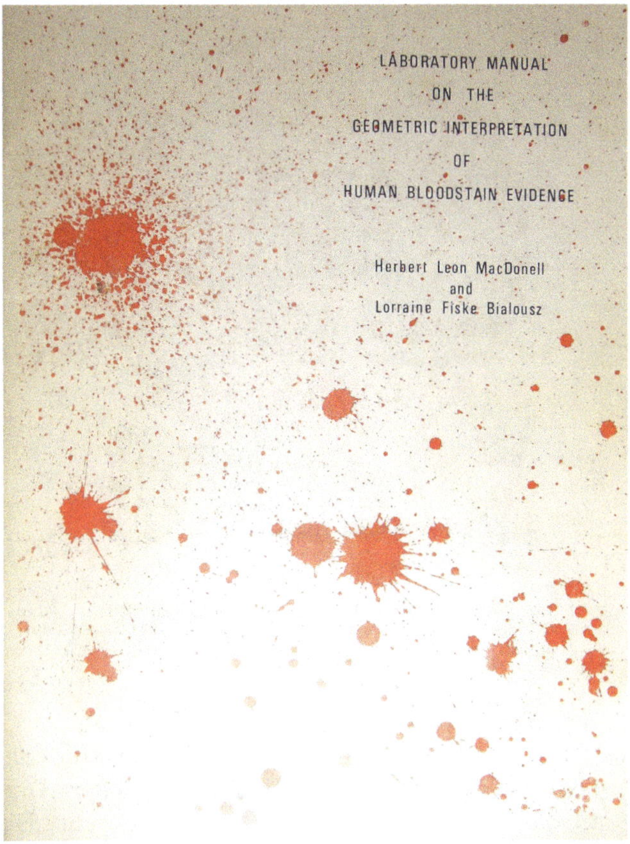

Figure 1.13 Copy of *Laboratory Manual on the Geometric Interpretation of Human Bloodstain Evidence* written by Herbert Leon MacDonell with the assistance of Lorraine Fiske Bialousz and published in 1973.

The International Association of Bloodstain Pattern Analysts and Related Organizations

MacDonell instructed the first advanced course in bloodstain pattern interpretation in 1983. The course was attended by 23 students who had successfully passed the basic course. The course was held at the Corning Hilton and included mock crime scenes set up in nearby abandoned apartments. Students also presented cases they had worked on for critique by the class. Late one evening, the group decided to form a BPA organization. Thus, the International Association of Bloodstain Pattern Analysts (IABPA) was created (Figure 1.14).

There were 22 charter members in 1983.

- Tom Bevel (Oklahoma City Police Department, Oklahoma)
- Joseph Dean (Sacramento County Sheriff's Department, California)
- Charles Edel (Broward County Sheriff's Office, Florida)
- Rod Englert (Multnomah County Sheriff's Office, Oregon)
- Robert Fitzer (San Francisco Police Department, California)
- Harry Holmes (Virginia Beach Police Department, Virginia)
- Stuart H. James (Forensic Consultant, New York)
- Michael L. Johnson (Ada County Coroner, Idaho)

Figure 1.14 Original logo of the International Association of Bloodstain Pattern Analysts (IABPA) in the form of a patch.

- Samuel Johnson (District 21 Medical Examiner's Office Fort Myers, Florida)
- Ronald Linhart (Los Angeles Medical Examiner/Coroner, California)
- Herbert Leon MacDonell (Laboratory of Forensic Science, Corning, New York)
- Sara Lea Moore (Laboratory of Forensic Science, Corning, New York)
- Robert W. Przygoda (Schuyler County Sheriff's Department, New York)
- Daniel Qyealy (Cook County Sheriff's Police, Illinois)
- Norman H. Reeves (Gloucester County Prosecutor's Office, New Jersey)
- James W. Rossi (Cook County Sheriff's Police, Illinois)
- Donald Ray Schuessler (Eugene Police Department, Oregon)
- Hal F. Sharp (US Army Criminal Investigation Laboratory)
- Casimer J. Smerecki (Middlesex County Prosecutor's Office, New Jersey)
- Anita K. Y. Wonder (Wonder Institute, California)
- Robert W. Young, Jr. (Columbus Police Department, Ohio)
- Deborah J. Wakida (San Francisco Police Crime Laboratory, California)

The first President of the IABPA was Sgt. Tom Bevel of the Oklahoma City Police Department (Figure 1.15).

The goals of the organization were:[28]

- To encourage research and further knowledge in Bloodstain Interpretation
- To standardize terminology and testing procedures in the discipline
- To keep its members apprised of the latest techniques, discoveries, and developments in bloodstain interpretation

The initial publication of the organization, the *International Association of Bloodstain Pattern Analysts News* appeared in 1984, with Anita K. Wonder as the first Editor.[28] The publication became the *Journal of Bloodstain Pattern Analysis* in 2011 and is currently online at www.iabpa.org (Figure 1.16a and b).

As a direct result of the efforts of MacDonell, the discipline of BPA has continued to grow considerably along with the IABPA both nationally and internationally. The IABPA has made great strides and growth in membership since the 23 charter members assembled in 1983.

Figure 1.15 Tom Bevel, retired Sergeant of the Oklahoma City Police Department and first President of the IABPA.

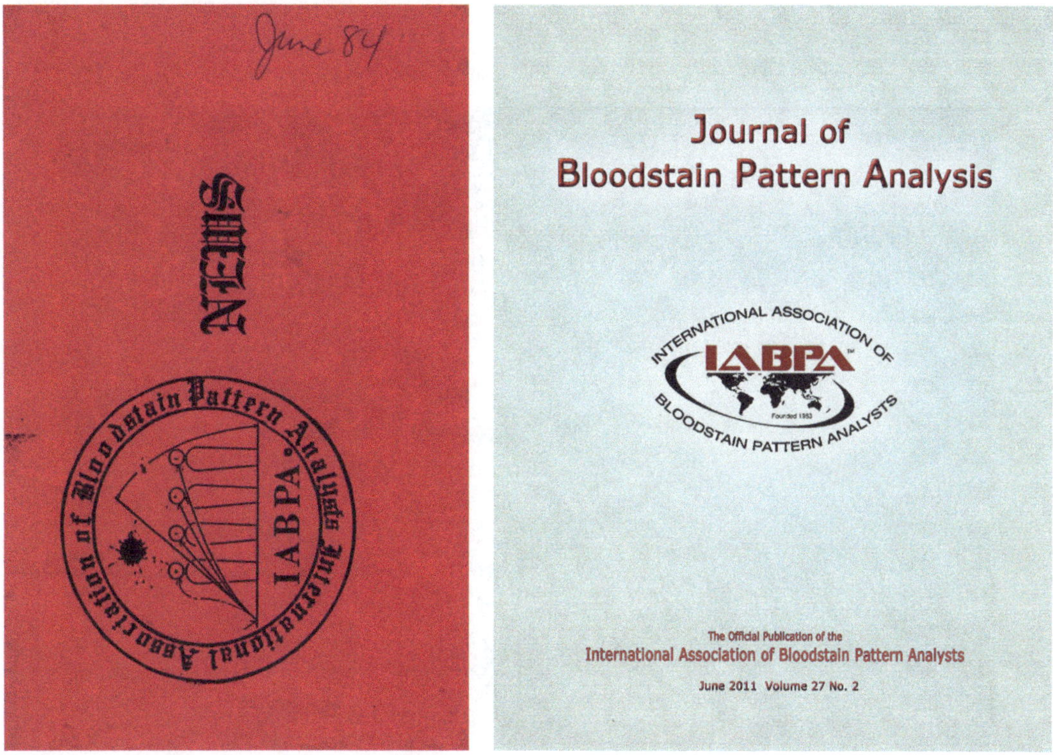

Figure 1.16 (a) Cover of the first edition of the *International Association of Bloodstain Pattern Analysts News* in published in June 1984 and (b) cover of the *Journal of Bloodstain Pattern Analysis* published in June 2011.

The organization currently has approximately 600 members from the United States, Canada, Europe, Australia, New Zealand, the Far East, and South America. The levels of membership are: associate, provisional, full member, and distinguished member. There are six designated regions of the IABPA based upon times zones, with an elected vice-president for each region.[29]

- Region I Pacific time zone
- Region II Mountain time zone
- Region III Central time zone
- Region IV Eastern time zone
- Region V Europe and the United Kingdom
- Region VI Pacific/Asia

Annual North American IABPA training conferences are held in the United States and Canada. The 2020 annual conference was held online via Zoom due to the COVID-19 pandemic, with presentations scheduled according to national and international time zones.

One of the first bloodstain pattern conferences developed in Europe was the Scandinavian conference in 2004 in Copenhagen, Denmark, where police and laboratory personnel from Denmark, Finland, Iceland, Norway, and Sweden would meet every other year. With a higher attention to methodology, the IABPA conferences in America would be attended by more European participants and out of this the European Bloodstain Network developed around 2005. The European Bloodstain Network was interdisciplinary, but it soon began to split into disciplines. European attendance at the annual IABPA conferences in the United States increased and an interest developed in Europe for IABPA training conferences.[30]

The first European IABPA training conference in Europe was held at the old city hall in Middleburg, the Netherlands in 2006 and hosted by André Hendrix and the Zeeland Police Force (Figure 1.17). They produced an outstanding, special full color publication of the conference entitled *Bloodstain Pattern Analysis* (Figure 1.18a and b).[31]

Figure 1.17 Old City Hall in Middleburg, the Netherlands, the venue of the first IABPA European training conference.

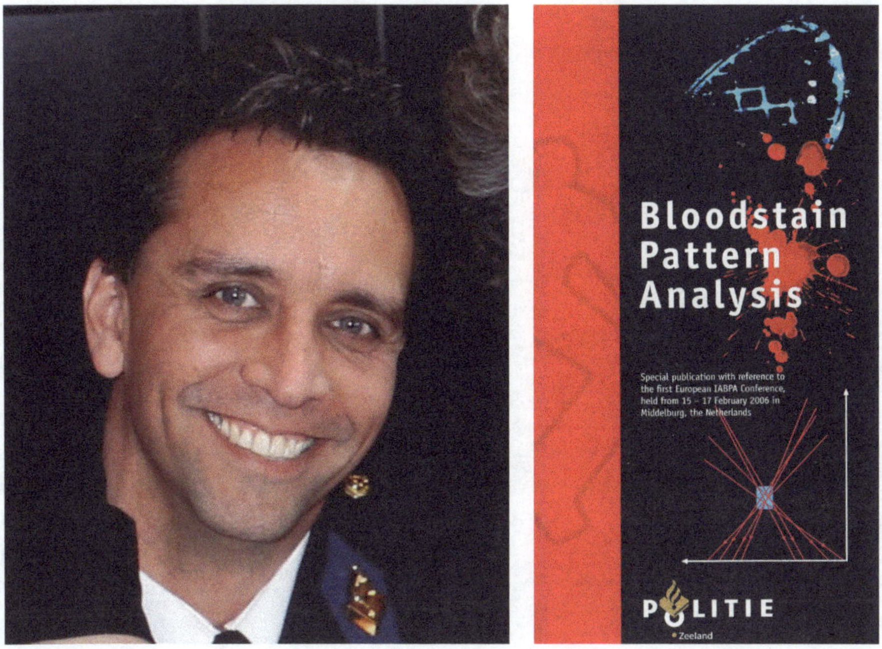

Figure 1.18 (a) Andre Hendrix, Dutch National Police Force, the Netherlands and (b) cover of *Bloodstain Pattern Analysis*, a special publication with reference to the first IABPA European training conference.

The second European IABPA training conference was held in Zurich, Switzerland in 2008 hosted by Sabine Hess and Andreas Schweizer from the Wissenschaftlicher Dienst (Scientific Services). The third was held in Lisbon, Portugal in 2010 hosted by Lino Henriques of the Polícia Judiciá – Laboratório de Policia Científica. The fourth was held in Edinburgh, Scotland in 2012 hosted by Amanda A. Pirio and Chris Gannicliffe from the Scottish Police Services Authority Forensic Services. A special venue for the conference in Edinburgh was the 500-year-old Royal College of Physicians (Figure 1.19). The fifth was held in Rome, Italy in 2015 hosted by Andrea Berti from the Arma dei Carabinieri Forensic Science Department. The sixth was held in Jachranka near Warsaw, Poland in 2017 hosted by Kamil Januszkiewicz from the Central Forensic Laboratory of the Police Research Institute in Warsaw. The seventh was held in Pontoise, France in 2019 hosted by Céline Nicloux from the Forensic Science Laboratory of the French Gendarmerie. The first South American IABPA Conference was held in Buenos Aires, Argentina in 2018 hosted by Pablo M. Núñes at the Instituto Universitario de la Policia Federal Argentina.

The Rocky Mountain Association of Bloodstain Pattern Analysts (RMABPA) was formed in 1988 for the purpose to meet informally to review, discuss, and critique specific bloodstain cases. The group began as an informal quarterly meeting among a few practitioners and grew to a formal organization of over 150 members. The meetings included case presentations, experiments, and demonstrations.[32]

The Association for Crime Scene Reconstruction (ACSR) was formed in 1991 with a group of professionals in Oklahoma and Texas, who investigated crime scenes, performed forensic analyses, and compared evidence from crime scenes. The organization publishes the Journal of the Association for Crime Scene Reconstruction. ACSR currently has approximately 225 members from the United States and abroad. Many members who are bloodstain pattern analysts are also affiliated with the IABPA.[33]

Figure 1.19 Royal College of Physicians in Edinburgh, Scotland, the venue of the second IABPA training conference.

Advances in Bloodstain Pattern Analysis Instruction and Training

Many of MacDonell's former students and other trained practitioners have made significant contributions to the discipline of BPA in teaching, research, and scientific publications. The basic and advanced BPA courses have been instructed by Tom Bevel and Ross Gardner from Bevel & Gardner Associates, Toby Wolson, Paul E. Kish, Stuart James, Bart Epstein, Terry Laber, and T. Paulette Sutton throughout the United States and abroad. The first basic BPA course in Italy was held in June of 2007 in Parma. It was organized by Colonel L. Garofano from the Reparto Carabinieri Investigazioni Scientifiche of Parma and by the State University of Parma. The course was instructed by Herbert Leon MacDonell and T. Paulette Sutton.[34]

The Korean Police and the National Forensic Service collaborated with each other to bring BPA to Korea. In 2005, Young-Seok Choi from Daegu and Woon Cha from Joennam traveled from Korea to Oklahoma to take a crime scene course from Bevel & Gardner Associates. They also were accepted into a BPA training program at the Ontario Police College in Ontario, Canada instructed by Pat Laturnus. Between 2006 and 2009, instructors from the United States and Canada, including Ross Gardner, Tom Bevel, Pat Laturnus and Jim Kileen, traveled to Korea to take BPA workshops. Since then, BPA terminology has been translated into Korean and the discipline has been used in the Korean Courts. The Korean Association of Bloodstain Pattern Analysis (KABPA) was established in 2008.[35] The third edition of the Bevel and Gardner text, *Bloodstain Pattern Analysis with an Introduction to Crime Scene Reconstruction* was translated into Korean as *Crime Scene Reconstruction through Bloodstain*.

Martin Eversdijk and René Gelderman from Loci Forensics, the Netherlands, instruct basic and advanced BPA courses, as well as courses in the use of luminol and chemical enhancement. Dr. Silke Brodbeck instructs basic and advanced BPA courses in Germany. Joanne Millington and Gillian Leak instruct BPA courses in the United Kingdom. They presented a workshop at the 2012 International IABPA training conference in Edinburgh, Scotland entitled "Simulated Projected

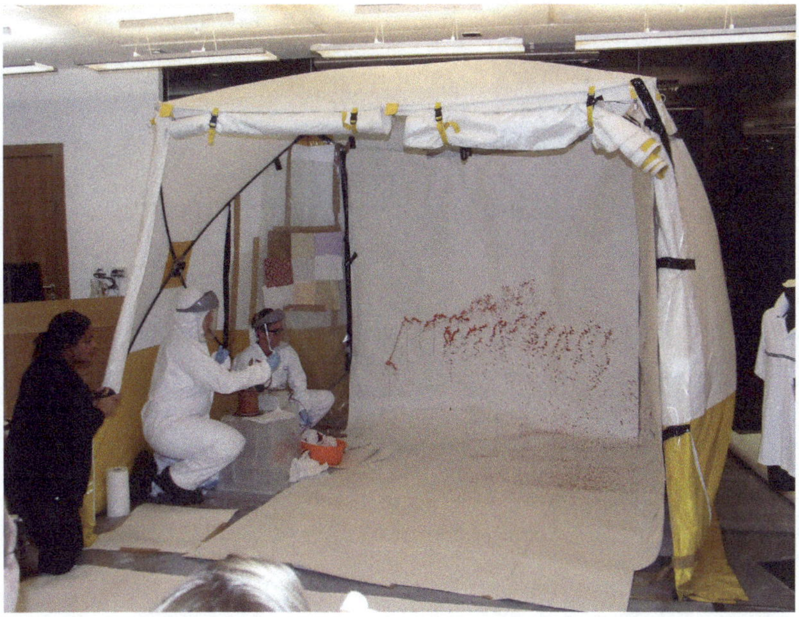

Figure 1.20 View of Joanne Millington and Gillian Leak from the United Kingdom demonstrating simulated projected bloodstain patterns using the arterial pump at the 2012 IABPA training conference held in Edinburgh, Scotland.

Bloodstain Patterns Using the Arterial Pump." The device relied on the use of various syringes and other props to simulate projected bloodstain patterns on surfaces and clothing (Figures 1.20 and 1.21).

Andre Anyon from Forensic Bodies in North Carolina created "Spatterhead" in 2004 as a tool to reproduce impact spatters for experiments and as a teaching aid. "Spatterhead" is a gypsum base

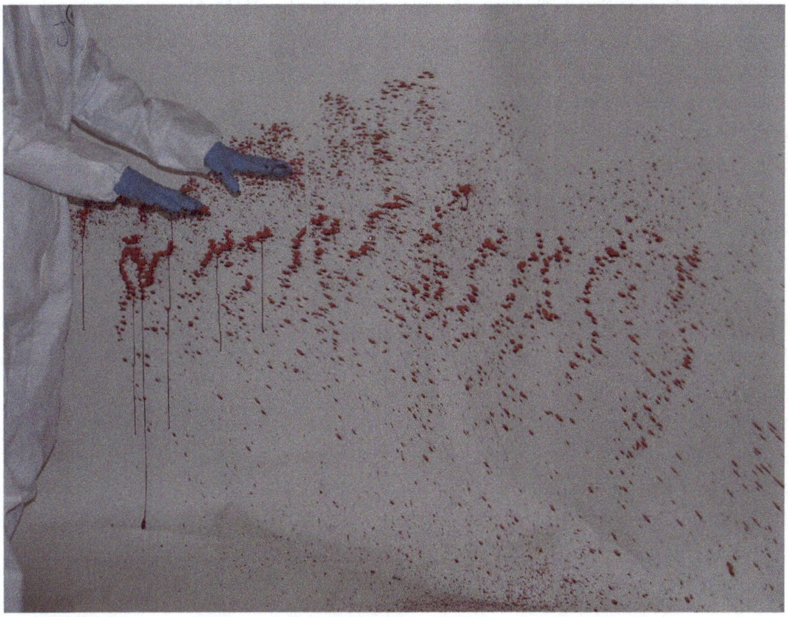

Figure 1.21 Closer view of the simulated projected bloodstain patterns produced with the arterial pump.

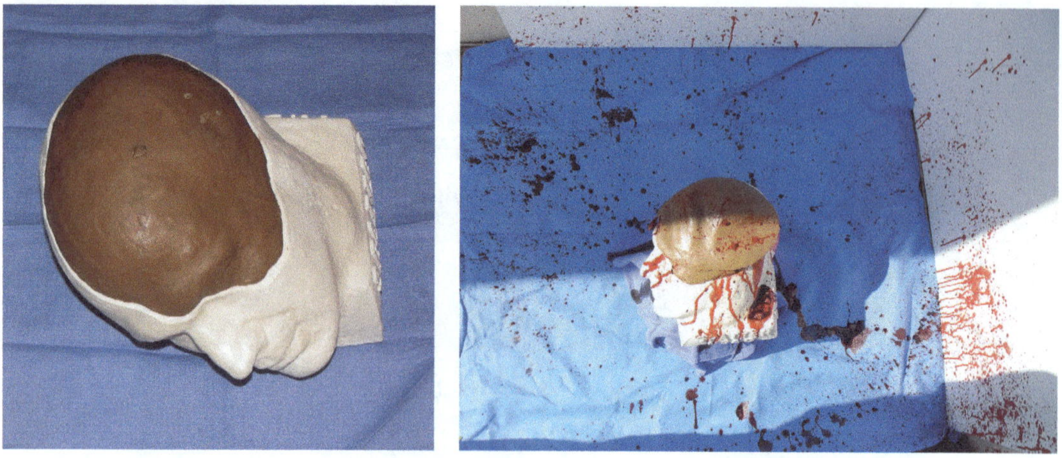

Figure 1.22 (a) View of the horizontally oriented "Spatterhead" with pre-filled wax cap for demonstration of impact spatter produced by blunt force and (b) view of "Spatterhead" and the production of impact spatters from blunt force.

that depicts the lower three-fourths of a human head. The upper one-fourth consists of a hollow wax cap that contains an absorbent interior. The wax cap serves as a well to hold blood, which is then subjected to blunt force with a horizontally oriented head or gunshot with a vertically oriented head (Figure 1.22a and b). He introduced it to the bloodstain community at a Scientific Working Group on Bloodstain Pattern Analysis (SWGSTAIN) meeting at the FBI Academy and the IABPA training conference held in Corning, New York in 2006. Over the years, he made improvements to "Spatterhead." In 2010, he moved from pre-filled caps with pig blood to empty caps that the users could fill themselves. Andre also created synthetic blood to use it in place of pig blood, eliminating the need of refrigeration and the hazard of using real blood.[36]

Dr. Mark Reynolds formerly with the Western Australia Police and Edmund "Ted" Silenieks formerly with Forensic Science SA in South Australia, who are both currently forensic consultants, developed an 80-hour advanced fabrics bloodstain pattern analysis training course in 2011. The purpose of the course was to present an understanding of basic textile properties and how they interact with blood to affect resultant bloodstain appearance on fabrics. They have instructed the course in Australia as well as in the United States, Canada, Europe, South Africa, and Asia.

Michael Taylor and Mark Jermy developed the first course on the fluid mechanics of bloodstain pattern formation at the Institute of Environmental Science and Research (ESR) in Christchurch, New Zealand. Michael wove together fundamental theory and hands-on practice to assist analysts understand and articulate the science of bloodstain formation. Roz Rough from ESR joined the teaching team in 2015. Currently, the 40-hour course entitled "The Fluid Dynamics of Bloodstain Pattern Formation" is instructed by Mark Jermy and Roz Rough has now run 20 times in 6 countries, training 216 analysts.

As a result of the expanded opportunities in basic and advanced BPA courses since the early 1970s, thousands of police, crime scene investigators, forensic scientists, and crime laboratory personnel have received training. This has also been the stimulus for additional scientific publications concerning BPA, as well as for several textbooks and manuals.

The Canadian Mentorship Program

Bloodstain pattern analysts in Canada participate in a mentorship program as part of their training. Analysts are members of a police service except for Quebec where they are part of their

Figure 1.23 Patrick Laturnus.

Forensic Laboratory. In 1990, the Royal Canadian Mounted Police (RCMP) positioned full-time analysts across Canada within their Forensic Laboratory system. Police officers were selected for training from experienced forensic identification personnel. These officers began their training with a program lasting approximately one year.[37]

Investigators recognized the value of BPA and its need grew. Given the value of this evidence, municipal and provincial police services wanted to have bloodstain analysts as part of their own forensic team. In 1995, Patrick Laturnus moved from a full-time analyst to an instructor's position at the Canadian Police College. While there he developed the beginnings of an understudy program that would work not only for the RCMP but also for other municipal and provincial police services (Figure 1.23).

In 2001, the Canadian Police College cancelled the Bloodstain Understudy Program and Laturnus moved the program to the Ontario Police College. It was during this time that other countries trained their analysts using the Canadian system.

The Ontario Police College program requirements for each candidate include the following:

- A minimum number of bloodletting cases is required prior to this training program.
- Successful completion of an IABPA recognized basic BPA course is required.
- The candidate must identify an active, qualified bloodstain analyst to act as mentor.
- The candidate must have an access to various bloodstain analysis books and articles.
- The candidate must be able to review relevant case files provided by mentor.
- The candidate must be able to conduct an analysis of mock scenes and provide a written report.
- The candidate has to attend actual scenes with mentor.
  - Level one: mentor conducts analysis while candidate observes
  - Level two: candidate takes a more active role such as documentation.
  - Level three: candidate conducts the analysis while mentor observes.
- Successful completion of an Advanced Bloodstain Course held at the Ontario Police College is required.

- Successful completion of Math/Physics course is required.
- The candidate must submit written reports to the mentor for all actual scenes attended.
- Successful completion of a written exam is required.
- Successful completion of an oral board examination, simulating a trial, is required.
- The candidate must continue to attend bloodstain training on an annual basis.

DEVELOPMENT OF ADDITIONAL TEXTS IN BLOODSTAIN PATTERN ANALYSIS

In 1983, an important text entitled *Forensic Science – An Introduction to Criminalistics*, authored by Peter R. DeForest, professor of criminalistics at the John Jay College of Criminal Justice in New York, R.E. Gaensslen, professor of forensic science at the University of New Haven in Connecticut, and Henry C. Lee, chief criminalist at the Connecticut State Police Forensic Science Laboratory, was published. In Chapter 11 entitled "Physical Patterns" of that book, they included bloodstain pattern evidence and reconstruction.[38]

Numerous BPA texts and laboratory manuals have been published during the period from 1983 through 2020. Scientific articles pertaining to aspects of bloodstain pattern interpretation are gaining increasing visibility in well-known forensic publications, including the Journal of Forensic Sciences, the American Journal of Forensic Medicine and Pathology, the Journal of the Canadian Society of Forensic Science, and the Journal of Forensic Identification.

Bart Epstein and Terry Laber from the Minnesota Bureau of Criminal Apprehension Laboratory in St. Paul published a laboratory manual for their basic BPA course entitled "Experiments and Practical Exercises in Bloodstain Pattern Analysis" in 1983. An important feature of this manual was the development of an experiment to study the drying time of blood using controlled blood volumes on various surface textures with various air flows, temperature, and humidity levels.[39]

The first edition of the text, *Bloodstain Pattern Analysis – with an Introduction to Crime Scene Reconstruction*, authored by Tom Bevel and Ross M. Gardner, was published in 1997. The second edition was published in 2001. Both editions provided a comprehensive text of the theory and practice of BPA.[40,41] This was the first time that the principles of BPA were merged with a logical effective methodology for crime scene reconstruction. The third edition of the book published in 2008 featured a classification of bloodstains based on the taxonomy of the physical characteristics of the patterns rather than the mechanisms that created them.[42]

The text, *Interpretation of Bloodstain Evidence at Crime Scenes*, authored by Dr. William G. Eckert, MD and Stuart H. James, was published in 1989, with a second edition published in 1998. The texts featured basic theory and numerous case studies.[43,44] James edited a text entitled *Scientific and Legal Applications of Bloodstain Pattern Analysis*, which was published in 1999. This text featured a chapter on the legal and ethical aspects of BPA authored by Attorney Carol Henderson of the Stetson University College of Law, and another by Cambridge Attorney Marie Saccoccio.[45]

In 2001, the text entitled *Henry Lee's Crime Scene Handbook* was authored by Henry C. Lee, Timothy M. Palmbach, and Marilyn T. Miller from the University of New Haven and the Henry C. Lee Institute of Forensic Science at the University in New Haven in Connecticut. Chapter 10 entitled "Crime Scene Reconstruction" of that book integrates BPA and reconstruction with other pattern evidence and physical matching.[46]

In 1993, T. Paulette Sutton from the department of pathology, University of Tennessee, produced a teaching manual for her classes on the theory of BPA entitled *Bloodstain Pattern Analysis in Violent Crimes*.[47] This manual was followed with a companion laboratory manual in 1995 entitled *Experiments – Bloodstain Pattern Analysis in Violent Crimes* that provided the instructions for 14 experiments utilizing blood.[48]

Anita K. Wonder (1943–2015) was the founder and director of the Wonder Institute, a forensic science consulting, training, and research association that specialized in bloodstain pattern evidence based in Carmichael, California. She provided training and assistance to law enforcement practitioners worldwide, private investigators, and attorneys for both the prosecution and defense. She authored three significant and comprehensive textbooks during her career. The first was entitled *Blood Dynamics* published in 2001. This textbook was followed by *Bloodstain Pattern Evidence – Objective Approaches and Case Applications* in 2007. Her third textbook entitled *Bloodstain Patterns – Identification, Interpretation and Application* was published in 2015, the year of her death.[49,50,51]

The text, *Principles of Bloodstain Pattern Analysis – Theory and Practice,* authored by Stuart H. James, Paul E. Kish, and T. Paulette Sutton, was published in 2005. The book was highlighted with numerous color photographs and graphics of bloodstains and patterns. The book introduced a classification system for bloodstains and patterns based on size, shape, distribution, and the mechanism that produced them.[52] The three main categories of bloodstains and patterns were *passive, spatter,* and *altered.*

Development of Scientific Organizations – SWGSTAIN and OSAC

For almost 20 years, the Federal Bureau of Investigation (FBI) had actively organized and sponsored technical working groups (TWGs). The purpose of these groups, later renamed scientific working groups (SWGs) to distinguish them from other similarly tasked groups sponsored by the United States Department of Justice, was then the establishment of professional forums in which local, state, and federal government experts, together with academic and commercial scientists, can operate to address operational issues arising within specific forensic disciplines.

The Scientific Working Group on Bloodstain Pattern Analysis (SWGSTAIN) was created in 2002 at a meeting held by the FBI Laboratory at the FBI Academy in Quantico, Virginia. The meeting was facilitated by the Laboratory's DNA Analysis Unit I (DNAUI) and its Forensic Science Research and Training Unit (FSRTU). DNA Analyst Anthony Onorato of the FBI Laboratory served as chairman. Biannual meetings were held at the FBI Academy and nearby locations in Virginia (Figure 1.24).

Figure 1.24 SWGSTAIN logo.

SWGSTAIN operated as a professional forum in which bloodstain pattern analysts and practitioners from law enforcement, federal, state, and local laboratories, private sector, and academia participated. The group comprised experts from North America, Europe, New Zealand, and Australia. Substantive and operational issues within the discipline of BPA were addressed in order to build consensus-based, or so-called "best practice" guidelines for the enhancement of BPA. Subcommittees were organized for:

- Terminology and taxonomy
- Quality assurance
- Education and training
- Research
- Legal issues

Documents were prepared by each subcommittee and made available for public review and then adopted as official protocols. The research subcommittee produced a bibliography of bloodstain references in April 2009 that consisted of 538 publications of scientific articles and texts.[53]

In the fall of 2008, the operation of SWGSTAIN transferred sponsorship and management to the Midwest Forensics Resource Center (MFRC), a National Institute of Justice (NIJ). MFRC was operated by Ames Laboratory under contract by Iowa State University in Ames, Iowa. Dr. David Baldwin served as chairman. Biannual meetings were then held in Salt Lake City, Utah. The final SWGSTAIN meeting was held in 2012.[54]

The Organization of Scientific Area Committees (OSAC) for Forensic Science was a joint venture of the Department of Justice (DOJ) and the Department of Commerce (DOC) and managed by the National Institute of Standards and Technology (NIST) in 2014 to address a lack of discipline-specific forensic science standards. OSAC was the government's response to the National Academy of Science (NAS) report in 2009 concerning forensic science in the United States. This organization is committed to strengthening the nation's use of forensic science by facilitating development and promoting the use of high-quality technically sound standards. Proposed standards are sent to standards development organizations (SDOs), which further develop and publish them. These standards define minimum requirements, best practices, standard protocols, and other guidance to help ensure that the results of forensic analysis are reliable.[55]

There are seven scientific area committees (SACs). The BPA subcommittee is under the Physics/Pattern Interpretation SAC (Figures 1.25 and 1.26).

This committee focuses on standards and guidelines of bloodstain patterns present at crime scenes and on associated evidence. Current BPA standards and a technical report of terms and definitions have been accredited by the American National Standards Institute (ANSI), published by the SDO and the American Academy of Forensic Sciences AAFS Standards Board (ASB), and are available on the website www.asbstandardsboard.org.

- ANSI/ASB Standard 030, Standard for a Quality Assurance Program in Bloodstain Pattern Analysis, First Edition, 2019
- ANSI/ASB Standard 031, Standards for Report Writing in Bloodstain Pattern Analysis, First Edition, 2020
- ANSI/ASB Standard 032, Standards for a Bloodstain Analyst's Training Program, First Edition, 2020
- ASB Technical Report 033, Terms and Definitions in Bloodstain Pattern Analysis, First Edition, 2017
- ANSI/ASB Standard 072, Standard for the Validation of Procedures in Bloodstain Pattern Analysis, First Edition, 2019

In January, 2021, the BPA research task group produced an updated Bloodstain Pattern Analysis Bibliography (Revision 3) that consisted of 1,326 bloodstain related articles and texts. This bibliography historically began as the Bibliography Project generated by SWGSTAIN and continues to be updated periodically.[56] This bibliography is available on the OSAC website, www.nist.gov.

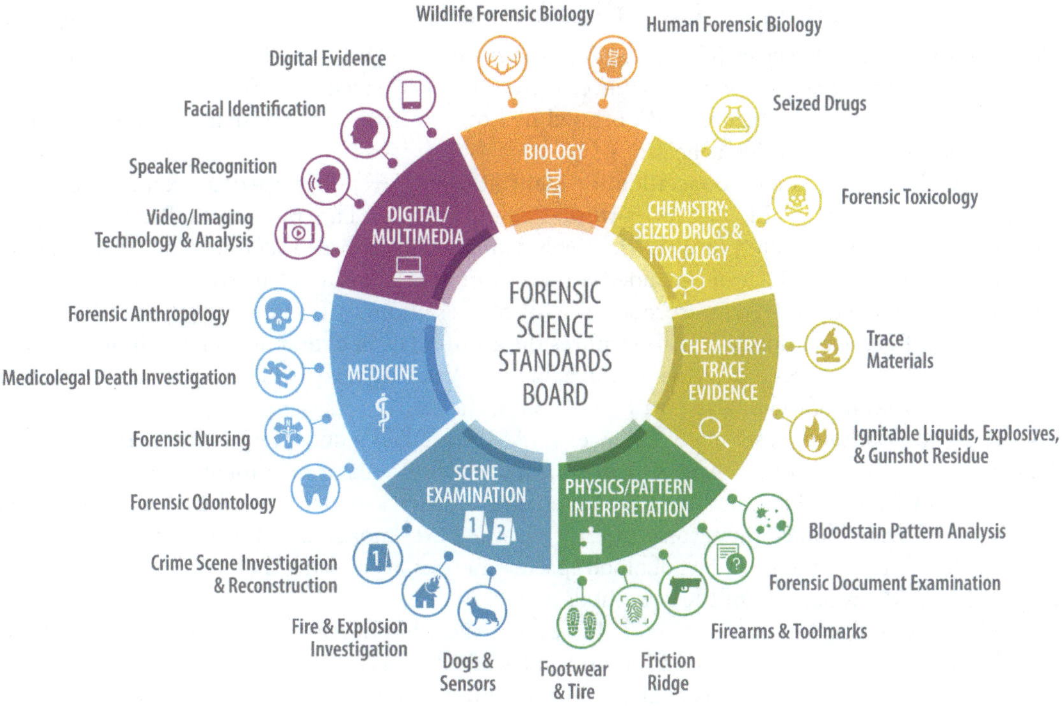

Figure 1.25 OSAC organizational structure.

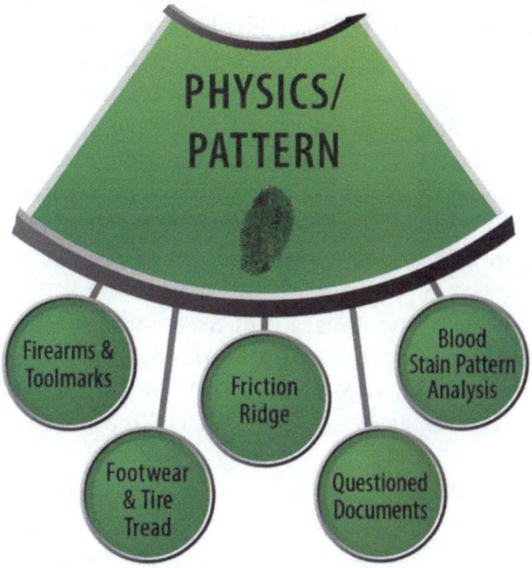

Figure 1.26 BPA as a subcommittee is under the Physics/Pattern Interpretation SAC.

In 2019, Gabriele Rotter from Gabinetto Regionale di Polizia Scientifica per la Calabria in Reggio Calabria, Italy coordinated a working group of five additional BPA specialists from various forensic laboratories of the Italian Police Forces and from the academic world. The ultimate goal of the group was to set standards and terminology, both in scientific and judicial fields. They translated the BPA list of terms and definitions recommended by (OSAC) into Italian. The Italian translation was published in January 2020 in the IABPA website.[57]

Proficiency Testing and Certification in Bloodstain Pattern Analysis

Collaborative Testing Services (CTS) and Forensic Assurance (FA) have been offering proficiency tests in numerous areas of forensic science, including BPA, since the 1970s and 2013, respectively.[58,59] The proficiency test for BPA offered by both organizations consists of angle of impact measurements and pattern identifications.

In 1998, the International Association for Identification (IAI) developed an examination protocol for certification as Bloodstain Pattern Examiner,1998. The Bloodstain Pattern Analyst Certification Test was created in 2012 that included an analysis-based section. The requirements for an applicant for certification included a minimum of 240 hours of instruction in associated fields of study related to BPA/interpretation. Out of those hours, 100 hours must be in BPA specific training. Recertification in 5 years requires the accumulation of 50 hours of continuing education/professional development credits in the field of BPA during the previous 5-year period as well as successful passing of the analysis-based portion of the test.[60]

In 2009, the National Academy of Sciences (NAS) published a document entitled *Strengthening Forensic Science in the United States: A Path Forward*. This important document included a critical assessment of BPA, which concluded that the uncertainties associated with BPA are enormous and that purported bloodstain pattern experts' opinions are "more subjective than scientific." The report highlighted several incidents of blood spatter analysts overstating their qualifications as well as questioning the reliability of their methods.[61]

The issues of cognitive and contextual biases and their implications for forensic practice have been hotly debated and researched in forensic and academic circles over the last decade. The 2009 NAS report on the state of forensic science in the United States and the 2016 President's Council of Advisors on Science and Technology (PCAST) report on forensic science recommended that forensic practitioners address issues relating to bias in forensic science and provide evidence to the fact finder that they have done so. The PCAST report referred to cognitive bias as ways in which human perceptions and judgments can be shaped by factors other than those relevant to the decision at hand. The report included cognitive bias where individuals are influenced by irrelevant background information, and confirmation bias where individuals look for new evidence in a way that conforms to their pre-existing beliefs or assumptions.[62]

In 2015, Rachel Zajac, Nikola Osborne, Lee Ann Singley, and Michael Taylor authored an article entitled "Contextual Bias: What Bloodstain Pattern Analysts Need to Know," which was published in the *Journal of Bloodstain Pattern Analysis*. They introduced the notion of the potential contextual bias in BPA and the implications of this bias as an expert witness in the courtroom.[63]

At the time, Dr. Nikola Osborne, was a full-time forensic research scientist at ESR in Christchurch, New Zealand. Dr. Osborne and Dr. Mark Reynolds currently instruct a course entitled "Contextual Bias in Forensic Science. What It Is, How Do We Detect It and What Can We Do about It" for bloodstain pattern analysts. This topic is discussed in more detail in Chapter 37.

Development of Directional Analysis Software for Bloodstain Pattern Analysis

Dr. Alfred L. Carter (1930–2014) was a professor of physics at Carleton University in Ottawa, Ontario, Canada. He received his PhD in physics from McGill University in Montreal, Quebec. He spent over 40 years in teaching, including 29 years at Carleton University, and was a pioneer in the development of BPA software. (Figure 1.27).

In 1982, the RCMP requested Dr. Carter's assistance to create a course in BPA to better understand the mathematics and physics involved. He studied what was known of the discipline and then introduced the first course. His course focused on the underpinning science and built the foundation of confident analysis. The Math/Physics course continues to be updated and is still taught today.

Figure 1.27 Dr. Alfred Carter at his office at Carleton University. (Courtesy of Pat Laturnus, Private Consultant, Ottawa, Ontario, Canada.)

In 1989, Dr. Carter had the vision to realize how computers could help BPA analysts with the tedious work of measuring impact patterns. The result was his advent of *BackTrack*™, a computer program that increased the accuracy of bloodstain measurements and the determination of areas of convergence and origin in 1992. His son, Brian Carter, was a computer programmer and they built this program together. The program was also extremely efficient in comparison to other methods such as the stringing technique.

Dr. Carter's article entitled "The Directional Analysis of Bloodstain Patterns – Theory and Experimental Validation" was published in the *Journal of the Canadian Society of Forensic Science* in 2001.[64] He contributed a chapter entitled "Bloodstain Pattern Analysis with a Computer" in the text entitled *Scientific and Legal Applications of Bloodstain Pattern Interpretation* in 1998.[65] His chapter "Directional Analysis of Bloodstain Patterns with a Computer" in the text *Principles of Bloodstain Pattern Analysis – Theory and Practice* was published in 2005.[66]

Dr. Carter continued to be exposed to the reality of bloodstain scenes and quickly realized the implications of his program. He attended IABPA conferences on a regular basis and was quick to share his knowledge and expertise. He was honored as a Distinguished Member of the IABPA in 1999.

Andy Maloney, a computer software programmer, and his brother, Kevin Maloney, a forensic identification officer at the Ottawa Police Services, collaborated on a project to improve software for impact pattern analysis. A prototype was developed to make a more modern tool based on the same principles as Dr. Carter's BackTrack™ that was accepted in the discipline of BPA.[67] The prototype was named *HemoSpat* and released in 2006 by the company FORident Software founded by Andy Maloney. Based on photographs of impact spatters and scene documentation, the program calculated angles of impact and areas of origin. The main focus of *HemoSpat* was on usability, data freedom, and open science. Ellipse fitting was improved and more usable and the program worked on any planar surface unlike *BackTrack*™. The program also allowed the analysis of multiple impact patterns within one project. It was important that the program was transparent (open science) as demonstrated in the publication of articles in scientific literature.[68] Building on the same methods within HemoSpat, research on cast-off patterns and how they might be analyzed and presented in a useful manner with 3D modeling software.[69] Its first version was released in 2006 and there have been 30 updates to HemoSpat through 2021. The second version of HemoSpat, with 3D viewing capabilities, new PDF reporting, and experimental cast-off analysis, is being developed. This topic is discussed in more detail in Chapter 31 of this textbook.

Development of High-Speed Videos of Bloodstain Producing Mechanisms

The use of video film cameras for the demonstration of bloodstain producing mechanisms was initiated in the early 1990s. Jerry Chisum from California Criminalistics Institute, a unit of California Department of Justice in Sacramento, produced a regular video entitled *Slow Motion Blood Drop Studies* in 1991. [70] This was followed by the work of Dan Rahn of the RCMP in Edmonton, Canada, who produced the first known high-speed video entitled *High Speed Photography on Bloodstains* in 1993.[71] The video entitled *Blood in Slow Motion* was produced at the Metropolitan Police Forensic Science Laboratory in London by Forensic Scientists, Adrian Emes and Chris Price in 1993.[72] The video demonstrated mechanisms, including spatter produced by a hammer striking blood, blood dripping into blood, and blood drops striking an angular surface accompanied with a musical background. This classical work was recognized as an important contribution to BPA.

The modern definitive work with high-speed video production began in 2007 and was completed in 2008 by Terry L. Laber from the Minnesota Bureau of Criminal Apprehension Forensic Science Laboratory, criminalist and forensic consultant, Bart P. Epstein, and Michael C. Taylor from ESR in Christchurch, New Zealand. Over 500 individual high-speed digital video clips were prepared that demonstrated impact spatter, gunshot spatter, expiration, cast-off, and projected and contact bloodstaining. The clips were primarily designed to be of assistance to instructors of bloodstain pattern courses. They were permitted to be used for any presentation or project with appropriate acknowledgement of their source. The project was primarily supported by an NIJ grant from the MFRC in Ames, Iowa and Crown Research Institute (CRI) Capability Funds from ESR in New Zealand.[73] High-speed videos are available and can be downloaded from the Resource section of the IABPA website, www.iabpa.org. This topic is discussed in more detail in Chapter 15, Article 1.

Laser Scanning Technology for the Determination of the Area of Origin of Bloodstains

Eugene Liscio is a professional engineer in the province of Ontario, Canada and is an adjunct professor at the University of Toronto, Mississauga, where he teaches a 3D forensic mapping and reconstruction course and supports student research projects. In 2015, an article by Liscio et al. entitled "A Preliminary Validation of the Use of 3D Scanning for Bloodstain Pattern Analysis" was published in the 2015 issue of the *Journal of Bloodstain Pattern Analysis*.[74] This article was followed another article entitled "Calculating Point of Origin of Blood Spatter Using Laser Scanning Technology" published in the *Journal of Forensic Sciences* in 2016.[75] One more article entitled "The Accuracy of Laser Scanning Technology on the Determination of Bloodstain Origin" was also published in 2016 in the *Canadian Society of Forensic Science*.[76]

Additional research was conducted to determine the accuracy of the Faro Focus 3D laser scanner paired with the Faro scene software for estimating the area of origin on a complex surface. The results were published in an article entitled "3D Bloodstain Pattern Analysis on Complex Surfaces Using the FARO Focus Laser Scanner" in the *Journal of Bloodstain Pattern Analysis* in 2016 (Figure 1.28).[77]

In 2020, Liscio et al. published an article entitled "Observations and 3D Analysis of Controlled Cast-off Stains" in the *Journal of Forensic Sciences*. In this article, he outlined a method of using 3D laser scanner and associated software to assist in determining the path volume envelope (PVE), which is a volume in space that encloses part of the object's swing path. He continues to pursue research and validation studies in this area.[78] This topic is discussed in more detail in Chapter 33.

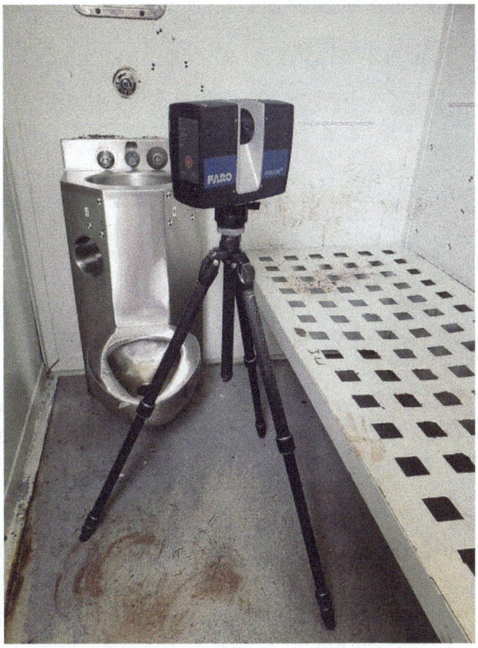

Figure 1.28 View of 3D laser scanner. (Courtesy of Eugene Liscio.)

Development of the Use of Infrared Photography for the Documentation of Bloodstains on Dark Surfaces and Clothing

Robert Williams Wood (1865–1955) was an optical physicist and a pioneer in the development of ultraviolet and infrared photography (Figure 1.29). He developed Wood's light or lamp that has medical and laboratory use. He earned several degrees in physics from Harvard University, the Massachusetts Institute of Technology, and the University of Chicago. Several of his photographs appeared in the October 1910 issue of the *Royal Photographic Society Journal*, including

Figure 1.29 Robert Williams Wood 1865–1955.

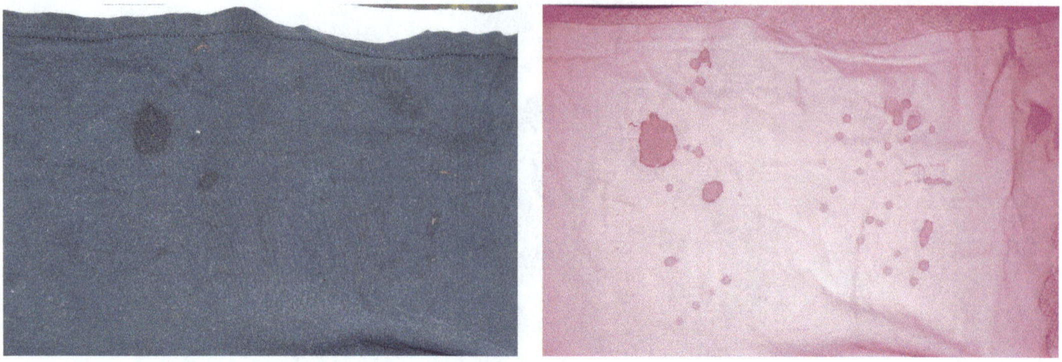

Figure 1.30 (a) Digital image of front bottom of black tank top (Courtesy of Anna Cox, Cox Forensic Consulting and Training, LLC, Brandon, Florida.) and (b) infrared image of bottom of black tank top showing visible enhancement of bloodstains. (Courtesy of Anna Cox, Cox Forensic Consulting and Training, LLC, Brandon, Florida.)

the so-called "Wood effect," which was a dream-like appearance of photographs in the infrared. By the 1960s, Kodak introduced 35 mm false-color infrared film and the popularity of infrared photography boomed. This popularity was driven in part by its use in pop music album covers by rock stars, Jimi Hendrix and Frank Zappa.[79]

In 2004, an article entitled "The Application of Infrared Photography in Bloodstain Pattern Documentation of Clothing" authored by Michael Perkins from the Las Vegas Metropolitan Police Department was published in the *Journal of Forensic Identification*. He noted that the procedure was specifically mentioned in texts as early as 1961 but noticeably absent until this publication. He also observed that the infrared technique worked best with solid dark-colored and patterned fabrics because color caused interference with the bloodstain visibility.[80]

In 2016, the *International Journal of Legal Medicine* published an article entitled "Reconstruction of Crimes by Infrared Photography" by Sterzik and Bohnert, which described the infrared photography of dark bloodstained clothing. Its authors emphasized the difficulty of the human eye to detect bloodstains because of the low contrast to the background. In the near infrared wavelength (beyond 830 nm), the contrast is considerably higher as blood absorbs the light and appears darker, whereas many dark fabrics reflect this light. The method was able to distinguish between spatter stains, drop stains, and contact stains, but only suitable to detect blood with little or no dilution.[81]An example of the use of infrared photography to detect bloodstains on dark clothing is shown in Figure 1.30a and b.

In 2020, an article entitled "An Evaluation of Infrared Photography for Detecting Bloodstains on Dark-Coloured Floor Coverings Commonly Encountered at Crime Scenes" by Arlie et al. was published in the *Australian Journal of Forensic Sciences*. Their results supported infrared photography as an effective, non-destructive method compared to tetramethylbenzidine (TMB) and luminol on several dark surfaces, including nylon carpet, tile, laminate, and vinyl.[82]

Research and Development of a Blood Substitute

In 2015, Theresa Stotesbury et al. provided a brief introduction to the importance of developing a synthetic blood substitute (SBS) for use in crime scene reconstruction, training, and research in the *Journal of Bloodstain Pattern Analysis*.[83] This would be an entirely separate class of SBS that has been created for medical purposes. The article described the features that an SBS can offer:

- Contains only non-hazardous components to meet the requirements of basic health and safety codes

- Uses components with long-term stability to avoid the effects of clotting, hemolysis, and/or acidosis for use at ambient temperatures
- Bypasses need for ethics approval
- Creates cost-effective alternatives to whole blood

Further research and development of SBS was described in the article entitled "The Application of Silicon Sol-Gel Technology to Forensic Blood Substitute Development: Mimicking Aspects of Whole Human Blood Rheology" by Stotesbury et al. that was published in *Forensic Science International* in 2016.[84]

ACKNOWLEDGMENTS FOR CONTRIBUTIONS OF REFERENCES AND PHOTOGRAPHS

Gabriele Rotter, Italian State Police Regional Forensic Science Office, Reggio Calabria, Italy

Philippe Esperanca, Laboratoire d'Analyses Criminalistiques, Marseille, France and Bibliotheque de France)

Tom Bevel, Oklahoma City, Oklahoma

Patrick Laturnus, Ottawa, Canada

David Baldwin, Midwest Forensics Resource Center, Iowa State University, Ames, Iowa

Silke Brodbeck, Blutspureninstitut, Usingen, Germany

Andy Maloney, Ottawa, Canada

Kacper Chromanski, University of Warsaw, Poland

Notes

1. Bayard, Enrico and Giovanni Duodo, *Manuale Pratico di Medicina Legale*, Cecchini Publishing Co., Venice, Italy, 1846, pp. 234–235.
2. Tidy, Charles M., *Legal Medicine*, Smith, Elder & Co., London, 1882, pp. 212–213.
3. Woodman, William Bathurst and Charles Meymott Tidy, *A Handy Book of Forensic Medicine and Toxicology*, J & A Churchill, London, 1877, p. 580.
4. Gross, Hans, *Handbuch für Untersuchungsrichter als System der Kriminalistik*, Richter, Munich, Germany, 1893.
5. Lapponi, Giuseppe, "Segni per Ladeterminazione Fiscio-biologica Della Identità", in *Compendio di Medicina Legale*, Tipo Poliglotta Publishing Co., Rome, Italy, 1894, pp. 265–208.
6. Damulewicz, Anna, "Doktor Eduard Piotrowski–Zapomniany Prekursor Badań nad Dynamiką Sadów Krwawych Paradygmaty Kryminalistyki", (Eduard Piotrowski, Forgotten Researcher of Research on the Dynamics of Bloody Traces) ed. Józef Wójcikiewicz, Violetta Kwiatkowska-Wójcikiewicz, Kraków, 2016. Thesis of Anna Damulewicz at Jagiellonian University.
7. MacDonell, Herbert Leon, "The Literature of Bloodstain Pattern Interpretation - Segments of History through the 1800's", *IABPA News*, 8 (1), March 1992, pp. 3–12.
8. Piotrowski, Eduard, *Uber Entstehung, Form, Richtung und Ausbreitung der Blutspuren nach Hibwundendes Kopfes*, K.K. Universitat, Wein, 1895.
9. MacDonell, Herbert Leon, "The Literature of Bloodstain Pattern Interpretation - Segments of History, 1901–1910", *IABPA News*, 8 (4), December 1992, pp. 5–22.
10. Glaister, John, *Jurisprudence, Toxicology and Public Health*, Livingston Publishing Co., Edinburgh, Scotland, 1902, pp. 234–241.
11. Florence, Albert, "Les Taches de Sang au Laboratories de Medicine Legal de Lyon", *Archives de Anthropologie Criminelle*, 16, 1901, pp. 255–269.
12. Wood, Edward S., "Medico-Legal Examination of Blood Stains", *Boston Medical and Surgical*, v. CXLV (20), 1901, pp. 533–537.
13. "Detection of Crime by Photography", *The Albany Law Journal*, 529, December 1893.
14. MacDonell, Herbert Leon, "The Literature of Bloodstain Pattern Interpretation - Segments of History, 1911–1920", *IABPA News*, 9 (2), June 1993, pp. 4–10.

15. Ziemke, Ernst, "Die Untersuchung von Blutspuren (The Investigation of Blood and Traces of Blood)", *Gerichtsärztliche und Polizerärzliche Technik (Forensic and Police Medical Technology)* by Theodore Lochte, Weisbaden, Germany, 1914.
16. Ziemke, Ernst, in Emil Abderhalden's, *Handbuch Biologischen Arbeitsmethoden (Handbook of Biological Working Methods)* v. 12, sect IV, Wein Urban und Schwarzenberg, Vienna, Austria,1924, pp. 179–122.
17. MacDonell, Herbert Leon, "The Literature of Bloodstain Pattern Interpretation - Segments of History 1921–1930", *IABPA News,* 10 (1), March 1994, pp. 6–14.
18. Balthazard, Victor, Renè Piedelièvre, Henry DeSoille, and Lèon DèRobert, *Etude des Gouttes de Sang Projecte.* Presented at the 22nd Congress of Forensic Medicine, Paris, France, 1939.
19. Balthazard, Victor, Renè Piedelievre, Henry DeSoille, and Lèon DèRobert, "Etude des Gouttes de Sang Projecte", *Annales de Medecine Legale, Criminologie, Police Scientifique et Toxicologie,* 19, 1939, pp. 265–323.
20. Esperanca, Phillippe Laboratoire d'Analyses Criminalistiques, Marseille, France, Personal Communication, February 2021.
21. Snyder, Lemoyne, "Chapter 4, Examination of Bloodstains", in *Homicide Investigation,* 2nd Edition, Charles C. Thomas, Springfield, Illinois, 1973, pp. 53–56.
22. Kirk, Paul L., *Crime Investigation,* 2nd Edition, John Wiley and Sons, New York, 1974, pp. 167–181.
23. Kirk, Paul L., Affidavit in the *State of Ohio v. Samuel Sheppard* in the Court of Common Pleas Criminal Branch No. 64571, 1955.
24. MacDonell, Herbert L. and Lorraine Fiske Bialousz, *Flight Characteristics and Stain Patterns of Human Blood,* United States Department of Justice, Law Enforcement Administration Assistance, Washington, DC, 1971.
25. MacDonell, Herbert L., *Bloodstain Patterns, 2nd Revised Edition,* Gola Printing Co., Elmira Heights, NY, 2005.
26. MacDonell, Herbert L. and Lorraine Fiske Bialousz, L., *Laboratory Manual on the Geometric Interpretation of Human Bloodstain Evidence,* Painted Post Press, Painted Post, New York, 1973.
27. MacDonell, Herbert L., "Institute on the Physical Significance of Bloodstain Evidence", *Identification News,* June 1973.
28. *IABPA News,* Issue 1, No. 1 June 1984, pp. 2–3.
29. www.iabpa.org
30. Brodbeck, Silke, Blutspureninstitut, Usingen, Germany – Personal communication.
31. Hendrix, Andre, *Bloodstain Pattern Analysis,* Department of Public Relations and Press, Zeeland Police Force, The Netherlands, 2006.
32. Rocky Mountain Association of Bloodstain Pattern Analysts www.rmabpa.org
33. Association of Crime Scene Reconstruction, www.acsr.org
34. Rotter, Gabriele, Italian State Police Regional Forensic Science Office, Reggio Calabria, Italy – Personal Communication.
35. Choi, Yong-Seok, Patrick Laturnus, Brian Yamashita, and Jim Killeen, "Korea's Approach to Bloodstain Pattern Analysis Training", *IABPA News,* 26 (3), September 2010, pp. 1–9.
36. Anyon, Andre, Personal communication, www.forensicbodies.com
37. Laturnus, Patrick, Ottawa, Canada – Personal Communication February 2021.
38. DeForest, Peter R., Robert E. Gaensslen, and Henry C. Lee, *Forensic Science – An Introduction to Criminalistics,* McGraw-Hill, New York, 1983, pp. 295–308.
39. Laber, Terry L. and Barton P. Epstein, *Experiments and Practical Exercises in Bloodstain Pattern Analysis,* Callen Publishing, Minneapolis, Minnesota, 1983, pp. 100–104.
40. Bevel, Tom and Ross M. Gardner, *Bloodstain Pattern Analysis with an Introduction to Crime Scene Reconstruction,* 1st Edition, CRC Press, Boca Raton, Florida, 1997.
41. Bevel, Tom and Ross M. Gardner, *Bloodstain Pattern Analysis with an Introduction to Crime Scene Reconstruction,* 2nd Edition, CRC Press, Boca Raton, Florida, 2001.
42. Bevel, Tom and Ross M. Gardner, *Bloodstain Pattern Analysis with an Introduction to Crime Scene Reconstruction,* 3rd Edition, CRC Press, Boca Raton, Florida, 2008.
43. Eckert, William G. and Stuart H. James, *Interpretation of Bloodstain Evidence at Crime Scenes,* CRC Press, Boca Raton, Florida, 1989.
44. Eckert, William G. and Stuart H. James, *Interpretation of Bloodstain Evidence at Crime Scenes,* 2nd Edition, CRC Press, Boca Raton, Florida, 1998.

45. James, Stuart H., Ed., *Scientific and Legal Applications of Bloodstain Pattern Analysis*, CRC Press, Boca Raton, Florida, 1999.
46. Lee, Henry C., Tim Palmbach, and T. Marilyn Miller, *Henry Lee's Crime Scene Handbook*, Elsevier Academic Press, New York, 2001, pp. 281–298.
47. Sutton, T. Paulette, *Bloodstain Pattern Analysis in Violent Crimes*, University of Tennessee, Memphis, Tennessee, 1993.
48. Sutton, T. Paulette, *Experiments - Bloodstain Pattern Analysis in Violent Crimes*, University of Tennessee, Memphis, Tennessee, 1993.
49. Wonder, Anita Y., *Blood Dynamics*, Academic Press, London, 2001.
50. Wonder, Anita Y., *Bloodstain Pattern Evidence—Objective Approaches and Case Applications*, Elsevier, New York, 2007.
51. Wonder, Anita Y., *Bloodstain Patterns – Identification, Interpretation and Application*, Elsevier, New York, 2015.
52. James, Stuart H., Paul E. Kish, and T. Paulette Sutton, *Principles of Bloodstain Pattern Analysis, Theory and Practice*, CRC Press, Boca Raton, Florida, 2005, pp. 3–7.
53. Scientific Working Group on Bloodstain Pattern Analysis (SWGSTAIN) Research Subcommittee, *Bibliography Project – Bloodstain Pattern Analysis*, 2009.
54. Baldwin, David, Midwest Forensics Resource Center, Iowa State University, Ames, Iow Personal Communication.
55. Organization of Scientific Area Subcommittees (OSAC) website, www.nist.gov
56. Bloodstain Pattern Analysis Research Task Group, Bloodstain Pattern Analysis Subcommittee, Organization of Scientific Area Subcommittees (OSAC) for Forensic Science, *Bloodstain Pattern Analysis Bibliography*—Revision 3, Updated in 2021.
57. IABPA website. www.iabpa.org
58. Collaborative Testing Services (CTS) website, www.cts-forensics.com
59. Forensic Assurance (FA) website, www.forensicassurance.com
60. International Association for Identification website, www.theiai.org
61. Committee on Identifying the Needs of the Forensic Sciences Community, National Research Council, *Strengthening Forensic Science in the United States: A Path Forward*, National Academy of Sciences, National Academies Press, 2009, pp. 24. 177–179.
62. President's Council of Advisors on Science and Technology Report to the President, *Forensic Science in Criminal Courts: Ensuring Scientific Validity of Feature-Comparison Methods*, 2016, p. 31.
63. Zajac, Rachel, Nikola K.P. Osborne, LeAnn Singley and Michael C. Taylor, "Contextual Bias: What Bloodstain Pattern Analysts Need to Know", *Journal of Bloodstain Pattern Analysis*, 31 (2), 2015, pp. 7–16.
64. Carter, Alfred L., "The Directional Analysis of Bloodstain Patterns- Theory and Experimental Validation", *Journal of the Canadian Society of Forensic Science*, 34 (4), 2001, pp. 173–179.
65. James, Stuart H., Ed., *Scientific and Legal Applications of Bloodstain Pattern Analysis*, CRC Press, Boca Raton, Florida, 1999, pp. 17–28.
66. James, Stuart H., Paul E. Kish and T. Paulette Sutton, "Chapter 12, Directional Analysis of Bloodstain Patterns with a Computer", A.L. Carter (Ed.), *Principles of Bloodstain Pattern Analysis – Theory and Practice*, 2005, pp. 241–261.
67. Maloney, Andy, Céline Nicloux, Kevin Maloney and Franck Heron, "One-sided Impact Spatter and Area of Origin Calculations", *Journal of Forensic Identification*, 61 (2), 2011, pp. 123–135.
68. Maloney, Kevin, Jim Killeen and Andy Maloney, "The Use of HemoSpat to Include Bloodstains Located on Nonorthogonal Surfaces in Area of Origin Calculations", *Journal of Forensic Identification*, 59 (5), 2009, pp. 513–524.
69. Maloney, Andy, Todd Campbell and Jim Killeen, "Visualization of Cast-off Patterns Using 3D Modelling Software, *Journal of the Association of Crime Scene Reconstruction*, 17 (4), 2011, pp. 49–56.
70. Chisum, Jerry, *High Speed Photography on Bloodstains*, California Criminalistics Institute, California Department of Justice, Sacramento, California, 1991.
71. Rahn, Dan, *High Speed Photography on Bloodstains*, RCMP, Edmonton, Alberta, Canada, 1993.
72. Emes, Adrian and Chris Price, *Blood in Slow Motion*, Metropolitan Police Forensic Science Laboratory, London, Video, 1994.
73. Laber, Terry L., Barton P. Epstein and Michael C. Taylor, "High Speed Digital Video Analysis of Bloodstain Pattern Formation from Common Bloodletting Mechanisms – Project Report", MFRC Project No. 06-S-02, *IABPA News*, 24 (2), June 2008, pp. 4–12.

74. Liscio, Eugene, Sandro, Bortat, John Frankcom, Tonya Hackenbrook, Jeffrey Inch, Robert Lamarche, Trevor Penney, Brian Allen, Fons Chafe and Brian Yamashita, "A Preliminary Validation of the Use of 3D Scanning for Bloodstain Pattern Analysis", *Journal of Bloodstain Pattern Analysis*, 31 (3), December 2015, pp. 3–10.
75. Hakim, Nashad and Eugene Liscio, "Calculating Point of Origin of Blood Spatter Using Laser Scanning Technology", *Journal of Forensic Sciences*, 60 (2), 2015, pp. 409–417.
76. Le, Rebecca and Eugene Liscio, "The Accuracy of Laser Scanning Technology on the Determination of Bloodstain Origin", *Canadian Society of Forensic Science Journal*, 49 (1) 2016, pp. 38–51.
77. Kwan, Nathan, Eugene Liscio and Tracy Rogers, "3D Bloodstain Pattern Analysis on Complex Surfaces Using the FARO Locus laser Scanner", *Journal of Bloodstain Pattern Analysis*, 32 (2), 2016, pp. 21–27.
78. Liscio, Eugene, Patrick Bosek, Helen Guryn and Quan Le, "Observations and 3D Analysis of Controlled Cast-off Stains", *Journal of Forensic Sciences*, 65 (4), July, 2020, pp. 1128–1140.
79. Vos, David, Ed., "This Month in Physics History—October 1910 – First Infrared Photographs Published", *American Physical Society (APS) News*, 26 (9), October 2017, p. 1.
80. Perkins, Michael, "The Application of Infrared Photography in Bloodstain Documentation of Clothing", *Journal of Forensic Identification*, 55 (1), 2005, pp. 1–9.
81. Sterzik, Vera and Michael Bohnert, "Reconstruction of Crimes by Infrared Photography", *International Journal of Legal Medicine*, 130 (5), September 2016, pp. 1379–1385.
82. Airlie, Melissa, Janet Chaseling, Matt N. Krosch and Kirsty Wright, "An Evaluation of Infrared Photography for Detecting Bloodstains on Dark-Coloured Floor Coverings Commonly Encountered at Crime Scenes", *Australian Journal of Forensic Sciences*, Online Abstract, 54 (2), August 2020, pp. 280–292.
83. Stotesbury, Theresa Michael Illes, Paul Wilson and Andrew J. Vreugdenhil, "A Commentary of Synthetic Blood Research and Development", *Journal of Bloodstain Pattern Analysis*, 31 (2), September 2015, pp. 3–6.
84. Stotesbury, Theresa, Michael Illes, Paul Wilson, and Andrew J. Vreugdenhil, A., "The Application of Silicon Sol-Gel Technology to Forensic Blood Substitute Development: Mimicking Aspects of Whole Human Blood Rheology", *Forensic Science International*, 270, 14 November 2016, pp. 12–19.

CHAPTER 2

HEALTH, SAFETY, AND BLOODBORNE PATHOGENS

Scene and Evidence Protocols

Amy Santoro

INTRODUCTION

The very thing that brings the bloodstain pattern analyst to a crime scene poses a significant threat to the analyst. Blood carries with it not only a large volume of useful information but also the threat of bloodborne pathogens. To operate safely at a crime scene, the bloodstain pattern analyst must be aware of bloodborne pathogens, universal precautions, and the proper use of personal protective equipment (PPE).

BLOODBORNE PATHOGENS

Bloodborne pathogens are viruses and microorganisms present in human blood which can cause disease.[1] In addition to blood, analysts must also use caution when faced with other potentially infectious materials (OPIM), which are human tissues, organs, and human body fluids, including but not limited to semen, vaginal secretions, cerebrospinal fluid, and saliva.[2] While there are many bloodborne pathogens, the primary concern of a bloodstain pattern analyst is related to two main threats when dealing with blood: HIV and hepatitis.

HIV

Human immunodeficiency virus (HIV) attacks the body's immune system and, when left untreated, leads to acquired immunodeficiency syndrome (AIDS). While there are medical treatments that can control HIV and allow people infected with HIV to live long, healthy lives, there is currently no cure for HIV.

The most likely route of transmission of HIV in the workplace is a needle stick or puncture from some other sharp object contaminated with HIV positive blood. Fortunately, HIV does not survive long outside the body, and it cannot reproduce outside a host body. However, with respect to blood contained within a used syringe, research indicates that HIV can survive for up to 42 days.[3]

There is no single answer for how long HIV can survive outside the body. The conditions of the blood (dry or wet), environmental temperature, exposure to sunlight and humidity, blood volume, and viral load all impact the survival time of HIV outside the body and therefore the potential for

DOI: 10.4324/9781003163695-2

infection following exposure. Additionally, HIV is transmitted not only through blood, but also through other body fluids that may be encountered at a crime scene, including semen, vaginal fluids, and breast milk. For these reasons, the analyst should exercise caution and always utilize universal precautions.

Hepatitis

Hepatitis, meaning inflammation of the liver, is caused by viral infection. Of most concern to the bloodstain pattern analyst are hepatitis A, B, and C. While perhaps less considered than HIV, the threat of hepatitis infection is quite real, with the Centers for Disease Control (CDC) estimating that over two million people in the United States live with hepatitis C.[4] There are tens of thousands of new hepatitis A, B, and C infections each year.[5]

Hepatitis A infections are often the result of foodborne outbreaks and are common in countries lacking modern sanitation. In more developed regions, hepatitis A outbreaks still occur and person-to-person transmission is possible. Hepatitis A is spread when a person ingests fecal material, which is usually the result of contact with contaminated food. The hepatitis A virus is capable of surviving outside the body for months. Hepatitis A infections can last for weeks to months, and while most patients recover with no lasting liver damage, death can occur. Fortunately, proper sanitation can reduce the risk of hepatitis A infection. Additionally, an effective vaccine to prevent against hepatitis A infection is available. The CDC recommends hepatitis A vaccination in childhood. Bloodstain pattern analysts should evaluate their vaccination history and seek inoculation against hepatitis A if they have not previously received proper doses of the vaccine. While the precise duration of protection from hepatitis A infection in the inoculated person is unknown, studies have shown that antibodies persist for at least 20 years.

Hepatitis B is spread by contact with infected body fluids, including blood and semen. The hepatitis B virus can survive outside the body and remain potentially infectious for at least seven days. Some patients infected with hepatitis B experience only a mild illness lasting a few weeks, but some infected patients develop chronic conditions and serious complications. The CDC reports that 15%–25% of chronically infected patients develop liver disease, liver failure, or liver cancer. In fact, hepatitis B infection is a leading cause of liver cancer.[6] Since hepatitis B is transmitted in blood, the analyst should be cautious when dealing with potentially contaminated objects, especially contaminated needles or other sharp objects, which are the prime routes of exposure. Fortunately, a safe and effective vaccine against hepatitis B is available. The Occupational Safety and Health Administration (OSHA) mandates that employers develop exposure control plans and make hepatitis B vaccinations available to all employees having occupational exposure. OSHA defines workers with occupational exposure as any worker who has a reasonably anticipated contact with blood during performance of their job duties. Due to OSHA mandates, the vaccine must be offered to employees in the United States at no cost. If not previously inoculated, bloodstain pattern analysts should refer to their department's exposure control plan for guidance on seeking vaccination. Studies have shown that protection from hepatitis B infection lasts for at least 30 years in healthy, previously vaccinated patients.[7]

Hepatitis C is spread via the blood of an infected person. When blood from an infected person enters the bloodstream of an uninfected person, transmission of the virus occurs. In the United States, hepatitis C infection is the most common bloodborne infection; so, the likelihood is great that bloodstain pattern analysts will be confronted with infected blood at some point in their career. Unfortunately, the CDC estimates that half of people infected with hepatitis C do not know they are infected. Hepatitis C can survive outside a host body for several days. If infected, patients may experience mild symptoms or chronic, lifelong infection, with most infected patients developing chronic hepatitis C. Hepatitis C infection is a leading cause of liver transplants and liver cancer. Fortunately, modern treatment options exist for patients dealing with chronic hepatitis C infections, with newer oral therapies offering curative effects to more than 90% of treated patients (CDC). Hepatitis C infection is of particular concern to the bloodstain pattern analyst not only because of the potential for chronic illness but also because there is no vaccine to protect against hepatitis C infection. To protect against exposure to hepatitis C, the bloodstain pattern analyst must employ caution, take universal precautions, and be especially aware of needle stick and other puncture hazards.

Other Diseases

Although hepatitis and HIV are of primary concern to the bloodstain pattern analyst, they are not the only disease risks posed when processing a crime scene. Leptospirosis is a zoonotic bacterial disease which is spread through the urine of infected animals, including rodents and domestic canines. Humans can be infected by contacting infected urine, either by ingestion or absorption through broken skin and mucous membranes.[8] While an uncommon hazard, the bloodstain pattern analyst should be especially aware of leptospirosis risk when processing crime scenes with evidence of rodent infestation. In these situations, as with all crime scenes, the bloodstain pattern analyst should take steps to ensure all areas of exposed skin are covered and any injuries or breaks in the skin are properly bandaged.

Like leptospirosis, hantaviruses are carried by rodents. Hantaviruses are primarily transmitted when humans inhale air contaminated with virus shed in urine, feces, and saliva. Infection with hantavirus can lead to hantavirus pulmonary syndrome (HPS) or hemorrhagic fever with renal syndrome (HFRS).[9] Cases of hantavirus in the United States are generally infrequent; however, the analyst should use caution in scenes where rodent infestation is evident. In these situations, a mask or respirator should be worn in addition to other appropriate PPE.

Tuberculosis (TB) is a potentially fatal disease spread by airborne particles. Since TB bacteria is put into the air when a person coughs, sneezes, or speaks, it is not usually a primary concern for the bloodstain pattern analyst, especially when dealing with deceased individuals. However, the World Health Organization (WHO) cautions that TB can be spread from dead bodies if residual air in the lungs is released, or fluid from the lungs is expelled from the nose or mouth during handling.[10] Screening for TB is recommended by the CDC for healthcare workers upon hire and after a potential exposure and is prudent for those analysts who may work closely with dead bodies. In the United States, most states have a tuberculosis control program, which can provide additional guidance for the analyst.[11]

UNIVERSAL PRECAUTIONS

Universal precautions is an approach to controlling infection. When following universal precautions, the analyst treats all blood and bodily fluids as if they were known to be infectious. Since the likelihood is extremely low that the analyst would be aware if a particular blood sample is infectious for HIV, hepatitis B or C, or other bloodborne pathogens, employing universal precautions requires the analyst to prevent contact with blood and other potentially infectious materials. Occasionally, there will be situations where the analyst is presented with a fluid that appears to be blood or a fluid of unknown origin. In these situations, the analyst should proceed with universal precautions until it is determined that the fluid in question is not a body fluid or other potentially infectious material. When using universal precautions, the analyst must employ careful work practices to limit exposure to potentially infectious materials and must ensure that proper PPE is worn at all times.

PERSONAL PROTECTIVE EQUIPMENT

PPE is the clothing or equipment worn by employees for protection against hazards. Depending on the type of hazard present at a scene, the bloodstain pattern analyst may need varying types and amounts of PPE.

While general work clothes, such as the uniform worn by a bloodstain pattern analyst in the field, are not considered PPE, a uniform does offer some protection from hazards. Despite the analyst's best efforts, the uniform may at times become contaminated with potentially infectious material. Contaminated uniforms should be removed as soon as possible. To reduce the risk of exposure, the uniform and footwear should be covered with PPE that can be easily removed, disposed of, and replaced when soiled. Care should be taken when wearing the same uniform and especially footwear both in a crime scene and at the home of a bloodstain pattern analyst. Generally, it is a good practice to avoid wearing crime scene worn footwear inside one's private residence. If shoes become contaminated with blood or other potentially infectious material, it may be possible to decontaminate them using a 10% bleach solution. A bleach solution containing one part bleach and nine parts water may be mixed and either sprayed on the soles of boots or placed in a shallow container into which the shoes may be placed.

The amount and type of PPE necessary depend on the hazards present at a crime scene. In general, at any scene where potentially infectious materials are present, universal precautions should be taken and gloves worn at all times. Best practices dictate that shoe covers also be worn inside all crime scenes, but certainly in scenes where the flooring is contaminated with blood. If a splash hazard exists from liquid blood, covering the eyes and face (either with goggles or a face shield) becomes necessary. At a scene with a large volume of liquid blood present, it is prudent to wear an outer garment such as a Tyvek suit or impermeable gown, along with goggles or a face shield and gloves.

In addition to protecting the analyst from hazards, PPE also serves to protect the evidence from contamination by the analyst. In modern forensic investigations, due to the sensitivity of DNA analysis, the bloodstain pattern analyst should always take steps to prevent introducing their own DNA to a sample. One way to do this while also protecting the analyst is to wear a facemask or respirator. Like all types of PPE, there are varying types of masks that are appropriate for different situations.

A surgical mask is a loose fitting, fluid-resistant, disposable face covering that is worn to protect the wearer from large droplets or splashes. In general, a surgical mask is suitable to protect the bloodstain pattern analyst from exposure to bloodborne pathogens on scene and to protect from respiratory irritants from chemicals used in processing, such as luminol. When used, surgical masks should be worn to cover the nose and mouth. An N95 mask is a tighter fitting disposable mask that filters out airborne particles and small aerosols; it may be more appropriate in some situations (for example, in a scene where an inhalation risk exists).[12] Although rarely necessary for protection against bloodborne pathogens, half face respirators, full face respirators, self-contained breathing apparatus (SCBA), and personalized air purifying respirators (PAPRs) offer more protection. In situations where an unknown biological or novel threat exists, it may be necessary to employ one of these more robust options. Respirators should also be considered in situations where an unknown chemical or environmental hazard exists. If there is a risk of an unknown chemical or environmental hazard, consult with a local hazardous materials (Hazmat) team.

Once a decision is made about what PPE is needed for the scene, the bloodstain pattern analyst should (in a clean area) prepare to enter the scene by donning the appropriate PPE. PPE should be donned with clean hands, starting with shoe and clothing covers, continuing with masks and eye protection, and ending with gloves. Most PPE can be worn throughout the entirety of scene processing unless it becomes visibly contaminated; however, gloves should be changed routinely.

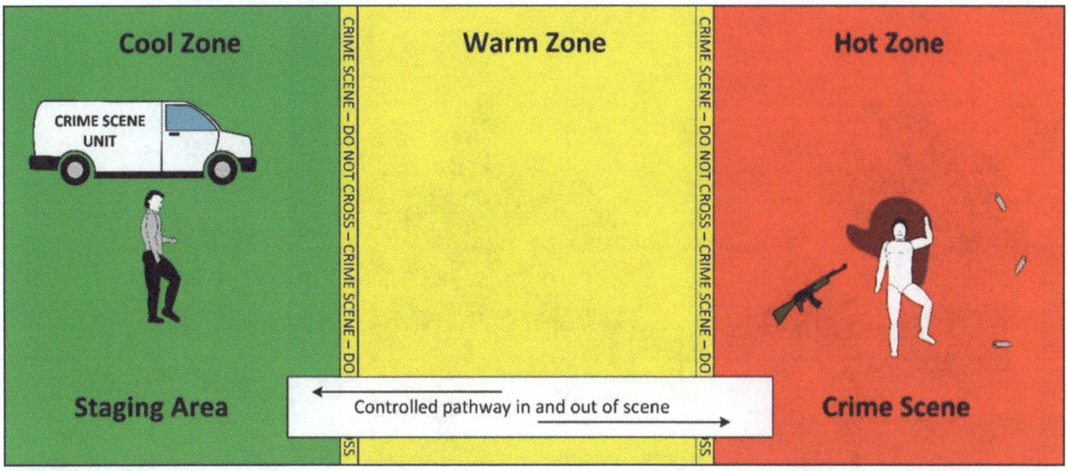

Figure 2.1 Hot, warm, and cool zones at a crime scene. The "hot zone" is the inner area of the crime scene where hazards exist and PPE must be worn. The "cool zone" is a staging area where the analyst can take breaks and safely work without PPE. The "warm zone" is a barrier space between the hot and cool zones where contaminated PPE can be removed prior to entering the clean staging area.

When the analyst leaves the scene, removal of PPE should occur in a designated area. Contaminated PPE should never be worn into the clean staging area utilized to store equipment, but removal of PPE should occur outside the area where there is a risk of infection and contamination. This necessitates use of a "warm zone" – a space between the contaminated "hot zone" of the scene and the clean "cool zone" of the staging area (Figure 2.1).

Once the bloodstain pattern analyst has entered the warm zone, they may begin removing their PPE. Typically, removal begins with doffing of outer garments, starting with shoe covers. Gloves should be worn during the removal of outer garments and shoe covers. After removal of an outer garment, it is prudent to remove gloves and perform hand hygiene (either by washing or sanitizing) prior to removing PPE covering the face, such as eye protection and masks. If hand hygiene stations are not feasible at a crime scene, clean gloves can be worn to remove eye and respiratory protection. Some analysts may choose to remove PPE covering the face prior to removing outer garments, which is also acceptable assuming PPE on the face is removed with clean gloves or hands. PPE should be disposed of in an appropriate biohazard receptacle and removed from the scene. After doffing all PPE, the analyst should perform hand hygiene by washing with soap and water as soon as possible.

It is important that analysts use proper doffing techniques when removing soiled gloves to avoid contaminating their skin with biohazardous material that may be on the outer surfaces of the gloves. To accomplish this, grasp the glove of one hand in an area of the palm near the wrist. Slowly and carefully remove this glove, pulling it off inside out and holding it in the fingers of the still gloved hand. Cautiously slip one or two fingers of the ungloved hand inside the wrist of the remaining glove and gently pull the glove off inside out. The first glove will become entrapped within the second glove and the second glove will be inside out, limiting exposure to the potentially contaminated outer surfaces. The soiled gloves can be safely disposed of, and the analyst should proceed with hand sanitization and further removal of PPE. When removing gloves soiled with blood, the analyst should be aware of the likelihood that liquid blood can be freed from the gloves during removal, so they should doff the gloves in a slow manner and in a safe direction to avoid creating artifactual bloodstains or flinging blood onto other personnel in the scene (Figure 2.2).

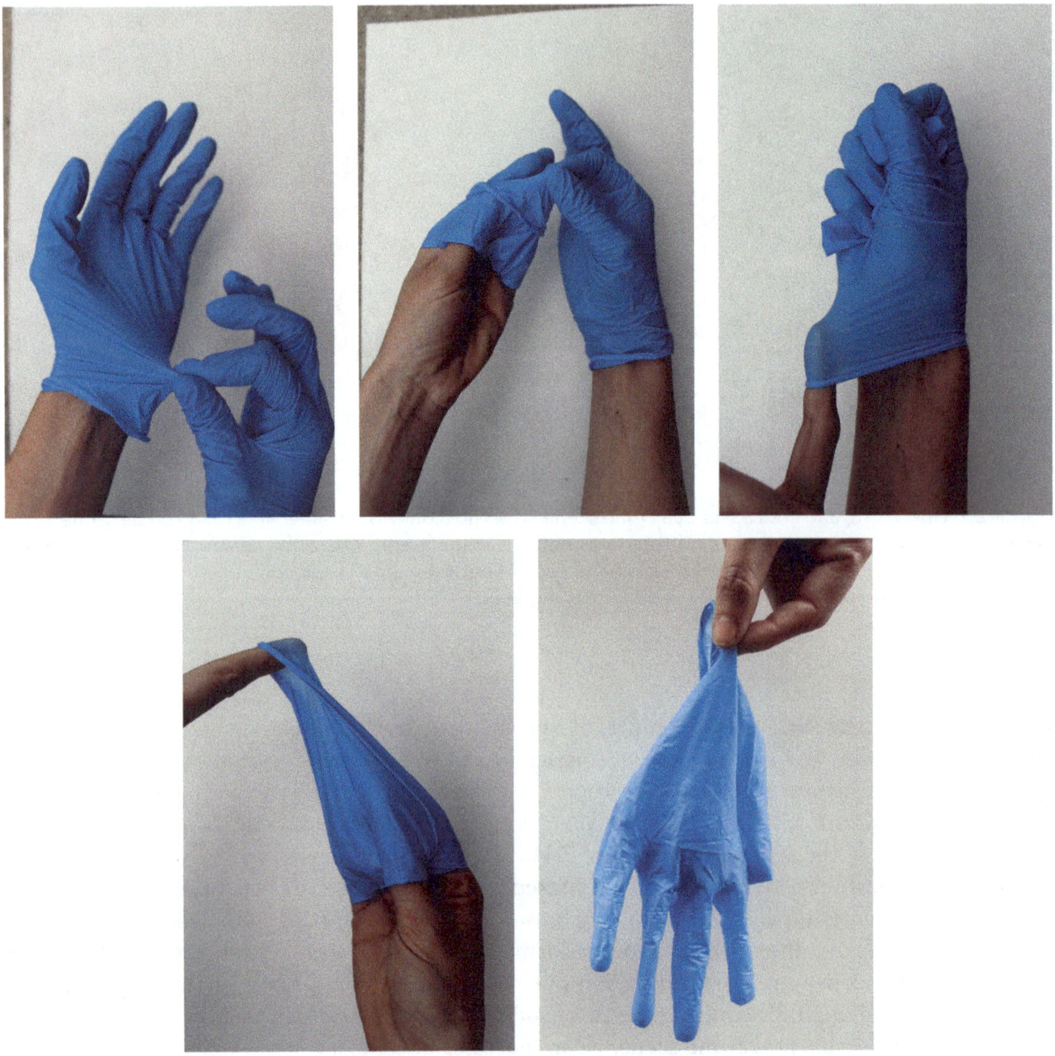

Figure 2.2 Proper glove doffing technique. This technique prevents material on the gloves from touching the skin.

ROUTES OF EXPOSURE AND WORK CONTROLS

While some hazards (such as HIV) require contact between blood sources, there are several potential routes of exposure that the bloodstain pattern analyst must be aware of. Ingestion, injection, absorption, and inhalation are all potential concerns for the bloodstain pattern analyst. To prevent against exposure by any route, work controls should be employed in addition to the use of PPE. To prevent against exposure, all actions which could result in ingestion, injection, absorption, and inhalation should be avoided within a crime scene and when dealing with blood or other potentially infectious material. Work controls are efforts which can be taken to adjust the way an analyst behaves on a scene and how they interact with potentially infectious material to limit possible exposures.

New bloodstain pattern analysts may find it unlikely that a hazard or bloodborne pathogen could be ingested. However, ingestion of hazards is not limited only to blatant consumption of infectious material. Most frequently, an ingestion risk exists when an analyst eats, drinks, or smokes within a crime scene or around contaminated materials. Fortunately, such actions are widely recognized to be careless in modern forensic investigations. However, the need to eat and drink during crime scene processing often arises, especially when on-scene processing occurs over a period of several hours. An ingestion risk can present itself when the analyst takes a break, even in a clean area, to eat or drink without properly doffing PPE and performing hand hygiene. Other potential ingestion risks exist when the analyst smokes, applies lip balms, or thoughtlessly puts equipment (such as pens) in their mouth. For this reason, all such activities should be avoided at the crime scene.

Accidental exposure via injection poses a risk to the bloodstain pattern analyst when dealing with contaminated sharps. The most likely route of infection from bloodborne pathogens generally comes from inadvertent injection, such as in cases of accidental needle sticks. Extreme caution should always be exercised when handling needles, syringes, and other sharp, hollow bore implements. While it is not common practice to wear puncture-resistant gloves, wearing thicker or multiple pairs of disposable gloves can offer a modicum of additional protection. Capping an uncapped needle is never recommended when collecting evidence. Needles and syringes should immediately be secured within an appropriate syringe collection tube to reduce the opportunity for accidental exposure. When dealing with other sharp objects of evidentiary value, consider puncture-resistant packaging such as plastic evidence tubes. Sharps used during scene processing that are not collected as evidence should be immediately disposed of in an appropriate biohazard sharps container.

The bloodstain pattern analyst should also be aware of potential routes of absorption. Some hazards may be absorbed through the skin or through contact with a mucous membrane. To prevent against exposure via absorption, bloodstain pattern analysts should be aware of all open sores or cuts in the skin and take precautions to cover these areas at all times. Ensuring a barrier is present between the skin and mucous membranes and potentially infectious material is a prudent way to reduce the risk of exposure via absorption. If a complete Tyvek suit is not required for the scene conditions, steps can still be taken to cover exposed skin, such as exposed arm skin for those analysts wearing short-sleeve uniform shirts. Tyvek sleeves can be worn to cover the skin between a sleeve and the glove. The most likely route of absorption is via a mucous membrane, such as the nasal passages, mouth, and conjunctiva of the eye. Precautions should be taken to limit contact with the mucous membranes; analysts should wear appropriate PPE and refrain from touching their eyes, nose, and mouth/lips when actively engaged in processing activities.

The final route of exposure to be aware of is inhalation. Biological hazards, chemical hazards, and environmental hazards can all pose a potential inhalation risk to bloodstain pattern analysts. While use of proper PPE can reduce the risk of exposure via inhalation, workplace controls and engineering controls should also be considered and employed when possible. Engineering controls are measures that protect an analyst by placing a physical barrier between the analyst and the hazardous material. Within the laboratory environment, engineering controls such as fume hoods and other ventilated cabinets are available to limit inhalation risk; however, these protections are not available at crime scenes. For this reason, limiting handling of some items while on scene may be advisable if the item can be collected and examined in the laboratory within a more controlled environment. If the item must be examined on scene, careful handling and efforts to avoid shaking an item can reduce the production of airborne particles, which can further serve to reduce inhalation risk. While an increased airflow, such as from an overhead fan or an open window, is generally considered problematic in forensic scene processing, increasing ventilation before entering a scene may be necessary if chemical or other environmental hazards exist. In these situations, the bloodstain pattern analyst should coordinate with local Hazmat teams for guidance.

WORKPLACE CONTROLS: EQUIPMENT

Work controls also need to be applied to the equipment utilized by an analyst when on scene or working with evidence. The bloodstain pattern analyst's equipment may become contaminated with potentially infectious material, and thus, it may itself become a route of possible exposure. An easy way to mitigate risk is to treat all equipment used during scene processing as "dirty" and only handle them when wearing gloves or other appropriate PPE. It is also wise to regularly clean equipment with a 10% bleach solution or use a single use, disposable option. Items that are disposable (such as pens, markers, cutting instruments, etc.) should be disposed of regularly if there is a risk of contamination. Like all forensic practitioners, the bloodstain pattern analysts would be wise to quickly break themselves of the habit of chewing on pens or writing implements to avoid accidentally putting a contaminated item in their mouth.

Some analysts may employ a clean hand/dirty hand methodology to limit contamination of commonly used equipment. Most typically, this technique is utilized with respect to camera equipment. One hand (usually the dominant hand) is the "clean hand" and is not used to touch anything potentially infectious (including bloodstains and decedents). The other hand is the "dirty hand" and is used to hold scales, touch or hold potentially contaminated evidence, and touch any decedents. The dirty hand does not touch the camera or other equipment. This technique requires the attention of the analyst to avoid using the "dirty hand" to touch or adjust the camera; however, it still requires the use and frequent changing of gloves, and may not always be feasible.

Another effective work control to limit contamination of equipment is to cover equipment with a disposable barrier. Just as the analyst wears gloves and shoe covers as PPE, equipment used on scene can be covered to avoid direct contact with blood or OPIM. For example, the feet of a tripod can be covered by securing Tyvek hand preservation bags or plastic evidence bags to the bottoms of the tripod legs before using the tripod in the scene. The coverings are easily removable and disposable and act as an effective barrier to prevent contact between reusable equipment and blood present within the scene.

Decontamination of equipment after working on a scene is a critical step in scene processing, as it not only ensures the safety of persons handling the equipment but also avoids cross-contamination between scenes. Decontamination strategies may vary based on the type of equipment used. Equipment that can be safely submerged, such as evidence marking placards and plastic scales, can be cleaned with a 10% bleach solution. Alternatively, a 10% bleach solution can be sprayed on objects which have been contaminated but cannot be submerged, such as the interior surfaces of a crime scene van or the legs of a tripod.

In some scenes, it may be difficult or unsafe to walk on the floor due to the presence of blood or OPIM. In scenes with extended downtime and severe decomposition, flooring surfaces may be slick and present slipping hazards. In situations like this, there are several measures that can be considered to reduce the risk of falling onto blood or OPIM. In the United Kingdom, stepping plates are commonly utilized to avoid stepping on evidence in a crime scene. Stepping plates, which are small, elevated platforms made of plastic or metal, may be deployed to create a safer surface on which to stand if blood covers the floor (Figure 2.3). However, the use of stepping plates may be impractical at some scenes as they can still be slick and are uncommon outside of Europe. Once the floor is documented and any evidence is collected, it may be appropriate to cover the slip hazard with an absorbent pad, tarp, or paper to provide a safe walkway. Such walkways not only reduce the chances of slipping in wet blood or decomposition material but also function as an additional barrier between the analyst and potentially hazardous fluids. In a very dire situation, it may be necessary to remove slick decomposition material from the floor or laydown kitty litter, sand, saw dust, or some other textured material to reduce the risk of falls, exposures, and injuries (Figure 2.4).

Figure 2.3 In the hallway, tarps were nailed to the floor over decomposition material to allow an analyst to safely walk through the scene. (Photos by Amy Santoro.)

Figure 2.4 Two crime scene investigators, Paul Stockdell and Amy Santoro, Johnson County, Kansas Sheriff's Office Criminalistics Laboratory, utilize blue absorbent pads known as "chux pads" to absorb a large, previously documented blood pool. The use of chux pads reduces exposure to bloodborne pathogens and lessens slipping hazards. (Photo by Tammy Ljungblad/The Kansas City Star.)

COLLECTION OF EVIDENCE

While avoiding contamination and cross-contamination of evidence is a typical concern for the forensic scientists, additional care must be taken to avoid exposure to blood or OPIM when collecting bloodstained evidence. For more information regarding evidence collection procedures, refer to Chapter 23. While dealing with bloodborne pathogens, there are special considerations with respect to health and safety, which must be taken into account. For example, when collecting blood and bloodstained items, one major consideration must be to avoid creating aerosols and minimize splashing, as both increase the risk of exposure to bloodborne pathogens. For this reason, scraping of bloodstains should be avoided and swabbing or cutting out stains is favored in most situations.

Packaging used to keep blood and bloodstained evidence needs to be suitable to avoid exposure to blood and OPIM present within the package. When collecting a bloodstained sharp object, such as a bloody knife or syringe, analyst's safety should be the primary concern. A cut from a bloodstained object or a needle stick from a contaminated needle is a huge exposure risk and must be avoided at all costs. Knives and other sharp bloody objects can be packaged in cardboard to avoid cuts and appropriately preserve biological evidence. Plastic knife tubes are also available and may be appropriate in some situations. The addition of desiccant packages to plastic knife tubes may be utilized in situations where moisture would be problematic. Syringes with needles should always be packaged in puncture-proof syringe tubes.

For the purposes of preservation of biological evidence, bloodstained evidence should be air-dried and packaged in a paper container. However, this is not always feasible when removing blood-soaked items from a crime scene. In these situations, temporary packaging (such as a plastic biohazard bag) may be necessary to avoid leaking. Alternatively, an absorbent pad may be placed inside a paper bag to absorb any wet blood and prevent leaking. Leakproof plastic packaging is not appropriate for long-term storage of bloodstained evidence but can be effectively utilized to transport evidence from a crime scene to the laboratory or station where it can be safely air-dried.

Bloodstained evidence should be dried in a designated drying area. Ideally, evidence should be dried within an evidence drying cabinet outfitted with a high efficiency particulate air (HEPA) filtration system. If an evidence drying cabinet is not available, evidence should be dried in a designated area away from other activities, as it is possible that drying blood may flake off and become airborne.

TRANSPORTATION OF EVIDENCE

Once the analyst is ready to depart the scene, collected evidence needs to be prepared for transport to the laboratory. Generally, evidence is transported in a crime scene vehicle. Before evidence is placed inside any transport vehicle, it should be packaged in a way to avoid leakage to reduce the risk that blood or OPIM could contaminate the transport vehicle. If items wet with liquid blood are not already packaged in leakproof convenience packaging, a leakproof plastic barrier may be laid inside the transport vehicle to protect against contamination. Alternatively, the surfaces of the vehicle may be periodically cleaned with a 10% bleach solution. Most analysts find it beneficial to keep cleaning supplies in their vehicles, including 10% bleach, paper towels, cleaning wipes, alcohol wipes, and hand sanitizer.

DISPOSAL OF WASTE

When dealing with blood or OPIM, it is not appropriate to use traditional disposal methods. In the United States, OSHA has published regulations on the storage and disposal of regulated waste. States within the United States may have their own, more specific guidelines, often maintained by the health department. Analysts should always familiarize themselves with the applicable state and local guidelines.

OSHA defines regulated waste as "liquid or semi-liquid blood or other potentially infectious materials; contaminated items that would release blood or other potentially infectious materials in a liquid or semi-liquid state if compressed; items that are caked with dried blood or other potentially infectious materials and are capable of releasing these materials during handling; contaminated sharps; and pathological and microbiological wastes containing blood or other potentially infectious materials."[13] OSHA regulations require that regulated waste be packaged in color-coded, leakproof, closeable containers that are designed to contain all the contents placed within. The most common types of waste receptacles are red plastic biohazard trash bags and red plastic puncture-proof sharps' containers. Whether working on scene or in laboratory, it is the analyst's responsibility to ensure that all biohazardous waste materials are disposed of in an appropriate receptacle. A commonly employed technique is to maintain a trash bag on scene for analysts to dispose of used gloves and other PPE or other items that become soiled with blood or OPIM and could be considered regulated waste. This designated trash bag should be removed from the scene upon the completion of processing and disposed of per regulated waste guidelines.

NOVEL THREATS

When novel viruses and threats emerge, it is incumbent upon the analyst to stay informed. Generally, agencies like local health departments, the CDC, or the WHO publish up to date information and resources. In early 2020, a novel coronavirus (COVID-19) spread around the world causing a global pandemic. During this time, scientists and healthcare workers faced critical PPE shortages. One of the most sought-after types of PPE during the beginning weeks of the COVID-19 crisis was N95 masks. While typically meant to be disposable, single-use assets, it became necessary to reuse N95 masks due to worldwide shortages. Some healthcare facilities and law enforcement agencies attempted to reduce the risk to analysts by utilizing UV irradiation to sanitize masks between uses (Figure 2.5). While there was little concern of transmission of COVID-19 in the blood, there was concern that analysts could be infected by the bodies of the recently deceased. It is beneficial for laboratories to maintain a sufficient stockpile of PPE to meet processing needs for several months. It may also be wise to invest in reusable PPE such as PAPRs and reusable face shields, which can be wiped down and reused several times.

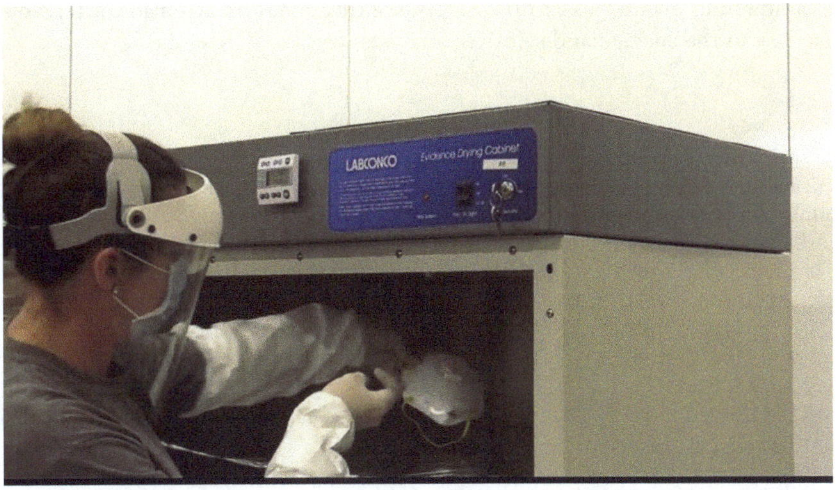

Figure 2.5 In the height of the COVID-19 crisis, the author uses an evidence drying cabinet outfitted with UV lights to irradiate N95 masks to allow for reuse. (Photo credit: Deputy Claire Canaan, Johnson County (Kansas) Sheriff's Office.)

EXPERIMENTATION AND TRAINING

In addition to blood encountered at crime scenes, bloodstain pattern analysts work with blood in training and during experimentation. As with all biological material, blood utilized during experimentation and training should be considered potentially infectious and universal precautions should be taken.

There are several measures to mitigate risk when dealing with blood in training and experimentation settings. Non-human blood sources are commercially available, and many analysts make use of these options and purchase defibrinated sheep's blood or other similar animal blood products to use in experimentation and training. Many analysts prefer to train and experiment with human blood, and in those situations, expired blood product is generally available from a local blood bank. Expired blood from the blood bank is pre-screened for infectious diseases (as it is intended for transfusion into human patients), so it is typically safe to work with. The blood products available from blood banks are typically lacking white blood cells, so the risk of DNA contamination of lab spaces is mitigated. If analysts are performing experiments or training exercises where their skin may contact liquid blood or are attempting to experiment with expirated patterns (where blood may be placed in or around the nose and mouth), it is wise to consider using one's own blood. For these situations, blood may be drawn into tubes by a qualified phlebotomist for use by analysts. All other persons involved in the experiment should be extremely cautious and utilize universal precautions.

SUMMARY

The reality of bloodstain pattern analysis demands that the analysts come in close contact with blood from unknown and unvetted sources. It is impossible to overstate the importance of universal precautions and awareness of the dangers faced at a crime scene by bloodstain pattern analysts. Constant care for reducing and avoiding accidental exposure is of paramount importance for analysts. Medical research is a rapidly evolving field and the guidelines for the treatment of individuals exposed to various pathogens can change as our understanding of these viruses deepens. Wearing proper PPE, remaining aware, and immediately seeking medical attention after any accidental exposures are key to the success and safety of analysts.

Notes

1. "Bloodborne Pathogens and Needlestick Prevention Overview | Occupational Safety and Health Administration." n.d. www.osha.gov. https://www.osha.gov/bloodborne-pathogens
2. "Hospital ETool: Healthcare Wide Hazards - Bloodborne Pathogens." n.d. www.osha.gov. https://www.osha.gov/SLTC/etools/hospital/hazards/bbp/bbp.html
3. "HIV and Injection Drug Use | HIV Transmission | HIV Basics | HIV/AIDS | CDC." 2021. www.cdc.gov. April 21, 2021. https://www.cdc.gov/hiv/basics/hiv-transmission/injection-drug-use.html#:~:text=Risk%20of%20HIV&text=HIV%20can%20survive%20in%20a.
4. "Hepatitis C Questions and Answers for Health Professionals." 2019. https://www.cdc.gov/hepatitis/hcv/hcvfaq.htm.
5. "Statistics & Surveillance of Viral Hepatitis | CDC." 2020. Www.cdc.gov. May 11, 2020. https://www.cdc.gov/hepatitis/statistics/index.htm.
6. CDC. 2020. "Hepatitis B FAQs for Health Professionals | CDC." Centers for Disease Control and Prevention. December 30, 2020. https://www.cdc.gov/hepatitis/hbv/hbvfaq.htm#C11
7. "OSHA Fact Sheet: Hepatitis B Vaccination Protection | Occupational Safety and Health Administration." 2011. Osha.gov. 2011. https://www.osha.gov/OshDoc/data_BloodborneFacts/bbfact05.html

8. "Leptospirosis | CDC." 2019. www.cdc.gov. March 13, 2019. https://www.cdc.gov/leptospirosis/
9. "CDC - Hantavirus." 2019. https://www.cdc.gov/hantavirus/index.html
10. "Risks Posed by Dead Bodies after Disasters." n.d. www.who.int. https://www.who.int/publications/m/item/risks-posed-by-dead-bodies-after-disasters
11. CDC. "Tuberculosis (TB)." Centers for Disease Control and Prevention. 2019. https://www.cdc.gov/tb/default.htm
12. "Centers for Disease Control and Prevention National Institute for Occupational Safety and Health Surgical Mask N95 Respirator Testing and Approval." n.d. https://www.cdc.gov/niosh/npptl/pdfs/UnderstandDifferenceInfographic-508.pdf
13. "1910.1030 - Bloodborne Pathogens. | Occupational Safety and Health Administration." 2011. Osha.gov. 2011. https://www.osha.gov/laws-regs/regulations/standardnumber/1910/1910.1030

Further Reading

Bevel, Tom, and Ross M. Gardner. *Bloodstain Pattern Analysis: With an Introduction to Crime Scene Reconstruction*. Boca Raton: CRC Press/Taylor & Francis, 2008.

James, Stuart H., Paul Erwin Kish, and T. Paulette Sutton. *Principles of Bloodstain Pattern Analysis: Theory and Practice*. Boca Raton: CRC Press/Taylor & Francis, 2005.

Masters, Nancy E. *Safety for the Forensic Identification Specialist*. Jacksonville: Lightning Powder Co, 2002.

Thompson, Sandra C., Clem R. Boughton, and Gregory J. Dore. "Blood-Borne Viruses and Their Survival in the Environment: Is Public Concern about Community Needlestick Exposures Justified?" *Australian and New Zealand Journal of Public Health* 27, no. 6 (2003): 602–7. https://doi.org/10.1111/j.1467-842x.2003.tb00606.x.

CHAPTER 3
PROPERTIES OF BLOOD

Elisabeth Williams and Natalia Kabaliuk

IMPORTANCE OF PHYSICAL PROPERTIES OF BLOOD IN BLOODSTAIN PATTERN ANALYSIS

To improve the quality of the science behind bloodstain pattern analysis (BPA) and advance the understanding of the fundamental principles, a controlled, systematic approach is necessary. Good experiments should be valid and repeatable to produce reliable results. To ensure the validity of BPA experimental results, the blood medium used must emulate the physical properties of fresh human blood as closely as possible. To ensure these results are repeatable, the physical properties of the blood medium should be replicable, at least within an acceptable margin of error. In this chapter, the composition of human blood is discussed as it relates to the physical properties of blood and the understanding of blood fluid dynamics in BPA. A thorough explanation of human blood composition can be found in Hoffbrand's *Essential Hematology, 8th edition*.[1] The composition section presented here is significantly reduced and only includes those components relevant to the BPA discipline. The physical forces at play during bloodstain pattern formation, which are influenced by blood properties, are covered in Chapters 4 and 5.

Blood is a unique and rheologically complex, shear-thinning, non-Newtonian fluid. The behavior of blood outside of the body is dependent on mainly three physical properties: viscosity, surface tension, and density,[2] in addition to external forces applied to liquid blood during dispersion, flight, and impact. Blood of different species is routinely used in BPA, with a range of chemical and mechanical treatments reported. A comparative hemorheology section is thus included in this chapter, evaluating the blood properties of different species. The effects of various procedures of handling, storage, and treatment on the physical properties of blood are also discussed.

HUMAN BLOOD COMPOSITION

Blood is a liquid connective tissue, transporting oxygen, nutrients, hormones, etc. to other tissues and organs and removing waste products as part of the cardiovascular system.[1] As a colloidal solution, blood represents a highly complex suspension of polydisperse, flexible, chemically, and electrostatically active cells suspended in blood plasma with proteins, urea, glucose and other organic substances.[3] The physical properties of blood as a complex fluid are thus the result of the combined effects of all its constituents. Blood plasma constitutes 50–60% and formed elements (blood cells) 40–50% of the whole blood volume, respectively. Formed elements of blood are erythrocytes (red blood cells or RBCs), leukocytes (white blood cells or WBCs), and thrombocytes (platelets). Typical whole blood volume is about 78 ml per 1 kg of body mass, and the whole blood is slightly alkaline (pH 7.35–7.4).

DOI: 10.4324/9781003163695-3

Red Blood Cells

RBCs constitute 95–99% of the cellular component of blood. The cells develop in the bone marrow and circulate in the body for about 100–120 days before they are recycled in the liver and spleen. RBCs are bereft of nucleus and most organelles; these are biconcave-disk-shaped cells with a disk diameter of approximately 6.2–8.2 μm, a thickness of about 2–2.5 μm, and a minimum thickness in the center of 0.8–1 μm,[4] being smaller than most other human cells. These cells have an average volume of approximately 90 fl with a surface area of about 136 μm.[5] Due to high membrane flexibility, erythrocytes can squeeze through capillaries as small as 3 μm in diameter. They carry iron-containing oxygen-binding protein, hemoglobin, which comprises about a third of the total cell volume and gives blood its specific red coloring.

RBCs are 1.098 times denser than pure water at 25/4°C. RBCs are also denser than blood plasma, causing them to naturally settle (or sediment) with time in a still blood sample. The rate at which RBCs settle in a period of an hour is called erythrocyte sedimentation rate (ESR) or just sedimentation rate. This process is governed by the combined effect of pro-sedimentation factors, mostly fibrinogen, and the factors resisting the sedimentation, including the negative electrical charge of erythrocytes. In humans, normal ESR for males is 1–10 mm/h and for females is 2–15 mm/h.[4]

The terms packed cell volume (PCV) and hematocrit (Ht) are both measures of the fraction of whole blood comprising erythrocytes. PCV refers to the measurement of packed RBCs in a capillary tube, having been spun in a centrifuge. By contrast, Ht is calculated using an automatic analyzer, where the RBC count is multiplied by the mean cell volume.[1] The normal human Ht range is approximately 40–50% for males and 35–45% for females.

Thrombocytes and Leukocytes

Platelets or thrombocytes are small, irregular-shaped, clear cell fragments (without nuclei), 0.5–3 μm in diameter with an average life span of ten days.[1] They comprise approximately 4.9% of the cell volume of blood and have an important role in hemostasis. WBCs or leukocytes are immune system cells comprising 0.1% of the cellular component of blood in an average healthy adult. They live for between six hours and several days in the human body and measure 12–20 μm in diameter. Leukocytes are either phagocytes (neutrophils, eosinophils, basophils, and monocytes) or lymphocytes (B-cells and T-cells).[1] As platelets and leukocytes make up only about 5% of the cellular component of blood, their effect on the macroscopic properties of blood is considered negligible.

Blood Plasma

Blood plasma is approximately Newtonian and comprises mainly water by volume (85–91%) with dissolved minerals, hormones, vitamins, enzymes, mediators, organic compounds, and gases (oxygen and carbon dioxide). Blood plasma has yellow or straw color due to the presence of bilirubin (a waste product of heme, part of hemoglobin degradation), and is slightly alkaline with a pH of 7.3–7.5 and a colloid osmotic pressure of 330 mm H_2O. Plasma is 1.0239 times more dense than pure water at 25/4°C and 1.019–1.022 times at 37/4°C.[6]

Cations (Na^+, K^+, Mg^{2+}, Ca^{2+}) and anions (HCO_3^-, Cl^-, PO_4^{3-}, SO_4^{2-}) account for approximately 2–3% of plasma by weight. Organic compounds correspond to 9% of plasma by weight. These are nitrogen-bearing substances (such as proteins, monoacids, urea, creatinine, ammonia, metabolic waste products) and anazotic or nitrogen-free glucose (70–130 mg/dl before meals and less than 180 mg/dl after meals), fatty acids, pyruvate, lactate, phospholipids, triacylglycerols, and cholesterin. Proteins represent 7–8% of plasma by weight and play a major role in molecular transport, osmotic pressure maintenance, and blood clotting. The most abundant proteins are albumins (4.5 g per 100 ml), globulins (2.5 g per 100 ml), and fibrinogen (0.3 g per 100 ml).[6] The liquid remaining after blood is allowed to clot is called **serum**, which is, in effect, plasma with clotting proteins (mostly fibrinogen) removed.

HUMAN BLOOD VISCOSITY

Viscous forces have an important role in determining the impact dynamics of falling blood droplets.[7] The viscosity of a fluid is defined as the fluid's resistance to deformation and flow. As a non-Newtonian fluid, blood viscosity, and hence flow behavior, varies with shear stress and shear rate.[8] The shear rate is the rate of application of the deforming shearing force, so the faster the force applied, the higher the rate. Blood viscosity decreases with the increase in the rate of its shearing deformation. In other words, blood gets less viscous or "runnier," the more rapidly it is deformed. Equivalently, blood gets more viscous or "thicker" if the deforming force is removed. Blood viscosity is calculated by dividing the shear stress (Pa) placed on a fluid by the shear rate (s^{-1}) using a viscometer.

Blood viscosity is determined by several factors and mechanisms, namely plasma viscosity, PCV (alternatively, Ht), RBC aggregation, RBC deformability, and blood temperature. PCV and RBC aggregation are the two main factors that contribute to the shear-thinning behavior of blood. Effects of other types of blood cells (leukocytes and platelets) are minimal mostly due to their small number relative to erythrocytes.

Red Blood Cell Aggregation

Studies measuring the viscosity of blood have found viscosity increases exponentially as the shear rate decreases below 100 s^{-1} (Figure 3.1).[9] For high shear rates above 100 s^{-1} (as for blood in small blood vessels), blood viscosity approaches its asymptotic limit (Newtonian plateau) with viscosity of approximately 4–6 mPa·s for average adult male and 3.5–5.8 mPa·s for average adult female normal populations, respectively.[10] At lower shear rates, such as 10 s^{-1}, viscosity increases to as much as about 10 mPa·s.[8] The whole blood viscosity values at different shear rates are plotted in Figure 3.1.

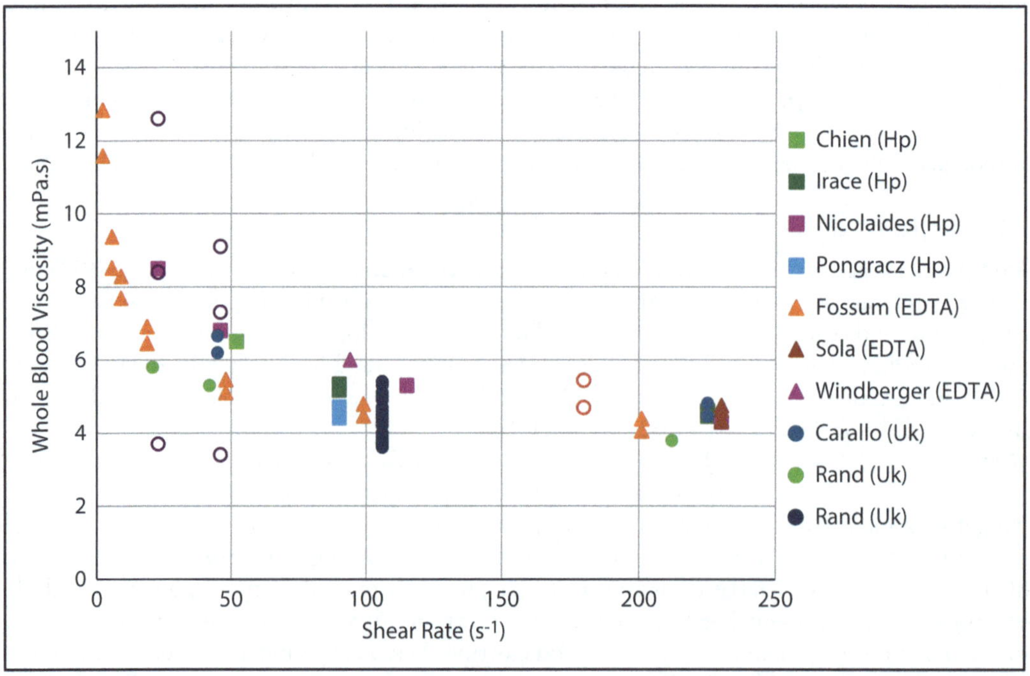

Figure 3.1 Whole human blood viscosity vs. shear rate showing values from 12 different studies. Anticoagulant use noted in legend: heparin (Hp), ethylenediaminetetraacetic acid (EDTA), unknown (Uk), and none (No).

The generally accepted main mechanism for the variation in blood viscosity with shear rate is the aggregation of RBCs, known as *rouleaux formation*.[9] Rouleaux formation is a reversible phenomenon, which occurs at zero or low shear rates. Rouleaux are stacks of human RBCs which "stick" together face-to-face due to both macromolecules in the blood plasma (primarily fibrinogen and globulins) and cellular factors. Rouleaux formation is dependent on the RBC surface charge.[9] Under normal conditions, the membranes of RBCs possess negative charge and repulsive electrostatic forces act between cells.[11] Indeed, they show no signs of aggregation in, for example, a saline solution. However, in the presence of plasma proteins, particularly fibrinogen and globulin, the cells tend to aggregate. This process depends on the concentration of proteins and increases with the decrease in shear rate. This in turn increases the effective cell volume resisting the flow and hence increases blood viscosity. Upon increasing the shear rate, the aggregates tend to break up causing a decrease in blood viscosity.

In normal human circulation, rouleaux formation or RBCs aggregation can be observed in the low-pressure venous system, where it has been hypothesized to have a host of important physiological functions. These include increasing vascular resistance, which plays a significant role in homeostasis of the vascular system.[9] Increased RBC aggregation in humans has for a long time been associated with illness and inflammation. Factors such as increased levels of plasma fibrinogen in acute phase response to trauma and changes to RBC morphology in conditions like diabetes have been cited as likely causes.[12]

Red Blood Cell Deformability

RBC rigidity or deformability has an influence on blood viscosity at high shear rates.[13] Human RBCs are biconcave discs with a strong and flexible plasma membrane, and a membrane cytoskeleton, allowing them to deform without rupturing to squeeze through capillaries. At high shear rates, the rouleaux break down. RBCs are dispersed and tend to deform from their normal resting shape into ellipsoids and move along flow streamlines. This explains much lower normal blood viscosity compared to, for example, the suspension of hardened red cells in plasma. In addition, it is believed that the reduction in the RBC membrane deformability inhibits rouleaux formation. This important property of RBCs allows blood to flow even at Ht of 98%.

Packed Cell Volume

Blood viscosity increases logarithmically with linear increase in PCV over the range of 0.2–0.6 and relatively linearly over the normal range of 0.35–0.55 for healthy humans.[14] The effect of PCV on blood viscosity is more pronounced at lower shear rates. This dependence of blood viscosity on PCV can be explained in terms of increase in RBCs aggregation with the increase in their concentration. This in turn causes an increase in the effective cell volume bringing higher level of energy dissipation during flow and, hence, higher blood viscosity. At high shear rates, however, the increase in cell concentration stimulates cell deformation, which decreases their effective size and so balances the increase in blood viscosity.[15]

Blood Plasma Viscosity

Blood plasma behaves like a Newtonian fluid with viscosity independent of the shear rate.[16] The contribution of plasma viscosity (PV) to that of the whole blood is believed to be more pronounced at high shear rates. PV is measured in a viscometer; capillary viscometers have been found to be particularly effective.[17] If a viscometer is unavailable, good correlations have been reported between PV and plasma protein concentration.[16] Plasma protein concentration can be easily measured with a refractometer.[18] PV is slightly higher than that of water due to molecules suspended in it, which cause additional energy dissipation during flow. Its viscosity at 37°C is 1.15–1.35 mPa·s with the average of 1.25 mPa·s as opposed to 0.69 mPa·s for water.[19] This difference is mainly due to the presence of high-molecular weight proteins in blood and only 1–2% contribution due to smaller molecules.

The proteins which have the greatest effect on plasma viscosity are the serum globulins (lipoproteins, immunoglobulins, etc.). Albumin due to its relatively low molecular weight and symmetry, and despite its weight percentage (3.4–5.4 g/dl), contributes only about 36% of the difference between plasma and water viscosities. Fibrinogen, which comprises only about 4% of plasma by weight, causes 22% difference in plasma and water viscosities due to its high molecular weight and asymmetry.[19]

PV increases linearly by about 2.4% with the decrease in temperature by one degree over the range of 20–40°C. At 25°C, it is in the range of 1.50–1.72 mPa·s, whereas at 20°C, it is 1.70–1.92 mPa·s. By comparison, the whole blood viscosity changes by approximately 3% per degree of Celsius.[20]

Blood Yield Stress

Due to RBC aggregation at low shear rates, some finite amount of stress needs to be exerted to break the aggregates and induce some bulk movement of blood. This stress is called yield stress. According to Merrill et al.,[21] the level of yield stress depends on fibrinogen concentration and Ht. For normal blood it is about 4–5 mPa and is relatively independent of temperature in the range of 10–37°C.[20]

Blood Thixotropy

Blood is also thixotropic, which means it exhibits a time-dependent change in viscosity at a constant shear rate. Blood viscosity has been shown to decrease with time during shearing at a constant rate.[22] In particular, it has been found that blood viscosity decreases over about 20 s during shearing at 10 s^{-1}. Upon increasing the shear rate to 100 s^{-1}, however, no time is needed to reach a steady viscosity value. This is primarily due to the breakdown of RBC aggregates at low shear rates with more rapid structural changes at high shear rates. In addition, Gaspar-Rosas and Thurston[23] found that approximately 50 s are needed to restore this internal structure at low shear rates compared to relatively instant disaggregation at high shear rates.

Viscoelasticity of Blood

Human blood also shows viscoelasticity in periodic or transient flow,[24] as blood exhibits both viscous and elastic behavior. Several factors contribute to the viscoelastic behavior of blood. The aggregates of RBCs, as well as human RBCs themselves, deform elastically under stress.[25] At low shear rates, the viscoelasticity is primarily due to the aggregation of RBCs. At intermediate shear rates, however, the progressive breakdown of the aggregates occurs together with the alignment and deformation of distinct cells. The latter is the predominant cause of viscoelasticity of blood at high shear rates. Moreover, the elastic behavior of blood increases significantly with the increase in Ht due to the increased number of the interactions between the cells.

Blood Viscosity Variability

The viscosity of human blood varies significantly and is affected by many different factors.[26] These include gender, various pathologies, obesity,[27] blood group and smoking,[28] alcoholism,[29] hydration status,[30] anticoagulant and other drugs in the body,[31] anxiety, and physiological responses to trauma.[28] Most of what is known about the physical properties of human blood specifically relates to blood behavior inside the body and how various pathologies change its flow properties. Blood viscosity is of particular relevance in the medical community as it is a risk factor in cardiovascular diseases and peripheral vascular diseases.[8]

Human Blood Surface Tension

Surface tension, or, more specifically, interfacial tension between two fluids at liquid–air interface (i.e. blood and air), is caused by greater cohesive forces between liquid molecules than the adhesion forces between the liquid molecules and the molecules of air. Molecules on the surface of a liquid are not completely surrounded by other liquid molecules, so are strongly drawn inward. This creates internal pressure which forces the liquid to contort to the shape with the least surface area; a sphere, forming into a droplet.[32] The internal pressure of a droplet is inversely proportional to its radius. Surface tension is, therefore, the greatest force acting on very small droplets, regardless of other competing forces.[2] The surface tension of liquids has been found to decrease with the addition of detergents or surfactants.[32] Surfactant compounds contain both hydrophilic and hydrophobic groups; so, having surfactants at the surface modifies the surface properties of the liquid.

Surface tension can be measured by various methods; the common is the sessile drop method.[2] This method involves a droplet being formed on a flat, concave or cup-shaped depression. The radius of curvature and height of the droplet are measured to calculate surface tension. The lesser used drop weight method involves filming a blood droplet being slowly formed at the end of a nozzle. The weight of the droplet forming under gravity overcomes the surface tension forces adhering the droplet to the liquid still in the tube. The maximum size of the droplet before it detaches is used in the surface tension calculation. Blood density must be known for this method to be used. Both these methods for blood density and surface tension measurement have been adequately described by Raymond.[2] Since about 50% of blood content is water, (liquid-vapor) interfacial properties of blood may be analyzed in terms of their deviation from (or relative to) that of pure water.

Harkins and Harkins[33] reported the mean surface tension of blood plasma to be about 52 and 48 mN/m at 20°C and 37°C, respectively, and a more recent study reported values within the range of 60–68 mN/m.[32]

Surface tension of the whole blood in healthy humans was measured by Hrncir and Rosina[34] to be 55.9 mN/m at 22°C with no correlation to age or sex. These authors also found no correlations between the surface tension of blood and basic hematological variables. A follow-up study assessed the effect of anticoagulant on the surface tension of blood and identified a linear correlation with the concentration of the anticoagulant compound sodium citrate.[32] Surface tension was found to rise from 62 mN/m at a blood-sodium citrate concentration of 10% to 67 mN/m at 90%. A 100% sodium citrate solution had a surface tension value of 68 mN/m, all measured at 22°C. A study examining the effects of blood temperature on surface tension found that surface tension decreases linearly with an increase in temperature from 20°C to 40°C (60.5 mN/m at 20°C to 51 mN/m at 40°C).[35]

The most important property of liquid water that has a crucial influence on all immersed molecules, particles, cells, and surfaces is its very strong energy of cohesion, which is 30% due to van der Waals attractions and 70% due to the hydrogen-bonding driven (i.e., polar) attraction of water molecules.[36] The polar attraction between water molecules causes strong attraction of all hydrophobic (non-polar) molecules and particles immersed in water (so-called "hydrophobic effect"), whereas polar attraction of water molecules and hydrophilic (polar) molecules and particles cause repulsion between such hydrophilic entities when immersed in water ("hydration pressure" effect). The latter effect causes repulsion of blood cells from each other, keeps them in stable suspension in blood, and prevents clot formation. Moreover, repulsion exists between serum protein molecules, which keeps them in a stable solution avoiding precipitation.

It is believed that single sugars such as glucose, some of the low-molecular weight amino acids (e.g., glycine),[37] and many salts (such as sodium chloride and potassium chloride) decrease the surface tension of water at very low concentrations. At high concentrations, however, these solutes increase the surface tension of water considerably. Dissolved glucose, in particular, has high energy of cohesion (or the amount of work that is needed to be performed in a system in order to separate two-unit areas of identical material (molecules) from contact to infinity) leading to a strong continuous attraction between these molecules' freely available electron acceptors and electron donors, and so, it increases surface tension of water to about 32%.[37] In aqueous solutions, the molecules of simple sugars are repelled from the free interface and move to the bulk fluid.

For salts, the change in surface tension is proportional to the concentration of salt and, provided the concentration is not too low, it is toward the increase in the surface tension of solvent (water) and depends on both the anions and the cations present, but usually more strongly on the anions.[29] Each ionic species experiences different forces near the free interface. These might be forces of attraction or repulsion, but all together they lead to an increase or decrease in concentration near the interface. It is this alteration in concentration that leads to the surface tension increment. The increase in the surface tension of water implies the increase in the free energy of cohesion, which enhances hydrophobicity of its aqueous solution. In the case of salts, for example, this leads to the decrease in solubility of proteins and their precipitation when added to a concentrated salt solution (so-called "salting out"). Despite the effects of glucose and salts dissolved in blood plasma (and/or serum), the surface tension of blood serum is much lower than that of pure water.[38]

Like serum, blood plasma is also a concentrated protein solution. Protein molecules consist of hydrophobic and hydrophilic amino acids. In aqueous solutions, hydrophobic amino acids of proteins usually form protected hydrophobic areas, while hydrophilic amino acids interact with the molecules of solvent and allow proteins to form hydrogen bonds with the surrounding water molecules. Several experimental studies suggest the controlling role of water in protein adsorption to the surface.[39] It is argued that liquid-vapor interface saturates with protein adsorbed from bulk solution at a fixed weight-volume concentration (~436 mg/ml) independently of protein type or proportions in a mixture. Accordingly, blood serum is not different from plasma in terms of the observed surface tension increments. Globular proteins such as human albumin and serum immunoglobulin-G (IgG) are attracted to the free interface when in aqueous solution. It causes a decrease of 17–18% in the apparent surface tension of the aqueous solvent.[40]

Human Blood Density

Blood density, the mass per unit volume, is proportional to Ht and plasma protein concentration.[41] Density is usually measured in a calibrated density flask on a calibrated scale. Published values for human blood density range from 1.043 g/cm^3 to 1.065 g/cm^3.[42,43] These values were measured using a number of different methods at different temperatures and PCV values.[41] Blood is 1.056 and 1.048–1.054 times denser than pure water at 25/4°C and 37/4°C, respectively.[6] Blood is assumed to be *incompressible*, i.e., its density does not change during blood transfer events. Blood, like other liquids, can be compressed, but it requires enormous pressure to change the density by more than a fraction of 1%.

The sensitivity of bloodstain characteristics to the viscosity and surface tension of blood has been highlighted in several studies.[44] These authors examined the effects of common therapeutic drugs on these physical properties and their theoretical effect on bloodstain dimensions based on the measurements taken from passive blood drops. These studies reported significant changes in these properties between unaltered and therapeutic to fatal doses of the respective substances. They hypothesized that this would lead to variations of up to 2.9%[44] and 5.93%[31] in the diameter of circular bloodstains.

Larkin and Banks[45] studied the effect of PCV on dried bloodstain appearance, reporting PCV to strongly affect viscosity, and hence the degree of spreading. PCV varies from individual to individual over a normal range of 35–50%. In extreme cases, this may range from 15–75%, which was the range used in this study. Larkin and Banks found PCV to have a significant effect on stain diameter, but not on stain aspect ratio (ellipticity). This is reassuring given aspect ratio is used to infer the direction (angle of impact) a spattered blood drop was traveling. Brownson and Banks[44] studied the effect of amphetamines in blood at concentrations from therapeutic to potentially lethal. Amphetamines affected blood viscosity by 0.5% (for therapeutic concentrations) to 11.0% (potentially lethal concentrations). At worst, this gives a 2.9% difference in stain diameter, which is impractical to perceive given the other unknowns at a crime scene. El-Sayed, Brownson, and Banks[31] studied the effect of warfarin at therapeutic to potentially lethal concentrations, finding a 3.6–20.4% change in viscosity, respectively, a 0.6–4.7% change in surface tension, and up to 6% change in stain diameter as a result. Larkin et al.[46] studied the effect of cocaine and one of its metabolites, as well as the effect of neurotransmitters dopamine, serotonin, and epinephrine. Cocaine affected blood viscosity by 1.1–7.8% and its metabolite by 6.4–9.5%, and surface tension altered by up to 14%. Neurotransmitters had no measurable effect on viscosity.

ANIMAL BLOOD COLLECTION, HANDLING, AND STORAGE METHODS FOR BPA

Despite the advantages of using human blood in BPA experimentation, substitutes are most often required. This is primarily due to the biohazard dangers associated with the handling of human blood. Ethical issues associated with human blood acquisition and the requirement of large blood volumes for BPA research are also limitations.[47] Many factors need to be taken into account when planning a BPA experiment using human blood, animal blood, or a synthetic blood substitute. Factors such as hematology, temperature, handling procedures, and the anticoagulant compound used to store blood can all have important effects. Even the properties of freshly drawn human blood can be altered if strict handling procedures are not adhered to.

There are currently no recommendations regarding what the physical properties of blood substitutes used in BPA should be. There is no standard or recommended method of measuring or reporting these values. There is no current protocol to manipulate the physical properties of blood or blood substitutes. No accepted methodology has been developed to determine or quantify the effect that these properties have on stain formation. There are no existing guidelines regarding which animal blood substitutes should be used in BPA research when human blood is not an option. There are no recommendations as to which anticoagulant or methods of animal blood collection should be used to avoid contamination and mechanical damage to RBCs. However, it is necessary to standardize the physical properties of blood used in BPA research.

Christman[48] compared the macro-characteristics of drop and spatter stains created with human, ovine, bovine, equine, and porcine blood, reporting negligible differences in stain presentation between blood samples. Raymond, Smith, and Liesegang[2] examined the validity of pig blood for use in BPA experimentation, reporting favorable comparisons between human and pig blood properties. These studies provided sufficient support for the use of pig blood in the majority of BPA research and scene reconstruction experiments at the time of their publication. This still holds true for macro-level experiments and teaching. Further investigation into the use of animal blood as a substitute is necessary as the requirements for precision in this field increases. Detailed studies considering the complex fluid dynamics of blood are increasingly being carried out by researchers in the field of BPA and this topic is covered in greater detail in Chapter 5.

BPA research has been performed using blood from a variety of species, at a range of temperatures and with a range of synthetic blood substitutes. Most published studies in the BPA literature use either human[49] or pig blood.[47] Whole bovine blood,[50] whole equine blood,[51] defibrinated equine blood,[44] and ovine blood[52] have also been used in a small number of studies. Using human blood, however, doesn't necessarily guarantee validity in terms of emulating human blood fresh from the source. Factors including blood temperature, agitation, and changes resulting from additives such as anticoagulants must be considered.

Anticoagulant Compounds

The effect of the anticoagulant used on the physical properties of blood is an important consideration. Anticoagulants are added to blood as it is collected to prevent clotting and ensure sample integrity. This is achieved by binding calcium ions or inhibiting thrombin, a protein essential in the coagulation process.[53] Many anticoagulant compounds are available and used for different purposes in medicine and analytical chemistry. Different anticoagulant compounds have been found to have different effects on the physical properties of blood.[54] The same anticoagulant has also been found to have different effects on the hematology of different animal species (sheep, cattle, dogs, and humans).[53] The ratio of anticoagulant to blood is important to control as solutions not isotonic to blood are likely to cause swelling (or conversely, shrinking) of erythrocytes. This, in addition to causing hemolysis, can have a noticeable effect on measurements of PCV and total plasma protein.[55]

Reporting of Blood Treatments in BPA

In the interests of establishing scientific repeatability in BPA research, reporting of the physical properties and measurements methods of blood, where possible, should be encouraged. Given the complexities and required equipment, however, at least the species of origin, PCV, the age of the blood sample, and ambient temperature during experimentation should be stated. It is also important to report the collection methods, treatment, and handling procedures used as they affect the physical properties of blood. Raymond et al.[2] measured the viscosity, density, and surface tension values of the blood they used when looking at oscillation and compared these to the published pig and human values. Orr et al.[50] reported sample preparation procedures, viscosity, density, surface tension, PCV, temperature, and the age of the sample, as did by de Castro et al.[56]. Most authors, however, do not measure these properties or PCV, but report the species of origin[49] and the anticoagulant used.[57] Some authors warm the blood to 37°C prior to experiments.[57] Others warm blood to room temperature but do not state the exact temperature.[49] Few studies report collection, treatment procedures,[49] and the age of the blood sample.[58] Two studies have reported published values of the physical properties of pig blood.[47]

Comparative Hemorheology and Physical Properties of Animal Blood

Studies in comparative hemorheology are generally undertaken to provide information on the structural and functional basis of RBCs.[59] Information regarding various adaptive features of blood of different species can help in determining the functional significance of various rheological characteristics.[60] This can have a plethora of applications in human health and disease. Findings from these studies can be applied to the context of BPA to evaluate the relative merits of different animal blood models.

Various comparative hemorheological studies have identified a number of factors affecting blood viscosity and flow characteristics in vitro. These have been found to differ significantly between human and animal blood. These include PCV, plasma protein concentration, RBC morphology, RBC aggregation, RBC flexibility, and RBC sedimentation rate (ESR).[9] These factors may also play a role in the behavior of blood outside of the body. The blood of different mammalian species

Table 3.1 Published values for whole blood viscosity (WBV) at 0.7, 2.4, and 94 s^{-1}; and plasma viscosity (PV)

	Shear rate	Human	Pig	Horse	Cattle	Sheep
WBV (mPa.s)	0.7 s^{-1}	33.49	24.69	38.17	6.57	6.59
	2.4 s^{-1}	18.53	14.86	20.18	6.29	6.09
	94 s^{-1}	5.99	4.94	5.18	4.80	4.37
PV (mPa.s)		1.24	1.58	1.66	1.72	1.49

Source: Windberger et al.[105]

has also been shown to exhibit different aggregation behaviors.[61] Variances in plasma components and RBC shape, size, and membrane composition could be largely responsible for these differences.[62]

Windberger et al.[14] compared the hematological and physical properties of nine mammalian species, including pig, horse, cattle, and sheep. In this study, 40 individual adult animals from each species were sampled. Of particular interest to the field of BPA was the comparison of whole blood viscosity (WBV) at three shear rates, plasma viscosity, and RBC aggregation. All blood samples were normalized to 40% PCV. Despite this PCV standardization, WBV values differed for different species, and to a lesser extent, within species. The blood of humans, pigs, and horses showed a rise in WBV values at the two lower shear rates, whereas the blood of cattle and sheep did not (Table 3.1). This finding is consistent with RBC aggregation (rouleaux formation) being a major factor contributing to increased blood viscosity at low shear rates.

Hematology of Animal Blood

Table 3.2 provides a literature summary of hematological properties for pig, horse, cattle, and sheep blood[14] compared with human.[63] Pig blood is shown to have Ht values mostly like human, followed by horse blood. Human RBC diameter is larger than any of these mammalian species. Pig, horse, and cattle have been shown to have similar sized RBCs to one another, while sheep RBCs are significantly smaller. Accordingly, the mean RBC volume (MCV) of humans is much greater than those of other species, with pig MCV being the closest, and sheep blood being the least similar. The plasma protein concentration of pig, horse, and cattle blood have a greater range than human blood.

Animal Red Blood Cells

Pig RBCs are of biconcave discoid shape, are relatively fragile, have been observed to hemolyze easily, and have a moderately high ESR.[64] Horse RBCs are biconcave discoid shape, form prominent rouleaux at low shear rates, considered "hyper- aggregating", and have a rapid ESR.[65] Cattle RBCs are biconcave, rouleaux formation is unusual, and ESR is thus low. Sheep have some of the

Table 3.2 Hematology, plasma protein concentration, and plasma fibrinogen for pig, horse, cattle, and sheep blood from Windberger et al.[14] compared with human values from Laurent et al.[63]

	Human	Pig	Horse	Cattle	Sheep
Ht (%)	38–52	36–43	27–43	21–30	27–45
RBC diameter (µm)	7–8	5–6	5–6	5–6	4–5
RBC (*10^{12}/l)	3.8–6.5	5–7	6–10.4	5–10	9–15
MCV (fl)	79–95	52–62	37–49	40–60	28–40
PP (g/dl)	7.0–7.5	6.0–8.0	6.0–8.5	6.0–8.0	6–7.5
Plasma fibrinogen (g/dl)	0.2–0.4	0.2–0.4	0.1–0.4	0.1–0.6	0.1–0.5

smallest of mammalian RBCs, which do not aggregate (form rouleaux) and do not deform as easily as the RBCs of other mammalian species.[66] The exponential increase seen in WBV as shear rates decrease below 100 s^{-1} is therefore lower in cattle or sheep.

The results from both the studies of Windberger et al.[14] and Weng et al.[66] show that for the purposes of emulating the physical properties of human blood for BPA research, pig blood is the most suitable. Thorough mixing of horse blood is required in hematology testing to prevent errors in lab measurements due to sedimentation[66] and the same applies to BPA experiments. Removing fibrinogen from horse blood will lower the ESR by removing the proteins that are needed for rouleaux formation and by changing the electrical charge on the surface of RBCs.[66] Due to rapid ESR of horse blood, it would require defibrinating or constant mixing during experimentation, which are additional steps, further limiting the practicality of its use in BPA. This finding, consistent with other studies,[61] further supports the use of pig blood in BPA activities.

Physical Properties of Pig Blood

Pigs size and physiological similarity to humans make them popular biomedical models for human health and disease.[67] The collection and handling of high-quality samples can be difficult, and thus, the literature validating normal pig hematology values is sparse.[64] Serum harvested from samples of whole pig blood is frequently used in veterinary practice for disease antibody quantification and virus detection. Whole blood, however, is seldom collected for hematological analysis as tissue biopsies are preferred for routine health checks. A wide range of WBV values have been reported for both whole blood and plasma between different breeds of pig and between studies performed in different parts of the world. These studies have used different anticoagulant compounds, collection methods, and measurement techniques. These are summarized in Table 3.3. Very little data is available regarding pig blood density or surface tension.

Hematological parameters vary considerably between breeds, age, growth phase, diet, and lifestyle of pigs.[64] While PCV (alternatively, Ht) is the main determinant of WBV and density, other contributing factors include plasma protein concentration (fibrinogen in particular), hemoglobin concentration, RBC volume, deformability, shape and aggregation, and ESR.[9] These factors may also play a significant role in the behavior of blood outside of the body. The significant differences in WBV seen at the lower shear rates have been attributed to the greater erythrocyte aggregation and plasma fibrinogen concentration measured in pigs.[61] Durussel et al.[61] found that higher WBV seen in pigs correlated with plasma fibrinogen concentration in a study where PCV values were significantly higher in humans (0.41 ± 0.28) than pigs (0.356 ± 5.4). Windberger et al.[14] also found that erythrocyte aggregation correlated with plasma fibrinogen in pigs but not in cattle or sheep.

The non-Newtonian characteristics of blood that govern the decrease in viscosity with an increase in shear rate also decrease the interspecies viscosity differences; however, many bloodstains are created at very low shear rates. These findings suggest that factors such as RBC morphology and plasma constituents may have an important role in explaining the viscosity differences observed between humans and pigs.

Table 3.3 Summary of published values for pig whole blood viscosity compared to human

Study	Shear rate (s^{-1})	Anticoagulant	WBV vs human blood
Laurent et al.[63]	10	Heparin	38.5% higher
Durussel[61]	10	Heparin	33% higher
Windberger et al.[14]	94	EDTA	17.5% lower
Wickham[60]	100	EDTA	15.5% higher
Raymond et al.[2]	230	EDTA	20% higher

Notes

1. Hoffbrand AV, Steensma DP. Hoffbrand's Essential Haematology. 8th ed. Hoffbrand AV, Steensma DP, editors. Oxford: Wiley-Blackwell; 2019.
2. Raymond MA, Smith ER, Liesegang J. The physical properties of blood – forensic considerations. Science & Justice. 1996 Jul;36(3):153–60.
3. Dzwinel W, Boryczko K, Yuen DA. A discrete-particle model of blood dynamics in capillary vessels. J Colloid Interface Sci. 2003 Feb;258(1):163–73.
4. Turgeon ML. Clinical Hematology : Theory and Procedures. 4th ed. Philadelphia: Lippincott Williams & Wilkins; 2004.
5. McLaren CE, Brittenham GM, Hasselblad V. Statistical and Graphical Evaluation of Erythrocyte Volume Distributions. American Journal of Physiology. 1987;252(4):857–66.
6. Trudnowski RJ, Rico RC. Specific Gravity of Blood and Plasma at 4 and 37 Degrees C. Clin Chem. 1974;20(5):615–6.
7. Kabaliuk N, Jermy MC, Morison K, Stotesbury T, Taylor MC, Williams E. Blood drop size in passive dripping from weapons. Forensic Sci Int. 2013 May;228(1–3):75–82.
8. Fossum E, Høieggen A, Moan A, Nordby G, Velund TL, Kjeldsen SE. Whole Blood Viscosity, Blood Pressure and Cardiovascular Risk Factors in Healthy Blood Donors. Blood Press. 1997 Jan 5;6(3):161–5.
9. Baskurt OK, Meiselman HJ. Hemodynamic Effects of Red Blood Cell Aggregation. Indian J Exp Biol. 2007;45(1):25–31.
10. Dintenfass L. Blood Viscosity. In: FIFTH INTERNATIONAL CONGRESS OF BIORHEOLOGY. Sydney; 2006. p. 191–206.
11. Rampling MW, Whittingstall P. The effect of temperature on the viscosity characteristics of erythrocyte suspensions. Clin Hemorheol Microcirc. 2016 Dec 22;7(6):745–55.
12. Chien S, Usami S, Taylor HM, Lundberg JL, Gregersen MI. Effects of hematocrit and plasma proteins on human blood rheology at low shear rates. J Appl Physiol. 1966 Jan;21(1):81–7.
13. Seiyama A, Suzuki Y, Maeda N. Increased viscosity of erythrocyte suspension upon hemolysis. Colloid Polym Sci. 1993 Jan;271(1):63–9.
14. Windberger U, Bartholovitsch A, Plasenzotti R, Korak KJ, Heinze G. Whole Blood Viscosity, Plasma Viscosity and Erythrocyte Aggregation in Nine Mammalian Species: Reference Values and Comparison of Data. Exp Physiol. 2003 May 4;88(3):431–40.
15. Dintenfass L. The Rheology of Blood in Vascular Disease. J R Coll Physicians Lond. 1971;5(3):231–40.
16. Késmárky G, Kenyeres P, Rábai M, Tóth K. Plasma viscosity: A forgotten variable. Clin Hemorheol Microcirc. 2008;39(1–4):243–6.
17. Dintenfass L, Kammer S. Re-evaluation of heat precipitation method for plasma fibrinogen estimation: effect of abnormal proteins and plasma viscosity. J Clin Pathol. 1976 Feb;29(2):130–4.
18. George JW. The Usefulness and Limitations of Hand-held Refractometers in Veterinary Laboratory Medicine: An Historical and Technical Review. Vet Clin Pathol. 2001 Dec 5;30(4):201–10.
19. Lowe GDO, Barbenel JC. Plasma and Blood Viscosity. In: Lowe GDO, editor. Clinical Blood Rheology. 1st ed. BocaRaton: CRC Press; 1988.
20. Barbee JH. The effect of temperature on the relative viscosity of human blood. Biorheology. 1973 Mar 1;10(1):1–5.
21. Merrill EW, Gilliland ER. Rheology of Blood. Physiol Rev. 1969;49(4):863–88.
22. Huang CR, Siskovic N, Robertson RW, Fabisiak W, Smitherberg EH, Copley AL. Quantitative characterization of thixotropy of whole human blood1. Biorheology. 1975 Oct 1;12(5):279–82.
23. Gaspar-Rosas A, Thurston GB. Erythrocyte aggregate rheology by transmitted and reflected light. Biorheology. 1988 Jun 1;25(3):471–87.
24. Thurston GB. Viscoelasticity of Human Blood. Biophys J. 1972 Sep;12(9):1205–17.
25. Puig-de-Morales-Marinkovic M, Turner KT, Butler JP, Fredberg JJ, Suresh S. Viscoelasticity of the human red blood cell. American Journal of Physiology-Cell Physiology. 2007 Aug;293(2):C597–605.
26. de Simone G, Devereux RB, Chien S, Alderman MH, Atlas SA, Laragh JH. Relation of blood viscosity to demographic and physiologic variables and to cardiovascular risk factors in apparently normal adults. Circulation. 1990 Jan;81(1):107–17.
27. Solá E, Vayá A, Simó M, Hernández-Mijares A, Morillas C, España F, et al. Fibrinogen, Plasma Viscosity and Blood Viscosity in Obesity. Relationship with Insulin Resistance. . Clin Hemorheol Microcirc. 2007;37(4):309–18.

28. Dintenfass L. Blood Viscosity, Hyperviscosity & Hyperviscosaemia. Dintenfass L, editor. Boston: Lancaster Lancashire, MTP Press; 1985.
29. Weissenborn PK, Pugh RJ. Surface Tension of Aqueous Solutions of Electrolytes: Relationship with Ion Hydration, Oxygen Solubility, and Bubble Coalescence. J Colloid Interface Sci. 1996;184:550–63.
30. Vlastos GA, Tangney CC, Rosenson RS. Effects of Hydration on Blood Rheology. Clin Hemorheol Microcirc. 2003;28(1):41–9.
31. El-Sayed M, Brownson DAC, Banks CE. Crime scene investigation II: The effect of warfarin on bloodstain pattern analysis. Analytical Methods. 2011;3(7):1521.
32. Kratochvíl A, Hrnčíř E. Correlation between the Blood Surface Tension and the Activity of Some Enzymes. Physiol Res. 1997;50(4):433–7.
33. Harkins HN, Harkins WD. The Surface Tension of Blood Serum, and the Determination of the Surface Tension of Biological Fluids. Journal of Clinical Investigation. 1929;7(2):263–81.
34. Hrnčíř E, Rosina J. Surface Tension of Blood. Physiol Res. 1997;46(4):319–21.
35. Rosina J, Kvašňák E, Šuta D, Kolářová H, Málek J, Krajčí L. Temperature dependence of blood surface tension. Physiol Res. 2007;S93–8.
36. Van Oss CJ. The Properties of Water and Their Role in Colloidal and Biological Systems. 1st ed. Van Oss CJ, editor. Vol. 16. Amsterdam: Elsevier Science; 2008.
37. Docoslis A, Giese RF, van Oss CJ. Influence of the water–air interface on the apparent surface tension of aqueous solutions of hydrophilic solutes. Colloids Surf B Biointerfaces. 2000 Dec;19(2):147–62.
38. Morgan JLR, Woodward HE. The Weight of a Falling Drop and the Laws of Tate. XI. The Drop Weight and Surface Tension of Blood Serum. J Am Chem Soc. 1913;35(9):1249–62.
39. Krishnan A, Wilson A, Sturgeon J, Siedlecki CA, Vogler EA. Liquid–vapor interfacial tension of blood plasma, serum and purified protein constituents thereof. Biomaterials. 2005 Jun;26(17):3445–53.
40. Absolom DR, Van Oss CJ, Zingg W, Neumann AW. Determination of surface tensions of proteins II. Surface tension of serum albumin, altered at the protein-air interface. Biochimica et Biophysica Acta (BBA) - Protein Structure. 1981 Aug 28;670(1):74–8.
41. Kenner T. The measurement of blood density and its meaning. Basic Res Cardiol. 1989 Mar;84(2):111–24.
42. Yamauchi T, Yanai M, Takahashi S, Man N. Blood Density Monitoring During Dialysis. Artif Organs. 1996 Sep 12;20(9):981–5.
43. Hinghofer-Szalkay H. Volume and density changes of biological fluids with temperature. J Appl Physiol. 1985 Dec 1;59(6):1686–9.
44. Brownson DAC, Banks CE. Crime Scene Investigation: The Effect of Drug Contaminated Bloodstains on Bloodstain Pattern Analysis. Analytical Methods. 2010;2(12):1885.
45. Larkin BAJ, Banks CE. Exploring the effect of specific packed cell volume upon bloodstain pattern analysis: blood drying and dry volume estimation. Canadian Society of Forensic Science Journal. 2015 Oct 2;48(4):167–89.
46. Larkin BAJ, El-Sayed M, Brownson DAC, Banks CE. Crime scene investigation III: Exploring the effects of drugs of abuse and neurotransmitters on Bloodstain Pattern Analysis. Analytical Methods. 2012;4(3):721.
47. Hulse-Smith L, Mehdizadeh N, Chandra S. Deducing Drop Size and Impact Velocity from Circular Bloodstains. J Forensic Sci. 2005 Jan 1;50(1):JFS2003224-10.
48. Christman D. A Study to Compare Animal Blood to Human Blood Product. In: International Association of Bloodstain Pattern Analysts and Association of Crime Scene Reconstruction Joint Training Conference. 1997.
49. Adam CD. Fundamental studies of bloodstain formation and characteristics. Forensic Sci Int. 2012 Jun 10;219(1–3):76–87.
50. Orr A, Gualdieri R, Cossette ML, Shafer ABA, Stotesbury T. Whole bovine blood use in forensic research: Sample preparation and storage considerations. Science & Justice. 2021 May;61(3):214–20.
51. Hill T. TECHNICAL REPORT Visualizing Bloodstain Patterns on Dark or Multi-Colored, Multi-Designed Clothing Using Luminol and Adobe Photoshop® Layers. Journal of Bloodstain Pattern Analysis. 2011;29(1):29–33.
52. Sweet MJ. Velocity Measurements of Projected Bloodstains from a Medium Velocity Impact Source. Canadian Society of Forensic Science Journal. 1993 Jan;26(3):103–10.

53. Mohri M, Rezapoor H. Effects of heparin, citrate, and EDTA on plasma biochemistry of sheep: Comparison with serum. Res Vet Sci. 2009 Feb;86(1):111–4.
54. Cerón JJ, Martínez-Subiela S, Hennemann C, Tecles F. The effects of different anticoagulants on routine canine plasma biochemistry. The Veterinary Journal. 2004 May;167(3):294–301.
55. Rapoport S, Wing M. Dimensional, Osmotic, and Chemical Changes of Erythrocytes in Stored Blood. I. Blood Preserved in Sodium Citrate, Neutral, and Acid Citrate-Glucose (ACD) Mixtures. Journal of Clinical Investigation. 1947 Jul 1;26(4):591–615.
56. de Castro TC, Taylor MC, Carr DJ, Athens J, Kieser JA. Storage life of whole porcine blood used for bloodstain pattern analysis. Canadian Society of Forensic Science Journal. 2016 Jan 2;49(1):26–37.
57. Knock C, Davison M. Predicting the Position of the Source of Blood Stains for Angled Impacts. J Forensic Sci. 2007 Sep 28;52(5):1044–9.
58. Pizzola PA, Roth S, De Forest PR. Blood Droplet Dynamics. I . J Forensic Sci. 1986;31(1):36–49.
59. Baskurt OK, Meiselman HJ. Lessons from Comparative Hemorheology Studies. Clin Hemorheol Microcirc. 2010;45(2–4):101–8.
60. Wickham LL, Bauersachs RM, Wenby RB, Sowemimo-Coker S, Meiselman HJ, Elsnerl R. Red Cell Aggregation and Viscoelasticity of Blood from Seals, Swine and Man. Biorheology. 1990;27:191–204.
61. Durussel JJ. Comparative Viscosity and Erythrocytes Disaggregation Shear Stress of Blood-Radiographic Contrast Media Mixtures in Three Mammalian Species. Clin Hemorheol Microcirc. 1997;17(4):261–9.
62. Plasenzotti R, Stoiber B, Posch M, Windberger U. Red Blood Cell Deformability and Aggregation Behaviour in Different Animal Species. Clin Hemorheol Microcirc. 2004;31(2):104–11.
63. Laurent A, Durussel JJ, Dufaux J, Penhouët L, Bailly AL, Bonneau M, et al. Effects of Contrast Media on Blood Rheology: Comparison in Humans, Pigs, and Sheep. Cardiovasc Intervent Radiol. 1999 Jan 30;22(1):62–6.
64. Thorn CE. Hematology of the Pig. In: Weiss DJ, Wardrop KJ, editors. Schlams Veterinary Hematology. 6th ed. Ames, Iowa: Wiley-Blackwell; 2010.
65. Fedde MR, Wood SC. Rheological characteristics of horse blood: significance during exercise. Respir Physiol. 1993 Dec;94(3):323–35.
66. Weng, X, Cloutier G, Pibarot P, Durand L. Comparison and simulation of different levels of erythrocyte aggregation with pig, horse, sheep, calf, and normal human blood. Biorheology. 1996 Jul 10;33(4–5):365–77.
67. Walters EM, Agca Y, Ganjam V, Evans T. Animal models got you puzzled?: think pig. Ann N Y Acad Sci. 2011 Dec 29;1245(1):63–4.

Further Reading

Absolom, D. R., C. J. van Oss, W. Zingg, and A. W. Neumann. "Determination of Surface Tensions of Proteins II. Surface Tension of Serum Albumin, Altered at the Protein-Air Interface." *Biochimica et Biophysica Acta* 670, no. 1 (1981): 74–78.

Adam, Craig D. "Fundamental Studies of Bloodstain Formation and Characteristics." *Forensic Science International* 219, no. 1–3 (2012): 76–87. https://doi.org/10.1016/j.forsciint.2011.12.002

Assendelft, O. W. Van, B. S. Bull, K. Fujimoto, W. Groner, B. Houwen, L. Van Hove, G. G. Klee, et al. "Recommendations for Reference Method for the Packed Cell Volume (ICSH Standard 2001)." *Laboratory Hematology* 7, no. 3 (2001): 148–70.

Barbee, James H. "The Effect of Temperature on the Relative Viscosity of Human Blood." *Biorheology* 10, no. 1 (1973): 1–5. https://doi.org/10.3233/BIR-1973-10101.

Baskurt, Oguz K. and Herbert J. Meiselman. "Hemodynamic Effects of Red Blood Cell Aggregation." *Indian Journal of Experimental Biology* 45, no. 1 (2007): 25–31.

Baskurt, Oguz K. and Herbert J. Meiselman. "Lessons from Comparative Hemorheology Studies." *Clinical Hemorheology and Microcirculation* 45, no. 2–4 (2010): 101–8. https://doi.org/10.3233/CH-2010-1287.

Bäumler, H., B. Neu, E. Donath, and H. Kiesewetter. "Basic Phenomena of Red Blood Cell Rouleaux Formation." *Biorheology* 36, no. 5–6 (1999): 439–42.

Brownson, Dale A. C. and Craig E. Banks. "Crime Scene Investigation: The Effect of Drug Contaminated Bloodstains on Bloodstain Pattern Analysis." *Analytical Methods* 2, no. 12 (2010): 1885–89. https://doi.org/10.1039/c0ay00537a.

Carallo, C., C. Irace, M. S. De Franceschi, F. Coppoletta, R. Tiriolo, C. Scicchitano, F. Scavelli, and C. Gnasso. "The Effect of Aging on Blood and Plasma Viscosity. An 11.6 Years Follow-up Study." *Clinical Hemorheology and Microcirculation* 47, no. 1 (2011): 67–74. https://doi.org/10.3233/CH-2010-1367.

Castro, Therese C. de, Michael C. Taylor, Debra J. Carr, Josie Athens, and Jules A. Kieser. "Storage Life of Whole Porcine Blood Used for Bloodstain Pattern Analysis." *Journal of the Canadian Society of Forensic Science* 49, no. 1 (2016): 26–37. https://doi.org/10.1080/00085030.2015.1108770.

Cerón, José J., Silvia Martínez-Subiela, Carla Hennemann, and Fernando Tecles. "The Effects of Different Anticoagulants on Routine Canine Plasma Biochemistry." *Veterinary Journal* 167, no. 3 (2004): 294–301. https://doi.org/10.1016/j.tvjl.2003.09.009.

Chien, Shu. "Determinants of Blood Viscosity and Red Cell Deformability." *Scandinavian Journal of Clinical and Laboratory Investigation* 41, no. S156 (1981): 7–12. https://doi.org/10.3109/00365518109097424.

Chien, S., S. Usami, H. M. Taylor, J. L. Lundberg, and M. I. Gregersen. "Effects of Hematocrit and Plasma Proteins on Human Blood Rheology at Low Shear Rates." *Journal of Applied Physiology* 21, no. 1 (1966): 81–87. https://doi.org/10.1152/jappl.1966.21.1.81.

Christman, D. V. "A Study to Compare Animal Blood to Human Blood Product." *International Association of Bloodstain Pattern Analysts and Association of Crime Scene Reconstruction Joint Training Conference*, 1997.

Dintenfass, Leopold. *Blood Viscosity. Hyperviscosity & Hyperviscosaemia*. Edited by Leopold Dintenfass. Lancaster, England: MTP Press, 1985.

Dintenfass, L. "The Rheology of Blood in Vascular Disease." *Journal of the Royal College of Physicians of London* 5, no. 3 (1971): 231–40.

Dintenfass, L. and S. Kammer. "Re Evaluation of Heat Precipitation Method for Plasma Fibrinogen Estimation: Effect of Abnormal Proteins and Plasma Viscosity." *Journal of Clinical Pathology* 29, no. 2 (1976): 130–34. https://doi.org/10.1136/jcp.29.2.130.

Dintenfass, L. "Influence of Plasma Proteins on the in Vivo and in Vitro Rheological Properties of Blood." The Proceedings of the Fifth International Congress of Biorheology, *Clinical Hemorheology and Microcirculation* 5, no. 3 (1985): 191–206.

Docoslis, A., R. F. Giese, and C. J. Van Oss. "Influence of the Water-Air Interface on the Apparent Surface Tension of Aqueous Solutions of Hydrophilic Solutes." *Colloids and Surfaces B: Biointerfaces* 19, no. 2 (2000): 147–62. https://doi.org/10.1016/S0927-7765(00)00137-5.

Durussel, J. J. "Comparative Viscosity and Erythrocytes Disaggregation Shear Stress of Blood-Radiographic Contrast Media Mixtures in Three Mammalian Species." *Clinical Hemorheology and Microcirculation* 17, no. 4 (1997): 261–69.

Dzwinel, Witold, Krzysztof Boryczko, and David A. Yuen. "A Discrete-Particle Model of Blood Dynamics in Capillary Vessels." *Journal of Colloid and Interface Science* 258, no. 1 (2003): 163–73. https://doi.org/10.1016/S0021-9797(02)00075-9.

El-Sayed, Meerna, Dale A. C. Brownson, and Craig E. Banks. "Crime Scene Investigation II: The Effect of Warfarin on Bloodstain Pattern Analysis." *Analytical Methods* 3, no. 7 (2011): 1521–24. https://doi.org/10.1039/c1ay05196b.

Fedde, M. R., and S. C. Wood. "Rheological Characteristics of Horse Blood: Significance During Exercise." *Respiration Physiology* 94, no. 3 (1993): 323–35. https://doi.org/10.1016/0034-5687(93)90027-8.

Fossum, Eigil, Aud Høieggen, Andreas Moan, Gudmund Nordby, Turid Lohne Velund, and Sverre E. Kjeldsen. "Whole Blood Viscosity, Blood Pressure and Cardiovascular Risk Factors in Healthy Blood Donors." *Blood Pressure* 6, no. 3 (1997): 161–65. https://doi.org/10.3109/08037059709061932.

Gaspar-Rosas, A., and G. B. Thurston. "Erythrocyte Aggregate Rheology by Transmitted and Reflected Light." *Biorheology* 25, no. 3 (1988): 471–87. https://doi.org/10.3233/bir-1988-25308.

George, Jeanne W. "The Usefulness and Limitations of Hand-Held Refractometers in Veterinary Laboratory Medicine: An Historical and Technical Review." *Veterinary Clinical Pathology* 30, no. 4 (2001): 201–10. https://doi.org/10.1111/j.1939-165X.2001.tb00432.x.

Harkins, Henry N., and William D. Harkins. "The Surface Tension of Blood Serum, and the Determination of the Surface Tension of Biological Fluids." *Journal of Clinical Investigation* 7, no. 2 (1929): 263–81.

Hill, Tom. "Technical Report Visualizing Bloodstain Patterns on Dark or Multi-Colored, Multi-Designed Clothing Using Luminol and Adobe Photoshop® Layers." *Journal of Bloodstain Pattern Analysis* 29, no. 1 (2011): 29–33.

Hinghofer-Szalkay, H. "Volume and Density Changes of Biological Fluids with Temperature." *Journal of Applied Physiology* 59, no. 6 (1985): 1686–89. https://doi.org/10.1152/jappl.1985.59.6.1686.

A. Hoffbrand, Victor, and David P. Steensma. *Hoffbrand's Essential Haematology*. 8th ed., Hoboken, NJ: Wiley-Blackwell, 2019.

Hrnčíř, E., and J. Rosina. "Surface Tension of Blood." *Physiological Research* 46, no. 4 (1997): 319–21.

Huang, C. R., N. Siskovic, R. W. Robertson, W. Fabisiak, E. H. Smitherberg, and A. L. Copley. "Quantitative Characterization of Thixotropy of Whole Human Blood." *Biorheology* 12, no. 5 (1975): 279–82. https://doi.org/10.3233/BIR-1975-12505.

Hulse-Smith, Lee, N. Z. Navid, Z. Mehdizadeh, and Sanjeev Chandra. "Deducing Drop Size and Impact Velocity from Circular Bloodstains." *Journal of Forensic Sciences* 50, no. 1 (2005): 1–10. https://doi.org/10.1520/jfs2003224.

Irace, Concetta, F. Scarinci, V. Scorcia, D. Bruzzichessi, R. Fiorentino, G. Randazzo, G. Scorcia, and A. Gnasso. "Association among Low Whole Blood Viscosity, Haematocrit, Haemoglobin and Diabetic Retinopathy in Subjects with Type 2 Diabetes." *British Journal of Ophthalmology* 95, no. 1 (2011): 94–98. https://doi.org/10.1136/bjo.2009.172601.

Kabaliuk, N., M. C. Jermy, K. Morison, T. Stotesbury, M. C. Taylor, and E. Williams. "Blood Drop Size in Passive Dripping from Weapons." *Forensic Science International* 228, no. 1–3 (2013): 75–82. https://doi.org/10.1016/j.forsciint.2013.02.023.

Kenner, T. "The Measurement of Blood Density and Its Meaning." *Basic Research in Cardiology* 84, no. 2 (1989): 111–24. https://doi.org/10.1007/BF01907921.

Késmárky, Gábor, Péter Kenyeres, Miklós Rábai, and Kálmán Tóth. "Plasma Viscosity: A Forgotten Variable." *Clinical Hemorheology and Microcirculation* 39, no. 1–4 (2008): 243–46. https://doi.org/10.3233/CH-2008-1088.

Knock, Clare, and Marie Davison. "Predicting the Position of the Source of Blood Stains for Angled Impacts." *Journal of Forensic Sciences* 52, no. 5 (2007): 1044–49. https://doi.org/10.1111/j.1556-4029.2007.00505.x.

Kratochvíl, A., and E. Hrnčíř. "Correlation between the Blood Surface Tension and the Activity of Some Enzymes." *Physiological Research* 50, no. 4 (2001): 433–37.

Krishnan, Anandi, Arwen Wilson, Jacqueline Sturgeon, Christopher A. Siedlecki, and Erwin A. Vogler. "Liquid-Vapor Interfacial Tension of Blood Plasma, Serum and Purified Protein Constituents Thereof." *Biomaterials* 26, no. 17 (2005): 3445–53. https://doi.org/10.1016/j.biomaterials.2004.09.016.

Laber, Terry L., Bart P. Epstein, and Michael C. Taylor. "High Speed Digital Video Analysis of Bloodstain Pattern Formation from Common Bloodletting Mechanisms." *IABPA News* 24, no. 2 (2008): 4–12.

Larkin, Bethany A. J. and Craig E. Banks. "Exploring the Effect of Specific Packed Cell Volume upon Bloodstain Pattern Analysis: Blood Drying and Dry Volume Estimation." *Journal of the Canadian Society of Forensic Science* 48, no. 4 (2015): 167–89. https://doi.org/10.1080/00085030.2015.1083161.

Larkin, Bethany A. J., Meerna El-Sayed, Dale A. C. Brownson, and Craig E. Banks. "Crime Scene Investigation III: Exploring the Effects of Drugs of Abuse and Neurotransmitters on Bloodstain Pattern Analysis." *Analytical Methods* 4, no. 3 (2012): 721–29. https://doi.org/10.1039/c2ay05762j.

Laurent, Alexandre, Jean Jacques Durussel, Jacques Dufaux, Laurence Penhouët, Anne Laure Bailly, Michel Bonneau, and Jean Jacques Merland. "Effects of Contrast Media on Blood Rheology: Comparison in Humans, Pigs, and Sheep." *Cardiovascular and Interventional Radiology* 22, no. 1 (1999): 62–66. https://doi.org/10.1007/s002709900330.

Lowe, Gordon. D. O., and J. C. Barbenel. "Plasma and Blood Viscosity." In *Clinical Blood Rheology*, edited by Gordon D. O. Lowe, 1st ed., 228. Boca Raton: CRC Press, 1988. https://doi.org/10.1201/9780429261176.

McLaren, C. E., G. M. Brittenham, and V. Hasselblad. "Statistical and Graphical Evaluation of Erythrocyte Volume Distributions." *American Journal of Physiology* 252, no. 4 Pt 2 (1987): 857–66.

Meiselman, H. J., B. Neu, M. W. Rampling, and O. K. Baskurt. "RBC Aggregation: Laboratory Data and Models." *Indian Journal of Experimental Biology* 45, no. 1 (2007): 9–17.

Merrill, Edward W. "Rheology of Blood. Physiological Reviews." *Physiological Reviews* 49, no. 4 (1969): 863–88.

Merrill, E. W., E. R. Gilliland, G. Cokelet, H. Shin, A. Britten, and R. E. Wells. "Rheology of Human Blood, Near and at Zero Flow: Effects of Temperature and Hematocrit Level." *Biophysical Journal* 3, no. 3 (1963): 199–213. https://doi.org/10.1016/S0006-3495(63)86816-2.

Mohri, M., L. Allahyari, and K. Sardari. "Effects of Common Anticoagulants on Routine Plasma Biochemistry of Horse and Comparison with Serum." *Journal of Equine Veterinary Science* 27, no. 7 (2007): 313–16. https://doi.org/10.1016/j.jevs.2007.05.004.

Mohri, M., and H. Rezapoor. "Effects of Heparin, Citrate, and EDTA on Plasma Biochemistry of Sheep: Comparison with Serum." *Research in Veterinary Science* 86, no. 1 (2009): 111–14. https://doi.org/10.1016/j.rvsc.2008.05.010.

Morgan, J. L. R., and H. E. Woodward. "The Weight of a Falling Drop and the Laws of Tate. XI. The Drop Weight and Surface Tension of Blood Serum." *Journal of the American Chemical Society* 35, no. 9 (1913): 1249–62.

Nemeth, N., O. K. Baskurt, H. J. Meiselman, and I. Miko. "Species-Specific Effects of Anticoagulants on Red Blood Cell Deformability." *Clinical Hemorheology and Microcirculation* 43, no. 3 (2009): 259–61. https://doi.org/10.3233/CH-2009-1213.

Nicolaides, A. N., Tikva Horbourne, Rosemary Bowers, P. H. Kidner, and E. M. Besterman. "Blood Viscosity, Red-Cell Flexibility, Haematocrit, and Plasma-Fibrinogen in Patients with Angina." *The Lancet* 310, no. 8045 (1977): 943–45.

Orr, Amanda, Rebecca Gualdieri, Marie Laurence Cossette, Aaron B.A. Shafer, and Theresa Stotesbury. "Whole Bovine Blood Use in Forensic Research: Sample Preparation and Storage Considerations." *Science and Justice* 61, no. 3 (2021): 214–20. https://doi.org/10.1016/j.scijus.2021.02.004.

Oss, Carel van. *The Properties of Water and Their Role in Colloidal and Biological Systems.* Edited by Carel van Oss. 1st ed. Amsterdam: Elsevier Ltd, 2008.

Pizzola, P. A., S. Roth, and P. R. De Forest. "Blood Droplet Dynamics. I." *Journal of Forensic Sciences* 31, no. 1 (1986): 36–49.

Pizzola, P. A., S. Roth, and P. R. De Forest. "Blood Droplet Dynamics. II." *Journal of Forensic Sciences* 31, no. 1 (1986): 50–64.

Plasenzotti, Robert, B. Stoiber, M. Posch, and U. Windberger. "Red Blood Cell Deformability and Aggregation Behaviour in Different Animal Species." *Clinical Hemorheology and Microcirculation* 31, no. 2 (2004): 105–11.

Pongrácz, Endre, Hajnalka Andrikovics, Iván S. Bernát, and Zoltán Nagy. "Connection between Genetically Determined Blood Coagulation Factors and Haemorheology." *Clinical Hemorheology and Microcirculation* 39, no. 1–4 (2008): 333–41. https://doi.org/10.3233/CH-2008-1099.

Puig-de-Morales-Marinkovic, Marina, Kevin T. Turner, James P. Butler, Jeffrey J. Fredberg, and Subra Suresh. "Viscoelasticity of the Human Red Blood Cell." *American Journal of Physiology - Cell Physiology* 293, no. 2 (2007): 597–605. https://doi.org/10.1152/ajpcell.00562.2006.

Rampling, M. W., and P. Whittingstall. "The Effect of Temperature on the Viscosity Characteristics of Erythrocyte Suspensions." *Clinical Hemorheology* 7, no. 6 (1987): 745–55. https://doi.org/10.3233/ch-1987-7602.

Rand, Peter W., and Eleanor Lacombe. "Hemodilution, Tonicity, and Blood Viscosity *" 43, no. 11 (1964): 2214–26.

Rand, P. W., E. Lacombe, H. E. Hunt, and W. H. Austin. "Viscosity of Normal Human Blood Under Normothermic and Hypothermic Conditions." *Journal of Applied Physiology* 19 (1964): 117–22. https://doi.org/10.1152/jappl.1964.19.1.117.

Rapoport, S. "Dimensional, Osmotic, and Chemical Changes of Erythrocytes in Stored Blood Preserved in Sodium Citrate, Neutral, and Acid Citrate-Glucose (ACD) Mixtures." *The Journal of Clinical Investigation* 26, no. 4 (1947): 591–615. https://doi.org/10.1172/JCI101843.

Raymond, M. A. A., E. R. R. Smith, and J. Liesegang. "The Physical Properties of Blood - Forensic Considerations." *Science and Justice - Journal of the Forensic Science Society* 36, no. 3 (1996): 153–60. https://doi.org/10.1016/S1355-0306(96)72590-X.

Reynolds, M. E., M. A. Raymond, and I. Dadour. "The Use of Small Bloodstains in Blood Source Area of Origin Determinations." *Journal of the Canadian Society of Forensic Science* 42, no. 2 (2009): 133–46. https://doi.org/10.1080/00085030.2009.10757602.

Rosina, Jozef, E. Kvašňák, D. Šuta, H. Kolářová, J. Málek, and L. Krajči. "Temperature Dependence of Blood Surface Tension." *Physiological Research* 56, no. SUPPL. 1 (2007). https://doi.org/10.33549/physiolres.931306.

Seiyama, A., Y. Suzuki, and N. Maeda. "Increased Viscosity of Erythrocyte Suspension upon Hemolysis." *Colloid and Polymer Science* 271, no. 1 (1993): 63–69. https://doi.org/10.1007/BF00652304.

Simone, Giovanni De, Richard B. Devereux, Shu Chien, Michael H. Alderman, Steven A. Atlas, and John H. Laragh. "Relation of Blood Viscosity to Demographic and Physiologic Variables and to Cardiovascular Risk Factors in Apparently Normal Adults." *Circulation* 81, no. 1 (1990): 107–17. https://doi.org/10.1161/01.CIR.81.1.107.

Sniegoski, Lorna T., and John R. Moody. "Determination of Serum and Blood Densities." *Analytical Chemistry* 51, no. 9 (1979): 1577–78.

Solá, E., A. Vayá, M. Simó, A. Hernández-Mijares, C. Morillas, F. España, A. Estellés, and D. Corella. "Fibrinogen, Plasma Viscosity and Blood Viscosity in Obesity. Relationship With Insulin Resistance." *Clinical Hemorheology and Microcirculation* 37, no. 4 (2007): 309–18.

Sweet, M. J. "Velocity Measurements of Projected Bloodstains from a Medium Velocity Impact Source." *Journal of the Canadian Society of Forensic Science* 26, no. 3 (1993): 103–10. https://doi.org/10.1080/00085030.1993.10757463.

Thorn, C. E. "Hematology of the Pig." In *Schlams Veterinary Hematology*, edited by D. J. Weiss and K. Jane Wardrop, 6th ed. Ames, Iowa: Wiley-Blackwell, 2010.

Thurston, G. B. "Viscoelasticity of Human Blood." *Biophysical Journal* 12, no. 9 (1972): 1205–17. https://doi.org/10.1016/S0006-3495(72)86156-3.

Trudnowski, R. J. and C. Rico. "Specific Gravity of Blood and Plasma at 4 and 37 Degrees C." *Clinical Chemistry* 20, no. 5 (1974): 615–16.

Turgeon, Mary Louise. *Clinical Hematology : Theory and Procedures*. 4th ed. Philadelphia: Lippincott Williams & Wilkins, 2004.

Usami, S., S. Chien, and M. I. Gregersen. "Viscometric Characteristics of Blood of the Elephant, Man, Dog, Sheep, and Goat." *The American Journal of Physiology* 217, no. 3 (1969): 884–90. https://doi.org/10.1152/ajplegacy.1969.217.3.884.

Vlastos, George A., Christine C. Tangney, and Robert S. Rosenson. "Effects of Hydration on Blood Rheology." *Clinical Hemorheology and Microcirculation* 28, no. 1 (2003): 41–49.

Walters, Eric M., Yuksel Agca, Venkataseshu Ganjam, and Tim Evans. "Animal Models Got You Puzzled?: Think Pig." *Annals of the New York Academy of Sciences* 1245, no. 1 (2011): 63–64. https://doi.org/10.1111/j.1749-6632.2011.06345.x.

Weissenborn, Peter K., and Robert J. Pugh. "Surface Tension of Aqueous Solutions of Electrolytes: Relationship with Ion Hydration, Oxygen Solubility, and Bubble Coalescence." *Journal of Colloid and Interface Science* 184 (1996): 550–63.

Wells, Roe E., and Edward W. Merrill. "Shear Rate Dependence of the Viscosity of Whole Blood and Plasma." *Science* 133, no. 3455 (1961): 763–64. https://doi.org/10.1126/science.133.3455.763.

Weng, X., G. Cloutier, P. Pibarot, and L. G. Durand. "Comparison and Simulation of Different Levels of Erythrocyte Aggregation with Pig, Horse, Sheep, Calf, and Normal Human Blood." *Biorheology* 33, no. 4–5 (1996): 365–77. https://doi.org/10.1016/0006-355X(96)00028-5.

Wickham, L. L., R. M. Bauersachs, R. B. Wenby, S. Sowemimo-Coker, H. J. Meiselman, and R. Elsnerl. "Red Cell Aggregation and Viscoelasticity of Blood from Seals, Swine and Man." *Biorheology* 27 (1990): 191–204.

Willis, Cordelia, Anna K. Piranian, John R. Donaggio, Robert J. Barnett, and Walter F. Rowe. "Errors in the Estimation of the Distance of Fall and Angles of Impact Blood Drops." *Forensic Science International* 123, no. 1 (2001): 1–4. https://doi.org/10.1016/S0379-0738(01)00506-0.

Windberger, Ursula, A. Bartholovitsch, R. Plasenzetti, K. J. Korak, and G. Heinze. "Whole Blood Viscosity, Plasma Viscosity and Erythrocyte Aggregation in Nine Mammalian Species: Reference Values and Comparison of Data." *Experimental Physiology* 88, no. 3 (2003): 431–40. https://doi.org/10.1113/eph8802496.

Windberger, Ursula, and Oguz K. Baskurt. "Comparative Hemorheology." In *Handbook of Hemorheology and Hemodynamics*, edited by O. K. Baskurt, M. R. Hardeman, M. W. Rampling, and H. J. Meiselman, Volume 69, Amsterdam: IOS Press, 2007: 267–85.

Yamauchi, Tatsuyuki, Mitsuru Yanai, Susumu Takahashi, and Nguyen Khoa Man. "Blood Density Monitoring During Dialysis." *Artificial Organs* 20, no. 9 (1996): 981–85. https://doi.org/10.1111/j.1525-1594.1996.tb04584.x.

CHAPTER 4

MATH AND PHYSICS OF DROPLET TRAJECTORIES

Brian Yamashita and Fons Chafe

INTRODUCTION

Bloodstain patterns created as a result of an impact, or impacts, can be analyzed in an attempt to determine a minimum number of blows that might have been struck, and approximately where in the room the source of the blood was located (the area of origin, AOO). See Chapter 13 for a more detailed discussion of impact patterns. Early techniques that were used to handle this type of problem relied on assuming that the trajectory of the droplet of blood was a straight line extending from the AOO to the wall or other surface where the stain was deposited. When a number of these straight-line trajectories are traced back from the wall, the area where they all intersect will be the approximate location of the source of blood. For this position, the conventional coordinate system generally used will designate X as the distance into the room out from the wall; Y will refer to the distance horizontally from the left side of the room; and Z will be the height of the blood source (Figure 4.1).

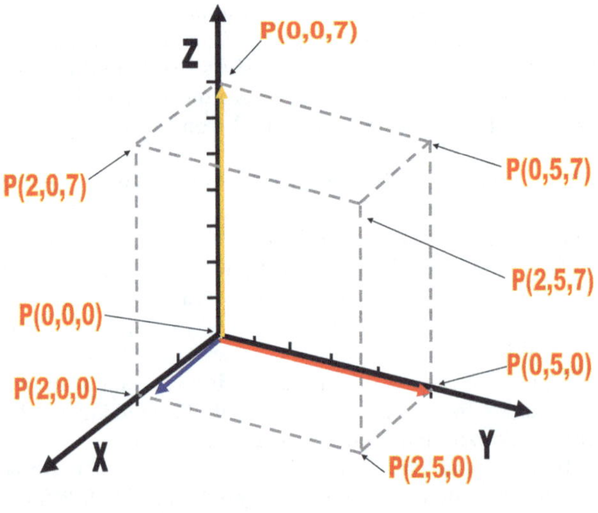

Figure 4.1 Coordinate system for a point P(X, Y, Z).

 DOI: 10.4324/9781003163695-4

STRINGING AN IMPACT PATTERN

A very visual method that can be used to trace trajectories of blood droplets emanating from an impact is the stringing method. Lengths of string are attached to the wall at the locations of the stains and are each extended into the room at the angle at which the droplet struck the wall. The angle at which the droplet struck the wall can be estimated by measuring the width and length of the elliptical stain. Imagine a flashlight shining on a wall. If the flashlight strikes the wall at 90°, the shape of the illumination will be circular. As the angle at which the flashlight is held changes, the illumination on the wall turns into an ellipse, and becomes longer as the angle decreases from 90°. The width (W) and length (L) of the bloodstain ellipse on the wall can be used to calculate this alpha (α) angle using the formula:

$$\alpha = \arcsin\ (W/L)$$

That is, the result of the width of the stain divided by the length of the stain will be the sine of the angle at which the droplet struck the wall (Figure 4.2). This can be done for several stains, from both the right and left sides of the pattern, and the approximate location where the strings cross will be the area of convergence (Figure 4.3).

While this method requires few calculations, the strings may interfere with one another making it a tedious procedure to carry out and could not be done single-handedly. However, in some cases, for example, when unusual surfaces are involved, stringing may be the best method to use to approximate from where the blood originated.

A slightly less tangled method of using strings begins by determining an area of convergence (AOC) in the Y-Z plane of the wall. The first step is to choose several stains on the wall, from both the left and right sides of the impact pattern. Lines drawn on the wall along the long axes of the ellipses will converge to a point on the wall that will correspond to the Y and Z coordinates of the blood source location, the AOC. A rod or dowel is then held in place, extending into the room at 90° from the AOC. The strings are then not extended until they reach the floor but are instead fastened to the rod while maintaining the correct α angle. Where the strings meet the rod, the rod will correspond to different estimates of the X value of the AOO. These values can be averaged and then combined with the Y and Z values from the AOC to determine the AOO (Figure 4.4).

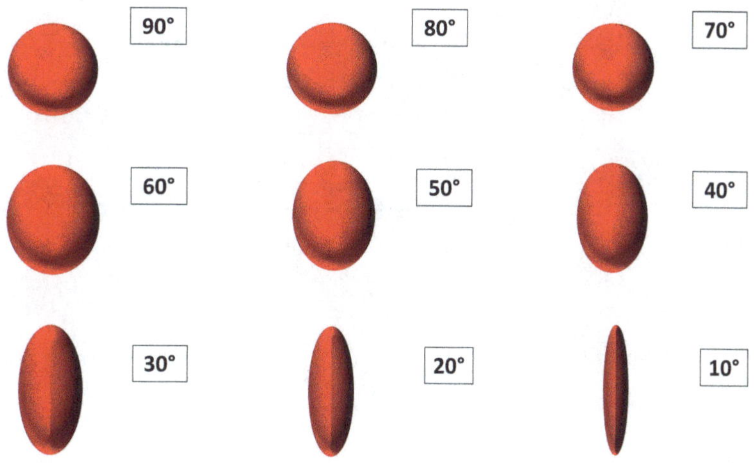

Figure 4.2 Ellipses created from different angles of impact.

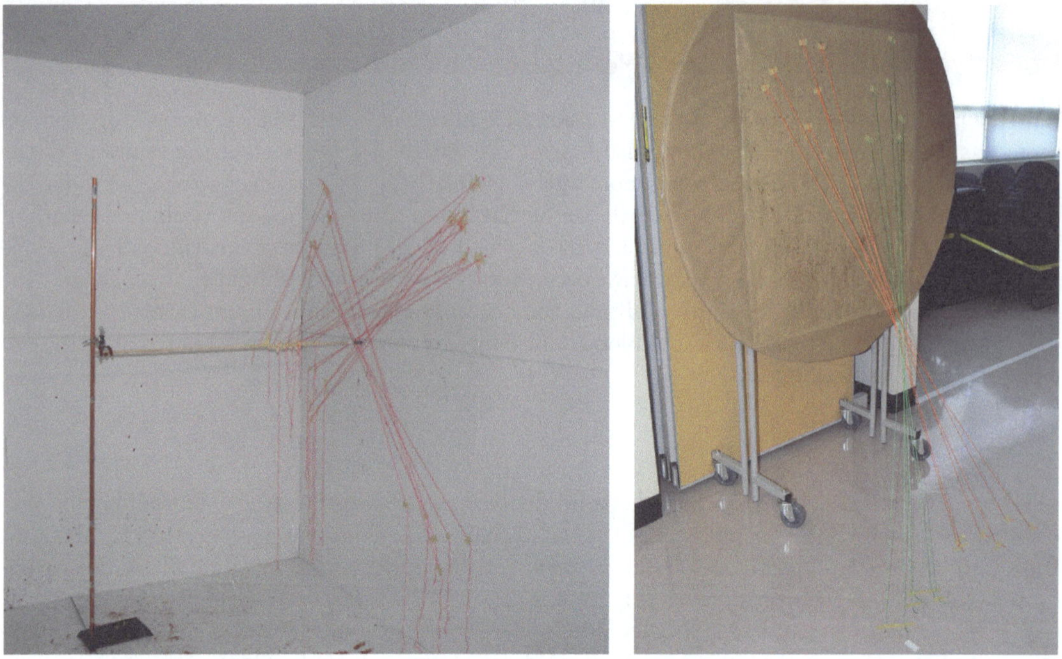

Figure 4.3 (a) Stringing of a pattern to a rod or dowel and (b) a variation involves stringing of a pattern to the floor.

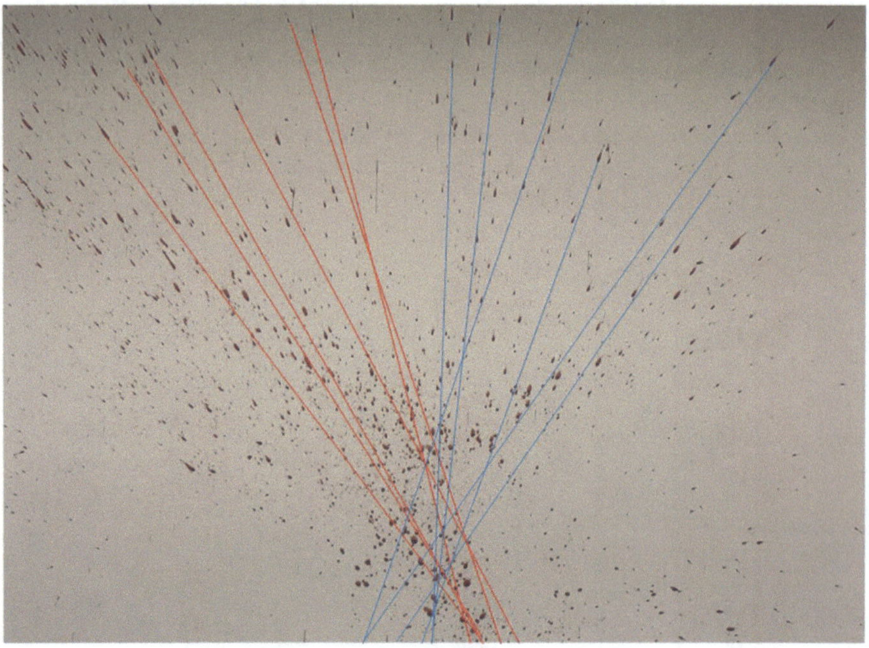

Figure 4.4 Lines drawn through ellipses on the wall.

THE TANGENT METHOD

Another method that relies on the straight-line trajectory assumption is the tangent method.[1,2] Recalling trigonometric functions (see **trigonometry, vectors, and components** below), in a right triangle, one with a 90° angle, the tangent of an angle Θ is defined as the length of the side of the triangle opposite to the angle, divided by the length of the side adjacent to the angle in question (see Figure 4.5):

$$\tan \Theta = \text{Length of opposite side/Length of adjacent side}$$

The tangent method requires the construction of a series of right triangles where the same α angle calculations described earlier are used; this time to determine one angle of each triangle. One vertex of the triangle will be at the bloodstain on the wall, while a second vertex will be at the right angle at the AOC, and the third will be at the AOO (the long side of the triangle, the hypotenuse, will correspond to a straight-line trajectory from the AOO to the stain). As in the second stringing method described earlier, the first step is to choose several stains on the wall, from both the left and right sides of the pattern. Again, lines drawn on the wall along the long axes of the ellipses will converge to a point on the wall that will correspond to the Y and Z coordinates of the AOC. For any bloodstain, a right triangle can be constructed with the distance to the (Y, Z) point as one side of the triangle, adjacent to angle α. The right angle means that the length of the second side of the triangle perpendicular to the wall can be calculated, and will correspond to the distance out from the wall, the X value **(denoted by a in Figure 4.6)**. That is, if the distance from the stain to the (Y, Z) point is D **(denoted by b in Figure 4.6),** then

$$\tan \alpha = X/D$$

$$\text{and } X = D \tan \alpha$$

Once this calculation is done for several stains and α angles, an average value for X can be calculated (Figures 4.6 and 4.7).

Technology involving 3D scanning techniques[3,4,5] also employ a version of the tangent method. Detailed digital photographic images that contain markers are used to determine coordinates and corresponding AOO and display this perspective in computer images. Another computer software method called "Sherlock" that uses parametric equations from linear algebra along with trigonometry has been developed at Trent University in Canada.[6] The "Sherlock" method acknowledges the directional analysis technique[7] first reported by A.L. Carter.[8]

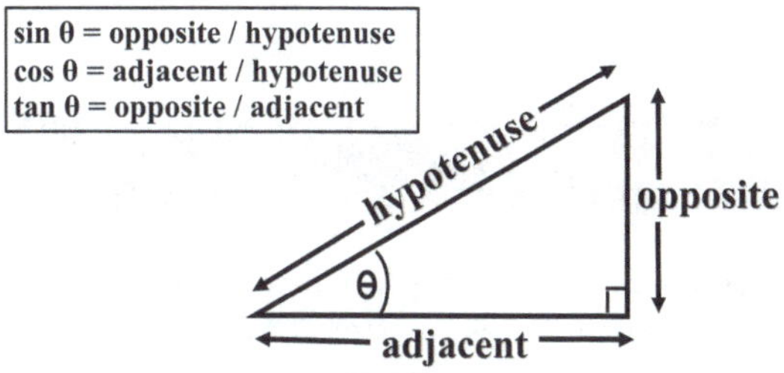

Figure 4.5 Showing angle Θ and corresponding sides of a triangle.

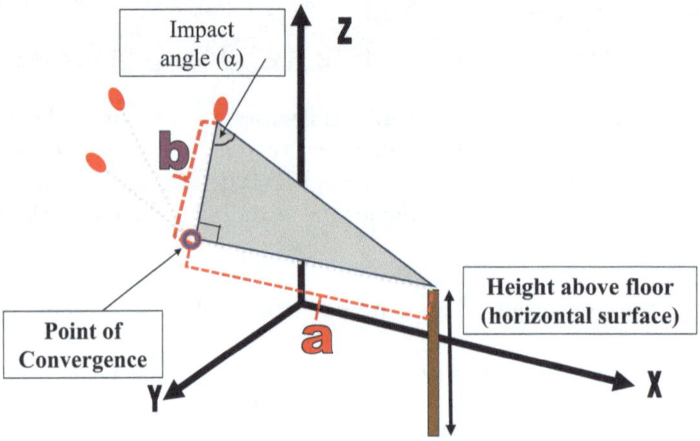

Figure 4.6 Tangent method for stains on a vertical surface. According to this method, a = b tan(α), where b = distance from leading edge to the 2D point of convergence.

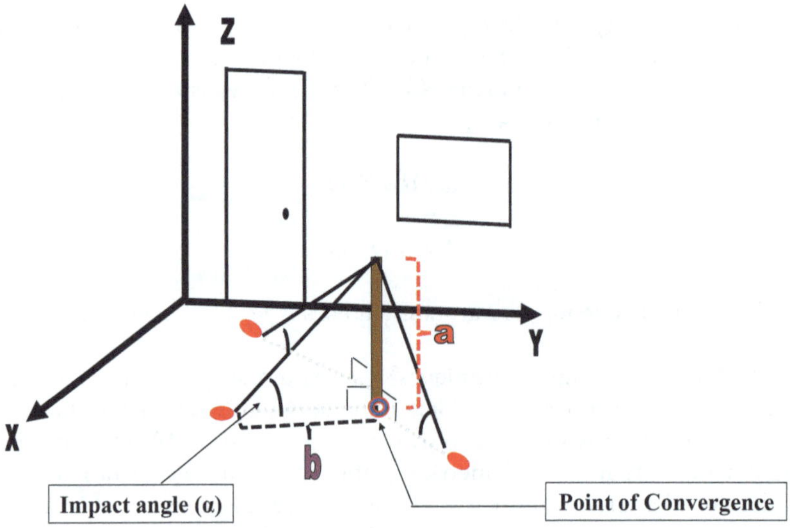

Figure 4.7 Tangent method for a horizontal surface.

DIRECTIONAL ANALYSIS

The term "directional analysis" was coined by A.L. Carter when he was developing the BackTrack computer program for the analysis of impact patterns,[9] and was also utilized by Maloney when he developed his HemoSpat software. In both computer programs, the bloodstain trajectories are seen as straight lines, when seen from above in a bird's-eye view. Where the trajectories cross will indicate the location of X and Y coordinates, while the Z coordinate will be determined on further analysis of the trajectories viewed from the side.[10]

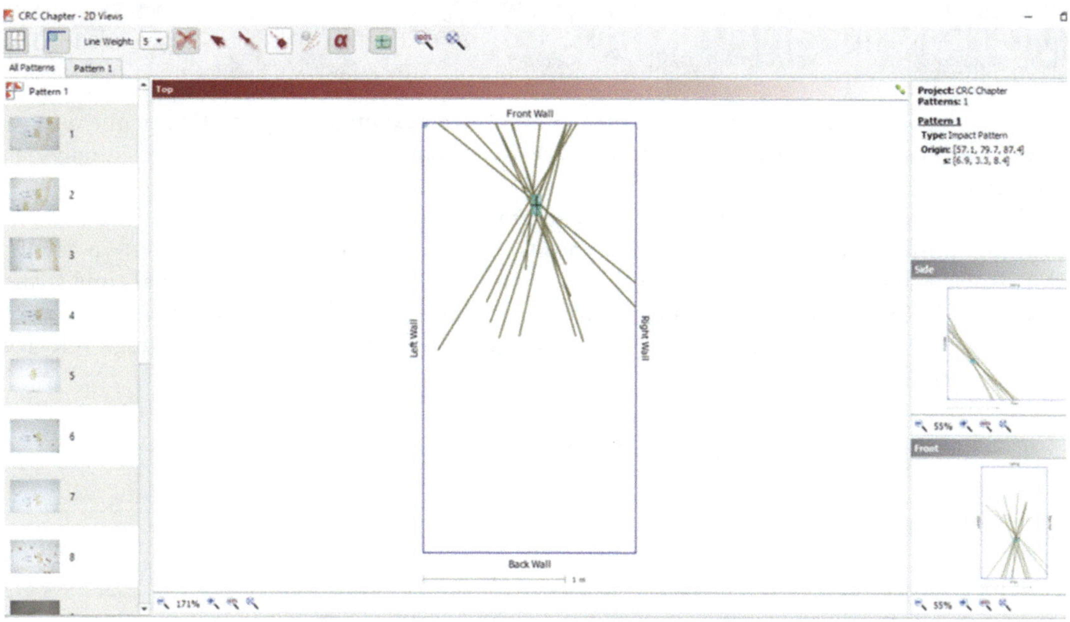

Figure 4.8 HemoSpat results for an impact pattern.

Since directional analysis depends on the bird's-eye view to determine X and Y coordinates, it can be used even when the droplets have been affected by gravity, when the straight-line trajectory does not have to be assumed.[11] However, the calculation of the height of the AOC is much more compromised (see Figure 4.8 showing an example of HemoSpat results).

While we are concentrating on impact patterns on a wall in this section, these techniques can also be applied in other situations like patterns on the floor, or spatter patterns created by other mechanisms such as firearms or expiration.

THE PHYSICS OF BLOOD DROPLET TRAJECTORIES

While the assumption that the trajectory of a blood droplet can often be approximated as a straight line under certain conditions, bloodstain pattern analysts have long recognized that the actual flight path will be curved. Unless a droplet of blood encounters a vertical surface, it will trace out a near-parabolic arc (parabolic, if drag is ignored in our calculations to follow) and eventually hit the ground. In this chapter, readers will familiarize themselves with the equations of motion, and then see how these can be used to calculate the flight path of a droplet of blood if certain initial conditions are known. This will be useful to an analyst in that it increases their basic understanding of the true movement of the droplet in flight and helps to explain why the trajectory can be approximated by a straight line in the early stage of the trajectory. The droplet of blood will travel in a curved path in two dimensions, where the plane in which it is traveling will look like a straight line when viewed from above, as utilized in directional analysis computations. While gravity will have a prominent role in the calculations that follow, air resistance (also called drag), which can have a profound effect on the flight path of a droplet of blood, will not be included (see Chapter 5).

MOTION IN ONE DIMENSION

The first important concept that has to be mastered is the examination of motion in one dimension. In this case, we are looking at an object that can move forward and backward in only one direction, X.

The Greek letter "delta" (Δ) is used in mathematics to indicate a difference. If we start at an initial position X_0 and end up at a final position X, the difference between the two values, the **displacement**, is given as ΔX. If we start at an initial time 0 and end at a final time t, the difference in time is Δt. For our object moving in X direction, the **velocity** – how fast we are moving – is given by ΔX/Δt (for example, if you travel 160 km in 2 hr, your average velocity is 80 km/h).

$$\text{Average velocity} = \underline{V} = \Delta X/\Delta t = (X_f - X_i)/(t_f - t_i) = (X - X_0)/t$$

Re-arranging:

$$\begin{aligned} \underline{V} &= (V - X_0)/t \\ X - X_0 &= \underline{V}t \\ X &= X_0 + \underline{V}t \end{aligned} \tag{4.1}$$

Acceleration is defined as the change in velocity as a function of time. If someone brags that their sports car can go from 0 to 100 km/h in 6 s, they are talking about the acceleration, the change in velocity over time. For velocity at time t = 0 given by V_0, and velocity V at time t

$$\begin{aligned} \text{Acceleration} = a &= \Delta V/\Delta t = (V - V_0)/t \\ a &= (V - V_0)/t \\ V - V_0 &= at \\ V &= V_0 + at \end{aligned} \tag{4.2}$$

For constant acceleration, the average velocity, $\underline{V}$, can be determined by simply averaging the initial and final velocities:

$$\underline{V} = (V_0 + V)/2 \tag{4.3}$$

For example, if you started at 10 km/h and increased with constant acceleration to 90 km/h, your average velocity was 50 km/h.

If you use equation (4.2) to replace V in equation (4.3), we get:

$$\underline{V} = (V_0 + [V_0 + at])/2 = (2V_0 + at)/2 = V_0 + at/2$$

Equation (4.1) becomes:

$$X = X_0 + \underline{V}t = X_0 + V_0t + \tfrac{1}{2}\,at^2 \tag{4.4}$$

For easy reference, and to help solve the exercises that follow, the four equations of motion are mentioned below:

$$X = X_0 + \underline{V}t \tag{4.1}$$

$$V = V_0 + at \tag{4.2}$$

$$\underline{V} = (V_0 + V)/2 \tag{4.3}$$

$$X = X_0 + \underline{V}t = X_0 + V_0 t + \tfrac{1}{2} at^2 \tag{4.4}$$

Solving a Quadratic Equation

Equation (4.4) is an important equation in our treatment of motion in one dimension. It can be described as determining the final position, X, given the initial position, X_0, the initial velocity, V_0, acceleration, a, and time, t. However, depending on the known variables given in a problem, a different variable other than X may need to be determined (see for example, exercise 4 below, where X is given and V_0 is to be determined.). In some cases, the unknown variable might be time t (see exercise 12 below). When this is the case, we note that equation (4.4) is a quadratic equation in variable, t. In order to determine t, we must solve a quadratic equation.

A quadratic equation is defined as one that can be written in the form:

$$ax^2 + bx + c = 0 \tag{4.5}$$

Although there are various methods that can be used to calculate x, the simplest is the quadratic formula:

$$x = \frac{-b \pm \sqrt{b^2 - 4ac}}{2a} \tag{4.6}$$

For example, for the quadratic equation $x^2 + x - 6 = 0$,

$$a = 1; \quad b = 1; \quad c = -6$$

$$x = \frac{-b \pm \sqrt{b^2 - 4ac}}{2a} = \frac{-1 \pm \sqrt{1^2 - 4(1)(-6)}}{2(1)} = \frac{-1 \pm 5}{2} = 2; -3$$

The occurrence of ± in the equation results in there being two final values.

Take another example of a quadratic equation $x^2 + 6x - 8 = 0$. For this,

$$a = 2; \quad b = 6; \quad c = -8$$

$$x = \frac{-b \pm \sqrt{b^2 - 4ac}}{2a} = \frac{-6 \pm \sqrt{6^2 - 4(2)(-8)}}{2(2)} = \frac{-6 \pm 10}{4} = 1; -4$$

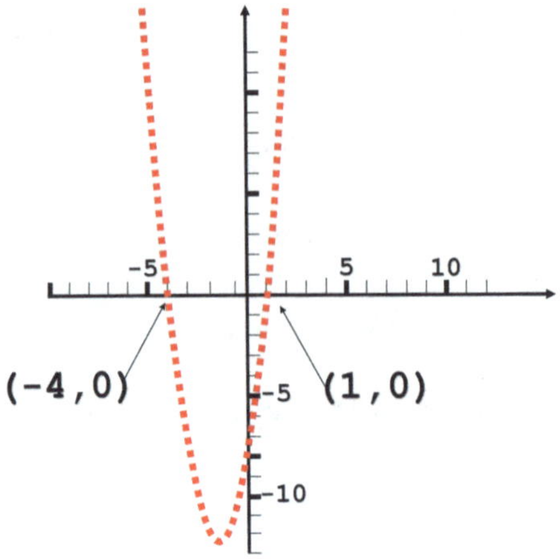

Figure 4.9 Graph of $y = 2x^2 + 6x - 8$.

If you draw a graph of points (x, y) for the quadratic equation

$$ax^2 + bx + c = y$$

the result will be a parabola. There will be two points where the parabola will cross the x-axis, where y = 0, which is why the solution to the quadratic equation gives us two results (Figure 4.9).

As we will see below, the flight path of a drop of blood will end up being a parabolic arc.

Exercises

1. If an object travels for 3.0 s at 10.0 m/s, then for 5.0 s at 5.0 m/s, and finally for 1.0 s at 7.0 m/s, what is $\underline{V}$, the average velocity?
2. If a snail starts at a position of $X_0 = 6$ in, and moves at a velocity of 8 in/h, where will it be at t = 7 h?
3. If the initial velocity of an object is 2.0 m/s and acceleration is given by 3.0 m/s², what will the velocity be after 5 s? If X_0 is 2.5 m, where will the object be at t = 5 s?
4. If $X_0 = 0$, a = 10 m/s², t = 5 s, and X = 145 m, what is V_0?
5. Given an initial velocity, $V_0 = 10$ m/s, and a final velocity, V = 80 m/s, what is the average velocity, $\underline{V}$? If t = 10 s, what is the acceleration?
6. If $X_0 = 0$, X = 270 km, and t = 4.5 h, what is the velocity (no acceleration)? Given that velocity, what is X at t = 7 h?
7. Given $V_0 = 0$ and V = 40 m/s at t = 10 s, what is the acceleration? What is the velocity 5 s later (at t = 15 s)?
8. If a = 8 m/s², $V_0 = 0$, and V = 24 m/s, what is t? What is X, assuming $X_0 = 0$?
9. If $X_0 = 8$ ft and V = 12.5 ft/s, what is X at t = 3 s.
10. If a = 10 m/s², $V_0 = 10$ m/s, what is t when V = 50 m/s?
11. Given $X_0 = 7$ m, $V_0 = 8$ m/s, and a = 6 m/s², what is X at t = 7 s?
12. If $V_0 = 30$ m/s, $X_0 = 0$, and a = 30 m/s², what is t when X = 300 m? (Hint: Quadratic equation)
13. Given $V_0 = 8$ m/s and a = 0, what is X at t = 9 s for $X_0 = 0$? If a = 2 m/s², what is X at t = 9 s? If a = 2 m/s² and X = 120 m, what is t?

TRIGONOMETRY, VECTORS, AND COMPONENTS

In order to make the extension from one dimension to two, it is necessary to re-familiarize ourselves with some trigonometry. First, for a right triangle (one with a 90° angle), the lengths of the three sides are related by the Pythagorean Theorem. The long side of the triangle is called hypotenuse. If we label it as "h," and the other two sides are "a" and "b," then

$$a^2 + b^2 = h^2 \tag{4.7}$$

For example, for a right triangle with sides of length 3 and 4 units, the hypotenuse will have a length of 5 units:

$$3^2 + 4^2 = 9 + 16 = 25 = 5^2$$

For one of the non-90° angles, called "theta" (Θ), the three main trigonometric functions, sine, cosine, and tangent, are defined by:

$$\text{Sin}(\Theta) = \text{Length of opposite side/Hypotenuse} = 3/5 = 0.60 \tag{4.8}$$

$$\text{Cos}(\Theta) = \text{Length of adjacent side/Hypotenuse} = 4/5 = 0.80 \tag{4.9}$$

$$\text{Tan}\ (\Theta) = \text{Length of opposite side/Adjacent side} = 3/4 = 0.75 \tag{4.10}$$

where the opposite side is the side of the triangle across from the angle, Θ. The adjacent side runs from Θ to the right angle (refer back to Figure 4.5).

The angle can be determined by calculating the inverse function, the arcsin (or $\sin^{-1}$), arccos ($\cos^{-1}$), or arctan ($\tan^{-1}$), from the sine, cosine, or tangent. For example, from equations (4.8)–(4.10), if the sine is 0.60, then

$$\text{angle}\ (\Theta) = \arcsin\ (0.60) = \sin^{-1}(0.60) = 36.9° \tag{4.11}$$

$$\Theta = \arccos\ (0.80) = \cos^{-1}(0.80) = 36.9° \tag{4.12}$$

$$\Theta = \arctan\ (0.75) = \tan^{-1}(0.75) = 36.9° \tag{4.13}$$

Using equations (4.7)–(4.13) makes it possible to solve a variety of trigonometry problems. Given only the lengths of two sides of a right triangle, or one angle and the length of one side, all other lengths and trigonometric functions can be determined. For example, given a right triangle with one angle of 30° and the side opposite the angle having a length of 7 units, the lengths of all sides of the triangle and the trigonometric functions for 30° can be calculated. The side opposite the 30° angle, with a length of 7 units, figures into equation (4.8) for sine or equation (4.10) for tangent.

$$\sin(30) = \text{Side opposite/Hypotenuse} = 0.50 = 7/\text{Hypotenuse}$$

$$\text{Hypotenuse} = 14\ \text{units}$$

Once the hypotenuse has been calculated, equations (4.7), (4.9), or (4.10) can be used to calculate the length of the third side of the triangle. Using equation (4.10),

$$\tan(30) = \text{Side opposite/Side adjacent} = 0.58 = 7/\text{Side adjacent}$$

$$\text{Side adjacent} = 12.1 \text{ units}$$

This can be verified using equation (4.7).

$$(12.1)^2 + (7)^2 = (14)^2$$

For another example, given a right triangle with a hypotenuse of 11 units and one other side of the triangle being 5 units, the third side can be calculated using equation (4.7), or the angles can first be calculated using equations (4.8)–(4.13). Using equation (4.8),

$$\sin(\Theta) = \text{Side opposite/Hypotenuse} = 5/11 = 0.454$$

$$\Theta = \arcsin(0.454) = 27.0°$$

Using equation (4.9),

$$\cos(\Theta) = \text{Side adjacent/Hypotenuse} = \cos(27.0) = 0.891$$

$$\text{Side adjacent (the third side)} = (0.891)(\text{Hypotenuse}) = 0.891 \times 11 = 9.8 \text{ units}$$

The angles of a triangle add up to 180, so the third angle is given by

$$180 - 90 - 27.0 = 63.0°$$

The right triangle has angles of 27.0°, 63.0°, and 90°, and sides measuring 5, 9.8, and 11 units.

Vectors and Components

In physics, **vectors** are defined as quantities that have both magnitude and direction, as opposed to **scalars**, which have only magnitude. Temperature and mass are examples of scalars. Displacement, velocity, and acceleration are vectors. A velocity can be given with a magnitude (30 m/s) and a direction (45° above the horizon). A different vector would correspond to 30 m/s in a horizontal direction. Speed is a scalar quantity and would be the same for two different velocity vectors, equal to the magnitude only, without direction.

Two vectors are added by placing the start of the second vector at the end of the first. The resultant straight-line vector, the sum, begins at the start of the first vector and ends at the end of the second vector. In a 2D coordinate system, for example, one vector could be a displacement of 4 units in X direction, a second vector could be a 3 units displacement in Y direction, and the resultant vector (which would be the hypotenuse of a right triangle) would be a vector of 5 units at an angle of 36.9° (Figure 4.10).

If we begin with a resultant vector and try to see what vectors will add up to this sum, there are an infinite number of vector combinations that will start at the beginning of the resultant vector and end up at the end of the resultant. However, if we consider the resultant vector to be the

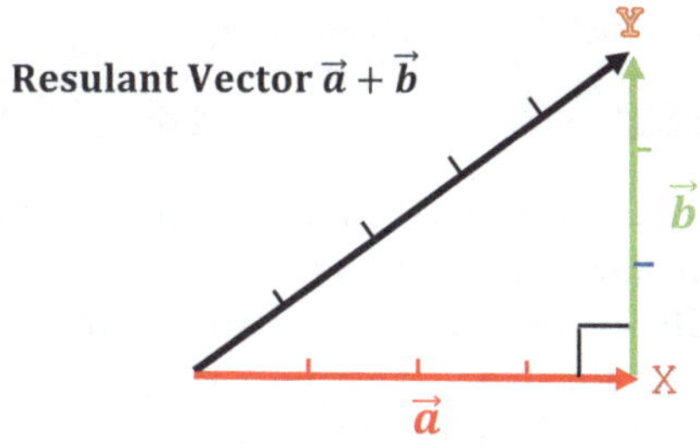

Figure 4.10 The addition of two perpendicular vectors to obtain the resultant vector.

hypotenuse of a right triangle, the two sides parallel to X-axis and Y-axis are called vector components of the resultant. Determining X and Y components of a vector, given its magnitude and direction, becomes a trigonometry problem where the hypotenuse and one angle are given.

For example, if a vector makes an angle of 55° with X-axis and has a length of 12 units, then the lengths of X and Y components can be calculated. The X component can be calculated using equation (4.9).

$$\cos(\Theta) = \text{Side adjacent/Hypotenuse} = \text{X component}/12 = \cos(55) = 0.57$$

$$\text{X component} = [\cos(\Theta)][\text{Hypotenuse}] = 0.57 \times 12 = 6.88\,\text{units}$$

For Y component, using equation (4.8),

$$\sin(\Theta) = \text{Side}\frac{\text{opposite}}{\text{Hypotenuse}} = \text{Y component}/12 = \sin(55) = 0.82$$

$$\text{Y component} = [\sin(\Theta)][\text{Hypotenuse}] = 0.82 \times 12 = 9.83\,\text{units}$$

In other words, a vector of length 9.83 units in Y direction added to a vector of length 6.88 units in X direction will result in a vector of length 12 units at an angle of 55° with respect to X-axis. For any given resultant vector, X and Y components can be determined using trigonometry.

If you have ever used the Etch-A-Sketch® toy, you will recall that one knob moves the line horizontally, while the second knob generates a line in the vertical direction. If you turn both knobs at the same time, you can create a line that traces out an angular path. One knob can be thought of as creating one component vector, while the other creates a perpendicular vector. Turning both knobs is like creating a resultant vector made up of two perpendicular components.

Exercises

14. If sin (Θ) = 5/13, determine the length of the third side of the triangle. Using these lengths, determine cos (Θ), tan (Θ), and Θ.
15. Given a right triangle with one angle of 35° and the side adjacent to the angle having a length of 100 units, what are the lengths of the other two sides? What are the lengths of the other two sides if it is the hypotenuse that has a length of 100 units?
16. Given a right triangle with two sides equal to 7 and 12 units, what is the length of the hypotenuse? What are the two angles? Calculate sin, cos, and tan for both angles.
17. For a vector of 16 units at an angle of 38° above X-axis, what two vectors are the X and Y components? What are the X and Y components if the angle of the resultant vector is 50° and the resultant vector has a length of 22 units?

MOTION IN TWO DIMENSIONS

A droplet of blood leaving a blood source location travels in a parabolic flight trajectory toward a wall or floor (or ceiling). When viewed from the side, the trajectory remains in a plane, that is, in two dimensions, if no extraordinary forces act on the droplet in flight. When viewed from above, the trajectory looks like a straight line from the source location toward the wall. HemoSpat uses this top view to determine the source location in the X-Y plane of the floor.

The way to treat a 2D problem is to simplify it into two problems in one dimension. This can be done using vector components to separate a vector into two perpendicular vectors that can be solved as two 1D problems.

As an example, consider an object starting at the origin (0, 0) of an X-Y coordinate system. If the object moves with a velocity vector of 100 m/s, with no acceleration, at an angle of 60° above the X-axis, where the object will be after 3 s can be determined. The first thing to do is to separate the velocity vector into its two X and Y components. For the Y component,

$$V_y = V\sin(\Theta) = [100\,\text{m/s}][0.866] = 86.6\,\text{m/s}$$

For the X component,

$$V_x = V\cos(\Theta) = [100\,\text{m/s}][0.5] = 50.0\,\text{m/s}$$

Instead of a single 2D problem, we now have two 1D problems, which we can solve using equations (4.1)–(4.4). From equation (4.1),

$$Y = Y_0 + V_y t = 0 + [86.6\,\text{m/s}][3\,\text{s}] = 259.8\,\text{m}$$

$$X = X_0 + V_x t = 0 + [50.0\,\text{m/s}][3\,\text{s}] = 150.0\,\text{m}$$

The object has moved 150.0 m in X direction and 259.8 m in Y direction. In terms of X-Y coordinates, it has moved from (0, 0) to (150.0, 259.8). To determine the actual distance traveled in two dimensions, it is necessary to solve for the hypotenuse of the triangle.

$$H^2 = [259.8]^2 + [150.0]^2 = 90000$$

$$H = 300\,\text{m (The object has moved a total of 300 m in 3 s.)}$$

In the example above, the object moved with constant velocity in both directions; so, equation (4.1) could be used for both 1D problems. Newton's first law states that an object in motion, with no external force acting on it, will continue moving in the same direction at a constant velocity. This would mean that a drop of blood would continue to travel in a straight line if gravity did not affect it.

The acceleration due to gravity, a_g, is a vector that has a magnitude of 9.8 m/s^2 and a direction always directed downward, and, for a droplet traveling through the air with no drag, represents the external force referred to by Newton. For velocity in X direction, gravity has no effect, and equation (4.1) will apply for determining displacement in X direction. For velocity in Y direction, acceleration will be acting in the negative Y direction, and equations (4.2) and (4.4) will apply. For two children throwing a ball back and forth, if you are in a balcony above the children, you will

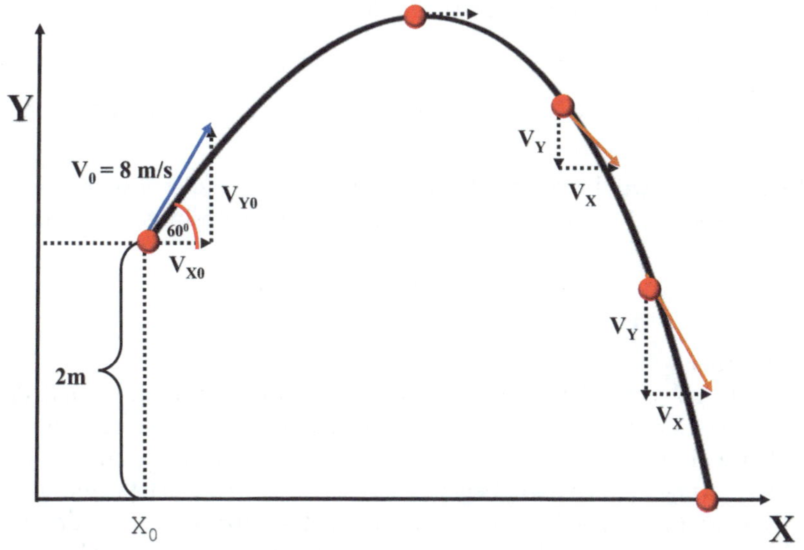

Figure 4.11 Curved flight trajectory and velocity vectors.

see the ball travels at a constant velocity in a straight line between the children (in X direction), without seeing the change in height. If you are standing behind the children, you will see the ball rise and fall with a varying velocity (in Y direction), but will not see the ball moving horizontally.

Consider an object 2.0 m above the ground on Y-axis, at an X position of 0, with an initial velocity of 8.0 m/s at an angle of 60° above horizontal (see Figure 4.11). The position and velocity of the object can be determined for any point in time. For velocity in X direction, the initial X component can be calculated using the cosine of the angle:

$$V_x = V_0 \cos(\Theta) = 8.0(0.5) = 4.0\,\text{m/s}$$

Initially, in Y direction,

$$V_y = V_0 \sin(\Theta) = 8.0(0.866) = 6.93\,\text{m/s}$$

As a function of time, the equations of motion in one dimension are

$$V_x = 4.0\,\text{m/s (No acceleration)}$$

$$X = X_0 + V_0(t) = 0 + (4.0)(t)\,\text{m}$$

$$V_y = [6.93 - 9.8(t)]\ \text{m/s (Acceleration is due to gravity)}$$

$$Y = Y_0 + V_0(t) + \tfrac{1}{2}\,a\,(t^2) = [2.0 + (6.93)(t) + \tfrac{1}{2}(-9.8)(t^2)]\ \text{m}$$

For example, the position of the object can be determined 1 s after it begins its flight. In X direction,

$$X = X_0 + V_0(t) = 0 + (4.0)(1) = 4.0\,\text{m}$$

That is, after 1 s, the object has moved 4.0 m in X direction.
In Y direction,

$$Y = Y_0 + V_0(t) + \frac{1}{2} a (t^2) = 2.0 + (6.93)(1) + \frac{1}{2}(-9.8)(1^2) = 4.03\,\text{m}$$

So, after 1 s, the object will have moved 4.0 m in X direction and be 4.03 m above the ground, or be at a point (4.0, 4.03). Note that if gravity is disregarded, Y position would instead be

$$Y = 2.0 + (6.93)(1) = 8.93\,\text{m}$$

Contrast this with Y = 4.03 m when gravity is involved.

If the position of an object is determined at a series of times, a plot of position at different times will have the shape of a parabolic arc. Because of gravity, a droplet of blood will not continue to rise endlessly, but will reach a maximum and then begin to fall to the ground. In fact, as soon as the droplet begins its flight, gravity will begin to have an effect. The straight-line assumption used in many calculations will be a good approximation of the trajectory only if the droplet impacts the wall very early in its travel. A bloodstain on the wall pointing in a downward direction indicates that the droplet has passed over the top of its parabolic path and fallen toward the ground when it impacts the wall. This is a valuable concept for a BPA expert to bear in mind if they have to explain which bloodstains were used in their analysis.

The velocity at any time can also be determined. For example, at t = 1.5 s, the velocity in X direction will be given by

$$V_x = V_0 + at = 4.0\,\text{m/s (Since there is no acceleration)}$$

There is acceleration due to gravity acting in Y direction, so the velocity will be given by

$$V_y = V_0 + at = 6.93 + (-9.8)(1.5) = -7.77\,\text{m/s}$$

(It is negative because it is going downward in Y direction.)

The resultant velocity vector can be calculated using the Pythagorean Theorem and trigonometric functions. For a right triangle with sides of length 4.0 and 7.77, the length of the hypotenuse will be 8.74. The angle of the velocity vector can be calculated from sine, cosine, or tangent.

$$\tan(\Theta) = \text{Side opposite/Side adjacent} = 7.77/4.0 = 1.94$$

$$\Theta = \arctan(1.94) = 62.8°$$

Therefore, after 1.5 s, an object that was initially traveling upward at an angle of 60° with a speed of 8.0 m/s will be traveling downward at an angle of 62.8° below horizontal with a speed of 8.74 m/s.

As seen above, as the drop of blood travels upward, its velocity in Y direction will decrease due to gravity. The point at which the drop reaches the top of its parabolic travel will be where the velocity in Y direction is equal to zero.

$$V_y = V_0 + at = 6.93 + (-9.8)t = 0$$

Solving for t,

$$t = 6.93/9.8 = 0.707\,s$$

From an initial velocity of 6.93 m/s in Y direction, the velocity will be at zero at the top of the parabola after 0.707 s.

At what time will the object hit the floor? For this problem, set Y = 0. The equation for Y becomes a quadratic equation in t.

$$Y = Y_0 + V_0(t) + \tfrac{1}{2}\,a\,(t^2) = 2.0 + (6.93)(t) + (-4.9)(t^2) = 0$$

Solving this quadratic equation, the two solutions are t = 1.66 s and t = −0.246 s. We choose the positive solution as the time of flight for the given mass point.

Exercises

18. For the example above, calculate the position and velocity of the object at 0.5 s, at 0.75 s, and at 1.20 s. At what time will the object be 1.0 m above the ground?
19. Given an object traveling with a velocity vector of 100 m/s at an angle of 50°, what are the two initial velocity vectors, V_x and V_y? Calculate X and Y positions of the object at t = 1, 3, 7, and 14 s, with no acceleration due to gravity. Repeat the same calculation for Y position, but with the addition of an acceleration vector due to gravity of $-9.8\ m/s^2$. Note the difference in Y position with and without the force of gravity.

AIR RESISTANCE, SURFACE TENSION, AND VISCOSITY

Air resistance (drag) is a force which has been ignored in the calculations carried out in this chapter, but it has a significant effect on the trajectory of a real blood droplet in flight. Unfortunately, it is a difficult property to include in our simple calculations above. The force of air resistance can be represented by a vector that is always pointing in the opposite direction of travel. As a body changes its direction, the air resistance vector also changes its direction to continue to be in the opposite direction of travel. Further complicating any calculation is the fact that the magnitude of the force increases with the increase in velocity. Think about the force of air upon your face increasing when you go from walking to riding a bike to sticking your head out the window of a moving car. As a droplet of blood flies through air, the air resistance vector continually changes in both magnitude and direction, which, when included, would make our calculations more complicated (Figure 4.12).

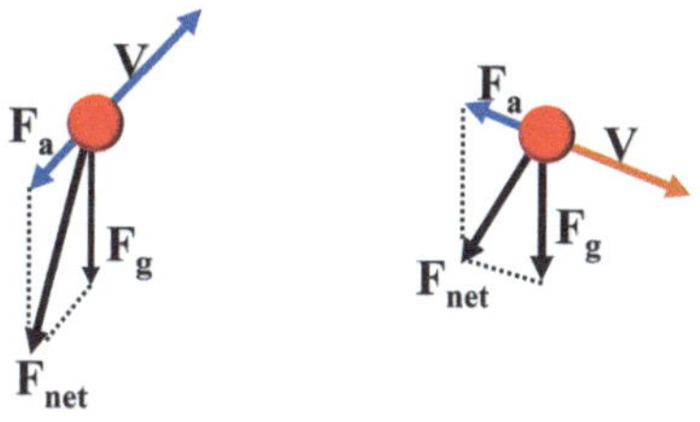

Figure 4.12 Net force, including the air resistance vector.

For an object that is falling straight down under the force of gravity, air resistance pushes it upward with a force that increases with the increase in the velocity of the object. At some point, the force of air resistance will exactly equal the force of gravity, and the net force acting on the object will be zero, meaning that the acceleration will be zero. According to Newton's second law, force is equal to mass times acceleration; so when the net force is zero, there will be no acceleration. The object will continue to fall, but at a constant velocity, known as **terminal velocity**.

When air resistance is taken into account, the droplet of blood will not travel as far as our gravity-only calculations would predict. Smaller droplets see a greater effect due to air resistance, which can be seen from examining the size of the small stains on the floor closest to the impact.

The strength of the air resistance force depends on the speed, size, and shape of the droplet. The shape, usually but not always a sphere, depends on the surface tension force. Surface tension and viscosity are treated in more detail in Chapter 5.

For a droplet of water, an individual water molecule experiences attractive intermolecular forces between it and its nearest neighbor molecules. For molecules on the surface, there will be neighboring molecules below the surface but none above, so the net attractive intermolecular forces will be pulling the surface molecules toward the interior of the liquid. Left to their own devices, this inward attraction will result in the water molecules trying to assume the shape with the smallest surface area. For a given volume, a sphere has the smallest surface area; so, drops of blood in air will always be trying to assume a spherical shape. Mercury is an example of a liquid that has very high surface tension compared to water or blood. When mercury is poured out on to a table, the surface tension is so strong that it will bead up into spheres instead of flowing and wetting the table.

The Weber Number (see Chapter 5 for a more complete treatment) is a dimensionless number that is proportional to the dynamic pressure force on the drop ($\frac{1}{2}\rho v^2$; that is, ½ times density of air times velocity squared) divided by the surface tension force. In simple terms, for a blood droplet in flight, surface tension tries to maintain the spherical shape of the droplet, while dynamic pressure tries to cause it to flatten or break up.

Viscosity refers to a fluid's ability to flow. Fluid like molasses flow more slowly than water and are said to be more viscous. Blood is more viscous than water but not as viscous as molasses. Air can be considered a very low viscosity fluid. However, this viscosity can still contribute significantly to air resistance as a drop of blood tries to travel through an ocean of air.

The Reynolds Number (see Chapter 5 for a more complete treatment) is another dimensionless number; this time related to viscosity. Originally developed to relate to the flow of fluids through pipes, it can help to predict if the flow of a fluid is smooth and laminar, or turbulent. For a blood droplet, the Reynolds number will address the flow, turbulent or laminar, of air while passing around a droplet of blood in flight, as it affects air resistance.

This section may give readers a better understanding of the trajectory of a droplet of blood from an impact pattern. Ignoring air resistance but including gravity, the flight path of a droplet of blood can be calculated if the initial conditions are known. The appropriateness of assuming a straight-line trajectory in order to determine the AOC should now be better understood.

Solutions to problems

1. $V = 6.9$ m/s
2. $X = 62$ in
3. $V = 17.0$ m/s; $X = 50$ m
4. $V_0 = 4$ m/s
5. $V = 45$ m/s; $a = 7$ m/s^2
6. $V = 60$ km/h; $X = 420$ km
7. $a = 4$ m/s^2; $V = 60$ m/s
8. $t = 3$ s; $X = 36$ m
9. $X = 45.5$ ft
10. $t = 4$ s

11. $X = 210$ m
12. $t = 3.58$ s
13. $X = 72$ m; $X = 153$ m; $t = 7.7$ s
14. Side#3 = 12 units; sine = 5/13; cosine = 12/13; tangent = 5/12
15. Side#2 = 70; Hypotenuse = 122
    Side#1 = 81.9; Side #2 = 57.4
16. Hypotenuse = 13.9; $\Theta_1 = 59.7°$; $\Theta_2 = 30.3°$
17. $X = 12.6$; $Y = 9.85$
    $X = 14.1$; $Y = 16.9$
18. At 0.5 s,
    $X = (4.0)(0.5) = 2.0\,\text{m}; Y = 2.0 + (6.93)(0.5) + \frac{1}{2}(-9.8)(0.5^2) = 4.24\,\text{m}$
    $V_x = 4.0\,\text{m/s}$; $V_y = 6.93 + (-9.8)(0.5) = 2.03\,\text{m/s}$
    $V = 4.49\,\text{m/s}; \Theta = 26.9°$
    For $Y = 1.0\,\text{m}$, $t = 1.54\,\text{s}$ (second solution $= -0.13\,\text{s}$)
19. $V_x = 64.3$ m/s; $V_y = 76.6$ m/s At $t = 3$ s,
    $X = 192.9\,\text{m}$; $Y = 229.8$ (no gravity); $Y = 0 + (76.6)(3) + \frac{1}{2}(-9.8)(3^2) = 185.7$

ACKNOWLEDGMENTS

We wish to acknowledge the immense contributions of Dr. Fred Carter, who was instrumental in the development of the BPA course upon which this chapter is largely based.

Notes

1. Chafe, F., "The Tangent Method and Spreadsheets: Determining Point or Area of Origin in Bloodstain Pattern Analysis," *International Association of Bloodstain Pattern Analysts News* 23, no. 3 (2007): 4–14, https://iabpa.org/docs/September_2007_News.pdf
2. Griffin, Tom and Anderson, John, "Out on a Tangent with Bloodstain Pattern Interpretation," *IABPA News* 9, no. 1 (1993): 3–5, https://static1.squarespace.com/static/543841fce4b0299b22e1956a/t/54be8fd0e4b07c132e42694b/1421774800627/Out+on+a+Tangent+Griffin+Anderson+1993.pdf
3. Liscio, E., Bortot, S., Frankcom, J., Hackenbrook, T., Inch, J., Lamarche, R., Penney, T., Allen, B., Chafe, F., and Yamashita, A.B., "A Preliminary Validation of the Use of 3D Scanning for Bloodstain Pattern Analysis," *Journal of Bloodstain Pattern Analysis* 31, no. 3 (2015): 3–10, https://iabpa.org/docs/December_2015_JBPA-2.pdf
4. Joris, P., Develter, W., Jenar, E., Suetens, P., Vandermeulen, D., Van de Voorde, W., and Claes, P., "HemoVision: An Automated and Virtual Approach to Bloodstain Pattern Analysis," *Forensic Science International* 251 (2015): 116–23, https://www.sciencedirect.com/science/article/abs/pii/S0379073815001243
5. Hakim, N. and Liscio, E., "Calculating Point of Origin of Blood Spatter Using Laser Scanning Technology," *Journal of Forensic Sciences* 60, no. 2 (2015): 409–17, https://doi.org/10.1111/1556-4029.12639
6. Orr, A., M. Illes, M., Beland, J., and Stotesbury, T., "Validation of Sherlock, a Linear Trajectory Analysis Program for Use in Bloodstain Pattern Analysis," *Canadian Society of Forensic Science Journal* 52, no. 2 (2019): 78–94, https://doi.org/10.1080/00085030.2019.1577793
7. Beland, Jacques, "The Math behind Sherlock," Trent University, Peterborough, ON, Canada, 2018, http://sherlock.trentu.ca/~forensics/The_Math_Behind_Sherlock_BSA.pdf
8. Carter, A.L., "The Directional Analysis of Bloodstain Patterns Theory and Experimental Validation," *Canadian Society of Forensic Science Journal* 34, no. 4 (2001): 173–89, http://dx.doi.org/10.1080/00085030.2001.10757527

9. Maloney, A., "Bloodstain Pattern Analysis Software," HemoSpat. FORident Software, 2021, https://hemospat.com/#/0
10. Carter, **A.L.,** Illes, M., Maloney, K., Yamashita, **A.B.,** Allen, B., Brown, B., Davidson, L., Ellis, G., Gallant, J., Gradkowski, A., Hignell, J., Jory, S., Laturnus, **P.L.,** Moore, **C.C.**, Pembroke, R., Richard, A., Spenard, R., and Stewart, C., "Further Validation of the BackTrack™ Computer Program for Bloodstain Pattern Analysis – Precision and Accuracy," *International Association of Bloodstain Pattern Analysts News* 21, no. 3 (2005): 15–22, https://iabpa.org/docs/September_2005_News.pdf
11. Carter, **A.L.** and Podworny, **E.J.,** "Bloodstain Pattern Analysis with a Scientific Calculator," *Canadian Society of Forensic Science Journal* 24, no.1 (1991): 37–42, https://doi.org/10.1080/00085030.1991.10756981

CHAPTER 5

FLUID DYNAMICS OF BLOODSTAIN PATTERN FORMATION

Mark Jermy and Natalia Kabaliuk

INTRODUCTION

Fluid dynamics is the field of physics that predicts the behavior of fluids. An understanding of fluid dynamics helps in understanding how blood leaves a wound, travels to a surface, and forms a stain there, and what shapes, sizes, and patterns the stains take. Understanding the physics correctly helps in arriving at correct interpretations of bloodstain patterns, in knowing what information can and cannot be correctly inferred from bloodstain patterns, and in giving clear explanations of the pattern analysis process during training, peer-review, and testimony.

Fluid dynamics (also called fluid mechanics) is a broad field, including aerodynamics, hydraulics, energy generation, weather prediction, and other sub-disciplines. It is a well-developed field with reliable quantitative theories for most phenomena (except turbulence, which retains some mystery!). The term "fluid" includes both liquids and gases.

Calculations in fluid dynamics rely heavily on calculus, which is not to everyone's taste. In this chapter, we describe only the fluid mechanics which is relevant to bloodstain pattern analysis (BPA), without excessive use of equations. Readers desiring a more mathematical approach may refer to the standard textbooks written for engineering undergraduates, for example White and Xue,[1] or any number of tutorials on YouTube.

Jermy and Taylor[2] summarized the fluid dynamics of BPA, which this chapter expands upon. Attinger et al.[3] reviewed the state-of-the-art research in the field as it stood in 2013, and have done much to expand knowledge in the field since then. Laber, Epstein, and Taylor produced a comprehensive library of slow motion videos of blood transfer events[4] hosted by the Midwest Forensic Resource Center (MFRC) at the Ames Laboratory and Iowa State University, which has been of great value to trainers and researchers.

KEY CONCEPTS IN FLUID DYNAMICS

Fluid mechanics is a quantitative science. It can be used to make verifiable predictions. Using the theories of fluid mechanics, repeatable experiments can be designed, executed, and analyzed. It is based on fundamental physical laws founded in Newton's laws of motion, and another set of physical laws called conservation laws.

Newton's laws of motion are:

- An object will not change its velocity unless a force acts on it (Newton's First Law).

DOI: 10.4324/9781003163695-5

- If a force does act on it, the rate at which its velocity changes is directly proportional to the force, and inversely proportional to its mass (force equals mass times acceleration or $F = ma$) (Newton's Second Law).
- When two objects interact, they apply forces on each other, equal in strength but opposite in direction (Newton's Third Law).

Velocity is a quantity which includes both speed and direction of motion.

Conservation laws are based on the idea that there are fundamental physical quantities, such as mass, momentum or energy, which are conserved, i.e. the amount present in a certain volume of space remains the same unless increased or decreased by some definite, measurable process. An example is the flow of water in a pipe. Water does not spontaneously appear or disappear, and the amount of water pumped in at one end, which can be measured, is equal to the amount which flows out at the other end, plus any leaks. Measuring the flow at both ends allows the calculation of any leaks. In this example, the leak rate can be worked out because mass is conserved (to be pedantic, it has also been assumed that there is no airspace in the pipe, and the flow is constant). The mass of the water in the pipe does not increase or decrease unless the water enters or leaves in a way that is observable and, at least in principle, measureable.

Momentum and energy are also conserved in fluid flow. The momentum of a given volume of water is the mass times the velocity. The momentum of the water in the pipe can't change, except by definite, measureable forces acting on the water, e.g. the pressure from the pump forcing water down the pipe, and friction at the walls.

Changes in a fluid's behavior can be described by the action of forces, or the conversion of energy from one type to another. Any process can be described either in terms of forces or energies. These are linked, as forces act to move things in a way that reduces the energy of some part of a system. Equations can be written to show how forces change energy over time. However, explanations are generally clearer when given in terms of either force or energy, but not both. Mixing the forces and energy in the same sentence can easily lead to confusion or incorrect statements. Therefore, we suggest that in reports and testimony, you talk only about forces, or only about energy, in any one sentence. Don't mix them. This chapter focuses on forces primarily. Energy is briefly described. Momentum is used very little in the present chapter, as it is a concept often misunderstood.

KEY FORCES ACTING ON BLOOD

There are four important forces which act on blood during blood transfer events: weight, pressure, viscous force, and interfacial tension.

Weight

Weight is the force due to gravity. Strictly, mass and weight are different quantities, but they are often confused with each other. For example, we weigh fruit and vegetables in kilograms (kg) or pounds (lb), which are units of mass and not weight.

The mass of an object is the quantity of substance in it. In SI units, it is expressed in kilograms. The mass remains the same wherever the object is: on Earth, on the moon, or in space. A person of 60 kg will be 60 kg in any of these places.

Weight is the force exerted on an object by gravity, and is measured in Newtons (N). The weight is equal to the mass times the strength of gravity. The standard strength of gravity on the Earth's surface is 9.81 Newtons per kilogram (N/kg); so a person with a mass of 100 kg has a weight of 981 N, and they exert this force on whatever they stand on. On the Moon, gravity is only 1.62 N/kg; so the 100 kg person still has a mass of 100 kg on the Moon, but only weighs 162 N.

The strength of gravity is also an acceleration and its units (N/kg) are exactly the same as the unit of acceleration, meters per second per second (m/s^2). An object falling in a vacuum toward the surface of the Earth will accelerate at 9.81 m/s^2. All objects, whatever their mass or shape, will accelerate at the same rate when falling in vacuum. In air, different objects will have different drag (air resistance), which reduces the acceleration during falling. Thus, a feather will accelerate more slowly than a rock.

Although it is a diversion from discussion of forces, now is a good time to describe inertia. Inertia is the tendency of an object to continue moving at the same speed in the same direction. Inertia is not a force. It is not like friction or drag. The amount of inertia an object has is equal to its mass, and like mass, inertia is measured in kilograms. The amount of inertia an object has doesn't change, unless its mass changes. The key idea behind inertia is that you don't have to look for a force to explain why something keeps moving. You only need to look for a force if something changes its speed or direction.

Pressure

Pressure is divided into two types: static pressure and dynamic pressure.

Static Pressure

Static pressure is the pressure we feel on our skin or in our ears. It is the pressure in water that increases as you dive toward the bottom of a swimming pool. It is the pressure in air that decreases as you climb toward the top of a mountain. Static pressure acts in all directions equally (it is *isotropic*) (Figure 5.1).

Dynamic Pressure

Dynamic pressure is the amount by which static pressure changes when a fluid changes its speed or direction. This change in pressure occurs because any part of the fluid has mass. To change the speed or direction of the fluid, a force has to be applied. This force F is proportional to the mass of fluid m and the rate of change of velocity (acceleration) a. These are related by Newton's Second Law, $F = ma$.

If the speed or direction of a part of the fluid changes, a force must be causing this. This force is felt as a change in static pressure. The amount of increase in the static pressure, near where this change in speed or direction happens, is called the dynamic pressure.

Think about standing on top of a hill facing into the wind. The air blowing toward you has to move around your face, either to the left, or right, or over the top of your head. It must change direction, and might change speed as well. Therefore, it accelerates. Something must cause it to accelerate. This something is the extra static pressure created in the air near your skin (Figure 5.2).

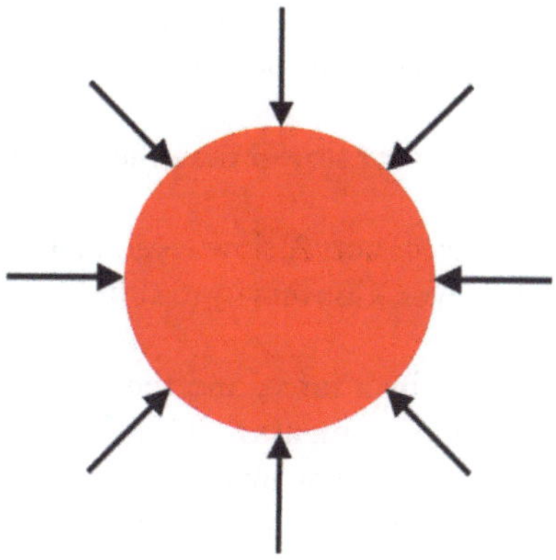

Figure 5.1 Static pressure acting equally in all directions on the outside of a droplet.

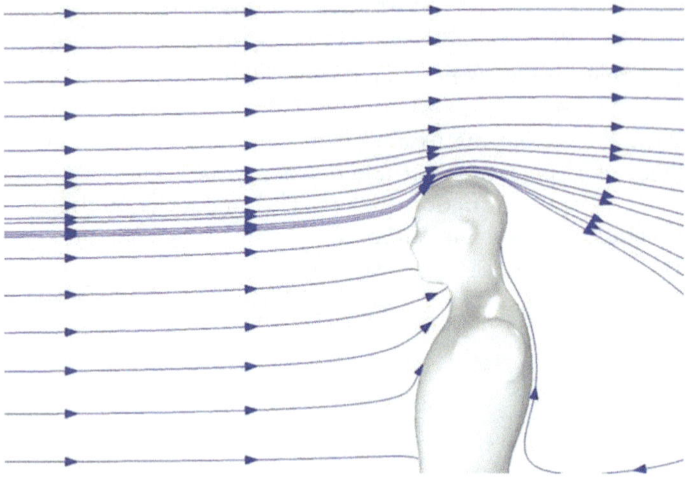

Figure 5.2 Air flowing toward a person's face, deflecting around it, and changing in pressure due to acceleration. (Courtesy: Dr. Jason Chen.)

This extra pressure pushes against your skin. A force equal in strength and opposite in direction (Newton's Third Law) changes the direction of the air. In this process, the static pressure has increased by an amount equal to the dynamic pressure. The dynamic pressure is given by $P_{dynamic} = \frac{1}{2}\rho V^2$, where ρ is the density of the fluid and V is the speed.

Dynamic pressure is sometimes called an inertial force. Dynamic pressure only exists because a force is needed to change the speed and direction of a fluid. This force is needed because the fluid has inertia. The amount of inertia is proportional to the mass of the fluid, which is why dynamic pressure depends on the density of the fluid.

Viscous Force

Viscous force appears in fluids when nearby parts of the fluid move at different speeds. It is analogous to friction in that it always opposes motion, and it dissipates energy ultimately as heat. When a fluid moves over a solid surface, e.g. air moves over a car roof, the layer closest to the surface is stationary, "stuck" to that surface. This is because of frequent collisions between the fluid molecules and the surface.

A layer of fluid further away from the surface will be moving, but slowly. The next layer out will be moving a little faster, and so on, until, at some distance from the surface, a constant speed is reached. This is the "free stream" speed, the speed the fluid would have if the solid surface was not present.

The set of layers of fluid which are moving slower than the free stream speed is collectively called the "boundary layer" (Figure 5.3).

Within a boundary layer, viscous forces act. A slow layer exerts a viscous force on a faster layer, which tends to slow down the faster layer. Conversely, fast fluid exerts a viscous force on neighboring slow fluid.

Any change in momentum is caused by a force, and the viscous force arises because molecules pass from one layer to another, carrying momentum with them from their old to their new layer. The molecules move from one layer to another by diffusion, or are carried by eddies. Jermy and Taylor[2] describe the physical origin of viscosity in a little more detail.

The description above uses the idea of distinct layers of fluid, but in practice, sharp boundaries are not present between them, and speed changes gradually with distance from the solid surface.

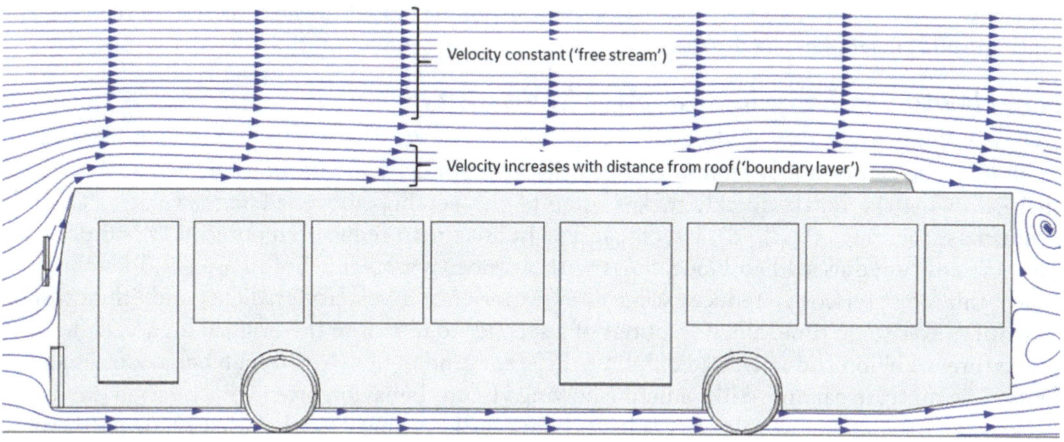

Figure 5.3 Boundary layer forming on a bus roof. (Courtesy: Dr. Jason Chen.)

We will use the symbol τ for the strength of the viscous force per unit area (force per unit area is stress) and is given by:

$$\tau = \mu \frac{\partial V}{\partial y}$$

So, the strength of the viscous force depends on two things:

1. The absolute viscosity μ (Greek letter pronounced "mu"), which is a physical property of the fluid. It varies from fluid to fluid, depending on the size, mass, and shape of the molecules. It is greater for "thick" fluids like honey and oil than for water. For liquids, μ decreases with temperature (hence asphalt, which is a very viscous liquid, is heated to spread it over a road surface). Note that there are two ways of expressing the physical property of viscosity: absolute viscosity (used in this chapter), which is also called dynamic viscosity, and kinematic viscosity, often represented as ν (Greek letter pronounced "nu"), which is the absolute viscosity divided by the fluid's density.
2. How fast velocity changes from place to place, which is expressed mathematically by $\frac{\partial V}{\partial y}$; it is the velocity gradient, also called shear rate. It is essentially the change in velocity ∂V over some distance perpendicular to a surface, ∂y. ∂ (pronounced "dau") means "the change in value of."

Viscous force can also develop at the interface between two different fluids. This is relevant to expirated blood. If a person has blood in their mouth, and exhales air, the air moving over the blood will exert a viscous force on the blood, driving it out of the mouth (Figure 5.4). The surface of the blood develops waves (see later for more about waves).

Figure 5.4 Air blowing over a liquid, exerting viscous force, creating waves, causing those waves to grow, until droplets pinch off from the crests. (Courtesy: Dr. Jason Chen.)

Viscosity is called a *shear force* because it typically acts parallel to the direction of motion, and pulls on solid surfaces in the direction of flow.

Non-Newtonian Behavior: Variation in Viscosity

For some fluids, the value of viscosity μ depends on the velocity gradient. Ketchup is one such fluid. Ketchup pours slowly from a glass bottle, but rapidly if the bottle is given a sharp slap or shake. Moving the bottle quickly makes some of the ketchup move, adding a velocity gradient (known as "shearing" the fluid), which causes viscosity μ to reduce temporarily. Blood does the same: viscosity reduces when blood flows with a velocity gradient. Both blood and ketchup are "shear thinning" (viscosity reduces when they experience a velocity gradient) and "thixotropic" (viscosity takes some time, albeit fractions of a second, to return to the original high value).

Mixtures of blood and saliva can exhibit a different kind of non-Newtonian behavior: viscoelasticity. The mixture can move like a fluid (showing viscous behavior, often with a very high viscosity). At low speeds and low velocity gradients, while still flowing, it can behave like an elastic solid, which changes its shape when a force acts on it but which regains its original shape when that force is removed. The combination of fluid and solid behaviors can cause it to form string-like bodies of fluid which hold together for a long time.

Drag

Drag is the combined effect of pressure and viscosity on an object moving through a fluid. When an object such as a droplet moves through a fluid such as air, the pressure on the front is greater than the pressure on the rear (Figure 5.5). This pressure difference is a part of drag, and is usually the greatest part. The other part of drag is viscous force caused by the boundary layer as the air moves over the surface of the droplet. The viscous force is strongest at the sides, where the velocity gradient is greatest (Figure 5.5). These forces add together to make the drag force, which always acts opposite to the direction the droplet is moving in relation to the air. The drag force F depends on the speed of the droplet V, the size of the droplet (measured as its cross-sectional area A), the density of the air ρ, and on a factor known as the drag coefficient C_d.

$$F = C_d A \frac{1}{2} \rho V^2$$

The drag coefficient depends on the size and shape of the droplet, in a way that is described later in this chapter.

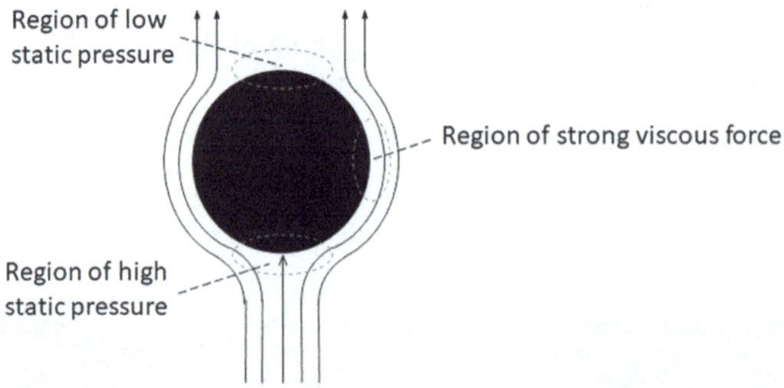

Figure 5.5 A droplet, with air moving upward past it. High pressure on the front face of the droplet and low pressure on the rear cause the pressure component of drag. Viscous force (strongest at the sides where the velocity gradient is greatest) adds to drag.

Interfacial Tension, Surface Tension, and Capillary Forces

Interfacial tension, surface tension, and capillary forces are overlapping terms, each describing aspects of the same physical phenomenon. An *interface* is where two different materials touch (Figure 5.6). Molecules of any stable material are in a negative energy state, i.e. energy has to be added to separate them from their neighbors. Molecules at an interface are in a higher energy state than molecules deep within the parent material. Those deeper molecules are surrounded by molecules of the same type, whereas those on the surface only have neighbors of the same type on one side.

To deform the material, the surface shape must be changed, and this may bring more molecules to the interface, or fewer. The energy required to bring enough molecules to the surface, raising their energy, is the *interfacial energy* and is expressed per unit area of new surface (Joules per square meter or J/m^2). The exact value of the interfacial energy depends on the nature of the two materials in contact.

Imagine that the two materials are the ingredients of a simple salad dressing: olive oil and vinegar. When put in the same container, there is an interface between the oil and vinegar (Figure 5.6). The interfacial energy between these two materials is high. Left alone, the materials will organize themselves into shapes with the smallest possible area of contact (the smallest interfacial area) and hence the lowest interfacial energy. A force arises (*interfacial force*) which pushes them toward a state of lower interfacial energy. Thus, over time, they separate out into a layer of oil floating on a layer of vinegar (Figure 5.6, top).

To mix the oil and vinegar again, energy has to be added, which is done by shaking or stirring. Commercial salad dressings don't need this as they have emulsifier added. The emulsifier changes the surface energy, so the separation doesn't happen (Figure 5.6, bottom).

A droplet of liquid sitting on a solid surface in air is called a sessile droplet (Figure 5.7). The edge of the droplet, where the droplet ends and dry surface begins, is called the *contact line*. The shape of the droplet depends on three interfacial energies:

- Interfacial energy between the liquid and the air (simply called "surface tension")
- Interfacial energy between the liquid and the solid
- Interfacial energy between the air and the solid (this is small, and has little influence on what happens).

If the liquid is water, and the surface is something like stainless steel (perhaps a kitchen sink), the droplet will spread out over the surface like a lens shape. The area over which water touches the steel is approximately the same as the area over which water touches the air. This spread-out state is called *wetting*. The degree of wetting is often described by the contact angle, which is the angle between the solid surface and a line which touches the liquid surface, just where it meets the solid (Figure 5.7).

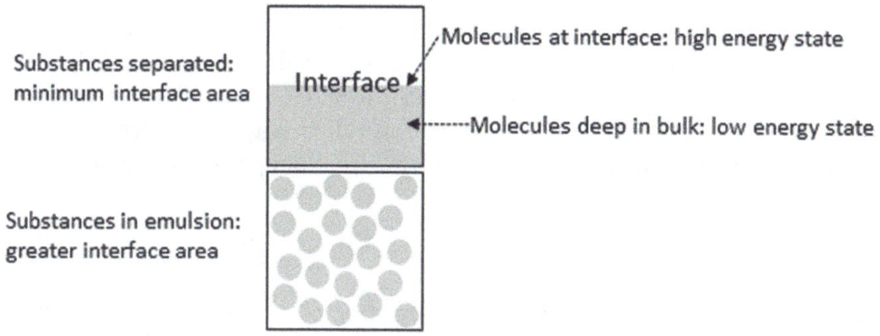

Figure 5.6 Top: two substances, separated as much as possible, with a single interface between them. Bottom: one substance is broken up into droplets and dispersed into the other substance to make an emulsion.

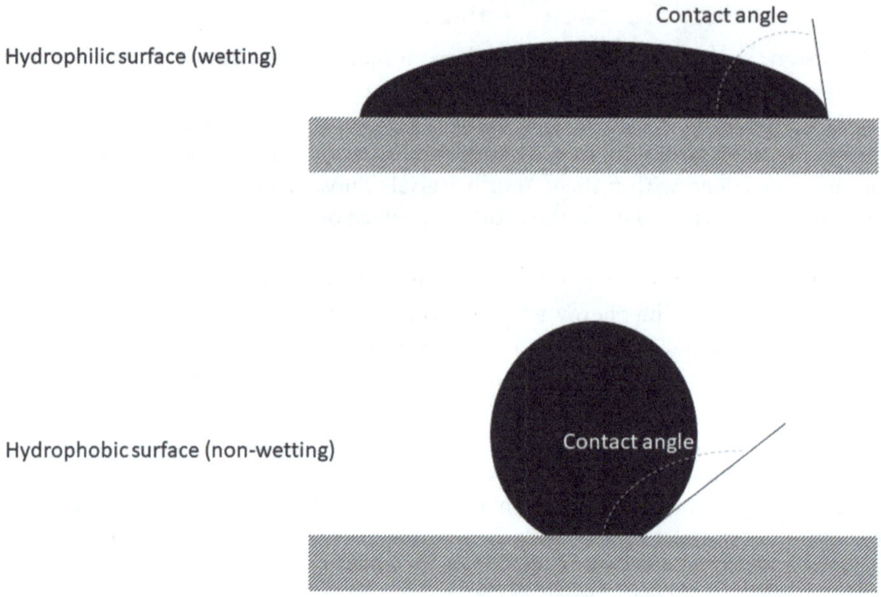

Figure 5.7 Droplets sitting on a surface (sessile drops). Top: wetting, small contact angle; bottom: non-wetting, large contact angle.

If the liquid is water, and the surface is something water-repelling (*hydrophobic*) like a feather, the droplet will take a near-spherical shape, with very little area of contact between the water and the feather. This is because the interfacial energy between water and water-repelling materials is very high. The system seeks a low-energy state, which is minimal area of contact with the solid, and more area of contact with the air, which requires little energy.

Forces act to move systems toward lower energy states. To achieve this low-energy state, forces appear in the outermost layer of the drop. This force is called *surface tension*, and acts parallel to the surface.

Note we have used the same term *surface tension* to describe both the force acting in the droplet (measured in Newtons) and the interfacial energy between liquid and air (measured in Joules per square meter or Newtons per meter). When describing an interfacial energy at an interface with air, surface tension is a physical property, and takes a value of about 0.072 J/m^2 for pure water and 0.055 J/m^2 for blood at room temperature.

Surface tension, the force, and other related forces which arise on interfaces (*interfacial forces*) are together sometimes called *capillary forces*.

Surface tension is not a skin on a droplet. The only special feature of the molecules that feel surface tension force is that they are on the outside of the droplet, in contact with a different fluid on one side. The set of molecules that experience this is only one or two molecules deep. Surface tension forces change as the surface changes shape, and there might be forces which are stronger than surface tension, and which oppose it to determine what happens to a droplet, but surface tension does not really "break" or "rupture."

Surface Tension and Spreading

Surface tension, the force, is important in the spreading of blood on surfaces. The strength of surface tension force depends on the physical property (surface tension, J/m^2) and how strongly curved the surface is, measured as the radius of curvature r (the radius of a circle that follows that part of the surface: Figure 5.8, left). The more curved the surface, the smaller the radius of

Figure 5.8 Left, the radius of curvature of a surface is the radius of a circle that fits that part of the surface. Right, a blood droplet spreading on a surface. The left side is spreading over a smooth part of the surface. The right side is spreading over a protrusion on a rough part of the surface. The radius of curvature of the blood surface is smaller in some parts of the right side, leading to stronger surface tension forces, which resist spreading.

curvature, and the higher the surface tension force (Figure 5.8). Rough surfaces have small protrusions which make the surface curve strongly, which is why liquids don't spread far on rough surfaces (Figure 5.8), compared to smooth surfaces. Some hydrophobic surfaces, like feathers, have many fine protrusions. Others may be smooth, but are made of materials with a naturally high interfacial energy with water, such as greases and fats.

One way of describing spreading is that the contact line moves. The contact line is the edge of the drop, and is the boundary between wetted surface and dry surface (Figure 5.9). Surface tension forces, and also viscous forces, are strong at the contact line, and act to slow down motion of the contact line. The combined effect of these surface tension and viscous forces at the contact line is called *contact line pinning*. This effect is stronger on rough surfaces (Figure 5.8, right).

Surface Tension and Wicking

Wicking is the spontaneous motion of a liquid through narrow pores in a material, such as a textile. Surface tension is responsible for wicking, as it accelerates the liquid so that it moves in a way that more of the material is covered in liquid. In some cases, wicking can pull the liquid up against gravity.

Surface Tension and the Sphericity of Droplets

Droplets traveling through the air usually take a nearly spherical shape, although there are exceptions, described below. Surface tension is the force responsible for the spherical shape, as a sphere

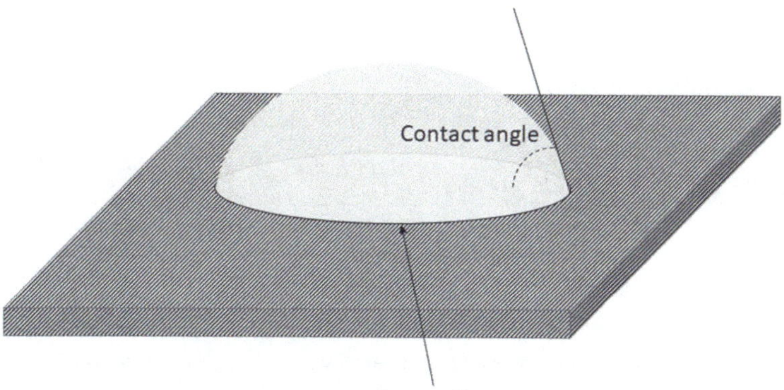

Figure 5.9 A sessile drop, showing the contact line.

has the same curvature everywhere, and also has the minimum surface area for a given volume of liquid. Air pressure varies over the surface of a droplet, which tends to push the droplet out of this spherical shape, but surface tension resists this change of shape. The air pressure force is not strong enough to make the droplet noticeably non-spherical, unless the droplet is very large, or is going fast. This competition between pressure and surface tension is described in more detail below.

Interfacial Tension and Adhesion

Interfacial tension is a term describing forces of the same type as surface tension, but is not limited to liquid-gas interfaces; so it also includes the forces at solid-gas and solid-liquid interfaces. Interfacial tension is responsible for sticking (adhering) a liquid to a solid surface. The interfacial tension forces, including surface tension, act to maintain a certain area of contact between the liquid and the solid. This is why blood can remain on the underside of an object, where it may remain, drip off, or be cast-off, depending on the amount of blood and the motion of the object. Due to a small contact area (non-wetting) and weak interfacial force, water adheres poorly to hydrophobic surfaces like feathers: this is why, with a quick shake, a duck can almost completely dry itself.

Summary of Key Forces

The key forces described above are summarized in Table 5.1.

Turbulent and Laminar Flows

If layers of fluid pass smoothly over each other, with different parts of the fluid moving in roughly parallel lines, the flow is called "laminar" (Figure 5.10, top). However, the viscous shear forces between layers of fluid tend to roll parcels of fluid into *vortices*. Vortices (also called *eddies*) are features in which the fluid spins about an axis. If vortices are allowed to develop, they naturally tend to break down into smaller vortices, which interact with each other. Thus a complex system of vortices, of different sizes, spinning in different directions about different axes develops (Figure 5.10, bottom). This is called turbulent flow.

Not all flows are turbulent. There must be some driving force which sets the fluid into motion with enough variation in speed from place to place that the vortices develop. The variation in speed is often caused by viscous forces, e.g. the strong viscous force where the fluid passes over a surface. If the driving force is not strong enough, viscous forces reduce the difference in speed between adjacent regions, and destroy the vortices. Thus, viscosity has a role in producing turbulence as well as in stopping it. If the driving force is weak compared to viscous forces, or if there has not been enough time for vortices to develop, there is no turbulence and the flow is laminar. Most flows in BPA are laminar, with the possible exception of arterial spurts of blood, air flow during expiration, and short-lived fast motion of blood in gunshot wounds.

Table 5.1 Summary of key forces in BPA

Force	Depends on	Formula
Weight	Mass m	Weight = Mass × g
Static pressure	Atmospheric pressure, and what is happening to dynamic pressure	
Dynamic pressure	Density ρ and speed V	Dynamic pressure = $\frac{1}{2}\rho V^2$
Viscous force	Absolute viscosity μ and velocity gradient $\frac{\partial V}{\partial y}$	$\tau = \mu \frac{\partial V}{\partial y}$ (τ is viscous force per unit area)
Interfacial tension (surface tension force)	Surface tension σ and radius of curvature r	Surface tension force per unit area is proportional to $\frac{\sigma}{r}$

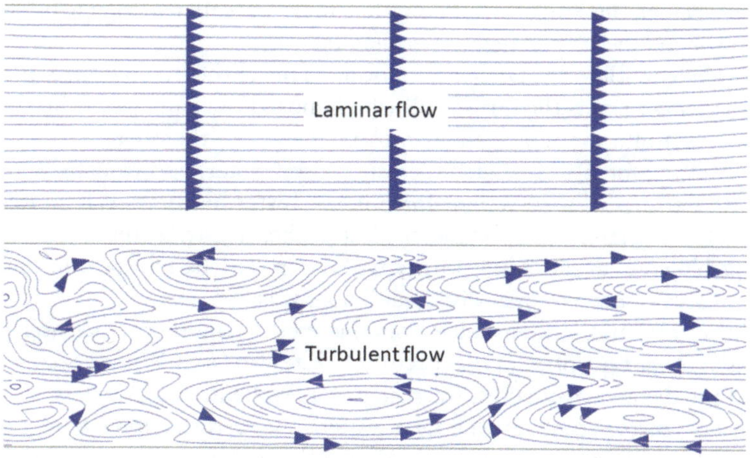

Figure 5.10 Laminar and turbulent flow. (Courtesy: Dr. Jason Chen.)

Wave Processes

Wave processes are important in the breakup of liquid into droplets. Waves are essentially cyclic, i.e. they go through a repeated cycle of back and forth, or up and down, or some other motion. Waves of any type are made possible by (i) inertia and (ii) a *restoring force*, a force that tends to move the system back to a position where all forces are in balance. An example is a pendulum made out of a ball on a string (Figure 5.11). The string always has some tension because of the weight of the ball. The ball is pulled to the left, and rises a little. Once it is released, tension in the string pulls the ball upward (balancing the weight) but also a little toward the right, i.e. toward the center. Tension in the string is the restoring force. When the ball gets to the center, the tension acts only upward, and there is no force to the left or right. However, the ball does not stop moving because it has inertia. It moves to the right of center. Tension now pulls the ball toward the left (toward the center). The ball swings left then right then left again in a cycle. The restoring force, tension, switches between left and right, but always acts toward the center. The cyclic motion does not continue forever, and eventually the ball stops moving. What stops it is the drag of the ball and the drag of the string moving through the air, plus a little friction in the string. The ball travels a little

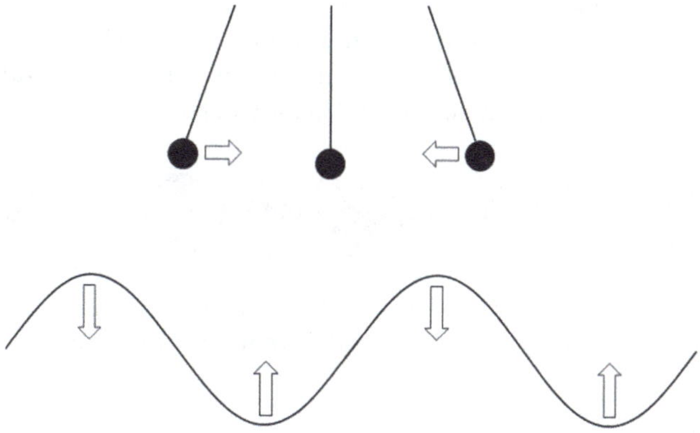

Figure 5.11 Wave motion in (top) a pendulum moving left to right and (bottom) on the surface of water, either an ocean wave or a capillary wave. Arrows indicate the direction of the restoring force.

less far each time. The gradual reduction in distance moved is called *damping* (or *dissipation*). How far the ball moves in one swing is called the *amplitude*.

Waves also need some force to start cyclic motion. This is the *exciting force*. In the case of the pendulum, the exciting force is the initial pull which moved the ball away from the center.

Ocean waves are set into motion by the wind blowing across the ocean (the viscous force from the wind is the exciting force). This sets up crests (raised water) and troughs. Weight force pulls water from crests into troughs, so weight force is the restoring force. When water flows into a trough, it does not stop there, due to its inertia, but pushes nearby water up to make a new crest. If the wind stops blowing, eventually viscosity will damp out the motion and the waves will die away, but ocean waves can travel great distances before this happens.

Such ocean waves are large (the distance from one crest to another, or *wavelength*, is of several meters). There is another type of wave that occurs on water surfaces. These are called *ripples* or *capillary waves*, and the distance from crest to crest is of a few centimeters or less. An example is the waves caused by dropping a stone into a pool of water. The restoring force here is surface tension, which acts in a way that would make the surface smooth and flat, pulling crests down and troughs up. Inertia prevents the surface from becoming flat and still, so the waves go on, until damped out by viscosity. Weight also plays a role, but is weaker than surface tension in capillary waves.

If wind blows across the crest of an ocean wave, it can make ripples (capillary waves on top of an ocean wave). If the wind blows fast enough, these crests grow until they break up into droplets (ocean spray). The growth and breakup of the crests is caused by viscous force from the air moving over the water, and also the pressure difference between the upwind and downwind sides of the crests (dynamic pressure). This process is similar to how blood breaks up into droplets in some types of expirated spatter.

PHYSICAL PROPERTIES OF FLUIDS AND INCOMPRESSIBILITY

For fluid dynamics, the most important physical properties of fluids are density, viscosity, and surface tension. The properties of air are important in droplet flight. At 20°C and typical sea-level atmospheric pressure, air has a density of 1.2 kg/m^3, absolute viscosity of 0.000018 Pa.s (Pascals times seconds), and no surface tension as it is a gas. The properties of blood are described in Chapter 3.

Blood is assumed to be *incompressible*, i.e. its density doesn't change during blood transfer events. In reality, blood, like other liquids, can be compressed, but it takes enormous pressures to change the density by more than a fraction of one percent.

If the blood is released from wounds in the mouth, nose, or elsewhere in the airway, the blood may be mixed with saliva and/or mucus, which can modify its viscosity and surface tension. Mucus is viscoelastic, which can strongly influence its behavior when it impacts a surface.

ENERGY

During blood transfer events, energy is converted from one type to another. The total amount of energy (added together over all types) is conserved. The important types of energy are:

Kinetic Energy

This is the energy associated with motion of an object of mass m at a speed V (magnitude of velocity) and is equal to $\frac{1}{2}mV^2$.

Gravitational Potential Energy

This is the energy associated with raising a mass m by a distance h above some reference level, in gravity of strength g and is equal to mgh.

Surface Energy

This is the energy associated with expanding the liquid-air interface by an area A, for a liquid of surface tension (the physical property) σ, and is equal to σA. The more energy that is concentrated into a fixed volume of blood, the more new surface area A can be created. The more surface area that is created, the more droplets a fixed volume of blood is broken up into, and since the total volume is fixed, each individual droplet is smaller. Hence, processes which are good at transferring a lot of energy into a small volume of blood (e.g. bullet or hammer impacts), create more, smaller droplets, compared to processes which transfer less energy, or transfer it into a larger volume (e.g. stomping into a pool of blood).

Heat

Heat is a form of internal energy. Temperature does not usually change very much during the formation of a bloodstain, except during the final stage when the blood, which starts at body-temperature, cools to ambient temperature, during the early phases of drying. Viscous force dissipates kinetic energy by turning it into heat, but typically with a very small (less than 1°C) change in temperature.

Pressure Energy

Pressure is another form of internal energy, which is important where blood experiences changes in pressure, e.g. when released from an artery into the air or when temporarily pressurized by colliding with an object.

DIMENSIONLESS NUMBERS RELEVANT TO BPA

The fluid dynamics of bloodstain pattern formation involves a large number of variables, e.g. droplet diameter d, density ρ, speed V, dynamic pressure $\frac{1}{2}\rho V^2$, viscosity μ, surface tension σ, and so on. Researchers in fluid dynamics frequently reduce the number of variables needed to be considered by making dimensionless numbers, achieved by forming fractions from these variables, e.g.:

$$Dimensionless\ number = \frac{abc}{def}$$

where $a,b,c,d,e,$ and f are important variables in the problem. The variables are chosen so that the units of the numerator (abc) are the same as the units of the denominator (def). Thus, the units cancel out and the resulting number has no units (i.e. no dimensions, hence "dimensionless number," also called a "nondimensional number" or "dimensionless group"). This example equation is written with three variables in the numerator and three in the denominator, but there may be any number in each.

A simple example is the Mach number:

$$Ma = \frac{V}{c}$$

where V is a speed, e.g. the speed of an airplane, and c is the speed of sound. Therefore, the Mach number is the speed of the airplane expressed as multiple of the speed of sound. If $Ma = 0.5$, the airplane is moving at half the speed of sound; if $Ma = 1$, it is going at exactly the speed of sound, and if Ma is bigger than 1, the plane is supersonic.

V and c are written in the same units, meters per second. Therefore, the units cancel out, and the Mach number has no units (it is dimensionless).

Using dimensionless numbers has several advantages:

- The value of the dimensionless numbers tells you something about the fluid dynamics immediately. For example, if the Mach number is greater than 1, you know that supersonic effects like shock waves might be important.
- Results from experiments carried out with different fluids (e.g. two different gases like helium and air, or two different liquids like water and blood) can be compared by using dimensionless numbers because physical properties like density, viscosity, or speed of sound appear in the formulas in a way which cancels out their effect.
- Many fluid dynamic equations are simpler when expressed using dimensionless numbers.
- It doesn't matter what system of units you use, providing you are consistent. The Mach number will have the same value if both speeds are in meters per second, or if both speeds are in miles per hour. People working with SI units (meters, kilograms, seconds) will get the same number as people working in English units (feet, pounds, seconds). (However for each calculation, a consistent set of units must be used for all of the variables, e.g. if using SI units to calculate one of the dimensionless numbers described below, distances must be in meters, velocities in meters per second, densities in kilograms per cubic meter, absolute viscosity in Pascal seconds, surface tension in Newtons per meter, and acceleration (e.g. due to gravity) in meters per second per second.)

In the fluid dynamics of bloodstain formation, the Mach number is rarely used, but other dimensionless numbers can be used to find out several important things:

- the shape of a droplet while it is traveling through the air (Weber number)
- the drag coefficient of a droplet while it is traveling through the air (Reynolds and Weber numbers)
- how far a droplet will spread when it impacts a surface (Reynolds and Weber numbers)
- whether a droplet will splash when spreading on a surface (Reynolds and Weber numbers)
- the shape a droplet will take when sitting on a surface, after spreading and splashing have stopped (Bond number)
- how far wicking will carry liquid inside a porous object (capillary number)

These dimensionless numbers are used frequently in the research literature. They are rarely, if ever, used in case reporting.

For a droplet traveling through the air, the Weber number is:

$$We = \frac{\rho_{air} V^2 d}{\sigma}$$

where ρ_{air} is the density of air, V is the speed of the droplet relative to air, d is the diameter of the droplet, and σ is the surface tension of blood. The Weber number is the ratio of the force caused by dynamic pressure (inertial force) to the surface tension force. If you write an equation for each of these two forces, divide one by the other, and erase some constants such as $\frac{1}{2}$, you get the equation for the Weber number above. This means that the Weber number tells us which of these forces is the stronger. If the Weber number has a large value, the force due to dynamic pressure is stronger than surface tension. Due to dynamic pressure, the pressure is higher on the front of the droplet than on any other side; so it tends to flatten droplets into a disk or bag shape as it travels through the air. Surface tension acts to keep droplets spherical. If the force due to dynamic pressure is stronger than surface tension, the droplet will flatten into a disk shape, and this will increase the drag on it. It may even break up in the air to leave smaller fragments of blood. If the Weber number takes a low value, surface tension is the stronger of the two forces, and the droplet will be spherical. It has been established by researchers studying droplets of different liquids, different sizes, and different speeds[5,6] that:

- If the Weber number is less than 2, the droplet is practically spherical.
- If the Weber number is greater than 2, the droplet is not spherical.
- If the droplet is suddenly exposed to a fast air flow in which the Weber number is greater than 13, the droplet will break up into smaller packets of liquid.
- If the droplet is slowly accelerated, it can reach a Weber number of 22 before breaking up.

The exact speed V at which this happens depends on the size of the droplet (d) and the properties of the air (ρ_{air}) and blood (σ).

The Reynolds number is the ratio of inertial (dynamic pressure) to viscous forces. Low Reynolds numbers indicate that viscous forces are dominant, and the fluid flow will be smooth with layers at different speeds passing smoothly over each other (*laminar flow*). At high Reynolds numbers, inertial forces are dominant with the fluid flow having a chaotic appearance with a constantly evolving set of vortices, i.e. *turbulent flow*.

The Reynolds number can be used to find the drag force on a droplet traveling through the air. The first step would be to find the droplet Reynolds number using the following formula:

$$Re = \frac{\rho_{air} V d}{\mu_{air}}$$

where μ_{air} is the absolute viscosity of the air, and the other variables have the same meaning as above. Note that in this version of the Reynolds number, the density and viscosity of the *air* are used. This number tells us about how the air is flowing over the surface of the droplet.

The drag force on a droplet depends on the drag coefficient. The drag coefficient is set by two things, one which depends on the Weber number, and one which depends on the Reynolds number:

- The shape of the droplet (is it a sphere, or is it a disk, or a bag shape, or something in between?) determined by the Weber number.
- The way air flows over the surface, particularly whether flow near the surface is laminar or turbulent. This is determined by the Reynolds number. The transition from laminar to turbulent flow in the air flowing over the surface of a droplet occurs at a Reynolds number between 300,000 and 500,000.

The drag coefficient of spheres has been measured by many different researchers. The results of all properly conducted experiments agree well, and there is a standard graph of sphere drag coefficient against Reynolds number.[7,8] The drag coefficient of a sphere varies from in excess of 100, to around 0.5 across much of the range of Reynolds numbers experienced by a moving blood droplet, to values of less than 0.1 for specific conditions.[7,8]

If the droplet changes from a spherical to a disk or bag shape, the drag coefficient depends on the exact shape it takes, i.e. on the Weber number as well as on the Reynolds number. There are a number of expressions for the drag coefficient of a droplet at various degrees of deformation.[9,10,11,12] One example assumes that a droplet reaches maximum deformation when it takes the form of a disk. The drag coefficient of the deformed droplet is then estimated by interpolating between that of a solid sphere C_d^{sphere} and of a disk C_d^{disk}.[11,12]

$$C_d = AR \cdot C_d^{sphere} + (1 - AR) C_D^{disk}$$

where AR is the droplet aspect ratio ($AR = 1$ for a sphere, whereas for a thin disk, $AR \approx 0$). The aspect ratio is estimated using an empirical correlation based on the Weber number. There are empirical expressions for the drag coefficient of disks for a wide range of Reynolds numbers.[7,8]

The drag coefficient is itself a dimensionless number. It is the ratio of the drag force on a particular object to the drag force on a hypothetical "reference" object which has a drag force exactly equal to the dynamic pressure multiplied by the area.

The Reynolds and Weber numbers can be defined a little differently to understand what happens when a droplet impacts a surface. For a blood droplet impacting a surface, these are:

$$Re_{impact} = \frac{\rho_{blood} V d}{\mu_{blood}}$$

$$We_{impact} = \frac{\rho_{blood} V^2 d}{\sigma}$$

i.e. the density and absolute viscosity of *blood* are used, instead of the air. In this case, V is the speed of the droplet relative to the solid surface.

The degree of droplet spreading, splashing, rebound, and the number of spines and satellite stains which form, all depend on Re_{impact} and We_{impact}. Surface characteristics like roughness and hydrophobicity also play a role.

From the equations for Re_{impact} and We_{impact}, it can be seen that both numbers increase when either the droplet is made bigger or made faster. As either droplet size or droplet speed increases, the impact behavior moves from simple spreading, to splashing, and then to more severe splash with more fingers and satellite spatter.

The Bond number is the ratio of the droplet weight to the interfacial tension forces. It is important when a droplet is sitting still on a surface, where its shape is determined by the competition between weight force and surface tension force. Weight force tends to cause it to spread, and surface tension force, which tends to minimize the surface area, works against spreading.

$$Bo = \frac{\rho_{blood} g d^2}{\sigma}$$

where g is the acceleration due to gravity (9.81 m/s^2).

Two additional dimensionless numbers which are sometimes used in research in the breakup of liquid into droplets are the Ohnesorge (Oh) and capillary (Ca) numbers.

The Ohnesorge number is the ratio of the viscous force to the combined effect of inertial and surface tension forces inside a sheet or jet of liquid, or a droplet:

$$Oh = \frac{\mu_{blood}}{\sqrt{\rho_{blood} d \sigma}}$$

It is effectively the viscous force divided by the square root of (inertial force times surface tension force). The Ohnesorge number is used in some descriptions of how liquid jets or sheets break up into droplets, and how droplets oscillate in shape.

If you take the square root of the Weber number and divide it by the Reynolds number, you will find the Ohnesorge number. However, don't stress about it: ohnesorge can be translated from German as "no worries."

The capillary number is the ratio of the viscous forces to the surface tension forces. It is used in describing how liquid sheets and jets break up, and how liquid moves by wicking through porous solids, like textiles. The capillary number is given by:

$$Ca = \frac{\mu V}{\sigma}$$

where μ is the absolute viscosity of the liquid. μ would be the viscosity of blood if wicking of blood in a textile is being studied.

THE DYNAMICS OF DROPLET FORMATION AND FLIGHT

This section is concerned with the mechanisms of breaking up bulk liquid into droplets. The initial formation of droplets at the blood source is termed primary breakup. Common examples include dripping faucets, shower heads, garden hoses, and paint sprays.

Breakup occurs when the disruptive forces acting on the liquid are stronger than the cohesive surface tension forces and dissipative viscous forces, which act to stabilize the liquid. The strength of the forces at play, the nature of the liquid source, and the physical properties of the liquid influence the sizes and velocities of the droplets which form.

The droplets produced as a result of the primary breakup may undergo shape oscillations, deform, and break up further into smaller droplets. Breakup in flight is called secondary breakup.

Droplets of blood traveling through the air are sometimes referred to as "stains," but this is not really correct: they are droplets at this stage, and do not become stains until they land on a surface.

Primary Breakup

The most elementary primary breakup mechanism is dripping of a liquid from a source, for example, water or blood dripping from an orifice or a wetted object.

In dripping of liquid at relatively low flow rates, when inertial forces are small and there is little or no air motion, the important forces are interfacial tension and weight. This results in the formation of relatively large (larger than 1 mm in diameter)[13] and uniform droplets, which periodically detach from the bulk liquid. This mode of droplet formation is called *dripping* or *periodic dripping*.

Dripping proceeds through the following general stages. The static stage is characterized by slow growth of a hanging mass of liquid. Interfacial tension forces hold it to the source. As soon as the weight of the hanging liquid exceeds interfacial tension forces, the droplet starts to elongate, forming a liquid neck (Figure 5.12a). The neck further elongates into an almost cylindrical column or ligament[14] (Figure 5.12b), which eventually becomes narrow enough to break in one or several places[15] (Figure 5.12c). In most cases, it breaks at the lower end near the detaching droplet, called "end-pinching." The main or primary droplet is formed and it continues to move downward experiencing large amplitude shape oscillations (alternately bulging and contracting: Figure 5.12c–e). These oscillations eventually stop (are damped out) due to viscous forces acting inside the liquid. At the same time, the ligament contracts vertically and experiences bulging-contracting oscillations due to surface tension (Figure 5.12d). In some cases, it may break at two or more places forming one or more smaller accompanying droplets (Figure 5.12e). They oscillate in shape. They may (due to the impulse given by surface tension forces just prior to breaking off) move upward

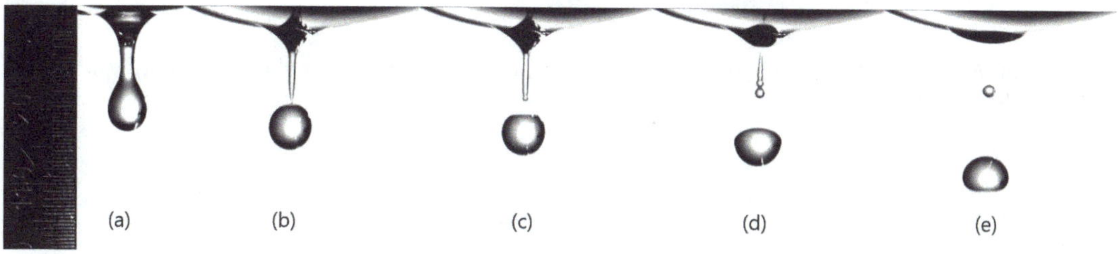

Figure 5.12 Dripping of distilled water: (a) neck, (b) ligament, (c) formation; ligament "end-pinching" and contraction, (d) consequent ligament breakup (d), and (e) accompanying drop formation. Shape oscillation of the primary droplet is seen (c–e).

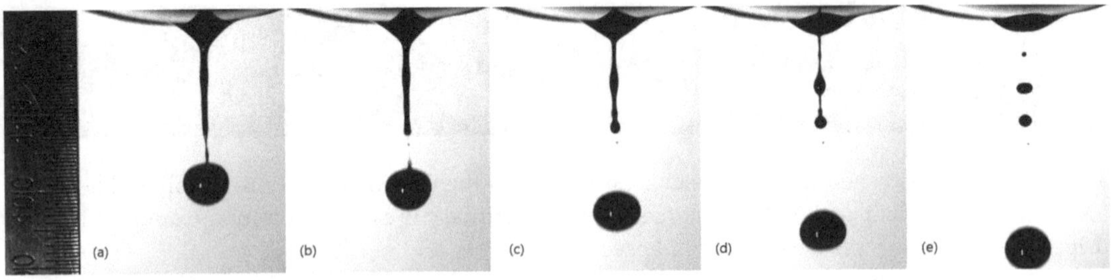

Figure 5.13 Dripping of porcine blood from the cylindrical object. The smallest scale division is 0.5 mm.[20]

and merge with, or bounce off, the residual liquid that is still adhering to the source. The falling droplets may also collide with or bounce off each other.[16] Figure 5.13 shows the dripping process in porcine blood.

The process is variable, and the dripping rate, size of the primary droplet, and sizes and number of accompanying droplets all depend on the geometry of the orifice or wetted object, on the physical properties of the liquid, and on temperature, wind or drafts, and any motion of the wetted object. In particular, the greater the radius of curvature of the wetted object, the larger the size of the falling primary droplet.[17] Very viscous fluids, or viscoelastic fluids, like mixtures of mucus and blood can develop extended, long-lived, stable ligaments.

As the flow rate of the liquid increases, inertial forces grow more important. The dripping process continues but the detaching droplets vary in size from one to another. The time between successive droplets also varies and the point of droplet detachment moves further down the hanging column of liquid. This regime of droplet formation is called *chaotic dripping*.

With further increase in flow rate, the balance between interfacial tension and gravitational forces can no longer be maintained and the liquid forms a cylindrical jet as it emerges from an orifice. Oscillations grow on the liquid's free surface and under favorable conditions, the jet disintegrates into droplets[14,15] (Figure 5.14). This process of droplet formation is called *jet breakup*. This phenomenon has been well studied due to its importance in a variety of industrial processes such as ink-jet printing, fuel combustion, and spray painting. For bloodstain formation, it can occur when an artery is breached.

The initial waves appear spontaneously, due to vibrations and viscous forces between the liquid and air. The waves grow leading to jet breakup. This is called the *varicose jet breakup mode* (Figure 5.15a). The restoring force of these waves is surface tension. The waves are damped out by viscosity, but if the liquid breaks up into droplets, this damping is not complete by the time breakup occurs.

Figure 5.14 Water jet breakup.[15] (Figure 3 in Lord Rayleigh "Some applications of photography," *Nature*, 44, 249–54, 1891, courtesy Springer.)

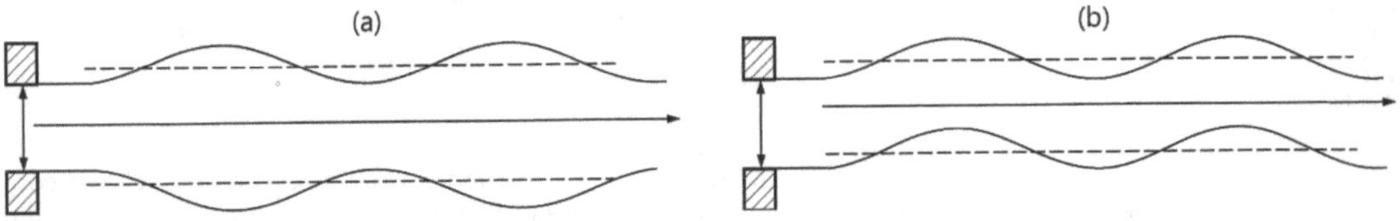

Figure 5.15 (a) Varicose (symmetric) and (b) sinuous (antisymmetric) jets.

If the jet speed is further increased, viscous and dynamic pressure forces dominate the surface tension forces, and a sinuous wave (Figure 5.15b) is formed. The jet disintegrates closer to the exit compared to a varicose jet.

For high-speed jets, the liquid starts to break up almost immediately producing a conical spray of small droplets (Figure 5.16).

Liquid properties play an important role in the jet breakup dynamics. Surface tension and viscosity both affect the droplet sizes.

The breakup process is broadly similar if, instead of a jet, the liquid first emerges as a sheet. Figure 5.17 shows this process in a type of spray nozzle that forms a conical sheet of liquid, which subsequently breaks up. In bloodstain pattern formation, sheet formation and breakup may occur during an arterial breach (leading to a projected pattern), when liquid is pushed out between two surfaces (leading to an impact pattern) or during the breakup of a raised rim during splash (drip patterns).

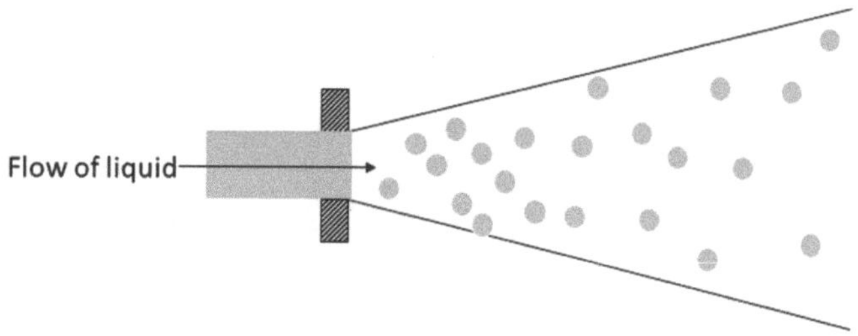

Figure 5.16 Breakup of a high speed jet.

Figure 5.17 Breakup of a conical liquid sheet formed by a spray nozzle. (Courtesy: Prof. Patrick Scheunemann, Fachhochschule Südwestfalen.)

The breakup of a liquid sheet depends on its initial speed, the physical properties of the liquid, and the physical properties of the surrounding air. Three modes of sheet breakup can be distinguished: rim, wavy-sheet, and perforated-sheet disintegration (Figure 5.18).

During *rim disintegration* (Figure 5.18a), the free edge of the liquid sheet contracts into a thicker rim due to surface tension forces tending to reduce the liquid surface area. The rim subsequently disintegrates into relatively large droplets similar to the breakup of a liquid jet. The breakup is caused by surface tension waves. The droplets move in the original flow direction. They may briefly remain connected to the main liquid body by thin ligaments, which eventually breakup into smaller satellite droplets. *Wave-sheet disintegration* (Figure 5.18b) occurs when aerodynamic forces induce rapidly growing waves on the surface of a sheet leading to its breakup. The detached pieces contract due to surface tension effects, but can further disintegrate into droplets of various sizes. In *perforated-sheet disintegration* (Figure 5.18c), holes form in the body of the sheet. The holes grow in size until a web of thin ligaments is left. These ligaments break into relatively uniform droplets. In practice, more than one of these modes may be seen in a given breakup event.

In all these processes, a range of droplet sizes is created.

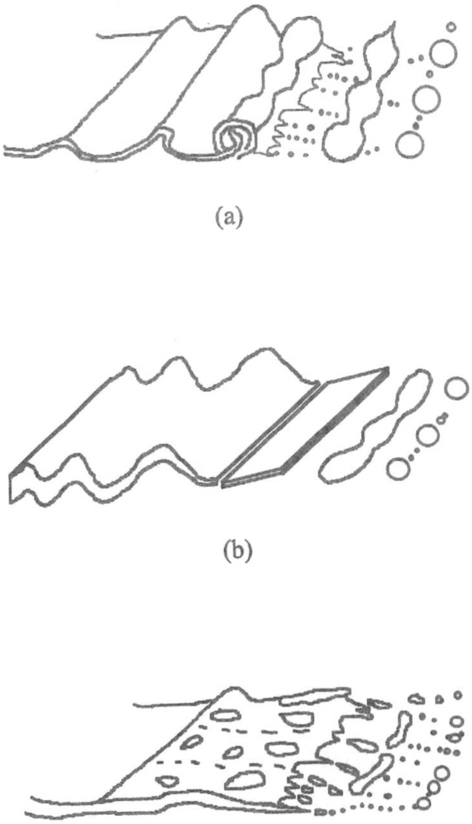

(a)

(b)

(c)

Figure 5.18 Liquid sheet breakup modes[18]: (a) rim, (b) wave-sheet, and (c) perforated-sheet. (Figure 3.8 in H. Liu, *Science and Engineering of Droplets: Fundamentals and Applications*, 2000, courtesy Noyes Publications/William Andrew Publishing.)

Droplet Deformation and Secondary Breakup

Once the droplets have been formed and are traveling through the air, further breakup may occur. This is called *secondary breakup*. Blood droplets can break up by one of three breakup mechanisms: *vibrational breakup*, *bag breakup*, and *shear breakup*.

If droplet oscillations trigger breakup, the process is vibrational breakup. The droplet first takes a dumbbell-like shape. The two bulges move alternately apart and together, moving a little further apart each time, until they separate altogether (Figure 5.19).

When vibrational breakup occurs in bloodstain formation, it is most often observed when a droplet, not having sufficient time to reach a spherical shape, is elongated and is tumbling. The tumbling prevents it reaching a stable spherical shape, and the neck between the two halves of the droplet pinches off to make two separate droplets. This is seen in some videos of impact spatter, and some videos of drip pattern formation. An example is seen in MFRC library[4] video 6Ad1c "Blood drop falling 100 cm to an existing blood drop," especially the dumbbell-shaped droplet, which breaks off from the main pool about the 12 o'clock position. This droplet takes a dumbbell-like shape from frame 16 onward (in the video, frame numbers are shown in the text block on the left-hand side of the image). It travels toward the top of the image and breaks apart in frame 35 just before it leaves the image.

An airborne droplet experiences unbalanced forces due to dynamic pressure that can deform it. Surface tension forces tend to resist the deformation. The competition between pressure force and surface tension force can be expressed by the Weber number. A large Weber number means the pressure force is strong compared to surface tension, leading to deformation of the droplet. Droplets can be considered effectively spherical for Weber numbers less than 2. As the droplet speed increases, so does the Weber number, and the droplet deforms. The front face (facing in the direction the droplet is traveling) flattens, and the rear face, where air pressure is lower, has a dome-like shape (Figure 5.20). These changes increase the cross-sectional area of the droplet, which in turn increases the drag on it.[19] As a result, the trajectory of the droplet is altered, compared to that of a droplet which remains spherical.

The degree of droplet deformation is not influenced by droplet liquid viscosity. Higher liquid viscosity, however, lowers the rate of droplet deformation without altering the final shape.

If the Weber number increases further, the droplet disintegrates into smaller or "child" droplets by the bag breakup mechanism. The droplet deforms into a hollow bag with a thick, roughly circular rim containing about 70–75% of the original droplet mass (Figure 5.21). The bag breaks up into smaller droplets first. The rim disintegrates subsequently into slightly larger droplets.

The level of droplet deformation and breakup depend both on the strength of the aerodynamic forces and how fast they are applied. In the case of slow, gradual loading, such as a rain droplet falling from a cloud, a droplet has sufficient time to adjust itself to the deforming dynamic pressure force, and the surface tension force keeps it together. Droplets exposed to slowly increasing aerodynamic forces can reach Weber numbers of 22 before breaking up. If suddenly exposed to

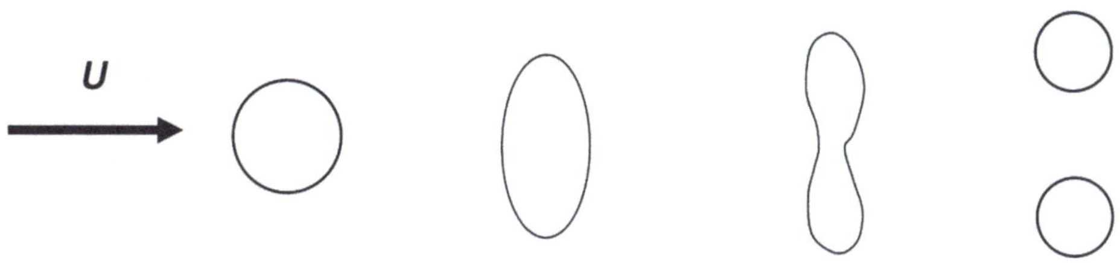

Figure 5.19 Vibrational droplet breakup.

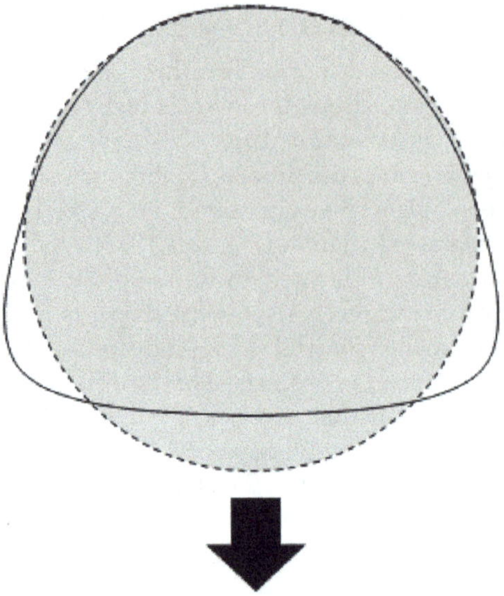

Figure 5.20 A droplet moving downward through the air and deforming from an undisturbed spherical shape (dashed line) under the action of aerodynamic pressure. The black arrow indicates the direction of travel.

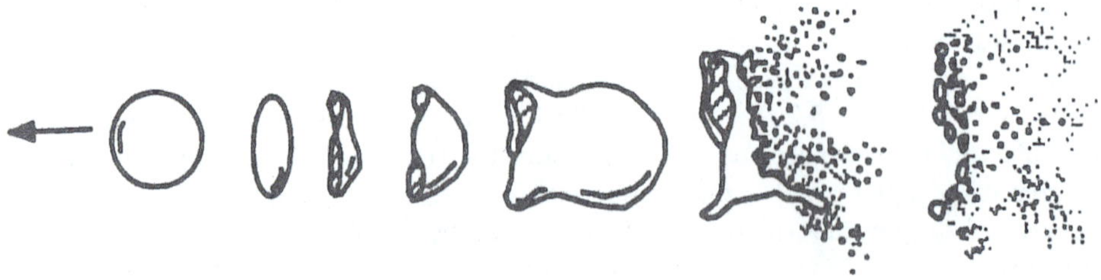

Figure 5.21 Droplet bag breakup mechanism.[18] Droplet movement is from right to left. (Figure 3.10 in H. Liu, *Science and Engineering of Droplets: Fundamentals and Applications*, 2000, courtesy Noyes Publications/William Andrew Publishing.)

the flow (e.g. a droplet experiencing a blast of muzzle gas e.g. from a firearm), droplets break up at a Weber number of 13.

Examples of vibrational and bag breakup of a porcine blood droplet are shown in Figure 5.22.

Shear breakup can occur when a droplet is exposed to a sudden change in air speed (e.g. a blast of air), in which the Weber number exceeds 100. The droplet first deforms to make a convex surface (curving away from the source of the air flow). The edges of the droplet extend into thin sheets and ligaments which break up into child droplets (Figure 5.23).

Figure 5.22 Vibrational (top) and bag (bottom) breakup of a porcine blood droplet (droplet movement is from left to right).[20]

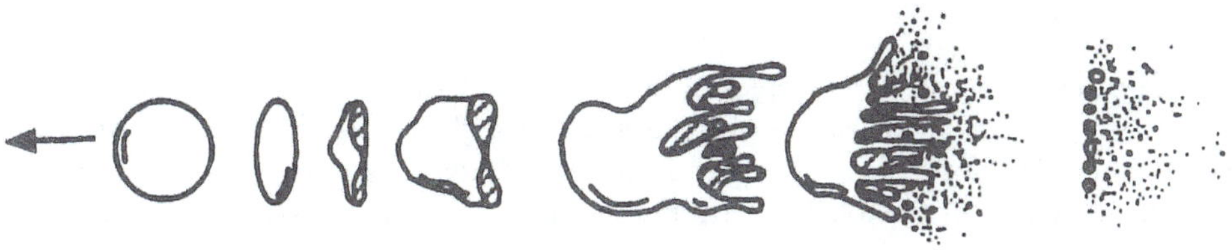

Figure 5.23 Shear breakup.[18] Droplet movement is from right to left. (Figure 3.10 in H. Liu, *Science and Engineering of Droplets: Fundamentals and Applications*, 2000, courtesy Noyes Publications/William Andrew Publishing.)

Summary of Breakup

In breakup, when some disrupting force is applied, the blood may extend into sheets, or directly into ligaments. A jet is similar to a ligament. Sheets break up into ligaments. Ligaments break up into droplets. Droplets may in some cases undergo further breakup into smaller droplets. The process of liquid breakup can be complete by the time the blood has traveled only a few millimeters, or it may need up to tens of centimeters to finish.

It should be noted that there is no "standard droplet size" formed as a result of liquid breakup. Most breakup processes produce a range of droplet sizes, with the average size being dependent on a number of factors, among which are the strength of the disturbing force, liquid properties, and the shape of the blood source.

Droplet Shape Oscillations

A droplet can oscillate in shape following its formation, due to the unbalanced surface tension forces at the time of release. Strong oscillations may lead to vibrational breakup, but often they are not strong enough and the droplet remains whole. If non-spherical, surface tension forces pull the droplet into a sphere: when it reaches that spherical shape, the parts of the droplet which are already moving keep moving (inertia) and it enters a new non-spherical shape. Thus, a droplet which starts as a prolate shape (like a football or egg standing on its point) becomes an oblate shape (like a football or egg sitting on its side). Surface tension forces stop and reverse the motion, and it passes briefly through a spherical shape to become prolate again, and so on (Figure 5.24).

The amplitude of oscillations dies away with time, damped by viscous forces. If there is enough time, the droplet settles into a stable spherical shape.

Smaller droplets oscillate at higher frequency (more complete cycles in each second or millisecond), but the oscillation damps out earlier (oscillation stops after less time has passed). Droplets of blood of 3–5 mm in diameter, dripping from an object, stop oscillating before they have fallen by 200 mm or so.

Figure 5.24 Droplet shape oscillations between oblate and prolate spheroids. The most oblate shapes are on the far left and the far right. The most prolate is the center image.

Droplet Flight

The drag force experienced by a droplet in flight plays a significant role in determining droplet trajectory. Using the known strengths of the drag and weight forces, the path of a droplet can be calculated, if the size of the droplet and its initial speed are known. A droplet traveling with no drag (e.g. in a vacuum) would follow a path that is a perfect parabola. With drag, the trajectory is no longer exactly a parabola.

If a small and a large blood droplets are launched at the same initial speed and direction, the small droplet experiences a weaker drag force because its area A is smaller. However, its mass is even smaller; so, by Newton's Second Law $F = ma$, a small drag force can result in a large change in speed. Therefore, although the drag on the small droplet is weaker, a small droplet loses more speed than a large droplet in the same time, all other things being equal. This is why small droplets don't travel as far horizontally, if launched with the same speed, when there is no wind (Figure 5.25: compare the "no wind" curves for the 0.5 mm and 2 mm diameter droplets).

Wind blowing in the direction the droplet is traveling will make it travel further. Wind affects small droplets more than large droplets[20] (Figure 5.25: compare the "2 m/s wind" curves for the 0.5 mm and 2 mm diameter droplets. The small droplet travels farther horizontally, as it is blown further by the wind. Wind or draft blowing in the opposite direction will make the droplets travel less far).

The effect of wind can be calculated, provided the speed and direction of the wind are known.[19] Of course, these quantities are not usually known by an analyst who arrives at the scene sometime after the droplets have stopped moving and formed stains.

Droplets experience some loss of water by evaporation during flight, but given the short time the droplet is in the air, this is negligible.[20]

Terminal Velocity

When an object falls in air, the downward force of gravity F_G, the buoyancy force F_B, and the aerodynamic drag force F_D act on it (Figure 5.26). (Buoyancy force is equal to the weight of the air which would be present if the droplet was not there, and is quite small for a droplet of water or blood in air.) As the object falls faster, the drag force increases, but weight and buoyancy forces

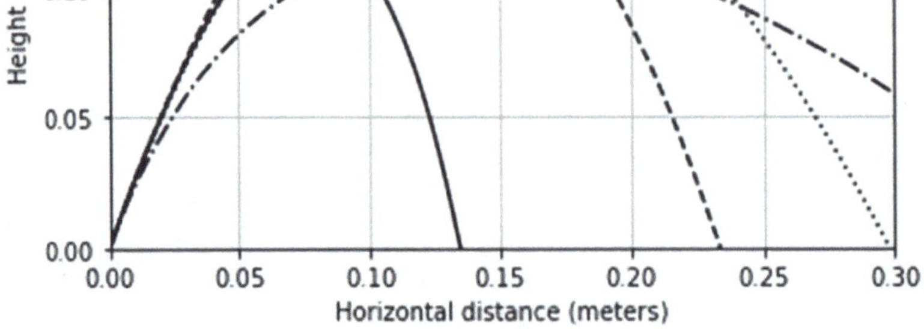

Figure 5.25 The trajectories of droplets with diameters of 0.5 mm and 2 mm, with and without wind. All droplets start at 2 m/s, aimed 70° above the horizontal. When the wind is blowing, it is from left to right at 2 m/s.

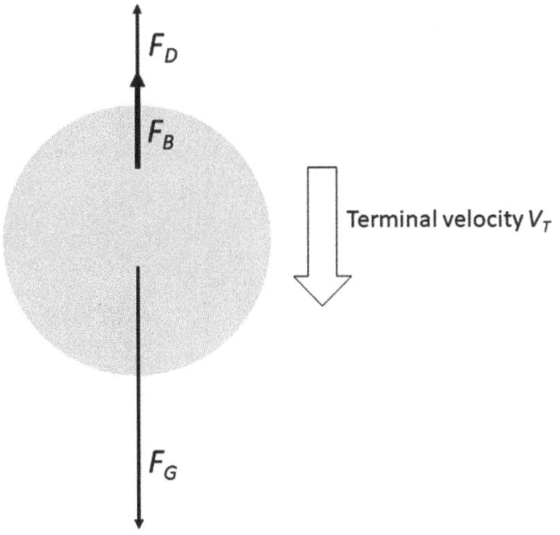

Figure 5.26 Forces acting on a free falling object.

stay the same. At some point, drag force will balance the gravitational and buoyancy forces so that $F_D = F_G - F_B$. There is now no net force, and the object no longer accelerates. Its velocity is now a constant, called the *terminal velocity* V_T.

The magnitude of terminal velocity for a spherical object can be calculated using the following expression:

$$V_T = \sqrt{\frac{4}{3} \frac{\rho_{droplet} dg}{\rho_{air} C_d}}$$

This formula gives you the magnitude of velocity, i.e. the speed. Velocity is speed *and* direction, and when we talk about "terminal velocity," we are usually talking about the speed, but we usually also know the direction (the droplet is moving straight down). d is the diameter of the sphere, and $\rho_{droplet} = \rho_{blood}$ if this sphere is a droplet of blood. The terminal velocity is faster for denser or larger objects. Objects with lower drag coefficients have higher terminal velocities.

There have been many experimental studies on the movement of water drops at terminal velocities in air, due to its importance for meteorological science. The phenomenon of droplet deformation in flight plays an important role in determining its terminal velocity. Data on terminal velocities of water droplets from various sources[21,22,23,24,25,26] are plotted below (Figure 5.27). As terminal velocity depends primarily on density, and blood has a similar density to water, the terminal velocity of blood droplets will be very similar.

A droplet falling from rest will never actually reach its terminal velocity exactly, as the accelerating force (weight minus drag and buoyancy) gets smaller and smaller, and the acceleration gets smaller all the time. van Boxel[27] investigated the distance needed for water droplets to reach given fractions of their terminal velocity. He showed that only droplets smaller than 1 mm would reach 95% of their terminal velocities, falling from rest, in less than 2 m. Larger drops need longer distances to reach 95% of their terminal velocity. For example, for a 2 mm droplet to attain 95% of its terminal velocity of 6.5 m/s, it needs to fall as much as 5.8 m. For the case of a droplet with initial velocity close to its terminal velocity, the distance needed will be shorter.

If a droplet is launched downward faster than its terminal velocity, perhaps by a gunshot or impact, it will slow down and approach its terminal velocity during its fall.

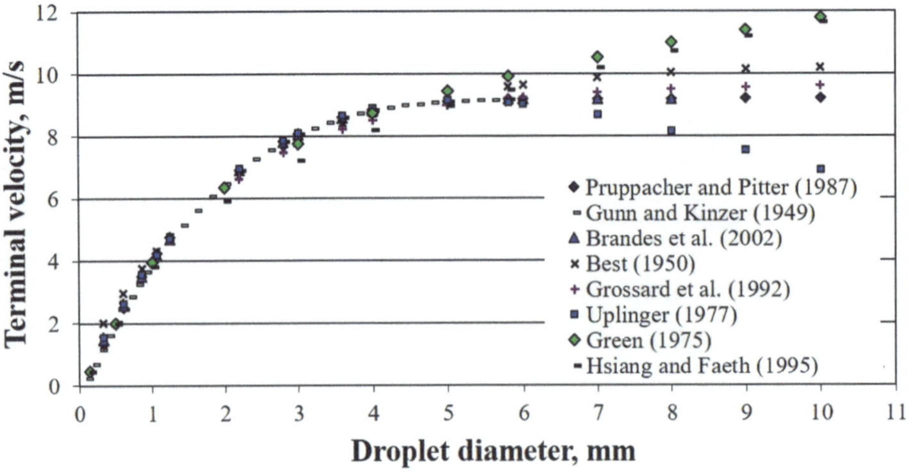

Figure 5.27 Terminal velocity of water drops in air.

BREAKUP OF BLOOD TO FORM AIRBORNE DROPLETS (SPATTER)

This section describes the sequence of events which lead to the formation of airborne droplets in several common spatter-producing mechanisms. The forces acting at each step are described. In general, all spatter-producing mechanisms produce sheets or lines (ligaments) of extended blood, which break up into smaller bodies of blood by the action of waves. Sheets break up into ligaments, and ligaments break up into droplets. The droplets may not be spherical initially, but if given time, they will take on a spherical shape. The waves responsible for breakup are made possible by surface tension force (it is the restoring force which must exist for cyclic wave motion to be possible). The waves are damped out by viscosity. Viscosity, and a second role for surface tension, ultimately limit the breakup process. Surface tension resists the deformation and extension of the blood, and thus ultimately stops the breakup process long before the blood has broken down into individual molecules and particles.

Thus, surface tension plays two opposing roles, one which leads to breakup, and one which limits it.

The processes involved in the impact of a droplet on a surface, and formation of the final stain, are covered later.

Drip Stains (Passive Dripping)

In dripping, the primary force causing separation of blood from the source is weight. Opposing this is interfacial tension (primarily surface tension). Viscosity acts to slow all motion. The sequence of phenomena is set out in Table 5.2. This is well-illustrated by a video in the MFRC video library, video "1Ab1 Blood dripping from a wrench handle pre-wet with blood." The table shows the frame numbers in the video which illustrate each stage (the frame number is shown in the text block to the left of the image. The videos play slower than real time so all the stages are clear). Timings are approximate as many of the processes are indistinct when they start, and occur simultaneously with other processes.

Table 5.2 Sequence of events in dripping in video 1Ab1

Phenomenon	Forces at play	Energy transfers	Frame number
Body of blood extends into downward-moving neck which is narrowing.	Weight accelerates blood. Surface tension and viscosity resist.	Gravitational potential energy converted into surface energy and kinetic energy.	0–16
Neck pinching off. Neck may break in multiple places, creating small drops from the neck ("accompanying drops"), as well as the large primary drop.	Surface tension is the restoring force for waves traveling along the neck. Viscosity damps.	Interchange between kinetic and surface energy, both ways, but minor.	Pinching off in frames 16–20. Accompanying drops formed in frames 19–24. Three accompanying drops merge in frame 25.
Fall.	Weight accelerates primary and accompanying drop. Drag resists, but its effect is minor.	Gravitational potential energy converted to kinetic energy. Drag dissipates some kinetic energy as heat, but this is minor.	Frame 17 to end of video.
Oscillation of droplet shape: cycling from oblate (football or egg on its side) to prolate (football or egg on its tip) and back.	Surface tension is the restoring force which causes this cyclic motion. Viscosity damps out the motion.	Surface to kinetic, and back.	17–39
Further breakup of primary drop.		Kinetic into surface.	Does not occur in this experiment.
Impact of drops on surfaces: spreading, splash, formation of spines and satellite stains according to impact Reynolds and Weber number.	(Covered later)	(Covered later)	Not shown in this video.

The size of the droplet released depends on the surface characteristics of the wetted object (material, roughness, and any coatings such as dirt or grease), the shape of the object (sharpness or surface curvature), and the rate of flow of blood onto the location where the drops are formed.[17]

The neck can break in more than one place, leaving one or more smaller droplets ("accompanying droplets") (frames 19–24 in the video). These may remain separate and land to form accompanying stains, or two or more may merge (frame 25). In some cases, they can merge with the primary drop.

Cast-off patterns and cessation patterns are formed by a similar sequence of events, but in cast-off, the primary force which causes separation of the blood from the source object is not weight but whatever force accelerates the source object. The acceleration is centripetal acceleration (always present when there is motion in a curved path) for swing cast-off, and linear acceleration for cessation cast-off. A good example is video 5Ac3 ("Cast-off from the vertical swing of a bloodied wrench").

Impact Spatter (E.g. Blunt Weapon Assault)

The sequence of events which lead to the formation of impact spatter is described in Table 5.3. The table refers to an example video of a hammer impacting a pool of blood on a surface (video 6Jb3e "Impact-hammer into blood on a hard surface" in the MFRC library.

Table 5.3 Sequence of events in impact spatter formation in video 6Jb3e

Phenomenon	Forces at play	Energy transfers	Frame number
Hammer squeezes blood.	Incompressible fluid extrudes.	Kinetic energy of hammer into pressure energy in blood.	56–57
First liquid sheet extruded, moving low, close to the table top.	"Jetting" under pressure.	Kinetic energy of blood and surface energy created.	57
First sheet breaks up.	Sheet breaks up into ligaments, which break up into droplets. Surface tension waves cause breakup: surface tension and viscosity resist breakup.	More surface energy created, then minimized.	57–64
Outgoing pressure wave accelerates second sheet behind hammer head.	Inertial force (dynamic pressure) causes acceleration.	Pressure energy into kinetic energy.	58
Second sheet extends.	Surface tension resists, viscosity also resists extension.	Kinetic into surface energy.	58–80
Second sheet breaks up. Droplets become spherical.	Sheet into ligaments into droplets. Surface tension waves cause breakup: surface tension & viscosity resist.	More surface energy created then minimised.	72–190
Droplets fly and impact nearby surfaces.	(Covered later)		58–end

Gunshot Spatter

The formation of gunshot spatter follows roughly the same sequence as impact, though the forces are typically stronger. Droplets are created by acceleration of the tissue due to bullet impact, due to the formation and collapse of the temporary cavity in the damaged tissue, and by shear (effectively viscous force between the bullet and blood) as the bullet passes through the blood-bearing tissue. The higher forces lead to smaller droplets, compared to the impact of blunt objects. These forces set the blood in motion in all directions, ultimately causing both forward and backspatter. A good example is video 7Ab1, ".44 cal bullet impacting bloodied sponge from 182 cm." The video shows backspatter starting from frame 4, and forward spatter from frame 5. Both processes continue to develop after the bullet has left the target.

Projected Patterns

The MFRC video library does not contain an example of the formation of a projected pattern, but the sequence of events is described in Table 5.4.

Expiration Patterns

The fluid dynamic processes which cause expiration patterns are amongst the most complex in BPA, and although there is some published work on the mechanisms,[28,29,30] there is much left to discover. What follows is the authors' best effort to explain the processes based on current knowledge. The language used does not necessarily follow a standard terminology.

The formation of expiration spatter might be divided into two classes of event: sudden and steady.

Table 5.4 Sequence of events in projected patterns

Phenomenon	Forces at play	Energy transfers
Formation of a jet.	Pressure in the blood vessels accelerates the blood through a breach.	Pressure energy to kinetic energy.
Disruption of the jet.	Viscous shear forces between the blood jet and the surrounding air initiate wave motion in the jet. Complex wave motion occurs, with waves of different wavelengths and directions passing through each other. Surface tension is the restoring force of the waves; viscosity damps them.	Kinetic energy into surface energy.
Breakup.	Jet breaks into sheets and/or ligaments; sheets break into ligaments; ligaments break up into droplets. Each breakup step is caused by wave motion. Surface tension is the restoring force that creates these waves. Surface tension and viscosity resist.	Kinetic energy into surface energy.
Falling (simultaneous with other processes).	Weight.	Gravitational potential energy to kinetic energy.

Sudden Generation of Expiration Spatter

Droplets can be formed and released into the exhaled air by short-lived, fast actions e.g. a spit, cough, sneeze, grunt, or certain speech sounds. These actions are all associated with either rapid chest motion to compress the lungs and drive airflow through the open airway (e.g. sneeze) or the opening of the mouth in which air pressure has been built up, e.g. spitting, coughing, or making *plosive* speech sounds like "p," "b," or "k." Here, the *airway* means the passages in the body through which air passes, such as the mouth, nasal cavity, pharynx, trachea, bronchi, and passages deeper in the lungs.

Spitting is an action optimized for expelling fluid from the airway, and can produce high volumes of expiration spatter.

In video 15Ac3, "Cough through bloodied lips," sudden generation of expiration spatter is seen, due to several occurrences of the film-burst mechanism (see later).

All exhalation actions release droplets of saliva and/or mucus, including normal or exertional breathing and speech.[31,32] However, in most actions, these droplets are small (mostly less than one micron in diameter) in low concentrations, and of course, contain no blood unless there is a wound to the airway.

Steady Generation of Expiration Spatter

Droplets can be formed and released by exhalations that occur over longer timescales, e.g. during exhalation, sighing, or pronouncing *fricative* sounds with high airflow like "ss" or "sh," or "ff." Vowel sounds do not generate much flow of air through the mouth, and are unlikely to produce much spatter, but this needs experimental confirmation.

In video 15Aa2, "Coughed blood," steady generation of expiration spatter causes some of the small, fast-moving droplets which are seen throughout the video.

Film-burst Mechanism

In either steady or sudden generation, but particularly in sudden generation, droplets may be produced by the bursting of films. Films of liquid may bridge the mouth, nose, or a wound in the airway. These films may form with blood from a wound, possibly mixed with saliva and/or mucus. A difference in pressure between the air behind and in front of the film will extend it, and then rupture it. This may happen within the airway, or at the lips and nose, or at the surface of a chest wound. Film burst is seen in video 15Ac3 "Cough through bloodied lips" from frames 6 onward. There are several films which form and burst, including those seen in frames 6, 11, 32, 38, a large one at about frame 46, and a couple of films later bursting from the corner of the mouth.

Wave Growth Mechanism

In either steady or sudden generation, as well as films which bridge the airway and burst, a coating of blood may form on the lining of the airway. Airflow parallel to this film may cause spatter generation. First, waves develop on the coating due to viscous force. Once waves start to grow, a pressure difference between the downwind and upwind side of the wave crests will develop (Figure 5.4). This is similar to the way wind breaks up seawater on ocean waves, to create spray. The wave crests extend into sheets, which break up by the sheet-ligament-droplet breakup sequence described earlier. Breakup may continue to occur after the liquid has left the airway and is traveling through the outside air.

Nature of the Fluid

Any wound in the airway causes blood to mix with the saliva and/or mucus already present on the airway lining. Expiration spatter is often formed from a mixture of these fluids. This leads to the characteristic features of expiration spatter:

- Diluted stains, where the red coloration of blood is diluted by the paler saliva and/or mucus.
- Strings (ligaments), where the viscoelastic nature of the mucus (and to a lesser degree saliva) inhibits breakup and leads to the formation of linear or dumbbell-shaped bodies of fluid, which hit the target without forming spheres. Persistent strings are seen in video 15Aa2, "Coughed blood."
- Bubble rings, where the air pressure, coupled with the viscoelastic behavior of blood/mucus/saliva mixtures, leads to strong bubbles that do not burst in the air.

The Effect of the Exhaled Air

Besides causing the breakup of blood into droplets, the exhaled air also influences where the droplets go (their trajectories). Small droplets follow the air more closely than large droplets, which drop out of the air stream earlier.

DROPLET IMPACT AND SPREADING

When a droplet strikes a dry, solid surface, the following events occur (Figure 5.28):

- The droplet makes first contact with the solid surface (impact). The liquid in the droplet begins to decelerate. The pressure in the liquid at the point of contact rises, as this part of the liquid is the first to decelerate (this is the action of dynamic pressure). This pressure causes liquid to accelerate sideways, outward from the point of contact, moving along the surface. This is *spreading*.
- The droplet deforms, by spreading. The liquid moves outward from the point of contact. The shape of the droplet changes from a sphere and starts to resemble a disk. During this deformation, liquid layers pass over each other, creating viscous forces, which resist the deformation. Surface tension forces increase in strength, as the droplet is no longer a sphere. These surface tension forces also resist spreading. Viscous force acts everywhere on the underside of the drop as the liquid moves over the solid surface. Viscous and surface tension forces are strong at the contact line, and their combined effect here is called *contact line pinning*.

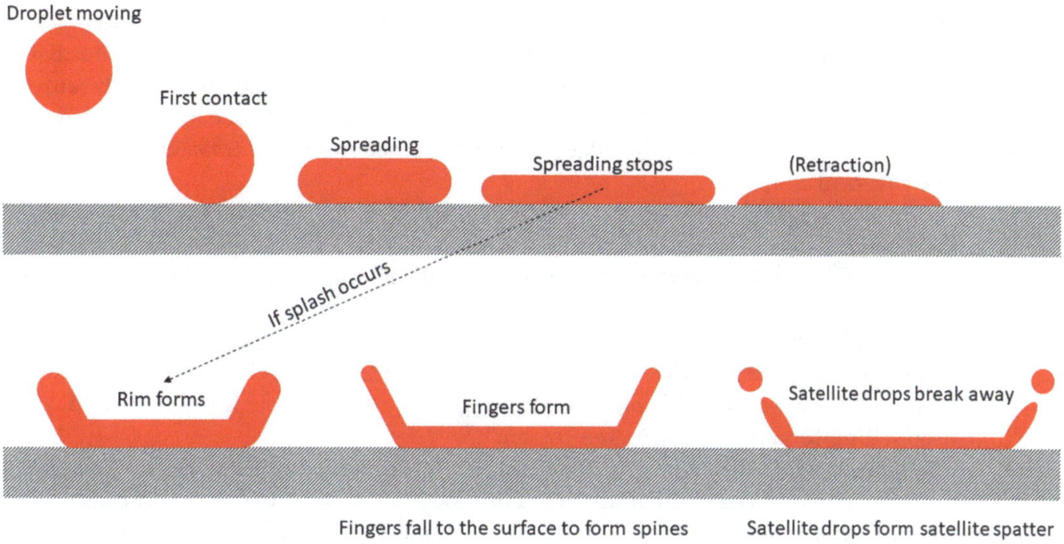

Figure 5.28 Sequence of events when a droplet impacts a surface.

The droplet continues to spread, and the pressure at the initial point of contact grows weaker, while the surface tension and viscous forces grow stronger. At some point, the surface tension and viscous forces are strong enough to stop spreading. The droplet has reached its maximum spread diameter. At this point, one of four things will happen:

a. *Rebound:* On hot or very hydrophobic surfaces, surface tension forces fully retract the droplet into a sphere, and it bounces off the surface, leaving nothing behind. This can be seen to happen on good waterproof clothing. It is rare at crime scenes, and if it happens, it leaves no bloodstain behind.

b. *Formation of a smooth-edged pool:* Viscous forces stop the spreading motion, leaving a circular or elliptical pool with a smooth edge (no spines or scallops). Waves of raised liquid may be seen moving out from the center to the rim, reflecting off the rim and returning to the center (ripples), and repeating until viscosity stops this motion. This may happen several times before the liquid comes to rest. The blood stays on the surface, taking the shape of a disk or ellipse. The diameter of the disk depends on the size of the droplet (mass), how fast it impacted, and the hydrophobicity of the surface. A good example is video 3Aa1a "Blood drop falling 10 cm onto cardboard." Surface tension forces may retract the droplet into a smaller disk or ellipse. Retraction is likely on a hydrophobic surface such as a smooth, greasy surface, but is unlikely on hydrophilic surfaces like used cotton textiles or concrete. Retraction does not occur in video 3A1a.

   A bigger stain is caused when either a bigger droplet impacts the surface at the same speed, or the same size droplet impacts at a faster speed, or both.

c. *Formation of rim and fingers, i.e. "mild splash":* If the outward acceleration is strong enough, and the resisting surface tension and viscous forces are weak enough, the liquid at the edge of the spreading disk becomes unstable. This instability (actually a kind of wave traveling around the rim) results in a series of protrusions or fingers at the rim. These protrusions move outward but don't break off, and leave visible fingers (spines) at the edge of the resulting pool. Mild splash happens if the droplet is bigger (more mass) or faster than a droplet which simply spreads. In terms of the dimensionless numbers used in the fluid dynamics literature, a larger or faster droplet will have a higher impact Reynolds number and a higher impact Weber number.[33,34] The formation of fingers can happen directly from the spreading disk (*prompt splash*, typically occurring in very small droplets), or a raised rim may form first, like a steep-sided dish, and fingers appear on the edge of this rim (called *corona splash* because it looks like a crown).

A bigger droplet, or a faster droplet, or one that is both bigger and faster, will create more fingers.

d. *Strong splash and the formation of satellite stains:* If the droplet is yet bigger, or faster, or both, the splashing process continues further and the fingers break off, and each finger may even break into multiple pieces. These pieces (*satellite droplets*) fly away from the central pool and land on the surface to become satellite stains. The forces that cause this are the same as in mild splash, just stronger. A good example is video 4Bi2 "Blood drop falling 100 cm to a 90 degree cotton."

When a satellite droplet lands to become a satellite stain, it is small (low mass) and slow, compared to the original droplet. The blood in the satellite droplet spreads over the surface, but does not spread far. Satellite droplets typically have a low impact angle, leading to the formation of elongated stains. They are often far from spherical when they land. The low impact angle, non-spherical shape, and any irregularities in the surface which limit their spreading in some directions, lead to irregular stains, which may not point back toward the original impact point.

A bigger droplet, or a faster droplet, or one that is both bigger and faster, will create more satellite spatter.

Some authors only call the process "splash" when the fingers break off. Others call it splash as long as fingers form. This difference occurs because there is no international body that agrees terminology for fluid dynamics in general. Also, many of the fluid dynamics terms used in BPA have not yet been standardized by the BPA community.

Soft surfaces, like carpet or clothing, slow down droplets progressively. This leads to less pronounced splash effects, compared to a droplet of the same size and speed impacting a hard surface.

Impact at an Angle

If the droplet strikes at an angle other than 90° (i.e. other than a right angle to the surface), spreading proceeds further in the direction of motion than in the sideways direction (Figure 5.29). This leads to an elliptical stain, which can be analyzed with the sine law.

During spreading, the conservation of momentum can lead to a wave rising at the advancing edge of the spreading pool, which may break up into new droplets (*wave cast-off*). This is seen in video 4Ac2 "Blood drop falling to a 30 degree target (front view)" and its counterpart 4Ac2 "Blood drop falling to a 30 degree target (side view)."

If splash occurs, it will occur to the greatest degree in the direction of motion. Thus, if there are fingers or satellite stains around only one part of the stain's edge, that edge may indicate the direction the droplet was moving in.

Droplets Impacting a Pool or Film of Liquid, and Splash Patterns

If a droplet impacts a film, or deep pool of liquid, whether of blood or some other liquid, the processes of splash differ a little to what is described above.

In a deep pool, a circular rim of liquid and/or central column of liquid may rise above the surface. The central column is called the **Worthington jet**. Either the rim or the jet may break up into satellite drops. These features subside into the pool, and may reappear again a few times, smaller each time, but eventually viscosity will bring all motion to a stop, leaving a flat liquid surface. No lasting stain is formed.

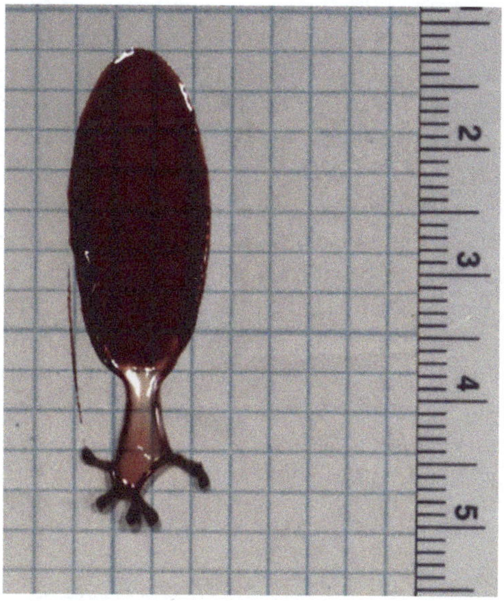

Figure 5.29 An elliptical stain is forming. At the bottom of the stain, wave cast-off is occurring, and the wave is breaking into fingers. (Taken from MFRC video 4Ac2 "Blood drop falling to a 30 degree target (front view).")

When droplets hit a shallow film of liquid, a raised rim is formed. A droplet which is too small or too slow to splash on a dry surface may splash on a wet surface. If satellite drops are formed, those that fall into the liquid film will leave no trace. However, any satellite drops which fall onto neighboring dry surfaces will form satellite stains. A good example is video 6Aa1c "Blood drop falling 50 cm (1st of three drops)." Repeated fall of droplets onto a film of blood may thus cause a dense pattern of satellite stains.

IMBIBITION, WICKING, DRYING, AND CLOTTING

After spreading (and splashing if it occurs), several processes may occur to complete the formation of a stain.

Imbibition and Wicking

Imbibition is the flow of blood into the pores of a surface. Weight and/or the high static pressure generated on first contact can accelerate the liquid into the pores (imbibition, or "drinking"). If the solid is hydrophilic, liquid is drawn into the pores by capillary forces (wicking). This is due to a combination of liquid-air and liquid-solid interfacial tension forces, increasing the area of contact between the liquid and the solid.

Wicking is the spread of blood beyond the initial area of contact, through the pores, driven by capillary forces, opposed by (and eventually stopped by) viscous forces. The effect of these processes on stain formation on textiles is described in detail in Chapter 20 of this book, and also in the book edited by Carr,[35] which focuses on textiles in forensic science. Whereas initial spreading on any surface occurs over about 0.01 s, wicking can continue over thousands of seconds in textiles. Wicking increases the area of a stain and can change the shape of the stain, as it can proceed faster in certain directions, e.g. along the yarns of a textile.

Drying

The drying of bloodstains proceeds principally by evaporation. On some porous substrates like textiles, it is speeded by wicking of serum into fibres to leave red blood cells behind. The rate of evaporation depends strongly on temperature, humidity, and air motion (wind and/or drafts). It also depends on the concentration of dissolved components in blood. This has little effect during the early stages of drying, but more effect when much of the water has been lost and a gel is formed. In common crime scene conditions, drying happens over a longer timescale than imbibition and wicking. A detailed description of the process is given by Jermy et al.[36] Drying occurs in several stages: loss of water, formation of a gel by the non-volatile components of the blood leading to a reduction in drying rate, solidification, sometimes crack formation due to shrinkage in the dried solids, and sometimes peeling of the dried solids from the surface, depending on the type of surface. The early stages can concentrate the red blood cells at the perimeter of a stain, which is important in skeletonization (perimeter stains).

Drying does not generally change the shape or size of a stain greatly. Drying proceeds at a different rate in small pools of blood (e.g. pools made by one or a few droplets) than in large pools.

Clotting (Coagulation)

Clotting is a complex cascade of processes, with at least 30 molecular species interacting in feedback processes. Clotting is initiated by biomolecules released when tissue is damaged, and the rate is variable. It is usually much slower than spreading, splashing, imbibition, and wicking processes. It can be either faster or slower than drying.

Separation of clear serum from the red blood cells may also occur, particularly in large pools. The conditions for separation are briefly reviewed by Jermy et al.[36]

FLUID DYNAMICS OF NON-SPATTER TRANSFER EVENTS

This section describes, briefly, the fluid dynamic processes in transfer of wet blood in events that do not involve isolated droplets traveling through the air (i.e. are not spatter).

Transfer Stains, Swipes, Prints, and Insect Stains

Common to all of these mechanisms is that blood is initially carried on one surface (e.g. a hand, clothing, an insect's feet, or some other item) which comes into contact with a second surface, with some blood being transferred onto that second surface. Interfacial forces (adhesion) are responsible for holding the blood onto the first surface. There may be pressure when the two surfaces come into contact, or a shear force (friction and viscous force in the blood) if the surfaces brush against each other, or there may be both pressure and shear. There does not have to be a lot of pressure or shear force to transfer blood, as once the blood has contacted the second surface, interfacial forces may draw it onto that surface. The amount of blood transferred depends on the surface area that is coated in blood. It also depends on properties of both surfaces: surface roughness and hydrophobicity, angle of inclination (which affects draining due to weight), and the speed and direction of the relative motion of the two surfaces. It may also depend on the state of drying and clotting of the blood which affect interfacial forces ("stickiness").

Interfacial forces then hold some of the blood onto the second surface. The blood on the second surface may spread in all directions (pressure) or predominantly in one (friction and viscous force). Imbibition and wicking may occur depending on the quantity of blood transferred, the pressure, the angle of the surfaces, and the nature of the second surface.

Wipes

A wipe through a pre-existing wet stain leads to spreading of the blood primarily in the direction the wiping object is moving, due to pressure and viscous force. Further wicking may occur.

Flows and Pools, Saturation Stains

In these processes, there is outward flow from a source, driven by gravity or blood pressure.

Spreading occurs, in which the forces are the same as in spreading of a droplet striking a surface, but inertial force is usually much weaker, and spreading can be caused by only gravity or blood pressure at the wound. The role of surface tension and viscosity in resisting the spread is the same as with the impact of spatter droplets on a surface, and the effects of surface roughness and hydrophobicity are also the same. Splashing may occur, but is rare unless the blood strikes the surface with sufficient speed, e.g. a flow from sufficient height or a jet from a breached artery hitting a surface. The effects of imbibition, wicking, drying, and clotting are the same.

Draining

When a mass of blood on a vertical or inclined surface drains, the weight force pulls downward, initiating a flow, and viscous force and surface tension resist. The physical process is much the same as spreading, except that weight is the driving force.

CONCLUSION

Many of the features observed in bloodstains can be explained using the science of fluid dynamics. Many of the relevant processes are the result of just four forces: weight, pressure, viscous force and surface (interfacial) tension. An analyst can use an understanding of fluid dynamics to help determine what information can be obtained from bloodstain patterns, and what cannot. Such an understanding can also be used to help give clear explanations in testimony. Of course, when addressing non-specialists, jargon should be avoided.

This chapter gives an outline of the areas of fluid dynamics which are most important for BPA. We have not attempted to review the literature in depth.

Areas in need of further research include the formation of bloodstains on textiles, automation of trajectory reconstruction in impact spatter, the mechanisms leading to expiration patterns (and how such patterns can be discriminated from other types of pattern), and the mechanisms leading to transfer stains.

ACKNOWLEDGMENTS

We are very grateful to Dr. Jason Chen for the illustrations he kindly prepared. We are indebted to Michael Taylor and Rosalyn Rough, who, with Mark Jermy, co-developed and co-taught the 40-hour course "Fluid Dynamics of Bloodstain Pattern Formation," and who greatly contributed to elucidating the fluid dynamics described in this chapter. We are grateful to the participants in that course, who contributed their insights, posed key questions, initiated discussion, and brought the lessons of their field experience to the discussions during the course.

Our current understanding of the fluid dynamics of BPA would be much poorer were it not for the work of Terry Laber, Bart Epstein, and Michael Taylor, who made a comprehensive library of high-quality high-speed videos of blood transfer events.

Glossary

This contains some terms used in the chapter, and other terms which may be encountered in fluid dynamics literature.

Atomization: The breaking up of a body of liquid into smaller bodies (usually droplets).

Bond number: A dimensionless number which is the ratio of the weight to the surface tension forces.

Boundary layer: The layer(s) of fluid located close to the surface of an object, in which the velocity of the fluid is affected by the presence of the object. Typically, the speed of the fluid increases with distance from the surface, up to the edge of the boundary layer, beyond which it is constant.

Capillary force: See surface tension (force).

Capillary number: A dimensionless number which is the ratio of viscous forces to surface tension forces.

Contact line: The edge of a sessile drop. The contact line is the line where the liquid, the solid, and the surrounding air all meet.

Contact line pinning: The strong surface tension and viscous forces at the contact line, which occur when liquid spreads over a surface, and which resist motion of the contact line.

Crown, coronet: A feature created when one droplet of fluid splashes into a surface or into a pool of liquid. The feature looks like a circular or conical wall, topped with fingers or spines.

Damping: Progressive reduction in the amplitude of some process, due to some energy-dissipating mechanism, e.g. the action of viscosity.

Dimensionless number (non-dimensional number, dimensionless group, non-dimensional group): A number formed by dividing a quantity by another quantity which has the same units of measurement. Dimensionless numbers are often ratios of forces, and can be used to understand which force is stronger. Dimensionless numbers themselves have no units, as the units cancel out in division.

Drag (aerodynamic): The retarding force that is experienced by an object as it passes through the air (or other fluid).

Drag coefficient: A dimensionless number that expresses the degree to which an object experiences drag force.

Drop, droplet: Interchangeable terms meaning a contiguous body of liquid in a gas (perhaps air), or in another liquid into which it does not mix.

Dynamics: A way of thinking about physical processes, in which the analyst describes all of the forces acting upon a body or fluid or process of interest.

Fingers: A feature created when one droplet of a fluid splashes onto a surface or into a pool of fluid, which takes the form of regular or semi-regular protuberances that extend outward from a body of fluid. (cf. spine)

Fluid: A liquid or a gas. Both these states of matter will flow in response to a shear force. Solids may deform in response to a shear, but don't flow. Solids develop elastic tension when deformed, which tends to pull them back to their original shape when the deforming force is released. Fluids do not do this.

Fluid dynamics/fluid mechanics: Interchangeable terms for the science which studies the response of fluids to forces.

Hydrophilic: "Water-loving." This term refers to a surface, substance, chemical species, or functional group which has low energy when hydrated or wetted with water.

Hydrophobic: "Water-hating." This term refers to a surface, substance, chemical species, or functional group which has high energy when hydrated or wetted with water.

Incompressible (fluid): A fluid which cannot be compressed, or whose density changes very little when compressed.

Inertia: Resistance to change in motion. A measure of the force required to achieve a given change in the motion or momentum of an object. The inertia of an object is measured by its mass.

Inertial forces: Forces related to the acceleration of masses. They are the forces which arise from a change in the momentum of a moving fluid or object (commonly caused by a change in speed). In fluids, the most important inertial force is that related to dynamic pressure.

Interfacial energy, surface energy: In general, interfacial energy is the potential energy of an area where two materials are in contact (the materials may be gas and liquid, gas and solid, two dissimilar solids, or two dissimilar and immiscible (won't mix without separating out) liquids).

Gas-liquid interfacial energy is called surface energy, and this is quantified with the surface tension of the liquid.

Interfacial force: A general term for forces like the surface tension force; while surface tension refers to liquid-gas interfaces, "interfacial force" is general to all interfaces.

Kinematics: A way of thinking about and analyzing physical processes in which the analyst describes the position and speed of the elements.

Ligaments: String-like bodies of fluid; may be straight or curved.

Momentum: Mass times velocity of an object.

Newtonian (when describing a fluid): A fluid whose viscosity does not change with shear rate.

Non-Newtonian: A fluid whose viscosity changes with shear rate. It may go up or down with shear rate depending on the type of fluid.

Oblate: A sphere-like shape which has a shorter diameter along the polar axis than across the equator. "Squished" along the polar axis.

Ohnesorge number: A dimensionless number which is the ratio of the viscous force to the inertial and surface tension forces together.

Pendant droplet: A droplet hanging from a surface.

Pressure drag, form drag: Drag due to the difference in fluid pressure between the leading (forward facing) and the trailing (backward facing) faces of an object. Pressure drag is strongly affected by the extent of flow separation. It is an inertial force.

Primary droplet: The largest droplet released in some breakup event.

Prolate: A sphere-like shape which has a longer diameter along the polar axis than across the equator.

Restoring force: The force that pulls something undergoing wave motion toward the center.

Reynolds number: A dimensionless number which is the ratio of the inertial force acting on a body to the viscous force acting on that body.

Rim: Either the rising circular or conical rising feature that is formed when an impacting droplet splashes onto a surface or into a pool of liquid, or the ring-like bead or lip along the top of this feature (like the rolled cuff of a disposable latex glove).

Satellite or secondary drop: A droplet, smaller than the primary droplet, released in some breakup event. Also, droplets released from a finger during the evolution of a crown, in a splash process.

Separation, flow separation: The phenomenon that occurs when a fluid flow, which has been following the surface of an object, moves away from that surface. As it moves away from the surface, a recirculation or vortex region forms behind the object.

Sessile droplet: A droplet sitting on a solid surface.

Shear: A motion or force acting parallel to a surface. As an example, the parallel blades of a pair of scissors shear the object they are cutting. By way of contrast, a hammer striking at 90° to an object applies a force normal to the surface, which is not a shear force.

Shear force, shear stress, viscous shear: A force (usually due to viscosity) which acts parallel to a surface or thing causing the force.

Shear rate: As a fluid flows, shear rate is the rate of deformation of an imaginary cube drawn in the fluid. It is also the degree to which fluid velocity increases with distance from a solid surface.

Sheet: A flat or curved sheet of liquid which may subsequently break up into ligaments.

Skin friction drag: The drag due to viscous shear on the surface of the object.

Speed: The magnitude of velocity, i.e. velocity without information on direction.

Spine: Radial protuberances of a stain. Spine and finger may be used interchangeably, or spine may be reserved for the feature of the stain after all motion has stopped, and finger for the feature formed during the splash process, which later becomes a spine.

Stress: Force per unit area. May be a normal stress (acts at right angle to a surface), like pressure, or a shear stress (see shear stress elsewhere in this list), such as viscous shear. Stress (N/m^2) is force (N) per unit area (m^2).

Surface tension (force) (also capillary force or interfacial force): A force (units of *N*) acting parallel to the liquid-gas surface (interface), dependent on the properties of the liquid, the properties of the gas, the local concentration of surfactant molecules at the surface, and the radius of curvature of the surface. Surface tension is related to surface energy. Surface tension forces are capillary forces (interfacial forces), but specific to liquid-gas interfaces.

Surface tension (physical property): A physical property (having units of N/m) of a liquid which determines how strong surface tension forces are.

Surfactant: A molecule which modifies the surface tension of a liquid. It usually has at least one hydrophilic functional group and at least one hydrophobic functional group.

Terminal velocity: The maximum velocity a falling object reaches, at which the weight and buoyancy forces are exactly balanced by the aerodynamic drag, and the object ceases to accelerate.

Velocity: A quantity that includes the speed and direction of an object.

Viscoelastic: This refers to the behavior of certain materials which behave partly as an elastic solid and partly as a fluid when a stress is applied. An elastic solid changes shape, but snaps back to its original shape when the stress is removed. Fluids change shape but do not return to their original shape when the stress is removed, i.e. they flow. Examples of viscoelastic fluids are mucus and saliva, and mixtures containing these.

Viscosity: This is a property of liquids. It measures the degree of shear stress that is required to initiate a motion with a given shear rate. It also refers to the degree of resistance to flow exhibited by a fluid that is exposed to a shear stress. It is measured as absolute viscosity or kinematic viscosity (kinematic viscosity is equal to absolute viscosity divided by density).

Weber number: A dimensionless number which is the ratio of the inertial forces acting on a droplet to the surface tension forces.

Notes

1. FM White and H Xue, "Fluid Mechanics", McGraw Hill, 2021.
2. MC Jermy and MC Taylor, "The mechanics of bloodstain pattern formation", Ch. 5 (pp 99–136) in *Forensic Biomechanics (Developments in Forensic Science)*, eds. J Kieser J, MC Taylor and DJ Carr, Wiley, 2013.
3. D Attinger, C Moore, A Donaldson, A Jafari, and HA Stone, "Fluid dynamics topics in bloodstain pattern analysis: Comparative review and research opportunities", *Forensic Science International* 231, 375–396, 2013.
4. T Laber, B Epstein, and MC Taylor, "High Speed Digital Video Analysis of Bloodstain Pattern Formation from Common Bloodletting Mechanisms", hosted by the Midwest Forensic Research Center at https://alvideo.ameslab.gov/archive/bpa-videos/ (accessed 4 May 2021).
5. A Wierzba, "Deformation and breakup of liquid drops in a gas stream at nearly critical Weber numbers", *Experiments in Fluids* 9, 59–64, 1990.
6. L-P Hsiang and GM Faeth, "Drop deformation and breakup due to shock wave and steady disturbances", *International Journal of Multiphase Flow*, 21(4), 545–560, 1995.
7. R Clift, JR Grace, and ME Weber, *Bubbles, Drops and Particles*, Academic Press, 1978.
8. BS Massey and J Ward-Smith, *Mechanics of fluids*, CRC Press, 2018.
9. A Haider and O Levenspiel, "Drag coefficient and terminal velocity of spherical and nonspherical particles", *Powder Technology* 58(1), 63–70, 1989.

10. AB Liu, D Mather, and RD Reitz, "Modeling the effects of drop drag and breakup on fuel sprays", SAE Technical Paper 930072, Society of Automotive Engineers, 1993.
11. R Schmehl, "Advanced modeling of droplet deformation and breakup for CFD analysis of mixture preparation", 1–10 in *Proceedings of the 18th Annual Conference on Liquid Atomization and Spray Systems (ILASS 2002)*, 2002.
12. G Luxford, "Experimental and Modelling Investigation of the Deformation, Drag and Breakup of Drizzle Droplets Subjected to Strong Aerodynamic Forces in Relation to SLD Aircraft Icing", PhD Thesis, Cranfield University, 2005.
13. WR Lane and HL Green, *Surveys in Mechanics.* edited by G Batchelor and R Davies, Cambridge University Press, 1956.
14. Lord Rayleigh, "Investigations in capillarity", *Philosophical Magazine* 48, 321–337, 1899.
15. Lord Rayleigh, "Some applications of photography", *Nature* 44, 249–254, 1891.
16. J Qian and C Law, "Regimes of coalescence and separation in droplet collision", *Journal of Fluid Mechanics* 331, 59–80, 1997.
17. N Kabaliuk, MC Jermy, K Morison, T Stotesbury, MC Taylor, and E Williams, "Blood drop size in passive dripping from weapons", *Forensic Science International* 228, 75–82, 2013.
18. H Liu, *Science and Engineering of Droplets: Fundamentals and Applications.* Noyes Publications/William Andrew Publishing, 2000.
19. N Kabaliuk, MC Jermy, E Williams, TL Laber, and MC Taylor, "Experimental validation of a numerical model for predicting the trajectory of blood drops in typical crime scene conditions, including droplet deformation and breakup, with a study of the effect of indoor air currents and wind on typical spatter drop trajectories", *Forensic Science International* 245, 107–120, 2014.
20. N Kabaliuk, "Dynamics of Blood Drop Formation and Flight", PhD thesis, University of Canterbury, 2014, https://ir.canterbury.ac.nz/handle/10092/8979
21. HR Pruppacher and RL Pitter, "A semi-empirical determination of the shape of cloud and rain drops", *Journal of Atmospheric Sciences* 28, 86–94, 1971.
22. R Gunn, and GD Kinzer, "The terminal velocity of fall for water droplets in stagnant air", *Journal of Meteorology* 54, 243–248, 1949.
23. E Brandes, G Zhang, and J Vivekanandan, "Experiments in rainfall estimation with a polarimetric radar in a subtropical environment", *Journal of Applied Meteorology* 41, 674–685, 2002.
24. AC Best, "Empirical formulae for the terminal velocity of water drops falling through the atmosphere", *Quarterly Journal of the Royal Meteorological Society*, 76, 302–311, 1950.
25. EE Gossard, RG Stauch, DC Welsh and SY Matrosov, "Cloud layer, particle identification, and rain rate profiles from Z. RV measurements by Doppler radars", *Journal of Atmospheric and Oceanic Technology* 9, 108–119, 1992.
26. WG Uplinger, "A New Formula for Raindrop Terminal Velocity", Preprints of the 20th Conference on Radar Meteorology, American Meteorological Society, Boston, 389–391, 1977.
27. JH van Boxel, "Numerical Model for the Fall Speed of Raindrops in a Rainfall Simulator", p. 77–85, Workshop on Wind and Water Erosion, November 17–18, Ghent Belgium, 1997.
28. D Denison, A Porter, M Mills, and RC Schroter, "Forensic implications of respiratory derived blood spatter distributions", *Forensic Science International* 204, 144–155, 2011.
29. AE Donaldson, NK Walker, IL Lamont, SJ Cordiner, and MC Taylor, "Characterising the dynamics of expirated bloodstain pattern formation using high-speed digital video imaging", *International Journal of Legal Medicine* 125, 757–762, 2011.
30. PH Geoghegan, AM Laffra, NK Hoogendorp, MC Taylor, and MC Jermy, "Experimental measurement of breath exit velocity and expirated bloodstain patterns produced under different exhalation mechanisms", *International Journal of Legal Medicine* 131(5), 1193–1201, 2017.
31. GR Johnson, L Morawska, ZD Ristovski, M Hargreaves, K Mengersen, CYH Chao, MP Wan, Y Li, X Xie, D Katoshevski, and S Corbett, "Modality of human expired aerosol size distributions", *Journal of Aerosol Science* 42(12), 839–851, 2011.
32. FKA Gregson, NA Watson, CM Orton, AE Haddrell, LP McCarthy, TJR Finnie, N Gent, GC Donaldson, PL Shah, JD Calder, BR. Bzdek, D Costello, and JP Reid, "Comparing aerosol concentrations and particle size distributions generated by singing, speaking and breathing", *Aerosol Science and Technology* 55(6), 681–691, 2021.
33. CD Stow and MG Hadfield, "An experimental investigation of fluid flow resulting from the impact of a water drop with an unyielding surface", *Proceedings of the Royal Society A*, 373, 419–441, 1981.

34. C Mundo, M Sommerfeld, and C Tropea, "Droplet-wall collisions: Experimental studies of the deformation and breakup process", *International Journal of Multiphase Flow* 21(2), 151–173, 1995.
35. DJ Carr, ed., "Forensic Textile Science", Woodhead Publishing, 2017.
36. M Jermy, C Knock, S Michielsen, F Smith, R Rough, T de Castro, L Dicken, and D Brutin, "Drying processes in the formation of bloodstains at crime scenes", in *Drying of Complex Fluid Drops*, eds. D Brutin and K Sefiane, Royal Society of Chemistry, 2022.

Further Reading

For further reading on the processes in bloodstain formation, we suggest the following literature.

For a general overview:

Attinger, D., C. Moore, A. Donaldson, A. Jafari, and H. A. Stone. "Fluid Dynamics Topics in Bloodstain Pattern Analysis: Comparative Review and Research Opportunities." *Forensic Science International* 231 (2013): 375–96.

Jermy, M. C., and M. C. Taylor. "The Mechanics of Bloodstain Pattern Formation." In *Forensic Biomechanics (Developments in Forensic Science)*, edited by J. Kieser, M. C. Taylor and D. J. Carr, 99–136. New Jersey: Wiley, 2013.

Kabaliuk, N. "*Dynamics of blood drop formation and flight*," PhD thesis, University of Canterbury, 2014. https://ir.canterbury.ac.nz/handle/10092/8979.

For bloodstain formation on textiles:

Carr, D.J. ed., *Forensic Textile Science*. Oxford: Woodhead Publishing, 2017.

Wang, F., V. Gallardo, S. Michielsen, and T. Fang. "Fundamental Study of Porcine Drip Bloodstains on Fabrics: Blood Droplet Impact and Wicking Dynamics." *Forensic Science International* 318 (2021): 110614.

These references also include other works by S. Michielsen and his co-authors.

For drying of bloodstains:

Jermy, M., C. Knock, S. Michielsen, F. Smith, R. Rough, T. de Castro, L. Dicken, and Brutin D.. "Drying Processes in the Formation of Bloodstains at Crime Scenes." In *Drying of Complex Fluid Drops*, edited by D. Brutin and K. Sefiane (pp. 171–90), London: Royal Society of Chemistry, 2022.

For a broad, technical description of the processes involving surface tension (not limited to blood):

de Gennes, P. G., F. Brochard-Wyart, and D. Quere. *Capillarity and Wetting Phenomena: Drops, Bubbles, Pearls, Waves Capillarity and Wetting Phenomena: Drops, Bubbles, Pearls, Waves*. New York: Springer-Verlag, 2004.

For a detailed technical description of liquid jet breakup:

Eggers, J., and E. Villermaux. "Physics of Liquid Jets." *Reports on Progress in Physics*, 71(2008): 036601.

On spreading and splashing in general:

Josserand, C., and S. T. Thoroddsen. "Drop Impact on a Solid Surface." *Annual Review of Fluid Mechanics* 48, no. 1 (2016): 365–91.

Yarin, A. L. "Drop Impact Dynamics: Splashing, Spreading, Receding, Bouncing." *Annual Review of Fluid Mechanics* 38, no. 1 (2005): 159–92.

On spreading and splashing, specifically for blood:

Smith, F. R., N. C. Buntsma, and D. Brutin. "Roughness Influence on Human Blood Drop Spreading and Splashing." *Langmuir* 34, no. 3 (2018): 1143–50.

CHAPTER 6

BLOOD AND THE MEDICAL EXAMINER

From the Crime Scene to the Autopsy Including a Discussion of Wounds and Bloodletting Injuries

Emma O. Lew

A coroner is an official who is generally elected and charged with the responsibility of investigating and certifying violent, suspicious, and sudden unexplained deaths. They may be a medical professional but may also have little or no medical training. A coroner determines the cause and manner of death but unless they are also a pathologist, the coroner will decide whether to send a case to a pathologist for an autopsy.

Chief medical examiners are appointed to investigate and certify violent, suspicious, and sudden unexplained deaths. In most jurisdictions in the United States, a medical examiner is a medical doctor who has undergone three to four years of specialty training in pathology and at least one year of subspecialty training in forensic pathology. The medical examiner is therefore qualified to conduct forensic/medicolegal autopsies. The medical examiner has the advantage of investigating a case fully from start to finish, from the scene to the autopsy, to include ancillary studies, witness statements, and recorded evidence in order to determine the cause and manner of death.

The cause of death is an event or entity that starts a chain of events leading to death. Examples of cause of death are ruptured cerebral and atherosclerotic aortic aneurysms, gunshot wounds, and diabetic ketoacidosis. Too often, mechanisms of death are confused with the cause of death. A mechanism is an entity that is not specific to a cause of death. For example, hemorrhagic shock is a mechanism and without further clarification, you do not know whether the hemorrhaging is due to a stab wound, a compound (open) fracture of the skull, or a perforated duodenal ulcer. There are five manners of death: natural, accident, suicide, homicide, and undetermined. The manner of death is determined by the totality of information, including the history, terminal events, scene findings, autopsy findings, toxicology results, and all pertinent ancillary studies. The undetermined manner is reserved for those cases where after a full investigation, complete autopsy, toxicological analyses, and ancillary studies, there is not a preponderance of evidence to support one manner of death over another, or there is inadequate information to determine a cause of death. In many cases where the manner of death is undetermined, the cause of death is also undetermined.

When news media report a death under suspicious circumstances, they frequently state that the body will be sent to the coroner or the medical examiner for an autopsy to determine the exact cause of death. The public's understanding, therefore, is that it takes an autopsy to determine the cause and manner of death and that an autopsy will always be able to determine the cause and manner of death. That may be true in many cases; however, death investigation is far more complex than just an autopsy. Suffice it to say that the cause and manner of death *can* be determined

DOI: 10.4324/9781003163695-6

without an autopsy and conversely, an autopsy *may not always* be able to determine the cause and manner of death.

Medical examiners are medical subspecialists who have graduated from medical school, undergone three or four years of residency training in the specialty of pathology and have had at least one year of subspecialty training in forensic pathology. An autopsy technician is fully capable of eviscerating or taking the organs out of the body but does not have the training or experience to recognize and interpret the anatomical findings. The process of evisceration is critically important. A pathologist sees, feels, and smells the organs, tissues, and fluids inside the body cavities and notes the relationship of the structures to each other. During evisceration, the pathologist specifically looks for certain findings based on the history and terminal events or is alert for anything unusual because there is no information about the body.

Let us start from the beginning. Death investigation does *not* begin at the autopsy table. It begins with the history, whatever history is available from family, coworkers, friends, or just witnesses. But history is not available in every case. Bodies may simply be found, many times unidentified, possibly decomposing, dismembered, partially skeletonized with postmortem animal activity to scatter body parts. Wherever there is a body, there is a scene. It may not be where the death occurred, but some information will always be there. The focus of this chapter is on scenes that have blood.

Blood is contained within the cardiovascular tree, in the heart and blood vessels, and is not normally seen on the external surfaces of the body. The appearance of blood indicates a disruption in blood vessels, whether it be capillaries in the skin or a major artery or vein in the body. Injury to tissues and organs will disrupt the cells and blood vessels, allowing blood to escape. Internal bleeding is when the leaking blood is contained within the body cavities but not evident from the outside. Internal bleeding may manifest as external bleeding once that blood exudes from an open wound or drains from a natural orifice such as the mouth. The blood at a scene may provide clues as to the source of the bleeding, the type of injury, the degree and manner of movement of the person, the interval between the beginning of the bleeding and time of death, and whether other people were at the scene besides the decedent.

The presence of blood may not indicate an injury. It may reflect a natural disease condition. Alternatively, injuries do not always manifest by visible external bleeding.

A perforating injury is when a weapon or object enters and exits the body. This is most applicable to gunshot wounds where the projectile enters and exits the body, as opposed to a penetrating injury when a weapon or object enters the body but does not exit the body, such as in stab wounds. Impaling injuries where the object remains in the body without being pulled out, may not bleed much externally because the wound is essentially plugged by the penetrating object. Therefore, injuries from impaling may not bleed initially. The bleeding occurs when the penetrating object is pulled out. A construction worker fell several stories and became impaled on reinforced bars. His small bowel was pushed out by the bars at the exit wound on the left side of the abdomen. He survived the trip to hospital but sustained nonsurvivable internal injuries. There is some blood on the shirt at the entrance and exit points because the skin and soft tissues were punctured but the shirt was not saturated with blood and the chest and abdominal cavities were not full of blood, containing only 300 ml of blood in total (see Figure 6.1).

Scenes of sharp force injuries frequently appear more bloody than scenes of gunshot wounds (see Figure 6.2). Stab wounds may not be immediately debilitating like some gunshot wounds. The wounds may not gape in the same way as gunshot wounds because the weapon creates a narrow or less expansive wound. The stabbing cannot be done from a distance so the assailant and the victim are in close proximity; there can be a prolonged struggle with movement, injuries on both the victim and assailant, and therefore potentially widespread blood patterns at the scene.

The head and neck are very vascular parts of the body. Gunshot wounds of the head are frequently immediately incapacitating and are exceptionally bloody. A head wound may lacerate skin/scalp, fracture bone/skull, and lacerate brain, releasing a torrential gush of blood and likely

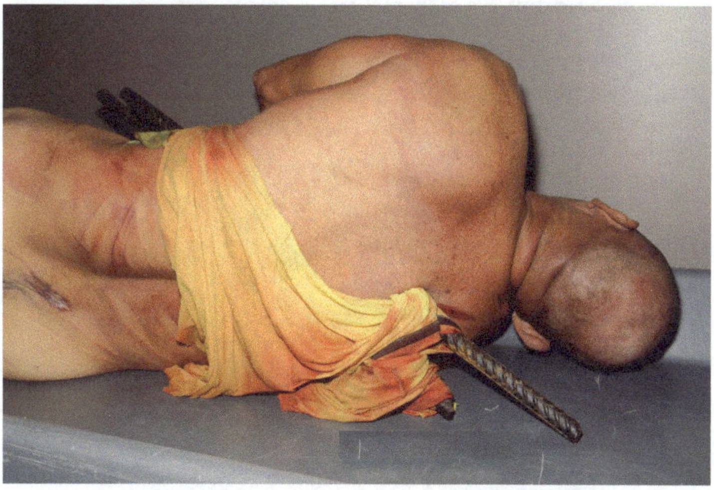

Figure 6.1 The rebar is seen entering the right shoulder area and exiting the left flank. There is blood on the shirt but it is not saturated with blood.

Figure 6.2 The victim is on the couch with extensive blood all over the room.

portions of brain tissue. It is not unusual to find a large pool of coagulated blood under and around the head, with no evidence that the decedent moved after collapsing. If the gunshot wound is too far forward, there will be facial lacerations and fractures, possibly avulsion of teeth, injury to the nose and eyes, fractures in the anterior (frontal) aspects of the skull, and laceration of the frontal lobes of the brain, but not necessarily immediate incapacitation or death (see Figure 6.3).

Internal bleeding from injuries to the organs and tissues can be fatal but do not necessarily manifest as obvious or external bleeding. Rapid blood loss can lead to hypovolemia (decreased or low blood volume), hypotension (decreased or low blood pressure), and death, while slow, steady bleeding also drains blood from the cardiovascular tree and left untreated, will lead to death. The length of time it takes to collapse/die from blood loss depends on what vessels, organs, and tissues are injured and the extent of injury.

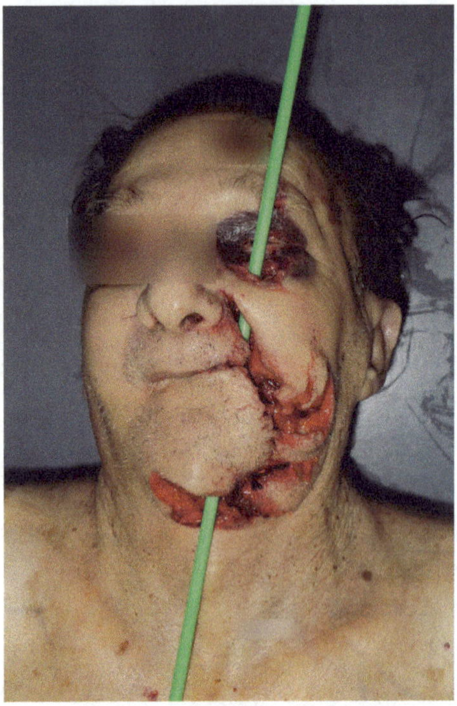

Figure 6.3 The first gunshot wound was under the chin, exiting below the left eye.

HEAD AND NECK

Injuries in the head and neck with open wounds will bleed externally because there are no large cavities to contain extravasated blood (see Figure 6.4). If an artery is disrupted, the blood under pressure within the artery may spurt with contraction of the left ventricle (pumping of the heart).

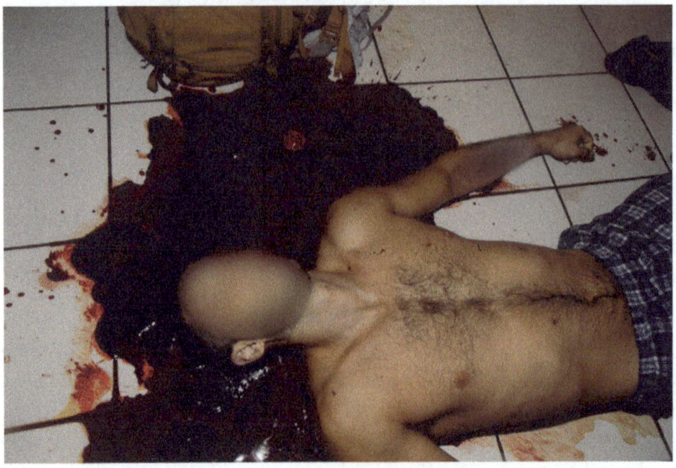

Figure 6.4 Note the large pool of coagulated blood around the head and a two-inch portion of brain one foot to the left of the head.

Therefore, a large amount of blood can be lost within a short period of time. Disruption of a vein where the blood is under less pressure will result in outward draining of blood, but less blood will be lost within a given period of time as compared with the blood coming out of the same size of disrupted artery. Large amounts of blood loss can occur with injury to veins only and result in hypovolemic shock and death, given that the wound is not closed and continues to bleed.

It is said that dead people do not bleed because the heart has stopped actively pumping blood to the body. That is true, but blood vessels of varying size are everywhere throughout the body. If the body is injured after death and tissues are disrupted, the blood vessels in those tissues may be lacerated (torn) and whatever blood is contained within those local vessels will leak out and that lost blood will not be replaced by the heart pumping more blood to the area. The "bleeding" or more accurately, leakage of blood then stops.

PATTERNS

The blood patterns at a scene may demonstrate movement, the possible type of injury, chronology of events, suggest whether more than one person was present, indicate whether the bleeding was related to injury (and whether it was intentional or inflicted injury), and provide clues as to whether it was the blood loss that more likely than not resulted in death (see Figure 6.5).

DRIPPED BLOOD

Dripped blood at a scene may be from multiple sources. The circumstances and the findings at the scene are critical factors.

Dripped blood on a body could be the victim's own blood, the assailant's blood, or someone else's blood. The dripped blood may not be from the victim dripping it on themselves unless it is on the legs or top of the feet. Round drips of blood onto a body may be from a bloody weapon held by the assailant and dripping the victim's own blood or blood from the injured assailant standing over the downed victim.

Cast-off spatter can be from a beating and multiple "passes" or swings may be discerned by analysis of the pattern. Multiple separate swings traced back to a common point of origin would be consistent with the victim not moving much.

Figure 6.5 (a) The orange pyramids mark the blood trail which follows a zig-zag pattern as the victim staggered from side to side and (b) the yellow markers are along a trail of dripped blood as the staggering victim fled the scene.

SPECIAL PATTERNS

In Figure 6.6a, the projected blood on the wall above the female victim is from a stab wound on the neck which perforated the internal jugular vein. In Figure 6.6b and c, the fine blood spatter behind and to the right of the victim was from multiple perforating gunshot wounds. The fine spatter is usually not seen unless the victim is close to a surface because minute blood droplets do not travel far enough to be deposited.

The bloody tire tracks on the concrete floor were close to a victim who was on the ground with gunshot wounds. The tracks represent a car backing up in the parking spot, then changing direction to leave the scene to the left (see Figure 6.6d).

Bloody head hair leaves an irregular transfer pattern with some hairline trails discernible and sometimes hair adherent to the blood (see Figure 6.7).

Writing with blood on walls is usually done with the blood of whoever is bleeding, usually the victim's blood. Unlike having an ink reservoir in a ballpoint pen, blood on a finger will wipe off and the blood needs to be replenished in order to write more than one swipe. Therefore, the writer is the assailant, or the injured person is conscious and capable of dipping a finger into blood again and again to complete the desired message (see Figure 6.8).

Figure 6.6 (a) The projected blood on the wall was from an injury to the internal jugular vein, (b) fine blood spatter is behind and to the right of the victim, above bullet holes in the wall, (c) note the void on the wall where the right shoulder was; exit wounds on the victim's back correspond with the bullet holes in the wall, and (d) the victim is in the background and bloody tire tracks are consistent with a vehicle backing up, changing direction, and driving off to the left.

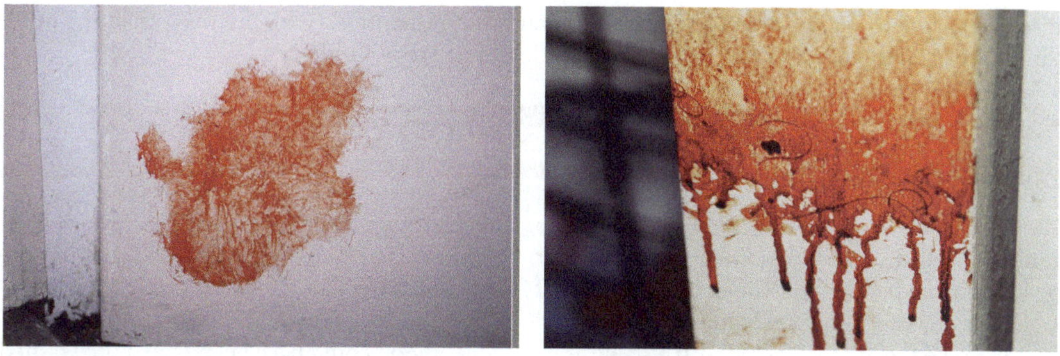

Figure 6.7 (a) Irregularly smudged stain from hair on a bloody head and (b) strands of hair are also within the smudged blood stain.

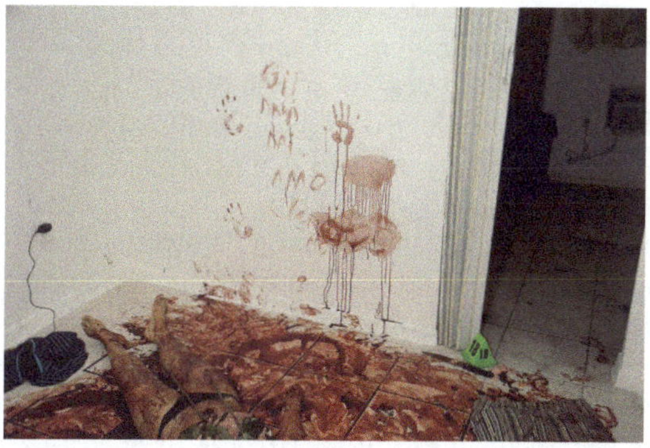

Figure 6.8 Words written by assailant using victim's blood.

DECOMPOSING BODIES

At the scene of a decomposed body, there may be loss of body fluids from the decomposition process (see Figure 6.9). There may also be blood at the scene. Decompositional fluid may vary in color, usually from yellow to brown to black and all shades in between. True blood will be red, contrasting with the various colors of decomposition. In the appropriate setting, the trick is to

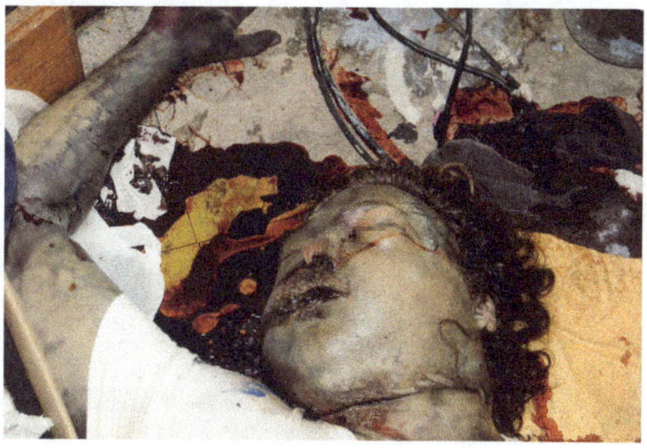

Figure 6.9 Red blood admixed with decompositional "purge" fluid draining from the bloated body.

discern that there is a different pattern of fluid and that it manifests a brighter red than the other fluids. Fly excrement may simulate droplets of blood but are not red.

INTERPRETATION AT THE SCENE

Look for blood on the doors, light switches, floor, furniture, walls, ceiling, in the bathroom sink, toilet and bathtub, in the kitchen utensil drawer, cupboards and sink, in the bedroom behind the head of the bed and under the bed, in the laundry room, in closets, in the garage, inside vehicles – essentially everywhere (see Figure 6.10a).

Don't take the amount of blood at a scene at face value. Blood could have been wiped up, washed away, flushed down the toilet, drained down an opening, or inhaled/aspirated and swallowed by the victim.

Voids in blood spatter can indicate an object shielding the area from blood spatter during the event.

Postmortem animal activity can smear blood on and around the body. Bloody paw prints may be seen (see Figure 6.10a and 6.10b). Blood may be on the muzzle and paws of the animal.

It takes an experienced forensic pathologist/medical examiner to differentiate intentional sadistic mutilation of a victim (by an assailant) from animal activity such as a dog mauling or bites from pets or turkey vultures after death (see Figure 6.11).

The scene should not be interpreted in a vacuum on its own without additional information.

One may be able to walk into a scene and start interpreting the scene findings because the scene is so obvious. Usually, there is some preliminary information such as a witness seeing or hearing something, or the decedent could not be contacted and the police are called for a welfare check. These clues frequently provide valuable evidence that allows more accurate interpretation of the scene findings. In practice, the medical examiner will not have the luxury of time to ponder the circumstances and the findings. Typically, the medical examiner arrives at the scene, gets briefed by detectives from the investigating agency, is walked through the scene, and then begins documentation with photographs and notes. In particular, the area around the body should be documented/photographed before the body is examined. As the body is examined in tandem (detectives, crime scene personnel, and medical examiner), valuables and property are photographed and impounded, clothing is examined then removed in layers, and the body is documented as the parts of the body are exposed. The visual and physical findings at any scene may be critical in the death investigative process (see Figure 6.12). Adequate photographs taken with good lighting and resolution at correct angles to the subject matter and enough angles of approach are invaluable. Basic scene investigation

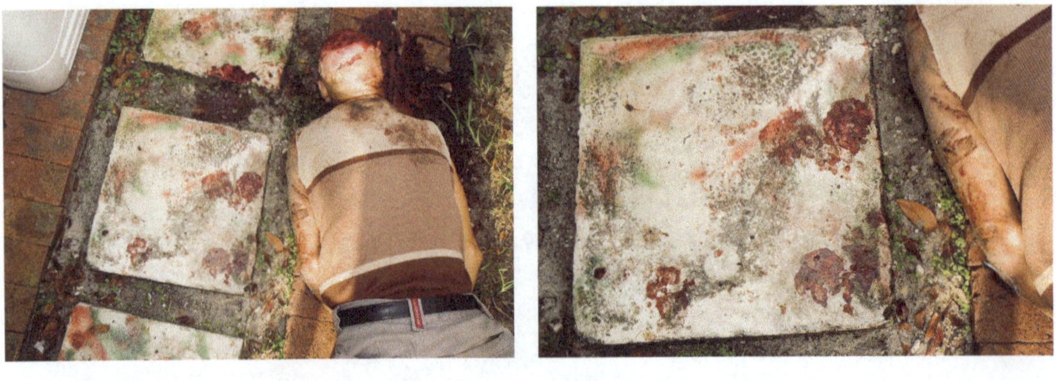

Figure 6.10 (a) Smeared blood on the back of the shirt and separate patches of blood on the ground and (b) the separate patches of blood are bloody paw prints from a dog.

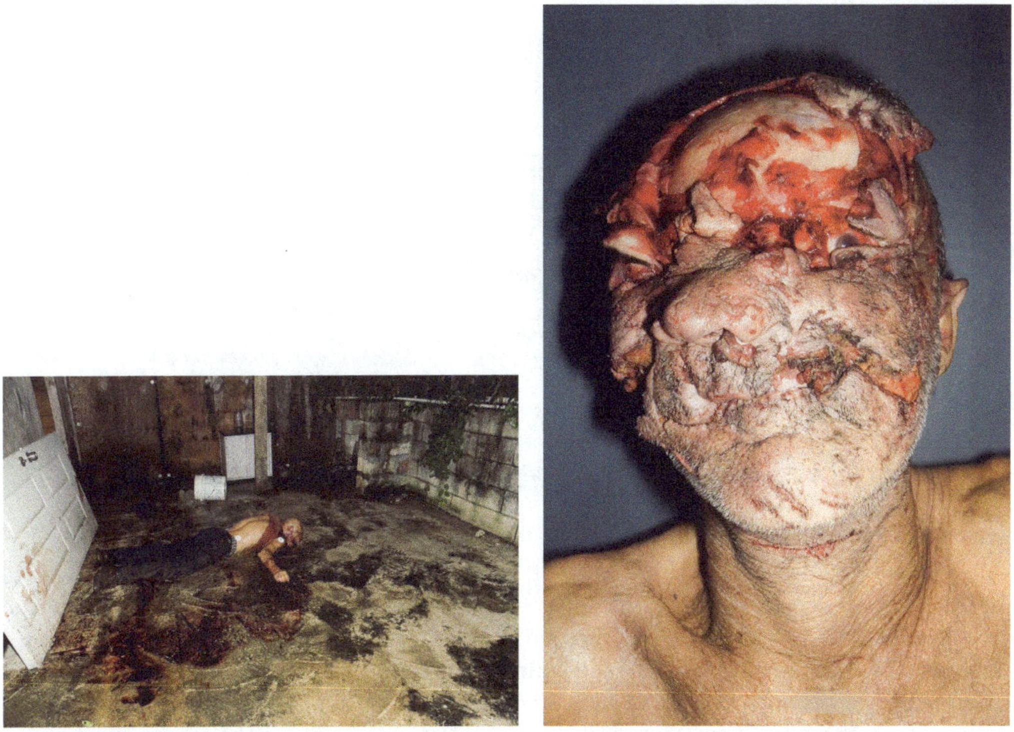

Figure 6.11 (a) Bloody scene of a dog mauling and (b) the face was avulsed by a dog but the soft tissues have been put back into place.

Figure 6.12 (a) Projectiles are in the blood on the gravel and (b) the four projectiles recovered from the blood on the gravel.

principles apply – make your perimeter larger than what you believe it to be because once a scene is altered, the evidence that was present may have been destroyed.

Remember that victims may not be immediately incapacitated after an injury and therefore do not always die immediately. They may be fully capable of moving and speaking, and actually struggling with the assailant. The pattern of blood at the scene can be significantly modified because of the movement and may not be representative of an expected blood pattern for the type of injury. Blood may *hold* evidence as well as *be* evidence.

The amount of blood in body cavities depends on what vessels, organs, and tissues were injured, the inherent state of health of the victim, and the length of survival after injury (see Figure 6.13).

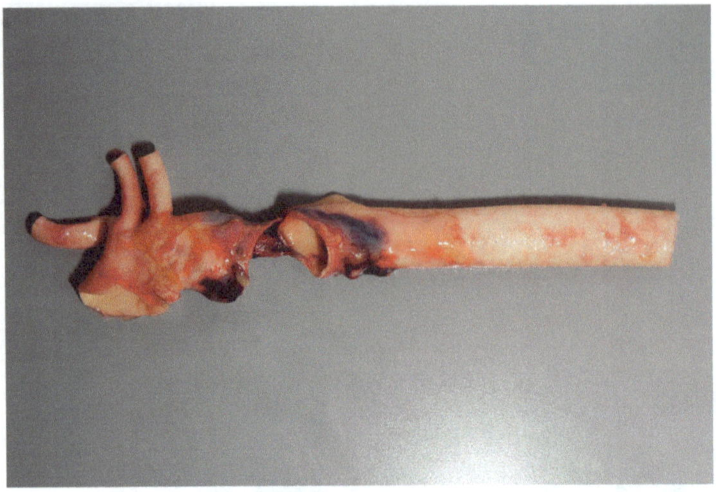

Figure 6.13 Laceration of the aorta (largest artery in the body) results in massive internal bleeding.

Catastrophic or devastating injuries and/or short survival times are frequently not associated with large collections of blood within the body cavities. On the other hand, a survival time of minutes could result in loss of greater than half the entire blood volume.

Blood collected on surfaces may change, depending on the type of material and the ambient conditions such as temperature, humidity, etc. With time, not only can the serum separate at the edges of the pool of blood but the blood may dry, crack, and curl (see Figure 6.14).

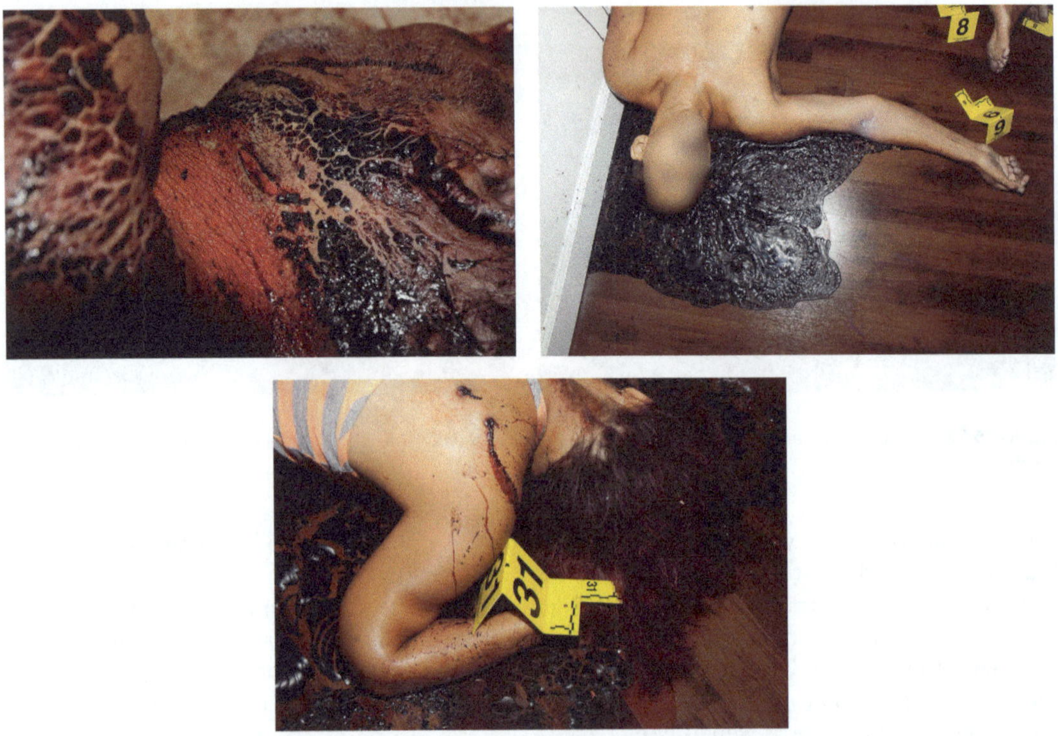

Figure 6.14 (a) Dried cracked blood on skin around a stab wound, (b) drying of the coagulated pooled blood resulted in a cobbled texture, and (c) the blood dried, cracked, and appeared contracted/shrunken (next to the elbow).

Homicide scenes may have little or no blood. Every scene and each body is different. The types of injuries that may leave minimal blood include asphyxial mechanisms such as suffocation, strangulation, smothering, and sitting on someone to restrict breathing (burking).

Drag marks frequently indicate some incapacitation of the victim, allowing the victim to be able to be moved by others.

BLUNT TRAUMA FROM BEATING

As shown in Figure 6.15a, blood spatter is originating from the area of the head and slightly above the head. It is evident on the wall behind and above the head. Photographs can document the point of origin of the spatter and when the photographs are taken at different locations around the point of origin, the direction of the spatter is easily demonstrated. In addition to the spatter from cast-off blood, there is passive drainage of blood from the injured head (see Figure 6.15b).

Dark brown fluid may represent altered blood, typically originating from the upper gastrointestinal tract (esophagus, stomach, and duodenum) from emesis or vomiting. Blood that has passed through the gastrointestinal tract to become melena stool can be black-red, thick, sticky, or tar-like. Melena stool takes time to form as blood makes its way through yards of bowel, although bright red blood may be admixed with the dark blood. The nature of the blood is dependent on the location and type of lesion in the gastrointestinal tract that caused bleeding. Altered blood may be found at the scene of a chronic alcoholic (see Figure 6.16).

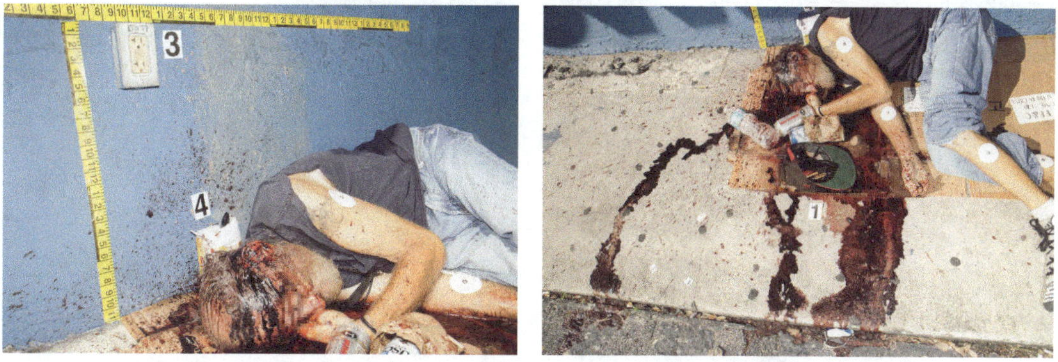

Figure 6.15 (a) Blood spatter is on the wall above and behind the head and (b) blood spatter on the sidewalk, originating from the head; blood also draining from the head.

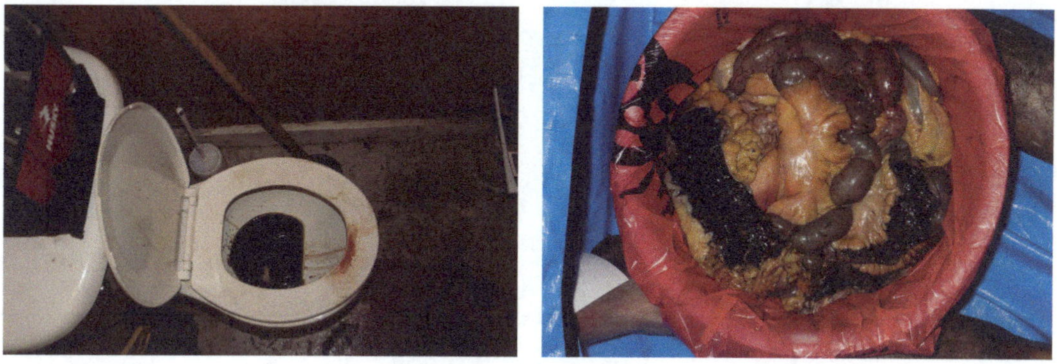

Figure 6.16 (a) Altered dark blood (melena stool) in the toilet and (b) melena stool in the colon at autopsy.

DESCENT FROM HEIGHT

The scene shown in Figure 6.17 was on an extended balcony on the tenth floor of a high-rise building. Blood and tissue were scattered over the balcony. Blood spatter was on the bent railing and glass of the far wall around the balcony. The body of a young woman was prone (face down) next to the bent railing. A compound (open) fracture exposed the inside of the head. The traumatically amputated right lower leg and foot were close to the building, across from the body. Several feet

Figure 6.17 (a) Blood and spatter on bent balcony railing and wall; point of impact for the head is to the left of the body (right side of image); fractured skull in body, (b) blood spatter from the point of impact; the trail of blood begins as the extruded brain lands on the ground and starts to slide across the floor, leaving the trail of blood as it travels, (c) the sliding brain impacts the wall of the building and ricochets off the wall after impact, (d) the cerebellum was flung to the far balcony wall as the body bounced, and (e) the cerebellum impacting the balcony wall and falling to the floor.

left of the body was an impact point, with blood spatter radiating away from the point of impact. A several-inch wide trail of smeared blood started from the edge of the blood spatter and continued toward the building. The trail of smeared blood led to an impact point on the wall of the building. The blood trail approached the wall at an approximate 45° angle and after the impact, the angle of the blood trail away from the wall was symmetrical. The trail of blood was left by the brain that was catapulted out of the head through the skull fracture.

The events were as follows. The woman was witnessed jumping off the 32nd floor. After the head impacted the floor of the balcony, the skull fractured, resulting in radiating blood spatter. The marked compression of the skull by the impact then expelled the brain out through the fractured skull, with enough momentum for the brain to be propelled several feet before landing on the floor and creating the trail of blood as it slid toward the wall and bounced off, leaving a hemispheric imprint that was of the same shape as the cerebral hemisphere. The impact point to the left of the body was from the head landing on the floor, however, the terminal location of the head was several feet to the right of the impact point. The reason for the head being in a different location from where it impacted the floor is that after dropping onto the floor of the tenth story balcony from the 32nd floor, the body bounced and flipped to the right. The cerebral hemispheres were extruded at the time of the head's impact on the floor. Now, as the body flipped, the cerebellum (smaller back portion of the brain) flew out of the open skull fracture in the direction that the body was flipping, and landed yards away on the balcony wall at the end of the balcony to the far right of the body. The cerebellum then dropped from the wall to the floor of the balcony.

ACCIDENTAL PENETRATING WOUND

A man found his mother's body in blood on her kitchen floor (see Figure 6.18). There was abundant blood leading away from her head. Footprints from a left foot were seen alongside the blood. Of importance is the fact that her left foot was bare and bloody, below a stool with blood and a left shoe. A sock was on her right foot. A large pool of blood was around her left foot and below the stool. A long barbeque fork and a cordless telephone were on the counter above the stool. The astute detective rinsed off her bloody left sock that was next to her left foot and found a small hole in the ankle area. A puncture wound is on the lateral aspect (outside) of the left ankle. The son explained that his mother had arthritis and used a fork to help get her socks off. That bit of information put the entire scene into logical context. She was using the fork to get her left sock off and accidentally punctured a varicose vein on her ankle. She could not stop the bleeding from the varicose vein and eventually bled to death. She tried calling her son but collapsed before she could finish entering the numbers. The first several digits of the son's telephone number were on her cordless telephone.

SELF-INFLICTED GUNSHOT WOUND

A man typed a suicide note and left it on his computer and laid out the contents of his wallet on the kitchen counter. Blood was on the doorway of the bathroom and dripped blood led from the bathroom into the walk-in closet next to the bathroom. Blood was on the corner of the bathtub and wet blood-stained sheets and blankets were in front of the toilet and bidet. A blood-soaked towel was on the toilet seat and blood was on the front of the toilet. Blood was smeared on the front of the bidet. A bullet hole was in the wall to the left of the bidet. Dripped and smeared blood was on the bathroom counter, in the sink, and on the floor in front of the counter and sink. A revolver was on the counter behind the sink. Where was the body? The naked male decedent was sitting on the bench in the shower with the hinged door closed. Prominent fixed livor mortis (postmortem

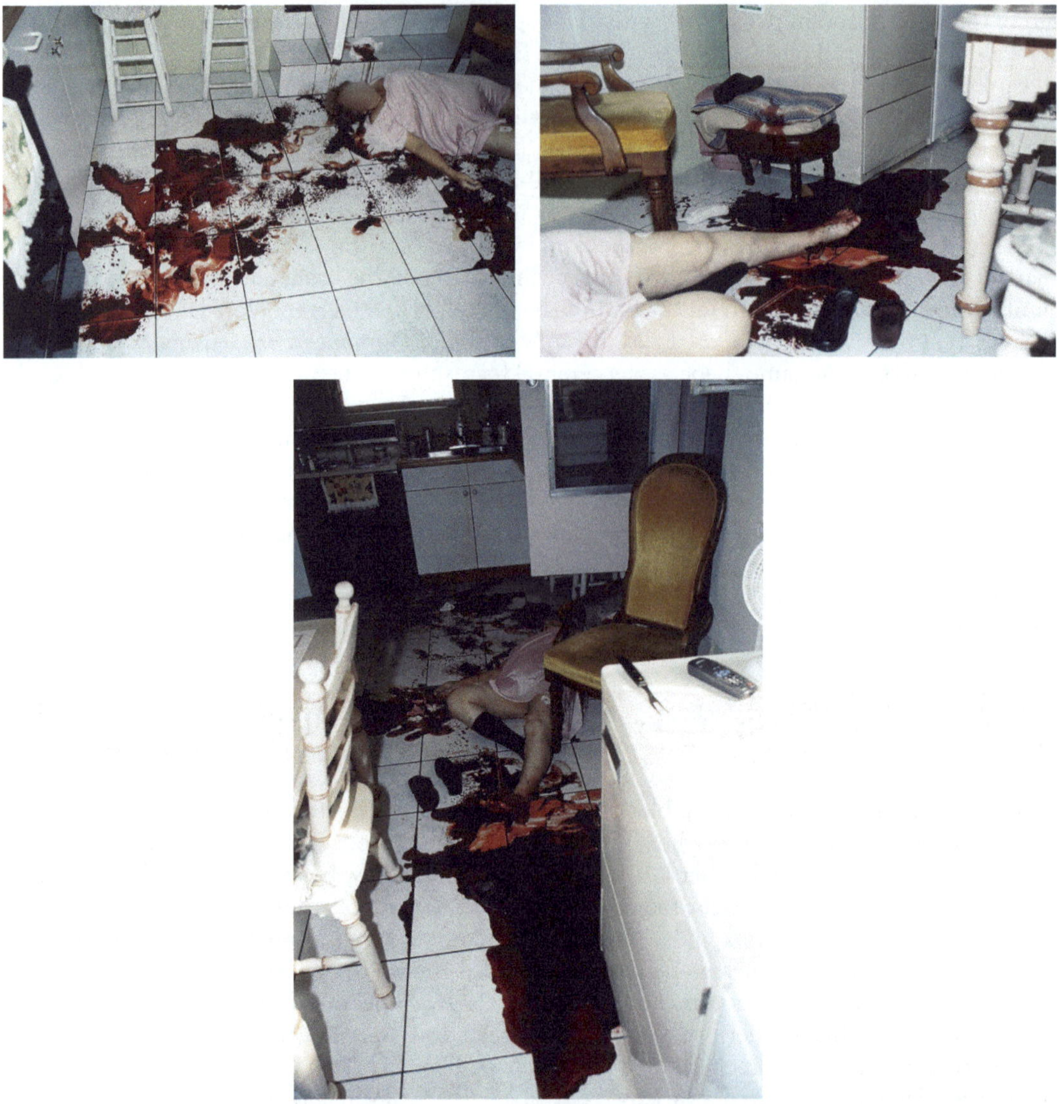

Figure 6.18 (a) A blood trail with left foot prints, (b) left shoe on the bloody stool and blood on and around the bare left foot, and (c) barbeque fork and telephone on counter above the left foot.

settling of blood) in the lower legs and feet provided evidence that the body had been there for hours (see Figure 6.19). Blood had drained out of the perforating (through and through) gunshot wound on the head. The entrance gunshot wound was under the chin and the exit gunshot wound was on the right side of the forehead. Although a significant amount of blood was on the floor of the shower, it did not appear as much as would be expected from a gunshot wound of the head. The slant of the floor in the shower was designed to allow water to drain. In identical fashion, the pool of blood on the floor followed gravity and flowed down the drain. The remaining blood on the shower floor then dried and cracked. The scene findings support that the decedent shot himself over the toilet but the projectile path was too far forward on the head to cause immediate incapacitation although the right eye was perforated. He was able to walk to the closet, return to the bathroom, get into the shower and close the door from inside, then possibly became unconscious,

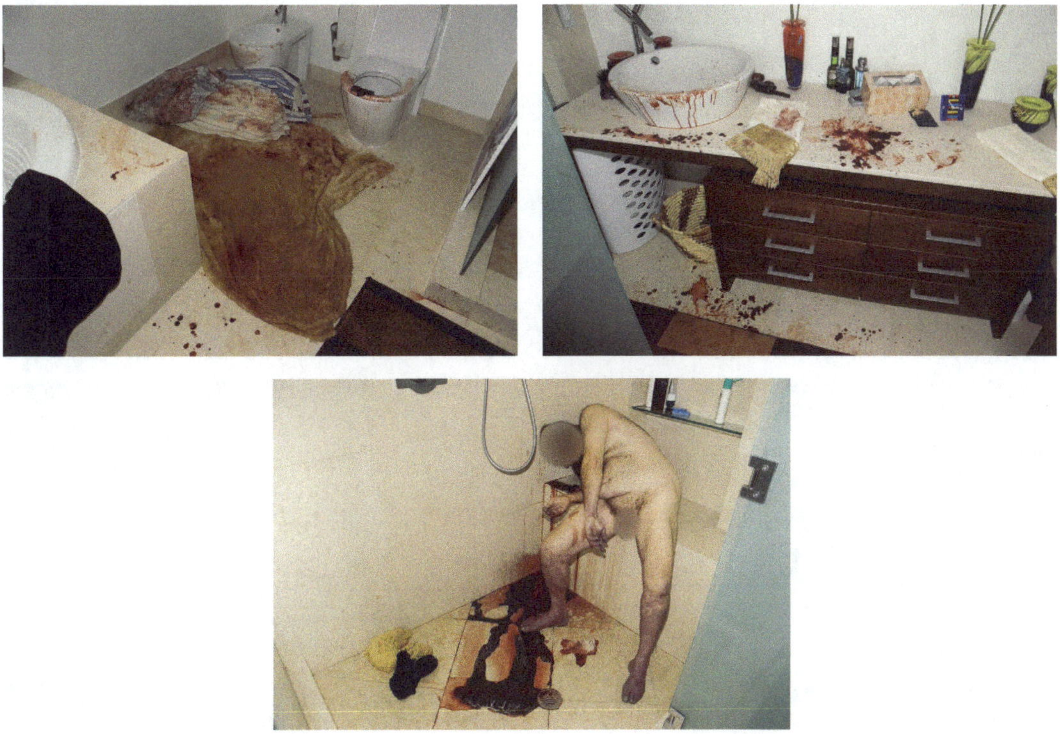

Figure 6.19 (a) Blood-soaked towel on the toilet and blood on the sheets and blanket, (b) blood on the floor, counter, and sink, and a revolver on the counter, and (c) body in the shower; pooled, dried blood on the floor, flowing to the drain; purple livor mortis in the lower legs and feet indicates the body had been there for hours.

and continued to bleed. At some point, he placed the revolver on the bathroom counter before getting into the shower.

ACCIDENTAL GUNSHOT WOUND

A 94-year-old man lived alone and was found by his daughter two days after she last spoke with him. In the kitchen, one-half of a torn brown gun pouch/holster was on the floor along the left cabinets. In the far left corner of the narrow kitchen, a 38 Special two-shot revolver was on its right side on the floor next to a white wastebasket with downward trails of blood. Blood spatter was located low down on the cabinets and the wastebasket. A dried, focally interrupted circle of blood was on the floor around a stool close to the handgun (see Figure 6.20). The other half of the holster was on the floor at the edge of the circle of blood. A trail of blood led from around the stool into and through the living room. The bloodstains were distinctly of left footprints with small drips of blood between the footprints heading toward the bedroom. Blood was on the left side of the bedroom door frame.

The bed was to the right, inside the bedroom. The body of an elderly white male was lying face up on the near side of the bed with the legs toward the bedroom door. The trail of blood from the kitchen and living room led to the left foot where the blood then formed a large pool on the carpet around the foot. The left lower pant leg was heavily saturated with blood. The blood-stained handset of a telephone rested on the right thigh, just under the right hand; the telephone cord was connected to a telephone that was dangling off the night table on the left side of the body.

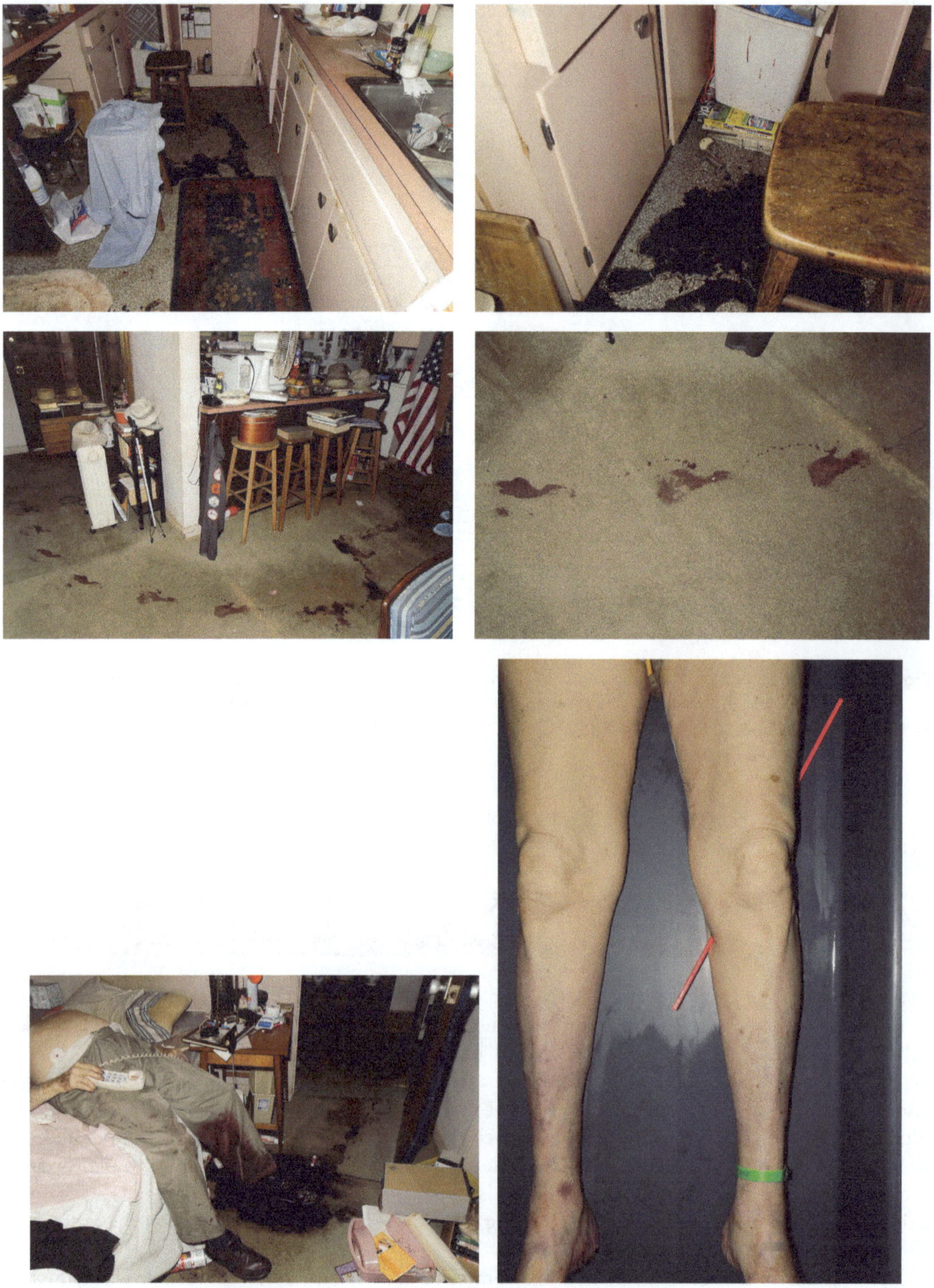

Figure 6.20 (a) Wide trail of blood on the floor around the stool, (b) revolver on the floor next to pooled blood; blood spatter on the white garbage container, (c) left footprints leading from the kitchen to the bedroom, (d) left footprints connected by a trail of dripped blood, (e) footprints led to a man on the bed with blood on the left pant leg and blood pooled around the left foot; note the telephone in his right hand, and (f) pink probe through the gunshot wound on the left leg; the bruise on inside front of the right ankle aligned with the projectile path.

A bullet hole on the inside of the left lower pant leg corresponded with a gunshot wound on the medial aspect (inside) of the left lower leg below the knee. An apparent exit gunshot wound on the posterolateral aspect (outside back) of the left knee was associated with a bullet hole on the outside knee region of the left pant leg; no blood was around the bullet hole on the outside of the pant leg.

Autopsy confirmed a gunshot wound on the medial aspect (inside) of the left lower leg below the knee, with features consistent with an indeterminate range gunshot wound that had a projectile path from right to left, upward, and slightly front to back, tearing the left popliteal vein before exiting the posterolateral aspect (outside back) of the left knee.

A 2 cm purple ecchymosis (bruise) on the inside front of the right ankle aligned (lined up) with the projectile path.

How was he shot? It is possible that he was holding the revolver in front of him with the muzzle pointed at his left lower leg while he was sitting on the stool; that could be consistent with the pathway of the gunshot wound. The son subsequently informed police that he found a bullet in the ceiling of the kitchen above the stool. Considering the history, circumstances, the findings at the scene, and the findings at autopsy, it was likely that the elderly man dropped the revolver while he was standing. The revolver struck the inside front of the right ankle before impacting the floor. The weapon fired upon striking the floor, tearing the holster at the muzzle. The revolver had to have been pointed upward and toward the left lower leg at the time it struck the floor. The fired projectile went through the left lower leg, going from right to left, upward, and slightly front to back. This scenario explains the torn holster at the scene, the projectile in the ceiling, the bruise on the inside front of the right ankle, and the projectile path in the left lower leg. The blood at the scene is consistent with the injured man walking around the stool in the kitchen before making his way to the bedroom to use the telephone to call for help.

SHARP FORCE INJURY

As shown in Figure 6.21, a blood trail began at the apartment with the open door. The trail passed around the open door and wound its way down the sidewalk. The trail meandered from side to side, turned the corner to go down a hallway to the right, and ended at the supine (face up) body of an elderly male at the exit to the hallway. Multiple stab wounds were on the torso. Incised (slicing) wounds were on the wrists and ankles where there was attempted disarticulation (dismemberment) of the hands and feet. The ankles were crossed. The most obvious wound was a deep incised wound across the front of the neck.

A father lived with his son in the apartment. Two large knives were in the kitchen sink, one of which was bloodstained. Beginning at the apartment door, the blood trail is a pattern characteristic of dragging. After stabbing the father, the son dragged the body of his father out of the apartment, most likely by the wrists. The crossed ankles of the body support that the body was initially dragged prone (face down). The meandering of the blood trail from side to side in an undulating or sinusoidal pattern was probably from the son shifting his weight from side to side, or foot to foot, as he pulled the heavy weight of the body backward along the sidewalk.

CRUSH INJURY

Injuries may result in the spatter of more than just blood, depending on the area of the body and the organs and tissues injured. This occurs not infrequently with injuries of the head, including penetrating, perforating, and crush injuries. As a heavy weight is placed suddenly on the head, such as a truck rolling over the body, the skin lacerates, the skull fractures, and the brain is squashed and extruded out the compound fracture of the skull. One picture tells it all (see Figure 6.22): the tire

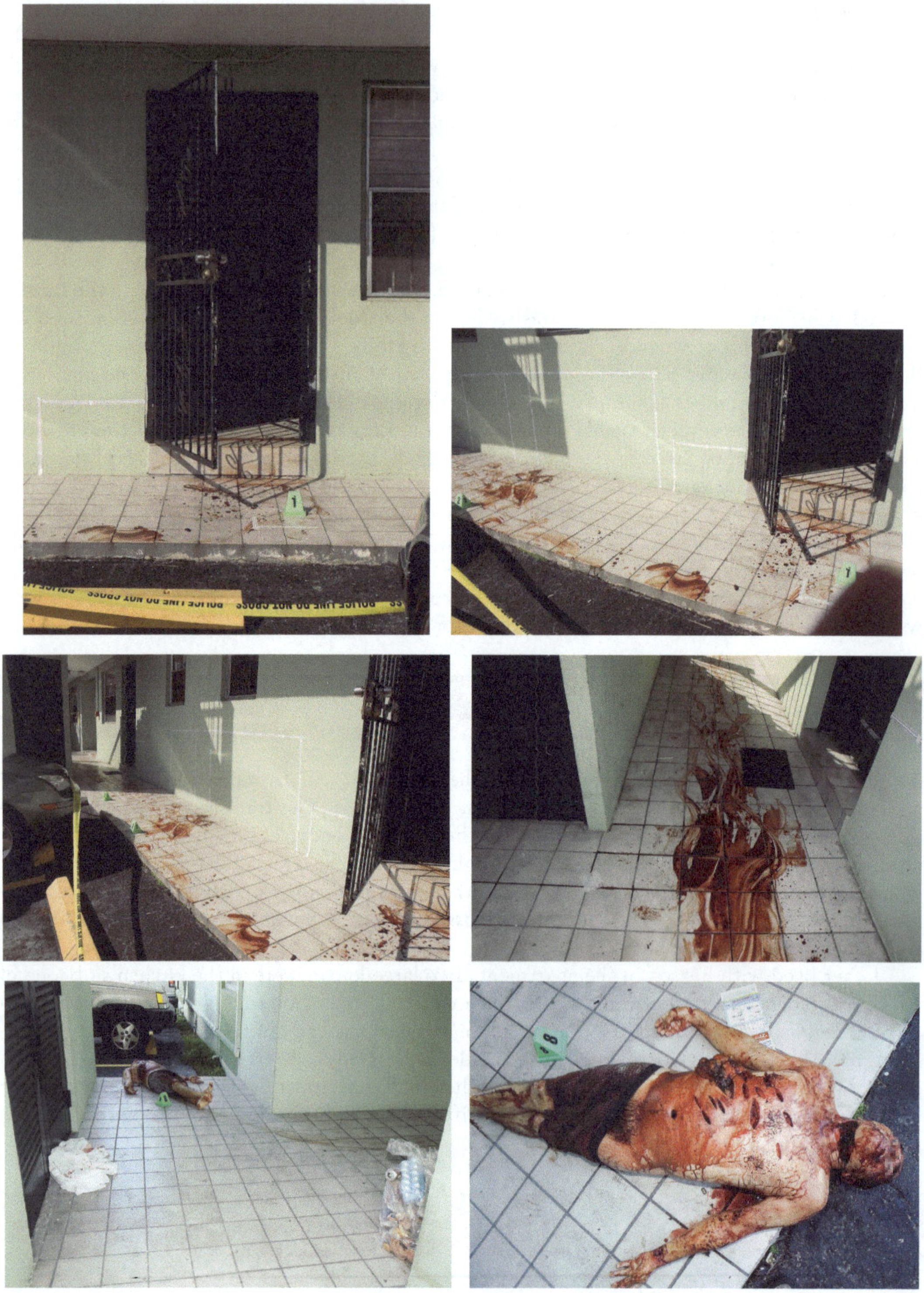

Figure 6.21 (a) Blood on the walkway below the open door; (b) the blood trail went around the door, off the walkway and back on the walkway; (c) the blood trail continued along the walkway away from the open door; (d) two trails within the blood describe a wavy, sinusoidal pattern, (e) the blood trail thinned out and stopped at a body with crossed ankles, and (f) the victim had been stabbed multiple times, and the neck and wrists incised (sliced).

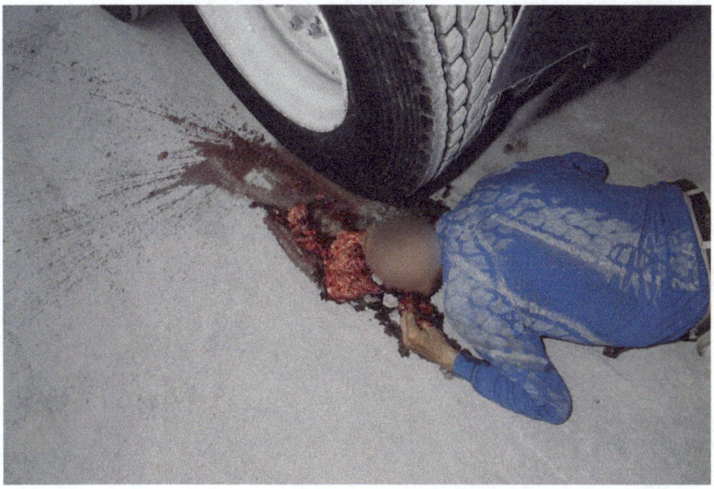

Figure 6.22 Note the tire tracks on the back, brain extruded from the head, and blood spatter from where the head was originally located.

marks on the back; the brain extruded through the mouth and the top of the head; the dentures beyond the major portion of brain; the extended spatter of blood and tissue from the tire rolling over the head.

EXAMPLE OF BLOOD SPATTER USED AS EVIDENCE FOR CONSISTENCY

A man sustained a gunshot wound on the right side of the face next to the nose while he was in the bedroom; he told police after he regained consciousness in the hospital that his female friend shot him. His female friend told police that she was eating in the dining room when she heard the gunshot. The police wanted to know who was telling the truth. The blood spatter on the wall above the bed was consistent with the man sitting on the edge of the bed, with the right side of his face toward the wall (see Figure 6.23). The female friend had blood spatter mostly on the right side of her face, right arm, and right leg. A police video showed that after the police arrived, she got onto the bed by the wall and was cradling his head in her lap as he lay on his back with his feet away from her. Therefore, both people were facing the same direction. The video showed him gasping and breathing heavily as she held his head and was looking down at him. Blood spewed from his mouth, nose, and the right-sided face wound as he gasped for air, depositing the blood on her right side, sparing the right groin area of her shorts and inner right thigh because her hips were flexed (bent) and his head was in her lap. Therefore, the blood on the female was expirated blood, which looked like blood originating from impact. She was right-handed and so was he. If she was facing him as she shot him, the blood spatter from the wound on the right side of his face would be expected to be on her left side and not her right side. Her mother was also in the residence and verified that her daughter was eating when they heard the gunshot. The circumstances and the physical evidence were consistent with the man shooting himself as he sat on the bed.

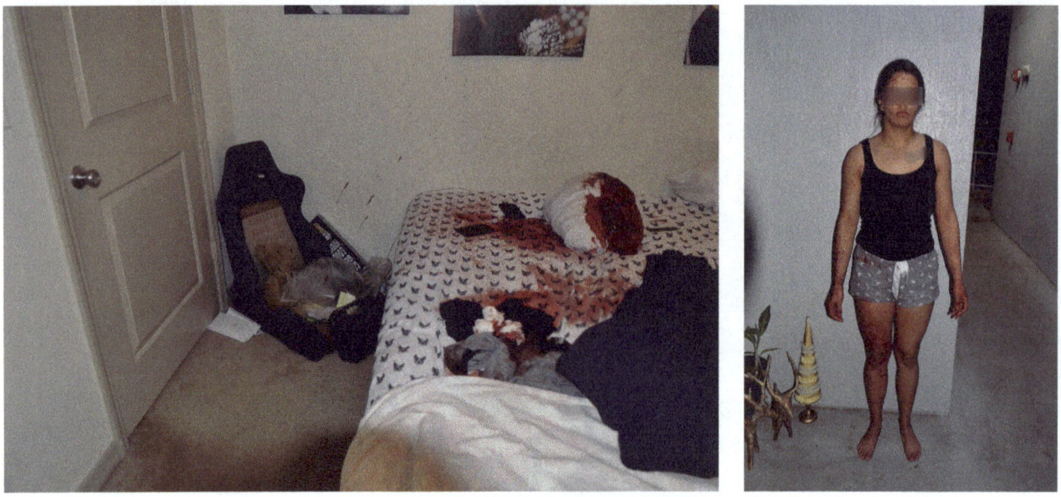

Figure 6.23 (a) Blood spatter on the wall beginning at the approximate height of the face of someone sitting on the bed and (b) blood spatter on the right side of the forehead, chin, right arm, right leg, and left wrist and hand.

AUTOPSY REPORTS

The autopsy report format differs from one department/office/jurisdiction to the other. The basic components covered by most reports include the external examination; evidence of medical intervention; evidence of injury; internal examination; autopsy findings; tissues submitted for histology.

The name of the department/office/jurisdiction and name of the pathologist are documented usually at the beginning of the report. All reports should have the decedent's name, age, sex, race, and date and time of the autopsy. The autopsy technician, photographer, and other attendees may also be listed.

The autopsy findings are listed at the end or, in some jurisdictions, at the beginning of the autopsy report. Some pathologists may write a paragraph to summarize the history and terminal events of the decedent, and/or conclusions drawn from the autopsy. Medical examiners frequently use the autopsy report as a descriptive, objective document rather than an interpretive document and list the findings as opposed to explaining the findings. In forensic pathology, it is accepted that the description of the findings does not change – it is the interpretation of the findings that may differ, depending on the pathologist.

The external examination provides details of the outside of the body (including but not restricted to length of the body, weight, hair, eyes, orifices, scars, and tattoos). Findings that are not inherent to the usual state of the body are usually described in sections that are designated for non-natural findings on the body, such as evidence of medical intervention and injuries.

Evidence of medical intervention usually refers to procedures that are acute or terminal, such as intravenous catheters, endotracheal tubes, electrocardiographic patches, and defibrillator pads. Scars from remote surgeries are considered inherent to the body and frequently described under external examination. Under more complex circumstances, if, for example, the decedent was admitted to a hospital, underwent surgical procedures, and never recovered to the point of being discharged, the procedures received during the entire hospitalization may be considered part of the terminal admission/medical intervention regardless of the duration because the patient never recovered.

Pathologists have different styles of writing to memorialize evidence of injury. Injuries may be described according to the type of injury, for example, blunt trauma, sharp force injuries, evidence of asphyxia, gunshot wounds, evidence of submersion in water, etc. Injuries may also be described according to the region of the body, such as the head and neck, chest, abdomen, torso, extremities, etc.

The internal examination is the examination of body cavities as well as organs and tissues inside the body cavities, from the brain inside the skull down to the pelvic organs. Forensic pathologists remove the tongue and neck structures, whereas a hospital pathologist may not. The organs are examined inside the cavities, then removed, weighed, and dissected.

Specimens for toxicology are taken during autopsy and include ocular fluid (from eyeballs), blood, bile, urine, and gastric contents. Other specimens include brain, liver, spleen, skeletal muscle, and fat. A molar tooth or segment of long bone may be needed from partially skeletonized bodies for DNA profiling to establish identity.

Specimens for a sexual battery kit include pulled head hair, pubic hair combings, pulled pubic hair, and swabs from the mouth, anus, and vagina or penis. Fingernail swabs or clippings may be included in the sexual battery kit or packaged separately. Swabs from additional areas of the body depend on the type of case.

The tissues submitted for histology (to be made into glass slides for examination under a microscope) are also listed in a separate section.

Photographs may be taken at any stage of autopsy from the time of external examination through to the end of autopsy, and include the specimens obtained during autopsy as well as evidence such as projectiles.

Further Reading

Dettmeyer, *Forensic Histopathology* – It is the only book about forensic histopathology.

DiMaio Forensic Pathology: https://www.amazon.com/Forensic-Pathology-Practical-Criminal-Investigations/dp/084930072X/ref=sr_1_1?dchild=1&keywords=dimaio&qid=1615216172&s=books&sr=1-1

DiMaio Gunshot Wounds: https://www.amazon.com/Gunshot-Wounds-Ballistics-Techniques-Investigations/dp/1498725694/ref=pd_bxgy_img_2/130-4931904-2060454?_encoding=UTF8&pd_rd_i=1498725694&pd_rd_r=89d60de1-505d-4f13-aabf-256a7aac8e9b&pd_rd_w=TQ5I8&pd_rd_wg=SN40S&pf_rd_p=f325d01c-4658-4593-be83-3e12ca663f0e&pf_rd_r=5YSA1B91AWNKM0Q61546&psc=1&refRID=5YSA1B91AWNKM0Q61546

Dolinak. Forensic Pathology: Principles and Practice

Dolinak Forensic Pathology: https://www.amazon.com/Forensic-Pathology-Principles-David-Dolinak/dp/0122199510/ref=sr_1_2?dchild=1&keywords=dolinak+forensic+pathology&qid=1615216127&s=books&sr=1-2

Essentials of Death Reporting and Death Certification: Practical Applications for the Clinical Practitioner by Erica J. Armstrong

Knight Forensic Pathology – It is a more "European" book, but contents, photos, and text are amazing. It also shows the different terminologies used in Europe compared to the United States.

Molina Toxicology: https://www.amazon.com/Handbook-Toxicology-Examiners-Practical-Investigations/dp/0815365446/ref=sr_1_1?dchild=1&keywords=Molina+toxicology&qid=1615216236&s=books&sr=1-1

Robbins Pathology: https://www.amazon.com/Robbins-Cotran-Pathologic-Diseas-Pathology-dp-032353113X/dp/032353113X/ref=dp_ob_title_bk

Spitz and Fisher's Medicolegal Investigation of Death: Guidelines for the Application of Pathology to Crime Investigation

Other books to consider are as follows:

Brogdon's Forensic Radiology – To learn the basics of virtopsy.
Clarke's Analytical Forensic Toxicology – A comprehensive, in-depth forensic toxicology book.
Handbook of Forensic Toxicology for Medical Examiners – Quick, good manual for basic forensic toxicology.

CHAPTER 7

TERMINOLOGY AND TAXONOMY IN BLOODSTAIN PATTERN ANALYSIS

Jeremy Morris

As discussed in Chapter 1, bloodstains have been studied extensively for well over 100 years. The purpose of these investigations always advanced the answer to the same question: "What story do the bloodstains tell regarding events which occurred during or after bloodshed?" The process of answering this question starts with an examination of the bloodstains themselves followed by a determination of what mechanisms are likely to have created those bloodstains.

But how exactly does an analyst express this determination? What words or phrases properly capture both the visual features observed within the patterns and the manner in which the pattern was created?

The terminology used in bloodstain pattern analysis (BPA) has changed over the past 100 years and until only recently varied significantly within the broader community of analysts. Individuals developed words or phrases of their own which became ingrained in their research, reports, and testimony. Other individuals, examining the exact same patterns, developed their own terms. Authors of books published their own terms. Even organizations such as the International Association for Identification[1] and the International Association of Bloodstain Pattern Analysts[2] published proposed terminologies for BPA. What resulted was an inconsistent and sometimes contradictory use of words and phrases to describe both the features and potential mechanisms of bloodstain patterns. While the work of Herbert MacDonnell resulted in the general preference of certain terms and phrases,[3] not all analysts used the terms proposed by him. As a result, investigators, attorneys, or triers of fact had to constantly adjust to slightly to widely different vocabularies for different analysts.

Bloodstain patterns determined to be the result of blood exiting a wound under hydraulic pressure were referred to as arterial gushing,[4] arterial spurts,[5] arterial fountain,[6] arterial rain,[7] and projected blood patterns.[8] But "projected" was also used by some to describe patterns which were the result of force (other than gravity) being applied to a liquid source of blood causing the blood to disperse into airborne droplets.[9] Bloodstains caused by blood-bearing objects touching a surface were referred to as smears, transfers,[10] transfer impressions,[11,12] transfer patterns,[13] transfer stains, compression transfer patterns,[14] and pressure patterns,[15] among others. Even when the same terms were used in the same general way, there were often very different definitions for those terms.

Additionally, certain terms were being used to classify bloodstain patterns which were factually inaccurate when the specific mechanism was studied in more detail. For example, "blowback effect" or "drawback effect" were used in reference to spatter stains found on the interior of a firearm's barrel near the muzzle.[16,17,18] These terms were variously defined as follows: "The presence of blood in the barrel of a firearm that has been drawn backward into the muzzle"[19] or "When blood is sucked back into the muzzle of a firearm due to the rapidly contracting gases in the firearm."[20] High-speed videos have conclusively demonstrated these explanations for bloodstains being on the inside of a barrel are fundamentally inaccurate. In fact, as will be discussed in the chapters on

DOI: 10.4324/9781003163695-7

forward spatter and backspatter patterns, muzzle gases have been shown to drive blood droplets *away* from the muzzle rather than pull them into the barrel.

The 2009 National Academy of Science's report on forensic science provided many recommendations to advance and improve forensic science.[21] Included was a recommendation to standardize the terminology used to report and testify about the results of examinations.[22] A few months later in 2009, the Scientific Working Group on Bloodstain Pattern Analysis (SWGSTAIN) published a list of 38 terms related to BPA.[23] These terms included those for bloodstain patterns, features of bloodstains, as well as various concepts related to BPA. This was the first step in the process of standardizing terms for describing and classifying bloodstain patterns.

Additionally, the SWGSTAIN terminology list abandoned the use of various terms which had become ingrained within the community but were problematic for a variety of reasons. SWGSTAIN recommended the single phrase "impact pattern" replaces what had been three commonly used terms: high-velocity impact spatter, medium-velocity impact spatter, and low-velocity impact spatter. The thinking at the time was the size of the spatter stains could be used to determine the speed of the object which impacted the liquid blood. As published by Herbert MacDonnell, medium-velocity impact spatter was the result of an impact of 5–25 ft/s. Low-velocity impact spatter was supposedly the result of an impact less than 5 ft/s, while high-velocity impact spatter was supposedly the result of an impact of greater than 25 ft/s.[24] As traditionally taught, a stain from dripping blood was an example of "low-velocity" spatter, stains created from a beating were "medium-velocity" spatter, and stains from gunshots were "high-velocity" impact spatter.

The recommendation from SWGSTAIN to discontinue the use of the distinctive terms low-, medium-, and high-velocity impact spatter, was based on a number of factors. First, a single event could create spatter stains from all three categories. Figure 7.1 is an impact of a pattern created by a single hammer strike into liquid blood on a wood block. When using past approaches to classify spatter stains based on size, this single event created stains which would be classified as high-velocity impact spatter (right side of the pattern), medium-velocity impact spatter (center of the pattern), and low-velocity impact spatter (left side of the pattern). Additionally, the phrase "high-velocity impact spatter" was routinely considered evidence of a gunshot injury. The presence of "mist-like" spatter stains was often considered diagnostic of bloodstains created from a gunshot despite the fact that "mist-like" spatter stains were known to be created by several other mechanisms. SWGSTAIN's recommendation of the single phrase "impact pattern" removed the confusion caused by the previous distinctive terms.

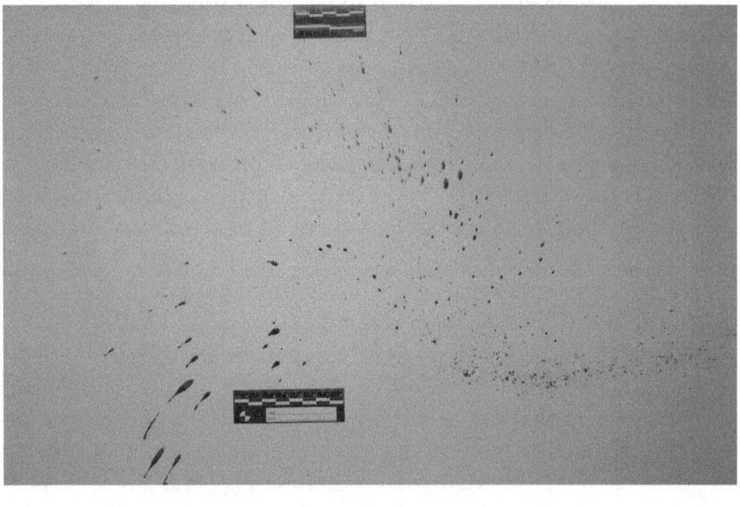

Figure 7.1 Impact pattern from a single hammer strike with a broad range of spatter stains sizes.

The process of solidifying a standard set of terms for BPA continued in 2017 when the American Academy of Forensic Sciences Academy Standards Board (ASB) published a revised version of SWGSTAIN's recommended terminology list.[25] The ASB terminology list contained all but one of the original SWGSTAIN terms with slight to moderate changes to the definitions of a handful of the terms. Only "mist pattern" was removed from the SWGSTAIN list based on similar reasons that high-velocity impact spatter was discontinued. Additionally, "cessation cast-off pattern" was replaced with "cessation pattern."

The ASB terminology list, like the SWGSTAIN list, contains a combination of mechanisms of deposition (i.e., pattern types), features of bloodstains, and a few other terms directed primarily toward training individuals in the science. Table 7.1 contains the various ASB terms separated into these three categories. "Bloodstain and pattern types" refer to those terms which would ultimately be used for classification purposes to describe mechanisms of deposition. "Features" are those terms which are visual characteristics of stains or patterns but which could be present within several patterns of differing mechanisms of deposition. "Miscellaneous terms" are those which are either largely restricted to training discussions (e.g., Accompanying drop) or the blood-bearing surface rather than the bloodstains (e.g., Target).

The following chapters will contain more thorough discussions on the specific types of bloodstains and bloodstain patterns; however, selecting the correct pattern type in the classification stage of the method always relies on an evaluation and understanding of the features of the bloodstains. The ASB terminology list contains some, but not all, possible features which could be observed in bloodstains at a scene or on evidence. For example, Figure 7.2 contains images of three circular bloodstains with very different edge characteristics. These edge characteristics are not only a function of both the forces involved at the time of impact as described in the chapter on fluid dynamics but also a function of the properties of the target surface (e.g., wettability

Table 7.1 Terminology in bloodstain pattern analysis

Bloodstain and pattern types	Features	Miscellaneous terms
Backspatter pattern	Altered stain	Accompanying drop
Bloodstain	Angle of impact	Target
Bloodstain pattern	Area of convergence	
Cast-off pattern	Area of origin	
Cessation pattern	Blood clot	
Drip pattern	Bubble ring	
Drip stain	Directionality	
Drip trail	Directional angle	
Expiration pattern	Edge characteristic	
Forward spatter pattern	Flow	
Impact pattern	Parent stain	
Insect stain	Perimeter stain	
Pool	Serum stain	
Projected pattern	Void	
Satellite stain	Wipe	
Saturation stain		
Spatter stain		
Splash pattern		
Swipe		
Transfer stain		

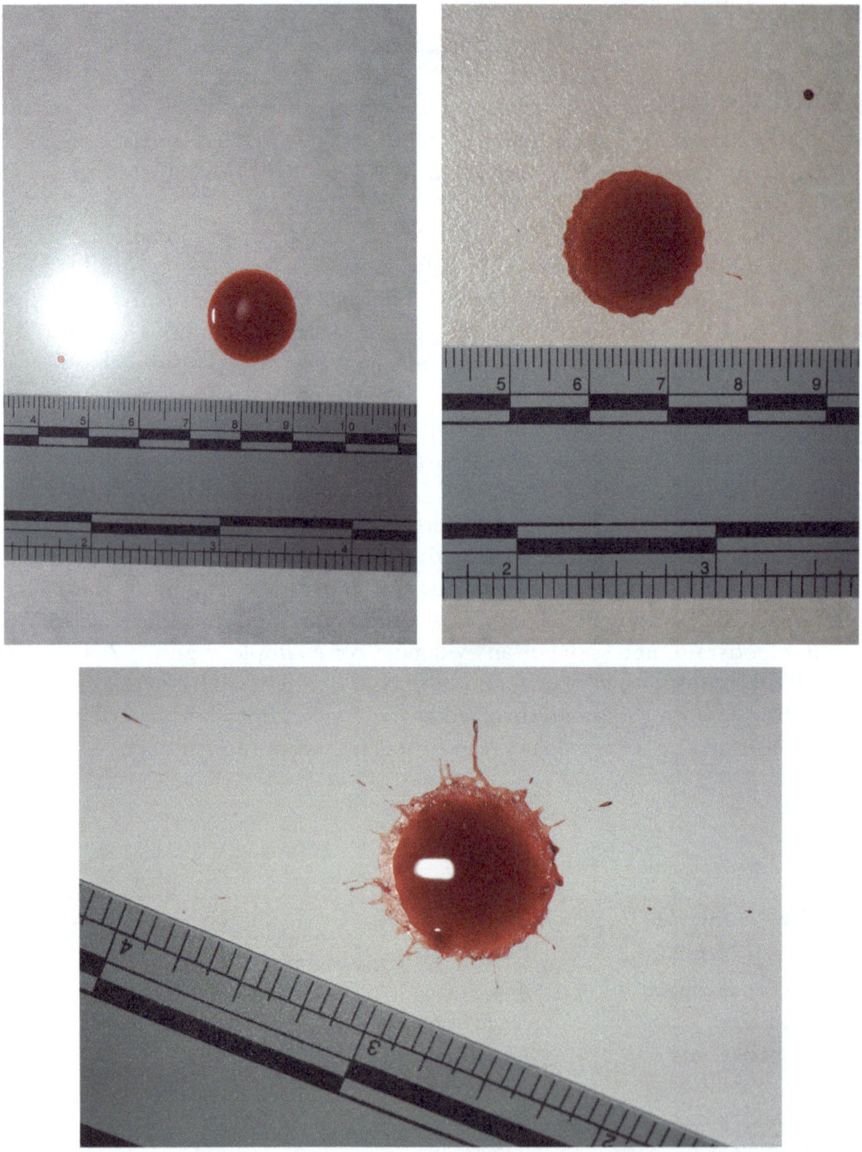

Figure 7.2 Different edge characteristics of circular bloodstains (a) smooth edges, (b) scalloped edges, and (c) spines or streaks.

and roughness). Analysts often describe these features as smooth edges (Figure 7.2a), scalloped edges (Figure 7.2b), and spines or streaks (Figure 7.2c). Although many prefer different descriptors for these edge characteristics, correct determination of the manner of deposition requires both a recognition of these specific edge characteristics and an understanding of how these edge characteristics correspond to concepts of fluid dynamics.

Other terms address changes which can occur in bloodstains after they were deposited. Referred to as altered stains, these stains have features which are the result of either a physical or biochemical change which has occurred in the blood.[26] These changes can occur when a portion of the blood is still liquid or after the stain has completely dried. Figures 7.3 and 7.4 both depict bloodstains where the center has been removed. When only the edges of the original bloodstain remain, this is called a perimeter stain. If the center was removed by movement of an object through the stain,

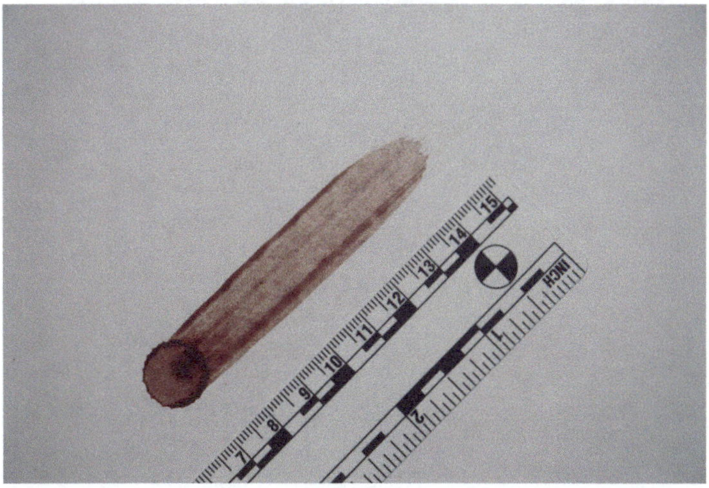

Figure 7.3 Circular bloodstain with a perimeter stain and features indicating the direction of the wiping movement.

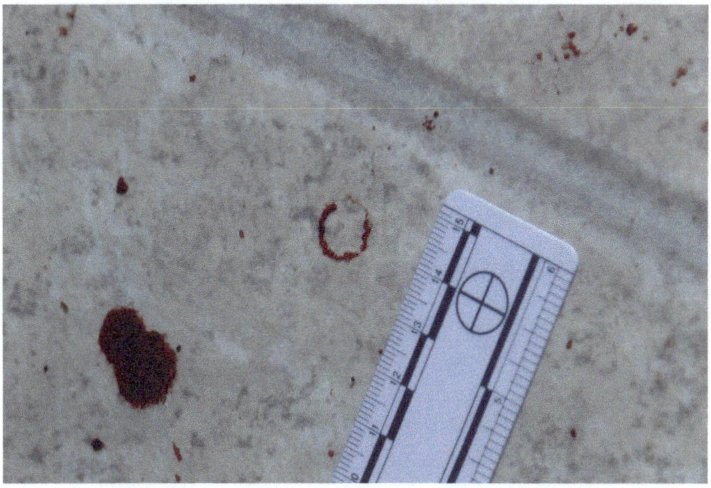

Figure 7.4 Perimeter stain where the center flaked away after drying.

the action pushes the remaining liquid blood along the target surface, as depicted in Figure 7.3. This form of alteration is referred to as a wipe.[27]

Biochemical changes can also occur in bloodstains after deposition. The primary change is the liquid portion of blood coagulating before it completely dries. This creates a blood clot, and in the case of larger pools on non-absorbent surfaces, serum separation (Figure 7.5). Forces can also be applied to clotted blood to create bloodstains which contain clotted blood at the time of deposition rather than developing after deposition.

Three other terms are related to situations when an airborne droplet strikes a surface at an inclined angle: directionality, angle of impact, and directional angle.[28] The directionality is determined by observing the "tail" or "spines" extending from a drop. These always extend in the direction the droplet was moving at the time of deposition. The angle of impact is the flight path of the droplet relative to the plane of the target surface. The directional angle is the flight path of the droplet relative to a plumb line on the target surface. Figure 7.6 depicts these concepts and they will be discussed in more detail in later chapters.

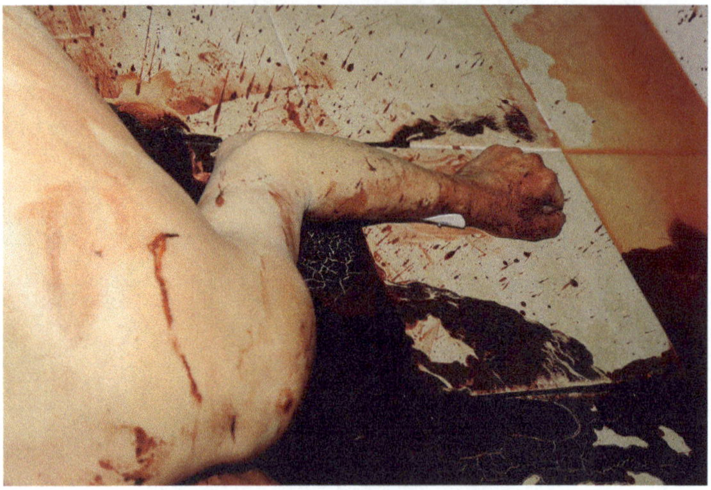

Figure 7.5 Blood pool which shows coagulation and serum separation while still liquid.

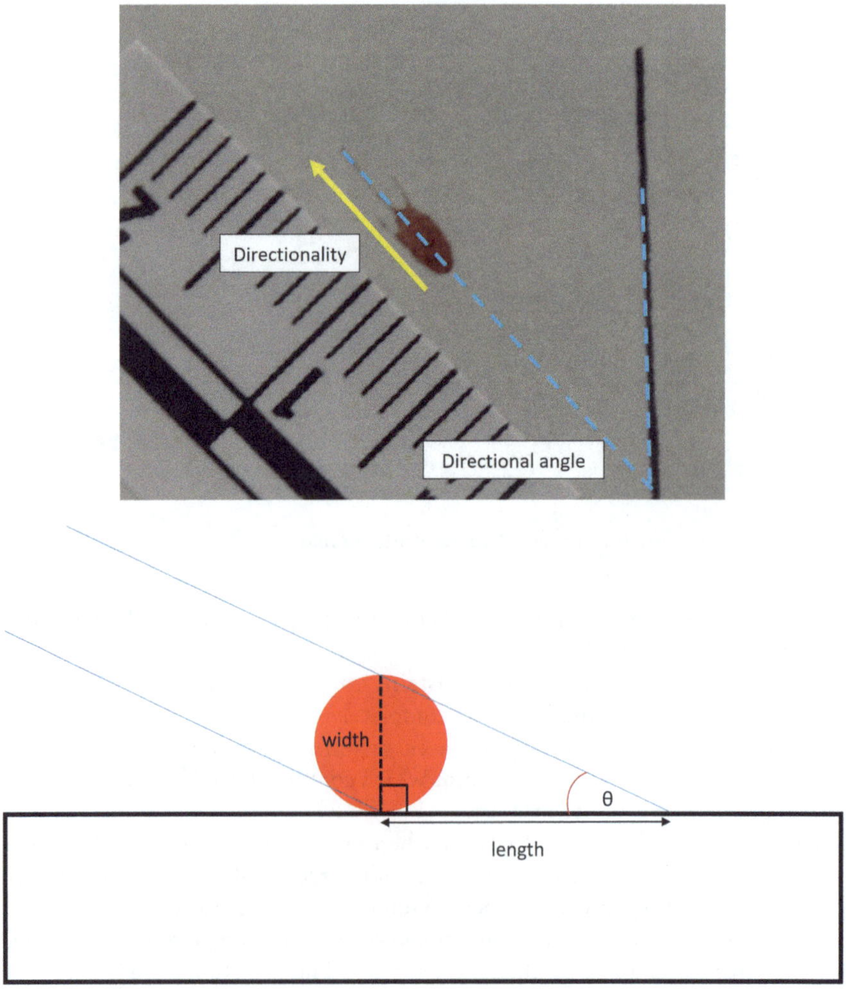

Figure 7.6 Directionality, directional angle, and angle of impact of a droplet in flight.

In addition to developing terms and definitions for bloodstains and bloodstain patterns, several past efforts have been made to place the various stains and patterns into different groups. This process of "grouping"-related items is referred to as taxonomy. The biological system of taxonomy developed by Carolus Linnaeus is a classic example of using features of organisms to place them in groups.[29] These groups progressed from a Domain down to a Species. By understanding the various groups, those familiar with biological classification can understand specific shared features of organisms placed within those groups. For example, if an organism is described to be in the Chordata phylum, it is known that at some point in its life cycle, it has developed a dorsal nerve cord.

The bloodstain community has taken various approaches to group the distinct bloodstain patterns. Over time, two primary approaches have come to the forefront: mechanism-based taxonomies and feature-based taxonomies.

Mechanism-based taxonomies group the various bloodstain patterns according to shared or similar actions which occurred to the liquid blood. For example, James, Kish, and Sutton, proposed three categories of bloodstains: passive, spatter, and transfer.[30] Bevel and Gardner also proposed three categories – spatter, non-spatter, and complex – before transitioning to a feature-based approach.[31] The classification system of Wonder had the primary categories of Spatter Groups, Spatters Not a Criteria, and Composites.[32]

As discussed in the chapter on fluid dynamics, the features of bloodstain patterns are directly related to the forces which are applied to liquid blood. Differences in the types of force applied, as well as the magnitude of those forces, affect these features. Table 7.2 contains a mechanism-based means of categorizing bloodstain patterns based upon the primary forces which are applied to liquid blood. This taxonomy shows some interesting relationships. For example, a drip stain and a splash pattern look very different even though the same forces are involved. Both are "a volume" of blood falling to the ground; however, because splash patterns contain a significantly larger volume of blood than a single droplet, significantly more kinetic energy is present within the falling blood which creates a splash pattern. The increased blood volume and kinetic energy are responsible for the significantly different features in a splash pattern. Additionally, an impact pattern and a backspatter pattern both are created when "an object" strikes a liquid source of blood. For a backspatter pattern, this object happens to be a projectile moving at a rapid speed.

Two stain types are absent from Table 7.2: satellite stains and spatter stains. Satellite stains are the result of secondary forces acting upon blood as it interacts with a target surface. Spatter stains are a broad category of stains which are simply the result of an external force being applied to liquid blood. This external force could be from another object, from an object's motion, or fluid forces.

Mechanism-based taxonomies have the advantage of being easily understood by analysts and non-analysts. This has been the traditional approach to categorizing the various bloodstain patterns and is a common approach used in teaching introductory courses. Despite these advantages, mechanism-based approaches toward categorizing bloodstains run the risk of developing a

Table 7.2 Categorizing bloodstain patterns based on the primary forces applied to liquid blood

Contact forces	Insect stain, transfer stain, swipe
Gravity	Drip pattern, drip stain, drip trail, pool, splash pattern
Forces from external objects	Backspatter pattern, forward spatter pattern, impact pattern
Forces from an object's motion	Cast-off pattern, cessation pattern
Fluid forces	Expiration pattern, projected pattern
Capillary forces	Saturation stain

top-down approach to evaluating patterns. The mechanism which created the pattern is emphasized first followed by a discussion of features within the pattern. This "top-down" approach with an emphasis on the mechanism rather than an emphasis on the features is susceptible to confirmation bias and other logical fallacies. As such, mechanism-based taxonomies are not suitable for scene work when attempting to classify a questioned bloodstain pattern.

The transition toward a feature-based taxonomy in BPA began with the work of Philippe Esperança. His bloodstain pattern identification key[33] provided a new approach toward evaluating and categorizing bloodstain patterns. He proposed a "bottom-up" approach toward bloodstain pattern evaluation with an emphasis on the features. His identification key follows a progression of features present within a pattern to lead to a decision regarding a manner of deposition. Following this development by Esperança, Bevel and Gardner published a Bloodstain Classification Decision Map of their own using the same general principles.[34] This bottom-up approach toward classification is better suited for scene work on questioned patterns.

Feature-based taxonomies also provide clarity regarding differences between different patterns which may not be obvious if one just used the definitions of the pattern types as a guide for classification. Consider the definitions below for drip stain, pool, and splash pattern as defined in the ASB Recommended Terminology list.[35]

- *Drip stain:* A bloodstain resulting from a falling drop that formed due to gravity
- *Pool:* A bloodstain resulting from an accumulation of liquid blood on a surface
- *Splash pattern:* A bloodstain pattern created from a large volume of liquid blood falling onto a surface

The definitions, while accurately describing *how* these patterns were created, contain an insufficient amount of information to differentiate between the three. As such, classifications which only use the definitions of patterns as the guide are inherently flawed. Feature-based taxonomies can highlight the specific features which allow for better differentiation between the three.

Two key concepts must be understood when developing and ultimately using any feature-based taxonomy. First, different mechanisms can create patterns which have very similar features. The taxonomy must recognize this and embrace the real (and common) possibility that a pattern simply does not have sufficient information within the features to limit the classification to a single pattern type. Second, bloodstain features are directly related to the target surface features. While surface roughness and wettability influence features to a degree, the most dramatic difference in bloodstain pattern features is between target surfaces which are non-absorbent and those which are absorbent. Figures 7.7 and 7.8 depict examples of two different feature-based taxonomies: one for non-absorbent target surfaces and one for absorbent surfaces like textiles. These taxonomies depict two different possible approaches to use features as a means of organizing and classifying the different patterns. While there are likely other valid feature-based taxonomies, they should all share similar themes.

Both taxonomies are constructed in the same manner. The broader classification of "bloodstain" contains multiple groups with broadly described features. Within the boundaries of these subgroups are various pattern types which may or may not be further grouped based on other specific features. At times, the most inner group contains a single pattern, but other times even the smallest group contains multiple pattern types. The organization of this taxonomy demonstrates how patterns created by different mechanisms can have very similar features. When looking closer at the taxonomy, there are times when a single pattern type appears more than once. This reflects how a single mechanism can create patterns with vastly different features.

Unlike mechanism-based taxonomies, feature-based taxonomies as depicted in Figures 7.7 and 7.8 could be used to guide classifications in casework. When progressing from a larger group to smaller group, all patterns contained within the boundaries of the larger group must be included as possible mechanisms unless they can be specifically excluded based on features or case-relevant information. For example, if a pattern is an irregularly shaped stain, greater than 30 mm wide, and

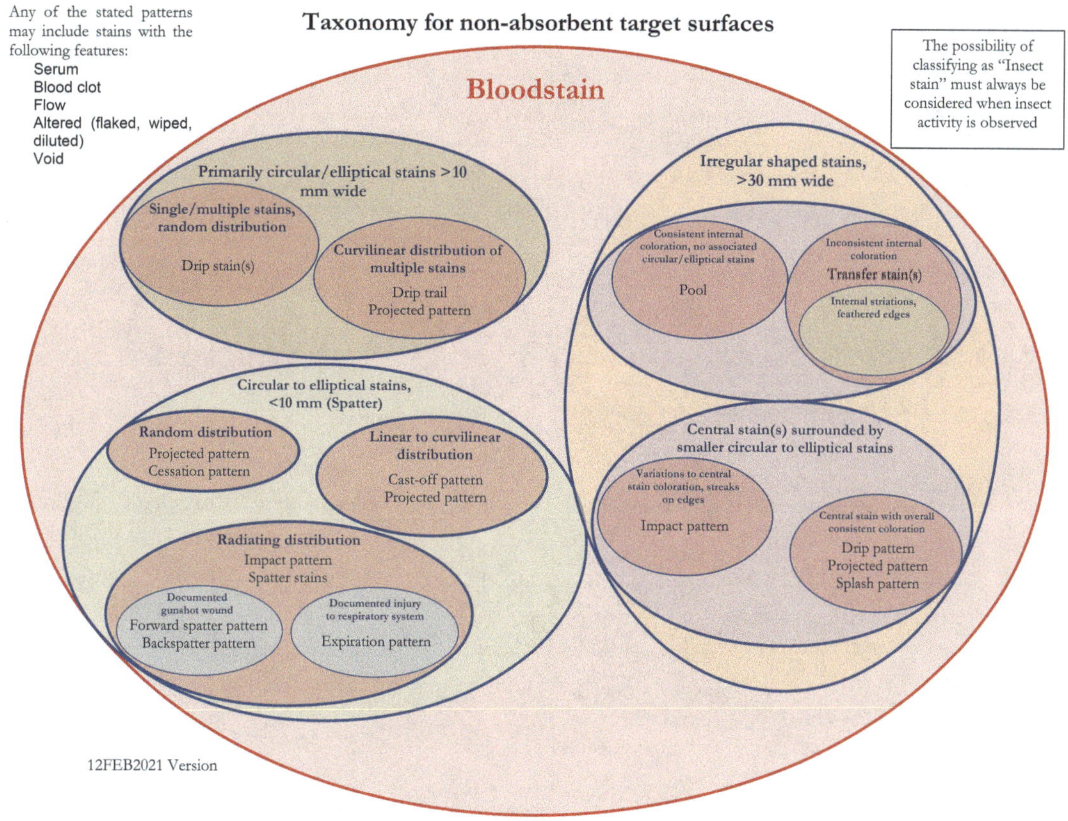

Figure 7.7 Possible feature-based taxonomy for bloodstains on non-absorbent surfaces.

is surrounded by smaller circular to elliptical stains, the analyst must consider impact patterns, drip patterns, projected patterns, and splash patterns as possibilities. If the central stain has consistent coloration, a feature indicating the central stain has not been disrupted, an impact pattern can be excluded; however, drip pattern, projected pattern, and splash pattern all must still be included as possibilities. If none of these can be excluded based on features or case-relevant information, then the final classification must include all three. For circular to elliptical stains on absorbent surfaces which are less than 5 mm wide, penetrate the fabric construction, and have a broad distribution, they may only have features sufficient to classify them as spatter. A more refined classification may not be possible. In fact, regardless of the nature of the target surface, there may be times when the classification is simply limited to "bloodstain."

Example 7.1

The image in Figure 7.9 will be used to demonstrate how the feature-based taxonomy in Figure 7.7 may be used. The primary stain on the floor is irregularly shaped and greater than 30 cm wide. This places the classification within the larger oval "Irregular shaped stains, >30 mm wide." Because numerous highly elliptical stains surround the larger stain, the classification continues to the "Central stain(s) surrounded by smaller circular to elliptical stains." This eliminates "Pool," "Transfer stain(s)," and "Swipe" as possibilities. Because the central stain has an inconsistent internal coloration as well as streaks on the edges, the classification can be further limited to "Impact pattern".

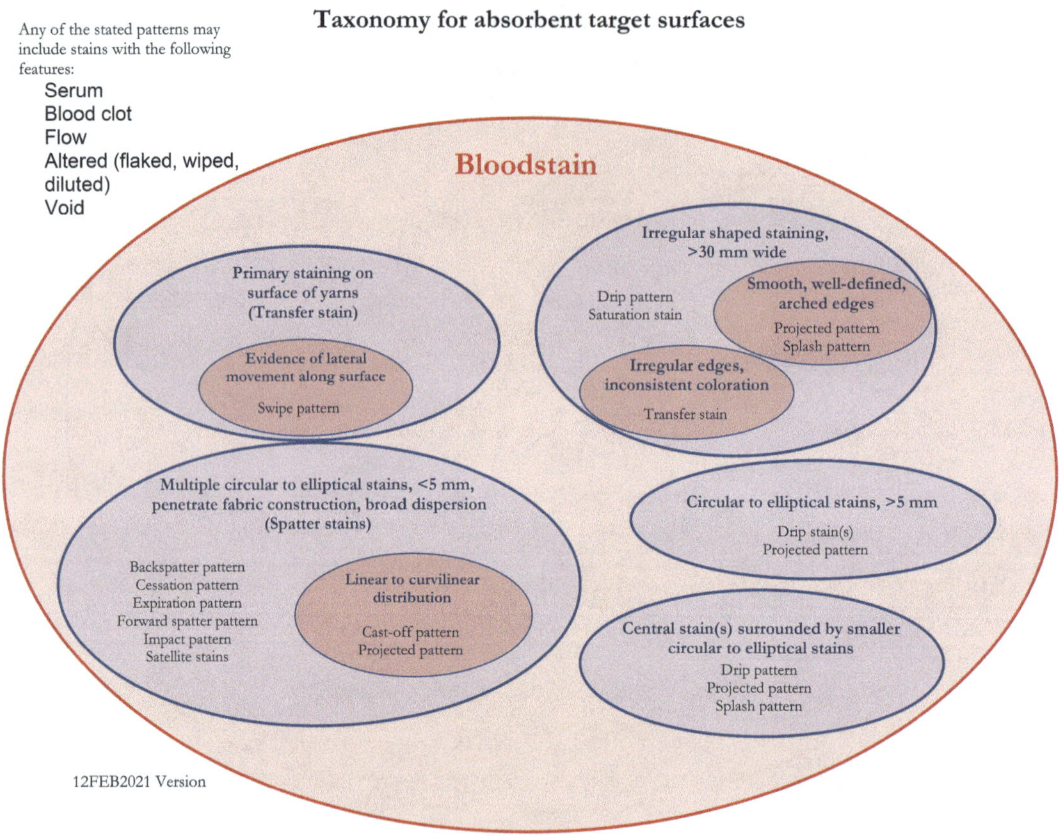

Figure 7.8 Possible feature-based taxonomy for bloodstains on absorbent surfaces such as textiles.

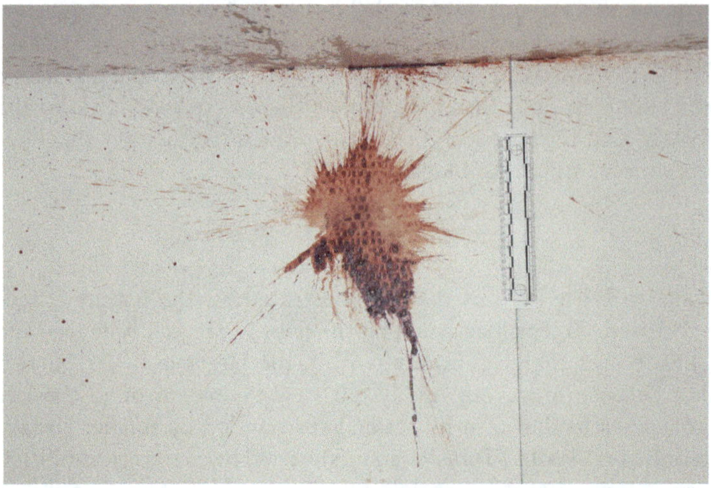

Figure 7.9 Bloodstain pattern on a non-absorbent, horizontal surface.

Example 7.2

The image in Figure 7.10 will be used to demonstrate how the feature-based taxonomy in Figure 7.8 may be used. The primary stain for pattern "B" is irregular in shape, larger than 30 mm wide, and the staining penetrates the construction of the fabric. This moves the classification to the "Irregular shaped staining, >30 mm wide" oval. The edges of the stain are both smooth and irregular. As such, all patterns within this oval are included within the initial classification – drip pattern, saturation stain, projected pattern, splash pattern, and transfer stain. The lack of circular to elliptical stains surrounding the parent stain could be used to exclude "drip pattern." While this is likely as far as the initial classification can progress, additional relevant case information (e.g., injury information) or adjacent patterns on the garment could potentially further refine this classification. It also may be that further refinement is not possible.

Although Figure 7.8 depicts an example of a feature-based taxonomy for absorbent surfaces like clothing, individuals using it as a guide to classify casework patterns must use extreme caution. Textiles like clothing are arguably the most complicated and challenging target surface to examine for BPA. The features of the patterns are affected by numerous factors such as fiber type, fabric construction, surface texture, chemical treatments to textiles, how the garment lays on the individual, and the three-dimensional nature of textiles while being worn. Additionally, research and published literature are only beginning to scratch the surface of our knowledge of how liquid blood interacts with textiles. The complicated nature of the target surface and a limited knowledge base are just two reasons why classifying bloodstains on textiles is extremely challenging. A more thorough discussion analyzing bloodstains on textiles is in Chapter 20. The proposed features in Figure 7.8 used for classification are largely generalities and there are numerous exceptions to the described features for the various patterns. The interaction of liquid blood on textiles still has many aspects which are not well understood. As such, the proposed taxonomy in Figure 7.8 is still a work in progress.

While feature-based approaches toward taxonomy can provide guidance with questioned bloodstain patterns, these approaches have their limitations. No feature-based classification can capture all possible features for all patterns on all target surfaces. The taxonomies will inherently be

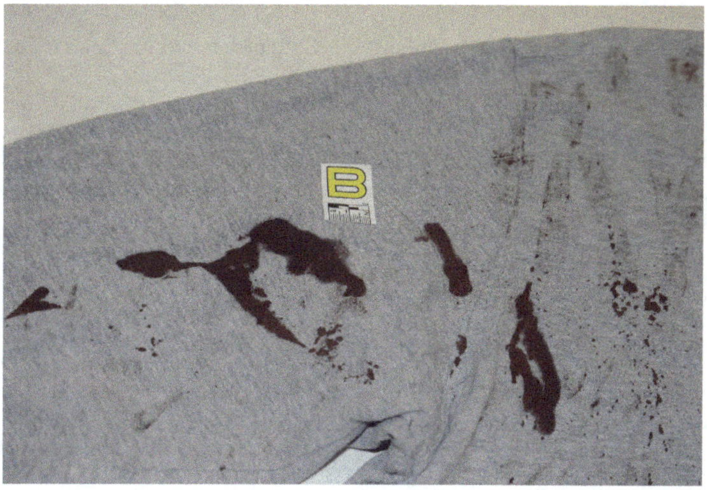

Figure 7.10 Bloodstain on the right sleeve of a sweatshirt.

limited to the most studied pattern–target surface combinations. Additionally, these taxonomies are not designed to be used as a guide for non-analysts. Because they do not contain the subtle features which differentiate two or more visually similar pattern types, feature-based taxonomies can only be used by individuals who have been trained to competency in BPA. As emphasized in the above paragraph, this is especially true for bloodstains on textiles.

The BPA community has made significant progress over the years in reducing the confusion over words and phrases used to describe the mechanisms which created specific stains or patterns. This progress has also resulted in the modification or abandonment of past terms based on a better understanding of how liquid blood responds to various forces. This refinement is a positive step. As discussed above, the manner in which the various pattern types are grouped continues to be modified as the community encourages the use of featured-based taxonomies which emphasize the features of the patterns rather than the mechanism. A solid understanding of these two concepts – terminology and taxonomy – is essential to developing a strong foundation for both interpreting bloodstains at scenes and effectively and accurately communicating these interpretations to others.

Notes

1. International Association for Identification, Bloodstain Pattern Identification Subcommittee, Proposed Terminology, 1993.
2. "BPA Terminology", https://bevelgardner.squarespace.com/s/BPATerminology.pdf (accessed 5/11/2021).
3. MacDonell, Herbert Leon, and Lorraine Fiske Bialousz. Flight characteristics and stain patterns of human blood. Washington, DC: National Institute of Law Enforcement and Criminal Justice, 1971.
4. Wonder, Anita Y. Blood dynamics. Academic Press, 2001.
5. "General Information on Bloodstain Pattern Analysis and Bloodstain Terminology," Royal Canadian Mounted Police Forensic Laboratory, Edmonton, Alberta.
6. Wonder, Anita Y. Blood dynamics. Academic Press, 2001.
7. Wonder, Anita Y. Blood dynamics. Academic Press, 2001.
8. Laber T.L. and Epstein B.P. "Experiments and Practical Exercises in Bloodstain Pattern Analysis," n.d.
9. "General Information on Bloodstain Pattern Analysis and Bloodstain Terminology," Royal Canadian Mounted Police Forensic Laboratory, Edmonton, Alberta.
10. International Association for Identification, Bloodstain Pattern Identification Subcommittee, Proposed Terminology, 1993.
11. International Association for Identification, Bloodstain Pattern Identification Subcommittee, Proposed Terminology, 1993.
12. J.L. Bunker, Blood Stain Evidence Manual, Vol. 3, Identification of stain and pattern characteristics. Doje's Press. 1998.
13. Eckert, William G., and Stuart H. James, eds. Interpretation of bloodstain evidence at crime scenes. CRC Press, 1998.
14. MacDonell H.L. Bloodstain patterns, 2nd edn. Golos Printing, New York, 2005.
15. J.L. Bunker, Blood Stain Evidence Manual, Vol. 3, Identification of Stain and Pattern Characteristics. Doje's Press. 1998.
16. International Association for Identification, Bloodstain Pattern Identification Subcommittee, Proposed Terminology, 1993.
17. Eckert, William G., and Stuart H. James, eds. Interpretation of bloodstain evidence at crime scenes. CRC Press, 1998.
18. MacDonell H.L. Bloodstain patterns, 2nd edn. Golos Printing, New York. 2005.
19. Eckert, William G., and Stuart H. James, eds. Interpretation of bloodstain evidence at crime scenes. CRC Press, 1998.
20. "General Information on Bloodstain Pattern Analysis and Bloodstain Terminology," Royal Canadian Mounted Police Forensic Laboratory, Edmonton, Alberta.
21. National Research Council. Strengthening forensic science in the United States: a path forward. National Academies Press, 2009.

22. National Research Council. Strengthening forensic science in the United States: a path forward. National Academies Press, 2009.
23. Scientific Working Group on Bloodstain Pattern Analysis (SWGSTAIN), and the United States of America. "Scientific Working Group on Bloodstain Pattern Analysis: Recommended Terminology." 2009. https://www.fbi.gov/about-us/lab/forensic-science-communications/fsc/april2009/standards/2009_04_standards01.htm
24. MacDonell, Herbert Leon, and Lorraine Fiske Bialousz. Flight characteristics and stain patterns of human blood. Washington, DC: National Institute of Law Enforcement and Criminal Justice, 1971.
25. Organization of Scientific Area Committees for Forensic Science. "Terms and definitions in bloodstain pattern analysis. ASB Technical Report 033." 2017.
26. Organization of Scientific Area Committees for Forensic Science. "Terms and definitions in bloodstain pattern analysis. ASB Technical Report 033." 2017.
27. Organization of Scientific Area Committees for Forensic Science. "Terms and definitions in bloodstain pattern analysis. ASB Technical Report 033." 2017.
28. Organization of Scientific Area Committees for Forensic Science. "Terms and definitions in bloodstain pattern analysis. ASB Technical Report 033." 2017.
29. Linnaeus, Carolus. Systema naturae. Vol. 1, no. Part 1. Laurentii Salvii: Stockholm, 1758.
30. James, Stuart H., Paul E. Kish, and T. Paulette Sutton. Principles of bloodstain pattern analysis: theory and practice. CRC Press, 2005.
31. Bevel, Tom, and Ross M. Gardner. Bloodstain pattern analysis: with an introduction to crime scene reconstruction, 2nd edition. CRC Press, 2001.
32. Wonder, Anita Y. Blood dynamics. Academic Press, 2001.
33. Esperança, Philippe. Bloodstain Pattern Identification Key. 2019. http://l-a-c.expert/wp-content/uploads/2019/01/Bloodstain_Pattern_Identification_Key_Philippe_Esperanca.pdf
34. Bevel, Tom, and Ross M. Gardner. Bloodstain pattern analysis with an introduction to crime scene reconstruction, 3rd edition. CRC Press, 2008.
35. Organization of Scientific Area Committees for Forensic Science. "Terms and definitions in bloodstain pattern analysis. ASB Technical Report 033." 2017.

CHAPTER 8

DRIPPING BLOOD

Stains, Patterns, and Trails

Rosalyn Rough

INTRODUCTION

In the field of bloodstain pattern analysis (BPA), drip stains, drip trails, and drip patterns refer to bloodstains or bloodstain patterns where the predominant action causing these stains is the formation of a falling blood drop or drops due to gravity. Often, blood found at a scene is the result of blood dripping from objects. These drops can occur in a variety of ways. Blood can drip from a wound, a weapon, clothing, hair, or from any other surface where sufficient blood has accumulated to form the drops.

A *drip stain* refers to an individual stain that results when a blood drop that formed due to gravity falls and lands onto a target surface. Drip stains are commonly deposited onto horizontal surfaces such as floors and pavements, but can also be deposited onto vertical surfaces close to a bleeding source. Drip stains can also be deposited onto the clothing of the bleeder as well as other individuals in close contact.

A *drip trail* is merely a combination of individual drip stains linked by a common blood source moving between two points. These are generally observed on horizontal surfaces at scenes. For instance, a person with a bleeding injury may deposit several drip stains on the floor as they walk along it, resulting in a drip trail.

A *drip pattern* is defined as a bloodstain pattern resulting from a liquid that has dripped into another liquid, at least one of which is blood.[1] Drip patterns are usually formed by a person bleeding onto a surface for a period of time, depositing multiple blood drops on the same area. The resultant blood drips overlap and pool to create a larger accumulation of blood. Although blood dripping into itself is the most common scenario at scenes, other liquids can be involved, such as rain falling into a preexisting wet bloodstain or blood drops falling into a pool of liquid such as water already present on a surface. In cases of blood interacting with a different liquid, it is likely the drip pattern will appear paler and dilute compared to a blood into blood drip pattern.

Drip stains and drip trails are useful for indicating movement of a bloodied object or bleeding person through the scene. Conversely, a drip pattern is useful for indicating that the source of the drops has become stationary depositing blood drops into the same localized area for a period of time.

BLOOD BEHAVIOR DURING DRIP STAIN FORMATION

The mechanical process relating to the formation of blood drops has been covered in detail in Chapter 5. As described in this chapter, the primary force causing separation of the blood from the source is weight. The body of blood flows to the lowest position on the surface of the object

DOI: 10.4324/9781003163695-8

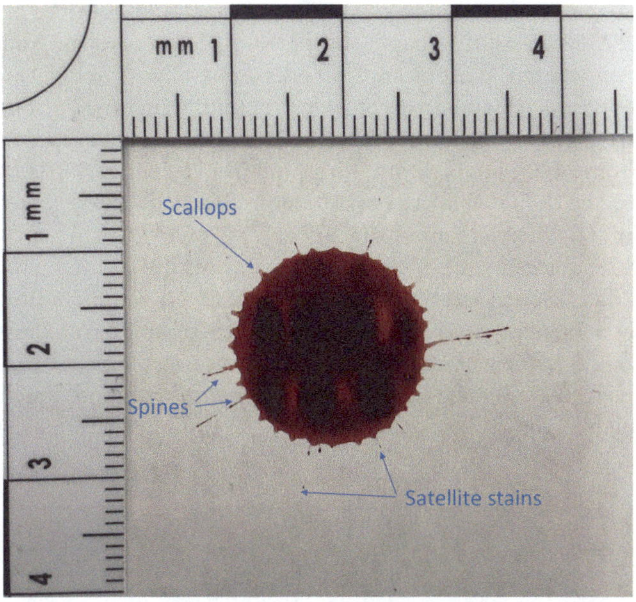

Figure 8.1 Drip stain displaying scallops, spines, and satellite stains formed when the falling drop impacted the target surface.

extends into a downward moving neck which then pinches off creating a primary drop. Sometimes smaller drops are formed as the neck breaks in multiple places (referred to as accompanying drops). The drop falls and as it lands onto the target surface, the drop collapses and spreads, as described in Chapter 5, resulting in individual stains.

The force created by the drop impacting the target surface causes the blood to spread with outward acceleration. As the blood reaches its maximum spread, a rim is formed at the boundary which then retracts back into the film of liquid blood. Simple spreading results in a regular edged stain as the rim is not disrupted. If there is enough outward acceleration, the rim is disrupted and splashing can occur. Mild splashing results in small fingers forming from the rim, and stronger splashing results in small droplets being released from these fingers. These fingers and droplets result in scallops, spines, and small satellite spatter stains around the final parent stain. Scallops describe the irregular wavy protrusions on the edge of the stain. Spines describe the thin protrusions extending from the parent stain boundary. Satellite stains are small stains which have fully detached from the parent stain (Figure 8.1).

Increasing the force of the impacting drop increases the chance of it splashing upon impact. This can be achieved in two ways: by increasing the size of the drop or the distance that it falls (thus increasing the velocity).[2] The other major influence that determines whether a drop will splash on impact is the roughness of the target surface, with rougher surfaces creating more disruption of the rim and more splashing.[3] A decrease in the stain diameter is also observed when the surface roughness increases.[4]

FEATURES OF A DRIP STAIN

Drip stains are characterized as single stains which are circular or roughly circular on horizontal surfaces and usually range 10–20 mm in diameter on a dry non-porous surface. The smaller diameter accompanying drops can result in smaller diameter stains close by or can be absorbed by the primary stain if the drop lands on top of it. The size of the drip stain is influenced by the size of the initial primary drop, the impact velocity, and the features of the surface it impacts.

The size of the initial drop depends on the surface characteristics of the object (material, coatings such as dirt, and roughness), the shape (sharpness, surface curvature), and the rate of flow of blood onto the location where the drops are formed.[5] Generally speaking, thin or sharply tapered objects such as knives produce blood drops of lower volumes than broader shaped objects such as a baseball bat. Typically, blood drops formed from everyday objects can range in size from 4.15 mm diameter (dripping from a knife) to 6.15 mm (dripping from a cylinder).[5] As the volume of a single blood drop increases, the diameter of the resultant stain will increase (providing the drops fall from the same height and onto the same surface).

Increasing the fall distance increases the velocity and results in more spreading of the blood on the impacting surface. So, a faster-moving drop of a given volume will create a larger stain. However, the diameter increase is asymptotic, that is, the diameter of the stain increases with velocity until it reaches a point when the increase becomes very small. At this stage, the drop is nearing its terminal velocity and a maximum stain diameter is reached. Smaller drops have lower terminal velocities than larger drops, so a maximum stain diameter is reached earlier for smaller drops (Figure 8.2).

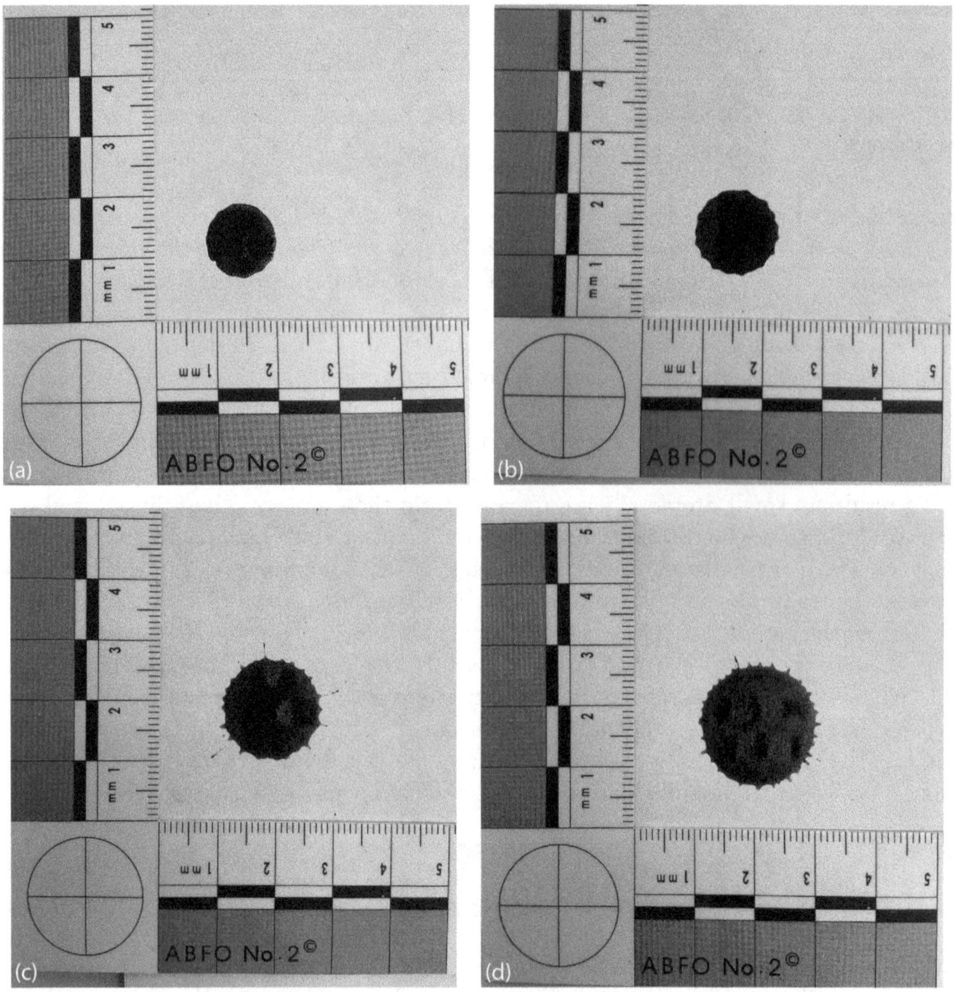

Figure 8.2 Drip stains formed dripping off a pipette at various heights above the card target. (a) Distance = 10 cm (~11 mm diameter), (b) Distance = 25 cm (~13 mm diameter), (c) Distance = 50 cm (~16 mm diameter), and (d) Distance = 200 cm (~19 mm diameter).

Depending on the strength of the splashing when the blood drop impacts the surface, scallops, spines, and satellite stains can be formed around the parent drip stain. The appearance of the resultant stain is also influenced by the surface it lands on as this directly effects the amount of splashing on impact. Smooth dry non-porous surfaces tend to result in the least splashing and produce smooth-edged and circular stains. Rough surfaces restrict spreading and therefore cause larger disruptions during the rim formation resulting in smaller and more irregular-shaped stains with increasing associated spines and satellite stains.[3] Absorbent surfaces such as carpet also result in smaller stain diameters as the volume of blood is absorbed into the structure of the textile rather than spreading on the surface[6] (Figure 8.3).

Previous research into the minimum size drops and the resultant stain formation has shown that the minimum volume required for a drop to form based on gravity (and some minor oscillations due to movement) was 0.008 ml which equated to approximately 3-mm diameter drop.[7] When

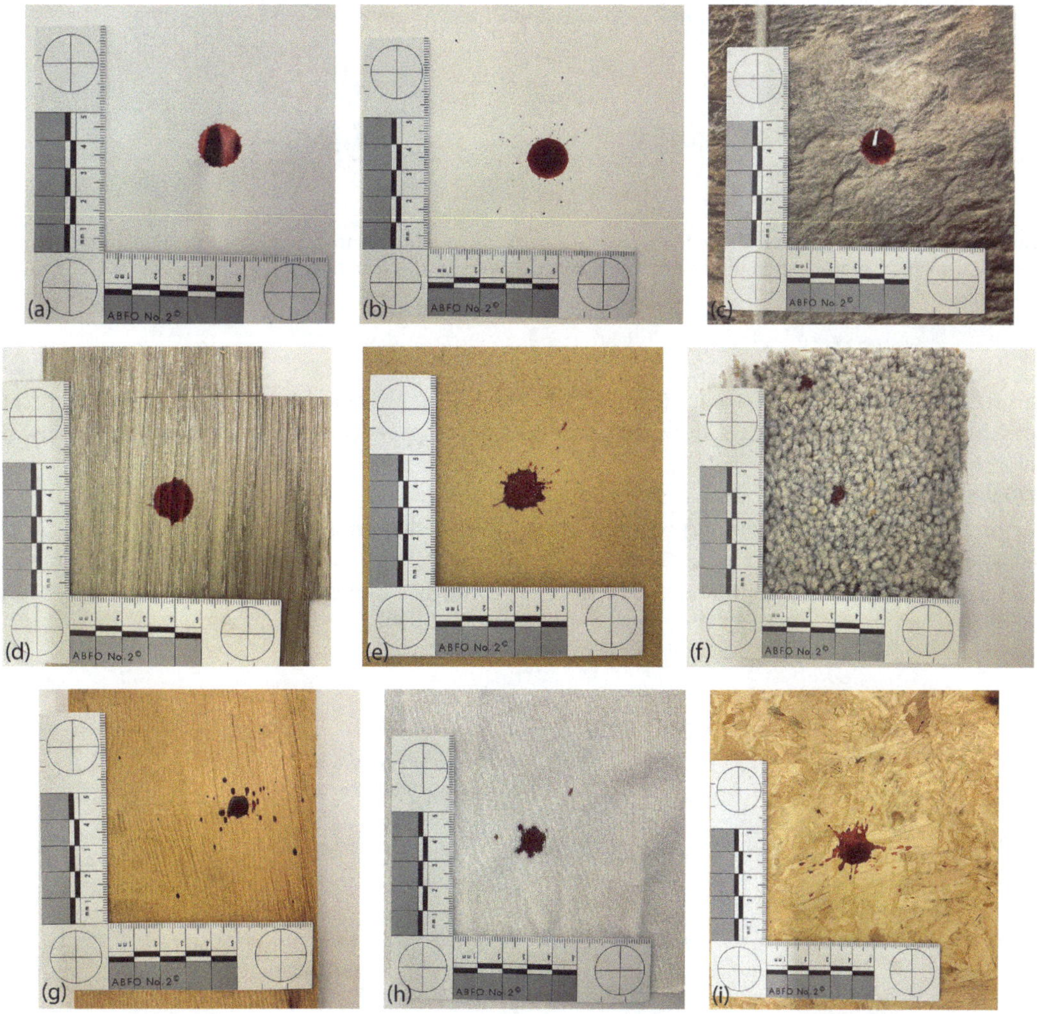

Figure 8.3 Images of drip stains formed under the same conditions (falling from a pipette at 50 cm from the target). The differences in the visual characteristics of the stains are due to the effects of the target surface. Note the variety in sizes and shapes and splashing created. (a) Paper, (b) cardstock, (c) linoleum, (d) laminate floor, (e) rough sandpaper, (f) carpet, (g) wood, (h) knitted polyester/cotton fabric, and (i) cork floor tile.

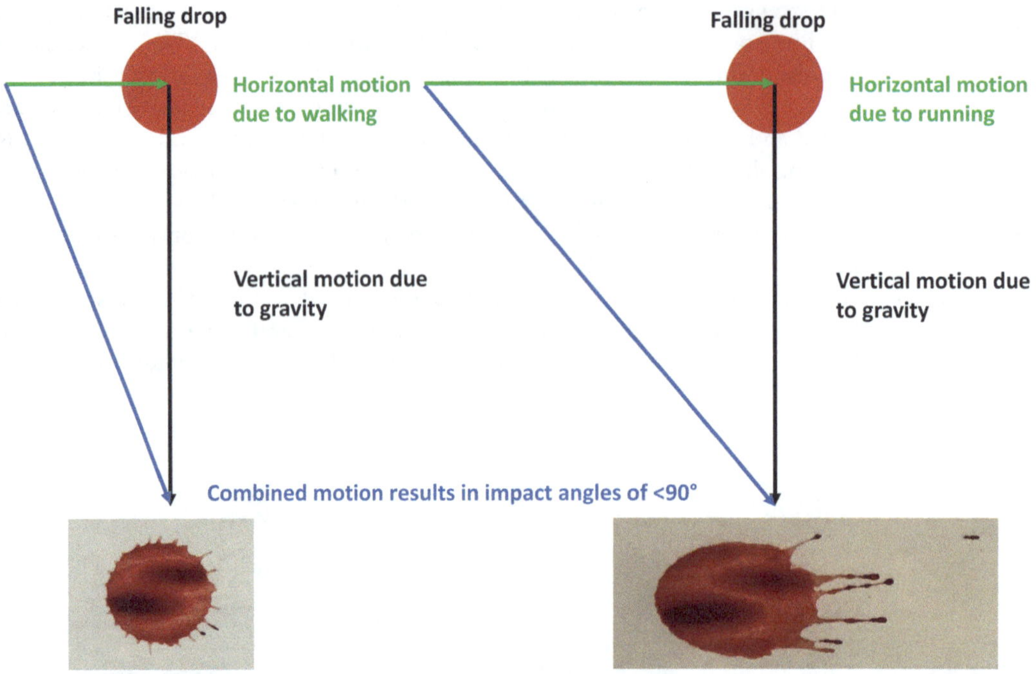

Figure 8.4 Schematic diagram showing resultant velocity vectors for falling drops with horizontal motion onto a horizontal surface. Note that as the horizontal velocity increases, the resulting impact angle decreases, forming more elliptical stains.

this sized drop fell a short distance (3 in. or 7.6 cm), the resultant stain size on a horizontal surface was always greater than 4 mm in diameter except on carpet where the smallest stain was always greater than 3 mm.

On a horizontal surface, drops falling with some horizontal motion (such as dripping from a person that is walking or running) will result in elliptical-shaped stains due to the impacting angle being less than 90°. Any irregularities such as scallops, spines, or satellite stains will be formed at the terminal edge of the stain and can be a reliable indication of direction of motion (Figures 8.4 and 8.5).

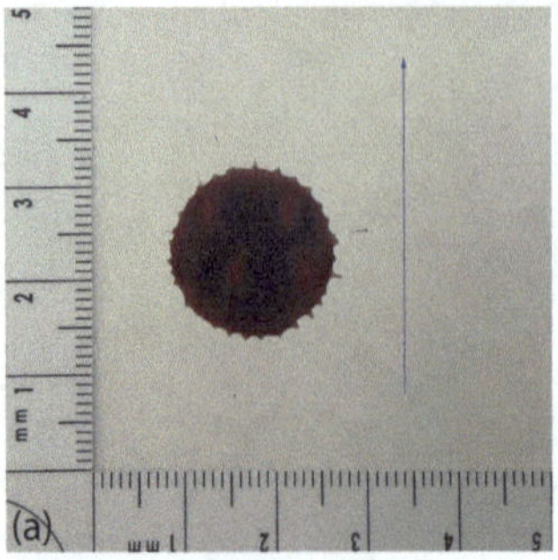

Slow walk
Scallops around entire edge of stain
No obvious directionality

Figure 8.5 Drip stains from a pipette formed during a slow walk, brisk walk, and running motion. Direction of travel is noted by the blue arrows. Note the directionality features in the stains become more pronounced (and therefore more reliable) with increasing velocity. *(Continued)*

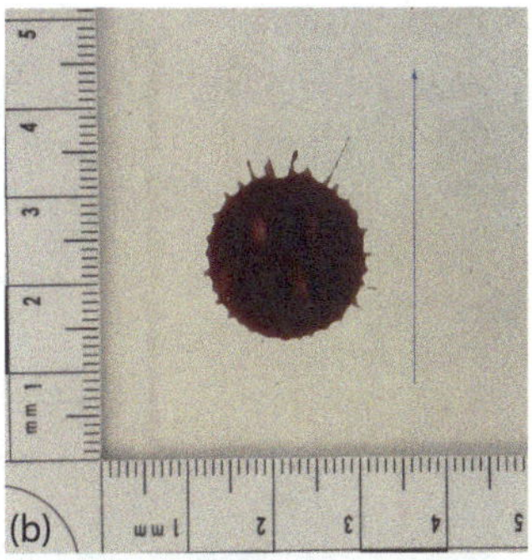

Brisk walk
Decreased scalloping on leading edge
More defined spines in line of travel
Directionally is clearer

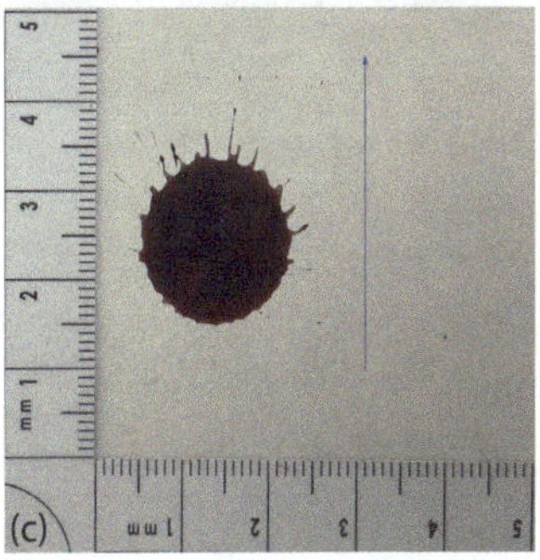

Run
No scalloping on leading edge
Well-defined spines in the direction of travel
Directionality is obvious

Figure 8.5 *(Continued)*

Drips with some horizontal motion can also impact vertical surfaces such as walls, doors, and fences. On these surfaces, the falling drops form large elliptical stains, typically greater than 7 mm in diameter. Directionality of these stains should always be downward if falling from gravity alone (gamma angle greater than 90° and less than 270°).

As discussed in Chapter 4, increasing elongation of the bloodstains is observed with decreasing angles of impact. That is, as the angle becomes more oblique or glancing, the subsequent stain becomes longer and narrower. As such, singular elongated elliptical downward directional stains on horizontal surfaces such as walls, etc. are likely to be drip stains.

DRIP TRAIL

The same characteristics and influencing factors that apply to drip stains apply to a drip trail. As a trail covers a distance between two points (Figure 8.6), there is the opportunity for the target surfaces to change. When this does, there is an expectation that the appearance of the stains will change as the size, shape, and amount of satellite stains and spines are influenced by the target surface. For instance, a trail of drip stains that crosses smooth tiled floor, then carpet, and then an outside surface such as a concrete path will result in quite different looking stains for each surface. Understanding the factors that influence the features of drip stains will enable the analyst to have some confidence in attributing these stains to the same pattern even though the appearance is varied.

As discussed, directionality in the drip stains is more likely to be observed when there is greater horizontal movement resulting in more elliptical-shaped stains with spines and satellite stains which define the terminal stain edge. So, for a slow-moving person or object dripping onto a smooth surface or an absorbent surface, it may be difficult to establish directionality of the trail by the stain features alone.

Figure 8.6 Example of drip trail on wooden floor in hallway. Close-up of drip stains near front door.

The source of the blood causing the drip stains is usually a bloodstained object or an individual with a bleeding injury. The number of drip stains present may indicate which of these is more likely. The amount of blood that can adhere to the surface of an object is restricted to a finite volume, thus limiting the number of stains that can be created. A bleeding injury can be regarded as a replenishing source of blood (until the bleeding is stemmed), so it has the potential to generate more drip stains, and potentially longer drip trails.

For a regularly dripping object (or person), the faster the object travels, the greater the distance there will be between stains. As the rate of dripping will never be known by the analyst, the speed the object was traveling cannot be estimated with any accuracy. However, the relative speed may be able to be derived, particularly if there is a significant change in distance between stains during the drip trail. For example, if the distance between drip stains decreases suddenly, then this may suggest the bleeding person or object has slowed down.

BLOOD BEHAVIOR DURING DRIP PATTERN FORMATION

As described in Chapter 5, when a falling blood drop lands on a surface covered in a shallow film of liquid blood, the splashing process is modified. A raised rim is formed which is a combination of the liquid from the collapsing drop as well as liquid from the preexisting film on the surface. The raised rim forms fingers which break up into satellite drops which create satellite stains on nearby surfaces. A drop which is too small or too slow to splash on a dry surface may splash on a wet surface; therefore, the expectation is that more satellite stains are created when a drop impacts a surface wet with blood compared to a dry surface. As further drops fall into the same area, a dense pattern of satellite stains is generated.

The formation of the satellite stains occurs at two different stages of the drip pattern formation. As the impacting primary drop collapses, the rim expands, and the first satellite droplets are released from the ends of the rim. These initial satellite drops are small and are released from the growing ends of the rim with outward pressure and travel further distances than subsequent satellite droplets. As these droplets are small and have a longer flight path; by the time they land on a target surface, they have usually formed spherical shapes and therefore create elliptical and circular stains which display directionality upon landing on a target.

Once the primary drop has collapsed into the liquid film, the surface tension of the blood retracts the rim and fingers. Satellite droplets formed during the retraction process are usually larger and have lower velocities than the initial droplets released. They are often irregular in shape and do not have time to retract into a sphere before landing. These satellite droplets often tumble in flight before falling close to the parent stain due to their irregular shapes and low outward force. As these droplets have low volume and low velocities, they do not spread very much once they land on a target; hence they often have raised profiles and can appear darker in color (due to the high concentration of hemoglobin in the area of the stain) compared to other small spatter stains.

FEATURES OF DRIP PATTERN

Blood drops repeatedly falling onto the same surface result in an accumulation of blood forming a larger central stain that is irregular in shape, but often with a continuous margin. Individual drip stains can be observed close to the central stain or overlapping at the edge. Small circular, elliptical, and irregular-shaped satellite spatter stains are usually distributed in a dense pattern, 360° around the periphery of the central stain on a horizontal surface and are also deposited onto vertical surfaces if nearby (Figure 8.7). The size of the satellite stains is usually <1–3 mm in diameter.

Satellite stains close to the central parent stain often display irregular shapes, non-coherent directionalities, and can have raised profiles (on smooth surfaces). Satellite stains further away from the central stain display more typical regular elliptical shapes and display directionality extending away from the large central stain. Satellite stains close to the central parent stain are usually larger in size and number, with the smaller satellite stains being further out and sparser on the periphery of the pattern.

The patterning of deposition of satellite stains on vertical surfaces can be described as "bow tied" or U-shaped depending on the distance the vertical surface is from the central stain. The pattern often has a distinct boundary within which most of the stains are located. The lowest height of this

Figure 8.7 Examples of drip patterns. (a) Small drip pattern on carpet with satellite stains on shelving. (b) Bird's-eye view of drip pattern on floor near cupboard door. Note drip stains on top edge of door.

boundary is located perpendicular to the location of the blood pool (the least distance), with the height of the boundary increasing as the stains are deposited further out from the center. A maximum height will be reached and then the height of the boundary will drop again as the distance further increases. This patterning is due to the satellite droplets being created under very similar conditions (being formed from repeated drops of blood impacting the target surface), which result in them having less variation in their flight trajectories compared to other spatter creating mechanisms, such as impact or expiration. At the center of the pattern, the vertical target is close enough to interrupt the upward trajectory path of the droplets resulting in the lowest height in the pattern boundary. Increasing the distance of the target from the source, by spreading outward, increases the height the droplet reaches in flight before it hits the target, until the maximum height of the flight path is achieved (this is represented by the highest portion of the boundary). Further away still, the droplets will then be on the downward trajectory path, thus landing on the vertical target at lower heights. This effect results in a "bow-tie"-shaped stain patterning (Figures 8.8 and 8.9).

Increasing the volume or height of the primary drops will increase the number of satellite drops created and the distance they can travel, resulting in more stains and a larger pattern of satellite stains. Increasing the number of drops will also lead to an increase in satellite stains formed as well as an increase to the central parent bloodstain size.[8]

The satellite stains that form can be deposited onto a range of surfaces near to the accumulated parent bloodstain, including footwear and clothing of individuals close by. It is possible that if the blood drops fall from a very low height, no splashing and hence no satellite stains are formed around the central stain.

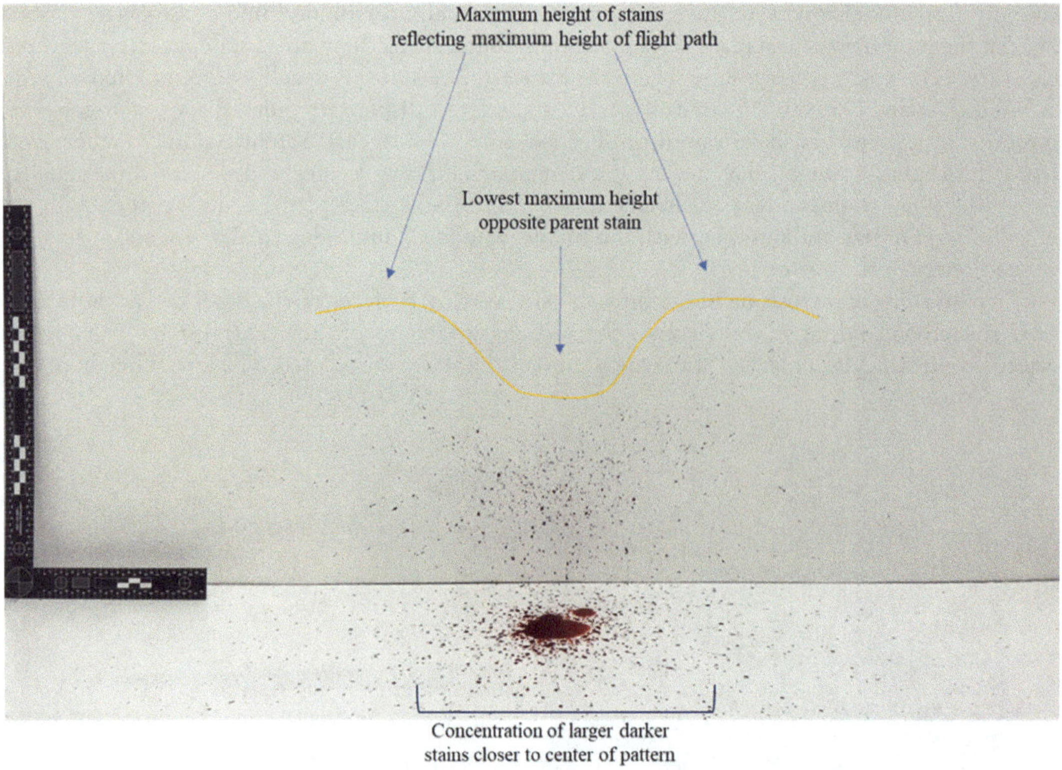

Figure 8.8 Laboratory-created drip pattern. Falling drops generated from a pipette at a height of 100 cm onto card surface. Distance from vertical surface is approximately 10 cm. Note the U-shaped distribution of satellite stains (boundary outlined in orange) on the wall with the lowest height perpendicular to the blood pool. A more dense patterning of stains is observed close to the blood source, with more sparse distribution further out.

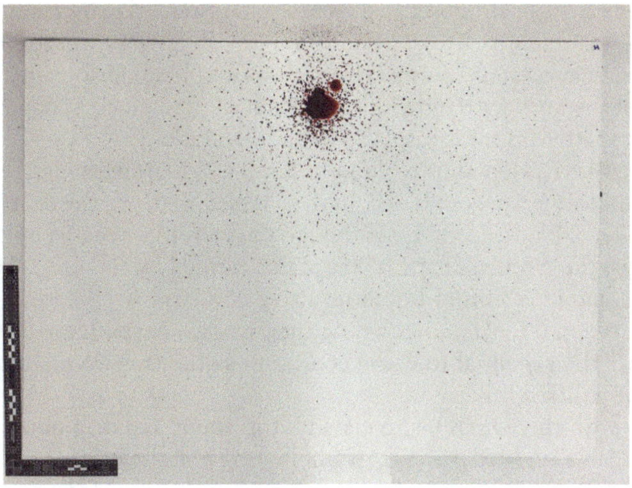

Figure 8.9 Bird's-eye view of the horizontal surface of drip pattern in Figure 8.8. Note the large, darker, and more irregular-shaped satellite stains closer to the center of the pattern.

TEXTILES

Different textiles have different properties and influence the formation of the drip stains differently. It has been noted that drip stains on fabrics can appear distorted, with this being attributed to the absorbency of the fabric and the rough texture.[9] Further research has noted that parent stains on some fabrics were not circular and were larger in the warp or wale direction, preferentially staining along the grain of the fabric.[10] Some very absorbent textiles result in smaller stains as the volume of blood is absorbed into the structure of the textile rather than spreading over its surface.[6] Increasing roughness of the textile results in an increase in satellite stains which can also result in smaller parent stains as less volume becomes available.[11] Some fabrics are designed to wick liquids away from the wearer. Wicking is a form of capillary action in fabrics. Drip stains formed on these types of fabrics often form larger stains sizes than would form on a non-porous surface.[12] Furthermore, the shape can be influenced by movement of the blood through the fabric after the initial collapse and spread of the drop, including preferential wicking along one portion of the fabric. This can result in non-circular stains being formed from vertical impacts with the shape of the final stains bearing little resemblance to the initial stain.[13]

The use of a stereo microscope is recommended when examining bloodstains on textiles to assist with visualizing all the features of the stains.[14] The influence of textiles on the characteristics of bloodstains is detailed further in Chapter 20.

LIMITATIONS/DISCUSSION

Drip stains and drip patterns have historically been categorized differently by different classification systems. James et al. (2005)[15] classified drip stains, trails, and patterns under their "passive" category based on the conditions that only passive bleeding and gravity are at play during their formation. The resulting small satellite stains, however, are classified under their spatter category (secondary mechanism). This has the potential for confusion as the two major components of these patterns (the large stain and the surrounding satellite stains) are rated under different categories.

Bevel and Gardner (2008)[16] proposed a different bloodstain classification taxonomy with two major classes – spatter and non-spatter; spatter stains are defined as where the primary stains are elliptical and circular-shaped stains formed from drops of blood. Drip stains are therefore classified under the spatter category with individual drip stains categorized as non-linear, and drip trails categorized as linear spatter (as trails display a linear orientation).

Drip patterns (described as blood into blood in Bevel and Gardner's classification map) are categorized into the non-spatter category based on the characteristics of the central stain which forms due to an accumulation of blood drops. Even though the pattern is created by the same mechanism of falling blood drops, the circular shape of the stains formed by the drops is either lost or never formed as the drops land on a film of liquid resulting in a large irregular-shaped stain. The non-spatter classification is noted for "not precluding the presence of spatter associated to the primary stain." Again, this has the potential to cause confusion as the two major components of the drip pattern are categorized differently.

An issue can arise with these systems to classify drip stains and drip patterns, if only a portion of the pattern is available for analysis. For example, it is not obvious for either system where to categorize satellite stains created from a drip pattern in the absence of the parent stain. A drip pattern consisting only of the satellite stains can occur if the target that was dripped onto is cleaned, moved, or altered. Such situations could include a mat or rug, being moved or removed from scene, or a shelf or table being tipped over after being bled on. If a person bleeds onto the tops of their shoes either while walking or in a stationary position before leaving the scene, numerous satellite stains may be deposited on surrounding surfaces with no evidence of a central parent stain. Another issue can arise when examining clothing worn by an individual who was standing nearby the creation of a drip pattern. Again, the satellite stains can be deposited onto the clothing and footwear of a bystander. Typically, these stains land on the footwear and lower legs when dripping occurs onto the floor or ground; however, if the drip pattern was formed elsewhere (such as bleeding onto a bench or table), the location of the satellite stains on the bystanders clothing may be in a location that is unexpected.

Satellite stains formed from drip stains or the repeated dripping of blood onto a surface are not always an obvious consideration when evaluating patterns of small spatter stains. In the absence of the parent stain, these spatter stains may be overlooked as satellite spatter and wrongly attributed as being formed from a higher energy event such as impact or expiration due to their small size. This may explain why this pattern type has a high rate of misclassification under previous reliability studies.[17]

Therefore, caution should be taken when analyzing bloodstain patterns that may involve more than one mechanism, or partial patterns where significant characteristics may be missing. Good documentation of the features observed in the pattern, including characteristics such as stain size, color, distribution, and directionality, can assist the analyst with evidence to support the likelihood of one pattern type over another.

Notes

1. ASB Technical Report 033, Terms and Definitions in Bloodstain Pattern Analysis, 1st edition, 2019.
2. Stotesbury, T.; Taylor, M. C.; Jermy, M. C. 2017. "Passive Drip Stain Formation Dynamics of Blood onto Hard Surfaces and Comparison with Simple Fluids for Blood Substitute Development and Assessment." *Journal of Forensic Sciences*, 62: 74–82.
3. Smith, Fiona R., Naomi C. Buntsma, and David Brutin. 2018. "Roughness Influence on Human Blood Drop Spreading and Splashing." *Langmuir*, 34(3): 1143–1150
4. Hulse-Smith, L., N. Z. Mehdizadeh, and S. Chandra. 2005. "Deducing Drop Size and Impact Velocity from Circular Bloodstains. *Journal of Forensic Science*, 50(1): 1–10.
5. Kabaliuk. N., M. C. Jermy, K. Morison, T. Stotesbury, M. C. Taylor, and E. Williams. 2013. "Blood Drop Size in Passive Dripping from Weapons." *Forensic Science International*, 228: 75–82. https://doi10.1016/j.forsciint.2013.02.023.

6. Feng, Chengcheng, Stephen Michielsen, and Daniel Attinger. 2018. "Impact of Carpet Construction on Fluid Penetration: The Case of Blood." *Forensic Science International*, 284:184–193. ISSN 0379-0738. https://doi.org/10.1016/j.forsciint.2018.01.009.
7. Gardner, Ross M. 2006. "Defining the Diameter of the Smallest Parent Stain Produced by a Drip." *Journal of Forensic Identification*, 58(2): 210–221.
8. Boos, Kristine, Amanda Orr, Mike Illes, and Theresa Stotesbury. 2019. "Characterizing Drip Patterns in Bloodstain Pattern Analysis: An Investigation of the Influence of Droplet Velocity and Number of Droplets on Static Pattern Features." *Forensic Science International*, 301: 55–66. https://doi.org/10.1016/j.forsciint.2019.05.002.
9. Slemko, Joseph A. 2003. "Bloodstains on Fabrics: The Effects of Droplet Veolocity and Fabric Construction." IABPA Newsletter, December 2003: 3–11.
10. De Castro, Therese, Tania Nickson, Debra Carr, and Clare Knock. 2013. "Interpreting the Formation of Bloodstains on Selected Apparel Fabrics." *International Journal of Legal Medicine*, 127(1): 251–258.
11. Miles, H. F., R. M. Morgan, and J. E Millington. 2014. "The Influence of Fabric Surface Characteristics on Satellite Bloodstain Morphology." *Science and Justice* 54(3): 262–266.
12. Williams, Elisabeth M. P., Margaret Dodds, Michael C. Taylor, Jingyao Li, and Stephen Michielsen. 2016. "Impact Dynamics of Porcine Drip Bloodstains on Fabrics." *Forensic Science International*, 262: 66–72.
13. Li, Xingyu, Jingyao Li, and Stephen Michielsen. 2017. *Forensic Science International*, 276: 41–50.
14. Cho Y., F. Springer, F. A. Tulleners, and W. D. Ristenpart. 2015. "Quantitative Bloodstain Analysis: Differentiation of Contact Transfer Patterns versus Spatter Patterns on Fabric via Microscopic Inspection." *Forensic Science International*; 249:233–240.
15. James, S. H., P. E. Kish, and T. P. Sutton. 2005. Principles of Bloodstain Pattern Analysis: Theory and Practice. CRC Press, Taylor & Francis Group, Boca Raton, FL.
16. Bevel, T. and M. Gardner. 2008. Bloodstain Pattern Analysis with an Introduction to Crime Scene Reconstruction. 3rd edition, CRC Press, Taylor & Francis Group, Boca Raton, FL.
17. Taylor, Michael C., Terry L. Laber, Paul E. Kish, Glynn Owens, and Nikola K. P. Osborne. 2016. "The Reliablilty of Pattern Classification in Bloodstain Pattern Analysis – Part 2: Bloodstain Patterns on Fabric Surfaces." *Journal of Forensic Sciences*, 61(6): 1461–1466.

CHAPTER 9

TRANSFER, SWIPE, AND WIPE BLOODSTAINS

Jeff Gurvis

When referring to the discipline of bloodstain pattern analysis, it is often associated strictly with blood traveling through the air and creating small stains on various surfaces throughout a crime scene. In fact, many incorrectly refer to the discipline as blood spatter analysis which neglects an entire category of pattern types that do not involve any airborne blood. This chapter will explore the various pattern types where the mechanism of deposition of blood involves the transfer of blood between two surfaces. This involves a long-standing forensic principle developed by Edmund Locard: when two objects come in contact with one another, there is an exchange of matter between them. In the current example, the matter is blood.[1]

This chapter will focus on two different modes of blood deposition:

1. Objects that contact each other without lateral motion during the contact
2. Objects that contact each other with lateral motion during the contact

TRANSFER STAINS

The first of the above modes results in transfer stains. The American Academy of Forensic Science, Academy Standards Board (ASB), defines a transfer stain as "A bloodstain resulting from contact between a blood-bearing surface and another surface."[2] Transfer stains are one of the most common bloodstains encountered at crime scenes and are akin to other forensic disciplines that involve other impression evidence such as paint transfers, fabric impressions, and, more commonly, footwear impressions and friction ridge impressions. Indeed, there is crossover with bloodstain pattern analysis and footwear impression examination and latent print (friction ridge) examination where the medium that these impressions are made is in blood. Chapter 11 of this book discusses bloody fingerprints in more detail.

TRANSFER STAIN CREATION

While it might seem considerably obvious, there are several factors that are involved for the creation of a transfer stain. First, blood must be present on the originating surface. How that deposition occurs determines how the blood is distributed on that surface. Then the bloodstained area must come in contact with the second surface. It is important to realize that the area of contact might not include the entire bloodstained portion of the originating surface. Hence, the resulting transfer stain may not be a complete mirror image of the original bloodstained area. In some instances, if the entire surface of the original object is coated in blood and the object makes significant contact with another surface, the transfer stain may appear to be in the shape of the original object.

DOI: 10.4324/9781003163695-9

This may make the determination of the donor of the transfer stain an easier task than with much less contact or less blood originating from the object. For example, if a hand is covered in blood and is placed on a table and removed, the entire shape of the hand may be visible, thus making it easier to conclude that a hand made the transfer stain. This, however, is rare. Due to the three-dimensional contours of objects and surfaces, it is more common that partial contact and blood transfer occur making the resulting transfer stain more ambiguous as to their donor.

TRANSFER STAIN CHARACTERISTICS

As a result of the creation process outlined above, transfer stains have an infinite number of sizes and shapes, largely due to the infinite number of sizes and shapes of objects and blood distributions. The porous nature of the surfaces can also play an important role in the stain's size and shape. As discussed in Chapters 19 and 20, clothing and fabrics can absorb blood in different ways, making the transfer from or to these surfaces result in more complex sizes and shapes. How wet or dry the blood is prior to transfer also adds a dynamic in overall appearance of transfers stains. The less wet the blood, the less likely the transfer of blood to occur.

There are several factors that contribute to a stain's shape and appearance. Pressure, duration of the contact, the distribution of blood that is on the initial surface, and what portion of that bloodstained area meets the opposing surface can influence the resulting stain shape. The texture of the initial object can also affect the appearance within the stain (e.g., fabric impressions).

In some instances, a recognizable shape is produced. There are a few of these shapes that can be determined with near certainty: friction ridge and footwear impressions. These stains are commonly found at crime scenes and are relatively easy to discern. However, there are an infinite number of other shapes due to the infinite number of objects and infinite blood distributions with infinite ways to make contact. Because of this, it is important to take great caution in speculating what the potential donor object/surfaces are. In these instances, which is much of the time, any bloodstained surfaces should be considered. Looking for surfaces with similar blood distribution as the transfer stain is one way to associate the two surfaces together.

From a reconstruction perspective, two surfaces must come in contact to create a transfer stain. Prior to any transfer of blood occurring, it is important to realize that blood had to have been deposited on the original surface some time prior to the transfer. While this point might seem to be minor, it can be incredibly important when putting together reconstruction event windows of actions that took place at the crime scene.

CAPILLARY SHIFTS

Transfer stains often exhibit distinct darker areas or linear formations within the stain indicating heavier volume distribution. These areas are created during the removal of the object from the surface, when blood is still trying to adhere to the departing object and is coalescing along the contours of the object. Ultimately, when the object breaks away, the coalesced blood returns and remains within the stain closest to the last area where the object last was in contact. These are called capillary shifts and may indicate the direction that the departing object was removed (Figure 9.1). For instance, if a bloodstained finger is placed on a surface and removed straight out from the surface, then the darkened areas will be present in the middle of the stain. If the finger is removed to the right, then these areas are *shifted* to the right and thus indicate the direction that the finger went. On its own, this information might not carry much significance, but it is another piece of information that might contribute to the reconstruction of events.

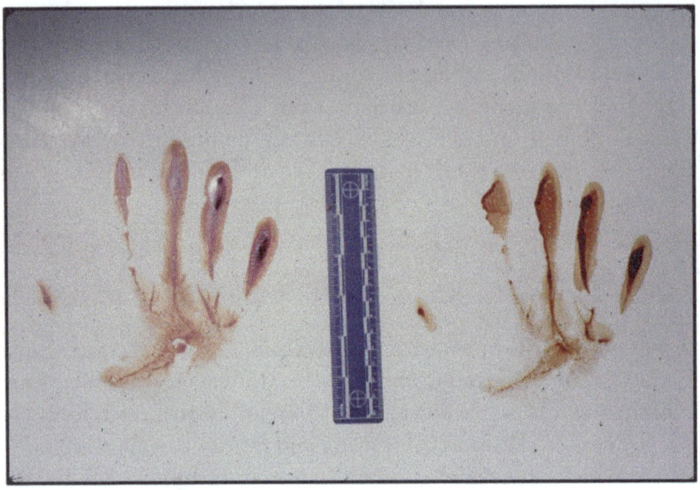

Figure 9.1 Capillary shifts are depicted by the heavier staining. The left stain shows the heavier staining in the middle, whereas the stain on the right shows heavier staining toward the left of the stain. This indicates that the hand was removed to the left.

REPETITIVE TRANSFER STAINS

If there are a series of transfer stains that have the same shape, distribution, and general appearance, these are referred to as repetitive transfer stains. A common example is someone walking across a floor leaving behind a series of bloody footwear impressions (Figure 9.2). This can also occur when hands repeatedly touch various surfaces within a scene. Another not so obvious example is when a cylindrical object with blood on it rolls across a surface.

In all these examples, the first transfer stain in a series will have the most blood deposited due to there being the most blood available on the object at the beginning of the sequence. Once the

Figure 9.2 The two footwear impressions are an example of repetitive transfer stains where the same object (shoes) comes in contact with a surface multiple times. The sequence of the stains is indicated by amount of blood transferred. The left impression was created first.

initial stain is deposited, there will be less blood left on the object and thus less blood available for the next stain. This makes it relatively simple to sequence and determines the direction of the series of repetitive transfer stains due to the diminishing amount of blood in successive stains. The transfer bloodstains may diminish to such a point that chemical enhancement may be needed to see the subsequent transfers.

SECONDARY TRANSFER

There is the notion of a secondary transfer whereby a surface is somewhat porous such as clothing or fabric and blood is transferred onto one side of the surface of the fabric, it may ultimately diffuse through the surface onto an underlying surface or another surface. This is the mechanism of secondary transfer. On its own, it is not possible to tell that it is a secondary transfer but if an object in a room is moved or even pulling in the room during the commission of the crime scene event, then it may be possible to place the fabric in the original location when the original deposition was made.

TRANSFER STAINS ON CLOTHING

Sometimes within a single layer of fabric, it is possible to determine the direction of blood that originated from one side of a fabric to the other, especially with clothing. If there is a transfer stain, the blood on the edges of the stain may not completely diffuse through to the other side of the fabric which leaves gaps in the otherwise contiguous area of blood. This aids in determining which side of the fabric the blood was originally deposited (see Figure 9.3a and b).

Wipes

Wipes are often grouped with transfer stains but are actually a form of altered stains. The ASB defines a wipe as "An altered stain resulting from an object moving through a preexisting wet bloodstain."[2] After the initial deposition, blood begins to dry. Typically, on non-porous surfaces, the drying process begins at the periphery of the initial stain(s) where the blood may be thinnest and progresses inward. If the distribution of blood is such that thinner areas exist within the initial stain, then drying may complete in those areas earlier than others.

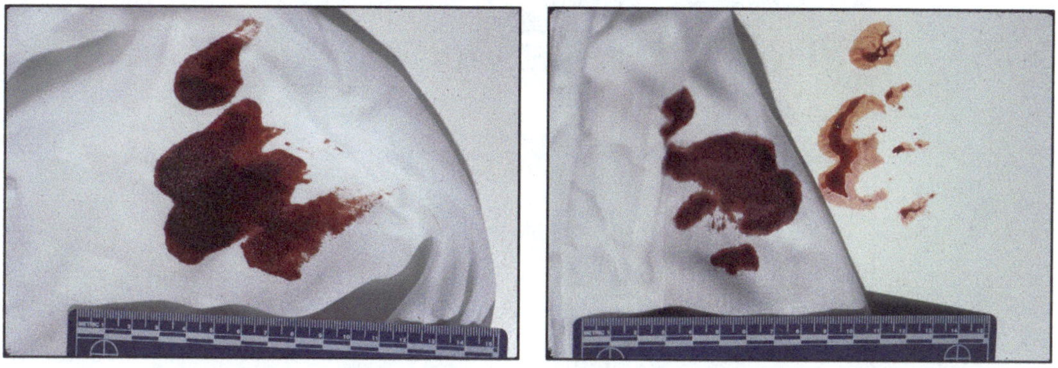

Figure 9.3 A bloody hand came into contact with a white shirt. Since the shirt is absorbent, the blood travels through the underside and onto the surface the shirt resting on. Through each of these layers, a diminishing amount of blood is transferred indicated by the gaps in the staining.

WIPE CHARACTERISTICS

When another surface subsequently moves across the blood, the dried areas will less likely be disturbed while the liquid areas will move in concert with the motion and produce streaks or striations. The dried portions of the original stain(s) may exhibit an outline of their original shape. These areas are referred to as skeletonization or periphery stains due to the drying occurring at their periphery (Figure 9.4). Since the original shapes and location may be preserved, it may be possible to classify the original stain(s) or patterns. Additionally, since the original location may be evident, the striations emanating from the original stain(s) will indicate the direction of the movement that disrupted them.

It is important to note that to exclusively classify a wipe, the skeletonized areas must be evident not only on the periphery of original stain but also in the area where the striations appear. There are situations where skeletonized areas are present without striations, hence the need for both characteristics to be present.

RECONSTRUCTIVE VALUE

Wipes can possess value when it comes to reconstruction. Each wipe consists of two separate actions: initial deposition and subsequent movement. This creates an event window that sequences two separate actions. Furthermore, and perhaps more significantly, the time differential between these two actions may be indicated by the thickness of the skeletonized area of the original deposition: the thicker this area, the longer the blood allowed to dry prior to any movement. Drying times of blood are impacted by many variables such as temperature, humidity, and airflow. This is one of the main reasons it is required that crime scene documentation must include information about the environmental conditions. Additionally, surface conditions are always a consideration in bloodstain pattern analysis and are important when considering how long blood might take to dry. Therefore, if it is an important aspect in a case, experimentation under similar conditions (surface, temperature, humidity, etc.) may be necessary to help in determining the rate of drying of blood on the surface in question.

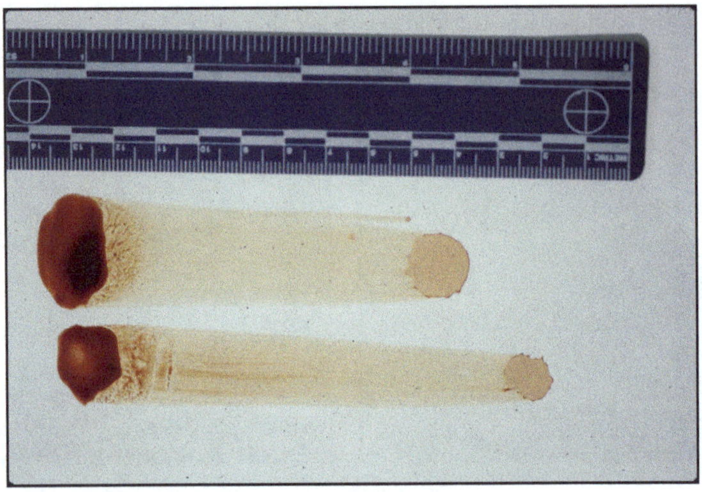

Figure 9.4 Wipes are characterized by the skeletonization of the periphery of the original stain on the right side and subsequent motion that displaces the blood to the left.

The direction of travel of a wipe may be important in the overall context of scene reconstruction. Due to the presence of skeletonization and the stria emanating from it, direction of travel of the wipe can easily be determined.

Swipes

When a wet, bloodstained object or surface comes in contact with another surface, moving laterally, a swipe is created. The ASB defines a swipe as "A bloodstain resulting from the transfer of blood from a blood-bearing surface onto another surface, with characteristics that indicate relative motion between the two surfaces."[2] These patterns are typically created by victims and perpetrators during the criminal events. Often, bloodstained hands, clothing, hair, and other areas of the body can brush up against various surfaces depositing blood and creating swipes.

SWIPE CHARACTERISTICS

Swipes can be of various sizes depending on the size of the area that comes in contact with the surface and the duration of this contact as it is moved. Typically, longer contact results in a longer and larger swipe. The shapes of swipes are also dependent on the contact area and the length of the swipe. When the length is greater that the size of the contact area of the depositing surface, the overall shape becomes linear or curvilinear based on the manner of the motion (e.g., straight). Similar to wipes, swipes also have striations indicating movement along the surface. Because the surface is clean prior to contact, there is no skeletonization present.

DIRECTION OF TRAVEL

On smooth non-porous surfaces, the direction of travel is indicated by the pushing or "plowing" of blood by the moving object. When the object pulls away from the surface, a heavier deposit of blood may be left at the end of the stain. This area appears to be a darkened border along the edges of the stria, which might need magnification to visualize (Figure 9.5).

Figure 9.5 Swipes are characterized by striations indicating motion. Darker deposits at the end of striations indicate directionality. This swipe indicates a left to right, down to up directionality.

Figure 9.6 Feathering is an indication of pressure and may exist on both ends of a swipe as depicted. However, the darkened borders show a right to left directionality.

Some references in other publications point to feathering or feathered edges as an indication of direction. However, this characteristic is an indication of pressure rather than directionality. All swipes are not created the same way. Some start with heavy pressure and leave lightly. Others may begin lightly and end with greater pressure before releasing. Some even are light throughout in which feathered edges appear on both sides of the stain. Figure 9.6 shows this phenomenon. Observing the areas of blood pushed to the edges provides a much more reliable characteristic for directionality determination.

Luckily, many surfaces found at crime scenes are textured and three dimensional. Swipes deposited on these types of surfaces have a more obvious characteristic that can be used for determining directionality. As blood is deposited on a textured surface, blood will collect on the leading edges and will be voided on the trailing edges of the textured areas as shown in Figure 9.7.

Swipes over door and floor thresholds are very common. Looking at the swipe at the bottom of the left door threshold shows the collection of blood on the surfaces facing the lens of the camera

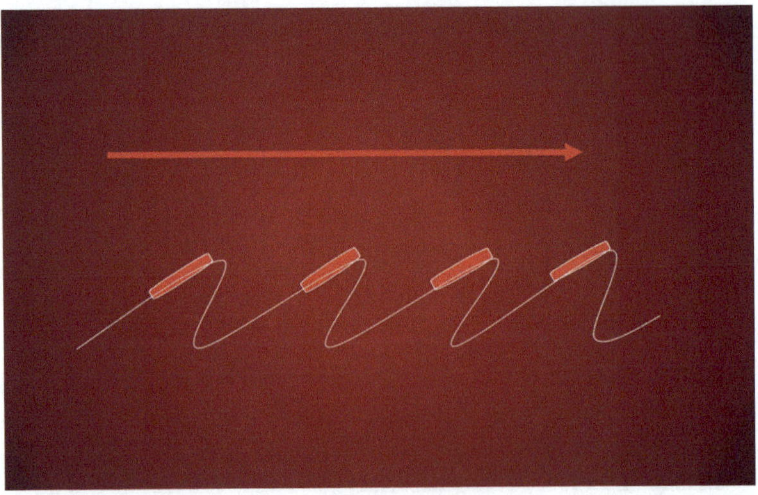

Figure 9.7 Blood collects on the leading edge of textured surfaces as a bloody object moves across. This illustrates a left to right motion where blood is deposited on the left side of textured areas.

Figure 9.8 Looking at the swipe at the bottom of the left door threshold shows the collection of blood on the surfaces facing the lens of the camera and some areas are voided on the planes perpendicular. This indicates the direction away from the camera and into the room.

and some areas are voided on the planes perpendicular. This indicates the direction away from the camera and into the room (Figure 9.8).

Similar characteristics can be found in carpeting, furniture, windows, and vehicles. It is important to note, however, that the direction of travel may not be determined, and it is ok to have a result of unknown directionality.

Summary

Transfers, wipes, and swipes are very common bloodstain patterns and can be quite helpful during the reconstruction of events. They may contain quite a bit of information relative to sequencing, source attribution, direction of events, and other aspects of actions that can take place during the commission of a crime.

Notes

1. Practical Crime Scene Analysis and Reconstruction, Gardner, Ross., Bevel, Tom, CRC Press, 2009, pp. 17–18.
2. *ASB Technical Report 033, Terms and Definitions in Bloodstain Pattern Analysis,* First Edition, 2017.

CHAPTER 10

ALTERED BLOODSTAINS

Stuart H. James

INTRODUCTION

An altered bloodstain is a bloodstain with characteristics that indicate a physical change has occurred.[1] The deposition of bloodstains at crime scenes occurs under many different environmental and physical conditions that may alter their appearance either initially or thereafter. Existing wet bloodstains may be altered and artefactual stains may be produced by activities during and after an assault by the victim or the assailant. Movement of the body by a medical and law enforcement personnel can also change the appearance of bloodstains and create additional stains at the scene and on the clothing of the victim. The handling of clothing and other items wet with blood can produce alterations. Packaging of wet bloody items should be avoided. Often, there are cleanup efforts used by the assailant to obliterate or remove bloodstains, which alter their appearance at the scene.

Common alterations of bloodstains include the following:

- Diffusion and capillarity
- Dilution
- Drying
- Coagulation
- Aging and color changes
- Sequencing
- Voids
- Effects of fire and soot
- Intentional alteration or attempts at the removal of bloodstains

DIFFUSION AND CAPILLARITY OF BLOODSTAINS

Diffusion is defined as the movement of a substance from an area of higher concentration to an area of lower concentration. Capillarity is a function of the ability of a liquid to wet a particular material, such as blood wetting a type of textile or fabric material. These materials possess a complex structure and their relative ability to wick liquids. Various types of textiles are commonly present at bloodshed events, including clothing of suspects and/or victims, carpets, bedding, and towels.

The effects of blood diffusion and capillarity are readily observed when blood saturates bedding and clothing, as demonstrated in Figures 10.1 and 10.2. The bloodstain analyst should be aware of the textile factors that can influence the appearance of blood on fabrics. The stains can be altered and be significantly larger or distorted and may not resemble the original stain or pattern.[2] The reader is referred to Chapter 20 for a comprehensive presentation of this topic.

 DOI: 10.4324/9781003163695-10

Figure 10.1 View of area of a bloodstain on a bedsheet that has diffused as the result of capillary action. Note the dark center area and the lighter periphery of the stain.

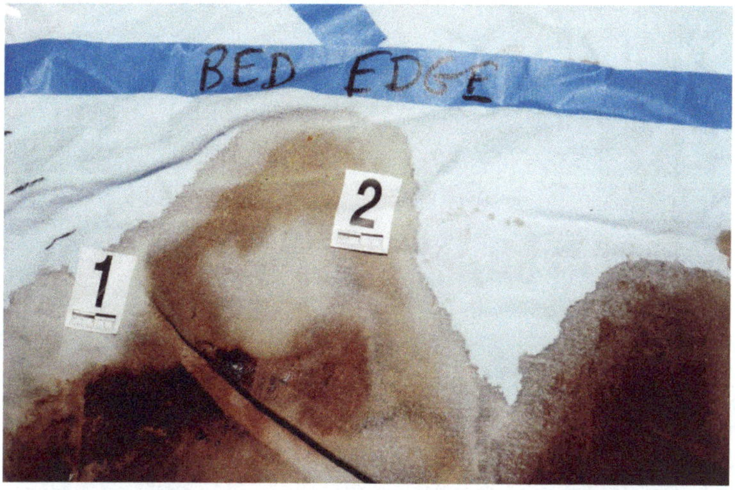

Figure 10.2 Closer view of diffusion of a bloodstain on a sheet.

DILUTED BLOODSTAINS

Diluted bloodstains may be present at scenes as a result of mixture with water or other fluids. In external environments involving rain or snow, the characteristics of the original stains may be altered to the point where analysis is difficult or impossible. Cleanup attempts at scenes, including the attempts at washing bloodstained clothing, often produce evidence of diluted bloodstains (Figures 10.3 and 10.4).

An interesting case involved the issue of diluted bloodstains in the form of small spatters on the sleeves of a husband's jacket accused of fatally beating and stabbing his three children and stabbing

Figure 10.3 Diluted bloodstains in the front of jeans.

Figure 10.4 Diluted bloodstains on front of blouse.

his wife to death. This became important evidence for the defense during his trial. The presence of blood spatters on the sleeves of the jacket was not apparent until a prosecution expert sprayed the jacket with luminol to identify the spatters of blood. The expert testified that the presence of these spatters was consistent with the defendant administering blows or stab wounds to the members of his family. The husband claimed that he had returned to his residence and found the bodies of his wife and children. He admitted carrying one of his children who was barely alive from a bathroom to the living room floor before calling for help. After police and medical personnel arrived, the husband, who had visible blood on his hands, began washing his hands under the faucet at the kitchen sink. A police officer testified that he observed this and directed the husband to stop washing his hands. The scene photographs clearly showed diluted blood in the sink and some blood transfer on a roll of paper towels near the sink. The force of the tap water on the bloodstained hands of the husband certainly could have produced spatters of diluted blood that would be deposited on the sleeves of the husband. This was presented to the jury in addition to other bloodstain and forensic pathology testimony that resulted in the acquittal of the husband on all charges. The defense presented convincing evidence to show that the wife had beaten and stabbed her children and then stabbed herself in the chest, resulting in a triple homicide and suicide.

A common feature of diluted bloodstains is a prominent dark outer rim with a lighter, washed out appearance in the center area referred to as perimeter stain (Figures 10.5 and 10.6). A perimeter stain is an altered stain that consists of the peripheral characteristics of the original stain.[3]

Damp clothing resulting from excessive perspiration may dilute bloodstains that are present on clothing worn by a victim or an assailant (Figure 10.7). In some cases, perimortem urination by the victim has caused dilution of blood on their clothing or on a surface such as a couch, bed, or floor. High levels of urea and creatinine in the stained areas can confirm the presence of urine. When

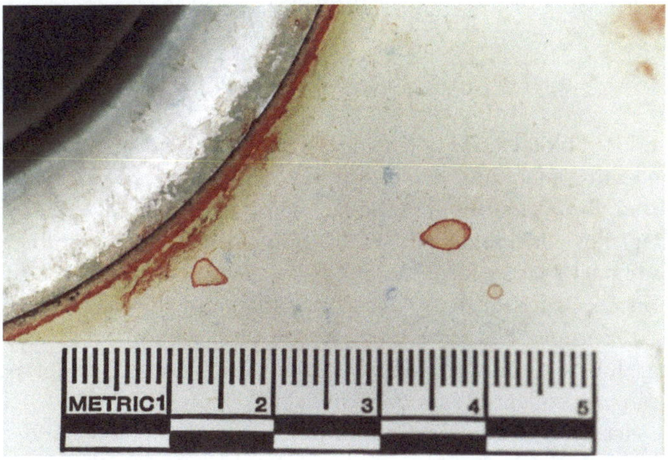

Figure 10.5 Diluted bloodstains on edge of sink.

Figure 10.6 Diluted bloodstains on floor of shower stall.

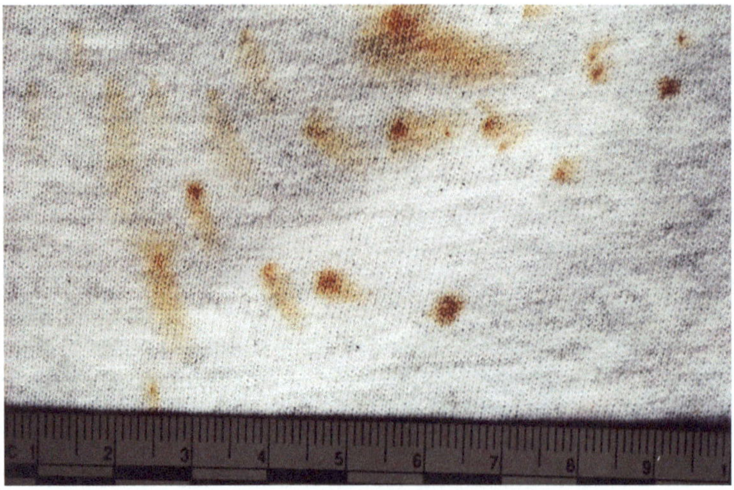

Figure 10.7 Diluted spatters on T-shirt as the result of excessive perspiration.

bloodstains that appear diluted are suspected to contain saliva, a test for the presence of amylase is recommended.

Another form of diluted bloodstains occurs occasionally with massive head trauma involving the combination of blood and spinal fluid. In a recent suicide, a young man sat on a bed and discharged a shotgun into his head. Brain tissue and blood were projected and spattered throughout the small room. On the ceiling tiles above and forward of the victim were seen numerous areas of blood tinged and colorless impact spatters of spinal fluid that were easily interpreted (Figure 10.8).

Bloodstain patterns deposited on snow or ice may maintain their size, shape, and distribution for a period of time. Occasionally, the blood deposits on surfaces in cold weather or on snow will have a reddish-orange hue to them. The stains should be documented, preserved photographically, and representative samples collected as soon as possible (Figures 10.9 and 10.10). Homicides have occurred where the victims are found in walk-in freezers, and the bloodstains have not presented problems with analysis in the author's experience. In those types of cases, often occurring in

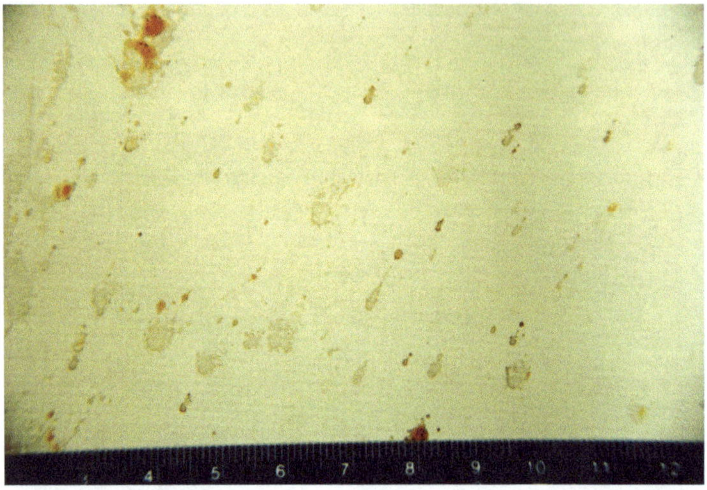

Figure 10.8 Impact spatters of blood intermixed with spinal fluid spatters on ceiling tile as the result of suicidal shotgun injury to head of victim sitting on a bed.

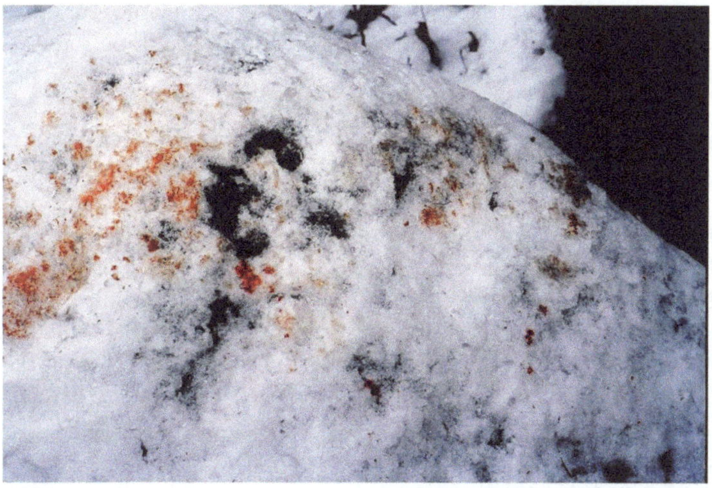

Figure 10.9 Blood deposits on snow. Note the orange color of the stains. (Courtesy of Jeremy Morris, Johnson County Sheriff's Office, Olathe, KS.)

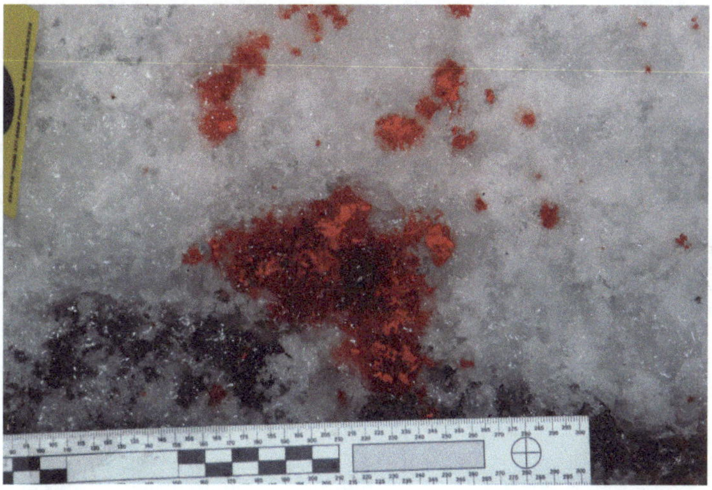

Figure 10.10 Closer view of orange color of blood deposits on snow. (Courtesy of Jeremy Morris, Johnson County Sheriff's Office, Olathe, KS.)

fast-food restaurants, the bloodstains may freeze to the surface even before they would have dried, and their characteristics may be less likely to be altered. The maintaining of the cold temperature within these walk-in freezers is critical until the stains have been thoroughly documented, photographed, and representative samples have been collected. Allowing the freezer to thaw will cause alteration and possible intermixing of stains with water.

DRYING OF BLOOD

When blood is exposed to an external environment, the drying process on various surfaces is initiated. During the process, water evaporates from the volume of blood leaving a residue of the cellular components of blood. The drying process is a function of the blood drop size, volume, thickness, exposed surface area, the texture of the target surface, and the influences or effects of the external environment. Large-volume pools on non-porous surfaces and saturation stains on carpet and bedding usually exhibit extended drying times. A high ambient temperature and decreased humidity will accelerate drying times of blood as will increased air currents such as wind, a fan, or a blowing air conditioner vent in proximity to the deposition of blood. It follows that humid environments, lower temperatures, and minimal airflow will produce longer drying times.

Small stains and spatters, light transfer stains, and thin flow patterns of blood may dry within a few minutes at normal conditions of temperature, humidity, and airflow on non-porous surfaces.

The drying of bloodstains is observed initially around their edges or periphery and proceeds inward to the central portion of the stain as the drying process continues. Cracks are often produced on the surface of the stains. Occasionally, the dried central area of a dried bloodstain will flake away, leaving an intact circular rim. This is referred to as a perimeter or skeletonized bloodstain (Figure 10.11a and b). Progressive drying of large pools of blood are demonstrated in Figures 10.12 and 10.13.

Laan et al. described five distinct phases of the drying of a blood pool deposited on a linoleum surface. It was emphasized that the duration of any one stage and complete desiccation can differ

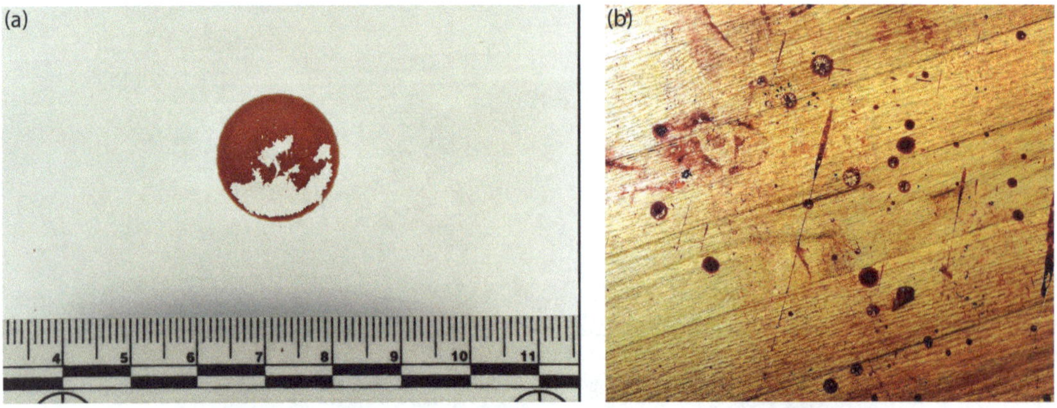

Figure 10.11 (a) Perimeter stain resulting from the flaking of dried blood. (Courtesy of Anna Cox, Cox Forensic Consulting and Training, LLC, Brandon, FL.) (b) Multiple perimeter stains on floor with flaking of dried blood.

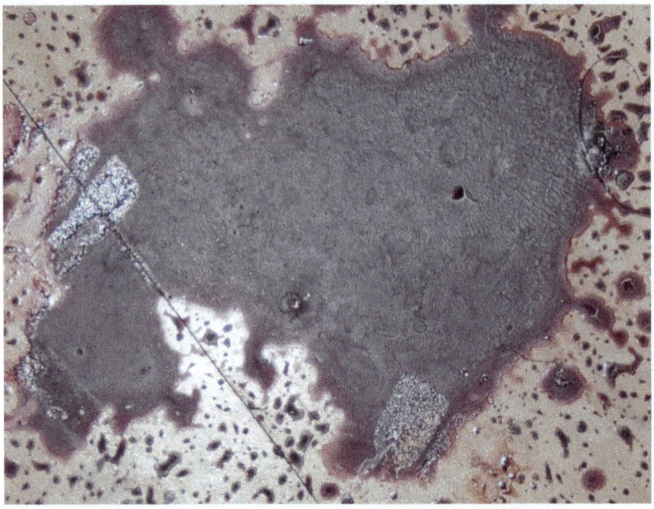

Figure 10.12 Partially dried pool of blood on a floor.

Figure 10.13 Completely dried pool of blood on tiled floor. Note the dark color and extensive cracking of the surface.

between blood pools depending on the humidity, temperature, shape and size of the pool, and the type of surface.[4]

i. Coagulation stage (color change from dark to lighter red)
ii. Gelation stage (red cells transported to rim of the stain)
iii. Rim desiccation stage (rim turns black and starts to crack)
iv. Center desiccation stage (drying and cracking propagates toward the center of stain)
v. Final desiccation stage (pool is desiccated with flakes separated and black in color)

An interesting dried bloodstain is shown in Figure 10.14. The air bubble in the center of the drip stain persisted for 24 hours surrounded by the dark cracking of the stain. Drying and cracking of

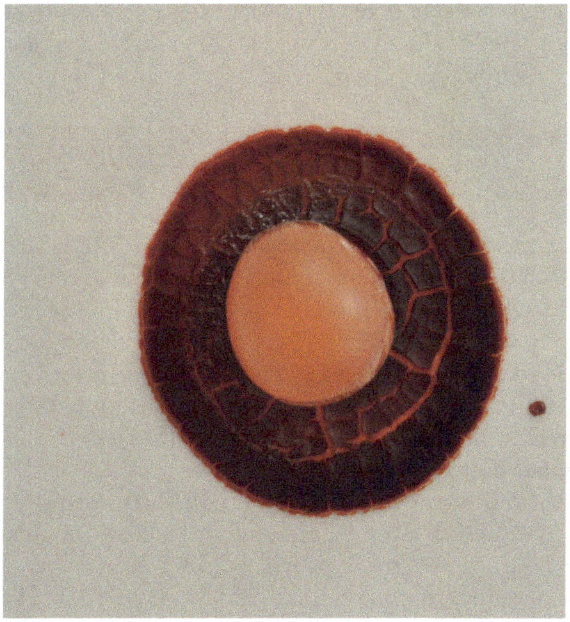

Figure 10.14 Dried drip stain of blood with air bubble that persisted for 24 hours. (Courtesy of Celestina Rossi, Montgomery County Sheriff's Office, Conroe, TX.)

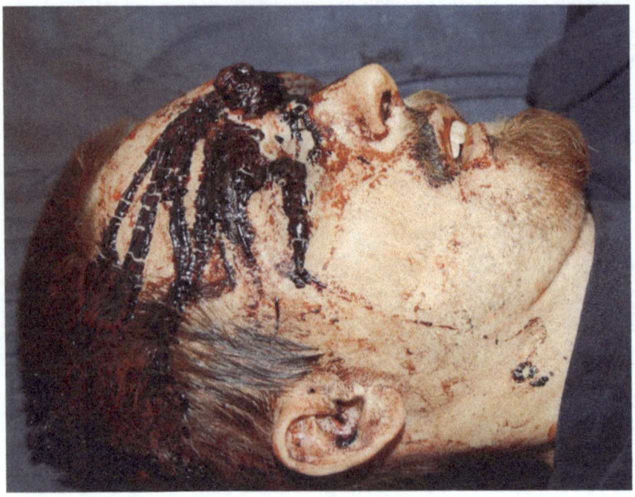

Figure 10.15 Dried flow patterns on right side of victim's face that originated from gunshot wound in forehead. (Courtesy of Todd A. Thorne, Retired-Kenosha Wisconsin Police Department – Forensic Unit.)

blood on victims is often observed. Figure 10.15 shows a victim with a gunshot wound in the forehead with dried blood and possible tissue protruding from the wound site and dried and cracked downward flow patterns on the right side of his head.

Research by Laber and Epstein published in their 1983 manual, *Experiments and Practical Exercises in Bloodstain Pattern Analysis,* contained significant data on the drying time of blood.[5] They studied the effect of temperature, humidity, airflow, and surface texture on the drying time of blood using a single drop, with 1 ml, 5 ml, and 10 ml volumes of blood to create the bloodstains. Their study can be used as a general guideline. However, when drying times are to be estimated in casework, they should be very conservative. When comparative experiments are considered, the bloodstain size should be estimated and the surface texture, airflow, and other environmental conditions should be duplicated as closely as possible. These parameters are difficult to achieve and there can be a significant error rate.

AGING AND COLOR OF BLOOD

Blood circulates through the circulatory system of the body. Arterial blood transports oxygen in the form of oxyhemoglobin throughout the body and is bright red in color. Venous blood is a darker red color since it is deoxygenated. After fresh blood is shed, the resultant bloodstains increase in age and progress through a series of color changes from red to reddish brown to green and eventually to dark brown and black. This change of color is attributable to environmental conditions, the drying process, and to the loss of oxygen from the oxyhemoglobin in the red cells on exposure to air. Exposure to the sun will hasten the darkening process (Figures 10.16 and 10.17).

A particularly warm and humid environment with the presence of bacteria and other microorganisms during the decomposition process will also affect the sequence and duration of color changes in bloodstains. The original red color of blood will usually progress to red brown and then to green within 24–48 hours at a warm temperature. This process may be hastened as a result of the growth of bacteria and the decomposition process (Figure 10.18). Postmortem growth of fungus can produce unusual changes to blood, as seen in Figure 10.19. This was a scene where the body had begun the decomposition process and the growth of the hair-like fungus was determined to be *Aspergillus* sp. It is important to recognize the limitation of the estimation of the aging of

Figure 10.16 Spattered blood on side of wooden fence with photograph taken shortly after deposition.

Figure 10.17 The darkened appearance of the spattered blood on the side of the wooden fence in photograph taken 24 hours later.

Figure 10.18 Decomposing saturation stain on mattress. Note the greenish discoloration around the periphery of the stain.

Figure 10.19 View of hair-like extensions on a pool of decomposing blood on a floor with hair-like extensions identified as the fungus, *Aspergillus* sp. (Courtesy of Martin Eversdjik, Loci Forensics, B.V., The Netherlands.)

blood based on their color and condition at the scene should be very conservative since there are many variables to be considered.

A review of the scientific literature has provided research articles on the estimation of the age of blood using various techniques.[6,7,8,9]

- RNA Degradation based on the ratio between different types of RNA (mRNA versus rRNA) that changes over time in a linear fashion
- Amino acid residues based on the decrease of tryptophan fluorescence decay over time

- Reflectance spectroscopy that measures the autoxidation of oxyhemoglobin to methemoglobin and its denaturation to hemichrome
- Near-infrared that measures the formation of methemoglobin and binding of water

Medical conditions such as peptic ulcer hemorrhage and vomiting often produce dark "coffee ground emesis" and resulting bloodstains that have the appearance of aged blood. The dark color is the result of the stomach acids denaturing the blood (Figure 10.20a and b). Bleeding within the lower gastrointestinal tract can produce loose, black, tarry stool that is the result of the breakdown of blood prior to evacuation (Figure 10.21).

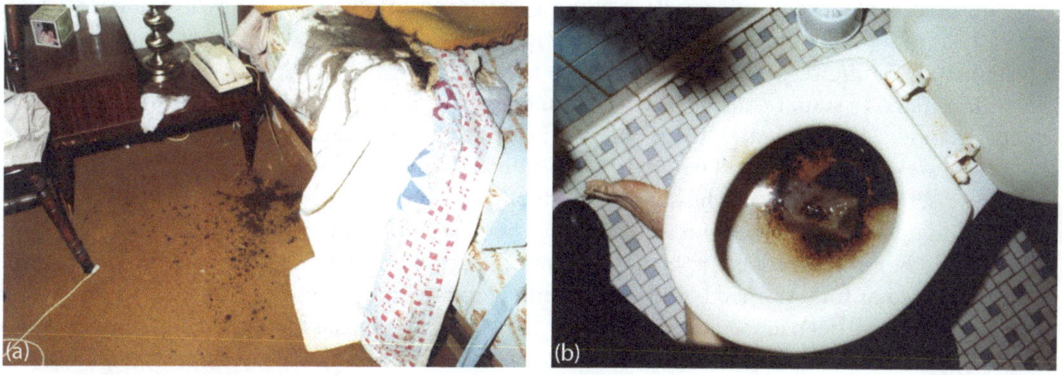

Figure 10.20 (a) Victim of fatal hemorrhaging peptic ulcer on floor of bathroom. Note the brownish color of the blood on the floor. (b) The victim vomited blood into the toilet prior to his death. Note the dark brown clumps of blood referred to as coffee ground emesis.

Figure 10.21 Black tarry blood and stool deposits on floor and toilet in the bathroom due to severe bleeding from the gastrointestinal tract of the victim.

COAGULATION OF BLOOD

The process of the coagulation of blood results in the formation of a blood clot and eventually clot retraction and serum separation. A blood clot is a gelatinous mass formed by a complex mechanism involving the red blood cells, fibrinogen, platelets, and other clotting factors.[10] Fibrin is integral to clotting. For fibrin to be available whenever an injury occurs, it is constantly being transported through the body by the circulating blood. Fibrin must be in a soluble form (called fibrinogen) when it is circulating in the blood, but it must change into an insoluble form for clotting to commence (Figure 10.22).[11]

An image of a blood clot taken with a scanning electron microscope is shown in Figure 10.23. The early appearance of the formation of a clot in a small pool of blood lifted with a pipette after approximately 7 minutes is demonstrated in Figure 10.24.

A serum stain is a stain resulting from the liquid portion of the blood (serum) that separates during coagulation.[12] Subsequently, the blood clot begins to retract, causing further separation of the serum (Figures 10.25–10.28). The observation of coagulated or clotted bloodstains and patterns and serum separation at scenes has been well documented by bloodstain pattern analysts in case work. Blood clots and serum stains surrounding them as well as the degree of observed drying of blood should be recognized as important information at crime scenes. In general, the presence of partially clotted or fully formed blood clots within bloodstain patterns and the presence of clotted impact spatter have been associated with a time lapse between initial bloodshed and the formation of the clots. This interval is variable, depending on the degree of clotting, source and quantity of blood, and environmental conditions existing at the time. It is also important to obtain a medical history of the victim and a record of medications.[13]

The serum separation resulting from clot formation and retraction may take an hour or more depending on the original blood volume, the surface or substrate where the blood is present, and environmental factors such as temperature and humidity. It is difficult to attempt to reproduce experimentally the degree of clotting and serum separation observed at a scene to estimate the time interval since bloodshed.

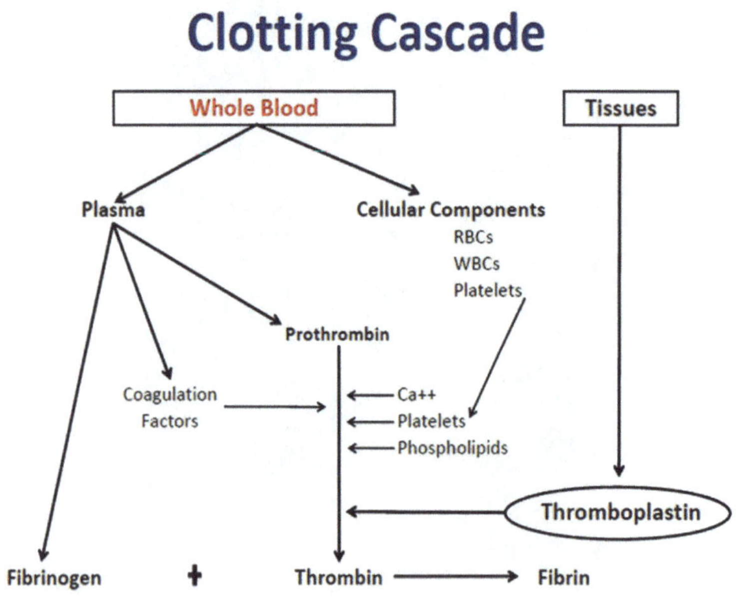

Figure 10.22 Diagrammatic representation of the clotting cascade.

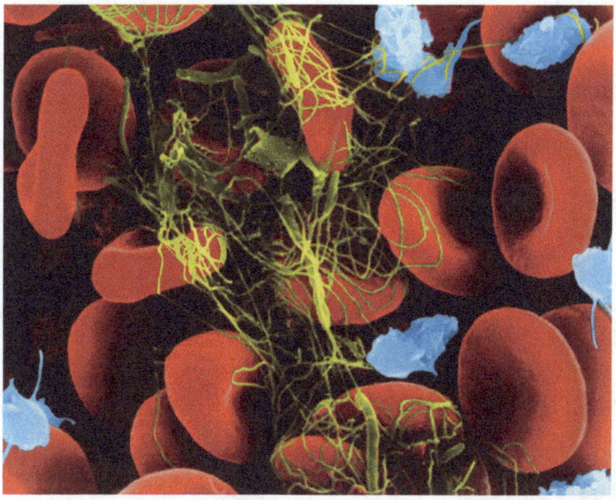

Figure 10.23 Formation of a blood clot taken with a Hitachi Field Emission Scanning Electron Microscope (FESEM). The red concave disks are red blood cells (RBC), the blue irregular cellular elements are activated platelets, intermixed with yellow strands of fibrin. The magnification was 1,445x for an image 24 mm in the narrow dimension. (Courtesy of Dennis Kunkel Microscopy, Kailua, Hawaii.)

Figure 10.24 Demonstration of initial clot formation with freshly drawn human blood in a laboratory setting.

Figure 10.25 Partially clotted pool of blood on the floor of vehicle.

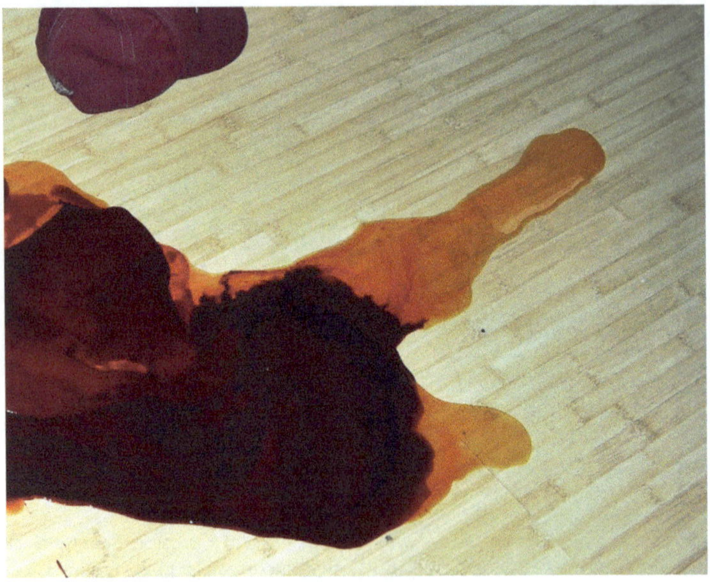

Figure 10.26 Pool of partially clotted blood with serum separation around the periphery of the pool.

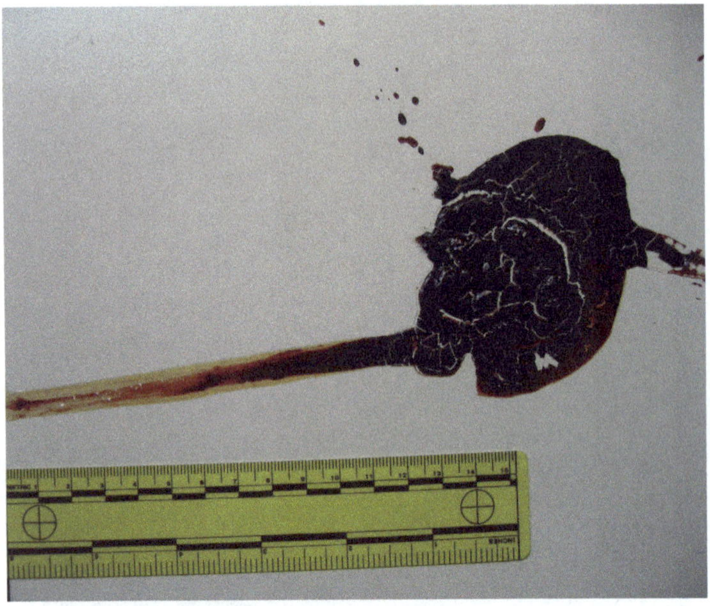

Figure 10.27 Pool of clotted and dried blood with serum separation around the periphery of an associated flow pattern.

There are a variety of clinical tests for the determination of clotting or coagulation times and a wide range of normal values. The whole blood is obtained by venipuncture or lancet puncture. The prothrombin and partial thromboplastin tests are performed on plasma not whole blood and the results are reported in seconds. The average normal values have been established for hospital and clinical laboratories by the testing of large sample populations in controlled laboratory studies,

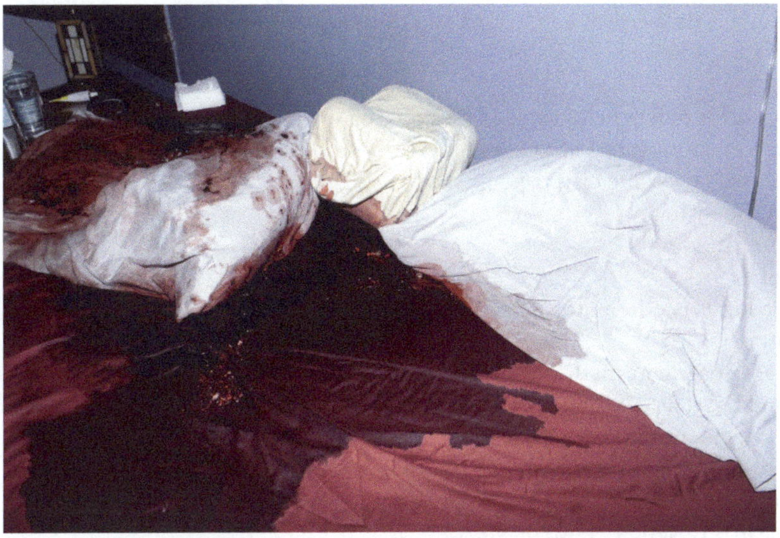

Figure 10.28 Pool of clotted blood on bed with diffusion and serum separation on pillows.

Table 10.1 Average Normal Values for Clinical Coagulation Tests

Test	Normal Value
Prothrombin time	9.5–12.0 seconds
Partial thromboplastin time	60–85 seconds
Activated partial thromboplastin time	20–35 seconds
Duke bleeding time (lancet in ear lobe)	1.0–3.0 minutes
Ivy bleeding time (incision in forearm)	Less than 9.0 minutes
Lee–White clotting time	3.0–15.0 minutes

as shown in Table 10.1.[14] In a forensic situation where injury has caused bloodshed, the bloodstain pattern analyst must consider the external factors that could affect the length of time required to form a clot. The values may vary depending on the diagnostic reagents used for the tests and the procedure utilized for the specific tests or external factors that could affect the length of time required to form a clot.

A normal range of 3–15 minutes for visible clots to appear has been utilized in BPA case work. This normal range was based upon the three-tube Lee–White clotting test performed at 37.5 °C that historically was utilized in hospital and clinical laboratories as a normal range for healthy individuals.[15]

In a forensic situation where injury has caused bloodshed, the bloodstain pattern analyst must consider the external factors that could affect the length of time required for a clot to form.

In 2001, Laber and Epstein published a research study "Substrate Effects on the Clotting Time of Human Blood" in the *Journal of the Canadian Society of Forensic Science.* They utilized 10 ml of freshly drawn human blood applied to substrates of human skin, glass, wool-polyester cloth, paper, and wood. They noted that clotting times varied among individuals and the surface upon which the blood was deposited.[16] Though not addressed in their paper, they recognized that environmental factors such as temperature and humidity as well as other conditions and circumstances will also have an effect on the clotting times of human blood.

There are numerous medical conditions and diseases that will lengthen the blood clotting time of individuals:

- Anemia
- Clotting factor deficiencies such as hemophilia
- Low platelet count (normal range is 150,000–400,000/mcL)
- Liver disease (alcoholic cirrhosis, hepatitis)
- Vitamin K deficiency
- Malignant tumors
- Leukemia
- Systemic lupus erythematosus
- Chemotherapy

Prescribed anticoagulant medications for the so-called blood thinning reduce the risk of recurrent strokes and heart attacks, and maintain patients at a controlled and lengthened clotting time. Common anticoagulant therapy medications are as follows:

- Warfarin – Coumadin®
- Heparin
- Enoxaparin – Lovenox® (clot blaster)

Patients prescribed these therapeutic medications are monitored and tested on a regular basis to ensure that the intended lengthened clotting times are not exceeded in order to avoid a serious bleeding episode. Aspirin will also increase the clotting time. Many adults are advised by their doctors to ingest a therapeutic dose of 81 mg of aspirin per day to reduce the risk of stroke or heart attack. It has been reported in *Circulation – The Journal of the American Heart Association* that the statin drug Simvastatin®, which acts to prevent coronary artery disease by reducing the cholesterol level, also lengthens the clotting time of blood.[17]

There are medical and physiological conditions that have the effect of shortening the clotting time of blood, which is referred to as hypercoagulability. High platelet count (in excess of 400,000 mcL) and excessive tissue factor (TF) will shorten the clotting time. Cerebrospinal fluid (CSF) is one of the triggers that may accelerate blood clotting. Head injuries or injuries to the spinal canal potentially release CSF into the site of the injury. As a result, the clotting times in such instances may be shortened.

A review of the scientific literature revealed studies that described an acceleration of the clotting time of blood when mixed with saliva.[18] This was due to a high level of TF present in saliva. An article, "Medical and Forensic Aspects of Blood Clot Formation in the Presence of Saliva" by Celestina Rossi et. al. was published in the September 2012 issue of the *Journal of Bloodstain Pattern Analysis.* [19] The results of their experiments are summarized in Table 10.2.

The article concluded that mixtures of saliva and blood significantly accelerated the clotting time of blood as demonstrated by Nour-Eldin and Wilkinson in their article "The Blood Clotting Factors in Human Saliva," published in the *Journal of Physiology* in 1957.[18] Therefore, the estimation of the elapsed time for the formation of blood clots in pooled blood or clotted spatters at scenes involving facial injuries and injuries to the airway may be reduced in the presence of tissue factor. This set of experiments has provided another factor to be considered for the estimation of clotting times in forensic casework and re-enforces the need for conservative conclusions. Another factor to consider is that the clotting times recorded in these experiments were based upon the "appearance of visible clots," which is a subjective visualization.

Small clotted spatters are often characterized by their "fried egg" appearance with a dark, dense center and lighter periphery of the stain (Figure 10.29). Clotted blood spatter on an assailant or a victim's clothing or surrounding surfaces associated with a beating death may indicate a significant interval between blows administered or possibly postmortem infliction of injury.

Coughing or exhalation of clotted blood by a victim may be associated with post-injury survival time. Usually small stains of freshly spattered blood will dry before they have the opportunity to

Table 10.2 Bar Graph of the Effects of Human Saliva on Human Blood Clotting Time

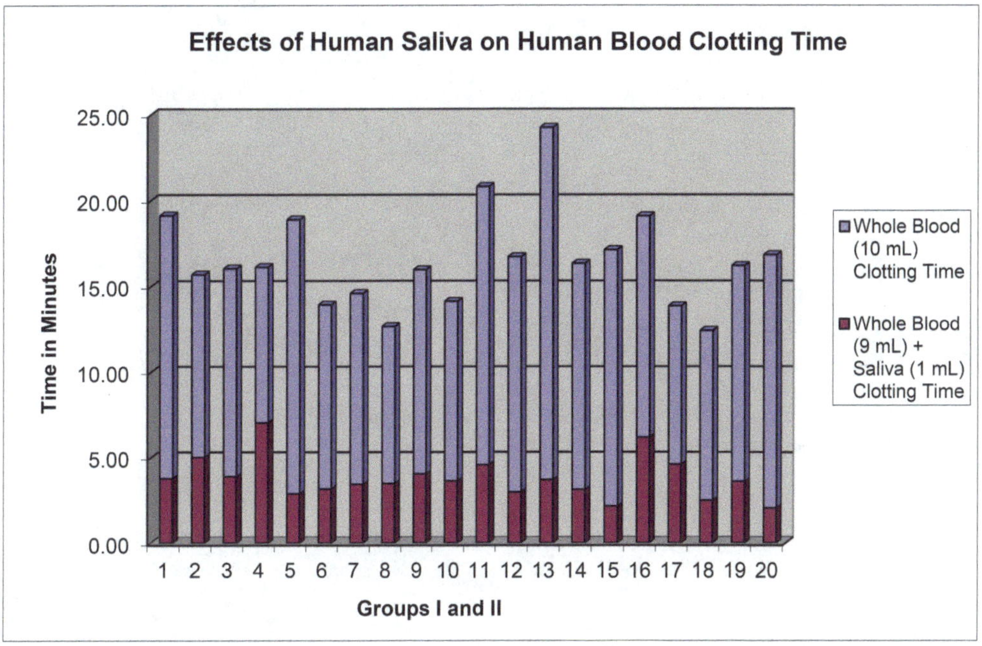

exhibit clots. An example of clotted spatter in the analysis of bloodstain patterns is demonstrated in the following case. A woman was found deceased in the bathroom of her cabin on a cruise ship. She had sustained multiple blunt force injuries to her head and abdomen. There was also evidence of strangulation. Her husband was arrested for her homicide. Examination of his shirt revealed spatters on the front of his shirt and shorts. A significant number of spatters on the shirt and shorts exhibited dark central areas surrounded by lighter reddish-brown staining. These spatters were consistent with clotted spatters. The mechanism for their production was likely a combination of impact spatters and small expiration stains (Figures 10.30a and b and 10.31a and b).

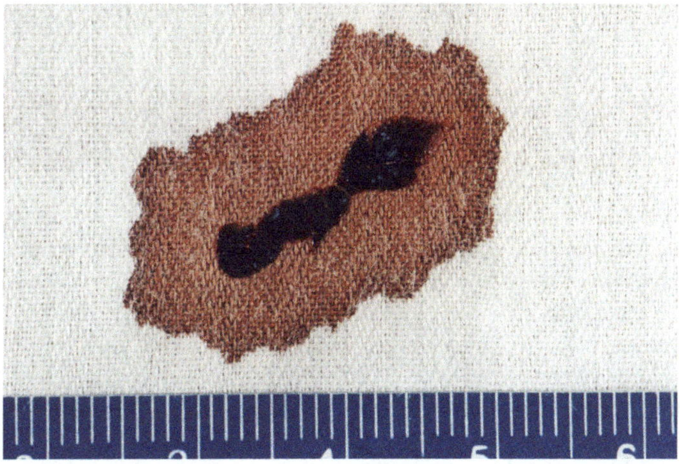

Figure 10.29 Clotted spatter produced in laboratory resulting from impact into partially clotted blood. Note the dark center and lighter periphery of the stain.

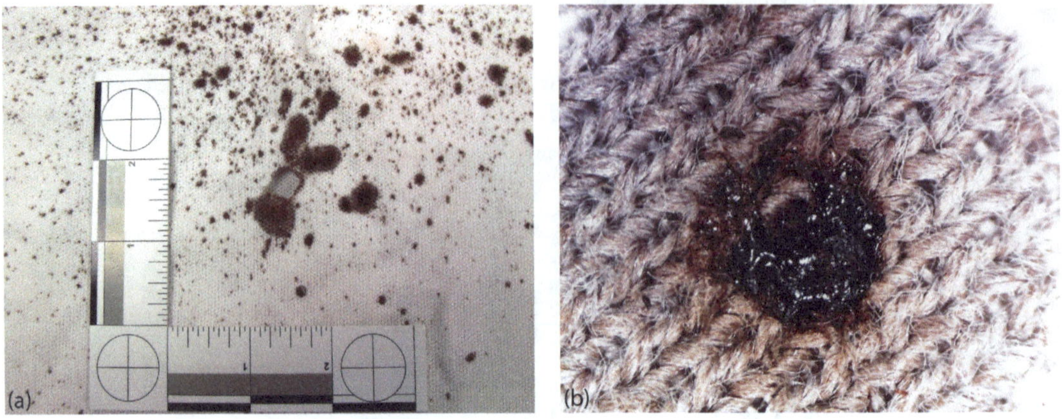

Figure 10.30 (a) Clotted spatters on front of white shirt of the assailant and (b) View of clotted spatter on white shirt with Celestron® digital microscope at approximately 10×.

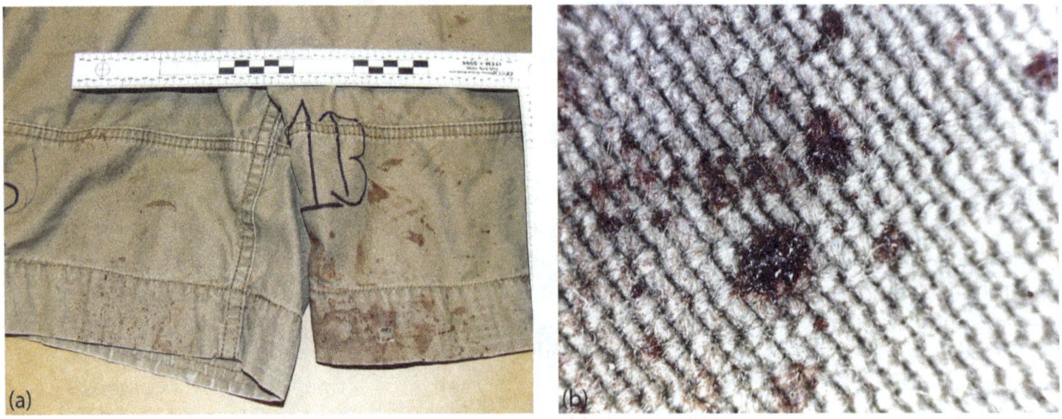

Figure 10.31 (a) View of clotted spatters on front of shorts of the assailant. (b) View of clotted spatters on front of shorts of the assailant with Celestron® digital microscope at approximately 10×.

SEQUENCING OF BLOODSTAINS

Sequencing is the placing of an order of events producing alterations of bloodstains which is possible in some cases. This could involve a significant amount of time with importance to the overall bloodstain reconstruction of the scene. The presence of clots in a drag pattern indicates the movement of a body at a time interval since the infliction of injury (Figure 10.32). A wipe through a partially dried stain leaving a perimeter stain indicates that more than a single event occurred sequentially with a lapse of time while the blood was still wet (Figure 10.33).

Experimentation by Hurley and Pex in 1990 has shown that the differentiation of blood spatter that has dried prior to being stepped on from a dried blood print with blood spatter on the top was difficult and not always possible.[20] Experiments conducted by the author and students in their advanced bloodstain pattern analysis classes have confirmed the study of Hurley and Pex. Caution should be exercised, especially if this analysis is attempted from photographs (Figures 10.34a and b and 10.35a and b).

Figure 10.32 Drag pattern with clotted blood indicating movement of a victim after a period of time after bloodshed

In 2014, Laber et al. published an article "The Reliability of Current Methods of Sequencing Bloodstain Patterns." They performed a study of superimposed spatter/transfer patterns on three different substrate surfaces where the spatter component consisted of small, medium, and a large number of stains. A total of 112 bloodstain patterns were prepared, half of which were spatter stains superimposed on transfer stains and half were transfer stains on spatter stains. They concluded that from this study on superimposed patterns, in general, analysts were reluctant to draw a firm conclusion in approximately half the samples. They incorrectly concluded the sequence of patterns in approximately 12% of pattern combinations where spatter stains were deposited on top of transfer stains and 17% for the reverse sequence.[21]

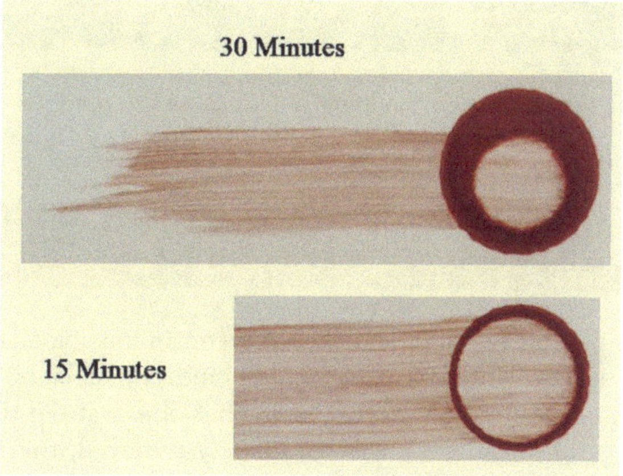

Figure 10.33 A wipe through drip stains indicating a lapse of time while the blood was wet

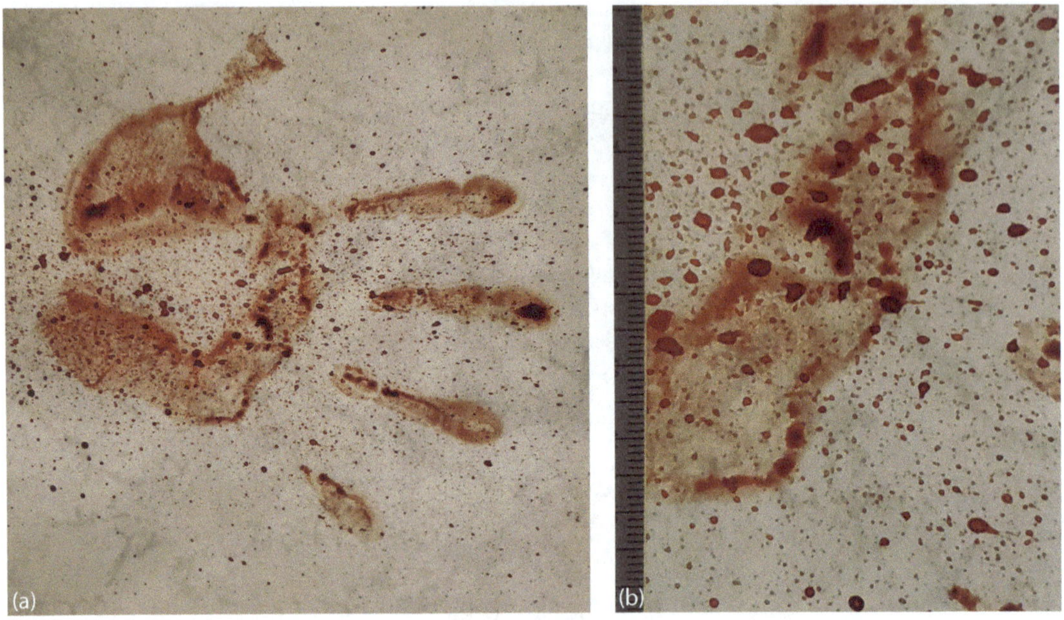

Figure 10.34 (a) View of bloody hand print over spatter on cardboard. (b) Close view of bloody hand print over spatter on cardboard.

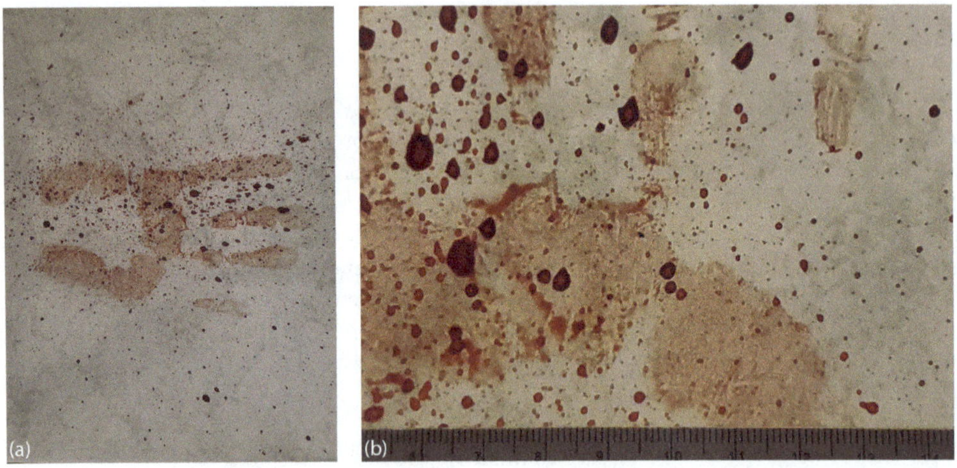

Figure 10.35 (a) View of spatter over bloody hand print. (b) Close view of spatter over bloody hand print.

VOID PATTERNS

A void is the absence of bloodstaining in an otherwise continuous bloodstain pattern.[22] A void is a result of the presence of intervening objects, victims, and/or assailants. Voids are functional for establishing the position of a victim, an assailant, or other object at the time of the event.[23] If the object or person is shifted in position or was completely removed, the resultant unstained void pattern remains and their original position can be reconstructed. The void may be a recognizable outline or may just show that someone or something interrupted the production of the bloodstain

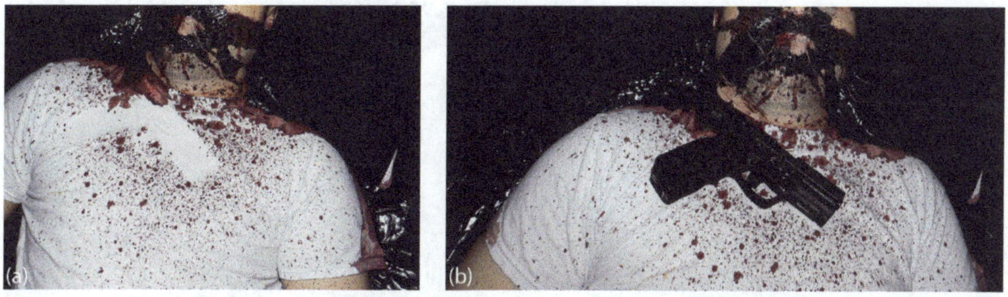

Figure 10.36 (a) Void within a pattern of expirated stains on the upper front of the shirt of a victim who sustained a self-inflicted gunshot wound to his right temple that exited his left temple. (Courtesy of Tiffany Fischer, Forensic Division, St. Charles County Police Department, O'Fallon, MO.) (b) Original location of the 9-mm firearm on the upper front of the shirt with expirated stains on the exposed right side of the weapon. (Courtesy of Tiffany Fischer, Forensic Division, St. Charles County Police Department, O'Fallon, MO.)

pattern. A void within a pattern of expirated bloodstains on the upper front shirt of a victim of a self-inflicted gunshot to the right temple that exited his left temple was produced by a 9-mm firearm that rested on his chest when the expirated pattern was produced (Figure 10.36a and b).

A void on the shirt of an assailant within a pattern of spattered bloodstains was created by folded eye glasses that were attached to the front collar of his shirt, as shown in Figure 10.37.

There was a pattern of spattered bloodstains with a void on a corner of a wall above a nightstand in a bedroom where a struggle and beating had occurred. There was a lamp on the bed with spatters on the underside of the shade. The void was created as the result of the lamp being overturned on the nightstand when the spatter was produced (Figure 10.38a–c).

Frequently, the position of a victim can be reconstructed by observation of a complete or partial outline of the victim or within a bloodstained area (Figure 10.39a and b). Voids may be present on victims that may indicate folding and the position of arms or hands or legs at the time of bloodshed (Figure 10.40). Folding of clothing and other fabrics while wet with blood often creates voids and additional stained areas that are referred to as mirror images, as shown in Figure 10.41.

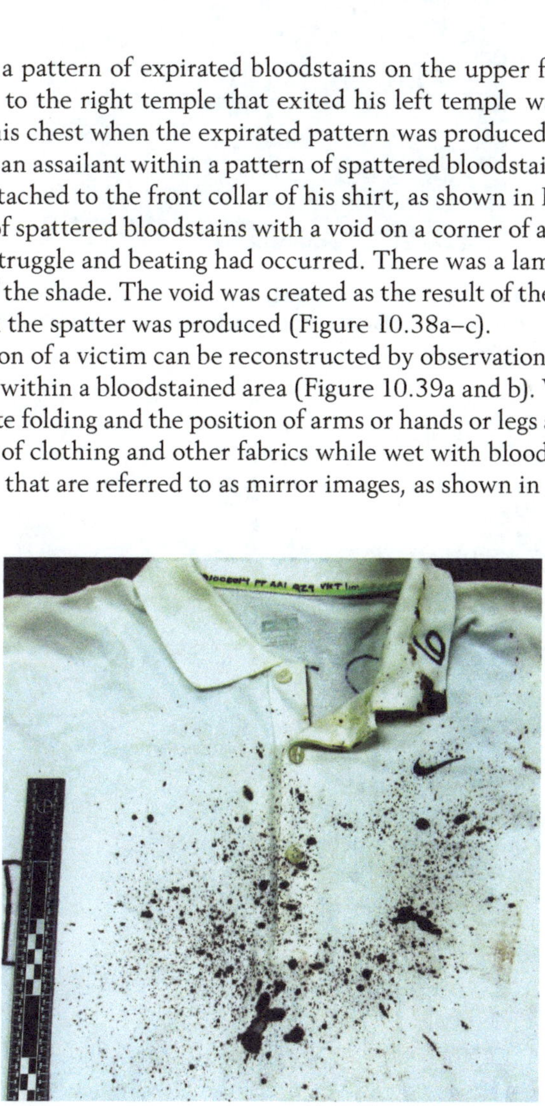

Figure 10.37 Void within a spatter pattern on the front of the shirt of an assailant created by folded glasses that were attached to the front collar of his shirt.

Figure 10.38 (a) Void within spatter pattern on the wall of a bedroom above a nightstand. (b) Overturned lamp with spatters on underside of the shade of a lamp on the bed near the nightstand. (c) Placement of the overturned lamp within the void on the bedroom wall.

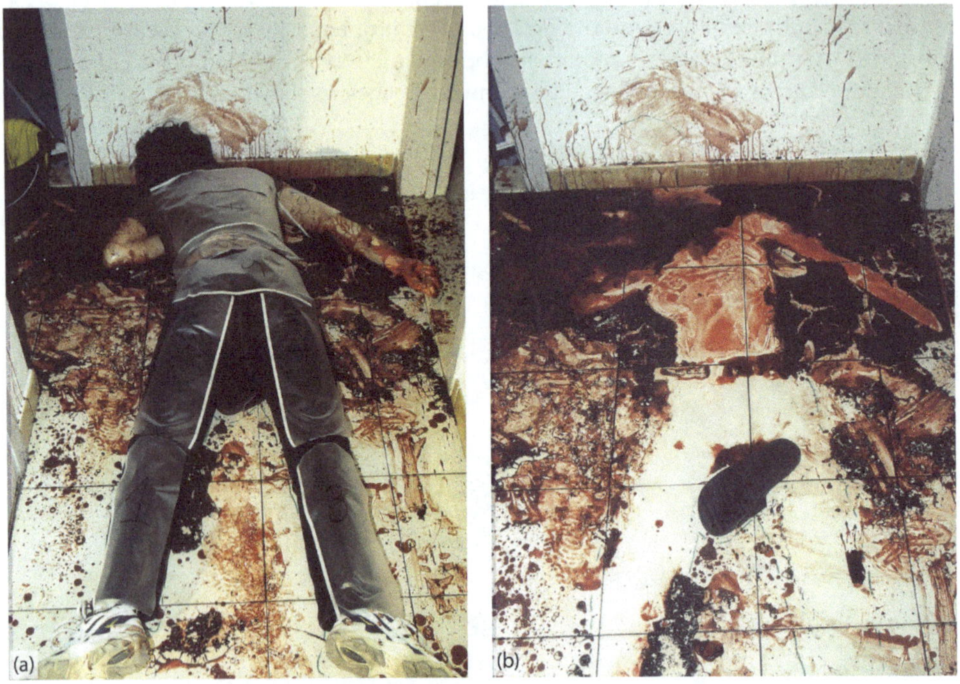

Figure 10.39 (a) View of a victim on the floor prior to removal. (Courtesy of Martin Eversdijk, Loci Forensics B.V., The Netherlands.) (b) Void on floor after removal of the victim. (Courtesy of Martin Eversdijk, Loci Forensics B.V., The Netherlands.)

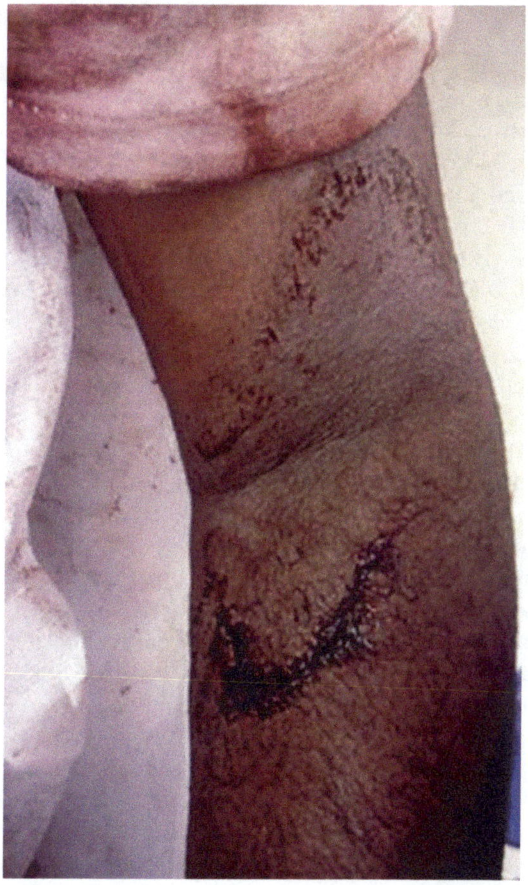

Figure 10.40 Void on arm in antecubital area indicating that the arm was folded during the deposition of blood.

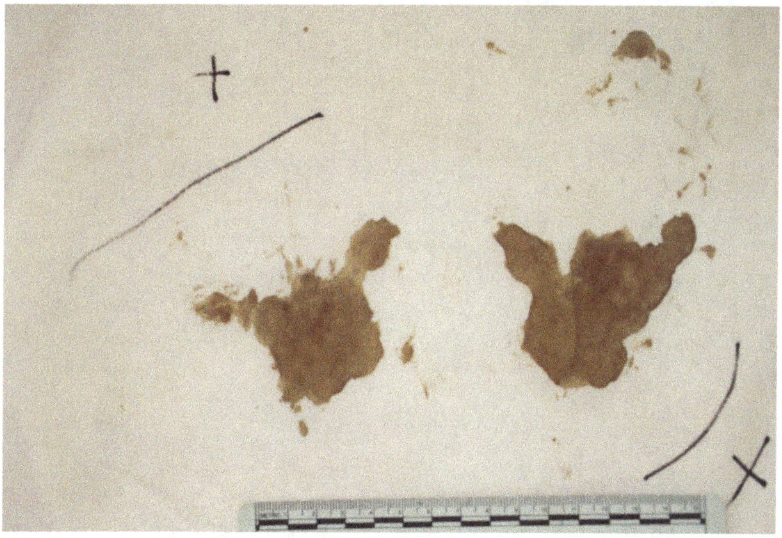

Figure 10.41 Void on fabric between mirror image of bloodstain created by the fold in the fabric prior to the deposition of the blood.

EFFECTS OF FIRE AND SOOT ON BLOODSTAINS

The alteration of bloodstains as the result of the effects of fire and soot is another consideration for analysis. In some cases, bloodstains may be covered by soot and be missed entirely at the scene of a homicide that preceded a fire. MacDonell, in his 1993 publication, *Bloodstain Patterns*, demonstrated that the outer layer of soot is easily removed with lifting tape.[24] The distinction of soot over bloodstains or conversely bloodstains over soot is helpful to determine the sequence of events.

In 1997, Redsicker and O'Connor coauthored the book, *Practical Fire and Arson Investigation*, 2nd edition. They discussed the effects of fire, heat, and smoke on bloodstains in their chapter "Investigating Fatal Fires." As would be expected, bloodstains undergo a variety of physical changes depending on their proximity to sources of heat, fire, and smoke. Bloodstains may darken due to the physical barrier created by the soot and fade (ghosting effect) or be totally destroyed, depending on the intensity and duration of a fire (Figures 10.42 and 10.43). It is also important to recognize alterations to bloodstains at fire scenes that may occur as a result of the diluting effects of water and the activities of firefighting personnel.[25]

The development of the latex technique of removing soot from bloodstains by Larkin et al. was the result of a case, in which a dismembered body was found in the Thames River. In correlation to a kidnapping, there was a suspicion that the victim had been staying in a flat that had been burned. The injuries to the victim indicated that a bloodletting event had taken place, so they searched for a technique to examine areas such as walls in the burned flat. In 2008, Larkin et al. reported their use of latex applied to soot covered surfaces to allow further fingerprint examinations in their article, "Using Liquid Latex to Remove Soot to Facilitate Fingerprint and Bloodstain Examinations: A Case Study," which was published in the *Journal of Forensic Identification*.[26]

In 2011, Luche et al. published an article, "Recovery of Bloodstain Patterns from Arson Scenes: Does Soot Removal Using Liquid Latex Damage Underlying Bloodstains?" in the *Canadian Society of Forensic Science Journal*. The liquid latex technique for soot removal facilitated bloodstain visualization as well as contaminant removal, aiding any subsequent presumptive testing or DNA

Figure 10.42 View of soot covering spatters and flow patterns on the wall.

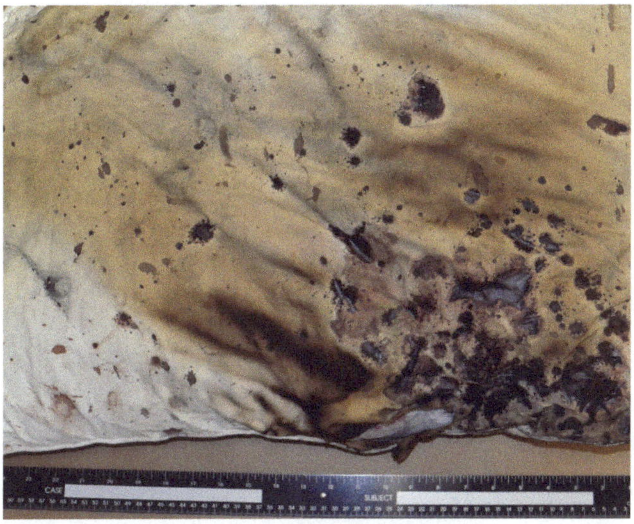

Figure 10.43 View of spatters and drip stains on a pillow exposed to fire.

analysis. They also noted that the circumstances upon which the success of the latex–soot removal methodology depends are primarily related to the nature of the surface.[27]

Detection of bloodstains covered with soot has been accomplished with the use of reflected infrared photography. The success of the technique is dependent on the reflective properties of the background surface, the spectral absorption properties of blood, and the ability of the infrared wavelengths to transmit through the soot layer.[28]

INTENTIONAL ALTERATION OR ATTEMPTS AT THE REMOVAL OF BLOODSTAINS

Attempts to eliminate bloodstain evidence at a scene or the washing of bloodstained clothing is often encountered during the course of an investigation. There have been many cases where attempts have been made to clean or obliterate bloodstains from surfaces at the scene and clothing by various methods that result in partial or complete alteration removal of the stained areas. These procedures include the use of detergent and water, bleach, pool acid (HCl), paint, fire, and even gouging. There is usually compelling evidence of the use of bleach and caustic agents. In a particular case, an assailant attempted to remove bloodstains from a brown carpet with bleach, which was clearly obvious (Figure 10.44). The same individual attempted to gouge out small impact blood spatters from a painted sheet rock wall but abandoned this effort because of the large number of blood spatters.

Paint has been used in an attempt to cover bloodstains on surfaces. Often bloodstains are partially visible through light-colored paint. Figure 10.45 and 10.46).

Detection of bloodstains that have been painted over up to six layers has been accomplished with reflective infrared photography.[29] However, the results vary depending upon the characteristics of the paint.

An attempt to cover bloodstains at the scene of a stabbing using "Quick Grits" taken from the kitchen cupboard at the scene is shown in Figure 10.47a and b).

In another case, a suspect was brought in for questioning by the police and provided a ballpoint pen to write a statement. While left alone for a period of time, he attempted to cover bloodstains

Figure 10.44 Attempted cleanup of blood trail on a carpet using bleach.

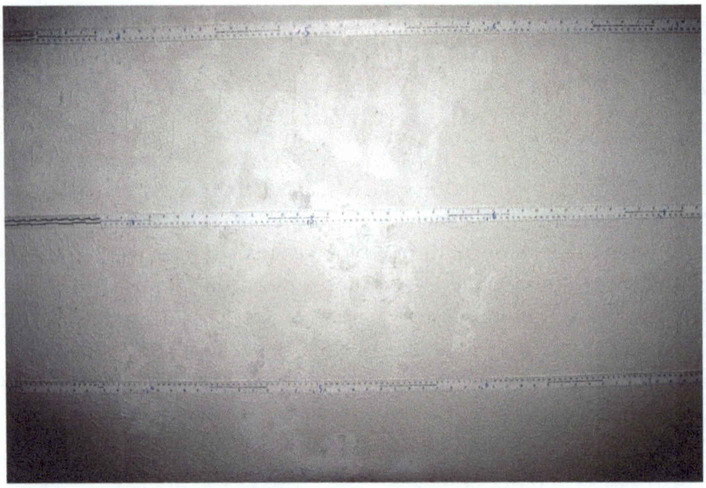

Figure 10.45 Attempted concealing of cast-off stains on ceiling using white poster paint.

on the front of his shirt with blue ink. The underside of the shirt below the inked areas showed blood that had soaked through the fabric (Figures 10.48–10.50).

As experience has shown, the cleaning procedures used often do not completely eliminate the presence of bloodstains. Occasionally, recognizable wipe patterns and diluted-appearing projected stains will be visible on nearby surfaces. Cast-off bloodstains and small spatters on furniture, walls, ceilings, and other objects often go unnoticed by the person attempting to clean up the scene.

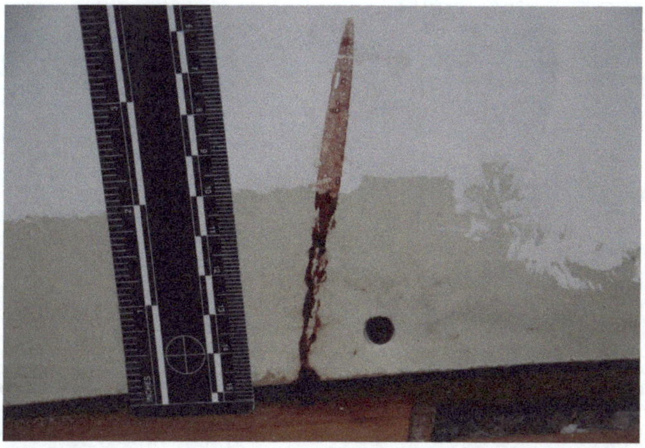

Figure 10.46 Attempted concealing of angular drip stain with white paint on the wall.

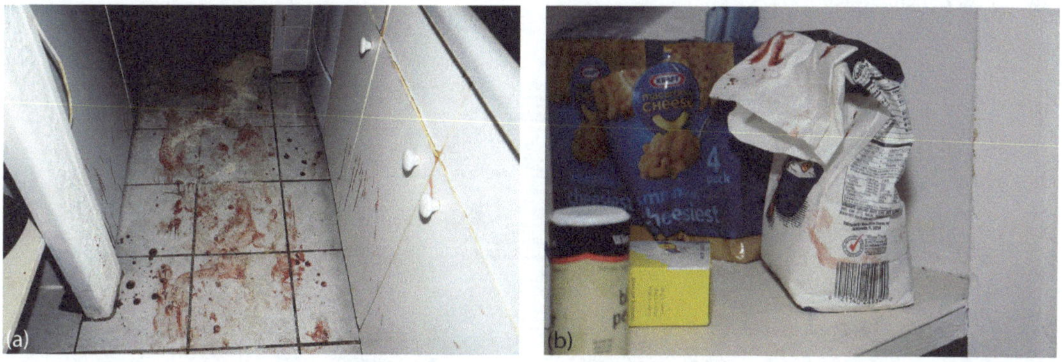

Figure 10.47 (a) Partial covering of bloodstains on the floor at scene with "Quick Grits." (Courtesy of Anna Cox, Cox Forensic Consulting and Training, LLC, Brandon, FL.) (b) Bag of "Quick Grits" in kitchen cupboard at scene that exhibited transfer stains and a few small spatters. (Courtesy of Anna Cox, Cox Forensic Consulting and Training, LLC, Brandon, FL.)

Figure 10.48 Outside of the front of the shirt with blue ink stains. (Courtesy of Andreas Schweizer, Zurich City Police, Zurich, Switzerland.)

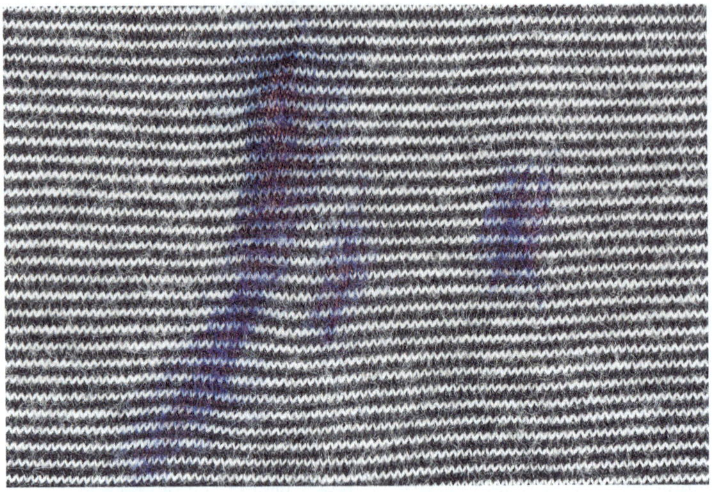

Figure 10.49 Close view of the blue ink stains on the front of the shirt. (Courtesy of Andreas Schweizer, Zurich City Police, Zurich, Switzerland.)

Figure 10.50 View of the underside of the front of the shirt with reddish-brown stains. (Courtesy of Andreas Schweizer, Zurich City Police, Zurich, Switzerland.)

Blood has been successfully removed from clothing by washing, but this depends on the quantity and age of the bloodstains, the type of fabric involved, and the washing procedure used. Gifford reported a case study in which diffused bloodstains were found on the denim jeans of a male gunshot victim who was found in a slow-flowing stream in Alaska six days after his death. He conducted experiments on bloodstained clothing in moving and stagnant water. The results of his experiments were that bloodstains did not survive in moving water for more than a few minutes. While in still water they lasted more than 3 hours. He concluded that the diffused blood was deposited on the victim's denim jeans after they had been removed at autopsy.[30]

Diluted bloodstains resulting from machine washing may not be visible especially on dark clothing. Research by Adair and Shaw showed the use of luminol as an effective blood reagent on many washed and unwashed surfaces. They cautioned in using LCV as this reagent did not yield acceptable results in their study. They also indicated that phenolphthalein will yield presumptively positive results on washed clothing even after the application of luminol and LCV.[31]

The ability of a fabric to retain blood after washing depends not only on the chemistry and manufacturing of the fabric but also on the type of detergent and the time of immersion. Research conducted by Mushtaq and Rasool showed that cotton polyester and khadder (a plain weaved cotton) showed maximum retention of blood after washing, whereas silk polyester had the minimum ability to hold bloodstains. They reported that Hemastix® was the most sensitive presumptive test for the presence of blood on washed stains.[32]

Standard dry cleaning procedures that immerse fabric in an organic solvent may not be effective for the removal of bloodstains from fabrics. William Best, a forensic scientist from North Carolina, demonstrated this in a case where a serologist testified that dry cleaning likely removed blood from a jacket that was negative on examination. Best applied his blood to a similar jacket and detected the blood on the jacket with luminol after the dry cleaning was completed.[33]

Another interesting case involving the alleged washing of bloody clothing was a triple homicide in which the victims were beaten and shot. A girlfriend of one of the co-defendants testified that she observed him washing his clothes in the washing machine the day after the homicides. He had used dishwashing detergent, causing soap bubbles to rise in the washer and overflow extensively onto the floor. She maintained that the bubbles were red, indicating that he must have been washing blood from his clothing. At the request of the defense attorney, experiments were designed to determine if an agitated mixture of the same brand dishwashing detergent, water, and blood would produce red suds or bubbles. Initial tests were performed in a beaker on a magnetic stirrer. The results indicated that the blood mixed with detergent and water quickly turned dark brown to black and the foam or suds remained white. The experiment was repeated in a washing machine using a heavily bloodstained blanket and the same brand dishwashing detergent. There were copious amounts of white foam and bubbles produced that overflowed onto the floor. There was no indication of red bubbles, as maintained by the witness.

In summary, the alterations of bloodstains by physical and environmental effects should always be considered when interpreting bloodstain patterns because they often affect the overall reconstruction of a case. If the appearance of the stains is out of the ordinary or atypical, then physical or physiological alteration should be considered.

ACKNOWLEDGMENTS

Jeremy Morris, Johnson County Sheriff's Office, Olathe, KS
Anna Cox, Cox Forensic Consulting and Training, LLC, Brandon, FL
Celestina Rossi, Montgomery County Sheriff's Office Conroe, TX
Todd A. Thorne, Retired – Kenosha Wisconsin Police Department – Forensic Unit, Kenosha, WI
Martin Eversdjik, Loci Forensics, B.V., The Netherlands
Dennis Kunkel Microscopy, Kailua, Hawaii
Andreas Schweizer, Zurich City Police, Zurich, Switzerland

Notes

1. American Academy of Forensic Sciences Academy Standards Board (ASB), Technical Report 033, Terms and Definitions in Bloodstain Pattern Analysis, 1st edition, 2017.
2. Michielson, Stephen, Michael Taylor, Namrata Parekh, and Feng Ji, "Bloodstain Patterns on Textile Surfaces: A Fundamental Analysis," United States Department of Justice, Document No: 248671, March 2015, pp. 2, 4, 33.
3. American Academy of Forensic Sciences Academy Standards Board (ASB), Technical Report 033, Terms and Definitions in Bloodstain Pattern Analysis, 1st edition, 2017.

4. Laan, Nick, Fiona Smith, Celine Nicloux, and David Brutin, "Morphology of Drying Blood Pools," *Forensic Science International*, 2016, 267, pp. 104–109. https://hal.archives-ouvertes,fr/hal-01770001, pp. 1–19.
5. Laber, Terry L., and Barton P. Epstein, *Experiments and Practical Exercises in Bloodstain Pattern Analysis*, Callen Publishing, Inc. Minneapolis, MN, 1983, pp. 100–104.
6. Anderson, Stacey, Brandi Howard, Gerald R. Hobbs, and Clifton P. Bishop, "A Method for Determining the Age of a Bloodstain," *Forensic Science International*, 2005, 148, pp. 37–45.
7. Guo, Kevin, Samuel Achilefu, and Mikhail Berezin, "Dating Bloodstains with Fluorescene, Lifetime Measurements," *Chemistry*, 18(5), 2012, pp. 1303–1305.
8. Bremmer, Rolf H., Annemarie Nadort, Ton G. van Leeuwen, Martin J. C. van Gernert, and Maurice C. G. Aalders, "Age Estimation of Bloodstains by Hemoglobin Derivative Determination Using Reflectance Spectroscopy," *Forensic Science International*, 206, 2011, pp. 166–171.
9. Botonjic-Sehic, Edita, Mary Tsaparikos, Chris W. Brown, and Marc Lamontagne "Forensic Application of Near-Infrared Spectroscopy: Aging of Bloodstains," *Spectroscopy*, 24 (2), 2009.
10. American Academy of Forensic Sciences Academy Standards Board (ASB), Technical Report 033, Terms and Definitions in Bloodstain Pattern Analysis, 1st edition, 2017.
11. James, Stuart H., Paul E. Kish, and T. Paulette Sutton, *Principles of Bloodstain Pattern Analysis: Theory and Practice*, CRC Press, Boca Raton, FL, 2005, pp. 188–189.
12. American Academy of Forensic Sciences Academy Standards Board (ASB), Technical Report 033, Terms and Definitions in Bloodstain Pattern Analysis, 1st edition, 2017.
13. James, Stuart H., Paul E. Kish, and T. Paulette Sutton, *Principles of Bloodstain Pattern Analysis: Theory and Practice*, CRC Press, Boca Raton, FL, 2005, pp. 190–192.
14. Malarkey, L. M., and M. E. McMorrow, *Laboratory Tests and Diagnostic Procedures*, 2nd edition, Mosby Company, St. Louis, MO, 2001.
15. United States National Library of Medicine, Bethesda, MD, 2011.
16. Laber, Terry L., and Barton P. Epstein, "Substrate Effects on the Clotting Time of Human Blood," *Canadian Society of Forensic Science Journal*, 34(4), 2001, pp. 209–214.
17. Undas,Anetta, Kathleen E. Brummel, J. Musial, Kenneth G. Mann, and A. Szczeklik, "Simvastin Depresses Blood Clotting by Inhibiting Activation of Prothrombin, Factor 5, and Factor 8 and by Enhancing Factor Va Inactivation," *Circulation: Journal of the American Heart Association*, 18, 2001, pp. 1–2.
18. Nour-Eldin, F., and John F. Wilkinson, "The Blood Clotting Factors in Human Saliva," *Journal of Physiology*, 136, 1957, pp. 324–332
19. Rossi Celestina, Misty Holbrook, Stuart H. James, and Daniel Mabel, "Medical and Forensic Aspects of Blood Clot Formation in the Presence of Saliva: A Preliminary Study," *Journal of Bloodstain Pattern Analysis*, 28(3), 2012, pp. 3–12.
20. Hurley, M., and James Pex, "Sequencing of Bloody Shoe Impressions by Blood Spatter and Blood Droplet Drying Times," *IABPA News*, December 1990.
21. Laber, Terry L., Michael C. Taylor, and Paul E. Kish, "The Reliability of Current Methods of Sequencing Bloodstain Patterns," *Journal of Bloodstain Pattern Analysis*, 2014, 30(1), pp. 3–10.
22. American Academy of Forensic Sciences Academy Standards Board (ASB), Technical Report 033, Terms and Definitions in Bloodstain Pattern Analysis, 1st edition, 2017.
23. Bevel, Tom, and Ross M. Gardner, *Bloodstain Pattern Analysis with an Introduction to Crime Scene Reconstruction*, CRC Press, Taylor & Francis Group, Boca Raton, FL, 2008, pp. 255–256.
24. MacDonell, Herbert Leon, *Bloodstain Patterns*, Golas Printing, Inc., Elmira Heights, NY, 1993, pp. 95–97.
25. Redsicker, David R., and John J. O'Conner, *Practical Fire and Arson Investigation*, 2nd edition, CRC Press, Boca Raton, FL, 1997, pp. 225–241.
26. Larkin, Tony, N. Marsh, and P. Larrigan, "Using Liquid Latex to Remove Soot to Facilitate Fingerprint and Bloodstain Examinations: A Case Study," *Journal of Forensic Identification*, 58(5), 2008, pp. 540–550.
27. Luche, Christopher, Ralph Jordan, and Tony Larkin, "Recovery of Bloodstain Patterns from Arson Scenes: Does Soot Removal Using Liquid Latex Damage Underlying Bloodstains?," *Canadian Society of Forensic Science Journal*, 44(2), 2011.
28. Bastide, Belinda, Glenn Porter, and Adrian Renshaw, "Detection of Latent Bloodstains at Fire Scenes Using Reflected Infrared Photography," Forensic *Science International*, 302, 2019.

29. Farrar, Andrew, Glenn Porter, and Adrian Renshaw, "Detection of Latent Bloodstains Beneath Painted Surfaces Using Reflective Infrared Photography," *Journal of Forensic Sciences*, 57(5), 2012.
30. Gifford, William D., "Bloodstain Survival in Water," *IABPA News*, 15(2), 1999, pp. 1–6.
31. Adair, Thomas W., and Rebecca L. Shaw, "Enhancement of Bloodstains on Washed Clothing Using Luminol and LCV Reagents," *IABPA News*, 2005, p. 9.
32. Mushtaq, Samreen, and Nouman Rasool, "Detection of Dry Bloodstains on Different Fabrics after Washing with Commercially Available Detergents," *Australian Journal of Forensic Sciences*, 48(1), 2015, pp. 1–8.
33. Best, William, North Carolina, Personal communication.

CHAPTER 11

INSECT STAINS

Elizabeth Richards

Forensic entomology is a broad discipline that encompasses the intersection of arthropod science and the judicial system with a focus on utilizing insect evidence to help solve criminal investigations, most often those involving violent crimes.[1,2] Insects, especially flies, are attracted to scenes where human remains, blood, and/or tissue are present. As the insects interact with those resources, their activities and movements can either alter existing bloodstains or create new ones. For example, Haglund and Sorg described what they termed "pseudo blood spatter" in their text, *Forensic Taphonomy: The Postmortem Fate of Human Remains*.[3] They described a case in which blood was observed "trailing in the wrong direction" from where the deceased was found. Blood was also observed underneath an exposed page of a calendar, but no blood was observed on the exposed page. This created some confusion during the bloodstain pattern analysis of the scene until a large cockroach was observed walking through a pool of blood and depositing stains on a nearby surface identical to those originally observed. In their 2003 paper, Benecke and Barksdale described three cases studies in which bloodstains were observed within crime scenes that also caused confusion during analytical and reconstructive efforts.[4] In one crime scene, a female was found deceased in her residence. She was located in her bedroom and there were no signs of a violent attack. However, what appeared to be spatter stains were observed in the kitchen (two rooms away) on the pull-chain of a ceiling fan. There was no visible evidence within the scene that linked the two locations. Through careful evaluation of the scene and an assessment of the fly activity present, they were able to determine those stains were actually deposited by flies. They were able to rule out the possibility of a violent event and her death was considered to be a result of self-neglect rather than homicide. Therefore, although insects can be of importance in resolving violent crimes, their presence and subsequent activities at a scene can be a complicating factor in bloodstain pattern analysis. Many types of insects are attracted to human remains and/or blood within a crime scene for a variety of reasons; however, this chapter will primarily focus on flies (Order Diptera) and will serve to increase a bloodstain pattern analyst's understanding of fly activity within a scene so that such factors can be properly accounted for during analytical and reconstructive efforts.

An insect stain is a bloodstain resulting from insect activity.[5] These stains have frequently been referred to as fly artifacts[4,6,7,8,9,10,11] and less frequently as fly specks or fly spots.[4,12,13] For the purpose of this chapter, bloodstains that have been newly created or altered by fly activity will be referred to as insect stains. Regarding flies, insect stains can be created a variety of ways and in this chapter, the focus will be on three mechanisms: regurgitation, defecation, and transfer. Adult flies ingest a liquid food source (blood) through their sponging mouthparts. They frequently regurgitate partially digested food from their crop (an enlarged area of an insect's gut) that can accumulate as a drop (or bubble) on the tips of their mouthparts.[6,14] The bubble will then either drop onto a surface or, if it is still adhering to the adult fly's mouthparts, be deposited onto a surface upon contact.[6] After ingesting a liquid food source, adult flies will also eliminate waste as liquid feces through defecation. Both processes, regurgitation and defecation, can create insect stains that are similar in appearance to bloodstains and bloodstain patterns. Insect stains are often a millimeter or less in diameter (although they can be over 2 mm in length) with no observable area

 DOI: 10.4324/9781003163695-11

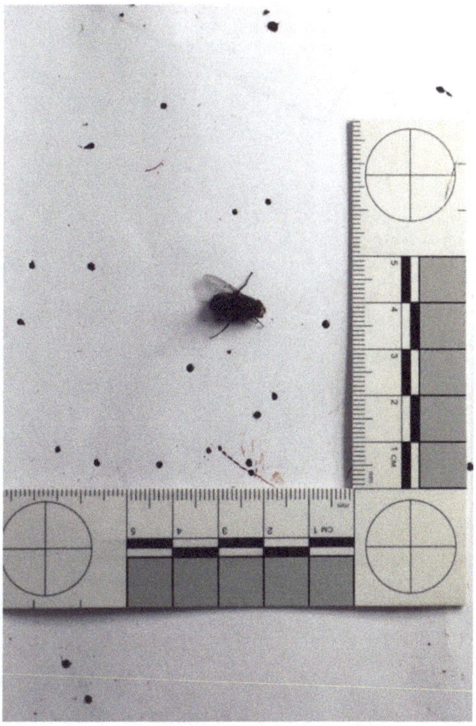

Figure 11.1 Circular/nearly circular insect (fly) stains with no tails on paper. (Photograph courtesy of Stuart James.)

of convergence or area of origin.[6,14] The stains are usually round or elliptical in shape and lack spiny edges (Figures 11.1 and 11.2); however, both regurgitate and defecatory insect stains can appear to have a tapered end or tail (Figures 11.3 and 11.4) giving the stain an appearance similar to that of a sperm, tadpole, or tear-drop.[4,6] The tapered end or tail is formed when the adult fly begins to move away as the regurgitate bubble is making contact with a surface or as the fly moves away prior to completing the defecation process. In some instances, the presence of a tail can indicate direction of fly movement.[6] Tails are also associated with defecate stains resulting from the forcible expulsion of feces.[15] With this type of stain, the tail can point in the direction the liquid feces traveled. Although observed as a characteristic of both regurgitate and defecatory insect stains, tails are most often associated with defecation.[6] The morphology as well as the color of regurgitate and

Figure 11.2 Circular/nearly circular insect stains (fly regurgitate stains) with no tails on window blinds. (Photograph courtesy of Todd A. Thorne, Kenosha, Wisconsin.)

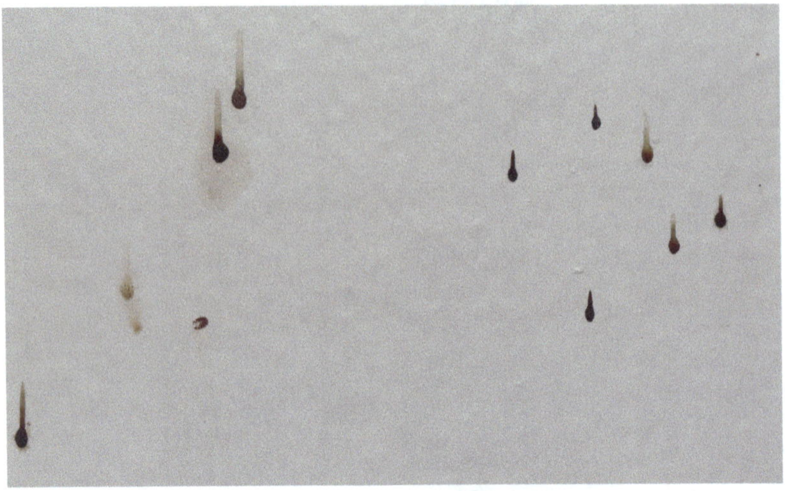

Figure 11.3 Insect stains (fly defecatory stains) with tails produced after feeding on human blood. (Photograph courtesy of Anna Cox, Cox Forensic Consulting and Training, LLC, Brandon, Florida.)

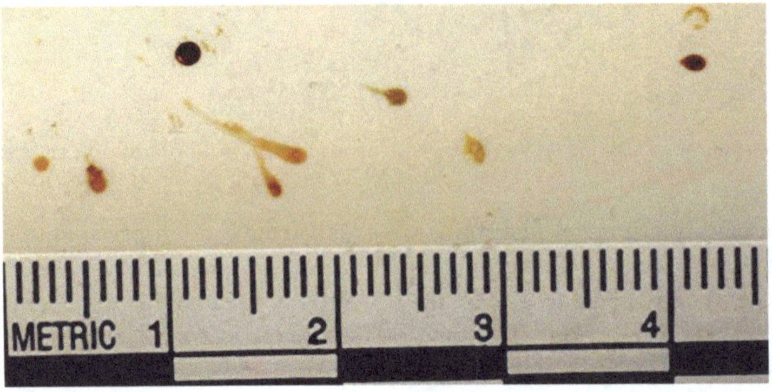

Figure 11.4 Insect stains (fly defecatory stains) with tails and circular/nearly circular regurgitate stains with no tails after feeding on human blood. (Photograph courtesy of Stuart James.)

defecatory insect stains can vary depending on the species of fly, diet, and deposition surface.[6,8,10] For a more in-depth discussion of the morphological characteristics of bloodstains and insect stains on non-porous surfaces, refer to Benecke and Barksdale,[4] Durdle et al.[8] and Parker et al.[16] All three offer insightful questions and guidance an analyst should consider when faced with the task of discerning insect stains from bloodstains. Research examining insect stains deposited on porous materials such as textiles is sparse in comparison to those deposited on non-porous surfaces. It can be much more challenging to distinguish insect stains from bloodstains on textiles such as clothing, especially if both are present. Rivers et al. determined the morphology of insect stains deposited on shirt fabrics was distorted in comparison to stains deposited on a smooth/non-porous surface.[15] Fabric color, type, tension (i.e., worn loose or tight fitting), and face (inside surface versus outside surface) all influenced their ability to visually distinguish insect stains from bloodstains. For example, on white or light-colored fabric, they were able to use morphology to distinguish between insect stains and bloodstains. However, on darker fabrics (low contrast with the stains), when satellite stains were absent (i.e., not associated with bloodstains on the fabrics in their study) or when substantial wicking occurred, it became more difficult to distinguish between insect stains and bloodstains. Bloodstain pattern analysts should therefore proceed with caution when

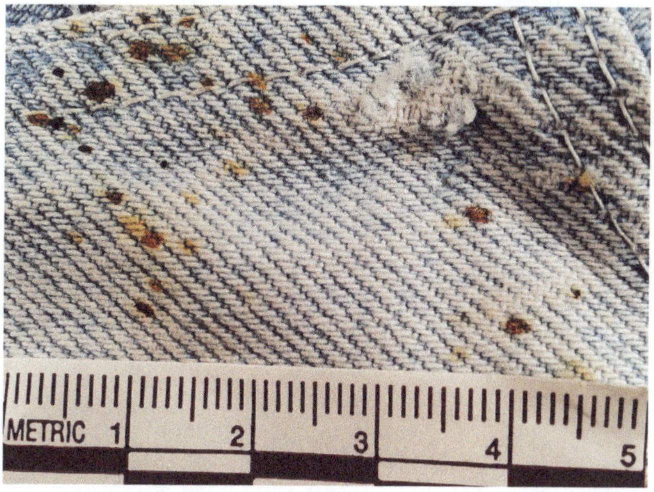

Figure 11.5 Insect (fly) stains on denim jeans. (Photograph courtesy of Stuart James.)

attempting to visually distinguish between insect stains and bloodstains on textiles based on morphological characteristics alone. Figures 11.5 and 11.6 represent insect stains on porous surfaces.

When adult flies (or other insects associated with human remains and/or blood) make contact with liquid blood, there is a possibility they will subsequently deposit that blood onto another surface, thus creating a transfer stain. If this happens, it is usually through their tarsi (feet)[13] and the resulting stains are sometimes referred to as "tarsal tracks" or "tarsal prints."[5,17] In some research studies, tarsal tracks were not observed even though the adult flies were observed with their tarsi in contact with liquid blood. In some of those studies, the researchers observed that the tarsi did not break the surface tension of the blood.[7,17,18] However, in Rivers and McGregor, they did observe tarsal tracks and further noted regurgitation stains were the most frequently observed type of stain with defecation stains the second most prevalent.[10] The frequency of tarsal tracks was dependent on species, and, interestingly, size as smaller (in terms of both length and mass) adult flies were more likely to produce stains from blood transference on the tarsi.[10]

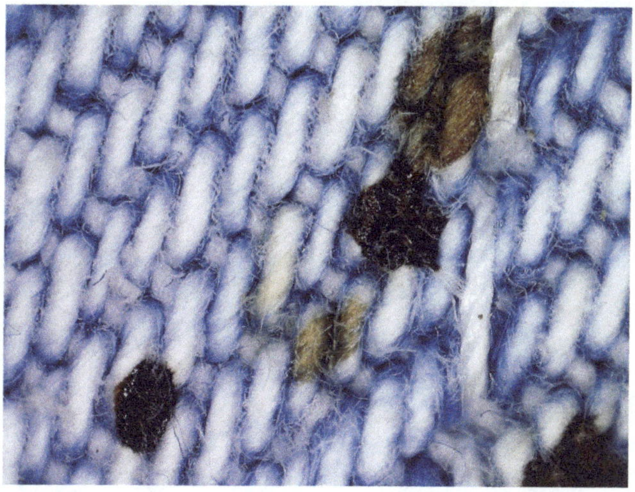

Figure 11.6 Insect (fly) stains on denim jeans with use of the digital microscope, Celestron®, at approximately 10x magnification. (Photograph courtesy of Stuart James.)

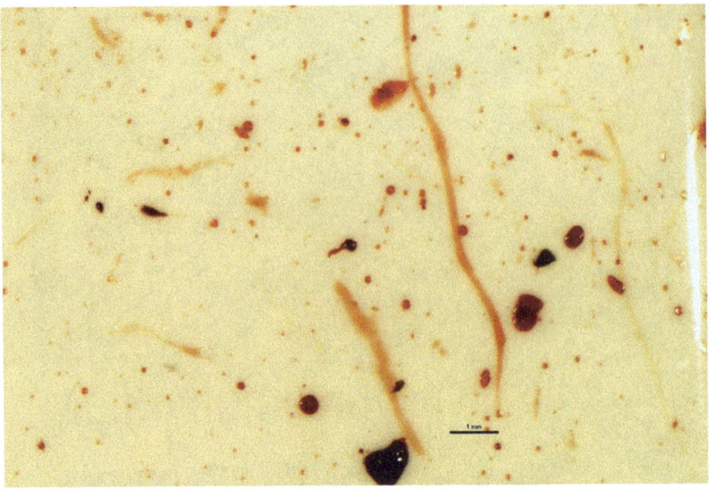

Figure 11.7 Several translocation stains (asymmetrical lines) intermixed with tarsal tracks and regurgitate stains. The stains were produced by adult *Calliphora vicina* walking through wet human blood and then dragging the leg (faint lines) or abdomen (darker stains) across ceramic tile. Images represent 6.3x magnification. (Photograph courtesy of David B. Rivers.)

Altered stains can potentially happen three ways due to fly activity: (1) As fly larvae (maggots) migrate away from their feeding source (which may be associated with liquid blood), they may create trails of blood or "larval trails" altering the appearance of that blood source.[7] (2) Adult insects, to include flies as well as roaches and ants, may drag their abdomens through a liquid blood source, causing linear, asymmetrical stains sometimes referred to as translocation stains (Figure 11.7).[6,10,13] (3) Through their feeding activity, adult flies may either entirely or partially consume a single bloodstain. If this happens with a wet bloodstain, very little of the stain may still be observed, leaving only the border or skeleton of the original bloodstain (Figure 11.8).[18] In bloodstain pattern analysis, this is known as a perimeter stain.[5] When adult flies feed on a dry bloodstain, small

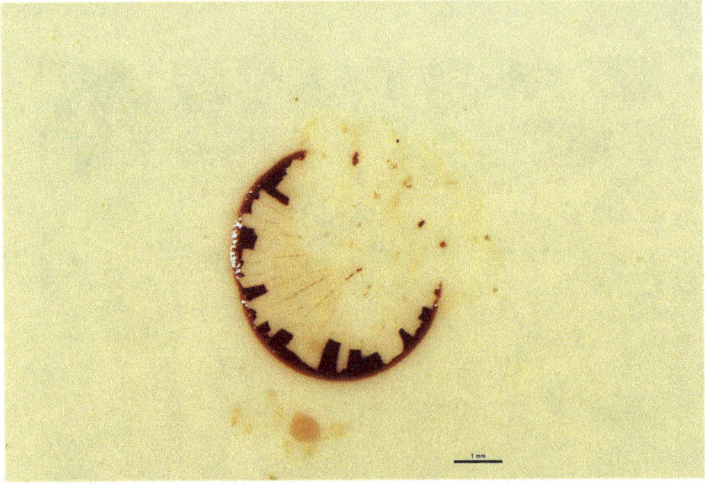

Figure 11.8 Perimeter stain generated after *C. vicina* partially consumed a dry bloodstain deposited on ceramic tile. Evidence of dried regurgitate is apparent with the stain. The regurgitate was used to moisten and digest the blood prior to imbibing the fluid with the mouthparts. Image represents 10x magnification. (Photograph courtesy of David B. Rivers.)

"wells" can be created in the center of those stains which can be similar in appearance to bloodstains that contained an air bubble at the time of deposition.[7] In bloodstain pattern analysis, this is known as a bubble ring[5] which can be observed in an expiration pattern created by blood forced by airflow out of the nose, mouth, or a wound.[7]

Since it can be challenging to rely on morphology alone to distinguish between insect stains and bloodstains, an analyst should be aware of other methods and/or techniques that have been explored to assist in this effort: some with more success than others. Presumptive testing has been investigated as a way to distinguish between insect stains and bloodstains. Common presumptive blood tests such as phenolphthalein, leucocrystal violet, Hemastix®, and fluorescien can return a positive test result for both insect stains and bloodstains.[7,18] Another research study demonstrated that in addition to Hemastix, the presumptive tests Hemident™ and Hemascein® also returned positive test results for both insect stains and bloodstains.[19] Similarly, positive test results also occurred with both insect stains and bloodstains when using the immunochromatographic strip assays Hematrace™ and Rapid Stain Identification of Human Blood (RSID Blood™).[20] These results should not be surprising since adult flies feeding on human blood will regurgitate partially digested blood and defecate either partially digested or even undigested blood as liquid feces.[13,18] Therefore, presumptive blood tests are not recommended for use as a method to distinguish between insect stains and bloodstains. The use of an alternate light source (ALS) has also been explored as a tool to distinguish between insect stains and bloodstains. Researchers found that applying a blue-green light (465 nm) in combination with the use of an orange filter to defecatory stains caused the stains to fluoresce.[17,18] In the same studies, however, regurgitate stains and bloodstains did not fluoresce under the same wavelength of light using the same orange filter. Conversely, in Rivers et al.,[20] both regurgitate and defecatory stains (collectively referred to as digestive artifacts by the authors) did fluoresce under an ALS equipped with a 450-nm light source in combination with the use of an orange filter. Therefore, analysts should proceed with caution when considering the use of an ALS to distinguish between insect stains and bloodstains.

Other research investigated the use of an immunoassay to distinguish between insect stains and bloodstains.[21,22] In those laboratory studies, it was possible to distinguish between insect stains and human bloodstains through the use of immunodetection of a digestive enzyme found in the foregut of the fly species selected for study. However, it was not possible to distinguish between insect regurgitate and defecatory stains using the same technique. The authors correctly pointed out that this should not be viewed as a weakness of the technique as the bloodstain pattern analyst's primary objective is to distinguish between insect stains (regardless if they originated from regurgitation or defecation) and bloodstains. The authors note in both publications that although immunodetection permits distinction between insect stains and bloodstains in their laboratory setting, further research is warranted to determine if this technique is suitable for non-laboratory conditions (such as with evidence recovered from crime scenes).

Scanning electron microscopy (SEM) has also been explored as a potential tool for distinguishing between bloodstains and insect stains. In one study, the authors reported that for one fly species, *Sarcophaga carnaria* (Diptera: Sarcophagidae), they were consistently unable to distinguish between bloodstains and insect stains visually and under low (40–300×) SEM magnification based on color, the presence/absence of a tail, and surface and edge characteristics of the stains.[23] However, when the stains were viewed under high magnification (1,200×), small, crystal-like deposits that were not present in their control samples (bloodstains) were observed in the insect stains. In addition, in the control stains at the same high magnification, red blood cells (RBC) in a rouleaux or stacked formation were observed. Stacked RBCs were not observed in the insect stains and, therefore, the authors offered high-magnification SEM as a means to distinguish between bloodstains and insect stains.

Although the previously discussed methods and techniques may be available to the bloodstain pattern analyst, the results should be carefully considered in the context of the presence or absence of insect activity within the scene as well as the location(s) of the stains in question.

Insect Stains

The analyst should look for indications of insect activity within the scene: from the presence of adult flies, eggs, and/or larvae to the presence of pupal cases (either those where the adult fly has not yet emerged or those that are empty [eclosed] showing a less recent history of insect activity in the scene). The location of insect stains must be documented thoroughly and cautiously considered in relation to other known facts and circumstances about the scene and/or events that took place. Insect stains may be found on items or in locations considered inconsistent with the location where a victim may have sustained an injury. Insect stains may be found on lights, lamp shades, ceilings, windows, the floor around the blood source, papers, clothing, as well as on the victim.[9,18] Insect stains can be found well away from the victim's location in the scene, for example, in other rooms or areas of a house, not just in windows, warm or well-lit areas where adult flies are commonly observed.[9] Under those circumstances, it is important for the analyst to be aware of this possibility so as not to erroneously attribute movement or action by a victim or subject based on an insect stain. For example, a bloodstain pattern analyst must keep in mind the potential for obtaining human DNA sufficient for profiling from insect stains (both regurgitation and defecation stains).[24] Since it can be difficult to distinguish between insect stains and bloodstains as outlined above, an analyst with limited experience could mistakenly sample an insect stain and make an erroneous reconstruction of events in a crime scene based on the DNA profile obtained from that stain. However, there are benefits in the ability to obtain a DNA profile from an insect stain. If a subject cleaned the immediate area of a scene or relocated the body, there might still be the potential to obtain a DNA profile from an insect stain located some distance away (i.e., in another room within the same scene) that went unnoticed by the subject. Research studies have documented the ability to obtain a human DNA profile from an insect stain up to 300 days post-deposition as well as after 750 days post-deposition.[22] As some crime/death scenes are not always readily located, this information may prove useful when searching a scene associated with a cold case or with delayed reporting. If suspected insect stains are located, it would be of benefit to collect those stains for analysis as the DNA results may place the victim/deceased in that location. Looking at this from another perspective, it is also possible for a fly (who previously consumed a human blood meal at a crime scene) to travel to a second, distinct location and deposit an insect stain through the regurgitation or defecation process, thus introducing a potential DNA sample into a completely unrelated location. Flies have the ability to retain a human blood-based meal in their crop for extended periods: more than three weeks as demonstrated in one study.[20] Therefore, it is important for an analyst to be aware of the potential for secondary transfer of DNA in this manner.

When faced with the possibility of insect stains or altered and/or transfer stains due to insect activity, a bloodstain pattern analyst should consider consulting with a forensic entomologist. The potential for insect activity to alter and/or create additional stains within a scene that are unrelated to the crime can add further complexity and ambiguity to the interpretation of bloodstain pattern evidence. Analysts should always proceed with caution in their analyses and consider and document all possibilities. Thorough documentation of the scene is of utmost importance and should include the presence as well as the absence of insect activity, the location(s) of stains (as well as notes/photographs detailing where a search for stains was conducted with negative results), the results of any visual observations regarding the stains such as size, shape, distribution, directionality, and/or convergence or lack thereof, and which stains were subjected to sampling for further testing. Once the analyst has thoroughly documented the scene and/or the item of evidence of interest, the analyst should then consider their answer to the following question posed by Benecke and Barksdale when evaluating stains in relationship to the context of the scene: Is there a logical relationship of stains (given the presence/absence of insect activity, the location and morphology of the stains, etc.) to events (i.e., what has been learned about actions/movements that took place within the scene, the nature of wounds to the victim, etc.)?[4] Doing so will enable the analyst to reduce ambiguity during their analysis and increase confidence in their interpretation and conclusions.

Notes

1. Benecke, Mark C., "A brief survey of the history of forensic entomology." *Acta Biologica Benrodis*, 14, 2008, pp. 15–38.
2. Byrd, Jason and Jeffery Tomberlin, *Forensic Entomology: The Utility of Arthropods in Legal Investigations*, CRC Press, Boca Raton, FL, 2020, p. xxiii.
3. Haglund, William D. and Marcella H. Sorg, *Forensic Taphonomy: The Postmortem Fate of Human Remains*, CRC Press, LLC, Boca Raton, FL, 1997, pp. 436–437.
4. Benecke, Mark and Larry Barksdale, "Distinction of bloodstain patterns from fly artifacts." *Forensic Science International*, 137, 2003. pp. 152–159.
5. American Academy of Forensic Sciences Standards Board (ASB), Technical Report 033, Terms and Definitions in Bloodstain Pattern Analysis, First Edition 2017.
6. Rivers, David and Theresa Geiman, "Insect artifacts are more than just altered bloodstains." *Insects*, 8, 37, 2017, pp. 1–12.
7. Striman, Becca, Armanda Fujikawa, Larry Barksdale, and David Carter, "Alteration of expirated bloodstain patterns by *Calliphora vicina* and *Lucilia sericata* (Diptera: Calliphoridae) through ingestion and deposition of artifacts." *Journal of Forensic Science*, 53, 2011, pp. S123–S127.
8. Durdle, Annalisa, Roland van Oorschot, and Robert John Mitchell, "The morphology of fecal and regurgitation artifacts deposited by the blow fly *Lucilia cuprina* fed a diet of human blood." *Journal of Forensic Science*, 58(4), 2013, pp. 897–903.
9. Durdle, Annalisa, Timothy J. Verdon, Robert John Mitchell, and Roland van Oorschot, "Location of artifacts deposited by the blow fly *Lucilia cuprina* after feeding on human blood at simulated indoor crime scenes." *Journal of Forensic Science*, 63(4), 2018, pp. 1261–1268.
10. Rivers, David B. and Andrew McGregor, "Morphological features of regurgitate and defecatory stains deposited by five species of necrophagous flies are influenced by adult diets and body size." *Journal of Forensic Science*, 63(1), 2018, pp. 154–161.
11. Rivers, David B., Gillian Acca, Mark Fink, Rebecca Brogan, Dorothy Chen, and Andrew Schoeffield, "Distinction of fly artifacts from human blood using immunodetection." *Journal of Forensic Science*, 63(6), 2018, pp. 1704–1711.
12. Bevel, Tom and Ross M. Gardner, *Bloodstain Pattern Analysis with an Introduction to Crime Scene Reconstruction*, CRC Press, Taylor and Francis Group, Boca Raton, FL, 2008, pp. 226–227.
13. Brown, Rosemary E., Roger I. Hawkes, M. Anderson Parker, and Jason Byrd, Forensic *Entomology: The Utility of Arthropods in Legal Investigations*, CRC Press, Boca Raton, FL, 2001, pp. 364–366.
14. James, Stuart H., Paul E. Kish, and T. Paulette Sutton, *Principles of Bloodstain Pattern Analysis, Theory and Practice*. CRC Press, Boca Raton, FL, 2005, p. 207.
15. Rivers, David, Brendan Dunphy, Claire Hammerschmidt, and Alexandra Carrigan, "Characterization of insect stains deposited by *Calliphora vicina* (Diptera: Calliphoridae) on shirt fabrics." *Journal of Medical Entomology*, 57(5), 2020, pp. 1399–1406.
16. Parker, M. Anderson, Stacey Sneider, Shayne Smithey, Mark Benecke, and Jason Byrd. *Forensic Entomology: The Utility of Arthropods in Legal Investigations*, CRC Press, Boca Raton, FL, 2020, pp. 399–403.
17. Fujikawa, Amanda, Larry Barksdale, Leon Higley, and David O. Carter, "Changes in the morphology and presumptive chemistry of impact and pooled bloodstain patterns by *Lucilia sericata* (Meigen) (Diptera: Calliphoridae)." *Journal of Forensic Science*, 56(5), 2011, pp. 1315–1318.
18. Fujikawa, Amanda, Larry Barksdale, and David O. Carter, "*Calliphora vicina* (Diptera: Calliphoridae) and their ability to alter the morphology and presumptive chemistry of bloodstain patterns." *Journal of Forensic Identification*, 59(5), 2009, pp. 502–512.
19. Durdle, Annalisa, Robert John Mitchell, and Roland van Oorschot, "The use of forensic tests to distinguish blowfly artifacts from human blood, semen and saliva." *Journal of Forensic Science*, 60(2), 2015, pp. 468–470.
20. Rivers, David B., Claire Hammerschmidt, Alexandra Carrigan, and Kayleen Melvin, "Retention of human body fluids in adults of *Calliphora vicina* (Diptera: Calliphoridae) following feeding." *Journal of Medical Entomology*, 2021, pp. 1–10. https://doi.10.1093/jme/tjab029
21. Rivers, David B., Gregory Cavanagh, Valerie Greisman, Rebecca Brogan, and Andrew Schoeffield, "Detection of fly artifacts from four species of necrophagous flies on household materials using immunoassays." *International Journal of Legal Medicine*, 134, 2019, pp. 1239–1253. https://doi.org/10.1007/s00414-019-02159-1

22. Rivers, David B., Gregory Cavanagh, Valerie Greisman, Andrew McGregor, Rebecca Brogan, and Andrew Schoeffield, "Immunoassay detection of fly artifacts produced by several species of necrophagous flies following feeding on human blood." *Forensic Science International: Synergy*, 233 (1), 2019, pp. 1–10.
23. Pelletti, Guido, Maria Carla Mazzotti, Paolo Fais, Desiree Martini, Laura Ingrà, Alberto Amadasi, Chiara Palazzo, Mirella Falconi, and Susi Pelotti, "Scanning electron microscopy in the identification of fly artifacts." *International Journal of Legal Medicine*, 133, 2019, pp. 1575–1580.
24. Durdle, Annalisa, Robert John Mitchell, and Roland van Oorschot, "The human DNA content in artifacts deposited by the blowfly *Lucilia cuprina* fed human blood, semen and saliva." *Forensic Science International*, 233, 2013. pp. 212–219.

Further Readings

Catts, E. Paul, and Neal H. Haskell (Eds.). *Entomology and Death, a Procedural Guide*. Clemson, SC: Joyce's Print Shop, 1990.

Goff, M. Lee. *A Fly for the Prosecution: How Insect Evidence Helps Solve Crimes*. London, Cambridge: Harvard University Press, 2000.

Rivers, David B., and Gregory A. Dahlem. *The Science of Forensic Entomology*. Wiley-Blackwell, U.K, 2014, pp. 237–250.

Smith, Kenneth G.V. *A Manual of Forensic Entomology*. London: Trustees of the British Museum (Natural History), 1986.

CHAPTER 12

BLOODY FRICTION RIDGE DETAIL EVIDENCE

Toby L. Wolson

Fingerprints in blood may be found during the processing of bloody crime scenes. This evidence item can be very important for identifying the individuals who were present during the activities that caused the injuries that resulted in bloodshed. The following discussion examines the subject of bloody fingerprints.

Fingerprints may be found on any substrate that is conducive to maintaining an impression of the finger's ridge and/or furrow pattern when touched by an individual. This is important because fingerprints can be associated with a specific individual due to the unique pattern of the ridges and furrows on each finger. It is an accepted principle that fingerprints are unique and individualized with no two people found to have the same patterns of ridges and furrows on their fingers.

Fingerprints can be divided into several types or categories. Plastic fingerprints are prints that occur when a finger is pressed against a plastic material resulting in a three-dimensional impression of the print. A negative print is an image of the furrows rather than the ridge pattern of the finger. Another type of fingerprint is a latent print. A latent print is the result of a transfer of the oils and dirt that may be present on the finger to a surface conducive for maintaining the impression of the print. These prints can be visible or invisible after being deposited on a surface. Invisible fingerprints are classified as latent prints and visible prints are classified as patent prints.

It is important to understand the sequence of events that result in bloody fingerprints occurring at a crime scene. Several types of analysis will be necessary when bloody fingerprints are recovered at a crime scene. The print will be examined to determine if the source of the fingerprint can be identified. In addition, the blood used to make the fingerprint can be analyzed to determine the source of the blood. Frequently, the result of the analysis identifies the suspect as the source of the print and the victim as the source of the blood that made the patent print. The suspect is then left in the position of having to explain how their fingerprint was found in the victim's blood at the crime scene. The two most common explanations are "I was not there but my fingerprints may have been present because I have been there before. The blood must have been deposited on the fingerprint, making it visible" or "I came in and found the victim. I must have touched some blood and left a fingerprint in the blood when I touched it." The following discussion examines the preceding scenarios and the scenario which would have resulted in a patent print: "I waxed the floors of the crime scene the day before and must have left my fingerprint in the sticky wax." The blood landing on a latent print and the wax image both were explanations provided to explain the presence of the defendant's fingerprint at the homicide scene in the case of the *State of Florida v. Ramirez*. Ramirez was the custodian at a Federal Express Office in Miami, Florida. He was accused of beating and stabbing to death another Federal Express employee while burglarizing the Federal Express office after it had closed for the evening. Two critical pieces of evidence in this case were presented during the trial. A knife recovered from the car Ramirez had been using the night of the homicide was used to make a positive toolmark comparison to the striations on the victim's ribs and a blood fingerprint that matched Ramirez. Ramirez was convicted of the homicide. However, his initial conviction was overturned, and he was given a new trial due to the toolmark evidence. The comparison of the toolmarks from the knife to the striations on the victim's ribs was novel

DOI: 10.4324/9781003163695-12

Table 12.1 Test surface descriptions and alphabetic identifiers

Identifier	Surface description
C	Glossy white glazed ceramic tile
G	Glass
H	White melamine bookshelf
K	Clear poplar wood
M	Galvanized flat sheet metal
P	Clear acrylic plastic
R	Residential vinyl tile
S	Marble threshold
T	Commercial vinyl tile
W	Clear white pine wood

science: meaning it had never been done or reported in the literature before this case. During the second trial, the bloody fingerprint and toolmark evidence were presented again. In addition, Ramirez testified that he was the custodian for the office and had waxed the floors. He said the wax was very sticky and he may have left his fingerprint when he touched a surface with his sticky fingers. Ramirez was convicted again. Ramirez's second conviction was overturned, and a new trial was ordered. During the third trial, the defense attempted to call a witness to testify that it was possible the fingerprint was preexisting and present on the surface and made visible when blood was deposited on top of the print. Ramirez was convicted of committing the homicide. As with the previous trials, Ramirez's conviction was overturned, and a fourth trial was ordered. The following study of bloody fingerprints was performed in preparation for the fourth trial.

Fingerprints were placed on a variety of surfaces that may be present in an office or residential environment (Table 12.1). The surfaces were all cleaned prior to use. Some of the surfaces were coated with paint before the addition of the fingerprints (Table 12.2).

The fingers of the participants were coated with an assortment of different substances (Table 12.3) and the fingerprints were applied to each surface using soft pressure or hard pressure (Table 12.4).

Table 12.2 Test surface coatings and alphabetic identifiers

Identifier	Surface coating
A	Oil-based glossy white paint
B	Oil-based flat white paint
C	Latex glossy white paint
D	Latex flat white paint
E	No coating applied

Table 12.3 Substances used to make the fingerprints and numeric identifiers

Identifier	Fingerprint substance
1	Motor oil
2	WD-40® lubricant
3	Floor wax
4	Skin oils (assumed to be sebaceous)
5	Hair oils (assumed to be sebaceous)
6	Silicone lubricant

Table 12.4 Fingerprint application pressures and alphabetic identifiers

Identifier	Fingerprint application pressure
Y	Low pressure
Z	Hard pressure

When a fingerprint is created by firm hard contact with a surface, the resulting print may be a negative print showing the furrows of the print rather than the ridge pattern. The test fingerprints were allowed to cure for several days at room temperature after application of the fingerprints on the test surfaces. Each surface was visually examined for the presence of latent and patent fingerprints before being used. A half-liter of fresh human blood was drawn from the author by a local blood bank via venous puncture using a citrate–phosphate–dextrose (CPD) preservative. The blood was stored at 4°C and allowed to warm to room temperature (22°C) prior to use. Blood was applied to all the surfaces and latent fingerprints by different mechanisms (Table 12.5) and allowed to air-dry before being photographed and examined by a qualified fingerprint examiner.

Table 12.5 Fingerprint application pressures and alphabetic identifiers

Identifier	Blood application method
DR	Dripping
FL	Flowing
SP	Impact spatter

Each fingerprint was assigned an alphanumeric identifier indicating the surface type, surface coating, print substance, application pressure, and the blood application method. A print deposited on glass (G), no coating (E), skin oil (4), low pressure (Y), and dripped blood (DR) would have an alphanumeric identification of GE4YDR. In addition to studying the questions posed by the Ramirez trial, two additional possibilities for the creation of a bloody fingerprint were tested. If the subject places their finger in a blood drop that has not completely dried, can a patent print happen? Droplets of blood with a volume of 50 µl were deposited on test surfaces and touched by a finger every 15 minutes starting at 0 minutes through 60 minutes. The final study involved touching the test surfaces with a finger that was coated with a thin layer of blood to examine the creation of positive bloody patent prints.

The studies did produce print images that were examined by a fingerprint examiner and compared to the fingerprint standards of the study participants. All the examined print images that were useful for possible comparison to the fingerprint standards were classified as negative impressions. The print images were of the furrows and not the ridges of the participant's finger. The surfaces that were smooth, non-porous, and non-absorbent were the surfaces in which print images were frequently observed. Surfaces that were porous, rough, and absorbent usually failed to produce print images upon addition of liquid blood. Fingerprints deposited with motor oil (1) and skin oils (4) excreted by sebaceous glands were the substances that produced the largest number of print images when blood was deposited on them.

Blood is a mixture of liquids and solids. The liquid portion of blood is predominantly water and accounts for slightly more than half of the blood volume. Oil and water do not mix. The blood was repelled away from the fingerprint ridge patterns that were made with oil and forced to flow into the areas between the oily ridges, causing an image of the fingerprint furrows. In the studies where blood was applied over the fingerprints made from oils, the blood usually flowed around the edges of the latent prints. When blood was deposited on the fingerprints made with floor wax (3), no print images were observed. More print images were obtained from the studies in which blood was dripped on the latent print or flowed over the latent fingerprints than with the impact spatter study. The study examining touching droplets of blood over time did produce some print impressions. However, the fingerprint examiner determined that they were not of sufficient quality for comparison to the fingerprint standards. The only positive prints obtained were the fingerprints made by coating the participant's finger with a thin coat of blood and touching the finger to a clean surface.

The enlightening observation from this study was the difficulty in making comparison quality patent prints. In order to obtain quality patent prints, it requires just the right amount of blood on the finger at just the right degree of drying (tackiness) to result in a patent print. These studies help explain why it is not the norm to find bloody fingerprints at bloody crime scenes. As areas and items are used, it is assumed that latent prints are deposited on surfaces and items because of use. It is also assumed that preexisting latent prints not associated with the activities that resulted in bloodshed are present in every crime scene. Yet bloody fingerprints are not found at every crime scene involving bloodshed. The absence of bloody fingerprints at every crime scene involving bloodshed suggests that the interaction of blood with preexisting latent prints and making them visible is an unusual occurrence. It is also possible to determine through the visible characteristics of the bloody impression what the mechanism for deposition of the blood was. Blood applied by impact spatter, flowing, and dripping on latent prints all exhibited visible characteristics consistent with the mechanism of blood application and all resulted in impressions that illustrated the patterns of the print furrows.

The only way to obtain bloody fingerprint impressions of the ridge pattern is for blood to be deposited on the finger before it is transferred to a surface by touch (Figures 12.1–12.21).

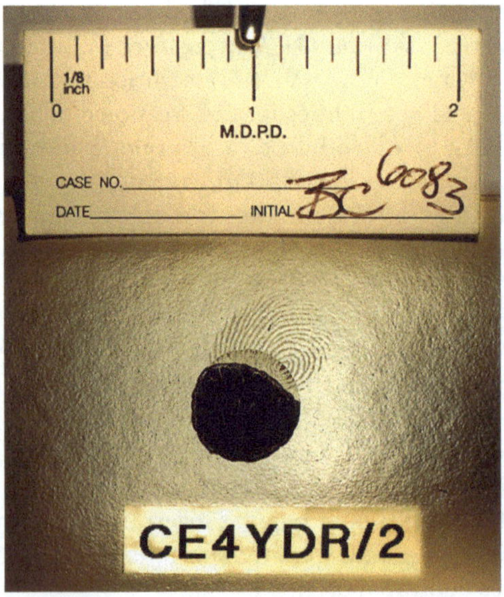

Figure 12.1 Blood dripped onto a latent print made with skin oil (sebaceous) and light pressure on the surface of an uncoated ceramic tile (CE4YDR/2). The "/2" indicates two tests were performed. The area at the top right side is the latent print that was deposited on the ceramic tile. The interface between the latent print and the drip of blood is the interaction of the blood with the latent print. The blood flowed into the gaps between the friction ridges making the furrows visible.

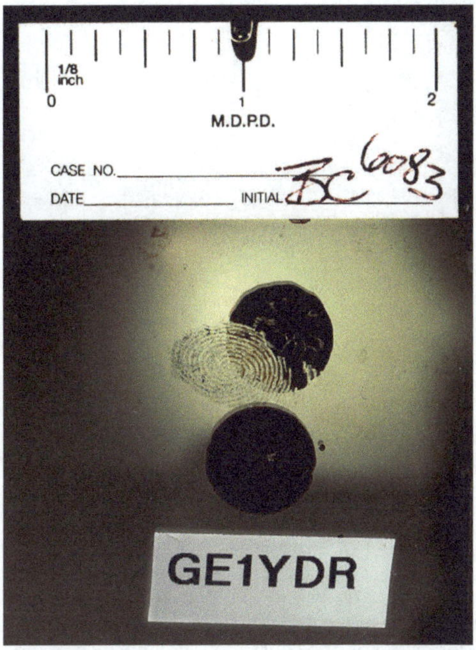

Figure 12.2 Blood dripped onto a latent print made with motor oil and light pressure on the surface of an uncoated piece of glass (GE1YDR). The area at the middle-left side between the two drips is the latent print that was deposited on the glass. The interface between the latent print and the drip of blood at the top shows the interaction of the blood with the latent print. The blood flowed into the gaps between the friction ridges making the furrows visible.

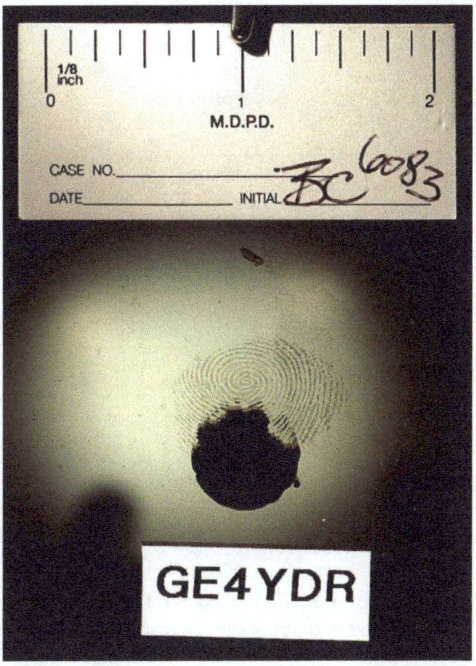

Figure 12.3 Blood dripped onto a latent print made with skin oil (sebaceous) and light pressure on the surface of an uncoated piece of glass (GE4YDR). The area at the top right side is the latent print that was deposited on the glass. The interface between the latent print and the drip of blood shows the interaction of the blood with the latent print. The blood flowed into the gaps between the friction ridges making the furrows visible.

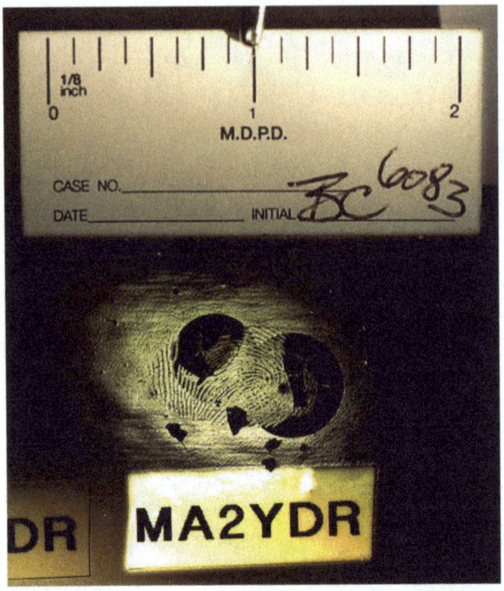

Figure 12.4 Blood dripped onto a latent print made with WD-40® lubricant and light pressure on the surface of a piece of galvanized sheet metal coated with oil-based glossy white paint (MA2YDR). The area at the bottom left side is the latent print that was deposited on the substrate. The interface of the latent print with the blood drips is the area in the center between the drips of blood. The blood flowed into the gaps between the friction ridges making the furrows visible.

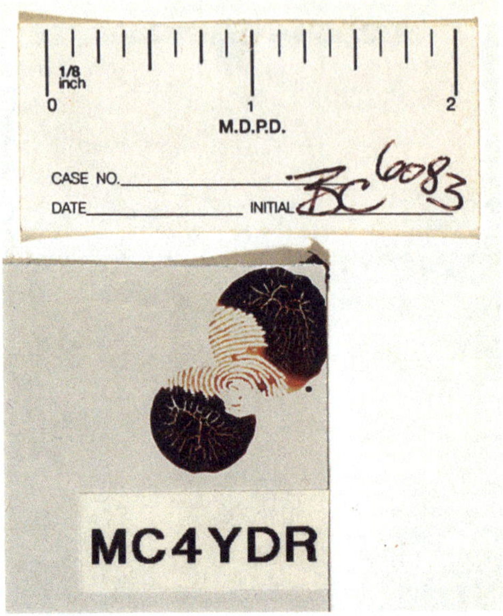

Figure 12.5 Blood dripped onto a latent print made with skin oil (sebaceous) and light pressure on the surface of a piece of galvanized sheet metal coated with latex glossy white paint (MC4YDR). The interface of the latent print with the blood drips is the area in the center between the drips of blood. The blood flowed into the gaps between the friction ridges making the furrows visible.

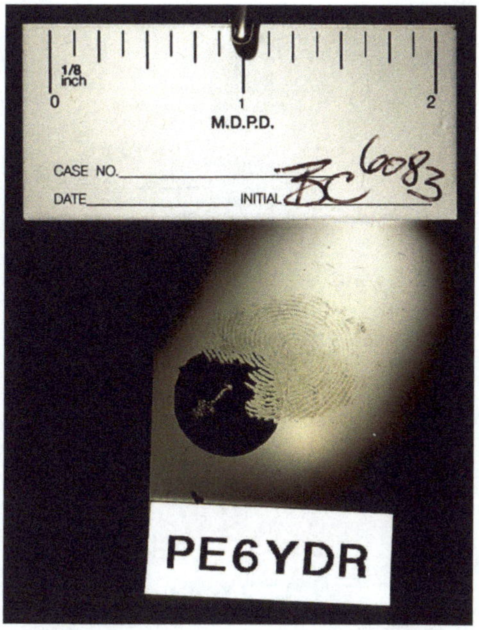

Figure 12.6 Blood dripped onto a latent print made with silicone lubricant and light pressure on the surface of an uncoated piece of acrylic plastic (PE6YDR). The area at the top right side is the latent print that was deposited on the glass. The interface between the latent print and the drip of blood shows the interaction of the blood with the latent print. The blood flowed into the gaps between the friction ridges making the furrows visible.

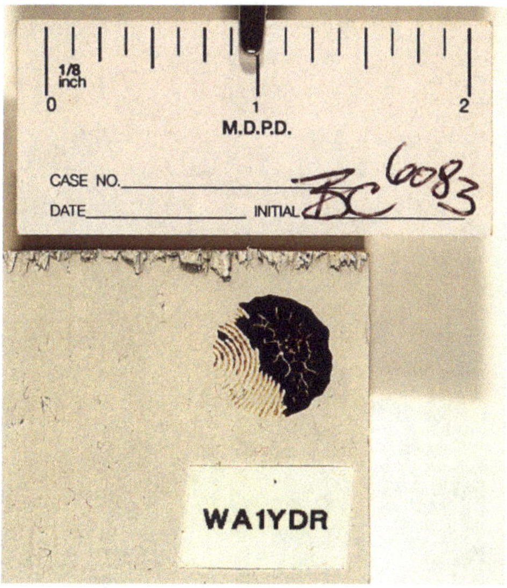

Figure 12.7 Blood dripped onto a latent print made with motor oil and light pressure on the surface of a piece of clear white pine wood coated with oil-based glossy white paint (WA1YDR). The interface between the latent print and the drip of blood is at the bottom left side and the blood flowed into the gaps between the friction ridges making the furrows visible.

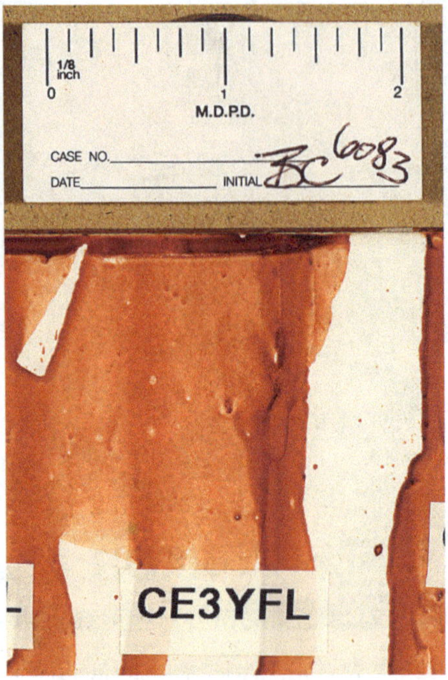

Figure 12.8 Blood flowed over a latent print made with floor wax and light pressure on the surface of an uncoated ceramic tile (CE3YFL). The blood did not react with the floor wax print making any details of the print or its location visible. This same result was observed for all the prints made with floor wax on all the test surfaces.

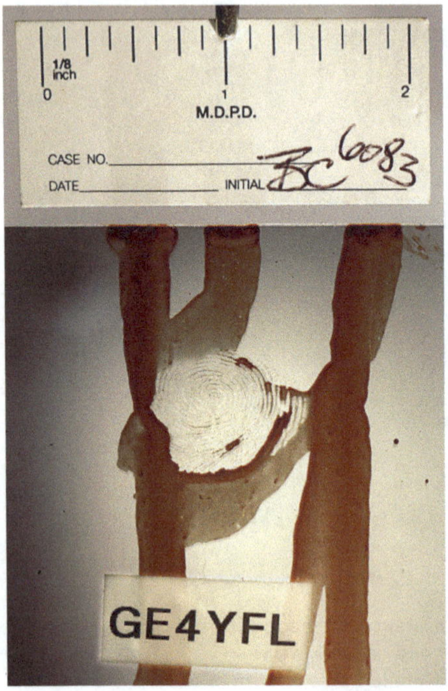

Figure 12.9 Blood flowed over a latent print made with skin oil (sebaceous) and light pressure on the surface of an uncoated piece of glass (GE4YFL). The blood flowed around the latent print and into the areas representing the furrows. The spikes along the lower edge of the print are the result of the blood flowing into the spaces between the friction ridge impression.

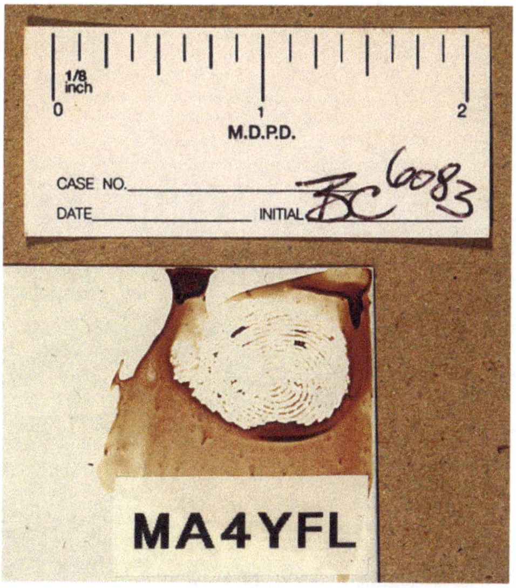

Figure 12.10 Blood flowed over a latent print made with skin oil (sebaceous) and light pressure on the surface of a piece of galvanized sheet metal coated with oil based glossy white paint (MA4YFL). The blood flowed around the latent print and into the areas representing the furrows. The spikes along the lower edge of the print are the result of the blood flowing into the spaces between the friction ridge impression.

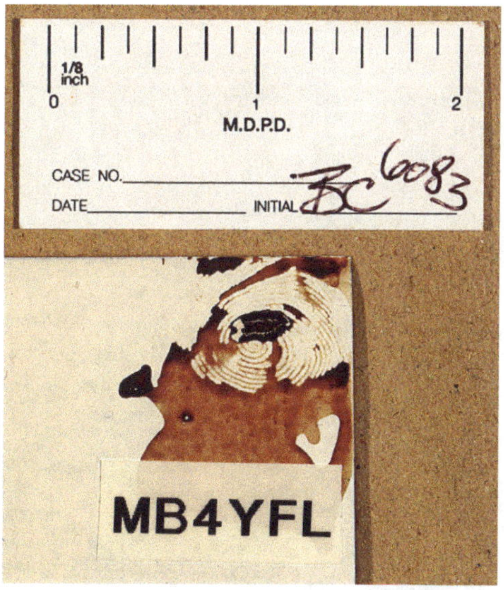

Figure 12.11 Blood flowed over a latent print made with skin oil (sebaceous) and light pressure on the surface of a piece of galvanized sheet metal coated with oil-based flat white paint (MB4YFL). The blood flowed around the latent print and into the areas representing the furrows. The spikes along the lower edge of the print are the result of the blood flowing into the spaces between the friction ridge impression.

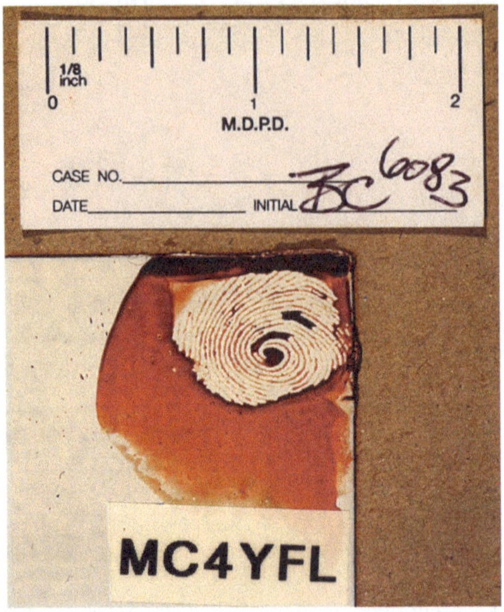

Figure 12.12 Blood flowed over a latent print made with skin oil (sebaceous) and light pressure on the surface of a piece of galvanized sheet metal coated with latex glossy white paint (MC4YFL). The blood flowed around the latent print and into the areas representing the furrows. The spikes along the lower edge of the print are the result of the blood flowing into the spaces between the friction ridge impression.

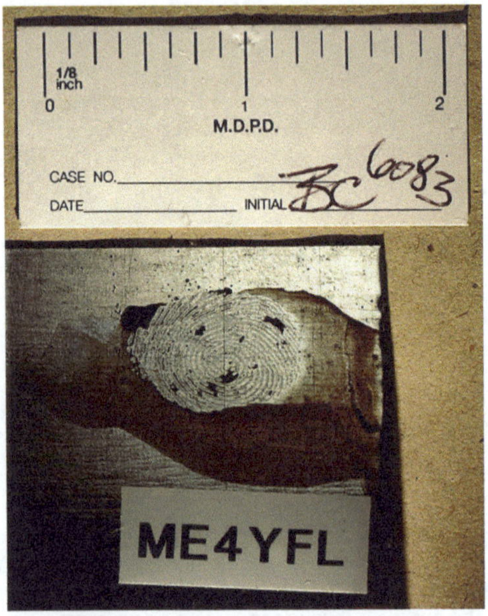

Figure 12.13 Blood flowed over a latent print made with skin oil (sebaceous) and light pressure on the surface of an uncoated piece of galvanized sheet metal (ME4YFL). The blood flowed around the latent print and into the areas representing the furrows along the top left side of the latent print.

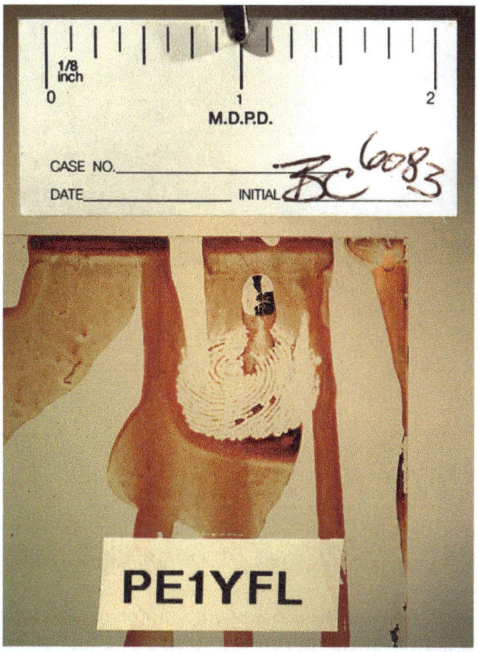

Figure 12.14 Blood flowed over a latent print made with motor oil and light pressure on the surface of an uncoated acrylic plastic (PE1YFL). The blood flowed around the latent print and into the areas representing the furrows. The spikes along the lower edge of the print are the result of the blood flowing into the spaces between the friction ridge impression.

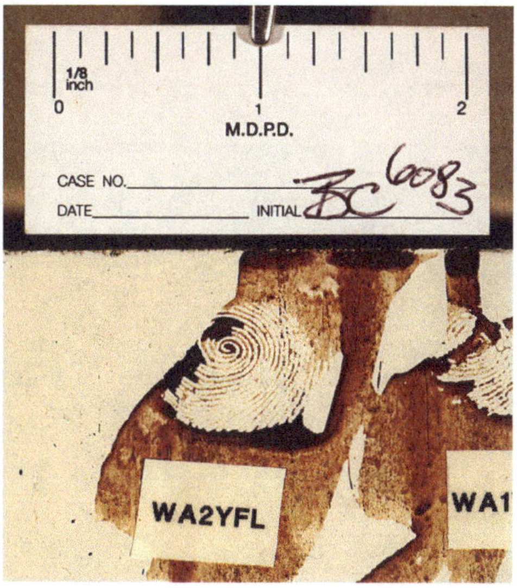

Figure 12.15 Blood flowed over a latent print made with WD-40® lubricant and light pressure on a piece of clear white pine wood coated with oil-based glossy white paint (WA2YDR). The blood flowed around the latent print and into the areas representing the furrows. The spikes along the lower edge of the print are the result of the blood flowing into the spaces between the friction ridge impression.

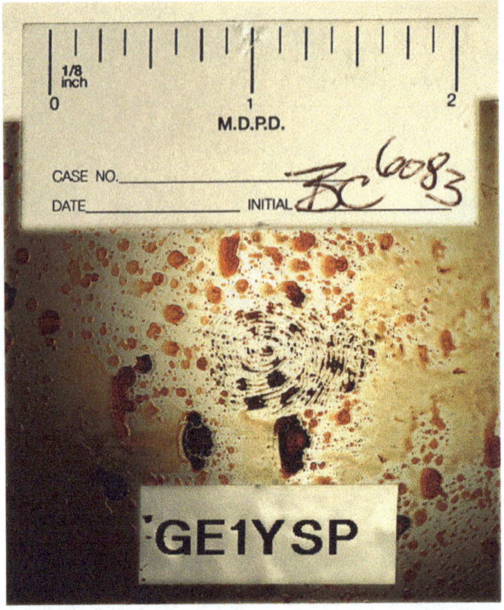

Figure 12.16 Blood spattered onto a latent print made with motor oil and light pressure on the surface of an uncoated piece of glass (GE1YSP). The spatter droplets of blood deposited on the latent print flowed outward along the areas of least resistance making small areas of the furrow pattern visible.

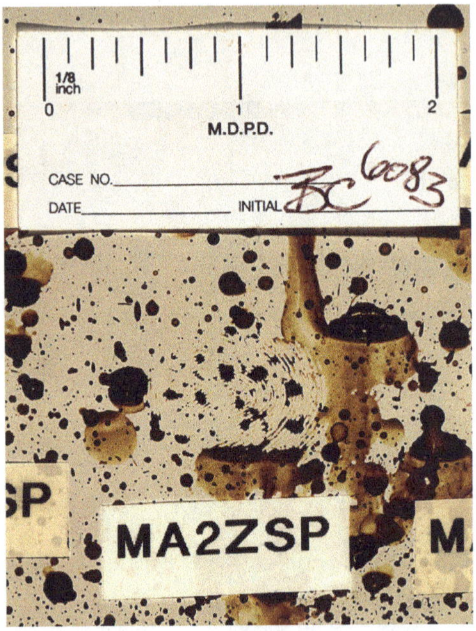

Figure 12.17 Blood spattered onto a latent print made with WD-40® lubricant and hard pressure on the surface of a piece of galvanized sheet metal coated with oil-based glossy white paint (MA2ZSP). The spatter droplets of blood deposited on the latent print flowed outward along the areas of least resistance making small areas of the pattern visible.

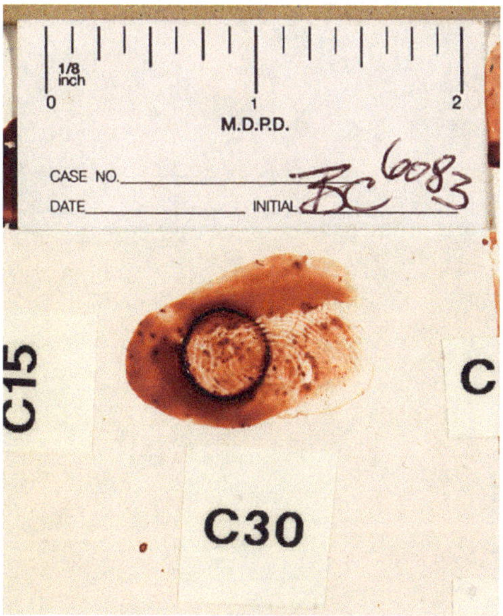

Figure 12.18 Blood placed on an uncoated piece of ceramic tile and touched after 30 minutes of drying (C30).

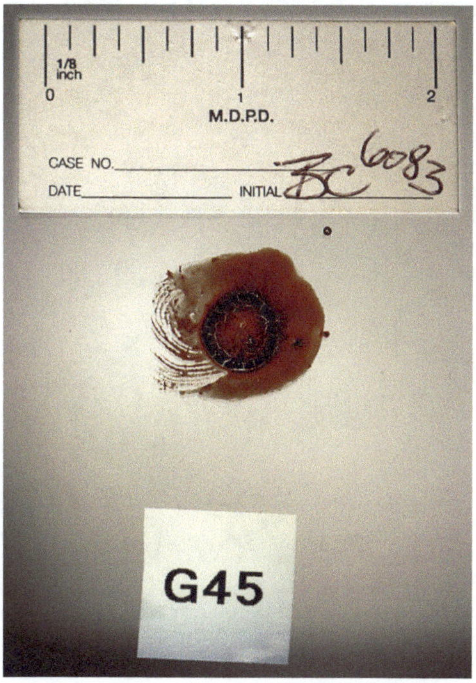

Figure 12.19 Blood placed on an uncoated piece of glass and touched after 45 minutes of drying. (G45).

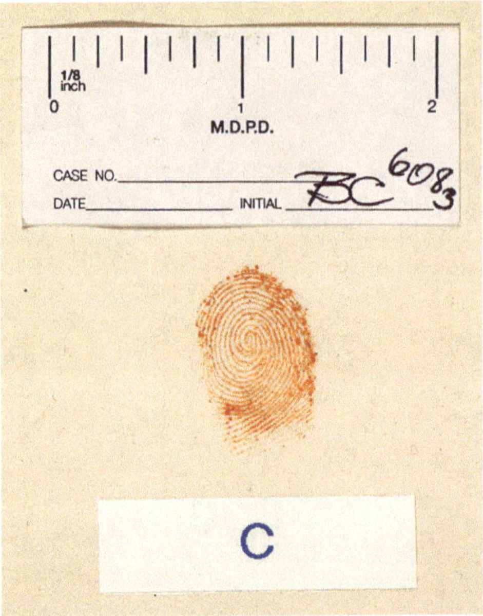

Figure 12.20 Patent print in blood on the surface of an uncoated ceramic tile (C) made by transfer from a blood-coated finger to the test surface.

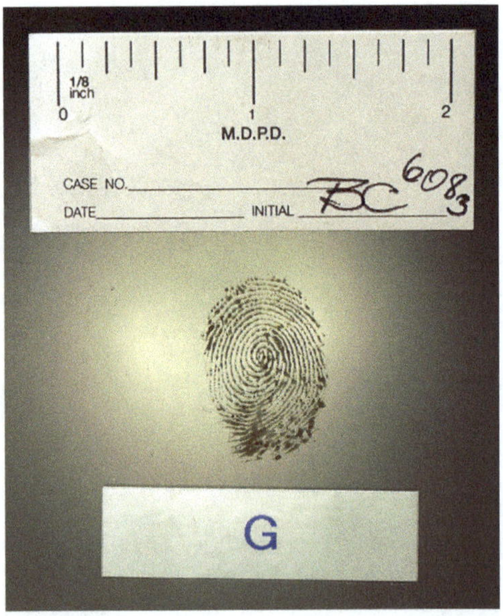

Figure 12.21 Patent print in blood on the surface of an uncoated piece of glass (g) made by transfer from a blood-coated finger to the test surface.

CHAPTER 13

IMPACT BLOOD PATTERNS

Rosalyn Rough

INTRODUCTION

Impact pattern is a well-used term to describe a pattern of spatter stains that have been created when an object strikes a source of liquid blood. Impact patterns are commonly observed as the result of beatings, in particular of the head region as this area is particularly vascular and therefore bleeds extensively when the circulatory system is breached. Although blunt force impacts are a common candidate for creating impact patterns, stabbing events can also cause the formation of impact patterns if the handle or the hand holding the stabbing implement strikes liquid blood. Impact patterns tend to be deposited on to a range of surfaces close to the impacting event, including walls, floors, and furniture. They can also be observed on the body and clothing of the victim. Portions of the pattern may also be deposited onto the perpetrator's skin or clothing or footwear. However, it is not unexpected to have minimal spatter stains deposited onto the perpetrator and their clothing, as the majority of blood travels in the direction of the applied force, which is often away from the position of the perpetrator.[1]

The finding of impact patterns at a scene can provide evidence that an assault has taken place. The inference is that the "source of liquid blood" being struck is an open wound or blood accumulation on an individual. In a beating or stabbing situation, a single blow alone is not generally considered destructive enough to create an impact pattern, as the creation of an impact pattern requires the circulatory system to be breached and an accumulation or volume of blood be struck. This implies an initial injury is required to generate a source of liquid blood to be impacted.

Analysis of the stains within impact patterns can sometimes indicate the location of the source of the blood when it was struck and therefore assist with the positioning of individuals within the scene (see Chapters 4 and 5 for details of this analysis). The distribution of the stains within the pattern(s) may also be able to assist with determining the direction of the impacting force(s).

Impact patterns can also be created from non-violent mechanisms such as medical interventions by first responders. Pools or accumulations of blood on horizontal surfaces such as floors can also be disturbed (such as by running and stomping through them) which can create impact patterns.[2]

BLOOD BEHAVIOR DURING AN IMPACT

Blood is an incompressible fluid, so when an object strikes a source of liquid blood, the blood is squeezed or pushed out of the way of the impacting object. This disturbance of the blood pool causes the blood to break up into sheets, ligaments, and finally droplets, as described in Chapter 5. The resulting droplets radiate out through the path(s) of least resistance away from the impacting

DOI: 10.4324/9781003163695-13

object, and travel through the air and land onto nearby surfaces forming small elliptical and circular spatter stains. The two unique elements of an impact pattern formation are as follows:

1. An object is involved and applies a force to the liquid blood.
2. At that moment in time, the source of the blood is relatively stationary.

This means that an impact pattern will have a single area of origin which may be able to be determined if the resulting stains display enough detail in their directionality and shape. Because the source of the blood is not moving and the droplets are released from the blood source within a short time frame, the resulting droplets form a radiating spatter pattern. This is characterized by a higher density of more circular stains in the central region of the pattern, and progressively less density of staining (which are more elliptical) toward the perimeter. The overall pattern shape is often "V" or fan-shaped but can also be asymmetrical or interrupted due the impacting object blocking the path of the liquid blood in some places.

FEATURES OF IMPACT PATTERNS

A large number of impact patterns have been made in research and training courses over the years. Anecdotally, impact patterns vary immensely, and patterns created under the same conditions do not produce exactly the same looking patterns. This is partly because there are many variables at play and not all variables can be exactly replicated. It is also because during the formation of the blood droplets, the forces involved have not reached equilibrium and there is a randomness to the mechanisms that break up the liquid blood into droplets. However, there are some repeatable features of impact patterns that you would expect to see, which include the size, shape, directionality, and density of the stains within the pattern, as well as the overall size, shape, and location of the pattern within a scene. Below is a list of features of impact patterns that may be observed on a non-porous vertical surface such as a wall:

- Many small spatter stains usually <1 mm to 9 mm in diameter (predominately <1 mm to 4 mm in diameter).
- Stain directionality converges in 2D and/or 3D space.
- "V"- or fan-shaped pattern can have interruptions or be asymmetrical.
- Radiating pattern features, i.e., progressive change from center to outward of pattern in the following:
  - Stain size (predominately small to larger)
  - Stain shape (circular to elliptical)
  - Stain density (more to less)
- A cluster of very small circular stains may be present in the center of the pattern.
- Stain color intensity can be light for small stains in the center.
- Wide range of gamma angles (potentially 0–360°) may be demonstrated.

Figures 13.1 and 13.2 illustrate the radiating pattern features often associated with impact patterns.

Impact patterns come in a range of pattern sizes, some patterns can be small; alternatively some impact patterns have been documented as covering more expansive areas with stains located some meters from the center of the pattern. The extent of the pattern may be constrained by the geometry of the scene, particularly indoors.

For impact patterns generated on a horizontal surface (such as a floor), there may be a central area of bloodstaining that appears disturbed, which may represent the pool of blood that was impacted. Spatter stains typically extend from this central staining and should display radiating pattern characteristics. Directionality of the stains will converge back to the central area, and progressive changes to the stain size and density are also observed (Figure 13.3).

The shape of the surrounding spatter stains will be different on a horizontal surface compared to a vertical surface. Stains present on the horizontal surface have originated from droplets that are

Figure 13.1 Laboratory prepared impact pattern using pigs blood. Photos supplied by ESR.

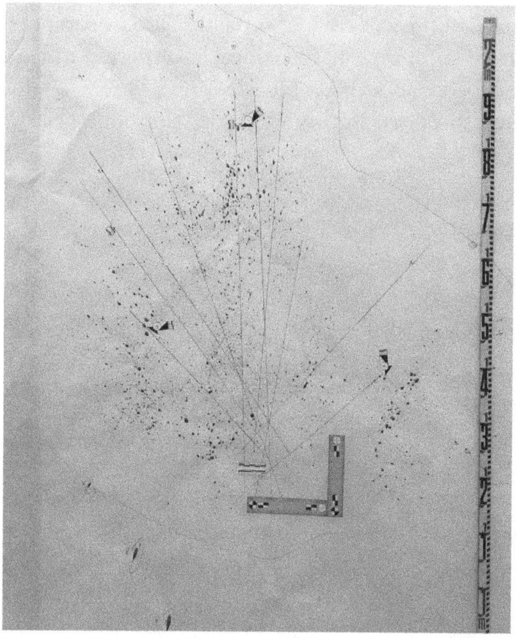

Figure 13.2 Close up of impact pattern with string lines indicating directionality of selected stains.

on the downward portion of their trajectory. As a result, more elliptical-shaped stains are observed close to the center of the pattern due to the initial droplets jetting directly outward, impacting the horizontal target at very oblique angles. Subsequent droplets formed by the second sheet break up travel further upward, resulting in more circular-shaped stains further away as gravity has more effect on their trajectory. This differs from a vertical surface where the circular stains are closer to

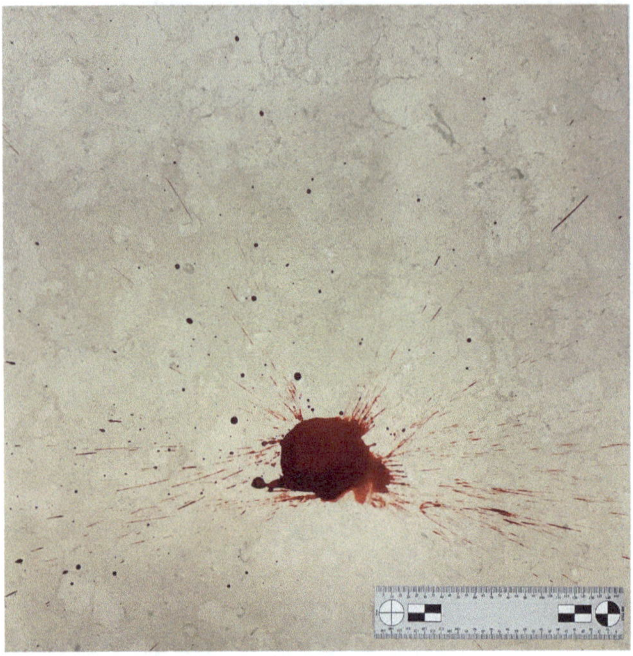

Figure 13.3 Laboratory-created impact pattern on a horizontal surface.

the blood source. A schematic representative of possible blood droplet trajectories and their subsequent stain shapes on vertical and horizontal surfaces is depicted in Figure 13.4.

Impact patterns can also be created by a bloodstained object contacting a surface (such as a bloodied head striking a wall or floor). In this situation, there may be evidence of transfer staining within the impact pattern.

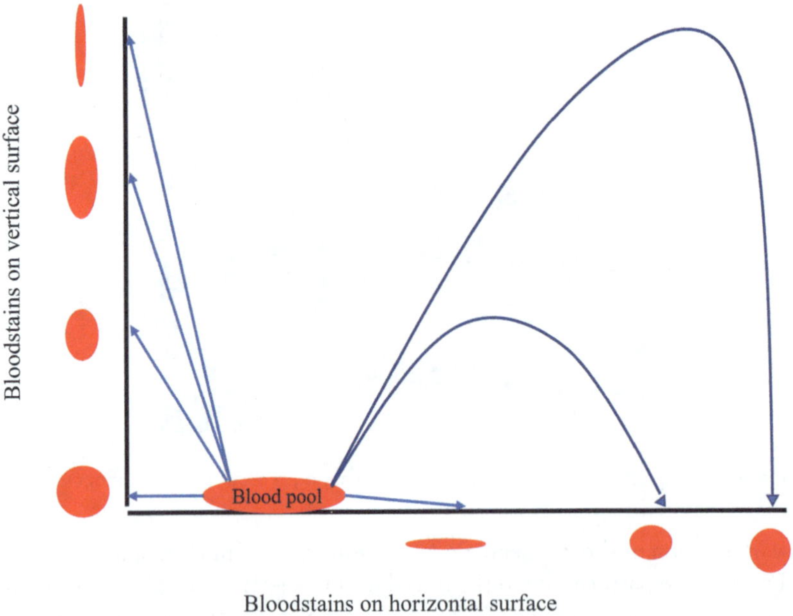

Figure 13.4 Schematic diagram showing different droplet trajectories and resulting stain shape for horizontal and vertical surfaces.

Multiple blows to the head can cause considerable quantities of spatter and sometimes other tissues and skull fragments if the injuries are severe.

EFFECTS ON STAIN SIZE

Individual stains can range in size from less than 0.5 mm diameter up to 8–9 mm diameter, with the majority of patterns having stains in the <1 mm to 4 mm range. Atomization of the blood into very small droplets can result when the striking object covers the pool of blood (or an edge of the pool). This forces the blood out sideways at high velocity resulting in almost instantaneous atomization often referred to as jetting under pressure. This results in a cluster of very small circular stains in the center of the pattern. These stains are often paler in color due to their high velocity causing them to spread very thinly across the target they deposit onto. These stains can give an approximate indication of the height of the blood source if they have jetted out straight from the blood source and the target is close (up to 50 cm) to the blood source.[3]

If the size of the blood pool is larger than the object, the blood can absorb some of the applied force, resulting in the formation of a larger second sheet that then extends and breaks up into droplets. The droplets formed from the larger second sheets tend to have larger diameters, resulting in larger stains. In reality, there is usually a combination of both jetting and sheet formation within the same impact resulting in a mixture of small and larger stains, with the small stains predominately closer to the center of the pattern.

As the volume of blood and therefore the surface area of the blood pool increases, there is more opportunity for the blood pool to form sheets, resulting in the formation of larger stains.

Conversely, as more energy is applied to the blood, more atomization occurs (the size of the droplets gets smaller) to dissipate this energy. This results in the formation of smaller stains (see Figure 13.5).

Figure 13.5 Laboratory-created impact patterns made under the same conditions (5 ml blood volume, 5 kg impactor) with varying fall heights and therefore velocities of the impacting object. Note the higher velocity in part b results in an increase in the number of stains and a decrease in the size of the stains. (a) Fall height = 30 cm (velocity = 2.21 m/s). (b) Fall height = 90 cm (velocity = 4.05 m/s).

Smaller droplets are affected by drag and gravity forces more quickly and do not travel as far. Therefore, as the distance increases between the blood source and the target, the number of small droplets reaching the target decreases, resulting in a pattern with less stains of generally larger size.

This effect of drag and gravity forces influences the distribution of stain sizes within an impact pattern in a predictable manner, with the smaller stains being located closer to the source of the blood (so usually in the "center" of the radiating pattern) with the preponderant stain size increasing further out the stains are located.

EFFECTS ON STAIN SHAPE

The droplets formed from impact are usually small (usually 0.1–2 mm diameter),[4] and when landing on targets result in stains which are circular to elliptical in shape. The trajectory angle of the droplets will define how far the droplets can travel before hitting the target, with more oblique trajectories resulting in stains further away from the source on vertical surfaces (as demonstrated in Figure 13.4). This results in a stain shape gradient for impact patterns with the stains close to the center being more circular and becoming more elliptical as the distance from the center increases on vertical surfaces. This is reflected in the width/length ratio of the stains which decreases from the center of the pattern out to the periphery.

If the target surface is very close to the impact site, the sheets and ligaments formed during the sheet break up may not have enough time to disengage to form spherical droplets before landing on the surface. This can result in larger irregular-shaped stains being present in the central area of the pattern along with smaller circular and elliptical stains. Likewise, when the target is close, the droplets do not have the opportunity to spread out from one another very far which can result in larger stains as the droplets land overlapping each other, as shown in Figure 13.6.

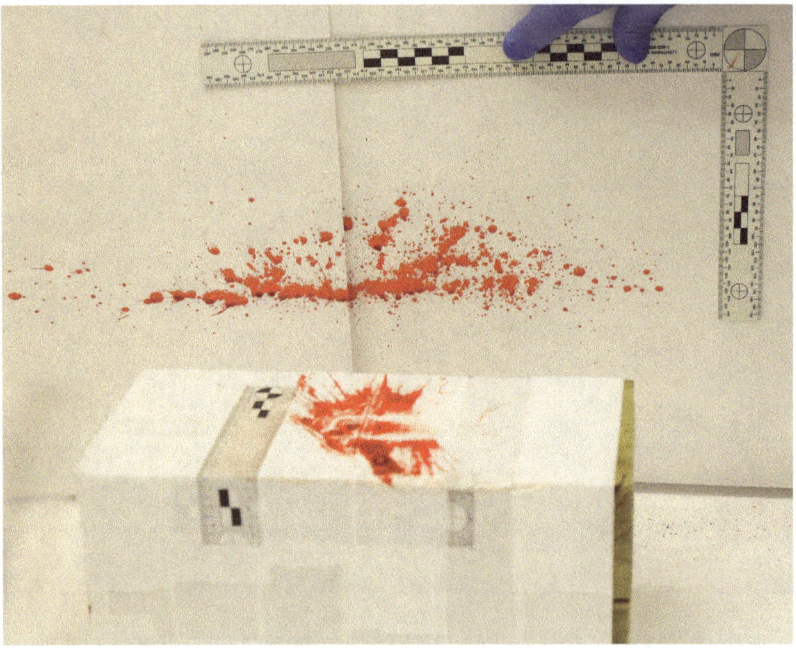

Figure 13.6 Impact pattern on card target created by striking a pool of blood with a fist. Note the overlapping and therefore larger stains present on the target due to the short distance between the blood source and target.

NUMBER OF STAINS

The number of stains in an impact pattern can vary immensely. Some patterns created only have a handful of stains, others can have thousands of stains. Again, there are a number of variables that will affect this. The distance between the blood source and the target is highly influential due to the influencing forces of drag and gravity.[5] The further the target from the blood source, the number of droplets that will reach it to make stains decreases. Conversely, as described above, if a target is very close to the blood, the sheets and ligaments may not have the opportunity to break up into individual droplets resulting in fewer but larger stains.[6] Droplets that do not have enough momentum to reach a vertical surface will land on the ground/floor where there is a high chance they will get disturbed or obliterated (often by being bled over).

The number of stains is also influenced by the volume of blood impacted. As the volume of blood increases, there is more opportunity for the blood pool to form larger sheets, resulting in more droplets and hence more stains, as demonstrated in Figure 13.7.

As discussed previously, increasing the energy applied to the blood pool results in smaller droplets being formed. So, for a given volume, a decrease in the size of the droplets will result in an increase in the number of stains. Therefore, increasing the energy applied to the blood (by increasing the velocity or mass of the impacting object) will result in more numerous but smaller stains.

SIZE OF PATTERN

Impact patterns can vary from a small cluster of spatter stains on a surface to expansive sizes that can span some meters across a room and up onto ceilings. High-energy impacts (either high velocity or large mass of object) onto large volumes of blood are likely to result in extensive patterns. As discussed earlier, the geometry of the space can also dictate the size of the pattern, larger spaces allow droplets to travel further.

Impacts onto soft surfaces such as beds, pillows, etc. may absorb some of the force applied by the object, resulting in less disruptive forces within the blood pool, limiting the formation of droplets and resulting in smaller patterns.

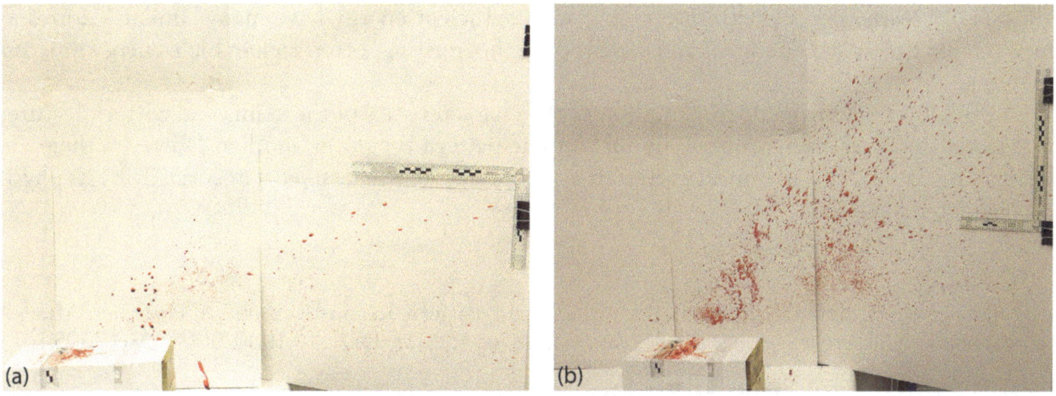

Figure 13.7 Laboratory-created impact patterns with increasing volumes of blood. Not the more extensive pattern in part b (larger volume), which has more stains, larger stains, and larger pattern distribution. (a) Laboratory impact pattern with 20 drops of blood using a metal pipe. (b) Laboratory impact pattern with 40 drops of blood using a metal pipe.

Other variables that can affect the size, shape, and distribution of impact spatter stains include the shape of the weapon, the weight and length of the weapon, the number of impacts, the location of the wounds, and the movement of the victim and perpetrator during the assault.

TEXTILES

Impact spatter stains on textiles can appear smaller in size due to the absorption of the material into the weave of the textile. Droplets may also break up when landing onto rougher textiles resulting in smaller stains and more satellite stains.[7] Directionality features may be difficult to interpret on textiles, again due to the interaction with the surface (splashing, wicking, absorption). For the examination of clothing and footwear, it is recommended that the visual examination of small stains be undertaken with the assistance of a low-power stereo microscope. This can assist with determining how the stain was deposited and clarify if the stain is due to spatter or a transfer mechanism.[8]

LIMITATIONS

It is not uncommon for impact events to create patterns with a limited number of stains and features. To be confident you are observing the expected features of an impact pattern, a reasonable number of stains is likely to be needed. It is important to consider other mechanisms that produce similar patterns such as forward spatter and backspatter patterns due to projectiles, drip pattern satellite stains, cessation pattern, and expiration, which may not be able to be excluded as a potential mechanism of the pattern.

In the absence of the parent stain, satellite stains from a drip pattern (blood dripping into blood) can appear very similar, especially on clothing. Previous reliability studies show that drip pattern satellite stains are likely to be misclassified as impact.[9]

Expirated patterns can also demonstrate radiating pattern characteristics. Dilution, air bubbles, and beading which are considered characteristic features of an expiration pattern are often present on non-porous surfaces, but can be obliterated on fabrics causing confusion in pattern classification.[9]

In a double blind study involving the classification of four different bloodstain patterns, over a third (37%) of the blunt force impact patterns were misclassified mostly as patterns resulting from gunshot.[10] Clearly, impact patterns created with sufficient energy have many similar features as forward and backspatter patterns and can produce the "misting" often seen in high-energy firearms patterns.

Careful observation and documentation of the characteristics of the stains and pattern features is essential and may offer stronger support for one pattern type over another. However, there are likely to be times when an impact pattern may not be able to be classified categorically by its physical characteristics alone.

Notes

1. Petricevic, S. and D. Elliot. 2005. "Bloodstain Pattern Reconstruction: A Hammer Attack." *Canadian Society of Forensic Science Journal*, 38, no.1: 9–19. DOI: 10.1080/00085030.2005.10757581
2. Goeghegan, Trudy. 2005. "A Comparison of Bloodstain Patterns Produced under Simulated Kicking, Stomping, Walking and Running." M.Sc. thesis. University of Auckland.
3. Kettner, M., A. Schmidt, M. Windgassen, P. Schmidt, C. Wagner, and F. Ramsthaler. 2015. "Impact Height and Wall Distance in Bloodstain Pattern Analysis: What Patterns of Round Bloodstains Can Tell Us." *International Journal of Legal Medicine*, 129: 133–140.

4. Kabaliuk, N., M.C. Jermy, E. Williams, T.L. Laber, and M.C Taylor. 2014. "Experimental Validation of a Numerical Model for Predicting the Trajectory of Blood Drops in Typical Crime Scene Conditions, Including Droplet Deformation and Breakup, with a Study of the Effect of Indoor Air Currents and Wind on Typical Spatter Drop Trajectories." *Forensic Science International*, 245: 107–120.
5. Siu, Sonya, Jennifer Pender, Frederic Tulleners, and William Ristenpart. 2017. "Quantitative Differentiation of Bloodstain Patterns Resulting from Gunshot and Blunt Force Impacts". *Journal of Forensic Sciences*: 62, no. 5: 1166–1179.
6. Liu, Yu, Daniel Attinger, and Kris De Brabanter. 2020. "Automatic Classification of Bloodstain Patterns Caused by Gunshot and Blunt Impact at Various Distances." *Journal of Forensic Sciences*, 65, issue 3: 729–743.
7. Wu, Jiaying, Stephen Michielsen, Ruksana Baby. 2018. "Impact Spatter Bloodstain Patterns on Textiles." *Journal of Forensic Sciences*: 64, no. 3: 702–710.
8. Cho Y., Springer F., Tulleners F.A., Ristenpart W.D. 2015. "Quantitative Bloodstain Analysis: Differentiation of Contact Transfer Patterns versus Spatter Patterns on Fabric via Microscopic Inspection." *Forensic Science International*, 249:233–240.
9. Taylor, Michael C., Terry L. Laber, Paul E. Kish, Glynn Owens, and Nikola K. P. Osborne. 2016. "The Reliability of Classification in Bloodstain Pattern Analysis – Part 2: Bloodstain Patterns on Fabric Surfaces." *Journal of Forensic Sciences*. 61: issue 6, 1461–1466.
10. Ristenpart, William, Fred Tulleners, Sonya Siu, Jennifer Saifi, and Faye Springer. 2013. "Quantitative Analysis of High Velocity Bloodstain Patterns." US National Institute of Justice Grant Report.

CHAPTER 14

CAST-OFF PATTERN ANALYSIS

Elisabeth Williams

The chapter reviews factors expected to influence cast-off patterns, such as the object shape and human wielding kinematics. It discusses competing theories on the formation of cast-off drops and establishes that the accepted mechanism involves drops detaching when centripetal forces are exceeded. High-speed video analysis of rotating devices and human swinging motions shows consistent blood migration and drop breakup behavior.

A four-stage process is proposed for cast-off analysis: measuring geometric pattern parameters; quantifying individual stain impact angles, sizes, and velocities; calculating droplet trajectories; and estimating object and human motion dynamics. Challenges around stain size, surface properties, and the variability of blood properties are also addressed. The chapter establishes cast-off patterns as a potential tool for crime reconstruction, given appropriate experimentation and analytical frameworks.

AN INTRODUCTION TO CAST-OFF BLOODSTAIN PATTERNS

Acts of physical violence, where victims are repeatedly beaten with human-wielded objects or body parts, are a prevalent means of homicide and serious assault.[1–3] Cast-off bloodstain patterns are frequently found at such crime scenes, where striking actions have been involved. Blood drops are formed and released from an object or body part being swung, creating characteristic trails of relatively small bloodstains in a linear or curvilinear distribution. Overall pattern and individual stain features depend on the trajectory, velocity, size, and shape of the striking object and available blood volume.[4] Individual stains within these patterns can have unique features, and by analysis of their directionality, the stains from the forward and backward swing movements can often be distinguished.

Cast-off is classified in the general bloodstain pattern class known as spatter, where forces other than gravity dictate blood breakup, flight, and impact dynamics. A *cast-off pattern* is defined as "a bloodstain pattern created when blood droplets are released from a weapon due to its motion."[5] While a cast-off pattern is often recognized, the mechanism by which it occurs is not so well understood. There are few scientific, peer-reviewed research papers dedicated to the understanding of this type of bloodstain pattern. Consequently, the question regarding whether the modern scene investigator is realizing the full potential of cast-off patterns arises.

The presence of correlating cast-off patterns on the clothing or body of an assailant can provide conclusive evidence regarding their positioning during the attack. Analysis of this type of bloodstain pattern is beyond the scope of this chapter and will not be addressed here.

DOI: 10.4324/9781003163695-14

EXPECTED CAST-OFF PATTERN CHARACTERISTICS

The typical features of cast-off patterns have been well described in previous textbooks. Three of these books indicated that a multi-surfaced or wider object will result in a distinctly different cast-off pattern than a single sharp edge or smooth edge.[6] These authors cautioned that the amount of blood available is of utmost importance as this can be a factor in the estimation of the velocity of the weapon. Regarding the individual stains in a pattern, these texts have stated that a larger weapon, such as a baseball bat, will result in larger cast-off stains. Conversely, a sharp-ended weapon may result in smaller blood drops due to the smaller surface area of the weapon end from which the blood is released.

Through the analysis of cast-off patterns, the minimum number of swings in an attack can sometimes be determined. This number is likely to be an underestimation, considering the first blow may not have been sufficient to draw blood. If it did, only the backswing cast-off would be present. This may refute a suspect's testimony if the individual had claimed, for example, to have only dealt one blow.[6] These authors advised that care must be taken when determining the number of blows as the weapon being swung may be multifaceted and leave a wide dispersion of stains. Cast-off from bloodied hair or a wide piece of timber, for example, being swung once could be mistaken for a smaller-tipped object being swung multiple times in the same plane. Authors stipulated that an experienced analyst could easily make this distinction; however, to the novice, this could be a significant source of error.

It has been suggested that the directionality of stains comprising the cast-off patterns may give an indication of the hand the assailant used to deal the blows. These, however, may not necessarily equate to the handedness of the assailant. Under controlled conditions, cast-off patterns produced weapons with the non-dominant hand were generally jerkier than those with the dominant hand.[6] These authors conceded that although this has been exhibited in experimental conditions, it is very unlikely that this could ever be established in casework.

Another important factor in the analysis of a cast-off pattern is the size of the individual droplets. The size of bloodstains is a function of volume and the impact velocity of the droplet. In falling drops, the volume can depend on the size of the object that it falls from,[7] so cast-off droplet size may also be a function of the size of the swinging weapon. The shape of individual stains is also known to vary within a pattern. The resulting bloodstains can be circular or elliptical depending on the orientation of the object with respect to the surface at the instant the blood drops are released. This will determine the angle at which they impact the target surface.[4] Photographs showing cast-off patterns created in a laboratory with a baseball bat during back swing on a vertical wall and on a ceiling are given in Figures 14.1 and 14.2, respectively.

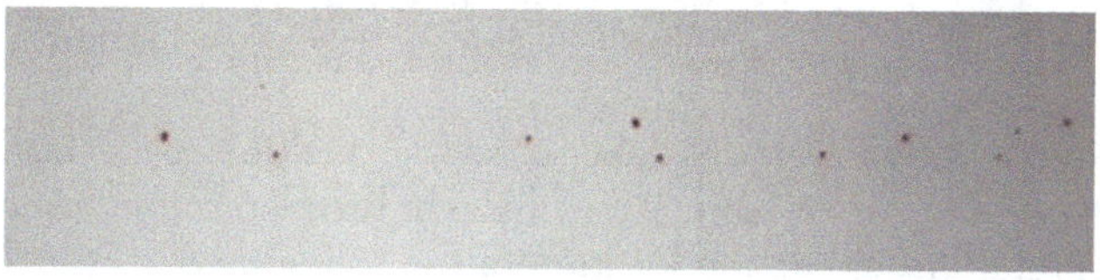

Figure 14.1 Photograph showing an example of a cast-off pattern on a vertical wall created during a back swing movement. (From Williams[4] Reproduced with permission.)

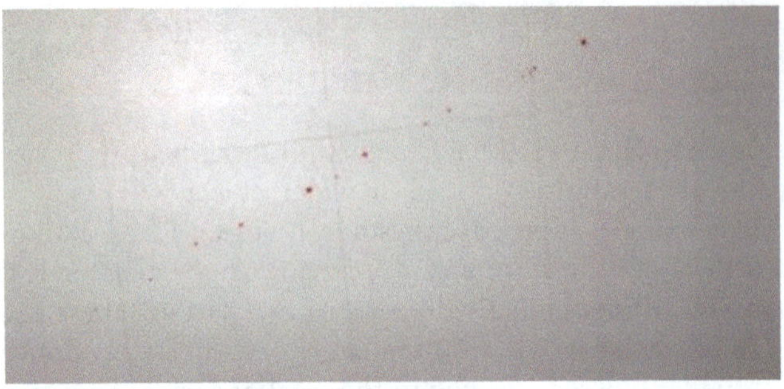

Figure 14.2 Photograph showing an example of a cast-off pattern on a horizontal ceiling surface, created during a back swing movement. (From Williams[4] Reproduced with permission.)

FACTORS AND VARIABLES AFFECTING CAST-OFF FORMATION

The overall presentation of a cast-off pattern is expected to reflect the weapon dynamics which created it.[8] To relate a cast-off pattern to the causative weapon dynamics, an understanding of blood behavior at the three stages of cast-off creation is required: drop formation and projection from the swinging object, droplet flight, and droplet impact.

Droplet formation, flight, and impact dynamics can be explained by the principles of fluid dynamics which are detailed in Chapter 5. These phenomena have a wide range of applications in industrial and engineering processes, to which extensive research has been dedicated for different liquids. Fundamentally, liquid droplet dynamics are dictated by the energy applied to a liquid resulting in droplet formation and dispersion and the forces acting on the liquid. The external forces acting on liquid droplets are gravity and aerodynamic drag and the liquid forces are viscosity and surface tension.

The study of blood droplet dynamics presents a unique set of conditions which need to be considered when applying any reconstructive techniques. It has been established in previous chapters that blood is a complex and variable biological fluid, the physical properties of which are affected by several factors. Bloodstain pattern analysts are interested in inferring the dynamic events leading to the deposition of bloodstains from analyzing stain presentation. That is to work backward from bloodstain to initial dispersion conditions, the so-called inverse problem. Stain presentation is a direct result of the balance of inertial forces present at the instant of droplet impact and the physical properties of the blood.[9]

FORMATION OF CAST-OFF BLOOD DROPS

Ambiguity still surrounds the cast-off creation process,[6,10] as this has previously been described in various contradictory ways. This ambiguity may have in turn led some crime scene examiners to draw incorrect interpretations about the location of the swinging object and the wielder. It may also have resulted in examiners overlooking potentially information within the pattern.

Some previous authors have described the formation of cast-off blood drops and disengagement from the swinging object in the non-inertial reference frame.[6,10] This means characterizing the blood drop formation process in the reference frame of the blood drop itself. These authors state that blood drops disengage from the swinging object due to "the generation of centrifugal force as a bloody weapon is swung in an arc",[6] or from the "generation of centrifugal force that overcomes the adhesive force that adheres the blood to the object".[10] This so-described centrifugal force acting on the blood drop, apparently acting away from the center of rotation, only appears to exist in this reference frame and does not correspond to a real force acting on the droplet. An explanation of this fictive centrifugal force is provided in Chapter 5.

The inertial reference frame is the reference frame of a stationary observer, also known as the laboratory reference frame.[9] Authors characterizing the cast-off blood drop formation process in this manner have stated:

> Blood droplets are thrown, by centripetal force, from a swinging object" when the "adhesion of blood to a transport medium is overcome by angular momentum".[11] Others have described "the angular momentum of the blood... is sufficient to overcome the surface tension of blood and small drops and droplets are released.[12]

The science of droplet breakup has been widely studied and is a phenomenon to which a vast body of literature has been dedicated. A review of the principles relevant to blood droplet breakup in cast-off pattern creation is provided in this section. As a complex process, an in-depth evaluation of the fluid dynamics principles regarding droplet formation is provided in Chapter 5. Briefly, however, a liquid droplet will separate from a liquid source when the disruptive external forces acting on the liquid exceed the cohesive surface energy forces of the liquid–air interface. The liquid surface tension draws the liquid molecules together into the form which minimizes surface energy, a sphere. The viscosity of the liquid has a stabilizing effect on the resulting droplet which opposes changes to the liquid geometry[13] The higher the viscosity of a liquid, the greater the stress required for the liquid to deform.[14] The greater the energy applied to the liquid, the greater the disruptive forces resulting in a larger number of smaller droplets. Five well-researched droplet generation mechanisms include dripping, sheet breakup, liquid column/jet breakup, liquid ligament breakup, and liquid free-surface breakup.[13] The most fundamental explanation of liquid droplet formation can be illustrated using the example of passive dripping, which is detailed in Chapters 5 and 7.

The science of droplet generation has a wide range of engineering and industrial applications. The generation of droplets in most of these applications involves atomization, where a bulk liquid is disintegrated into fine droplets. The basic principle of atomization can be described by an energy conservation model. Kinetic energy is imparted on the bulk liquid for the liquid to deform and disintegrate into fine droplets. The kinetic energy of the bulk liquid is dissipated in overcoming the viscous forces which resist deformation, and the surface tension forces which resist free surface creation.[15] Smaller droplets are likely to result from higher velocity or higher energy systems due to the magnitude of external fluid flow relative to that of the developing droplet. The generation of cast-off droplets can be compared to the process of rotary atomization. Rotary atomization is described as "centrifugal" atomization (in the non-inertial reference frame), where liquid is introduced to a rotating surface and droplets are generated via a liquid jet breakup mechanism. The liquid spreads out over the surface and disintegrates into droplets. This disintegration is due to a complex interaction between liquid and air and relies on large velocity differences between the two phases. The rotating surface can be a flat disk, vaned disk, or a cup.[15] Droplet formation has been described to result from several different mechanisms or regimes in rotary atomization depending on liquid flow rate and disk rotational speed: direct droplet formation, direct droplet and ligament formation, and sheet/film formation.[13]

At low velocities and flow rates, droplet generation is generally discontinuous and in the direct droplet regime. With increasing centripetal force due to increased disk velocity, droplets are projected at more regular intervals and may draw ligaments behind them, the direct droplet and ligament formation regime. Further increases in velocity and/or flow rate cause droplet generation to move into the ligament formation regime. Ligaments are formed around the disk periphery, which

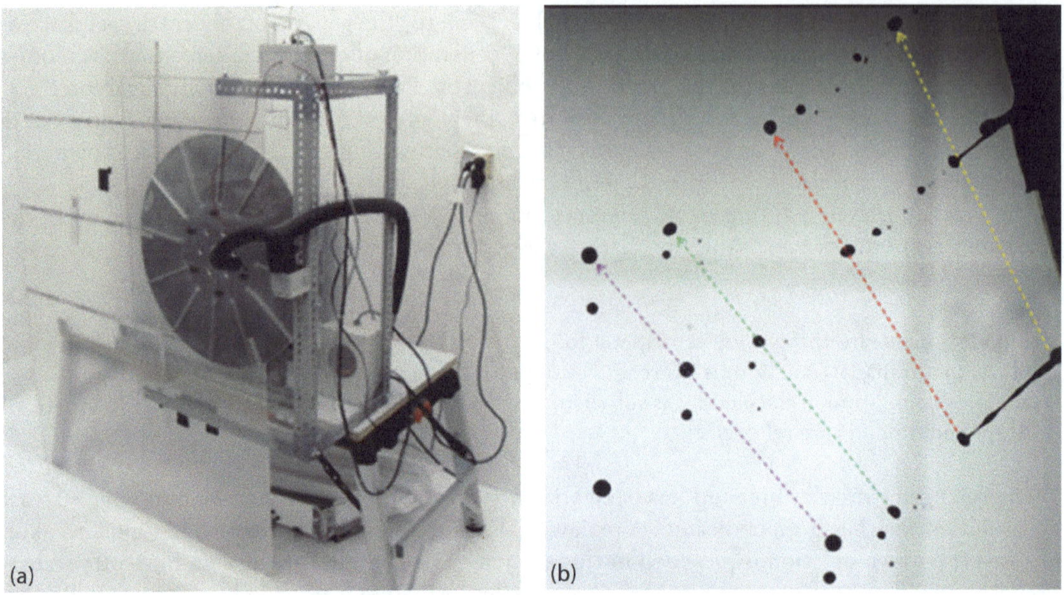

Figure 14.3 The motorized blood droplet generation device by Williams and Taylor[16] (a); and three superimposed still images (b) from high-speed video footage taken 0.009 second apart showing blood-forming ligaments at the periphery of the motorized, rotating disk. (Reproduced with permission from authors.)

disintegrate into droplets when exposed to the airflow around the disk. By increasing the speed of the disk periphery, liquid radiating out to the disk edge can be immediately atomized due to the high relative velocity between the disk and surrounding air.[15]

Williams and Taylor[16] developed a mechanical device constituting a motorized, rotating aluminum disk to specifically test this phenomenon with blood, to improve understanding of cast-off patterns Figure 14.3(a). These authors' observations were consistent with those of previous studies with other fluids.[13,15] Volumes of liquid blood were applied to the rotating disk, and blood behavior recorded with a high-speed video camera. Figure 14.3(b) shows overlaid still images, taken every 0.009 second, of the liquid blood having gravitated to the periphery of the rotating disk, forming ligaments which subsequently broke up into oscillating, individual blood drops.[16]

To overcome the previous ambiguity regarding blood drop formation and disengagement from swinging objects, the following technical description has been offered:[4]

> Cast-off patterns occur when blood present on a swinging object detaches and is projected onto nearby surfaces. This occurs if the wielder of the object swings the object in such a way that the surface tension forces holding the blood on the object are insufficient to provide the centripetal force necessary to keep the blood moving on the same arc as the object tip. Under these conditions, the liquid extends outwards in the form of a ligament, which subsequently breaks up and drops form. The now separated blood drops continue to travel (initially) in the same direction as that at the time of release, which is in near-straight lines tangential to the object-end trajectory.

This has been further supported by both Kunz, Adamec, and Grove[17] using a knife on a fixed hinge, and Liscio et al.[18] using a fixed device named "Castanova." The instant the blood drop becomes a projectile, the effects of gravity and air resistance will dictate the subsequent trajectory.[14] Blood drop flight is discussed in detail in Chapter 4 and briefly outlined below as it relates specifically to cast-off. A proper understanding of these phenomena is the first step in the development of a reliable method to objectively assess feasible crime dynamics based on cast-off patterns.

HUMAN-WIELDED OBJECTS

The preceding discussion on rotary atomization theory assumes uniform circular motion, where the rotation of an object with a fixed-length radius occurs around a fixed pivot point, at a constant rotational velocity.[4] Based on findings in sports biomechanics, a human-wielded object will undergo non-uniform circular motion. In actions such as striking or throwing, humans generally adopt a coordinated proximal-to-distal kinematic chain strategy whereby many body segments undergo linear and rotational motion.[19] Momentum is typically developed by the legs and transferred up the chain, progressing through the hips, torso, shoulder, upper arm, forearm, and hand.[20–22] Accordingly, neither the swing radius length nor pivot point will remain fixed, resulting in an elliptical object-end trajectory. The object's tangential velocity changes throughout the back and forward swing movements.

Williams et al.[4] compared blood drop formation and disengagement between a fixed, rotating device (uniform circular motion) and human volunteers wielding typical weapons found at crime scenes (non-uniform circular motion). The same pattern of blood migration to the most distal point of the weapon, formation of ligaments, and subsequent blood drop breakup were observed in both cases. A comparable volume of blood was applied to the fixed knife apparatus and human-wielded weapons, which were the same knife from the fixed device and an aluminum baseball bat. Figure 14.4 shows still, overlaid images from the fixed knife apparatus with blood drop trajectories notated. Figure 14.5 shows the impact angle of blood drops, calculated from resulting stains for the fixed knife experiment. Figure 14.6 shows still images of a knife being swung in an upward direction (back swing) with resulting blood drop trajectories indicated, with the corresponding knife tip and blood trajectories plotted on a graph. Figure 14.7 shows a graph of the same knife tip and two blood drop trajectories being swung downward (forward swing). Figures 14.8 and 14.9 show the same for a baseball bat. These images demonstrate that the blood behavior observed in rotary atomization and fixed devices with uniform circular motion also occur during non-uniform circular motion. Blood migrates to the most distal point of the swinging object and forms ligaments. These ligaments subsequently separate into individual blood drops, with the initial trajectory being at a tangent to the arcing trajectory of the object. This is also the case regardless of whether the object is swinging in a vertical or horizontal plane or whether the movement is traveling upward (back swing) or in a downward direction (forward swing).

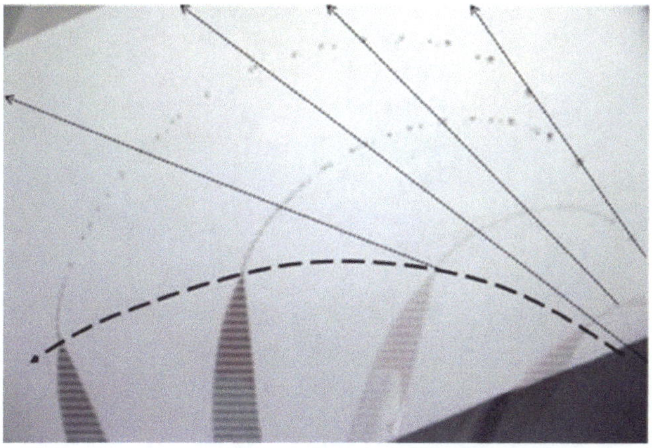

Figure 14.4 Overlaid still images of the trajectory of a fixed kitchen knife spinning on a fixed tripod and blood drops released from the knife. Trajectories of individual blood drops are indicated. (From Williams et al.[4] Reproduced with permission.)

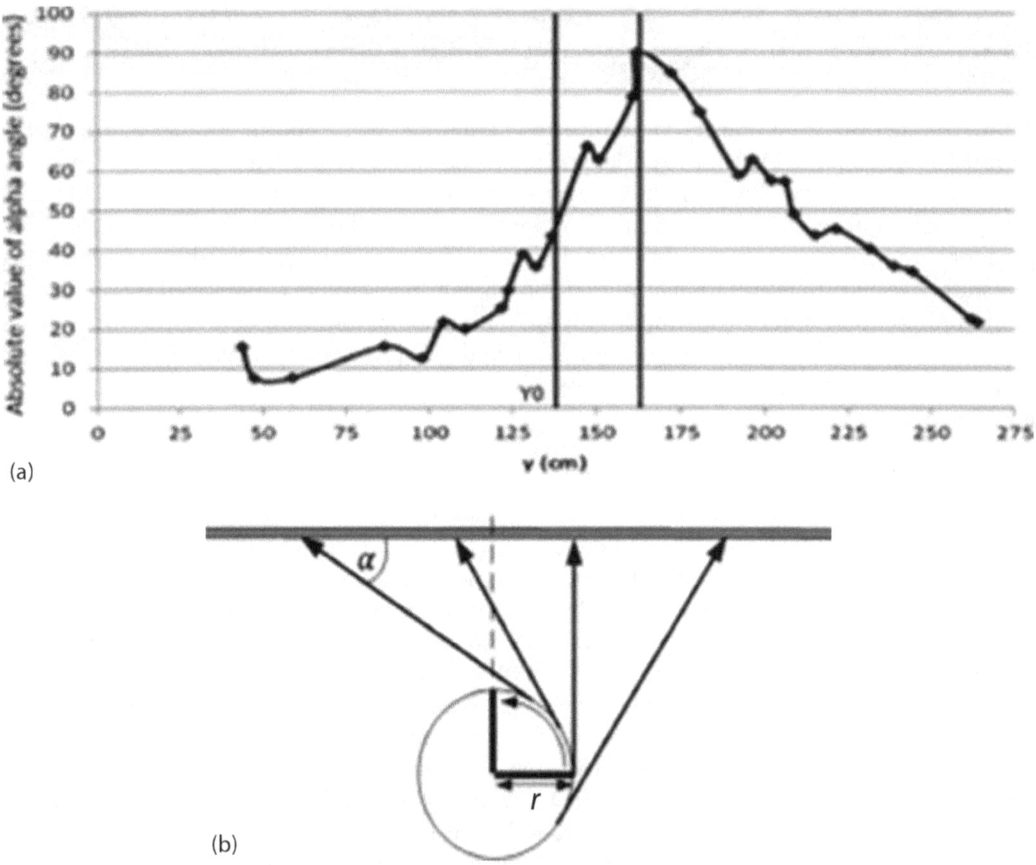

Figure 14.5 Graph showing calculated blood drop impact angle relative to position from knife pivot point (a) and a diagrammatic representation of the fixed knife tip trajectory and those of blood drops following disengagement from the knife (b). (From Williams et al.[4] Reproduced with permission.)

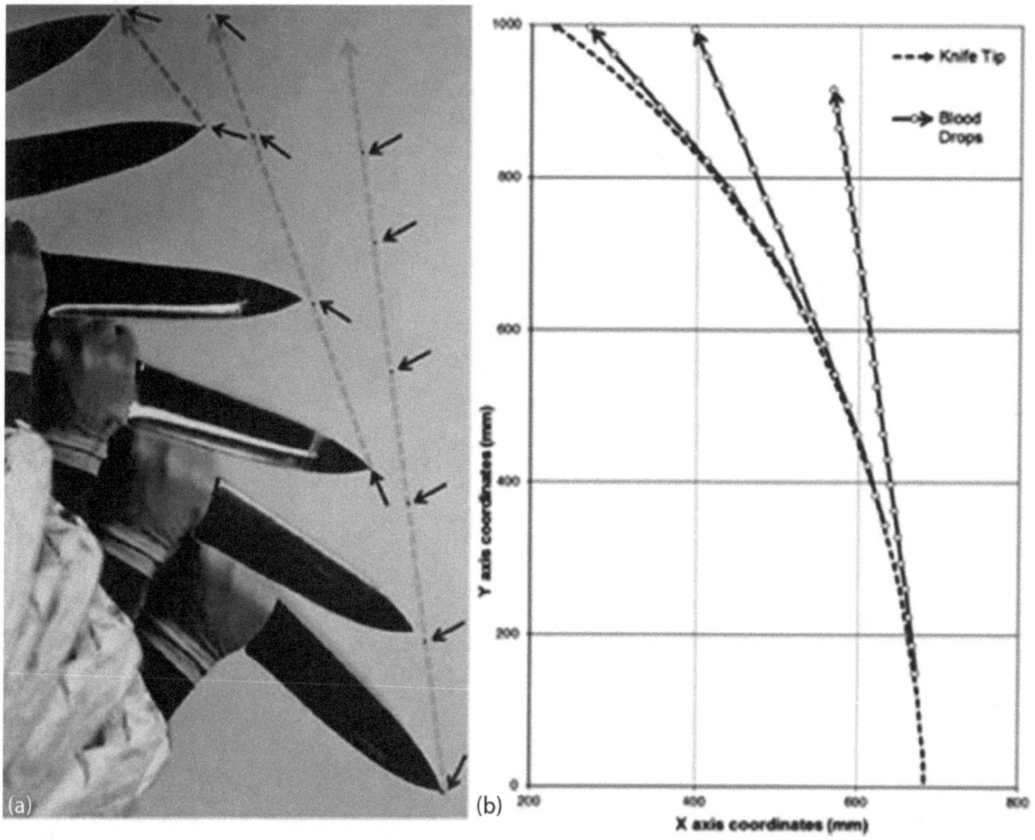

Figure 14.6 Overlaid still images of a human-wielded knife tip trajectory and corresponding blood drops during backswing (a) and the plotted knife tip and blood drop trajectories (b). (From Williams et al.[4] Reproduced with permission.)

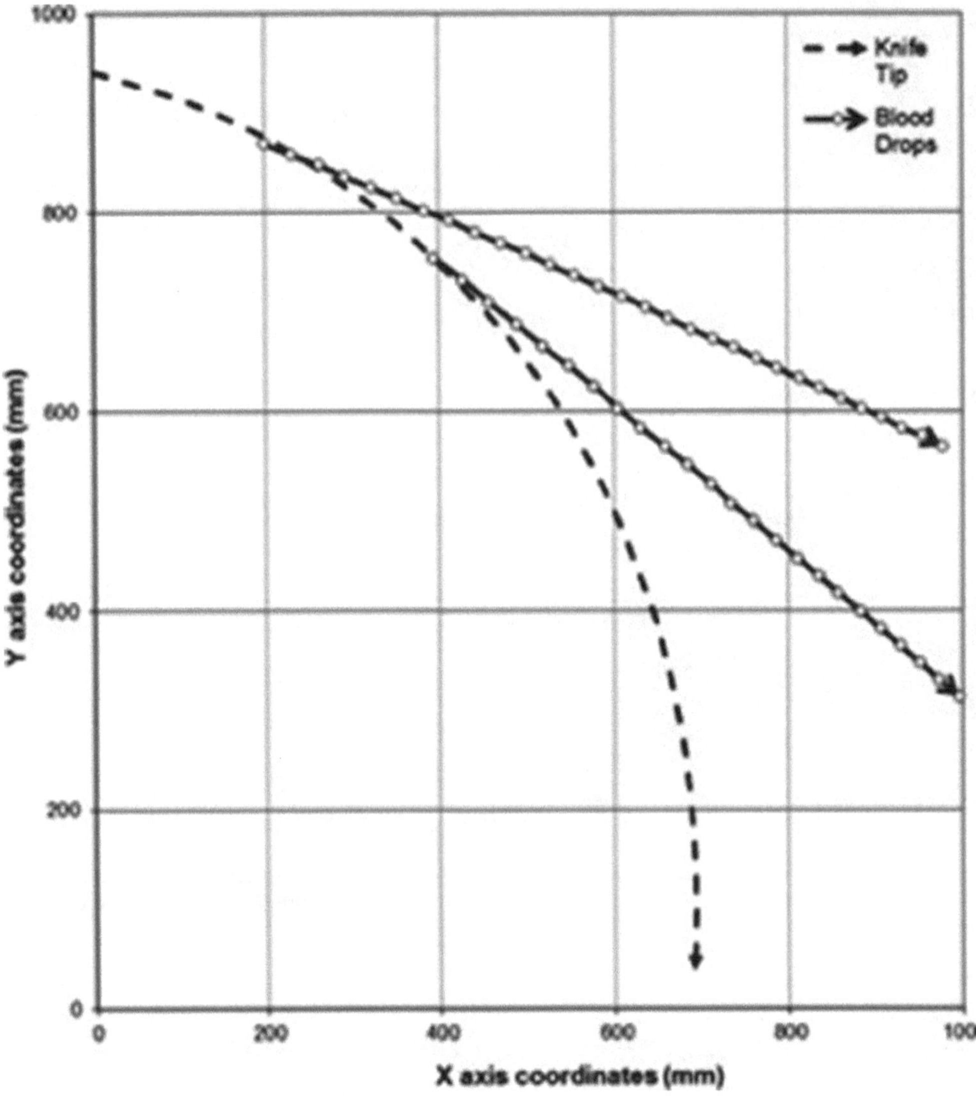

Figure 14.7 Plotted trajectories of the human-wielded knife tip trajectory and two corresponding blood drops during a forward swing motion. (From Williams et al.[4] Reproduced with permission.)

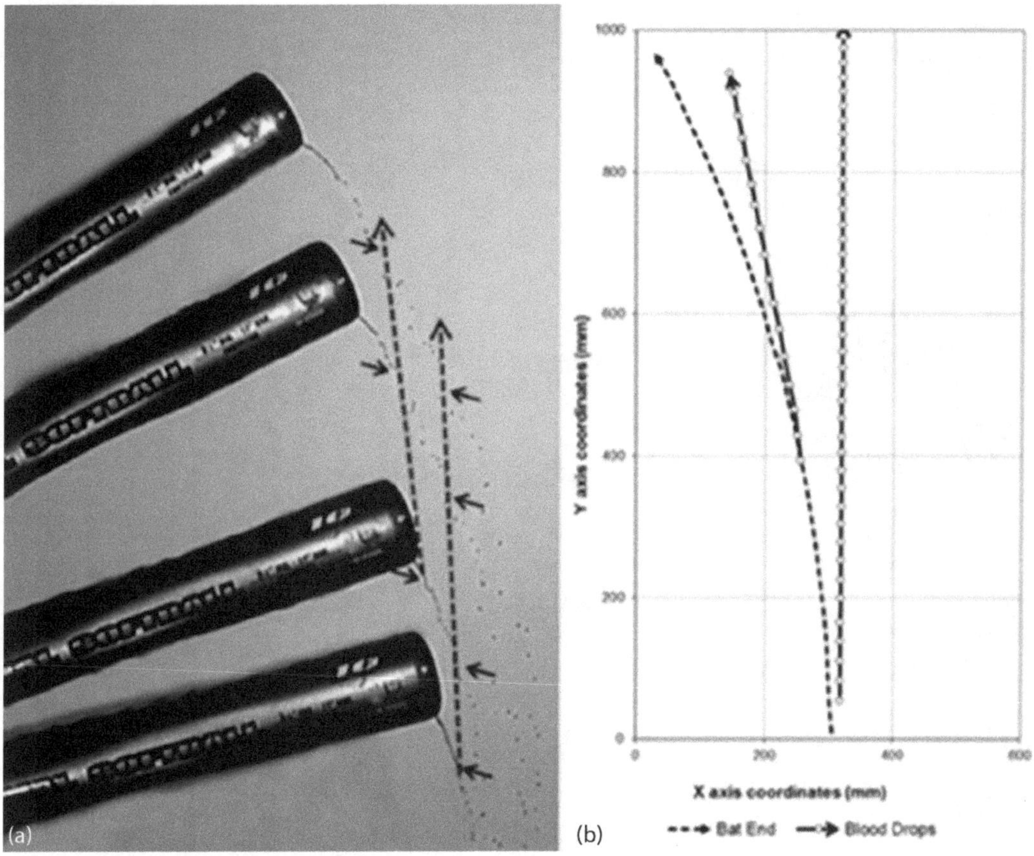

Figure 14.8 Overlaid still images of a human-wielded baseball bat tip trajectory and corresponding blood drops during backswing (a) and the plotted baseball bat tip and blood drop trajectories (b). (From Williams et al.[4] Reproduced with permission.)

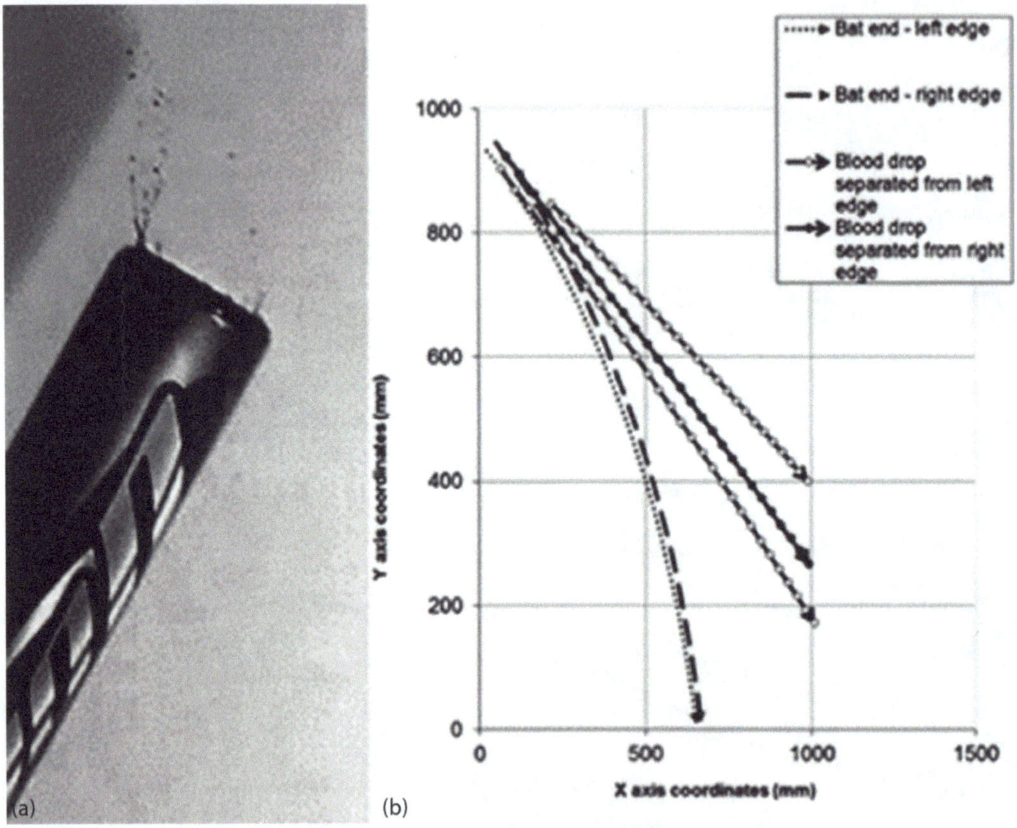

Figure 14.9 Overlaid still images of a human-wielded baseball bat tip trajectory and corresponding blood drops during forward swing (a) and the plotted baseball bat tip and blood drop trajectories (b). (From Williams et al.[4] Reproduced with permission.)

ASSAILANT KINEMATICS

In creating a cast-off pattern, the objective of the criminal assailant is to deliver a forceful blow to the victim. Hence there are elements of commonality between the assailant and the sports person trying to generate a high bat, racket, or club velocity.[23] Accordingly, the kinematics of the latter should be applicable when trying to understand the former. A human assailant may innately adopt a kinematic strategy to optimize the effectiveness of the swing for a given weapon. The weapon dynamics are a direct consequence of the human kinematic strategy used to swing the weapon. The possibility of cast-off patterns having certain features typical of distinctive weapon characteristics needed to be investigated. Patterns created with long weapons, for example, may differ from those created with short weapons. Weapons of different shapes and sizes may be swung in certain ways depending on their length, mass, and mass distribution.

The anatomical arrangement of the arms and shoulder joints effectively acts as levers around a central pivot point. In the case of swinging a weapon, it follows that the weapon will travel in some form of elliptical path. The centripetal force exerted on the weapon by the assailant keeps pulling it in this path. In kicking and hitting movements, there is generally a back swing phase followed by a forward swing phase culminating in the event of contact. The main purposes for the back swing movement are to increase the distance over which velocity can be developed during the forward swing and increase elastic energy in the muscle required to generate maximum downward force.[20,24]

Segmental coordination essential to develop velocity in a swinging object is consistent in all striking movements. Larger objects are typically swung with two hands, smaller, shorter objects with one. The relative magnitude of given kinematic parameters changes according to the length, shape, and mass of the object. Essentially, the principles of length-tension, force-velocity and the stretch-shorten cycle are all optimized when an individual is focused on swinging a given object at maximum velocity.

The objectives of each phase of the weapon swing are also expected to be reflected in the weapon velocity. The objective of the forward stroke or "forward swing" phase is to deliver force to a target. The objective of the backward pre-stretch movement or "back swing" is to develop distance between the object and the target to generate a faster forward swing. Sporting studies have reported that the fastest racket/bat/golf club velocities were recorded at the instant prior to contact with a ball or target. This is due to the strong, powerful muscles generating the momentum as well as the configuration of body segments. Velocities are usually slower during the backward pre-stretch movement due to smaller, weaker muscles being the prime movers. These same patterns have been observed in a laboratory-based pilot simulation of an individual swinging two improvised weapons, identical apart from in length.[8] Figures 14.10 and 14.11 show the experimental setup from this study.

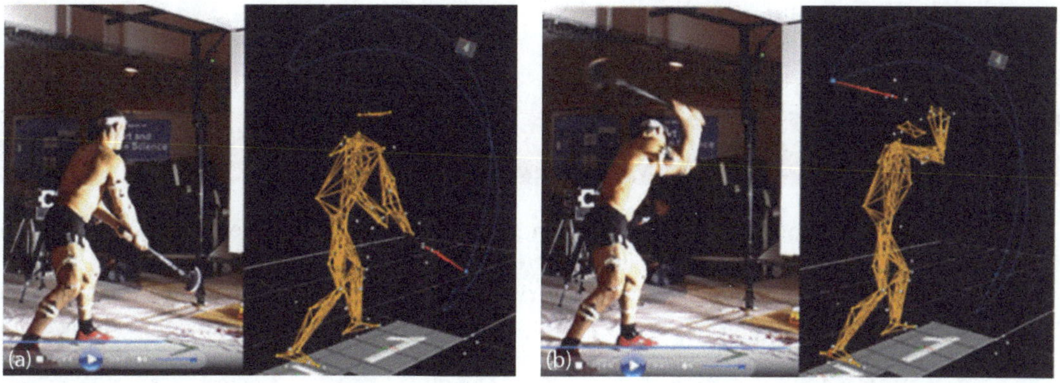

Figure 14.10 A laboratory simulation of an individual swinging a baseball bat-length bespoke weapon using two hands (a), and corresponding three-dimensional biomechanical reconstructions of the person and the weapon (b). (From Williams.[8] Reproduced with permission).

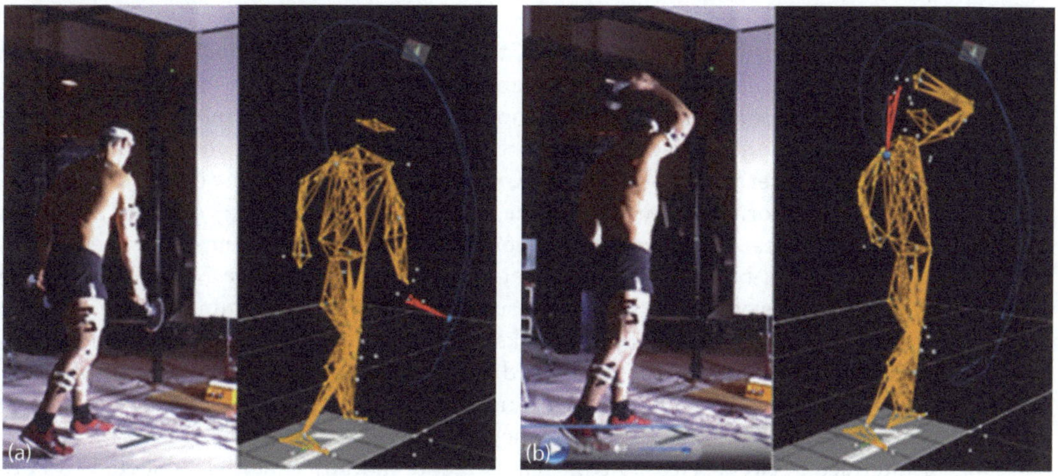

Figure 14.11 A laboratory simulation of an individual swinging a hammer-length bespoke weapon using one hand (a), and corresponding three-dimensional biomechanical reconstructions of the person and the weapon (b). (From Williams.[8] Reproduced with permission.)

BLOOD DROP FLIGHT

The resulting blood droplet trajectories and impact dynamics of typically small blood droplets must be considered when analyzing cast-off patterns. A comprehensive explanation of blood droplet trajectory has been provided by Kabaliuk et al.[14] and in Chapter 4. Kabaliuk et al. used the motorized blood droplet generation device[16] and high-speed digital video to validate numerical models for blood droplet breakup and trajectory. These authors demonstrated that the subsequent trajectory of blood droplets released from an object can be predicted using a numerical model, validated for blood droplets with experimental data. Droplets exhibited significant levels of deformation in the initial stages of flight, which dampened very quickly and did not affect droplet trajectory for the data in these experiments. The distance droplets were projected increase with an increase in disk velocity, and the velocity of smaller satellite droplets decreased rapidly relative to the larger drops released at the same speed. Depending on the distance traveled, blood droplet trajectories were found to deviate significantly from a straight line, immediately acted on by the forces of air resistance and gravity. Straight-line trajectories were thus not suitable to predict blood droplet flight in the conditions tested.

BLOOD DROP IMPACT

The phenomenon of liquid droplet impact on solid surfaces has received much attention in the fluid mechanics literature. The complexities of this process, including bouncing, spreading, and splashing, have been reviewed by Yarin.[25] The dynamics of the complex transfer of energy during stain formation when any liquid strikes a surface will dictate the resulting stain formation. The features of the resulting stain depend on the impact velocity, the direction of droplet travel, the characteristics of the surface, droplet size, and the physical properties of the fluid.[26–28] The impact velocity and angle of the impacting droplet will dictate the dynamics of the early phases, with the surface tension and viscosity limiting the spread of the liquid on the surface, and eventually bringing the liquid in the stain to a resting equilibrium.[25] A detailed explanation of the dynamics of blood droplet impact has been provided in Chapter 4.

Relative to the attention given to large, passive blood droplets in the development of reconstructive equations, very little has been given to small droplets. Reynolds et al.[28] studied bloodstains created by blunt impact force (≤3 mm in length) with regard to impact angle and region of origin calculations. These authors emphasized the largely unknown specific influences of inertial, viscous, and surface tension forces dictating impact dynamics of small droplets. Recommendations were made for further work to be done in this area before small stains should be used in area of origin calculations. The work of Raymond et al.[29] demonstrated that consistent with the classical fluid mechanics theory described by the Young-Laplace equation, the internal pressure of a blood droplet is inversely proportional to the radius. It has been established that regardless of competing forces, surface tension is the dominant force in liquid behavior in submillimeter droplets.[30] These works demonstrate that surface tension has a dominant influence on blood droplet shape for small droplets, regardless of other competing forces. The principle of capillary length may be useful in explaining any differences in the spreading dynamics between small and large droplets. The capillary length is the characteristic length scale for an interface between two fluids, such as blood and air, which is subjected to both gravitational acceleration and to surface force due to surface tension at the interface. Thus, blood droplets with diameters less than 2.45 mm may exhibit different spreading dynamics than larger droplets.

KEY CONSIDERATIONS FOR CAST-OFF PATTERN ANALYSIS

An understanding of the process of typical cast-off pattern creation presented in this chapter may aid practitioners in maximizing the evidential value of some cast-off patterns for reconstructive purposes. It has been established that the stain size, shape, directionality, and distribution will be a direct result of the trajectory, velocity, size, shape, and physical characteristics of the bloodied object being swung and the blood volume available. Therefore, the four-step systematic approach to cast-off pattern analysis described below offers increasing levels of complexity and precision relative to the evidence quality, and technology, expertise, and time available for analysis:

1. Measurement of geometric pattern parameters
2. Measurement of stain impact parameters
3. Calculation of droplet trajectories
4. Calculation of weapon dynamics and human kinematics

Some fundamental movement parameters could be calculated from the geometric pattern parameters alone. This may be the extent of the analysis possible for some cast-off patterns. Once these parameters have been carefully analyzed and evaluated within the context of the scene, subsequent steps may or may not be feasible and logical to undertake.

Step 1: Measurement of Geometric Pattern Parameters

In many cases, establishing the fundamental geometric parameters of a cast-off pattern is a logical first step. These can be measured for most cast-off patterns, including those where the quality of the stains is compromised by rough or hydrophobic surface characteristics, tampering, or contamination. The geometric parameters and potential measures these may provide include the following:

- *Stain Locations:* The location within a crime scene of cast-off stains may provide preliminary information about the location and plane of the object being swung. Depending on case circumstances, this may also imply the location of the individual performing the striking movement. The surfaces on which stains are found, such as walls and ceilings, may indicate a vertical or horizontal swing.
- *The Number and Density of Stains in the Pattern:* These may provide indications of the object velocity throughout the swing. The density of stains in a given location may indicate a higher object swinging velocity at the instant the corresponding blood droplets disengaged from the swinging object.
- *Stain Directionality:* Back swing stains on the front wall may provide information about the minimum object swinging velocity required during the initial stages of the back swing for stains to be created on the front wall. Stains on the ceiling created during back swing could yield the most valuable information about the object swing speed.
- *Length of the Pattern:* The length of patterns on the ceiling created during back swing may be indicative of the distance of travel of the swinging object during the back swing phase.
- *The Distance between Consecutive Stains:* The distance between consecutive ceiling stains created during back swing may be useful in determining the location of the center of rotation: the approximate position the assailant may have been standing.
- *Linearity of the Pattern:* The linearity of the pattern, particularly for ceiling patterns, created during back swing can indicate the lateral deviation of a swinging object trajectory. A high degree of lateral deviation may be indicative of a longer object being swung with two hands. This is due to the human kinematic chain involving trunk rotation during the back swing movement, to build distance over which to develop impact force during the subsequent forward swing.

If the individual stains lack sufficient detail for further analysis, or if further analysis is not required for a particular case, the analysis would stop at Stage 1. Without further calculations, a semiquantitative analysis of the geometric pattern characteristics can still provide objective information regarding the swinging object dynamics. The swinging object dynamics can be indicative of assailant biomechanics, as illustrated in Figures 14.10 and 14.11

Step 2: Measurement of Stain Impact Parameters

Following Step 1, increasingly detailed stain measurements could improve the accuracy of the cast-off movement reconstruction. For Stage 2 to be considered, the quality of the individual stains within the pattern must be adequate for the accurate measurement of stain characteristics. This will be largely dependent on the physical characteristics of the impact surface and the size of the stains. The stain impact parameters and the information they may provide are as follows:

- ***Aspect Ratio:*** The ratio of stain width to stain length can be used to calculate droplet impact angle. The sine equation ($\sin\Theta = W/L$) used to calculate droplet impact angle in BPA should be cautiously applied to stains with a diameter of <2 mm.
- *Stain Area and Splashing Characteristics.* Stain area is well correlated with droplet diameter. Droplet diameter and impact velocity can be calculated from stain area and the number of spines.[26] Should droplet impact angle, droplet diameter, and impact velocity be accurately calculated (within a small range), these can be used to calculate droplet flight trajectories based on the numerical code by Kabaliuk et al.[14]
- The variability in blood physical properties, particularly viscosity, for living humans can be used to estimate the uncertainty in droplet size and velocity calculated from prediction equations.

Step 3: Calculation of Droplet Trajectories

Where sensible outcomes have been calculated from Steps 1 and 2, droplet flight trajectory can be estimated, within a range consistent with the uncertainty of droplet impact calculations using the numerical model of Kabaliuk et al.[14] If a 3D workspace, such as a laser scan of the crime scene, is available, multiple droplet flight paths could be visualized to calculate aspects of the weapon trajectory and velocity. For this technique to be utilized, the practitioner must have extensive training in 3D laser scanning and relevant software applications, as well as an in-depth understanding of the fluid dynamics of blood. McCleary et al.[31] used straight lines to plot the trajectories of at least three cast-off blood droplets with merging arcs to escribe a weapon swing path using a probabilistic approach. Figure 14.12 shows an escribed arc for a fixed mechanical cast-off device, Castanova, and how the merged straight-line blood drop trajectories were used to plot this in the study of McCleary et al.[31]

Step 4: Calculation of Weapon Dynamics and Human Kinematics.

Based on the droplet trajectories calculated in Step 3, combined with knowledge of what a human-wielded object trajectory is likely to look like, aspects of this trajectory can be estimated based on the plotted trajectories of a number of blood droplets. The data shown in Figures 14.4–14.9 and Figure 14.12 show that aspects of a human-wielded weapon swing can be reconstructed in a similar but possibly limited manner. Based on these weapon swing dynamics and human kinematic knowledge, some sensible predictions of the assailant kinematics to produce such a trajectory could be made. An example of this by McCleary et al.[31] is given in Figure 14.13.

The increasing use of 3D laser scanning of crime scenes provides distinct advantages for the utilization of reconstructive frameworks. Integrating these data into a virtual replica of the crime scene facilitates effective visualization of the reconstruction data within the confines of the scene.

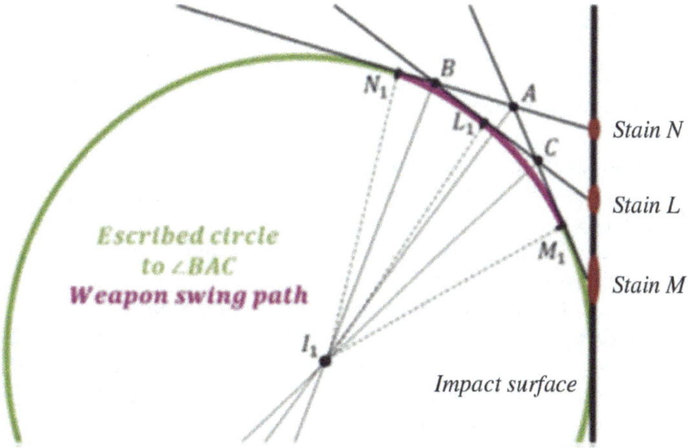

Figure 14.12 Diagram showing escribed arc of probabilistic weapon swing path and the straight-line trajectories and positions of three cast-off stains. (From McCleary et al.[31] Reproduced with permission).

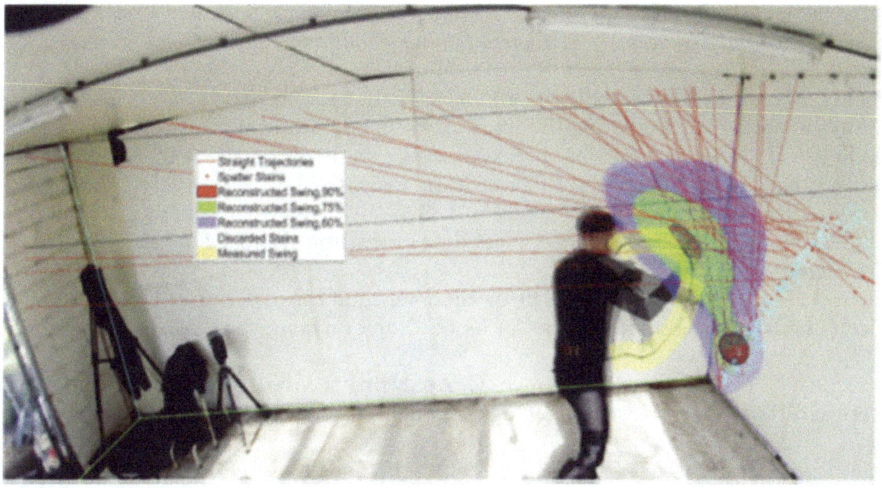

Figure 14.13 Image from McCleary et al.[31] showing a laboratory-based cast-off reconstruction for a human swinging motion. Overland are calculated straight-line blood drop trajectories, the measured swing trajectory (black line with yellow shading), and reconstructed swings with different levels of uncertainty. (Reproduced with permission from authors).

Hypothesis testing regarding the human and weapon/object kinematics which may have been used to create a particular weapon trajectory can include the consideration of any obstacles and structures. While substantial research is required to further develop and validate reconstructive frameworks such as these for forensic casework, the pilot studies cited here provide promising results.

Notes

1. Berlet, A. C., Talenti, D. P. & Carroll, S. F. The baseball bat: A popular mechanism of urban injury. J Trauma – *Injury, Infection and Critical Care* **33**, 167–170 (1992).
2. Lightbody, C. J. & MacIver, C. The baseball bat: A modern day cudgel. *J Emerg Med* **24**, 112 (2007).

3. Dujovny, M., Onyekachi, I. & Perez-Arjona, E. Baseball bats: A silent weapon. *Neurol Res* **31**, 1005–1011 (2009).
4. Williams, E. M. P., Graham, E. S., Jermy, M. C., Kieser, D. C. & Taylor, M. C. The dynamics of blood drop release from swinging objects in the creation of cast-off bloodstain patterns. *J Forensic Sci* **64**, 413–421 (2019).
5. AAFS Academy Standards Board. *ASB Technical Report 033, First Edition Terms and Definitions in Bloodstain Pattern Analysis*. https://www.aafs.org/asb-standard/terms-and-definitions-bloodstain-pattern-analysis (2017).
6. Bevel, T. & Gardner, R. *Bloodstain Pattern Analysis with an Introduction to Crime Acene Reconstruction*. (CRC Press, Boca Raton, FL, 2008).
7. Kabaliuk, N., *Jermy, M. C., Morison, K., Stotesbury, T., Taylor, M. C. T., Williams, E. M. P.* Blood drop size in passive dripping from weapons. *Forensic Sci Int* **228**, 75–82 (2013).
8. Williams, E. M. P. *From Weapon to Wall: Investigating the Link Between Cast-Off Bloodstain Patterns, Blood Dynamics and Assailant Kinematics* (University of Auckland, 2014).
9. Attinger, D., Moore, C., Donaldson, A., Jafari, A. & Stone, H. A. Fluid dynamics topics in bloodstain pattern analysis: Comparative review and research opportunities. *Forensic Sci Int* **231**, 375–396 (2013).
10. James, S. H., Kish, P. E. & Sutton, T. P. *Principles of Bloodstain Pattern Analysis: Theory and Practice*. (CRC Press, Taylor and Francis Group, Boca Raton, FL, 2005).
11. Wonder, A. *Blood Dynamics* (Academic Press, San Diego, CA, 2008).
12. MacDonnell, H. L. *Bloodstain Patterns* (Laboratory of Forensic Sciences, Corning, NY, 2005).
13. Liu, H. *Science and Engineering of Droplets. Fundamentals and Applications* (Noyes, Park Ridge, NJ, 2002).
14. Kabaliuk, N., Jermy, M. C., Williams, E., Laber, T. L. & Taylor, M. C. Experimental validation of a numerical model for predicting the trajectory of blood drops in typical crime scene conditions, including droplet deformation and breakup, with a study of the effect of indoor air currents and wind on typical spatter drop traj. *Forensic Sci Int* **245**, 107–120 (2014).
15. Lavernia, E. J., Gutierrez, E. M., Szekely, J. & Grant, N. J. Mathematical model of the liquid dynamic compaction process. Part 1: Heat flow in gas atomization. *International Journal of Rapid Solidification* **4**, 89–124 (1988).
16. Williams, E. M. P. & Taylor, M. C. The development and construction of blood droplet generation device (BDGD) for detailed analysis of blood droplet dynamics. *Forensic. Sci. SEM.* **3**, 95–104 (2013).
17. Kunz, S. N. S. N., Adamec, J. & Grove, C. Analyzing the dynamics and morphology of cast-off pattern at different speed levels using high-speed digital video imaging. *J Forensic Sci* **62**, 428–434 (2017).
18. Liscio, E., Bozek, P., Guryn, H. & Le, Q. Observations and 3D analysis of controlled cast-off stains. *J Forensic Sci* **65**, 1128–1140 (2020).
19. Welch, C. M., Banks, S. A., Cook, F. F. & Draovitch, P. Hitting a baseball: A biomechanical description. J Orthop Sports Phys Ther **22**, 193–201 (1995).
20. Roach, N. T., Venkadesan, M., Rainbow, M. J. & Lieberman, D. E. Elastic energy storage in the shoulder and the evolution of high-speed throwing in Homo. *Nature* **498**, 483–486 (2013).
21. Escamilla, R. F. *et al.* A comparison of age level on baseball hitting kinematics. *J Appl Biomech* **25**, 210–218 (2009).
22. Putnam, C. A. Sequential motions of body segments in striking and throwing skills: Descriptions and explanations. *J Biomech* **26**, 125–135 (1993).
23. Gervais, P., Baudin, P., Cruikshank, B. & Dahlstedt, D. L. Comparative analysis between police batons. *Forensic Sci Int* **91**, 7–17 (1998).
24. Elliott, B., Reid, M., & Crespo, M. (Eds.). *Biomechanics of Advanced Tennis* (pp. 33-47) (International Tennis Federation, London, 2003).
25. Yarin, A. L. Drop impact dynamics: Splashing, spreading, receding, bouncing. *Annu Rev Fluid Mech* **38**, 159–192 (2006).
26. Hulse-Smith, L., Mehdizadeh, N. Z. N. Z. & Chandra, S. Deducing drop size and impact velocity from circular bloodstains. *J Forensic Sci* **50**, 1–10 (2005).
27. Knock, C. & Davison, M. Predicting the position of the source of blood stains for angled impacts. *J Forensic Sci* **52**, 1044–1049 (2007).

28. Reynolds, M. E., Raymond, M. A. & Dadour, I. The use of small bloodstains in blood source area of origin determinations. *Can. Soc. Forensic Sci. J.* **42**, 133–146 (2009).
29. Raymond, M. A. A., Smith, E. R. R. & Liesegang, J. The physical properties of blood – Forensic considerations. *Sci Justice* **36**, 153–160 (1996).
30. Lu, H. M. & Jiang, Q. Size-dependent surface tension and Tolman's length of droplets. *Langmuir* **21**, 779–781 (2005).
31. McCleary, S., Liscio, E., De Brabanter, K. & Attinger, D. Automated reconstruction of cast-off blood spatter patterns based on Euclidean geometry and statistical likelihood. *Forensic Sci Int* **319**, (2021).

Further Readings

AAFS Academy Standards Board. "ASB Technical Report 033, First Edition Terms and Definitions in Bloodstain Pattern Analysis." Washington DC, 2017. https://www.aafs.org/asb-standard/terms-and-definitions-bloodstain-pattern-analysis.

Adam, Craig D. "Fundamental Studies of Bloodstain Formation and Characteristics." *Forensic Science International* 219, no. 1–3 (2012): 76–87. https://doi.org/10.1016/j.forsciint.2011.12.002.

Attinger, D., C. Moore, A. Donaldson, A. Jafari, and H.A. Stone. "Fluid Dynamics Topics in Bloodstain Pattern Analysis: Comparative Review and Research Opportunities." *Forensic Science International* 231, no. 1–3 (2013): 375–96. https://doi.org/10.1016/j.forsciint.2013.04.018.

Berlet, A. C., D. P. Talenti, and S. F. Carroll. "The Baseball Bat: A Popular Mechanism of Urban Injury." *Journal of Trauma: Injury, Infection and Critical Care* 33, no. 2 (1992): 167–70. https://doi.org/10.1097/00005373-199208000-00001.

Bevel, Tom, and Ross Gardner (Eds.). *Bloodstain Pattern Analysis with an Introduction to Crime Acene Reconstruction*. 3rd ed. Boca Raton, FL: CRC Press, 2008.

Dujovny, M., I. Onyekachi, and E. Perez-Arjona. "Baseball Bats: A Silent Weapon." *Neurological Research* 31, no. 10 (2009): 1005–11. https://doi.org/10.1179/174313209X385716.

Elliott, Bruce, Machar Reid, and M. Crespo. *Biomechanics of Advanced Tennis*. London: ITF Limited, 2003, p. 221.

Escamilla, R. F., G. S. Fleisig, C. DeRenne, M. K. Taylor, C. T. Moorman III, R. Imamura, E. Barakatt, and J. R. Andrews. "A Comparison of Age Level on Baseball Hitting Kinematics." *Journal of Applied Biomechanics* 25, no. 3 (2009): 210–18. https://doi.org/10.1123/jab.25.3.210.

Gervais, Pierre, Pierre Baudin, Bruce Cruikshank, and Dennis L. Dahlstedt. "Comparative Analysis between Police Batons." *Forensic Science International* 91, no. 1 (1998): 7–17. https://doi.org/10.1016/S0379-0738(97)00177-1.

Hulse-Smith, Lee, Navid Z. Mehdizadeh, and Sanjeev Chandra. "Deducing Drop Size and Impact Velocity from Circular Bloodstains." *Journal of Forensic Sciences* 50, no. 1 (2005): 1–10. https://doi.org/10.1520/jfs2003224.

James, S. H., P. E. Kish, and T. P. Sutton. *Principles of Bloodstain Pattern Analysis: Theory and Practice*. Boca Raton, FL: CRC Press, Taylor & Francis Group, 2005.

Kabaliuk, N., M. C. Jermy, K. Morison, T. Stotesbury, M. C. Taylor, and E. Williams. "Blood Drop Size in Passive Dripping from Weapons." *Forensic Science International* 228, no. 1–3 (2013): 75–82. https://doi.org/10.1016/j.forsciint.2013.02.023.

Kabaliuk, N., M. C. Jermy, E. Williams, T. L. Laber, and M. C. Taylor. "Experimental Validation of a Numerical Model for Predicting the Trajectory of Blood Drops in Typical Crime Scene Conditions, Including Droplet Deformation and Breakup, with a Study of the Effect of Indoor Air Currents and Wind on Typical Spatter Drop Trajectories." *Forensic Science International* 245 (2014): 107–20. https://doi.org/10.1016/j.forsciint.2014.10.020.

Knock, Clare, and Marie Davison. "Predicting the Position of the Source of Blood Stains for Angled Impacts." *Journal of Forensic Sciences* 52, no. 5 (2007): 1044–49. https://doi.org/10.1111/j.1556-4029.2007.00505.x.

Kunz, N. Sebastian, Jiri Adamec, and Christina Grove. "Analyzing the Dynamics and Morphology of Cast-off Pattern at Different Speed Levels Using High-Speed Digital Video Imaging." *Journal of Forensic Sciences* 62, no. 2 (2017): 428–34. https://doi.org/10.1111/1556-4029.13299.

Lavernia, E. J., E. M. Gutierrez, J. Szekely, and N. J. Grant. "Mathematical Model of the Liquid Dynamic Compaction Process. Part 1: Heat Flow in Gas Atomization." *International Journal of Rapid Solidification* 4, no. 1–2 (1988): 89–124.

Lightbody, C. J., and C. MacIver. "The Baseball Bat: A Modern Day Cudgel." *Emergency Medicine Journal* 24, no. 2 (2007): 112. https://doi.org/10.1136/emj.2006.042929.
Liscio, E., P. Bozek, H. Guryn, and Q. Le. "Observations and 3D Analysis of Controlled Cast-Off Stains." *Journal of Forensic Sciences* 65, no. 4 (2020): 1128–40. https://doi.org/10.1111/1556-4029.14301.
Liu, Huimin. *Science and Engineering of Droplets: Fundamentals and Applications*. Park Ridge, NJ: Noyes, 2002.
Lu, Hai Ming, and Qing Jiang. "Size-Dependent Surface Tension and Tolman's Length of Droplets." *Langmuir* 21, no. 2 (2005): 779–81. https://doi.org/10.1021/la0489817.
MacDonnell, H. L. *Bloodstain Patterns*. 2nd ed. Corning, NY: Laboratory of Forensic Sciences, 2005.
McCleary, S., E. Liscio, K. De Brabanter, and D. Attinger. "Automated Reconstruction of Cast-Off Blood Spatter Patterns Based on Euclidean Geometry and Statistical Likelihood." *Forensic Science International* 319 (2021). https://doi.org/10.1016/j.forsciint.2020.110628.
Putnam, C.A. "Sequential Motions of Body Segments in Striking and Throwing Skills: Descriptions and Explanations." *Journal of Biomechanics* 26, no. 1 (1993): 125–35. https://doi.org/10.1016/0021-9290(93)90084-R.
Raymond, M. A., E. R. Smith, and J. Liesegang. "The Physical Properties of Blood: Forensic Considerations." *Science and Justice: Journal of the Forensic Science Society* 36, no. 3 (1996): 153–60. https://doi.org/10.1016/S1355-0306(96)72590-X.
Reynolds, M. E., M. A. Raymond, and I. Dadour. "The Use of Small Bloodstains in Blood Source Area of Origin Determinations." *Journal of the Canadian Society of Forensic Science* 42, no. 2 (2009): 133–46. https://doi.org/10.1080/00085030.2009.10757602.
Roach, N. T., M. Venkadesan, M. J. Rainbow, and D. E. Lieberman. "Elastic Energy Storage in the Shoulder and the Evolution of High-Speed Throwing in Homo." *Nature* 498, no. 7455 (2013): 483–86. https://doi.org/10.1038/nature12267.
Welch, C. M., S. A. Banks, F. F. Cook, and P. Draovitch. "Hitting a Baseball: A Biomechanical Description." *Journal of Orthopaedic and Sports Physical Therapy* 22, no. 5 (1995): 193–201. https://doi.org/10.2519/jospt.1995.22.5.193.
Williams, E.M.P. *From Weapon to Wall: Investigating the Link between Cast-Off Bloodstain Patterns, Blood Dynamics and Assailant Kinematics*. University of Auckland, 2014.
Williams, E. M. P., and M. C. Taylor. "The Development and Construction of Blood Droplet Generation Device (BDGD) for Detailed Analysis of Blood Droplet Dynamics." *Forensic Science SEM*. 3, no. 2 (2013): 95–104. http://fss.xxyy.info/home/sites/default/files/2157118X.3.2.4_0.pdf.
Williams, E. M. P., Emma S. Graham, Mark C. Jermy, David C. Kieser, and Michael C. Taylor. "The Dynamics of Blood Drop Release from Swinging Objects in the Creation of Cast-Off Bloodstain Patterns." *Journal of Forensic Sciences* 64, no. 2 (2019): 413–21. https://doi.org/10.1111/1556-4029.13855.
Wonder, A. *Blood Dynamics*. San Diego, CA: Academic Press, 2008.
Yarin, A. L. "Drop Impact Dynamics: Splashing, Spreading, Receding, Bouncing." *Annual Review of Fluid Mechanics* 38 (2006): 159–92. https://doi.org/10.1146/annurev.fluid.38.050304.092144.

CHAPTER 15

GUNSHOT PATTERNS

Silke M.C. Brodbeck

INTRODUCTION

To understand how bloodstains are mechanically produced in cases of gunshots, we must first examine how gunshots create bloodstain patterns.

When we look at a typical firearm, the mechanical ignition of an exothermic reaction is triggered, producing a gas in the casing which expands and propels the projectile out of the casing. Through this reaction, the projectile is pressed into the barrel. Much of the barrel is equipped with grooves and lands. They are responsible for the projectile spinning, while angular momentum stabilizes the projectile in flight.

In a close-up view of a gunshot, we can recognize four potential structures leaving the firearm based on this mechanism (Figure 15.1):

- Primer flash
- Firearm discharge residue
- Projectile
- Ejected casing

The impact of the projectile on the target and the resultant destruction (additionally caused also by a pressure wave) are the main factors in the creation of bloodstains in firearm injuries.

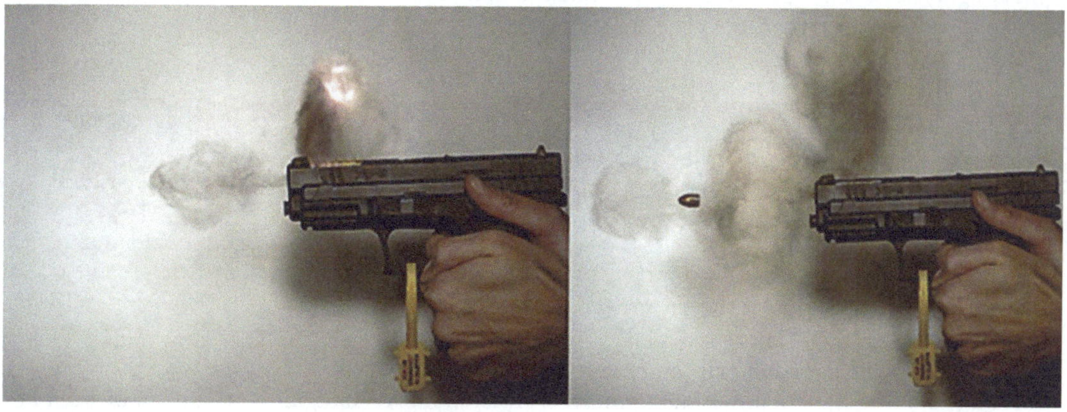

Figure 15.1 *Left:* Primer flash and firearm discharge residue in a sporting pistol. *Right:* Firearm discharge residue and projectile approximately 300 ms later. (*Credit:* MFRC blood pattern analysis videos, accessed via https://alvideo.ameslab.gov/archive/bpa-videos/. Used with permission.)

DOI: 10.4324/9781003163695-15

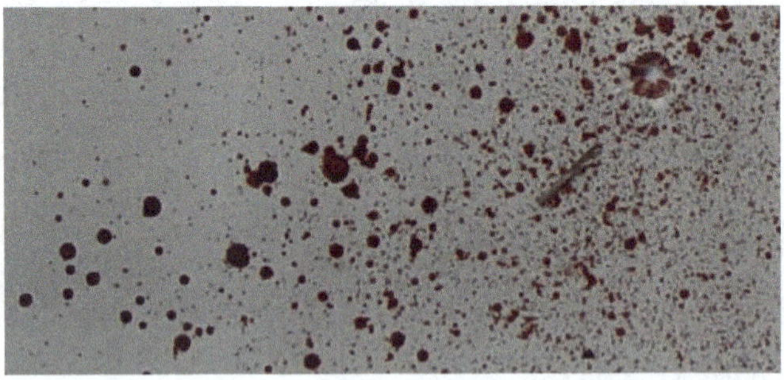

Figure 15.2 Forward Spatter in a single shot experiment with a 9x19 mm full metal jacket munition. Spatter of all sizes occur. The amount of blood is primary dependent from the size of the injured vessels and not from the wound morphology.

The primary pattern associated with gunshot is spatter. Gunshot is associated with high energies in the projectiles and can cause spatters of all sizes, which can be seen in Figure 15.2.

Two additional factors are of primary importance in the creation of bloodstains in gunshot cases. The first one is the influence of the shooting distance on the exiting blood; the second one is that in gunshot cases several injuries may be created, for example, through a multi-segmental gunshot.

THE INFLUENCE OF THE SHOOTING DISTANCE ON THE EXITING BLOOD

Blood, as long as it is liquid, can be affected by additional factors (e.g., wind, overlaying of transfer patterns due to changes of the body position, and so on). Some of them are different for cases of close-range shots and long-distance shots.

As can be seen in high-speed videos, firearm discharge residue can strongly impact the flight direction in cases of close-range shots, an effect that cannot be observed in long-distance shots. This insight, however, is primarily of scientific importance and does not have any practical use in bloodstain pattern analysis (BPA) at crime scenes.

SEVERAL BLEEDING INJURIES CAUSED BY ONE GUNSHOT

In comparison to other types of injuries, such as blunt force, gunshots can often create several injuries through one shot. All three variants are possible:

1. One shot–entrance injury only.
2. One shot–entrance and exit injury.
3. One shot–multiple injuries due to multi-segmental hits or shotgun shots, as can be seen in Figure 15.3.

If this one gunshot passes through different segments of the human body, it is called a multi-segmental hit – often yielding a combination of four, six, or more bleeding injuries.

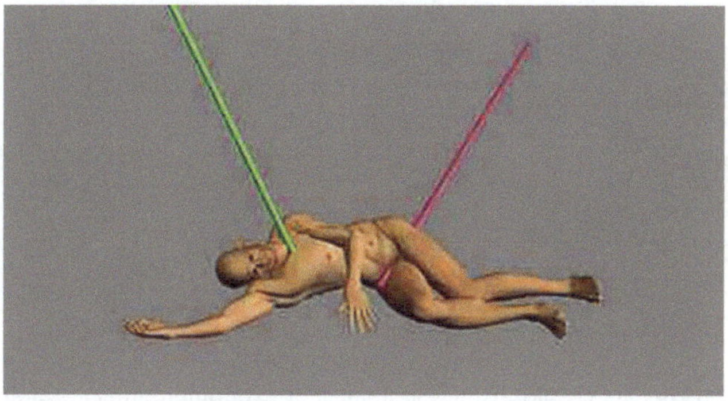

Figure 15.3 Reconstruction of two gunshots. The pink one shows a three-segment shot through the left and right thigh and the genital area, resulting in six massively bleeding injuries. (*Source:* Blutspureninstitut.)

BLOODSTAIN PATTERNS CREATED BY GUNSHOT WOUNDS

Shooting-Created Spatter in Relation to Projectile Movement

Spatter can be distributed in all the directions which are three-dimensionally possible for airborne flight after an injury to a blood source. For that reason, gunshot-created spatter is named in relation to the flight direction of the projectile (see Figures 15.4). Spatter which exits the body in the flight direction of the projectile is called "forward spatter," whereas spatter which exits the body opposite the flight direction is referred to as "backward spatter" (Figure 15.5).

However, it is important to understand that these definitions are derived solely from the movement direction of the projectile.

Often backward spatter, for example, has been described in cases of suicide as the blood on the hands of a person who took their own life with a firearm. But it must be understood that there

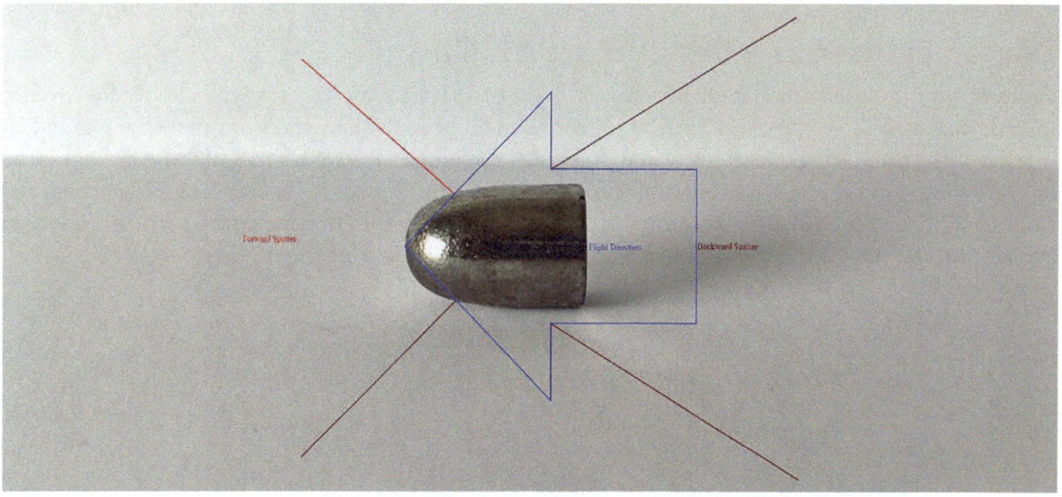

Figure 15.4 Movement direction of the projectile in relation to the naming of the exiting spatter. (*Source:* Blutspureninstitut/Frank Jost.)

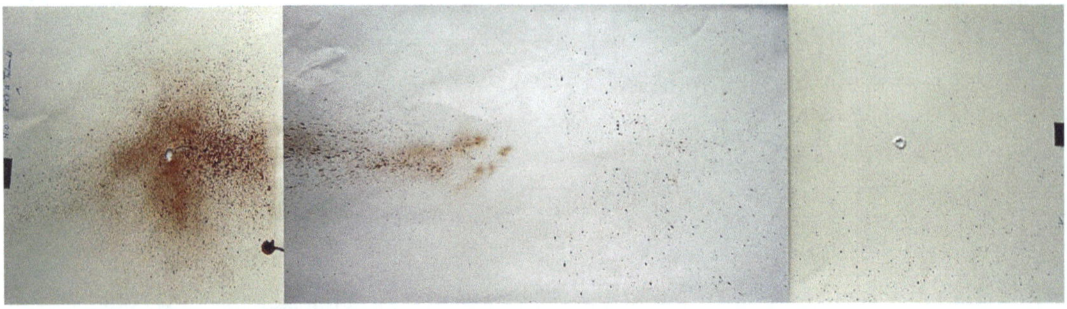

Figure 15.5 Experimental results for bloodstains in a gunshot experiment. Results of an 8 × 57 mm (SAAMI)/8 × 57 IS (CIP) in the bloodstain-creating experiment. Three sides of the box are shown here: on the right, the entrance side, in the middle, a sidewall of the box; and on the left, the exit. Notice a small drop with flow pattern on the lower part of the exit target as a result of a change in position afterward, when the blood was still liquid. (*Source:* Blutspureninstitut.)

are also situations in homicide cases where a victim or shooter does have a hand near an occurring shot and that backspatter, therefore, can be found on the hands. For that reason, the occurrence of backspatter is not specific to suicides.

Differentiating suicide and homicide cannot be based on the diagnosis of BPA alone but must be the result of an investigation. That said, the reconstruction of, for example, a position is a valid diagnosis of BPA.

The amount of blood set free depends primarily on the available volume of blood, which can be large when there is impact, for example, to a large vessel such as the superior sagittal sinus or the internal carotid artery in cases of gunshot wounds to the head. The morphology of the wound plays only a minor role in the creation of bloodstain patterns; more important is the location of the injury and what size vessel was injured (Figure 15.6).

The forming of bloodstain patterns after exiting the body strongly depends on additional factors, including head hair, clothing worn, body position at the time of the shot, and the complete surfaces in the area of exit presented at the scene.

Diluted Spatter as a Result of Head Injury

Cases of head injuries can also yield a special kind of spatter which is not typical only for firearm injuries but also for other bloodletting injuries of the head. When the dura mater is opened, it often results in a mixing of cerebrospinal fluid with the blood. Therefore, the blood may be diluted in these cases, and diluted spatter can also occur. The dilution of the spatter can be morphologically seen in the reduced color intensity of the spatter, while the morphological form is preserved because the mixing of the two liquids occurs prior to the impact of the liquid upon the surface.

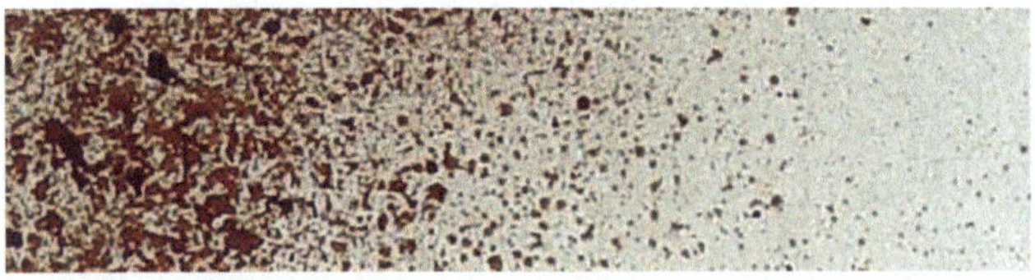

Figure 15.6 Spatter of all sizes that can occur in gunshots. Although the high energy of the projectile might cause misting, misting is not specific to gunshots. (*Source:* Blutspureninstitut.)

Misting

When a projectile leaves the muzzle, the area in the flight path with the highest bullet energy can usually be found at the muzzle. Frequently, the impact energy is reduced just a bit due to external factors (for example, air resistance) acting upon the projectile during flight.

Despite this effect the kinetic energy of a projectile upon impact is still very high in comparison to the energy which causes, for example, blunt trauma to the head. The energy of a 9mm cartridge is between 400 and 500 joule; the energy reached in a 5.56x45 NATO ammunition for assault rifles is much higher, ranging from 1.200 to 1.900 joule and in a .223 Remington ammunition is 1.700 joule; topping the list is .408 Chey Tac ammunition with 10.500 joule.

In comparison to that, a golf ball physically reaches around 150 Joule, which can be compared to severe blunt-force trauma, among other impacts.

Due to the high impact energy of the projectile (not the blood!), this often leads to a very fine dispersion of the blood set free as well as in a pattern, which is called misting (see Figure 15.7). Almost like a spray, the blood is dispersed in extremely small droplets. While this pattern is not specific to gunshots, it can be found in bloodstains related to gunshots. Sometimes, it can also be found as a result of expirated blood or in blunt-force trauma.

Secondary Patterns

It is important to understand that gunshot can create all types of bloodstains, often resulting secondarily from the shot person's position or movement.

Gunshot wounds of the head, for example, can often be correlated to a fast incapacitation of the injured; so in some cases of single head shots, the original position remains for most of the body parts obtained directly after the shot. When, for example, the blood is dripping out of the head, many types of bloodstains can be found, including dripping, pooling, saturation, splashing, and other patterns as a result of the gunshot, although in that position these are primarily produced by gravity. All this depends on the specific structure of the scene. Spatter is the primary pattern created by a gunshot, but all other types of bloodstain patterns can be secondarily created in gunshot cases. Especially when the heart stops beating, the blood will follow gravity.

The range of patterns which can be found at a gunshot scene is wide. The upshot: there are no gunshot-specific bloodstains, although gunshot-related bloodstains can be described.

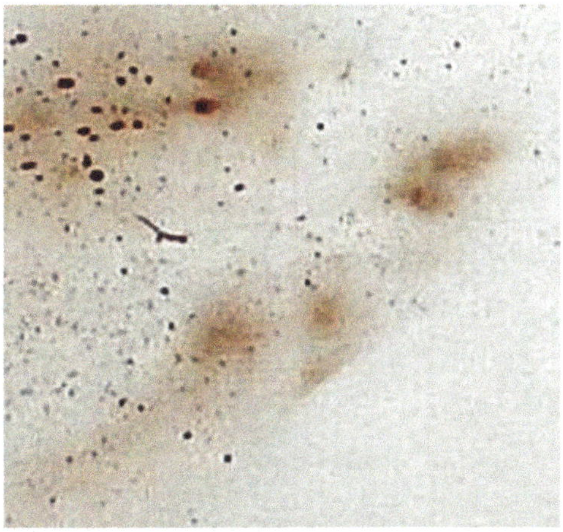

Figure 15.7 Misting in comparison to spatter in a gunshot on a paper surface. (*Source:* Blutspureninstitut.)

EXPERIMENTAL APPROACHES TO GUNSHOTS

Experiments

The classic experimental approach to gunshot patterns is a shot through a spongiform substance, usually a sponge. The spongiform substance is required to hold the blood, and although it shows a different order than vessels in a tissue supplied with blood does, in a good experimental setup, it can produce a reasonable result.

Often a blooded sponge is used in a box, where the walls are covered with interchangeable white paper. Prior to the shot, the sponge is soaked in blood and then hanged inside the box. Then the box and the sponge are shot through. In areas where it is unnecessary to protect the walls, the box can be left out.

Biomodeling

In biomodeling for gunshots, two different types of models are used. The spongiform bleeding models are used for the simulation of bloodstains. Here it is important to match the blood volume stored in the spongiform substance to that of the body part one tries to model. This can be seen in Figure 15.8. A hand model was produced for a series of experiments with explosives. The sponge is covered with several materials for the presentation of the skin and soft tissue of the hand. The liquid volume of this model was matched to the blood volume in a regular hand. These models do not need to be in the actual shape, but their buildup should be matched to the simulated structures.

Contrasting types of models are used for the demonstration of form, for example, a trajectory through a body. These models are built differently. The problem here is the many different materials in the human body, with different physical material properties; so there are no models which come close to, for example, the behavior of a skull.

In gunshot wounds to the skull, one can find, among other things, internal ricochet on the tabula interna of the neuro-skull. This means that in some cases the bullet ricocheted on the inside of the skull, which can lead to extending destruction of the skull bone and the brain portion. These problems cannot be simulated easily through models.

Figure 15.8 Bloodletting model for the simulation of a hand on top of an explosive charge loaded with non-Newtonian experimental blood liquid built by the Blutspureninstitut for the Carabinieri in Italy. (*Source:* Blutspureninstitut.)

For a plain trajectory reconstruction, however, a setup with body parts formed out of expanded polystyrene (EPS, Styrofoam) covered with additional layers of gypsum for the simulation of the bone and additional layers of polyethylene for the simulation of the skin layers has proven useful. Among these models' benefits is the ability to reconstruct trajectories through, for example, the head.

CONCLUSIONS

The primary type of bloodstain patterns produced through gunshots is spatter. Gunshot spatters are named after their relation to the movement direction of the projectile. Spatter which is moving in the opposite direction of the projectile movement is called backward spatter. Spatter moving into the direction of the projectile is called forward spatter.

The existence of backspatter on a hand cannot be used to diagnose a suicide because backspatter on a hand can also occur in positions of homicide victims who have their hand in a close position to the injury at the time of the shot.

There is no correlation of spatter size and the pattern created by a gunshot. Gunshot patterns can create all sizes of spatters.

Only relying on bloodstains, it is not possible to diagnose whether any given bloodstain pattern was created by a gunshot; nor can the weapon or the type of weapon be identified through BPA.

Gunshots can produce more than one bleeding injury, with one shot producing more massive bleeding injuries than blunt trauma, for example, through multi-segmental shots.

In case of death and once the heart stops beating due to cardiac arrest, the blood will follow gravity. Often this will result in pooling, splashing, transfer, or other patterns or in additional spatter.

All types of patterns can be found in injuries of gunshots as secondary patterns.

Although spatter is the primary pattern linked to the shotgun mechanism, all types of bloodstain patterns can appear at a crime scene where firearms were used.

Further Reading

Bevel, Tom, and Gardner Ross. *Bloodstain Pattern Analysis*. CRC Press, Boca Raton, 2008. ISBN 978-1420052688.

Brodbeck, Silke M. C. *Postmortale Computertomographie von Schussverletzungen im Vergleich zu Obduktionsbefunden*. Verlag für Polizei und Wissenschaft, Frankfurt am Main, 2008. ISBN 978-3-86676-039-4.

Brodbeck, Silke M. C. "Introduction to Bloodstain Pattern Analysis." *SIAK Journal: Journal for Police Science and Practice* 2 (2012), 51–57. https://doi.org/10.7396/IE_2012_E

Brodbeck, Silke M. C. "The Formation of Bloodstains Following Head Injuries: Gross, Piotrowski and the First Blow." *SIAK-Journal: Journal for Police Science and Practice*, International Edition, 11 (2021), 4–11. ISSN 1813-3495.

Brodbeck, Silke M. C., M. Brodbeck Sinikka, and J. Öhman. "The Grasp Reflex in Adults: The Forensic Significance of Other Neurosurgical and Neurological Subjects." *SIAK Journal: Journal for Police Science and Practice*, International Edition, 8 (2018), 48–56. https://www.bmi.gv.at/104/Wissenschaft_und_Forschung/SIAK-Journal/internationalEdition/files/Brodbeck_IE_2018.pdf

DiMaio, Vincent J. *Gunshot Wounds: Practical Aspects of Firearms, Ballistics, and Forensic Techniques*. 3rd ed. (Practical Aspects of Criminal and Forensic Investigations). Taylor & Francis Inc., Boca Raton, 2015. ISBN 78-1498725699.

James, Stuart H., Paul E. Kish, and T. Paulette Sutton. *Principles and Theory of Bloodstain Pattern Analysis*. CRC Press, Boca Raton, 2005. ISBN 978-0849320149.

Kneubühl, Beat P. Das Abprallen von Geschossen aus forensischer Sicht = Le ricochet des projectiles en sciences forensiques. Thèse. Droit. Sciences criminelles. Administration publique, Lausanne, 1999.

Kneubühl, Beat P. *Geschosse – Gesamtausgabe*. Motorbuch, Stuttgart, 1st ed., 2013.

CHAPTER 16

PROJECTED BLOOD PATTERNS

Cristina Gonzalez

A projected pattern is a bloodstain pattern resulting from the ejection of blood under hydraulic pressure, typically from a breach in the circulatory system.[1] Historically, hydraulics is a fluid mechanics term used to describe the applied or experimental aspects of real fluid behavior.[2] In bloodstain pattern analysis, hydraulic pressure refers to the force exerted by the pumping of the heart on the blood in the circulatory vessels.

The currently accepted term and definition have evolved over time. With the acquisition of empirical data and with a greater understanding of human anatomy, physiology, and fluid dynamics, this evolution became necessary. Historically, arterial spurting was the term that was generally used. This term specifies that the generated pattern originated from a breached artery; however, it has been shown that similar patterns can be generated from veins.[3,4,5]

Projected patterns are unique in that the pattern can be associated with a specific wound, usually a damaged heart, artery, or vein. There is usually no ambiguity that the pattern resulted from any mechanism other than a breach in the circulatory system. This can be extremely helpful in providing positional, locational, and movement information for reconstruction purposes.[6,7]

Capillary bleeding results in passive bleeding and can generate drip stains, drip patterns, or drip trails. Venous and arterial bleeding are more dangerous and can be fatal. This is mainly due to pressure and blood volume within the vessel. Figure 16.1 helps to illustrate this.

One of the disadvantages in studying projected patterns in the laboratory is that the mechanisms that generate these patterns cannot be easily duplicated as the severing of a blood vessel would be necessary. Researchers have developed and used an arterial pump to simulate and study projected blood patterns.[8]

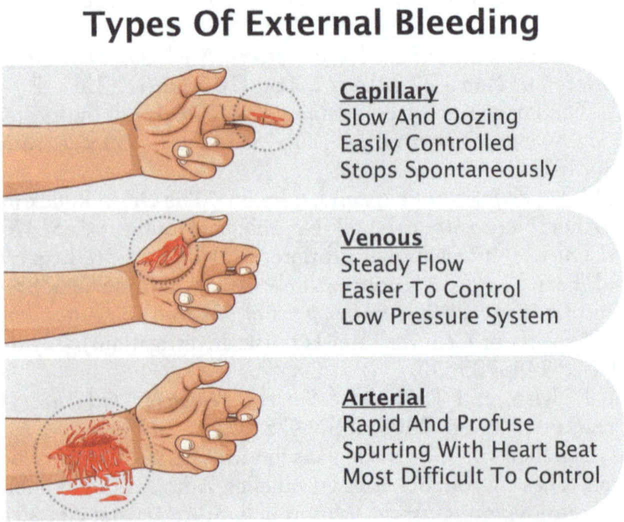

Figure 16.1 Arterial and venous bleeding are more dangerous than capillary bleeding.

DOI: 10.4324/9781003163695-16

ANATOMY AND PHYSIOLOGY

The cardiovascular system (or the circulatory system) in the human body functions to transport oxygenated and deoxygenated blood throughout the body. This system is made up of the heart, arteries, veins, arterioles, and capillaries. Veins and arteries are the major vessels through which the blood travels. Arterioles are small arteries and capillaries are the smallest of the blood vessels. Figure 16.2 shows the cardiovascular system.

Blood is carried away from the heart through the main artery, the aorta. As blood travels away from the heart, arteries branch out to supply blood to different parts of the body. The more distant the artery is from the aorta, the smaller the diameter of the blood vessel.[9] The greatest pressure of blood flow occurs in the large arteries. For this reason, artery walls are thicker and more elastic than veins. Arterioles face a smaller pressure and thus are not as elastic. Capillaries consist of a single cell layer allowing for the exchange of gases and other substances. Veins transport blood

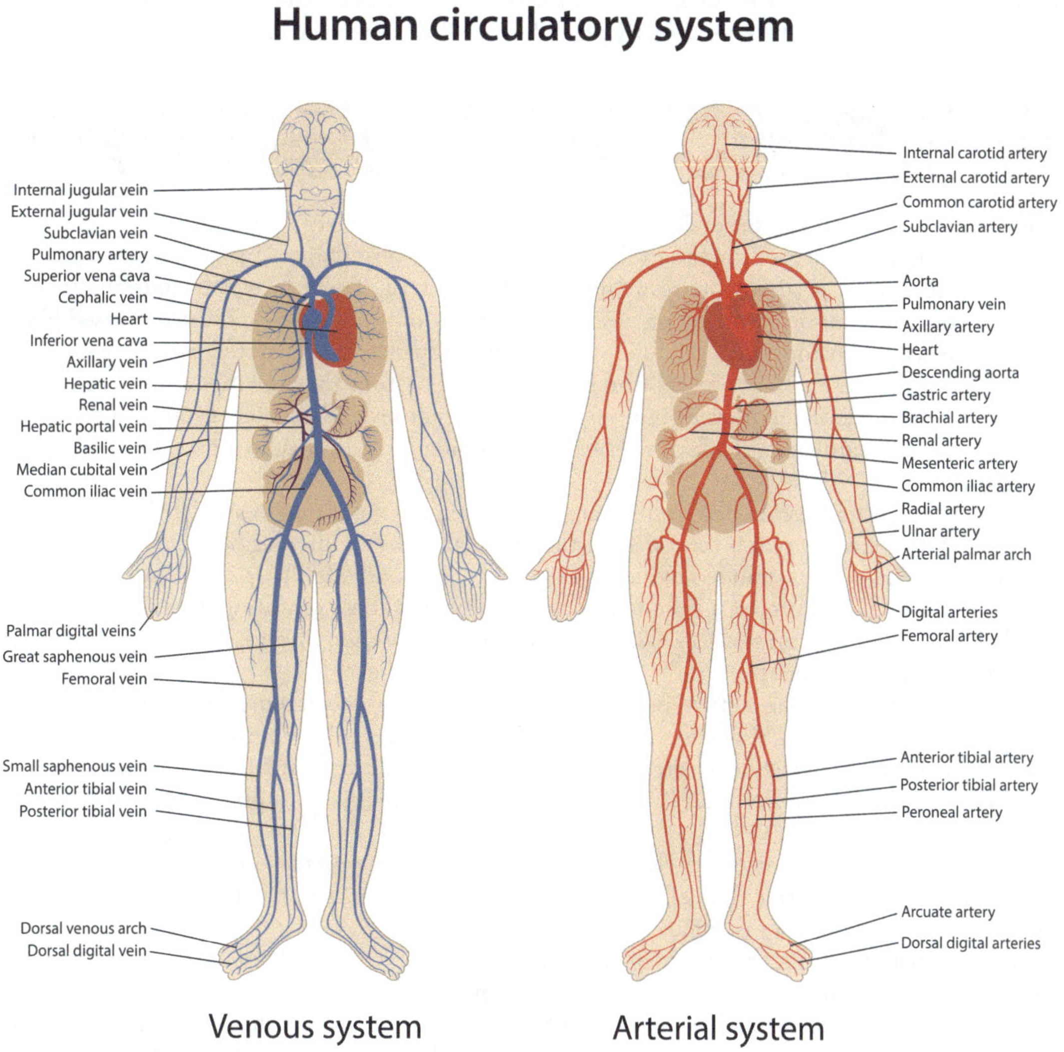

Figure 16.2 Cardiovascular system.

back to the heart and receive less pressure of blood flow than arteries. They also contain valves to prevent backflow. In contrast to arteries, venial walls are thinner and less elastic. The blood flow in veins is under reduced pressure and are not able to actively pump blood.[10] Figure 16.3 shows the differences in the structures of veins and arteries.

The arterial system is a high-pressure system and the venous system is low-pressure system. Veins store more blood volume than arteries do. Table 16.1 illustrates these and other differences.

Since arteries bear greater pressure than veins, the patterns generated from artery damage tend to be more striking than those from venial damage. This is especially true when a large artery like the aorta is involved. When damage to an artery does occur, the appearance of the generated pattern may be dependent on the location of the damaged part of artery. Table 16.2 shows common arteries and their general location on the human body.

The arterial blood pressure is also a contributing factor. This pressure drops to atmospheric pressure almost as soon as the blood exits the wound, but the momentum imparted by the pressure difference can transport the blood some meters in an arcing trajectory as gravity accelerates the blood toward the ground.[12] Diameters of the blood vessels may also affect the generated pattern. The size range in the human body is 12.5 mm in the aorta to 20 μm in the arterial capillaries; in the venous system, the size range is 15 mm to 30 μm.[13] An understanding of fluid dynamics is important as these diameters are directly related to the flow resistance of the system.

FEATURES OBSERVED

The features discussed will generally pertain to non-absorbent surfaces. As with any pattern type, caution needs to be applied in the evaluation of blood on absorbent targets. There are several wound factors that can affect the resultant projected pattern. These factors include the type of blood vessel, the location of the blood vessel, the severity of the wound, and the dispersed blood volume. As with all bloodstains, the following can also influence the generated pattern: the target, the presence of intermediary objects, the position of the victim, the activities and movement of the victim, the sequence of multiple injuries, overlapping patterns, alteration of stains, and medical intervention.[14] Regardless of the factors, there are common features that are observed in projected patterns.

In projected patterns generated from an arterial breach, the repetition of similar shaped stains is observed. Generally, there is a central stain that is usually oval or circular but can also be irregularly shaped. This central stain has radiating elongated spines and satellite spatter may also be present, as is depicted in Figure 16.4. Frequently, the alignment of these repeating stains can occur in a parallel manner on vertical surfaces. The stains under the doorknob in Figure 16.5 are an example of this parallel arrangement.

In arterial spurting, the nature of the wounds affects the projected pattern. If the wound through which the blood flows has an irregular shape, there will be an unsteady flow due to the varying pressure of the heart through the cardiac cycle. This results in an irregular breakup with a wide range of droplet sizes.[15] This wide range of droplet sizes is observed on the floor in Figure 16.5.

With enough volume, downward flow can also be present. The pattern may show undulation or pulsation which is representative of the pressure variation and victim movement. These features are also present on the door in Figure 16.5.

Projected patterns from an arterial breach can also be observed as a dense distribution of stains of similar size. On horizontal surfaces, these stains tend to be somewhat circular. The phrase, arterial rain, has been used to describe this type of pattern.[16] Although significant damage to a blood vessel can be fatal, this type of pattern has been observed from subjects with non-fatal injuries to the brachial or radial arteries (Figure 16.6).

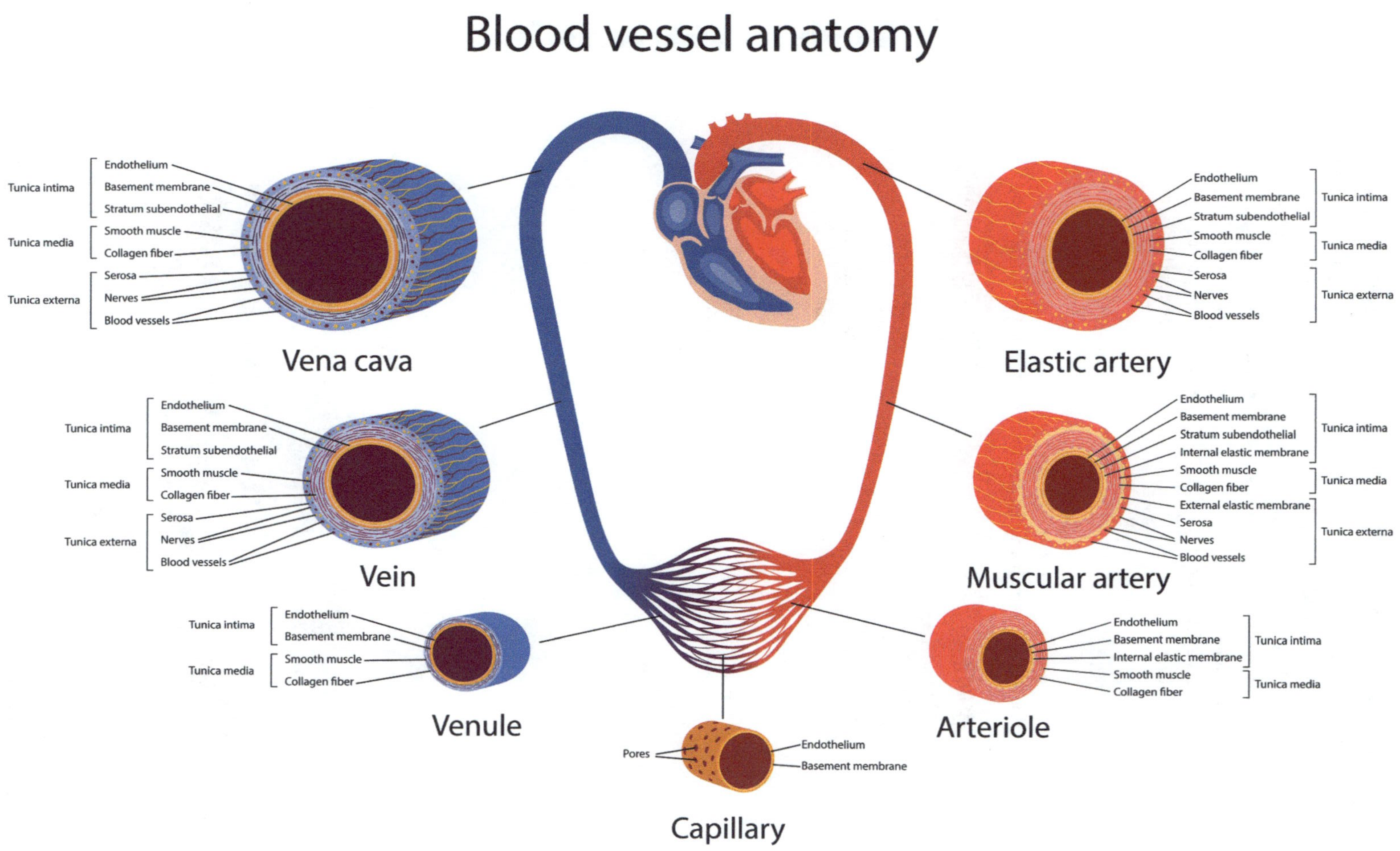

Figure 16.3 Differences between an artery and a vein.

Table 16.1 Comparison of the features of the venous and arterial systems[11]

Venous system	Arterial system
• Volume system	• Pressure-regulating system
• 80% of total blood volume	• 20% of blood volume
• Lower blood flow velocities	• Higher blood flow velocities
• Pressure levels lower to negative	• Pressure levels high to lower
• Venous pulse	• Pulse wave
• Connective tissue loose	• Connective tissue tight
• Outer layer	• Inner and middle layers

Table 16.2 Common arteries and their location in the human body

Artery	General location
Aorta	Chest
Temporal	Temples
Carotid	Neck
Subclavian	Under clavicles
Axilla	Armpit
Brachial	Arms
Radial	Wrists
Iliac	Pelvic area
Femoral	Thighs
Renal	Kidneys
Popliteal	Knees
Tibial	Lower legs

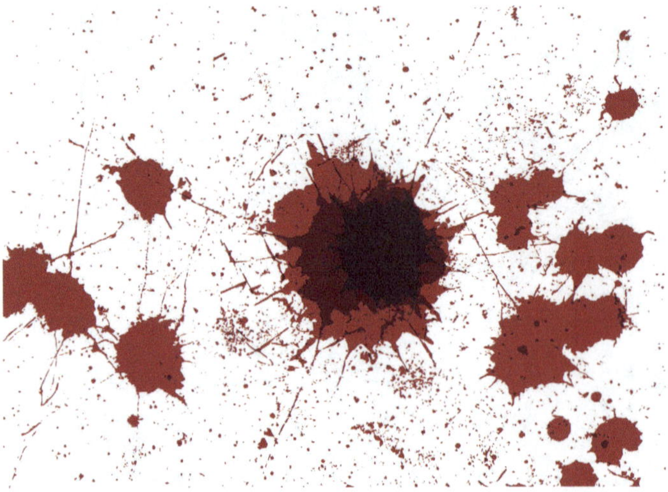

Figure 16.4 Example of features of projected stains on a horizontal surface. Generally, there is a large central stain with radiating elongated spines.

Figure 16.5 Projected patterns on the floor and on the door.

Figure 16.6 Features observed in arterial rain are similar shaped and sized stains in a dense distribution.

A venial breach can exhibit similar features. This has been observed in ruptures of varicose veins and can result in hemorrhage.[17,18,19] Usually this is non-fatal; however, in one specific case, incorrect first aid resulted in death.[20] Since these ruptures generally originate from the legs and are a result of a medical condition, there may not be a criminal component associated with these patterns. This can also be true of arterial bleeding. Medical conditions such as lung cancers, peptic ulcers, and ulcers in the gastrointestinal tract can produce projected type patterns from artery eruption.[21]

AUTOPSY OR MEDICAL INFORMATION

Although stain morphology and pattern distribution are significant features to consider in the classification of projected patterns, it is desirable that a breach of a blood vessel or the heart be confirmed with medical or autopsy information. This may not always be possible as exemplified in a situation where the victim is transported to a hospital. In this case, saving a life is of primary importance; thus, specific wound information may not be recorded.

This may also be the case when an autopsy is performed. This is especially true in decomposition cases, arson cases, or in cases where the victim sustained multiple wounds. In the latter case, a breached, minor blood vessel may generate projected patterns but may not be the cause of death. Again, this breach in a minor blood vessel may not be specifically recorded in the examination. The lack of specific information of a vessel breach should not exclude the possibility of the presence of a projected pattern.

The location of and the damage to the vessel may affect the pattern. Arteries that are closer to the surface may be more likely to produce patterns as opposed to arteries deeper in the body. Also, severe damage to the blood vessel may cause more internal bleeding than outward projected bleeding.

AN INTERESTING CASE

In one interesting case, the classification of a projected pattern was significant in that it provided an explanation for the generation of a secondary pattern type. The case involved a shooting in which the decedent was shot in the upper torso. Patterns observed are depicted in Figures 16.7 and 16.8.

These patterns were classified as projected patterns. This classification was supported by the autopsy finding that the arterial arch was breached. The decedent was found holding a taser which bore a fingerprint in blood. The fingerprint was identified as being from the decedent and can be seen in Figure 16.9. As part of bloodstain pattern analysis, investigators requested if it could be determined how that fingerprint was created. To address this question, latent prints experts were consulted, and experimentation was performed.

Figure 16.7 Projected stains on a vertical surface resulting from an aortic breach. (Image courtesy of LAPD detective Dimitri Kort.)

Figure 16.8 Projected stains on a horizontal surface resulting from an aortic breach. (Image courtesy of LAPD detective Dimitri Kort.)

Figure 16.9 Tonal reversal fingerprint impression caused by projected and flow mechanisms. (Image courtesy of LAPD detective Dimitri Kort.)

The fingerprint in blood was a tonal reversal which is defined as a transferred impression representing the furrows of a friction ridge impression rather than the ridges.[22] In this case, the blood in the fingerprint impression on the taser represented the furrows and the ridges were represented by the lack of blood.

With this understanding, it was hypothesized that the impression was generated when blood was projected onto the hand and the held taser. Blood would have traveled into the space between the finger and the taser. The blood would have settled in the furrows and dried. To test this, experiments were conducted in which the subject held a similar object and blood was projected onto the area between the hand and the object. The blood was allowed to dry. Generated bloodstains on the hand and the object were observed and examined. The result was a totally reversed, identifiable impression. It was determined that the fingerprint pattern was generated by projected blood possessing enough volume to flow into the furrows, thus creating an impression (see Chapter 12).

One lesson learned from this case is to recognize one's limitations. This type of pattern could be incorrectly classified as a transfer pattern which can lead to misinterpretations in reconstructions. To avoid this, it was necessary to understand specifically where the blood was deposited in relation to the furrows and the ridges. This understanding came to fruition after latent print experts were consulted.

Notes

1. ASB Technical Report 033, *Terms and Definitions in Bloodstain Pattern Analysis*, 1st edition, 2017.
2. Bruce R. Munson, Theodore H. Okiishi, Wade W. Huebsch, and Alric P. Rothmayer, *Fundamentals of Fluid Mechanics*, 7th edition, John Wiley and Sons, Inc., Hoboken, NJ, 2013, p. 27.
3. Stuart H. James, Paul E. Kish, and T. Paulette Sutton, *Principles of Bloodstain Pattern Analysis: Theory and Practice*, CRC Press, Boca Raton, FL, 2005, pp. 158–160.
4. Rex T. Sparks, *Chronic Venous Insufficiency Syndrome: Case Report*, IABPA News, Vol. 20, No. 3, September 2004, pp. 4–9.

5. Silke MC and Brodbeck MD, Reflections upon Arteries and Veins: A Plea for "Spurt Patterns", IABPA News, June 2007, pp. 4–14.
6. L. Allyn DiMeo, CSCSA, and Jane Taupin, M.A., Arterial Bloodstain Patterns on Clothing: An Interesting Case Linking the Accused to the Scene, *Journal of Bloodstain Pattern Analysis*, Vol. 28, No. 2, 2012, pp. 3–10.
7. Samir Kumar Bandyopadadhyay and Goutam Roy Chowdhury, Analysis of Bloodstain Patterns at the Crime Scene due to Arterial Bleeding, *International Journal of Development Research*, Vol. 7, Issue 1, 2017, pp. 10978–10983.
8. Jo Millington and Gillian Leak, *Simulated Projected Blood Patterns Using the "Arterial Pump"*, Fort Worth Texas, 2015, IABPA Training Conference Workshop, September 29–October 2, 2015.
9. Brodbeck, *Reflections upon Arteries and Veins: A Plea for "Spurt Patterns"*, p. 5.
10. Ibid, p. 7.
11. Ibid, p. 13.
12. Jules Kieser, Michael Taylor, and Debra Carr, *Developments in Forensic Science: Forensic Biomechanics*, John Wiley & Sons, Inc., 2013, p. 105.
13. Brodbeck, *Reflections upon Arteries and Veins: A Plea for "Spurt Patterns"*, p. 10.
14. James et al., *Principles of Bloodstain Pattern Analysis: Theory and Practice*, pp. 152–153.
15. Kieser et al., *Developments in Forensic Science: Forensic Biomechanics*, p. 124.
16. Millington et al., *Simulated Projected Blood Patterns Using the "Arterial Pump"*, 2015.
17. Sparks, *Chronic Venous Insufficiency Syndrome: Case Report*, pp. 4–9.
18. Peter Hejna M.D., A Case of Fatal Spontaneous Varicose Vein Rupture: An Example of Incorrect First Aid, *Journal of Forensic Science*, 2009, Vol. 54, No. 5, pp. 1146–1148.
19. Roger W. Byard, David Veldhoen, Colin Manock, and John D. Gilbert, *Journal of Forensic and Legal Medicine*, 2007, Vol. 14, No. 3, pp. 155–158. doi: 10.1016/j.jcfm.2006.02.025.
20. Henja, *A Case of Fatal Spontaneous Varicose Vein Rupture: An Example of Incorrect First Aid*, pp. 1146–1148.
21. James et al., *Principles of Bloodstain Pattern Analysis: Theory and Practice*, p. 154.
22. Sergio Castellon, Clues in Friction Ridge Comparisons: Tonal Reversals Technical Note, *Journal of Forensic Identification*, Vol. 64, No. 3, 2014, pp. 223–237.

CHAPTER 17

SPLASH PATTERNS

Susan Rinehart

A splash pattern is a bloodstain pattern created from a large volume of liquid blood falling onto a surface.[1] A large volume would be considered a larger volume than the volume of blood typically spattered by a single blunt-weapon impact or gunshot and the distance fallen would be far enough to create satellite stains. Splash patterns are not commonly observed or classified in bloodstain pattern analysis. If present, they may be overlooked or misclassified. A splash pattern is created by a passive mechanism where the dominant force involved is gravity, yet splash patterns may share similar features with some impact spatter patterns, drip patterns, and even some projected patterns on a horizontal surface. Drip patterns and, on occasion, projected patterns also involve a large volume of blood falling to a horizontal surface, so this is not an unexpected result. Often projected blood results in a linear distribution of closely spaced circular stains on a horizontal surface, but that is not always the case. Depending on the nature of the ejection of blood, projected blood may present itself as a large volume of blood that is eventually overtaken by gravity and falls to the ground. When there is ambiguity in the specific pattern type, some analysts prefer to report 'a pattern created by a large volume of free-falling blood.'

In everyday language, "splash" usually describes liquid moving away from what impacted into it, such as stomping into a puddle of water or jumping into a swimming pool. In bloodstain pattern analysis, that is an impact pattern.

In fluid dynamics, splash is the process of liquid drops impacting a surface and forming fingers (spines) and/or satellite droplets.

The Academy Standards Board (ASB) definition is more general and describes splash as the result of a large volume of blood falling to a surface due to gravity and rapidly decelerating. Often it is used to describe the situation created by someone who is cupping their hands over a wound with blood pooling into their hands, followed by reaching out and having the accumulated blood fall to the ground. A splash has also been documented as a final type of pattern that may exit the mouth from expirated bloodstain mechanisms.[2]

On impact with a surface from a sufficient height, a splash produces a large primary stain as well as numerous satellite spatter and spine-like stains radiating out from the primary stain.[3] A splash will have related spatter and spine-like stains radiating all around the perimeter of the primary stain. Some drip stains may also be observed on the periphery of the primary stain. One characteristic seen in a splash pattern that may occur, but is not always present, are elliptical stains that appear to have directionality toward the primary stain versus the majority that will have directionality directed away from the primary stain. This is due to the irregular shape and tumbling motion of some satellite droplets, before they hit the surface. The fluid dynamics for explaining how these stains are formed can be found in Chapter 5. Since a splash pattern is created by blood falling onto a surface, the distance between the surface and the blood source can affect the appearance of the resulting pattern. The greater the distance, the smaller and more numerous the satellite spatter and spine-like stains may appear (Figure 17.1).

A bloodstain pattern that may physically resemble a splash and may be confused with a splash is an impact into a pool of blood. Even though an impact pattern is created when an external force

DOI: 10.4324/9781003163695-17

Figure 17.1 A splash of approximately 30 ml of porcine blood released from a height of approximately 2.3 m.

other than gravity is applied to liquid blood, these two pattern types share characteristic features. They both involve satellite spatter that may include long spine-like stains radiating out from the primary stain. An impact, however, does not always occur truly perpendicular to the pool of blood all at once, so pressure differences from the impact cause radiating stains to occur in particular directions away from the primary stain but rarely surround the entire primary stain. Also, the edges of the primary stain from this type of impact pattern typically are more disrupted than with a splash. Instead of the circular stains seen with drip stains, large elliptical stains may be observed on the periphery of the primary stain of the impact pattern. Figure 17.2 illustrates a splash of 30 ml

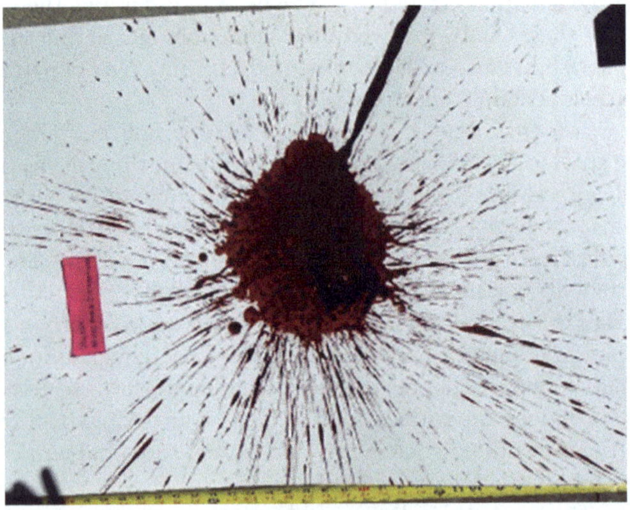

Figure 17.2 Approximately 30 ml of porcine blood released from a 61-cm vertical distance.

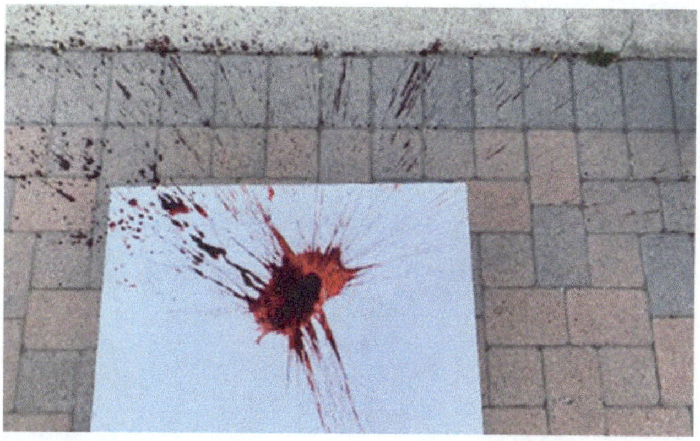

Figure 17.3 Approximately 30 ml of porcine blood pooled onto white board and stomped into.

of blood dropped from a height of 61 cm as compared to an impact by a stomp into a pool of blood (Figure 17.3).

Splash patterns and drip patterns involve large volumes of blood affected by gravity. The differentiation of these two patterns may be dependent on the wound. With a small wound, a drip pattern might be generated when multiple successive blood drops fall onto a surface. With a larger wound, especially one where blood can accumulate such as in the nose or mouth, a splash pattern might be created when a volume larger than several drops falls onto the surface. The major feature differences to be observed between a drip pattern and a splash pattern exist in the edge characteristics of the two patterns. Splash patterns typically have a large primary stain with long radiating spines. Drip patterns often have overlapping circular edges with surrounding satellite stains and lack the long radiating spines. In addition, for splash patterns and drip patterns that occur low to the ground, distinguishing between the two types of patterns may not be possible. Figure 17.4 illustrates a drip pattern using 5 ml of porcine blood dropped from a disposable pipet, from a height of approximately 15 cm. Figure 17.5 illustrates a splash pattern from the release of 5 ml of porcine blood from a conical tube, from a height of approximately 15 cm.

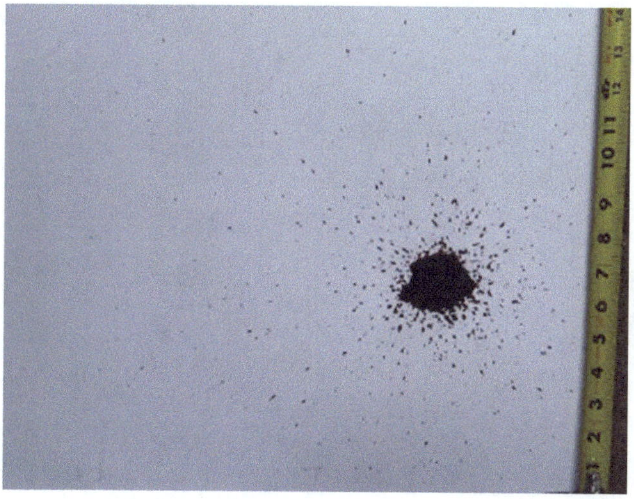

Figure 17.4 Drip pattern of 5 ml of porcine blood from a disposable pipet, from a height of approximately 15 cm.

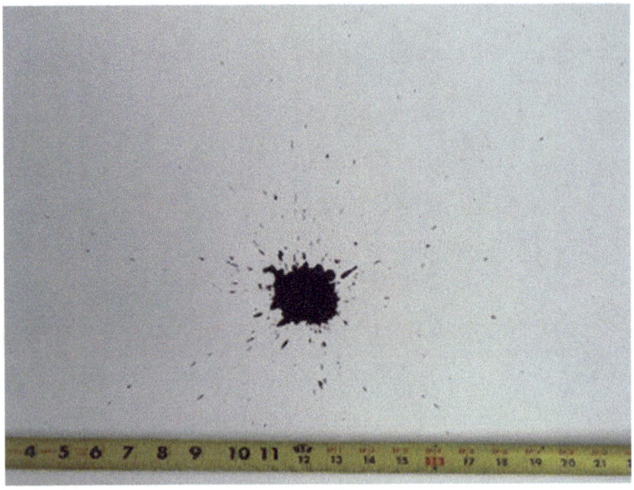

Figure 17.5 Splash pattern of 5 ml of porcine blood released from a height of approximately 15 cm.

In addition, with absorbent or rough surfaces, distinguishing these types of patterns may not be possible. The features observed in Figure 17.6 (drip pattern) and Figure 17.7 (splash) appear very similar on carpet.

At one crime scene, it was determined that one of the patterns was most likely a splash pattern. The pattern consisted of a large primary stain with long spines surrounding and radiating away from the primary stain. Contextual information was necessary to make the classification. The location of the pattern and absence of blood near the pattern, the nature of the victim's wounds, and the presence of bloodstains in other locations lead to the classification of a splash pattern. The case involved a victim who was stabbed multiple times. One of the wounds was a gaping wound that dissected one side of the mouth and cheek. The assault started on the first floor near the stairs of a two-story house. The bleeding victim traveled up the stairs and eventually died at the top of the stairs. There were multiple bloodstains and patterns on the stairs and on surrounding areas. On the floor, below the stair railing, there was a pattern that was similar in appearance to that

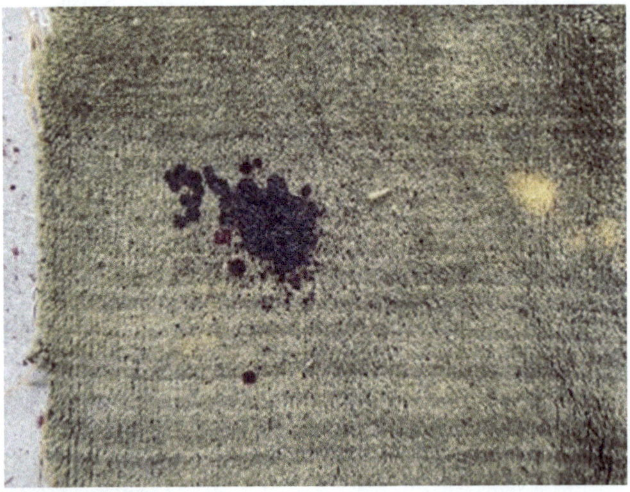

Figure 17.6 Drip pattern on carpet.

Figure 17.7 Splash pattern on carpet.

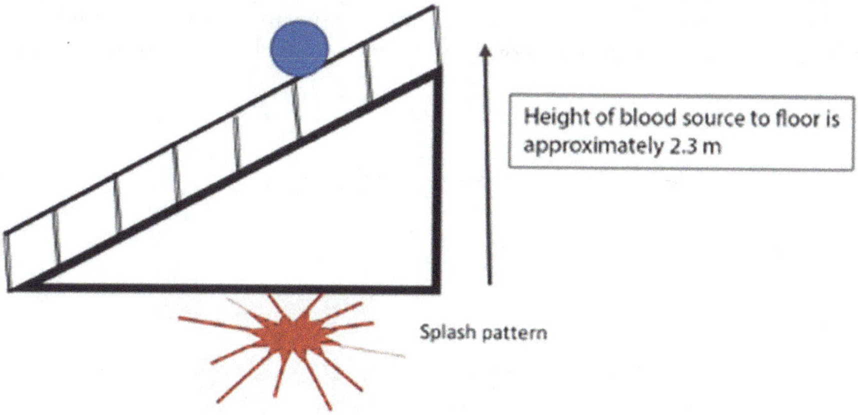

Figure 17.8 Diagram of the crime scene.

depicted in Figure 17.8. There were no other bloodstains in that area. It was determined that the pattern was probably a splash pattern created by blood from the mouth wound falling onto that floor area from a height of approximately 2.3 m.

The implications of a splash pattern are similar to those of a drip stain. A source of blood was located at a position above the target surface when it was created.

Notes

1. ASB Technical Report 033, *Terms and Definitions in Bloodstain Pattern Analysis*, 1st edition (2017).
2. Trönnberg, Rebecca, Edmund Silenieks, and Katrin Both, *The Recognition of Expirated Bloodstain Patterns on Cotton Fabrics*, R&D Report: #R 82, Government of South Australia, Forensic Science SA, February 2007, pp. 10–11.
3. Bevel, Tom, and Ross M. Gardner, *Bloodstain Pattern Analysis, Third Edition with an Introduction to Crime Scene Reconstruction*, CRC Press, 2008, p. 56.

CHAPTER 18

EXPIRATION PATTERNS

Susan Rinehart

An expiration pattern is a bloodstain pattern resulting from blood forced by airflow out of the nose, mouth, or a wound.[1]

Respiration is the act of breathing. The respiratory system delivers oxygen to the cells in your body. This is accomplished by air entering the respiratory system through the nose or mouth. The respiratory system also removes waste, including carbon dioxide, from your body during exhalation.[2] The respiratory system includes the nose, mouth, throat (pharynx), voice box (larynx), windpipe (trachea), the large airways (bronchi), and the lungs (Figure 18.1).

Physical trauma to the respiratory system can cause blood to accumulate. Any injury that causes blood to accumulate in the respiratory system can result in blood being forced out of the wound or by exhalation through the mouth or the nose, coughing, sneezing, cardiopulmonary

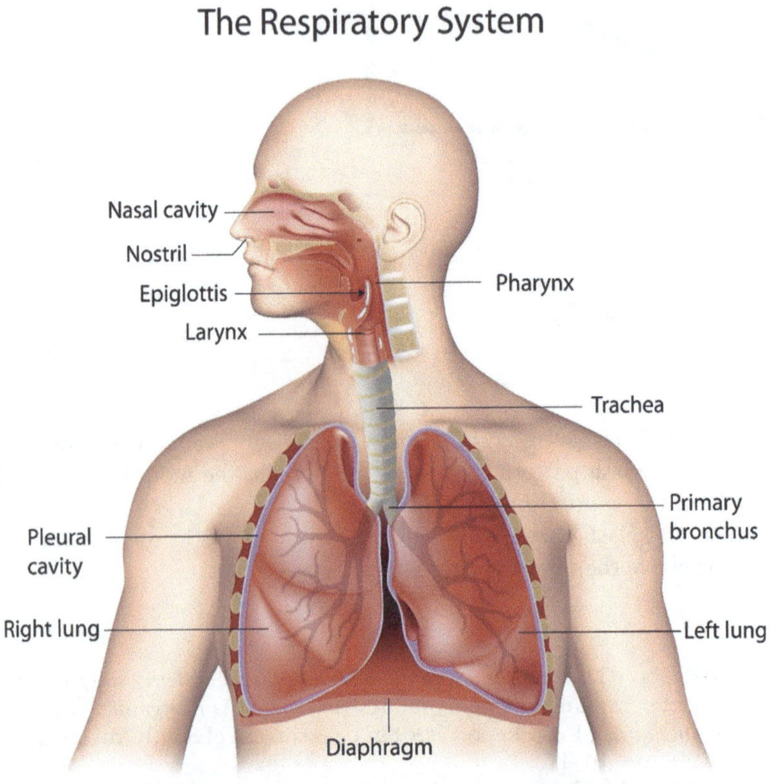

Figure 18.1 A diagram of the respiratory system.

DOI: 10.4324/9781003163695-18

resuscitation (CPR), or head injuries that cause internal bleeding that enters the back of the nasal cavity.[3] Resulting patterns that occur onto nearby surfaces will be produced from expirated blood and will consist of a distribution of spatter stains. Expirated bloodstain patterns can also occur from an external facial injury that results in blood accumulation into the mouth or nose that is then forcefully expelled out.[4] A requirement for an expirated bloodstain pattern classification is that there must be blood in the respiratory system to produce it. The analyst will usually review medical or autopsy reports for documentation of this information or converse directly with the medical person who examined the subject for this clarification. Analysts should be aware that the presence of blood in the airway may not be documented by emergency or medical personnel. In these situations, the analyst will depend on the features of the pattern and the wounds, or the lack of external injuries, for pattern classification. An expiration pattern can be classified in the broader category of a spatter pattern if this information cannot be obtained.

An injury or wound to the respiratory system allows air or mucous to intermix with blood that, upon ejection from the body, may contain some key features consistent with expirated blood. Possible features in bloodstain patterns produced from expirated blood include air bubbles, bubble rings, mucous strands, linked bloodstains, dilution, mist patterns, and large, irregular-shaped stains. Some of these features are not unique to expirated bloodstain patterns.[5,6]

Air Bubbles or Bubble Rings (Figure 18.2): Air bubbles are the result of blood being mixed with air as it is being expelled. Bubble rings are a circular outline of where an air bubble previously existed within a stain before it dried, but subsequently bursted and left behind a vacuole.[7,8] This feature may be present on non-absorbent surfaces. It is not usually seen on fabric due to absorption into the fabric.[9]

Mucous Strands (Figure 18.3): Airway mucous, found in the trachea, bronchi, and bronchioles, is an extracellular gel in which water and mucins (proteins) are the most important components.[10] Mucous strands, a characteristic feature of expirated blood, are likely produced due to the presence of the mucin proteins. The viscoelastic properties of mucous are due to the major mucins which are secreted as large polymers.[11]

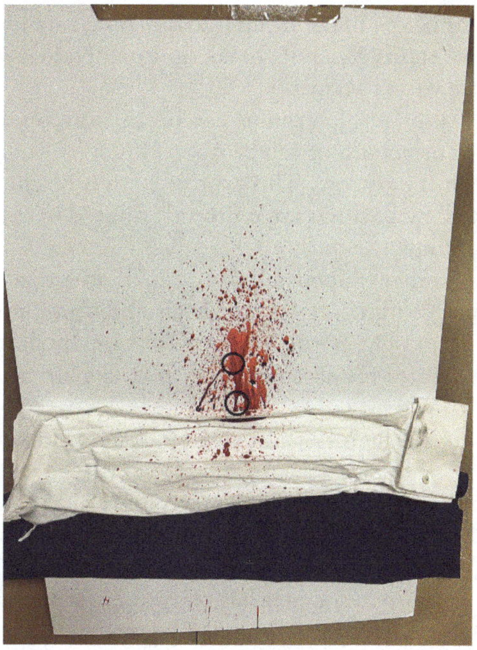

Figure 18.2 An air bubble is present within each of the circled bloodstains.

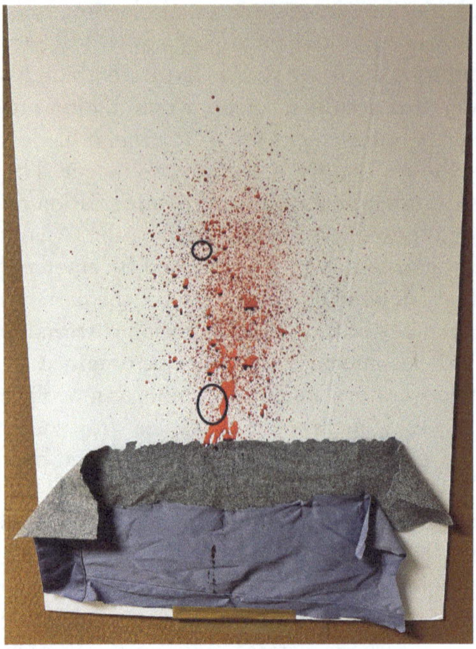

Figure 18.3 Linear blood–saliva strands linking multiple stains together.

Linked (Beaded) Bloodstains: Bloodstains may be linked together by a mucous or salivary strand. They appear to be beads on a string, a characteristic feature of expirated blood, and are caused by blood droplets in flight linked by a mucous or salivary strand that strike a target before the distance necessary to fragment into small droplets. The strands may be linear or non-linear. Strands of beaded stains do not travel far before breaking up into individual stains. High-speed video imaging has shown that these types of stains generally break up to individual stains within approximately 300 mm (11.8 in.) or less of a vertical target.[12]

Dilution (Figure 18.4): Dilution of bloodstains can occur from mixture with other body fluids such as saliva, mucous, lung surfactant, or cerebrospinal fluid.[13] Resulting stains appear lighter in color than other stains within the pattern. This type of stain is often seen on both non-absorbent and absorbent surfaces. Not all bloodstains are uniformly diluted in expirated patterns due to non-homogeneous mixing of the fluids.

Mist Patterns: A grouping of many bloodstains in a small area that are 0.5 mm in diameter or less, with fewer stains in the 1–3 mm diameter range also present. Some of the stains may appear diluted, or lighter in color than neighboring stains. Occasionally, larger stains may be observed within a mist pattern. The greater the force exerted from the airways, the smaller the resulting stain size in the pattern.

Large, Irregular-Shaped Stains: The result of many bloodstains linked together by thick strands of mucous.[14]

Amylase Testing: If blood leaves the mouth, it may be possible to detect saliva by testing for amylase using presumptive tests. Amylase is an enzyme that promotes digestion by breaking down carbohydrates (starch and glycogen) into simple sugars. It is found in saliva and later in the digestive process in pancreatic fluid. It is also found in other body fluids at significantly lower levels, such as serum, urine, sweat, semen, breast milk, and feces.[15] The concentration of amylase in saliva is variable among individuals and within the same individual at different times. If an amylase test is negative, it does not mean an expirated bloodstain is excluded as a possibility. Saliva could be present

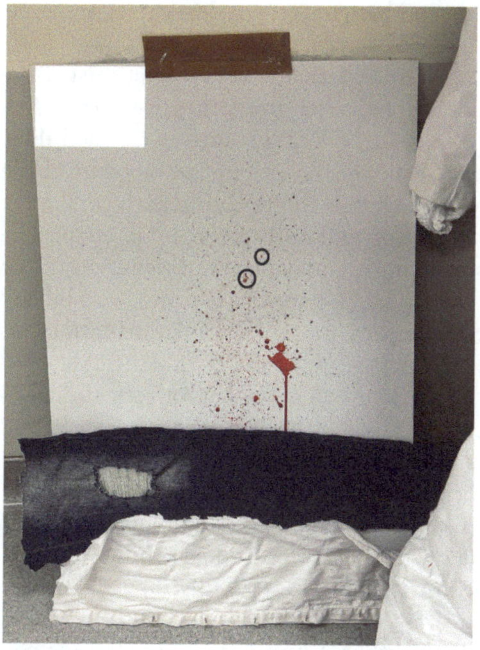

Figure 18.4 The circled bloodstains are lighter in color compared to other bloodstains in the pattern, indicating dilution.

at a lower level than the limit of detection of the test, or it may not be present in the specific area tested since its mixture with blood may be variable. One recommendation for screening with an amylase test is to test more than one area within a bloodstain pattern. One test, the SALIgAE® saliva test, was found to detect human saliva up to a 2,000-fold dilution with sterile water.[16] The sensitivity of the test when saliva is mixed with blood may be reduced due to discoloration of the test solution by blood. Overall, various studies have found this test to be sensitive, simple to perform, and accurate.

When using a screening test for saliva, the target surface should be considered. Bedding and clothing items may produce a positive amylase result due to historical use rather than from the bloodletting incident. The analyst may consider amylase testing outside of the bloodstain pattern area, and DNA testing to assist with classification.

The process of expiration causes blood to expel in a radial fashion initially, with the resulting shape of the overall expiration pattern being variable.[17] Different body motions and different initial velocities create different patterns.[18] One study found that blood expirated from the back of the mouth produced irregular shaped stains and droplet sizes that varied from 1 mm to 5 mm, while blood expirated from the front of the mouth produced regular shaped stains (circular and oval) and smaller droplets from 0.5 mm to 3 mm.[19] There also may be flow stains present if enough blood is available.

High-speed video imaging experiments have been conducted on coughing, spitting, and breathing or blowing mechanisms onto various types of target surfaces after subjects placed either a volume of their own blood or a synthetic blood substitute into their mouths. Peak expiration velocity occurred near the beginning of the expiration mechanisms for all subjects and appeared to control the various types of stains produced. Blowing and spitting produced the highest air velocities, followed by coughing. Peak air velocities were measured at 6–64 m/s for blowing, 1–64 m/s for spitting, and 1–47 m/s for coughing. Spitting resulted in blood droplets observed at 1,600 mm

(5 ft 3 in.), whereas coughing and blowing resulted in drops observed at approximately 500 mm (19.6 in.).[20]

Blood droplets left the mouth in a particular order. First mist size droplets (less than 1 mm in diameter) were expelled, followed by larger droplets (greater than 1 mm in diameter) and strands of liquid. The smaller the droplet, the less distance it traveled due to a higher drag (from air resistance) to mass ratio, and the larger the amount of blood available for expiration, the greater the variation in droplet size produced in the resulting pattern. Common sizes of stains observed ranged from less than 1 mm up to several millimeters in diameter.[21]

In forensic investigations utilizing bloodstain pattern analysis, it can become important to distinguish expiration spatter (a bloodstain pattern resulting from blood forced by airflow out of the nose, mouth, or a wound) from impact spatter (a bloodstain pattern resulting from an object striking liquid blood).

These two types of spatter mechanisms may contain very similar types of overall distribution, size ranges of bloodstains, and shapes of bloodstains. The location of the pattern, the injuries received by the subject, blood present in airways or not, and amylase testing help to distinguish which type of pattern may be present. The location of the pattern must also be considered because some locations might be unlikely to contain expirated blood, such as high up on a surface in relation to the height or position of the subject, positional limitations, or a wide distribution of bloodstains. The two types of patterns cannot always be distinguished from each other however, and in those instances both mechanisms should be considered as possibilities.

Small bloodstains, typically less than 1 mm in size, on clothing could indicate that the subject wearing the clothing was in close proximity to a spatter-producing event, such as delivering blows to a victim. If, however, the small stains were due to expirated blood, this could indicate the subject instead was rendering aid to an injured person. Differentiating these two types of patterns is obviously crucial for an investigation.[22]

On absorbent targets like fabric, characteristic stains may include mist stains, spatter stains, altered stains, irregular shaped stains, linked stains, haloed stains, and/or a possible splash.[23] Altered stains would include diluted stains or haloed stains which are stains with a lighter edge around the perimeter of the stain from blood not mixing thoroughly with saliva. This could also be due to an effect of the fabric composition itself which could be determined from experimentation. Bubble rings may or may not be observed. Linked stains may be present still connected from a mucous or salivary strand. From coughing experiments, where an upright individual placed blood in their mouth and coughed toward the front surface of a shirt worn by a mannequin, larger stains (5 mm diameter and above) were present and were typically located at a position below the smaller stains. These larger stains could also be intermixed with the smaller stains. A final splash stain was observed due to the head movement at the end of the cough and blood spilling from the mouth.[24] In this positional configuration, the splash stain may be produced onto the fabric or may end up on nearby targets or on the ground, which could subsequently be separated from the other types of stains previously mentioned on the shirt (Figure 18.5).

Expiration bloodstain patterns may be part of complex patterns by being intermixed with other impact patterns from impact mechanisms. In one case, an intoxicated man received multiple impact blows to the head with an object during a struggle with another man. The only injuries he received were internal head injuries, with external bleeding occurring through the mouth, nose, and ears. The blood was from expirated blood, as it was coming from airways; however, the mechanism of injury was from multiple impacts to the head. In this case, neither expirated blood nor the impact spatter could be eliminated as possible mechanisms for the bloodstain patterns produced (Figures 18.6 and 18.7).

The classification of expiration spatter should be considered when there are spatter patterns, but there are no external bleeding injuries. In several homicide cases involving children, there were no external bleeding injuries on the victims; however, patterns classified as expiration patterns were observed at the crime scenes. The victims in these cases succumbed to internal bleeding and

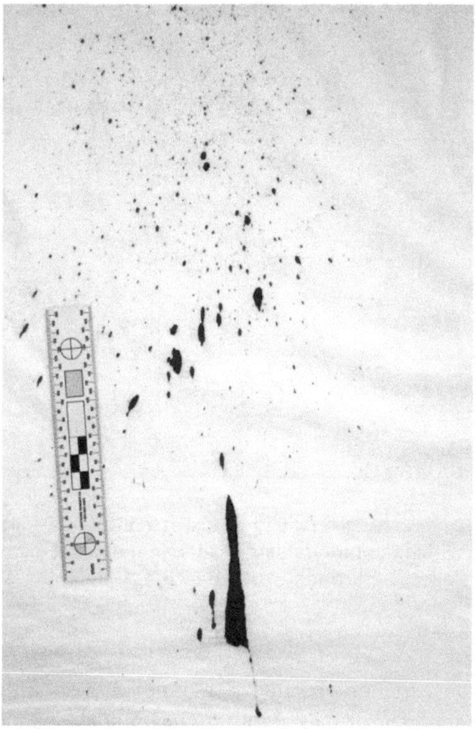

Figure 18.5 Expiration stains produced onto a white T-shirt from coughing experiments where the individual was upright and coughing toward the front surface of a shirt worn by a mannequin. (Image courtesy of Edmund Silenieks from *The Recognition of Expirated Bloodstain Patterns on Cotton Fabrics*, R&D report: #R 82, Government of South Australia, Forensic Science, SA, February 2007.)

Figure 18.6 The stains were from a combination of expirated and impact spatter mechanisms. The victim received repeated blows to the head. The stains were all located within the bottom 3 ft on the garage door and on the ground in front of the garage door. (Image courtesy of Long Beach Police Department, Long Beach, CA, detective Mark Mattia.)

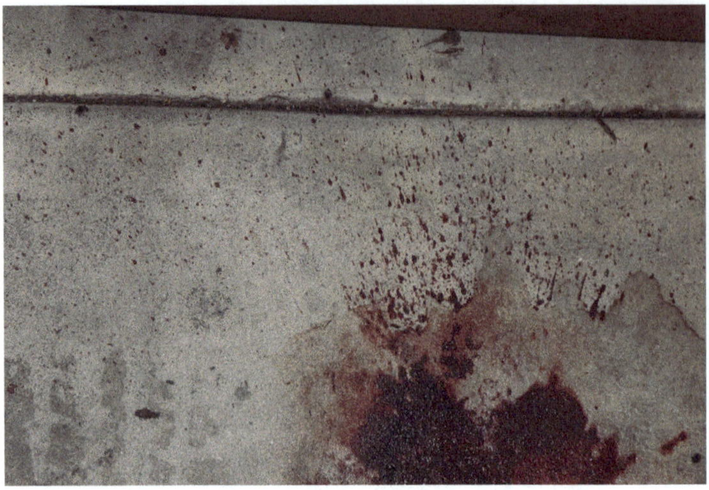

Figure 18.7 The location of the victim's head on the ground was in the pooled area. Air bubbles and various stain sizes and shapes could be seen within the bloodstains located in the radial distribution of stains on the ground. (Image courtesy of Long Beach Police Department, Long Beach, CA, detective Mark Mattia.

non-bleeding injuries. In one case, emergency personnel did document that blood was present in the nose of the victim. In another case, a young victim suffered a beating which resulted in a broken bloody nose and internal head injuries. The victim had lost consciousness and had blood in the airway. Being in a supine position and unable to move, the victim died from complications resulting from fluid in the airway.

Depending on the distance from the target, the amount of blood available in an airway, and the nature of the target itself, very few of the characteristic features may be present. The presence of diluted bloodstains or a positive screening test for amylase might be more commonly observed. One study found that the most reliable way to distinguish between small impact bloodstains and expirated bloodstains on clothing was to test for amylase.[25] It is not uncommon for a bloodstain pattern from an expirated mechanism to not contain any physical stain features such as bubble rings, mucous strands, or beaded stains. Other information should be considered to determine the possibility of a pattern resulting from expirated blood.

Notes

1. ASB Technical Report 033, *Terms and Definitions in Bloodstain Pattern Analysis*, 1st edition (2017).
2. James, Stuart H., Paul E. Kish, and T. Paulette Sutton, *Principles of Bloodstain Pattern Analysis: Theory and Practice*, CRC Press, Boca Raton, FL, 2005, p. 20.
3. Emes, A. (2001) Expirated blood: A review. *Journal of the Forensic Science Society*, 34(4):p. 200.
4. Ibid.
5. Trönnberg, Rebecca, Edmund Silenieks, and Katrin Both, *The Recognition of Expirated Bloodstain Patterns on Cotton Fabrics*, R&D Report: #R 82, Government of South Australia, Forensic Science, SA, February 2007, p. 28.
6. Geoghegan, P.H., A.M. Laffra, N.K. Hoogendorp, M.C. Taylor, and M.C. Jermy, Experimental measurement of breath exit velocity and expirated bloodstain patterns produced under different exhalation mechanisms, *International Journal of Legal Medicine*, 2017, 131:1194. doi: 10.1007/s00414-017-1545-2.
7. James, Kish, Sutton, *Principles of Bloodstain Pattern Analysis*, pp. 162–163.
8. Bevel, Tom, and Ross M. Gardner, *Bloodstain Pattern Analysis, Third Edition with an Introduction to Crime Scene Reconstruction*, CRC Press, p. 52.
9. Emes, A (2001) *Expirated Blood: A Review*, p. 201.

10. Fahy, John V., and Burton F. Dickey, Airway mucus function and dysfunction, *New England Journal of Medicine* 2010, 363(23):2233–2247. doi: 10.1056/NEJMra0910061.
11. Donaldson et al., *Characterising the Dynamics*, p. 758.
12. Donaldson et al., *Characterising the Dynamics*, p. 759.
13. Emes, A. (2001) *Expirated Blood: A Review*, p. 200.
14. Trönnberg, Silenieks, and Both, *The Recognition of Expirated*, 2007, p. 30.
15. Pang, Benjamin C.M., and Bobbie K.K. Cheung, Applicability of two commercially available kits for forensic identification of saliva stains, *Journal of the Forensic Science*, 2008, 53(5):s1120. doi: 10.1111/j.1556-4029.2008.00814.x.
16. Ibid, p. 1119.
17. Donaldson et al., *Characterising the Dynamics*, p. 758.
18. Geoghegan et al., *Experimental Measurement of Breath*, p. 1194.
19. Carter, G.S. A consideration of coughed or spat-out blood, Forensic Science Service Report No. TN 817, 1996, referred to in Geoghegan et al., *Experimental Measurement of Breath*, p. 1194.
20. Geoghegan et al., *Experimental Measurement of Breath*, p. 1197.
21. Ibid, p. 1201.
22. Donaldson et al., *Characterising the Dynamics*, p. 757.
23. Trönnberg, Silenieks, and Both, *The Recognition of Expirated*, 2007, p. 6.
24. Ibid, p. 11.
25. Ibid, p. 33.

CHAPTER 19

UNDERSTANDING TEXTILES

Stephen Michielsen

PREAMBLE

Bloodstains are commonly deposited on textiles during violent crimes and those bloodstains, particularly when deposited on clothing and footwear, can provide important evidence connecting the wearer to a crime scene or to a victim of crime and provide insight to the mechanisms that led to the bloodstain deposition. In many cases, the established criteria commonly used to classify bloodstains on non-porous surfaces typically found at crime scenes may not apply to certain textiles. Textiles generally have a textured surface and are porous, so blood will react differently when compared to how blood reacts with smooth, non-porous surfaces. Resultant bloodstains on textiles will often vary in shape and appearance when compared to similar bloodstains caused by the same deposition mechanism but deposited on non-porous surfaces.

This chapter introduces the reader to the basic structure and properties of textiles, their complexity, and how liquids, typically blood, can interact with textiles and potentially affect resultant bloodstain shape. This interaction can influence the analyst's ability to successfully classify bloodstains and interpret bloodstain patterns on textiles. An overview of the limitations associated with the examination and interpretation of bloodstains deposited on clothing is also discussed.

UNDERSTANDING TEXTILES

Textile materials are some of the most common items found at crime scenes. When they interact with blood, they may strongly repel blood or strongly absorb it; they may alter the appearance of a blood drop or even hide the blood within the textile structure; they may cause a blood droplet to break into many satellite drops or they may absorb the energy of the drop hitting the textile, thus preventing drop breakup. To understand how textile materials (textiles) interact with blood, it is necessary to understand a little about the structure of textiles and modifications to the textile surface, which is one of the subjects of this chapter.

FIBER

The most fundamental component of a textile is a fiber, which is defined as follows:

> A unit of matter, either natural or manufactured, that forms the basic element of fabrics and other textile structures. A fiber is characterized by having a length at least 100 times its diameter or width. The term refers to units that can be spun into a yarn or made into a fabric by various

 DOI: 10.4324/9781003163695-19

> methods including weaving, knitting, braiding, felting, and twisting. The essential requirements for fibers to be spun into yarn include a length of at least 5 millimeters, flexibility, cohesiveness, and sufficient strength.[1]

Fibers can be natural, such as cotton, wool, and silk, or manufactured. Manufactured fibers are broken down into two more categories, synthetic and regenerated. Common synthetic fibers include acrylic, nylon, polyester, polypropylene, spandex, and Kevlar, while common regenerated fibers include acetate, Lyocel or Tencel, and rayon or viscose. In each case, the fiber is long, 5 mm to many kilometers, and thin, typically 1–100 μm in width or diameter. Fibers thinner than this range are very delicate and tend to be used only in specialty applications, such as the filtration layer of surgical masks. Fibers thicker than this range are very stiff, such as the bristles of a toothbrush. Extremely long fibers are most common as manufactured fibers and silk. They are usually referred to as "filaments":

> A fiber of an indefinite or extreme length such as found naturally in silk. Manufactured fibers are extruded into filaments that are converted into filament yarn, staple or tow.[1]

These filaments can be used directly as yarn (filament yarn), cut into "staple" with lengths in the range of 2.5–4.5 cm for blending with cotton or to mimic cotton or longer to blend with or to mimic wool. Several filament yarns can be gathered together to form "tow," which is then cut into staple. The term "staple" is used to distinguish the shorter fibers (0.025–1 m) from filaments (many meters to many kilometers long).

Figure 19.1 shows a schematic of textile structures from fiber to final product. Fibers may be converted directly into nonwoven materials, such as surgical masks, diapers, incontinence garments, wipes, and so on or they may be converted into yarns for subsequent processing into other materials. Their interaction with blood or other liquids depends on the fiber properties as well as how the fibers were converted into the final product and any surface treatments, which are referred to as "finishes." Each of these will be discussed in the following sections.

Chemical Composition

The properties of fibers relevant to this chapter are their chemical composition, their shape, their length, and their interaction with liquids. The most common *natural* fibers are cotton, followed by other plant, i.e., cellulosic, fibers such as linen, jute, and hemp. Each of these fibers is hydrophilic and is easily wet by water if all oils and waxes are removed. Another class of natural fibers is "protein fibers" exemplified by wool, camel hair, alpaca, and silk. Again, if all waxes and oils are

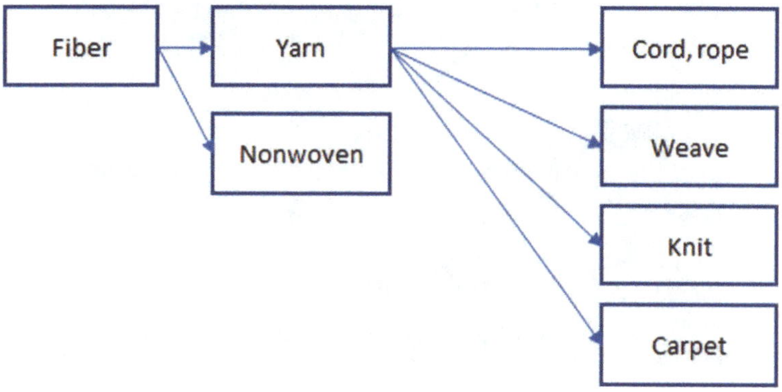

Figure 19.1 Schematic of textile structure formation.

removed, they are hydrophilic, but they often contain waxes and oils that render them hydrophobic. (Hydrophilic means that the fibers are spontaneously wet by liquid water, while hydrophobic means they repel liquid water.) With the exception of silk, all natural fibers are staple fibers. The most common manufactured fibers are polyester (usually polyethylene terephthalate but other polyesters are also used), viscose (rayon), acrylic, nylon, and polypropylene. Some manufactured fibers in their pure form are hydrophilic, e.g., viscose, while others are hydrophobic, for example, polypropylene. All manufactured fibers are made in filament form, but they may be cut in an additional process to make staple fibers, often to blend them with cotton or wool or to simulate the behavior of cotton or wool. Approximately 60% of worldwide production of polyester filaments are cut into staple fibers and blended with cotton, while the remaining 40% are used in filament form.

Shape

Although we often think of fibers as being round, this is often incorrect. Cotton has twisted ribbon shape (Figure 19.2); silk has a distorted triangular shape; wool is essentially round, but has scales on its surface; viscose has a kidney-shaped cross section; while the synthetic fibers can have nearly any shape the manufacturer desires, including round, trilobal, channeled, hollow, dog-bone shaped, and so on. For natural fibers, microscopic images can be used to identify the type of fibers, while for synthetic fibers this is not the case.

Interaction with Liquids

Liquid interacts with fibers in two ways, by wetting or not wetting the fiber surface and by being absorbed or not absorbed by the fiber. If the liquid is water-based and wets the fiber, we say the fiber is hydrophilic, i.e., "loves water"; if it repels water, we say it is hydrophobic. If the liquid is oil-based, we use the terms "oleophilic" and "oleophobic." If cotton and wool are perfectly cleaned of all contaminants and have not been chemically treated, they are hydrophilic. Polyester and polypropylene are naturally hydrophobic and oleophilic. However, fibers at a bloodstain scene are rarely cleaned to this extent and often the fibers have been treated by industry to give them special properties. In these cases, the interaction of liquids with the fibers may not be characteristic of the fiber type.

Another way that fibers interact with liquids is in the absorption of liquid in which the molecules of the liquid are taken into the fiber structure. This is quite different from how yarns absorb liquid discussed below. At 65% RH (relative humidity) and 20°C, cotton contains about 7% water by

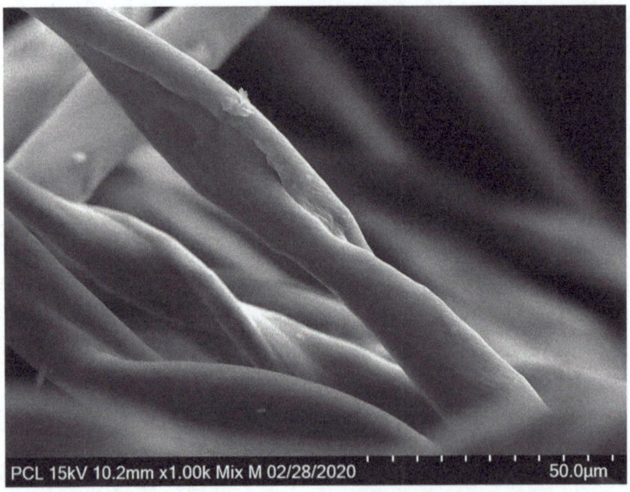

Figure 19.2 Cotton fibers have a twisted ribbon shape. (RMIT Materials Database, SEM photograph by Sebastian Nordstrom, 2019.)

weight while wool and viscose will contain about 12%. On the other hand, polyester will contain only about 0.4% and polypropylene contains less than 0.2%. Often, this is referred to as moisture regain, which is defined as follows:

$$\frac{W_{\mathrm{RH},T} - W_{\mathrm{RH}\,=\,0,T}}{W_{\mathrm{RH}\,=\,0,T}}$$

where W is the weight and the subscripts indicate the environmental conditions. T is the temperature and RH is the relative humidity. Moisture regain is usually measured under "standard conditions," i.e., at 65% RH and 20°C for textiles. The impact of moisture regain on bloodstains is poorly understood.

In summary, fibers are the fundamental form of textiles. They may be made by nature or manufactured; they may be short, discontinuous "staple" fibers or long, continuous filaments; and filaments may be cut to create staple fibers. The cross-sectional shape of natural fibers is dictated by nature, but for synthetic fibers, the cross-sectional shape is dictated by the manufacturer. Finally, the interaction of liquids with the fibers depends on the fiber and liquid chemical compositions and any surface contamination or surface treatment.

NONWOVENS

Raw fibers are not particularly useful by themselves. Instead, they are combined into yarns for further processing, or converted directly into finished products, referred to as "nonwoven fabrics" or simply "nonwovens":

> An assembly of textile fibers held together by mechanical interlocking [hydroentangling or needle punching] in a random web or mat, by fusing of the fibers (in case of thermoplastic fibers), or by bonding with a cementing medium such as starch, glue, casein, rubber, latex.[1]

Nonwoven product classes divide about equally into three areas: medical and related applications (disposable surgical gowns, face masks, diapers, etc.), wipes and filters for household and industrial applications, and various industrial applications such as insulation, geotextiles, agricultural textiles, and building products. To give nonwovens strength, the fibers must be bonded together. This may be through application of heat to partially melt the fibers so that they stick together, through application of adhesives, or by entangling the fibers by needle punching them or using high-pressure water jets to entangle them. The interaction of liquids with nonwovens depends primarily on the type of fiber used to make the nonwoven, on the arrangement or packing of the fibers, and on any surface chemistry or treatments applied to them (Figure 19.3).

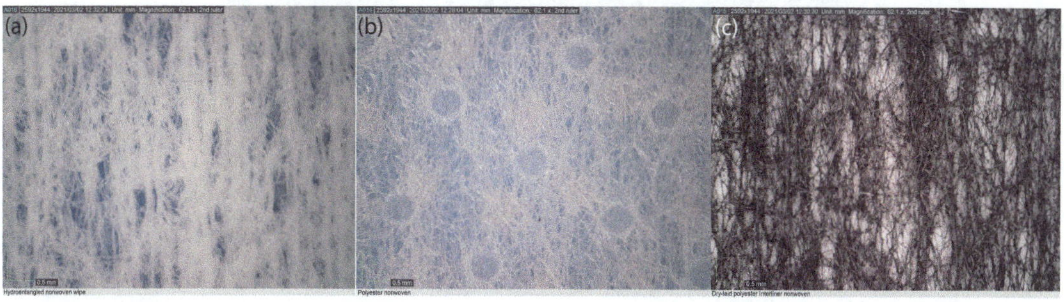

Figure 19.3 Nonwoven fabrics. (a) A hydroentangled wipe. (b) A thermally bonded polyester sheet. (c) A dry-laid nonwoven interlining.

Nonwovens tend to be either flat sheets or fabrics, which can be formed into garments, wipes, or other forms, or they may be formed into thick batts, typically for insulation such as the interior layers of quilts or sound deadening panels inside car doors, as a trunk or hood liner, and so forth. Nonwovens are highly engineered for their application, so it is difficult to give general rules about their behavior. Surgical gowns and gowns used by investigators at scenes strongly repel liquids, including blood to protect the wearer, but household wipes often absorb large amounts of liquid to clean up spills. Diaper inner linings will allow liquid to pass through quickly but will remain dry on the child's skin, while the superabsorbent middle layer can absorb more than six times its weight in water. Polypropylene and polyester are the most common nonwovens because these polymers are relatively inexpensive. Both strongly repel water and blood. However, polyester nonwovens can easily be modified to strongly absorb water or blood.

Summarizing the behavior of blood on nonwovens, it is difficult to draw general conclusions. Some nonwovens will strongly repel blood, others will absorb large quantities of blood, while others will allow blood to pass through unimpeded. Even when two nonwovens look identical, such as for two types of wipes, one may repel blood while the other may absorb it.

YARNS

As seen in Figure 19.1, if fibers are not converted into nonwovens, they are usually converted into yarns. A yarn is a collection of one or more filaments or a collection of fibers suitable for converting into cords, ropes, or fabrics. A yarn is defined as follows:

> A generic term for a continuous strand of textile fibers, filaments, or material in a form suitable for knitting, weaving, or otherwise intertwining to form a textile fabric. Yarn occurs in the following forms: (1) a number of fibers twisted together (spun yarn); (2) a number of filaments laid together without twist (a zero twist yarn); (3) a number of filaments laid together with a degree of twist; (4) a single filament with or without twist (a monofilament).[1]

A collection of untwisted staple fibers has very little strength; however, when the fibers are twisted together, they develop lateral forces which force the fibers together; the friction between the fibers then gives the yarn its strength. The yarn shown in Figure 19.4 is formed by twisting two staple

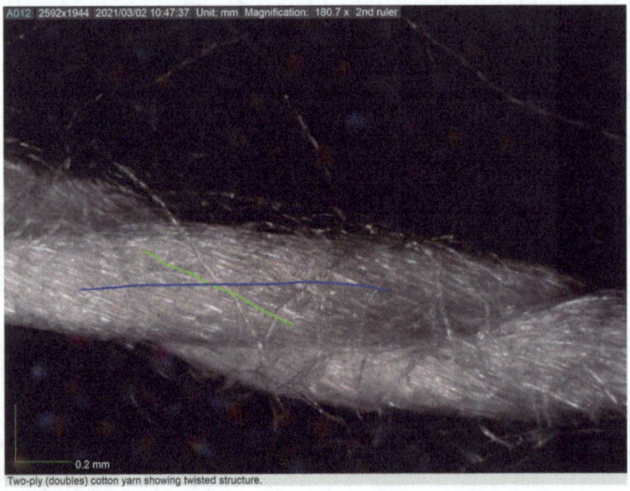

Figure 19.4 Micrograph of a two-ply cotton yarn showing the twisted structure, the yarn direction for one of the yarns (blue arrow) and the fiber direction (green arrow).

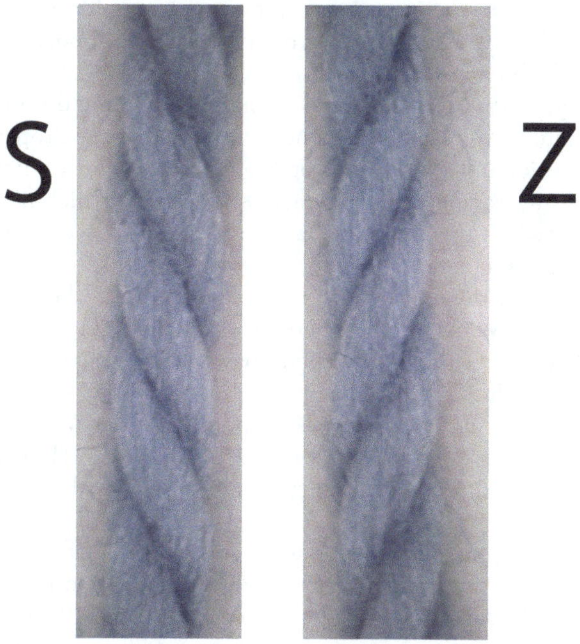

Figure 19.5 Two doubles yarns are shown with "S-twist" where the yarn is shown to follow the central section of the letter S and "Z-twist" where the yarn follows the central section of the letter Z.

or "spun" yarns together to form a two-ply or "doubles" yarn. Each of the two yarns is formed by twisting cotton staple fibers together. Note that the direction of the fibers is different from the direction of the yarn.

Staple fibers are twisted together to form a yarn in a process called spinning to form "spun" yarns. There are three main processes used: ring-spinning, rotor spinning, and air-jet spinning. A discussion of these processes is beyond the scope of this chapter, but the spinning method can influence the nature of a bloodstain.[2] When twisting fibers or yarns together (Figure 19.5), they can be twisted in a clockwise direction (S-twist) or counterclockwise direction (Z-twist). Two or more yarns can be twisted together to form cords, ropes, or cables. Cables can have sufficient strength to moor ocean liners to a dock. Thus, a collection of weak fibers can form a very strong cable by twisting the fibers together.

If a yarn consists of filaments, twist is not needed to give it strength, but often a small amount of twist is applied to keep the filaments together to avoid entangling or to prevent snagging. In other words, nearly all yarns contain some twist.

Yarns may also be "texturized" where texturing is

> [t]he process of crimping, imparting random loops, or otherwise modifying continuous filament yarn to increase cover, resilience, abrasion resistance, warmth, insulation, and moisture absorption or to provide different surface texture.[1]

The purpose of texturizing a filament yarn is to give it properties similar to spun yarn without the need of cutting the filaments to form staple and then processing the staple to form spun yarn.

As discussed above, water can be absorbed by fibers as molecular water, but not as liquid water. Liquid water as well as blood cells remains outside of the fibers but may reside in the spaces *between* fibers within the yarn. A typical cotton yarn used to weave fabric is 50–55% fiber by volume and 45–50% air, while filament and high twist staple yarn may be up to about 70% fiber but 30% of the volume of a yarn is still air. On the other hand, a low twist yarn for use in sweaters may contain less than 5% fiber and more than 95% air. When blood or water is applied to the yarn, or to a fabric containing these yarns, the liquid may displace air and fill these void spaces. As blood enters a yarn, it spreads along the fibers within the yarn, thus changing small round drops into elongated blood drops or strips. The amount of elongation depends on the size of the drop and the amount of void space within the yarn, which in turn depends on the amount of twist. High levels of twist essentially "squeezes out" the air, leaving long, thin channels for blood which must spread out along the length of the yarn. Low twist yarns generally have considerable space for air and hence for blood, so a small blood drop may remain nearly round on low twist yarns.

If blood wets the surface of the fibers and spreads along them in the spaces between the fibers, the process is call "wicking." Wicking can only occur after the liquid, e.g., blood, wets the fibers, although the time between wetting and wicking may be extremely short. The spaces between fibers are referred to as capillaries and wicking occurs through capillary action. As noted above, the size of the capillaries depends inversely on the amount of twist. When all else are equal (same fiber, same liquid, etc.), wicking is faster in large capillaries (low twist) but extends further in small capillaries (high twist). This results in a competition between fast but limited wicking and slow but extended wicking.

Besides twist, the capillary size also depends on the packing efficiency of the fibers. Round fibers can pack to about 90% of the yarn volume, while odd-shaped fibers and texturized fibers may be able to pack to only a few percent of the volume (Figure 19.6). In addition, if the fiber contains channels along its length, these channels form additional capillaries. Wool has scales on its surface and these scales prevent the fibers from packing tightly. In other words, the fiber's cross-sectional shape as well as the twist affects the capillary sizes and thus the extent of wicking. This, in turn, affects the resultant shape of a blood drop as it wicks into the yarn. Another complicating factor in the case of blood drops is that the size of red blood cells is comparable to the size of the capillary channels between fibers, which may exclude the red blood cells from the smaller capillaries while serum and plasma may easily wick into these regions. It is not currently known how this affects bloodstain patterns, but it could lead to serum separation even for small blood drops.

Most fabrics are made from yarn, which is made from fibers or filaments held together by twist. The amount of twist and the fiber's cross-sectional shape affects how tightly the fibers pack and thus the capillary structure. The capillary structure and the degree of wetting of the fiber by a liquid affects the amount of spreading of the liquid within the yarn and thus within the fabric. Finally, the amount of spreading of the liquid affects the distortion of the drop shape or staining. After nearly 100 years of research into moisture management for comfort in textiles, these factors are well understood qualitatively. However, even today they are poorly understood quantitatively, especially for bloodstain patterns.

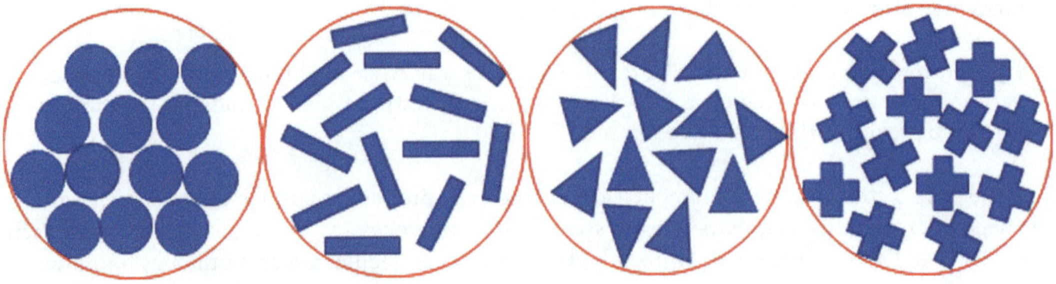

Figure 19.6 Packing of fibers of different shapes and the circumscribed circle. Note that the amount of space between the fibers is quite different in each case.

ROPES AND CORDS

As mentioned above, when two yarns are twisted together, they form a "plied" yarn. When plied yarns are twisted together, they form cords or ropes. When the yarn is plied together to form a "doubles" yarn, it is twisted in the opposite direction as the fibers were twisted to form the initial "singles" yarn. The doubles yarns are then twisted together, again in the opposite direction to form a cable or a rope. This process is repeated, alternating the twist direction for each layer until the desired size rope or cable is formed. By alternating the twist direction, the rope structure is stabilized to reduce unraveling. Once the rope or cord is built up to the appropriate size, it may be heat set to further stabilize its structure. The yarns can be put under high tension while tightly twisting them to give a compact stiff rope, or they can be held under low tension and twisted loosely. This results in quite different properties. The compact rope has much less space within the rope for blood, while the looser structure can easily accommodate blood in its structure.

WEAVES OR WOVEN FABRICS

Woven fabrics are formed from yarn that is interlaced at right angles (see Figure 19.7). In a plain weave, the simplest weave, a weft yarn, also called a pick or a filling yarn, runs across the width of the fabric passing over then under a warp yarn, or end, that runs the length of the fabric. Each subsequent pick follows the same pattern of over–under but offset by one yarn, i.e., the next weft yarn runs under–over and the next runs over–under, and so forth. Although this simple pattern is repeated in all plain weaves, there are still hundreds of variations. The yarns in the warp and weft directions may be the same or different. Even in a single direction, different yarn sizes, colors, and fiber types may be varied. This can result in ribs, color bands, puckering (e.g., seersucker), and many other effects. Another variation is to treat two or more yarns (picks or ends) as a single yarn to form basket weaves. A half-basket weave such as a 1 × 2 basket weave exemplified as an oxford weave used for shirting (Figure 19.8). The same oxford weave can be made with finer yarns, in which case it is called a "pinpoint oxford." Another variation of the plain weave is rip-stop fabric which was developed during World War II to prevent lightweight parachute canopies from tearing. They use

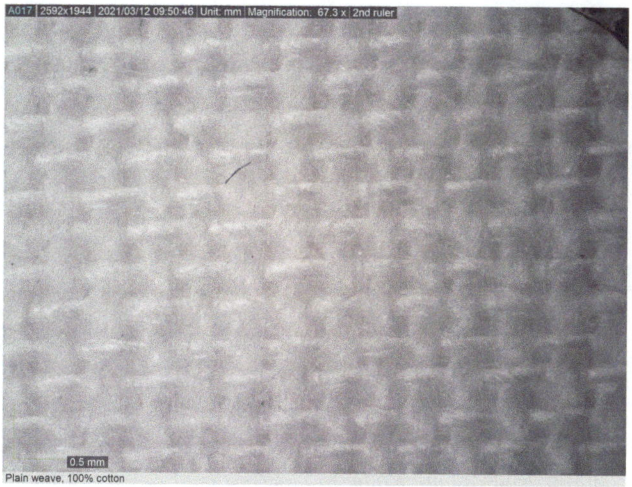

Figure 19.7 Plain weave.

Figure 19.8 Oxford weave is a ½-basket weave in which two yarns are woven as if they are one.

relatively thin yarns to reduce the weight, but about every five to ten yarns, a thin yarn is replaced by a thick yarn. If the fabric began to tear, it stopped when the tear ran into the thicker yarn.

Plain weave structures can also be varied by varying the types of yarns (natural, synthetic), their sizes, and their twist level. If the yarns are highly twisted and packed tightly, the fabric will be stiff; but if they are packed loosely and have low twist, the fabric will be softer and more flexible. Low twist staple yarns can also be brushed to loosen the fiber ends to make soft, warm fabrics such as flannel. Manufactured fibers with low twist but packed tightly into a plain weave can block wind; so they are often used for windbreakers or in the shell of outerwear.

More complicated but still simple weaves include twills, e.g., denim, and satins. These are made in a manner similar to a plain weave, but their interlacing patterns are different. Plain weaves and their derivatives are the most common types of weave, while the twill weave is the second most common weave. Common twill fabrics include denim, chino, and gabardine. Twills are characterized by a "twill line" that runs at an angle to the fabric edges or "selvedge," also spelled "selvage" (Figure 19.9). They are made by "floating" a pick over x ends, then passing under y ends, where x and y are small integers (typically 1, 2, or 3); e.g., in Figure 19.9, $x = 3$ and $y = 1$. Each subsequent

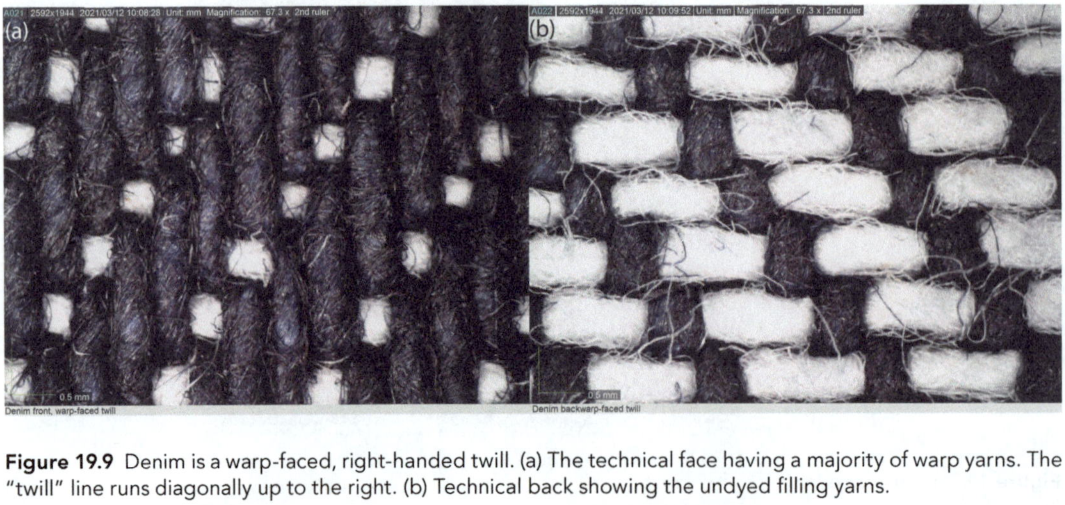

Figure 19.9 Denim is a warp-faced, right-handed twill. (a) The technical face having a majority of warp yarns. The "twill" line runs diagonally up to the right. (b) Technical back showing the undyed filling yarns.

pick follows the same pattern, but its interlacing point (point where it shifts from the front to the back of the fabric, and vice versa) is shifted by one end. This allows for more yarns to be packed into the fabric to make a more durable fabric, often used for trousers and jackets. The warp yarns are usually much stronger than the weft yarns, so they often appear on the fabric face to form a warp-faced twill which provides better abrasion resistance. Many of the variations found in plain weaves can also be used in twill weaves, but the variations are less common (Figure 19.9).

The third type of simple weave is the satin weave (Figure 19.10) and its related sateen weave. They are characterized by long floats with few interlace points which are scattered. This gives a smooth fabric. Satins are often used in formal wear, whereas sateens are used in upholstery. The long floats result is a smooth fabric, but they are prone to snagging, which can cause the fabric to distort. If non-texturized filament yarn is used, the satin tends to be shiny, which is easily recognized as satin. However, if spun yarn is used, the fabric will be less shiny, but still form a smooth surface.

Although they are less common, more complicated weaves such as dobby weaves (Figure 19.11) and jacquard weaves use more complicated interlacing patterns, but the properties are similar

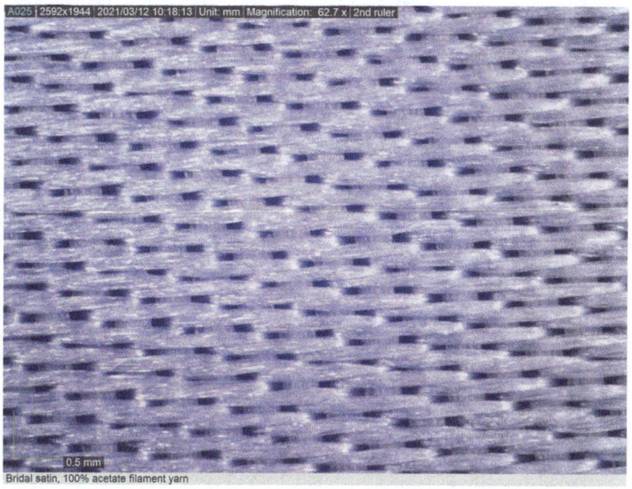

Figure 19.10 Technical face of bridal satin made from acetate filament yarns. Note the long floats in the crosswise direction.

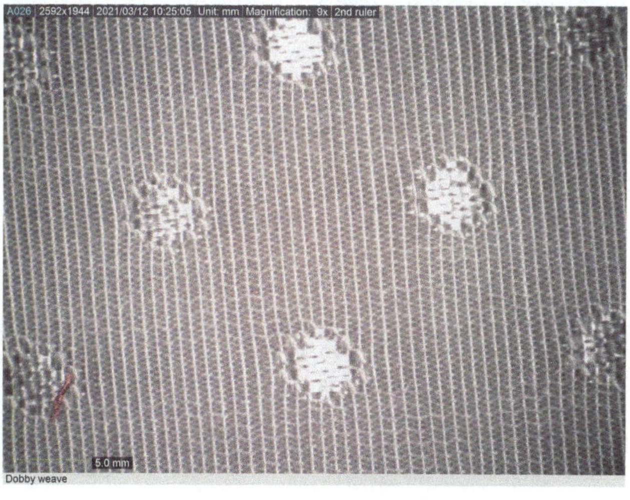

Figure 19.11 Technical face of dobby weave with a dot-pattern woven into the fabric.

to plain weaves. Thus, with minor variations in the yarn structures and the interlacing patterns, thousands of different weave structures can be generated. Although this is a daunting number, only a relatively few patterns are common: a plain weave common in bed sheeting, an oxford or pinpoint oxford weave in dress shirting, twills in trousers and denim jackets, and satins used in formal dresswear and in upholstery fabric.

Woven fabrics are generally dimensionally stable with little shrinkage, stretch, or distortion unless elastic yarns are used, e.g., made with spandex. If printed with a pattern, the pattern maintains its size and shape. Plain weaves often wrinkle easily but twills can be nearly wrinkle-free.

As discussed in the section on yarns, there are capillary channels within the yarns used to make woven fabrics. In addition to these intra-yarn capillaries, there are also inter-yarn capillaries. The capillary channels between the yarns are even larger than those within the yarns, thus liquids such as blood will move rapidly within these inter-yarn capillaries. However, for small liquid drops, such as from a single drip stain, once the blood has filled these inter-yarn spaces, it will wick into the intra-yarn capillaries and spread along the fibers while simultaneously draining blood from the inter-yarn spaces. This can lead to substantial distortions of the original bloodstain. With the thousands of variations possible in woven fabrics and the yarns from which they are made, it would seem to be an impossible task to learn anything from a bloodstain on a woven fabric. Fortunately, most woven fabrics have a similar underlying structure and are made from similar yarns. Thus, it is possible to understand how a stain evolved from impingement of a drop on the fabric based on the wicking properties of the yarn and the fabric construction. However, in many cases, it is not currently possible to reverse the process, going from the observed stain back to the original blood drop on the textile. Many different paths can lead to the same final pattern. Due to the importance of textiles in forensic investigations and their complex interactions with blood, bloodstain pattern analysis on textiles is an active area of research. Nevertheless, great progress in many areas has been made, as will be shown later in this chapter.

KNIT FABRICS

Knit fabrics are made by interlooping yarns. There are two major classes of knit fabrics: weft knits which are knitted one row at a time across the width (weft) of the fabric, and warp knits where the fabric is knitted lengthwise (warp) and the entire width of the fabric is knitted simultaneously. In general, knitting is faster than weaving and warp knitting is much faster than weft knitting. Most T-shirts, sweaters, and hand-knitted fabrics are weft knits, while cloth car seats and lace-like fabrics are warp knitted. Figure 19.12 shows a single jersey weft knit typical of a T-shirt, and Figure 19.13

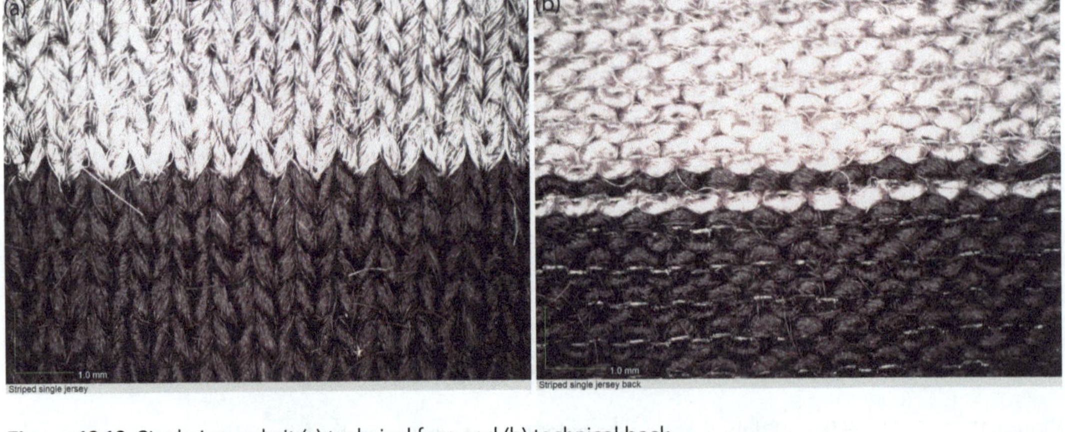

Figure 19.12 Single jersey knit (a) technical face and (b) technical back.

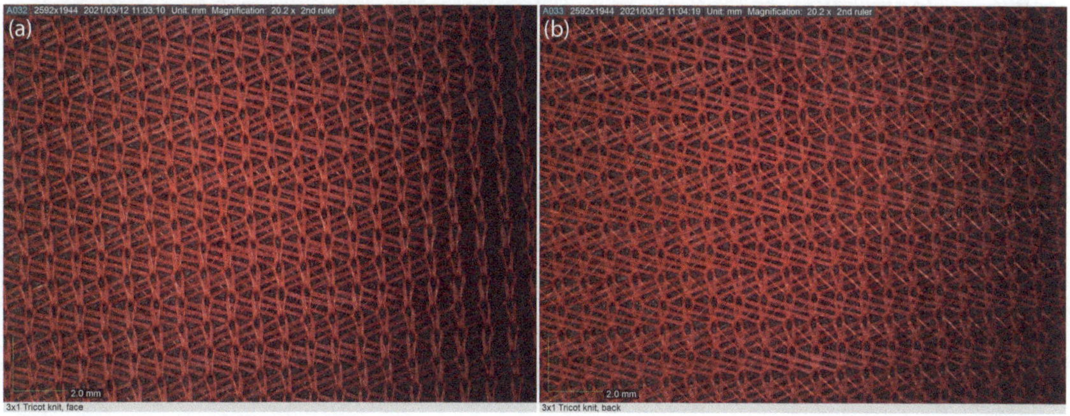

Figure 19.13 Tricot knit (a) technical face and (b) technical back.

shows a simple tricot warp knit, typical of cloth car seats and performance sportswear. As with weaving, there are many variations in knit fabrics. Weft knits are usually made with staple or spun yarns, while warp knits are usually made with filament yarns due to processing considerations.

The simplest knit is the "single jersey" knit, sometimes referred to as basic knit, plain knit, or, if hand-knitted, stockinette. To form a single jersey knit, a previously knitted loop of yarn is held, a length of yarn is fed into a needle which pulls this yarn through the previous loop. Thus, as the yarn moves across the fabric, it also moves up and down. Each row of loops is called a "course," while a column of loops is called a "wale." In a weave, every yarn lies only in the width direction or the length direction. In a weft knit, each yarn moves in both the width- and lengthwise directions. As seen in Figure 19.12, the face (or front) of the knit is different from the back. The face consists of "legs" forming a V-shape running primarily in the warp (vertical) direction. The back consists of "smiles and frowns" or "sinker loops" (the smiles) and "needle loops" (the frowns). A single yarn moves vertically on one leg, then forms the needle loop, and finally goes back down on the other leg before forming the sinker loop. For small quantities of liquid, the liquid moves within the yarns, thus moving in this same manner – up (or down) one leg, across through a needle (or sinker) loop, then back down, and finally into the sinker loop. Variations in the weft knit structure include "tuck" and "miss" stitches, which are used to control the fabric dimensions and stretch; rib knits, which use two sets of needles with the yarns knitting first on the fabric front and then on the back. Rib knits include the 1 × 1 ribs (typically found in T-shirt collars) and cardigans. Interlock weft knit fabrics are formed from two rib knit fabrics that are interknitted crossing through each other as one fabric passes front-to-back while the other passes back-to-front.

The simplest warp knit is a tricot fabric. Tricot knits are made at high speed as an entire course is knitted all at once and up to 4,000 courses can be knitted in 1 minute. A single course may be 215 in. wide with 8,000 needles and 16,000 yarns that are all being knitted simultaneously, i.e., several million loops may be knitted per minute. Each yarn forms a loop on the fabric face, then moves across the fabric 0–9 wales in the back and up one course before knitting another loop on the fabric face. The fabric shown in Figure 19.13 knits one loop, then moves across three wales in the back forming a "three needle underlap" before knitting another loop in the next course. The structure of warp knits is beyond the scope of this chapter; however, an analyst should be aware that they often occur in cloth car seats and sportswear due to their durability and low cost.

Knitwear tends to be much less dimensionally stable than weaves and may shrink or grow when laundered. Even when no elastic yarns are used, some knitwear can stretch many times their initial width or shrink several sizes if not laundered properly. This elastic behavior gives knits their excellent drape, shape fitting, and comfort properties. However, when analyzing bloodstains on knitwear, the analyst should be aware that a knit can look very different when hanging up or lying

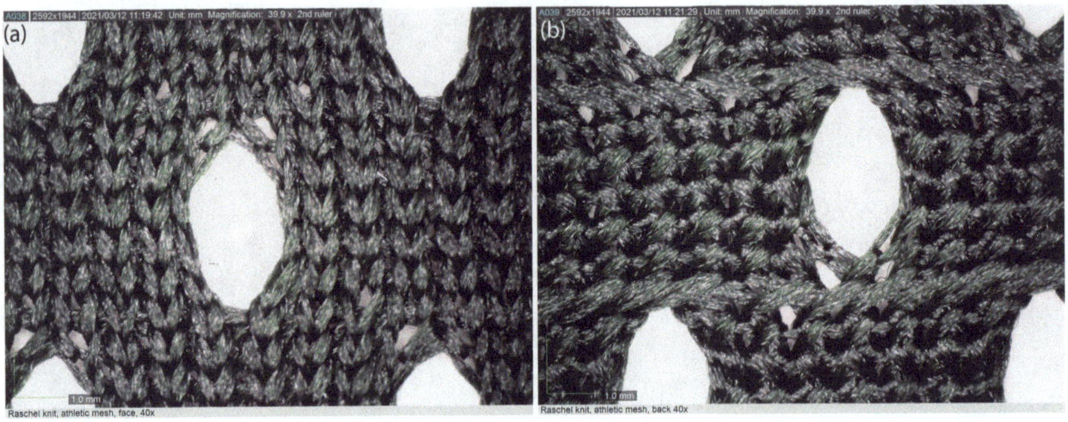

Figure 19.14 Openings knitted into a weft knit showing the face (a) and back (b) of the knit.

on the floor or a table versus when worn. This is especially true for stretch knits using spandex yarns where the same garment may be worn by people of vastly different sizes and shapes.

Another aspect of knits is that they contain many small holes wherever one loop passes through the loop of a previous course. This can be seen in Figure 19.12. In addition, many knit patterns also contain openings for comfort and design (Figure 19.14). When airborne blood lands on a knit surface, some or all of a blood drop may pass through these holes and stain whatever is behind the knit. The stain shape may be highly distorted by the presence of holes.

CARPET

Another type of textile often found at scenes is carpeting. Carpets may be woven or tufted (Figure 19.15), but most carpets in the United States are tufted. Tufted carpets are made by pushing a yarn through a base fabric to form a looped pile. The base fabric may be woven, nonwoven, or knit. If the looped pile yarn is cut, it is called a "tufted carpet"; if they are left uncut, it is called a looped or loop

Figure 19.15 Loop-pile carpet. If these loops were cut, it would be called a "tufted" carpet. Notice that the fiber and yarn sizes are much larger than in common apparel. (Compare scale bar and yarn sizes with those in Figure 19.10.)

pile carpet. The fibers or filaments in a carpet have a larger cross section than apparel grade fibers to prevent crushing when stepped on. Tufted carpets consist of the pile yarn forming the tufts or loops, the primary backing fabric, a binding layer made of adhesive and filler to keep the pile yarns in place, and a secondary backing, which is the material often seen on the back of a carpet. Carpet is frequently treated with an anti-stain finish (see finish below). Such carpets tend to repel water and blood, which may remain on the surface. If no finish is present, either because it was never applied or it was removed by cleaning, the carpet may rapidly absorb water or blood, which can penetrate deeply into the carpet. Outdoor carpets are often made from polypropylene and are naturally water repellent, but their structure may allow water or blood to drain through them.

COLORATION: DYEING AND PRINTING

Many textiles are colored or covered with patterns, although in their natural state they would be colorless, white, or off-white. Color is added to enhance a textile's appearance and may be imparted by dyeing, printing, or adding pigments before creating fibers. Color can be added to a textile at nearly any point in the manufacturing process. The addition of color can make it difficult to observe blood on a textile, especially when dark colors are used.

For manufactured fibers, pigments can be added to the polymer solution or the polymer melt prior to spinning the fiber. In fact, most synthetic fibers contain titanium dioxide (TiO_2) particles to reduce their shine or brightness. When colored pigments are added at this point, the process is called "dope dyeing" or "solution dyeing." In this case, the colored pigments are encapsulated by the fiber polymer and are durable to bleach or other chemicals. Fibers such as polyethylene or polypropylene can only be colored using this process. Another common use of dope dyeing is in carpets since the pigment colors are stable for many years.

Color may also be added by dyeing, where a colored dye is dissolved, usually in water, and applied to fibers, yarns, or fabrics. Different types of dyes are used for different types of fibers; their durability depends on the type of dye and the type of fiber to which it is applied. The dye solution is most frequently applied at elevated temperatures to speed the dyeing process. During the dyeing process, the dye diffuses into the fiber structure and becomes part of the fiber and is thus difficult to remove, although excess dye can be washed or rubbed off. Dyed fabrics usually have a uniform color; however, a fabric can be printed with dye solutions or specialized dyeing processes, such as tie-dyeing can be used to impart localized colors. Digital printing of textiles uses dye solutions that are sprayed onto the textile as single droplets and dye only the location at which the dye droplet lands on the fabric.

The third major process for coloring a fabric is printing with a pigment and binder in the form of a print paste, or ink. The print paste is applied to fabric in various patterns and the printed fabric is "cured", i.e., the fabric is exposed to heat which causes the binder to bind to the fabric while also encapsulating the pigment. The cured binder may be stiff and after multiple washings, the binder may crack or even delaminate from the fabric. The surface properties of the binders are quite different than the fiber properties and may alter the formation of bloodstains. The binders may even make the printed region impervious to blood or other liquids.

The most common coloration methods are through dyeing or printing the fabric. However, individual yarns can be dyed before converting to fabrics, as shown in Figures 19.8, 19.12, 19.15, and 19.16, such that patterns can be woven or knitted into the fabric. In addition, dyeing can be performed at the fiber stage, as in Figure 19.9. This allows for blending fibers of different colors such that each yarn may contain multiple colors. When a piece of fabric is dyed, the front and back have the same color. By using different types of yarn or different amounts of yarn, piece dyeing can also introduce patterns (Figure 19.17) because different fiber types absorb dye differently, but the front and back will have the same color(s). On the other hand, when a fabric is printed, great detail can be achieved, but the back is usually left uncolored or colored non-uniformly (Figure 19.18).

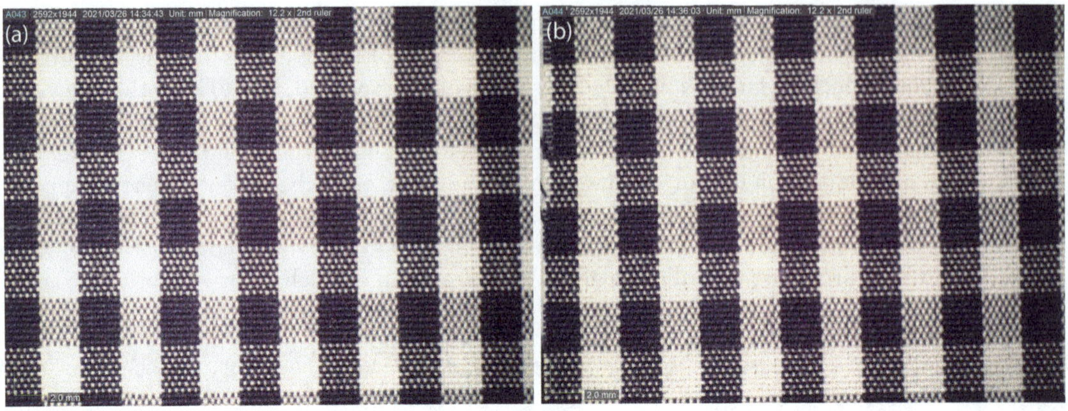

Figure 19.16 Yarn dyed then woven: front (a) and back (bs).

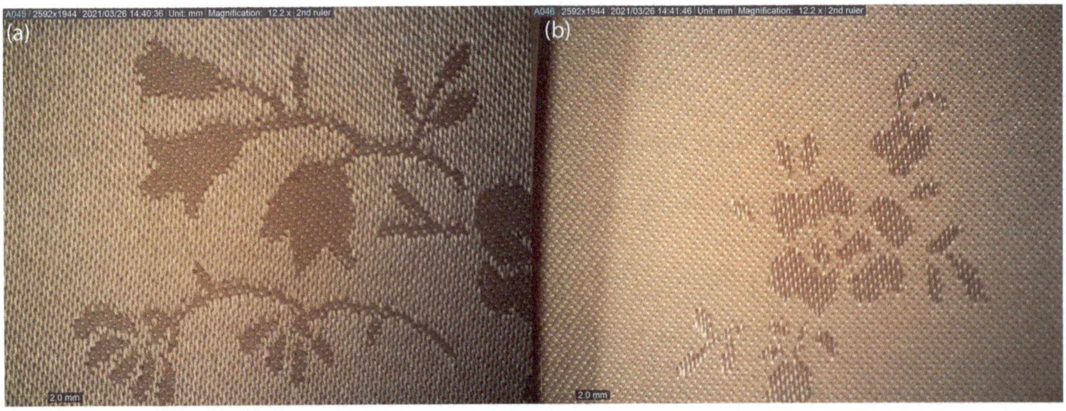

Figure 19.17 Piece dyed fabric: front (a) and back (b).

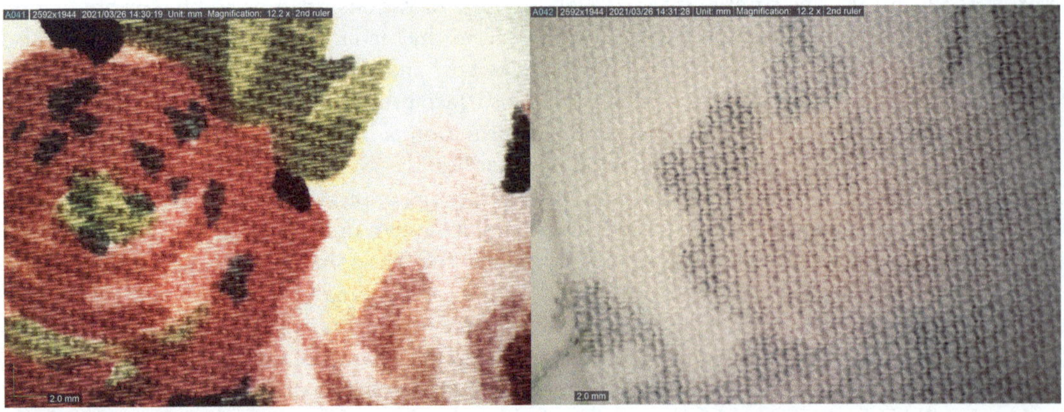

Figure 19.18 Printed fabric: front (a) and back (bs).

FINISHES AND FINISHING

Finishings are various processes that are applied to textiles near the end of their production to impart desired properties. A finish is defined as follows:

> Finish: 1. A substance or mixture of substances added to textile materials to impart desired properties. 2. A process, physical or chemical, performed on textile materials to produce a desired effect. 3. A property, such as smoothness, drape, luster, water repellency, flame retardancy, or crease resistance that is produced by 1 and/or 2 above. 4. The state of a textile materials as it leaves a process.[1]

And Finishing is defined as follows:

> Finishing: All the processes through which a fabric is passed after bleaching, dyeing, or printing in preparation for the market or use. Finishing includes such operations as heat-setting, napping, embossing, pressing, calendaring, and the application of chemicals that change the character of the fabric. The term finishing is also sometimes used to refer collectively to all processing operations above, including bleaching, dyeing, printing, etc.[1]

There are hundreds of finishing processes and finishes. Their purpose is to alter the properties, which means that they may also alter bloodstains. Napping is used to make a fuzzy fabric from a smooth one, while shearing is used to make a fuzzy fabric smooth. Both would be expected to change the formation of bloodstains. A softening finish can absorb the impact energy of blood landing on a fabric, thus reducing secondary spatter, while a fabric stiffening finish can increase secondary spatter. Often, a softening finish lubricates the fibers by applying an oil; this can alter the wettability of the fibers. Likewise, water-repellent and stain-resistant finishes may prevent blood from staining a fabric, while an enhanced wicking finish can change a water repellent fabric to one that will strongly absorb and wick liquids, such as blood. Sportswear is often made from polyester, a naturally water-repellent fiber, that is finished with an enhanced wicking finish creating a fabric that absorbs and wicks water and blood easily. On the flip side, cotton, a naturally water-absorbing fabric, can be finished to strongly repel water. Many of the properties of textiles can be changed, and even made to behave oppositely to our expectations, by finishing.

Unfortunately, hangtags on apparel or other fabrics rarely mention finishes or finishing apart from wrinkle resistance and sometimes stain resistance. In addition, finishes are rarely visible even under high magnification microscopy and can be difficult to analyze for in a non-destructive manner. In addition, new finishes are continually being developed to improve some function of the textile. The result is that very little is known about how finishes affect bloodstains on textiles even though they are likely to have a large impact on the stains observed.

MECHANICS

Another aspect of textiles is that they are often highly deformable. When an airborne blood drop lands on a plain weave pillowcase that is on a pillow, the impact energy can be absorbed and little to no secondary spatter may occur. On the other hand, the same pillowcase lying flat on a hard table or floor can cause a large amount of secondary spatter. The fibers in a napped fabric or the pile yarns in carpet can deform, thus absorbing the impact energy and reducing secondary spatter. Although textile mechanics has been the subject of intense research for over 100 years, very little is known about how this affects bloodstains. Nevertheless, the environment in which a textile is found should be noted as it may provide clues to how the bloodstain formed.

SUMMARY

Although bloodstained textiles are some of the most common pieces of evidence collected or documented at crime scenes, the way in which blood interacts with different textiles to form bloodstains and bloodstain patterns on those textiles is still unresearched. Without an understanding of this interaction and how this influences resultant bloodstain shapes on textiles, there is potential for wrongly classifying bloodstains deposited on textiles. This is partly due to the wide variety of fibers, yarns, textile structures, textile finishes, and complex mechanical interactions of textiles with blood. However, in favorable cases, considerable insight into the bloodletting event can be gleaned from stained textiles, as discussed in Chapter 20.

Supplemental Reading

Kadolph, Sara J. *Textiles*, 11th edition, Prentice Hall, Upper Saddle River, NJ, 2010.
Fibers and yarn: http://www.madehow.com/Volume-3/Yarn.htmlFabric
Kissa, Erik. Wetting and wicking. *Textile Research Journal*, 1996, 66, p. 660–668.
ASTM 123-19, Standard Terminology Relating to Textiles. West Conshohocken, PA, 2019.

Glossary

For a more complete list of terms, the reader should refer to ASTM 123-19, Standard Terminology Relating to Textiles. West Conshohocken, PA, 2019. The terms below are simplified or paraphrased from *Dictionary of Fiber & Textile Technology*. 1990, Hoechst Celanese Corporation, Charlotte, NC.

Absorption: Taking a liquid or gas *into* a material's *interior.*

Adsorption: Taking a liquid or gas *onto* a material's *surface.*

Basket weave: A variation of a plain weave in which two or more yarns are woven as if they were a single yarn. In a full basket weave, this substitution occurs in both the warp and weft directions, e.g., monk's cloth. In a half-basket, the substitution occurs in only one direction, e.g., oxford or pinpoint oxford weave.

Batt: A thick nonwoven fabric.

Binder: (1) A resin or glue-like material used to attach pigment particles to the surface of a textile, e.g., in printing. (2) A resin or glue-like material used to hold fibers together, e.g., in nonwovens. (3) A fabric with adhesive properties to hold multiple layers of fabric together.

Capillary: A channel or tube capable of transporting liquid.

Capillarity: The ability to or the action of moving a liquid through a tube, along a channel or between two surfaces under the forces of surface tension.

Carpet: A textile material often used as a floor covering made by (1) weaving, e.g., an oriental carpet, or (2) by pushing loops of yarn through a backing material to form pile loops of this yarn on the surface. These loops can be cut to form tufts.

Cord: A long, relatively thin textile structure made by twisting two or more yarns together where each of these yarns consist of two or more yarns.

Course: A row of loops in the weft direction of a knit fabric.

Dye: A colored substance that dissolves in a suitable solvent, usually water, to impart color to a textile material.

Dyeing: The process of coloring a textile material by the application of dyes.

End: A single warp yarn in weaving.

Fabric: A two-dimensional textile material. A fabric can be used as is, e.g., a bedsheet, or converted into other materials, such as apparel, e.g., by cutting and sewing.

Fiber: A solid material whose length is much larger than other dimensions, typically more than 100× larger. Fibers may be natural, such as cotton, wool, or silk, or manufactured, such as rayon, nylon, and polyester fibers.

Filament: A continuous fiber of extreme length, typically many meters to many kilometers in length.

Filling yarn: Also called a "weft yarn" or a "pick." In weaving, a yarn that interlaces with ends and perpendicular to the fabric length. Filling yarns "fill in" the weave.

Finish(es): Any treatment to a textile after dyeing or printing. Finishes may be chemical treatments, also known as functional finishes, such as enhanced wicking treatments or stain resistance; they may be thermal treatments, e.g., heat setting or embossing; or they may be mechanical treatments such as brushing or napping. In addition, more than one finish may be applied to the same fabric.

Finishing: The process(es) of applying a finish or performing the finish treatment.

Float: (in weaving) The section of yarn on a fabric surface between interlacing points. The yarn "floats" on the surface. Long floats are prone to snagging.

Hydrophilic: "Water loving." A material that spontaneously wets with water.

Hydrophobic: "Water hating." A material that resists wetting with water.

Interlace: Passing a yarn above, then below other yarns at approximately 90° to form a fabric.

Interloop: Passing a loop of yarn through an existing loop to form a fabric.

Knit: A fabric formed by interlooping yarns.

Manufactured fibers: Fibers formed by industrial processes. They may be regenerated from natural materials or they may be made from synthetic materials.

Monofilament: A yarn consisting of a single filament.

Napping: A finishing process where fiber ends are pulled out of a fabric by passing small wires across the fabric surface. This results in a soft, fuzzy fabric surface.

Natural fibers: Fibers created by nature, e.g. cotton, linen, wool, cashmere, silk, etc.

Nonwoven: A fabric made directly from fibers and bound together by heat, resin, or entangling.

Oleophilic: "Oil loving." A material that spontaneously wets with oil.

Oleophobic: "Oil hating." A material that resists wetting with oil.

Pick: A filling or weft yarn in weaves.

Pigment: A small, solid, colored particle (1) used to add color to a liquid polymer prior to forming a fiber or (2) added to a print paste to print onto textiles or other media.

Pile: Fibers or yarns that rise perpendicular to the plane of a fabric.

Plain weave: The simplest weave structure where a single filling yarn passes over a single end (yarn), then passes under a single end, and continuing to alternate above and below the adjacent yarns. The next filling yarn follows the same pattern, but is offset by one end, i.e., passing under then over subsequent ends.

Printing: Application of color to specific locations on a fabric or other substrate.

Regain: The weight of water molecules contained *within* the *fibers* of a textile under specific conditions of relative humidity and temperature divided by the perfectly dry weight of these fibers: $\left(W_{RH,T} - W_{RH=0,T}\right) / W_{RH=0,T}$

Repellent: The ability of a fabric to *resist wetting* by the selected liquid, usually water.

Resistant: The ability of a fabric to resist wetting *and penetration* by the selected liquid, usually water.

Satin: A simple weave with long floats and few interlacing points.

Selvedge/selvage: The finished or unfinished edge of a woven fabric that runs parallel to the warp.

Spin/spinning: (1) The conversion of a liquified polymer into filaments by passing the liquified polymer through thin capillaries and then solidifying the filaments by cooling (melt spinning), evaporation of solvent (dry spinning), or coagulation in a liquid bath (wet spinning). (2) The conversion of staple fibers into yarn by first paralyzing the fibers and then twisting the resultant material to bind the fibers together by friction. There are three major staple fiber spinning processes: ring spinning, rotor spinning, and air-jet spinning. They generate yarns with different internal structures.

Spun yarn: Yarn made from staple fibers.

Standard moisture regain: Moisture regain measured under standard conditions. For apparel, standard conditions are defined as 65 ± 2% RH (relative humidity) and 21 ± 1°C, while for industrial applications, the standard conditions are 55 ± 2% RH (relative humidity) and 24 ± 1°C.

Staple: Discontinuous fibers with typical lengths of 2–20 cm. They may be from natural fibers, e.g., cotton, wool, etc., or they may be made from filament yarn cut to specified lengths, often to simulate cotton (length ~3–4 cm) or wool (8–20 cm)

Textile materials: Fibers, filaments, yarns, and materials made from fibers, filaments, or yarns that retain the strength and flexibility of the original fibers or filaments. Examples include ropes, fabrics, carpets, nonwovens, apparel, etc.

Texturizing: Processing a filament yarn to introduce bulk into the yarn by creating crimps or otherwise creating disorder in the yarn.

Tuft: (in carpet) (cut) Loops of pile yarn that forms the face of a carpet.

Twill: A simple weave in which warp (or weft) yarns float over two or more weft (or warp) between interlacings. The pattern shifts by one yarn as the fabric progresses.

Twist: (S-, Z-) Yarn, especially spun yarn, is rotated in the clockwise (S-twist) or counterclockwise (Z-twist) direction to bind the fibers through yarn compression and friction.

Wale: A column of loops in the lengthwise direction, i.e., warp direction, of a knit fabric.

Warp: The length direction of a fabric, especially for a woven fabric, but also used for knits.

Weave: n. A fabric formed by the interlacing of yarns at right angles. v. The process of making woven fabric.

Weft: The crosswise direction of a fabric, especially for a woven fabric, but also used for knits.

Wet: To replace a vapor–solid interface with a liquid–solid interface. Usually the vapor is air and the liquid is water.

Wicking: Moving a liquid–solid interface along a surface through capillary forces.

Yarn: A long, thin assembly of fibers, or of one or more filaments suitable for knitting or weaving.

Notes

1. *Dictionary of Fiber & Textile Technology*, 1990, Charlotte, NC: Hoechst Celanese Corporation, p. 59.
2. Li, X., J. Li, and S. Michielsen, Effect of yarn structure on wicking and its impact on bloodstain pattern analysis (BPA) on woven cotton fabrics. *Forensic Science International*, 2017, 276: p. 41–50.

CHAPTER 20

BLOODSTAIN PATTERN ANALYSIS ON TEXTILES

Edmund Silenieks

The interpretation of bloodstains and bloodstain patterns on textiles is arguably the most difficult aspect of bloodstain pattern analysis. The variable absorbency, texture, and fiber composition of different textiles can have a significant influence on the resultant bloodstain shape, irrespective of whether the deposition was caused by a spatter, transfer, or other mechanism. The shape and appearance of a bloodstain deposited on a textile surface can be dramatically different when compared to a bloodstain deposited on a static, non-porous surface and created by the same mechanism.

The resultant shape of bloodstains deposited on static, non-porous surfaces has been well documented, in particular spatter impacting at varying angles. Piotrowski, Balthazard, and MacDonell all documented the consistent and repeatable circular and elliptical stain shapes associated with known blood droplet trajectories, which is the basis for impact angle and area of origin calculations.[1,2,3] Using high-speed photography, Pizzola recorded and documented blood droplets impacting static, non-porous surfaces at different known angles and associated resultant bloodstain shape.[4] Pizzola also observed the repeatable dynamics associated with the collapse of a blood droplet impacting a static, non-porous surface. Bevel and Gardner assigned the four terms contact/collapse, displacement, dispersion, and retraction to describe the dynamics of a blood droplet impacting a smooth, hard surface.[5]

While past research has underpinned bloodstain interpretation on smooth, non-porous, and semi-porous static surfaces, bloodstain formation on textiles clearly undergoes a different dynamic compared to deposition on smooth, static non-porous surfaces and currently remains under-researched. Using high-speed video, Michielsen et al. observed that when a blood droplet impacts a fabric surface, it undergoes inertial spreading (with subsequent breakup of the droplet), retraction, and then it wicks into the fabric.[6] Williams et al. later observed a similar dynamic and proposed that drip bloodstains deposited on fabric surfaces undergo three stages; (1) inertial spread, (2) retraction (with splashing at the periphery), followed by (3) wicking into the fabric, with wicking being the most significant stage that affected resultant bloodstain shape.[7] This research has shown that while they share some commonalities, the dynamics of bloodstain formation on porous textiles is notably different to the dynamics of bloodstain formation on non-porous surfaces.

While textiles are commonly encountered at crime scenes, the most common bloodstained textiles analyzed are clothing items. Although this chapter will focus on the interpretation of bloodstains deposited on clothing, the principles discussed apply to all textiles. The intention is to give the reader a basic understanding of textiles, how they interact with blood to affect the resultant bloodstain shape, and an understanding of the complexities involved when interpreting bloodstains on textiles.

DOI: 10.4324/9781003163695-20

INTERACTION OF BLOOD WITH TEXTILES

When blood or another liquid comes into contact with a textile, a series of physical interactions occur. These interactions allow the blood to coat the textile surface (wetting), penetrate the textile (capillary action), and migrate through the textile (wicking) to ultimately form a stain. These interactions will occur for bloodstains produced by both spatter and non-spatter mechanisms.

The wettability of a textile is dependent on the chemical properties of its fibers, the type of construction used, the degree of surface texture, and the use of any surface treatments. Essentially, wetting is the physical interaction that occurs when a liquid first comes into contact with a textile and this interaction leads directly to the wicking phase. Wicking is the movement of the bulk of the liquid *through* the textile and is driven by capillarity action. Capillarity action describes the process where blood flows along or migrates through the minute spaces between individual fibers and the small spaces between yarns. It is prominent at, but not restricted to, the expanding perimeter of a stain as it is forming.

Wetting

When liquid blood or another liquid comes into contact with a textile, the first interaction between the blood and the textile is wetting. Wetting is the process where the textile–vapor interface (where the textile surface and air interact) is displaced by a textile–liquid interface.[8] There are four wetting mechanisms that can describe blood's interaction with a textile: immersion, adhesion, spreading, and capillary penetration.[9] These mechanisms can occur individually or simultaneously dependent on the deposition mechanism and the textile characteristics.

Immersion occurs when a textile is saturated by a volume of blood large enough to completely submerge part of the, or the entire, textile. One surface of the textile initially contacts a significant volume of blood and as the contact increases, the textile becomes saturated with blood. Adhesion defines the attraction between two dissimilar surfaces that are in contact with each other. Adhesion is dependent on the physical and chemical properties of each contacting surface and these properties will influence how these surfaces will interact. An example of this is when a blood droplet impacts a non-porous target surface; the blood will not penetrate and depending on the target surface properties and the adhesion between the two surfaces, the blood potentially runs off. A blood droplet that impacts a porous textile, such as a cotton T-shirt, will penetrate and share a stronger adhesion to form a distinct bloodstain. The flow of blood over a textile surface is regarded as a spreading mechanism. Spreading is dependent on blood volume and generally occurs with larger volumes of blood. It describes the increase of the blood's contact with the surface as it moves across a textile surface.[10]

Capillary Penetration

Capillary penetration is the final wetting mechanism that encompasses the dispersion of the blood through the yarns and fibers within the body of the textile. This complex mechanism describes the movement of the liquid blood into and along the small capillary spaces between the fibers and yarns, wetting both the fibers and the yarns which allows the blood to then wick through the textile.[11] The narrow spaces within the construction of a textile, that is, between the fibers and between yarns, act as ductwork that facilitate the capillary action.[12]

Natural textiles, such as those made from cotton, are comprised of short staple fibers with a defined length. Natural staple fibers generally have some degree of absorbency and as blood wicks through a natural textile, the blood will also penetrate or *absorb* into the staple fiber itself. This inhibits the capillary penetration and hence the wicking of the blood through a natural textile.[13]

Synthetic textiles, such as polyester, are generally comprised of long filament fibers which, when first manufactured, are of indefinite length. When used alone in textile construction, filament fibers are usually much longer than natural fibers, but often they are cut to the same length as cotton fibers and blended with cotton to produced yarn used in, for example, cotton/polyester shirts. The length used is determined by the textile manufacturer's requirements. Synthetic fibers have a very low degree of absorbency and as blood wicks through a synthetic textile, the blood will coat or adhere to the surface of the fibers rather than penetrate them. The coating of fibers is known as *adsorption* and as blood has not been absorbed into the fiber, more remains in the ductwork and available to wick through the textile. Adsorption promotes the capillary penetration and hence the wicking of blood through a synthetic textile and can also occur in textiles made with natural staple fibers, particularly those that have been treated with surfactants, such as water repellents. Absorption and adsorption may occur simultaneously, particularly in blended textiles comprised of both synthetic and natural fibers which can ultimately affect the resultant stain shape.

Wicking

Wicking occurs immediately after wetting and describes the flow of the blood through the textile substrate by capillary action and can occur in both the longitudinal and transverse planes of a textile. Longitudinal wicking is the flow or spread of blood through the length and across the width of a textile and transverse wicking is the flow or spread of blood through the thickness of the textile.[14] Blood will wick between yarns, between fibers within the yarns, and will fill the pore spaces between the yarns as it migrates through the textile. The amount of wicking that occurs is determined by the blood volume available and the textile properties. These properties typically include how the textile was constructed (knitted or woven), yarns characteristics (e.g., thickness and how they were spun), the type of fiber used to make the yarns (natural, synthetic, or blended), and the absorbency of the fibers, and these properties ultimately determine the size and shape of the resultant bloodstain.

BLOODSTAIN FORMATION ON TEXTILES

The Influence of Textile Construction on Wicking

Textiles, in particular clothing, are commonly constructed using either a woven or a knitted process and the different constructions have an influence on how blood wicks through a textile. Blood, like any liquid, will flow in the path of least resistance; so the less complicated the yarn or textile structure is, the easier it is for the blood to wick through that yarn or textile. While the construction clearly influences the wicking process, it is the combination of construction and the absorbency of the fibers that ultimately determines the amount of wicking. Blood wicking through a fabric constructed of adsorbent (i.e., non-absorbent) synthetic fibers will generally migrate further compared to those constructed of absorbent, natural fibers. This is particularly so for simple woven fabrics compared to knitted fabrics. As the blood will only coat the surface of synthetic fibers rather than penetrate the fibers, more blood will remain in the fiber/yarn ductwork and hence is available to wick along the yarn. This results in a larger bloodstain compared to a similar bloodstain on a fabric made from natural fibers. The adsorption properties of synthetics enable the blood to migrate preferentially between the filament fibers rather than across them, wicking the blood both through and along the synthetic yarns resulting in an abnormal stain shape.[15]

As discussed in the previous chapter, woven fabrics are constructed from at least two yarns that are interlaced at right angles to each other (Figure 20.1). The woven yarns lay next to each other in essentially long straight lines along the length (warp) and across the width (weft) of a fabric, usually with very little gap or pore space between the yarns. These factors generally

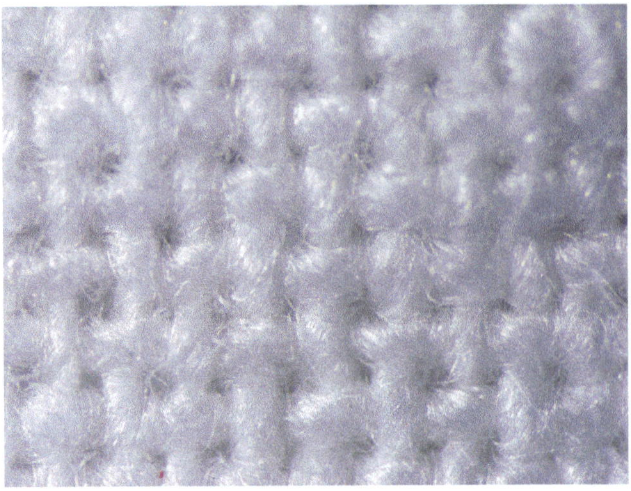

Figure 20.1 Plain woven fabric using yarns comprised of staple cotton fibers.

promote the preferential wicking of blood along the long straight ductwork created by woven yarns and there is minimal resistance to impede the migration of blood. This is particularly true for simple woven fabrics and in particular those constructed of long, synthetic filament fibers.

Knitted fabrics are constructed by the inter-looping of a single yarn or multiple yarns. This results in a series of loops where the yarn is constantly changing direction and loops back upon itself (Figure 20.2). The semicircular assembly produced by a knitted construction creates pore spaces within and between the yarn loops. The pore size will be dependent on the type of knit and the thickness of the yarns used. As blood spreads and wicks through a knitted garment, it will progressively fill the pore spaces and wick along the curved loops of yarn. This more complex structure provides more resistance and generally impedes the migration and hence the wicking of blood through a fabric.

Figure 20.2 Plain or jersey-knitted fabric.

The Influence of Texture on Bloodstain Formation

The texture of textiles is a design- or fashion-based feature and is influenced by the size, shape, and arrangement of the fibers and yarns used in its construction. Texture in a sense defines the build and surface characteristics of a textile; the surface roughness and thickness of a fabric is due to the texture of the yarns used to construct it. The surface texture of textiles can vary immensely, for example, from a relatively smooth surface on a pair of polyester business trousers to a coarse surface texture on a thick, woolen cable-knitted sweater. Therefore, it seems logical to conclude that blood deposited by the same mechanism on either of these two surfaces would result in stains that have different appearances. The major factor that affects the disruption of a blood droplet impacting a textile surface is its texture. Slemko concluded that the texture (and absorbance) of a fabric contributed to the distorted appearance of a bloodstain on fabrics, and de Castro et al. surmised that fabric texture effected the dynamics of an impacting blood droplet, causing the droplet to break apart.[16,17]

The construction of the fabric, that is, whether it is woven or knitted, obviously influences the roughness or surface texture of a fabric. Similar to rough non-porous surfaces, the rougher the textile surface, the more an impacting blood droplet will be disrupted. Surface roughness is not only due to fabric construction but is also influenced by the type of fiber used and how those fibers are arranged within the yarn. As discussed in the previous section, the shape and surface features of different fibers can vary enormously, from the twisted ribbon shape of a natural cotton fiber to the straight, smooth cylindrical structure of some synthetic fibers. When a yarn is constructed, textile manufacturers twist together a fiber bundle and the amount of twist used can vary from yarn to yarn. The type of fibers used and the way in which a yarn is spun contribute to fabric texture and adds yet another variable that can alter the wicking properties of a fabric.[18]

Generally, heavily twisting a yarn will result in greater texture as the yarn can buckle under the tension of a heavy twist, resulting in distortion along the length of a yarn. Yarns that are heavily twisted are no longer straight and will have a reduced space between the fibers, which will impede the migration of blood through the yarn. When woven together, heavily twisted yarns create a textured surface and develop spaces or pores between the yarns (Figure 20.3). The pores will hold a defined volume of blood which will be dependent on the size of the pore. The more pores available or the larger the pore, the more blood will be retained which will restrict the migration of blood, influencing the resultant stain size and its shape.

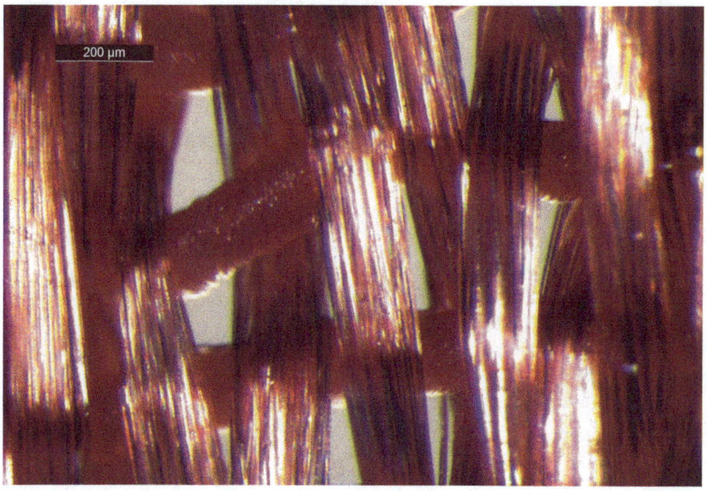

Figure 20.3 A woven polyester fabric constructed using heavily twisted weft yarns and low twist warp yarns, creating texture and pore spaces between yarns.

The thickness of yarns used in the construction of a fabric will influence the migration of blood through that fabric. The more fibers that are used or the thicker the fibers used, the thicker the yarn and hence a textile with an increased amount of surface texture will be produced. A blood droplet deposited on thinner fabric will wick further and produce a larger stain, compared to a heavy, thicker fabric. The thicker yarns will retain more blood and hence reduce the distance the blood will flow through the yarn and fabric.

Yarns comprised of natural staple fibers will have a coarse, "fuzzy" surface appearance. This is because the ends of the staple fibers protrude from the surface of the yarn, which results in a textile surface also having a fuzzy appearance (Figure 20.1). This can be easily observed by simply looking horizontally across the surface of a cotton T-shirt. The staple fiber ends can be seen extending upward from the T-shirt surface. As has been discussed, when blood is deposited on fabrics constructed of natural fibers, the absorbent properties of the fiber will inhibit blood wicking through the yarn, but the fuzzy surface created by the extended staple fiber ends also provides surface resistance to spreading blood. The surface tension and adhesive properties of blood combine to inhibit the spread of blood across the coarse, fuzzy surface of a natural textile. The absorption properties and consequent wicking inhibition of blood through fabrics comprised of natural fibers generally result in a bloodstain shape that closely correlates to the shape expected from the applied deposition mechanism.[19]

Consider denim as an example. It is constructed of tightly twisted cotton yarns which are woven together using a twill construction. The yarns used are thicker than for most other fabrics and are used to create a durable, hard-wearing garment. The thicker yarns, the tightness of the twist in the yarns, and the absorbent nature of the staple cotton fibers all provide resistance to blood flow resulting in a bloodstain that can usually be correlated to the deposition mechanism (Figure 20.4).

In contrast, fabrics made from synthetic filament fibers often have relatively smooth surfaces, with texture dependent on how the yarns and fabric have been constructed. As discussed earlier, when blood is deposited on a synthetic fabric, the migrating blood adsorbs rather than absorbs into synthetic fibers. The adsorption promotes blood to preferentially wick along synthetic yarns and the resultant stain shape generally will not correlate to the stain shape expected from the applied deposition mechanism.

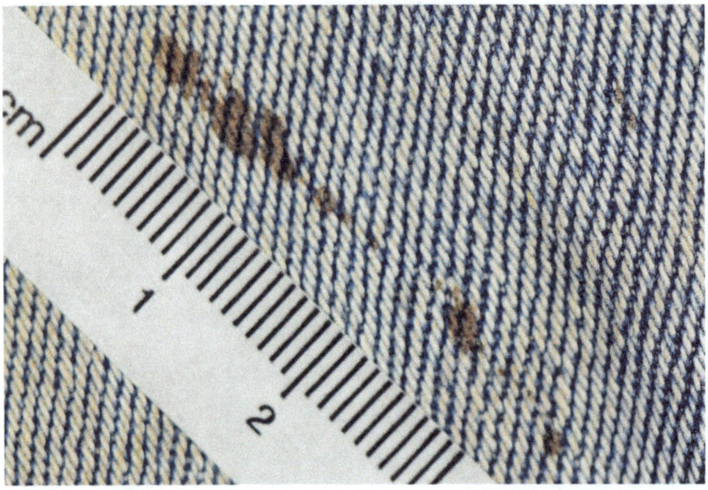

Figure 20.4 An elliptical spatter stain deposited on denim jeans. Although disrupted by the fabric surface texture, the stain is still recognizable as spatter.

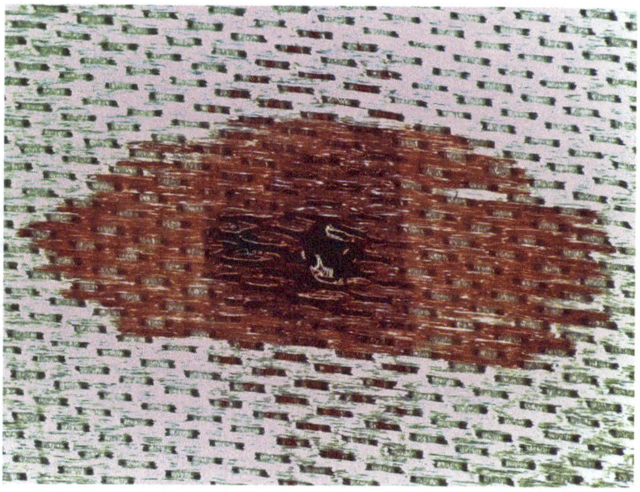

Figure 20.5 A drip stain deposited on a shiny, polyester satin weave. The blood has preferentially wicked along the yarns to form a bizarre shape.

Consider polyester satin woven fabric as an example, which is commonly used for pajamas, blouses, and evening gowns. Satin is a complex twill weave usually constructed using low twist synthetic yarns, with four weft yarns being covered by a single warp yarn, resulting in short "floats" of unrestricted yarn on the fabric surface. This pattern is repeated to construct the fabric and the floats contribute to the shininess of a satin fabric (Figure 20.5). The thin polyester yarns, the low degree of twist in the yarns, the reduced amount of interlacing, the unrestricted floats of yarn, and the adsorbent nature of the filament polyester fibers all combine to provide minimal resistance to blood flow, resulting in a bloodstain that cannot be correlated to its deposition mechanism (Figure 20.5). The wicking properties and direction of blood migration through blended fabrics may differ yet again and will be dependent on the type and percentage of fibers used, presenting an added challenge in the interpretation of bloodstains on fabrics.[20]

Interpreting Spatter Bloodstains on Textiles

The successful analysis and subsequent classification of spatter deposited on textiles is entirely dependent on the type of textile the spatter has been deposited on. The enormous variability in the type of textiles used by the fashion industry and the different ways in which clothing is constructed makes the analysis of spatter on textiles arguably the most complex aspect of bloodstain pattern analysis. When spatter is deposited on a static, smooth non-porous surface, it is classified based on the physical characteristics of the stain. The shape of spatter stains can vary from circular to elliptical, they will have a defined, uniform perimeter, and there may be spines and/or satellite spatter present. The preponderant stain size is dependent on the mechanism, the degree of force, and the target surface characteristics, and the spatter stains may have an approximate size range of perhaps 2–8 mm. Some of those characteristics used to classify spatter deposited on a flat, static surface can also be used to determine directionality and the angle of impact of a spatter stain, but when deposited on non-porous textiles, particularly worn clothing, the assessment of spatter directionality is unreliable. This is discussed further in the section below regarding the two- and three-dimensional analyses of clothing.

When deposited on a textile, the physical characteristics of spatter will be dramatically different compared to those deposited on non-porous surfaces. The appearance of the resultant stain is influenced by several factors, including the size and velocity of the blood droplet, the construction of the textile, the fiber composition of the textile, and the wetting and wicking properties of the textile. When a blood droplet impacts a textile at an angle approximately perpendicular to the textile surface, the inertial energy aids the droplet's ability to penetrate the textile surface to not only thoroughly wet the upper exposed surface of the yarns but also penetrate the lower surfaces protected within the valleys between yarns. Penetration of the droplet into the textile is a key feature when identifying spatter. Chang and Michielsen demonstrated that the degree of droplet collapse and penetration can be dependent on how taut the textile surface is and whether there is an underlaying surface present.[21] These factors will affect the wetting and subsequent wicking of the droplet through the textile.

When an airborne droplet impacts a textile surface, tiny satellite spatter may break away and be deposited close to the perimeter of the parent droplet. The production of satellite spatter is dependent on several different factors, which may include droplet velocity, tautness of the fabric, and the roughness of the surface. As the contact angle of a droplet increases, the roughness of the surface texture can increase droplet breakup and affect its penetration into the textile, affecting the wetting ability of the droplet, any satellite spatter production, and their subsequent wicking into the fabric. The presence of satellite spatter is a key feature that can be used to classify spatter stains deposited on textiles.

The construction of the textile, that is, the type of knit or weave used, and the thickness of yarns used will influence the wicking ability and the resultant shape of spatter. As discussed earlier, the wicking ability of a fabric is influenced by the type of fiber used, the absorbency of the fibers, and how those fibers have been spun to create a yarn. As a droplet wicks through a textile, the perimeter features commonly associated with spatter deposited on non-porous surfaces are often absorbed by the wicking blood. Yarns within a textile are not necessarily uniform, and a spreading droplet will wick along each yarn at a different rate, and the resultant shape of a spatter stain is dependent on each yarn. The variability of yarn wicking properties within a fabric and the position of yarns within the fabric construction influence the appearance of the perimeter which ultimately defines the shape of the stain. Hence, spatter stains deposited on a textile are seldom a true circular or elliptical shape, but rather they may form a vaguely circular shape (Figure 20.6). Dependent on the type of fabric, other spatter stains may form a geometric shape as the wicking blood flows along the yarns at different rates, with the degree of stain distortion dependent on the textile yarns and fibers (Figures 20.7 and 20.8).

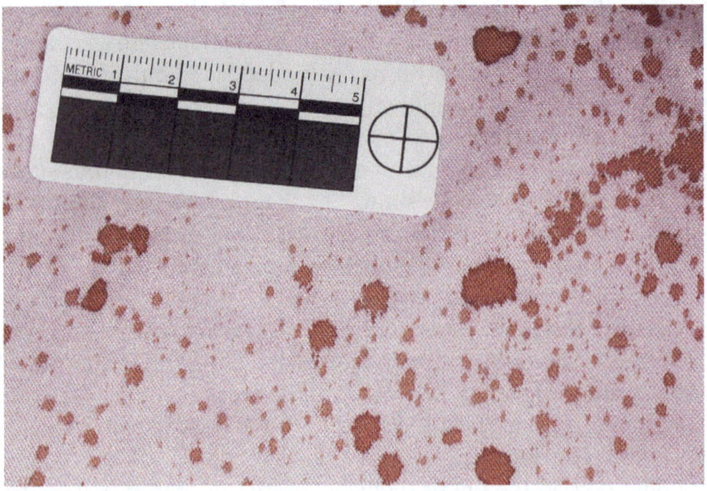

Figure 20.6 Spatter stains deposited on plain woven cotton fabric. The stains are broadly circular in shape and have fully penetrated the fabric.

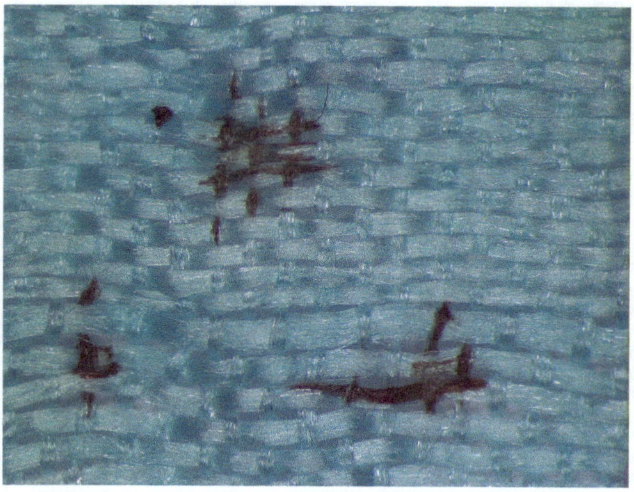

Figure 20.7 All bloodstains in the image are spatter, deposited on a loosely woven, polyester fabric. The different wicking properties of the thin and thicker yarns have distorted the resultant shape.

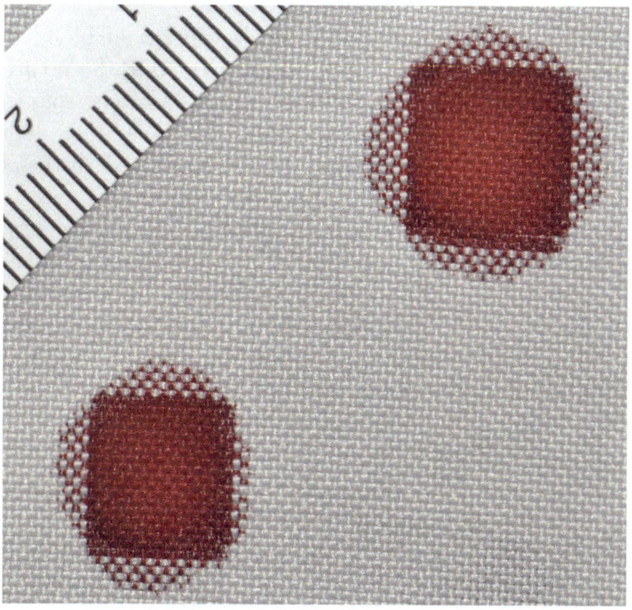

Figure 20.8 Drip stains deposited on plain woven polyester fabric. The blood has preferentially wicked along the yarns to form a near square shape that does not resemble the expected shape of a drip stain.

Interpreting Transfer Bloodstains on Textiles

Transfer bloodstains are created when one surface comes into contact with another bloodied surface. The transfer mechanisms involve either some degree of direct compression between two surfaces (contact bloodstains) or the lateral movement of one surface across the other (typically swipe or wipe bloodstains) that may or may not also include some degree of compression during blood deposition. The interpretation of transfer bloodstains on textiles is generally less complex than interpreting spatter, particularly for larger bloodstains. The physical features typically used to classify a transfer bloodstain deposited on a textile include the size, irregular

Figure 20.9 A transfer bloodstain on denim, displaying the irregular stain perimeter and variable deposition of blood across the surface of the denim, with the spaces or valleys between yarns remaining unstained.

shape, discontinuous stain perimeter, and variable deposition of blood across the surface of the fabric, and in particular at the stain perimeter (Figure 20.9). Some areas within a transfer bloodstain may be completely saturated where a volume of blood has soaked and penetrated the fabric, whereas other areas within the same stain may only have blood deposited on the upper, exposed surface yarns, with the protected yarns within the valleys of the construction remaining unstained.

When a bloodied surface comes into contact with a fabric surface, the amount of contact and/or compression between the contacting surfaces can vary, particularly when the contact involves the dynamics of human movement. The amount of contact can also be influenced by surface texture, the presence of fabric folds or creases, and curvature of the surface, as a worn garment follows the contours of the body and limbs. Any fabric folds within the contact area can produce voids within a transfer stain. If two items of clothing (while being worn) come into contact, the possible surface irregularities associated with each fabric can also affect the amount of contact between the two surfaces and the appearance of the transfer stain. Hence, the uneven deposition of blood across the fabric surface and the lack of penetration within the perimeter of a transfer stain are key features used to classify transfer. Where complete contact and an even penetration of blood has occurred across the entire transfer stain, examining the perimeter edges will often reveal sections where the blood has been deposited only on the upper surface of yarns, indicative of a transfer mechanism.

A violent assault is a dynamic event involving two or more people, where the parties involved are constantly moving and interacting with each other. Transfer bloodstains deposited on clothing during such an assault often exhibit characteristics indicative of lateral motion, and those characteristics can be used to classify both swipe and wipe bloodstains. Blood is deposited across the exposed parts of the surface yarns resulting in a feathered appearance across the fabric surface, with the amount of blood deposited generally decreasing along the length of the stain. This feature is typically used to indicate the direction of movement of swipes deposited on non-porous surfaces; however, due to the curvature of worn clothing, feathering can occur at both the beginning and the end of the swipe deposition. The analyst needs to be mindful that the directionality features typically used to classify transfer bloodstains on non-porous surfaces may not necessarily apply to those deposited on a curved textile surface, such as those associated with worn clothing, and may lead to erroneous assessment of directionality.

Discriminating between Spatter and Small Transfer Stains

The correct classification of spatter and small transfer bloodstains deposited on textiles can sometimes be complex and may not always be attainable. When assessing small-volume bloodstains, the small volume of blood involved and the size of the subsequent bloodstain may give rise to insufficient discernible characteristics to confidently classify a bloodstain. The influence of wicking and other fabric influences previously discussed may also eliminate characteristics that may have been otherwise visible on a non-porous surface. In general, the classification of spatter and small transfer bloodstains tends to be more reliable on natural fabrics when compared to synthetic fabrics.

When assessing small bloodstains, the analyst should begin by considering the physical characteristics that are visible to the eye, such as size, shape, appearance, and whether the blood has penetrated into the textile or just been deposited on top of the surface yarns. Small bloodstains can often be classified using those characteristics. Where doubt still remains, the analyst should then use a microscope to closely examine any questioned bloodstains. When examined microscopically, spatter and transfer bloodstains deposited on textiles can exhibit characteristics that potentially assist in classifying the stain. While further research is required to validate the use of these microscopic characteristics, it is the author's experience that these characteristics offer some probative value when distinguishing between spatter and transfer.

Microscopic characteristics are more commonly found on textiles comprised of natural, staple fibers than synthetics comprised of filament fibers. This is simply due to the fact that staple fiber ends protruding from yarns and fabric surfaces are able to receive and retain microscopic amounts of blood. When viewed with a microscope, the staple fibers on a natural fabric surface appear as a disarrayed network of tangled fibers. When blood is deposited on a natural fabric, such as cotton, in addition to the parent stain, a minute quantity of blood may be deposited on this tangled network of surface fibers with the blood suspended above the fabric surface. The surface tension holds the tiny blood volume together which, combined with the lack of direct contact with the actual yarns, impedes or negates the wetting/wicking process as there is insufficient blood volume to wet and wick into the fabric.

The key microscopic characteristic used to assist in the classification of a potential spatter stain is the presence of tiny micro-satellite spatter (Figure 20.10). The micro-satellites may present as submillimeter bloodstains staining just a small portion of a yarn, or as submillimeter globules of

Figure 20.10 A spatter stain deposited on a knitted cotton fabric. The blood has penetrated the textile and a micro-satellite spatter is visible in the top left of the image, immediately adjacent to the stain and adhering to staple fibers protruding from the fabric surface.

dried blood suspended above the fabric surface and adhering to fibers adjacent to the parent stain. The presence of micro-satellites immediately adjacent to a small bloodstain do not on their own confirm a bloodstain as spatter, but when used in conjunction with other spatter stain characteristics, such as size, shape, and penetration, they add support for the classification of a bloodstain as spatter.

The key characteristic used to aid the classification of a small transfer stain is the presence of coated fibers within the perimeter of or immediately adjacent to a bloodstain (Figure 20.11). The majority of transfer mechanisms involve some degree of movement, with the greater the amount of lateral movement, the greater the likelihood of blood deposition across the surface of a textile. The lateral movement generally results in blood coating some of the upper exposed surface yarns and fibers. For small transfer bloodstains, the coated yarns, and in particular coated fibers, may not be clearly visible to the eye. Microscopic examination can reveal fibers that have been coated with blood and are suspended above the fabric surface. The coated fibers may exhibit feathering characteristics, indicative of movement, and when used in conjunction with other transfer bloodstain characteristics, such as irregular perimeter, shape, and variable surface deposition, they add support for the classification of a bloodstain as transfer.

Bevel and Gardner use the term "painted" fibers to describe blood that has coated fibers on the surfaced of fabrics.[22] The term coated fiber is preferred by this author as it is an objective description of a bloodstain characteristic, without implying a deposition mechanism. Bevel and Gardner also observed that "painted" fibers can be present in both spatter and contact bloodstains. The presence of coated fibers in a spatter stain can be explained by considering the dynamics of stain deposition. Spatter deposition on natural textiles requires a blood droplet to pass though the upper network of tangled surface fibers to impact the yarns underneath. The amount of contact that droplet makes with the surface fibers will depend on the velocity and angle the droplet strikes the textile surface, so a moving blood droplet can potentially coat some of the fibers it comes contact with. When a droplet of blood strikes a textile surface at 90°, the liquid blood initially balloons as part of the dispersion process, and then retracts and wicks into the fabric to form the stain. As the droplet expands during dispersion, blood at the perimeter moves over the surface fibers immediately surrounding the impact site contacting nearby surface fibers. After the blood retracts, coated surface fibers can be observed outside the perimeter of the stain. This effect can

Figure 20.11 A transfer bloodstain deposited on a knitted cotton fabric. Although broadly circular, the coated fibers are indicative of a transfer mechanism.

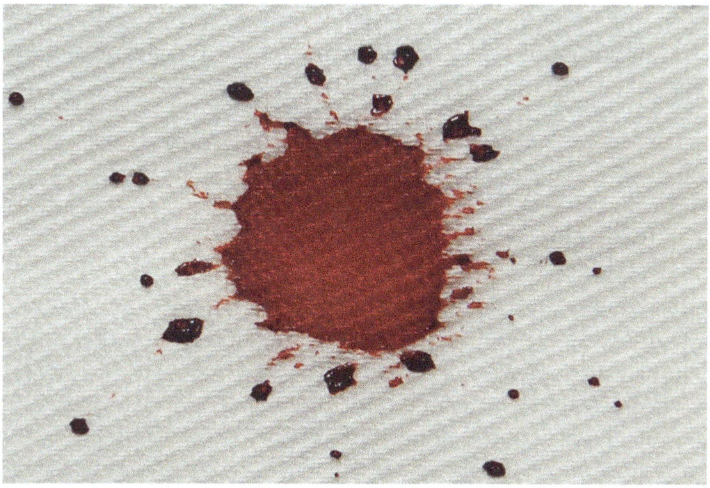

Figure 20.12 A drip stain deposited on a twill woven cotton fabric. Satellite spatter of varying sizes surround the stain, with smaller stains suspended on the fibers above the fabric surface. Coated fibers caused by droplet retraction are present at the perimeter of the stain.

be seen in Figure 20.12. For blood droplets striking the textile at an angle, the droplet can potentially skim over and coat the protruding staple fibers and the surface of yarns before penetrating the fabric (Figure 20.13). The more acute the angle, the more likely this will occur.

There are many variables associated with both the textiles and the dynamics of bloodstain deposition on textiles that need to be considered when classifying spatter and small transfer bloodstains, and it is not always possible to classify a bloodstain deposited on a textile. Micro-characteristics potentially offer the analyst additional data to assist in stain classification, but they should only be used in conjunction with existing known characteristics when classifying bloodstains in textiles. The interpretation and use of micro-satellite spatter and coated fibers to assist in the discrimination of spatter and small transfer bloodstains should only be undertaken by experienced analysts

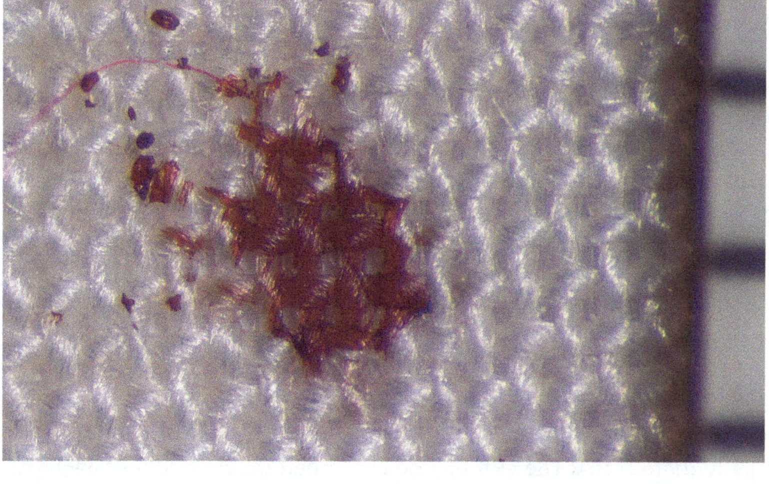

Figure 20.13 A spatter stain deposited at an acute angle on a woven 65% polyester/35% cotton blended fabric. Satellite spatter and coated surface fibers and yarns are present, with the coated fibers caused by the droplet moving across the fabric surface.

with appropriate training in textile structure and composition, the interaction of blood with textiles, and the interpretation of bloodstains on textiles. Where doubt remains, the analyst should exercise caution and take a conservative approach.

THE TWO- AND THREE-DIMENSIONAL ANALYSES OF BLOODSTAINS ON CLOTHING

The interpretation of bloodstains and bloodstain patterns on clothing is a complex process where the analyst not only needs to understand how blood interacts with textiles but must also consider the dynamics of human movement involved in a bloodletting event. Reynolds noted that many variables will influence the appearance and shape of a bloodstain deposited on clothing.[23] Those variables include fabric construction, composition, history, treatment(s), moisture content, fabric surface curvature, folding, and resultant vector influences. Reynolds demonstrated that the directionality features of bloodstains produced by blood droplets deposited on a curved surface can be dramatically altered due to the curvature of the target surface.[24] Surface curvature on clothing is caused by the way worn clothing drapes and follows the contours of the body and limbs. The analyst must be mindful of the movement associated with individuals during a blood deposition event. Pizzola et al. demonstrated that when a blood droplet was deposited onto a moving surface, the shape of the resultant stain dramatically changed and falsified the angle of impact.[25] The faster the target surface moved, the more oblique the resultant bloodstain became. These are important factors to consider when analyzing and classifying bloodstains on clothing.

When assessing bloodstains on clothing, the analysis undergoes two key phases: the first being a two-dimensional examination where the physical characteristics of the significant bloodstains or bloodstain patterns are assessed, recorded, and documented. The data recorded should include the size, number, distribution, and the location of bloodstains on the garment. This is an objective process which ideally should be completed without access to scene or injury information, which may bias the analyst's approach and interpretations. Once the bloodstains on the garment have been recorded, the analyst begins the second subjective phase which involves classifying the bloodstains, assigning deposition mechanisms, and forming opinions. It is in this second phase that the analyst should access and consider information available from the crime scene examination, DNA results, injuries to those involved, and potential weapons used. This information is essential to correctly classify bloodstains and correlate the findings with events that occurred and the bloodstains located at the crime scene. If available, the analyst should view photographs of the bloodstained clothing items taken from the crime scene or being worn by individuals at the time of apprehension and compare the bloodstains seen in photographs to those identified during the laboratory examination to ensure unrelated bloodstain artefacts have not occurred.

The examination of bloodstained clothing in the laboratory nearly always begins with the garment being laid flat on an examination table (Figure 20.14). This initial two-dimensional examination typically considers two sides of the garment, the front and the back, and whether deposition is on the inner or outer surfaces. While this two-dimensional approach is common practice, the analyst should consider not only the front and the back surfaces but also the left and right sides of the garment, and the top or upper aspect of the garment, for example, on top of the shoulders of a T-shirt or jacket. The location of any bloodstains should be recorded as being on the front, back, left side, right side, and uppermost surface, rather than just the front or the back. Where multiple items of clothing worn by the same individual have been submitted, laboratory protocols normally dictate that the exhibits be examined independent of each other. While this approach is necessary to avoid (DNA) contamination or evidence transfer between items, correlating bloodstain patterns deposited on the different garments worn by that individual may be difficult to achieve.

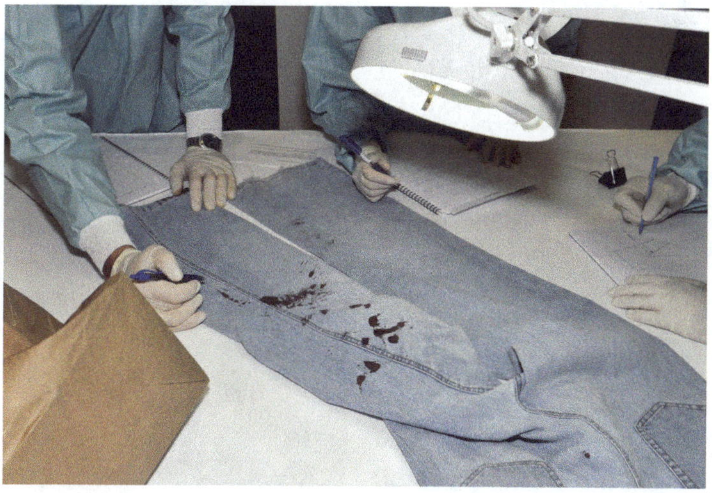

Figure 20.14 Students, conducting a two-dimensional examination, document bloodstains on the inside right leg of the jeans.

To assess the deposition and distribution of bloodstains on one or more garments, a three-dimensional examination is necessary and is particularly useful if the analyst needs to reconstruct the bloodletting event. After the two-dimensional examination is completed, a three-dimensional examination can provide a better understanding as to how the garments, and hence the wearer, were situated at the time of blood deposition and assist in probative DNA sample selection. This can be achieved by placing the item of clothing on a mannequin or on another individual. The individual must wear the appropriate personal protective equipment (PPE) and DNA contamination prevention measures must be employed.

Where multiple items of clothing (all from the same individual) are to be worn, the DNA sampling must be completed and the DNA profiles generated before commencing a three-dimensional examination. Preferably, an individual of similar height, weight, and build to the original wearer will wear the clothing, rather than using a mannequin. This gives the advantage of flexibility as the individual can easily move and assume different positions to best explain bloodstain deposition. Bloodstain patterns such as impact, castoff, transfer, and flow can potentially be deposited on two or more garments worn by the same individual and those bloodstain patterns that have been deposited on two or more garments can be easily identified during a three-dimensional examination (Figure 20.15a and b). This can provide useful information regarding the orientation of the individual at the time the blood was deposited. For example, a vertical flow pattern can indicate the individual was upright at the time of deposition, and may indicate the potential location of an injury or a source of the blood.

Where possible, the analyst should find out how the garment was worn by the individual. The way clothing is worn differs vastly from person to person, garment to garment, and is influenced by fashion and personal preference. Some garments can be tightly worn, some loosely, and some drape from the body. For example, there can be vast differences between individuals in how they wear jeans; some fitting tightly and others wear the jeans hanging low from their hips. The way clothing is worn can affect tautness and cause fabric folds and creases, all of which can influence resultant bloodstain shapes. Fabric folds and creases commonly occur on clothing close to joints, such as the elbow and knee, particularly when they are bent. Blood deposition across fabric folds creates voids in bloodstain patterns and can indicate how a limb was situated at the time of deposition (Figure 20.16a and b). All the factors mentioned here highlight the complexities and limitations associated with the bloodstain pattern analysis of clothing.

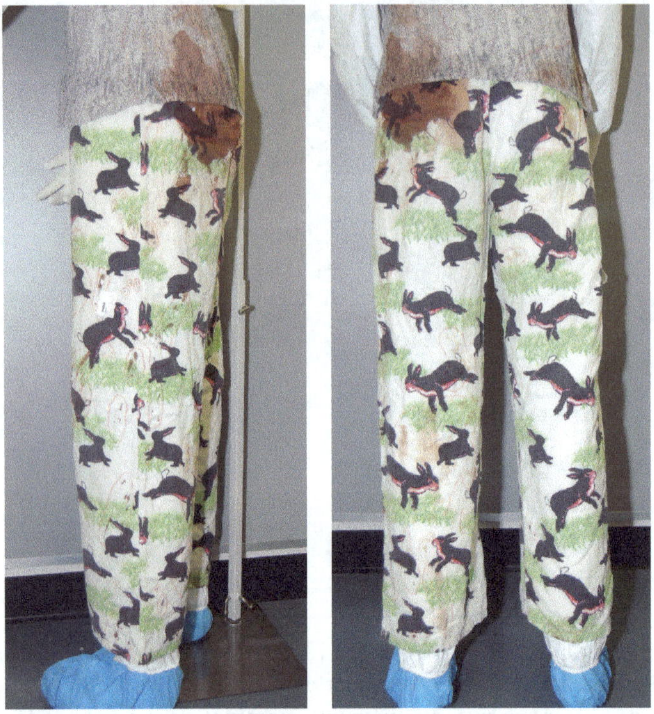

Figure 20.15 A three-dimensional examination showing overlapping bloodstain patterns between upper and lower garments.

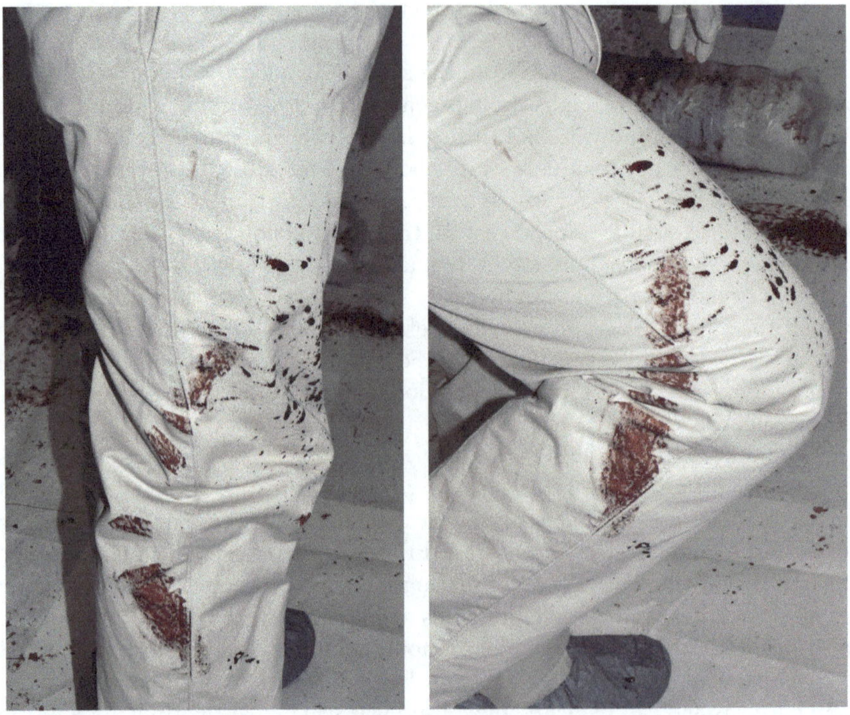

Figure 20.16 Three-dimensional examination of transfer bloodstains deposited on a trouser leg. When the voids are brought together, it demonstrates the knee was bent at the time of deposition.

SUMMARY

This chapter has demonstrated the intricacies associated with bloodstain pattern analysis of bloodied clothing. The analysis should be undertaken by those with appropriate training not only in bloodstain pattern analysis but also in textile composition and construction, and how blood will interact with different textiles. Taylor investigated error rates associated with the interpretation of bloodstains and bloodstain patterns on fabrics.[26] He observed high error rates by the bloodstain analysts who examined and classified selected bloodstains on fabrics. Where doubt remains on the classification of a bloodstain deposited on a textile, the analyst should opt for a conservative opinion and acknowledge the limitations associated with classifying bloodstains on textiles. In some cases, it is just not possible to classify a bloodstain or correctly assign a deposition mechanism. Given there are so many variables that can influence how blood will interact with different textiles, and the resultant bloodstain shape on textiles, analysts should exercise caution when examining and classifying bloodstains on textiles, particularly where only a few stains have been deposited on an exhibit.

Notes

1. Piotrowski, E. (1895). Uber Entstehung, Form, Richtung und Ausbreitung der Blutspuren nach Heibwundendes Kopfes (On the formation, form, direction, and spreading of blood stains after blunt trauma to the head), Wein: K.K. Universitat.
2. Balthazard, V., R. Piedlievre, H. Desoille, and L. DeRobert. (1939). Etude des gouttes de sang projete (Study of projected drops of blood). *Annual Medecine Legale Criminol Police Science Toxicology.* Paris, France, 22nd Congress of Forensic Medicine. 19, 265–323.
3. MacDonell, H. (1971). *Flight Characteristics and Stain Patterns of Human Blood*, 1st edition. Washington, DC.: National Institute of Law Enforcement and Criminal Justice.
4. Pizzola, P.A., S. Roth, and P.R. De Forest (1986). Blood droplet dynamics – I. *Journal of Forensic Sciences*, 31(1), 36–49.
5. Bevel, T., and R.M. Gardner. (2008). *Bloodstain Pattern Analysis: With an Introduction to Crime Scene Reconstruction*, 3rd edition. CRC Press.
6. Michielsen, S., M. Taylor, N. Parekh, and F. Ji. (2015). *Bloodstain Patterns on Textile Surfaces: A Fundamental Analysis.* National Institute of Justice, Award No.: 2012-DN-BX-K052. https://www.ojp.gov/pdffiles1/nij/grants/248671.pdf (accessed May 7, 2021).
7. Williams, E. M. P., M. Dodds, M.C. Taylor, J. Li, and S. Michielsen. (2016). Impact dynamics of porcine drip bloodstains on fabrics. *Forensic Science International*, 262, 66–72.
8. Kissa, E., (1996). Wetting and wicking. *Textile Research Journal*, 66(10), 660–668.
9. Patnaik, A., R.S. Rengasamy, V.K. Kothari, and A. Ghish. (2006). Wetting and wicking in fibrous materials. *Textile Progress*, 38(1), 101–105.
10. Hasan, M.M.B., A. Calvimontes, and V. Dutschk. (2008). Effects of topographic structure on wettability of differently woven fabrics. *Textile Research Journal*, 78(11), 996–1003.
11. Patnaik, A., R.S. Rengasamy, V.K. Kothari, and A. Ghish. (2006).
12. Kissa, E., (1996).
13. Reynolds, M. and E. Silenieks. (2016). Considerations for the assessment of bloodstains on fabrics. *Journal of Bloodstain Pattern Analysis*, 32(2), 17–22.
14. Carr, D. (2017). *Forensic Textile Science.* Cambridge: Matthew Deans.
15. Carr, D. (2017)
16. Slemko, J.A. (2003). Bloodstains on fabric: The effects of droplet velocity and fabric composition. *I.A.B.P.A. Newsletter*, December, 3–11.
17. de Castro, T., T. Nickson, D. Carr, and C. Knock. (2012). Interpreting the formation of bloodstains on selected apparel fabrics. *International Journal of Legal Medicine*, 127(1), 251–258.
18. Li, X., J. Li, and S. Michielsen. (2017). Effect of yarn structure on wicking and its impact on bloodstain pattern analysis (BPA) on woven cotton fabrics. *Forensic Science International*, 276 (April), 41–50.
19. Reynolds, M., and E. Silenieks. (2016).

20. Reynolds, M., and E. Silenieks. (2016).
21. Chang, J.Y.M. and S. Michielsen. (2016). Effect of fabric mounting method and backing material on bloodstain patterns of drip stains on textiles. *International Journal of Legal Medicine*, 130, 649–659.
22. Bevel, T. and R.M. Gardner. (2008).
23. Reynolds, M., and E. Silenieks. (2016).
24. Reynolds, M., and E. Silenieks. (2016).
25. Pizzola, P.A., S. Roth, and P.R. De Forest (1986). Blood droplet dynamics – II. *Journal of Forensic Sciences*, 31(1), 50–64.
26. Taylor M.C., T.L. Laber, P.E. Kish, G. Owens, and N.K.P. Osborne. (2016). The reliability of pattern classification in bloodstain pattern analysis – Part 2: Bloodstain patterns on fabric surfaces. *Journal of Forensic Sciences*, 61(6), 1461–1466.

CHAPTER 21

BLOODSTAIN PATTERN ANALYSIS METHODOLOGY

Holly Latham

The application of science and the scientific method to what we observe around us regarding bloodstain pattern analysis leads us to an understanding and knowledge of the limitations and potentials of what can be inferred from the observable information and data. The methodology put forth is the process of the observations and interpretations that occur and the progression toward classification, scene interpretations, and reconstruction opinions. This process is imperative to bias minimization by uncovering and applying task-relevant information[1] at designated moments to reduce the biasing effects of contextual information. This is done by mirroring the concept of linear sequential unmasking-expanded put forth by Dror and Kukucka.[2] This chapter discusses the process of examining bloodstains and their patterns to determine the importance of their presence or absence, what potential forces or mechanisms could result in those bloodstains or their patterns, and the significance of those determinations in regard to the scope or reason for the examinations.

The analyst should begin by defining the scope or reason for performing the examination. Is there a specific question being asked, or a scenario or statement to be evaluated? Or is everything unknown at the beginning of the examination and the analyst is trying to determine what may have happened. Knowing the scope or reason for the examination will allow the analyst to determine the suitability or utility of bloodstains and their patterns based on the focus of the examination and can guide the level of documentation and determination of task-relevant information during the examination. When determining or addressing the scope, the analyst should be careful to minimize exposure to biasing information. For example, any statements provided by the victim, suspect, or witnesses should not be read prior to examining the evidence, but knowing the scope or area of contention may help reduce unnecessary attention to other areas. The analyst may know that a statement or interview exists, but not know what was revealed. In this instance, the scope might be to analyze the veracity of a statement but would not require the analyst know what was in the statement at this particular point.

The analyst begins by making observations and collecting objective data and information. The observation and data collection begins as a search for blood, not only noting where it is present but also where it is notably absent. Observations are recorded utilizing imaging, notes, and sketches. Those images are used to support characterization of blood. Characterization is the process of making observations regarding the recognizable characteristics of bloodstains and their patterns. Analysts can use images they recorded or they can utilize images and documentation provided to them. Characteristics that should be noted and recorded are stain and pattern size, shape, distribution, appearance, and location. Stains that share characteristics and proximity may be grouped into patterns. Unique identifiers should be assigned to those groupings and stains that are determined to be from an event or mechanism to aid the documentation.

Bloodstain shape is characterized and documented. Possible shapes may include circular, elliptical, irregular, linear, or curvilinear. Shapes described can be those associated with an individual stain or can be the variety of shapes associated with the grouping or pattern. While interpreting

DOI: 10.4324/9781003163695-21

the shape of the stain, the edge characteristics are examined to determine whether the edges are smooth, disrupted, scalloped, exhibit spinning, or are feathered. Edge characteristics can be a result of the surface type or texture the blood was deposited on, the force or energy associated with the blood to surface interaction, or a combination of surface and energy.

When recording characteristics regarding size, the analyst notes individual stain measurements in millimeters and when referring to stains within a pattern, they may offer a range of the sizes of the stains by recording the minimum and maximum size. Circular and near circular stains are measured utilizing the diameter; elliptical stains are measured utilizing the width; and for those stains that are irregularly shaped, the overall general stain size is recorded.

The stains or patterns are characterized in terms of appearance. Consideration is given to observations that provide additional information about the origin of the blood, including the color or hue of the blood and whether it appears to be dilute. Characteristics such as whether the blood appears clotted or is wet or dry could also be noted.

Characterization of the distribution can refer to the arrangement of bloodstains including whether the stains appear to be radiating, are in a linear or curvilinear formation, and can include exhibited directionality indicating the flight path relative to the surface. Distribution could also include stains that have enough volume to exhibit flow, and any recognizable impressions that may include fabric, footwear, and patent prints. It can also be recognized that there may be a repeating pattern occurring with diminishing volume.

The last description to assist in characterization is the location and surface the stains are present on. This can be a roadmapped location within the scene or as simple as indicating the photo number containing the stains or pattern being described. It is important to know orientation regarding whether the stains are present on a ceiling versus a wall versus a floor. This alone will assist the analyst with excluding potential pattern types. For example, stains observed on a ceiling will not be from a gravity mechanism. Also important is to know details regarding the surface, whether it be smooth or rough, porous or nonporous, and whether it is a movable object or its location is fixed. For stains observed on fabrics, recording and considering the fabric composition, the weave, and potential treatments could also affect or play a part in distribution, appearance, and ultimate classification.

Once all of the potential elements of characterization have been considered, stains are generally grouped or organized with a presumption that they were deposited by the same mechanism and are then traditionally referred to as a "pattern." The characterization and collection of observed data allows for a classification to occur. As Bevel and Gardner point out, the classification should be based on observed criteria collected during characterization.[3] These are the physical characteristics that allow the analyst to interpret the resulting classification possibilities. At this point, the analyst determines the suitability/utility of stains and patterns based on the amount of information from characterization, and/or the reason or scope of the examination. Not all bloodstains or grouping of stains observed must be classified and used for reconstruction. Examples of reasons for not classifying a stain or pattern could include that there is not enough quantity of information present to make any definitive reconstruction statements or there may not be enough information to narrow down to a meaningful list of mechanisms. There may also be too much information in the case of overlapping or complex patterns. If asked, an analyst should be able to articulate why they chose not to consider a stain or pattern further in the analysis.

Occurring concurrently is the recognition of potential interrelationships of patterns and stains. Considering the general proximity that patterns and stains have with each other, the analysts can use that information during classification refinement to determine more likely pattern types. The directionality of stains previously noted during characterization can aid with determining flight path characteristics to assist in determining area of convergence or area of origin.

The next step is to determine what particular forces or mechanisms may have resulted in the observed bloodstains and their patterns and is more commonly referred to as classification. In making this decision, the analyst must consider the quantity and quality of data from the characterization that is present. The more data that is available, the more definitive the interpretation or classification may be. When considering mechanism or force, the analyst should start by considering all possibilities and narrow down to those most likely based on the presence of observable characteristics from characterization. The focus should start with mechanisms and forces that can be excluded as resulting in the observed stains and patterns. For example, are the resulting bloodstains consistent with blood traveling through the air before striking the target surface or are they consistent with being displaced or transferred due to contact? The inclusion of patterns should only be based on the observed characteristics in stains and patterns in conjunction with the surfaces they are on and should not consider scene context and what the scene might infer.[4] The list of potential mechanisms or forces should start broad and should be narrowed down through refinement by applying additional data and contextual information. This may help guide further exclusion of mechanisms.

Moving forward, a refinement of the list of potential classifications occurs that allows the analyst to eliminate mechanisms and forces based on the addition of task-relevant contextual information. Prior to the addition of contextual information, all decisions are based on the observed data and characteristics of bloodstains and their patterns. The observed data and the characteristics described would not change unless an error was effected. The resulting opinions and conclusions, however, can change in the presence of new task-relevant contextual information.[5] The contextual information can lead to refinement and logical exclusion of pattern types and mechanisms to follow. This information may include wounds and their locations, which can be retrieved from autopsy reports or injury reports, as well as testing to confirm that the substance is blood and the results of whose blood it is. Additional information could include officers and first responders' reports and statements that offer information for consideration of how or why a stain or pattern may be present. For example, if the first responders rolled the body to its side to render aid, it may assist in explaining a flow pattern that is present. It doesn't change the fact that it is a flow pattern but rather explains how it came to be. Another example would be the presence of a spatter pattern and if autopsy and injury information indicated that there was no bleeding in the airway and there was no potential for expirated blood to occur, it could be eliminated as a pattern type. This is a product of refinement of classifications, logical elimination of mechanisms and pattern types based on the application of contextual information. It is first determined what characteristics the bloodstains and their patterns have and then elimination of some of those patterns takes place based on the application of contextual information.

Complexity of the scene and the bloodstained areas should be considered. Examples of aspects that would add to the complexity would be if patterns appear to be overlapping, if there are multiple people bleeding within the scene, if alteration or clean-up may have occurred, or if the surfaces may not allow for definitive interpretation.

Finally, the classifications of patterns along with the application of interrelationships of the patterns within the scene or on the item of evidence and the task-relevant contextual information allow the analyst to form opinions as to how the stains were deposited and potentially the sequencing of possible events that occurred. This is commonly referred to as the reconstruction component of the bloodstain pattern analysis report (Figure 21.1). In this methodology, the analyst observes data and characteristics of bloodstains and their patterns, uses those characteristics to classify the patterns interpreting the potential mechanisms and forces used to result in the characteristics, applies task-relevant contextual information to eliminate or refine the classification choices, then applies scene or evidence context to determine the significance of bloodstains, and ultimately forms opinions or conclusions as to the reconstructive aspects of the scene or evidence.[6]

In instances when the methodology could not be followed as prescribed, it should be documented. There are times when task-irrelevant information is exposed to the analyst or the analyst is exposed to knowledge of the case or scene through general working of the scene itself. The analyst should document when they accessed or were exposed to information that could potentially be biasing.

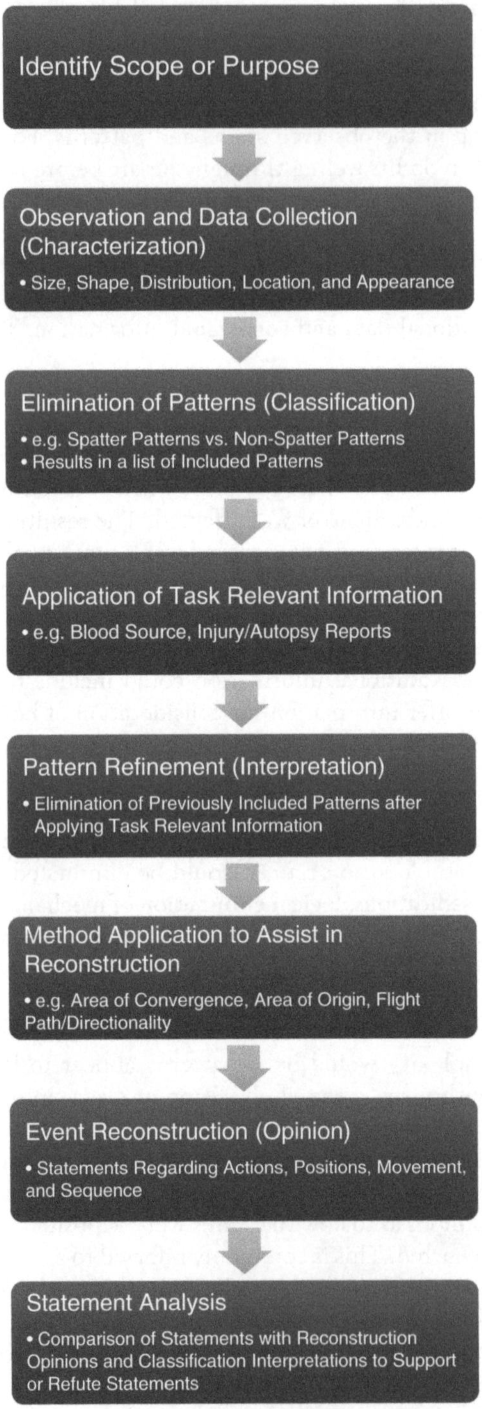

Figure 21.1 A visual depiction of the bloodstain pattern analysis methodology as described.

If statements are to be evaluated, it is at this point that the statements should be compared to determined classifications. The analyst must determine if the provided statement of actions, movement, or sequence is accounted for given the product of the classification and classification refinement. In some instances, it may be appropriate to report which portions of the statement are supported by the reconstruction opinions and classification interpretations and which are not.

Notes

1. National Commission of Forensic Science, *Ensuring the forensic analysis is based upon task-relevant information.* https://www.justice.gov/archives/ncfs/page/file/641676/download
2. Dror, Itiel E. and Jeff Kukucka. "Linear Sequential Unmasking-Expanded (LSU-E): A General Approach for Improving Decision Making as Well as Minimizing Noise and Bias." *Forensic Science International Synergy* vol. 3,. 13 Aug. 2021, p. 100161.
3. Bevel, Tom, and Ross Gardner. *Bloodstain Pattern Analysis with an Introduction to Crime Scene Reconstruction.* CRC Press, Boca Raton, FL, 2008, p. 99.
4. Saviano, Jeff. "Articulating a Concise Scientific Methodology for Bloodstain Pattern Analysis." *Journal of Forensic Identification* vol. 55, No. 4, 2005, p. 466.
5. Taupin, Jane, and Chesterene Cwiklik. *Scientific Protocols for Forensic Examination of Clothing.* CRC Press, Boca Raton FL, 2011, p. 11.
6. Bevel, Tom, and Ross Gardner. *Bloodstain Pattern Analysis with an Introduction to Crime Scene Reconstruction.* CRC Press, Boca Raton, FL, 2008, p. 105.

CHAPTER 22

FORENSIC DIGITAL PHOTOGRAPHY

Steve Sklavounos

Bloodstain pattern analysis (BPA) is an intricate process that requires knowledge and skill. The ultimate goal of the BPA analyst is to assist investigators, litigators, judges, and juries in understanding the crime scene in question. Whether it's identifying patterns, following a drip trail from beginning to end, or reconstructing events from impact patterns, the easiest way to show others who were not on scene is through photography. In this chapter, digital camera operation and settings are discussed to obtain quality results. No particular brand of camera is discussed, as there are too many to discuss in detail. However, all major brands of 35 mm DSLR camera should allow manipulation of the settings discussed in this chapter. Ultimately, the camera used is decided by the individual investigator and/or department. Regardless of brand, a good quality lens is arguably the most important consideration in purchasing a camera. A poor quality lens will almost always result in a poor-quality photo.

In order to understand the concepts discussed, it is important to understand the basics of how a camera works. Photography is all about light. Light enters the body of a camera through lens. The light strikes a digital sensor, capturing the image in front of the lens on some form of digital medium, such as an SD card or compact flash card. If too much light reaches the sensor, the photo will appear washed out or overexposed (see Figure 22.1).

If the amount of light that reaches the sensor is not enough, the photo will be too dark or underexposed (see Figure 22.2).

The goal is to get the correct amount of light to reach the sensor (see Figure 22.3).

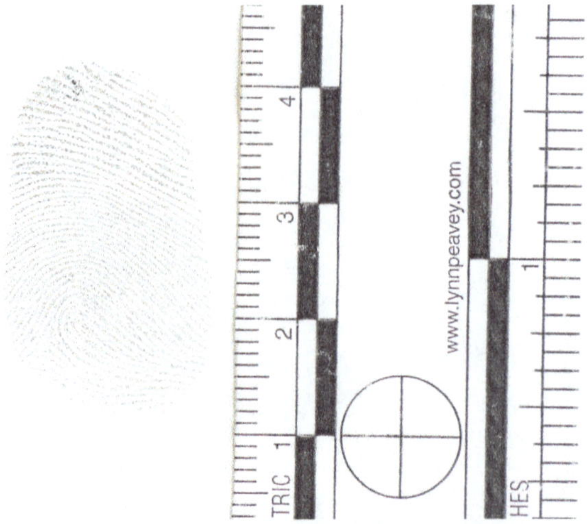

Figure 22.1 An example of an overexposed fingerprint (f/5.6, ISO 400, 1/6 second).

DOI: 10.4324/9781003163695-22

Figure 22.2 An example of an underexposed fingerprint (f/5.6, ISO 400, 1/200 second).

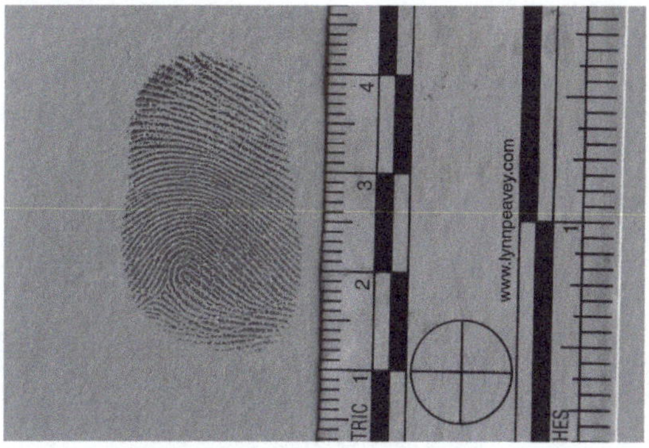

Figure 22.3 An example of a properly exposed fingerprint (f/5.6, ISO 400, 1/50 second).

By manipulating the following three controls of your camera, the amount of light reaching the sensor can be adjusted to obtain a correct exposure. The first control is *f-stop*, the second is *shutter speed*, and the third is *ISO*. These three controls are interdependent. This means if any one of the three is changed, one or both of the others can be altered to allow the same amount of light to reach the sensor. Each control is discussed separately, and then the relationship of how the three affect each other is discussed.

F-STOP

A shutter inside the lens opens and closes, allowing light through the lens. The size of the opening in the shutter, or *aperture*, is determined by the f-stop setting. A quality lens has f-stop settings of between f/2.8 and f/22. Macro lenses, used for close-up photography, allow for an f-stop of f/40 or higher. The f-stop numbers are inversely proportional to the size of aperture. In other words, at f/2.8 (see Figure 22.4), the aperture is at its widest opening, allowing the maximum amount of light to reach the sensor.

An f-stop between f/5.6 and f/8 allows a moderate amount of light to reach the sensor. At f/22, the aperture is at its smallest opening, allowing much less light to reach the sensor (see Figures 22.5–22.7).

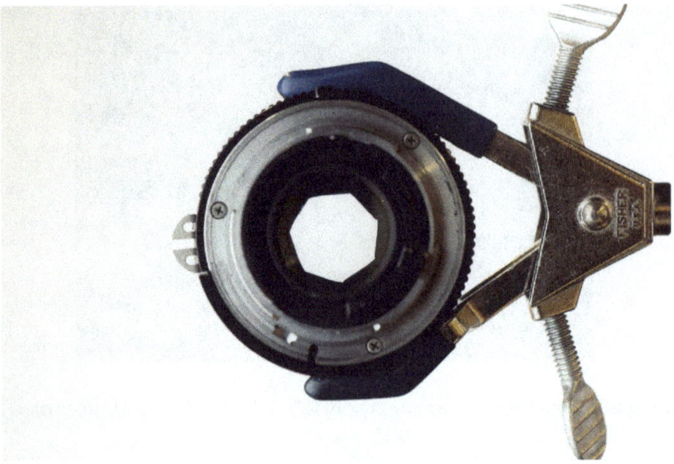

Figure 22.4 Aperture at f/2.8.

Figure 22.5 Aperture at f/5.6.

Figure 22.6 Aperture at f/8.

Figure 22.7 Aperture at f/22.

The size of the aperture also affects the *depth of field*. Depth of field can be thought of as how much of the image or scene is in sharp focus. At f/2.8, the largest aperture, depth of field will be the narrowest (see Figure 22.8). In other words, a very thin slice of the image will be in focus.

At f/22, the smallest aperture, depth of field will be the widest. In other words, most or all of the image will be in focus (see Figure 22.9).

In general, images in crime scene photography should have a wide depth of field to show as much of the item or scene as possible. Narrow depth of field has limited application in crime scene photography. An aperture of between f/5.6 and f/8 usually results in an acceptable depth of field for most crime scene situations.

Figure 22.8 Photograph of a casing taken at f/2.8 (ISO 100, 1/30 second) showing narrow depth of field.

Figure 22.9 Photograph of a casing taken at f/22 (ISO 100, 1/2 second) showing wide depth of field.

SHUTTER SPEED

Prior to taking a photo, the shutter in the lens is in closed state. When the shutter release button is pressed, the shutter opens to allow light in, then closes again. The amount of time the shutter remains open is called the *shutter speed*. Shutter speeds can range from 1/8000th of a second to 30 s. Most DSLR cameras have a "bulb" setting to allow for shutter speeds longer than 30 s. On the "bulb" setting, the shutter will remain open as long as the shutter release button is depressed. Faster shutter speeds between 1/500th and 1/8000th of a second are good for stopping motion, such as when taking pictures at a sporting event. When the aperture is open for such a short period of time, a very limited amount of light reaches the sensor. Since crime scenes are static, there is no need to use such a fast shutter speed. The longer the shutter is open, the more the amount of light that reaches the sensor. The photographer needs to take into account the amount of ambient light. The time of day (dawn, full daylight, dusk, or night), significant amounts of sun and shade, cloud cover in the sky, indoor v. outdoor scenes, etc. all affect the amount of ambient light. So how does one determine if photograph will be properly exposed? Most cameras have an integrated *light meter*. The light meter display can be seen through the viewfinder. Use this light meter display as a guide or starting point. If the photo appears underexposed, adjust by decreasing the shutter speed, thus leaving the shutter open longer. If the photo appears overexposed, increase the shutter speed. It is important to note that the view screen on the back of a camera may show the image either darker or lighter than a computer screen. Some view screens are adjustable. Refer to the operator's manual to determine how to change screen brightness.

Some cameras show the shutter speed as a fraction. If the camera shows a shutter speed of 1/120, then the shutter will remain open for 1/120th of a second. Most cameras show shutter speed as a whole number. For cameras that show shutter speed as a whole number, a shutter speed of 120 will actually be 1/120th of a second. If there is a quotation mark after the number, then that is the time the shutter will be open in seconds. For example, if the shutter speed is shown as 5", the shutter will remain open for five seconds.

The longer the shutter remains open, the more likely *camera shake* will be introduced. Camera shake occurs when the shutter is open and the camera moves, however slightly. This can be caused by the camera being bumped or resting the camera on an unsteady surface like a vehicle with the engine turned on. Physiological processes, such as breathing, heart beating, or shaky hands can also cause a handheld camera to shake. It is very difficult to hold a camera steady with a shutter speed of less than 1/50th of a second. If the shutter speed is fast enough, faster than about 1/60th of a second, camera shake can be minimized or eliminated.

ISO

ISO is a holdover from the days of film photography. Prior to the advent of digital photography, ISO referred to the sensitivity of the film. A photographer had to plan what type of photography was going to occur so as to load the proper type of film. If the photographer was going to take landscape photos or portraits, or photos in bright daylight, s/he would load a slower film such as ISO 100 or 200. If the photographer was going to a sporting event and wanted to stop the action, or take photos at night, s/he would load a faster film, such as ISO 800 or 1600. The benefit of having a slower film was that there would be less *grain* or noise, making a sharper, cleaner image. Having a lower ISO (slower) film meant needing to get more light to the film by adjusting either the f-stop, the shutter speed, or both. Having a higher ISO (faster) film meant less light was needed to get the image, and also meant that there would be significant grain.

The convention of ISO has been kept in digital photography, but it works in a slightly different way than film. Changing the ISO of the digital camera does not change the sensitivity of digital sensor. Lowering the ISO will darken the image, and raising the ISO will brighten the image. But like film, a higher ISO adds graininess and makes the image less sharp. As a general rule, the lower the ISO setting, the sharper the image. It is not always possible to photograph at a low ISO. The scene, equipment, and the ability of a photographer usually dictate the settings of a camera.

INTERACTION OF F-Stop, SHUTTER SPEED, AND ISO

The three controls, f-stop, shutter speed, and ISO are all interdependent. Changing any one will alter how much light reaches the sensor. Changing one or both of the others can bring the light reaching the sensor back to the original amount. For example, changing the f-stop from f/16 to f/5.6 will increase the amount of light reaching the sensor. This may cause overexposure in the image. Therefore, either the shutter speed needs to be faster or the ISO needs to be reduced, or both, in order to compensate for the extra light reaching the sensor. Similarly, if the shutter speed is changed from 1/30th of a second to 1/60th of a second, there will be less light reaching the sensor. Either the shutter needs to be opened wider (f-stop lowered) or the ISO needs to be raised to compensate for the decreased amount of light. Most DSLR cameras have a built-in light meter that is fairly accurate. The built-in light meter is a good starting place to determine if the photo will be properly exposed. In the days of film, photographers were never certain of how the exposure would turn out. A handheld light meter was used, and the camera settings were based off the reading. Photographers would have to bracket their photos. Bracketing involved taking the same photo several times while changing one setting, trying to increase the odds of getting a properly exposed image. The benefit of digital photography is that the photo is available immediately. Take a look at the photograph. If it is not the image that is desired, change the settings and take the photo again.

FLASH AND TRIPOD

Crime scenes rarely have ideal conditions. The strength and angle of light vary throughout the day, and there is no sunlight at night. Often times, a flash must be used to get a proper exposure. Some cameras have an *integrated flash*. The integrated flash is a part of the camera that pops up from the top. Many cameras have a *hot shoe*, which allows for an *external flash* to be mounted to the top of the camera. In general, an external flash gives better results than an integrated flash. Using a flash introduces light in a controlled way that is synced with the camera to produce a precise burst of light to be captured by the sensor. It is a simple way to increase the amount of light on an indoor scene or small outdoor scene. However, a flash can produce unwanted side effects. A flash can produce harsh shadows within the scene. Light from a flash that is aimed directly at the object being photographed will leave the flash, strike the object, then return directly to the lens. Anything behind the object will be in dark shadow. If the flash is directed toward the ceiling or a nearby wall, light will bounce off the ceiling or wall, striking the object at an angle before returning to the lens. It also illuminates behind the object, either softening shadows or eliminating them altogether. This is called a *bounce flash*. A flash may also produce a bright spot, especially from flat reflective surfaces like painted walls, vehicles, or mirrors. A bounce flash can help reduce bright spots.

Light from a flash is limited to approximately 12–15 ft (4–5 m) (see Figure 22.10).

If the scene is large, especially outdoors, using a tripod might be the best way to obtain the desired photograph under poor lighting conditions (see Figure 22.11).

A tripod allows the photographer to keep the camera stable, thus eliminating camera shake. It also allows for a lower ISO setting and a shutter speed as long as necessary to get a proper exposure. Keep in mind that a shutter release cable or remote should be used to avoid touching the camera while the shutter is open. Tripods are made from a variety of materials, including wood, metal, and even carbon fiber. When purchasing a tripod, there are many factors to consider. A lighter tripod is easier to carry, especially over long distances or uneven terrain. A heavier tripod is more stable and will give more consistent results under less-than-optimal conditions. Ultimately, the decision on which tripod to purchase will have to be made by the individual investigator or department depending on their needs.

Figure 22.10 Photograph at night using flash to illuminate the scene (f/5.6, ISO 400, 1/60 second).

Figure 22.11 Photograph at night using ambient light and a long exposure time to illuminate the scene (f/5.6, ISO 400, 60 seconds).

AUTO, SHUTTER PRIORITY, APERTURE PRIORITY, AND MANUAL

So how does one change the f-stop, shutter speed, or ISO? All major brands of DSLR camera have at least four modes. The four major modes are auto, shutter priority (S), aperture priority (A), and manual (M). Refer to the operator's manual for any particular camera to learn how to switch between modes. Auto is the most convenient of the modes. The camera chooses the f-stop, shutter speed, and ISO. S, or shutter priority, allows the photographer to set the shutter speed and ISO. The camera then selects the f-stop. A, or aperture priority, allows the photographer to set the f-stop and ISO. The camera then selects the shutter speed. Manual allows the photographer to set the f-stop, shutter speed, and ISO. Generally speaking, the auto mode setting produces poor results for crime scene photography. Auto mode may give a proper exposure, but usually at the expense of depth of field and graininess. When photographing a crime scene, the preference is to show as much of the scene as possible in a single overall photograph. Juries are in a stressful situation and tend to have a limited attention span. It is much easier to show a jury one or two photos encompassing the entire scene rather than a series of five, ten, or more photos, to give an overall impression of the scene. As such, photographing scenes in either aperture priority, where depth of field can be controlled, or manual, where all settings can be controlled, is preferable.

CONCLUSION

As mentioned earlier, the ultimate goal of the BPA analyst is to assist investigators, litigators, judges, and juries in understanding the crime scene in question. Since the only way others will be able to see the scene is via the photographs introduced as evidence, they need to be of high quality. In the eyes of others, poor-quality photographs mean a poor-quality investigator. Learning to use the camera to take high-quality photographs is as important as collecting fingerprints or DNA, or properly interpreting bloodstain patterns.

CHAPTER 23

CRIME SCENE PROCESSING AND EVIDENCE HANDLING

Rebecca Hooks

Bloodstain observations can and should be documented in multiple formats such as with notes, diagrams, sketches, and videos. Multiple forms of documentation are completed in order to provide a comprehensive and thorough account of the analyst's thought process, methodology, and observations. These items will be useful later for technical reviews and court proceedings. All observations, regardless of how they are recorded, should be retained indefinitely as part of the analyst's casefile.

NOTES

The recording of notes begins upon notification of the case and continues through the completion of the analyst's case responsibilities.[1] Notes should be taken in real time and provide a detailed and accurate record of the analyst's observations. The standardization of note forms is highly recommended and can provide consistency throughout a work unit. Even seasoned bloodstain pattern analysts can be overwhelmed by a large or especially complex scene. Standardized notes help the analyst stay focused and manage the scene in a way that ensures valuable observations are recorded and not forgotten. When standardizing forms, a *can't versus don't* mindset should be utilized. Developing forms with this mindset means including a checklist or blank on the form which doesn't allow the analyst the possibility of forgetting to record a valuable piece of information. For example, you *can't* forget to record the weather and environmental conditions when there is a designated area on the form for such information.

Upon notification of the case, at a minimum, the initial notes should include the following general information:

- Date contacted and by whom (Requestor)
- Requestor's analysis expectations
- Details of the initial briefing
- Case location
- First Responder/Crime Scene Investigator's actions prior to analyst's arrival
- Time of arrival, final walkthrough, and departure
- Who was present upon arrival[2]
- Justification for entering the scene

Bloodstains documented in notes should be referred to as "blood-like stain," "bloodlike," "red-brown stain," etc. until laboratory testing can be completed. An additional option is to address the term "blood" at the beginning of the notes. An analyst can specify that each time the word blood or bloodstain is used, they are referring to stains that have not been confirmed as blood yet.[3]

Often, the bloodstain workup of a scene is done after general crime scene processing. If this is the case, the condition of the bloodstains should be preserved in anticipation of the analyst's later arrival. Any measures taken to preserve the stains, such as the overlying of cardboard for

DOI: 10.4324/9781003163695-23

protection, should be thoroughly documented using photography and notetaking. These photographs, in addition to the original scene photographs, should be provided to the bloodstain analyst.

Whether the analyst is examining the scene through photographs or in person, a helpful initial step is to document all areas of visible blood. The list of these initial areas can serve as a guide or outline of areas to revisit and expand upon. Bloodstain analysts have long been taught to *simply* document size, shape, distribution, appearance, and location; with only slight explanation as to what this means and the detail it should entail. However, it is not simple at all and requires much deeper thought and discussion. The notes, along with other forms of documentation, must serve as a map to the analyst's conclusions. When broken down even further, the notes on bloodstain pattern characteristics become the map to the pattern identification. Let's take a look at size, shape, distribution, appearance, and location and build a *can't versus don't* form.

Size

The size of the individual spatters can aid in ascertaining the pattern mechanism.

- *Predominate Stain Size:* Predominate stain size can give an indication as to the level of force utilized and aid in identifying which mechanism produced the pattern.[4] A range can be listed; however, it should not be documented based on the smallest and the largest stain observed. All patterns will have variations due to unequal distribution of force; therefore, the predominate size will be the most probative information reference force and mechanism.
- *Approximate Number of Stains:* If too large to count, the approximate number of stains can be reported as >500 or >1000. The number of stains present can also aid in determining the mechanism which produced the pattern.[5]
- *Highest Stain/Directionality:* The highest stain and its directionality can aid the analyst in determining the height or position of the blood source. For example, if the highest stain is elliptical in shape, has an upward directionality, and is 2 ft above the floor, the analyst may be able to deduce the blood source had to have come from less than 2 ft above the floor.
- *Lowest Stain/Directionality:* The lowest stain and its directionality can also aid the analyst in determining the height or position of the blood source.
- *Surface Area/Overall Pattern Size:* The surface area and overall pattern size can aid in determining if the pattern is from a single event or multiple bloodletting events.

Shape

The overall stain or pattern shape can be used to determine if the bloodstain(s) are spatter or non-spatter.

- *Elliptical*
- *Circular*
- *Other:* If the shape does not fit in the "elliptical" or "circular" description, it can be described under "other." For example, irregular in shape with feathered edges on both ends.

Distribution

The distribution of spatter stains can aid in ascertaining the mechanism by which the pattern was produced.[6]

- *How are the stains arranged relative to one another?* Individual spatter stains should have similar directionalities and lead back to a common area of convergence.[7]
- *Where is the heaviest distribution of stains located?* The heaviest distribution can aid in determining where the blood source was located.
- *Where are the stains located within the overall pattern?* The individual stain location, such as height, can aid in determining the location of the blood source as well as potential limiting angles or voids.

- *How are the sizes of the stains distributed throughout the pattern?* The individual stain size distribution can aid in determining the pattern mechanism and if there is more than one bloodletting event.
- *How are the angles of impact and the directionality of the stains distributed throughout the pattern?* The varying angles of impact and directionality can aid in determining if there is more than one area of origin.
- *What is the overall arrangement of the stains (radiating, linear, etc.)?* The overall arrangement aids in ascertaining the mechanism by which the pattern was produced.

Appearance

This section of the notes documents the physical characteristics of the pattern or stain.

- Wet
- Dry
- Diluted
- Altered
- Flow
- Air Bubbles
- Flaking
- Color
- Patterned (This does not mean pattern identification; this merely means to ask if the pattern resembles something. For example, does the pattern resemble a footwear or fabric impression? Or does the pattern contain ridge detail?)

Location

- *Physical Location:* Where is the pattern located? For example, northwest corner of the kitchen or on the living room recliner and partially on the south wall behind the recliner.
- *Surface Description:* The texture of the target surface as well as the shape and/or angle of the surface can influence the shape of the individual spatter stains.[8]

Other

This portion of notes can include external factors, presumptive testing efforts, collection efforts, etc.

- External factors (temperature/airflow/humidity) (External factors can influence drying times. Observations such as running fans or open windows should be recorded.)
- Chemicals utilized and control test results
- Presumptive blood test type utilized
- Bloodstains tested with a presumptive test and the results
- Stains collected as evidence

Additional notes to consider taking are the following:

- *Has the autopsy taken place yet?*
- *What are the known injuries?* Once characteristics documentation is completed, injuries are known, and laboratory tests are received, a correlation to the observed patterns can occur. An important factor that is often overlooked is the shape of a wound can influence the shape of the pattern.
- *What limitations did the analyst have?* For example, the analyst was not able to directly examine the physical evidence, or the analyst completed the analysis through photographs only.

Figure 23.1 shows a representative bloodstain characteristic form that could be utilized for scene bloodstain documentation. When it comes to notes, a good rule to follow is: if you aren't sure, write it down! It's always better to have too many notes rather than not enough.

Analyst:

Date: ____________

Case #: ________________

Bloodstain Pattern Analysis- Pattern Characteristic Documentation

Pattern Identifier: ______________________________

Size	Predominate stain size: Approx. # of stains: Highest stain/directionality: Lowest stain/directionality: Surface area/overall pattern size:	**Shape**	Elliptical Circular Other:
Distribution (Heaviest distribution of stains, where stains are located within pattern, overall arrangement, radiating, linear, etc)			
Appearance	Wet Dry Diluted Altered Flow Air bubbles Flaking Color: ____________ Patterned (describe): Other: External factors (temp/air flow/humidity): Directionalities observed:		
Location	Surface description:		
Chemicals: LCV Bluestar Other: **Presumptive blood test:** Yes No **Test type:** **Stains tested (results):**		**Stains collected as evidence:**	

Page ___ of ___

Figure 23.1 A representative bloodstain characteristic form that could be used for scene documentation. (Courtesy of Illinois State Police, Scene and Evidence Services Command.)

SKETCHES AND DIAGRAMS

Photographs and notes alone may not always depict the spatial relationship between items of evidence, including bloodstains, at a crime scene. In addition, it can be difficult to understand the overall layout of the scene or the importance that distance may play from these types of documentation alone. A sketch allows the analyst to visually document only essential items, whereas photographs may be overcrowded or contain unnecessary details.[9] Sketches and diagrams help clear away the visual clutter and help focus on important details. A rough or field sketch is a hand-drawn or computer-aided representation of conditions at a crime scene and is completed while on scene. The finished diagram is the finalized version of the field sketch and is usually completed later, often in preparation for court or based upon the policy of the agency.

Including bloodstains and bloodstain patterns in a sketch should not be looked at as different than measuring and documenting other types of evidence. In both instances, enough exact measurements need to be taken not only to allow recreation of the overall scene layout to include pertinent surroundings or furniture but also to include the relevant items of evidence, i.e. bloodstain patterns. One of the main aspects of sketching through the scope of a bloodstain analyst is consideration of the size and location of stains. Can all the bloodstains be covered in one diagram? Are multiple sketches from varying views necessary? Often, a bird's-eye view is helpful for overall scene layout, but it does not easily or clearly depict bloodstains on walls. In such cases, individual diagrams of separate walls may be necessary in order to give the complete picture and ensure overall understanding. Figures 23.2 and 23.3 show examples of how bloodstains can be documented overall using a bird's-eye view and in more detail by using an individual wall diagram. In unique cases, a pattern may be so complex that it requires its own diagram. For example, a pattern located on a recliner chair in a living room may be so complex that the entire diagram consists of an enlarged picture of the chair with detailed bloodstain information and details.

Just as in general scene diagramming, the analyst would utilize a reference point to place the bloodstain(s) or pattern in the room. Measurements not placed directly on the sketch should

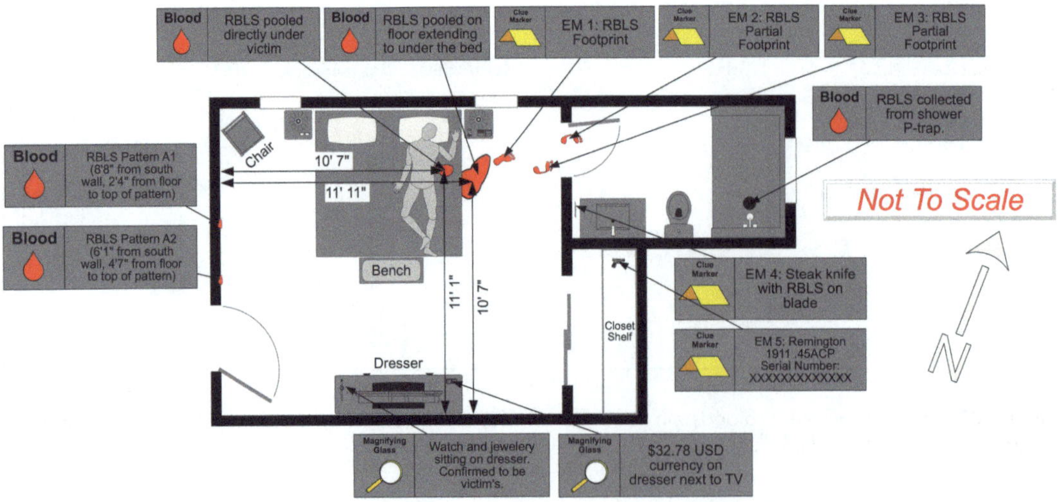

Figure 23.2 A representative bird's-eye view computer-generated diagram showing the overall scene layout. (Courtesy of Dan Johnson, Illinois State Police.)

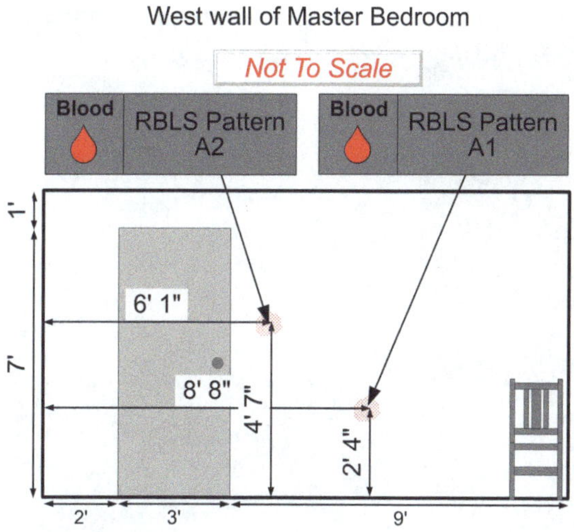

Figure 23.3 A representative computer-generated diagram of an individual wall (West wall of master bedroom) from the diagram depicted in Figure 23.2. (Courtesy of Dan Johnson, Illinois State Police.)

be included in the analyst's notes on a separate page or on a measurement coordinate form. In general, most patterns can be measured to the center of the pattern, such as a blood pool. Some pattern types, such as impact patterns, may need exact measurements to individual spatter stains if an area of origin software program is utilized. Drip trails can be documented by referencing both "ends" of the trail and a representative sample of stains throughout. Bloodstains can be documented using a red-colored pencil in paper drawings or by utilizing the red color in computer-aided diagrams. In addition, they should also be labeled with their assigned pattern identifier for clarification.

Another useful tool is the utilization of a photo to sketch program. Many photo programs and applications are now available as standard issue or affordable downloads. A photo to sketch program allows the user to convert a photograph into a depiction that resembles a black and white line drawing. Photo to sketch diagrams are easy to label with measurements and are a timesaver. They can also be especially useful in court where photographs depicting bloodstained scenes are considered prejudicial. A photograph of a bloody hallway turned into a black and white line drawing can easily depict scene measurements and is much less shocking. Figure 23.4a–d shows examples of photographs before and after utilizing a photo to sketch program.

VIDEOS

Digital video capture is a great supplement to regular crime scene photographs. However, it should never be used as the sole source of visual representation. Video documentation is utilized to augment the documentation of bloodstains when it would be beneficial to the investigation and is best performed prior to scene processing in order to capture the scene in situ.[10] Additional video documentation can also be completed later to specifically highlight portions of the scene such as bloodstain roadmapping.

The following is a list of guidelines for digital video capture:

- Utilize the highest resolution for general documentation.
- The sound port should be plugged or disabled to prohibit sound on the video.
- Video should be taken in a slow pan motion or in stop motion images.

Figure 23.4 (a) A scene photograph of a bloody hallway, (b) a depiction of the bloody hallway after it was converted to a black and white line drawing utilizing a photo to sketch program, (c) a scene photograph of blood in a bedroom, and (d) a depiction of the bedroom after it was converted to a black and white line drawing utilizing a photo to sketch program. (Courtesy of Jeff Gurvis, Illinois.)

- Movement should be extremely slow and limited.
- Documentation of evidence or points of interest should be recorded as stop motion images from long range, medium range, and close range.
- Ensure adequate lighting is available.[11]
- All personnel should be cleared from the scene prior to video recording.[12]
- The tape should not be altered in any way and the recorder should be documented in the notes.[13]

EVIDENCE PRESERVATION AND SCENE CONTEXT

It is important to ensure that bloodstain exhibits, and crime scene exhibits in general, are labeled and packaged using a methodology that preserves the evidentiary context and integrity of the crime scene. The method of preservation needs to be organized in such a way that leaves no question as to the exhibit's original location within the scene.

Convenience packaging may be utilized when packaging related items with similar scene context. This type of packaging typically consists of an exterior sealed container with smaller, individually packaged items located inside. The individually packaged items are labeled and packaged in a manner that prevents cross-contamination and ensures preservation of the evidentiary context of the scene. The description of the exhibit should include mention of the exterior packaging and the individual items located within.

For example, convenience packaging for swabs collected from an impact pattern would look like the following: *Sealed bag containing eight swabs collected from Bloodstain Pattern A (living room west wall), individually packaged and sealed (labeled A1–A8)*. In this example, the exterior bag would contain the labeling information described above. The swabs would be placed in separate swab boxes and placed inside individual paper bags. The bags would be properly sealed and labeled with the case number and associated identifier (A1, A2, etc.).

A representative sample from each bloodstain pattern should be collected. Exactly how many swabs per pattern this means should be based on information available at the time of collection and sound reasoning.[14] In general, a minimum of two swabs per pattern is acceptable. However, when dealing with complex patterns or patterns spread over a considerable distance, additional swabs above the two should be collected. For example, when dealing with an impact pattern, consideration should be given to the collection of a sample from each of the individual spatter stains utilized to perform the area of origin reconstruction. An important note to remember is that not all collected stains have to be analyzed by the laboratory.

While an analyst should consult with a specific forensic laboratory to ensure the proper laboratory protocols and procedures are adhered to, the following guidelines generally apply when dealing with the collection of bloodstain evidence:

- Liquid blood can be collected using a sterile cotton swab which is then packaged loosely to allow for air drying. Attempting to hasten the drying with heat or sunlight should not be done. If a liquid sample must be collected, it should be placed in a clean container using clean tools/equipment. The sample should be refrigerated as soon as possible.
- Dry bloodstains can be collected in two ways:
  - Scraping the stain with a sterile, disposable scalpel into a paper fold and then packaging the fold in an envelope.
  - Moistening a sterile cotton swab with distilled water and swabbing the stain. If the stain is small in size/limited in volume, swab the stain in a manner that concentrates the stain on one area of the swab, such as spinning the tip of the swab on the stain.
- When possible, the entire bloodstained item, such as clothing, should be collected. When appropriate and feasible, consider collecting large items of evidence such as bathtubs, shower installs, furniture, cabinets, rugs, or large sections of a wall or floor.
- Items such as clothing or bedding should not be folded or packaged wet due to potentially altering and/or destroying bloodstains present. Bloody items may require temporary packaging to avoid leaking and contamination while transporting to a drying cabinet. However, transporting the bloody item in plastic should only be done for a short period of time. Regardless of whether the temporary packaging is paper or plastic, the packaging should be dried and made an exhibit. In addition, it should be noted that if packaging has the potential to alter the bloodstains present, the item should be thoroughly photographed prior to the packaging taking place.

Notes

1. James, Stuart H., Paul E. Kish, and T. Paulette Sutton. *Principles of Bloodstain Pattern Analysis*, (Boca Raton, FL: CRC Press, 2005), 264.
2. James, Stuart H., Paul E. Kish, and T. Paulette Sutton. *Principles of Bloodstain Pattern Analysis*, (Boca Raton, FL: CRC Press, 2005), 264.
3. James, Stuart H., Paul E. Kish, and T. Paulette Sutton. *Principles of Bloodstain Pattern Analysis*, (Boca Raton, FL: CRC Press, 2005), 265.
4. James, Stuart H., Paul E. Kish, and T. Paulette Sutton. *Principles of Bloodstain Pattern Analysis*, (Boca Raton, FL: CRC Press, 2005), 100.
5. James, Stuart H., Paul E. Kish, and T. Paulette Sutton. *Principles of Bloodstain Pattern Analysis*, (Boca Raton, FL: CRC Press, 2005), 100.
6. James, Stuart H., Paul E. Kish, and T. Paulette Sutton. *Principles of Bloodstain Pattern Analysis*, (Boca Raton, FL: CRC Press, 2005), 100.
7. James, Stuart H., Paul E. Kish, and T. Paulette Sutton. *Principles of Bloodstain Pattern Analysis*, (Boca Raton, FL: CRC Press, 2005), 100.
8. James, Stuart H., Paul E. Kish, and T. Paulette Sutton. *Principles of Bloodstain Pattern Analysis*, (Boca Raton, FL: CRC Press, 2005), 103.

9. James, Stuart H., Paul E. Kish, and T. Paulette Sutton. *Principles of Bloodstain Pattern Analysis*, (Boca Raton, FL: CRC Press, 2005), 265.
10. Bevel, Tom and Ross M. Gardner. *Bloodstain Pattern Analysis: With an Introduction to Crime Scene Reconstruction*, (Boca Raton, FL: CRC Press, 2008), 311.
11. James Stuart H., Paul E. Kish, and T. Paulette Sutton. *Principles of Bloodstain Pattern Analysis*, (Boca Raton, FL: CRC Press, 2005), 265.
12. James, Stuart H., Paul E. Kish, and T. Paulette Sutton. *Principles of Bloodstain Pattern Analysis*, (Boca Raton, FL: CRC Press, 2005), 265.
13. James, Stuart H., Paul E. Kish, and T. Paulette Sutton. *Principles of Bloodstain Pattern Analysis*, (Boca Raton, FL: CRC Press, 2005), 265.
14. James, Stuart H., Paul E. Kish, and T. Paulette Sutton. *Principles of Bloodstain Pattern Analysis*, (Boca Raton, FL: CRC Press, 205), 343.

Further Reading

Gardner, Ross M. *Practical Crime Scene Processing and Investigation*. Boca Raton, FL: CRC Press, 2011.

CHAPTER 24

ROAD MAPPING FOR BLOODSTAIN PATTERN ANALYSIS SCENE AND EVIDENCE DOCUMENTATION

Toby L. Wolson

"Road mapping" is a method frequently used by bloodstain pattern analysts for the photographic preservation and documentation of bloodstain patterns at crime scenes and on physical items of evidence. The concept of road mapping was originated by the author in December 1988 during the documentation, reconstruction, and analysis of a death investigation scene in which a known drug dealer was alleged to have had a physical confrontation with six police officers in his apartment, resulting in his death. The process in its simplest form provides photographic documentation of the bloodstain patterns that can be used as a visual map while doing analysis of the data, report writing, and presentation in court. Over time, road mapping has been modified and adapted by bloodstain pattern analysts to fit their needs and methodologies. What is discussed in this chapter is the basic minimum process for scene documentation using road mapping. Procedure modifications above and beyond these basic procedures are acceptable if they work for the analyst documenting the bloodstain evidence. In addition to photographic documentation of the bloodstain scene, the analyst should memorialize their entire work product as written notes.

The length of time needed to document a bloodstain scene and complexity of using road mapping is variable and depends on the physical characteristics of the scene (indoor, outdoor, cluttered, neat, scene size…), the substrates the blood is deposited on (carpet, wood, painted surfaces, tile, glass, curved surfaces…), how much blood is present, length of time since the blood was deposited, and any previous processing of the scene prior to bloodstain pattern analysis (BPA). It is always preferred that the bloodstain analyst be allowed into the crime scene as early as possible after the arrival of police investigators and crime scene personnel. Early access to the crime scene by the bloodstain analyst allows them to see the original appearance of the bloodstains and observe the original condition of the crime scene prior to other personnel performing their processing functions. Documentation and reconstruction of the bloodstain scene can be an invasive process that may result in alterations and changes to the bloodstain pattern evidence. It is important to have a full and complete photographic record of all the bloodstain evidence prior to starting the road map documentation process. Photographs should show the blood scene from a general overall perspective (Figure 24.1 (a–c)) and through a series of close-ups that show the characteristics of the bloodstains being documented (Figures 24.2 (a–c)). All photographs should be captured as large raw, bitmap, or tiff image files. The larger the size of the image files, the more the images can be enlarged without beginning to pixilate and lose resolution. If the images are captured as jpg image files, it is important to know that jpg image files can lose image resolution each time the file is opened and closed. It is recommended that copies of the jpg images files be made and that those copies are used by the bloodstain analyst during analysis.

These images serve as a record demonstrating that a minimum number of bloodstains were altered or covered from view by the scales and materials used while documenting the bloodstain evidence.

DOI: 10.4324/9781003163695-24

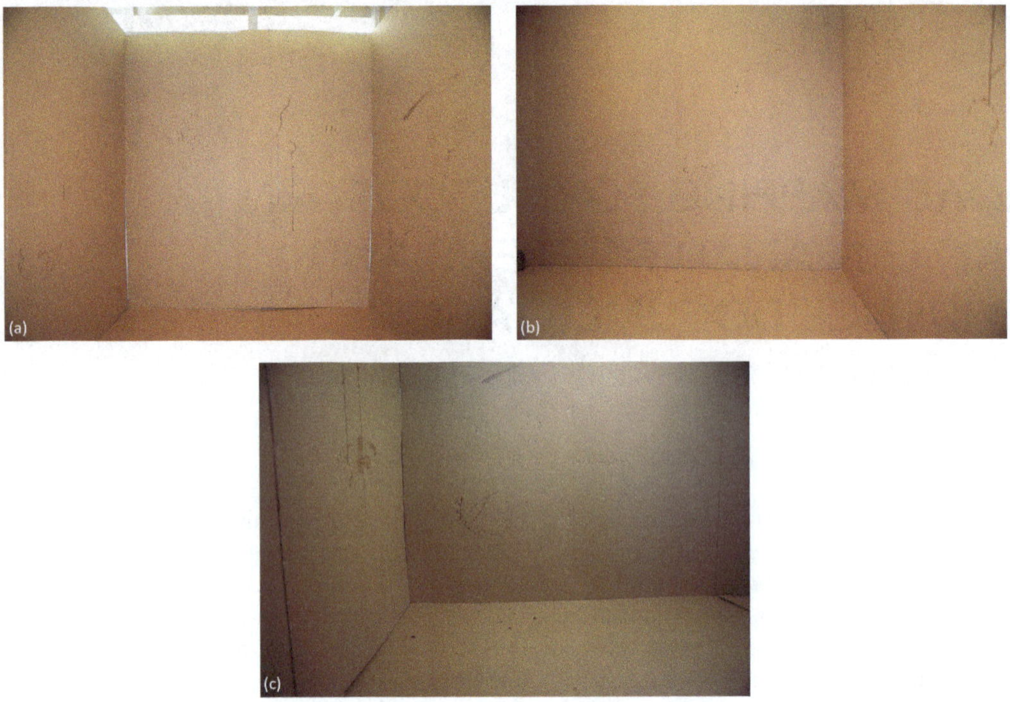

Figure 24.1 General overall pictures of the bloodstained surfaces before the start of the road mapping documentation procedure, (a) front wall, (b) left side wall, and (c) right side wall.

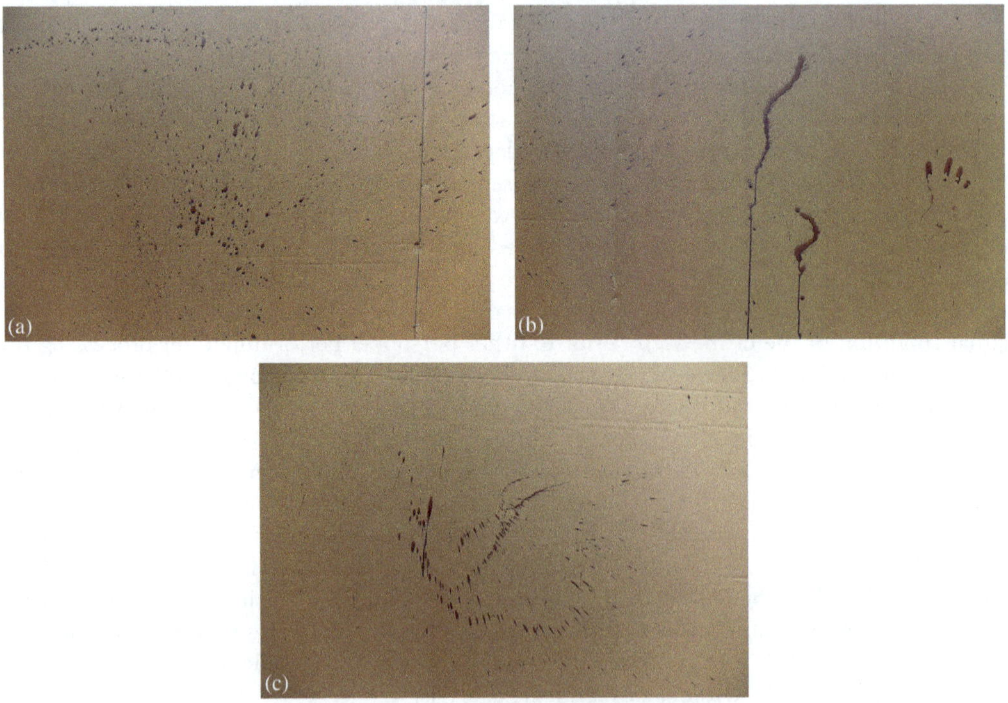

Figure 24.2 Close-up pictures of the bloodstained surfaces before the start of the road mapping documentation procedure, (a) left side wall, (b) front wall, and (c) right side wall.

It is important that the camera be positioned as close to perpendicular to the center of the bloodstained surfaces as possible. This limits distortion of the bloodstains and their patterns in the images. Use of a camera tripod is recommended for the documentation process. It is also very important while photographing the bloodstain evidence to have even lighting across the entire surface, which allows all the blood evidence to be seen in clear and crisp detail when viewing the photographs (Figures 24.3 and 24.4).

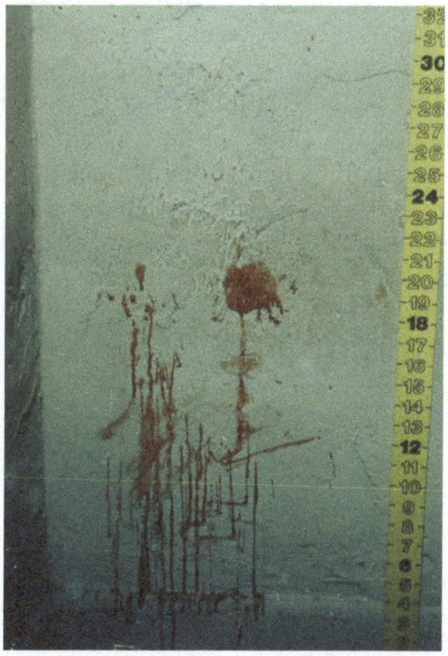

Figure 24.3 Close-up picture showing a bloodstained area with uneven lighting.

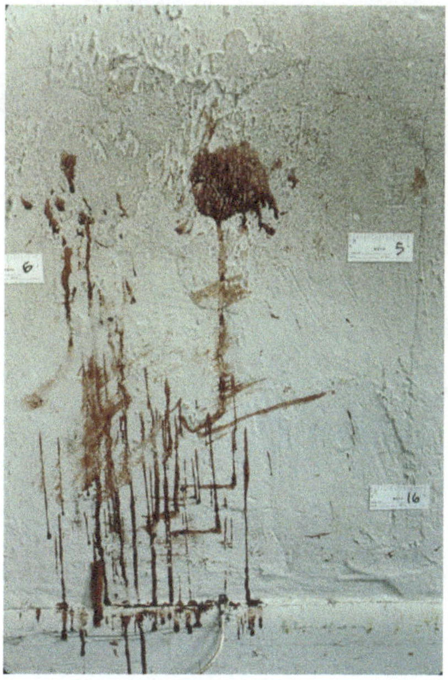

Figure 24.4 Close-up picture showing the bloodstained area from Figure 24.3 with even lighting.

This was a much more difficult process during the days when film cameras were used to photographically document bloodstain evidence. Digital cameras give the bloodstain analyst the ability to see the preserved images instantly and make changes to the camera orientation and surface lighting as needed.

After completing the photographic documentation of the unprocessed bloodstain evidence, the next processing step can start. Place vertical and horizontal scales to illustrate the location of the bloodstains and their patterns on the surfaces being photographed. The vertical scales should originate at a fixed location on the left or right side of the bloodstained surface, and the horizontal scales should originate at a fixed location from the top or bottom of the bloodstained surface. These scales can have metric or imperial measurement markings. Attachment of the scales to the bloodstained surface is dependent on the substrate properties. On many surfaces, the analyst can use adhesive scales, double-sided tape, and pins to attach the scales. However, some surfaces will not be amenable to using adhesives and pins for scale attachment. This will require the bloodstain analyst to improvise and use alternate methods for scale attachment. Photograph the surfaces with the camera perpendicular to the center of the surface, showing the entire surface, including the vertical and horizontal scales (Figure 24.5 (a–c)). Comparison of these images to the pre-documentation images serve as a record of the analyst's work product showing what alterations (if any) or bloodstains may have been hidden from view by the overlaying scales.

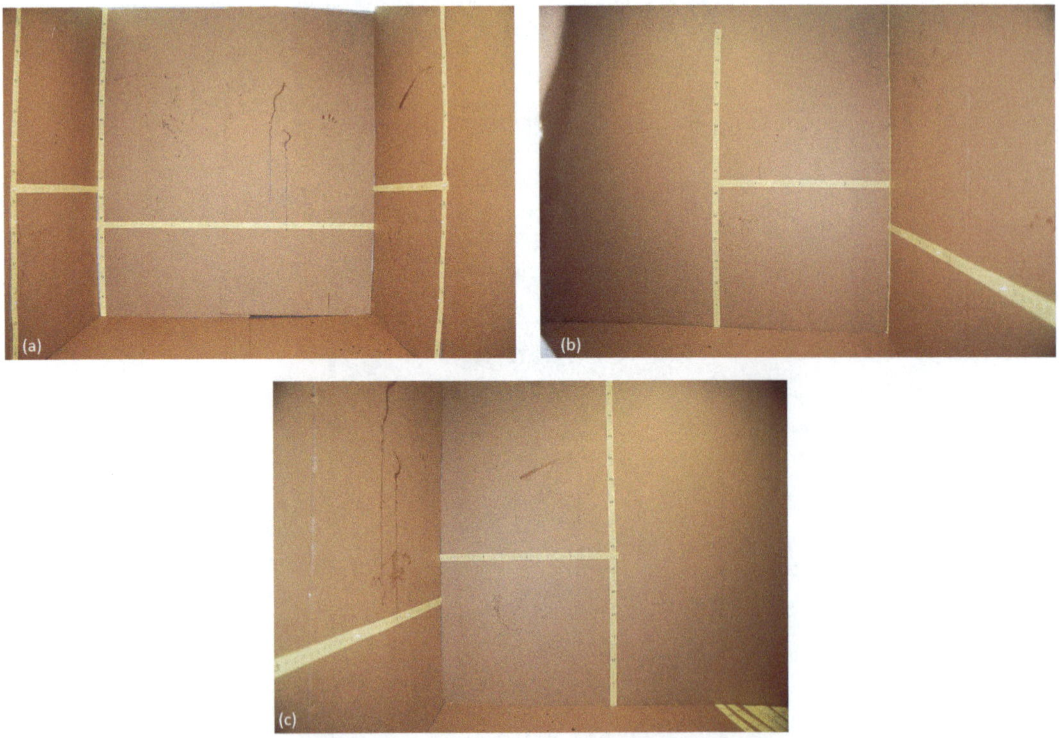

Figure 24.5 General overall pictures of the bloodstained surfaces after placement of vertical and horizontal scales originating from fixed points within the blood scene, (a) front wall, (b) left side wall, and (c) right side wall.

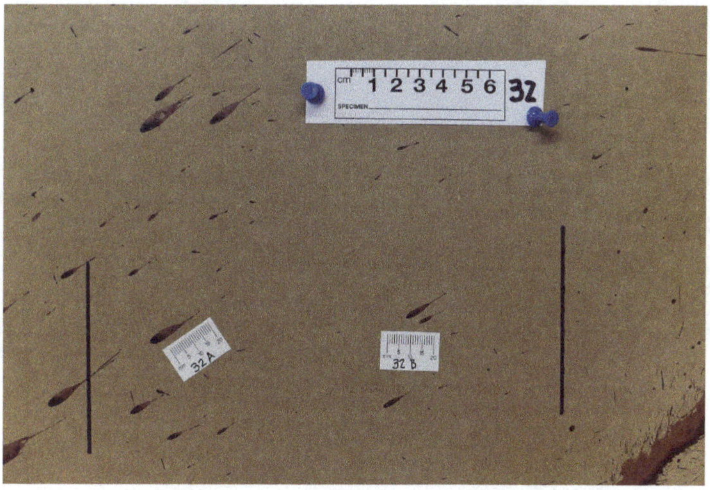

Figure 24.6 Picture of metric scales with numeric labels.

The next step in the road mapping process is the application of metric scales near the bloodstains and their patterns. The size of the metric scales depends on the provider of the forensic equipment. Large metric scales have the advantage of being easier to see in the images than small metric scales. However, the larger the metric scale, the more difficult it may be to place it on the bloodstained surface without covering bloodstains. The orientation and location of the metric scales is determined by the bloodstain analyst as they are placed on the surface. The analyst should use as many metric scales as necessary to ensure that all close-up images of the bloodstains will have a minimum of one metric scale in each image. Each metric scale should have a letter and/or numeric identifier written on or near it. This identifier should be bold, dark, and large to maximize visibility in the photographic images (Figure 24.6). The bloodstains and patterns are photographed after all the metric scales are in place. The photographs should start with general overall images showing the entire surfaces of interest. These initial photographs showing all the labeled metric scales are the mapping images. The mapping images are used to show the locations of bloodstains and their patterns that are documented using close-up photography (Figure 24.7 (a–c)). As with the previous photographic documentation, the camera should be positioned perpendicular to the center of the surface being photographed.

After the mapping photographs have been completed, close-up photography of all the bloodstains and their patterns should be done. This process should be thorough and complete so that all the bloodstains and their patterns are documented in the photographic record. It is essential that each close-up image contains a minimum of one labeled metric scale. This allows the analyst to show the location of the bloodstains and their patterns in the close-up images by using the labeled metric scale to locate the same labeled scale in the mapping images. Start by capturing images that show complete bloodstain patterns and then, if needed, follow these close-up photographs with additional close-up photographs showing the shapes and sizes of the bloodstains in the pattern (Figures 24.8 and 24.9).

If a bloodstain pattern is reconstructed using a "hands-on" procedure, such as stringing, to determine the area of convergence and the area of origin, the bloodstain pattern analyst should create a written and photographic record of their work product for each step of the reconstruction (Figures 24.10 and 24.11).

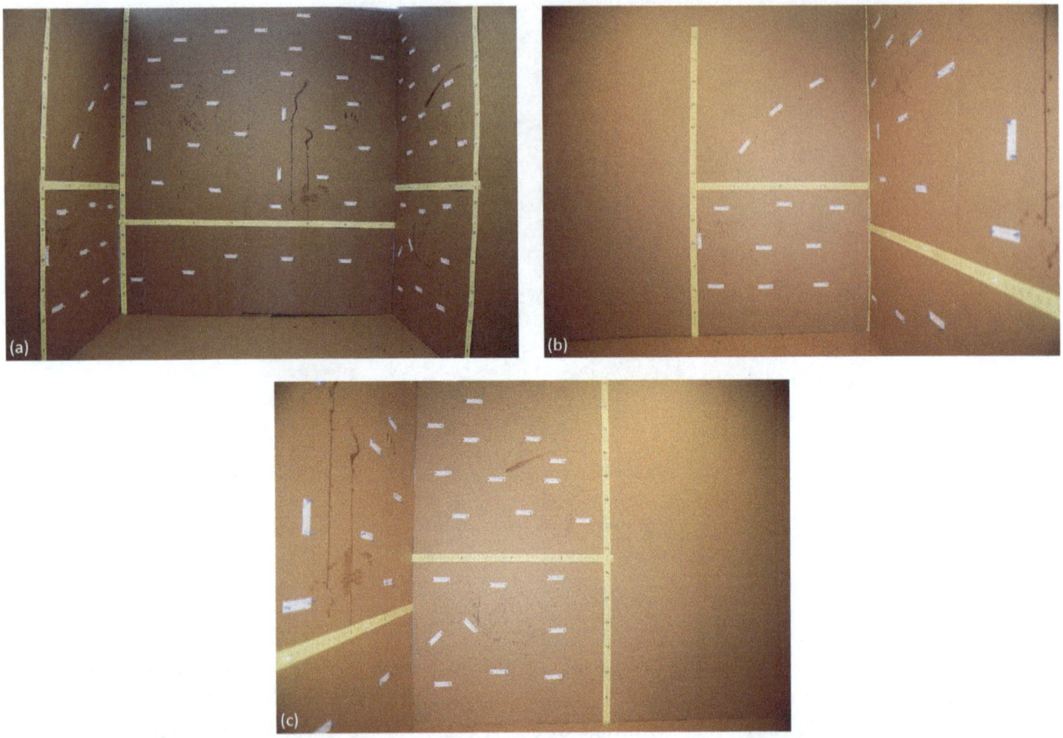

Figure 24.7 (a–c) General overall pictures of the bloodstained surfaces after placement of all the labeled metric scales, (a) front wall, (b) left side wall, and (c) right side wall.

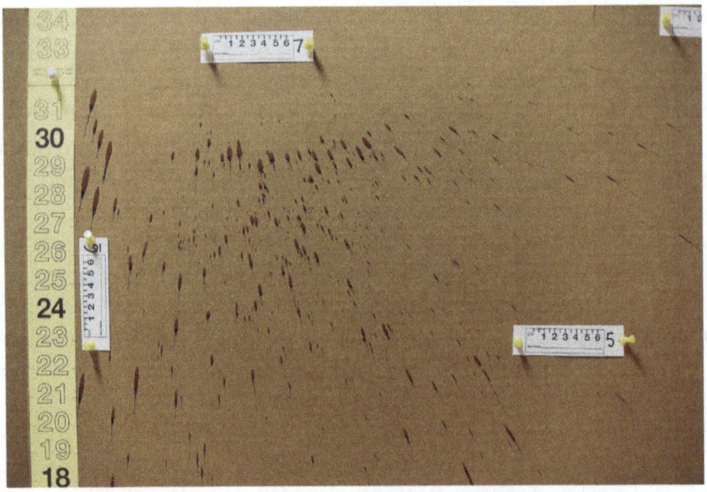

Figure 24.8 Overall picture of a bloodstain pattern with labeled metric scales.

Figure 24.9 Close-up picture of the bloodstains in the pattern illustrated in Figure 24.8.

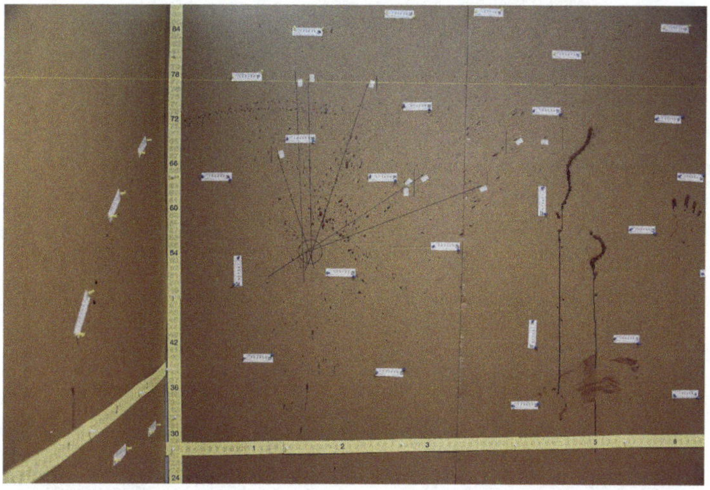

Figure 24.10 Overall picture showing an area of convergence determination.

If the area of convergence and the area of origin are determined using a computer program, additional steps must be added to the road map and the analyst's notes. It is necessary to photograph each individual bloodstain used for the reconstruction. Each close-up image of the reconstructed bloodstains should have a labeled metric scale positioned near the bloodstain. In addition, if the area of origin determination is to be done using a computer program, it will be necessary to include a line that shows the vertical axis of the bloodstains (Figure 24.12), and it will be necessary for the analyst to measure each bloodstain's distance away from the fixed vertical and horizontal planes that were previously documented.

The use of road mapping will assist the bloodstain analyst in their analysis of the bloodstain scene and the individual bloodstain patterns. It will also provide the bloodstain analyst with documentation that can be reviewed by other qualified bloodstain analysts and for visual presentation of their findings and opinions in their written report and trial testimony.

Figure 24.11 Overall picture showing an area of origin determination.

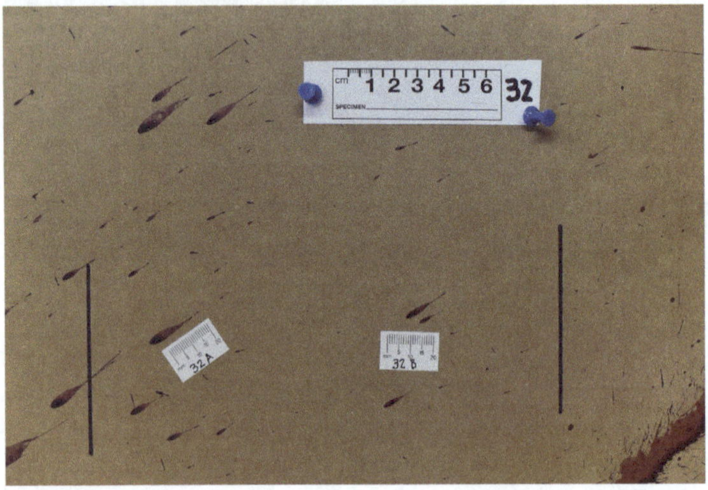

Figure 24.12 Picture showing the placement of metric scales near individual bloodstains and the placement of vertical lines to demonstrate the vertical axis of bloodstains.

CHAPTER 25

CHEMICAL VISUAL ENHANCEMENT AND SEARCHING TECHNIQUES FOR BLOOD

Martin Eversdijk and Theresa Stotesbury

INTRODUCTION

Chemical enhancement and searching techniques play an important role in crime scene investigation, including in the process of bloodstain pattern analysis (BPA). The goal of chemical visual enhancement is to create a visible contrast between the evidence (e.g. bloodstain) and the surface that it is deposited on. In this chapter, chemical enhancement refers to the visualization of latent bloodstains and bloodied impressions found at crime scenes. Latent or trace bloodstains are those that are invisible to the human eye without modification (e.g. chemical enhancement) and/or amplification (e.g. microscopy). These can include diluted, microscopic, and/or camouflaged bloodstains and their patterns typically in the form of bloodied impressions. The purpose of this chapter is to describe the basic mechanisms involved in chemical enhancement of blood, and, in addition, provide methods and tips for the chemical enhancement of and search techniques for blood deposited at a crime scene. A working knowledge of chemical reagents and their application to searching and/or enhancing bloodstains during crime scene investigations is essential for a bloodstain pattern analyst.

CHEMICAL ENHANCEMENT AND SEARCHING FOR BLOOD: THE BASICS

As we learned from Chapters 3, 4, and 5, bloodstains are a complex type of forensic evidence composed of a variety of biomolecules, including proteins, lipids, hormones, immunoglobulins, clotting factors, and more. Chemical enhancement reagents for blood react with these biomolecular components to produce products with a visible, and usually bright, color contrast compared to its initial deposition at the crime scene. Many chemical enhancement and searching methods for blood usually occur through the reagents' reactions with proteins. Generally, there are three types of chemical enhancement and searching reagents for blood which will be referred to in this chapter and include protein and amino acid staining, peroxidase, and other. A brief summary of each type is described in Table 25.1.

Staining reagents contain dyes that react with proteins, amino acids, and/or their degradation products to create (brightly) colored and sometimes fluorescent products. These reagents typically require fixing, staining, and rinsing steps. Staining reagents are often used to enhance bloodied impression evidence.[1,2,3,4]

DOI: 10.4324/9781003163695-25

Table 25.1 General classification of types of chemical enhancement and searching reagents for bloodstains

Reagent	Definition	Examples
Protein and amino acid staining	Solutions that contain dyes that will react with proteins, amino acids, and/or their degradation products to form (brightly) colored and/or fluorescent products. These typically require fixing, staining, and rinsing steps.	*Protein:* Acid black 1 (amido black), acid violet 19 (fuchsin/Hungarian red), acid yellow 7 (brilliant sulfoflavine), acid blue 83 (Coomassie brilliant blue R) *Amino acid:* Ninhydrin
Peroxidase	Solutions where the dye is oxidized to form (brightly) colored, fluorescent, and/or chemiluminescent products. In these reactions, typically hemoglobin and its derivatives catalyze the oxidation.	Aqueous leucocrystal violet (ALCV), leucomalachite green (LMG), 3-aminophthalhydrazide (luminol), acid yellow 73 (fluorescein)
Other	Contains compounds that promote physical and/or chemical interactions with components of the bloodstain to enhance its visual contrast with the target surface.	Suspension dyes, novel nanoparticle, and polymer solutions

Peroxidase reagents are basic and colorless dye solutions that become brightly colored and/or even fluorescent or chemiluminescent after oxidation. When enhancing bloodstains, hemoglobin, a key biomolecule found in the red blood cells responsible for oxygen transport throughout the body, is responsible for catalyzing the oxidation of these dyes. These reagents are typically more selective than protein staining reagents and do not react with other bodily fluids (unless they are contaminated with trace amounts of blood). These reagents are excellent to use for searching and presumptive testing at crime scenes as they have a high sensitivity for reactions with significantly diluted bloodstains.[5,6,7]

Other solutions that contain particulate suspensions[8] nanoparticles,[9,10] and other polymer solutions[11] have also demonstrated effectiveness in the chemical enhancement of bloodstains and bloodied impression evidence. These solutions promote physical and/or chemical interactions with components of the bloodstain to enhance its visual contrast from the target surface.

While many chemical enhancement and searching reagents exist for blood, the solutions discussed in this chapter are chosen for safety of use at a crime scene as well as for ease of reagent preparation, stability, and application to a wide range of surfaces. The following chemical enhancement reagents and visualization techniques for blood are discussed in detail:

- Amido black
- Acid fuchsin (Hungarian red)
- Aqueous leucocrystal violet (ALCV)
- Suspension dyes
- Luminol
- Fluorescein

Please note these formulations are **water-based**, described as aqueous, unless otherwise specified. Water-based formulations are important for general crime scene and laboratory use because they are not flammable or made from toxic solvents, and are generally more cost-efficient. For the purposes of this chapter, distilled water is written as the solvent choice for reasons of accessibility and availability; however, high-quality purified water (e.g. Millipore-Q®) is also used.

First, a scenario is described to put the role of chemical enhancement and searching for blood into perspective in the field of BPA and in overall crime scene investigation. Then, each enhancement and searching reagent is described in more detail with a focus on practical crime scene application.

SCENARIO

In the bedroom of a residential dwelling, the body of the deceased was found on the bed. On the floor and wall of this room, there were multiple transfer patterns, visibly made with blood, in the form of footwear and fingerprint impressions. Other bloodstain patterns, like drip and impact, were also observed. Beyond the visible bloodstains, what else could be at the crime scene that could be of importance? Without chemical enhancement and appropriate searching methods, what could be missed? Take some time to think about these questions and then draft your approach to process the scene.

SOME THOUGHTS ON THIS SCENARIO (WITH SUPPORTING INFORMATION FOUND THROUGHOUT THIS CHAPTER)

Latent Impression Enhancement

Impression evidence can help identify individuals and provide context as to the events of the crime. Visible bloodstains and transfer patterns present at crime scenes can often be accompanied by partial and latent impressions. These impressions can include footwear, bare feet, palm and fingerprints, and other objects such as weapons and fabrics that may be critical to the crime scene investigation. For example, some parts of a bloodied fingerprint impression may be visible and recognizable, but lack enough ridge detail and/or individual characteristics to make the impression suitable for comparison. Often partial or latent fingerprint impressions made with blood can contain class and individual characteristics useful for identification, and often these are visualized after chemical enhancement.[12] In these circumstances, a protein staining reagent that uses a fixative for blood like amido black, acid fuchsin, or ALCV should be considered for use.

Chemical Enhancement of Blood Versus Searching for Blood

Searching for latent bloodstains can help provide context to the events of the crime. Peroxidase reagents like luminol and fluorescein are generally used to search for latent bloodstains and bloodied impressions, which could be present at the scenario described above. These reagents can easily be sprayed over large areas of a crime scene and have very high sensitivity to detect diluted bloodstains (1:~10^6 dilution). A major limitation of luminol and fluorescein is the absence of a fixative. Latent bloodstains on non-absorbent substrates can quickly become distorted and run-off the surface when over-sprayed, causing changes in the impressions and dilution/spreading of genetic material (e.g. DNA and RNA). Therefore, although these reagents are useful for searching for latent bloodstains, they are not the best choice for chemically enhancing ridge detail and individual characteristics.

Approach: Considerations for the Bloodstain Analyst

A bloodstain pattern analyst who is considering the use of chemical enhancement and searching techniques for blood at a crime scene and in the laboratory should have considerable knowledge and experience of using and preparing chemical reagents. Beyond preparing the reagents, the bloodstain pattern analyst should be aware of the nature of the substrate on which the bloodstain or bloodied impression exists, the properties of the enhanced (color, fluorescence, etc.) bloodstains in relation to the substrate, the compatibility of the enhancement reagent with that substrate that the bloodstain is deposited on (e.g. porous vs non-porous), the sensitivity and selectivity of the chemical reagent for the enhancement, and the effect of the chemical reagent(s) on DNA extraction and analysis. For example, fluorescent protein stains are useful for enhancing bloodied footwear impressions on textiles.[13,14] Luminol has a greater sensitivity than hydrogen peroxide for diluted blood detection on dark surfaces; however, both can be useful to the analyst.[15] Compatibility of the reagents with each other for sequential treatment of the bloodstain or bloodied impression is also an important factor to consider. This is particularly true for bloodied impressions like footwear and fingerprints where amino acid enhancement reagents can also be applied to the impression.[16,17,18] Before starting any chemical enhancement or searching technique for blood, the bloodstain pattern analyst should practice:

- Following the safety data sheets (SDS), laboratory standard operating procedures (SOPs), and any known health and safety precautions for *every* reagent used in the chemical enhancement and searching process;
- Wearing appropriate personal protective equipment (PPE) during reagent preparation, documentation, reagent application, and subsequent analyses;
- Familiarizing themselves with past casework and the reported effectiveness of the anticipated technique used for the type of chemical enhancement or searching desired;
- Optimizing the color contrast between the enhancement reagent relative to the surface on which the bloodstain and/or bloodied impression may exist;
- Choosing an appropriate reagent for the porosity (porous, semi-porous, non-porous) of the surface on which the bloodstain and/or bloodied impression exists;
- Assessing the feasibility of optimizing and lifting the enhanced impression from the surface if required;
- Understanding the importance of reagent preparation, including the influence of pH, temperature, and room humidity on the effectiveness of subsequent enhancements in sequence with other techniques;
- Conducting the proper method for the collection of DNA depending on chosen enhancement technique; and,
- Applying the proper techniques for documentation of the enhancement with a focus on photography.

STEPS PRIOR TO CHEMICAL ENHANCEMENT OR SEARCHING REAGENT APPLICATION

Preliminary procedures should be performed prior to the application of the aqueous chemical enhancement and/or searching reagents for blood at a crime scene or within the laboratory. The evidence or surface that may contain the bloodstain and/or bloodied impression should be examined visually, preferably with the use of an alternative light source or bright light. For example, using infrared radiation is an effective spectroscopic method for the visualization of blood,[19] and, if accessible, so is hyperspectral imaging[20]. *Documentation is a critical step in the chemical enhancement and searching processes.* It serves as the analyst's record of any chemical modification conducted on the evidence. It is incredibly useful to record when the reagents and/or sampling techniques (e.g. swabbing for DNA) enhance or eliminate any details of the bloodied evidence (e.g. minutiae on fingerprints). If other evidence like a hair (Figure 25.1), fiber, or gunshot residue are also collected upon examination of the bloodied evidence, they must also be documented. After visual examination of the bloodied evidence, the analyst must then photograph the visible area of the impression.

After documentation and photography, the collection of serological and DNA samples should be taken prior to the application of any blood enhancement techniques, especially if this can be performed without risking damage to class or individual characteristics of a bloodied impression. A preferred method to keep the integrity of the bloodstain's features is to take such a sample by using

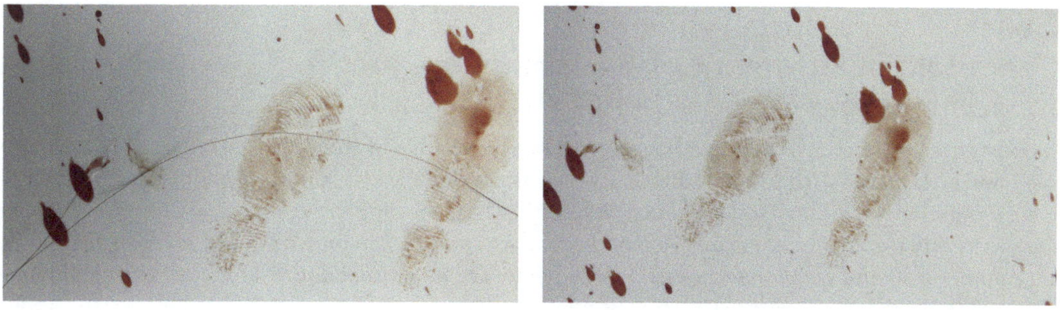

Figure 25.1 (a) Example of a hair found within a bloodied fingerprint and (b) the remaining bloodied impression when the hair is removed.

a swab with a micro tip. The swab should be taken from areas that lack visible detail, including the most heavily bloodstained portion of the impression. After taking a serological and DNA sample, the analyst should perform a confirmatory test for the presence of (human) blood in the impression (see Chapter 26).[21,22] False-positive reactions can occur! The impression may have the appearance of blood, even after the chemical enhancement when it may not be, making it very important to complete confirmatory testing. Presumptive reagents like the chemical enhancement and searching reagents mentioned in this chapter can also provide false-positive reactions with compounds that are not blood[23] – for example with bleach, copper, and/or with the protein albumin present in eggs.

There is scientific literature that demonstrates successful DNA profiles being generated *after* chemical enhancement and/or searching for bloodstains and bloodied impressions from aqueous amido black, acid fuchsin, ALCV, luminol, and suspension dyes for blood. The success of DNA recovery is influenced by the type of chemical enhancement and searching reagent used, the method of application, the dilution and alteration (e.g. bleaching) of the bloodstain, and the substrate which it is deposited on.[24,25,26,27,28] Even with using a fixative, subsequent applications of chemical enhancement and searching reagents can partially dissolve bloodstains[29] and can reduce the amount of DNA collected due to dilution. This can lead to false-negative results for confirmatory tests.[30] There are always risks for DNA and RNA degradation; however, there is research that has demonstrated that DNA profile generation post enhancement can be successful.[31,32,33,34,35,36] This process can also affect the resolution of impression evidence like bloodied fingerprints, so the application of the chemical enhancement or searching reagent is critical.[37] While beyond the scope of this chapter, working knowledge of fingerprint deposition is helpful for chemical enhancement considerations (Figure 25.2).

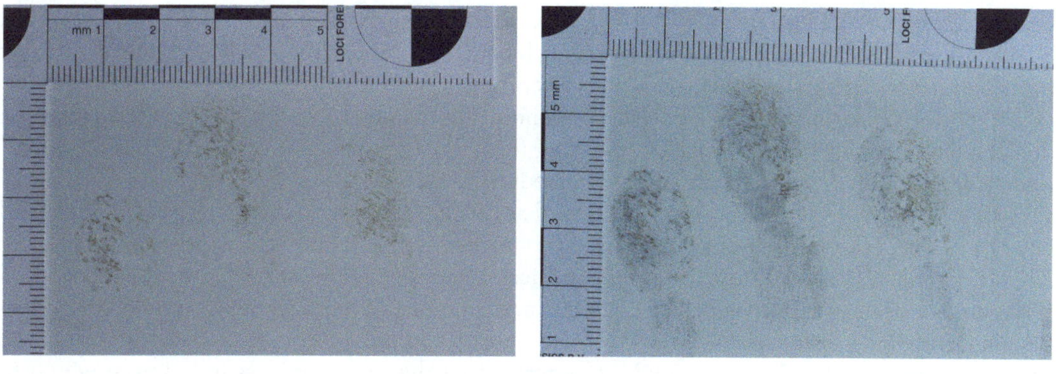

Figure 25.2 Bloodied fingerprints (a) before and (b) after enhancement.

General Information When Preparing and Using a Chemical Enhancement or Searching Reagent for Bloodstains and Bloodied Impressions

Bloodstain pattern analysts should have a working knowledge of the principles of analytical chemistry and be familiar with proper laboratory techniques for the safe handling and processing of biological materials and chemical reagents. While this chapter emphasizes aqueous solutions, *health and safety still needs to be at the forefront of the analyst's mind when preparing and applying the chemical enhancement and searching reagents.* Listed below are recommendations for preparing and using chemical reagents:

- All appropriate PPE should be used when preparing or applying the chemical enhancement reagents (e.g. gloves, face mask, goggles, protective clothing);
- Use only dry, clean, and high-purity starting materials and glassware when preparing your solutions;
- Use a fume hood when preparing and/or using enhancement reagents where appropriate;
- Run appropriate positive and negative controls to ensure the enhancement solution is working properly;
- The appropriate information should be recorded on the reagent bottle (e.g. chemical contents, date, reliability test results, preparer's initials) as well as in a log book;
- When processing has been completed, all chemicals should be disposed according to federal, state, and local environmental laws.

AQUEOUS FIXATIVE SOLUTIONS

Recall, some chemical enhancement techniques require a fixative solution to be applied prior to the enhancement reagent themselves. Aqueous chemical enhancement techniques for blood use 5-sulfosalicylic acid (5-SSA) to minimize blood from being diluted, washed away, or otherwise destroyed when coming in contact with the enhancement reagent. The fixative preserves the bloodstains features, with minimal and insignificant change in size and shape.[38]

Working aqueous amido black and acid fuchsin solutions for the enhancement of blood can be formulated *with or without* the fixative 5-SSA. When using an amido black or acid fuchsin solution without 5-SSA, prior fixation with an approximately 2% weight per volume (g/mL) aqueous solution of 5-SSA is necessary. *Excess fixative solution should be removed before application of the dye solution* for more selective (sharper) results. ALCV and aqueous suspension dyes should always contain 5-SSA as a fixative.

The fixing time and the amount of fixative are not standardized and vary based on the age, thickness, and perceived adhesion of blood to the surface. If the analyst is unsure how to fix an observed bloodstain or area presumed to contain latent bloodstains, experiment with similar conditions in the laboratory first, if possible. Also, it is important to note that fixing with aqueous solutions should not be performed by the analyst unless both the bloodied impression and the surface are dry. It is not recommended to accelerate drying (e.g. blowing heat over the surface) as this could lead to degradation, fracture, and flaking of bloodstain.

The application of the fixative solution as well as the dye solution to the surface or bloodstained object can be performed through immersion, pouring, spraying, or filter paper contact. Figure 25.3 (a–d) visually shows points of each application process. The application method chosen is dependent upon the nature of the evidence and goal of the enhancement. Immersion, pouring, and spraying should be conducted in short intervals across 3 minutes. A visual examination should be performed every 30 seconds to observe how the fixing process is progressing and to prevent over-spraying. Larger volumes of blood deposits will require longer fixing times. When

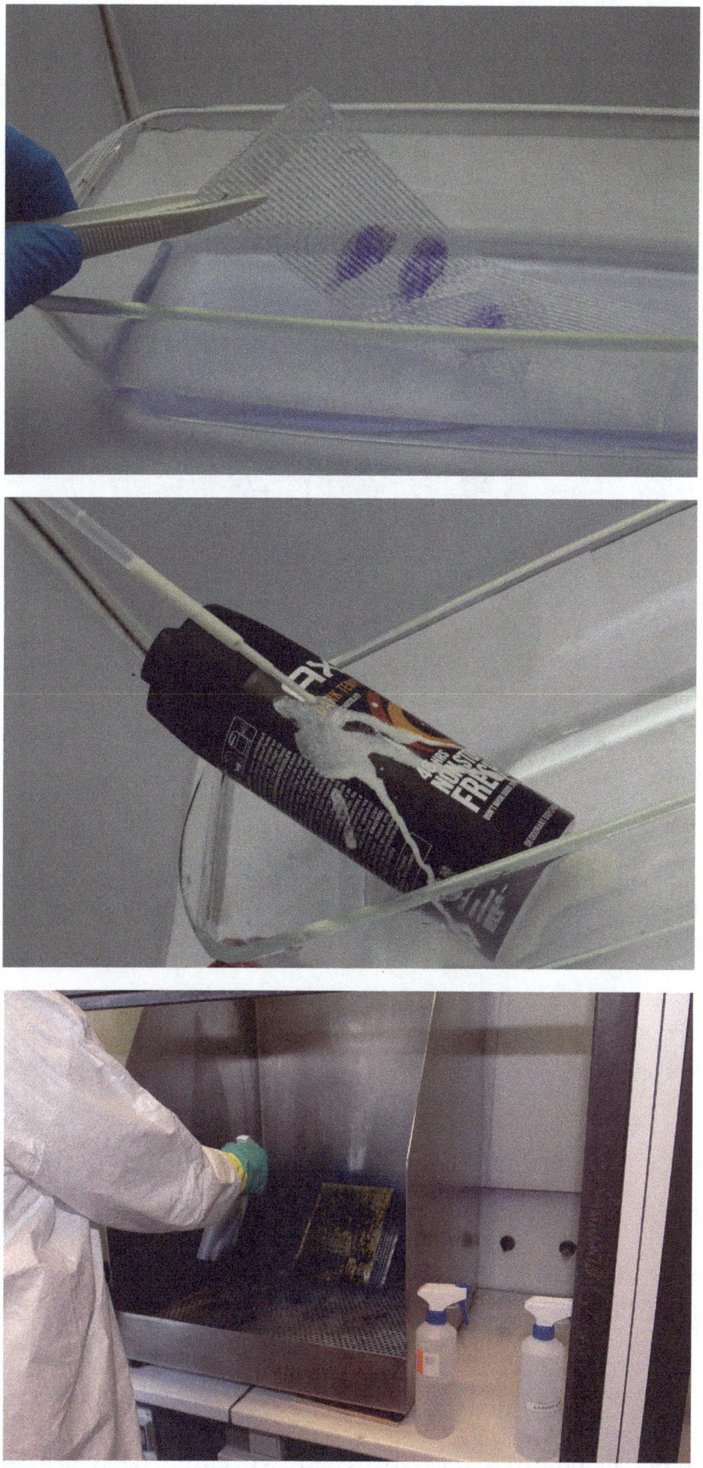

Figure 25.3 (a) Demonstration of the immersion method using a 2% w/v solution of 5-sulfosalicylic acid to fix latent bloodstains to the surface, (b) demonstration of the pouring method using a solution of titanium dioxide to fix latent bloodstains to the surface, (c) demonstration of the spraying method using a solution of fuchsine (Hungarian red) to enhance bloodstains on ceramic, and (d) demonstration of the filter paper method using a solution of amido black to enhance latent bloodstains. *(continued)*

Figure 25.3 *(Continued)*

using a 2% w/v aqueous solution of 5-SSA solution, fresh blood can change from a bright red color to brown. This color change may be a visual indication to the analyst that the surface of the bloodstain is "fixed."

Preparing the 2% w/v Aqueous 5-Sulfosalicylic Acid (5-SSA) Fixative Solution

2% w/v aqueous 5-SSA fixation for blood
10 g 5-SSA
500 mL distilled water

Protocol

- Weigh out 10 g of 5-SSA on a balance and add into it 50 mL of distilled water in a 500 mL volumetric flask.
- Fill with the rest of the distilled water to the 500 mL mark on the flask.
- Invert the flask (cap beforehand) or stir the solution with a magnetic stirring device for at least 15 minutes. A clear transparent solution will result.
- Run the appropriate positive and negative controls to ensure the reagent solution is working properly.
- Pour the solution using a clean funnel into a 500 mL dark (amber) bottle.
- Label and date the bottle, store at room temperature, and complete the log book.

Pending glassware availability, you could also add the 5-SSA to 500 mL of distilled water in a clean, dry beaker but it will still require stirring, not inverting.

Fixative and Chemical Enhancement Reagent Application Methods

As mentioned, there are four common application techniques for fixative and dye solutions; immersion, pouring, spraying, and filter paper contact.

Method 1: Immersion

- Pour sufficient volume of the fixative/dye solution into a clean dry dish that is large enough to cover and submerge the bloodstained surface.
- Submerge the surface or bloodstained object into the fixative/dye solution with the stained side facing upward and rock the dish side to side gently for 90 seconds or up to 3 minutes. Check the impression regularly during the fixing/dyeing process.
  - When dyeing, the solution must contain a fixative or the blood on the object must be pre-fixed.

Method 2: Pouring

- Pour the fixative/dye solution over the surface or bloodstained object by using a wash bottle or pipette (for smaller evidence) for at least 30 seconds. This procedure may need to be repeated and the enhancement should be visually inspected regularly during the fixing/dyeing process.
  - When dyeing, the solution must contain a fixative or the blood on the object must be pre-fixed.

Method 3: Spraying

- Use a spraying device that can create a fine mist (e.g. spray bottle) and lightly spray the fixative/dye solution multiple times over the surface or bloodstained objects for 90 seconds or up to 3 minutes.
  - When dyeing, the solution must contain a fixative or the blood on the object must be pre-fixed.

Method 4: Filter Paper

- Cover the surface or bloodstained object with filter paper and spray or pour the fixative/dye solution over the back of the filter paper. The fixative/dye solution must come in contact with the surface or bloodstained object.
- Remove the filter paper off the surface or bloodstained object after 90 seconds or up to 3 minutes.
  - When dyeing, the solution must contain fixative or the blood on the object must be pre-fixed.

RINSING PROCEDURES

Once the bloodied impression is fixed and enhanced, it can then be rinsed. Rinsing removes the excess dye solution that has not reacted with anything and therefore creates an enhanced impression that has selective (sharper) details (e.g. edges, boundary lines). For aqueous visual chemical enhancement techniques for blood, a citric acid and distilled water in a 5:1000 solution delivers excellent results. Dilute acetic acid solutions also work well (Figure 25.4).

Preparing the Rinse Solution for Aqueous Chemical Dyes

0.5% v/v aqueous rinse solution
2.5 mL glacial acetic acid
497.5 mL distilled water

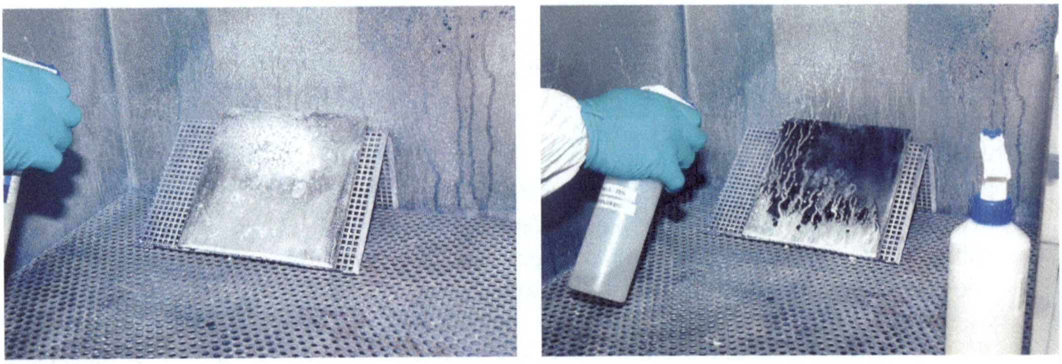

Figure 25.4 Example of spraying the rinsing procedure on a titanium dioxide dyed surface.

Protocol

- Add 2.5 mL of acetic acid into 100 mL of distilled water in a 500 mL volumetric flask.
- Fill with the rest of the distilled water to the 500 mL mark on the flask.
- Invert the flask (once capped) or stir the solution with a magnetic stirring device for at least 15 minutes. A clear transparent solution will result.
- Pour the solution using a clean funnel into the 500 mL dark (amber) bottle.
- Label and date the bottle, store at room temperature, and complete the log book.

Pending glassware availability, you could also add glacial acid to 500 mL of distilled water in a clean, dry beaker.

AMIDO BLACK

In the early 1970s, an amido black solution based on methanol and acetic acid was first used as a method for visual blood enhancement during forensic investigations. Using a solvent such as methanol/water/acetic acid is also possible and effective[39]; however, a safer, aqueous solution was introduced in 1989 for use in crime scene investigation and laboratory analysis. Amido black solutions stain the proteins present in the blood a blue-black color. In order to prevent blood traces from being washed away by the aqueous solution, a fixing agent 5-SSA is used in conjunction with or applied before the amido black dye solution. After staining, a rinsing solution of distilled water and a 0.5% v/v acetic acid can be applied to remove excess reagent. The aqueous amido black dye solution is suitable for non-porous surfaces. Amido black staining on porous surfaces can cause significant background staining. Amido black is also commonly known as amido black 10, acid black 1, or naphthol blue black (Figure 25.5).

Figure 25.5 A bloodied footwear impression on a bag (a) prior to enhancement and (b) after enhancement with water-based amido black.

Advantages of Using the Aqueous Amido Black solution

- The solution can be applied to evidence found on scene and at the laboratory when appropriate health and safety considerations are implemented.
- The solution is straightforward and inexpensive to prepare and apply.
- The solution is selective for blood proteins and does not enhance other common chemical compounds found in fingerprints.[40]
- Subsequent enhancement techniques like physical powders, vacuum metal deposition, and ALCV can be used after enhancement with amido black.
- Amido black enhancement has not been shown to interfere with subsequent DNA profiling, including after mass spectrometry imaging.[41]
- It demonstrated effectiveness on complex surfaces like thermal paper.[42]
- Application of the solution is versatile and can be applied by spraying, pouring, immersion, or filter paper methods.

Disadvantages of Using Aqueous Amido Black Solution

- The solution is not recommended for use on porous surfaces.
- Requires subsequent enhancement techniques for the detection of fingerprint and/or footwear residues.
- The solution is not suitable at freezing temperatures because of ice formation due to using water as solvent.

Preparing the Aqueous Amido Black Dye Solution without Fixative

Amido Black dye solution for blood
11 mL 10% citric acid solution
1 g amido black 10 or acid black 1 or naphthol blue black ≥ 85%
489 mL distilled water

Protocol

- Add 100 mL distilled water to a clean, dry 500 mL volumetric flask.
- Add 11 mL of citric acid solution (10% is recommended) to the flask.
- Weigh out 1 g of amido black 10 or acid black 1 or naphthol blue black ≤85% on a balance and add to the flask.
- Stir the solution with a magnetic stirring device for at least 10 minutes.
- Add the rest of the distilled water to the 500 mL mark and stir for at least 20 more minutes. A black aqueous solution is produced.
- Run the appropriate positive and negative controls to ensure the reagent solution is working properly.
- Pour the solution using a clean funnel into a 500 mL dark (amber) bottle.
- Label and date the bottle, store at room temperature, and complete the log book.

Pending glassware availability, you could also add the components to water in a clean, dry 1000 mL beaker. Although the dye is prepared for immediate use, leaving the solution to sit for several days prior to use is recommended.

Preparing the Aqueous Amido Black Dye Solution with Fixative

Amido black dye solution with fixative for blood
11 g 5-SSA
11 mL citric acid solution
1.5 g amido black 10B or acid black 1 or naphthol blue black ≥85%
489 mL distilled water

Protocol

- Add 100 mL distilled water in a clean, dry 500 mL volumetric flask.
- Add 11 mL of citric acid solution (10% is recommended) to the flask.
- Add 11 g 5-SSA to the flask.
- Weigh out 1.5 g of amido black 10B or acid black 1 or naphthol blue black ≤85% on a balance and add to the flask.
- Stir the solution with a magnetic stirring device for at least 10 minutes.
- Add the rest of the distilled water to the 500 mL mark and stir for at least 20 more minutes. A black aqueous solution is produced.
- Run the appropriate positive and negative controls to ensure the reagent solution is working properly.
- Pour the solution using a clean funnel into the 500 mL dark bottle.
- Label and date the bottle, store at room temperature, and complete the log book.

Pending glassware availability, you could also add the components to water in a clean, dry 1000 mL beaker. Although the dye is prepared for immediate use, leaving the solution to sit for several days prior to use is recommended.

Cautions

- Since the amido black solution uses a fixative, scraping of the enhanced bloodstain may be required for DNA analysis. Swabbing may be ineffective.
- Cyanoacrylate fuming can be detrimental to amido black enhancement.
- Amido black can be used subsequent to ALCV if different contrast with the substrate is desired. Refixing the bloodstain is not necessary between dyes.

ACID FUCHSIN (HUNGARIAN RED)

The aqueous acid fuchsin solution is another popular chemical enhancement technique for dyeing proteins in latent bloodstains and bloodied impressions. Like the aqueous amido black solution, the aqueous acid fuchsin solution is also suitable for non-porous surfaces. The resulting enhancement is a reddish-purple color, and more importantly, will fluoresce under an alternate light source. Enhanced bloodstains will be observed when excited with green light (515–560 nm) and viewed with red goggles. This is important for visualization on complex and multicolored surfaces. Fluorescence can also be visualized after the impression is lifted with a white gelatin lifter. Fluorescent dyes offer a significant advantage when dealing with multicolored, dark, and/or curved surfaces. Also, fluorescent visualization techniques post-lift can sometimes lead to observing more detail or characteristics compared to the enhanced stain or impression directly on the surface. Research also suggests it can be used to develop bloodied fingerprints on human skin (Figure 25.6).[43,44]

Figure 25.6 Bloodied fingerprint enhancement on a glass bottle using acid fuchsin.

Advantages of Aqueous Acid Fuchsin Solution

- The solution can be applied to evidence found on scene and in the laboratory when appropriate health and safety considerations are implemented.
- The solution is straightforward and inexpensive to prepare and apply.
- The solution is selective for blood proteins and does not enhance other common chemical compounds found in fingerprints.
- The enhancement is fluorescent which is useful for dark, multicolored, and/or curved surfaces.
- Traces made visible with acid fuchsin can be lifted with a white gelatin lifter for further analysis under an alternate light source.
- Subsequent enhancement techniques like physical powders, vacuum metal deposition, and ALCV can be used after enhancement with acid fuchsin.
- Acid fuchsin enhancement has not been shown to interfere with subsequent DNA profiling.
- Application of the solution is versatile and can be applied by spraying, pouring, immersion, or filter paper method.

Disadvantages of Aqueous Acid Fuchsin Solution

- The solution is not recommended for use on porous surfaces.
- This requires subsequent enhancement techniques for the detection of fingerprint and/or footwear residues.
- The solution is not suitable at freezing temperatures because of ice formation due to using water as solvent.

Preparing the Aqueous Acid Fuchsin Dye Solution without Fixative

Acid fuchsin dye solution
11 mL citric acid
1 g acid fuchsin
489 mL distilled water

Protocol

- Add 100 mL distilled water in a clean, dry 500 mL volumetric flask.
- Add 11 mL of citric acid and add to the flask.
- Weigh out 1g of acid fuchsin on a balance and add to the flask.
- Stir the solution with a magnetic stirring device for at least 10 minutes.
- Add the remaining distilled water to the 500 mL mark and stir for at least 20 more minutes. A red aqueous solution is produced.
- Run the appropriate positive and negative controls to ensure the reagent solution is working properly.
- Pour the solution using a clean funnel into the 500 mL dark (amber) bottle.
- Label and date the bottle, store at room temperature, and complete the log book.

Pending glassware availability, you could also add the components to water in a clean, dry 1000 mL beaker. Although the dye is prepared for immediate use, leaving the solution to sit for several days prior to use is recommended.

Preparing the Aqueous Acid Fuchsin Dye Solution with Fixative

Acid fuchsin dye solution with fixative
11 g 5-SSA
11 mL citric acid solution
1.5 g acid fuchsin
489 mL distilled water

Protocol

- Add 100 mL distilled water in a clean, dry 500 mL volumetric flask.
- Add 11 mL of citric acid solution (10% is recommended) to the flask.
- Add 11 g 5-SSA to the flask.
- Stir the solution with a magnetic stirring device for at least 5 minutes.
- Weigh out 1.5 g acid fuchsin on a balance and add to the flask.
- Stir the solution with a magnetic stirring device for at least 5 minutes.
- Add the remaining distilled water to the 500 mL mark and stir for at least 20 more minutes. A red aqueous solution is produced.
- Run the appropriate positive and negative controls to ensure the reagent solution is working properly.
- Pour the solution using a clean funnel into the 500 mL dark (amber) bottle.
- Label and date the bottle, store at room temperature, and complete the log book.

Pending glassware availability, you could also add the components to water in a clean, dry 1000 mL beaker. Although the dye is prepared for immediate use, leaving the solution to sit for several days prior to use is recommended (Figure 25.7).

Lifting Acid Fuchsin Enhanced Bloodied Impressions

- The enhanced bloodied impression and the surface must be completely dry.
- It is always important to photograph the impression before lifting.
- To optimize the results, the white gelatin lift has to be at least at room temperature, and the foil should not be too old and/or discolored.
- Starting at one end of the impression, lay the gel lift slowly over the area of interest. You can also use a roller to help smooth out the lifter and remove air bubbles.
- Leave the lift on the bloodied impression for 30–45 minutes. The optimal time is dependent on the level of the coloration of the enhanced bloodstain. In some cases, very faint

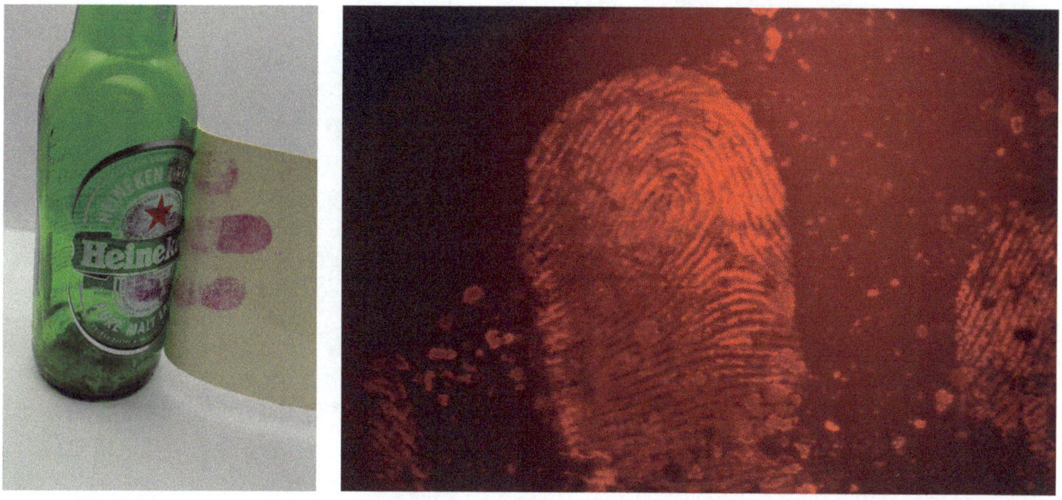

Figure 25.7 (a) The acid fuchsin solution can be lifted with a white gelatin lifter and (b) this lift can fluoresce when excited with green light (515–560 nm) and viewed with red goggles/filter.

bloodstains can be lifted after leaving the gelatin lift on the trace for more than 2 hours. After removing the gelatin lift from the bloodied impression, the protective transparent layer can be placed back over the lift surface for protection during transportation and storage.

- Lifting the acid fuchsin stained impression can be done more than once with or without re-staining. Heavily blood-stained impressions may, however, require additional fixative before re-staining.
- The blood impression on the gelatin lift must be photographed within several hours after lifting because the lift is not a permanent record. The dye will slowly spread in to and over the gelatin surface of the lift, causing loss of clarity.
- Bloodied impressions on a white gelatin lift enhanced with acid fuchsin can fluoresce when excited with green light (515–560 nm) and this can be viewed with red goggles.
- The fluorescence can be photographed with a red filter, such as Kodak Wratten 25, used on the camera lens. If the surface is dark or multicolored, the fluorescence can be very helpful in examining the impression and enhancing the photographic contrast.
- Be aware that a bloodied print lifted with a gelatin lifter is a mirror image.
- Be aware that cyanoacrylate fuming can be detrimental to this process.
- If not satisfied with the achieved contrast, it is possible to re-dye and rinse the bloodstain. It is not necessary to apply additional fixing solution between the first and the second enhancement, except in the case of heavily stained blood impressions. After the desired contrast is achieved, a final rinse should be conducted.

AQUEOUS LEUCOCRYSTAL VIOLET (ALCV)

Aqueous leucocrystal violet (ALCV) is a peroxidase chemical enhancement reagent. When ALCV solution comes into contact with heme, a redox reaction occurs, which rapidly generates a purplish-blue product. Specifically, in these reactions leucocrystal violet (colorless) is oxidized by the hydrogen peroxide that is commonly found in ALCV formulations. This is a reversible and time-sensitive reaction. ALCV enhancement of bloodstain evidence is a popular choice for bloodstain

Figure 25.8 Bloodied fingerprint impressions (a) pre- and (b) post-enhancement with ALCV on the sticky side of tape.

analysts because it is a quick, straightforward, and rather safe method of enhancing the visualization of faint or latent bloodstains. It is also suitable for both porous and non-porous surfaces. Most commercially available ALCV solutions contain a fixative and often the application of a rinse solution is not necessary. When applying to bloodied impressions on a non-porous surface, it is possible to apply amido black or acid fuchsin aqueous solution after the use of ALCV to further enhance the impression by staining the proteins in blood (Figure 25.8).

Advantages of ALCV

- The solution can be applied to evidence found on scene and in the laboratory when appropriate health and safety considerations are implemented.
- The solution is straightforward and inexpensive to prepare and apply.
- ALCV can be used on porous and nonporous surfaces.
- ALCV causes minimal background discoloration.
- ALCV will not enhance the common chemical compounds found in fingerprints.[45]
- Application of fingerprint powder before the application of ALCV does not interfere with the ability of the dye to stain heme present in blood; however, apply ninhydrin afterward.[46]
- Vacuum metal deposition does not interfere with the ability of the dye to stain heme present in blood.
- After ALCV is used for the staining of the proteins present in blood, amido black or acid fuchsin can be used in sequence to stain the protein.
- ALCV enhancement has not been shown to interfere with subsequent DNA profiling.
- Application of the solution is versatile and can be applied by spraying, pouring, immersion, or the filter paper methods.
- It is suitable for the use on human skin of deceased individuals.
- It can be used on the sticky side of adhesive tape.

Disadvantages of ALCV

- ALCV is not suitable for the detection of the normal constituents of latent fingerprints and footprints. Appropriate sequencing of enhancement reagents is required.
- The ALCV solution can have a negative influence on the enhancement of common components in latent fingerprints and footprints.
- The solution is not suitable at freezing temperatures because of ice formation due to using water as solvent.

Preparing the ALCV Solution

ALCV solution
11 g 5-SSA
1 g leucocrystal violet
3.7 g sodium acetate
Hydrogen tablets dissolved in 500 mL of distilled water or 500 mL of 3% hydrogen peroxide solution

Protocol

- Add 100 mL distilled water (hydrogen tablet included) or 3% hydrogen peroxide solution in a clean, 500 mL volumetric flask.
- Weigh out 3.7 g sodium acetate on a balance and add to the flask.
- Add 11 g 5-SSA to the flask.
- Stir the solution with a magnetic stirring device for at least 5 minutes.
- Weigh out 1 g leucocrystal violet on a balance and add to the flask.
- Stir the solution with a magnetic stirring device for at least 20 minutes.
- Add the remaining solvent and stir for at least 10 more minutes. The solution will appear reddish.
- Run the appropriate positive and negative controls to ensure the reagent solution is working properly.
- Pour the solution using a clean funnel into the 500 mL dark (amber) bottle.
- Label and date the bottle and complete the log book.
- Store the solution in a refrigerator.

Pending glassware availability, you could also add the components to water in a clean, dry 1000 mL beaker.

Although the dye is prepared for immediate use, it is recommended to allow the mixture to stand for 60 minutes prior to use. After activation, it is recommended to use it within 5 days. A working solution has a shelf life of approximately 30 days; remember to write the expiration date on the working solution and in the log book.

Cautions

- Spraying or pouring ALCV on the bloodied evidence is the recommended application of choice to control the intensity of enhancement and contrast with the background.
- In cases where sharp features are important for enhancement, consider prefixing the bloodied impression with 2% 5-SSA. Although the ALCV solution contains fixative, prefixing can create sharper boundary lines in enhancement, particularly in cases when enhancing on a porous surface.
- Amido black application does not require a subsequent fixing step after ALCV application.
- Always use the ALCV solution within its shelf life of 30 days in order to maximize the intensity and efficiency of enhancement. Create a new ALCV solution if a visible color change from clear to yellow is observed in the working solution.
- ALCV enhancement is not permanent and undesired background development can occur; therefore, make sure to document (e.g. photograph) the enhancement as soon as possible. Over time, the enhanced area will turn blue-purple and detail can be lost largely as a result of photoionization if the treatment is in direct sunlight, as well as through oxidation in ambient conditions.
- Impressions should be photographed immediately as well as during different time intervals. ALCV enhancement can change in intensity and specificity over time.

AQUEOUS SUSPENSION DYES

In contrast to amido black, acid fuchsin, and ALCV, suspension dyes do not chemically react with proteins or the heme portion of blood. Instead, (nano)particles will physically interact with bloodstain or bloodied impression in a way similar to how a powder would interact for latent fingerprint enhancement. These solutions sometimes still require a fixing reagent. Mixtures with titanium oxide powder, which produces a white enhancement, and iron oxide, which produces a black enhancement, are popular solutions. After staining, a rinsing solution of distilled water and a 0.5% v/v acetic acid is applied to remove excess reagent. Small particles of powder will be fixed by the 5-SSA to the faint or latent bloodstain. After drying, the "powdered" bloodstain can then be lifted with a gelatin lift. Similar to the ALCV technique, this offers a significant advantage when dealing with multicolored, dark, or curved surfaces. Also, by using this technique, there is the potential to see more detail or characteristics in the lifted blood trace compared to the enhanced one still on the surface or article. Using an aqueous suspension dye is a quick, straightforward, and safe method of enhancing the visualization of faint or latent blood and is suitable for non-porous surfaces. When applying to bloodied impressions on a non-porous surface, it is possible to apply amido black, acid fuchsin, or ALCV aqueous solutions after the use of a suspension dye to enhance the impression further by coloring the proteins/heme in the blood (Figure 25.9).

Advantages of Aqueous Suspension Dyes

- The solution can be applied to evidence found on scene and in the laboratory when appropriate health and safety considerations are implemented.
- The solution is straightforward and inexpensive to prepare and apply.
- The color of the dye can be adjusted with the use of fluorescent powder to provide the best contrast.
- Dry traces made visible with suspension dyes can then be lifted with gelatin lifts.
- After a suspension dye is used to stain the blood, ALCV, acid fuchsin, or amido black can be used in sequence to stain the heme/proteins in the blood.

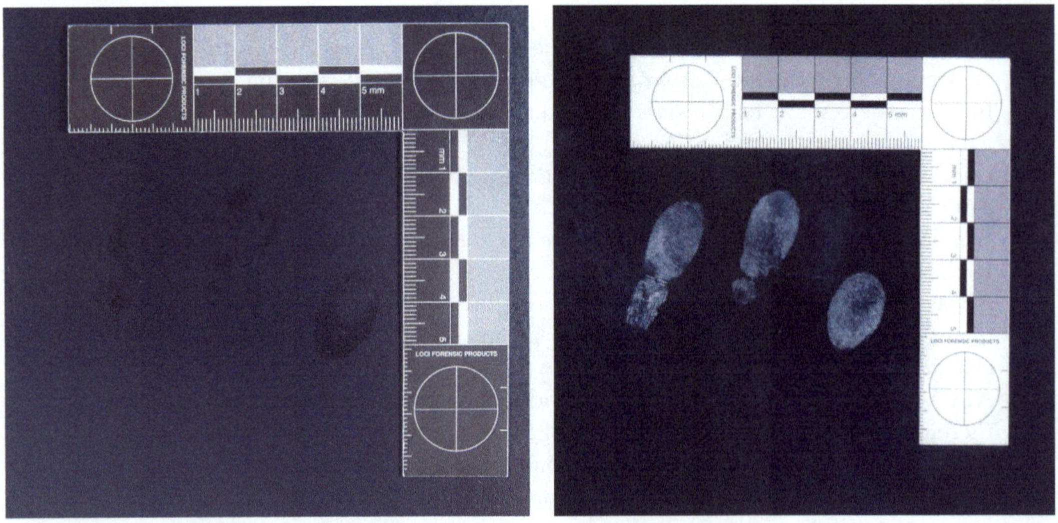

Figure 25.9 Bloodied fingerprint impressions (a) pre- and (b) post-enhancement with titanium dioxide and detail of enhance fingerprint.

- Suspension dyes can be used on non-porous surfaces.
- Application of fingerprint powder before the application of a suspension dye does not interfere with the dyes ability to stain, however apply ninhydrin afterward.

Disadvantages of Aqueous Suspension Dyes

- The solution is not recommended for use on porous surfaces.
- Suspension dyes are not suitable for the detection of the normal constituents of latent fingerprints and footprints. Appropriate sequencing of enhancement reagents is required.
- The technique is not suitable for use on human skin.
- The nozzle of sprayer/applicator can become clogged by the powder.
- The solution is not suitable at freezing temperatures because of ice formation due to the water solvent.

Preparing the Suspension Dye Solution

Titanium oxide or iron oxide suspension dye
11 g 5-SSA
8 g titanium oxide or 8 g iron(II) oxide
500 mL distilled water

Protocol

- Add 100 mL distilled water to a clean, 500 mL volumetric flask.
- Weigh out 11 g 5-SSA and add it to the flask.
- Stir the solution with a magnetic stirring device for at least 5 minutes.
- Weigh out 8 g titanium oxide or iron(II) oxide on a balance and add to the flask.
- Fill the rest of the flask to the 500 mL mark with distilled water.
- Stir the solution with a magnetic stirring device for at least 10 minutes.
- Run the appropriate positive and negative controls to ensure the reagent solution is working properly.
- Pour the solution using a clean funnel in to the 500 mL dark (amber) bottle.
- Label and date the bottle, store at room temperature, and complete the log book.

Pending glassware availability, you could also add the components to water in a clean, dry 1000 mL beaker. The dye is prepared for immediate use and must be shaken prior to use to ensure the powder is mixed in the solution.

Note: Suspension dyes based on titanium oxide or iron oxide can be made fluorescent by replacing 1 g of the powder used with 1 g fine fluorescent fingerprint powder (Figure 25.10).

Cautions

- If suspension dyes are used prior to the collection of DNA, sampling for DNA by swabbing may be ineffective. In these circumstances samples for subsequent DNA analysis should be collected by scraping.
- Be aware that cyanoacrylate fuming can be detrimental to suspension dye enhancement.
- After the use of a suspension dye, ALCV and/or amido black can be applied to create a higher contrast, without the necessity to refix.
- Blood impressions which are enhanced with suspension dyes can be lifted with a gelatin lift.
- If used in combination with other enhancement chemicals, titanium dioxide suspension solutions will not generate the same clarity or intensity as it would normally create when used by itself.

Figure 25.10 The iron oxide solution can be lifted with a white gelatin lifter.

- If titanium dioxide suspension solution is used prior to other blood enhancement chemicals, the titanium dioxide, once dried, will create an effective shell over the ridges and stains. This shell decreases the enhancement potential of other chemicals.

Luminol

Luminol is arguably one of the most useful investigative chemical searching techniques for latent bloodstains deposited at a crime scene. The luminol solution is applied directly to crime scenes in order to reveal latent bloodstains, and is particularly useful in scenarios where there is reason to believe that blood has been shed and an attempt has been made to conceal (wash) bloodied evidence. The luminol reaction is a very sensitive presumptive testing reagent for blood[47,48] and it will react with both fresh and aged blood of various dilutions.[49] The most striking feature of the luminol reaction is the bright blue chemiluminescence emitted, a spectacular observation when viewed in total darkness. The mechanism for blood detection using luminol and its derivatives has been well-documented in the literature.[50,51] The peroxidase-like activity of the hemoglobin catalyzes the oxidation of the luminol solution, driving the emission of the bright blue light in this chemiluminescent reaction. In fresh blood, the normal valence for iron of the hemoglobin in the red blood cells is the Fe(II) ferrous state. Upon degradation through time, humidity, and/or temperature, hemoglobin is converted to methemoglobin and the iron is oxidized to the Fe(III) ferric state, the catalyst in the luminol reaction. This means that since hemoglobin is a catalyst, it does not get consumed in this reaction – very advantageous for multiple applications of luminol to an area. To enhance the intensity and duration of the chemiluminescence, consider using a humidifier to increase the humidity in the room prior to luminol application.

The luminol solution is alkaline and contains an oxidizing agent like sodium peroxide or sodium perborate. The hemoglobin essentially decomposes the oxidizing agent which in turn oxidizes luminol and excites it. Upon dropping back to the ground state, a characteristic blue light is emitted at a wavelength of approximately 425 nm. The kinetics of the reaction is relatively rapid – analysts will see a bright emission that decays quickly. The decay is dependent upon many variables including the solution, method of application, and age/state of the bloodstaining. Luminol solutions need to be alkaline (pH ≥ 9) and as a result will not contain a fixative (e.g. 5-SSA is acidic). Therefore, luminol is not recommended for enhancing fine detail of bloodied impressions because

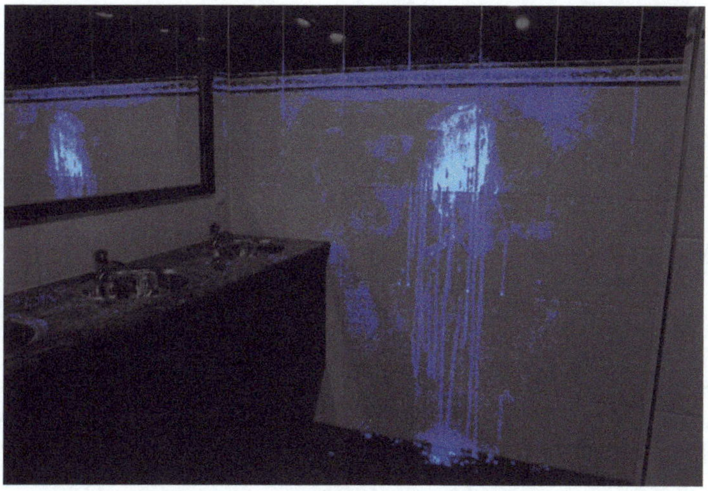

Figure 25.11 Luminol reaction photographed using a digital-overlay technique.

of the potential dilution and distortion of the enhanced impression. The edges can be blurred which can result in pattern, class, and individual characteristic loss as well as diffuse ridge detail distortion. Research suggests that using different solutions of luminol or commercial luminol-based products like Bluestar and Lumiscene showed that bloodstains contaminated with luminol did not adversely affect polymerase chain reaction (PCR) analysis of DNA.[52,53,54,55,56] Luminol is preferred for searching for minute bloodstains as well as detecting laundered bloodstains.[57,58] The ability to apply the solution by a fine mist throughout large areas of a crime scene is advantageous, and luminol's sensitivity makes it a far superior technique when compared to amido black, acid fuchsin, or ALCV solutions for searching (Figure 25.11).

Advantages of Luminol

- Luminol is unique in its reaction with blood compared to most other blood enhancement techniques because it results in chemiluminescence through the temporary emission of blue light.
- The solution can be sprayed over large areas of a crime scene and on exhibits in the laboratory when appropriate health and safety considerations are implemented.
- The solution is straightforward and inexpensive to prepare.
- The solution can be adjusted to accommodate any sensitivity issues.
- Luminol is highly sensitive and reveals bloodstains that are not detectable with the naked eye.
- To confirm if the luminated stain is blood, a more blood-specific presumptive test can be performed. Luminol does not interfere with the commonly used presumptive tests such as phenolphthalein, o-Tolidine or Combur-Test® strips/Hemastix™.
- DNA analysis of samples taken from the chemiluminescent area can further confirm the origin of the blood donor, as no measurable adverse effects have been observed on DNA stability and extraction or PCR of bloodstains pre-treated with luminol.
- Luminol can be used on porous and non-porous surfaces.
- Luminol causes minimal background discoloration.
- Luminol does not react with the common compounds found in fingerprints.
- Application of fingerprint powder before the application of luminol does not interfere with the chemiluminescent reaction.

- The chemiluminescence reaction can be photographed and/or filmed.
- The luminescence reaction can be reactivated by applying more luminol to the surface; however, the brightness diminishes with subsequent treatments.
- Luminol does not appear to be mutagenic by the Ames test.
- Luminol does not react with other body fluids such as urine, semen, and saliva (unless contaminated with blood).

Disadvantages of Luminol

- Luminol can only be used in a darkened environment, which can make maneuvering in unfamiliar and often crowded areas difficult.
- Luminol can cause traces to dilute and spread which has the potential to interfere with other forensic analyses.
- Luminol reacts non-specifically to any blood source regardless of species origin.
- Activated luminol solution can only be used for 2–4 hours after mixing for maximum effectiveness.
- Recording the observed reaction with photography requires experience and appropriate equipment.
- Training in use and documentation from a qualified forensic examiner with case experience is strongly recommended.
- Luminol is a presumptive test, meaning it is not specific to blood, and is susceptible to false-positive reactions. False-positive test results have been reported for peroxidases (e.g. horseradish, turnip), metal ions (e.g. copper, iron), and other oxidants (e.g. hypochlorite, iodine). Also, some furniture polishes, enamel paint, and interior fabrics in motor vehicles can produce chemiluminescent intensities comparable with that of hemoglobin.

Preliminary Procedures and Information for the Use of Luminol

Luminol is an excellent blood searching technique because it is applied as a spray and therefore large areas may be quickly screened for blood. It is relatively non-destructive to the surroundings (it is non-corrosive and non-staining). Before applying, it is important to know that luminol *could* interfere with other forensic examinations like DNA, fingerprint, hair, and fiber analyses. As mentioned, studies have demonstrated that DNA can be obtained after luminol application. Regardless, luminol should be applied once all other forensic investigations have been completed.

For the visualization of the luminol reaction, total darkness gives the best results. It is also important to allow the eyes to adjust to the darkness (typically a couple of minutes will suffice) in order to aid with determining where to spray in the scene. The presence of excess light, even from LEDs of electronic devices, can make it difficult to observe the chemiluminescent reaction of luminol, potentially resulting in missed blood staining. It will also impact the quality of the photography if there is too much ambient light present. Experience in low-light and luminol photography is essential.

It is recommended that protective clothing (including shoe covers) should be worn before and during the luminol procedure, which helps reduce the risk of contamination. As luminol is sprayed throughout a scene under darkened conditions, the use of face masks or ventilators is also required. Also be cautious of slipping hazards if spraying luminol on hard non-porous flooring.

- Make the scene dark – for example, black agriculture foil or garbage bags and tape can be used to cover windows or door bottoms to reduce light from the outside. Unplugging electronic devices can remove LED light interference.
- After mixing the luminol, the analyst must ensure that the luminol solution is working properly. The solution should be tested on scene prior to use using a known blood sample made of animal blood or a synthetic reference material of known dilution.

- First, spray the walls and then the floor. Use of floor protection is recommended when spraying the walls, whether it be craft paper or stepping plates, and pre-determining a route that prevents walking over pre-moistened areas to avoid cross-contamination.
- Minimize the number of people in the scene when applying the luminol reagent. This is for safety, efficiency, and minimizing contamination.

Preparation instructions for the stock luminol solution (Weber) are given here. This luminol solution is primarily used for recovering latent blood with the goal of recovering the DNA from these bloodstains.

Luminol stock solution (Weber)
1 g sodium hydroxide
0.8 g luminol
500 mL distilled water

Protocol

- Add 100 mL distilled water to a clean, dry 500 mL volumetric flask.
- Weigh out 1 g sodium hydroxide on a balance and add to the flask.
- Weigh out 0.4 g luminol on a balance and add to the flask.
- Stir the solution with a magnetic stirring device for at least 10 minutes.
- Fill the rest of the flask to the 500 mL mark with distilled water.
- Stir the solution with a magnetic stirring device for 20 more minutes.
- A faint yellow to transparent solution will result.
- Run the appropriate positive and negative controls to ensure the reagent solution is working properly.
- Pour the solution using a clean funnel into the 500 mL dark (amber) bottle.
- Label and date the bottle and complete the log book.
- Store the solution in a refrigerator.

The luminol stock luminol solution is ready for use after adding 5 mL 30% hydrogen peroxide solution or five 30% hydroxide urea tablets. The solution must then be shaken or stirred with a magnetic stirring device for at least 15 minutes. The mixed solution is relatively stable for 2–4 hours. After 2–4 hours, the sensitivity of the detection declines and it is advisable to make a new solution. Do not attempt to re-activate the solution by adding more 30% hydrogen peroxide.

Preparation instructions for the luminol photo/reconstruction stock solution are given here. This luminol solution is primarily used for photographing and reconstruction. The higher concentration of chemicals can have a negative effect on recovering the DNA from these bloodstains.

Luminol photo/reconstruction stock solution
2 g sodium hydroxide
1.6 g luminol
500 mL distilled water

Protocol

- Add 100 mL distilled water to a clean, dry 500 mL volumetric flask.
- Weigh out 2 g sodium hydroxide on a balance and add to the flask.
- Weigh out 0.8 g luminol on a balance and add to the flask.
- Stir the solution with a magnetic stirring device for at least 10 minutes.
- Fill the rest of the flask to the 500 mL mark with distilled water.
- Stir the solution with a magnetic stirring device for 20 more minutes.
- A faint yellow to transparent solution will result.

- Run the appropriate positive and negative controls to ensure the reagent solution is working properly.
- Pour the solution using a clean funnel into the 500 mL dark (amber) bottle.
- Label and date the bottle and complete the log book.
- Store the solution in a refrigerator.

The luminol stock solution is ready for use after adding 10 mL 30% hydrogen peroxide solution or ten 30% hydroxide urea tablets. The solution must then be shaken or stirred with a magnetic stirring device for at least 15 minutes. The mixed solution is relatively stable for 2–4 hours. After 2–4 hours, the sensitivity of the detection rate declines and it is advisable to prepare a new solution.

Preparing an Alternate Luminol Solution (Grodsky)

Luminol solution
3.5 g sodium perborate
0.5 g luminol
25 g sodium carbonate
500 mL distilled water

Note: Luminol solutions have been reported to visualize blood dilutions that are greater than 1:500,000. The analyst can adjust the quantity of the ingredients used to affect the dilution of the stock solution and hence modify the sensitivity.

Protocol

- Add 250 mL distilled water in a clean, dry 500 mL volumetric flask.
- Weigh out 3.5 g sodium perborate on a balance and add into the 500 mL flask.
- Weigh out 0.5 g luminol on a balance and add into the 500 mL flask.
- Stir the solution with a magnetic stirring device for at least 10 minutes.
- Add 250 mL distilled water into another 500 mL volumetric flask.
- Weigh out 25 g sodium carbonate on a balance and add into the 500 mL flask.
- Stir the solution with a magnetic stirring device for at least 10 minutes.
- Combine the two solutions and stir for 5 more minutes.
- A light yellow to clear transparent solution will result and is ready to be used.
- Run the appropriate positive and negative controls to ensure the reagent solution is working properly.
- Label and date the bottle (Figure 25.12).

Luminol Application

One of the greatest advantages of using luminol is that it is applied by spraying, making it capable of searching large areas for latent bloodstains without leaving visible staining. Since the aqueous luminol solution does not have a fixative, excess solution has the potential to lead to spreading or saturation of the latent bloodstain patterns and DNA material. The spreading or saturation of latent bloodstains caused by the application of luminol can lead to misinterpretation of the pattern (see Figure 25.13) and dilution of DNA material. Handpump trigger sprayers are very popular for applying luminol based on the ease of use and price. However, the application of luminol with these types of sprayers has several drawbacks. It can be difficult to control the volume sprayed and avoid uneven spreading of solution on the surface. The nonuniform spreading will lead to higher local concentration of the luminol solution which can then produce a higher local luminescence, adversely affecting the correct interpretation of bloodstaining.

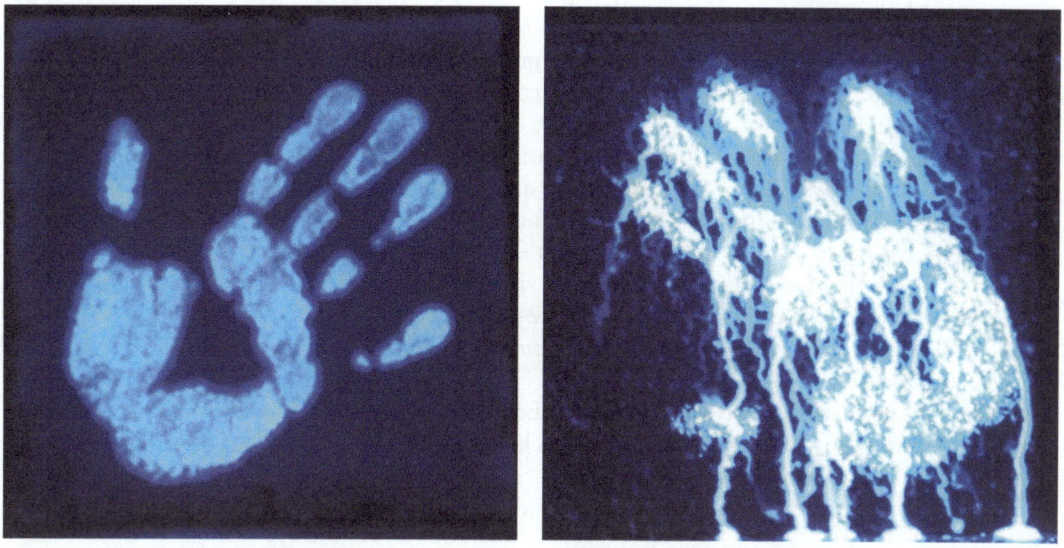

Figure 25.12 Application of a luminol solution with the use of (a) a special paint sprayer and (b) a handpump trigger sprayer. The handpump sprayer caused distortion and dilution of the bloodstain pattern.

Figure 25.13 Luminol reaction made visible with the use a special paint sprayer, the "running" trace is caused by the cleaning and not by the sprayer.

Since 1996, portable compressors with stainless steel aqueous paint sprayer nozzles have been used for the application of luminol by the Dutch police force. The lightweight compressor and sprayer are made of stainless steel and materials that have no adverse effect on the luminol solutions. Also, the nozzle of the sprayer is adjustable; so it produces a very even spray with negligible droplet formation and hence no excess luminol on the surface.

Reagent Application

- All appropriate PPE should be used when preparing and using luminol.
- Run the appropriate positive and negative controls just prior to use to ensure that the activated luminol solution is working properly.
- The area must be as dark as possible to maximize the visibility of the luminescence reaction of luminol with blood for observation and photographic purposes.
- Areas exhibiting the luminol reaction should be marked appropriately since the chemiluminescence is short-lived, i.e. chalk on carpet or pencil on walls, as once the lights are turned on, the area that reacted will no longer be visible.
- Use the activated luminol solution within 2–4 hours of mixing.
- Perform a more specific presumptive test on areas identified with chemiluminescence prior to sampling for DNA.
- Respray the marked/identified areas and photograph.
- When processing has been completed, all chemicals should be disposed of properly according to the appropriate federal, state, and local environmental laws.

Photographing Luminol

There is no standard setting for photographing the luminol reaction, since the emission of light produced by the reaction between luminol and blood is dependent on many variables. Recording the patterns and locations of blood traces identified by the luminol reaction may be just as important as the detection of blood itself. Photographing the luminol reaction has become a much simpler exercise with the advent of the digital (DSLR) camera. The analyst can take a photograph and see the results of various exposures on scene in real time and make adjustments to the camera settings and placement, if necessary. Photographing the luminol reaction occurs in almost total darkness and long exposure times are sometimes necessary to document the observations, often in combination with respraying the area. These blue and black pictures have a lack of reference; so a photograph of the same area under regular lighting conditions from the exact same position can be vital. The overlapping of these photographs introduces reference. There are several different methods for obtaining these results and two of them are explained here (Figure 25.14).

Figure 25.14 Luminol reaction photographed in total darkness using "long exposure time."

Photographing the Luminol Reaction with the Use of an In-Fill Flash

- Typical camera settings: ISO 1600, aperture of 2.8, shutter speed of 15 seconds, distance from area of interest approximately 1.5 meters.
- Place the camera on a tripod and focus the camera to the object or area of interest.
- Keep the focus setting on manual on both the lens and camera body.
- Darken the environment and allow your eyes to adjust (couple minutes).
- Start spraying the area with luminol while avoiding crossing between the camera and area of interest and when the luminol reaction starts, start the exposure.
- During exposure (15 seconds), a burst of light from the camera flash or a flashlight must be used to introduce the reference point on the photograph.
- Once the exposure is complete, check the photograph. If the luminescence reaction is not visible, a longer exposure time, higher ISO setting, less direct burst of light, or a different luminol solution should be considered.

Another way of photographing the luminol reaction involves overlapping the long exposure photograph of the luminol reaction in total darkness, with an ambient light photograph of the crime scene taken from the exact same location using software such as Adobe Photoshop (Figure 25.15).

Photographing the Luminol with Digital-Overlay

- Place the camera on a tripod and focus the camera to the object or surface to approximately 1.5 meters.
- Keep the focus setting on manual and take an exposure with ambient light or with the help of a flash light.
- Adjust the camera settings; ISO 1600, aperture of 2.8, shutter speed of 15 seconds, without changing the camera location.
- Darken the environment and allow the eyes to adjust (couple of minutes).
- Start spraying luminol over the area of interest and when the luminol reaction begins, start the exposure.
- Check the photographs. If the luminescence reaction is not visible on the second picture, longer exposure times, high ISO setting, multiple luminol applications, or a different luminol solution should be considered (Figure 25.16).

Figure 25.15 Luminol reaction photographed with the use of an in-fill flash technique.

Figure 25.16 Luminol reaction photographed with the use of digital-overlay.

Fluorescin

The use of fluorescin as a blood searching technique was introduced in 1995 by Cheeseman for the detection of latent bloodstains. Fluorescein is reduced in an aqueous alkaline sodium hydroxide solution with zinc powder to fluorescin. This reduced colorless fluorescin solution without the zinc powder is first sprayed over the surface, followed by a 3% aqueous hydrogen peroxide solution. The catalytic activity of heme is accelerated by hydrogen peroxide changing the colorless fluorescin to the yellow/green color of fluorescein. After both solutions are sprayed, visualization of the fluorescence of fluorescein requires the use of an alternate light source operating between 445 and 455 nm with a yellow barrier filter or at 485 nm with an orange barrier filter. Although the fluorescence of the latent bloodstains can fluorescence for up to 10 or more minutes, photographing and sampling have to be done as soon as possible. The fluorescin on the surface will change over time to fluorescein making it impossible to see the difference in fluorescence with latent bloodstains, making respraying unsuccessful.

Like luminol, there are a number of different materials that can interfere with the fluorescin reaction too. False-positive test reactions have been reported for peroxidases (e.g. horseradish, beet juice), metal irons (e.g. copper), and urine. In addition, many household products, paints, fabrics, and other materials produce fluorescence when illuminated with an alternate light source (ALS) at 445–485 nm. Pre-investigation of the object, surface, or crime scene with the help of an ALS and marking these false positives is a must before the application of fluorescin. Although studies regarding the interference of fluorescein with subsequent short tandem repeat (STR) testing of blood for DNA showed no evidence of DNA degradation,[59] it is important to remember fluorescein is a double solution application, which can increase the dilution, spreading, and running of potential DNA material in latent bloodstains when compared to luminol. As with luminol, fluorescin solutions need to be alkaline (pH 9 plus) and have therefore no fixative in the form of 5-SSA. As a result, fluorescin is also not recommended for detecting patent and latent prints because of the potential blurring effect of the chemical luminescence, which can result in pattern, class, and individual characteristic loss as well as diffuse ridge detail loss and dilution/spreading of DNA material (Figure 25.17).

Figure 25.17 Fluorescin enhancement of a bloodied footwear impression on black carpet.

Advantages of Fluorescin

- The solution can be sprayed at crime scenes and in the laboratory when appropriate health and safety considerations are implemented.
- Fluorescin does not have to be applied in total darkness.
- The fluorescence can be seen with the use of an ALS for up to 10minutes or more after application.
- The solution is inexpensive to prepare.
- The solution can be adjusted to sensitivity issues.
- Fluorescin is highly sensitive and shows bloodstains that are not detectable with the naked eye.
- Fluorescin solutions have not been shown to interfere with subsequent DNA profiling.
- Fluorescin can be used on porous and nonporous surfaces.
- Fluorescin will not react with common compounds found in fingerprints.
- Application of fingerprint powder before the application of fluorescein does not interfere with the dye to react with heme present in blood.
- The reaction can be photographed and/or filmed.

Disadvantages of Fluorescin

- Items and surfaces have to be screened and areas marked that give a false-positive fluorescent with the use of an ALS at 445–485 nm.
- The fluorescin reaction cannot be reactivated by applying new solution on the trace.
- Fluorescin is not blood-specific and can produce false-positive reactions.
- Fluorescin can cause traces to spread and can interfere with other forensic investigations.
- Fluorescin is extremely sensitive; it reacts non-specifically to any blood regardless of its species origin.
- Fluorescin can cause background discoloration when changed into fluorescein.
- Recording the observed reaction by photography needs experience.
- Training from a qualified forensic examinator with case experience is strongly recommended.
- For the preparation of fluorescin, zinc powder is used.
- Fluorescin is more sensitive than commonly used presumptive tests.

Preparing the Fluorescin Solution

Fluorescin solution
2 g sodium hydroxide
2 g zinc powder
0.2 g fluorescein
550 mL distilled water

Protocol

- Weigh out 2 g sodium hydroxide on a balance and add to the 100 mL volumetric flask.
- Weigh out 2 g zinc powder on a balance and add into the flask.
- Weigh out 0.2 g fluorescein on a balance and add into the flask.
- Pour 50 mL of distilled water into the flask.
- Stir the solution with a magnetic stirring device for at least 20 minutes and let it rest for 10 more minutes.
- A faint yellow to transparent stock solution with zinc powder on the bottom will result.
- Pour 500 mL of distilled water into a 1000 mL volumetric flask or glass beaker.

- Decant or pipette 5 mL of the stock solution, without zinc powder, into the 1000 mL flask or beaker.
- Stir the solution with a magnetic stirring device for at least 10 minutes.
- Run the appropriate positive and negative controls to ensure the reagent solution is working properly.
- Label and date the bottle and complete the log book. It is advisable to store the solution in refrigerator.

Note: Special care has to be taken when disposing of or using zinc powder because as zinc dries, it generates heat and can start combusting.

Preparation of 3% Hydrogen Peroxide Solution

3% hydrogen peroxide solution
5 mL 30% hydrogen peroxide
500 mL distilled water

Notes

1. Farrugia, Kevin J, Kathleen Savage, Helen Bandey, and Niamh Nic Daeid, 'Chemical Enhancement of Footwear Impressions in Blood on Fabric–Part 1: Protein Stains', Science & Justice 51, no. 3 (2011): 99–109.
2. Farrugia, Kevin J, Helen Bandey, Kathleen Savage, and Niamh Nic Daeid, 'Chemical Enhancement of Footwear Impressions in Blood on Fabric—Part 3: Amino Acid Staining', Science & Justice 53, no. 1 (2013): 8–13.
3. Bossers, Lydia, Claude Roux, Michael Bell, and Andrew McDonagh, 'Methods for the Enhancement of Fingermarks in Blood', Forensic Science International 210, no. 1–3 (2011): 1–11.
4. Sears, Vaughn, Colin PG Butcher, and Tania M Prizeman, 'Enhancement of Fingerprints in Blood–Part 2: Protein Dyes', Journal of Forensic Identification 51, no. 1 (2001): 28.
5. Barni, Filippo, Simon Lewis, Andrea Berti, Gordon Miskelly, and Giampietro Lago, 'Forensic Application of the Luminol Reaction as a Presumptive Test for Latent Blood Detection', Talanta 72, no. 3 (2007): 896–913.
6. Polacco, Sumiko, Paul Wilson, Mike Illes, and Theresa Stotesbury, 'Quantifying Chemiluminescence of the Forensic Luminol Test for Ovine Blood in a Dilution and Time Series', Forensic Science International 290 (2018): 36–41.
7. Hofmann, Michaela, Jiri Adamec, Katja Anslinger, Birgit Bayer, Matthias Graw, Oliver Peschel, and Martin Schulz, 'Detectability of Bloodstains after Machine Washing', International Journal of Legal Medicine 133, no. 1 (2019): 3–16.
8. Au, Catherine, Hayley Jackson-Smith, Ignacio Quinones, BJ Jones, and Barbara Daniel, 'Wet Powder Suspensions as an Additional Technique for the Enhancement of Bloodied Marks', Forensic Science International 204, no. 1–3 (2011): 13–18.
9. Barros, Hélio, Thayse Mikeski, Crisle Dillenburg, and Valter Stefai, 'Fluorescent Benzazole Dyes for Bloodstain Detection and Bloody Fingermark Enhancement', Forensic Chemistry 5(2017): 16–25.
10. Becue, Andy, Sébastien Moret, Christophe Champod, and Pierre Margo, 'Use of Quantum Dots in Aqueous Solution to Detect Blood Fingermarks on Non-Porous Surfaces', Forensic Science International 191, no. 1–3 (2009): 36–41.
11. Fan, Zhinan, Chi Zhang, Jiajun Chen, Rongliang Ma, Yaoqi Lu, Jia-Wei Wu, and Li-Juan Fan, 'Highly Stable, Nondestructive, and Simple Visualization of Latent Blood Fingerprints Based on Covalent Bonding between the Fluorescent Conjugated Polymer and Proteins in Blood', ACS Applied Materials & Interfaces 13(2021): 15621–32.
12. Yamashita, Brian, and Mike French, '*Fingerprint Sourcebook-Chapter 7: Latent Print Development*', US Dept. of Justice, Office of Justice Programs, National Institute of Justice, 2010.
13. Farrugia, Kevin J, Kathleen Savage, Helen Bandey, and Niamh Nic Daeid, 'Chemical Enhancement of Footwear Impressions in Blood on Fabric–Part 1: Protein Stains', Science & Justice 51, no. 3 (2011): 99–109.

14. Farrugia, Kevin J, Helen Bandey, Lorna Dawson, and Niamn Nic Daeid, 'A Comparison of Enhancement Techniques for Footwear Impressions on Dark and Patterned Fabrics', Journal of Forensic Sciences 58, no. 6 (2013): 1472–85.
15. Finnis, Jonathan, Jennie Lewis, and Andrew Davidson, 'Comparison of Methods for Visualizing Blood on Dark Surfaces', Science & Justice 53, no. 2 (2013): 178–86.
16. Farrugia, Kevin J, Helen Bandey, Kathleen Savage, and Niamh Nic Daeid, 'Chemical Enhancement of Footwear Impressions in Blood on Fabric—Part 3: Amino Acid Staining', Science & Justice 53, no. 1 (2013): 8–13.
17. Bossers, Lydia, Claude Roux, Michael Bell, and Andrew McDonagh, 'Methods for the Enhancement of Fingermarks in Blood', Forensic Science International 210, no. 1–3 (2011): 1–11.
18. Barni, Filippo, Simon Lewis, Andrea Berti, Gordon Miskelly, and Giampietro Lago, 'Forensic Application of the Luminol Reaction as a Presumptive Test for Latent Blood Detection', Talanta 72, no. 3 (2007): 896–913.
19. Varela Morillas, Alvaro, James Gooch, and Nunzianda Frascione, 'Feasibility of a Handheld near Infrared Device for the Qualitative Analysis of Bloodstains', Talanta 184(2018): 1–6.
20. Edelman, Gerda J, Ton G van Leeuwen, and Maurice C Aalders, 'Visualization of Latent Blood Stains Using Visible Reflectance Hyperspectral Imaging and Chemometrics', Journal of Forensic Sciences 60(2015): S188–S92.
21. Stewart, Vanessa, Paul Decon, Nathalie Zahra, Mari Uchimoto, and Kevin J Farrugia, 'The Effect of Mark Enhancement Techniques on the Presumptive and Confirmatory Tests for Blood', Science & Justice 58, no. 6 (2018): 386–96.
22. Streeting, Carl A, Janet Chaseling, Matt N Krosch, and Kristy Wright, 'A Comparison of Abacard® Hematrace® and Rsidtm-Blood Tests on Dried, Diluted Bloodstains Treated with Leucocrystal Violet or Luminol', Australian Journal of Forensic Sciences 54, no. 1 (2020):108–18.
23. Seashols, Sarah J, Heather D Cross, Danielle L Shrader, and Ashley Rief, 'A Comparison of Chemical Enhancements for the Detection of Latent Blood', Journal of Forensic Sciences 58, no. 1 (2013): 130–3.
24. Seashols, Sarah J, Heather D Cross, Danielle L Shrader, and Ashley Rief, 'A Comparison of Chemical Enhancements for the Detection of Latent Blood', Journal of Forensic Sciences 58, no. 1 (2013): 130–3.
25. Hartley, Gabrielle, and Claire L Glynn, 'A Comparative Analysis of Protein and Peroxidase Blood Enhancement Reagents Following Laundering and Their Impact on DNA Recovery', (2017).
26. Frégeau, Chantal J, Olivier Germain, and Ron M Fourney, 'Fingerprint Enhancement Revisited and the Effects of Blood Enhancement Chemicals on Subsequent Profiler Plus™ Fluorescent Short Tandem Repeat DNA Analysis of Fresh and Aged Bloody Fingerprints', Journal of Forensic Sciences 45, no. 2 (2000): 354–80.
27. Grubwieser, Petra, Alexandra Thaler, Silvano Köchl, Roger Teissl, Walter Rabl, and Walther Parson, 'Systematic Study on Str Profiling on Blood and Saliva Traces after Visualization of Fingerprint Marks', Journal of Forensic Sciences 48, no. 4 (2003): 733–41.
28. Passi, Neha, Rakeshh Kumar Garg, Mukesh Yadav, Ram Sarup Singh, and Magdy A Kharoshah, 'Effect of Luminol and Bleaching Agent on the Serological and DNA Analysis from Bloodstain', Egyptian Journal of Forensic Sciences 2, no. 2 (2012): 54–61.
29. Stotesbury, Theresa, Mike Illes, and Andrew Vreugdenhil, 'Investigation of Physical Effects of Acid Yellow 7® Enhancement on Dark and Non-Porous Surfaces in Impact Pattern Area of Origin Estimation', Canadian Society of Forensic Science Journal 45, no. 1 (2012): 22–35.
30. Streeting, Carl A, Janet Chaseling, Matt N Krosch, and Kristy Wright, 'A Comparison of Abacard® Hematrace® and Rsidtm-Blood Tests on Dried, Diluted Bloodstains Treated with Leucocrystal Violet or Luminol', Australian Journal of Forensic Sciences 2;54, no. 1 (2022 Jan):108–18.
31. Stewart, Vanessa, Paul Decon, Nathalie Zahra, Mari Uchimoto, and Kevin J Farrugia, 'The Effect of Mark Enhancement Techniques on the Presumptive and Confirmatory Tests for Blood', Science & Justice 58, no. 6 (2018): 386–96.
32. Frégeau, Chantal J, Olivier Germain, and Ron M Fourney, 'Fingerprint Enhancement Revisited and the Effects of Blood Enhancement Chemicals on Subsequent Profiler Plus™ Fluorescent Short Tandem Repeat DNA Analysis of Fresh and Aged Bloody Fingerprints', Journal of Forensic Sciences 45, no. 2 (2000): 354–80.

33. Fox, Ashleigh, M Gittos, SallyAnn Harbison, Rachel Fleming, and Richard Wivell, 'Exploring the Recovery and Detection of Messenger RNA and DNA from Enhanced Fingermarks in Blood', Science & Justice 54, no. 3 (2014): 192–8.
34. Budowle, Bruce, Jeffrey L Leggitt, Debra Defenbaugh, Kathleen M Keys, and Steven F Malkiewicz, 'The Presumptive Reagent Fluorescein for Detection of Dilute Bloodstains and Subsequent STR Typing of Recovered DNA', Journal of Forensic Science 45, no. 5 (2000): 1090–2.
35. De Almeida, Juliana Piva, Nadine Glesse, and Cristina Bonorino, 'Effect of Presumptive Tests Reagents on Human Blood Confirmatory Tests and DNA Analysis Using Real Time Polymerase Chain Reaction', Forensic science international 206, no. 1–3 (2011): 58–61.
36. Tontarski, Karolyn L, Kyle A Hoskins, Tani G Watkins, Leanora Burn-Conti, and Amy L Michaud, 'Chemical Enhancement Techniques of Bloodstain Patterns and DNA Recovery after Fire Exposure', Journal of Forensic Sciences 54, no. 1 (2009): 37–48.
37. Sears, Vaughn, Colin PG Butcher, and Tania M Prizeman, 'Enhancement of Fingerprints in Blood–Part 2: Protein Dyes', Journal of Forensic Identification 51, no. 1 (2001): 28.
38. Stotesbury, Theresa, Mike Illes, and Andrew Vreugdenhil, 'Investigation of Physical Effects of Acid Yellow 7® Enhancement on Dark and Non-Porous Surfaces in Impact Pattern Area of Origin Estimation', Canadian Society of Forensic Science Journal 45, no. 1 (2012): 22–35.
39. Sears, Vaughn G, and Tania M Prizeman, 'Enhancement of Fingerprints in Blood–Part 1: The Optimization of Amido Black', Journal of Forensic Identification 50, no. 5 (2000): 470.
40. Praska, Nicole, and Glenn Langenburg, 'Reactions of Latent Prints Exposed to Blood', Forensic Science International 224, no. 1–3 (2013): 51–8.
41. Kennedy, Katie, Ravell Bengiat, Cameron Heaton, Yael Herman, Carlo Oz, Michael Levin Elad, Laura Cole, and Simona Francese, '"MALDI-CSI": A Proposed Method for the Tandem Detection of Human Blood and DNA Typing from Enhanced Fingermarks', Forensic Science International 323(2021): 110774.
42. Hong, Sungwook, and Jin Yi Seo, 'Chemical Enhancement of Fingermark in Blood on Thermal Paper', Forensic Science International 257 (2015): 379–84.
43. Lawley, Rodney, 'Application of Amido Black Mixture for the Development of Blood-Based Fingerprints on Human Skin', Journal of Forensic Identification 53, no. 4 (2003): 404.
44. Petretei, David, and Miklos Angyal, 'Recovering Bloody Fingerprints from Skin', Journal of Forensic Identification 65, no. 5 (2015): 813–27.
45. Praska, Nicole, and Glenn Langenburg, 'Reactions of Latent Prints Exposed to Blood', Forensic Science International 224, no. 1–3 (2013): 51–8.
46. Miskelly, Gordon M, and Marmix Kelderman, 'Interference of Ninhydrin Pretreatment on Leuco Crystal Violet Visualization of Bloodstains', Canadian Society of Forensic Science Journal 34, no. 3 (2001): 109–16.
47. Webb, Joanne L, Jonathan I Creamer, and Terence I Quickenden, 'A Comparison of the Presumptive Luminol Test for Blood with Four Non-Chemiluminescent Forensic Techniques', Luminescence: The Journal of Biological and Chemical Luminescence 21, no. 4 (2006): 214–20.
48. Cassidy, Brianna M, Zhenyu Lu, Jennifer P Martin, Shawna K Tazik, Katie Q Kellogg, Stephanie A DeJong, Elle O Belliveau, Katherine E Kilgore, Samantha M Ervin, Mackenzie Meece-Rayle, Alyssa M Abraham, Michael L Myrick, and Stephen L Morgan, 'A Quantitative Method for Determining a Representative Detection Limit of the Forensic Luminol Test for Latent Bloodstains', Forensic Science International 278 (2017): 396–403.
49. Polacco, Sumiko, Paul Wilson, Mike Illes, and Theresa Stotesbury, 'Quantifying Chemiluminescence of the Forensic Luminol Test for Ovine Blood in a Dilution and Time Series', Forensic Science International 290 (2018): 36–41.
50. Barni, Filippo, Simon Lewis, Andrea Berti, Gordon Miskelly, and Giampietro Lago, 'Forensic Application of the Luminol Reaction as a Presumptive Test for Latent Blood Detection', Talanta 72, no. 3 (2007): 896–913.
51. Laux, Dale, 'The Detection of Blood Using Luminol', in *Principles of Bloodstain Pattern Analysis: Theory and Practice*, eds. Stuart H James, Paul E Kish, and T Paulette Sutton (CRC press, 2005).
52. Tobe, Shanan S, Nigel Watson, and Niamh Nic Daeid, 'Evaluation of Six Presumptive Tests for Blood, Their Specificity, Sensitivity, and Effect on High Molecular-Weight DNA', Journal of Forensic Science 52, no. 1 (2007): 102–9.

53. Manna, A Dell, and Shawn Montpetit, 'A Novel Approach to Obtaining Reliable PCR Results from Luminol Treated Bloodstains', Journal of Forensic Sciences 45, no. 4 (2000): 886–90.
54. Jakovich, Cathy J, 'STR Analysis Following Latent Blood Detection by Luminol, Fluorescein, and Bluestar', Journal of Forensic Identification 57, no. 2 (2007): 193.
55. Patel, Gnyaneshwari, and Andy Hopwood, 'An Evaluation of Luminol Formulations and Their Effect on DNA Profiling', International Journal of Legal Medicine 127, no. 4 (2013): 723–9.
56. Quinones, Ignacio, Dion Sheppard, SallyAnn Harbison, and Douglas Elliot, 'Comparative Analysis of Luminol Formulations', Canadian Society of Forensic Science Journal 40, no. 2 (2007): 53–63.
57. Hofmann, Michaela, Jiri Adamec, Katja Anslinger, Birgit Bayer, Matthias Graw, Oliver Peschel, and, Martin Schulz, 'Detectability of Bloodstains after Machine Washing', International Journal of Legal Medicine 133, no. 1 (2019): 3–16.
58. Nakanishi, Hiroaki, Takeshi Ohmori, Katsumi Yoneyama, Masaaki Hara, Aya Takada, and Kazuyuki Saito, 'Bloodstain Examination and DNA Typing from Hand-Washed Bloodstains on Clothes', Legal Medicine 47(2020): 101758.
59. Budowle, Bruce, Jeffrey L Leggitt, Debra Defenbaugh, Kathleen M Keys, and Steven F Malkiewicz, 'The Presumptive Reagent Fluorescein for Detection of Dilute Bloodstains and Subsequent STR Typing of Recovered DNA', Journal of Forensic Science 45, no. 5 (2000): 1090–2.

CHAPTER 26

PRESUMPTIVE TESTS, ENHANCEMENTS, AND DETECTION OF BLOODSTAINS AND BLOODSTAIN PATTERNS

Celestina Rossi

Presumptive tests, enhancement, and search chemicals, for the most part, can be used interchangeably. While some chemicals may have multiple uses, it is important to note that they may not be equally effective in all situations. For example, Luminol may be effective as a search and an enhancement chemical, but it may not be the best choice as a presumptive test or the best choice for certain surfaces or situations. It is important for forensic scientists to choose the appropriate chemical based on the specific circumstances of each case in order to obtain the most accurate results. The analyst should consider certain parameters before choosing a particular chemical:

- The surface that the stain or pattern is deposited on (i.e., is it porous or non-porous)
- The background color of the substrate versus the color reaction of the chemical being used
- The chemical reaction to the substrate (i.e., methanol on oil-based paint)
- The benefit of enhanced visualization by using alternate light
- The sensitivity of the test
- The ease of use, cost, and availability of the chemical
- Ability to ventilate the area and the use of personal protective equipment (e.g., gloves, air-filtration mask, laboratory coat, or polyethylene style suit) while using any chemical discussed in this chapter as some may be classified as irritants.

Presumptive testing is a cost-effective and time-efficient way to determine if a substance or stain is likely to be blood. In most cases, it is impractical to test every stain or substance for DNA that has the appearance of blood which is why presumptive testing is so important. If the presumptive test is positive, further testing such as confirmatory testing and DNA analysis can be performed to determine if the substance or stain is indeed blood and to obtain a DNA profile. If the presumptive test is negative, it indicates that the substance or stain is unlikely to be blood, and resources can be allocated to other evidence.

Some of the chemical enhancement techniques discussed in this chapter are chosen based on their effectiveness in detecting and enhancing bloodstains, as well as their practicality and safety in processing crime scenes and physical evidence. It is essential to perform a quality check on the reagent each day before use. This quality check involves testing the reagent using a known blood source as a positive control and a blank source as a negative control. The QC check should be noted in lab or field notes.

Prior to making any modifications or enhancements to a bloodstained area or item, it is crucial to record its initial state. This documentation is essential in order to show what it looked like in situ and can provide valuable evidence in analyzing the results obtained from any subsequent chemical or alternate light examinations. Infrared (IR) photography can be particularly beneficial in identifying bloodstains that are not discernible to the naked eye, as IR has the ability to penetrate some materials that visible light cannot.

 DOI: 10.4324/9781003163695-26

Figure 26.1 Application of Leucocrystal Violet (LCV) to the underside of carpet while wearing a respirator.

To preserve the quality and quantity of DNA samples, it is advisable to obtain a DNA sample prior to using any blood-enhancement reagent. Some of these reagents can degrade DNA, making it difficult to obtain an accurate and reliable DNA profile. Collecting the DNA sample before applying the chemical reagent can help ensure that the DNA evidence remains intact and can be used for further analysis.

The Material Safety Data Sheet (MSDS) is a crucial resource for understanding the potential hazards of a chemical. It contains important information about the physical and chemical properties of the substance, as well as its toxicity and recommended safety precautions. Analysts should carefully review the MSDS prior to working with any chemical and must follow the safety precautions specified. Additionally, chemical container labels provide essential safety information, such as hazard warnings, safe handling instructions, and first-aid measures in the event of accidental exposure or ingestion. It is important to adhere to the instructions and warnings provided on the MSDS and container labels to ensure the safe handling and use of chemicals (Figure 26.1).

CATALYTIC COLOR TESTS

Chromogenic substances are often utilized in catalytic tests that involve the chemical oxidation process to identify the existence of hemoglobin in blood specimens. The chromogenic substance can be a compound or molecule that is capable of generating a noticeable color change in response to a specific stimulus. The dye that is frequently employed in these tests changes its color when oxidized, with hydrogen peroxide commonly serving as the oxidizing agent. The intensity of the color alteration is directly proportional to the quantity of hemoglobin present in the sample.

The two-step process of color reaction tests typically involves the application of a drop of chromogen solution containing the dye that reacts with the target substance to change color, followed by the addition of a drop of oxidizing agent such as hydrogen peroxide to the suspected stain. Hydrogen peroxide is a preferred oxidizing agent due to its availability and wide range of reactivity. A 3% hydrogen peroxide solution is often used as it is strong enough to produce a reaction without damaging the sample or interfering with test results. The oxidizing agent catalyzes the reaction between the chromogen and the target substance in the stain. A positive result is indicated by a color change of the chromogen, with the intensity of the color change providing an estimate of the amount of the target substance present in the sample.

One-step tests or direct tests for detecting the presence of blood use a single solution containing both the chromogen and the oxidizing agent. These tests simplify the procedure and save time but may have a disadvantage: the order of adding reagents is crucial. Adding the color reagent first to a sample without the target substance may lead to a color reaction due to non-specific interactions between reagents and hemoglobin. Consequently, the oxidizing agent may not cause any additional color change, resulting in a false-positive result.

Catalytic color tests are widely used in bloodstain pattern analysis, clinical laboratories, and other fields for the detection and identification of various substances, including blood, saliva, drugs, and explosives. They are simple, rapid, and can be performed with minimal equipment and training, making them a valuable tool in many applications. However, it is important to note that color reaction tests are often presumptive and require confirmatory testing to confirm the results. Using both positive and negative controls in a test helps to ensure that the results are accurate and reliable. By including controls, any potential issues with the test, such as contamination or non-specific reactions, can be identified and addressed, minimizing false positives and false negatives.

Tetramethylbenzidine and Hemastix®

Tetramethylbenzidine (TMB) is used to catalyze the reaction with hemoglobin in blood and produce a visible color change. It is utilized with an acidic medium, such as acetic acid, to stabilize the solution and prevent the substrate from getting oxidized. The acidic medium also boosts color development by reducing the pH of the reaction, which promotes the formation of the blue-green-colored product. It should be kept in mind that TMB is light-sensitive and must be shielded from direct sunlight or bright light sources to avoid degradation and maintain the accuracy of the results.

Hemastix®

The Hemastix® test is a simple color reaction test utilizing a plastic strip with a reagent tab that is treated with tetramethylbenzadine (TMB) mentioned above. To conduct the Hemastix® test, first, a sample of the suspected bloodstain is gathered using a cotton swab that has been dampened with distilled water. The moistened swab is then placed onto the reagent tab located on the strip. If the stain contains hemoglobin, the TMB present in the reagent will catalyze a reaction with it and cause a color change from yellow to green or blue-green, which serves as a presumptive indication of blood (Figures 26.2 and 26.3). Other substances, such as plant material or certain metals, can also produce a positive result due to their ability to catalyze the TMB reaction.

Phenolphthalein (Kastle-Meyer Test)

Phenolphthalein is a simple acid-based presumptive test (Figure 26.4). The test involves applying a small amount of phenolphthalein solution to a sample of the suspected bloodstain. If the sample contains blood, the iron in the hemoglobin molecules will catalyze the breakdown of hydrogen peroxide, which is then used to oxidize phenolphthalein. This causes a color change in the solution from colorless to pink, indicating the presence of blood.

Phenolphthalein is not specific to blood and can be affected by other substances that contain catalytic agents such as copper, bleach, and certain types of organic matter such as horseradish, potatoes, and certain types of fungi. After the addition of the phenolphthalein and the hydrogen peroxide, a color change reaction should occur immediately (within 60 s) if blood is present (Figure 26.5).

It is crucial to observe and interpret the color change of any catalytic color test within a few seconds of adding the reagents. Delaying the observation can cause background color formation, which can make it challenging to interpret the result correctly. Thus, it is essential to read the manufacturer's instructions for the specific test being used and interpret the outcome promptly after the reaction occurs to obtain precise and dependable results.

Figure 26.2 Testing a spatter stain with Hemastix®.

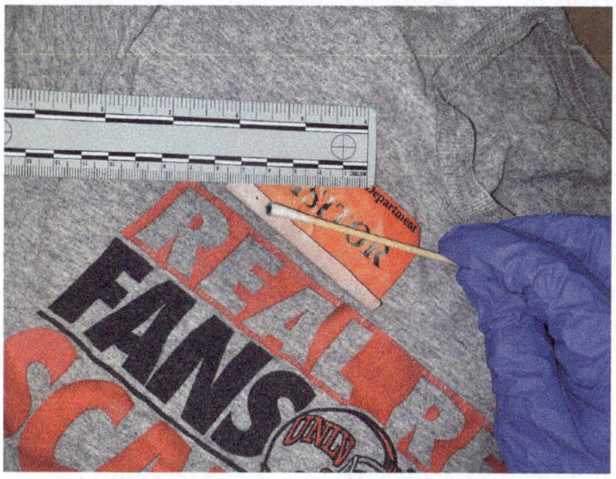

Figure 26.3 Color reaction after testing a bloodstain with Hemastix®.

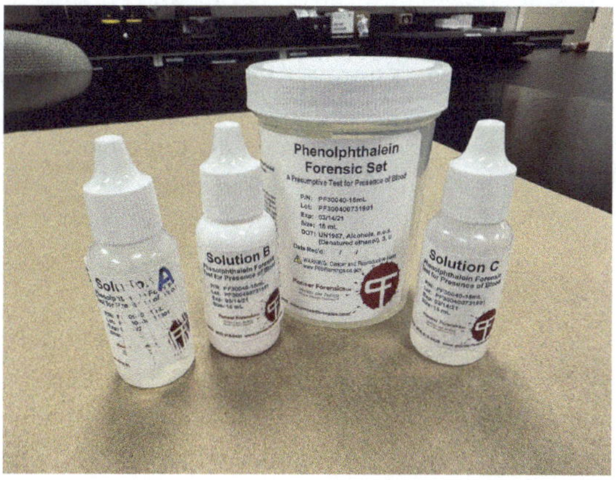

Figure 26.4 Commercially available Phenolphthalein 3-part kit.

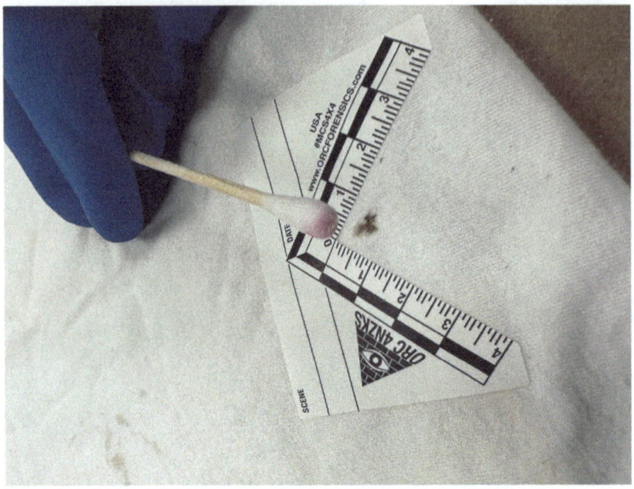

Figure 26.5 Color reaction after testing a bloodstain with Phenolphthalein.

CHEMILUMINESCENCE AND FLUORESCENCE

Chemiluminescence

To detect bloodstains, chemiluminescent bloodstain detection chemicals offer several advantages due to their high sensitivity and ability to detect bloodstains that have been diluted or wiped clean. Additionally, they can detect bloodstains that are invisible under normal lighting conditions. Chemiluminescence is a process that involves the emission of light as a result of a chemical reaction. In the context of bloodstain analysis, a chemical reagent is used to react with the hemoglobin in blood and produce a light indicator for visualization. Typically, the reagent is sprayed or applied to the surface suspected of containing blood, and a chemiluminescent reaction occurs, resulting in a visible reaction.

However, there are also some limitations to the use of chemiluminescence, including the potential for false positives from non-blood sources, the potential for contamination of the evidence, and the need for specialized training and expertise to use the technique effectively.

Luminol is a chemiluminescent reagent for the detection and enhancement of latent bloodstains, where a chemical reaction between luminol and an oxidizing agent (such as hydrogen peroxide) produces a pale blue light in the presence of blood (Figures 26.6 and 26.7). Excessive spraying will usually result in stain pattern diffusion. Additionally, luminol can interfere with subsequent DNA analysis, making it important to use appropriate sampling and preservation techniques.

In recent years, there have been several adaptations of the original luminol formulation, including the commercial products **BlueStar®** and **Lumiscene**. These products use similar chemical reactions to luminol but may have different properties or enhancements that make them more suitable for specific applications or scenarios.

Fluorescence

When a fluorescent substance is exposed to a specific wavelength of light, the atoms or molecules in the substance absorb energy and move to an excited state. As the atoms or molecules return to their ground state, they release the excess energy as light of a longer wavelength, typically in the visible or near-visible range.

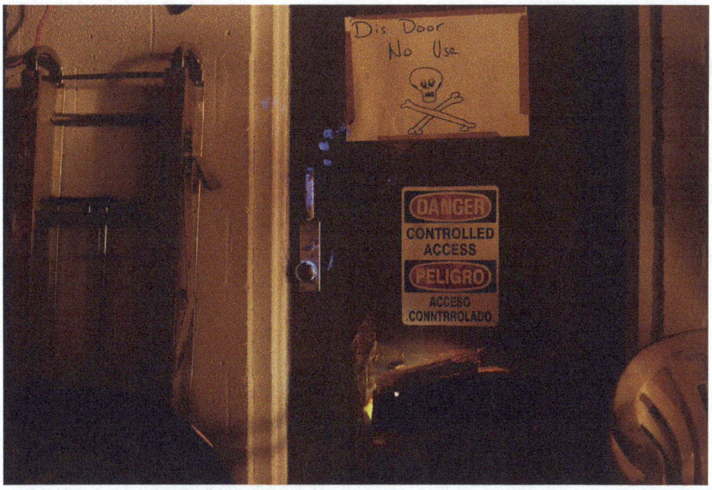

Figure 26.6 BlueStar® chemiluminescent reaction to bloodstains on the back of a door (photograph courtesy of Jennifer Karscher, Montgomery County Police Department, Maryland).

Figure 26.7 BlueStar® chemiluminescent reaction to bloodstains on carpet in a bedroom with a void pattern created by a cat tree (photograph courtesy of Ashleigh Berg, Denton County Sheriff's Office, Denton, Texas).

The use of fluorescein was introduced as a fluorescent alternative to luminol in 1995 by Rob Cheeseman.[1] Fluorescein can be used as a presumptive test for the detection of latent bloodstains. When fluorescein is applied to a suspected bloodstain, it binds to the heme group in hemoglobin and then when illuminated with ultraviolet or blue light (425–485 nm), it emits a bright green light, indicating the presence of blood. One of the advantages of fluorescein is that it can continue to emit light for several hours after application, which allows investigators to observe bloodstains in low-light conditions. Studies regarding the interference of fluorescein with subsequent DNA testing showed no evidence of DNA degradation.[2] However, like other presumptive tests, fluorescein is not specific to blood and can also react with other substances.

Bloodstain Dyes

Another type of bloodstain presumptive test is where the reagent interacts with blood proteins, specifically with the amino acids.

Leucocrystal violet (LCV) is a sensitive test and can detect bloodstains that are not visible to the naked eye. It is a one-step process that involves applying a solution of leucocrystal violet to the suspected bloodstain. LCV and the presence of hydrogen peroxide reacts with the heme group of hemoglobin, which is found in red blood cells, causing the stain to turn to a deep purple color (Figures 26.8–26.10). Additionally, LCV works well on porous items such as clothing and carpet.

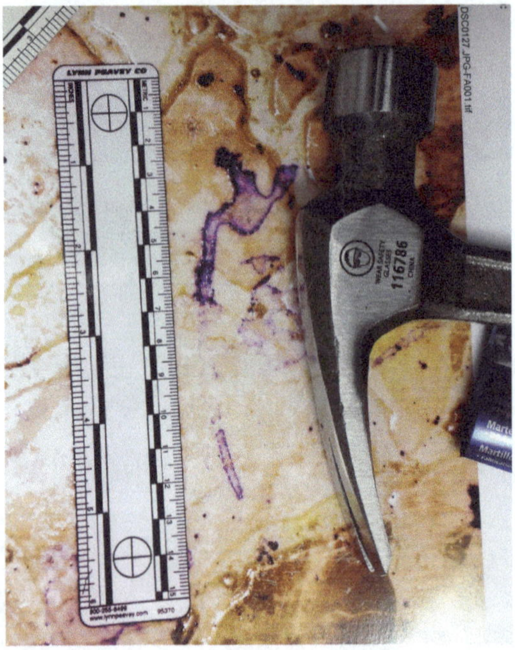

Figure 26.8 1:1 photograph of a bloodstain impression developed on linoleum floor with Leucocrystal Violet (LCV) in the shape of a roofing hammer.

Figure 26.9 Ceramic tile floor after treatment with Leucocrystal Violet (LCV).

Figure 26.10 Swipe bloodstains enhanced with Leucocrystal Violet (LCV) on ceramic tile.

Amido black is a synthetic dye that is commonly used as a protein stain. It is particularly useful for enhancing the visibility of bloodstains on various surfaces such as walls and floors as it selectively binds to proteins and forms a blue-black-colored complex with them (Figure 26.11). The use of amido black is a two-step process and requires a rinse with methanol or water to remove excess dye and improve contrast, which can damage or alter certain types of surfaces. As a result, it is not recommended for use on clothing or porous materials such as carpets or untreated wood.

Figure 26.11 Ceramic tile treated with Amido Black with a methanol rinse to enhance bloody shoe prints.

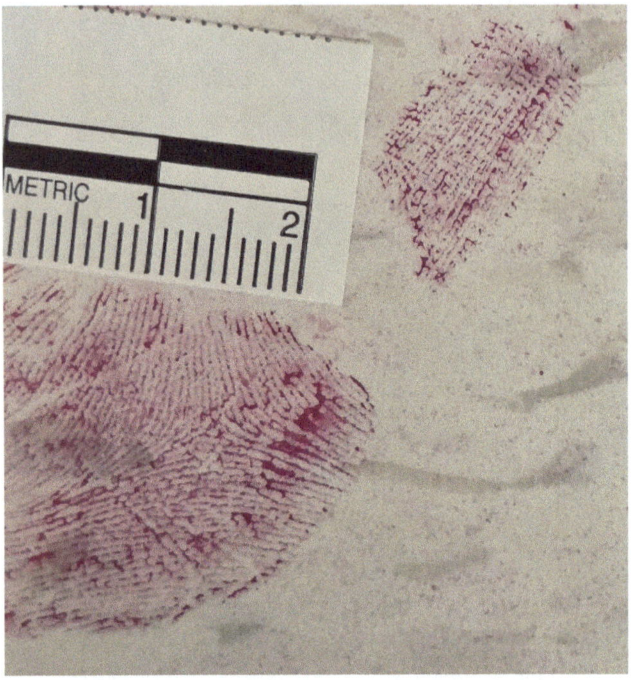

Figure 26.12 Vinyl flooring treated with Hungarian Red (Acid Fuchsin) (photograph courtesy of Dr. Casie Parish-Fisher).

Amido black can be used secondarily after the application of LCV to establish more contrast. This is especially useful in cases where the bloodstain is very faint or has been partially or completely washed away. Amido black reacts with the proteins in blood, producing a blue-black color. By using both LCV and amido black in combination, analysts can increase sensitivity and specificity of their analysis and get a more accurate picture of the bloodstain pattern. It should be noted that methanol is considered a hazardous material that can cause optical nerve damage and it is imperative that when dealing with such chemicals, you refer to the MSDS and wear proper personal protective equipment.

Hungarian Red (also known as **Acid Fuchsin**) is a dye that reacts with the iron present in hemoglobin, the protein in blood that carries oxygen, to produce a distinctive red-violet color (Figure 26.12). However, it is important to note that Hungarian Red is not a presumptive test for blood and should only be used after blood has been identified through a presumptive test. Hungarian Red will fluoresce with an alternate light source (515–560 nm with a red barrier filter), particularly when used in conjunction with a white gelatin lifter. This fluorescence can help to enhance the visibility of bloodstain pattern on multicolor or dark surfaces, which can be difficult to see with the naked eye or with conventional illumination.

Leucomalachite green (LMG) (Figure 26.13) interacts directly with the iron in hemoglobin in blood to produce a green color (Figure 26.14). This reaction is not specific to amino acids and does not involve catalytic activity like some other bloodstain presumptive tests, such as luminol or hemascein. LMG is primarily used as a confirmatory test for the presence of blood, but it may also produce a false positive result in the presence of certain metals or oxidizing agents.

Coomassie brilliant blue (CBB) is a blue-violet chemical dye that is commonly used for staining and visualizing proteins present in blood and other body fluids (Figures 26.15 and 26.16). CBB can be prepared in both aqueous and methanol-based solutions. The methanol-based solution is comparable in use with amido black previously discussed in this chapter.

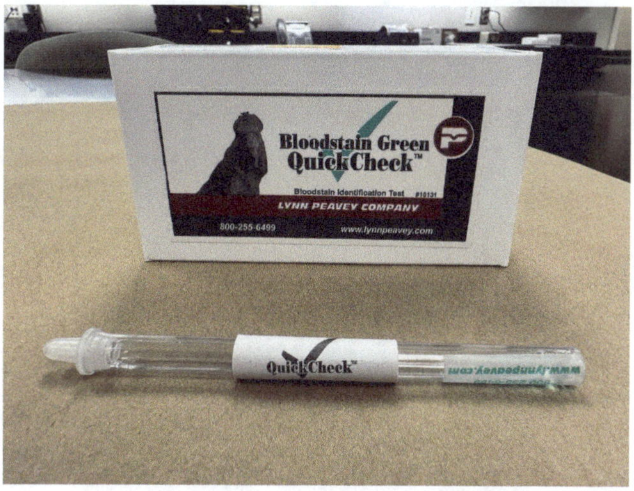

Figure 26.13 Commercially available Leucomalachite green (LMG).

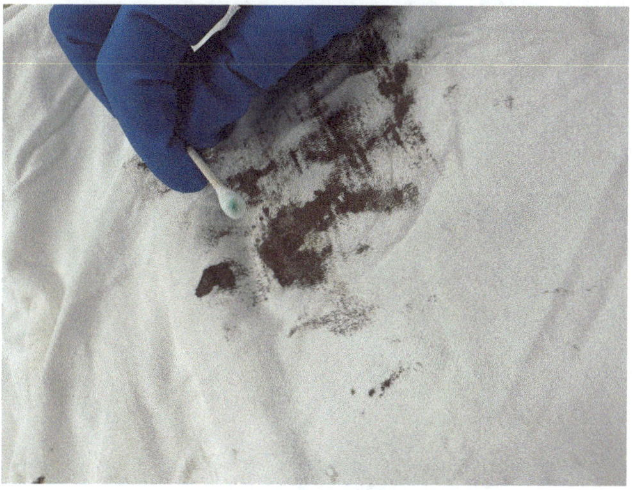

Figure 26.14 Color reaction after testing a bloodstain with Leucomalachite green.

Ninhydrin is a common chemical used for the detection of latent fingerprints on porous surfaces. However, since it reacts with amino acids, it can also be used as a purple dye for bloodstains and their patterns (Figure 26.17). Ninhydrin would be a good reagent choice for analysts who are processing for both latent and patent fingerprints.

Titanium dioxide (TiO_2) is a naturally harvested chemical powder used as a pigment in paints, plastics, papers, and other materials to provide a bright, white color. It is also used as a sunscreen agent in cosmetic and skincare products due to its ability to reflect and scatter UV radiation. Titanium dioxide can be used as a solution to enhance blood prints on dark surfaces. When dissolved in methanol, it forms a white suspension that can be sprayed or applied to a target surface. The TiO_2 particles adhere to bloodstains and create a white contrast against the dark background where other enhancement methods may not be effective, making the stains more visible for documentation and analysis (Figure 26.18).

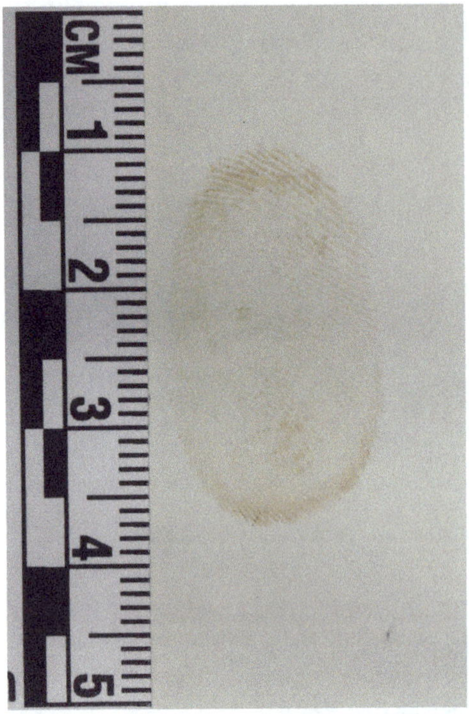

Figure 26.15 Untreated bloody fingerprint on glossy cardboard (photograph courtesy of Elise Crosswhite, Winston-Salem Police Department, North Carolina).

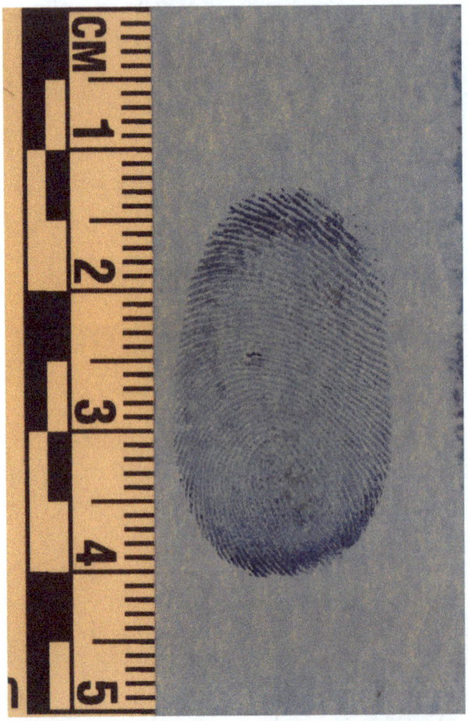

Figure 26.16 Bloody fingerprint after treatment with Coomassie Brilliant Blue (CBB) on glossy cardboard (photograph courtesy of Elise Crosswhite, Winston-Salem Police Department, North Carolina).

Figure 26.17 Bloody left palm print treated with Ninhydrin (photograph courtesy of Ashleigh Berg, Denton County Sheriff's Office, Denton, Texas).

Figure 26.18 Bloody fingerprint on a black trash bag treated with titanium dioxide (TiO_2) (photograph courtesy of Dr. Casie Parish-Fisher).

Crystal Tests

Crystal tests involve the use of chemicals that react with the nonprotein heme group of hemoglobin, which is the oxygen-carrying protein in erythrocytes. The nonprotein heme group belongs to a class of compounds called porphyrins. When certain chemicals are added to a bloodstain containing hemoglobin, they can cause the heme group to form distinctive crystal structures, which can be observed under a microscope. These crystal structures can help confirm the presence of blood in a sample. Some examples of crystal tests include Teichmann test and Takayama test or hemochromogen crystal test.

The Teichmann test is a chemical test used to detect the presence of hemoglobin in a sample. It involves heating a dried blood sample with glacial acetic acid and sodium chloride to form hemin crystals, which are then observed under a microscope. The hemin crystals are typically rhombic in shape and have a brownish color. The Teichmann test was developed by German chemist Julius Teichmann in 1853 and remains an important technique in forensic science.[3]

The Takayama test, also known as the hemochromogen crystal test, was initially developed by Japanese chemist Shiro Takayama in 1901 and later examined by Takayama in 1912.[4] This is a chemical test used for the detection of hemoglobin in bloodstains. The test involves gently heating the bloodstain in the presence of pyridine, an alkaline solution, and glucose. This reaction leads to the formation of pyridine ferriprotoporphyrin or hemochromogen crystals, which are the characteristic of hemoglobin and can be observed under a microscope.

Of interesting note, Dr. Paul Leland Kirk was an American forensic scientist and professor at the University of California, Berkeley. He is considered a pioneer in the field of forensic science and is known for his contributions to the development of techniques and methods for analyzing evidence in criminal investigations. According to Kirk (1953), both the specificity and sensitivity of the hemochromogen test are about the same as those of the hematin crystal test.[5] He also noted that a negative crystal test, however, should not necessarily be interpreted as meaning that blood is absent.

Species Origin Determination

Ring precipitin test is a serological method for identifying the species origin of blood or other biological samples. It is based on the principle of antigen-antibody reactions, where antibodies produced in one species react specifically with the antigens of another species. To perform the test, a small amount of the sample is mixed with an antiserum (antihuman) from a known species. If the sample is from the same species as the antiserum, a ring of precipitated immune complexes will form at the interface of the two fluids. The ring is visible to the naked eye and can be used to identify the species of origin of the sample. The test is typically performed with a series of antisera from different animal species to confirm the species identity of the sample. It is a sensitive and specific test, but it requires skilled interpretation and can be affected by the quality of the antiserum used. In the case where the bloodstain extract is not of human, there should be no reaction. If there are multiple precipitin bands, it can indicate the presence of different proteins in the blood sample or cross-reactivity with other species.

DNA-based tests use DNA analysis to determine the species origin of the blood. DNA markers specific to certain species can be identified and used to match the DNA from the blood sample to a particular species.

Crossed-over electrophoretic analysis is a method used for detecting and identifying proteins in a mixture. It involves two separate electrophoresis runs that are performed simultaneously, with the sample being loaded onto two different gel strips. The first gel strip is typically an agarose gel that is run horizontally, while the second gel strip is a polyacrylamide gel that is run vertically. Both gels contain a pH gradient, which allows proteins to migrate based on their isoelectric point (pI). During electrophoresis, the proteins move through the gels until they reach their pI, at which point they become stationary. The gel strips are then placed on top of each other, with the agarose gel on top of the polyacrylamide gel. The two gels are then sealed together, and an electrical current is applied perpendicular to the direction of the original electrophoresis runs. As a result of the perpendicular current, the proteins from the first gel strip diffuse into the second gel strip, where they encounter a new pH gradient. The proteins continue to migrate based on their pI until they reach their stationary point in the new gel strip. After electrophoresis, the gel strips are stained to visualize the protein bands. The bands that appear in both gels represent the same protein, allowing for identification of specific proteins in the mixture. Crossed-over electrophoresis can be used for species origin determination of bloodstains by comparing the protein band patterns of the unknown sample to those of known standards of different species.

Nonserum Protein Analysis

An immunochromatographic system, also known as a lateral flow test or strip test, is a diagnostic test that uses a membrane-based technology for the detection of a target analyte in a sample. It works on the principle of immunoassay, where a specific antibody is used to capture and detect the analyte of interest. The sample is applied to one end of a membrane strip that contains the immobilized antibody. The sample then flows along the membrane by capillary action and interacts with the immobilized antibody. If the analyte is present in the sample, it binds to the antibody and forms a visible colored band or line, indicating a positive result. The test is simple to use, rapid, and does not require any specialized equipment. Commercially, several products are available that are specific to human, higher primate, and ferret blood.

Hexagon OBTI® is a two-part test that includes a collection tube for the blood sample and a test bar. A sample of the presumed human blood is transferred into the tube with the transport medium. This mixture is then added to the test bar. Typically, a positive reaction will be detected within 2–3 minutes. This test is useful for identifying the presence of blood on surfaces and materials that may have been aged or degraded, and it is not affected by many common environmental factors except for detergents, household bleaches, and prolonged exposure to luminol.

The ABAcard® HemaTrace® test device shares similarities with the Hexagon OBTI® in appearance and procedure. It is designed to assist in identifying human blood by detecting the presence of human hemoglobin. The test works by detecting the reaction of human hemoglobin antigens with mobile monoclonal antihuman Hb antibodies in the "S" area. This creates a mobile antibody-antigen complex, which migrates toward the "T" area where stationary polyclonal antihuman antibodies capture the complex. The stationary antibodies are labeled with a pink dye, and when they aggregate, they form a pink line in the "T" zone, indicating the presence of human hemoglobin in the sample. The test also contains an internal positive control in the "C" area, which captures excess antihuman Hb monoclonal antibodies that do not bind to the antibodies in the "T" area. A pink line in the "C" area indicates that the test functioned properly. A positive result is indicated by two pink lines, one in the "T" area and one in the "C" area. A negative result is indicated by only one pink line in the "C" area, and an invalid test result is indicated by the absence of a pink line in the "C" area. However, the test may produce false positives with ferret blood.

SERATEC® HemDirect Hemoglobin Assay is a rapid and sensitive presumptive test for the presence of human hemoglobin in forensic samples (Figure 26.19). The test works by detecting the presence of human-specific globin chains that are present in hemoglobin. The HemDirect test uses a membrane-based technology that incorporates human-specific monoclonal antibodies. When a sample is applied to the test membrane (Figure 26.20), any human hemoglobin present in the sample reacts with the monoclonal antibodies to form a complex. The complex is then detected by a secondary antibody conjugated to a colored particle. If the test is positive, a visible line will appear on the test membrane (Figure 26.21). The HemDirect test is easy to use and provides results within minutes, making it a useful tool for preliminary screening of forensic samples. It is important to note that the HemDirect test is a presumptive test and should always be followed up with confirmatory testing, such as DNA analysis, to ensure accurate identification of human blood. As with the other two tests mentioned, the SERATEC® HemDirect test will react with the blood of primates and ferrets.

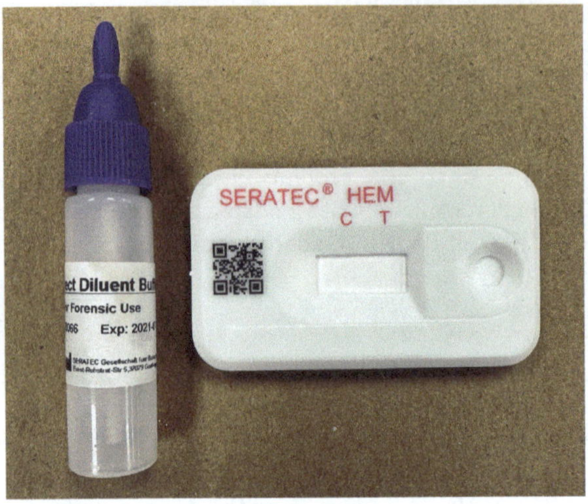

Figure 26.19 SERATEC® HemDirect buffer solution and test card.

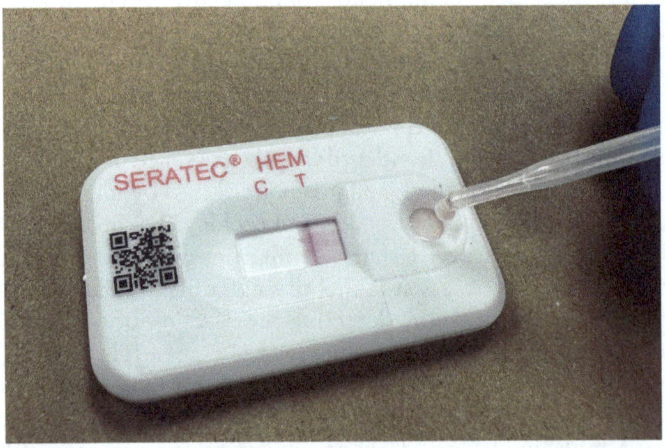

Figure 26.20 SERATEC® HemDirect buffer solution with suspected blood added to the test card well.

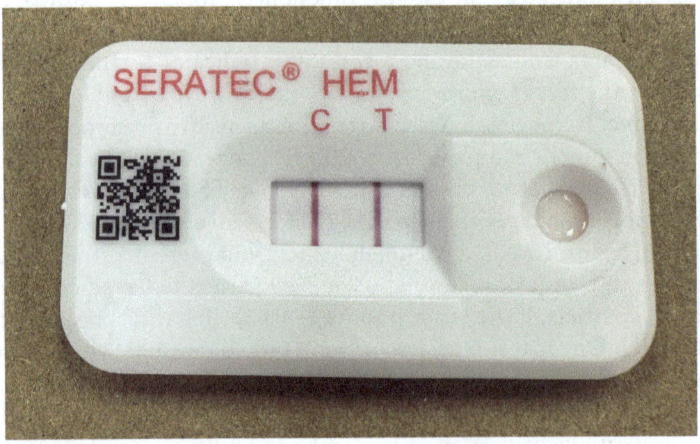

Figure 26.21 SERATEC® HemDirect test card resulting in a positive result.

CONCLUSION

During the initial testing phase, it is of utmost importance for an analyst to have a clear understanding of the available follow-up or confirmatory tests. DNA laboratories and their analysts not only provide confirmatory tests but also possess the capability to conduct highly sensitive and intricate testing methods such as the crystal test, DNA-based test, and crossed-over electrophoretic analysis. In addition to being proficient in presumptive testing, an analyst should also be well-versed in utilizing enhancement and search chemicals to aid in their examinations. However, it is crucial for an analyst to carefully assess the significance of the crime scene and/or evidence before initiating any unnecessary testing that could impede further analysis by other analysts. This evaluation helps prevent potential hindrances and ensures the optimal utilization of resources within the laboratory.

Notes

1. Cheeseman R, DiMeo LA. Fluorescein as a Field-Worthy Latent Bloodstain Detection System. *J Forensic Ident* 1985;45(6):631.
2. Budowle B, Leggitt J, Defenbaugh D, Keys K, Malkiewicz S. The Presumptive Reagent Fluorescein for Detection of Dilute Bloodstains and Subsequent STR Typing of Recovered DNA. *J Forensic Sci* 2000;45(5):1090–1092.
3. James SH, Nordby JJ, Bell S. *Forensic Science: An Introduction to Scientific and Investigative Techniques*, 4th ed. Florida: CRC Press, 2014.
4. Gaensslen RE. *Sourcebook in Forensic Serology, Immunology, and Biochemistry.* US DOJ NIJ 1983, p. 86.
5. Gaensslen RE. *Sourcebook in Forensic Serology, Immunology, and Biochemistry.* US DOJ NIJ 1983, pp. 86–87.

Further Reading

Adair, T., and R. Shaw. Enhancement of Bloodstains on Washed Clothing Using Luminol and LCV Reagents. IABPA News. December 2005.

Bergeron, J. "Development of Bloody Prints on Dark Surfaces with Titanium Dioxide and Methanol." *Journal of Forensic Identification* 53, no. 2 (2003): 149.

Bevel, T., and R.M. Gardner. *Bloodstain Pattern Analysis: With an Introduction to Crime Scene Reconstruction.* 3rd ed. Boca Raton, FL CRC Press, 2008.

Cox, M. "A Study of the Sensitivity and Specificity of Four Presumptive Tests for Blood." *Journal of Forensic Sciences* 36, no. 5 (1991): 1503–11.

Donachie, G., N. Dawnay, R. Ahmed, S. Naif, N. Duxbury, and N. Tribble. "Assessing the Impact of Common Forensic Presumptive Tests on the Ability to Obtain Results Using a Novel Rapid DNA Platform." *Forensic Science International: Genetics* 17 (2015): 87–90.

Forsythe-Erman, J. "A Comparison of Blood Enhancement Techniques." *Canadian Society of Forensic Science Journal* 34, no. 4: 159–65.

Gardner, R. M. *Practical Crime Scene Processing and Investigation.* CRC Press, 2012.

Gardner, R. M., and T. Bevel. *Practical Crime Scene Analysis and Reconstruction.* CRC Press, 2009.

James, S. H., P. E. Kish, and T. P. Sutton. *Principles of Bloodstain Pattern Analysis Theory and Practice.* CRC Press, 2005.

Kirk, P. L. *Crime Investigation.* 2nd ed. New York, John Wiley and Sons, 1974.

Maloney, M. S., and D. G. Housman. *Crime Scene Investigation Procedural Guide.* CRC Press, 2014.

Miller, R. Leuco Crystal Violet: A Simple, Effective Blood Enhancement Reagent. Arizona Identification Council Oct/Dec 1995.

Montgomery County Department of Police, MD: Forensic Services Section. Bloodstain Pattern Procedures Manual.

Reynolds, M. The ABAcard HemaTrace – A Confirmatory Identification of Human Blood Located at Crime Scenes IABPA News. June 2004, pp. 4–10

SERATEC HemDirect Hemoglobin Assay Technical Information Sheet (rev: June 2009). Gottingen, Germany.

Tobe, S., N. Watson, and N. Daeid. "Evaluation of Six Presumptive Tests for Blood, Their Specificity, Sensitivity, and Effect on High Molecular-Weight DNA." *Journal of Forensic Science* 52, no. 1 (January 2007): 102–9.

CHAPTER 27

FORENSIC ANALYSIS OF BLOOD (DNA) AND THE APPLICATION TO BLOODSTAIN PATTERN ANALYSIS

Cecilia Hageman

The investigative tasks of attributing biological evidence to a particular person, and correspondingly of excluding a person as a source of biological evidence, are presently within the almost exclusive realm of forensic DNA (deoxyribonucleic acid) analysis. There are myriad facets to forensic DNA analysis, from the purely technical aspects of producing DNA profiles in the laboratory to interpreting and comparing these profiles within the context of a criminal, civil, or regulatory case. The focus of this chapter is on forensic DNA analysis in aid of, or in combination with, bloodstain pattern analysis. In criminal casework where bloodstain patterns are produced and interpreted, the primary question to be answered by the bloodstain pattern analyst is not necessarily the potential source of the blood, but rather what actions could or couldn't have occurred to produce the observed bloodstain patterns – this is especially true if victim/deceased in the bloodletting event is already known or not in question, and if there is only one known bleeder at a crime scene. However, forensic DNA analysis may still be a key component of bloodstain pattern analysis work to address case-relevant questions of blood source identity. This analysis is especially crucial in bloodstain analysis cases that involve unknown victims or an unknown number of bleeders. In addition, DNA analysis assists the investigation of cases with samples from overlapping bloodstain patterns involving multiple bleeders, and also the investigation of cases with evidence samples that are mixtures of DNA from blood and other sources of body fluids and tissues.

This chapter is not a fulsome treatment of all things forensic DNA – Forensic DNA is an extensive and multi-faceted field – the reader is invited to avail themselves of numerous texts, websites, and journals that cover this massive topic[1]. Rather, this chapter will guide the bloodstain pattern analyst through topics pertinent to their forensic applications of the technique – how DNA profiles are produced and what they look like, how DNA analysis results and conclusions are reported for single source, multiple source, or mixed, evidence samples, and the kinds of questions may be addressed by forensic DNA analysis that may complement or inform about the bloodstain pattern analysis case.

Before describing the process of forensic DNA analysis, or even DNA itself, it may be useful to start with a picture of the forensic DNA data at completion of the laboratory and interpretive processes, explained with minimal scientific jargon. And with that picture in mind, the description of technical and interpretive aspects of the forensic DNA process becomes clearer.

Using the current forensic industry standard technology, short tandem repeat (STR) analysis, a person's forensic DNA profile is reduced to a simple set of number pairs. Different humans will display different sets of number pairs and can therefore be distinguished from each other. Therefore, in a typical case, reference (known) samples and biological evidence samples are labeled by number sets, rather than letters, as previously found in, for example, ABO blood testing. Today's technology does not examine the entirety of the DNA in a sample. It targets only particular genetic

 DOI: 10.4324/9781003163695-27

addresses in order to determine the length of DNA at each of these special addresses, interspersed among various locations throughout a person's DNA. These locations, or "loci" (singular "locus"), are known to exhibit significant variation in the lengths of DNA strands among humans. The number components in each profile are therefore descriptions that signify DNA strand lengths – the higher a number, the longer that particular strand of DNA. The numbers come in pairs because humans have two parents, and for each genetic location tested, each person will have a length of DNA inherited from each parent. What a person inherits from their parents determines the numeric content of their entire forensic DNA profile.

Here are forensic data from a typical criminal case, with one evidence blood sample and reference samples from two persons of interest. The fundamental forensic question is: Who could (or could not) be the source of blood evidence?

In Table 27.1, the first column lists all the genetic addresses tested. While there is a tremendous amount of information in a person/sample's DNA, forensic analysis targets only a tiny portion at these types of genetic addresses. The addresses fulfill a role akin to postal codes, in that they allow scientists to zero in on known locations within the DNA to the exclusion of all other locations. Column 2 describes a DNA profile from an evidence blood sample, with the entire profile showing the pairs of DNA strand lengths, in the form of numbers, found at 15 addresses in the DNA, as well as one special area, called amelogenin, which tests for the presence of the sex chromosomes. The "X,Y" result in the Column 2 evidence sample, as well as Column 3's Person A, denotes profiles attributable to a male, while the X,X result in Column 4, the profile from Person B, shows a profile attributable to a female. From a comparison of these three profiles, the question of potential attribution of the evidence profile can be answered quite straightforwardly. Person B's profile is different from the evidence blood profile – while she shares a few numbers at some of the genetic addresses, she does not exhibit all of the same numbers, and therefore the same lengths of DNA, as that of the blood evidence profile. She is therefore excluded as the source of that blood evidence. Indeed, even if there was only one number difference with the evidence profile, Person B would still be excluded as the evidence source. Person A, however, has the same profile as that of the

Table 27.1 Three forensic DNA profiles in a case involving the comparison of a blood evidence sample (Column 2) to two persons of interest (A and B, Columns 3 and 4, respectively). These profiles were produced using a PowerPlex®16 kit, one of many commercially available testing kits for forensic purposes

DNA test site "locus"	Blood evidence	Person A	Person B
Amelogenin	XY	XY	XX
D3S1358	16,16	16,16	12,16
THO1	8,8	8,8	9.3,9.3
D21S11	30.2,31	30.2,31	28,29
D18S51	17,18	17,18	12,16
Penta E	12,12	12,12	10,15
D5S818	12,12	12,12	12,13
D13S317	8,13	8,13	12,12
D7S820	8,9	8,9	10,11
D16S539	12,12	12,12	13,13
CSF1PO	12,12	12,12	10,11
Penta D	9,12	9,12	10,12
vWA	15,19	15,19	16,17
D8S1179	10,12	10,12	10,13
TPOX	8,11	8,11	8,8
FGA	20,24	20,24	21,24

evidence for all the test locations. There are no qualitative differences in the numbers found for Person A's profile and that of the evidence profile. Therefore, Person A is either the source of the blood evidence, or a coincidental genetic match happened. Because the sizes of the DNA at these chosen testing locations are known to vary widely within human populations, and the actual rarity of each piece of DNA is known and tabulated in databases, scientists are able to calculate the probability of two genetic profiles matching just by chance. With today's forensic DNA technology, using kits that examine anywhere from approximately 16 to over 20 addresses on the DNA, this probability tends to be an extremely low estimate, even for related persons.

With that short summary of forensic DNA analysis completed, the remainder of this chapter will describe some DNA basics, how forensic DNA profiles are produced, what they look like, and then, in the form of questions and answers, address how forensic DNA analysis is used in casework, with a special focus on casework involving bloodstain pattern analysis.

A DNA PRIMER

DNA, or deoxyribonucleic acid, is the biological substance containing the information that functions as the blueprint for the biochemical processes that define and maintain a living organism. Every human (indeed, every animal) begins life as a fertilized egg, with contributions of DNA from a mother and father. These contributions are in the form of chromosomes, the cellular structures that contain DNA. For humans, a fertilized cell contains 23 pairs of chromosomes, 23 chromosomes from the mother and 23 from the father, for a total of 46 chromosomes. Because all cells in a body are traced back to, and therefore copied from, this first fertilized egg, the DNA content of 23 pairs of chromosomes in all the cells of one body is the same. A person's forensic DNA profile from their blood would be the same as that obtained from their skin, hair roots, saliva, or any other body tissue.

DNA consists of extremely long, linear chains of just four chemical bases, the "letters" of the genetic alphabet: A (Adenine), T (Thymine), G (Guanine), and C (Cytosine). These chains run millions of bases/letters long within the individual chromosomes. The molecular information necessary for biological life functions is coded within sequences using just these four bases/letters. Most of the DNA sequence information is exactly the same for all humans across the over six billion bases/letters in human DNA, but a small portion differs among humans. Forensic scientists exploit this last fact by producing DNA profiles that target a tiny selection of just those locations in the DNA known to exhibit differences. A forensic DNA profile is therefore simply a portrait of some of these genetic differences.

Genetic differences of forensic significance take one of the two forms. There are *sequence variations*, where single base/letter at particular locations may differ among humans. For example, a stretch of human DNA might take one of the two forms: one form could exhibit an **A** base/letter at particular location (–ATAGCCGAGG**A**CCATTTATTT–), where another form would show a **G** base/letter at that same address (–ATAGCCGAGG**G**CCATTTATTT–). There are millions of these locations, known as "single nucleotide polymorphisms" or "SNPs" throughout human DNA, and these single base differences form the basis of testing for ancestry, skin, hair and eye color, disease susceptibility, and other inherited physical features.

While SNP-based analyses are surely the future of forensic DNA methodologies, most forensic DNA analyses, especially in criminal casework, currently exploit DNA *length variations*. Imagine a short sequence of four bases/letters, such as TATG, repeated end-to-end, a number of times at an address along a chromosome. The more of these repeats, end-to-end, the longer the stretch of DNA at that genetic address. This is a short tandem repeat, or STR – a short piece of DNA, repeated in tandem. Millions of STR locations are found throughout all 23 pairs of chromosomes in the human genome. If, for example, at one genetic STR address, a person shows five repeats in a stretch of DNA inherited from his father (TATGTATGTATGTATGTATG) and seven repeats of DNA from his mother (TATGTATGTATGTATGTATGTATGTATG) at the same genetic address, his/her type at that location would be interpreted as, and labeled, "5,7." This is the basis of the numbers shown in Table 27.1 – each number is a measure of the number of repeats of a particular small stretch of DNA; where there is a fraction, (for example, 30.2), there is a small portion of a repeat unit missing. And that is the essence of today's forensic DNA typing – targeting multiple STR locations on numerous chromosomes, determining the lengths of the strands of STRs at each of those locations in terms of the number of times a small sequence is repeated, compiling these STR sizing results at multiple genetic addresses to produce DNA profiles, and using those profiles to compare to other profiles in a case or in a databank.

IN THE LABORATORY: PRODUCING AND COMPARING FORENSIC DNA PROFILES

Typical criminal case exhibits sampled for bloodstain pattern analysis purposes include swabs, scrapings, and cut-outs from blood patterns on walls, items, and clothing. Testing a bloodied exhibit for DNA analysis may also include sampling a non-bloody background area on items where extraneous DNA may be expected, such as dirty floors or intimate clothing, in order to address the possibility of the presence of contaminating DNA on a blood sample medium.

The first step in the laboratory process is to mechanically and chemically remove, and then purify, the DNA from a physical sample. This can be accomplished in a number of ways, and in most forensic laboratories, it is performed using an automated or robotic system. The extraction process for a sample culminates in a small tube containing a liquid extract of purified DNA, if present, in solution. A tiny portion of the extracted liquid is applied to the second part of the process, quantification. The amount of DNA in that small liquid portion is determined, and from that the total amount of DNA in the remaining original liquid sample can be deduced. If there is insufficient or no DNA at this stage, the process stops, and the report will typically state something to the effect that an insufficient amount of DNA was detected in the sample and no further work was either attempted or completed.

If the sample contains a sufficient quantity of DNA, the third step in the process is amplification. This term means copying, and in scientific terms, it is known as the polymerase chain reaction or PCR. In this critical step, the technique zeroes in solely on the genetic STR addresses of interest, to the exclusion of all other parts of the DNA, and makes millions of copies of each of these areas so that they can be detected and measured in the fourth step. Amplification is accomplished using commercially available kits that contain all the ingredients to set the DNA copying process in motion. These kits typically target and make copies of 16 or more STR addresses in one test. Different commercial kits, such as PowerPlex®16 and PowerPlex®Fusion (Promega) and IdentilerPlus™ and GlobalFiler™ (ThermoFisher), among others, share common STR test locations necessary for inter-laboratory comparisons and uploads to government databanks, but differ with respect to the incorporation of other STR addresses into the testing.[2]

The final technical step is the visualization of the profile, and incorporates separation, detection, and measurement of millions of copies of DNA produced in the amplification step. Each sample is subjected to a process where the DNA copies are forced to travel through a small, gel-filled tube – the longer the piece of DNA, the more time it takes to emerge from the tube. The time that each piece of DNA takes to travel the tube is captured and then compared to known STR size standards. This leads to the final product, in scientific terms an "electropherogram", but more simply considered a genetic portrait. Figure 27.1 provides an example of such a genetic portrait, and is the basis of the profile described in Table 27.1 for the blood evidence (in Column 2).

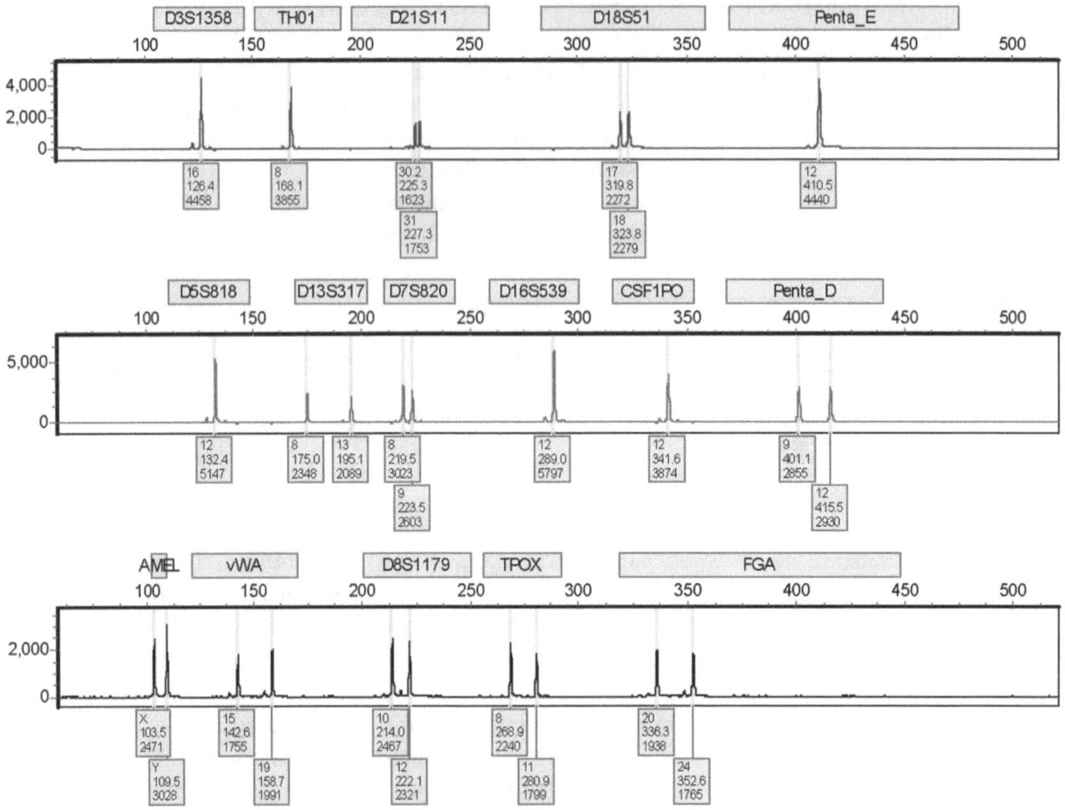

Figure 27.1 Short tandem repeat (STR) profile from a single male source of DNA, produced using a PowerPlex®16 kit. (Courtesy Wyndham Forensic Group, Guelph, Ontario, Canada.)

This particular electropherogram shows genetic results of a biological sample from a single source, at 16 addresses on their DNA. Each genetic address is provided in rectangles, with the actual DNA profile below the address rectangle in the form of "peaks." Each peak represents the amplified copies of strand of DNA of particular length, and is also called a variant or an allele. As presented in Figure 27.1, the first number in the box underneath the peak provides the STR variant label, the length of the strand of DNA defined by how many times a small STR sequence of DNA was repeated in tandem.

Starting with the first address on the top row, D3S1358, an address on the third pair of chromosomes, there is one "peak" – and underneath that peak is a set of numbers. The key number is the first one, "16." What this means is that this person has, at this address, one type of DNA, labeled STR size 16. It represents a STR strand that has been repeated 16 times. This "16" variant/allele is one of many possibilities at this location – common variants at this location include STR sizes 12 to 20, inclusive. Because there is only one piece of DNA found at this location in this sample, this person inherited the size 16 variant from both parents, and is therefore type 16,16 at the D3S1358 address.

At another address shown on the top row, D18S51, an address on the 18th pair of chromosomes, the person's genetic portrait displays two pieces of DNA, sizes 17 and 18. Again, there are many other different possibilities for DNA sizes at this location, where common variants include STR sizes 8 to 27, inclusive. This particular sample came from a person who is STR type "17,18"; he inherited the 17 from one parent and the 18 from the other.

At yet another address, "Am" (Amelogenin), the person's portrait displays two pieces of DNA, labeled X and Y. With the presence of DNA from both the X the Y chromosome, this portrait is that of a male source. A female source would only display the X peak at this location.

This simple analysis is done for each of the addresses, and the final interpretation is the set of number pairs found in Table 27.1.

The interpretation of samples from single sources is usually quite straightforward and unambiguous. However, scientists may be challenged with degraded samples that are missing some of the data at one or more of the test locations, or mixture profiles containing DNA from two or more contributors.

Samples from bloodstain patterns may, due to the way these patterns were formed, contain DNA from more than one person. Consider a situation where a person has blood from another person in their mouth or lips, and then spits onto a surface. The following profile could be developed from a swab of a portion of the resulting expirated bloodstain pattern:

Keeping in mind that a person can only have two parents, and therefore a maximum of two pieces of DNA at any genetic test address, the presence of more than one contributor to this profile is obvious. There are three or four peaks at a number of test locations on this electropherogram, signaling the presence of at least two contributors of DNA to the profile. Consider, for example, the test results at one genetic location, FGA, on the third line of the profile in Figure 27.2. There are four peaks, STR sizes 20, 22, 24, and 26 – this result is expected from a mixture of two people, and there are a number of ways to logically explain this. There could roughly equal contributions from a type 20,22 person plus a type 24,26 person, or from a type 20,24 person plus a type 22,26 person, or a type 20,26 person plus a type 22,24 person. At the genetic location D16S539, there is a large size 12 peak and a smaller size 13 peak. Because the height of a peak is informed by the amount of underlying DNA of that particular type in the sample, this result would be explained by roughly equal contributions from a type 12,12 source plus a type 12,13 source at that D16S539 address. Similarly, at the location TPOX, the results could be explained by the combination of a type 8,8 and a type 11,12, or a combination of a type 8,11 plus a 9,11. At the location CSF1P0, the presence of just a single peak in this profile points to the presence of two persons, both type 12,12. This type of analysis is performed for all of the test locations, and the role of the DNA scientist is to deconvolute, as much as possible, the possible contributors to a mixture profile. For some locations, there is only one explanation, but for other addresses, there may be multiple possibilities.

It is at this juncture in the interpretation that assumptions, based on case facts, may be appropriate. If, in the expirated bloodstain pattern scenario, the DNA profile of the "spitter" is known, then that profile might be "dialed out" of the mixture to find the remaining contribution that had to originate from the blood. In the above example, at the FGA location, if the spitter was type 20,26, then the remainder attributable to the blood would be type 22,24. Similarly, if the spitter was type 12,12 at the D16S539 location, then the blood would be attributable to a type 12,13 person at that location. This logical analysis would be performed at every location to deduce the profile attributable to blood. The same "dialing out" logic can also be used in a situation where a substrate control sample was taken along with the blood sample, perhaps on clothing or on a dirty floor. A profile attributable to the background sample may be dialed out of a blood mixture sample to logically reveal and clarify the DNA profile necessarily attributable to the blood itself.

The interpretation of mixture profiles is a very extensive and complex topic and also includes a careful consideration of the underlying amplification technology. Complex DNA profile types include mixtures of DNA from both equal and unequal sources (in terms of amounts of DNA), samples degraded to such an extent that some data are missing, as well as mixtures of even three or more biological sources. DNA profile interpretations, and in particular the more complex ones, should be accomplished with a consideration of the laboratory's validation data, where the laboratory has evaluated the DNA analysis technology in order to establish its reliability over a range of casework conditions. The interpretation of mixture DNA profiles is increasingly accomplished using probabilistic genotyping software, where complex algorithms are used to provide a range of possibilities for the deconvolution of mixture profile contributors.[3]

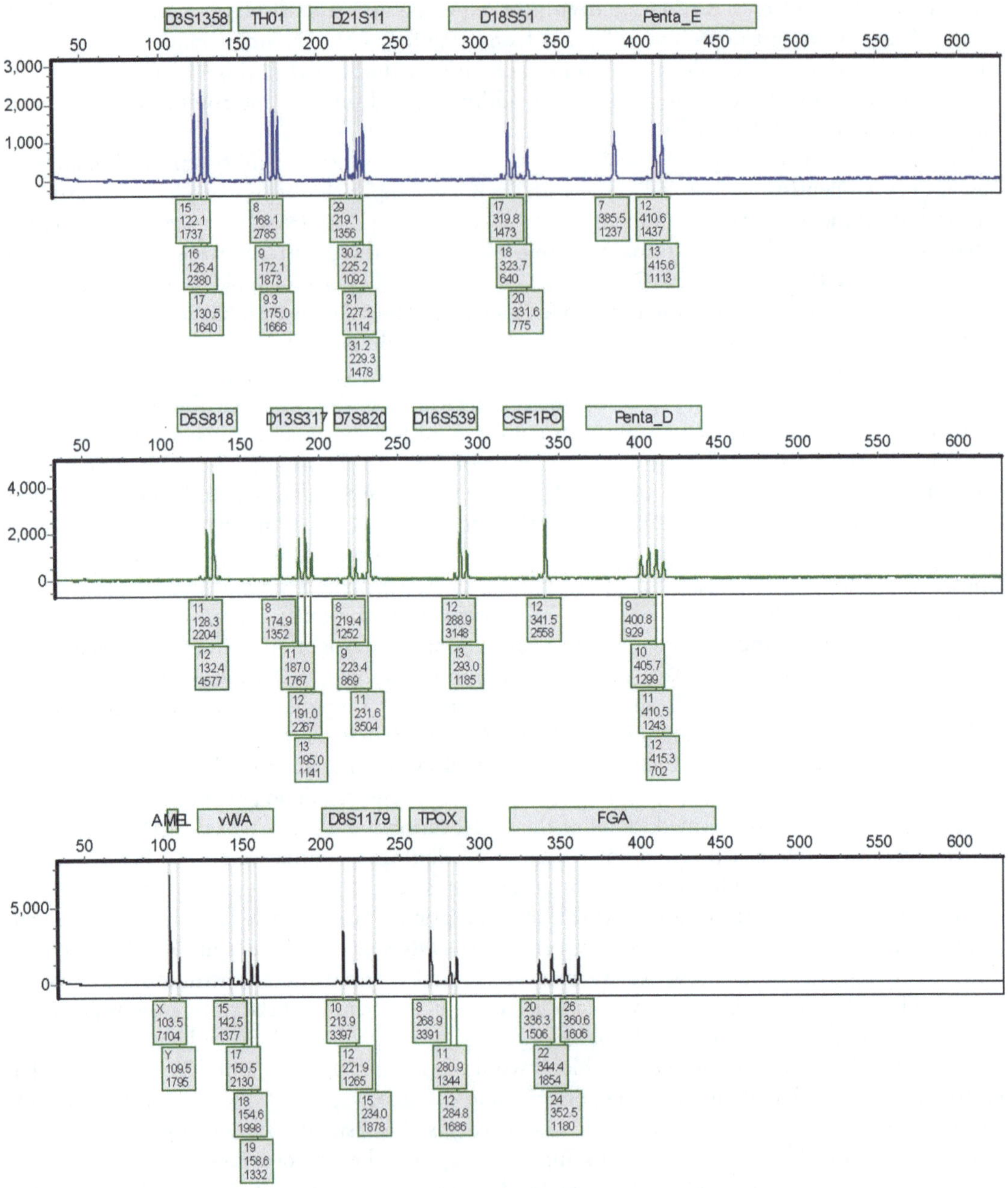

Figure 27.2 Short tandem repeat (STR) profile from a mixture of two sources of DNA, a male and a female, produced using a PowerPlex®16 kit. (Courtesy Wyndham Forensic Group, Guelph, Ontario, Canada.)

FORENSIC DNA ANALYSIS IN CASEWORK

What Is a DNA Profile Match?

Where there are no qualitative differences between two DNA profiles, they match. There are two explanations for such a match result. Either the two profiles came from the same source, or a coincidence occurred. A calculation called a random match probability (RMP) provides an estimate of the probability of the second hypothesis, a chance profile match.

Take as an example the match result between the STR profiles from the blood evidence and person A in Table 27.1. Either Person A is the source of the blood or he is not. If he is not, then the blood evidence profile came from someone else. What is the probability of finding that profile, by chance, in the population? That is the RMP calculated through the application of the principles of population genetics – determining how often each STR component ("allele") of the profile is found in a population, and then calculating how many times the whole STR profile would be expected to occur. For example, at the STR location vWA, both profiles have the result "15,19." The "15" variant is known to occur in a particular database at a level of 12% compared to all possibilities at the vWA location, while the "19" vWA variant is a bit rarer at 9%.[4] The probability of finding a vWA 15,19 type, by chance in the evidence sample, is simply twice the multiplied database figures: $2 \times 0.12 \times 0.09 = 2.2\%$ (or 0.022); the frequencies are multiplied by two because there are two ways that a 15,19 type can happen, where the 15 comes from the mother and the 19 from the father, or *vice versa*. Moving to another genetic location, TH01, the probability of finding an "8,8" type by chance is the frequency of that variant (10.4%)[5] multiplied by itself: $0.104 \times 0.104 = 1.1\%$ (or 0.011).[6] The extraordinary discriminatory power of forensic DNA analysis is found in the consideration of many genetic locations at once; even with just the two STR locations in this example, the probability of finding a vWA type 15,19 at the same time as TH01 type 8,8 in a single profile is calculated by multiplying the individual probability estimates together: $0.022 \times 0.011 = 0.024\%$ (or 0.00024). In other words, such a chance match considering only these two locations would be expected to occur once in approximately 4166 randomly chosen people. When such a calculation is done for all of the STR test location results, the probability of a chance match is extraordinarily low, typically with match probabilities in the range of one in billions to even more discriminating values.

In a case where the RMP is calculated for a whole STR profile to be, for example, one in one billion, a profile match result is typically reported in the following manner: Person A cannot be excluded as the source of the blood evidence at the scene. The probability of a randomly selected individual, unrelated to Person A, sharing the same profile is estimated to be one in one billion.

Some laboratories report the match statistics in a slightly different format than the better known (at least to date) RMP. A likelihood ratio (LR) compares the probability of the DNA evidence under competing hypotheses in the form of a ratio (a numerical comparison). In the two genetic locations example described above, where the RMP was reported as one in approximately 4166 randomly chosen people, the LR would involve the competing hypotheses of Person A being the source of the evidence and not being the source of the evidence and would provide, at the two genetic addresses considered, an LR of 4166. In other words, the DNA evidence at two STR locations from the blood at the scene is 4166 times more likely if Person A is the source of the blood than if a random person is the source of the blood.

The RMP and the LR estimates each speak to the probability of the DNA evidence, not the probability of source attribution, or guilt, or innocence. It is a fallacy to confuse the logically sound probabilities of the DNA evidence under the hypotheses that a person is or is not the source of evidence, with the probabilities of the hypotheses themselves, that a person is not guilty or not the source of the DNA evidence. The latter statistical mistake is commonly referred to as the "prosecutor's fallacy." For example, in a case with matching STR profiles and an RMP of one in a billion, it would be a fallacy to claim that, for example, "the blood came from Person A," or "there is only a one in a billion chance that the blood didn't come from Person A." Correctly stated, "the DNA evidence is a billion times more likely under the scenario that Person A is the source than if a random person is the source," or "the probability that a randomly selected individual, unrelated to Person A, coincidentally shares the profile estimated to be one in one billion."

Most RMP and the LR estimates are calculated under the competing, and mutually exclusive, hypotheses of a particular person being the source of the DNA or a random person being the source. These estimates assume that the random person is not related to the particular person in question. If case circumstances dictate the consideration of relatives also being the potential source of the DNA at a scene, then specialized calculations for the RMP or LR are made to take into account the potential of increased sharing of DNA variants among relatives.

How Are Non-Matches Reported?

If two profiles are qualitatively different, they do not match. This means that they came from different people. No statistical calculations are necessary.

Can Forensic DNA Analysis Provide an Estimate of the Time of Deposition of a Bloodstain?

While the quality of a forensic DNA profile may be adversely affected by the age of a blood sample and environmental challenges, including heat and humidity, there is currently no validated and commercially available testing system to reliably relate a forensic STR profile with the time of deposition of the blood. Potential DNA-based tests to address this time of deposition issue will not likely involve STR analyses, but rather next generation sequencing and epigenetic approaches.

How Long Does the Process of Forensic DNA Analysis Take? Can It Be Performed at the Scene?

From sample extraction to the production of an STR profile may take from 24 to 48 hours and includes not just processing the actual samples but also performing various quality control measures necessary to ensure a reliable result.

STR profiles may be obtained in a much quicker way with technology, which allows for the production and interpretation of STR profiles from a sample within approximately a few hours. There are numerous commercial providers of "rapid DNA" testing equipment, portable instruments that perform a fully automated process of developing a rudimentary STR profile from a sample without the technical need for a forensic DNA laboratory or even human intervention (aside from sample insertion) or interpretation. This technology has been developed primarily for the analysis of reference samples, known blood or buccal swabs that can be quickly processed for purposes of intelligence, military security, police booking stations and disaster victim identification, with STR profiles sent automatically to DNA profile databanks for comparison (but not upload) purposes. While not generally recommended for forensic evidence and scene samples,[7] rapid DNA technology can provide relatively quick assistance at crime scenes for investigative leads, and in particular to distinguish blood samples from more than one source in bloodstain pattern analysis cases, but cannot provide statistical estimates of profile rarity or allow for uploads to official profile databanks.

Can Animal Blood Be Distinguished from Human Blood?

Forensic STR kits for human DNA testing are human DNA-specific, and will therefore not produce profiles from biological samples from other species. If there is an issue of attribution of blood at a scene to a non-human species, there are numerous commercial kits available to detect either particular animal species or to screen for a number of animal species at once (for example, GeneScan DNAnimal kit, Eurofins). If the case issue is attribution to a particular dog, commercial STR kits are also available for addressing this question in the same way it is addressed for humans (for example, Canine Genotypes Panel, The`rmo Scientific).

Can a DNA Profile Sampled from a Bloodstain Be Necessarily Attributed to Blood?

A DNA profile, or a portion of a DNA profile, obtained from a sample containing blood may or may not be attributable to the actual blood deposition. The attribution of a DNA profile to a particular body fluid is usually not an issue with samples that provide sufficient quantities of extracted DNA coincident with expectations from body fluid samples. However, DNA profiles obtained from small amounts of DNA, and especially DNA mixture profiles from two or more sources, may require greater scrutiny.

Forensic DNA analysis addresses three general types of case questions, known as sub-source, source, and activity hypotheses.[8] Activity level hypotheses address questions of how the DNA at a scene or on evidence could have been transferred, and these questions are at the heart of the analyses of bloodstain patterns. Source and sub-source hypotheses address more fundamental questions regarding the potential individual source, or sources, of the DNA.

When a DNA profile is attributable to a particular person but cannot be attributed to a particular body fluid deposition, then the hypothesis level is considered "sub-source." This may occur, for example, where there are no body fluid testing results for the sample in question, or when the relatively small amount of DNA in a sample cannot be reliably attributed to a particular body fluid or tissue deposition. Consider, for example, a swab of a bloodstain that produces a mixed DNA profile from two sources. The DNA analyst may or may not be able to reliably attribute one or either source as the donor of blood in the sample. This exercise in DNA profile attribution would be informed by the quantitation data (the amount of DNA recovered in a sample) as well as the individual laboratory's internal validation data. A "sub-source" DNA profile would be reported as, for example, "the DNA profile from the sample" or "the DNA profile from the minor source of the mixture profile" rather than, for example, "the DNA profile from the blood."

Sub-source hypotheses are distinguished from "source" level hypotheses, where, for the latter, the DNA profile can be reliably attributed to a blood, saliva, semen, or other particular tissue deposition. Such an attribution would be based on DNA quantitation data from a sample, along with body fluid analysis testing results from that sample. A single source DNA profile, or major DNA profile from a mixture, from a sample with a coincident positive chemical blood test result could be reported as, for example, "the DNA profile from the blood." Where a DNA report is not clear as to the attribution (or not) of a particular DNA profile to a blood or other body fluid deposition, the bloodstain pattern analyst should request clarification from the DNA analyst.

THE FUTURE OF STR TECHNOLOGY

STR technology, now in its third decade of forensic use, provides bloodstain pattern analysts and crime scene investigators, in general, with reliable answers to questions regarding the potential sources of blood and body fluids left at scenes and on evidence items. While next generation sequencing (NGS) forensic technologies based primarily on the analyses of SNPs will eventually overtake, or at least supplement, the current industry standard of STRs, this change will not occur in the foreseeable future. STR technology provides investigators with extremely sensitive and highly discriminating forensic evidence that address the key question of the potential source of biological evidence. Indeed, STR technology's hardware and software, as well as commercially available STR kit chemistries and protocols, are firmly entrenched in modern forensic DNA laboratories worldwide. Forensic DNA databanks contain hundreds of thousands (in, for example, Canada[9]) to millions (for example, in the United States of America[10]) of STR DNA profiles of convicted offenders and evidence from on-going cases. As forensic biologists eventually begin to adapt NGS technologies into casework, it is likely that STR technologies will still be used, and will be incorporated into new NGS protocols.[11]

Notes

1. Some primary sources of forensic DNA analysis include the Journal Forensic Science International: Genetics, various texts by John M. Butler on *Forensic DNA Typing* (2001, 2005, 2010, 2012, and 2015), and the National Institute of Standards and Technology (NIST) website Short Tandem Repeat DNA Internet DataBase STRbase.

2. Forensic STR testing kits specifically targeting the Y chromosome are also available for forensic casework, including PowerPlex Y23 (Promega) and Y-filer Plus (ThermoFisher). These kits are used mostly in cases with evidence samples of small amounts of male DNA within mixtures of larger amounts of female DNA (typical samples in sexual assault cases), and also in kinship analysis cases.
3. Software products include STRmix (ESR), TruAllele (Cybergenetics), and EuroForMix (open source software).
4. These data come from a database of STR allele frequencies of Canadian Caucasians; each jurisdiction will use databases relevant to the geographical situation of the case. Database from various geographical regions and racial groups can be found via the STRbase website (endnote 1).
5. This estimate comes from a database of STR allele frequencies of Canadian Caucasians.
6. Note that slight adjustments to this calculation are made to account for slight increases in the number of homozygotes (a homozygote describes a result where the same variant is found at a test location) due to small deviations from non-random mating (National Research Council Committee, National Academy of Sciences, The *Evaluation of Forensic DNA Evidence*, 1996).
7. US Department of Justice, Federal Bureau of Investigation, Science and Technology Branch *Guide to All Things Rapid DNA*, Version 1.0, January 27, 2022.
8. John M. Butler, *Advanced Topics in Forensic DNA Typing: Interpretation* (Academic Press, 2014).
9. The National DNA Databank (NDDB) of Canada is maintained by the Royal Canadian Mounted Police.
10. The Combined DNA Index System (CoDIS) is maintained by the US Federal Bureau of Investigation.
11. For example, The ForenSeq DNA Signature Prep Kit (Verogen) is a kit that incorporates both SNPs and STRs for forensic purposes.

CHAPTER 28

THE SCIENTIFIC METHOD AND RESEARCH DESIGN IN BLOODSTAIN PATTERN ANALYSIS

Mike Illes, Theresa Stotesbury, and Brian Yamashita

INTRODUCTION

When a bloodstain pattern analyst attends a crime scene, it goes without saying that they will examine and record the scene, analyze and interpret the evidence, and testify as to what possibly occurred, following logical, scientific, and unbiased procedures. This chapter describes the Scientific Method, which underlies the philosophy that drives this way of proceeding. Besides using scientific thinking at the crime scene, the same fundamental ideas apply to research in BPA, both to answer fundamental questions and to address case-specific issues that arise.

THE SCIENTIFIC METHOD

In recent years, forensic science has come under increasing scrutiny by the courts, the public, and the media. Forensic disciplines that had been accepted by the courts for years are now being questioned. How do we know that fingerprints are unique? How much variability is there in striations on a bullet? How do we know that the deoxyribonucleic acid (DNA) statistics are being applied accurately to determine the values relevant to the general population?

Not long ago, the National Academies of Science (NAS) in the United States published a very critical report on forensic sciences, "Strengthening Forensic Science in the United States: A Path Forward."[1] The writers of the report felt that forensic science was not "scientific" enough and relied too much on subjective interpretations. The report recommended more research into the areas of accuracy, reliability, and validity of forensic science disciplines, and into human error and bias. Specific areas of forensic examination such as friction ridge analysis, shoeprints and tire tracks, toolmarks, and bloodstain pattern analysis (BPA) were looked at individually and critiqued.[2]

The techniques used in BPA, and the analysts themselves, are increasingly being scrutinized by the courts. Is crime scene investigation being done "scientifically"? Mohan, Frye, and Daubert challenges all have specific criteria against which a forensic discipline is measured, to determine if it should be allowed in court.[3,4,5] The original thinking was that so-called "junk science" had to be stopped at the courtroom door. Unfortunately, some traditionally accepted forensic sciences do not easily satisfy these criteria, which has led to numerous court challenges and criticisms. The criteria for definition as a science seem to be based on "hard" numerical sciences like chemistry and physics, where a temperature could be $21.0 \pm 0.6°$ C, rather than the "softer" sciences, where a

DOI: 10.4324/9781003163695-28

numerical result is not generated. By the Daubert criteria, some conventional sciences might have a hard time being accepted in court!

What does it mean to be scientific? What is the Scientific Method, and how does it apply to forensic science?[6] Does non-numerical necessarily mean non-scientific? Would a bloodstain pattern analyst ever be able to say that they are 82% certain about the mechanism that created the bloodstains found at a crime scene? Even if your scientific education is not extensive, it is hoped that going through this chapter will help to convince you that a bloodstain pattern analyst can and does think like a scientist when they are at a crime scene.

What Is Science? Forensic Science and Paleontology

When people think about what they would define a science to be, they think about areas of study like chemistry, physics, or mathematics where things tend to be very numerical or measurable. What is the distance to the moon? How many grams of sodium will react with 24 grams of chlorine to form NaCl? Other sciences like geology may be less numerical, but still have rules that have to be followed and obeyed. An applied science, where the theories put forward by other scientists are applied to practical problems, are still considered to be scientific. Why is forensic science being criticized?

Some people compare what forensic scientists do to what paleontologists do. Investigators arrive at the crime scene after the fact, and then try to reconstruct what happened, based on what evidence is left behind. A paleontologist looks at fossil records, found bones, and recovered artefacts and then tries to reconstruct what a dinosaur looked like millions of years ago. Without a fossil of the whole body, who can confirm that a dinosaur looked like the animal suggested by today's scientist? Today's scientist depends on the evidence gathered plus previous knowledge and experience to speculate on what an unknown dinosaur looked like, what it ate, and what ate it. Similarly, without a confession, who can confirm that a crime occurred the way the forensic investigator described it? Again, based on the evidence collected and previous knowledge and experience, the crime scene investigator tries to develop the scenario that best describes what might have occurred. In forensic science, how much is hard objective science and how much is subjective interpretation? In paleontology, how much is hard science and how much is subjective interpretation? Could some of the same criticisms of forensic science be leveled at accepted sciences that rely just as much on experience and interpretation and not on numerical results?

Some medical tests are very concrete and simple to interpret, but other diagnoses depend on the doctor's training and experience to interpret test results and patients' symptoms to try to determine what is wrong. Every person is different, and there are always a multitude of different variables involved, so there is always a combination of objective and subjective thinking that has to be applied to each individual case. It is not uncommon to seek a second opinion, meaning that patients are not always expecting all doctors to agree in their conclusions. Does this make the practice of medicine unscientific?

Early "scientists" were philosophers like Aristotle. They did not conduct experiments, but instead relied on their observations of the world around them to come up with theories about nature.[7] They liked to use "Deductive Reasoning." In deductive reasoning, conclusions about a specific case rely on generalizing from a large number of cases. "All swans are white. That is a swan, so of course it is white." The drawback of using deductive reasoning is that it depends on what is already known, and is less useful for speculating about the unknown. The other problem is that the existing general rule may not be true. What if all swans are not white, and you come across the proverbial black swan? What if all fingerprints are not unique?

Someone like Sherlock Holmes could look at a person's hands and deduce if they were a general laborer or an office worker, based on the premise that a laborer would have dirty, calloused, tanned hands, and an office worker would have clean, smooth hands. As long as the premise is correct, Mr. Holmes could correctly declare the occupation of the person he was confronting.

Everyone engages in some kind of deductive reasoning whenever they walk down the street. A gang approaching you on the street might raise some alarm, but, based on your past experience, not if they are seven-year-olds all wearing the same soccer uniforms.

In BPA, for example, an expert will look at bloodstains at a crime scene and decide, based on deductive reasoning, what kind of pattern is being observed. They would have learned the difference in appearance between blood dripping from a blood source as opposed to bloodstains created by an impact. Has the blood at the scene been cast-off a swinging weapon, or is it blood dripping from a moving victim? Based on what they see, and some "rules" based on past collective experience, the bloodstain pattern analyst comes to an opinion as to what caused the bloodstains being observed.

Experimental Science

It was not all that long ago, in the 13th century, when people started talking about the idea of using observation, hypothesis, and experimentation, as well as verification, when trying to better understand the world around us.[8] This could be seen as the early beginnings of what we now call the Scientific Method. In the late 16th and early 17th centuries, Sir Francis Bacon talked about the idea of using controlled experiments to determine what was really going on. The concept of "Inductive Reasoning" was introduced at this time. In inductive reasoning, our knowledge of specific cases is used to extrapolate to develop conclusions about general cases. "All swans I have seen so far are large and white, therefore, all swans will be large and white." You might propose that all fingerprints are unique because you have so far never seen any two alike. The problem is that the observations you are using for establishing your reasoning may be incorrect. Perhaps you have not seen enough swans or fingerprints. You can appear to be correct until you are confronted with a counter-example that shows you were wrong. All snowflakes can be considered unique until you find two that are the same.

Robert Boyle was one of the first to declare that experiments should be repeatable.[9] If two scientists do the same experiment, they should get the same results. Or if a scientist repeats their own experiment, they should get the same result on the second try. The basis for the Scientific Method is being established.

If someone examines a bloodstain pattern at a crime scene and proposes the mechanism that created it, according to Boyle, a colleague should be able to look at the same pattern and reach the same conclusion. But what happens if there is a disagreement? In the case of a chemical reaction, it can mean that the experiments were not done in exactly the same way, or one result was an anomalous fluke, or something is being misinterpreted. More people can do the experiment to try to figure out which is the correct result. Once several similar results are produced, by inductive reasoning, that would be the predicted result for all future experiments. Unfortunately, when two forensic investigators do not agree, critics claim that this demonstrates that the procedure being used is not scientific. When two chemists disagree, no such criticism is leveled. And again, what does it mean when you get a second medical opinion? In some of those cases, you are actually hoping that the second doctor disagrees with the first.

Karl Popper, in the 1920s, wrote extensively on the philosophy of science.[10] He came to the conclusion that, while negative results could immediately refute a theory, positive outcomes of experiments could never confirm a theory. No matter how many times the result was produced, you could never say for sure that the next experiment would not produce a counter-example. In other words, no matter how many snowflakes you look at, you can never prove that they are all unique. After you have seen a billion snowflakes and found no two the same, the billionth-and-first might be the same as a previous one.

Popper also promoted the idea of "falsifiability." A scientific theory must have the possibility of being proven false. "All fingerprints are unique" can be proven false by finding two fingerprints that are the same.[11,12,13]

The Scientific Method

The Scientific Method can be described as being a critical and logical way of looking at a problem and trying to understand it.[14] The researcher begins by developing a hypothesis to explain why something happened. The next step is to devise an experiment or a series of experiments meant to test the hypothesis. If the hypothesis is correct, the experiment should produce the expected results. On the other hand, if the results do not agree with the hypothesis, then a new hypothesis has to be proposed. Careful design of an experiment attempts to keep as many variables constant as possible. One variable (the independent variable) is then varied in a controlled manner, and the effect on a second variable (the dependent variable) is monitored. If more than one independent variable is altered, the investigator will not know which one is causing the observed effect on the dependent variable.

As an example, if the effects of temperature (T) and pressure (P) on the volume of a gas (V) were not known, they could be investigated by using the Scientific Method to devise appropriate experiments. One hypothesis could be that the volume of the gas will decrease when the pressure goes up. If the temperature is held constant and the pressure is increased, the volume will decrease (Boyle's Law), meaning that the proposed hypothesis was correct. A similar hypothesis could be proposed for the effect of temperature on volume. If the hypothesis was that the volume would decrease with an increase in temperature, it would be shown to be false, and a new hypothesis would be required. If the pressure is held constant and the temperature is raised, the volume will actually increase (The Law of Gay-Lussac and Charles). Only one independent variable, pressure, or temperature should be varied at a time to see what the effect is on the dependent variable, the volume of the gas. If both are varied at the same time, it would be impossible to know what their individual effects on the dependent variable would be.

The idea of developing a hypothesis and testing it is something non-scientists do all the time. A mechanic faced with a vehicle that will not start might hypothesize that the battery is dead. To test the hypothesis, they could try to turn on the lights or sound the horn. If the lights go on, the hypothesis is rejected, and a new hypothesis has to be developed. If the next hypothesis is that the fuel pump is broken, the next experiment might be to replace the fuel pump and then see if the vehicle will start. Every time a hypothesis is shown to be incorrect, a new hypothesis has to be developed and tested. We do it all the time.

If the kitchen lights suddenly go out, your first hypothesis might be that a fuse has blown. However, if all of the lights in the house have also gone out, then the first hypothesis is very likely incorrect. If all of the lights in the neighborhood have gone out, then the hypothesis would be that there has been a more widespread power failure. On the other hand, if the lights have not gone out in the neighbor's house, then the problem is probably confined to your house. Without sitting down and writing out hypotheses and experimental procedures, we are using the Scientific Method without really thinking about it.

As a further example, any time journalists produce articles or programs in which consumer products are compared, the method used to do the comparison must be logical and scientific. As many variables as possible should be kept the same, so the comparison would not have one brand of battery in a flashlight, another brand in a radio, and another in a calculator. TV commercials also use the Scientific Method to try to demonstrate that one product is better than another. To compare laundry detergents, a commercial will start with two garments that are exactly the same, stained in exactly the same manner. The only independent variable will be the detergent, and the dependent variable will be the appearance of the garments after washing. The "new and improved" detergent will produce cleaner shirts and socks than "another leading brand." If the experiment has not been done correctly and the comparison not done fairly, consumers will recognize that immediately. Everyone is automatically applying the Scientific Method without even thinking about it.

Validation

Another criticism raised in the NAS Report was the idea that techniques used in forensic science were not scientific in that they had not all been properly validated. The claim was that methods used by forensic scientists had not been proven to actually work, and were simply assumed to be correct, and then handed down from generation to generation of forensic investigators. Until recently, many techniques used in forensic science were developed outside of conventional educational research institutions and were criticized for their lack of scientific pedigree. Fingerprint comparison, for example, is difficult to explain numerically and thus can be problematic to defend in court. This question of validation is being addressed by researchers in some areas by carrying out so-called "black box" or "white box" studies where cases in which the ground truth is known can be examined "blind" by participants, and the results compared to the correct answ ers.[15,16,17,18,19] In BPA, experiments are being carried out where examiners are being given unknown bloodstain patterns and are asked to describe the possible cause, to see if the majority of them will report the same opinion. Does the fact that you can get the correct answer really mean that the method is valid?

Bias

The concept of bias is one that is recently being used to criticize forensic sciences (see Chapter 37). If you are given too much information, will it skew your interpretation of the facts? Dror has conducted some very interesting and disturbing experiments that seem to show that people can be influenced to state the "wrong" conclusion, or to change their conclusion based on information that has nothing to do with the actual evidence being examined.[20,21] Rather than claim that one is never biased and could never be swayed one way or the other, it is better to acknowledge that this type of bias can exist and to consciously guard against it.[22,23]

SCIENTIFIC RESEARCH DESIGN

Scientific research supports the foundations of a discipline, and forensic science is no exception. Controlled experimental studies are necessary to understand the objective and reproducible elements of pattern identification disciplines, including BPA. Analyses from meticulously designed experiments improve the scientific merit of BPA. Empirical data collected from well-designed research studies have serious implications for casework and can help to set, improve, and implement validated and standardized methodologies for BPA practices.[24] The purpose of this section of the chapter is to explore the basics of scientific research design as it relates to BPA by discussing (i) types of data, (ii) scientific research design, (iii) scientific communication, and, (iv) research collaboration. A bloodstain pattern analyst may be tasked with interpreting scientific research studies in the courtroom; and while they may not have been the person who conducted the experiment, they must be able to understand how the research study was designed, conducted, and communicated.

Types of Data

Broadly speaking, types of data commonly encountered in BPA research are either quantitative or qualitative. Quantitative data is numerical and can be objectively measured, whereas qualitative data is descriptive and can be subjectively observed. Scientific research design in BPA is not strictly limited to either type of study (qualitative or quantitative); and in fact, mixed-method approaches can be used. Mixed-method approaches are described in more detail in the section on case-specific research design.

Table 28.1 Examples of bloodstain variables and their classification

Variable	Classification
Number of bloodstains created in a cast-off pattern	Discrete
Number of bloodstain patterns observed at a crime scene	Discrete
Diameter of a 90° drip stain	Continuous
Viscosity of whole blood	Continuous
Level of education or years of experience	Ordinal
Zone a bloodstain is in an impact pattern[23]	Ordinal
Visible reaction with luminol (yes/no)	Nominal
Color of a bloodstain	Nominal

Quantitative and qualitative variables can be further categorized. For example, quantitative variables can be described as discrete and continuous, and qualitative variables can be described as nominal and ordinal. Discrete variables are countable and finite, whereas continuous variables are infinite and unlimited. Ordinal variables are ranked according to some sort of order and nominal variables are labeled according to some sort of system. The classification of variables is important as it prescribes the type of data analysis that can be performed on the variable. Table 28.1 provides some BPA-specific examples of variable classification.

Take some time to think about other variables relevant to BPA and classify them. For further details on data types and data analysis, the reader should consult texts written by statisticians.[25]

BPA Scientific Research Design

Scientific research can be performed in academic and applied settings; in either case, research design is of critical importance to the success of the study. The way an experiment is designed is directly related to how the research question can be answered and with what degree of certainty. At all points during the design process, it is important to keep the research question in mind. Research design, while critical, is one of many stages in the Scientific Method process. This process visualized in Figure 28.1 is non-linear and often iterative.

Research design relevant to BPA can take the form of experiments with repetitions, without repetitions, exploratory, cohort, descriptive, case studies, historical, sequential, or sampling from patterns.[26] The general process for these types of experiments include:

1. Planning the experiment
    a. Define the problem and construct a research question
    b. Conduct a literature search
    c. Develop hypotheses and prediction statements
2. Design the experiment
    a. Choose the type of experiment
    b. Define variables
    c. Plan methodologies to conduct your experiment
    d. Choose appropriate methods for data analysis*
3. Conduct the experiment
4. Collect data and interpret the results
    a. Analyze your data
    b. Draw conclusions – particularly as it relates to the hypotheses
    c. Describe limitations and suggest future works

*Statisticians have knowledge of research design and the use of statistical models. Therefore, it is always advisable to consult a statistician prior to commencing your experimentation.[27,28]

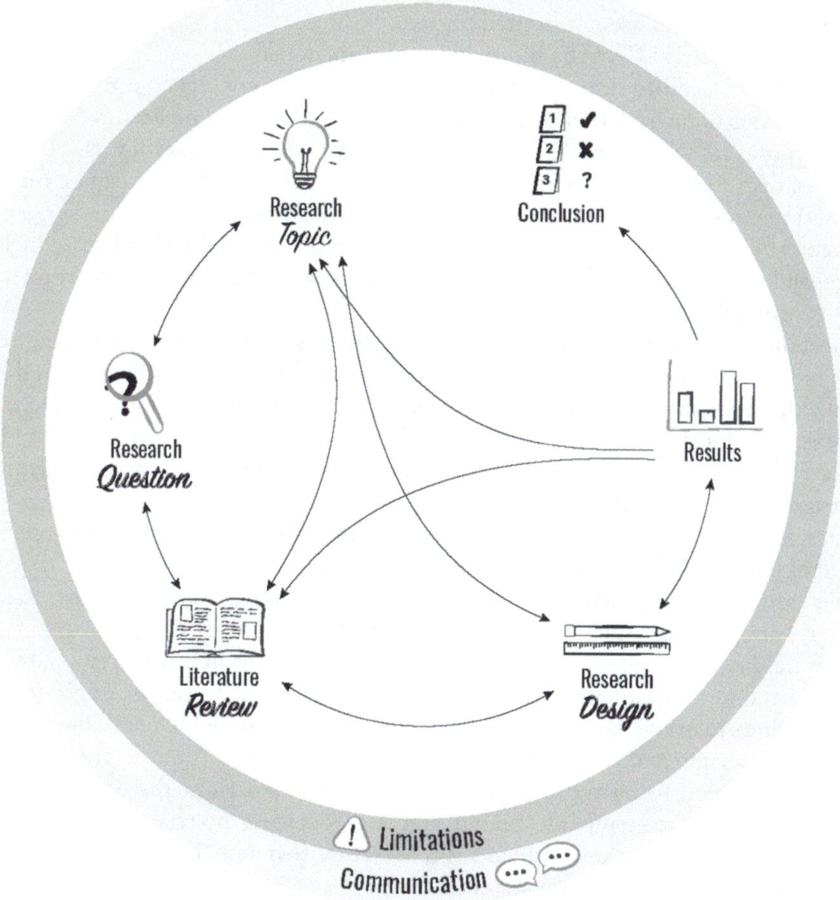

Figure 28.1 The scientific process is non-linear in nature composed of many steps, including having curiosity for a research topic, developing a research question, conducting a literature review, designing a research study, collecting data, interpreting these data, and communicating findings. (This figure was designed by Sonia Seto, Sonia Seto Studios, www.soniaseto.com, in *The Scientific Method in Forensic Science: A Canadian Handbook*, p. 161, Figure 7.1, and sourced with permission; courtesy of Canadian Scholars' Press Inc. and Dr. Mike Illes.)

Example of a Research Project Using Experiments with Repetitions: Drip Stain Formation in Sub-zero Conditions

Let us go through the process of scientific research design using an example to understand how sub-zero (<0°C) temperatures affect the features of a bloodstain. This is a broad research topic and can be approached in many ways. Before you go any further, it is important to scope the scientific literature on bloodstain formation in extreme temperatures[29] and see what knowledge has been published and where opportunities for new research lies. At the time the authors were writing this chapter, there was limited literature on how drip stains form on ice and snow,[30,31,32,33] suggesting basic fundamental research on drip stain formation in sub-zero conditions is still required.

Then, create a testable research question that will contribute to the growing body of knowledge of BPA. Some preliminary testable research questions that can address elements of your overall curiosity could include, but are not limited to:

Do sub-zero conditions effect the morphology of drip stains?

Where (if any) do satellite stains form when a blood droplet contacts a sub-zero surface?

What biomarkers of degradation in a bloodstain are affected by temperature?

For the purposes of this example, let us proceed with the first question that focuses on the morphology of drip stains. This is a broad and testable research question. It can be further divided into more testable research questions where *experiments with repetitions* can be designed and conducted in controlled laboratory settings. Morphological features in a bloodstain, including size, shape, edge, and surface characteristics, can be measured as a function of blood droplets impacting surfaces at controlled temperatures.[34,35,36,37]

It is important to set your null and alternative hypotheses early, before conducting your experiment. The null hypothesis should be designed in a way that it can be falsified. A null hypothesis, H_0, is formed in a way that the researcher's predictions are not true; in this case, that temperature does not affect the morphology of a drip stain. The opposite is true for the alternate hypothesis, H_1. A researcher tests the hypotheses and either accepts or rejects them after analyzing the data collected from the experiments.

H_0 = decreasing sub-zero surface temperatures do not affect the size of a drip stain

H_1 = decreasing sub-zero surface temperatures affect the size of a drip stain

H_0 = decreasing sub-zero surface temperatures do not affect the shape of a drip stain

H_1 = decreasing sub-zero surface temperatures affect the shape of a drip stain

Prediction statements are useful, particularly upon conducting a literature review, to incorporate key theories, laws, and explanations related to the topic at hand. In our example, you could discuss how temperature influences relevant fluid properties of blood which have been demonstrated to affect the size, shape, and distribution of bloodstains. You may want to predict a relationship that can be determined using the experimental data collected from the experiment: <increasing/decreasing> the surface temperature will <increase/decrease/no change> the <morphological feature of interest> because <key findings from literature review>. Take some time to look in the literature to complete this prediction statement.

Design your experimental methods meticulously – this is the framework of your experiment. If you miss any supportive beam (controlled variable), then the house (experiment) may collapse. Independent variables are controlled and dependent variables are measured. In our scenario, the dependent variables are size and shape. The independent variable is the temperature of the surface. Other independent variables that can be tested for future experiments can include, but are not limited to, the droplet volume, dripping height, angle of impact, humidity, fluid properties of the blood source, and surface features like roughness and porosity. For now, these variables will be controlled and this first experiment will only test the relationship between surface temperature and drip stain size and shape.

Conduct your experiment and collect your data. For size and shape characteristics, high-resolution images of the stains with a scale should be taken at a defined time point after stain formation. Stain size and shape can be determined manually, or more preferably using image processing software. Data analysis can take the form of linear regression analysis on stain size/shape as a function of surface temperature. You can plot these data to visualize the observed trends, if any. These data and observed trends can then be used to refute or support your hypotheses. Limitations should be described and future works (many of which we have described) can be recommended.

And the process continues...! It is important to remember that experiments are typically conducted in series to address a research question. The findings from each experiment incrementally contribute to our growing knowledge in BPA. Addressing "the big questions" often takes time and these types of repetition studies to provide a robust answer.

Scientific Communication

Scientific communication is an important aspect of the Scientific Method. It is important to communicate the results of an experiment clearly, concisely, and objectively. The primary results of a scientific study are commonly published in scientific journals. They can also be included in secondary and tertiary sources, including literature reviews on a topic, textbooks, news/media releases, and other resources.

Common sources to find research studies in BPA include, but are not limited to, Forensic Science International, Journal of Forensic Sciences, Science & Justice, International Journal of Legal Medicine, Canadian Society of Forensic Science, Australian Journal of Forensic Science, and the Journal of Bloodstain Pattern Analysis. For cross-disciplinary research studies, you may find articles relevant to BPA in a variety of other scientific journals. It is important to understand the publication process for each journal, as standards for peer-review, research design types, and readership focus vary.

Research Collaboration

Collaboration between academics and practitioners is an important aspect of scientific research in BPA. If collaborating, it is important that all stakeholders are aware of the expectations of the research project and the expertise that they can contribute. For scientific studies, it is important to include as many accepted and standardized approaches as possible to the research design. This will help downstream when comparing your results and putting your research into perspective with other studies. An in-depth discussion on the importance of collaboration and limitations is given in the next section of this chapter on case-specific research design.

CASE-SPECIFIC RESEARCH DESIGN

This section explores the case-specific research design, which is used to answer a case question that is pertinent to an investigation or the courts.[38,39] A bloodstain pattern analyst may be tasked with answering a research question during an investigation. A typical case-specific question could be – what type of mechanism(s) could have made a bloodstain pattern during a bloodletting event. The following provides some insight into bloodstain pattern case-specific design, specifically: (i) the need for collaboration and limitations, (ii) types of data, (iii) BPA case-specific research design, and (iv) case-specific research process: an example.

The Need for Collaboration and Limitations

The previous discussion on academic research design is fundamentally different than case-specific research because case-specific research examines past events. This can make case-specific research more complex because of issues such as:

- Unknown or uncontrollable variables
- Limited sample sets
- Limited research time
- Time since event
- Different types of data sets
- Other unknowns

There is limited research on how to conduct case-specific research in forensic science but other academic disciplines do have some guidelines.[40,41] The fundamental difference between case-specific research in these disciplines and forensic science is that in forensic science, we have no or very limited knowledge of past events.[42] These limitations can make forensic case-specific research more complex, even for an experienced researcher. Therefore, we emphasize the importance of research collaboration between practitioners and academics when conducting these projects.

The Canadian court case R. v. Millard[43] provides an example of how an expert's opinion of a shooting reconstruction was ruled inadmissible due to improper scientific experimentation. The witness reconstructed a shooting incident so that they could opine on orientation, position, and location of a gun and how the discharge may have happened. The judge would not allow parts of the testimony based on unsuitable case-specific research, specifically the lack of replication, quantitative data, and hypotheses development. Beyond this, the witness did not control variables, did not falsify hypotheses, and rejected evidence that did not support his opinion.

In the Supreme Court of Arizona an appeal was launched, State v. Romero,[44] to consider if the trial court abused its discretion by not allowing a defense expert witness to testify. The witness was being offered as an expert in experimental design and was challenging methods used by forensic firearm examiners. The Supreme Court decision specified that the expert was qualified as an expert in experimental design and the assessment of methods used by firearms examiner, that the witness testimony would help the jury in understanding the differences between comparison analysis and the Scientific Method, and that the witness testimony would help the jury with assessing the weight of the scientific evidence. The Supreme Court found that the lower court decision for preclusion of the expert witness was an error of law.[45] These examples are evidence that the expertise of the researcher is being assessed within judicial systems.

Historically, research collaboration between practitioners and universities has been slow in development. The literature has suggested that partnerships between practitioners and academics are low (although possible), citing issues of organizational structure variances, different perspectives on the value of the research, philosophical orientations, and the need for a trusting relationship.[46,47,48,49,50] In addition, Illes and Wilson[51] have suggested that there may be a research knowledge gap for forensic science practitioners and that case-specific research could be considered a separate type of expert evidence by courts. The expert would have to be qualified to give evidence in research design. It will be important for the bloodstain pattern experts to overcome these issues and successfully provide scientifically robust case-specific evidence in the court of law.

Types of Data

Research data can come in three forms: quantitative (e.g. numbers), qualitative (e.g. observations), or mixed method, which is a combination of quantitative and quantitative data. The selection of a research design in case-specific research and the statistical model used in that design will depend on the type of data to be collected. For the most part, bloodstain pattern analysts depend on both quantitative and qualitative data within their field analyses and this may direct how case-specific research is completed in this discipline. Therefore, a mixed method model for single case BPA experimental research may be most suitable and even critical so that qualitative information can give context to quantitative data.[52] The use of mixed method data involves the collection and analysis of different data types and the researcher must understand the complexity of these processes.[53] The research design and statistical model should be reviewed by a statistician before initiating the research.

BPA Case-Specific Research Design

Scientific discovery is not a predetermined linear path and research design can be a complicated endeavor. In fact, research design comes in many forms, having been developed from the different disciplines of academia. This can range from experimental design with repetitions, which provides information on causation, to a correlational study, which can only indicate a relationship between variables. Below is a list of common research designs that could be used in a BPA case-specific study framework:

- Experimental with repetitions
- Experimental without repetitions

- Correlational study
- Mixed methods single case research
- Exploratory
- Historical or archival design[54]

Reports such as "Strengthening Forensic Science in the United States: A Path Forward" and "Report to the President – Forensic Science in Criminal Courts: Ensuring Scientific Validity of Feature – Comparison Methods" made it clear that there is a need for quantitative experimental design research in forensic science.[55,56] The best practice, when possible, is that quantitative experimental design with repetitions should be used in BPA case-specific research. However, due to the nature of BPA work (qualitative and quantitative methods), case-specific research may lend itself to different types of research design, as noted earlier. Although experimental design in an academic setting has been discussed, the following presents one example of how this could be accomplished when answering a case-specific question.

Case-Specific Research Process: An Example

Stages of Case-Specific Research Design

1. Planning the experiment
    a. The researcher should define the case-related problem that needs to be addressed. At this stage, the problem may be broadly formulated and may consist of different sub-questions with many variables.
        i. What mechanism(s) created this bloodstain pattern?
    b. Obtain case-specific details and background.
        i. Obtain as much objective information concerning the problem as possible. All variables relevant to the problem should be identified.
            1. Observational information
                a. Method of measure
                b. Images
                c. Written notes
            2. Police reports
            3. Autopsy reports
    c. Define the significance of a solution to the problem.
        i. Consider Type I (rejecting a true hypothesis) and Type II (failing to reject a hypothesis that is false) errors.[57]
    d. State how a solution to the problem could further the investigation.
        i. At this point, a decision can be made on whether to continue with the research.
        ii. It could provide support for an alternative defense explanation.
    e. Literature search.
        i. Review scientific literature relevant to the case-related problem to see if a solution already exists. Identify any limitations or gaps in literature.
    f. Formulate a hypothesis.
    g. Give a clear statement of the expected outcome of the experiment (falsification).
        i. That the bloodstain pattern can be attributed to a mechanism which was [a]
    h. Formulate alternative hypotheses.
        i. That the bloodstain pattern can be attributed to a mechanism which was [b]
        ii. That the bloodstain pattern can be attributed to a mechanism which was [c]
    i. List other possible outcomes of the experiment.
        i. This may help in breaking the problem down into different sub-questions. It may also help to recognize different parameters/variables that are important to consider while performing the experiment.
    j. Formulate specific research questions.

        i. This is the most important part of planning the experiment. The research question must be:
            1. Narrowly defined
            2. answerable by doing experiments with a minimum number of unknown variables
            3. defined in such a way that it is possible to answer it by experiments
            4. Get help – colleague/seasoned researcher/statistician
2. Design of the experiment
    a. Variables
        i. When there are too many uncontrolled variables that cannot be accounted for in the experiment, the experiment should not be carried out
    b. Materials
        i. Case simulation materials
        ii. Evidence material
        iii. Physical parameters (Size of scene)
    c. Design of the experiment
        i. Research design
        ii. Data types
        iii. Statistical model(s) to be used
    d. Document steps
    e. Results
        i. Empirical data that was used to test the hypotheses
    f. Conclusion
        i. In the conclusion, a short, summarized answer to the specific research question should be written. It should make clear the contribution of the experimentation to the investigation. If the experiment does not answer, or only partly answers, the question, the reason for this should be stated.
        ii. Discuss limitations of the study.
            1. If the experiment did not wholly answer the specific research question, future experiments may be mentioned in this section that could help answer similar questions in future.
3. Technical review
    a. Appropriately qualified reviewers
    b. Provides a final review that considers organizational policy, spelling, grammar, and peer review of the scientific concepts/conclusions
4. Reporting
    a. Report regardless of outcome
    b. If scientifically robust and interesting, the results should be published in a peer-reviewed journal upon completion of the court proceedings.*

SUMMARY

The information provided in this chapter should help with understanding how the Scientific Method can be used in BPA. First, the difference between science and scientific philosophy and their relevance to BPA are discussed. In addition, the use of the Scientific Method, evidence-based

* This is the integration of information on case-specific research design from the Scientific Working Group on Bloodstain Pattern Analysis (SWGSTAIN) Research Subcommittee discussion notes, FRSC 2020 Scientific Methodology in Forensic Science, Trent University, course lecture notes, and The Scientific Method in Forensic Science: A Canadian Handbook.

analysis, logic and reasoning, and how observations alone are insufficient in BPA are emphasized. Second, how scientific research and case-specific research can be conducted in BPA is examined. Topics such as research design, data types, literature review, stages of research design suitable for BPA, limitations, and the need for a collaborative approach are discussed. Each section has provided experience-based learning by blending the concepts with case examples.

Notes

1. NAS, *Strengthening Forensic Science in the United States: A Path Forward,* (Washington: National Academy of Sciences, 2009).
2. PCAST, *Report to the President Forensic Science in Criminal Courts: Ensuring Scientific Validity of Feature - Comparison Methods (Executive Summary),* (USA, 2016).
3. 'R. V. Mohan', (Supreme Court of Canada, File no. 23063, 1994).
4. Daubert et al., V. Merrell Dow Pharmaceuticals Inc., '113 S Ct 2786', (1993).
5. 'Frye V. United States', in *3968,* (1923).
6. PCAST, *Report to the President Forensic Science in Criminal Courts: Ensuring Scientific Validity of Feature - Comparison Methods (Executive Summary),* (USA, 2016).
7. Gauch, Hugh G., *Scientific Method in Brief,* (New York: Cambridge University Press, 2012).
8. Gauch, Hugh G *Scientific Method in Practice,* (New York: Cambridge University Press, 2003).
9. Oster, Malcolm, 'Biography, Culture, and Science: The Formative Years of Robert Boyle', *History of Science* 31:2, no. June (1993): 195.
10. Popper, Karl, *Popper: The Logic of Scientific Discovery,* ed. Routledge (New York: Routledge, 1959).
11. Popper, Karl, *Popper: The Logic of Scientific Discovery,* ed. Routledge (New York: Routledge, 1959).
12. Swan, Liz Stillwaggon, 'Karl Popper, Forensic Science, and Nested Codes', *Biosemiotics* 7, no. 2 (2014): 309–19.
13. Popper, Karl R., *Normal Science and Its Dangers,* (Cambridge: Cambridge University Press, 1970).
14. Illes, M. and P. Wilson, *The Scientific Method in Forensic Science: A Canadian Handbook,* (Toronto: Canadian Scholars' Press Inc., 2020).
15. Maltais, Luc and A Brian Yamashita, 'A Validation Study of Barefoot Morphology Comparison', *Journal of Forensic Identification* 60, no. 3 (2010): 362–370.
16. Eldridge, Heidi, Marco De Donno, and Christophe Champod, 'Testing the Accuracy and Reliability of Palmar Friction Ridge Comparisons–A Black Box Study', *Forensic Science International* 318(2021): 110457.
17. Orr, Amanda, Mike Illes, Jacques Beland, and Theresa Stotesbury, 'Validation of Sherlock, a Linear Trajectory Analysis Program for Use in Bloodstain Pattern Analysis', *Canadian Society of Forensic Science Journal* 52 (2019): 1–17.
18. Bettison, A., M. N. Krosch, J. Chaseling, and K. Wright, 'Bloodstain Pattern Analysis: Does Experience Equate to Expertise?', *Journal of Forensic Sciences* (2021), https://www.ncbi.nlm.nih.gov/pubmed/33394513 (accessed Jan 4).
19. Carter, A. L., M. Illes, K. Maloney, A. B. Yamashita, B. Allen, B. Brown, L. Davidson, G. Ellis, J. Gallant, and A. Gradkowski, 'Further Validation of the Backtrack (Tm) Computer Program for Bloodstain Pattern Analysis: Precision and Accuracy', *IABPA News* 21, no. 3 (2005): 15–22.
20. Dror, Itiel E., David Charlton, and Ailsa E. Péron, 'Contextual Information Renders Experts Vulnerable to Making Erroneous Identifications', *Forensic Science International* 156, no. 1 (2006): 74–8.
21. Dror, Itiel E. and David Charlton, 'Why Experts Make Errors', *Journal of Forensic Identification* 56, no. 4 (2006): 600.
22. Dror, I. E., 'Cognitive and Human Factors in Expert Decision Making: Six Fallacies and the Eight Sources of Bias', *Analytical Chemistry* 92, no. 12 (2020): 7998–8004, https://www.ncbi.nlm.nih.gov/pubmed/32508089 (accessed Jun 16).
23. Zapf, Patricia A. and Itiel E. Dror, 'Understanding and Mitigating Bias in Forensic Evaluation: Lessons from Forensic Science', *International Journal of Forensic Mental Health* 16, no. 3 (2017): 227–38.
24. Morrison, Geoffrey Stewart, Cedric Neumann, and Patrick Henry Geoghegan, *Vacuous Standards–Subversion of the OSAC Standards-Development Process,* Forensics Science International: Synergy, 2 (2020): 206–09.

25. Curran, James Michael, *Introduction to Data Analysis with R for Forensic Scientists,* (Boca Raton, CRC Press, 2010).
26. Illes, M. and P. Wilson, *The Scientific Method in Forensic Science: A Canadian Handbook,* (Toronto: Canadian Scholars' Press Inc., 2020).
27. Curran, James Michael, *Introduction to Data Analysis with R for Forensic Scientists,* (Boca Raton, CRC Press, 2010).
28. Banks, David L., Karen Kafadar, David H. Kaye, and Maria Tackett, *Handbook of Forensic Statistics,* (Boca Raton, CRC Press, 2020).
29. Larkin, Bethany A. J. and Craig E. Banks, 'Preliminary Study on the Effect of Heated Surfaces upon Bloodstain Pattern Analysis', *Journal of Forensic Sciences* 58, no. 5 (2013): 1289–96.
30. J. D., North, 'Bloodstain Pattern Analysis in Snow - Examination of Bloodstain Patterns in Icy and Soft Powder Snow Conditions', *Journal of Bloodstain Pattern Analysis* 32, no. 1 (2016): 7–14.
31. Miles, Hester F., 'Bloodstain Pattern Analysis: Developing Quantitative Methods of Crime Scene Reconstruction through the Interpretation and Analysis of Environmentally Altered Bloodstains', Thesis, (UCL (University College London), 2014).
32. Kundan, P., 'Passive Drip Stain Formation on Ice Cold Surfaces', BSc thesis, (Oshawa, Ontario Tech University, 2020).
33. Illes, Mike and Paul Wilson, 'Forensic Epistemology: Exploring Case-Specific Research in Forensic Science', *Canadian Society of Forensic Science Journal* 53 (1), (2020): 26–40.
34. Adam, Craig D., 'Fundamental Studies of Bloodstain Formation and Characteristics', *Forensic Science International* 219, no. 1–3 (2012): 76–87.
35. Attinger, Daniel, Craig Moore, Adam Donaldson, Arian Jafari, and Howard A. Stone, 'Fluid Dynamics Topics in Bloodstain Pattern Analysis: Comparative Review and Research Opportunities', *Forensic Science International* 231, no. 1–3 (2013): 375–96.
36. Laan, Nick, Karla G. de Bruin, Denis Bartolo, Christophe Josserand, and Daniel Bonn, 'Maximum Diameter of Impacting Liquid Droplets', *Physical Review Applied* 2, no. 4 (2014): 044018.
37. De Castro, Therese, Tania Nickson, Debra Carr, and Clare Knock, 'Interpreting the Formation of Bloodstains on Selected Apparel Fabrics', *International Journal of Legal Medicine* 127, no. 1 (2013): 251–8.
38. Illes, M. and P. Wilson, *The Scientific Method in Forensic Science: A Canadian Handbook,* (Toronto: Canadian Scholars' Press Inc., 2020).
39. Illes, Mike and Paul Wilson, 'Forensic Epistemology: Exploring Case-Specific Research in Forensic Science', *Canadian Society of Forensic Science Journal* 53 (1), (2020): 26–40.
40. Kueffer, Christoph, 'Integrative Ecological Research: Case-Specific Validation of Ecological Knowledge for Environmental Problem Solving', *GAIA - Ecological Perspectives for Science and Society* 15, no. 2 (2006): 115–20, http://www.ingentaconnect.com/content/oekom/gaia/2006/00000015/00000002/art00010.
41. Mitchell, Gregory, Laurens Walker, and John Monahan, 'Beyond Context: Social Facts as Case-Specific Evidence', Emory LJ 60(2010): 1109.
42. Illes, M. and P. Wilson, *The Scientific Method in Forensic Science: A Canadian Handbook,* (Toronto: Canadian Scholars' Press Inc., 2020).
43. 'R. V. Millard', (2018).
44. 'State V. Romero', in *P. 3d,* vol. 365, (Ariz: Supreme Court, 2016).
45. ''State V. Romero', in *P. 3d,* vol. 365, (Ariz: Supreme Court, 2016).
46. Alpert, Geoffrey P., Jeff Rojek, and J. Andrew Hansen, 'Building Bridges between Police Researchers and Practitioners: Agents of Change in a Complex World', Washington, DC: US Department of Justice, National Institute of Justice (2013).
47. Graner, R. and O. Kronkvist, *The Past, the Present and the Future of Police Research: Proceedings from the Fifth Nordic Police Research Seminar,* (Växjö. Linnæus University Studies in Policing, 2015).
48. Datta, Ajoy, 'Deliberation, Dialogue and Debate: Why Researchers Need to Engage with Others to Address Complex Issues', *IDS Bulletin* 43, no. 5 (2012): 9–16, https://onlinelibrary.wiley.com/doi/abs/10.1111/j.1759-5436.2012.00357.x.
49. Beresford, D. V., T. Stotesbury, S. V. Langer, M. Illes, C. Kyle, and B. Yamashita, 'Bridging the Gap between Academia and Practice: Perspectives from Two Large-Scale and Niche Research Projects in Canada', *Science & Justice* (2019)**, [60, 95–98]** http://www.sciencedirect.com/science/article/pii/S1355030619300231 (accessed 2019/10/31/).

50. Steinheider, Brigitte, Todd Wuestewald, Richard E. Boyatzis, and Paul Kroutter, 'In Search of a Methodology of Collaboration: Understanding Researcher–Practitioner Philosophical Differences in Policing', *Police Practice and Research* 13, no. 4 (2012): 357–74, http://dx.doi.org/10.1080/15614263.2012.671620.
51. Illes, Mike and Paul Wilson, 'Forensic Epistemology: Exploring Case-Specific Research in Forensic Science', *Canadian Society of Forensic Science Journal* 53 (1), (2020): 26–40.
52. Onghena, Patrick, Bea Maes, and Mieke Heyvaert, 'Mixed Methods Single Case Research: State of the Art and Future Directions', *Journal of Mixed Methods Research*. 13 (4), (2018): 461–480.
53. Lanier, Mark and Lisa T Briggs, *Research Methods in Criminal Justice and Criminology: A Mixed Methods Approach*, (Oxford, Oxford University Press, 2014).
54. Illes, M. and P. Wilson, *The Scientific Method in Forensic Science: A Canadian Handbook*, (Toronto: Canadian Scholars' Press Inc., 2020).
55. NAS, *Strengthening Forensic Science in the United States: A Path Forward*, (Washington: National Academy of Sciences, 2009).
56. PCAST, *Report to the President Forensic Science in Criminal Courts: Ensuring Scientific Validity of Feature - Comparison Methods (Executive Summary)*, (USA, 2016).
57. Triola, Mario F., *Elementary Statistics*, (New Jersey, Pearson Higher Education, 2014).

Further Reading

Baechler Simon, "Do We Need to Know Each Other? Bridging the Gap between the University and the Professional Field." *Policing: A Journal of Policy and Practice,13(1)* (2017), 102–104.

Creswell, John W., and J. David Creswell, *Research Design: Qualitative, Quantitative, and Mixed Methods Approaches*. Sage Publications, Thousand Oaks, CA 2017.

Walliman, Nicholas, *Research Methods: The Basics*. London, Routledge, 2017.

CHAPTER 29

REPORT WRITING

Elizabeth Richards and Jeremy Morris

The purpose of a bloodstain pattern analyst's report is to convey scientifically substantiated conclusions and opinions prior to actually providing testimony. The analyst's report should effectively and accurately convey scientifically sound opinions such that they are well-understood by those completely unfamiliar with the discipline.[1] Consider this quote from Eldridge (2019): "While the practitioners and academics are embroiled in a scientific debate over the most logically, mathematically, or reliably 'correct' or 'accurate' way to present forensic evidence, they often forget to stop and consider the consumer of this information - the fact-finder. While the goal of providing accurate and logically cohesive evidence is a laudable one, if juries cannot understand or appropriately apply the testimony that is given, then forensic science has not been effective, transparent, or ultimately, useful to the trier of fact."[2]

BACKGROUND/HISTORY

In 2005, Congress tasked the National Academy of Sciences (NAS) to establish an independent committee to conduct a comprehensive review of the practice of forensic science in the United States in order to "improve the forensic science disciplines and to allow the forensic science community to serve society more effectively."[3] In 2009, the NAS report was published, which outlined 13 recommendations to strengthen the forensic science community overall, and among those recommendations was the following: "standardize terminology and report writing practices." In the 2009 report, report writing was specifically addressed in two sections. The first was the "improving methods, practice, and performance" section, which cited a critical need to raise the standards for report writing and to use consistent terminology with a consensus around the meaning of those terms.

The second was the "continuing education" section, which was recognized as an essential component for all forensic science service providers as they enter into and continue their professional practice. Six core elements of a continuing education program were outlined, one of which was communication. Within that core element, report writing was specifically listed as an essential topic.[3] Therefore, report writing is recognized as a key component of the continuing education program for forensic science service providers as well as a fundamental means to convey their findings and opinions in a manner that is well-understood by other experts, non-experts, judges, and juries.

REPORT STANDARDS/GUIDELINES

In response to the NAS report, the National Institute of Standards and Technology (NIST) established the Organization of Scientific Area Committees for Forensic Science (OSAC) to generate discipline-based standards within the forensic science community. Through the American Academy of Forensic Sciences (AAFS), AAFS Standards Board (ASB) (see website

 DOI: 10.4324/9781003163695-29

Table 29.1 Sample standards or legal requirements that contain either recommendations or requirements for the administrative and technical content of forensic science reports

Standard or legal requirement	Agencies affected
ISO/IEC 17025:2017 General requirements for the competence of testing and calibration laboratories[8]	Agencies seeking or possessing accreditation according to ISO 17025 standards
Forensic Science Regulator Guidance, Expert Report Guidance[7]	Agencies issuing reports in the United Kingdom
Australian "Federal Register of Legislation" Rule 23.13. Contents of an expert report[9]	Agencies issuing reports in Australia
"ENFSI Guideline for Evaluative Reporting in Forensic Science"[6]	Agencies issuing reports in Europe
National Commission on Forensic Science "Recommendation to the Attorney General Documentation, Case Record, and Report Contents"[10]	Federal agencies issuing reports in the United States

www.asbstandardsboard.org), the OSAC Bloodstain Pattern Analysis (BPA) subcommittee published the Approved American National Standard ANSI/ASB Standard 031, Standard for Report Writing in Bloodstain Pattern Analysis, First Edition 2020.[4] The United States is not the only country with established guidelines for report writing in forensic science; other countries have also provided recommendations for report writing. For example, Australia published an Expert Evidence Practice Note (GPN-EXPT) detailing what every report prepared by an expert witness should contain.[5] The European Network of Forensic Science Institutes (ENFSI) published a guideline for evaluative report writing in forensic science that outlines what reports should include.[6] The United Kingdom has expert report guidance detailed in the UK Forensic Science Regulator©, which establishes the requirements for reports which will be admitted as evidence as well as for reports produced for investigative purposes only (not admissible in court).[7] Additionally, numerous forensic science laboratories around the world are accredited according to the International Organization for Standardization (ISO) standard 17025, General Requirements for the Competence of Testing and Calibration Laboratories. Among other things, ISO 17025 includes a section on report writing that details the specific content that must be included within a report.[8]

When a bloodstain pattern analyst renders an opinion, it should be in the form of a written report. The content and arrangement of the report will vary based on the combination of standards and local legal requirements placed upon the analyst issuing the report. Table 29.1 contains examples of various standards or legal requirements and the agency affected by those standards. A report written by an analyst in the United Kingdom may have significantly different content than a report issued by an analyst in the United States working in an ISO 17025 accredited laboratory. Because there is substantial variation among standards and legal requirements regarding the specific content required in reports, analysts must know and adhere to their local requirements to ensure their reports are admissible and not excluded by courts because they do not contain the necessary information.

REPORT CONTENT

Two BPA-specific guidelines have been published regarding report content and other recommendations. The first by the Scientific Working Group on Bloodstain Pattern Analysis (SWGSTAIN) was issued in 2012.[11] This document was updated and re-published as the ANSI/ASB Standard 031 in 2020.[4] Because a number of bloodstain pattern analysts perform work outside of traditional forensic science laboratories, the original SWGSTAIN document and the ANSI/ASB update in 2020 were created to assist analysts in the development of standardized bloodstain reports.

The content of a bloodstain report can be broken down into administrative and technical content. Administrative content includes information such as (but not limited to) the report date, the submitting agency, the agency case number, and the author's signature. Technical content includes information such as (but not limited to) observations, results of serological tests, photographs of bloodstains or bloodstain patterns, and various conclusions.

Although it may seem the technical information of a bloodstain report is the most critical, analysts cannot neglect the administrative information. The administrative content links the report to a specific case number, identifies the reporting analyst, and identifies the date the report was issued. Without this information, the report and the conclusions contained within may not be admissible in court. Additionally, in some jurisdictions, the analyst will not be called to testify in court. Instead, the issued report is read into the court record. In these situations, it may be necessary for the report to contain significantly more information on the analyst's qualifications (i.e., training, education, competency) as well as a lengthy discussion about the science of bloodstain pattern analysis (BPA). Table 29.2 contains various types of administrative and technical content that may be in a report based on ANSI/ASB Standard 031.[4] Depending on jurisdiction as well as on the nature of the analysis, a report may or may not include every type of content listed in Table 29.2.

The manner and order in which various types of content appear within the report may be dictated by the analyst's agency or by individual preference (for those in private practice, for example).

Table 29.2 Administrative and technical content of a BPA report. Reference ASB Standard 031 for additional guidance on content that is a "shall" (mandatory) and "should" (not mandatory but recommended as a best practice)

Administrative content	Technical content
Title to identify the subject of the report	Case information to include relevant background information provided to the analyst
Case identifier (included on each page of the report)	Methods used such as chemical tests, infrared photography, or the application of forensic software used for calculations in the analysis
Name and address of reporting agency or individual (if in private practice)	Limitations and assumptions relevant to the analysis; may also include clarifying statements
Date of report	Case observations to include general descriptions of scene or evidence
List of evidence and/or materials reviewed	Descriptions of observed bloodstains and/or bloodstain patterns (can be supported by photographs and/or sketches included in the report)
Identification of location(s) where the analyst's examinations took place (for example, at the scene or in the laboratory)	Description of the absence of bloodstains or bloodstain patterns when relevant to the opinion provided by the analyst
Analyst's qualifications and duty to the court	Bloodstain and/or bloodstain pattern classifications
Statement by the analyst that if information changes after the date of the report, the opinions of the analyst may change	Results of chemical tests utilized at the scene or on the evidence
Name and signature of reporting analyst	Identifiers of samples collected for analysis (to include the location of stains sampled by the analyst)
Name of technical reviewer and date of review	Case conclusions
References cited during the analysis	

Much of the administrative content (e.g., names, addresses, dates, case information, items/references reviewed, etc.) could be listed before the technical content (e.g., observations, classifications, case conclusions, etc.). The content can be included within headers, text within the body of the report, footnotes, endnotes, or appendices. Some analysts include certain supporting technical content such as features of the observed bloodstains or the results of serological tests within their notes rather than within their report. This is acceptable as long as the analyst's notes are permanently retained and always available. For example, analysts working in ISO accredited laboratories are required to retain all notes in their case files. For those analysts working in private practice, it is highly recommended that they also adopt the practice of retaining their notes in their permanent records.

Regardless of the manner in which the content (both administrative and technical) is included within the report, the order in which it is presented must follow a logical process. The order of the report content must assist a reader in understanding the bloodstains or bloodstain patterns that were observed and the analyst's opinion of the meaning and/or interpretation of those observations. Even when the report is constructed in a logical manner and contains the required content, if the report is not written in a way that is understandable to the reader, who is often a non-scientist, then the analyst has failed the judicial system. Any observations and/or interpretations must be scientifically supported; however, the wording of those observations and interpretations should not be in "scientific language."

It is often appropriate for an analyst to include statements that address limitations and assumptions made during analysis that are relevant to the opinions/conclusions provided by the analyst. An analyst may also need to include clarifying statements to assist a reader of their report in fully understanding their observations or case conclusions. The next three sections discuss reporting limitations, assumptions, and clarifying statements in more detail.

Reporting Limitations

Table 29.3 contains a list of examples of limitation statements that can be used in bloodstain reports as case circumstances dictate. A way of prefacing these limitations could include a statement such as "The observations and conclusions contained in this report are limited in the following way(s)."

Reporting Assumptions

There may be times when the analyst must make certain assumptions or presumptions in order to proceed with the analysis or to make meaningful conclusions. Table 29.4 includes assumptions that should be included in a report when applicable to the specific case under investigation.

Table 29.3 Examples of limitation statements that can be included in a bloodstain report

- Analysis of bloodstains documented at the scene was performed solely from photographs and video. Some of the provided photographs were limited in aspects specific to bloodstain documentation (e.g., no scales, measurements not recorded, no close-up photographs).
- Resolution of the photography equipment was not adequate to provide detailed analysis of stain appearance in many photographs.
- Scales were not included in some of the photographs, specifically those photographs of bloodstains on the body of (the victim).
- At no time has the author attended (scene address).
- No presumptive or confirmatory tests for the presence of blood were performed. None of the stains observed were collected or preserved.

Table 29.4 Examples of assumption statements that can be included in a report

- All stains, which have the visual appearance of blood are in fact blood and will be referred to as blood for the purpose of this report.
- The (victim) was the primary contributor to bloodstains observed at the scene.
- All bloodstains observed were deposited contemporaneously to the event under investigation, unless otherwise stated.
- For samples where DNA reports stated that only (individual) could not be excluded as the source of the major STR DNA profiles, the blood was that of (individual).
- The majority of the observed bloodstains were deposited during or after (the victim) sustained bloodletting injuries.

Clarifying Statements

There may be situations in which an analyst needs to provide clarifying information beyond what might be covered in the limitations and assumptions sections of their report. Table 29.5 provides examples of various clarifying statements that may be of use to the analyst.

Observations

The section of the report containing observations of bloodstains and/or bloodstain patterns can contain a wide variety of information. However, according to ANSI/ASB Standard 031, the ASB Technical Report 033, Terms and Definitions in Bloodstain Pattern Analysis, First Edition, 2017[12] must be followed when producing a report. Further, the terms must be defined which can be accomplished through the use of footnotes, an appendix, or a glossary.

Observations can include the following:

- Overall statements about the scene or item(s) of evidence
- Statements about the locations and types of bloodstains and/or bloodstain patterns observed at a scene or on evidence; as well as locations without bloodstains and/or bloodstain patterns
- Features of the bloodstains and/or bloodstain patterns that were used for classification
- Type and results of serological testing of bloodstains
- Type and results of presumptive testing of bloodstains
- Locations of samples or items that were collected by analyst
- Results of other forensic examinations of bloodstains and/or bloodstain patterns (e.g. DNA analyses, impression comparisons)

There are multiple ways for an analyst to include the observed features of a bloodstain and/or bloodstain patterns upon which the classification is based. One approach is to include all of the relevant features within the body of the text. Although transparent, this approach runs the risk

Table 29.5 Examples of clarifying statements that can be included in a report

- Statements of "blood" or "bloodstain" refer to red-brown stains of apparent blood. These stains were consistent in physical appearance with known bloodstains and, unless stated otherwise, tested positive for the indication of blood using phenolphthalein or leucocrystal violet reagents.
- Any references to conclusions from other forensic reports are to be considered summary statements only. Refer to the referenced forensic report for a more complete discussion of the specific conclusion.
- This report is not intended to discuss every bloodstain present at the scene or on the examined items of evidence. Additional bloodstains were observed which are not discussed in this report.
- Unless otherwise noted, statements of "spatter stains" indicate these stains were observed on a particular item; however, they were not deposited in a manner to be able to determine the specific mechanism of deposition. Spatter stains do not necessarily indicate a violent act occurred near a particular item, only that airborne droplets of blood were created when force was applied to liquid blood.

of making it difficult for a non-bloodstain analyst to read and comprehend the report. A second option is to report the stain and/or pattern classification in the observations section of the report and place the detailed discussion of the observed features in an appendix. Some analysts choose not to include these features in the report in any manner and just keep them in their notes. If this approach is taken, the report must contain a clear statement that additional supporting information is available and the analyst's notes must be permanently retained.

Another approach to including the features of bloodstains and/or bloodstain patterns in a report is by including photographs or diagrams within the body of the report. Photographs serve to further the reader's understanding of the report's content. The adage "a picture is worth a thousand words" certainly rings true in a visual-based science such as BPA. When used appropriately, photographs of bloodstains or bloodstain patterns can assist readers of the report in understanding the extent of bloodstains, the location of a specific pattern within the context of the scene, and other case conclusion concepts such as position and directionality.

In addition, the analyst can annotate the photograph to focus on specific aspects of a stain or pattern, to differentiate between adjacent or overlapping patterns, or to identify other key aspects of the bloodstains or the scene. Figure 29.1 is an example of how annotations to an inserted photograph provide the reader with a better understanding of the pattern. In this example, text associated with the inserted image provides additional information regarding the identified patterns. This additional information could include the features used for classification, the results of latent print comparisons, or the results of DNA examinations of swabs collected from each pattern. If an analyst elects to include photographs or diagrams in their report, they can fix photographs within the report (as shown in Figure 29.1) or include them in an appendix to the report. Either way, when including photographs in a report, the analyst should always follow their agency's written policies and procedures.

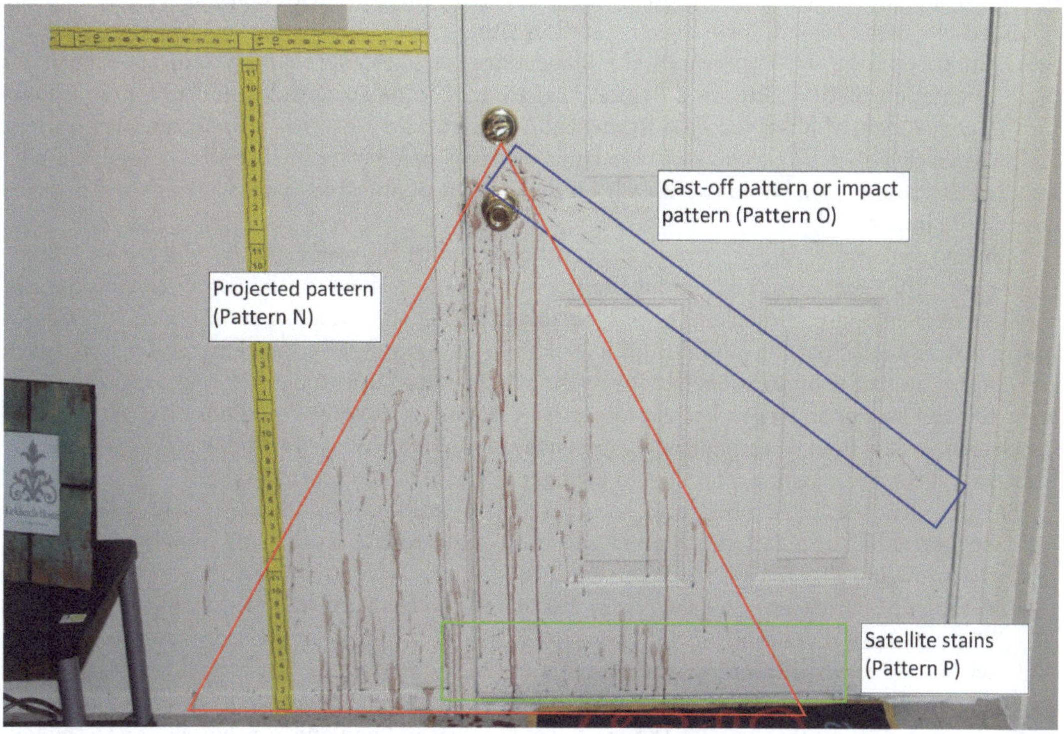

Figure 29.1 Example of an annotated image that can be inserted into a bloodstain report.

Bloodstain pattern analysis reports are unique in that they are often the last of the expert reports published. This is because bloodstain pattern analysts rely on reported results from other scientific disciplines to generate a complete and thorough report.[1] Bloodstain pattern analysts routinely use additional, relevant case information as part of their examinations and when forming their conclusions. Often this includes the results of other forensic examinations (e.g., latent print comparisons or DNA analyses) or observations of injuries detailed in autopsy reports. If it is appropriate to include relevant conclusions or observations from outside sources, these sources must be appropriately referenced and the analyst is strongly encouraged to quote the material verbatim from the report rather than summarize the content. Quoting the statements verbatim eliminates, or at least minimizes, the chance the analyst will misconstrue the referenced conclusion or observation. This is especially important when discussing DNA results, as BPA analysts frequently rely on the opinions of DNA analysts when forming their conclusions.

Case Conclusions

One of the most challenging aspects of producing a bloodstain report is writing case conclusions. Conclusions must be rooted in objective observations of the bloodstains and logically valid, scientific reasoning. Additionally, case conclusions must be worded in a manner that accurately conveys the intended meaning. Conclusions, like the rest of the report, must be concise, unbiased, and based on the analyst's area of expertise without including any unsubstantiated opinions or biased language.

At times, the analyst is requested to consider specific propositions (or hypotheses) by either investigators or attorneys. When requested to consider a specific proposition, the report must include not only the supplied proposition(s) but also any alternative propositions developed by the analyst. For example, if the analyst is requested to evaluate bloodstains on clothing to determine if any impact spatter stains are present, an alternative proposition to consider is whether any observed bloodstains could have been created by other spatter-producing mechanisms. Another proposition could be whether or not the bloodstains on a decedent's body indicate movement or re-orientation of the body. In all situations, an analyst must consider multiple propositions for the explanation of observed bloodstains and/or bloodstain patterns. Propositions can only be addressed if there are bloodstains or bloodstain patterns present for analysis. In general, support for a specific proposition based exclusively on the absence of objective data is a dangerous practice that should be avoided.

As mentioned earlier, all reported case conclusions must be supported by objective evidence and/or sound logical reasoning. Simply stating in the report that "the following conclusions are the best explanation of the events which occurred during the event" may not adequately demonstrate the specific pathway used by the analyst to develop certain conclusions. One approach to educate the reader on the specific observations that were used to develop the conclusion is to state the conclusion and then list the objective evidence and/or observations that support the conclusion. Below is an example of this approach. Observations based on additional case-specific information would include a reference to the source, possibly as a footnote.

"The decedent was in an upright to near upright orientation near the west wall of the master bedroom when he sustained at least one gunshot wound to the head." This conclusion is based upon the following observations:

- A forward spatter pattern (pattern L) was located on the west wall of the master bedroom. The pattern was centered ~5'11" above the floor. A circular defect was observed in the wall within the forward spatter pattern.
- The decedent was included as a source of DNA on a sample collected from pattern L.
- The decedent was reportedly 185 cm tall at autopsy and had one gunshot wound to the left temporal region of the head as well as one gunshot wound to the left side of his neck.

Case conclusions, as well as all other aspects of the report, must be free of statements which are either misleading, targeted to result in an emotional response, unsubstantiated, or outside the expertise of the analyst. For example, the phrase, "to a reasonable degree of scientific certainty" has been commonly used in the past; however, there is no way to demonstrate how this threshold can be met. At what point is there sufficient information to make this statement? In reality, this statement is simply an expression of the analyst's confidence in a conclusion. Words like "brutal," "vicious," or "violent" are unnecessary and run the risk of persuading readers based on emotional responses rather than objective evidence. An unsubstantiated conclusion is one which lacks any objective evidence at all for support. Conclusions which address an individual's intentions or mental state are outside the scope of a bloodstain report and most likely outside the expertise of the analyst.

The report content does not necessarily need to stop after listing/describing the observations and case conclusions. The use of appendices at the end of the report is an effective way to communicate additional details not included in the body of the report. Appendices allow the analyst to include important information without "cluttering" the report and making it difficult for the audience to read. Appendices can include the full list of bloodstain terms and their associated definitions, a list of all evidence examined and collected during the examination, a list of all materials supplied to the analyst for review, a list of the features observed within observed patterns which support the ultimate classification, or even information regarding the training and education of the analyst.

TECHNICAL REVIEW

According to ANSI/ASB Standard 031, each report produced by a bloodstain pattern analyst shall be subjected to a technical review prior to release.[4] The OSAC BPA subcommittee proposed a standard for the technical review of report writing in BPA.[13] In that draft standard, 2021-S-0011 Standards for the Technical Review of Bloodstain Pattern Analysis Reporting, a technical review is defined as "a qualified second party's evaluation of reports, notes, data, and other documents to ensure there is appropriate and sufficient support for the actions, conclusions, opinions and interpretations" made by the analyst and contained in their report. The purpose of a technical review is then two-fold: (i) to ensure the analyst utilized and correctly applied accepted BPA methods, and (ii) to ensure the analyst came to appropriate conclusions given the facts and circumstances of the specific case.

Bloodstain pattern analysts, whether in private practice or employed by laboratory or law enforcement agency, are highly encouraged to establish a process for conducting technical reviews as well as guidelines on how to document the review process. The person selected to conduct the technical review is just as important as establishing standards for the review process itself. According to the ANSI/ASB Standards for a Bloodstain Pattern Analyst's Training Program, Standard 032, the person conducting the review must be a bloodstain pattern analyst trained to competency.[14] Furthermore, the person selected to conduct the review should be objective, without prior knowledge of the case (when possible), and without any undue pressure to reach a certain conclusion during the review process. This, along with establishing an order in which case materials will be examined, will help minimize bias on the part of the reviewer and afford that person an opportunity to generate conclusions independent of those provided in the analyst's report. According to the OSAC draft standard, 2021-S-0011, the technical reviewer shall examine case materials in the following order:

1. Scene/evidence documentation
2. Forensic/medical reports
3. The analyst's supporting documentation

4. Other relevant documentation; for example, police reports or court transcripts
5. Outside forensic science service provider's BPA report if that report is referenced by the analyst authoring the report under review
6. Analyst's report

It is important to emphasize that the analyst's report is the last document examined in the technical review process. Again, the purpose of this is to minimize bias and allow the reviewer to form independent conclusions prior to reading the opinions rendered by the analyst.[13]

The technical review process must be documented and should include the case file identification, the name and signature (digital or otherwise) of the person conducting the review, the date(s) the review took place, and the case materials that were reviewed and in what sequence those materials were reviewed.[13] If the technical reviewer identifies any discrepancies with the analyst's procedures, observations, classifications, or case conclusions, the reviewer shall bring this information to the attention of the analyst and if the analyst makes any amendments as a result of the review, those amendments must be documented.[13] If discrepancies identified during the technical review process cannot be resolved, the following recommendations should be considered:[13]

1. "If a discrepancy occurs over the observation/classification of a specific stain pattern, the resolution shall be to report the most specific classification that results in an agreement. For instance, this may mean reporting a higher level of classification *(i.e., less specific)* or reporting as inconclusive/no conclusion."
2. "If a discrepancy occurs over a case conclusion, the resolution shall be to report the most specific case conclusion in which both the analyst and the technical reviewer agree."
3. "If the discrepancy cannot be resolved, a third, qualified analyst may be consulted to assist with a resolution. If this occurs, the details of that consultation must be documented."

In addition to a technical review, an administrative review should also be performed on all reports prior to their release. While technical reviews focus on the technical content and scientific validity of the analyst's conclusions, the administrative review checks the accuracy of the content listed in Table 29.2 as well as the format, grammar, and readability of the report. Additionally, administrative reviews verify that all pages are identified and correctly numbered as well as other non-technical requirements are satisfied. Whether or not the individual who performs the technical review also performs the administrative review is often left to agency policies or best practices established for those in private practice. Agency policies or best practices should also be established for which is conducted first, the administrative review or the technical review.

SUMMARY

Every forensic science service provider has the responsibility of articulating their findings and opinions in a science-based report that can be well-understood by both non-experts and non-scientists. The report should be objective and unbiased and follow established guidelines/standards set for that particular discipline in addition to the policy requirements for that forensic science service provider's agency. Practitioners of BPA are not exempt from these responsibilities. Following the guidance and recommendations in this chapter will enable a bloodstain pattern analyst to publish a report that is based on objective evidence and/or sound logical reasoning and is organized in a way that will assist the reader in gaining a suitable understanding of the foundation and significance of the analyst's opinions; ultimately enabling the reader (judges, jurors, triers of fact) to appropriately apply testimony based on the analyst's report.

Notes

1. James, Stuart H., Paul E. Kish, and T. Paulette Sutton, Principles of Bloodstain Pattern Analysis, Theory and Practice, CRC Press, Boca Raton, Florida, 2005, p. 433.

2. Eldridge, Heidi, Juror comprehension of forensic expert testimony: A literature review and gap analysis. Forensic Science International: Synergy 2019, Volume 1, pp. 24–34.
3. National Research Council, Strengthening Forensic Science in the United States: A Path Forward, The National Academies Press, Washington, D.C., 2009. https://doi.org/10.17226/12589.
4. American Academy of Forensic Sciences Standards Board (ASB), Technical Report 031, Standard for Report Writing in Bloodstain Pattern Analysis, First Edition 2020.
5. Allsop, James. L. B., Chief Justice, Expert Evidence Practice Note (GPN-EXPT), Federal Court of Australia, Canberra, 2016.
6. Champod, C., A. Biedermann, J. Vuille and J. Kinder, European Network of Forensic Science Institutes (ENFSI), Guideline for Evaluative Reporting in Forensic Science, 2015.
7. Forensic Science Regulator Guidance, Expert Report Guidance, FSR-G-200, 2020. (https://assets.publishing.service.gov.uk/government/uploads/system/uploads/attachment_data/file/881550/Statement_and_Report_Guidance_Appendix_Issue_4.pdf)
8. International Organization for Standardization, General Requirements for the Competence of Testing and Calibration Laboratories (ISO/IEC Standard No. 17025), 2017.
9. Australian "Federal register of legislation". Rule 23.13. Contents of an expert report. (https://www.legislation.gov.au/Details/F2019C00426, accessed on 3/22/2021)
10. National Commission on Forensic Science, "Recommendation to the Attorney General Documentation, Case Record, and Report Contents." 2016. (https://www.justice.gov/archives/ncfs/page/file/905536/download, accessed on 4/5/2021)
11. Scientific Working Group on Bloodstain Pattern Analysis: Guidelines for Report Writing in Bloodstain Pattern Analysis, issue date July 7, 2012.
12. American Academy of Forensic Sciences Standards Board (ASB) Technical Report 033, Terms and Definitions in Bloodstain Pattern Analysis, First Edition, 2017.
13. National Institute of Standards and Technology (NIST), Office of the Scientific Area Committees (OSAC), "Standard for Technical Review of Bloodstain Pattern Analysis Reports," 2021-S-0011 (under development).
14. American Academy of Forensic Sciences Standards Board (ASB), Technical Report 032, Standards for a Bloodstain Pattern Analyst's Training Program, First Edition 2020.

Further Reading

1. Hackman, Lucina. "Communication, Forensic Science, and the Law." *WIREs Forensic Science* 3 (2021):e1396. https://doi.org/10.1002/wfs2.1396.
2. Passalacqua, N. V., M. A. Pilloud, and W. R. Belcher. "Scientific Integrity in the Forensic Sciences: Consumerism, Conflicts of Interest, and Transparency." *Science & Justice* 59 (2019): 573–9.
3. President's Council of Advisors on Science and Technology (U.S.) and United States. Executive Office of the President. *Report to the President*, Forensic Science in Criminal Courts: Ensuring Scientific Validity of Feature-comparison Methods. Executive Office of the President, President's Council of Advisors on Science and Technology, Washington, D.C. 2016.
4. Schnackenberg, Andrew K., and Edward C. Tomlinson. "Organizational Transparency: A New Perspective on Managing Trust in Organization-Stakeholder Relationships." *Journal of Management* 42, no. 7 (2016): 1784–1810.
5. Howes, L. M., K. P. Kirkbride, S. F. Kelty, R. Julian, and N. Kemp. "Forensic scientists' Conclusions: How Readable Are They for Nonscientist Report-Users?" *Forensic Science International* 231, no. 1–3 (2013): 102–112.
6. Bevel, Tom, and Ross M. Gardner, *Bloodstain Pattern Analysis with an Introduction to Crime Scene Reconstruction*. Boca Raton, Florida: CRC Press, 2008, pp. 286–96.

CHAPTER 30

HIGH-SPEED DIGITAL VIDEO ANALYSIS OF BLOODSTAIN PATTERN FORMATION

Terry Laber

INTRODUCTION

The analysis of bloodstain patterns is used by criminal investigators to draw inferences about the events that created the pattern. Understanding the dynamics of a bloodstain pattern producing event is critical to the sound interpretation of the resultant bloodstain pattern. Until recently, the primary approach to bloodstain pattern analyses was experimentation. Under this approach, analysts conduct a series of experiments to identify actions that generate key features of an observed pattern and, potentially, identify actions that generate patterns that are distinct from the observed pattern. While experimentation can be an effective tool for creating bloodstain patterns, it can be difficult to identify how a given experiment generates a particular pattern. High-speed digital video (HSDV) allows analysts to observe how blood spatter forms, how it travels and interacts in flight, and what occurs during deposition.[1] This chapter presents the results of a systematic study of the formation of common bloodstain patterns using HSDV to record the bloodstain pattern producing events as they occur.

Over 300 individual HSDV clips were made of common bloodstain pattern producing events, such as single blood drop formation, impact, gunshot, expiration of blood, cast-off, projected, and transfer blood staining.[2] These were based on experiments typically performed by students in a basic bloodstain pattern analysis (BPA) course.[3] Segments of the video sequences are presented and discussed to illustrate the basic dynamics of bloodletting events, the formation of bloodstain patterns, and the dynamics of the collision between a blood drop and surfaces. Videos are referenced preceding captions derived from video sequences.

The goal of this section is to increase the understanding of the dynamics of bloodstain pattern producing events that produce specific bloodstain patterns, to contribute to the underlying science behind BPA methods, to contribute to the validation of the current bloodstain pattern recognition methods, and to strengthen the foundations upon which expert BPA opinion evidence is given in court.

DRIP STAINS

Drip stains are bloodstains resulting from a falling drop that formed due to gravity. Often bloodstains found at a scene are the result of blood dripping from objects. These drops can occur in a variety of ways. Blood can drip from a wound, a weapon, clothing, hair or from any other surface where sufficient blood has accumulated to form the drops. The diameter of a drip stain will depend upon the volume of the individual drop, the distance the drop falls, and the surface the drop strikes on impact.[4]

In basic BPA analysis classes, a common exercise is to examine the diameter of drip stains as a function of origin. In this exercise, students slowly apply blood to a variety of objects, e.g., crescent

DOI: 10.4324/9781003163695-30

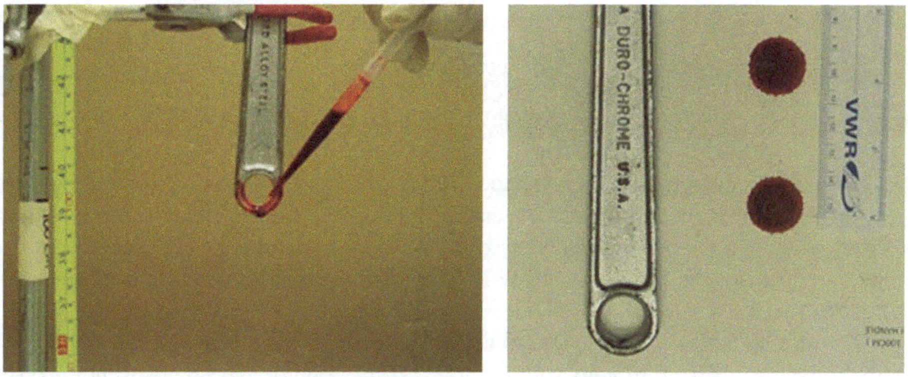

Figure 30.1 (a) Blood being applied to wrench handle to observe drop formation and (b) bloodstains produced by blood drops falling 100 cm from a wrench handle to a cardboard target.

wrenches, knives, etc., until blood drops fall from the object. Students observe the blood drop forming and falling, and how the resulting bloodstain varies across objects. Frequently, they observe a very small bloodstain deposited near the main drip stain. What students do not see is how complex drop formation is, how accompanying drops are formed, and the many stages a drop undergoes on impact. Understanding the bloodstain dynamics that occurs in this simple exercise forms the foundation of all drop formations that occur in BPA.

With the use of HSDV, students can observe in slow motion exactly how drops are formed, what happens when they are released, and how the small accompanying drops are formed. They can also observe blood drop oscillation, the effects of drop collisions, and what effect the target surface has on the resultant stain.

Figure 30.1a shows blood being applied slowly to a wrench handle to observe drop formation and release. The blood spreads out over the available surface area; so more surface area generally results in larger drops. Figure 30.1b shows the resultant bloodstains from drops of blood falling 100 cm from a wrench handle to a smooth cardboard surface. The experimenter observes that the resultant bloodstain diameters (volume of the drop) vary from object to object. A small accompanying drop is sometimes observed next to the parent drop (Figure 30.5e).

When this same demonstration is studied using HSDV, the amount of information gained is greatly increased. HSDV imaging was conducted using a Photron Fastcam-SA1, HSDV camera, two ellipsoid beam 750-watt light sources, and two photon beam 1000-watt light sources. The camera and two of the light sources are shown in Figure 30.2.

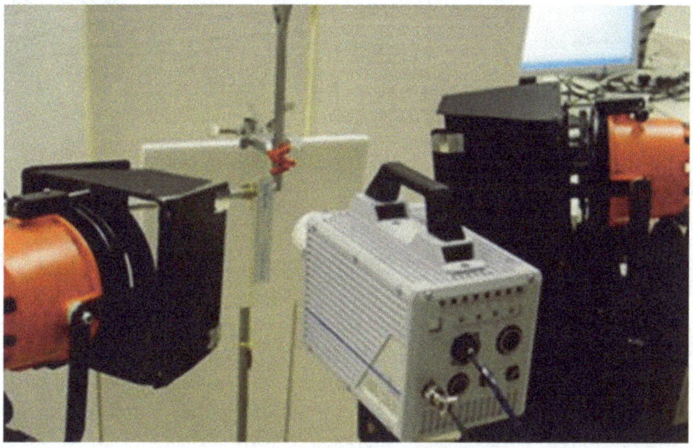

Figure 30.2 Photron Fastcam-SA1, HSDV camera, and lights for observing blood drops falling from a wrench.

HIGH-SPEED DIGITAL VIDEO SEQUENCES OF DROP FORMATION

The main drop goes through a series of shape changes from when it is forming, to just before it is released, and just after the column snaps and it is released. This is clearly seen in (Figure 30.3 b–d). Note the distance change between the two middle small drops by comparing (Figure 30.3e and f). The smallest drop is pulled back toward the wrench handle when it is released and then starts to fall again.

Figures 30.4 and 30.5 show interactions that can occur between drops. In Figures 30.4a–c, two micro drops traveling at different velocities collide and the smaller drop is absorbed into the larger drop. In Figures 30.5a–d, a micro drop bounces off the main drop causing it deflect sufficiently to be deposited as a small stain to the side of the main drip stain (Figure 30.5e).

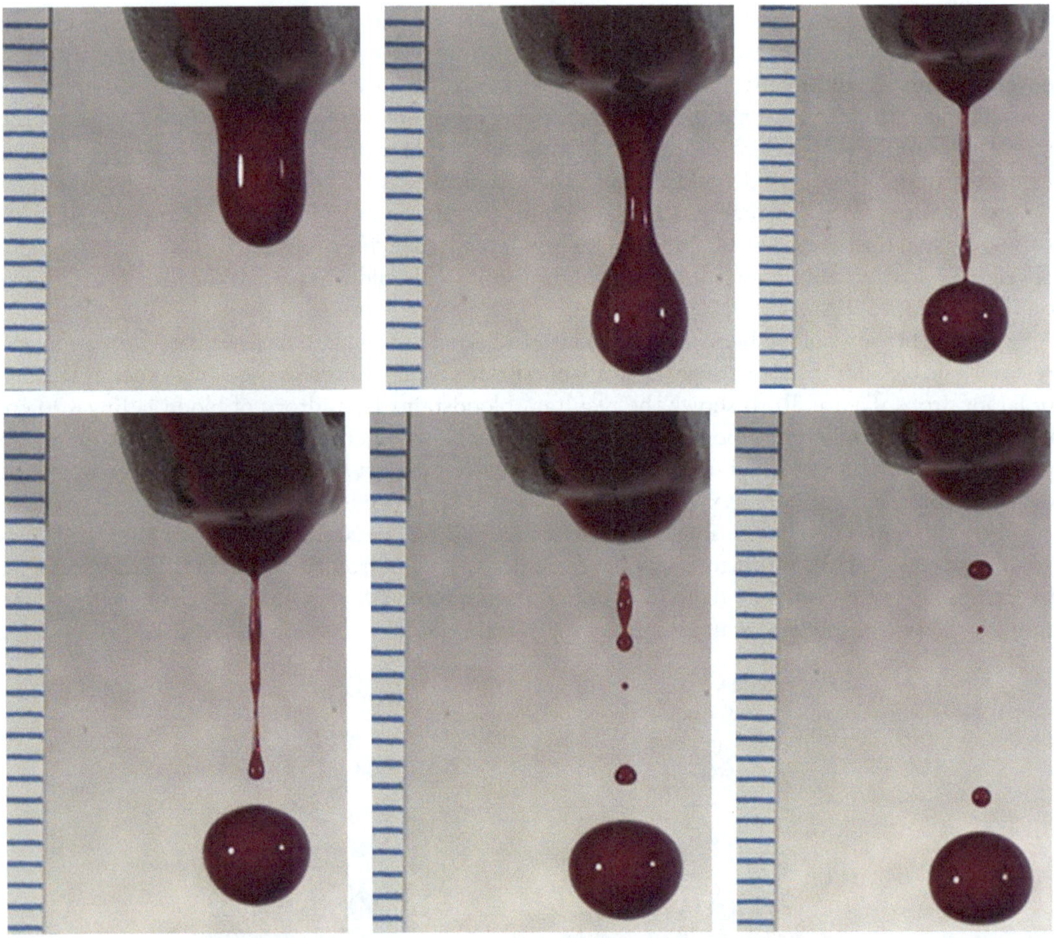

Figure 30.3 (Video 1Ab1) (a) Drop formation on the handle of a wrench, (b) the spindle shaft narrows as gravity pulls the drop away from the wrench, (c) the spindle continues to narrow as the drop pulls downward, (d) the spindle severs or "snaps" at specific locations, (e) the column has severed at four locations; part of the column remains preceded by a micro drop, a small drop, and the main drop; the small drop and large drop show significant oscillation, and (f) the remaining column has collapsed to form a drop which shows considerable oscillation due to the surface tension forces pulling the blood into a spherical shape; the oscillations of the smaller droplets appear to dampen within 5 mm of fall.

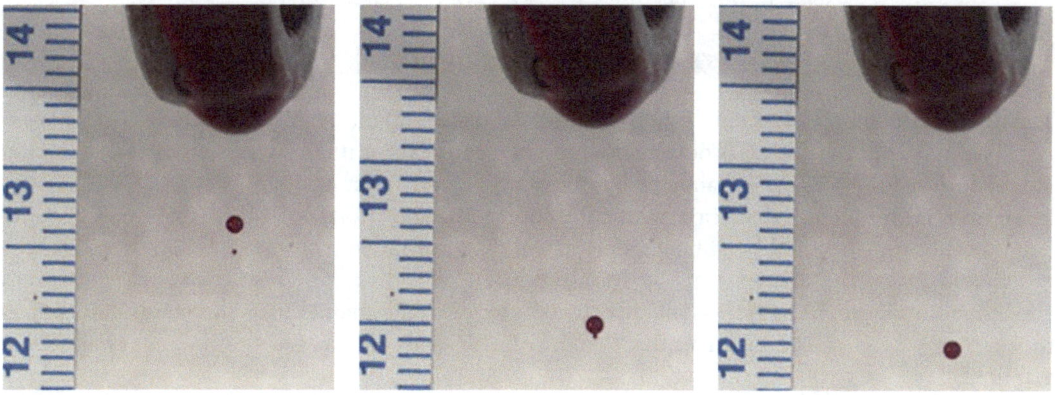

Figure 30.4 (Video 1Ab1) (a) Two droplets have different velocities due to the snapping of the column and size, (b) some drops may actually travel upward initially after they snap from the column; very small drops appear to be pulled upward to a greater extent than larger drops, and (c) these velocity differences result in some droplets catching up to others and the two drops combining.

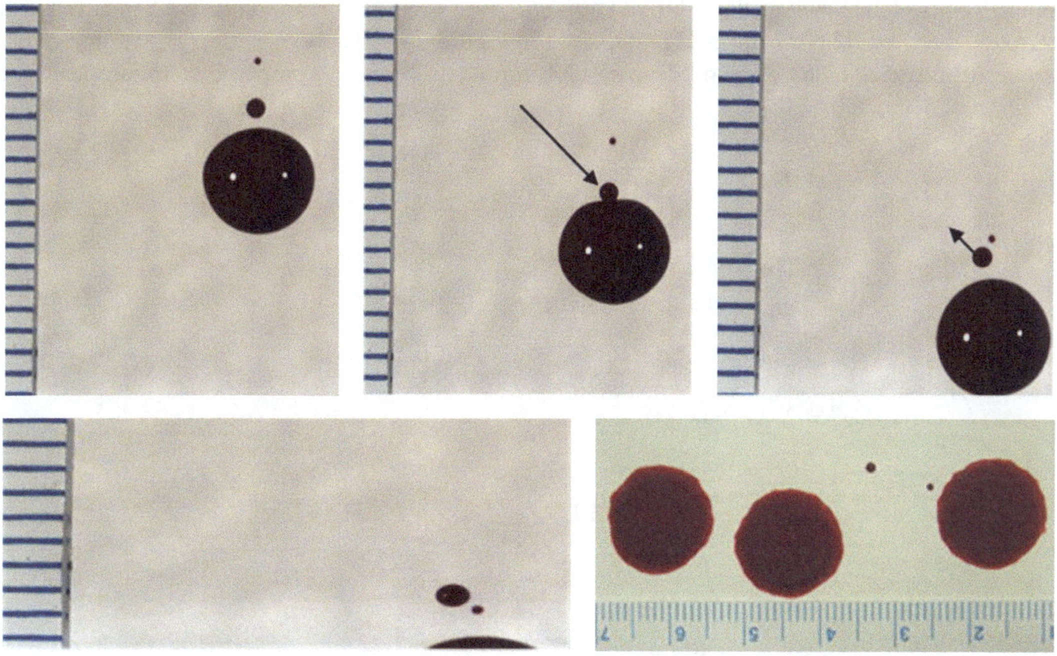

Figure 30.5 (Video 1Ab2) (a) Three drops of different sizes are traveling at different velocities, (b) one of the smaller drops collides with a larger drop and bounces off to the left causing a loss of downward velocity; if this deflection is great enough to cause the smaller drop to land outside the main drip stain, it will be seen as a small accompanying stain, (c) a micro droplet is about to pass the deflected drop, (d) oscillation appears to be the greatest when two drops collide, following snapping of a spindle, and coalesce of drops, and (e) three drip stains and two accompanying stains.

TERMINAL VELOCITY DETERMINATIONS

The diameter of bloodstains resulting from drops of constant volume increase with the distance of fall. The maximum diameter is obtained when the drop reaches its terminal velocity, i.e., the rate at which the pull of gravity is balanced by buoyancy and air resistance.

An exercise frequently done in a basic BPA course involves drops of different volumes dropped from a set of pre-specified heights. The effects of distance fallen, volume of blood drop, and terminal velocity on the diameter of the stain produced is studied. The results of such an exercise are shown in Figure 30.6. Across all three drop volumes, the diameter of the stains can be seen to increase with distance fallen until a height of 300–400 cm, where the diameters appear to stabilize.

Though the diameters of the drops are visually indistinguishable at 300 cm and 400 cm, the drops have not reached terminal velocity at this height. Since diameter of stain changes so slightly at these heights, the diameter of stain is not a viable method of determining actual terminal velocity. However, for most BPA applications, the diameter of stains produced by drops falling from heights greater than 300–400 cm does not change sufficiently to affect most BPA determinations.

The terminal velocity of blood drops of three different volumes was determined using HSDV. The drop volume was calculated via HSDV software and compared to the volumetric determination. The blood drops were allowed to fall 900 cm in a stairwell to obtain sufficient height to reach terminal velocity. The set up used is depicted in Figure 30.7. The experimental data for velocity versus distance fallen of blood drops of 3.4 mm and 4.3 mm is compared to theoretical data (Figure 30.8 and Table 30.1).

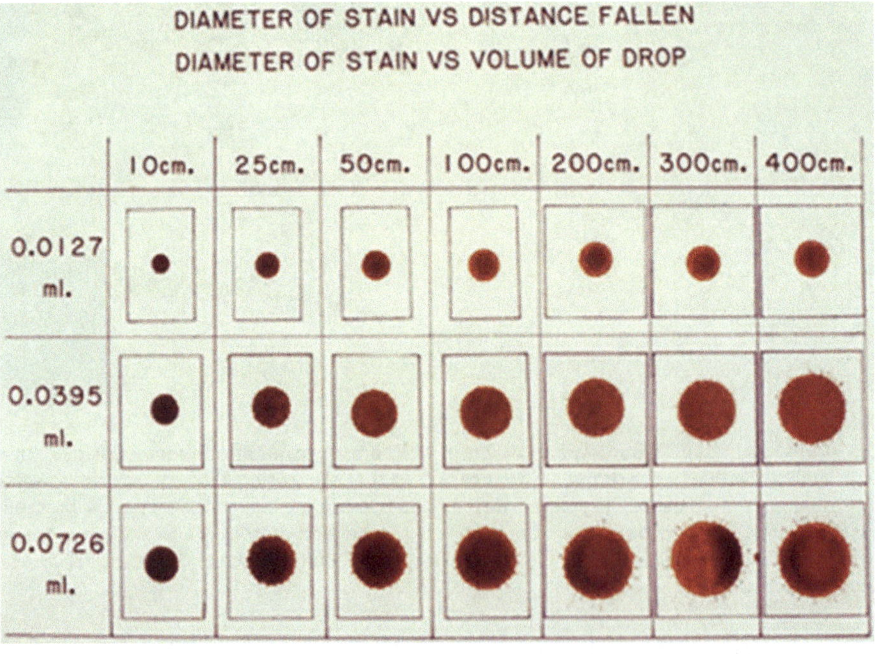

Figure 30.6 Display of experimental data of individual drip stains illustrating the effect of drop volume and distance fallen on drop stain size.

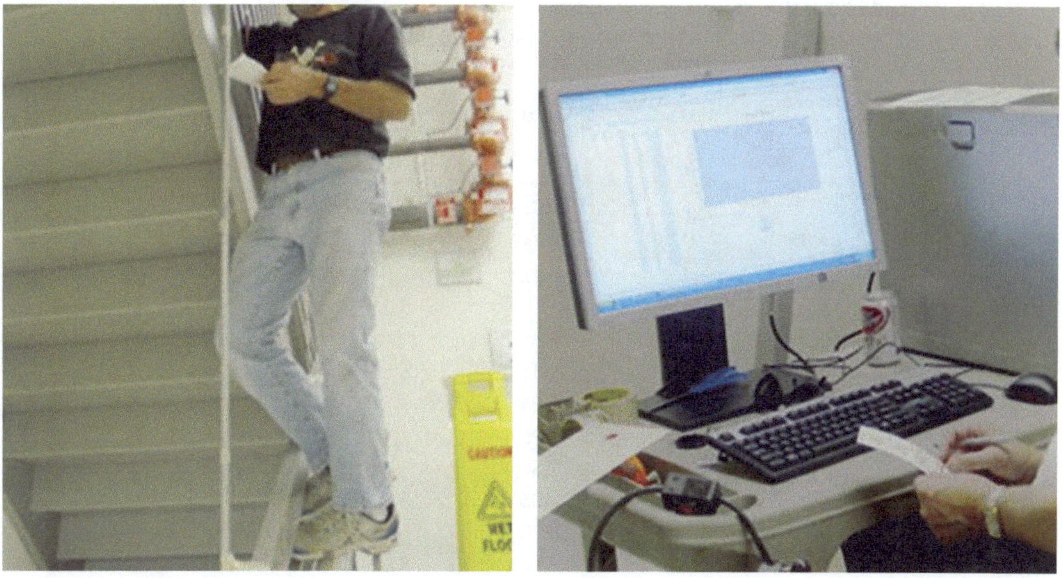

Figure 30.7 (a) A pole was set up in a stairway and blood drops of know volume allowed to fall from desired heights up to 900 cm and (b) HSDV measured the velocity of the falling drop over a 50 cm interval and the diameter of the falling drop.

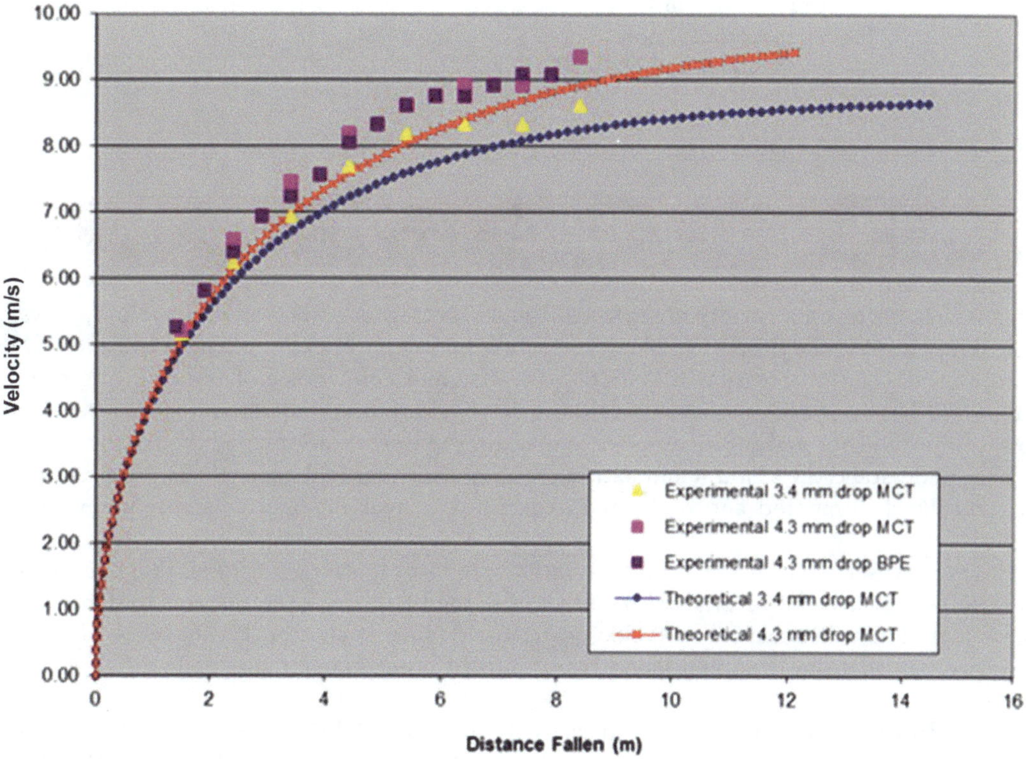

Figure 30.8 The diameter of falling blood drops was determined as was the velocity of the drops at various distances fallen from experimental data obtained utilizing HSDV. Experimental data (participants MCT and BPE) and theoretical data are shown.

Table 30.1 Velocity of medium and small blood drops at various distances of fall. It can be seen that at 8.4 m drops are approaching terminal velocity but have not quite made it to the theoretical terminal velocity

Height		Medium-sized drop		Small drop
		BPE	MCT	
(cm)	(m)	velocity (m/s)	velocity (m/s)	velocity
140	1.4	5.26		
150	1.5		5.21	5.15
190	1.9	5.81		
240	2.4	6.41	6.58	6.25
290	2.9	6.94		
340	3.4	7.25	7.46	6.94
390	3.9	7.58		
440	4.4	8.06	8.20	7.69
490	4.9	8.33		
540	5.4	8.62	8.62	8.20
590	5.9	8.77		
640	6.4	8.77	8.93	8.33
690	6.9	8.93		
740	7.4	9.09	8.93	8.33
790	7.9	9.09		
840	8.4		9.35	8.62
Theoretical terminal velocity		9.65	9.84	8.76

TARGET SURFACE EFFECTS

Bloodstains occur on a variety of surfaces, e.g., carpet, wood, tile, wallpaper, cloth, newspaper, skin, etc. When a droplet of blood impacts a surface, properties of the surface, e.g., how hard, porous, and/or irregular it is dictate the size and appearance of the resulting stain as well as the behavior and amount of satellite spatter. Therefore, understanding surface properties is important for making a complete and accurate interpretation of a bloodstain. One way to help understand the amount and nature of the spatter that will occur is to have a repository of carefully documented and replicated experiments involving spatter across many surface types.

HSDV was used to study surface effects on the degree of spatter using items that had a variety of different surface characteristics. Blood was dropped from different heights to demonstrate the effect of the distance fallen (velocity) on the degree of spatter. Figure 30.9b shows the results obtained from dropping blood from four different heights onto four different target surfaces.

Figure 30.10a–f shows time-lapsed images collected using HSDV, displaying a drop of blood impacting a pine board after falling 100 cm (Figure 30.10a–c) and 10 cm (Figure 30.10d–f). The time (t) is the time elapsed since drop impact.

HSDV sequence of images in Figure 30.11 shows the target surface effects on a drop of blood falling 100 cm to a fluffy sweatshirt fabric.

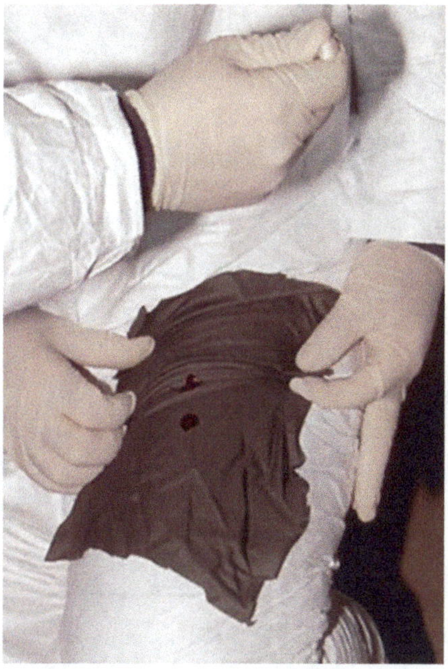
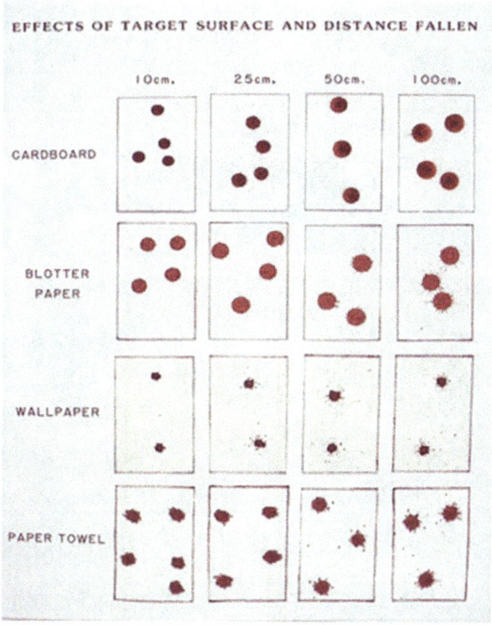

Figure 30.9 (a) Effects of cloth and a curved surface on the appearance of bloodstains and (b) summary display of the target surface effects when blood drops fall 10, 25, 50, and 100 cm to the target surface.

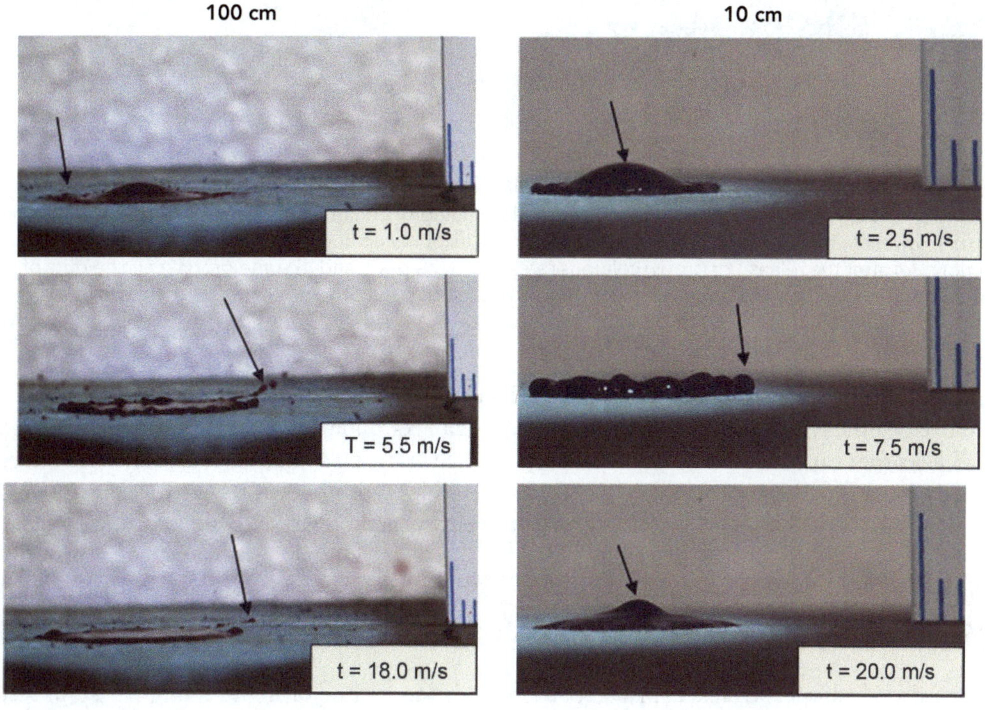

Figure 30.10 (Videos 3Fb2a and 3Fa1a) (a) Drop impacts and spreads to the edges in a wave form, (b) drop collapses and wave breaks into columns and droplets are released in the form of spatter, (c) drop has flattened out and spatter is seen as beads on the surface of the wood, (d) drop falling 10 cm takes longer to flatten out and edges are thicker from blood flow instead of a wave as seen in a 100 cm drop, (e) drop spreads and flattens but does not have sufficient force to leave the main stain and no spatter is observed, and (f) blood from the edges of the pool retract to the center resulting in a similar appearance as the initial impact drop.

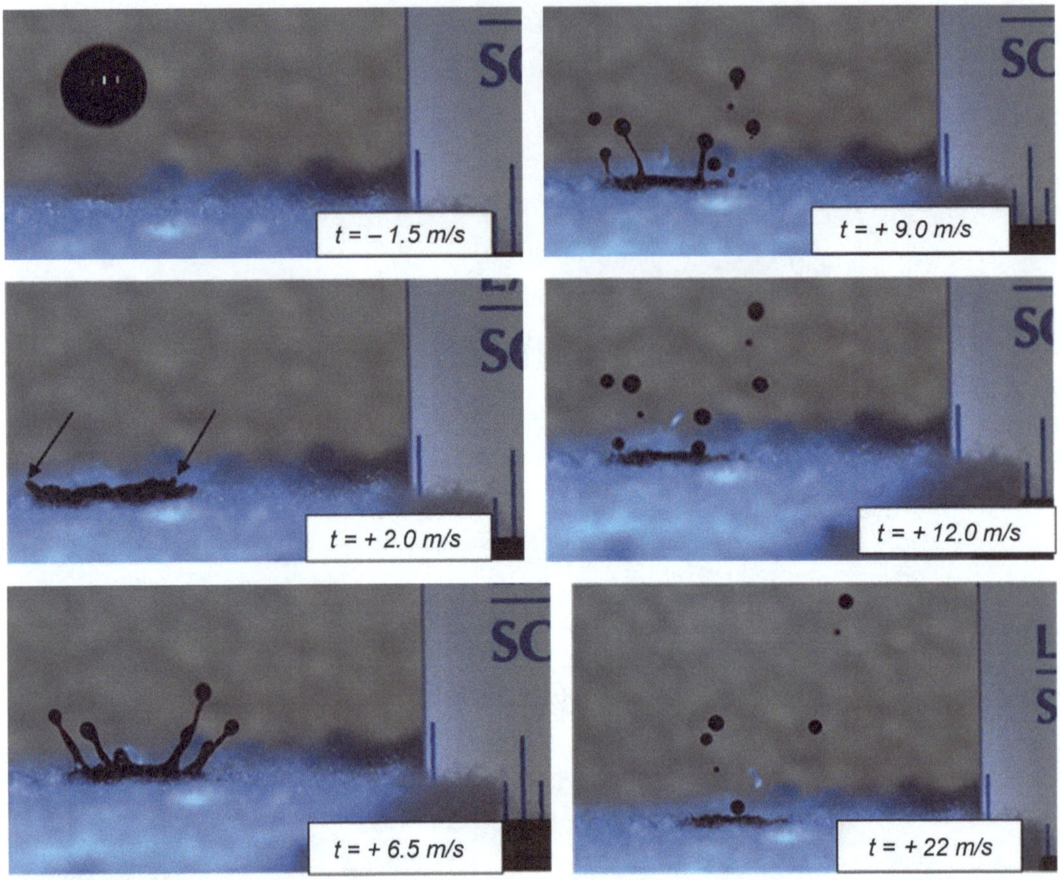

Figure 30.11 (Video 3Eb2a) (a) Blood drop falling 100 cm to fluffy sweatshirt fabric (1.5 ms before impact), (b) blood drop 2.0 ms after impact; arrows show the beginning of column formation, (c) drop disrupts, columns form, narrow, snap, and produce drops, (d) satellite drops disperse up and away from parent stain traveling in all directions, (e) after the release of drops, columns retract into the pool, and (f) some drops reach heights of about 3 cm, some drops land on the target surface while others fall back into the pool and are reabsorbed.

Frames taken from HSDV for three surfaces (Figure 30.9, 30.10 and 30.11), however, this does not begin to cover the wide variety of blood spatter across all commonly encountered surfaces. For example, some carpet surfaces absorb the blood drop with virtually no spatter and resultant stain sizes are generally much smaller compared to hard surfaces and less absorbing surfaces. Readers are encouraged to watch all the HSDV clips on target surface effects and on all other bloodletting events.[5]

IMPACT ANGLE VERSUS STAIN SHAPE

When a drop of blood strikes a surface perpendicular to its line of flight, a circular stain results. When a blood drop strikes a surface at an angle to its line of flight, an elongated stain will result. Stains impacting surfaces perpendicular were observed in the previous sections. In this section, the sequence of events in the formation of an elongated stain on an angle surface will be observed in HSDV sequences and discussed.

At one time or another, most, if not all, BPA analysts have dropped blood onto targets set at angles from 10° to 90° and measured the length and width of the resulting stains to determine

Figure 30.12 (a) Two HSDV cameras captured drops of blood falling approximately 100 cm to various surfaces. Each surface was impacted at increments from 10° to 90°. The events were filmed by one camera normal to the surface of the cardboard and by a second camera focused just above the plane of the cardboard surface and (b) resultant bloodstain from a drop of blood that fell 100 cm to a cardboard target that was set at 30°.

their impact angles. It is likely that the first-time analysts did this, most did not comprehend the complex sequence of events that occurred to form the stain. To capture this sequence of events, two HSDV cameras were used. One was filming normal to the target surface and the other camera was focused just above the plane of the target surface (Figure 30.12a). Figure 30.12b shows a bloodstain resulting from a drop of blood falling 100cm onto a target surface at 30°.

The following HSDV sequence (Figure 30.13) shows a drop of blood falling 100 cm to a 30° cardboard target. The sequence shows the drop deposition from a front view and a side view.

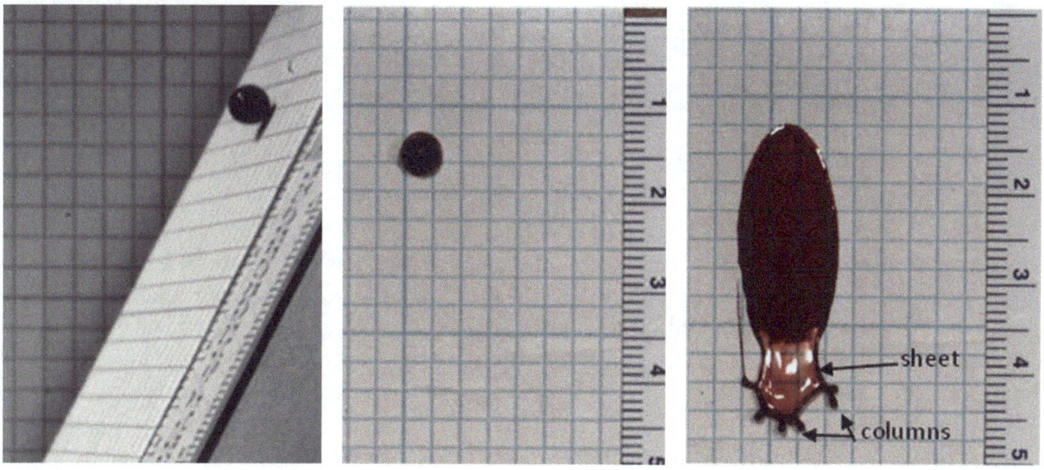

Figure 30.13 (Video 3Ac2) (a) Side view of a blood drop near impact to a 30° target, (b) front view of a blood drop near impact to a 30° target. (c) blood drop starting to spread out on the target surface (Note the tail is in the form of a sheet of blood. This sheet formation plays a fundamental role in drop formation.), (d) the sheet thins and elongates into spindles and columns, (e) blood has left the surface of the target and the sheet formation has collapsed into columns in subsequent sequences, (f) a blood spindle between the main blood deposit and tail is elongating, (g) part of the spindle has fallen to the target and drops are forming from the airborne blood tail, (h) small drops and a larger blood formation continue to travel over the target, and (i) the larger volume of blood is still airborne and is deposited beyond the view of the camera. *(Continued)*

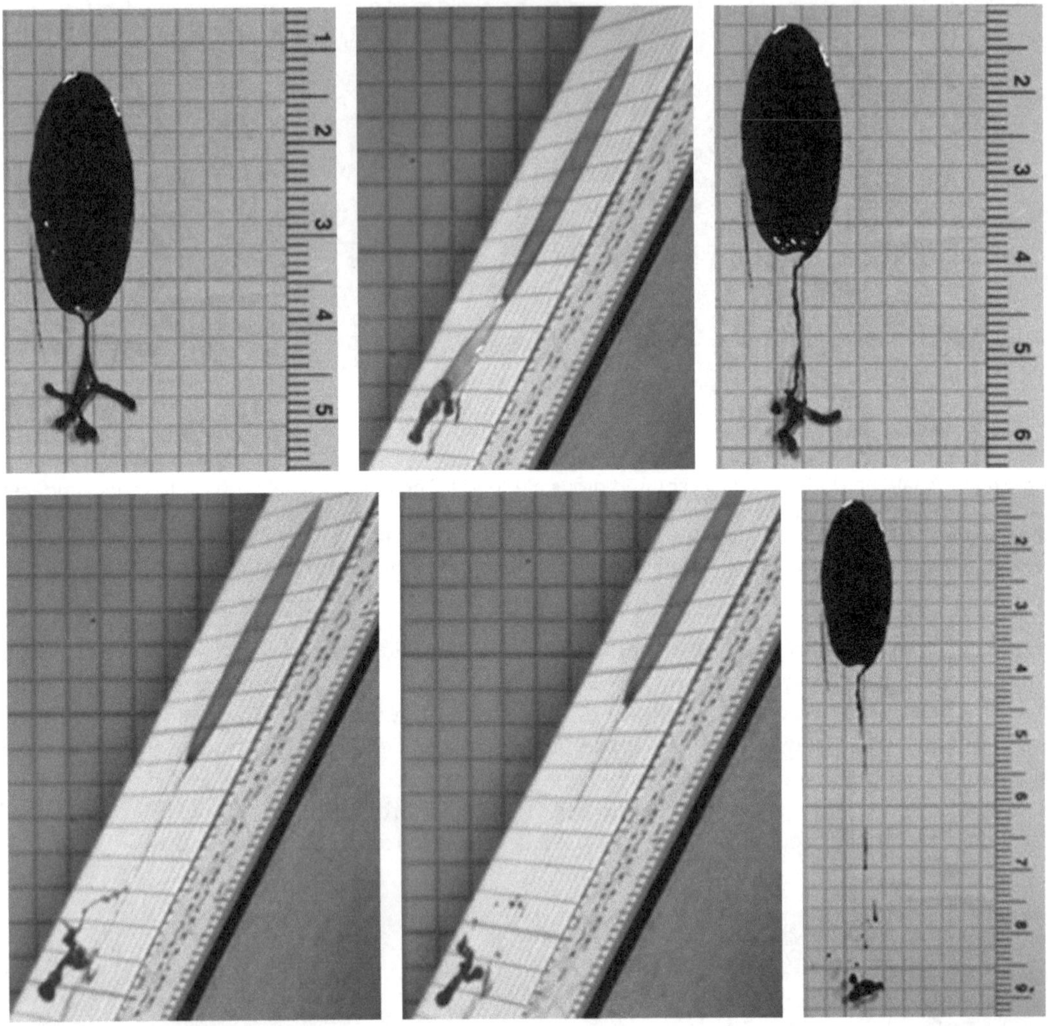

Figure 30.13 *(Continued)*

When blood impacts at acute angles on some surfaces such as the cotton t-shirt and cotton denim jeans material as shown in Figure 30.14b and c, the blood does not spread out over the surface as it did with the cardboard target Figure 30.14a. The blood may instead leave the surface of the target and form sheets and/or columns which break into drops. The drops may roll down the surface of the cloth leaving an inline stain pattern that can be traced back to the parent stain (Figure 30.15).

In the previous sections, it was demonstrated how drops form from columns and columns form from sheets of blood. The following sections will demonstrate that drop formation, whether it be from blood falling from an object, blood being impacted, expirated blood, or blood being cast-off an object, occurs by the same sequence of events. Blood forms a sheet, the sheet being the least stable thins to form an irregular lattice or forms columns directly. Columns are not stable and snap to form drops which is the most stable form. The formation of a sheet is dependent on the quantity of blood and the force applied to the blood; so sheet formation does not always occur, but it appears that all drop formations originate from columns. Sometimes, the columns appear as flows along the surface of an object.

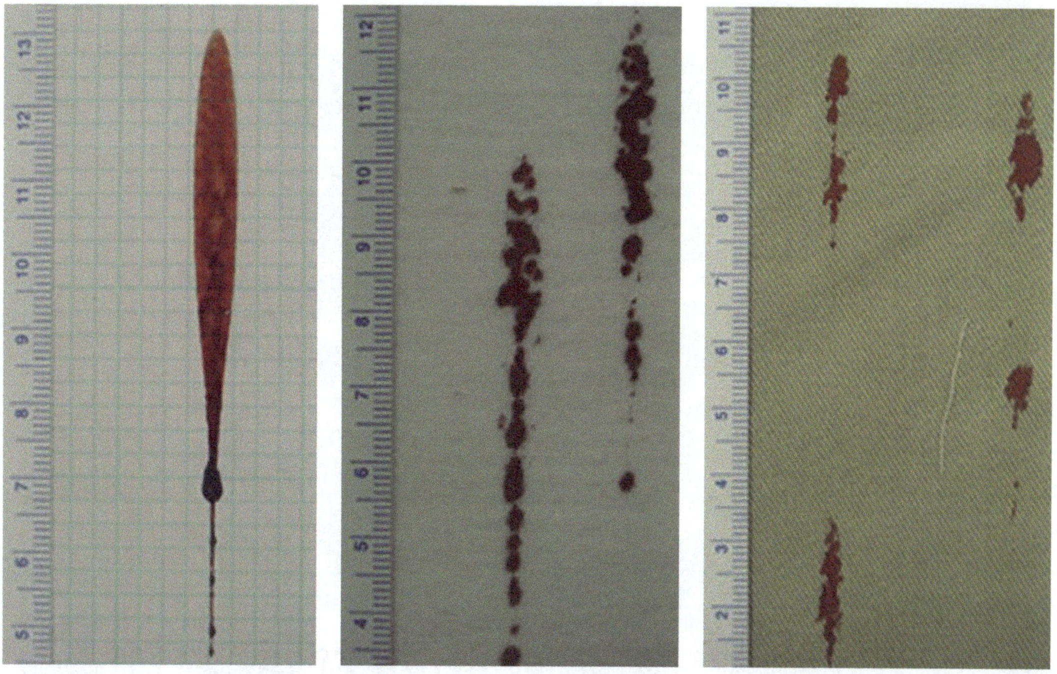

Figure 30.14 Blood drops falling 100 cm and impacting at 10° on (a) smooth cardboard, (b) cotton t-shirt material, and (c) cotton denim jeans material.

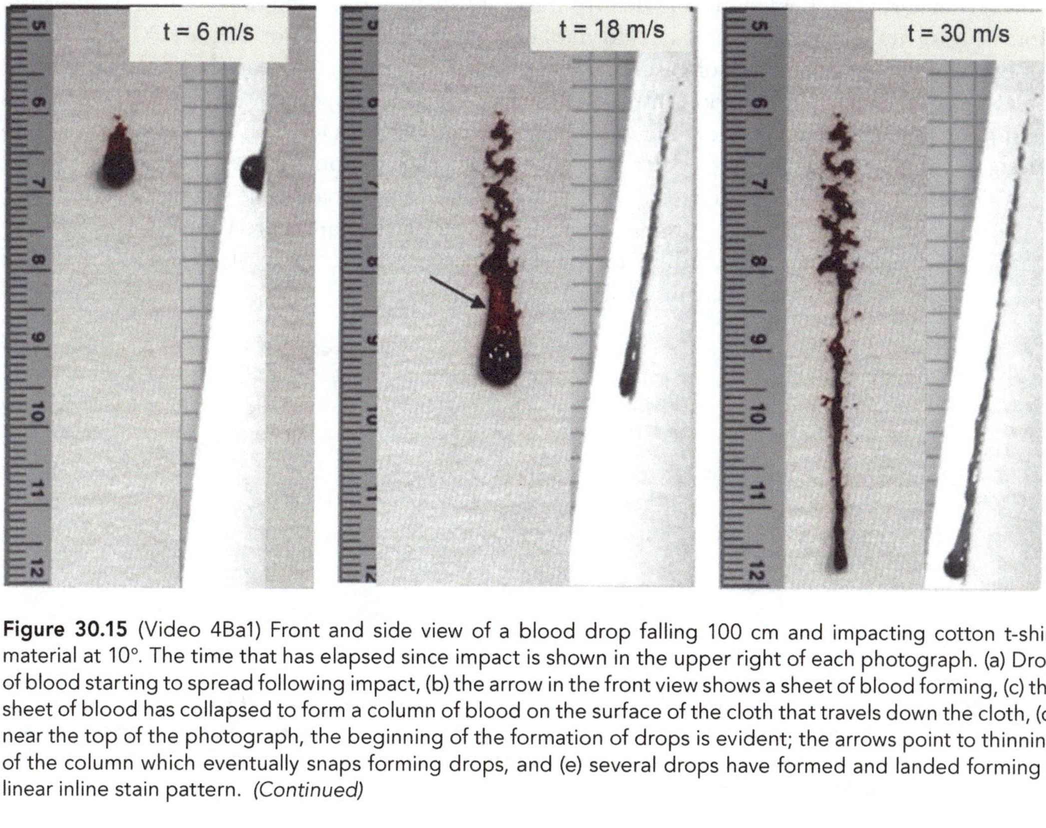

Figure 30.15 (Video 4Ba1) Front and side view of a blood drop falling 100 cm and impacting cotton t-shirt material at 10°. The time that has elapsed since impact is shown in the upper right of each photograph. (a) Drop of blood starting to spread following impact, (b) the arrow in the front view shows a sheet of blood forming, (c) the sheet of blood has collapsed to form a column of blood on the surface of the cloth that travels down the cloth, (d) near the top of the photograph, the beginning of the formation of drops is evident; the arrows point to thinning of the column which eventually snaps forming drops, and (e) several drops have formed and landed forming a linear inline stain pattern. *(Continued)*

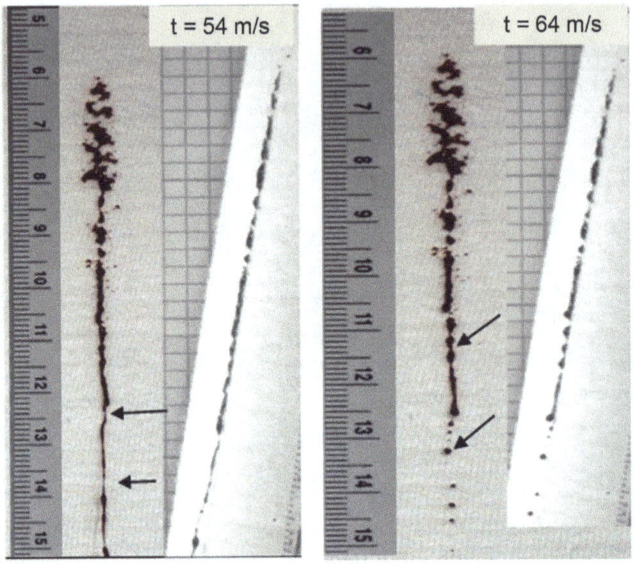

Figure 30.15 *(Continued)*

CAST-OFF BLOODSTAIN PATTERNS

A bloody object in motion, such as the swinging of a hand (Figure 30.16a) or weapon with sufficient blood and motion, results in blood being flung from or cast-off the object. If a bloody object comes to an abrupt stop, blood is released from the object all at once and the released drops travel more or less parallel to each other. This form of cast-off is called cessation (Figure 30.16b).

Observing HSDV sequences of cast-off events, cessation events, and the object that produced the events can give valuable insight into how the droplets form, how they travel, and what occurs on impact. HSDV sequences allow the study of how blood patterns form on objects when they are swung in various ways, change direction, or come to an abrupt stop. Figure 30.17 shows cast-off from a bloody hand, and cast-off and cessation from a bloody cardboard tube swung back, forward, and when it stopped abruptly Figure 30.18. The patterns on the cardboard tube clearly show the changes in direction of the bloody tube, the patterns that resulted due to cast-off, and the patterns that resulted due to cessation (Figure 30.19).

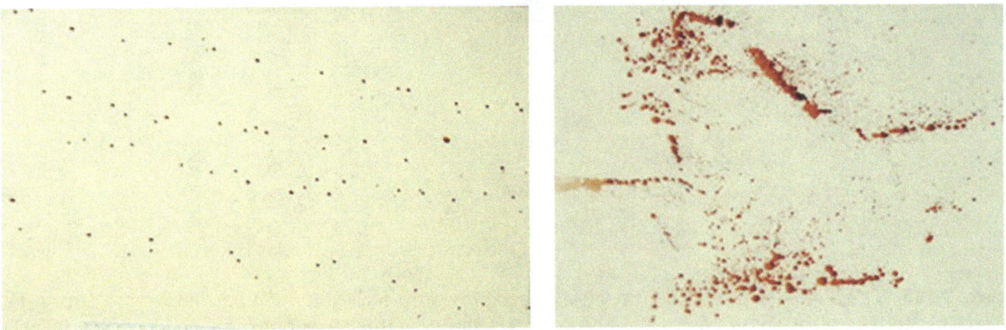

Figure 30.16 (a) Cast-off pattern produced by a bloody hand. Four distinct cast-off lines are observed. One line of cast-off was produced by each finger. The pattern was made by swinging the hand from right to left and (b) cessation pattern collected on a vertical target positioned below where a bloody cylinder struck the wall at the termination of its forward swing.

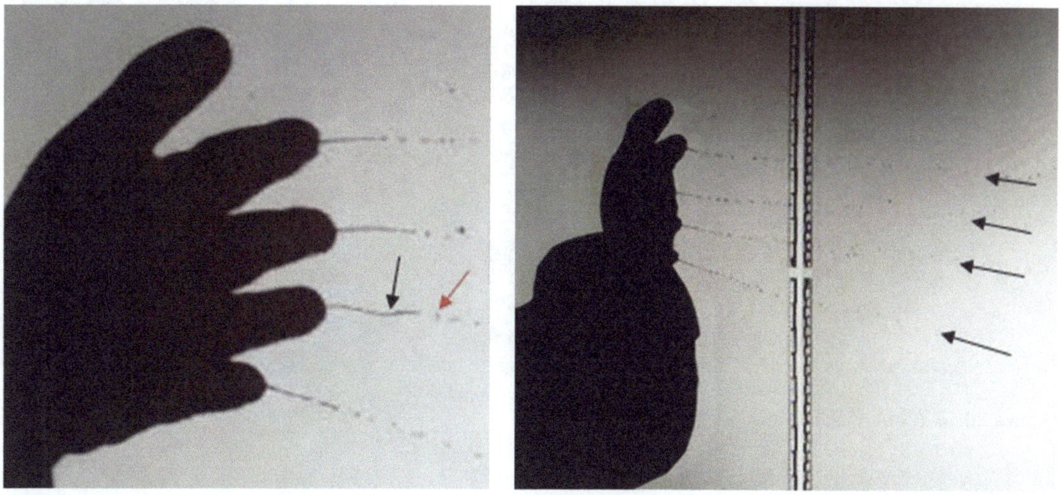

Figure 30.17 (Video 5Cj1) (a) Blood flows toward the ends of the fingers due to the movement of the hand from right to left. The blood flows off the fingers in columns that sever to form the drops, which eventually impact the wall leaving a cast-off stain pattern, (b) the four lines of cast-off remain parallel to each other as long as the hand does not rotate during the swing. If it rotates, the four cast-off lines may converge or cross each other.

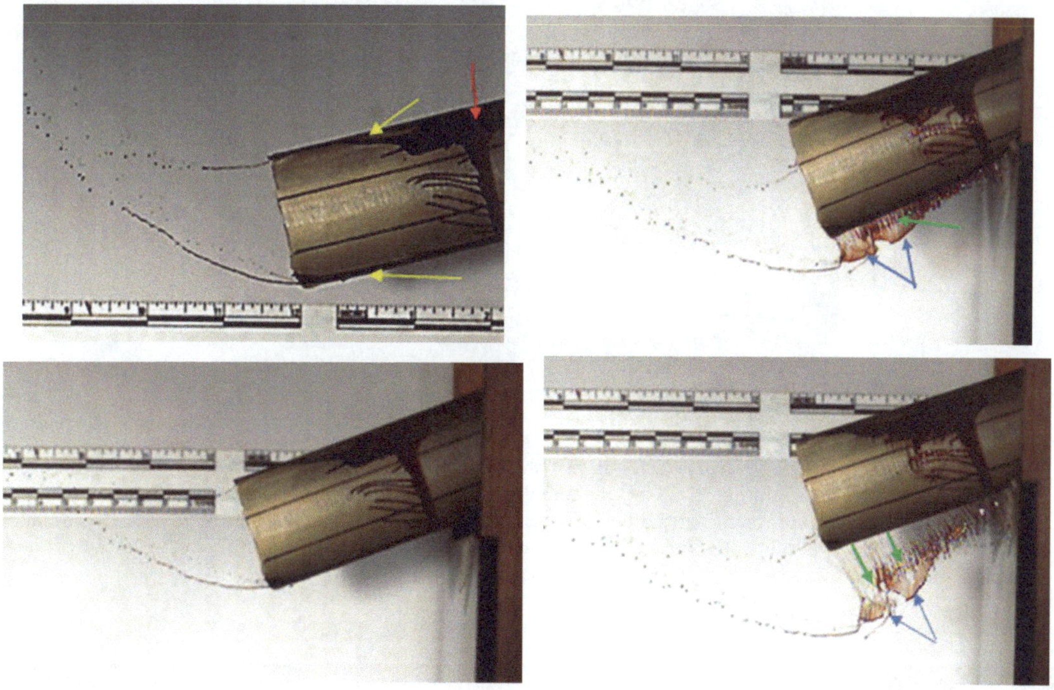

Figure 30.18 (Video 5Be1) (a) The red arrow shows the blood deposited on the tube at the start of the demonstration. The yellow arrows point to blood flows toward the end of the tube due to the forward swing of the tube. Blood flows from the tube and leaves as columns which sever to form drops, (b) two columns of blood forming drops are leaving the end of the tube, (c) the tube has impacted an object and rebounded slightly; the blue arrows point to blood sheets that formed from the bottom blood flow; the green arrows point to a line of parallel columns forming drops, (d) the green arrows point to parallel lines of cessation spatter; the blood sheets are thinning (blue arrows) and forming columns, (e) cessation spatter continues to travel in parallel lines (green arrows) toward the target; the blood sheets have formed columns which are forming drops in a random pattern, and (f) all the blood is now in the form of drops which are impacting the vertical target (yellow arrow) that is also shown in (Figure 30.16b). *(Continued)*

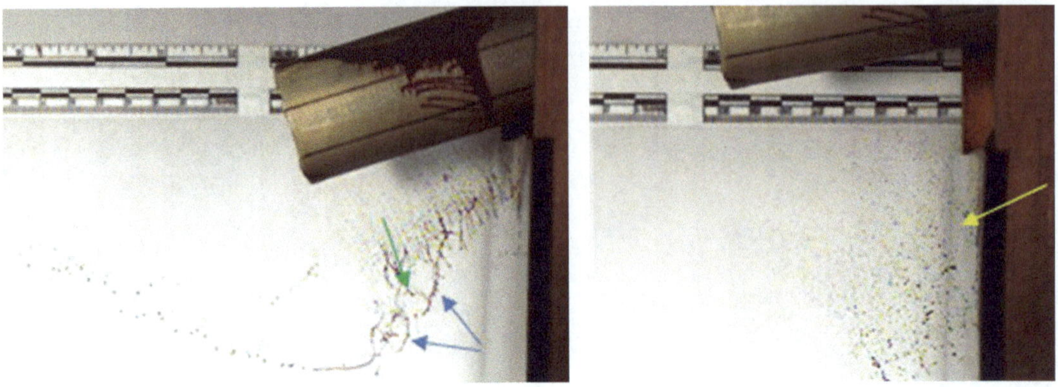

Figure 30.18 *(Continued)*

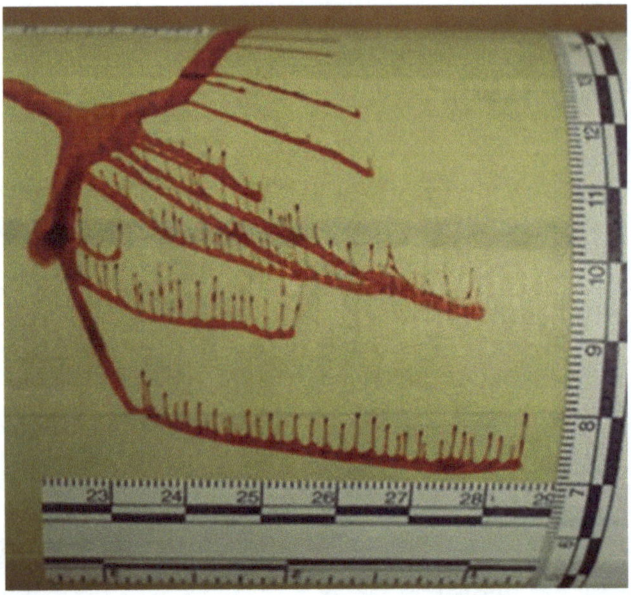

Figure 30.19 The narrow blood flows from left to right were produced during the swinging of the tube and resulted in cast-off stains when the blood left the ends of the blood flows. The spikes in the blood traveling up from the blood flows were produced at the time of impact of the tube with an object and resulted in cessation spatter. This clearly shows that the examination of objects and weapons for bloodstain patterns can produce valuable information as to how the object or weapon may have been used.

IMPACT SPATTER PATTERNS

When liquid blood receives a blow, it gets broken into small drops and dispersed in many directions. The number, size, dispersion, and shape of the resulting bloodstains will depend largely upon the amount of blood available for spatter, the force of the impact, the surface the blood is on, and the shape and nature of the object striking the blood. Because impact spatter is influenced by several different factors, the impact stain patterns produced can vary from a few spatters to many, from 6–7 mm stains to barely visible stains, and from round to elongated stains.

In general, if all other factors affecting the impact spatter are constant, increasing the force of impact increases the quantity of small diameter spatters. Care must be exercised in attempting to relate the size of the stain to the amount of force because several other factors significantly affect the stain size.[6] It is the purpose of this section to observe and describe the characteristics of impact spatter patterns and to note the possible range of patterns produced.

One component that often gets overlooked is the examination of the actual implement creating the spatter. Having an understanding of how impacting blood creates, often unique, bloodstain patterns on these implements can assist in the reconstruction of the crime. Often it is the spatter pattern or patterns on the impacting device, e.g., hair swipes, wipe/swipe patterns, blood flows, etc. on the instrument itself that can provide valuable information. Often one can determine, e.g., which side of a hammer was used, if the same instrument created multiple impacts, or if the object was wiped or washed in an attempt to clean it. In BPA, as in many other things, nothing is as simple as it seems. However, conducting experiments with multiple objects in a variety of ways gives the analyst a broader understanding of the conclusions that can be made and even more importantly their limitations. Two commonly conducted experiments producing impact spatter are blood dripping into blood and a foot stomping in blood (Figure 30.20).

It is hoped that viewing HSDV sequences of impact producing events will assist the BPA analyst in the identification of impact patterns and in recognizing patterns left on objects used to create the impact.

Spatter patterns produced by blood drops impacting liquid blood on a surface is a very common type of pattern that can be observed at crime scenes and on the clothing of suspects and victims. If the blood drops impacting the existing blood on a surface have sufficient energy to disrupt the blood pool, considerable spatter can result. If there is insufficient energy in the impacting drop(s), no spatter will be produced (Figure 30.21).

In order for blood to spatter from blood dripping into blood, the drop impacting the blood pool must fall from a height sufficient to provide enough energy to overcome surface tension of the pool. The next sequence (Figure 30.22) shows a drop falling from a height sufficient to cause spatter.

Drops impacting the surface prior to reaching equilibrium (spheres) are often observed near blood dripping into blood patterns. These drops appear as tear drop or dumbbell-shaped stains. The spatter stains surrounding blood dripping into blood have a beaded up or thick appearance not only because they have low energy but also because some of the drops are more than a single

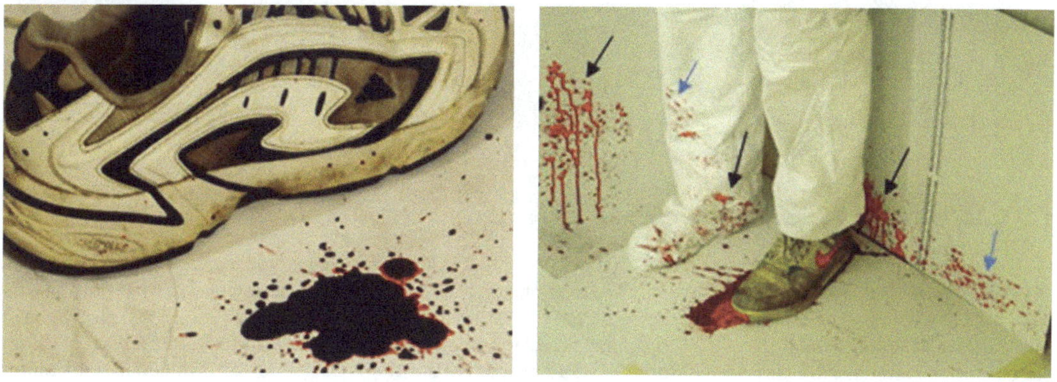

Figure 30.20 (a) Blood drops impacting a blood pool. Small spatter stains that resulted are observed on the shoe. HSDV shows the complicated sequence of events resulting in the spatter. (b) a foot stomp to a pool of blood results in spatter stains (blue arrows) and what appears to be splashed blood (black arrows). HSDV shows what occurs to cause these stain patterns.

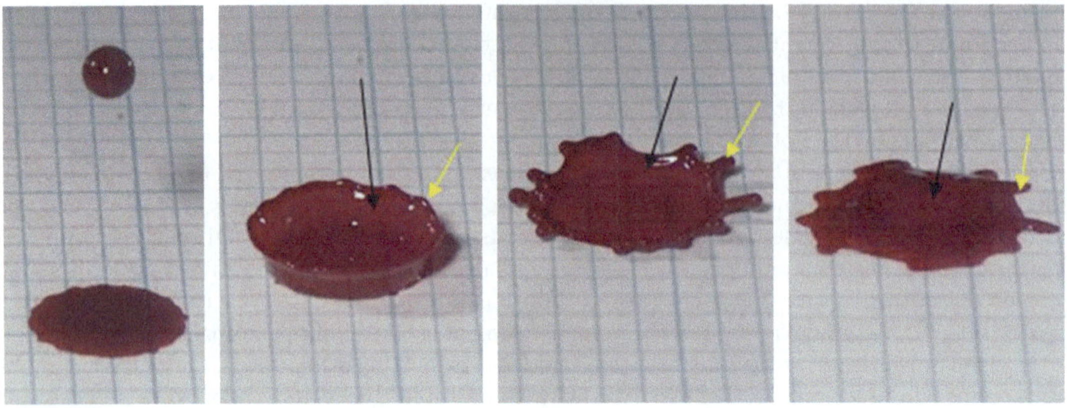

Figure 30.21 (Video 6Ab1a) (a) Drop of blood falling 25 cm to a drop of liquid blood deposited on graph paper, (b) drop impacts existing blood pool and forms a bowl like structure; the black arrow points to a blood sheet and yellow arrow to the beginning of a column formation, (c) sheet formation and columns collapse due to the lack of energy to overcome surface tension, and (d) during collapse, the columns start to retract but some fall to the surface before they completely retract back into the blood pool. This explains the shape of the resulting blood pool.

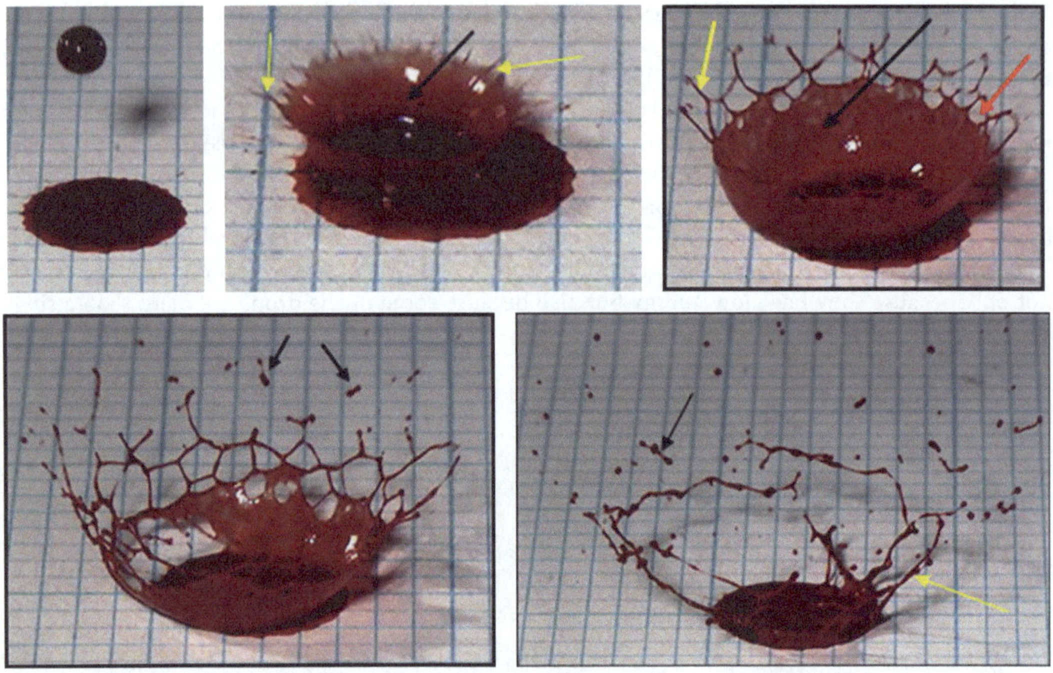

Figure 30.22 (Video 6Ad1a) (a) Drop falling 100 cm into a drop of liquid blood on graph paper, (b) after impact, a sheet of blood (black arrow) forms a bowl upward from the pool and columns of blood (yellow arrows) are seen at the top of the sheet, (c) yellow arrow indicates column formation from the blood irregular lattice (red arrow) that is formed from the blood sheet thinning and collapsing (black arrow), (d) sheet is thinning and retracting forming a larger irregular lattice; the black arrows point to blood drops that are dumbbell-shaped produced by the column snapping but not having time to form spheres, (e) blood sheet has collapsed and/or retracted to form columns and drops; yellow arrows indicate columns that will snap to form drops or be absorbed back into the pool, (f) yellow arrow shows area where columns have retracted into the pool; red arrow points to drop that has just separated from a column, and (g) red arrow points to drop just released and it is still oscillating. The connected drops (black arrow) show a piece of column that eventually will form a single drop prior to impact. *(Continued)*

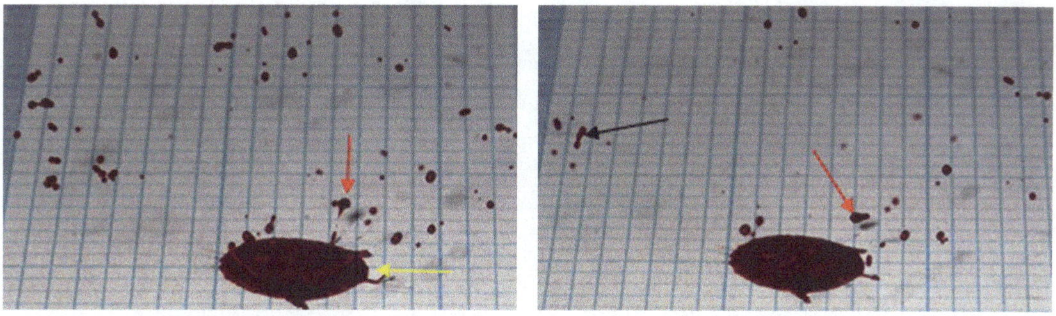

Figure 30.22 *(Continued)*

spatter drop. This is due to insufficient energy for the column to snap completely at some locations where it has thinned and/or two or more spatter drops combine before or upon impact. An example of this is shown by the black arrow in Figure 30.22g.

When objects, e.g., hammer, baseball bat, foot, etc. impact a blood pool, the result is often spatter stains and larger deposits of splashed blood. Whether all impact stains or a combination of impact stains and splash stains are produced will depend largely upon the force, the quantity of blood, and the distance from the impact site to the target surface. Upon impact to a pool of blood, the blood leaves the impact site as a sheet of blood, which thins to form an irregular lattice. The lattices separate into columns, which thin and sever to form drops of various sizes. In general, increase in force will impart more energy and columns sever in shorter pieces forming smaller drops. Splashed blood is observed around an impact site if a sheet of blood, lattices, or columns impact the target surface before forming individual drops. The following HSDV sequences of a hammer impacting blood (Figure 30.23) and a foot stomp (Figure 30.24) show the production of impact and splash stains on the target surfaces.

Most of the blood from the hammer impact broke into drops prior to impacting the target surface. Some splashed blood is observed in close proximity to the blood pool. Had the columns or sheets shown in Figure 30.23d struck a target, they would be seen as splash stains.

The filming of blood impacting cloth was found to be quite challenging. The area that could be filmed was very small and depth of field minimal. The following setup (Figure 30.25) was used to spatter blood onto various cloth surfaces (Figures 30.26, 30.27, and 30.28).

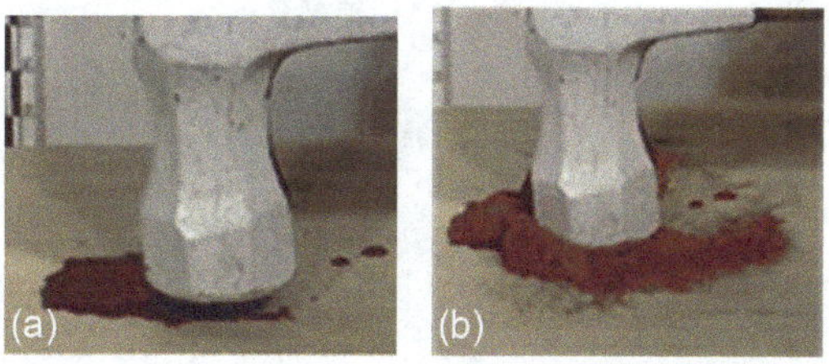

Figure 30.23 (Video 6Jb3e) (a) Hammer just prior to impacting blood pool. Note the impact will be to the right side of the pool and the hammer at a slight angle to the surface, (b) the initial impact sends a sheet of blood outward consistent with the slightly angled impact, (c) the sheet hits folds in the paper (black arrows) creating splash stains; the yellow arrow shows the sheet has now broken into columns and drops, (d) a large sheet of blood (blue arrow) rises upward from the pool to the left of the impact; a red arrow points to a column forming from the sheet, (e) the sheet begins to collapse back into the pool; almost all of the columns have severed into drops, and (f) the sheet has mostly been pulled back into the pool by the surface tension of the blood. The blue arrow points to blood from the sheet collapsing that did not make it back to the pool. *(Continued)*

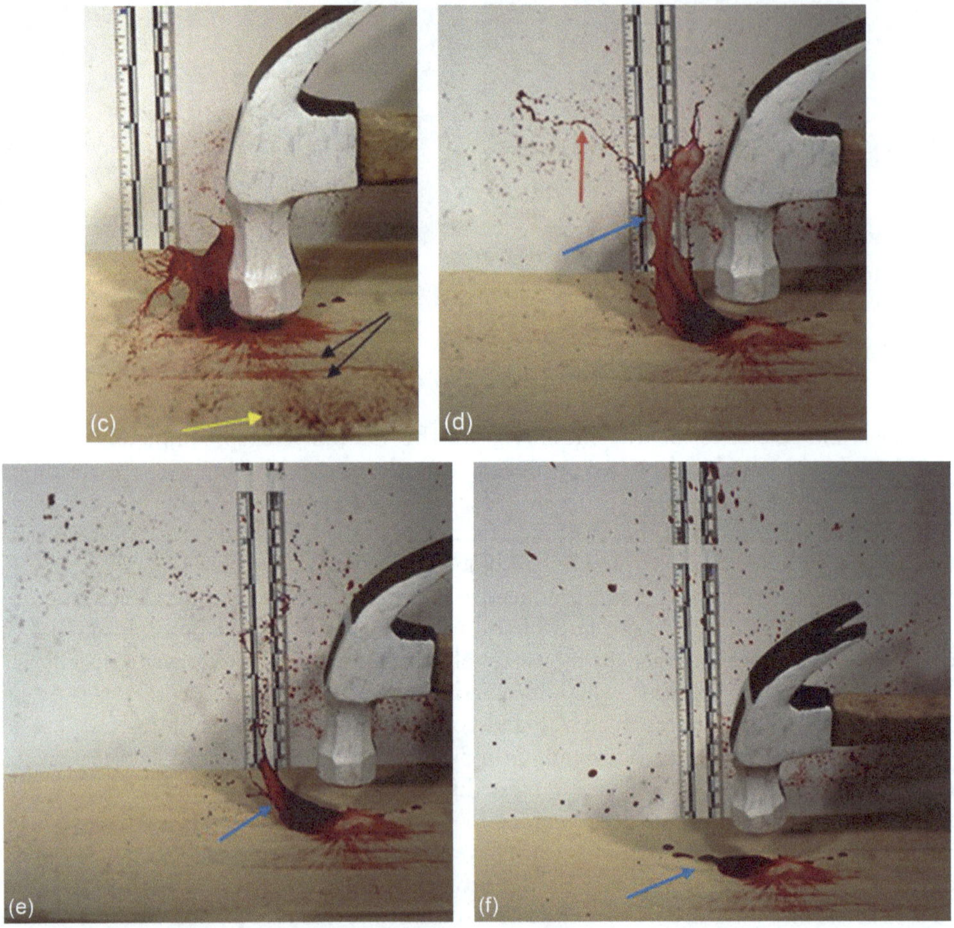

Figure 30.23 *(Continued)*

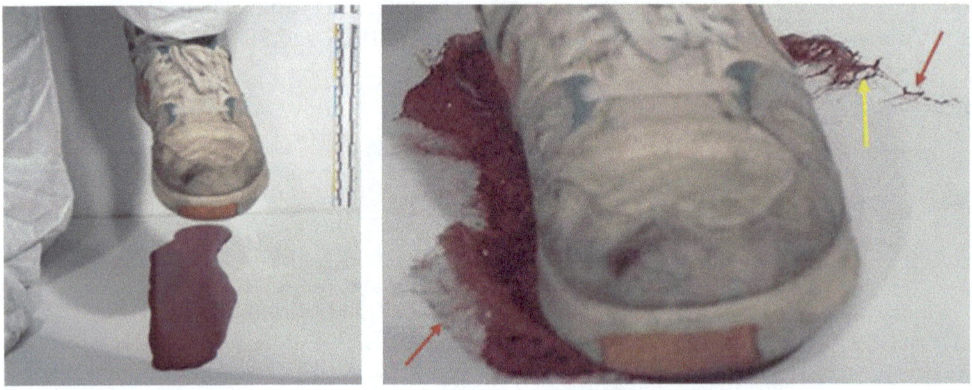

Figure 30.24 (Video 6Jb1f) (a) A forceful foot stomp to a blood pool, (b) yellow arrow points to an irregular blood lattice; red arrows show column formations, (c) yellow arrow shows blood sheet thinning to form the irregular lattice; red arrow shows a piece of lattice about to break into columns; black arrow to the left points to a column segment about to impact the target; This is what produces larger stains such as shown by the right black arrow, (d) red arrow shows an inline stain pattern that resulted from a column impacting just after severing into drops; blue arrow shows the blood sheets and columns retracting back into the blood pool, and (e) black arrows show larger blood deposits (splash stains) that resulted from columns and/or lattices impacting the target before breaking into individual drops. *(Continued)*

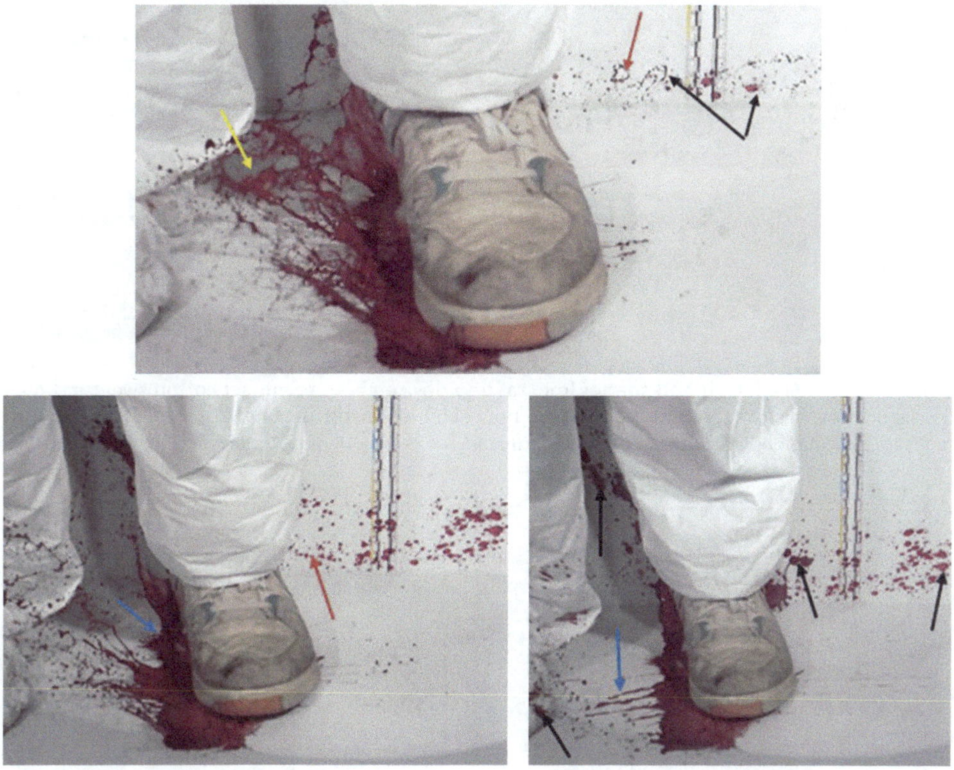

Figure 30.24 *(Continued)*

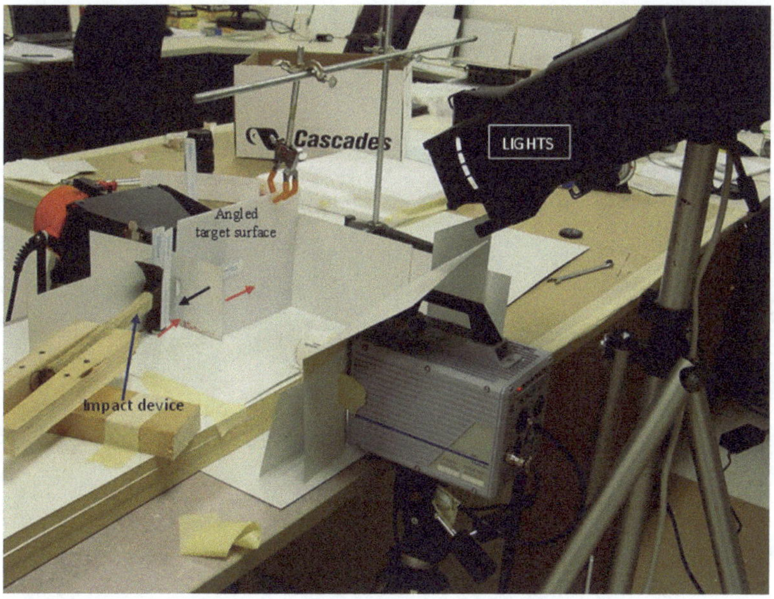

Figure 30.25 Setup for HSDV filming of blood impacting various surfaces at designated angles. A narrow slit in front of the impact site (black arrow) allowed only a small line of blood to pass onto the target as indicated by the red arrows. Moving the slit and impact device and filming a small area on the target allowed the impact angle to be controlled and the impacting spatter filmed. Several surfaces were spattered at various angles, including several types of cloth surfaces.

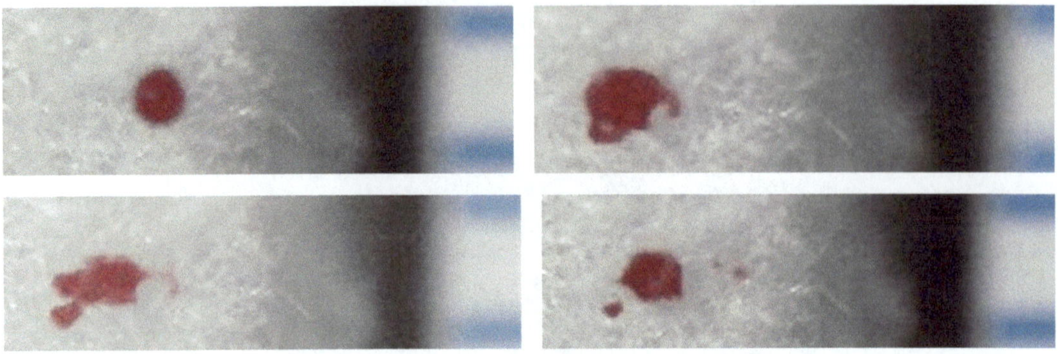

Figure 30.26 (Video 6la2f) (a) blood spatter from rat trap device about to impact cotton sweatshirt material at 30°. View is under a microscope and the distance between blue marks is 1 mm, (b) stain formation 1 ms after impact, (c) stain formation 2 ms after impact, and (d) stain formation 14 ms after impact.

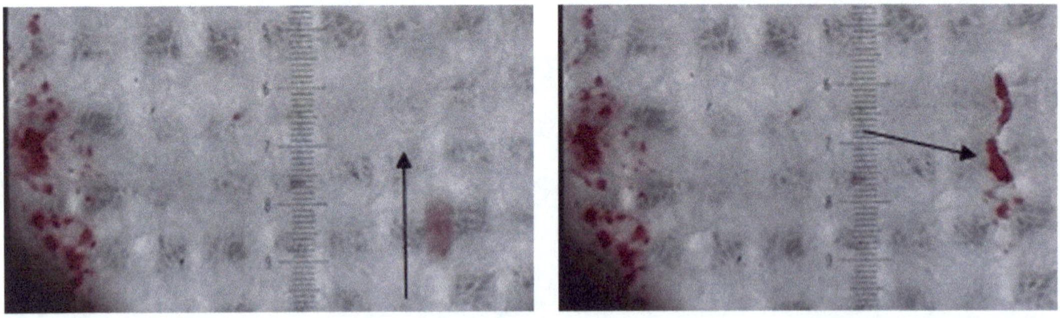

Figure 30.27 (Video 6La2a) (a) Black arrow shows direction of a spatter drop about to impact cotton cloth under a microscope at an angle of 8° and (b) spatter stain that impacted at 8° on cotton cloth.

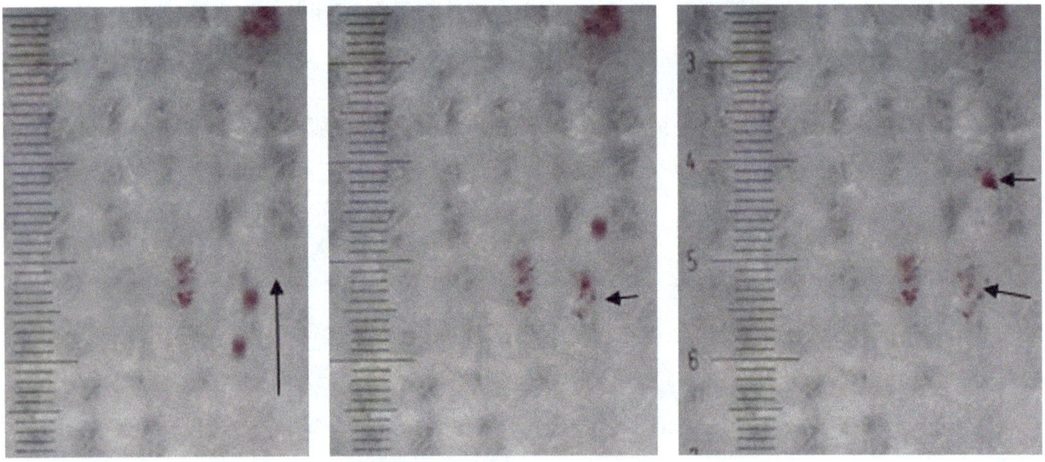

Figure 30.28 (a) Impact spatter (45°) to cotton cloth under a microscope. Scale divisions are 0.1 mm. Two spatters about to impact the cloth are just to the left of the arrow, (b) the arrow points to a spatter that has just impacted the cloth; the leading spatter drop has not impacted yet, and (c) two arrows show the two spatters that have impacted at 45°. The stain nearer the center and the stain at the top right are also 45° impacts of impact spatter.

GUNSHOT IMPACT SPATTER PATTERNS

Impact spatter patterns resulting from gunshots can be indicated by certain characteristics. The most noticeable of these is the formation of a fine "mist-like" spray of blood. This mist is produced by the high energy of the projectile breaking the blood into small drops. The resulting stains are very small (0.2 mm or less). This fine mist, because of its small mass, travels only a short distance. The size of spatter including mist produced by a gunshot overlaps many other impact spatter patterns. Therefore, great care must be taken when interpreting this type of spatter pattern. When the bullet impacts with the blood, droplets get dispersed in a cone-shape manner from the impact site. In some cases, the bloodstain pattern produced shows directionality, allowing the impact site to be determined by calculating the impact angles and projecting back to the source of origin.

When a bullet exits a body, the spatter that results is called forward spatter. The spatter that results when a bullet enters a body is called back spatter. The amount of spatter from an exit wound is usually greater than the amount of spatter from an entrance wound because blood is carried forward with the bullet as well as expelled particulates. Clothing, hair, and the amount of blood in the bullet's path will all affect the amount of spatter produced from either an exit or entrance wound.

Individuals studying gunshot spatter frequently used a setup which could produce forward and back spatter with a single projectile (Figure 30.29). This was accomplished by allowing the projectile to pass through the back target, strike a blood source and then exit the forward target. By this method, gunshot gases were blocked which greatly affected the gunshot back spatter.

In this study, to allow the gunshot gases to pass through the back target, a hole was made in the back target the size of the weapon's muzzle and the muzzle positioned flush with or through the hole (Figure 30.30). This allowed the gases to interact with the back spatter. To record the effects of the muzzle gases, a HSDV camera was set up perpendicular to the bullet trajectory and events filmed at 10,000 frames per second (Figure 30.31).

HSDV imaging of the discharge of several firearms (.44 caliber revolver, .22 caliber revolver, .50 caliber muzzle loader, and .308 caliber rifle) and the impact of bullets on a blood source were recorded (Figures 30.32, 30.33, 30.34, 30.35, and 30.36). Reflected light and shadowgraph imaging techniques were used to observe spatter, muzzle gases, and ballistic shock waves.[7] A significant interaction was observed between back spattered blood, muzzle gases, and particulate material from the firearm's discharge. Back spatter, initially traveling toward the firearm and the shooter, was observed to reverse direction under the influence of firearm muzzle gases and was blown back beyond its original source location.

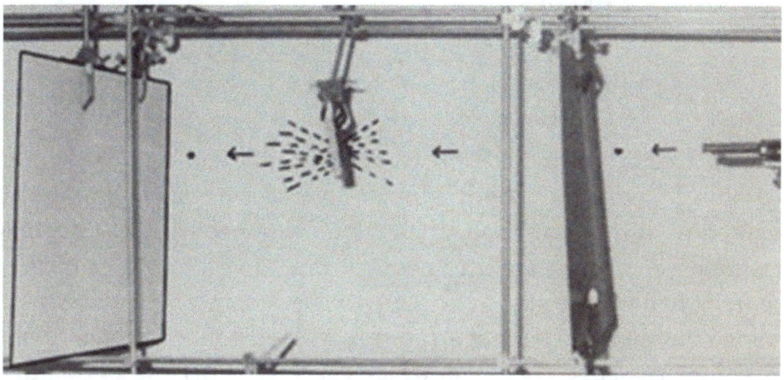

Figure 30.29 A setup that was commonly used by BPA analysts for producing forward spatter and back spatter targets. The gases were blocked by the back target greatly affecting the back spatter observed. This may have contributed to misinterpretations of back spatter evidence in case work.

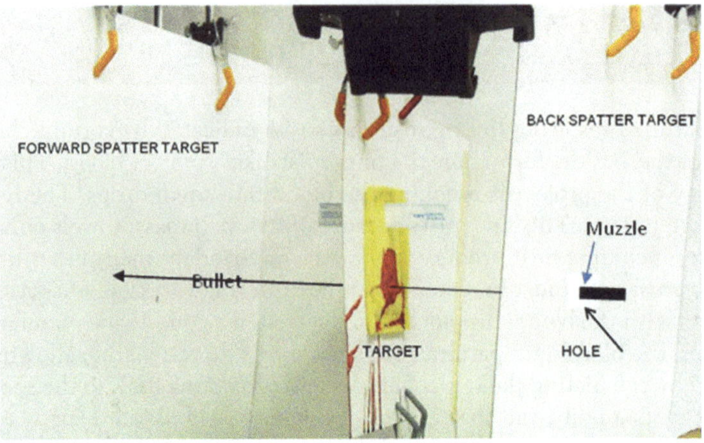

Figure 30.30 Setup used to create back and forward spatter targets with a single shot through a bloody sponge target. The muzzle of the weapon must be even with or slightly inside of a hole made in the back spatter target. If the shot is fired through the back target without a hole, the muzzle gases will be blocked. Muzzle gases can have a significant effect on the back spatter depending upon the muzzle to target distance.

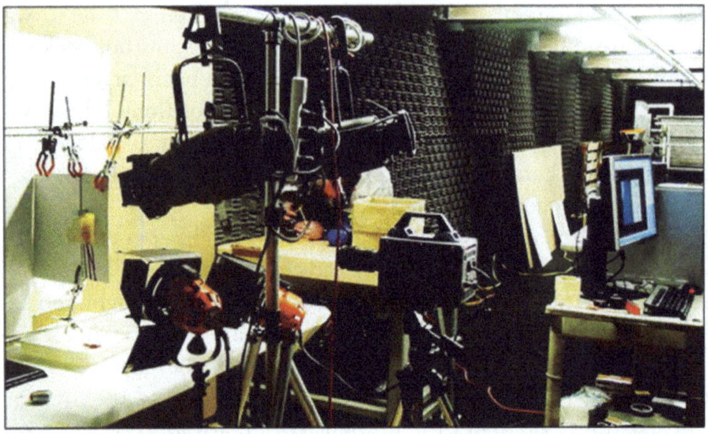

Figure 30.31 Camera and light setup for HSDV imaging of forward spatter, back spatter, and the effects of muzzle gases on the spatter. There were four light sources and the camera was set up perpendicular to the bullet trajectory. Events were filmed at 10,000 frames per second.

Figure 30.32 shows a comparison of forward spatter and back spatter produced by a .44 cal bullet impacting a bloody sponge, a bloody sponge covered with a single layer of cotton t-shirt, a bloody sponge covered with masking tape, and a bloody sponge encased in silicone. In this set of tests, the bullets were fired through an intermediate target to block the muzzle gases so that spatter could be compared without the gases affecting the back spatter.

Figure 30.32b shows forward and back spatter from a blood-soaked sponge. The two black arrows on the entrance site show the large area from which the spatter originates due to blood being compressed and squeezed out of the sponge by the bullet impact. The width of the spatter is considerably greater than the bullet hole. In Figure 30.32d–f, there is virtually no back spatter from a bullet of the same caliber impacting a bloody sponge covered with a t-shirt, masking tape, and silicone gel.

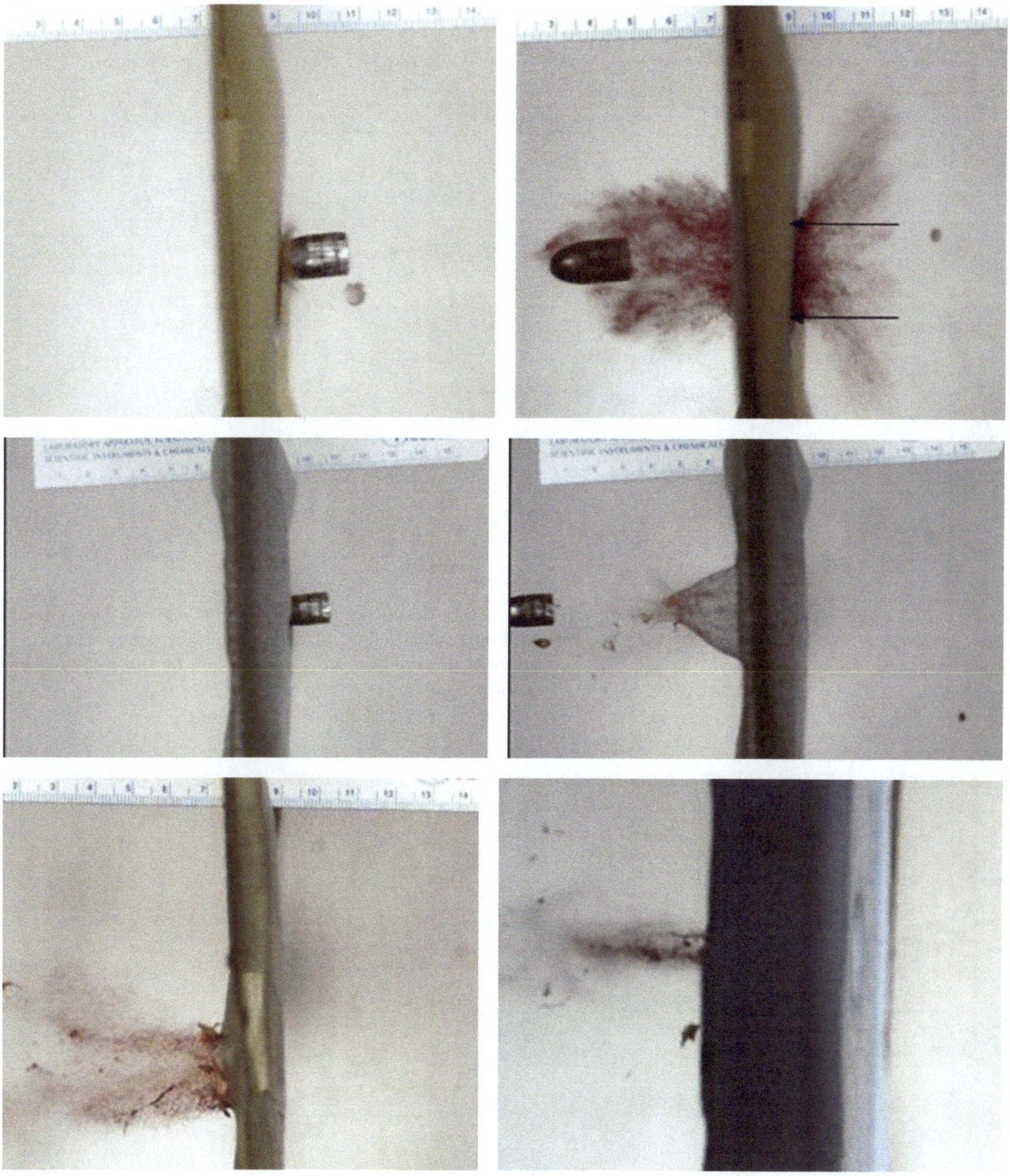

Figure 30.32 (Videos 7Ab1, 7Bb1, 7Cb3, and 7Eb1) A .44 cal bullet fired from a distance of 182 cm from the target. The bullet was fired through an intermediate target to stop muzzle gases so that spatter patterns could be compared without muzzle gas interference. (a) .44 cal bullet impacting a blood-soaked sponge, (b) forward and back spatter from .44 cal bullet impacting and exiting blood-soaked sponge, (c) .44 cal. bullet impacting a blood-soaked sponge covered with cotton t-shirt material, (d) forward and back spatter from .44 cal bullet impacting a blood-soaked sponge covered with a t-shirt, (e) forward and back spatter from .44 cal bullet impacting a blood-soaked sponge covered with masking tape, and (f) forward and back spatter from .44 cal bullet impacting a silicone encased blood-soaked sponge.

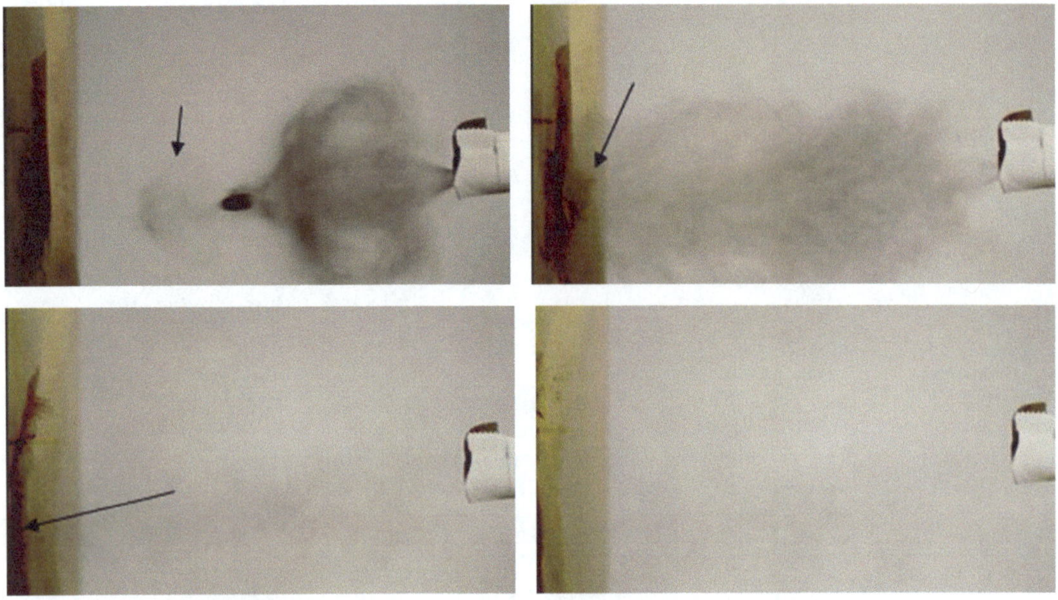

Figure 30.33 (Video 7Aa4) A .22 cal bullet impacting a blood-soaked sponge from 15 cm. (a) Arrow shows the primer gases, which are followed by the bullet and muzzle gases, (b) arrow shows back spatter starting to leave the target surface; the muzzle gas front is just short of reaching the back spatter, (c) the muzzle gases have reversed the back spatter and pushed it back to the target surface, and (d) the muzzle gases have not only reversed the back spatter but have also compressed the sponge out of view of the camera.

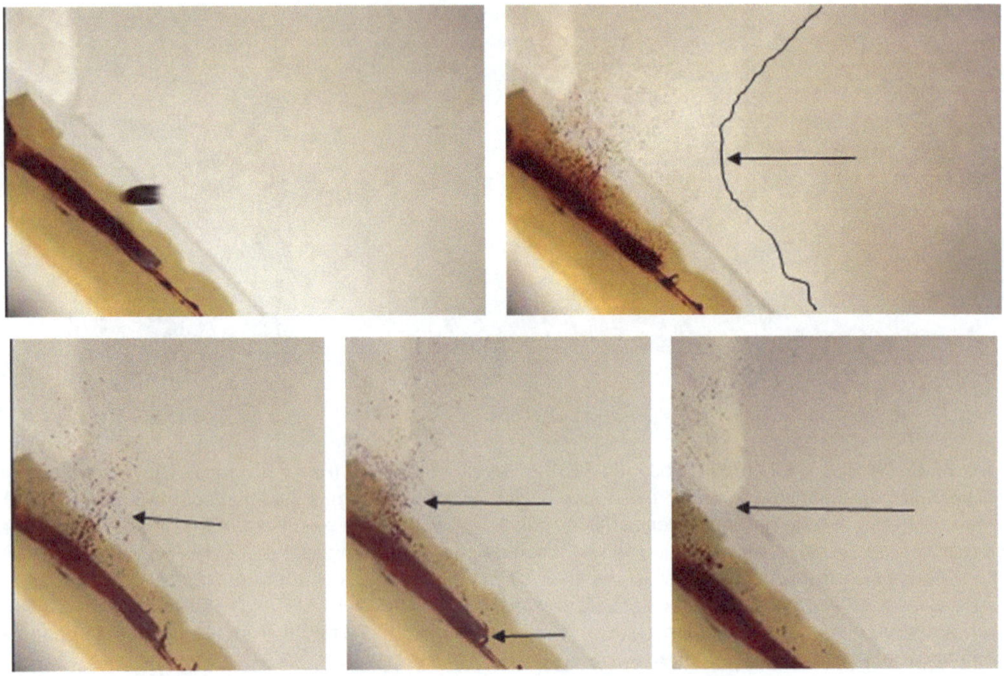

Figure 30.34 (Video 7Aa7) A .22 cal bullet impacting an angled blood-soaked sponge from 50 cm. (a) .22 cal bullet just prior to impacting a blood-soaked sponge, (b) back spatter starting to leave the target surface; the muzzle gas front (black arrow and outline) is just short of reaching the back spatter, (c) the muzzle gases have reversed some of the back spatter, (d) the muzzle gases continue to sweep the back spatter away from the shooter, and (e) most of the back spatter has been reversed away from the shooter.

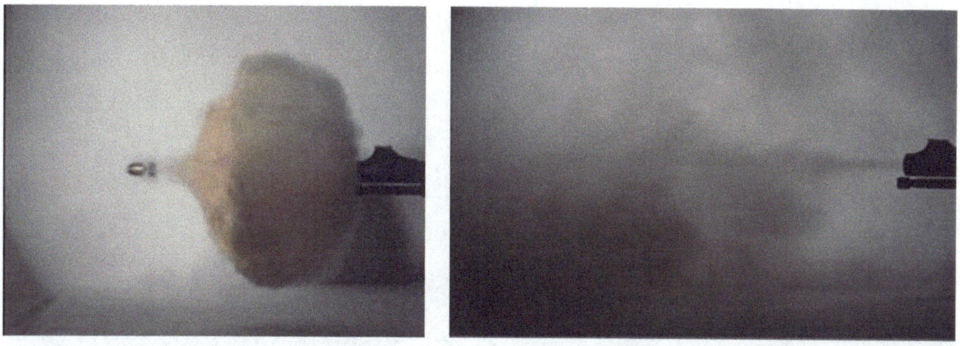

Figure 30.35 (Video 7Ge2) (a) A .50 cal CVC muzzle loader was fired. The bullet, followed by the sabot, and then the muzzle blast can be seen and (b) the muzzle gases continued to flow from the muzzle for about 14 ms, which was 5–6 times longer than all other weapons tested.

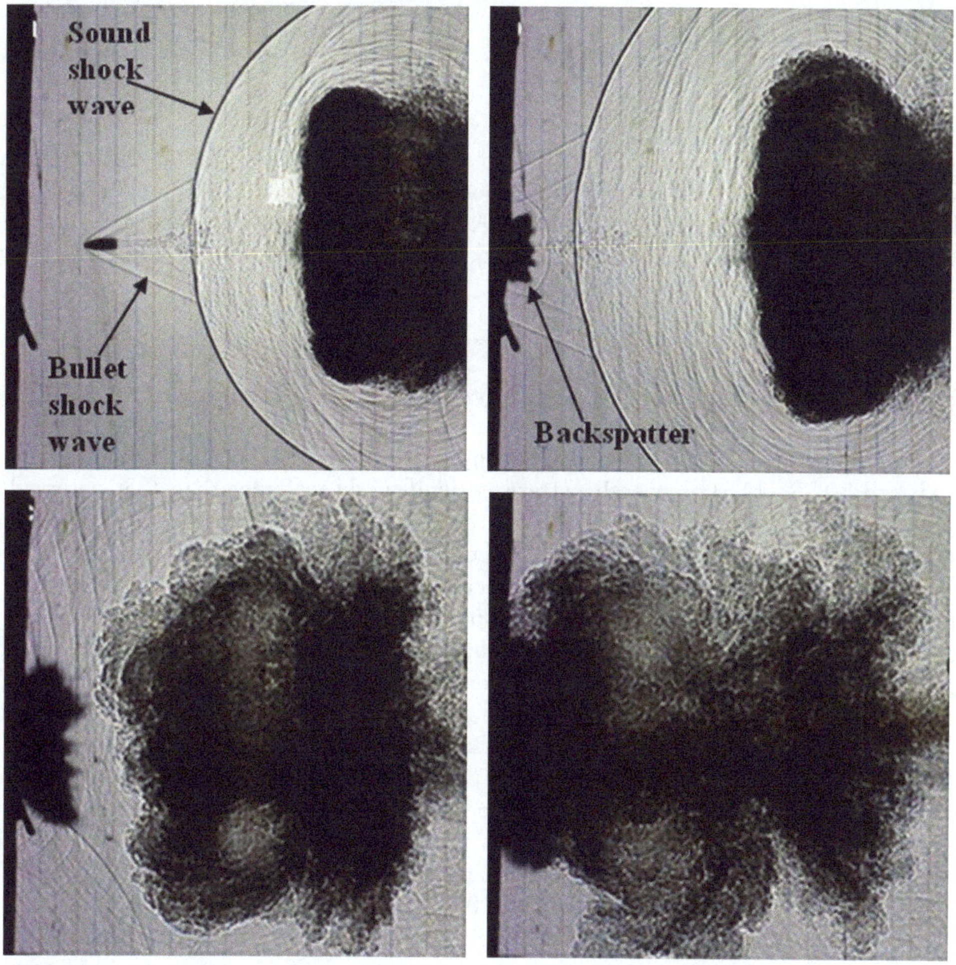

Figure 30.36 Sequence of shadowgraph images of the impact of a .308 Winchester caliber bullet striking a blood-soaked sponge (firearm to blood source distance was 45 cm with no intermediate target). (a) t = −0.2 ms; supersonic bullet and gases emerging from barrel, along with ballistic shock waves, (b) t = 0.3 ms; bullet strikes the blood source, initiating back spatter, (c) t = 0.8 ms; back spatter disperses ahead of approaching muzzle gases; shock waves appear to have no effect on the back spatter, (d) t = 1.4 ms; gases begin to interact with back spatter, (e) t = 2.2 ms; gases set up an interaction with back spattered blood droplets, and (f) t = 4.2 ms; violent backward dispersion of blood droplets occurs near the target. *(Continued)*

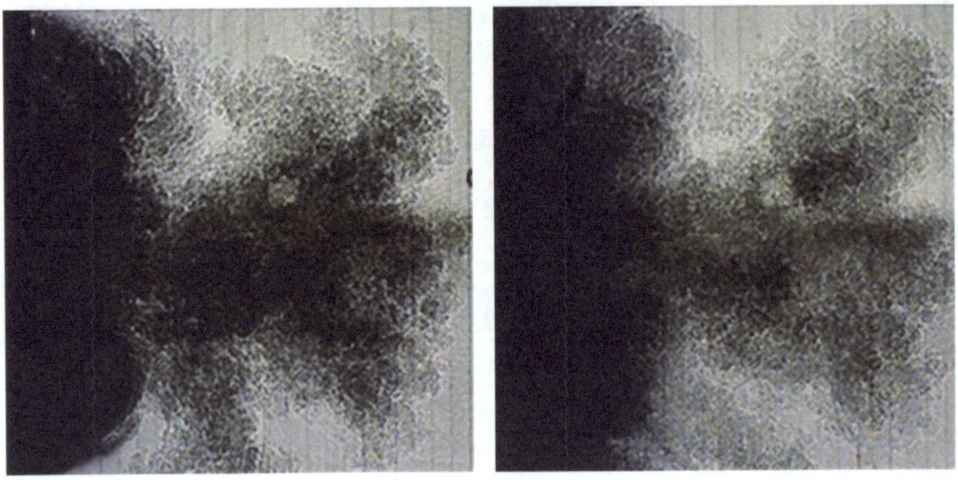

Figure 30.36 *(Continued)*

Several other bloody silicone gel targets were fired into all with similar spatter results. This tends to indicate that a blood-soaked sponge is not a good model for predicting the amount of spatter one would expect from a gunshot to an individual. A blood-soaked sponge is, however, a good model for studying the effects of muzzle gases on back spatter because of the large amount of spatter available to interact with the gases.

SPLASH PATTERNS AND PROJECTED BLOOD

When a volume of blood, 1 ml or larger, falls on a surface, a splash pattern is produced (Figures 30.37a,b and 30.38e–h). The overall pattern is significantly different than that observed from single drops of blood. The greater the distance the blood volume falls, the greater the velocity of the impact, and the more the blood volume will be separated into drops of varying sizes. At a 50 cm fall, the blood volume does not separate significantly and the resultant stain pattern has a large central "circular" stain area with many thick appearing drops surrounding the central stain. At a 175 cm fall, the blood volume separates significantly and the resultant stain pattern has some blood dripping into blood characteristics as well as many spines surrounding the central stain area.

Large volumes of blood can be projected from the body. Arterial spurting is an example of projected blood that can be encountered at a crime scene. The stain pattern resulting from projecting blood downward 175 cm to a target surface can be similar to the pattern produced by a large volume of blood falling from 175 cm because the projected blood velocity slows down over distance traveled and the falling blood velocity increases over distance fallen. In most cases, however, the projected blood has a greater number of radiating stains, which streak away from the central stain in a more dramatic fashion (Figures 30.37 and 30.38).

In this section, falling blood and projected blood impacting the target surface from various distances will be evaluated and compared. Still photographs and HSDV sequences will be employed.

Patterns produced by volumes of falling blood and projected blood can overlap due to the velocities that each have upon impact. Because the blood breaks up in flight and not all the blood can be released at exactly the same time, much of the pattern is the result of blood impacting blood. The mechanisms by which poured and projected blood patterns are produced are attempts to mimic events that can occur at crime scenes, but there is no substitute for studying these types of patterns in real crime scene situations when it is apparent how the patterns were produced.

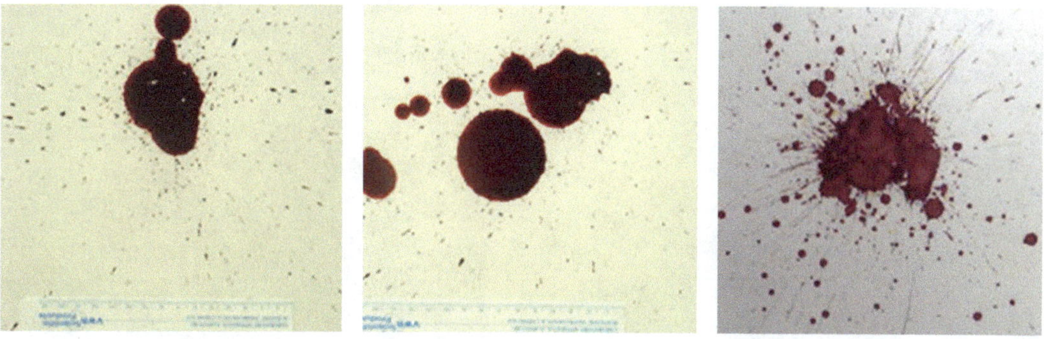

Figure 30.37 (a) 1 ml of blood poured all at once onto a cardboard target from a height of 100 cm. Some of the blood separated into drops during the fall. The spatter pattern produced resulted from large and small drops impacting the target surface and the blood pool that forms before some of the drops impact the surface, (b) 1 ml of blood poured all at once onto a cardboard target from a height of 175 cm; blood separates into more drops than from 100 cm fall, and; (c) 1 ml of blood projected with a syringe to a cardboard target from a height of 100 cm; blood has greater velocity, breaks into smaller drops, and the stain pattern has more spines than blood falling from heights of 100 cm or 175 cm.

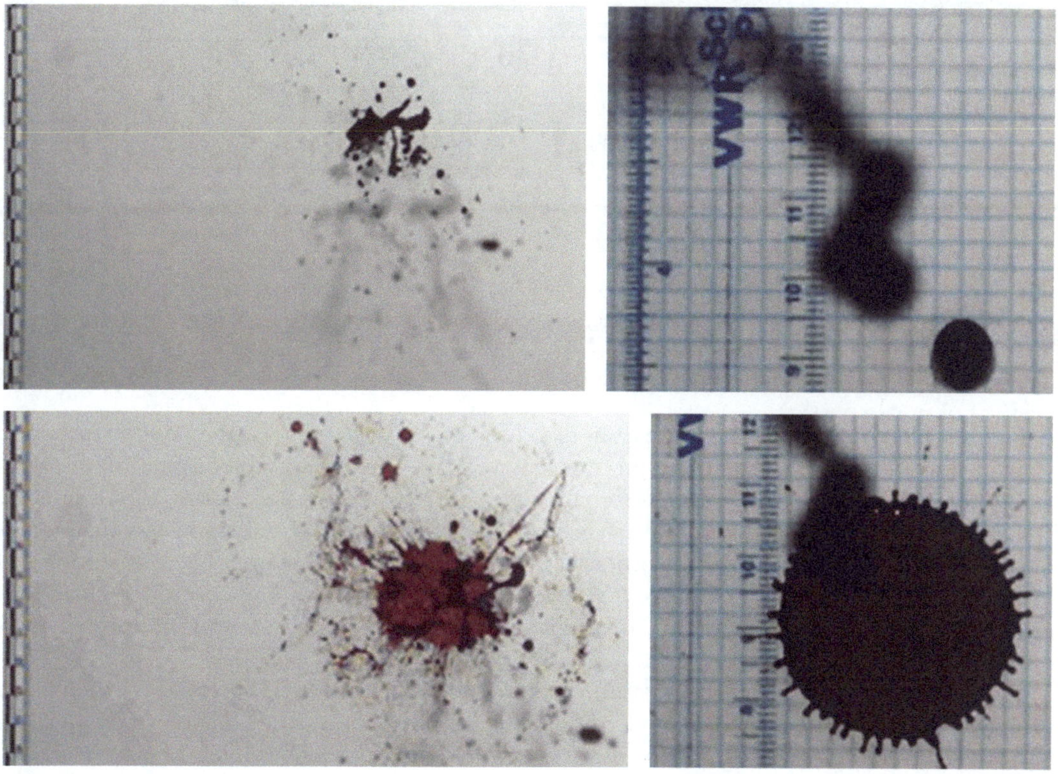

Figure 30.38 (Video 9Bb1and 8Ad1) HSDV images comparing 1 ml of blood projected with a plastic syringe (a–d) downward from a height of 100 cm to a cardboard target surface to 1 ml of blood poured from a beaker (e–h) from a height of 120 cm to graph paper adhering to cardboard. (a) Projected blood just prior to impact, (b) projected blood just after first blood impact, (c) projected blood after additional blood impacts the target surface and existing blood pool, (d) final pattern of the projected blood, (e) poured blood just prior to impact, (f) a large central stain made by a large leading drop; additional blood is shown to the upper left which has not impacted the target, (g) blood is impacting existing blood and target; sheets of blood and columns produced are similar to blood dripping into blood patterns shown in (Figure 30.22c), and (h) all blood has impacted the target or existing blood. The arrow points to an irregular lattice or arc-shaped column that resulted from blood impacting blood. This blood has not reached the target surface. *(Continued)*

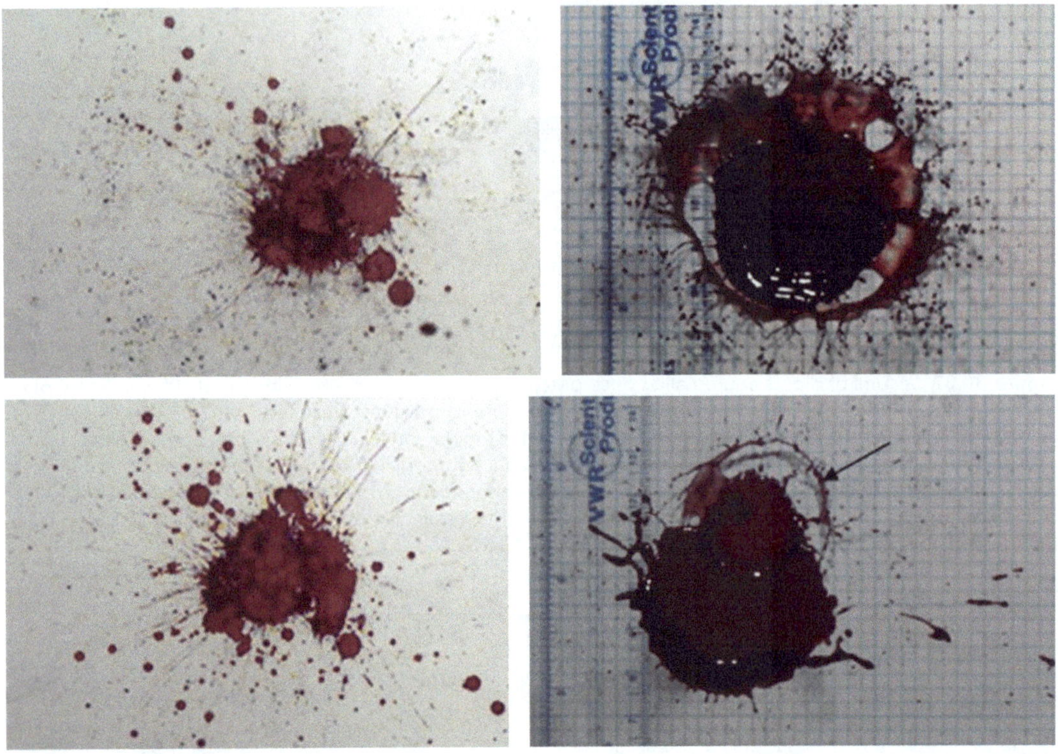

Figure 30.38 *(Continued)*

EXPIRATORY BLOODSTAIN PATTERNS

Expiratory bloodstain patterns result from blood forced by airflow out of the nose, mouth, or a wound. Some of the more common mechanisms that cause expiratory bloodstain patterns are exhalation with a bloody lip or tongue, coughing, sneezing, wounds penetrating the respiratory system, and resuscitation efforts. Expirated blood ranges from patterns of stains less than a millimeter to patterns of 1–5 mm stains to patterns of mostly 3–6 mm stains. The recognition and interpretation of expiratory bloodstain patterns require extreme caution because the small random stain patterns produced by this mechanism overlaps with and can be misinterpreted as an impact bloodstain pattern.

In searching the fluid dynamics literature, little was found related to air current effects on blood drop formation. However, air current effects on rain drops have been studied extensively. In 2007, Villermaux published research on processes that give rise to drops.[8] The effects of air currents on the distortion and fragmentation of a rain drop were included in this work. The sequence of events that occurred when a rain drop was subjected to air currents closely resembles the fragmentation and formation of small blood drops that occur when blood is placed on the lips and a gentle exhalation fragments the blood. The effect of an ascending stream of air on a falling water drop is shown in (Figure 30.39). The sequence of events from 30 ms to 60 ms are very similar to the blood drop formation by exhalation.

For expiratory stain patterns to occur, there must be a mechanism. Therefore, it is critical to view the body for blood in the nose and mouth or for wounds that may have penetrated the respiratory system. Autopsy reports should be reviewed for information.

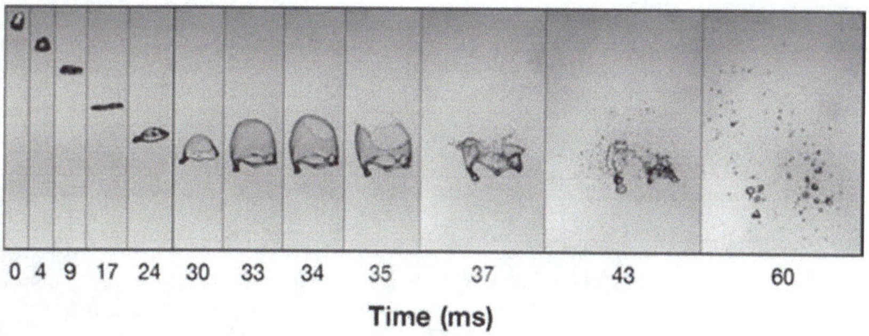

Figure 30.39 Fragmentation of a 5 mm water drop falling relative to an ascending stream of air.

The production of expiratory bloodstain patterns for the purpose of studying the stain patterns is not an easy task. Most often tests are conducted by a person having their blood drawn, putting the blood in their mouth, swishing it around, and more or less spitting it out with some force. These types of produced patterns most often consist of larger stain sizes and saliva strands. These can be observed in case work, but are not typical of what is most often observed. In case work, often the blood is expelled from a wound or projected from the lungs and not simply from the mouth. It frequently can consist of hundreds, if not thousands, of stains predominately less than 1 mm in size. It is not uncommon for these stain patterns to lack mucus strands. Air vacuoles may or may not be observed in an expiratory pattern and they can be found in non-expiratory pattern as well. Tests for the presence of amylase in a stain pattern can assist in determining if the pattern may be expirated; however, the lack of amylase in a bloodstain does not preclude it from being an expiratory bloodstain pattern. Spatter patterns from impact and expiration can have similar or overlapping characteristics (Figure 30.40). In the absence of finding mucus strands, air vacuoles and/or amylase if may not be possible to distinguish impact spatter from expiration spatter,

In this section, case examples, where it was known that the pattern resulted from expiration, will be presented and discussed. HSDV sequences will be used to visualize the production of expiration from the nose and mouth.

Figures 30.41 and 30.42 are the examples of expiratory spatter patterns that consist of small stain sizes and microscopic analysis of the stain patterns failed to reveal vacuoles or mucus strands.

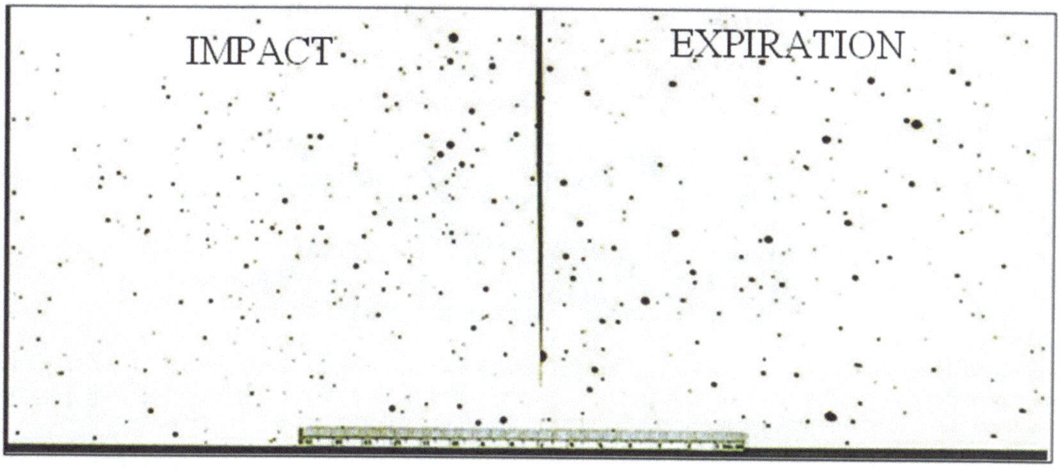

Figure 30.40 Impact spatter and expiration spatter can have similar or overlapping characteristics. In the absence of finding mucus strands, air vacuoles and/or amylase if may not be possible to distinguish impact spatter from expiration spatter.

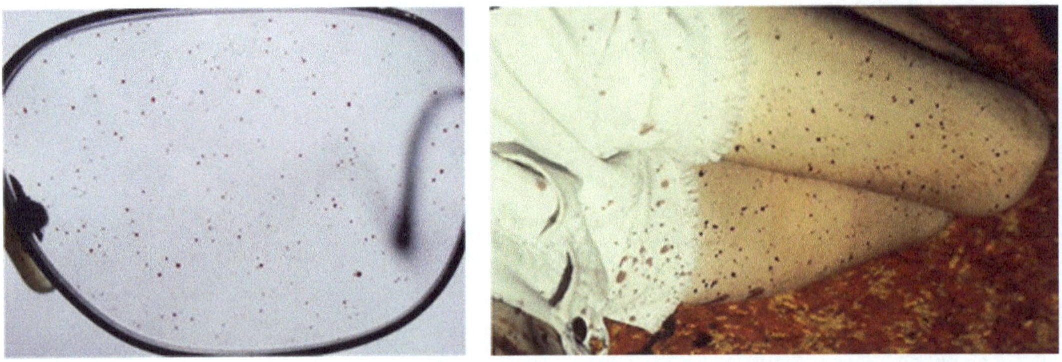

Figure 30.41 (a) A lens from a pair of glasses with an expiration pattern and (b) victim of a homicide who was drunk and asleep when he was stabbed one time in the chest which perforated his lung. The expiration pattern in the folds of his cut-offs and on his legs indicate he did not change his body position after the stab wound.

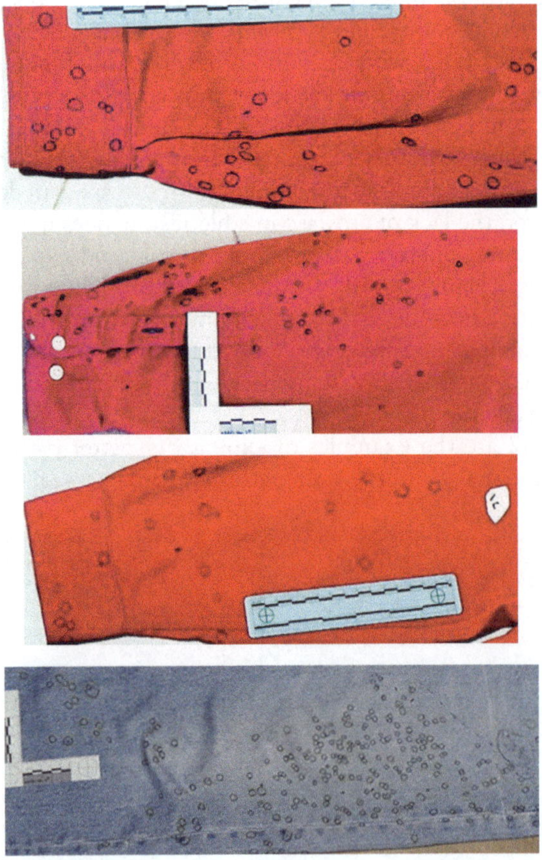

Figure 30.42 Spatter on the shirt sleeves and jeans of a suspect accused of punching a person. Forensic autopsy determined the victim was punched no more than twice and died as a result of falling and striking his head on the concrete. Suspect maintained he found the victim on the ground, started rescue efforts including chest compressions, and that was the source of the spatter. Blood spatter experts for the defense testified the spatter was consistent with expirated blood. Blood spatter experts for the prosecution testified the spatter was consistent with a punch and not expiration. The suspect was convicted. A few months after his conviction, an eye witness came forward and the suspect was cleared, released, and compensated for being wrongfully imprisoned. (a) front of left sleeve, (b) back of left sleeve, (c) front of right sleeve, and (d) left pant leg.

The patterns overlap with patterns frequently observed from impact spatter. The spatter in an expiration is the result of air being expelled and blood drops being carried by the air flow. Impact spatter results from a force dispersing the blood from an impact site. In each instance, the mechanism for the formation of the drops is basically the same. Figures 30.43 and 30.44 show HSDV images of expiration being produced, which should be compared to those presented in the impact spatter section.

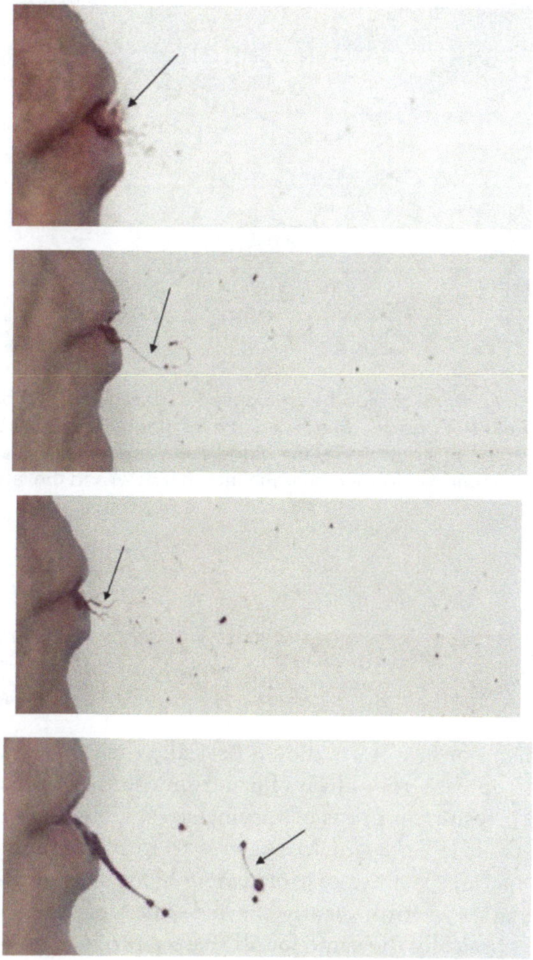

Figure 30.43 (Video 15Aa2) Expiration of blood after blood was forced into the back of the throat using a pipette. (a) A small sheet of blood in the form of a bubble (arrow) forms near the lips, then emerges as columns and drops, (b) a thin column of blood (arrow) breaks into drops and travels away from the lips, (c) two columns of blood are leaving the lips and other columns have separated into drops, and (d) near the end of the cough, the blood is more or less spit out which produces mucus strands.

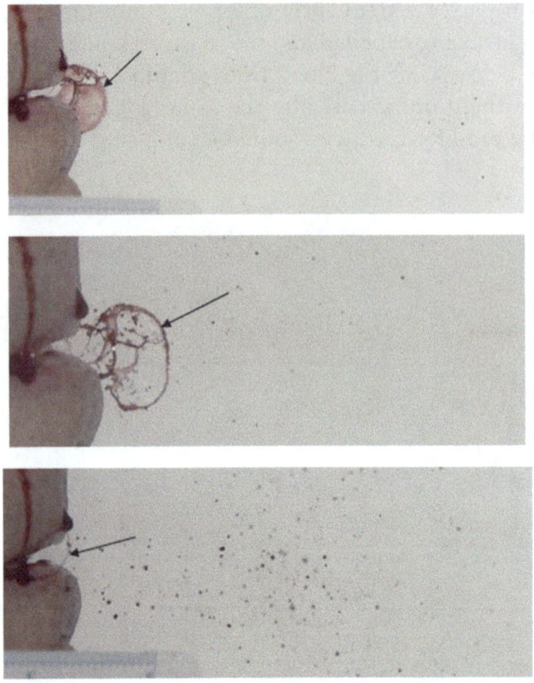

Figure 30.44 (Video 15Ac3) Two drops of blood were applied under the nose and allowed to flow down onto the lips. The expiration was the result of a gentle exhalation over bloody lips. (a) At the start of the exhalation, a sheet-like film formed in the shape of a bubble, (b) the blood sheet separates into an irregular lattice consisting of columns of blood, and (c) a column has formed near the mouth (arrow) and the lattice/columns observed in (b) have separated into drops.

CONCLUSION

In summary, the mechanism for drop formation is basically the same regardless of the action that acts upon the blood to disrupt it. Drops always form from columns of blood that narrow and snap at various locations, which results in drops of varying sizes. Columns form from sheets of blood that thin to form an irregular lattice, which separates to form columns. The sheets and lattices are not apparent in some actions such as cast-off where blood flows down an object and appears to leave as columns. Cessation cast-off clearly showed sheets of blood prior to drop formation. Because drop formation is basically the same for all spatter-producing events, there is likely to be overlap of pattern characteristics from one spatter-producing event to another. For this reason, analysts need to be cautious and conservative in identifying a pattern as having been the result of one specific action.

Notes

1. Laber, Terry L., Barton P. Epstein, and Michael C. Taylor, "High Speed Digital Video Analysis of Bloodstain Pattern Formation from Common Bloodletting Mechanisms," *IABPA News*, Vol. 24, No. 2, June 2008, pp. 4–12.
2. Laber, Terry L., Barton P. Epstein, and Michael C. Taylor, "High Speed Digital Video Analysis of Bloodstain Pattern Formation from Common Bloodletting Mechanisms," MFRC Project No. 06-S-02

3. Laber, Terry L. and Barton P. Epstein, *Experiments and Practical Exercises in Bloodstain Pattern Analysis,* Callan Publishing, Inc., St. Paul, Minnesota, 1983.
4. Laber, Terry L., "Diameter of Bloodstain as a Function of Origin, Distance Fallen and Volume of Drop," *IABPA News,* Vol. 2, No. 4, February, 1985, pp. 12–16.
5. https://alvideo.ameslab.gov/archive/bpa-videos/
6. Laber, Terry L., "Bloodspatter Classification," *IABPA News,* Vol. 2, No. 4, December 1985, pp. 44–55.
7. Taylor, Michael C., Terry L. Laber, Barton P. Epstein, Dan S. Zamzow, and David P. Baldwin, "The Effect of Firearm Gases on the Backspatter of Blood," *International Journal of Legal Medicine,* Vol. 125, No. 5, September 2011, pp.617–28. doi: 10.1007/s00414-010-0462-4. Epub 2010 May 12.
8. Villermaux, Emmanuel, "Fragmentation," *Annual Review of Fluid Mechanics,* Vol. 39, 2007, 419–46. doi: 10.1146 2007.

CHAPTER 31

HEMOSPAT BPA SOFTWARE

Andy Maloney

USING SOFTWARE FOR ANALYSIS

Over the last two decades, software has become an important part of almost every field and forensic science is no exception. In the first section of this chapter, we will look at how software fits in with the process of analyzing a bloodstain pattern, why we should use software and some of the advantages it confers, and some of the limitations of using software. In the second section, we will look at the specific example of HemoSpat bloodstain pattern analysis (BPA) software – what it is designed to do, how it works, and the different ways to use the results of an analysis.

HOW SOFTWARE FITS INTO THE PROCESS

To understand why we should use software for analysis of bloodstain patterns, we need to first look at how it fits in with the whole process of BPA – from identifying a pattern to generating data to using the results of the analysis (Figure 31.1). We will use impact patterns as an example, but this process is applicable to any other kind of pattern. At the time of writing (2021), generally only

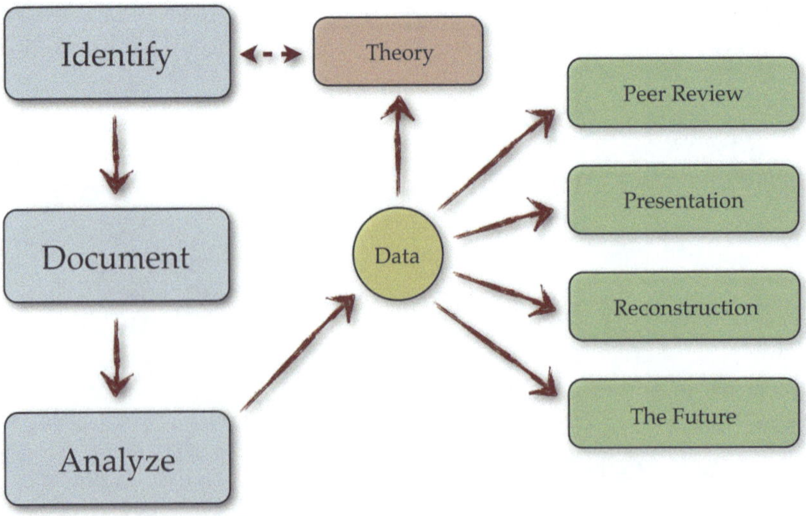

Figure 31.1 The process of generating results from an initial identification. (This image by the author is licensed under CC BY 4.0. To view a copy of this license, visit https://creativecommons.org/licenses/by/4.0/.)

DOI: 10.4324/9781003163695-31

impact patterns are analyzed mathematically, though some research has been conducted on cast-off patterns.

Identify the Pattern

The analyst sees some blood at the scene, looks at the characteristics, number of bloodstains, size, distribution, etc., and generates a theory about what kind of bloodstain pattern or patterns they are dealing with, e.g. "This is an impact pattern."

Document the Pattern

The analyst documents the bloodstains, usually by photographing them and measuring their locations in three-dimensional space so that their positions within the scene are recorded. This measurement may be carried out using anything from a simple measuring tape to a laser scanner (Chapter 33).

Analyze the Pattern

The analysis will depend on what type of bloodstain pattern is involved, so we will use an impact pattern as an example. The calculation of the area or origin may be completed in one or more ways: using physical strings (Chapter 4), crunching the numbers by hand using the mathematical formulas of the tangent method (Chapter 4), or by using software. The first two methods are essentially the same except that in one, mathematics takes the place of the physical strings, so it may be slightly less labor intensive. Both of these types of analysis must be completed on scene and create limitations on the use of the results as we will see below. Using software limits the time spent on scene as the analysis may be performed back in the lab or office.

This analysis generates data. Simply "doing the math" or using physical stringing will result in numbers which describe the area of origin in 3D space as well as a visual representation which may then be photographed in situ. Using software will result in the numbers as well as opening it up for a variety of visual representations of the analysis.

Use the Data

The results (data) feed back into the original theory about the bloodstain pattern to confirm or refute the original identification. For example, if after analysis what was thought to be an impact pattern looks more like multiple cast-off patterns, then a reevaluation from the beginning is in order.

The documentation that was performed and the method used to generate the data determines how these results may be used.

Peer review is a critical part of BPA, so one needs to consider how to peer-review each of the methods. Physical stringing of the scene (and the mathematical equivalent), for example, is difficult and time-consuming to review. This may involve bringing an analyst who did not participate in the stringing process to the scene to review the data. This may not be feasible and, if it is, it is certainly both costly and time-consuming.

Using software, however, allows the analyst to pass the entire project, including the documentation and their analysis, to another analyst to review it. This allows reviewers from anywhere in the world to peer-review another analyst's work. If the scene was well documented, using software also allows reviewers to review the analysts' stain selection and, if necessary, recommend using more (or different) stains for analysis. This is not easy to do with the other methods when the analysis is performed on scene.

The type of data also impacts how the analysis may be presented. Using a stringing method, for example, provides a nice visual of the results directly in the scene as photos, but it is limited to the photos the analyst decided to take and limited to a two-dimensional presentation. The analyst cannot pick another viewing angle to include in a report if there are no photos of it. The analysis using software, on the other hand, allows for presentation from any angle, in 2D and in 3D.

This flexibility is useful when performing a reconstruction of the scene. Typically, this process involves using software to build a 2D or 3D representation of the scene within which to place objects of interest and the results of analysis. This is easy to do when you have data from using software but quite difficult when you only have some photos from stringing.

Finally, we need to consider future analysis. It is possible that new methods may be developed to work with the data, or new formats might be required to import the data into other software. Stringing results are effectively a dead end as you cannot do much more with them. Having data results from software, however, at least opens up the possibility of conducting some other form of analysis on them.

WHY USE SOFTWARE?

The previous section covered several reasons why using software should be preferred over the older method of using stringing or mathematical methods at the scene. Generally, these revolve around flexibility of the resulting product. With stringing, the analyst is locked into a specific presentation (photos), whereas software provides the opportunity to use the results in many ways, including 2D and 3D views, integrating with a scene reconstruction, and even animations of the scene. Software methods also provide a much easier and cost-effective way to perform peer review of an analysis.

Using software can also prevent some types of error. Software is very good at doing the same thing over and over again with predictable results, for example, running numbers through a mathematical formula. After the algorithm has been implemented and tested, given a specific input it will always produce the same result. Doing these mathematical calculations by hand is tedious and error-prone. Software helps eliminate these kinds of errors.

Another benefit of using a software method is time. Using a software method is much faster than stringing. Physical stringing takes a lot of time on-scene and requires more than one person to do it effectively. This increases not only the cost of the work but also adds to the risk of contamination of the scene as well as potential additional health risks to the analysts. With software methods, documentation is performed at the scene but analysis is done in the safety and comfort of the lab or office.

Some software methods also work using resources already being used for scene documentation: a camera and a measuring device. This saves on the cost of disposables used in the stringing method and means less gear to store and carry into and out of the scene.

CONSIDERATIONS WHEN USING SOFTWARE

There are many issues to consider when using software for any kind of analysis (not just BPA). Ultimately, the analyst is the one who must stand behind their report and possibly testify to their results. So it is imperative that the analyst understands what the software is doing. This means that the software cannot be a "black box" where the user only knows the inputs and the outputs, but not what is happening inside. This implies that any software used for forensic analysis should publish or make available the algorithms and methods they are using to perform such analysis.

Knowing what the software is doing is also very important in the case that it is manipulating the inputs used for analysis. For example, using perspective correction on an image (aka orthorectification), rotating an image by anything other than a multiple of 90°, or even correcting for lens distortion adds and removes pixels from an image using some form of interpolation. If this image is subsequently used for analysis, the analyst should be able to answer these questions: "Which pixels in this image were added? Which were removed? What interpolation method was used? How does that affect your analysis? What is the error rate of this type of manipulation?" These are not easy questions to answer, so these types of manipulations are best avoided if possible. (For an overview of image interpolation techniques, see Fadnavis 2014.)

Software should simply be a tool to aid an analyst in their work, not replace their judgment. Any software used in forensic analysis should be scrutinized to determine what control is being taken away from the user. If it forces the user down one path, that path must be understood and accepted by the analyst and it should be thoroughly researched and vetted though a peer-review process.

Another consideration is access to, and use of, the resulting data. As outlined in the section above, there are many potential uses for the results. If the software, however, does not permit access to the results in common file formats, the user will be locked-in and reliant on a specific software package. The results of an analysis belong to the analyst and they should be able to use them however they like.

LIMITATIONS OF SOFTWARE

Software, like techniques used in any other analysis, has limitations. The notion that software is mathematical and therefore unbiased or infallible is flat-out incorrect. Take neural networks used in image analysis, for example. They work by training a computer model based on (hopefully) thousands of input images. Their effectiveness is completely dependent on the inputs, so if the image data used to train them is faulty, biased, or incomplete, the results will be as well. They are trained to recognize specific features and cannot handle exceptions – even things a human can see as blatantly obvious. This is problematic not only because of the potentially biased results, but because there is no way to "ask" the neural network how it came to a specific conclusion so as to assign some kind of weight to its result. If these kinds of tools are used, they should be used to augment the analyst's decision-making, not replace it. This is why it is critical that an analyst understands what their software is doing and not treat it as a "black box". (For an introduction to algorithms, artificial intelligence, and bias, see Osoba and Welser, 2017.)

All software has bugs. Software is designed and written by humans, so it is prone to flaws just like any other human endeavor. This can be a problem if the software tools being used for analysis have bugs that prevent the user from completing their analysis. By using software, users are putting themselves in a position where they are dependent on the software vendor to fix any problems within a reasonable amount of time.

Another drawback to using software is that the resulting data are often in a proprietary file format (meaning the specification of the file format is not publicly available and freely usable by anyone). In the short term, this might be fine because the software that produced the file can read it back. If, however, the data is required months or years later, it is possible that the software no longer works or no longer exists, in which case the data is useless. This problem can mostly be overcome by avoiding proprietary file formats in favor of open file formats. In an open file format, the specification is publicly available, so any software can implement reading and writing that type of file. These formats are also very useful for flexibility – the analyst can choose what software they want to use instead of being locked-in to a specific vendor.

HEMOSPAT

HemoSpat[1] is a software application designed to determine the area of origin of impact patterns as a 3D location in space. It was preceded by two other software tools: BackTrack (made up of BackTrack/Images and BackTrack/Win) by Forensic Computing of Ottawa, and No More Strings by Millar Forensic Software (Chapter 1). All three rely on the same methods of documentation and analysis of individual stains using the tangent method; however, No More Strings used a different method of pattern-level calculation.[2]

HemoSpat added several capabilities not found in these older tools, including being able to add and analyze patterns on multiple planar surfaces in any orientation, the ability to export data to multiple formats, providing multiple methods for viewing data and reporting on it, allowing the use of "one-sided" patterns,[3] and an intuitive user interface designed for analysts. Since HemoSpat's original implementation in 2005, the ability to analyze cast-off patterns has also been added in an experimental capacity.[4]

While developing HemoSpat, the focus was on usability, data freedom, and open science. Usability of software is important not only in making it easier for analysts to do their work but also to help prevent errors. Users should not have to relearn how to use software every time they use it and if it is too complicated, it leaves more room to make errors. It was also important to not lock the user into using HemoSpat after completing their analysis because the data that is generated belongs to the analyst. This meant keeping the data in a human-readable form – Extensible Markup Language (XML) which is an open, structured text format – and allowing the user to export their data to several common file formats for use in other software. Finally, the analysis itself had to be open and transparent – the algorithms/methods were published and made available, so analysts know what the software is doing. This is a critical aspect of using any software for analysis (as outlined in the first part of this chapter) because the analyst is the one who must stand behind the analysis in their report and possibly testify to the results in court.

The following discussion is based on HemoSpat version 2.0 which was released in 2024. Writing about specific software versions is generally difficult because user interfaces tend to change a lot, so a higher-level description of some of the concepts is included for illustration purposes.

DOCUMENTATION

Documentation of an impact or a cast-off pattern for HemoSpat only requires a digital camera, a measuring device, and a way to record stain location information (pen and paper, spreadsheet, etc.). First the surfaces to be used for analysis are identified and documented. Any planar surface may be used for analysis. These are typically the target surfaces that have the bloodstains deposited on them, but other surfaces may be included for reference. Once the pattern is identified, groups of stains are chosen based on their location within the pattern (Figure 31.2). Each of these groups of stains is photographed separately (Figure 31.3); these are known as *reference images*. Within these, one stain is chosen to be the *reference stain*. This reference stain is documented by adding a scale, a line to indicate the vertical called a *plumb line* (used to adjust for camera rotation), and a label to uniquely identify the bloodstain.

Measurement of surface and stain locations may be done using any kind of measuring device, from a simple tape measure to a laser distance measurer. First the analyst needs to establish a global 3D coordinate system by designating a *room origin*, where (x, y, z) is $(0, 0, 0)$, and an *orientation* – which direction is x, which is y, and which is z. This is used as an anchor point for all measurements in the room. The analyst then records the room's length, width, and height. These are used to make the floor, ceiling, and four walls of the room when creating the project in HemoSpat. Next, the analyst determines which other surfaces are required for analysis – this includes surfaces with bloodstains on them and any surfaces useful for visual orientation of the scene. The location of each of these target surfaces is recorded by measuring the (x, y, z) location of each of the corners of the surface. Finally, the location of each reference stain is determined by measuring the 2D location from the bottom-left corner of the target surface to the leading edge of the bloodstain.

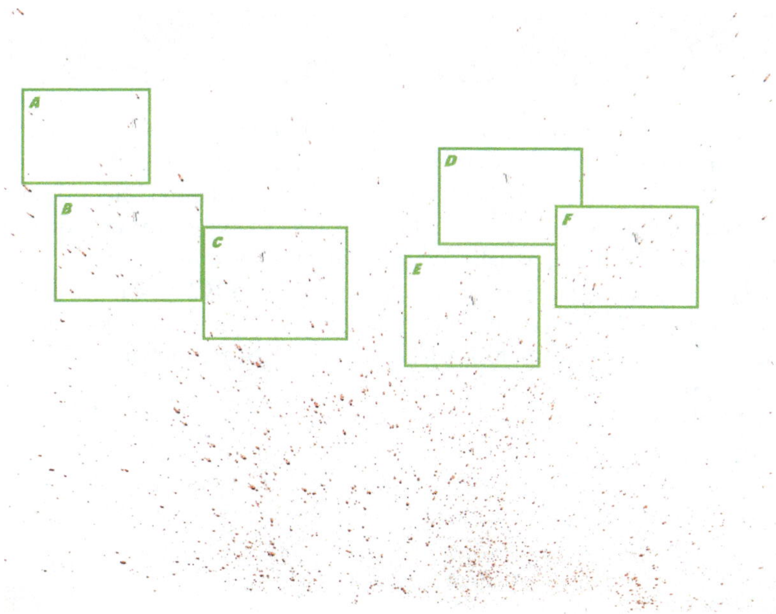

Figure 31.2 An overall photo of an impact pattern with groups highlighted. Separate photos are taken of each of these groups. (Image courtesy of Gord Lefebvre, Ontario Provincial Police, Retired.)

This establishes the location of the stain on the surface, which HemoSpat uses to calculate the 3D location of the stain in the room.

Note that all photos used in an analysis must be taken with the camera's focal plane parallel to the target surface. While HemoSpat adjusts for camera rotation using the plumb line, it does not alter the image by adjusting for any tilting of the camera (see the discussion of perspective correction in the section "Considerations When Using Software").

Figure 31.3 A photo showing a group of bloodstains with a reference stain marked with a scale. (Image courtesy of Gord Lefebvre, Ontario Provincial Police, Retired.)

ANALYSIS

The high-level process of analysis is as follows: the analyst creates a new HemoSpat project for the scene, creates any required surfaces, imports the reference photos, and analyzes the reference stain and any other stains in the photo they wish to use. From this input, HemoSpat calculates and outputs the area of origin of the pattern, and allows the user to export the data or generate reports.

Surfaces may be entered either manually by specifying the locations of the four corners of a surface (Figure 31.4) or imported using a comma-separated values (CSV) file with a specific layout. The surface editor also provides a way to remove one surface (or all the surfaces) and to create standard room surfaces (floor, ceiling, and four walls). The surfaces are shown in a 2D or 3D viewer to verify they were imported or input correctly.

There are two levels to the actual pattern analysis: stain level and pattern level. The analyst carries out the analysis at the stain level and the pattern-level analysis is performed by the software.

At the stain level, the angle of impact of each bloodstain is calculated based on the ellipse's width (minor axis) and length (major axis) using the well-known angle of impact formula:

$$\alpha = \mathit{arcsin}(\mathit{width}/\mathit{length})$$

This is calculated by entering the stain's location and then marking up the image with several tools. First, the scale tool is used to mark a specified length on the scale in the image. This will

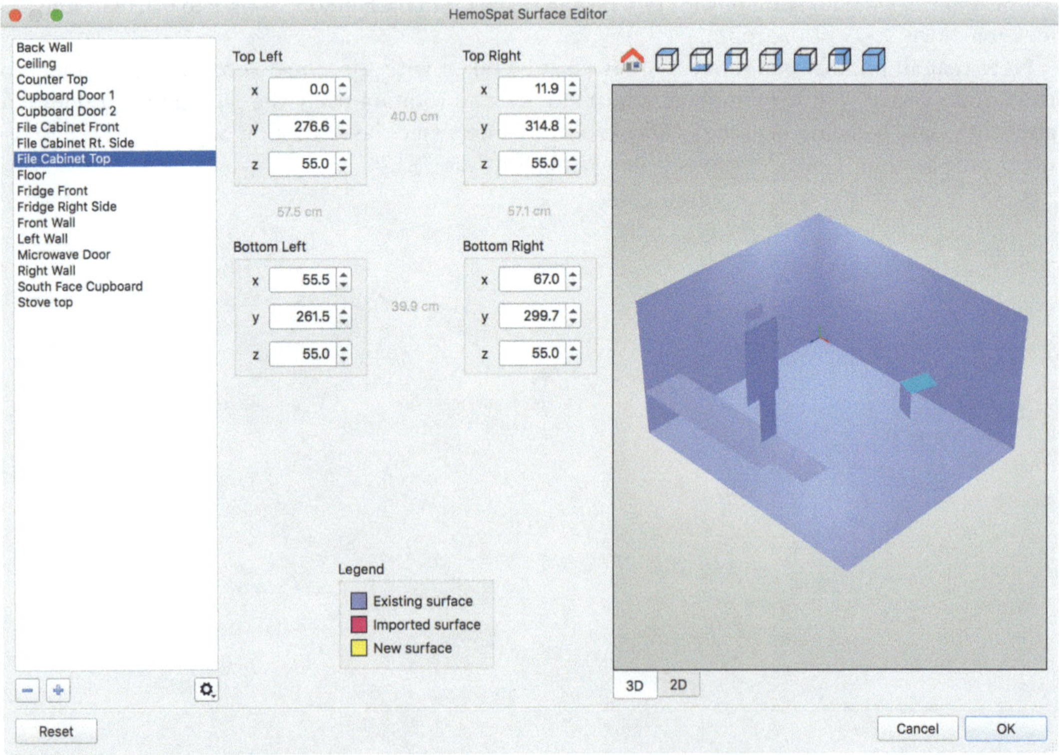

Figure 31.4 The surface editor allows the creation and editing of additional surfaces for analysis. (This image by the author is licensed under CC BY 4.0. To view a copy of this license, visit https://creativecommons.org/licenses/by/4.0/.)

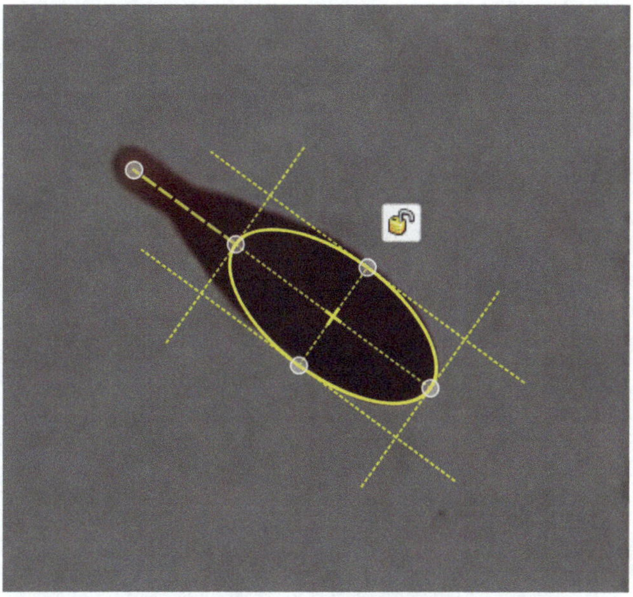

Figure 31.5 The ellipse tool allows the user to manually adjust the ellipse to fit it to the bloodstain. (This image by the author is licensed under CC BY 4.0. To view a copy of this license, visit https://creativecommons.org/licenses/by/4.0/.)

calibrate the image so that HemoSpat can locate other stains within the image. Next, the plumb line tool is used to identify the vertical. This will account for any camera rotation by adjusting the stain's gamma angle. (Note that HemoSpat does not alter the image by adjusting for any pitch or yaw of the camera. See the discussion of perspective correction in the section "Considerations When Using Software".) Finally, the ellipse tool is used to fit an ellipse to the bloodstain. Clicking a stain with this tool will use an algorithm to look for the edges of the stain, fit an ellipse to these points, and then propose this ellipse to the user (Figure 31.5). The user may then adjust the ellipse until they are satisfied with the placement.

Once these four pieces of information are available, HemoSpat will calculate the angle of impact (alpha), the gamma, the tangent line, and where the tangent intersects other surfaces within the scene.

Once the stain in a reference image is fully analyzed in HemoSpat (Figure 31.6), any other stain in the reference image (Figure 31.3) may be chosen using the point-select tool. With this tool, clicking the leading edge of another stain in the reference image will create a new stain to analyze with the ellipse tool. The location, scale, and plumb line for the new stain are all filled in from the reference image. This makes it very fast to add multiple stains from one reference image.

Once two or more stains have been analyzed in the project, HemoSpat uses all of their tangent lines to calculate the *area of origin* of the pattern. This follows the methods outlined in Carter,[5] generalized for planar surfaces in any orientation.[6] First an x–y projection is performed (top-down view), and the points where the tangent lines from either side intersect are averaged to determine a 2D convergence point. Then the height is calculated for each tangent by first creating a plane perpendicular to the tangent vector containing the 2D convergence point, and then intersecting the tangent with that plane. These heights are averaged to produce the height (z). The results are presented as the calculated point of origin and the standard deviations for each axis (x, y, z), which all together make up the *area of origin*.

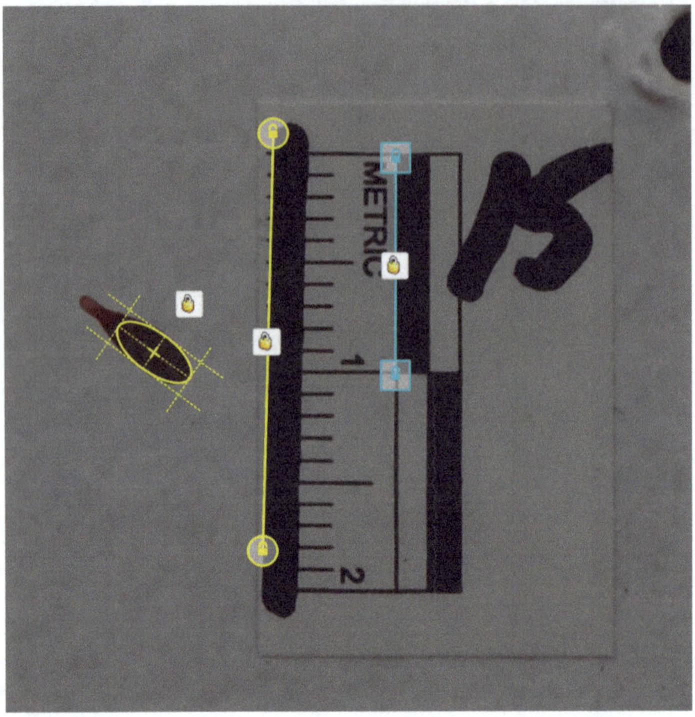

Figure 31.6 In addition to the stain's location, a fully analyzed stain has a fitted ellipse, a plumb line (yellow line), and a scale (cyan line). (This image by the author is licensed under CC BY 4.0. To view a copy of this license, visit https://creativecommons.org/licenses/by/4.0/.)

VIEWING DATA

Once the patterns have been analyzed, HemoSpat has several ways of examining the results. The first is simply the calculated point of origin and its associated standard deviation in numbers, which together make up the *area of origin*. The data in Figure 31.7 shows the calculated point of origin and the standard deviation (s) and also shows information about the known origin (using *experiment mode* – see below), including the known origin itself, how far the calculated origin is from the known origin in absolute distance, and how far the points are in the x, y, and z directions.

Second, 2D views are available to show the surfaces, the impact pattern's tangent line, the calculated area of origin, and the known origin (if running an experiment). The views show top-down, side, and front-on line drawings of the impacts (Figure 31.8). The tools at the top allow modification of the views such as how the lines are drawn (thickness, arrows or not, full lines or truncated at the origin, end caps), whether to show excluded stains, whether to highlight stains with an alpha higher than a specific angle (as the error increases with the alpha angle)[7], and whether to show the origin's colored box and the known origin.

Finally, HemoSpat offers a 3D viewer to explore the project in 3D (Figure 31.9). This allows the analyst to rotate and zoom the scene, save the scene as an image, and jump to a standard view (top, left side, right-side, etc.). The analyst may also set the virtual camera to a view they like and save it as a custom view (Figure 31.10). This makes it easy to save specific camera positions and orientations to return to at a later time.

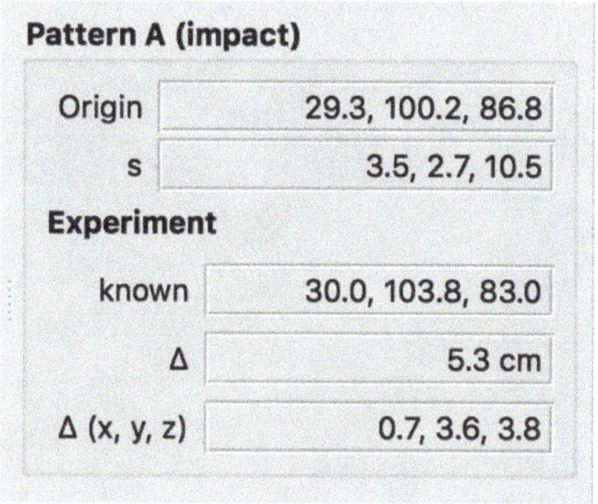

Figure 31.7 Results of an impact pattern analysis showing the calculated area of origin as well as the experiment results. (This image by the author is licensed under CC BY 4.0. To view a copy of this license, visit https://creativecommons.org/licenses/by/4.0/.)

Both the 2D and 3D views are interactive and the analyst may select a tangent line or a group of tangent lines for exclusion, to edit the stains, to flip the direction if they are in an incorrect orientation, to move them from one pattern to another, or to move them to a new pattern. If the user has a scene with two impact patterns close to each other, these views provide an intuitive way to separate the patterns by analyzing all the bloodstains as one pattern and then separating them visually.

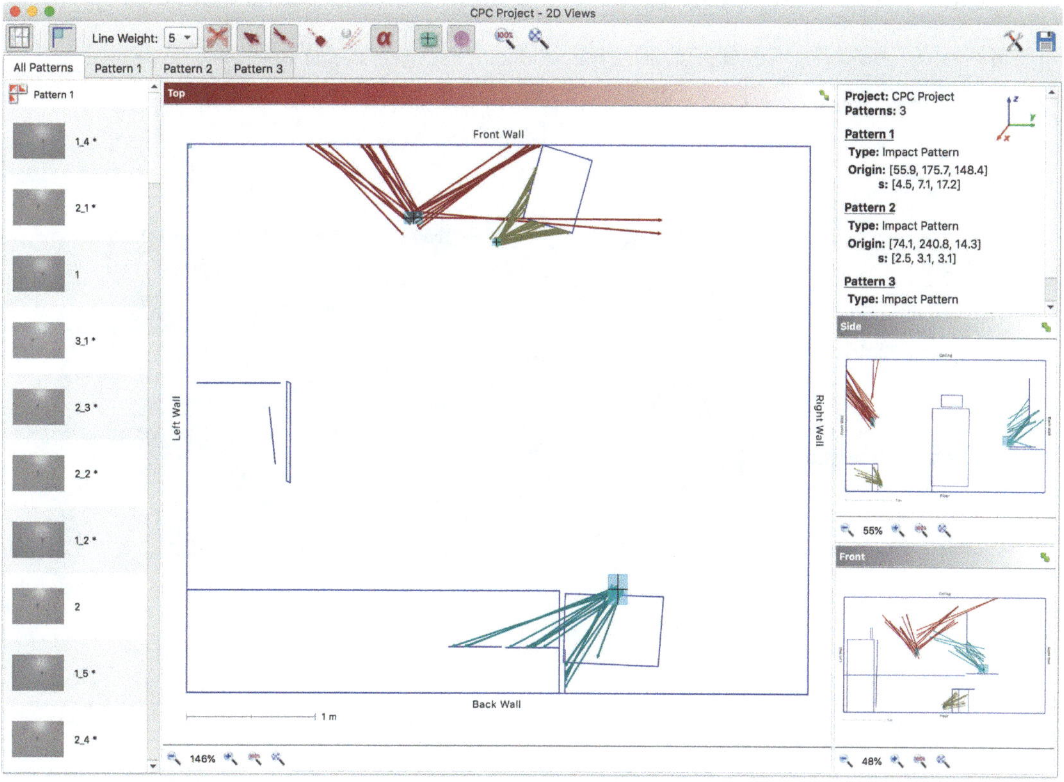

Figure 31.8 Three impact patterns from one scene displayed using 2D views. (This image by the author is licensed under CC BY 4.0. To view a copy of this license, visit https://creativecommons.org/licenses/by/4.0/.)

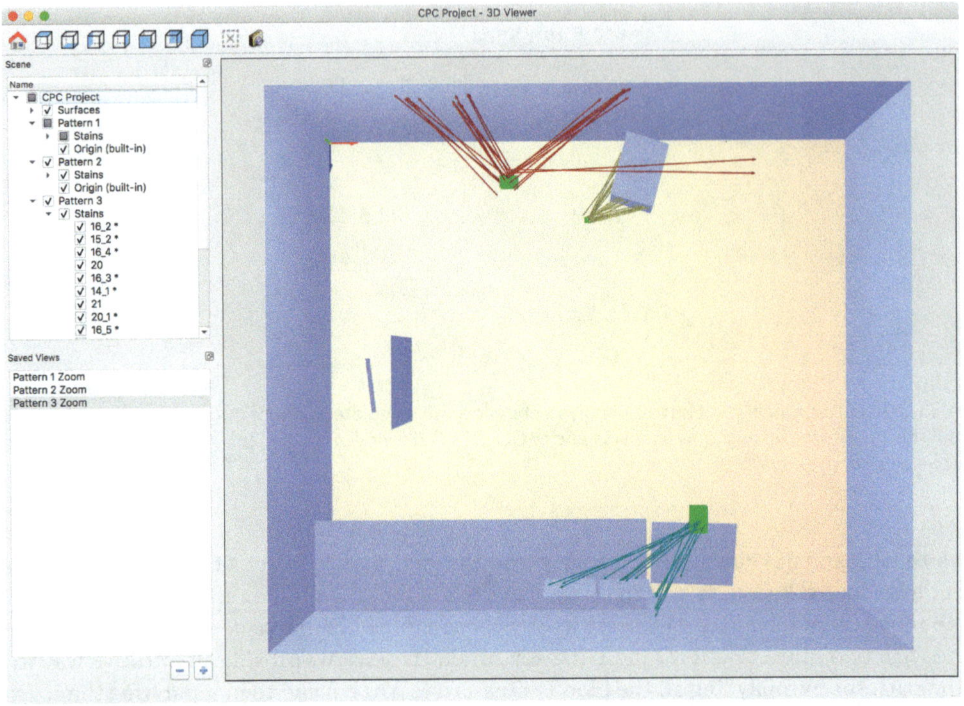

Figure 31.9 The scene displayed top-down using an interactive 3D view. (This image by the author is licensed under CC BY 4.0. To view a copy of this license, visit https://creativecommons.org/licenses/by/4.0/.)

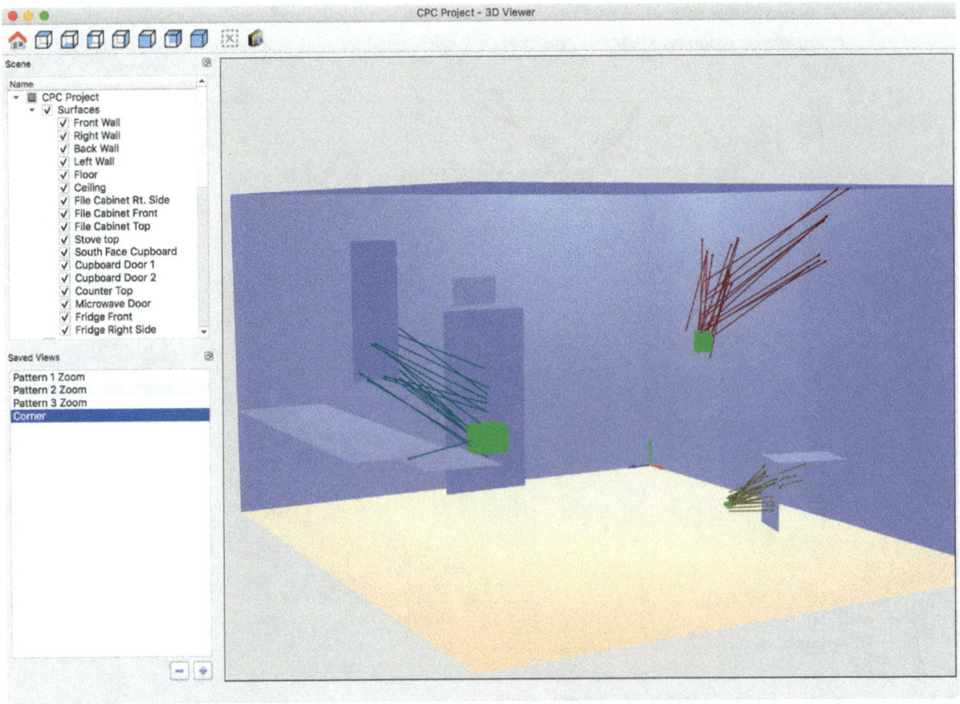

Figure 31.10 The scene rotated to show the three impact patterns from a different angle. The saved view is called "Corner" and clicking it will return the view to this orientation. (This image by the author is licensed under CC BY 4.0. To view a copy of this license, visit https://creativecommons.org/licenses/by/4.0/.)

REPORTS

In addition to exporting the analyst's data (see next section), HemoSpat provides reports which can be included on their own as addenda to a BPA report or used to copy-paste information into an organization's standard report template.

The first is the *Basic Report* which – as the name implies – is a very straightforward listing of the information from a project in a text format. This includes project information as entered by the analyst – file number, investigator, location of the scene, and date. Following that is a section for each pattern: a list of the stains analyzed and their name, location, surface, major axis length, minor axis length, alpha, beta, and gamma angles, a list of excluded stains and the reason why they were excluded (if this information was entered by the user), the calculated area of origin, the known origin (if it is an experiment), and some statistics about the analysis. The statistics include how many x–y intersections were used, how many stains were used to calculate the height (z), and the minimum and maximum values in the (x, y, z) directions

The second report is a *Summary Report*. This is a PDF which includes very similar data to the basic report. The main difference – other than being a much nicer format – is the information that is included in the table of stains for each pattern. This table includes the stain's name, surface, location, major axis length, minor axis length, area of the bloodstain, and the calculated alpha and gamma angles.

The final report – the *Full Report* – is the most comprehensive. The first part of this PDF includes an overall project summary with a list of patterns, how many stains were on each surface, and 2D top and front views of the overall scene. In the second part, the same analysis information and table from the summary report is included for each pattern, as well as all three 2D views (top, front, and side). Finally, a page is included for each stain used in the analysis with its image indicating the stain itself, followed by its location, measurements, and calculated alpha and gamma angles.

EXPORTING DATA

One of the initial goals when designing HemoSpat was to ensure that the analyst's data is not locked-in. That is to say that the analyst owns their data and should be able to use it however they like. To this end, HemoSpat has a flexible system which allows users to export the project's data to several popular file formats. This not only prevents lock-in, but it allows the user to integrate the data from their analysis into other software tools (see next section).

Comma-Separated Values (.csv)

This very common format may be used to input the data into spreadsheets, any text editor, or any word processor. For each stain, it includes fields for the project name, pattern name, stain name, location (x, y, z), surface name, major and minor axis lengths (in mm), stain area, pixels/mm, major and minor axis lengths (in pixels), alpha, beta, gamma, and the location the tangent line intersects with another surface (x, y, z). This depth of information is useful when performing analysis on the data using other software.

COLLADA Digital Asset Exchange (.dae) and GL Transmission Format (.gltf)

These open, standard file formats describe complete 3D scenes – surfaces, lines, textures, lighting, cameras, etc. They are used to exchange 3D modeling data between different programs. These formats are used for game engines, some CAD software, and most 3D modeling software.

Drawing Interchange Format (.dxf)

This is a widely used CAD format that is readable by many programs. HemoSpat takes advantage of several different features in the DXF format. It allows you to arrange how the data is separated by layers, choose which parts of the impact patterns to export, and export all the surfaces created with the Surface Editor. This format is useful for importing into CAD software.

OBJ Format (.obj)

This is a simple but powerful file format. Because it is an open format and an easy one to work with, it has been adopted by many 3D tools. This is useful for some point cloud software and most 3D modeling tools.

Polygon File Format (.ply)

This is another very simple 3D format readable by most 3D modeling and point cloud tools.

Virtual Reality Modeling Language 2.0 (VRML) (.wrl)

This is an old format not widely used by modern 3D software, but it is useful for one of the main scanner vendor's point cloud software.

The 3D exporters have many options to customize how the data is output, including selecting which surfaces are included, conversion to different measurement units, colors of the different components, and more. This allows for visual refinement as well as better compatibility with other software. These exporters also include a way to automatically modify the scale, location, and orientation of the output so that it can be imported into other software without having to modify it each time.

INTEGRATING WITH OTHER SOFTWARE

Using the export capability, a project's data can be brought into many other software packages. Usually this is a 3D software package – a CAD program, a 3D modeling tool, a crime-scene–specific program, or a point cloud software solution. How this is accomplished depends on which tools are being used.

Given an existing diagram or point cloud in some other software, one of the issues is how to match the scale, position, and orientation of HemoSpat's data with that of the other software. HemoSpat solves this by using some information to translate from HemoSpat's coordinate system to that of the other software while exporting the data. This is supported in two ways – having the other software produce a file that HemoSpat can load, or having the analyst enter some data manually.

HemoSpat defines the HemoSpat Coordinate Exchange Format[8] which is used to map the HemoSpat coordinate system to the coordinate system of the importing software. This is an open JSON-based format, meaning its specification is available to anyone who wants to use it. This file allows HemoSpat to modify the model on export so that when it is imported into other software, it appears in the correct location with the correct orientation and scale. Some point cloud software include facilities for creating this file automatically.

If the software is not able to produce this file, the information may be gathered and entered manually. For example, CloudCompare is freely available open-source software,[9] but it does not include a specialized tool for HemoSpat. Using a series of steps, the user can gather the information necessary to integrate HemoSpat data with point clouds in CloudCompare (Figure 31.11).

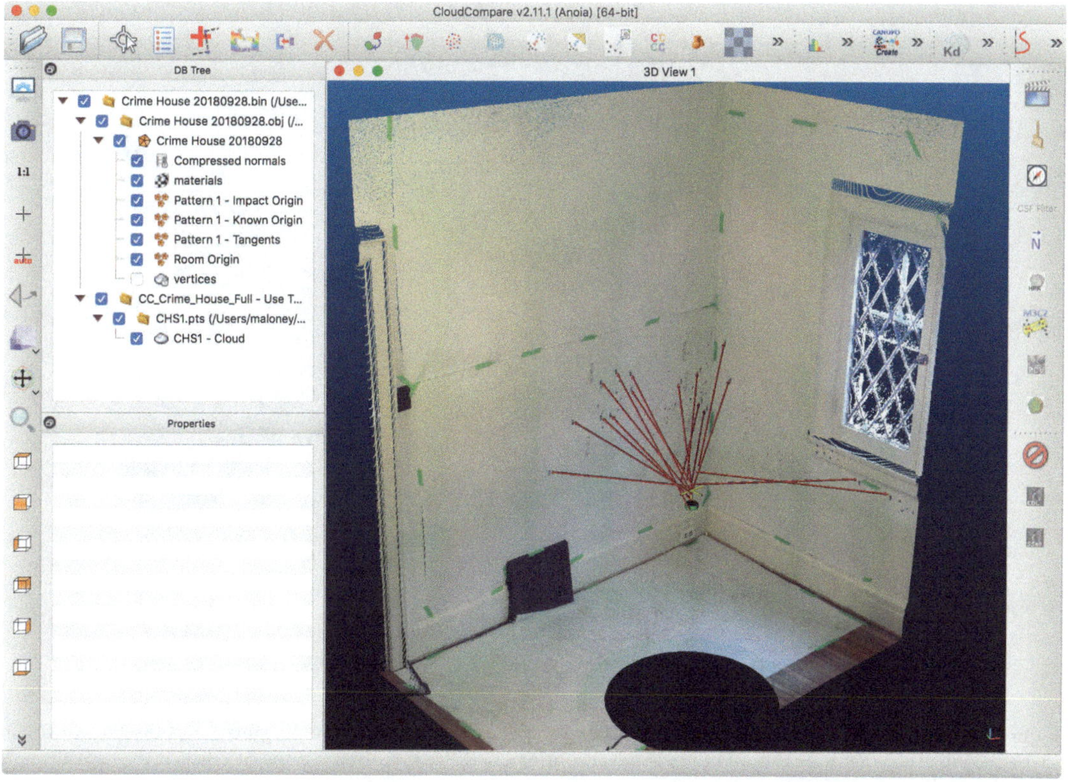

Figure 31.11 HemoSpat data imported into CloudCompare 2.11.1 (open source). (This image by the author is licensed under CC BY 4.0. To view a copy of this license, visit https://creativecommons.org/licenses/by/4.0/.)

Once this mapping has been created, any changes to the HemoSpat analysis can be imported into the point cloud software without having to reposition and scale the models. This makes collaboration easier when working on a crime scene reconstruction – a point cloud expert can work with the point cloud data and a bloodstain analyst can focus on their impact pattern analysis, for example.

Any of HemoSpat's 3D exporters (COLLADA, DXF, OBJ, PLY, and VRML) can use this data format.

EXPERIMENT MODE

HemoSpat provides an experiment mode – which must be turned on explicitly per project – that adds some capabilities which are not intended to be used in casework. With this mode on, a *known origin* may be added to an impact pattern when training or running experiments. With this additional information, HemoSpat will calculate the difference from its calculated origin to the known origin and present this both as a series of numbers (Figure 31.7), and visually in the 2D and 3D viewers (Figure 31.12).

Because the method is not yet validated, cast-off patterns may only be analyzed in experiment mode. The result of a cast-off analysis is an *approximate plane of motion*[4] and is presented visually in the 2D viewer, and, more usefully, in the 3D viewer. These approximate planes of motion may also be exported to any of the 3D formats HemoSpat supports to be imported into other 3D software (Figure 31.13).

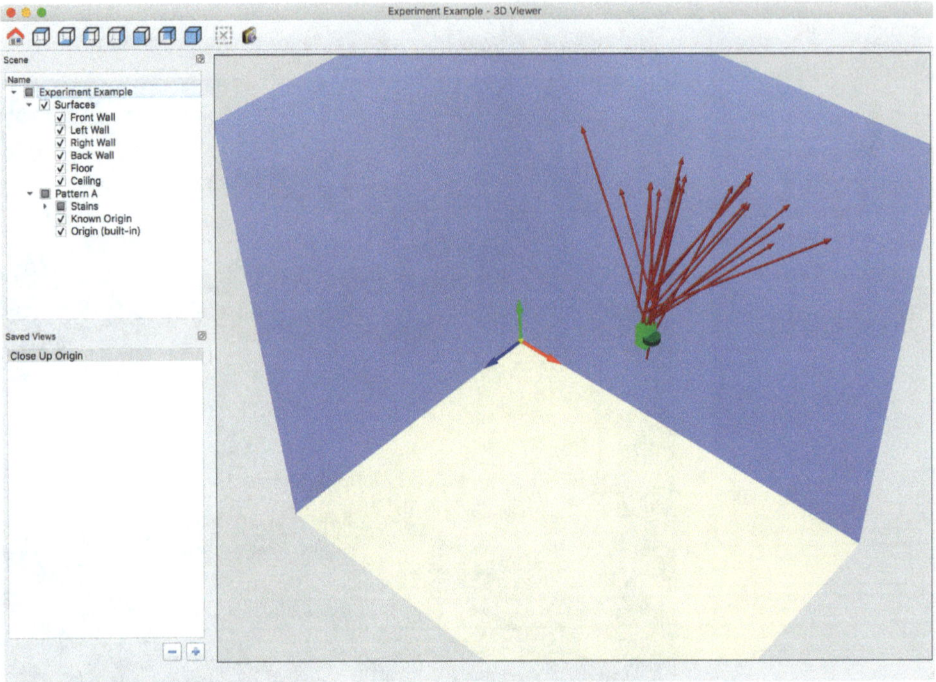

Figure 31.12 A 3D view of an impact pattern showing the calculated origin (light green) and the known origin (dark green). (This image by the author is licensed under CC BY 4.0. To view a copy of this license, visit https://creativecommons.org/licenses/by/4.0/.)

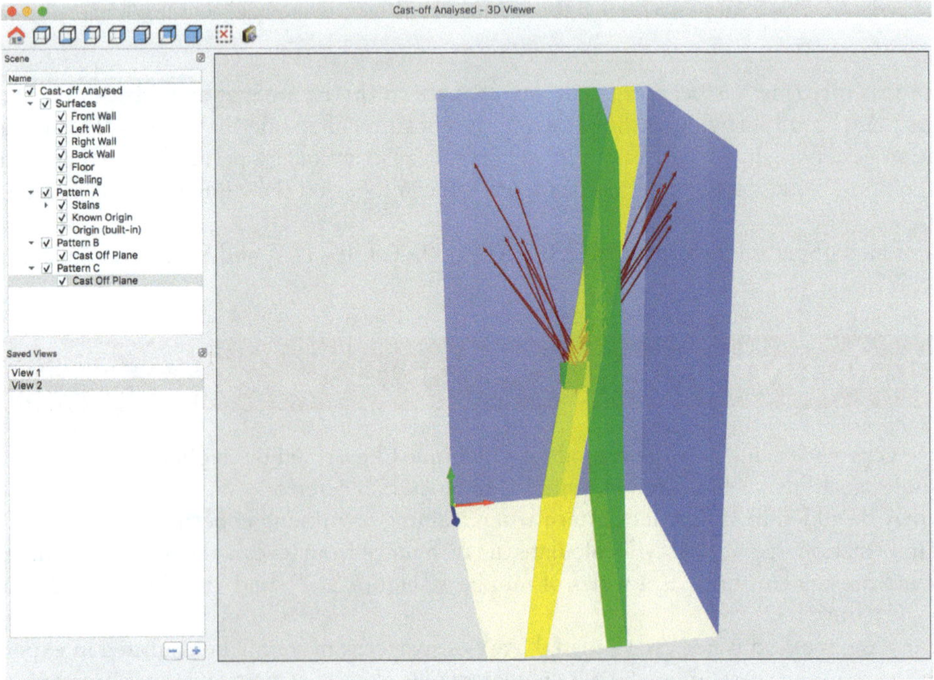

Figure 31.13 A 3D view of two cast-off patterns (green and yellow) and one impact pattern (red lines). (This image by the author is licensed under CC BY 4.0. To view a copy of this license, visit https://creativecommons.org/licenses/by/4.0/.)

Experiment mode not only provides users with support for training and experimentation, but it also provides a way to add new, experimental techniques to HemoSpat in the future without impacting casework.

CONCLUSION

Software is a very important tool for any kind of mathematical analysis and provides many benefits over analog methods. It provides data that may be used in many different ways, and can help prevent certain kinds of errors. It is, however, very important that users of software for any type of analysis understand what the software is doing and not just take the results and use them without this understanding.

HemoSpat is a specialized tool for BPA that provides a quick and flexible way to analyze impact patterns (and cast-off patterns in an experimental capacity). It was written with a focus on usability, transparency of the algorithms, and the freedom to use the resulting data in an open fashion, and provides several ways to integrate with other software. Chapters 31 and 32 will look at other software and tools which may be used to perform different kinds of analysis in the field of BPA.

Notes

1. Maloney, Andy, *HemoSpat*, v2.0, FORident Software, Windows and macOS, 2024, https://hemospat.com.
2. Gardner, Ross, "Computer Aided Analysis: Capabilities and Limitations Part I," *International Association of Bloodstain Pattern Analysts News* 11, no. 3 (1995): 15–22.
3. Maloney, Andy, Céline Nicloux, Kevin Maloney, and Franck Heron, "One-Sided Impact Spatter and Area-of-Origin Calculations," *Journal of Forensic Identification* 61, no. 2 (2011): 123–135.
4. Maloney, Andy, Todd Campbell, and Jim Killeen, "Visualization of Cast-Off Patterns Using 3D Modelling Software," *Journal of the Association for Crime Scene Reconstruction* 17, no. 4 (2011): 49–56.
5. Carter, A.L., "The Directional Analysis of Bloodstain Patterns: Theory and Experimental Validation," *Journal of the Canadian Society of Forensic Science* 34, no. 4 (2001): 173–189.
6. Maloney, Kevin, Jim Killeen, and Andy Maloney, "The Use of HemoSpat to Include Bloodstains Located on Nonorthogonal Surfaces in Area-of-Origin Calculations," *Journal of Forensic Identification* 59, no. 5 (2009): 513–524.
7. Willis, C., Piranian, A. K., Donaggio, J. R., Barnett, R. J., and Rowe, W. F., "Errors in the estimation of the distance of fall and angles of impact blood drops", Forensic Science International (2001) 123:1–4.
8. "HemoSpat Coordinate Exchange Format," FORident Software. https://hemospat.com/hemospat-coordinate-exchange-format/ (last modified September 20, 2016).
9. CloudCompare Contributors, *CloudCompare*, v2.11.1, Open Source, Windows, macOS, and Linux, 2020, https://github.com/CloudCompare/CloudCompare.

Further Reading

Fadnavis, Shreyas. "Image Interpolation Techniques in Digital Image Processing." *International Journal of Engineering Research and Applications* 4, no. 10 (2014): 70–73.

Maloney, Andy, "FORident Software Technical Paper – HemoSpat Validation." FORident Software, 2009. https://hemospat.com/hemospat-validation-technical-paper/.

Osoba, Osonde A., and William Welser IV, "An Intelligence in Our Image: The Risks of Bias and Errors in Artificial Intelligence." RAND Corporation, 2017. https://www.rand.org/pubs/research_reports/RR1744.html. Also available in print form.

CHAPTER 32

AUTOMATED METHODS FOR ANALYZING BLOODSTAINS

Ravishka Arthur

Pattern recognition forms the basis of the forensic discipline of bloodstain pattern analysis (BPA). Recognizing bloodstain patterns involves careful observation of bloodstains, identification of diagnostic features such as their size, shape, and orientation, and an evaluation of these features within the context of possible mechanisms that may have led to their deposition at a crime scene. Together, these form the process of *pattern classification*, which is often carried out by bloodstain pattern analysts to facilitate crime scene reconstruction.

Automated pattern recognition has been used in several disciplines for several reasons, for example, in the development of automated diagnosis systems for the detection of disease,[1,2,3] to identify characteristics of fluids,[4] or to organize/retrieve large amounts of electronic data.[5,6] In the wider forensic science disciplines, it is evident that tasks that were once manually conducted have now become efficient automated processes. Examples of this include bullet comparison,[7] fingerprint recognition,[8] facial recognition,[9] speech emotion recognition,[10] and handwriting recognition.[11] Certain components of pattern recognition systems (e.g., pre-processing, feature extraction,[12] and classification) have even been integrated into studies involving bloodstain patterns.[13,14,15,16,17,18,19] Software now takes the place of previously used manual methods for the calculation of important BPA parameters at the crime scene. For example, "stringing"[20] traditionally used by analysts to estimate the area of origin[21] involved using string to create straight lines along the long axis of a bloodstain. To that end, there have been advances in the research involving computer-assisted methods in BPA[22,23] demonstrating the value of automation and the utility of technology as crime scenes become more complex and pattern recognition a more demanding process.

Like many forensic disciplines, human expertise forms the primary instrument of analysis in BPA. However, it has been suggested that the interpretations of bloodstain patterns by analysts are often mainly guided by their experience, rather than the product of a benchmarked, discipline-standard methodology. Relying on experience alone poses the risk that subjective statements might be made about a bloodstain pattern potentially rendering the opinions of a BPA analyst unreliable for expert testimony. Despite extensive dialogue in the BPA community[24,25,26] around pattern classification, no single and fully validated method has emerged.

As currently practiced, pattern characterization can be considered largely the result of the subjective visual evaluation of a bloodstain pattern combined with analyst experience. However, there are several inherent issues with bloodstain patterns and their analysis that appear to encourage this practice. These issues are discussed as follows.

BLOODSTAIN PATTERNS CAN APPEAR AMBIGUOUS

It is well accepted that different bloodletting mechanisms may give rise to bloodstain patterns that exhibit similar or indistinguishable features.[27,28] This can lead to ambiguity in distinguishing

DOI: 10.4324/9781003163695-32

different bloodstain pattern types. For example, impact spatter and expiration bloodstain patterns both may feature small bloodstains. However, in the absence of additional features, expiration bloodstain patterns could be considered impact spatter bloodstain patterns.[29] Making distinctions between different bloodstain pattern types may be further complicated by patterns that comprise only a few bloodstains or are the result of blood that has been deposited on complex surfaces.[30] In both cases, analysts need to determine whether there is sufficient information available to reliably characterize and interpret the bloodstain pattern evidence. Substrate composition and absorbency are among other compounding factors that may need to be taken into further consideration and have subsequently formed the basis for ongoing research on bloodstains formed on fabrics.[31,32] Ambiguous bloodstain patterns, therefore, provide several logistical challenges for an analyst, especially in the absence of sophisticated automated tools that may be employed to visualize and/or enhance the appearance of a complex bloodstain pattern.

BPA TERMINOLOGY HAS THE TENDENCY TO RESULT IN A DESCRIPTION OF THE MECHANISM RATHER THAN A DESCRIPTION OF THE PATTERN CHARACTERISTICS

Terminology has continued to be an area of contention with certain terms having evolved (e.g., terms listed in the ASB technical report[33]), while particular terms have been embedded into existing classification systems (e.g., Bevel and Gardner[27] features categorical terms: spatter, non-spatter, and complex). One persistent challenge that all these systems appear to share is the tendency to describe patterns using terminology that relates to a mechanism rather than terminology that describes the physical attributes of a pattern. For example, "Expiration Pattern" and "Cast-off Pattern" elicit a description while simultaneously assigning a mechanism. It has been argued that this may potentially result in the formation of early conclusions before a full set of observations has been made.[34] A study conducted by Arthur et al.[35] addressed this issue of terminology proposing a range of tested terms that could be used instead to describe patterns at a more fundamental level. The main goal of this study was to encourage analysts to treat bloodstains as individual, discrete, and potentially measurable units termed *Elements*. Furthermore, the study suggested that bloodstain patterns could be broken down into components with descriptions provided in a way that avoided the use of mechanistic nomenclature. As recommended, having automated tools that can break patterns down into individual labeled components would be of immeasurable value in the way of visualization of the spatial distributions of bloodstains. Additionally, the study demonstrated that the use of high-speed video footage to complement the fluid dynamic underpinnings of bloodstain formation could greatly enhance expert interpretation by providing a scientific and visual foundation to pattern formation. Indeed, several BPA studies now commonly employ high-speed videography to visualize blood droplets,[36] to measure droplet velocities and trajectories,[37] to distinguish between different bloodstain pattern types[38] and to evaluate the underlying error in BPA calculations.[39] This technology has vastly improved our understanding of complex bloodstain pattern formation and has provided a platform for the development of other automated methods of analysis. Mechanism-free terminology is central to the interpretation of bloodstain patterns, therefore, in combination with appropriate technology, bloodstain pattern characterization is continuing to evolve into a more objective, reliable, and well-defined task.

THERE IS A LACK OF A RIGOROUS AND STANDARDIZED METHODOLOGY

BPA training courses are valuable and equip BPA analysts with the necessary pattern recognition skills. However, it has been contended that these courses do not provide an appropriate framework which analysts can use to apply these skills.[27] This problem has been demonstrated in criminal trials, where experts have arrived at completely different conclusions about the same bloodstain pattern.[40] Of greatest concern is the fact that some analysts may experience difficulty in articulating the rationale behind their decisions.[27] Bevel and Gardner's BPA taxonomy[27] appears to be the most comprehensive classification methodology currently available to BPA practitioners. Applying their taxonomy requires BPA analysts to make systematic choices about the appearance of a bloodstain pattern using criteria that has been grouped according to a specific mechanism. Some issues have been noted. For example, certain criteria remain vague, and potentially introduce ambiguity. To that end, quantitative pattern measures have been suggested as one method of combatting this.[38] On the other hand, it has also been argued that using quantitative pattern measures might itself lead to uncertainties in the boundaries between groups, thus, making them subject to attack.[41] Considering the complex decision-making that these current taxonomies introduce, it is reasonable to contend that automated tools have the potential to play an even greater role in assisting analysts in decision-making, particularly when analysts are required to group or classify bloodstain patterns based on shared characteristics.

HUMAN EXPERT INTERPRETATION OF BLOODSTAIN PATTERNS MAY BE VULNERABLE TO CONTEXTUAL BIAS

Encountering contextual information is generally unavoidable for a BPA analyst, especially when crime scene attendance is expected. Extraneous information present at the crime scene or information that is communicated by law enforcement may unintentionally exert an influence on the interpretation of bloodstain pattern evidence. Studies have produced compelling evidence to show that BPA analysts are indeed susceptible to the effects of contextual bias[42,43] and this is not limited to forensic comparison disciplines such as fingerprints[44,45] and bitemarks[46] alone. By learning from large sets of bloodstain pattern data, and with improved objectivity that automated methods could bring to the BPA discipline, it has been suggested that human factors such as bias could be mitigated.[47] To that end, Chapter 37 outlines further the role of contextual bias in BPA.

Research effort has already been directed toward the need to make forensic pattern comparison tasks more objective, especially considering the importance and magnitude that objectivity plays in criminal proceedings.[48] This has generally involved the application of suitable image-processing methods to enhance video-surveillance data,[49,50] for latent fingerprint recognition[51,52] and for shoeprint comparisons.[53,54,55] In most cases, the aim has been to improve the resolution of images and enhance human interpretation. Techniques such as cropping and grayscale conversion has been used to process infrared images of bloodstains on clothing substrates,[56] while binarization,[13,57] edge detection,[58] contour extraction,[59] and object recognition[17] have also been used as pre-processing steps where refining bloodstain pattern images has been desirable.

Pattern recognition is defined as the study of how computers observe the environment, learn to distinguish patterns of interest, and make reasonable decisions about different categories of patterns.[60] A pattern recognition system generally consists of the following stages: defining pattern classes, data collection, selecting the distinguishing features, specifying classification algorithms, and estimating the classification error.[61]

The concept of using automated pattern recognition to distinguish different bloodstain patterns was first documented by Arthur et al.[47] To develop the proposed system, a reference bloodstain pattern dataset was generated consisting of 30 impact spatter and 30 cast-off laboratory manufactured bloodstain patterns that were deposited on paint and wallpaper and specifically digitized for the study. An image-processing methodology[14] was then applied to all the patterns and used to extract features that were representative of common bloodstain pattern properties. Following the identification of the optimal set of features, an automated classifier (i.e., Fisher Quadratic Discriminant Classifier[62]) was trained and tested with separate groups of patterns from the reference pattern dataset. The performance of the classifier was finally evaluated with an independent dataset consisting of bloodstain patterns that were generated on paint and wallpaper. A high classification precision (2% error rate) was achieved when these bloodstain patterns were tested with the trained classifier illustrating that an automated system could be used to distinguish different bloodstain patterns. Furthermore, this system appears to rely on the direct measurement of pattern features thereby generating quantitative pattern data, an area that has previously lacked research. The authors suggested that this quantitative information could provide objective pattern data to support/complement statements made by an analyst regarding the appearance of a pattern. To that extent, objective pattern data should be an absolute necessity in any method used to distinguish the properties of bloodstain patterns and it has been shown that this can clearly be done with the application of automated methods.

Eye tracking technology has been shown to be a valuable tool in evaluating the expertise of crime scene investigators and their ability to recognize pertinent evidence relevant to an investigation.[63] Furthermore, eye tracking has been applied to studies concerned with differentiating experts and novices in tasks involving the comparison of fingerprints[64] and handwriting specimens.[65,66] Eye movements are therefore an important physiological mechanism that bring a small fraction of the visual field into high resolution, thus enabling the perception of fine detail. Most often, eye movements will also bring focused attention to the area in which an observer is looking. Therefore, it is presumed that by tracking eye movements, it may be possible to follow the path of attention that was deployed by the observer.[67] This may provide useful information about what an observer found interesting and potentially offer insight into their train of thought, otherwise defined as the eye-mind hypothesis.[68] This hypothesis was employed in a first of its kind, eye tracking study[69] to understand how analysts assess bloodstain patterns and the regions of a pattern that they spend time fixating given that visual evaluation forms the fundamental basis to BPA.

The gaze of 24 bloodstain pattern analysts was recorded during an assigned task of classifying a single impact spatter bloodstain pattern. The properties of selected features of the pattern were quantified leading to the delineation of areas of interest (AOIs). Eye tracking data was collected for each AOI and combined with verbal statements made by analysts after the classification task to determine the critical range of values for relevant diagnostic features. The eye tracking data indicated that there were four main regions of the impact pattern that analysts were most interested in. These regions comprised either upward moving elliptical bloodstains, small (0.5 mm^2) circular bloodstains, or large, irregular bloodstains. Specific terminology referencing the directionality, size, color, and shape was used by analysts, thus highlighting pertinent bloodstain pattern characteristics. Overall, the study showed that the eye movements of trained bloodstain pattern experts and their verbal descriptions of a pattern were well correlated. It is acknowledged that this study offers only a limited window into the classification task, and more complexity is involved in the thought process of bloodstain pattern analysts. However, the application of eye tracking in this novel context highlights potential advantages in keeping up with current and evolving technology, to better understand the requirements of BPA.

As has been emphasized in this chapter, automated methods offer advantages in areas such as pattern classification and pattern pre-processing, where human expertise and the complexities of pattern deposition are known to influence the reliability of expert pattern classifications. Automated methods such as a trained classifier or the use of eye tracking technology provide an original and invaluable contribution to the discipline by putting forward the means to characterize patterns via the generation of quantitative pattern data and better understand the mindset of bloodstain pattern analysts in their decision-making. Automated classification methods have the potential to become part of well-established BPA software or a useful addition to virtual BPA approaches.[70] Indeed, automated classification methods have begun to feature as exampled in a recent study involving the novel application of machine learning methods to pattern classification.[71]

Moving forward, automation could become invaluable when dealing with mixed bloodstain patterns deposited on a range of surfaces. The portability of automated methods of analysis also highlights the distinct advantage that analysts could gain when required to attend a crime scene. Finally, in addition to the expediency that automated tools could provide, the availability of some initial pattern data might help analysts take early decisions that will benefit a more objective and reliable interpretation of bloodstain pattern evidence.

Notes

1. Yu, S., and L. Guan. 2000. "A CAD System for the Automatic Detection of Clustered Microcalcifications in Digitized Mammogram Films." *IEEE Transactions on Medical Imaging* 19 no. 2, 115–126. https://doi.org/10.1109/42.836371.
2. Gurcan Metin, Laura Boucheron, Ali Can, Anant Madabhushi, Nasir Rajpoot, and Bulent Yener. 2009. "Histopathological Image Analysis: A Review." *IEEE Reviews in Biomedical Engineering* 2, 147–171. https://doi.org/10.1109/RBME.2009.2034865.
3. Constantinidis Alex, Michael Fairhurst, and A.F.R. Rahman. 2001. "A New Multi-Expert Decision Combination Algorithm and Its Application to the Detection of Circumscribed Masses in Digital Mammograms." *Pattern Recognition* 34, 1527–1537. https://doi.org/10.1016/S0031-3203(00)00088-1.
4. Kim Namwon, Zhenguo Li, Cedric Hurth, Frederic Zenhausern, Shih-Fu Chang, and Daniel Attinger. 2012. "Identification of Fluid and Substrate Chemistry Based on Automatic Pattern Recognition of Stains." *Analytical Methods* 4, 50–57. https://doi.org/10.1039/C1AY05338H.
5. Uysal, Alper Kursat. 2016. "An Improved Global Feature Selection Scheme for Text Classification." *Expert Systems with Applications*, no. 43, 82–92. https://doi.org/10.1016/j.eswa.2015.08.050.
6. Antani, Sameer, Rangachar Kasturi, and Ramesh Jain. 2002. "A Survey on the Use of Pattern Recognition Methods for Abstraction, Indexing and Retrieval of Images and Video." *Pattern Recognition* 35, 945–965. https://www.sciencedirect.com/science/article/abs/pii/S0031320301000863.
7. Leon, Fernando Puente. 2006. "Automated Comparison of Firearm Bullets." *Forensic Science International* 156, 40–50. https://doi.org/10.1016/j.forsciint.2004.12.016.
8. Jain Anil, Arun Ross, and Salil Prabhakar. 2004. "An Introduction to Biometric Recognition." *IEEE Transactions on Circuits and Systems for Video Technology* 14, no. 1, 4–19. https://doi.org/10.1109/TCSVT.2003.818349.
9. Zhao Wenyi, Rama Chellappa R., P. Jonathon Phillips, and Azriel Rosenfeld. 2003. "Face Recognition: A Literature Survey." *ACM Computing Surveys* 35, no. 4, 399–458. https://doi.org/10.1145/954339.954342.
10. El Ayadi Moataz, Mohamed Kamel, and Fakhri Karray. 2011. "Survey on Speech Emotion Recognition: Features, Classification Schemes, and Databases." *Pattern Recognition* 44, 572–587. https://doi.org/10.1016/j.patcog.2010.09.020.
11. Plamondon Rejean and Sargur N. Srihari. 2000. "On-Line and Off-Line Handwriting Recognition: A Comprehensive Survey." *IEEE Transactions on Pattern Analysis and Machine Intelligence* 22, no. 1, 63–84. https://doi.org/10.1109/34.824821.
12. In pattern recognition literature feature extraction can be used to describe algorithms that create new features based on transformations or combinations of the original feature set (Solomon Chris, and Toby Breckon. 2010. Fundamentals of Digital Image Processing: A Practical Approach with Examples in Matlab, West Sussex, UK: John Wiley & Sons. https://doi.org/10.1002/9780470689776).

13. Siu Sonya, Jennifer Pender, Faye Springer, Frederic Tulleners, and William Ristenpart. 2017. "Quantitative Differentiation of Bloodstain Patterns Resulting from Gunshot and Blunt Force Impacts." *Journal of Forensic Sciences* 62, no. 5, 1166–1179. https://doi.org/10.1111/1556-4029.13418.
14. Arthur Ravishka, Martin Baiker, Philomena J. Humburg, Jerry Hoogenboom, Michael C. Taylor, and Karla G. de Bruin. 2017. "An Image-Processing Methodology for Extracting Bloodstain Pattern Features." *Forensic Science International* 277, 122–132. http://dx.doi.org/10.1016/j.forsciint.2017.05.022.
15. Cho Yuen, Faye Springer, Frederic A. Tulleners, and William D. Ristenpart. 2015. "Quantitative Bloodstain Pattern Analysis: Differentiation of Contact Transfer Patterns versus Spatter Patterns on Fabric via Microscopic Inspection." *Forensic Science International* 249, 233–240. http://dx.doi.org/10.1016/j.forsciint.2015.01.021.
16. Chen S. L., Yang C., Zhu C., and Yin X. C. 2016. *Bloody Image Classification with Global and Local Features*. In: Tan T., Li X., Chen X., Zhou J., Yang J., and Cheng H. (Eds.) *Pattern Recognition*. CCPR 2016. Communications in Computer and Information Science, vol. 663. Springer, Singapore.
17. Shoumy Nusrat Jahan, Phaklen Ehkan, Shahrul Nizam Yaakob, Md. Shawkat Ali, and Sabira Khatun. 2016. "Feature Extraction for Neural Network Pattern Recognition for Bloodstain Analysis." *International Journal of Applied Engineering Research* 11, no. 15, 8583–8589.
18. Laber Terry, Paul Kish, Michael Taylor, Glynn Owens, Nikola Osborne, and James Curran. 2014. "Reliability Assessment of Current Methods in Bloodstain Pattern Analysis." U.S. Department of Justice Grant Report.
19. Ristenpart William, Fred Tulleners, Sonya Siu, Jennifer Saifi, and Faye Springer. 2013. "Quantitative Analysis of High Velocity Bloodstain Patterns." U.S. Department of Justice Grant Report.
20. Carter A. L. 2001. "The Directional Analysis of Bloodstain Patterns: Theory and Experimental Validation." *Canadian Society of Forensic Science* 34, no. 4, 173–189.
21. Area of origin is defined as the space in three dimensions to which the trajectories of spatter can be utilized to determine the location of the spatter producing event (ASB Technical Report 2017).
22. Reynolds Mark, Daniel Franklin, Michael Raymond, and Ian Dadour. 2008. "Bloodstain Measurement Using Computer Fitted Theoretical Ellipses: A Study in Accuracy and Precision." *Journal of Forensic Identification* 58, no. 4, 469–484.
23. de Bruin Karla, Reinoud Stoel, and Josita Limborgh. 2011. "Improving the Point of Origin Determination in Bloodstain Pattern Analysis." *Journal of Forensic Sciences* 56, no. 6, 1476–1482. https://doi.org/10.1111/j.1556-4029.2011.01841.x.
24. Saviano Jeffrey. 2005. "Articulating a Concise Scientific Methodology for Bloodstain Pattern Analysis." *Journal of Forensic Identification* 55, no. 4, 461–470.
25. Gardner Ross. 2005. "Defining a Methodology for Bloodstain Pattern Analysis." *Journal of Forensic Identification* 56, no. 4, 549–556.
26. Latham Holly. 2011. "Using and Articulating the Scientific Method in Bloodstain Pattern Analysis." *Journal of Forensic Identification* 61, no. 5, 487–494.
27. Bevel Tom, and Ross Gardner. 2008. *Bloodstain Pattern Analysis with an Introduction to Crime Scene Reconstruction*, Boca Raton, FL: CRC Press.
28. James Stuart, Paul Kish, Paulette Sutton. 2005. *Principles of Bloodstain Pattern Analysis: Theory and Practice*. Florida: Taylor & Francis Group.
29. Geoghegan Patrick, Albert Laffra, Nathan Hoogendorp, Michael Taylor, and Mark Jermy. 2017. "Experimental Measurement of Breath Exit Velocity and Expirated Bloodstain Patterns Produced under Different Exhalation Mechanisms." *International Journal of Legal Medicine* 131, no. 5. https://doi.org/10.1007/s00414-017-1545-2.
30. Peschel O., S. Kunz, M. Rothschild, and E. Mutzel. 2011. "Blood Stain Pattern Analysis." *Forensic Science, Medicine and Pathology* 7, 257–270. https://doi.org/10.1007/s12024-010-9198-1.
31. de Castro Therese, Tania Nickson, Debra Carr, and Clare Knock. 2013. "Interpreting the Formation of Bloodstains on Selected Apparel Fabrics." *International Journal of Legal Medicine* 127, no. 1, 251–258. https://doi.org/10.1007/s00414-012-0717-3.
32. Li Xingyu, Jingyao Li, and Stephen Michielsen. 2017. "Effect of Yarn Structure on Wicking and Its Impact on Bloodstain Pattern Analysis (BPA) on Woven Cotton Fabrics." *Forensic Science International* 276, 41–50. https://doi.org/10.1016/j.forsciint.2017.04.011
33. American Academy of Forensic Sciences. 2017. ASB Technical Report 033, "Terms and Definitions in Bloodstain Pattern Analysis," 1st edition. http://asb.aafs.org/.

34. Bernstein, E. 2005. "Science in Bloodstain Pattern Analysis." *International Association of Bloodstain Pattern Analysis News*, 16–19.
35. Arthur Ravishka, Sarah Cockerton, Karla de Bruin, and Michael Taylor. 2015. "A Novel Element-Based Approach for the Objective Classification of Bloodstain Patterns." *Forensic Science International* 257, 220–228. https://doi.org/10.1016/j.forsciint.2015.08.028.
36. Kunz Sebastian, Jiri Adamec, and Christina Grove. 2017. "Analyzing the Dynamics and Morphology of Cast-Off Pattern at Different Speed Levels Using High-Speed Digital Video Imaging." *Journal of Forensic Sciences* 62, no. 2, 428–434. https://doi.org/10.1111/1556-4029.13299.
37. Comiskey P. M, A. L. Yarin, and D. Attinger. 2017. "High-Speed Video Analysis of Forward and Backward Spattered Blood Droplets." *Forensic Science International*, 276, 134–141. doi: 10.1016/j.forsciint.2017.04.016.
38. Donaldson Andrea, Nicole Walker, Iain Lamont, Stephen Cordiner, and Michael Taylor. 2011. "Characterising the Dynamics of Expirated Bloodstain Pattern Formation Using High-Speed Digital Video Imaging." *International Journal of Legal Medicine* 125, no. 6, 757–762. https://doi.org/10.1007/s00414-010-0498-5.
39. Behrooz Nima, Lee Hulse-Smith, and Sanjeev Chandra. 2011. "An Evaluation of the Underlying Mechanisms of Bloodstain Pattern Analysis Error. *Journal of Forensic Sciences* 56, no. 5, 1136–1142. https://doi.org/10.1111/j.1556-4029.2011.01835.x.
40. *Indiana v. David Camm*, 812N.E.2d 1127, (Ind. App., 2004).
41. Cooper, Antony. 2003. Thoughts on Categorising Bloodstain Patterns. Technical Report No. 0442-0001-701-A1. *Council for Scientific and Industrial Research.*
42. Osborne Nikola, Michael Taylor, and Rachel Zajac. 2016. "Exploring the Role of Contextual Information in Bloodstain Pattern Analysis: A Qualitative Approach." *Forensic Science International* 260, 1–8. http://dx.doi.org/10.1016/j.forsciint.2015.12.039.
43. Osborne Nikola, Michael Taylor, Matthew Healey, and Rachel Zajac. 2016. "Bloodstain Pattern Classification: Accuracy, Effect of Contextual Information and the Role of Analyst Characteristics." *Science & Justice* 56, no. 2, 1–8. http://dx.doi.org/10.1016/j.scijus.2015.12.005.
44. Dror Itiel, David Charlton, and Ailsa Péron. 2006. "Contextual Information Renders Experts Vulnerable to Making Erroneous Identifications." *Forensic Science International* 156, no. 1, 74–78. http://dx.doi.org/10.1016/j.forsciint.2005.10.017.
45. Osborne Nikola, and Rachel Zajac. 2016. "An Imperfect Match? Crime-Related Context Influences Fingerprint Decisions." *Applied Cognitive Psychology* 30, 126–134. https://doi.org/10.1002/acp.3180.
46. Osborne Nikola, Sally Woods, Jules Kieser, and Rachel Zajac. 2014. "Does Contextual Information Bias Bitemark Comparisons?" *Science and Justice* 54, no. 4, 267–273. http://dx.doi.org/10.1016/j.scijus.2013.12.005.
47. Arthur Ravishka, Jerry Hoogenboom, Martin Baiker, Michael Taylor, and Karla de Bruin. 2018. "An Automated Approach to the Classification of Impact Spatter and Cast-Off Bloodstain Patterns." *Forensic Science International* 289, 310–319. https://doi.org/10.1016/j.forsciint.2018.05.019.
48. Saviano Jeffrey. 2005. "The Pursuit of Objectivity in the Examination of Forensic Evidence." *Journal of Forensic Identification* 56, no. 6, 877–884.
49. Jerian M., S. Paolino, F. Cervelli, S. Carrato, A. Mattei, and L. Garofano. 2007. "A Forensic Image Processing Environment for Investigation of Surveillance Video." *Forensic Science International* 167, no. 2–3, 207–212. https://doi.org/10.1016/j.forsciint.2006.06.048
50. Rocha Anderson, Walter Scheirer, Terrance Boult, and Siome Goldenstein. 2011. "Vision of the Unseen: Current Trends and Challenges in Digital Image and Video Forensics" *ACM Computing Surveys* 43, no. 4, 26:1–26:42. https://doi.org/10.1145/1978802.1978805.
51. Coetzee Louis and Elizabeth Botha. 1993. "Fingerprint Recognition in Low Quality Images." *Pattern Recognition* 26, no. 10, 1441–1460. https://doi.org/10.1016/0031-3203(93)90151-L.
52. Mehtre B. M. 1993. "Fingerprint Image Analysis for Automatic Identification." *Machine Vision and Applications* 6, 124–139. https://doi.org/10.1007/BF01211936
53. de Chazal Philip, John Flynn, and Richard Reilly. 2005. "Automated Processing of Shoeprint Images Based on the Fourier Transform for Use in Forensic Science." *IEEE Transactions on Pattern Analysis and Machine Intelligence* 27, no. 3, 341–350. https://doi.org/10.1109/TPAMI.2005.48.
54. AlGarni Gharsa and Madina Hamiane. 2008. "A Novel Technique for Automatic Shoeprint Image Retrieval." *Forensic Science International* 181, no. 1–3, 10–14. https://doi.org/10.1016/j.forsciint.2008.07.004.

55. Speir Jacqueline, Nicole Richetelli, Michael Fagert, Michael Hite, and William Bodziak. 2016. "Quantifying Randomly Acquired Characteristics on Outsoles in Terms of Shape and Position." *Forensic Science International* 266, 399–411. https://doi.org/10.1016/j.forsciint.2016.06.012.
56. Perkins Michael. 2005. "The Application of Infrared Photography in Bloodstain Pattern Documentation of Clothing." *Journal of Forensic Identification* 55, no. 1, 1–9.
57. Boonkhong Kittipat, Montri Karnjanadecha, and Pattara Aiyarak. 2010. "Impact Angle Analysis of Bloodstains Using a Simple Image Processing Technique." *Songklanakarin Journal of Science and Technology* 32, no. 2, 169–173.
58. Hulse-Smith Lee, Navid Mehdizadeh, and Sanjeev Chandra. 2005. "Deducing Drop Size and Impact Velocity from Circular Bloodstains." *Journal of Forensic Sciences* 50, no. 1, 54–63.
59. Joris Philip, Wim Develter, Els Jenar, Paul Suetens, Dirk Vandermeulen, Wim van de Voorde, and Peter Claes. 2014. "Calculation of Bloodstain Impact Angles Using an Active Bloodstain Shape Model." *Journal of Forensic Radiology and Imaging* 2, no. 4, 188–198. https://doi.org/10.1016/j.jofri.2014.09.004.
60. Jain Anil, Robert P. W. Duin, and Jianchang Mao. 2000. "Statistical Pattern Recognition: A Review." *IEEE Transactions on Pattern Analysis and Machine Intelligence* 22, no. 1, 4–37. https://doi.org/10.1109/34.824819.
61. Raudys Sarunas, and Anil Jain. 1991. "Small Sample Size Effects in Statistical Pattern Recognition: Recommendations for Practitioners." *IEEE Transactions on Pattern Analysis and Machine Intelligence* 13, no. 3, 252–264. https://doi.org/10.1109/34.75512.
62. Linear discriminant analysis is a statistical method used in classification to separate classes by projecting all data to a linear discriminant subspace thereby simplifying the process of classification (Ronald Fisher. 1936. The Use of Multiple Measurements in Taxonomic Problems. *Annals of Eugenics* 7 (2): 179–188. https://doi.org/10.1111/j.1469-1809.1936.tb02137.x).
63. Watalingam Renuka. 2016. "Eye Tracking to Evaluate Proficiency of Crime Scene Investigators with Varying Levels of Expertise: The Ability to Recognize Evidence and Understand Its Significance." Masters diss., Eberly College of Arts and Sciences at West Virginia University.
64. Busey Tom, Chen Yu, Dean Wyatte, John Vanderkolk, Francisco Parada, and Ruj Akavipat. 2011. "Consistency and Variability among Latent Print Examiners as Revealed by Eye Tracking Methodologies." *Journal of Forensic Identification* 61, no. 1, 60–91.
65. Dyer Adrian, Brian Found, and Doug Rogers. 2006. "Visual Attention and Expertise for Forensic Signature Analysis." *Journal of Forensic Science* 51, no. 6, 1397–1404. https://doi.org/10.1111/j.1556-4029.2006.00269.x.
66. Merlino Mara. 2015. "Validity, Reliability, Accuracy and Bias in Forensic Signature Identification." Report no. 2010-DN-BX-K271. National Institute of Justice, U.S. Department of Justice.
67. Duchowski Andrew. 2003. *Eye Tracking Methodology: Theory and Practice*, Springer Verlag.
68. Just Marcel and Patricia Carpenter. 1976. "Eye Fixations and Cognitive Processes." *Cognitive Psychology* 8, 441–480.
69. Arthur Ravishka, Jerry Hoogenboom, Richard Green, Michael Taylor, and Karla de Bruin. 2017. "An Eye Tracking Study of Bloodstain Pattern Analysts during Pattern Classification." *International Journal of Legal Medicine* 132, 875–885. https://doi.org/10.1007/s00414-017-1711-6.
70. Joris Philip, Wim Develter, Els Jenar, Paul Suetens, Dirk Vandermeulen, Wim Van de Voorde, and Peter Claes. 2015. "HemoVision: An Automated and Virtual Approach to Bloodstain Pattern Analysis." *Forensic Science International* 251, 116–123. https://doi.org/10.1016/j.forsciint.2015.03.018.
71. Liu Yu, Daniel Attinger, and Kris de Brabanter. 2020. "Automatic Classification of Bloodstain Patterns Caused by Gunshot and Blunt Impact at Various Distances." *Journal of Forensic Sciences* 65, no. 3, 729–743. https://doi.org/10.1111/1556-4029.14262.

CHAPTER 33

CAPTURE, ANALYSIS, AND VISUALIZATION OF BLOODSTAIN PATTERNS USING 3D TECHNOLOGIES

Eugene Liscio and Jason Keller

INTRODUCTION TO 3D TECHNOLOGIES FOR BPA

Bloodstain patterns and the mechanisms that create them are often quite dynamic and complex in nature. When compounded by a complex environment and a multitude of surfaces on which blood may be deposited, it comes as no surprise that the types of patterns which can be produced by blood are also complex in their form. Regardless of how repeatable a bloodstain pattern may be, it would not be a difficult argument to suggest that each bloodstain pattern is unique in size, shape, and form for which it cannot be identically replicated. As such, creating hand-drawn sketches or taking photographs, which can accurately record a complex bloodstain pattern, is often a difficult task. This is especially so when an investigator attempts to perform a specific quantitative analysis and not just document the general bloodstain pattern for demonstrative purposes.

The digital camera is by far the most utilized tool for documenting bloodstain patterns, but whenever a three-dimensional (3D) environment is reduced to a two-dimensional (2D) image, something is lost in the process. Photographs are extremely useful, but they may also give a false sense of perspective, provide limited information of the surroundings, distort the size of a surface, and introduce other artifacts that are not true to form. Certainly, taking a photograph of an impact pattern on a flat wall is one thing, but trying to show a series of bloodstains dispersed on a curved, organic shape is a difficult task with photography. This is where 3D technologies excel.

When most people think of modern-day 3D documentation technologies, the laser scanner is likely to be one of the first things to come to mind. The laser scanner has made great strides and contributions to the BPA discipline in the past decade, but this is not the first 3D technology to present itself as an option to scene investigators. Photogrammetry is one of the earliest 3D technologies that has its roots tied to the development of the very first cameras starting from about the 1850s.[1] However, it was not until the 1980s when the digital era of computing allowed for simplified solutions of photogrammetry which permitted the development of large 3D data sets. Today, photogrammetry is much more developed and can produce very dense data sets showing the true shape and form of a piece of evidence. This "true to form" digital model can then be used for all types of analysis or visualization.[2]

Handheld 3D scanners are also making a lot of headway in the forensics discipline. These lower-cost units can capture highly accurate data sets that are perfectly suited to documenting a small scenes where blood has been deposited. They are not intended for large, outdoor areas, but are well-suited when the analysis is limited to one room or an area of several square meters in size. Like all technologies, handheld scanners have their limitations, but they have been shown

DOI: 10.4324/9781003163695-33

to provide acceptable data when compared to a terrestrial laser scanner. In general, handheld scanners can be broken into two categories: those which utilize visible structured light and those which utilize invisible structured light. Many handheld scanners work in the infrared range and utilize laser light above the 700 nm range while structured light scanners that work in the visible range emit a series of rapidly changing striped patterns which can generate 3D point data. In each of these categories, there are a range of accuracies that be found. Typically, higher cost units provide more accurate data while lower cost units come with lower accuracy and sometimes other limitations as well.

The terrestrial laser scanner is the modern-day workhorse for documenting scenes and can be applied to applications such as, bullet trajectories, suspect height analysis, witness perspectives, and BPA.[3] It is extremely versatile and offers the investigator a flexible tool for documenting small scenes on the order of a few square meters, right up to large, outdoor scenes which may be thousands of meters long. Currently, the terrestrial laser scanner is the most studied 3D technology for impact and cast-off pattern analysis. This is in part due to the terrestrial laser scanner's ability to rapidly collect accurate data in complex scenarios, saving time at a scene and allowing for visualizations, which make it easy and more accurate for investigators, judges, and juries to comprehend and draw conclusions.

DIFFICULTIES WITH TRADITIONAL DOCUMENTATION

Not all scenes are simple to document and for the most part, they can be quite complex in nature. One only has to imagine the infinite number of ways in which blood can be deposited on walls and furniture to note that any measurement that is not planar, like a floor or wall becomes much more complex to record. The use of baseline-offset or triangulation manual measurement methods to record a bloodstain pattern on a tiled floor may be reasonable enough; however, a similar bloodstain pattern on the inside of a vehicle or a cluttered garage where surfaces and objects are not orthogonal to one another makes the documentation process slower and much more difficult.

There are several difficulties with baseline-offset and triangulation manual measurement methods. These are often due to human error, carelessness, limitations of tools, environmental issues, weather, or difficulties working within confined or complex spaces. Baseline-offset measurements of bloodstains require that the offset measurement is at 90° to the baseline. This method may be useful on floors or walls and is often a requirement when doing an area of origin analysis of an impact pattern using programs like HemoSpat. In the case of impact patterns, the overall size of an individual pattern is usually on the order of a few square centimeters up to a few square meters, which is normally not problematic in terms of size. However, the difficulty in recording bloodstain patterns arises when the surfaces are not flat and orthogonal to one another. Thus, curved or angled walls increase the complexity of documentation and when intermediary objects are considered, they can make for a very difficult task. In some cases, such as an impact pattern created inside a vehicle, the task of recording the location of the resulting spatter stains is practically impossible to do with any reasonable accuracy and thus, is rarely attempted using conventional manual measurement methods. The documentation and subsequent analysis of these difficult scenarios are better suited to 3D technologies.

3D TECHNOLOGY OVERVIEW

The application of 3D technologies to forensic documentation has revolutionized the visualization and analysis of elements within a scene, particularly as it relates to BPA. The benefit of employing these 3D tools during the processing of a scene can vary depending on the chosen instrument. This section compares the categories of 3D technologies which can be used in documentation and analysis of bloodstain patterns.

Laser Scan Data

Properly capturing a scene using a 3D laser scanner ensures the entirety of the scene will be documented, to include contextual information that may be missed or not readily apparent by a responding scene investigator. Once captured, the scene is "frozen" in both time and scale, allowing a scene to be virtually revisited or reanalyzed years later. The resulting scene data can be visualized from an infinite number of angles and perspectives, many of which would not be possible from a 2D image or diagram. Along with the permanence of the resulting 3D model, because the 3D laser scanner objectively captures laser measurement data from every surface within the scanner's range and line of sight, the subjectivity a scene investigator is burdened with, choosing what to measure, photograph, and analyze, is significantly reduced. Because laser scanners are precision measurement instruments, the measurement error common among traditional crime scene diagramming techniques is also minimized. Figure 33.1 depicts the scope of a large scene captured by a terrestrial laser scanner.

The capturing of laser scanner data on a scale relative to BPA can be accomplished by using one of the two categories of 3D laser scanner or a combination of both: handheld 3D scanners and terrestrial LiDAR scanners (TLS), also known as "terrestrial laser scanners." Each type of laser scanner has its benefits and limitations; however, when analyzing bloodstain patterns specifically, these are the two types of laser scanner technologies employed. Other larger-scale laser scan collection devices exist in the market, such as mobile-mapping and simultaneous localization and mapping (SLAM) devices; however, for smaller, confined areas and the required accuracy for most bloodstain patterns, these technologies will not be discussed, as they are not suitable for the collection of bloodstain pattern data.

Capturing bloodstain evidence with a laser scanner alone is not sufficient to produce results with a high enough degree of accuracy to analyze individual bloodstains. Due to the reported accuracy of 3D laser scan devices, high-resolution digital photographs of the bloodstains must also be captured for an accurate analysis to be performed using 3D data. These high-resolution photographs are aligned with the point cloud data to affect an analysis of the individual bloodstain patterns. This process will be discussed in detail in a subsequent section but is worth mentioning here. Therefore, the main role of a 3D laser scanner in the capture of bloodstain pattern evidence is to document the overall context of a scene to a high degree of accuracy and to have the ability

Figure 33.1 Large-scale outdoor scene captured with a terrestrial LiDAR scanner (TLS).

to scale and align the high-resolution photographs of the bloodstains within the 3D scan data for subsequent analysis and visualization.

Handheld 3D Scanners

Due to the relatively condensed size of a single bloodstain pattern and the breadth of different surfaces on which blood may be deposited, one of the most useful tools in the 3D documentation of these patterns is a handheld 3D scanner. As the name implies, a handheld 3D scanner is a laser scanning device that is small enough to be held in the operator's hand(s). Due to its compact size, relatively light weight, and portable nature, it allows for the capture of contextual data from a multitude of angles and orientations. As mentioned earlier, handheld 3D scanners are exceptional for capturing data in small, confined spaces such as vehicle exteriors and interiors, below items of furniture, within cabinets or closets, and for documenting clandestine graves, as depicted in Figure 33.2. An increasing number of handheld 3D scanners allow for the capture of larger and larger data sets, in some cases up to several average-sized residential rooms in one scan.

Unlike a TLS which is typically stationary throughout the data capture of a single scan, handheld 3D scanners rely on structured light technology and internal inertial sensors to capture data, which allows the device to be rotated and moved around in 3D space while scanning to ensure relevant surfaces are adequately captured. Most handheld 3D scanners are either connected to or integrated with a computer processing unit and visual display, allowing the real-time processing of collected data, which provides instantaneous feedback to the operator so they can visualize the coverage and resolution of data captured.

As mentioned earlier, structured light technology used by many handheld scanners involves the projection of either an infrared (IR) pattern of dots, typically above the 700 nm wavelength, onto the scanned surface or in the visible spectrum, a series of rapidly changing striped patterns, onto the scanned surface. Cameras detect the projected patterns and measure the differences in the known pattern when projected onto 3D objects. This results in measurement data, which is processed into a 3D point cloud – a digital 3D representation of the area scanned. Most handheld 3D scanners also use an integrated color camera to capture color data, which in turn assigns RGB (red, green, and blue) values to each measured point, thereby colorizing the point cloud data.

Figure 33.2 Handheld 3D scanner being used to document a clandestine grave.

Accuracy

The structured light technology used by handheld 3D scanners sometimes requires a reference measurement (i.e. known length artifact) to be placed somewhere within the area scanned to help verify the accuracy of the measurements. At the time of the publication of this book, handheld 3D scanners range in minimum accuracy from 0.05 mm, which are designed for scanning small objects with a working distance on average of 0.2–0.3 m, to an accuracy of ≤0.5 mm, which are capable of scanning larger objects and areas such as vehicles and rooms with a working distance of 0.4–5.0 m. One thing to note on manufacturer-published accuracy is the fact that accuracy decreases as the distance from scanner to target increases. Therefore, depending on the area to be scanned and the accuracy required, one handheld 3D scanner might be more appropriate for the given task than another.

Limitations

There is no one perfect scanner for every scenario. Each scanner model, type, and manufacturer has its pros and cons. One limitation to most handheld 3D scanners is their ability to scan in bright daylight. Because most handheld scanners rely on a structured light pattern, intense light, such as that emitted by the sun, can create problems for handheld scanners to detect the projected pattern and thus decreases the amount and quality of data captured in bright conditions. One solution is to block the light source by placing a canopy over the area to be scanned or by blocking light emitting sources in the area to be scanned, such as sunlight coming in through a window. Some scanners are beginning to take advantage of smaller, compact LiDAR technology, which helps overcome this limitation outdoors.

Considerations

As discussed earlier, one huge benefit handheld scanners have over TLS is their ability to capture data in confined areas or complex surfaces, which would be difficult to capture using a tripod-based TLS. However, some handheld 3D scanners generate very large file sizes during capture. Therefore, considerations should be made with respect to the duration and size of the area scanned with a handheld device. Depending on the instrument and requirements for a specific scene, a handheld device may be used to capture a portion of a room and the rest of the scene context can be captured by a TLS. The data can then be aligned or "registered" in the laser scanner's software. To ensure a proper alignment of the two data sets, common reference markers such as spheres, checkerboards or April Tags may be placed in the scene prior to data collection with both devices and not moved throughout data collection. The subsequent data set ensures adequate coverage of the overall scene, while also ensuring coverage of the small, confined, or complex surfaces, resulting in a complete and "true to form" depiction of the scene. Figure 33.3 depicts a mock scene captured using a handheld 3D scanner, focusing on the bed and victim's location. In contrast, Figure 33.4 depicts the same scene captured using a TLS, which encompasses the entirety of the room, but lacks data in the areas below the bed and behind the victim.

Another consideration when using a handheld 3D scanner is the resolution or density of data points collected in the area containing bloodstain evidence. The scanner-to-target distance impacts the point density of data points collected on the target surface; the further the scanner is from the surface, the lower the point density and vice versa. Most handheld devices have an effective operating range with a minimum and maximum distance from the target surface; therefore, a handheld scanner will not capture points if the device is too close or too far away from the surface. The effective range of each device varies and must be tailored to the requirements of the specific project. For instance, if bloodstain data are to be collected on the ceiling of a room, the handheld scanner operator must either utilize a handheld 3D scanner with a larger effective range to adequately capture data on the ceiling or the operator must move closer to the ceiling, decreasing the scanner-to-target distance.

Figure 33.3 Handheld 3D scanner data focused around bed and victim location; common reference markers allow the registration of handheld data with TLS data.

Figure 33.4 TLS data capturing context surrounding area of interest, previously scanned with handheld 3D scanner.

Terrestrial LiDAR Scanners

One of the most prevalent 3D data capture tools for the documentation of scenes is the terrestrial LiDAR scanner (TLS). These scanners are typically larger and heavier than a handheld 3D scanner and are mounted atop a tripod or mounted to a base plate that sits on the ground. TLSs use LiDAR (Light Detection and Ranging) technology, such that the device takes measurements by emitting a laser pulse from the center of the device. The scanner rotates around the vertical axis while a mirror at the center of the device rotates around the horizontal axis and emits millions of laser measurement pulses with each scan. Each laser measurement pulse is reflected off the object or surface and a portion of the pulse is returned to the scanner. With the speed of light as a constant variable, the scanner can then calculate the time it takes for the laser pulse to be emitted from the scanner, travel to and reflect off the object, and travel back to the laser sensor. This is called time-of-flight (ToF) measurement. Many TLSs on the market today use ToF measurement to gather 3D data from their surroundings. Unlike a typical total station measuring device used traditionally by survey crews and accident reconstructionists, wherein one laser measurement point is captured at a time, a TLS captures millions of laser measurement points with every scan.

Like the handheld 3D scanners, most TLSs also capture color data using either an internal color camera or external supplementary camera, mounted atop the scanner. The color data captured by a TLS is typically better than that of handheld 3D scanners for a few reasons. First, the camera is typically more sophisticated, capturing high-resolution, spherical photographs with each scan position. Second, because the TLS is stationary during each scan, mounted atop a tripod, the color camera has the opportunity to meter the surrounding environment and properly expose for changes in lighting from one context to another. And third, many of the newer TLSs now have the ability to capture high dynamic range (HDR) photographs, which results in greater detail being captured in over-exposed and under-exposed areas of the photographs. This, in turn, creates more accurate color data and a truer depiction of the 3D environment, which is imperative in forensics.

Accuracy

One major advantage TLSs have over handheld 3D scanners is their range. Most TLSs have an effective measurement range of less than one meter to several thousand meters (in the longer-range TLS). This allows for the collection of a more thorough and complete 3D data set with every scan. Thus, entire rooms, roadways, building façades, and outdoor areas can be captured by a TLS; hence, they are popular and utilized in documenting entire scenes, crash scenes, and areas pertinent to an investigation. Figure 33.5 depicts the interior and exterior of an entire residence captured with a TLS using multiple scan positions throughout the house and around the exterior of the home.

Like handheld 3D scanners, the scanner-to-target distance directly affects the density of the laser scan data. The closer to the surface to be scanned, the closer the point spacing and thus, the more data points collected, barring some limitations that will be discussed in the next section.

Most TLSs have the ability to increase or decrease the "resolution" of a given scan. By increasing or decreasing the resolution, the point density or point spacing at a given distance also changes. The resolution also significantly changes the amount of time required to complete a scan. Therefore, a

Figure 33.5 Point cloud depicting entirety of interior and exterior scene captured using TLS; roof of residence hidden to allow viewer to visualize interior layout of structure.

trained laser scanner operator will choose the appropriate settings to adequately capture a given scene or object. The scanner operator must balance the collection of dense point cloud data at a very slow scan speed or the collection of sparse point cloud data at a faster scan speed. Each scenario, time constraints, and subsequent use of the point cloud data will dictate the resolution settings for each scan.

Each laser scanner manufacturer publishes the accuracy of the particular model of laser scanner in the scanner's specification sheet. The typical accuracy of most TLSs on the market at the time of this publication ranges from ±1 mm to ±5 mm at 10 m, meaning the measurement of a given point 10 m away from the scanner is accurate in 3D space to ±1 mm to ±5 mm. One factor that affects this published measurement accuracy is the reflectance of the object. Many TLS manufacturers publish the scanner's accuracy based on the reflectivity of the surface. Therefore, a scanner's reported accuracy is not all that simple to quantify without knowing the other variables involved.

One other part of a laser scan data set's accuracy comes when multiple scans are stitched together or "registered." Since the scanner is a line-of-sight device, the scanner will only capture laser measurement points on surfaces and objects the laser can "see" from the scan position. For example, if a scanner is placed in an office setting atop a 2 m tripod, the laser scanner will likely not capture data below desks, behind cubicle walls, and around corners. Therefore, the scanner must be moved into multiple positions in order to capture the data required for that environment. It is incumbent upon the laser scanner operator to ensure that with each scan position, there is sufficient overlap between scan positions such that all scans can be later registered together. Registration is the alignment of two or more scans into one coordinate system. This process of registration, using complex algorithms in the registration software, will produce a mathematical result of how well all scans are registered or fit together. How well the scans fit together is dependent on several factors, but largely dependent on the percentage of overlap between scans as well as on the presence of common geometry or surfaces between scans. If no common geometry exists in the environment or where there is very little overlap, artificial reference objects such as spheres or checkerboard targets must be used. These reference objects should be sufficient in number to be captured by the scanner in overlapping scan positions. The registration result, either by aligning the scans using organic common surfaces, called cloud-to-cloud or targetless registration, or by aligning the scans using artificial reference objects, called targeted registration, produces an accuracy for the overall scan project. Thus, one can deduce the accuracy of one point at the very far limit of the scan project to another point at the opposite end of the scan project. The overall project accuracy can vary from less than 1 mm to well over 10 cm depending on the aforementioned variables, overall scale and complexity of the project, and thresholds within the program.

Lastly, like handheld 3D scanners, an artificial reference or length measurement should be placed somewhere within the scene such as a known or traceable artifact like a calibrated scale bar or target pole, the length of which has been certified by an independent measurement device or organization like the National Institute of Standards and Technology (NIST). Placing an artificial reference object within the scene allows the analyst to determine whether the laser scanner was operating correctly on the day the scans were taken. This is done by comparing the measurement of the artifact in the laser scan data to the known measurement of the artifact. Any difference would be reported as an uncertainty of measurement.

Limitations

No TLS is perfect for every scenario. Each scanner has its own limitations, effective ranges, published accuracies, and physical constraints. Some TLSs are small and compact and can sit atop a standard camera tripod or even on the ground, while other TLSs are larger and require a sturdier survey-grade tripod, which much be leveled with each scan. Due to the relative size, weight, and stationary position of TLS with each scan, the physical position in which a TLS can be placed is limited. As mentioned earlier, the TLS is a line-of-sight device; therefore, the scanner will not capture data on surfaces or objects behind or below objects that are in the way of the laser beam

Figure 33.6 Reflective surface on top surface of stove, depicting TLS limitation of scanning reflective surfaces.

being emitted from scanner. Therefore, multiple individual scans must be performed to capture a given scene or object completely. Still, some areas may not be captured by the TLS, depending on the limiting angles and relative size of the space to be scanned. For example, a small, cluttered closet or trunk of a vehicle may be difficult environments for a TLS to thoroughly capture data due to tight spaces and blind spots.

Not all surfaces are captured the same with a TLS. Reflective and transparent surfaces are difficult surfaces to accurately capture with a TLS, as depicted in Figure 33.6, with the chrome cooking pans of the stovetop. When the laser beam from the scanner hits a reflective surface, the beam may reflect, refract, or otherwise be misdirected or scattered upon returning to the scanner. Reflective surfaces commonly create digital noise or artifacts within scan data that can either be corrected with filters within the scanning software or manually in the post-processing phase. Additionally, laser scanner operators can apply a coating to any reflective surface, taking into consideration any contamination of the surface for forensic purposes. Common coatings include a solution of baby powder and alcohol, dry shampoo, or laser scan-specific sprays that are designed to sublimate after a given amount of time. Reflective surfaces can also be covered with non-reflective materials, such as brown paper, to reduce the reflective artifacts in the point cloud.

Sharp edges of objects are another difficult surface captured by the TLS. When a laser beam hits a sharp edge in the environment, due to the thickness of the laser beam, a portion of the beam travels beyond the edge and a portion of the beam reflects off the surface with the edge. This returns a signal to the scanner that may be inaccurate and the scanner may calculate that measurement somewhere between the edge and the surface beyond the edge. This results in "edge artifacts" as depicted in Figure 33.7 along the edge of the furnace, which can also be corrected using filters in the scanning software or manually in post-processing.

Weather and precipitation can be a significant limitation when using TLS technology. Some TLSs are rated for scanning in precipitation and dust; however, some are not. Depending on the manufacturer's recommendations and specifications, a severe weather event could impact a scan project significantly and require a laser scanner operator to triage important areas to be scanned first, or somehow protect the scanner from those environmental variables. The secondary limitation of the laser scanner actually returning a signal from precipitation or particulates in the air should also be considered. This can result in a snow globe-like effect in the resulting point cloud.

One additional limitation, specifically as it relates to scanning wet surfaces, is the scanner's inability to capture data through pooled or puddles of liquid. Due to the laser wavelength of

Figure 33.7 TLS data depicting edge artifacts along the edge of a furnace.

1550 nm used by most laser scanner manufactures and the subsequent absorption of that wavelength by water, a void often exists in scan data with the presence of pooled liquids. The laser beam is absorbed by water and does not return a signal to the scanner; therefore, no data will exist in the area where pooled liquid was in the scene, rather a lack of data will be apparent, as depicted in Figure 33.8 with the void created by scanning wet liquid on the floor of a warehouse. The scanner's camera still captures the color data of the liquid, but laser scan data points do not exist in the final point cloud on which to assign the color data. In typical BPA, the bloodstains are largely dry by the time the analysis is completed; therefore, this is rarely a limitation worth considering in BPA, but worth noting when documenting larger, wet blood pools, flow patterns, altered stains, or serum stains.

Figure 33.8 TLS data depicting void created by scanning wet liquid on the floor of a warehouse.

Considerations

Knowledge of the aforementioned limitations and careful planning by the laser scanner operator is paramount to the successful capture of laser scan data at a given scene. The scope of the scene, the potential investigative question to be answered with the scan data, weather limitations, registration concerns are all factors that go into the pre-planning of where to place the scanner and what settings to use on the scanner for each scan position. Objects moving through the scan such as people walking or vehicles driving through a scene should be avoided, if possible. The laser scanner will capture data from those moving objects and subsequently create artifacts which will later need to be corrected in post-processing. It is best to limit personnel and/or vehicle traffic in the scene while laser scanning to the greatest extent possible; this may require closing hallways, sidewalks, roadways, etc.

As it relates to bloodstain evidence specifically, in addition to ensuring the entire surrounding context of the area containing the bloodstain evidence is properly captured, considerations for the size and scope of the bloodstained area or object should be taken into account. In addition, the type of bloodstains present and the potential for subsequent analysis should also be considered. A larger area with largely drip stains and/or transfer patterns may be able to be captured at a lower resolution to depict the overall distribution and stain pattern. Whereas the area and/or surfaces containing impact or cast-off pattern stains may need to be scanned at a higher resolution and more scans may need to be performed to capture the area in great detail.

As mentioned earlier, laser scan data alone are not sufficient to adequately perform an analysis on an impact or cast-off pattern. High-resolution photographs must also be taken of the patterns along with high-resolution scan data, on top of which the photographs will be aligned. In order to align the photographs with the scan data, artificial reference markers must be placed around the stains to be documented and those markers must be visible in both the scan data and photographs to align the two media. This process will be described in depth in following sections, but the selection of which area of stains and the orientation of the reference markers surrounding those stains are of utmost importance.

In order to obtain high-quality, accurate laser scan data on the target surface containing bloodstain evidence, the laser scanner operator must choose a scanner resolution high enough and scanner-to-target distance close enough to capture laser scan data at an approximately 1 mm or lower point spacing. This ensures accurate alignment of the high-resolution photographs with the scanned surface, minimizing error in the subsequent analysis. Additional steps and considerations for the analysis of impact patterns and cast-off patterns will be discussed in depth in the following sections.

Photogrammetry

Photogrammetry has a long history that arose soon after the first cameras were invented in the 1850s. At the time, it was discovered that by taking overlapping images, the camera could be used for terrestrial mapping and aerial surveying. The methods used at that early time were all manual and required that geometric perspective lines were drawn directly on plate photographs to calculate elevation and positional data. Of course, analytical methods and computing have played an enormous role in the advancement of photogrammetry over the years. Today, many people know that photogrammetry is a process of taking several overlapping photographs of an object, loading them into a software program, and then having some sort of 3D output as a dense point cloud or colored, meshed model. This process is the basis of most modern-day photogrammetry programs and although there are a lot of high-tech algorithms, vector algebra, and heavy computing happening behind the scenes, the users simply need to perform some basic operations and they can produce some stunning results.

The basic process of photogrammetry can be summarized as follows:

1. Images are acquired and uploaded to a software program.
2. Photographs are automatically processed to find "matches" between similar photographs.

3. The camera positions are reconstructed and a sparse set of points is established.
4. A dense point cloud reconstruction is performed.
5. A meshed object is created from the dense points.
6. A high-resolution texture is applied to the meshed object.
7. The model is exported to other programs for analysis or inspection.

These steps are common to many photogrammetry programs but omit items such as editing, scaling, or choosing the area of interest. Of particular importance is the scaling step which sets the scale of the entire model.

Unlike laser scanners, photogrammetry has no fixed scale. It is up to the user to enter some sort of reference scale. This can be both problematic and beneficial at the same time since it's possible to photograph objects of extreme sizes. The only limitations are the camera, lens, equipment, and accessibility to the object. For example, a large scene on the order of 200 m is best photographed from an elevated position using a drone, thus, access is important. On the other hand, a small bloodstain of less than 1 mm in diameter may require a macro lens and a very stable setup. This varying scale makes photogrammetry a very flexible technology and maximizes its use in many different scenarios.

In contrast, an instrument such as a laser scanner is often provided by the manufacturer with a range of optimal scanning distances and set accuracy. Most scanners fall into a range of accuracy on the order of a few millimeters at short distances and this is often reported on a manufacturer's specification sheet, which is a convenient and simple way for an analyst to communicate the accuracy of an instrument. However, objects which fall below the manufacturer's stated accuracy may not be practical (or even possible) to scan with sufficient accuracy. Digital cameras can interchange lenses from typical zoom lenses to fixed focal length macro lenses and thus, investigators can capture smaller pieces of evidence with finer details so that they can be recreated in 3D. Figure 33.9 shows a three-dimensional model of a hiking boot which was created using photogrammetry. Small spatter stains on the surface of the boot can be visualized and measured in a 3D analysis for directionality.

There are different ways to scale a photogrammetry model, but one of the simplest ways is to use reference points. These reference points may be established by using specific, artificial targets that are placed around the model, or by simply selecting two existing points on the model with known distances between them. Thus, an external scale or ruler can be placed on a wall or by the

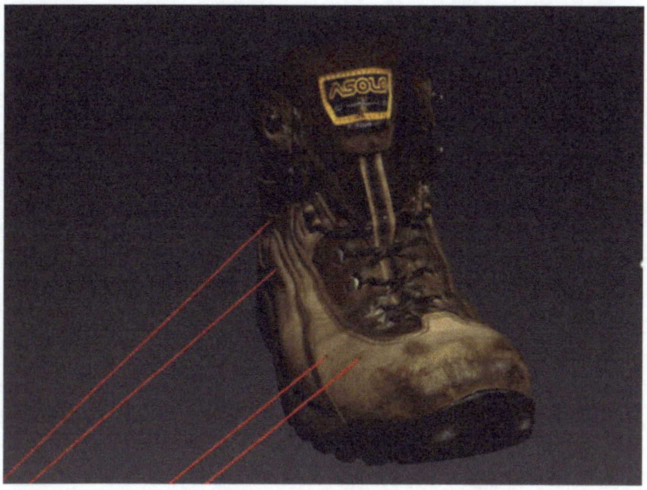

Figure 33.9 Hiking boot with reconstructed bloodstain trajectories visualized with red vector lines.

side of a weapon for example, as a known measurement. So long as the scale is included and visible in several photographs, it is usually possible to scale the model accurately. Any errors in setting the reference scale for a photogrammetry model propagate throughout the entire model. Thus, it is important to take this step seriously and accurately select the exact location of each reference point for determining the most accurate measurement between the reference points, whether it be by tape measure or other device. Also, it is often best to make the scale larger than the object being measured. This way, the error does not extrapolate with the measurement. As an example, assume a bloodstain pattern on a wall is approximately 30 cm in length and a small 1 cm scale is placed in the middle of the pattern as a reference measurement. Should the analyst make a 1 mm error in selecting the points on the scale, a measurement across a distance of 50 cm would be scaled 50 times, thus introducing a measurement error on the order of 5 cm. On the other hand, when measuring the same pattern and using a larger 50 cm reference scale, a 1 mm error does not increase within the 50 cm region. Thus, scale placement and reference point location can have a large impact on the overall accuracy of a photogrammetry model, as depicted in Figure 33.10.

The application of photogrammetry in forensics has many uses since it has some advantages as compared to other 3D technologies. Perhaps the most obvious advantage is that most people already own or have access to a digital camera, whether it be in their mobile phones, tablets, or a professional DSLR or mirrorless camera kit. Thus, the availability and investment cost for the hardware is already within reach of most people/agencies. Regardless as to whether people are familiar or not with photogrammetry software, having some knowledge of how to take photographs for photogrammetry means that one is able to "freeze" a scene in photographs. Should the need arise in the future to extract any measurement data or 3D models, the opportunity has not been lost.

There are several techniques for capturing photographs for a good 3D reconstruction. In general, the best photogrammetry models get reconstructed when the layout and structure of the photographs is based on the "ring method." This means that the camera operator takes photographs in an organized and controlled fashion around the object of interest. Contrary to what is often taught in typical forensic photography courses, the photographs should not all be taken at 90° to the surface of an object. In fact, photogrammetry benefits from having multiple, overlapping images

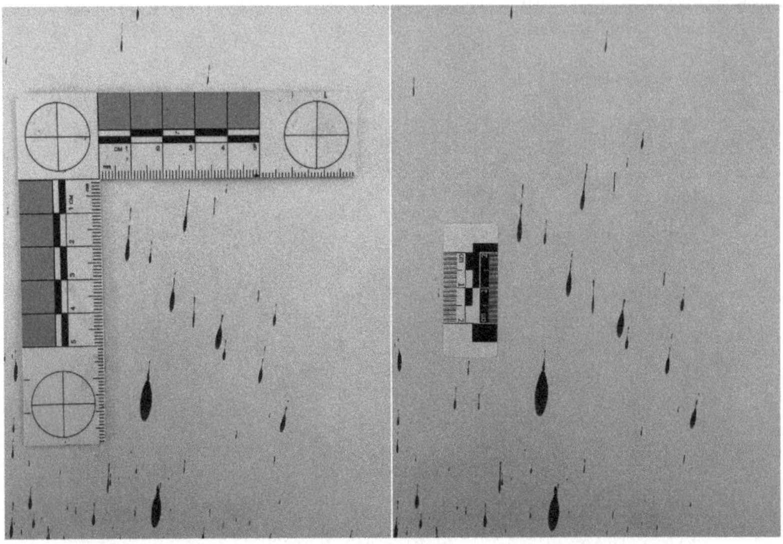

Figure 33.10 Image on left shows a large scale which is beneficial for measuring the smaller bloodstains and minimizes errors when measuring across the image. Image on right shows a small scale that will cause measurement errors to be extrapolated when measuring bloodstains across the image.

from differing angles. A typical strategy example for a piece of evidence on the ground would be to try and photograph all around the object in a 360° circle. Keeping the camera at a constant focal length (i.e., zoom setting) and a similar distance around the object is helpful. Also, using small angles of separation between each photograph, approximately 15° or less, ensures that plenty of overlap between photographs is available for the reconstruction process. Sufficient overlap is an important aspect for a successful photogrammetry model as only the areas which are overlapping can be reconstructed into a 3D model.

Of course, there are many scenarios where it is not possible to get completely around an object due to confined spaces, obstructions, furniture, walls, etc.; however, it is still important to take multiple images of the object of interest. Sometimes, using elevation can help by photographing overlapping images in a different direction instead of moving horizontally around an object. Often, tripods, poles, and other accessories may be helpful in getting the right photographs. It's important to remember that since photographs are the basis of the photogrammetry reconstruction, all photographic best practices apply. This means setting the correct exposure, shutter speed, depth of field, focus and ISO on the camera to get the best photographs possible.

Another advantage of photogrammetry has to do with the speed of acquisition. Under most daylight or indoor conditions where lighting is sufficient, the digital camera can work incredibly fast. Since the digital camera is a non-contact device, it also lessens the risk of evidence contamination. So long as the photographer can get access to the evidence by moving closer to the object or by using different lenses, the camera is an extremely capable tool. Additionally, the photographer needs to be able to take photographs from different angles for the best 3D reconstruction results. This can be challenging at times in confined spaces, but certainly not impossible with additional accessories such as camera poles, tripods, and even drones. However, when considering bloodstains, a typical tripod is all that is necessary since the area for documentation remains relatively small.

Visually, photogrammetry 3D models are often photorealistic and appealing to the eye. This is due to the fact that sensors in most modern-day DSLR and mirrorless cameras are relatively robust in resolution, accuracy, and resultant image quality. This is not always the case when dealing with terrestrial laser scanners where the on-board camera is of relatively lower resolution and quality. Many of the terrestrial laser scanners do not allow for full control of the camera and are limited by presets. Thus, laser scanner point cloud data often falls short of being photorealistic when compared to a photogrammetry model.

Time is always a factor and must be given some consideration. The entire photogrammetry process from image capture to a basic reconstructed model can be rather significant when the number of high-resolution photographs is greater than 100 images. Fortunately, smaller evidence or smaller portions of a scene often require less than 100 images. However, most photogrammetry packages require a significant amount of time to process large sets of photographs since there are additional factors such as editing, cleaning, scaling, meshing, and texturing before a final model is complete. These activities can equate to a few hours of work. However, the actual time to gather the photos at the crime scene is minimal and quite an efficient process. This can be demonstrated by the rapid surge in the use of drones to map large crime and accident scenes. The ability to get the drone and camera into an elevated position means that large areas can be photographed in minutes as opposed to hours. Crash and crime scene documentation has become a very popular application of photogrammetry since drones and unmanned aerial vehicles (UAVs) allow for quick access to an overall outdoor scene with perspectives only possible with aerial platforms. However, since the digital camera is available to many people in many forms (e.g., high-end digital camera, phone camera, tablet camera), the ability to capture smaller pieces of evidence such as bloodstain patterns, clothing, weapons, and other objects on the order of several meters is easily achievable. The resulting data set can be processed to provide a fully textured 3D model with sufficient accuracy to do an analysis (where necessary) for the investigator. Thus, there are many situations when photogrammetry is the right choice for speed, quality of data, and accuracy, especially when considering small pieces of evidence or very large, outdoor scenes.

Figure 33.11 Left: Photograph of bathroom wall with targets. Right: Reconstructed dense point cloud showing noise and limited data on walls where lack of texture causes problems with the photogrammetric reconstruction.

Some typical limitations of photogrammetry have to do with the types of surfaces on which blood may be deposited. A key point for a good photogrammetry reconstruction is that the object requires a lot of random texture. A photograph of a white wall with very small bloodstains does not make for a good photogrammetric reconstruction. In fact, white walls will often produce voids in the data or a lot of noise. This is quite common on plain textured surfaces since the photogrammetry algorithm has difficulties trying to pinpoint exactly where a point is located in 3D space. Figure 33.11 shows a reconstructed model of a bathroom wall and how noise presents itself around the flat areas of the wall which are devoid of any random patterns.

There are currently many photogrammetry software packages available in the market today which range in price from free to several thousands of dollars. However, many developers allow for monthly licensing and there are often different levels for each package that can fit varying budgets, operating systems, and needs. This is partly why photogrammetry is such a flexible option for many agencies.

SPATTER PATTERN ANALYSIS

The two most commonly analyzed bloodstain patterns using 3D data are *impact patterns* and *cast-off patterns*. The general workflow behind capturing complete and accurate data using 3D technologies for the analysis of these two types of bloodstain patterns involves the following steps, generally:

1. The identification and labeling of individual stain areas to be documented and analyzed
2. Affixing common reference markers (such as circular checkerboard targets) to the bloodstained surface(s) surrounding the stain to be analyzed
3. Capturing 3D data of the bloodstained surface(s), including the common reference markers
4. Capturing close-up, high-quality, in-focus digital 2D images of each area of the target bloodstain area, ensuring a minimum of three reference markers are captured in each 2D image
5. Scaling and aligning the 2D digital images on top of the resulting 3D data, using the common reference markers as alignment points
6. Using 3D analysis software to analyze the resulting stains in three dimensions

Impact Pattern Analysis

The mechanisms and characteristics of an impact pattern are discussed elsewhere within this text. One major advantage of 3D technologies is the ability to analyze and subsequently visualize impact patterns on surfaces within the 3D environment. Traditional analysis techniques for the calculation of area of convergence and area of origin involve time-consuming and laborious manual measurement techniques on scene using tape measures and string. Proper capturing of 3D data for an impact pattern on scene allows the analyst to calculate the area of origin back at the office rather than spending time at a scene. Additionally, because 3D measurement data of the entire scene is possible, analysis and conclusions can be drawn from the area of origin to its surrounding context and this can be done days, weeks, months and years after leaving the scene.

The collection of data to conduct an analysis of an impact pattern starts with the proper identification and labeling of individual stain areas within the impact pattern to be documented and analyzed. The selection of these stains follows the same principles as area of origin analysis using the manual measurement method. Studies have shown that the selection and subsequent analysis of longer and more elliptical stains resulted in the lowest error when compared to the selection and analysis of more circular stains.[4] In addition, upward-traveling stains, which are less likely to have been influenced by gravity, should be selected. Figures 33.12 and 33.13 depict a section of a 3D point cloud containing an impact pattern on two perpendicular walls in the corner of a room.

Once a cluster of representative stains has been selected, common reference markers must be placed surrounding the cluster of stains. These reference markers serve as common points between the 2D photographs and 3D point cloud data. Three of the markers should be placed in an "L" shape such that two markers are roughly parallel to a horizontal surface (i.e. the floor) and the third marker is perpendicular to these other two markers, as depicted in Figure 33.14. Different software programs may have different requirements for the markers. Each stain area to be documented and photographed can be labeled to differentiate one stain area from another when aligning the photographs to the point cloud.

Following the placement of the reference markers and labeling of stain clusters, high-resolution photographs must be taken of each cluster of stains to be analyzed as part of the impact pattern. These photographs are typically taken with high enough resolution and level of detail to enlarge on a computer screen and identify the margins of the bloodstain ellipses to be analyzed. The photograph should encompass at least three of the common reference markers, typically in three corners

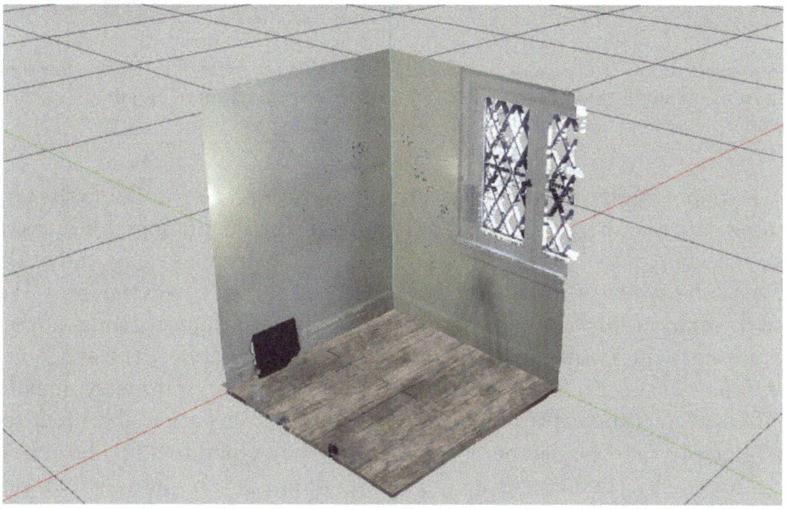

Figure 33.12 Section of a 3D point cloud containing an impact pattern in the corner of a room to be reconstructed in 3D space.

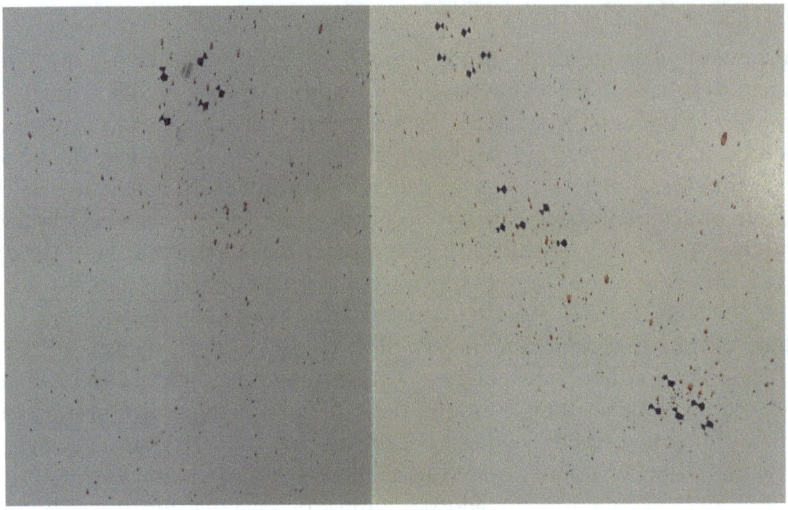

Figure 33.13 Close-up view of 3D data containing an impact pattern in the corner of a room.

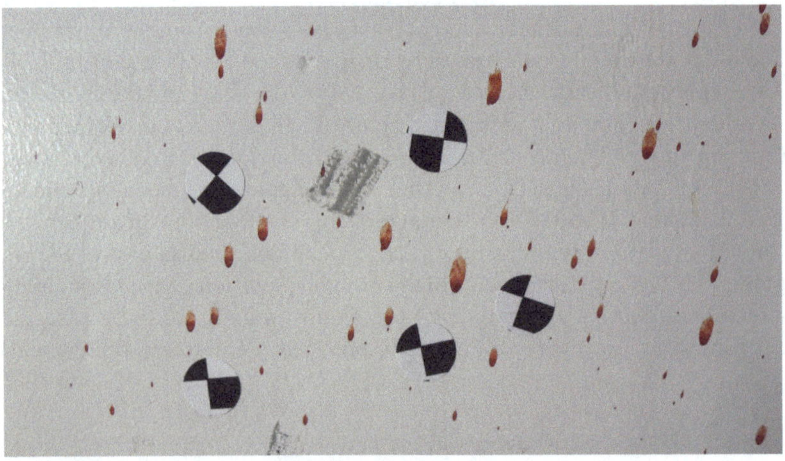

Figure 33.14 High-resolution 2D image of one section of an impact pattern including three circular checkerboard targets used as common reference markers for scaling and subsequent alignment of the photograph to the 3D point cloud.

of the image. The photographs must be taken with the sensor plane parallel to the target surface to ensure no distortion in the image. The further from parallel the photograph is taken, the greater the error in the subsequent analysis. The photographs must be properly exposed so the bloodstains can be visualized in contrast with the target surface and the photographs must also be in clear, sharp focus, so the margins of the ellipses are clearly defined for later marking in the software.

Once the reference markers and labels are in place and photographed, the area must be captured with the appropriate 3D technology, whether that's using photogrammetry, handheld 3D scanner, or TLS. 3D data must be captured with a high enough resolution and point spacing so that the individual reference markers can be selected in the point cloud to allow for proper scaling and alignment of photographs. The better quality of 3D data and 2D photographs captured at the scene will minimize error in the subsequent analysis. The same 3D capture principles apply to the capture of 3D data, such as using reference measurements, minimizing registration error, and using appropriate resolution and point spacing.

Once the 2D and 3D data have been captured of the impact pattern, the rest of the analysis is done in the bloodstain analysis software. At the time of publication, only two software packages are known to these authors, which allow for the analysis of impact patterns using 3D data. In both instances, the 3D data are imported, processed, and registered (if necessary) inside the 3D software package. That data, along with the 2D photographs, are then imported into one of the two aforementioned software packages to analyze the impact pattern.

Inside the analysis software, the 2D photographs are enlarged and the exact center of the common reference markers within the photographs are selected as depicted in Figure 33.15. The same is performed on the corresponding reference markers within the 3D point cloud. Once the center of all three markers are marked in the photographs and scan data, the software program scales the photographs and aligns the photographs to the 3D surface using the reference markers for alignment. It is imperative that the analyst take care in the selection of the reference markers, as a small selection error can affect the alignment of the photo to the 3D surface and therefore the subsequent analysis of the impact pattern.

Once all photographs are aligned to the 3D surface, as depicted in Figure 33.16, the process of marking the individual bloodstain ellipses can start. Within the analysis software, each photograph

Figure 33.15 Alignment process by picking the center of the common reference marker checkerboards.

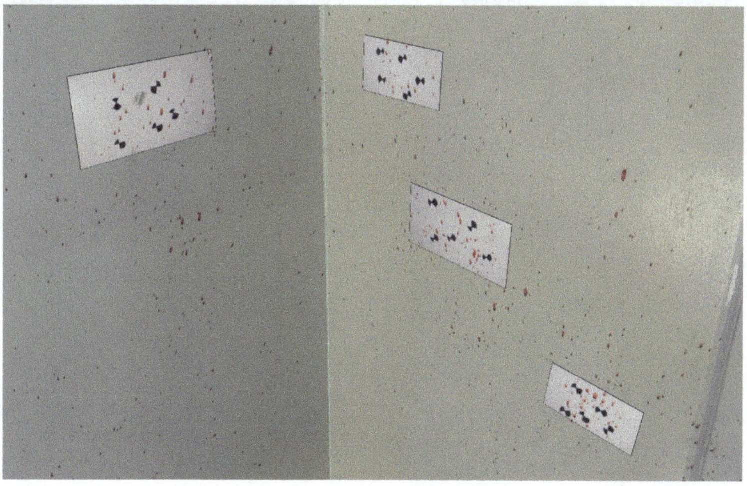

Figure 33.16 3D point cloud with 2D images aligned using common reference markers.

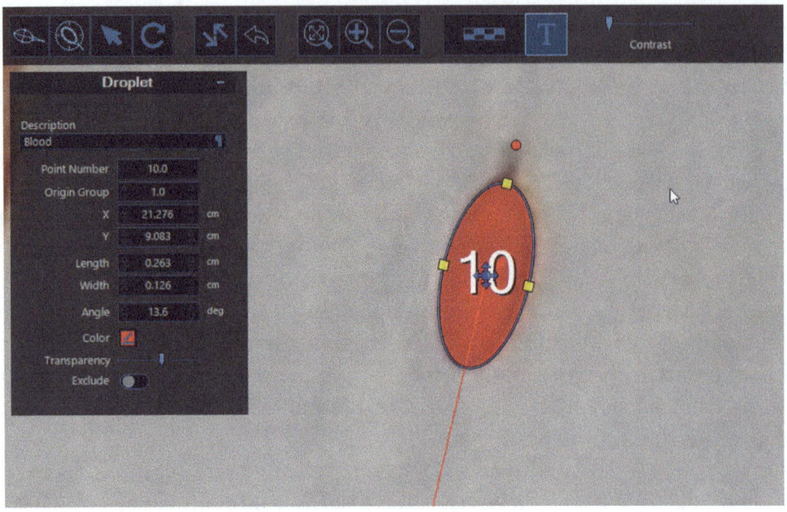

Figure 33.17 Ellipse marking tool within software program depicting semi-transparent virtual ellipse overlaid on top of actual bloodstain ellipse from photograph.

is enlarged so the margins of each ellipse to be analyzed are clearly defined. A digital ellipse marking tool is used to overlay virtual bloodstain ellipses on top of the actual bloodstain ellipses depicted in the photographs. The analyst first selects the leading edge of the bloodstain ellipse, followed by the trailing edge of the ellipse and then adjusts the width of the ellipse using the mouse scroll wheel to increase and decrease the width until the ellipse matches the shape of the bloodstain ellipse in the photograph, as depicted in Figure 33.17. As many bloodstain ellipses can be marked in this manner as the analyst wishes. Marking more bloodstain ellipses will increase the accuracy of the subsequent area of origin analysis. Figure 33.18 depicts multiple bloodstain ellipses marked within the software.

For each bloodstain marked, much like the manual measurement method, the software analyzes the length and width of the ellipse and reports an impact (alpha) angle for each ellipse. In addition, since the exact 3D location of each ellipse is known based on the 3D data, the directional (gamma)

Figure 33.18 Multiple ellipses marked for analysis within software on original photograph.

angle is calculated. The alpha and gamma angle are visually represented by a red 3D trajectory line for each bloodstain ellipse.

Once a sufficient number of bloodstain ellipses from all photographs captured are marked in the analysis software, an area of origin is calculated based on the intersection of the individual trajectory lines from the bloodstain ellipses. In addition, an ellipsoid, representing the calculated area of origin is created based on the selected standard deviation within the analysis software, as depicted in Figure 33.19. This 3D ellipsoid can now be visualized from any angle within the 3D point cloud and in relation to the other objects and context within the scanned scene, as depicted in Figure 33.20. In addition, because every point within the point cloud has an X, Y, Z value, the center of the area of origin ellipsoid can be measured from any point within the 3D scene, including the typical measurements of height off the floor and distance from the target surface(s), as depicted in Figure 33.21.

Lastly, once the area of origin is analyzed and depicted in 3D using the aforementioned methods, that data can be included in subsequent 3D visualizations to accurately depict the scene to the viewer. In Figures 33.22 and 33.23, the common X, Y, Z (0, 0, 0) origin at the corner of the room can be aligned in 3D software and 3D models can be imported to depict a demonstrative representation of the scene in relation to the 3D area of origin.

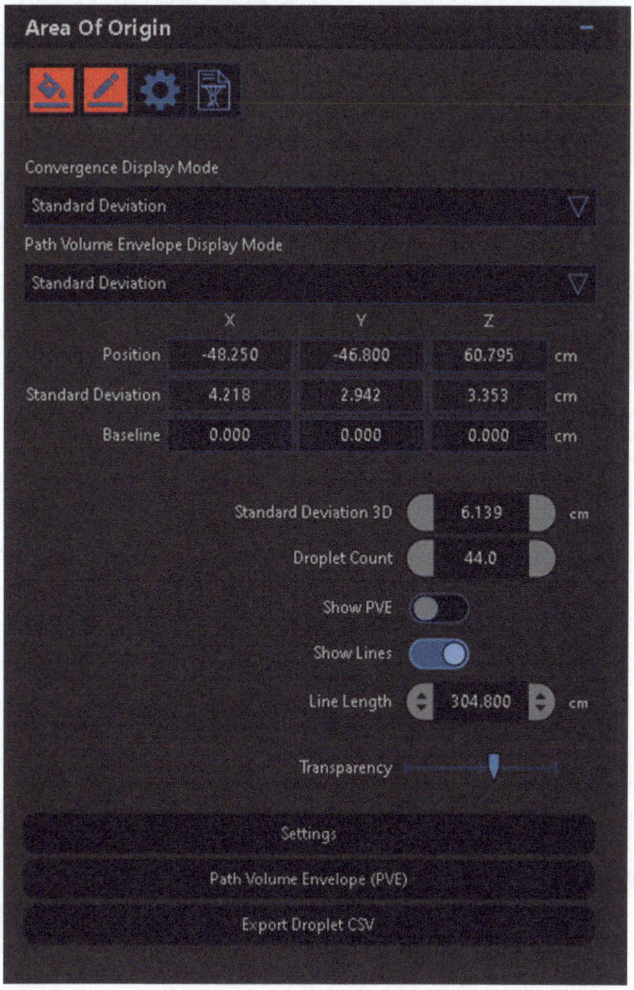

Figure 33.19 Area of origin analysis output after marking bloodstain ellipses on multiple 2D images.

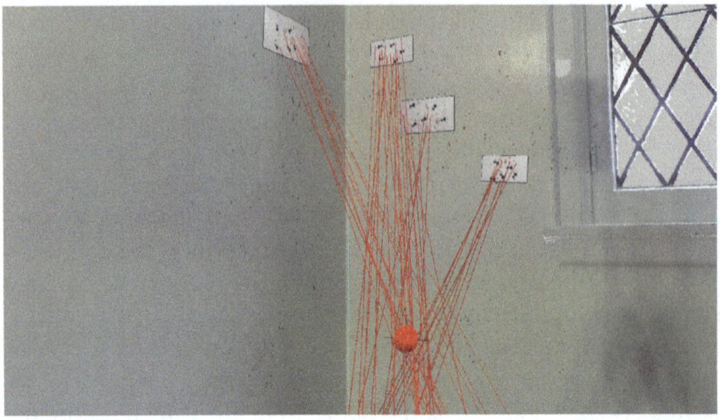

Figure 33.20 Resulting visualization of individual bloodstain calculated trajectories and resulting area of origin depiction as an ellipsoid.

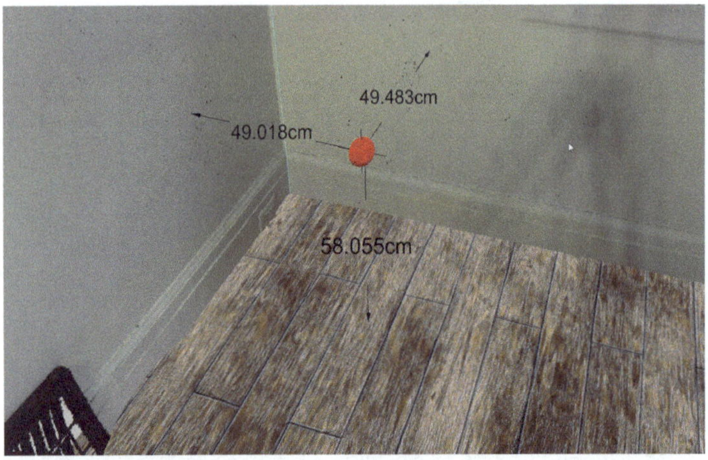

Figure 33.21 Ellipsoid representing one standard deviation of error surrounding area of origin with measurements to each adjacent wall and the floor.

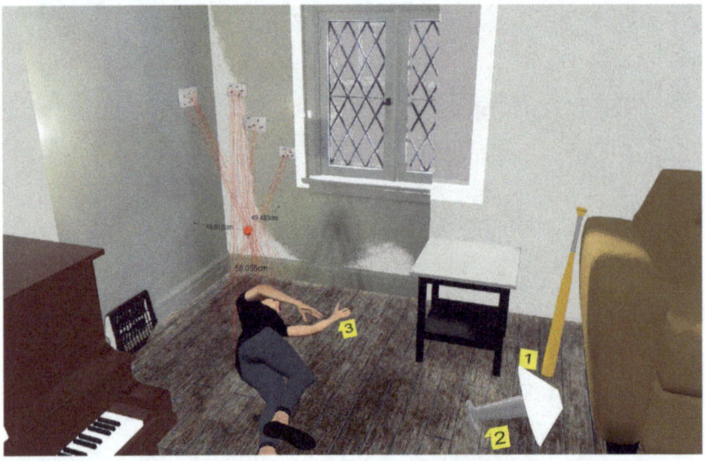

Figure 33.22 Impact pattern visualization inserted into a rendered 3D depiction of a scene using the common X, Y, Z (0, 0, 0) origin of the corner of the room.

Figure 33.23 Area of origin depicted with representative human 3D model placed into scene for context.

Cast-off Pattern Analysis

There are many mechanisms which can produce a cast-off pattern and many objects from which blood may be released. Cast-off patterns are the result of blood drops released from an object due to its motion. This motion must provide sufficient acceleration to overcome the adhesion forces of blood so that a portion of the blood breaks away from the source and is then free to move under the influence of gravity and air resistance. One can imagine a very typical scenario where a beating is taking place with a weapon such as a hammer or a baseball bat. Once the weapon breaks the surface of skin and meets a blood source, the blood adheres to the weapon, and when swung with sufficient force, blood is then projected onto another surface.

Cast-off patterns tend to make linear or slightly curvilinear paths of individual bloodstains. These paths may be long or short depending on the object's path, location of surfaces, intermediate objects (which may cause voids), and the stability of the weapon or object being swung. In addition, the distribution of bloodstains along the projected path may be broken or non-uniform with varying overall widths. Thus, there could be more bloodstains at the initial part of a cast-off pattern and less near the end. The variation in blood drops deposited through a cast-off pattern is great and thus, in real scene scenarios, where the quantity of bloodstains may be scarce, it is up to the analyst to determine whether these drops are part of a cast-off pattern, whether they are from a single event, and whether they are suitable for an analysis.

The size of cast-off stains often varies with the amount of blood deposited on the swung object and the force or acceleration, among other factors. There is normally a change in the elliptical shape of bloodstains as the swing path passes by a surface and creates an increasing or decreasing angle. As is typical in area of origin analysis, selection of the longer and more elliptical stains for analysis is desirable for minimizing errors. This has been shown in a large-scale study by Moore & Liscio[5] where blood drops tend to be more accurately marked when they are longer and more elliptical in nature. This is true for both the impact (alpha) angle and directional (gamma) angle.

The benefit of using 3D technologies to analyze a cast-off pattern is that it is now possible to determine a path volume envelope (PVE), which is a region of 3D space that encloses part of the object's swing path. Currently published studies are still exploring how to refine the analysis and determine typical uncertainties under laboratory conditions. The analysis of cast-off patterns is an extension of the area of origin analysis and requires all the same steps and procedures, including the calculation of the area of origin. This may not seem intuitive at first since the cast-off mechanism is quite different in nature from an impact, however, studies have shown that there is a benefit of using the area of origin in cast-off analysis.[6,7]

At the time of writing, there are only two known software packages available which have implemented the PVE as an option for BPA. This implementation is still relatively new and does not take advantage of more recent developments which help to refine the "envelope" from which an object was swung. The workflow is the same as the area of origin analysis, which involves selecting bloodstains and marking ellipses. Once this is complete, the user simply opts to show the PVE, which displays a rectangular prism that encompasses the majority of the swing path which formed the resultant bloodstains. The calculation and considerations of the PVE are different from those of an area of origin analysis since the position of the bloodstain and gamma angle play a bigger role in cast-off pattern analysis than the alpha angle. The study published by Liscio and Le shows that in a blind test, analysts were able to locate the lateral position of the PVE within a ±15 cm range.

Current studies are looking at typical errors and uncertainties of how to refine the PVE to provide greater confidence in the result as well as using statistical likelihoods to determine the area from which the swing path originated (see McCleary et al.).[8] It should be noted that although most studies include some form of 3D technology for the documentation portion of analysis, it is possible to document a cast-off pattern using traditional tools such as a camera and tape measure, without the use of a laser scanner. However, the risk of introducing human error, especially in complex scenarios, increases, as does the time to document a scene (Figure 33.24).

For the moment, the PVE method is a simplistic analysis, which provides an objective way to refine and state the position from where an object may have been swung. However, it is limited to a general area and is currently not possible to trace an accurate swing path in space. Although there is some suggestion that the current methods may be refined in the future, the PVE method is similar to the area of origin analysis in that it provides enough information to discern where an event may have occurred to a reasonable degree of certainty.

Figure 33.24 3D analysis of a cast-off pattern showing the overall path volume envelope (PVE). The object's swing path (shown as blue line) is enclosed inside of the PVE, and the red, linear trajectories of bloodstains are shown coming from adjacent walls.

VISUALIZATION

One of the benefits of working with 3D technologies is that the captured data are visual in nature. Large point clouds or 3D meshed objects with textures give a very good representation of relative scale and represent evidence "true to form." In many cases, the results of a documented piece of evidence can be immediately shown as a 3D render, animated model, or as a camera "fly through," whereby the user is given a small tour of the scene. This can be useful at trial as demonstrative evidence and can enhance the understanding of judges, juries, or analysts with respect to the overall form of a larger scene or smaller piece of evidence.

The most common type of 3D instrument used in BPA cases is the terrestrial laser scanner although photogrammetry and hand scanners are also being utilized. Thus, there are more and more sources of 3D digital data, which allow for different types of analysis. Whether it is used for a directional analysis of bloodstains, area of origin, or a cast-off pattern analysis, the results of a 3D analysis are easily visualized, which can be useful when trying to explain difficult concepts or when the scene is complex in nature.

Most bloodstain pattern analysis software programs that work with 3D data also provide reports and different perspectives of the results overlaid on top of the 3D data. However, simply presenting results as a list of numbers, coordinates, or positions is not always intuitive for people to understand. The more complex the scene, the better it is to visualize the results directly with the collected 3D data. Jurors can then see the results of the analysis directly overlaid in the virtual scene and gain a better perspective with context.

2D Renderings

With respect to BPA, perhaps the most common type of visualization is a 2D rendering of the data, which shows marked bloodstains, bloodstain trajectories, and the result overlaid on the 3D data. This is quite powerful when one can see the results of analysis in the context of the scene and simple screen captures can be easily included in reports, PDF documents, and shown on large screens for judges and juries to ponder without the need for any special technology.

Animated Flythroughs

Animated flythroughs are also possible and useful for a few reasons. However, it's useful to discern that animated flythroughs are not the same as a crime scene animation where people or other objects are shown to be moving. When providing a scene flythrough, only the camera is moving, and the scene remains static. It is as if a moment has been frozen in time and it's possible to move and inspect the scene without any influence of moving objects, people, or other items. This is useful in that an animated flythrough can give people a very strong sense of spatial relationships and provides many different perspectives of a scene from different angles. This is a good alternative to showing individual still images when it may be important to demonstrate a particular aspect of the scene or BPA from different angles.

Interactive 3D Models

Interactive 3D models such as the one depicted in Figure 33.25, have also been used as demonstrative evidence and although less common, can be a powerful tool. The interactive models are packaged in a player and once launched, allow the user to interact with a computer mouse and to show different angles based on their own input. As with animations, interactive 3D models may be static or animated; although for most BPA uses, the models would likely be static. However, animations have preset camera paths that are fixed once they are rendered and presented. Additional angles require that the user complete a different animation or that they alter their original animation to

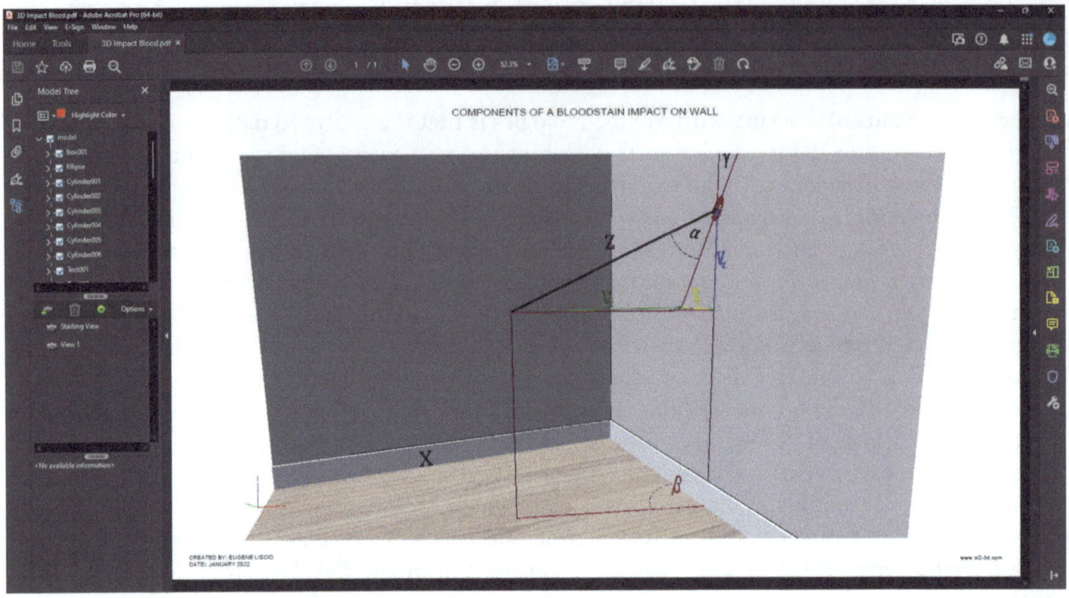

Figure 33.25 Interactive 3D PDF model of a bloodstain on a wall showing the components of the trajectory and angles. The user can rotate and pan the image to move into any view.

include the new camera positions. Interactive 3D models allow for the user to move to any position around the virtual model, zoom, pan, turn items on and off, and make screen captures that can be entered as evidence at trial. Perhaps the greatest benefit here is that the user has much flexibility during a presentation, and it keeps judges and juries interested.

Virtual Reality

Virtual reality (VR) has been a topic of great discussion on social media in recent times due to the development of new technologies and the large companies investing in VR as a new social media platform. More and more young people are becoming comfortable and educated on the immersive experience. Currently, the greatest use of VR in the forensics and law enforcement area is for training as depicted in the screenshot of a VR training environment in Figure 33.26, with limited use

Figure 33.26 Screen capture taken from a VR immersive training package. (Courtesy of RiVR.)

in actual cases and at trial. The idea with VR is that detectives, attorneys, judges, and juries can all be taken back to the scene of the crime and given a virtual tour of the environment. In some cases, this may be unnecessary as the use of photographs and other 3D technologies provide enough for a judge or juror to understand the spatial aspects of a scene. However, there are scenarios where a witness perspective cannot be accurately recreated or when an important spatial aspect such as height or depth has not been accurately depicted in photographs or animated flythroughs. Thus, it is in these situations where VR may provide the greatest benefit.

There is currently much interest in VR although there is also some "VR hesitancy" in the forensics world with respect to its adoption at trials. There are many reasons for this but some of the more important points have to do with financial, technical, and logistical issues. To begin with, setting up a VR experience is no trivial matter. The effort required to provide a realistic and professional looking VR experience is likely beyond the capabilities of most law enforcement agencies. Hiring an external company to provide this type of experience is also quite costly since it is a custom setup and experience. Thus, this may dissuade some law enforcement agencies from using this type of visualization. There are some software programs that make it simpler to import 3D data from different sources and then become immersed in the data set. However, this does not provide any interactivity other than basic movement around the virtual space and perhaps some basic measurements. It also does not provide any type of analysis such as area of origin or cast-off pattern analysis.

From a technical standpoint, there are different types of VR experiences often classified and they can be classified as three degrees of freedom (3DoF) or six degrees of freedom (6DoF). This is an important distinction because each changes the experience, technical requirements, and logistics.

A 3DoF experience is much like what people are used to seeing in Google Street View or in a typical real estate virtual tour. There are a series of preset 360° images that the user can move to within the tour, and it usually starts with being at a central position of any one of the 360° images. This can be imagined as being at the center of a "bubble." The viewer has the ability to look around in all directions and even interact with links that could trigger videos, documents, audio, or other media. However, the user can only be at the center of a single 360° image at one time, although they can move into the view of another bubble (i.e., another 360° image). It is not possible to move into a position between these preset locations. Thus, it is not a fully immersive experience where people can walk about a scene.

These types of 3DoF experiences have some advantages as they require less hardware and can be simultaneously broadcast to a judge or jury at trial. For example, if an attorney wished to take jurors on a tour of a scene to show a bloodstain pattern, it would be possible to outfit each juror, judge, attorney, defense, and others with a VR headset where they could see the scene while being seated comfortably in their chairs. The attorney could act as a guide and point out different locations of interest as they moved from one position to another. Jurors would be able to look around at will but would not have the ability to move to a different position until the guide (i.e., attorney) moved to a new part of the scene. This solution is a simple implementation that is currently possible without a lot of technical hurdles.

A 6DoF experience, such as that depicted in Figure 33.27, can work in a similar manner to the above except that the viewers can also walk around the immersive environment and are not limited to any one fixed position in space. Thus, for using this type of setup at trial requires a large space such that people could experience the full scene by looking, walking, and interacting with any relevant links/media that were in place. Currently, the technology to provide a large scale 6DoF experience is rather limited and is not easily deployed at trial. In addition, there are issues with the viewers' experience using controls, whereby moving around in a 3D VR environment has some associated risks of motion sickness which would lead to an unpleasant experience. Thus, for the moment, the 3DoF is a simpler solution for implementation at trial as the technology is readily available, has lower cost, and the user experience is effective. It is likely that 3DoF is a good starting point for using VR at trials.

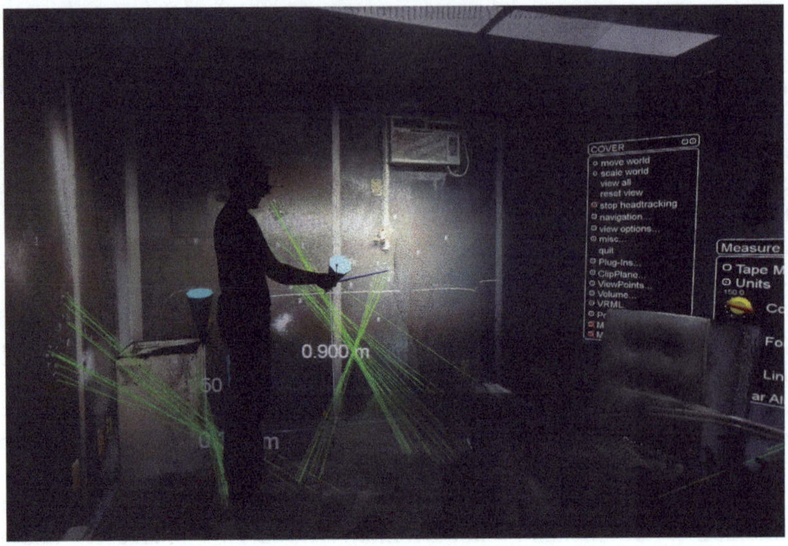

Figure 33.27 Dr. Uwe Woessner from the University of Stuttgart in "The Cave." This is a virtual environment with 6DoF. The results of a BPA are overlaid on a point cloud and the user is able to interact with the environment.

Notes

1. American Society for Photogrammetry and Remote Sensing (ASPRS), *Manual of Photogrammetry*, 6th ed. Bethesda: ASPRS, 2013.
2. Le, Quan; Liscio, Eugene P. "FARO Zone 3D Area of Origin Tools with Handheld 3D Data." *Journal of the Association of Crime Scene Reconstruction*, no. 23 (2019): 1–10. https://d7922adf-f499-4a26-96d4-8ab2d521fa35.usrfiles.com/ugd/d7922a_cf292e36c80e490083eff413faed6045.pdf
3. Ropero-Miller, Jeri. "Landscape Study on 3D Crime Scene Scanning Devices." *National Institute of Justice* (2016):1–53. https://www.ojp.gov/library/publications/landscape-study-3d-crime-scene-scanning-devices
4. Liscio, Eugene P.; Moore, Craig C. "A Large-Scale Study of Bloodstain Ellipse Marking." *Journal of Bloodstain Pattern Analysis*, vol. 36, no. 3 (2021): 22–36.
5. Ibid.
6. Liscio, Eugene; Le, Quan. "Inter Observer Errors of Cast-Off Stains Using FARO Zone 3D." *Forensic Science International*, vol. 330 (2022). https://doi.org/10.1016/j.forsciint.2021.111098
7. Liscio, Eugene; Bozek, Patrick; Guryn, Helen; Le, Quan. "Observations and 3D Analysis of Controlled Cast-Off Stains." *Journal of Forensic Sciences*, vol. 65, no. 4 (2020): 1556–4029. https://doi.org/10.1111/1556-4029.14301
8. McCleary, Scott; Liscio, Eugene, De Brabanter, Kris, Attinger, Daniel. "Automated Reconstruction of Cast-Off Blood Spatter Patterns Based on Euclidean Geometry and Statistical Likelihood." *Forensic Science International*, vol. 319 (2021): 110628. http://dx.doi.org/10.1016/j.forsciint.2020.110628

CHAPTER 34

QUALITY ASSURANCE IN BLOODSTAIN PATTERN ANALYSIS

LeeAnn Singley

Quality assurance (QA) can be defined as "a program for the systemic monitoring and evaluation of the various aspects of a project, service, or facility to ensure that standards of quality are being met."[1] A variety of fields, such as medicine, manufacturing, engineering, hotel management, etc., utilize quality control (QC) and QA measures to provide confidence to the consumer that a quality product has been produced. Having a *documented* program establishes not only the framework for the monitoring processes but also a mode of accountability as to whether those processes are being followed.

The phrases quality control and quality assurance are often used interchangeably, although each holds a different meaning and purpose. QC refers to processes that are employed to determine the quality measures for a product or service have been met. In the forensic arena, an example of this might be standard drug samples used in gas chromatography or quality checks to ensure a reagent is working properly. QA, on the other hand, refers to an organized system of quality measures that establish confidence in the product outcomes.[2] This chapter will focus on the QA program aspects for bloodstain pattern analysis (BPA).

A QA program in BPA carries particular importance since the work product, the written report, can influence life-changing positive or negative outcomes for a defendant or victim. It is for this reason that all forensic agencies providing BPA services, including laboratories, private consultants, and police departments, ensure the establishment of sound, documented QA programs.

The first step in establishing a program is determining the specific components which apply to the agency and will be addressed within the QA system. As stated previously, the system is designed as a means of accountability for the consumer, so it is crucial that the agency is actually doing what they say they are doing. As a result, a QA component, or part thereof, should not be included merely because it is what is expected, but because it works within the framework of that agency. Additionally, agencies with already established QA programs for other forensic disciplines should guard against overlooking the special needs of BPA when seeking to offer this service as a function of their agency. A reliable resource for establishing a QA program specific to BPA can be found in the ANSI/ASB Standard 030, *Standard for a Quality Assurance Program in Bloodstain Pattern Analysis*.[3] The components addressed within this resource will be expanded upon here.

TERMS AND DEFINITIONS

Establishing a QA program begins with defining the levels of adherence each component will be expected to meet. Words matter – therefore, it is important for terms like "shall," "must," "should," "recommend" to be defined in the context of the program and that the agency is realistic in its ability to meet the component. For example, if an agency defines the word "shall" as a provision that is mandatory, one might guard against stating that each analyst "shall" attend training every

DOI: 10.4324/9781003163695-34

six months if budgetary restrictions will not allow for it. This does not mean an agency should set the bar arbitrarily low either. Thoughtful consideration should be undertaken when choosing the level of adherence so as to meet the highest quality possible.

PERSONNEL AND QUALIFICATIONS

The quality of a work product is dependent on the training and qualifications of the individuals producing that product. An agency's QA program should establish the minimum education, training, and experience required to perform BPA in that agency. This starts with establishing the prerequisite education necessary to enter into the BPA training program. The training program itself must be well-documented and comprehensive to include the specific training goals and objectives. The criteria for demonstrating competency in each of the training objectives must also be included. Furthermore, given the interpretive elements of BPA, training under a qualified analyst in a mentorship component is also vital. Finally, an agency should emphasize continuing education through ongoing training and conference attendance as an important part of a QA program. Guidance for establishing educational and training requirements can be found in ANSI/ASB Standard 032, *Standards for a Bloodstain Pattern Analyst's Training Program.*[4]

While the appropriate training and education of individuals is essential, equally important is the opportunity for the analyst to employ that training. An agency should evaluate their personnel and the demand for BPA within their agency; and then establish the number of analysts necessary to meet those demands. Too many will limit the opportunity to engage in BPA; too few may place undue demands on the analysts.

STANDARD OPERATING PROCEDURES

A critical component of a QA program is establishing the overarching framework for *how* the BPA will be performed within that agency. Standard Operating Procedures (SOP) will create that framework and will likely be the most expansive element of a documented QA program. Agencies can refer to ANSI/ASB Standard 031, *Standard for Developing Standard Operating Procedures in Bloodstain Pattern Analysis,*[5] for guidance in developing their own SOP.

At the outset, agencies must first establish the *scope* of BPA services it will offer. Will BPA be performed at both crime scenes and in the laboratory? Will analysis also include photographic review? Each of these circumstances will carry different needs regarding training, staffing, equipment, etc. Once the scope of the agency's BPA operations has been determined, the methodology – or the description of the steps used to carry out the BPA – should be incorporated as part of the SOP. The methodology should initially consider how an agency will triage pre-analysis information, and the sequential unmasking of that information, so as to mitigate bias to the analyst.

Appropriate *documentation* and *data collection* are critical to the final analysis. The agency must therefore establish the means for documentation and the steps for data collection as part of the SOP. Documentation will take the form of photographic records, notes, and sketches. This section of the SOP will set forth the agency-specific elements for each form of documentation. Regarding data collection, the criteria for pattern recognition and classification, a critical piece of the BPA, will be considered in this part of the SOP. Furthermore, specific processes for determining angle of impact and area of origin calculations should also be addressed here.

In addition to necessary BPA data collection, certain forms of supporting testing relevant to the BPA may also be the responsibility of the bloodstain pattern analyst as part of an agency's protocols. This supporting testing may include, but is not limited to, presumptive blood testing, species identification, and collection for DNA analysis. Subsequently, written procedures associated with supportive testing must also be established.

During the *data review and analysis* stage of the examination, the collected data is analyzed in conjunction with other associated information in order to generate conclusions with regard to the BPA. Ultimately, this may assist in the reconstruction of events surrounding the case. It is therefore important for the agency to establish the process for data review and analysis as part of their SOP. The gathering of all the documentation generated in the course of the analysis and the correlation of this information with other reports which are relevant to the BPA will begin this review. These reports include autopsy reports, forensic biology reports, and crime scene diagrams, to name but a few. It is essential that the agency acknowledge within the SOP that during this stage, it may be necessary to reevaluate the previous classification of the bloodstain patterns in light of this relevant information. As the analysis unfolds, *reconstruction experimentation* may also be necessary and the agency should ensure that the steps for designing appropriate experimentation are captured in the SOP. The final steps to be addressed in the SOP include the analyst's drawing upon all information and data to form conclusions/opinions based on the facts of the case. The communication of these conclusions will come in the form of a written final report.

A sound BPA QA program will have documented and defined measures for report generation, review, and approval. The report is the final work product provided by the bloodstain pattern analyst to its stakeholders. It is the document that will often be referred to in preliminary hearings or during testimony in court, and in so doing, carries with it tremendous amount of weight. Therefore, the established criteria for report writing within the SOP should not be taken lightly. Guidance for report writing can be found in ANSI/ASB Standard 031, *Standard for Report Writing in Bloodstain Pattern Analysis*.[6] While reports may vary from agency to agency, it is important that reports generated *within* an agency follow a standard format. This would include the use of consistent and standard terminology. The Organization of Scientific Area Committees (OSAC) has established a listing of terms and definitions in BPA which has been subsequently published for reference in a technical report through the American Academy of Forensic Sciences (AAFS) Academy Standards Board (ASB).[7]

All completed reports must be subjected to both an administrative and a technical review and therefore it is vital that the SOP address the steps in this undertaking. The administrative review will address editorial correctness within the report, while the technical review is designed to ensure the correct application of the methodology and whether the conclusions are appropriate for the data presented. The technical review must be conducted by a qualified second party and include the evaluation of the reports, notes, data, and other relevant documentation. The technical review is a critical piece of the QA process because it is the final step in providing confidence to the stakeholders that quality measures have been followed. Consequently, it is vitally important that both reviews are documented to include at minimum the signature of the reviewer, the date of review, and the case file identification.

Finally, it is important for an agency to acknowledge within the SOP that certain situational *limitations* may exist that can affect the analysis of the bloodstains and subsequent conclusions. These factors are often case dependent and may include, but are not limited to the following:

- Lack of blood source information
- Environmental factors (e.g., weather conditions)
- Scene integrity and prior access
- Evidence item history and condition
- Cleaned or altered scenes
- Bloodstain patterns on movable objects
- Quality of documentation or photography

CASE FILES AND CONFORMANCE

The case file not only houses the information and documentation associated with the case which ultimately supports and includes the analyst's conclusions, but it is also the record to which the analyst and agency will refer in years to come. It is therefore essential that an agency includes as part of its QA program written procedures for the content and maintenance of BPA case files. Agencies should address what information must be included in the case file and where and for how long the files will be maintained. Additionally, a provider must incorporate a documented program for the periodic review of the case files to ensure their adherence to the agency's QA program with regard to content and maintenance. This can be accomplished through an annual audit of a set number of randomly selected case files reviewed for conformance.

ASSESSMENTS

A customer should not only have confidence in an agency's training program, but also that a trained analyst's skills and knowledge are being maintained year after year. Consequently, a BPA QA system should include a documented program of ongoing skill assessment. Two methods agencies can use to assess analysts are annual proficiency testing and the evaluation of courtroom testimony. Proficiency testing is a formal evaluation of an analyst's skills in specific areas of BPA. This type of assessment is made available externally through reputable outside vendors or can be produced by the agency internally. Guidance in BPA proficiency testing can be found in ANSI/ASB Standard 157, *Required Components for a Proficiency Testing Program in Bloodstain Pattern Analysis*.[8] Apart from proficiency testing, courtroom testimony evaluation provides a twofold benefit. This assessment evaluates both the analyst's ability to convey technical information to a layperson jury and the analyst's understanding of the legal process.

CORRECTIVE ACTION

It is not enough to simply create an agency BPA QA program. Documented policies and procedures only serve their purpose if they are being followed. Agencies should build into their quality framework written procedures for the identification of deficiencies as they pertain to the QA program and for the implementation of corrective action. These deficiencies may arise from the noting of administrative failures, analytical or interpretive errors, or skill assessment errors.

FACILITIES AND EVIDENCE CONTROL

In forensic science, the integrity of forensic evidence is paramount. Often expert testimony questioning revolves around the chain of custody of evidence and conditions that evidence is maintained, particularly regarding the avoidance of tampering, contamination, or evidence destruction. To that end, agencies must establish documented programs with safeguards for evidence integrity. This begins with ensuring that a facility, or part thereof, is secured from unauthorized access. Additionally, an agency must establish an evidence control system that addresses the steps to protect evidence integrity. This may look quite different from agency to agency, so it is important that this program is agency-specific. What applies to a multi-section crime laboratory may not be appropriate for a single-employee consulting agency. Either way, evidence integrity must be maintained.

EQUIPMENT, REAGENTS, AND PROCEDURE VALIDATION

Confidence in the results of the forensic analysis is dependent on the equipment, reagents, and the procedures used to conduct those analyses. To ensure these components are performing properly, the agency must have in place a program to monitor them. Initially, agencies must establish a systematic review of the maintenance and calibration of equipment or instrumentation that may affect the accuracy or the validity of the final outcome of the BPA. This would include logs recording when a piece of equipment is placed in service along with the regular maintenance and calibration schedule. Additionally, the functionality of individual reagents must be tested. A complete QA program will establish the testing schedule and the process for documentation.

Finally, all procedures and techniques that are new to an agency must undergo a validation process. This documented program component will not only determine if the procedure is working as intended but will also help to establish it is valid in the hands of the individual user. Additional guidance for procedure validation can be found in ANSI/ASB Standard 072, *Standard for Validation of Procedures in Bloodstain Pattern Analysis*.[9]

SUMMARY

As emphasized previously, the work of a forensic scientist carries a tremendous amount of responsibility. Each day they engage in literal life and death issues. In some cases, the outcome of their work contributes to justice for the victim of a crime; and in other cases, it assists in the exoneration of someone wrongfully accused. In either situation, these are profound circumstances and the forensic analyst's work addresses them constantly. Forensic service agencies, in particular those offering BPA, owe it to their stakeholders – the victims, the defendants, the law enforcement agencies, the attorneys, and the juries – the confidence all measures have been put in place which will establish to the greatest extent possible that the analytical results are valid. This begins and ends with a well-constructed and reliable BPA QA program.

Notes

1. "Quality Assurance." In *Merriam-Webster.com Dictionary*. https://www.merriam-webster.com/dictionary/quality%20assurance#:~:text=%3A%20a%20program%20for%20the%20systematic,of%20quality%20are%20being%20met.
2. "Ensuring High Standards of Laboratory Performance." In *The Evaluation of Forensic DNA Evidence*, compiled by National Research Council (US) Committee on DNA Forensic Science: An Update. Washington, DC: National Academies Press, 1996. https://www.ncbi.nlm.nih.gov/books/NBK232602/#ddd00089.
3. "Standard for a Quality Assurance Program in Bloodstain Pattern Analysis, ANSI/ASB 030." American Academy of Forensic Sciences. https://www.aafs.org/asb-standard/standard-quality-assurance-program-bloodstain-pattern-analysis. Last modified 2019.
4. "Standards for a Bloodstain Pattern Analyst's Training Program, ANSI/ASB 032." American Academy of Forensic Sciences. https://www.aafs.org/asb-standard/standards-bloodstain-pattern-analysts-training-program. Last modified 2020.
5. "Standard for Developing Standard Operating Procedures in Bloodstain Pattern Analysis, ANSI/ASB 157." American Academy of Forensic Sciences. https://www.aafs.org/asb-standard/standard-developing-standard-operating-procedures-bloodstain-pattern-analysis. Last modified 2023.

6. "Standard for Report Writing in Bloodstain Pattern Analysis, ANSI/ASB 031." American Academy of Forensic Sciences. https://www.aafs.org/asb-standard/standard-report-writing-bloodstain-pattern-analysis. Last modified 2020.
7. "Terms and Definitions in Bloodstain Pattern Analysis ASB Technical Report 033." American Academy of Forensic Sciences. https://www.aafs.org/asb-standard/terms-and-definitions-bloodstain-pattern-analysis. Last modified 2017.
8. "Required Components for a Proficiency Testing Program in Bloodstain Pattern Analysis, ANSI/ASB 157." American Academy of Forensic Sciences. https://www.aafs.org/asb-standard/required-components-proficiency-testing-program-bloodstain-pattern-analysis. Last modified 2023.
9. "Standard for the Validation of Procedures in Bloodstain Pattern Analysis, ANSI/ASB 072." American Academy of Forensic Sciences. https://www.aafs.org/asb-standard/standard-validation-procedures-bloodstain-pattern-analysis. Last modified 2019.

CHAPTER 35

ERROR AND ERROR RATES IN BLOODSTAIN PATTERN ANALYSIS

Jeremy Morris

In criminal proceedings in the United States, a two-fold examination is applied to evidence and testimony to determine admissibility. First, the evidence or testimony must be relevant to the case at hand. It must directly relate to specific concepts or events under investigation. Second, the evidence or testimony must be reliable. In essence, the material being presented to the court should be dependable.

Various court rulings in the United States have created criteria for evaluating the reliability of expert testimony. In 1923, when considering the systolic blood pressure deception test, the United States Supreme Court created what was known as the *general acceptance criteria*.[1] Specifically, "the thing from which the deduction is made must be sufficiently established to have gained general acceptance in the particular field in which it belongs." This "general acceptance" criteria remained the primary standard until 1993 when the Supreme Court expanded the criteria which must be satisfied for evidence to be deemed reliable.[2] In *Daubert*, the Court suggested the following factors be considered:

1. Has the technique been tested in actual field conditions (and not just in a laboratory)?
2. Has the technique been subject to peer review and publication?
3. What is the known or potential rate of error?
4. Do standards exist for the control of the technique's operation?
5. Has the technique been generally accepted within the relevant scientific community?

While much can be said, and has been said, regarding each of these criteria, the "potential rate of error" will be the specific focus of this discussion since many consider this to be a specific measure of reliability. In addition to *Daubert* in the United States, using rates of error to assess the reliability of scientific testimony is also part of case law in Canada.[3]

What is the known or potential rate of error for bloodstain pattern analysis (BPA)? Perhaps a different question is a better starting point: What is meant by reliability?

Like many concepts, the meaning of reliability changes slightly with different perspectives. When restricted to mathematics and statistics, reliability is "consistency of results as demonstrated by reproducibility or repeatability."[4] If a measurement is performed 100 times on the same material, how consistent are the results? With this perspective, a reliable technique or method is one in which the 100 measures are very similar to one another, but those 100 results may still be different than the actual value. In mathematics and statistics, the difference between the measured value and the true value is not reliability, it is accuracy.

Evaluating qualitative conclusions in pattern classifications requires a different approach to assess the reliability. The legal concept of reliability, the one most critical to this discussion, is different. For the courts, reliability is "credibility and trustworthiness of proffered evidence."[5] In essence, did the technique obtain the correct result? In this light, an incorrect result is an error.

Using this understanding of reliability allows us to address the first question above: What is the known or potential rate of error for PBA? How often does a technique provide an incorrect result?

DOI: 10.4324/9781003163695-35

BPA is not a single technique like measuring the mass of a powder or measuring the length of a gun barrel. Instead, it consists of multiple processes which are used together to find the answer to the singular question: What story do the bloodstains tell? Some of these processes involve taking actual measurements which result in numerical values. Other processes rely primarily upon qualitative observations and logic. Because BPA is truly a collection of multiple processes, the meaning of "error," and by extension, "error rate" differs. This concept is critical because it means there is no single "rate of error" for BPA.

Another critical concept regarding "rate of error" which must be discussed is determining the source of the error. When an incorrect result is reported, what is the true cause of this erroneous result? In forensic science, at least four different sources of error have been proposed. They are practitioner error, instrument error, statistical error, and method error.[6] Of these, instrument error is really not applicable to BPA and statistical error has limited applicability to area of convergence/origin determinations. Thus, practitioner error and method error are the main sources of potential erroneous qualitative conclusions, but they are not equal. Practitioner errors occur when an appropriate method is used but the analyst makes mistake. This could be a mistake in either the application of the method leading to an erroneous result or in the interpretation of the data. Either way, the fault is with the analyst and not the method. Method errors occur because there is some inherent shortcoming or failure within the process. Method errors occur regardless of the training and abilities of the analysts.

This last distinction is important. Multiple studies have evaluated various conclusions provided by bloodstain analysts and compared these with the ground truth. When evaluating areas of convergence and origin conclusions, the studies typically include a detailed discussion and evaluation of the specific method utilized in the process as well as the difference between the calculated location and the known location. For studies focusing on pattern classification conclusions, any conclusion which did not include the known mechanism as a possibility was considered erroneous; however, none of the current studies on the reliability of pattern classification conclusions investigated the specific methods used by analysts nor did any of the studies require analysts to follow a specific method. The impact of this critical aspect of pattern classification studies will be discussed later.

ERROR IN AREA OF CONVERGENCE AND ORIGIN CALCULATIONS

Determinations for the areas of convergence or origin are typically the only calculations performed and reported by bloodstain pattern analysts. As discussed in Chapters 4, 31, and 33, there are multiple methods which can be used to calculate the area of convergence or the area of origin for patterns containing radiating distributions of spatter stains. Although there are differences in the technologies used for the various methods regularly used in casework, each method uses a straight-line assumption to calculate the flight paths of droplets which created the selected spatter stains. As discussed in Chapter 5 on fluid dynamics, gravity immediately affects the flight paths of upward moving droplets of blood as soon as they are generated. Because gravity and drag cause the actual flight path to be curved, the straight-line assumption will always result in an overestimation of the height of the spatter-producing event (Figure 35.1). This systematic error of area of origin calculations using the straight-line assumption is a form of error (i.e., measurement bias) which is inherent within all current area of origin methods. Since overestimation of the height is inherent when using the straight-light assumption, the calculated height component can be considered the upper limit of the location of the spatter-producing event.[7]

But how close are the measurements compared to known locations of spatter-producing events? Even with this inherent form of measurement bias, areas of convergence and origin calculations

Figure 35.1 Demonstration of how the straight-line assumption of spatter stains created by droplets affected by gravity and drag will always result in an overestimation of the height of an event. The green line depicts the true flight path of a blood droplet when accounting for gravity and drag. If the droplet were to strike a wall located at the blue line, the red line depicts the calculated height estimation using the straight-line assumption which is obviously higher than the height of the actual event (green line).

have been demonstrated numerous times to have suitable accuracy. The stringing method has been shown to provide an area of origin within 10–20 cm of the known location.[8] While this may initially appear concerning, when it's understood that the real question is to determine the general location and orientation (e.g., upright or non-upright) of an individual, this level of accuracy is still sufficient for a proper interpretation of the events which occurred at the scene.[9] Numerous studies have demonstrated that the results of area of origin calculations for the tangent method,[10] computer-assisted directional analysis,[11,12,13] and three-dimensional laser scanning[14,15] are all much closer to the known location than the stringing method. In some situations, the calculated locations are within a few centimeters of the known locations. Additional discussions can be found in Chapter 4 for the tangent method, Chapter 31 for computer-assisted directional analysis, and Chapter 33 for three-dimensional laser scanning techniques.

The majority of the previously cited studies were based on analyzing ideal, two-sided patterns with cardboard as the target surface and numerous stains to search for those with ideal shapes. In addition, these ideal patterns are typically created with the event location less than 100 cm from the target surface. Casework patterns are significantly different. They can be one-sided, contain only a few stains, contain even fewer ideal stains, be on textured or other problematic target surfaces, and occur at distances greater than 100 cm from the target surface. Each of these complicating factors potentially has a negative effect on the calculated area of convergence or origin. When the method uses a software program, this negative effect is reflected in an increased standard deviation for the calculated area of convergence or origin. The standard deviation is a measure of the variation or "spread" of the intersections of pairs of straight-line flight paths selected for analysis. When the standard deviation is small, it means the volume of possible locations for the area of

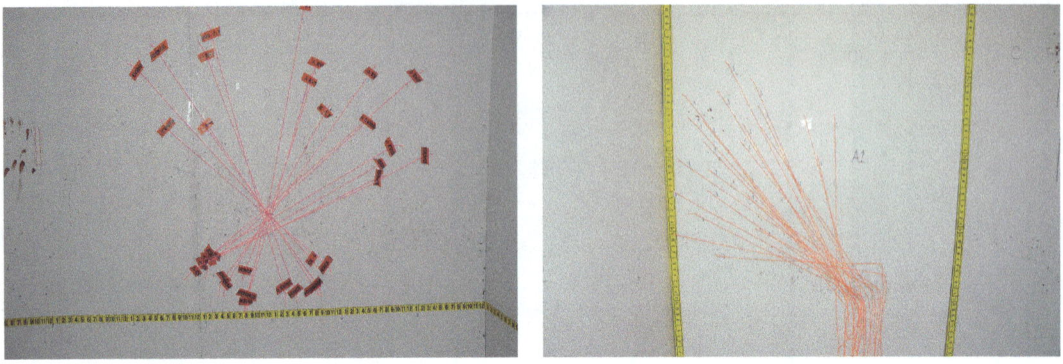

Figure 35.2 The strings demonstrate that the intersections for straight-line trajectories of the selected stains have different variations or "spreads."

origin is relatively small. When the standard deviation is large, it means there is significantly more variation within the data and therefore a larger volume of possible locations. As such, the size of the standard deviation is a measure of the uncertainty within the calculation.

Consider one-sided patterns as an example. Although computer-assisted analyses demonstrated the calculated area of origin is sufficiently close to the known location, one-sided patterns had much higher standard deviations and therefore significantly higher uncertainty regarding the actual location of the event.[16] The same effect is observed as the distance out from the vertical surface increases.[17]

Although a "standard deviation" is not calculated, per se, when using the stringing and tangent methods, the variation or "spread" of the intersection is visually apparent after documenting the straight-line trajectories of the selected stains. In Figure 35.2, the intersections of the straight-line trajectories of the pattern on the right side have a greater spread than the pattern on the left side. Selecting better stains may sometimes improve this variation; however, this is not always possible if the pattern has limited stains, low-quality stains, or if the spatter-producing event was far away from the target surface. In addition, analyst error could be the cause of a large spread of intersecting lines.

A large standard deviation can directly impact the interpretation of the results. For example, if the standard deviation of the height was calculated as +/– 45 cm, this is a possible range of 34 inches which may cast doubt on the ability to determine if an individual was in an upright or non-upright position at the time an impact occurred. A failure to consider the standard deviation of the calculated location can potentially result in an error in the interpretation.

Because the straight-line trajectory assumption is known to result in overestimation of the height component of an area of convergence or area of origin, some research has been performed to calculate the ballistic trajectory of the droplets associated with the selected stains.[18] This has been coupled with an attempt to depict the area of origin in more probabilistic terms to account for statistical uncertainties associated with stain measurements as well as ballistic trajectory calculations.[19,20] Probabilistic approaches have also been proposed to estimate the origin of cast-off patterns.[21] At the present time, these concepts largely remain within the research realm and have little to no validation work to make them suitable for casework examinations.

In addition to estimating the areas of convergence and origin for radiating spatter patterns, there are times when a single area may contain multiple, overlapping patterns. While individuals may desire to determine how many overlapping patterns are present in a single area, this is not always possible. Preliminary research demonstrated trained analysts could reliably differentiate between multiple, overlapping impact patterns when there was at least 6–8 inches of separation in at least one direction between the two events.[22] Based on this research, analysts should use extreme caution when reporting a specific number of overlapping spatter-producing events beyond "at least one."

ERROR IN PATTERN CLASSIFICATION

Besides areas of convergence and origin, the most studied process of BPA is pattern classification. As mentioned before, despite a growing body of research into classification conclusions, no study to date has either controlled the specific methodology used by participants or attempted to link the methods used to the reported pattern classifications – either correct classifications or erroneous classifications. As a result, while these studies provide some helpful insight into the discussion of "known or potential rate of error" in BPA pattern classifications, because the specific methods of analysis were neither controlled nor studied, erroneous results could be practitioner error or method error. Regardless, a brief examination of these studies on erroneous classifications is beneficial.

Although it wasn't the first study to evaluate error in pattern classifications, one of the most significant was a 2016 study examining the reliability of pattern classification on rigid, nonporous surfaces.[23] Twenty-seven, court-qualified bloodstain pattern analysts with advanced training were provided examples of multiple patterns from different spatter-producing mechanisms. The study examined multiple variables including amount of detail present within the pattern, different target surfaces, as well as case information. The case information was designed to lean toward the correct classification, an incorrect classification, or have no effect at all. Across all variables, the study found 13% of the classifications to be erroneous. While some variables affected the relative magnitudes of correct and inconclusive classifications, the single factor which corresponded to an increase in erroneous classifications was contextual information. While insightful, a rate of 13% erroneous conclusions for spatter-only patterns is limited. As the authors stated, these numbers "are based, in part, on the conditions chosen for examination ... Had other more easily recognized pattern types, such as drip stains, drip patterns, transferred blood, and saturation patterns been included, the proportion of correct classifications may have been higher."[24]

The same research group examined the reliability of pattern classification on fabric surfaces, specifically clothing.[25] Thirty-seven analysts with the same qualifications as described above were provided multiple pairs of pants with different bloodstains deposited on them. Four different spatter-producing mechanisms were studied as well as one transfer mechanism. Besides the pants, analysts were also provided case information, which was designed to lean towards the correct classification, an incorrect classification, or have no effect at all. Across all variables, the study found 23% of the classifications to be erroneous; however, the majority of the misclassifications (51%) were misclassifications of satellite stains from a drip pattern. According to the authors, "given the construction of the satellite stains in this study, it could be argued that an overall error rate that excludes this pattern type (14%) is more appropriate."[26] Like the previous study, contextual information also affected erroneous classifications.

Both of these studies focused primarily on spatter-producing mechanisms. Prior to both of these, an unpublished study from 2012 examined the accuracy of classifying ten different patterns which included various spatter and non-spatter mechanisms.[27] For 92 self-identified bloodstain experts, only 2% of pattern classifications were erroneous while 79% of conclusions by nonexperts were erroneous. This dramatic difference in erroneous conclusions was repeated in a 2016 study which compared the responses of court-qualified analysts with advanced training (i.e., experts) and the individuals with only a basic training in BPA (i.e., novices).[28] When examining a cast-off pattern, 4% of the classification conclusions provided by the expert analysts were erroneous while 44% of the novices provided an erroneous classification.

A more extensive study evaluating all pattern types was published in 2021.[29] The study examined 75 practicing bloodstain pattern analysts evaluating 192 bloodstain patterns. The patterns were a mix of lab-generated patterns with known mechanisms and crime scene patterns where the ground truth was not known. Analysts were allowed to provide definitive classification conclusions or less restrictive "possible" conclusions. When the ground truth was known, the study found 11.2% of the responses were incorrect. A full discussion of various findings of the study is beyond the scope of this review; however, two key points are worth noting. First, no clear correlation was found in the study between the rate of incorrect classifications and length of casework experience or the type of educational degree possessed by the analyst. Second, the study found analysts who had a tendency to provide more "definitive" classifications had a higher percentage of incorrect classifications. This specific finding may suggest different mechanisms can create very similar patterns.

A 2021 study expanded upon the differences between trained analysts and non-practitioners.[30] In this study, eight different mechanisms were studied (i.e., transfer stain, swipe pattern, drip pattern, flow, cessation cast-off pattern, impact pattern, perimeter stain, and void). For all pattern types, 15.44% of classifications by trained analysts were erroneous while 67.43% were erroneous for non-practitioners with no bloodstain training. But the amount of training analysts received also influenced the rate of erroneous classifications. Individuals classified as junior analysts submitted specific pattern classifications which were erroneous 31.25% of the time. For intermediate analysts, erroneous conclusions rate dropped to 15.63%. For senior practitioners, the rate of erroneous classification conclusions was 9.38%. Across all experience levels, patterns of spatter stains had a higher rate of erroneous conclusions than those of non-spatter stains.

Another means of evaluating erroneous pattern classification conclusions is to study the published results of proficiency tests in BPA. An unpublished study evaluated submitted responses for tests between 2005 and 2020.[31] During this time period, erroneous conclusions were submitted 6.2% of the time across all pattern types. When breaking these down to spatter patterns and non-spatter patterns, 10.4% of conclusions for patterns of spatter stains were erroneous but only 2.2% of conclusions for non-spatter patterns were erroneous. Interestingly, two published studies evaluating the submitted proficiency tests for Australian government service providers reported no erroneous conclusions were submitted on bloodstain proficiency tests between 2005 and 2017.[32,33] The highly accurate responses of bloodstain analysts from Australia on tests provided by the Collaborative Testing Services (CTS) could be a result of the extensive training program the reporting analysts are required to complete,[34] the use of a defined methodology for these examinations, or both. Although there are several valid reasons results of proficiency tests should not be used to establish error rates,[35] the information is insightful and agrees with the general observations of the previously described studies. Table 35.1 summarizes the rates of erroneous conclusions for all these studies.

While these studies provide interesting and valuable information, the field of BPA must learn from the results and make the necessary accommodations within the methodology to minimize the rate of erroneous conclusions. A closer examination of the studies reveals some critical trends for consideration.

First, across all studies which examined spatter and non-spatter patterns, more erroneous conclusions occurred for patterns of spatter stains. This is important because patterns of spatter stains are often considered one of the most important patterns within a scene or on evidence even though there are numerous nonviolent mechanisms to create spatter. Regardless, the higher rate of erroneous conclusions for patterns of spatter stains is a reflection of a fundamental concept that different mechanisms can produce patterns with very similar features. This was previously addressed in the feature-based taxonomies presented in Chapter 7. Because different spatter-producing mechanisms can create very similar patterns, this increases the uncertainty for pattern classification. Rather than limiting the classification to a single pattern type, it may be more appropriate to include multiple mechanisms as options for patterns of spatter stains.

While the current number of studies comparing conclusions of analysts with different experience levels is low, there are indications that individuals with limited training in BPA have increased likelihoods of reporting erroneous conclusions than individuals with advanced training. This makes sense considering the critical importance for individuals to appreciate various features

Table 35.1 Summaries of all research on erroneous pattern classification conclusions

Study	Pattern types examined	Primary variable(s)	Erroneous conclusions
Patterns on rigid, non-porous surfaces	Spatter-only patterns (impact, cast-off, forward spatter, expiration)	Pattern type and influence of contextual information	13%
Patterns on absorbent surfaces	Spatter-only patterns (impact, cast-off, expiration, satellite stains) and transfer	Pattern type and influence of contextual information	23% (but only 14% if satellite stains removed)
Experts and nonexperts	Ten various pattern types	Self-identified expertise	2% for experts 79% for nonexperts
Analyst characteristics	Cast-off pattern	Degree of training	4% for experts 44% for novices
Overall accuracy and reproducibility	All pattern types	None	11.2% for all pattern types
Experience level	Eight different pattern types	Degree of training	15.44% for all levels 31.25% for junior analysts 15.63% for intermediate analysts 9.38% for senior analysts
Proficiency tests	All pattern types	None	6.2% for all pattern types 10.4% for spatter patterns 2.2% for non-spatter patterns

of bloodstains created by different mechanisms, how a single mechanism can create two patterns with vastly different features, how two patterns created by different mechanisms can look very similar, and how target surface properties dramatically affect the features of the resultant bloodstains. Individuals with limited experience should recognize this tendency and adjust the specificity of pattern classification conclusions accordingly as well as subject all conclusions to peer review.

Finally, classifications are affected when analysts are provided, or seek out, information other than the features of the bloodstain patterns. While there are times when additional, relevant case information is arguably helpful, if not essential, for correct classifications of certain bloodstain patterns, multiple studies within BPA[36,37] and outside of BPA[38,39,40,41,42] have demonstrated that some case information can be the source of erroneous conclusions. Research has also shown that various forms of relevant and irrelevant information have shifted classifications by analysts after they examine the features of patterns.[43] Analysts must use caution to examine and document the features of the bloodstains prior to accessing case information. Even then, the information which the analyst accesses, must only be information which is relevant to either determining how the bloodstains were created or their meaning in the context of the scene.

Some work has been done researching the possibility of using machine-learning techniques for automated classifications of bloodstain patterns. The goal of this research is to develop methods for pattern classification which are objective, based entirely on features of the patterns, and free of other cognitive fallacies which can occur by analysts. Image processing techniques are used to extract and process features of the bloodstains.[44] These techniques have been used to differentiate impact patterns from gunshot-related patterns[45,46] as well as impact patterns from cast-off patterns.[47] At the present time, all automated processes for pattern classifications are still under development and lack the necessary validation studies to use them in casework.

ERROR IN RECONSTRUCTION CONCLUSIONS

Very little is currently known regarding the rate of error for reconstruction conclusions, also called the case conclusions, in BPA. Despite the value of these conclusions, there is very little information regarding the rate of error for this category of conclusion due to the scarcity of published research. To date, the only published studies related to reconstructive conclusions involve sequencing the order of deposition of overlapping patterns, estimating clotting times of blood, and determining the direction of movement for swipes and wipes. Of these, only sequencing patterns and determining the direction of movement for swipes and wipes have been evaluated for erroneous conclusions.

Multiple studies have been published attempting to determine features of overlapping bloodstains which can be used to determine which pattern was deposited first on the target surfaces. These features include a "halo" around the edges of the first pattern[48] or disturbances in the blood of the original pattern.[49] Only two studies have attempted to determine the rate of erroneous conclusions. In a study of 27 experienced analysts evaluating overlapping swipe and spatter stains, 52.9% of the responses were inconclusive. Of the responses which provided a definitive order of deposition, 32.7% provided the correct order while 14.4% provided erroneous conclusions.[50] Like the previous studies on pattern classification, this study did not evaluate the methods used by analysts or define a specific approach. In a later study evaluating drip and transfer stains, the authors provided participants guidance of features of bloodstains which could be used to assist in the sequencing conclusions. In addition, some participants were provided the actual patterns while others were provided only photographs of the patterns. When analysts were provided target features to use for classification, the number of correct conclusions increased from 57 to 79%. The percentage of erroneous conclusions decreased from 23% to 8%. Surprisingly, there was no correlation between erroneous conclusions and whether the analyst examined a photograph or the actual pattern.[51] The results of these two studies should encourage analysts to use caution when attempting to sequence overlapping patterns and to also establish objective criteria to increase the reliability of sequencing conclusions.

Direction of movement is also a common type of reconstruction conclusion included in reports. Direction of movement can be determined in a number of ways – examining the location of spines on individual stains within a drip trail; evaluating the orientation of transfer stains with features indicative of footwear; or evaluating the features of swipe patterns. Of these three, only swipe patterns have been studied regarding rates of error for directionality conclusions. Features useful to determine the directionalities of swipes have been recommended for nonporous surfaces[52] as well as fabrics.[53] In the only study evaluating the reliability of directionality conclusions, experienced analysts examined a total of 36 swipe and wipe patterns. Of the 216 conclusions provided, 33% of the definitive directionality conclusions were erroneous. The highest percentage of erroneous directionality conclusions involved swipe patterns created with fabric.[54] While determining the directionality of a swipe pattern may appear relatively easy, this preliminary research indicates it would be wise for analysts to use caution when making these conclusions.

SUMMARY

The reliability of conclusions provided by bloodstain pattern analysts is critical when determining the admissibility of bloodstain evidence in criminal proceedings. Like many other forensic disciplines, BPA includes a variety of conclusion categories and the rate of error must be evaluated for each separately; in addition, not all errors are equal. Errors committed by unqualified analysts, errors committed by misapplication of the method, and errors inherent within a defined methodology should not be grouped together when determining the rate of erroneous conclusions within a specific area of BPA. Errors committed by unqualified analysts, those committed by the misapplication of the method, and those committed when an inappropriate method was used, are fundamentally different than errors which occur when a valid method is correctly applied by a competent analyst. The multiple studies discussed above clearly show incorrect conclusions were submitted; however, the specific root cause for the errors was not investigated. Even then, the studies demonstrate the trustworthiness of BPA conclusions while also providing insight in how the discipline and individual analysts can move forward to reduce the number of incorrect conclusions in the future. Extensive training, using a defined methodology, and embracing uncertainty when appropriate, are the three critical takeaways from these studies.

Notes

1. *Frye v. United States*, 293 F. 1013 (1923).
2. *Daubert v. Merrell Dow Pharmaceuticals, Inc.*, 509 U.S. 579 (1993).
3. *R. v. J-L.* J [2000]2 S.C.R. 600.
4. OSAC Lexicon, accessed March 15, 2021. https://lexicon.forensicosac.org/
5. OSAC Lexicon, accessed March 15, 2021. https://lexicon.forensicosac.org/
6. Christensen, A. M., C. M. Crowder, S. D. Ousley, and M. M. Houck, "Error and Its Meaning in Forensic Science", *Journal of Forensic Sciences*, 59 (1), 2014, pp. 123–126
7. Carter, A. L., "The Directional Analysis of Bloodstain Patterns Theory and Experimental Validation", *Canadian Society of Forensic Science Journal*, 34 (4), 2001, pp. 173–189.
8. Carter, A. L., J. Forsythe-Erman, V. Hawkes, M. Illes, P. Laturnus, G. Lefebvre, C. Stewart, B. Yamashita, "Validation of the BackTrack Suite of Programs for Bloodstain Pattern Analysis", *Journal of Forensic Identification*, 56 (2), 2006, pp. 242–254.
9. Carter, "Validation of the BackTrack Suite of Programs for Bloodstain Pattern Analysis." 242–254.
10. Carter, "Validation of the BackTrack Suite of Programs for Bloodstain Pattern Analysis." 242–254.
11. Carter, "The Directional Analysis of Bloodstain Patterns Theory and Experimental Validation."
12. FORident Software I, "FORident Software Technical Paper-HemoSpat Validation", 2009.
13. Orr, Amanda, Mike Illes, Jacques Beland, and Theresa Stotesbury. "Validation of Sherlock, a Linear Trajectory Analysis Program for use in Bloodstain Pattern Analysis", *Canadian Society of Forensic Science Journal*, 52 (2), 2019, pp. 78–94.
14. Dubyk, Michael and Eugene Liscio, "Using a 3D Laser Scanner to Determine the Area of Origin of an Impact Pattern", *Journal of Forensic Identification*, 66 (3), 2016.
15. Santoro, Amy, "Leica Map360: Bloodstain Pattern Analysis", Leica Geosystems, 2020.
16. Maloney, Andy, Céline Nicloux, Kevin Maloney, and Franck Heron, "One-sided Impact Spatter and Area-of-Origin Calculations", *Journal of Forensic Identification*, 61 (2), 2011, pp. 123–135.
17. Hakim, Nashad and Eugene Liscio, "Calculating Point of Origin of Blood Spatter Using Laser Scanning Technology", *Journal of Forensic Sciences*, 60 (2), 2015, pp. 409–417.
18. Buck, Ursula, Beat Kneubuehl, Silvio Näther, Nicola Albertini, Lars Schmidt, and Michael Thali, "3D Bloodstain Pattern Analysis: Ballistic Reconstruction of the Trajectories of Blood Drops and Determination of the Centres of Origin of the Bloodstains", *Forensic Science International*, 206 (1-3), 2011, pp. 22–28.
19. Attinger, Daniel, Patrick M. Comiskey, Alexander L. Yarin, and Kris De Brabanter, "Determining the Region of Origin of Blood Spatter Patterns Considering Fluid Dynamics and Statistical Uncertainties", *Forensic Science International*, 298, 2019, pp. 323–331.
20. Camana, Francesco, "Determining the Area of Convergence in Bloodstain Pattern Analysis: A Probabilistic Approach", *Forensic Science International*, 231 (1-3), 2013, pp. 131–136.
21. McCleary, Scott, Eugene Liscio, Kris De Brabanter, and Daniel Attinger, "Automated Reconstruction of Cast-off Blood Spatter Patterns Based on Euclidean Geometry and Statistical Likelihood", *Forensic Science International*, 319, 2021, pp. 110628.
22. Doller, Donald, "An Assessment of the Minimum Distance between Impact Sites Necessary to Differentiate Bloodstain Patterns Created by Multiple Impacts", Master's Thesis (Pace University, 2007).
23. Taylor, Michael C., Terry L. Laber, Paul E. Kish, Glynn Owens, and Nikola KP Osborne, "The Reliability of Pattern Classification in Bloodstain Pattern Analysis, Part 1: Bloodstain Patterns on Rigid Non-absorbent Surfaces", *Journal of Forensic Sciences*, 61 (4), 2016, pp. 922–927.

24. Taylor, "The Reliability of Pattern Classification in Bloodstain Pattern Analysis, Part 1: Bloodstain Patterns on Rigid Non-Absorbent Surfaces." 922–927.
25. Taylor, Michael C., Terry L. Laber, Paul E. Kish, Glynn Owens, and Nikola KP Osborne, "The Reliability of Pattern Classification in Bloodstain Pattern Analysis, Part 2: Bloodstain Patterns on Fabric Surfaces", *Journal of Forensic Sciences*, 61 (6), 2016, pp. 1461–1466.
26. Taylor, "The Reliability of Pattern Classification in Bloodstain Pattern Analysis—Part 2: Bloodstain Patterns on Fabric Surfaces." 1461–1466.
27. Meneses, B. N., P. E. Kish, and B. J. Gestring, "A Preliminary Study of the Error Rate Associated with Bloodstain Pattern Analysis", in 61st Annual Meeting of the American Academy of Forensic Sciences: Denver, CO. 2009.
28. Osborne, Nikola KP, Michael C. Taylor, Matthew Healey, and Rachel Zajac, "Bloodstain Pattern Classification: Accuracy, Effect of Contextual Information and the Role of Analyst Characteristics", *Science & Justice*, 56 (2), 2016, pp. 123–128.
29. Hicklin, R. Austin, Kevin R. Winer, Paul E. Kish, Connie L. Parks, William Chapman, Kensley Dunagan, Nicole Richetelli, Eric G. Epstein, Madeline A. Ausdemore, and Thomas A. Busey, "Accuracy and Reproducibility of Conclusions by Forensic Bloodstain Pattern Analysts", *Forensic Science International*, 2021, pp. 110856.
30. Bettison, Alexandra, Matt N. Krosch, Janet Chaseling, and Kirsty Wright, "Bloodstain Pattern Analysis: Does Experience Equate to Expertise?", *Journal of Forensic Sciences.*
31. Morris, Jeremiah, "Lessons Learned from Proficiency Test Results in Bloodstain Pattern Analysis", Forensic Technology Center of Excellence, National Institute of Justice, 2021.
32. Wilson-Wilde, Linzi, Stephen Smith, and Eva Bruenisholz, "The Analysis of Australian Proficiency Test Data Over a Ten-Year Period", *Forensic Science Policy & Management: An International Journal*, 8 (1-2), 2017, pp. 55–63.
33. Wilson-Wilde, Linzi, Hannah Romano, and Stephen Smith, "Error Rates in Proficiency Testing in Australia", *Australian Journal of Forensic Sciences*, 51 (supl), 2019, pp. S268–S271.
34. Bloodstain Pattern Analysis Scientific Working Group, ANZPAA/NIFS, "Bloodstain Pattern Analysis (Level 2 and 3) Training Program", ver. 1, 2009.
35. Gardner, Brett O., Sharon Kelley, and Karen DH Pan, "Latent Print Proficiency Testing: An Examination of Test Respondents, Test-Taking Procedures, and Test Characteristics", *Journal of Forensic Sciences*, 65 (2), 2020, pp. 450–457.
36. Taylor, "The Reliability of Pattern Classification in Bloodstain Pattern Analysis, Part 1: Bloodstain Patterns on Rigid Non-absorbent Surfaces", pp. 922–927.
37. Taylor, " The Reliability of Pattern Classification in Bloodstain Pattern Analysis, Part 2: Bloodstain Patterns on Fabric Surfaces", pp. 1461–1466.
38. Stevenage, Sarah V. and Alice Bennett, "A Biased Opinion: Demonstration of Cognitive Bias on a Fingerprint Matching Task through Knowledge of DNA Test Results", *Forensic Science International*, 276, 2017, pp. 93–106.
39. Nakhaeizadeh, Sherry, Itiel E. Dror, and Ruth M. Morgan, "Cognitive Bias in Forensic Anthropology: Visual Assessment of Skeletal Remains is Susceptible to Confirmation Bias", *Science & Justice*, 54 (3), 2014, 208–214.
40. Mattijssen, Erwin JAT, Cilia LM Witteman, Charles EH Berger, and Reinoud D. Stoel, "Cognitive Biases in the Peer Review of Bullet and Cartridge Case Comparison Casework: A Field Study", *Science & Justice*, 60 (4), 2020, pp. 337–346.
41. Dror, Itiel E. and Greg Hampikian, "Subjectivity and Bias in Forensic DNA Mixture Interpretation", *Science & Justice*, 51 (4), 2011, pp. 204–208.
42. Elaad, Eitan, "Psychological Contamination in Forensic Decisions", 2013.
43. Osborne, "Bloodstain Pattern Classification: Accuracy, Effect of Contextual Information and the Role of Analyst Characteristics", 123–128.
44. Arthur, Ravishka M., Philomena J. Humburg, Jerry Hoogenboom, Martin Baiker, Michael C. Taylor, and Karla G. de Bruin, "An Image-processing Methodology for Extracting Bloodstain Pattern Features", *Forensic Science International*, 277, 2017, pp. 122–132.
45. Siu, Sonya, Jennifer Pender, Faye Springer, Frederic Tulleners, and William Ristenpart, "Quantitative Differentiation of Bloodstain Patterns Resulting from Gunshot and Blunt Force Impacts", *Journal of Forensic Sciences*, 62 (5), 2017, pp. 1166–1179.

46. Liu, Yu, Daniel Attinger, and Kris De Brabanter, "Automatic Classification of Bloodstain Patterns Caused by Gunshot and Blunt Impact at Various Distances", *Journal of Forensic Sciences*, 65 (3), 2020, pp. 729–743.
47. Arthur, R. M., J. Hoogenboom, M. Baiker, M. C. Taylor, and K. G. De Bruin, "An Automated Approach to the Classification of Impact Spatter and Cast-off Bloodstain Patterns", *Forensic Science International*, 289, 2018, pp. 310–319.
48. Corby, Christen, Caitlyn Hauke, Brian Gestring, and Lawrence Quarino, "Preliminary Study Analyzing the Halo Effect: Factors Involved in Sequencing the Deposition of Overlapping Bloodstains Caused by Wipe Patterns and Blood Droplets", *Investigative Sciences Journal*, 4, 2012.
49. Hurley, N. M. and J. O. Pex, "Sequencing of Bloody Shoe Impressions by Blood Spatter and Blood Droplet Drying Times", *International Association of Bloodstain Pattern Analysts News*, 6 (4), 1990, pp. 1–8.
50. Laber, Terry L., Michael C. Taylor, and Paul E. Kish, "The Reliability of Current Methods of Sequencing Bloodstain Patterns", *Journal of Bloodstain Pattern Analysis*, 30 (1), 2014, pp. 3–10.
51. van Steijn, L. J., J. C. M. Limborgh, and G. J. Edelman. "Visual Characteristics for Sequencing of Overlapping Bloodstain Patterns", *Forensic Science International*, 286, 2018, pp. 166–176.
52. Gardner, R., "Directionality in Swipe Patterns", *Journal of Forensic Identification*, 52 (5), 2002, pp. 579–594.
53. Dozier, Jayme, "Investigating Directional Characteristics in Swipe Patterns on Fabrics", *Journal of Forensic Identification*, 70 (2), 2020.
54. Yuen, Sita K. Y., Michael C. Taylor, Glynn Owens, and Douglas A. Elliot, "The Reliability of Swipe/Wipe Classification and Directionality Determination Methods in Bloodstain Pattern Analysis", *Journal of Forensic Sciences*, 62 (4), 2017, pp. 1037–1042.

Further Reading

Behrooz, Nima, Lee Hulse-Smith, and Sanjeev Chandra. "An Evaluation of the Underlying Mechanisms of Bloodstain Pattern Analysis Error." *Journal of Forensic Sciences* 56, no. 5 (2011): 1136–1142.

Connolly, Candace, Mike Illes, and Jim Fraser. "Affect of Impact Angle Variations on Area of Origin Determination in Bloodstain Pattern Analysis." *Forensic Science International* 223, no. 1–3 (2012): 233–240.

de Bruin, Karla G., Reinoud D. Stoel, and Josita CM Limborgh. "Improving the Point of Origin Determination in Bloodstain Pattern Analysis." *Journal of Forensic Sciences* 56, no. 6 (2011): 1476–1482.

Esaias, Owen, Grant W. Noonan, Shane Everist, Michell Roberts, Cassie Thompson, and Matt N. Krosch. "Improved Area of Origin Estimation for Bloodstain Pattern Analysis Using 3D Scanning." *Journal of Forensic Sciences* 65, no. 3 (2020): 722–728.

Griffiths, Gareth, Eugene Lisco, and Dean NORTHFIELD. "Accuracy of Area of Origin Analysis on Textured, Wallpaper Surfaces." *Journal of Bloodstain Pattern Analysis* 35, no. 1 (2020): 1–11.

Illes, M., and M. Boué. "Robust Estimation for Area of Origin in Bloodstain Pattern Analysis via Directional Analysis." *Forensic Science International* 226, no. 1-3 (2013): 223–229.

Illes, M. B., A. L. Carter, P. L. Laturnus, and A. B. Yamashita. "Use of the Backtrack™ Computer Program for Bloodstain Pattern Analysis of Stains from Downward-Moving Drops." *Canadian Society of Forensic Science Journal* 38, no. 4 (2005): 213–217.

Illes, M., and T. Stotesbury. "Development of an Application Method for a Zone Stain Selection Model in Bloodstain Pattern Analysis." *Canadian Society of Forensic Science Journal* 49, no. 1 (2016): 19–25.

Knock, Clare, and Marie Davison. "Predicting the Position of the Source of Blood Stains for Angled Impacts." *Journal of Forensic Sciences* 52, no. 5 (2007): 1044–1049.

Kwan, N., E. Liscio, and T. Rogers. "3D Bloodstain Pattern Analysis on Complex Surfaces Using the FARO Focus Laser Scanner." *Journal of Bloodstain Pattern Analysis* 32, no. 2 (2016): 21–7.

Larkin, Bethany AJ, and Craig E. Banks. "Bloodstain Pattern Analysis: Looking at Impacting Blood from a Different Angle." *Australian Journal of Forensic Sciences* 45, no. 1 (2013): 85–102.

Le, Quan and Eugene Liscio. "FARO Zone 3D Area of Origin Tools with Handheld 3D Data." *Journal of the Association of Crime Scene Reconstruction* 23 (2019): 1–10.

Lee, Rebecca, and Eugene Liscio. "The Accuracy of Laser Scanning Technology on the Determination of Bloodstain Origin." *Canadian Society of Forensic Science Journal* 49, no. 1 (2016): 38–51.

Liesegang, John. "Bloodstain Pattern Analysis—blood Source Location." *Canadian Society of Forensic Science Journal* 37, no. 4 (2004): 215–222.

Maloney, Kevin, Jim Killeen, and Andy Maloney. "The Use of HemoSpat to Include Bloodstains Located on Nonorthogonal Surfaces in Area-of-Origin Calculations." *Journal of Forensic Identification* 59, no. 5 (2009): 513–524.

March, Jack. "Determining the location of an impact site from bloodstain spatter patterns: computer-based analysis of estimate uncertainty." PhD diss., University of Nottingham, 2005.

Rowe, Walter F. "Errors in the Determination of the Point of Origin of Bloodstains." *Forensic Science International* 161, no. 1 (2006): 47–51.

CHAPTER 36

BLOODSTAIN PATTERN ANALYSIS TRAINING AND EDUCATION

Holly Latham

The journey to become a competent expert in bloodstain pattern analysis (BPA) cannot be accomplished by enrolling in a few workshops at a conference, by reading a few books, or by attending a few courses at a university alone. Rather, the path to become an expert involves study, research, experimentation, education, experience, and mentorship. This can be accomplished by a combination of attending conference workshops, reading books, and university courses but must be supplemented with research and experimentation guided by an experienced competent bloodstain pattern analyst with a mentorship component to give the trainee experience at the journeyman level while they develop expertise. The proposed training components put forth mirrors and/or complements the published standard ANSI/ASB Standard 032, Standards for a Bloodstain Pattern Analyst's Training Program, that can be found published on the Organization of Scientific Area Committee's (OSAC) Registry.[1]

Traditionally, most training begins by attending an introductory course on BPA taught by a competent expert in BPA. Historically, these courses have been taught in a "40-hour" format that includes lecture and experimentation with a heavy hands-on component. However, the concepts and segments studied during these introductory courses could be broken down and delivered in smaller segments to achieve the same goal. These initial concepts delivered will be the scientific foundations the trainee will use to develop expertise as they navigate more advanced concepts and scenarios. In no way is a "40-hour" "introductory" BPA course enough instruction to prepare a student to classify bloodstains, form reconstruction opinions, author reports, or testify in court. Rather, these beginner courses introduce the student to terminology, basic fluid dynamic concepts when dealing with stationary targets, and methods to accurately document a BPA scene.

At the beginning of a BPA training program, the trainee will build and learn foundational and informative knowledge. Informative knowledge includes knowing the history of the discipline: who were key researchers and what concepts did they contribute to, what were important legal cases and rulings that developed where we are today, and what are the professional organizations to which bloodstain pattern analysts belong. Also important are health and safety issues associated with BPA. Since BPA is dealing with scenes and evidence that contain bodily fluids including blood, concepts to be familiar with are bloodborne pathogens and associated health hazards, equipment and procedures dealing with biohazard safety, and methods for protection and remediation of chemical hazards when exposures occur.

Foundational knowledge begins with an understanding of blood itself: what components make up blood and what functions do those components serve and the physical laws that apply to blood itself as a fluid such as surface tension, molecular forces, and viscosity. Because BPA deals with the distribution, movement, and transfer of blood, it is important to understand the physics behind how a drop of blood is formed and the forces acting on and causing drop formation. Once a drop is formed, how does it travel through the air, what is the flight path, what effect do the forces applied

DOI: 10.4324/9781003163695-36

to blood have, including gravity, air resistance, and velocity. Also to consider is how the mass of the droplet in conjunction with the force applied affect the potential flight path.

The trainee also needs to study and understand the effects a surface can have on the resulting appearance and deposition of blood and bloodstains. How does the surface texture, rigidity, and absorption affect the appearance of the deposited bloodstain. Trainees should take part in experimentation and research regarding the relationship between blood and the surfaces it is deposited on while varying the velocity and flight path. At this stage of training, most of the surfaces studied by the trainee are in fixed positions and are flat, for example, walls, floors, and ceilings. However, advanced training regarding surfaces that are mobile or are in motion during deposition should also be studied and understood. In addition to the potential motion of the receptive surface, the movement of the surface the blood is originating from during disbursement should also be considered. This component of the training is imperative to exposing the trainee to the limitations of BPA and effects that surface and movement can have on resulting deposition characteristics.

Aside from understanding blood and the surfaces it is deposited on, another variable to appreciate is the environment and how it affects pattern formation and drying time. Studying, researching, and experimenting with air movement, temperature, humidity, post-incident activity, and surface characteristics will give the trainee an awareness of the affect these variables can have on expectations regarding drying time and pattern formation.

All of this foundational knowledge will assist the trainee with learning and understanding how the application of different forces to varying volumes of blood results in recognizable pattern formation and deposition. The trainee should experiment with applying different forces to volumes of blood to gain experience on resulting deposition. Once blood has traveled through the air and struck the target surfaces, the trainee should learn the proper way to measure bloodstains and how the measurements can be used to determine angle of impact of the individual stains. The limitations of the measurements and calculations should be discussed and how it could affect the resulting pattern deposition interpretations. The trainee should also learn and be familiar with the different methods and limitations of determining area of origin in stain deposition. This includes mathematical formulas, software programs, and theories which allow for areas to be eliminated such as in using limiting angles.

Once the trainee understands how blood acts and what happens to blood when forces are applied, they will be able to apply all of the characteristics of the individual bloodstains and their distribution and use that to accurately classify bloodstains and bloodstain patterns. This classification should be based on stain and pattern characteristics alone and not take into account contextual information. Classifying a bloodstain pattern and determining what stains make a bloodstain pattern will allow the trainee to accurately collect the bloodstains and assist in documentation.

Being able to document bloodstains and bloodstain patterns is important so that case notes accurately reflect the observations and interpretations of the analyst for the case record. Documentation includes notes, photographs or imaging techniques, and sketches. This proper documentation includes searching for blood using enhancement chemicals and techniques and testing for blood using presumptive testing. The trainee should understand how these chemicals function and how they are appropriately applied to include any limitations the test methods have. The trainee should have an understanding of other forensic testing available and the knowledge to know what testing to request to assist with furthering the classification refinement and reconstruction.

The trainee needs to have a basic understanding of human anatomy and physiology and accurately associate wound location with potential patterns produced by injuries. This will assist not only with classification refinement but also in sequencing and/or injury location within a scene during reconstruction. It is also important to know how clotting can affect resulting bloodstain patterns and understand the limitations associated with clotting and determining time to clot.

All of this information can assist the trainee with learning to reconstruct events, but just as important as knowing what one can say about bloodstains and bloodstain patterns is knowing what one cannot say about bloodstains and bloodstain patterns. Having a thorough understanding of the limitations and uncertainties of the discipline is important to make sure that the opinions and conclusions reached are well supported through research and experimentation.

The information discussed up to this point is usually covered to some degree in what is referred to as basic or introductory courses. But there are many more advanced topics to be learned and understood before an analyst can be an expert. In the introductory courses, trainees are explained concepts by doing experimentation and showing examples on fixed flat immovable surfaces such as walls, ceilings, and floors. In advanced courses and workshops, the trainees will explore concepts and surfaces that are not fixed, are not flat, and are often moveable. For example, the field of textiles and the amount of variability that exists among them have resulted in entire 40- and 80-hour courses just exploring the limitations, uncertainties, and variability. Before an analyst interprets bloodstains and bloodstain patterns on clothing, it is highly suggested that the analyst take part in intensive research and training regarding textiles and the interaction blood has with them. This exposure includes composition and construction of the textile, treatments that the fabric may have, the condition of the fabric, and the effects of the fabric moving during interaction with the blood.

Other advanced topics include experimental design and understanding how to design and implement a case-specific experiment, including how to identify and control variables and how to interpret and report on results of the experiments. This includes an understanding of the scientific method and how it pertains to BPA and is utilized in methodology and case-specific experimental design.

Advanced study is also available on fluid dynamics to provide an understanding of how forces are applied to liquid blood and how those forces affect bloodstain and bloodstain pattern formation and potential flight path. Paired with advanced topics on math and physics as they relate to Newton's laws of motion and potential blood drop flight paths give the trainee an understanding of the possibilities of flight paths and expectations of blood in motion.

The trainee must have knowledge of cognitive biases and the potential effect they can have during an analysis. This includes understanding contextual bias, confirmation bias, motivational bias, and expectation bias. The analyst should understand and apply methods that assist with minimizing potential biases and be able to articulate when information was accessed or known and how that information may have affected the interpretation or opinions reached.

The bloodstain pattern analyst will be able to not only document their observations and interpretations regarding the scene and evidence but will also be able to objectively communicate the interpretations and opinions that result from the analysis in the form of a written report and will be able to accurately and objectively testify to their interpretations and opinions.

A mentorship program should be participated in allowing the trainee to work with a qualified bloodstain pattern analyst. The mentor observes the trainee document and interpret bloodstains and bloodstain patterns on evidence and at scenes. This can be done by creating mock evidence and scenes or utilizing previous cases. Competency tests may be administered in small increments along the way over portions of the training, or one final competency may be administered at the end of training that encompasses all of the components trained on. It is highly suggested that the trainee keep documentation of training received, practical exercises and experimentation, mock scenes worked, and tests taken as evidence of their training program. At the successful completion of training as determined by the mentor, the bloodstain pattern analyst would be determined to be competent in those areas that training was received and successfully passed.

Bloodstain pattern analysts must be devoted to a continual learning process. It is critical to remain engaged on current topics and research in BPA. Participation in organizations, attending meetings, seminars, and workshops, and continuing to experiment and research are required to maintain proficiency and growth throughout one's career.

Suggested reading to complement and enhance the BPA training can be found at the BPA Bibliography published on the OSAC Bloodstain Pattern Analysis Subcommittee website at https://www.nist.gov/system/files/documents/2021/05/17/BPA_Bibliography_by_topic_2021.pdf

This list will provide the trainee and mentor with available published articles organized by topic. It is also highly suggested that the trainee read and be familiar with 2009 National Academy of Sciences' Committee report on Strengthening Forensic Science in the United States.

ADDITIONAL SUGGESTED READING

Hicklin RA, Winer KR, Kish PE, Parks CL, Chapman W, Dunagan K, Richetelli N, Epstein EG, Ausdemore MA, Busey TA (2021) "Accuracy and Reproducibility of Conclusions by Forensic Bloodstain Pattern Analysts," Forensic Science International 2021, 110856, ISSN 0379-0738, https://doi.org/10.1016/j.forsciint.2021.110856

Note

1. ANSI/ASB Standard 032, *Standards for a Bloodstain Analyst's Training Program*, 2020, 1st edition. https://www.nist.gov/organization-scientific-area-committees-forensic-science/osac-registry

CHAPTER 37

BIAS IN BLOODSTAIN PATTERN ANALYSIS

Nikola Osborne

INTRODUCTION TO COGNITIVE BIAS

Cognitive biases are the result of subconscious decision-making shortcuts by humans.[1] They are a way of "filling in the gaps" when data are missing or ambiguous. When considering crime scene evidence, ambiguous, distorted, or missing data are the norm rather than the exception. Bloodstain patterns, for example, may only contain a few stains; there may be voids, alterations, or distortions in the pattern; or the features of the stains may represent those found in multiple pattern types with different underlying mechanistic causes. It is the role of the bloodstain pattern analyst, then, to make interpretations and derive opinions based on incomplete data. It is here that analysts must consider the potential for bias.

Although various definitions of bias and its related terms exist, this chapter chooses to align with the Organization of Scientific Area Committees for Forensic Science (OSAC)-preferred definitions[2] (Table 37.1). In general, bias occurs when information extraneous to the data that a decision should be based on subconsciously informs the decision-making process and, ultimately, the decision. Biasing information or influences may be tangible (e.g., knowledge of a confession prior to performing a fingerprint comparison, exposure to a reference DNA profile before examining a complex DNA mixture) or intangible (e.g., a gut feeling based on experience, expectations). A biased decision is not necessarily something one can easily "see" or identify. Indeed, an analyst can reach a "correct decision" through biased decision-making (albeit through an incorrect method) or reach an "incorrect decision" through unbiased decision-making.

Training and experience are not enough to overcome the potential for cognitive bias to affect the expert's decision-making process.[3] Because expertise increases automaticity, which can shortcut objective data-driven decision-making, experts may be more susceptible to bias in some circumstances than nonexperts.[4]

Dror[5] discusses six fallacies about cognitive bias that forensic experts commonly hold. These are ethical issues, bad apples, expert immunity, technological protection, blind spots, and the illusion of control. A description of each of these beliefs is listed in Table 37.2.[5] The common theme within these beliefs is the idea that bias (or the effect of bias) occurs outside of us, to other people, or is something that we have control over. However, the reality is that cognitive biases occur as a function of being human and are not easily controlled or minimized through sheer willpower alone.

According to Dror,[6] the strength of biasing effects will depend on three factors: (1) the strength of the information, (2) the difficulty of the decision, and (3) the direction of the bias. In a later paper,[5] he further describes eight sources of bias that might affect a forensic expert throughout an examination (Figure 37.1). These fall into three main categories: case-specific; environment, culture, and experience; and human nature.

DOI: 10.4324/9781003163695-37

Table 37.1 Definition of cognitive, confirmation, and contextual bias, as preferred by the Organization of Scientific Area Committees for Forensic Science (OSAC)[2]

Term	Definition
Cognitive bias	A set of influences that may affect the reliability and validity of one's observations and conclusions.
Confirmation bias	The tendency to search for data or interpret information in a manner that supports one's preconceptions, expectations, or desires.
Contextual bias	A deviation in human judgment caused by exposure to information that is either irrelevant to the judgmental task or inappropriate for consideration.

Table 37.2 Six fallacies about cognitive bias commonly held by experts

Fallacy	Incorrect belief
Ethical issues	It only happens to corrupt and unscrupulous individuals, an issue of morals and personal integrity, a question of personal character.
Bad apples	It is a question of competency and happens to experts who do not know how to do their job correctly.
Expert immunity	Experts are impartial and are not affected because bias does not impact competent experts doing their job with integrity.
Technological protection	Using technology, instrumentation, automation, or artificial intelligence guarantees protection from human biases.
Blind spot	Other experts are affected by bias, but not me. I am not biased; it is the other experts who are biased.
Illusion of control	I am aware that bias impacts me, and therefore, I can control and counter its effect. I can overcome bias by mere willpower.

Source: This table originally appeared in Dror[5] and is reproduced with permission.

Bias in Forensic Science and Bloodstain Pattern Analysis

Evidence for bias in forensic science is seen across almost all forensic disciplines,[7] including latent print comparison,[8–13] bitemark analysis,[14,15] shoeprint comparison,[16] ballistics,[17] anthropology,[18,19] DNA interpretation,[20] and bloodstain pattern analysis (BPA).[21–24]

Although researchers can theorize about bias in BPA based on what they know from other forensic disciplines and decision-making in general, it is essential to research the extent to which it might be an issue. Taylor and colleagues conducted the first two studies[21,22] to examine baseline rates of reliability and the role of contextual information in bloodstain pattern classification decisions. In their first study,[21] 27 bloodstain pattern analysts (considered experienced analysts based on training and casework experience) examined bloodstain patterns on rigid, nonabsorbent surfaces. Patterns were paired with contextual case information that was neutral (i.e., non-biasing), suggested the correct pattern type (i.e., positively biasing), or suggested a pattern type other than the correct type (i.e., negatively biasing). In total, 13% of the classifications (across over 400 unique target patterns) were erroneous when the contextual information was neutral. This rate increased to 20% when the patterns were paired with negatively biasing information and decreased to 8% when paired with positively biasing information. The error rate* was 11% when the patterns were paired with neutral contextual information. In general, as the patterns became more difficult to analyze (due to the substrate or limited pattern availability), analysts tended to be less conclusive in their decision-making rather than more erroneous.

Another study by Taylor and colleagues[22] followed the same general methodology but assessed judgments on fabric surfaces, resulting in similar findings. Erroneous classifications occurred for

26% of the pattern classifications paired with neutral contextual information; this dropped to 14% paired with positively biasing contextual information and increased to 30% with the negatively biasing contextual information.

Notably, Taylor and colleagues' second study[22] has higher overall error rate than the study examining patterns on rigid nonporous surfaces (23% vs. 13%).[21] A closer look at the data found that most incorrect classifications occurred when the ground truth pattern type was *satellite stains from dripped blood* – participants primarily incorrectly classified the pattern as a *blunt-force impact pattern*. In designing the stimuli, the researchers created these patterns whereby the stains appeared approximately at knee height or above the knee. They theorize that participants in the study likely used the location of the stains to rule out satellite stains. That is, if the parent stain (not available in the study) was assumed to be on the floor (as you might expect in casework), then satellite stains above the knee height are unlikely. It appears then that an expectation bias was enough to override an observation-based classification. Indeed, these findings highlight that bloodstain patterns with different underlying mechanistic causes can appear similar and their interpretation can be influenced (both positively and negatively) by contextual information such as the location of the staining.

In the first two studies,[21,22] each participant was sent a unique target pattern. Although this allowed for a large dataset across various patterns and pattern types, it does not speak to whether different analysts will reach the same opinion when looking at the same target pattern (i.e., inter-rater reliability). Osborne and colleagues[24] examined inter-rater reliability in a study comparing expert ($n = 23$) and novice ($n = 16$) participants. Those in the expert group had advanced training in BPA and were currently presenting BPA testimony in court. The novice analysts had basic BPA training and were not active in court.

Participants were given a pattern to examine and were able to ask for additional contextual information (i.e., medical findings, DNA statement, police briefing, other bloodstain patterns, other forensic evidence, and a witness statement) if they believed it would assist in their classification of the pattern. Overall, 70% of the participants were correct in classifying the pattern as cast-off. Half of these participants classified the pattern as cast-off with no other pattern types selected, and half included cast-off within a conservation classification that included other potential spatter patterns (e.g., blunt force impact or gunshot spatter). Eight participants (20.5%) incorrectly classified the pattern – only one of these participants was in the expert group.

Researchers in that study measured the effect of contextual information via a shift score.[24] That is, participants indicated their confidence in various classification possibilities by providing a score out of 10. This score could then shift as they examined contextual information if the information changed their opinion or their confidence in the opinion. All the available contextual information, except witness statements, influenced participants' decision-making. Only four participants were not influenced in some way by the contextual information. A series of individual characteristic measures also revealed that participants who scored higher on the *intuitive* construct of the General Decision-Making Style (GDMS) scale[25] also tended to have higher shift scores. Osborne and colleagues' study[24] demonstrated differences between experts and novices, and that different analysts (including experts) can and do reach different opinions when presented with the same data.

Although all forensic disciplines are at risk of bias in analysts' opinions, there are several reasons why BPA may be particularly vulnerable. These can be separated into factors relating to the task of BPA itself (Levels 1–4 of Figure 37.1),[5] and system in which BPA analysts operate (Levels 5–7 of Figure 37.1).[5]

Nature of the Task

When considering the nature of the task: first, as explained earlier in the chapter, there is often ambiguity in the evidence. Patterns with different underlying mechanistic causes can exhibit

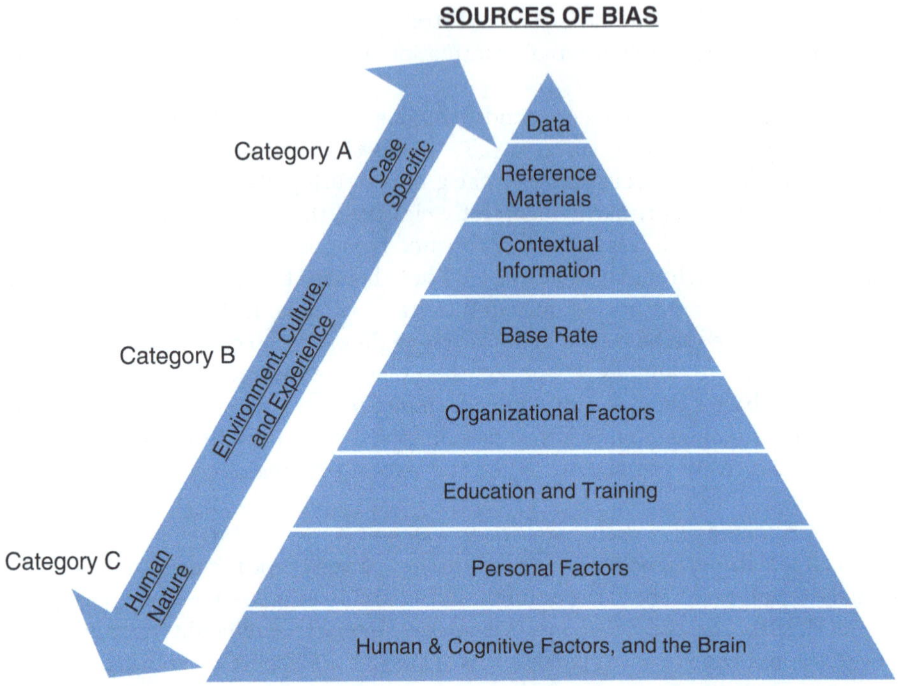

Figure 37.1 Eight sources of bias that may cognitively contaminate sampling, observations, testing strategies, analysis, and conclusions, even by experts.[5] (This figure is reproduced with permission.)

similar characteristics and may not be easily distinguishable. Alternatively, a pattern may contain only a few stains or be altered somehow. Furthermore, BP analysts will frequently conduct their examination through photographs rather than being present at the scene. All these factors can increase ambiguity and therefore increase the potential for bias.[26,27]

Second, analysts conduct BPA in an environment rich with contextual information. It is not a discipline that can operate within a vacuum separate from other elements of the investigation. It is unrealistic to expect that an analyst spending days at a scene could shield themselves from information that could be potentially biasing. Furthermore, some of that information may be relevant to their task. For example, witness accounts that could bias an analyst may also inform hypotheses for an analyst to test.

Third, the decision-making process in BPA is inherently subjective due to the interpretive and reconstructive nature of the discipline. The BPA analyst examines a static pattern and "fills in the gap" about actions that may have happened between the blood exiting a wound (or a source of blood being disrupted) and the final presentation of that blood on a surface (i.e., what was the mechanistic cause of the static pattern, and what can that tell us about the events that took place?).

There is no mandated or generally accepted methodology for BPA that prioritizes the presentation of objective, observable data over the interpretation of that data. Interpretation in any forensic discipline is *required* to make sense of the observable data. In BPA, however, interpretations and descriptions of those interpretations tend to precede descriptions of observable characteristics of patterns. This methodological limitation is most clearly evidenced by the mechanistic-based terms used to classify and describe static patterns. In 2018, Taylor and Osborne[28] wrote a letter to the editor in which they asked the BPA community to help contribute to a methodology for BPA that clearly delineates observations from interpretations. The author of this chapter is aware that discussions within OSAC about this issue are ongoing, and a multi-step BPA classification methodology is under development to address these concerns. Such a methodology will have a positive contribution to the discipline moving forward.

Finally, analysts are operating in an environment that is inherently emotive and may result in vicarious trauma (VT), secondary traumatic stress (STS), compassion fatigue (CF), or posttraumatic stress disorder (PTSD).[29] These afflictions can be caused by exposure to traumatic material or events[29] and can manifest in many ways, including stress, burnout, anxiety, or depression, which can all affect cognitive processing. A decline in cognitive processing may also decrease critical thought processing and increase vulnerability to bias. Although researchers have considered VT and other conditions in mental health experts for over 30 years, it is only in the past decade that researchers have explored this in the context of forensic practitioners.[30] This issue is not unique to BPA and must be considered across all forensic disciplines.

Nature of the System

There are several vulnerabilities to consider in understanding the potential for systematic bias in BPA. First, as identified earlier in this chapter, the terminology used to classify patterns in BPA frequently describes the mechanism for deposition, not the observable characteristics. This terminology is limiting in nature and may lead to a cart-before-the-horse type decision-making process (or, more aptly, *circular* or *backward reasoning*).[31,32] Although the BPA community is active in its discussions[33] to remedy this limitation, current terminology still encompasses mechanistic language.

Second, given that bloodstain patterns result from violent events, it is not ethical to produce ground truth training materials that accurately represent all the variables encountered in casework. Instead, patterns are created in research laboratories using mimicking techniques that can only represent a small proportion of the variables encountered in casework (e.g., shooting a blood-soaked sponge to mimic a firearms-related pattern,[34,35] or hitting a hammer into a blood source to mimic an impact pattern[21,22]). Attempts to address stimuli limitations using cadaver[36] and animal models[37–39] exist, but still cannot perfectly represent the complexity of variables in casework. Laboratory-based training materials are necessary, however, to measure against ground truth.

Third, when using casework examples for training, the ground truth cannot be known, so obtaining feedback on the reliability of the interpretation is problematic. Correlating CCTV footage of crimes with the resulting bloodstains may help in this endeavor but will come with its challenges if trainee analysts cannot attend the scene directly. There is no obvious solution to the training bias in BPA, and as such, analysts must instead be cognizant of and transparent about the limitations that it brings.

Third, analysts' adversarial position (e.g., whether the prosecution or defense hires them) may influence how they approach the case.[40] This issue is not unique to BPA but rather a function of working in an adversarial justice system. Inquisitorial justice systems, such as those seen in France or Italy, attempt to circumvent this type of bias by calling experts to account to the court, rather than representing a side, per se.

Adversarial position bias as a systematic issue for BPA may be further compounded by unequal scene access for defense versus prosecution positioned analysts. Generally, the prosecution-positioned analysts are called to the scene in the first instance (by virtue of being aligned with law enforcement). A longer period may have passed when (and if) the defense retains an analyst, and the scene may not be available for analysis outside of photographs.

Finally, although not unique to BPA, time and resource pressures can influence the speed and thoroughness at which a scene or case can be analyzed. These factors, along with fatigue from shift work or extended working hours, may impact cognitive capacity and vulnerability to bias.

CONTEXTUAL INFORMATION MANAGEMENT

The first step in addressing bias in forensic science is to be aware of it. Awareness on its own, however, is not enough to overcome bias. The next step is to actively engage in methods designed to minimize the potential for cognitive bias. There are several different contextual information management (CIM) methods that analysts and agencies can employ to address the potential for bias in BPA.[28,41–48] At the core of CIM is the restriction of task-irrelevant and potentially biasing information, while still allowing the analyst access to that information which is necessary to perform their task(s). Regardless of the CIM method employed, transparency and documentation should be the foundation of every analysis and subsequent report.[49]

Before deciding which CIM method is appropriate for an analyst or laboratory to employ, it is critical to determine which types of information are task-relevant and which are task-irrelevant. The National Commission on Forensic Science (NCFS)[50] states that:

> information is task-relevant if it is necessary for drawing conclusions: (i) about the propositions in question, (ii) from the physical evidence that has been designated for examination, (iii) through the correct application of an accepted analytic method by a qualified analyst. Information is task-irrelevant if it is not necessary for drawing conclusions about the propositions in question, or if it assists only in drawing conclusions from something other than the physical evidence designated for testing, or assists only in drawing conclusions by some means other than an appropriate analytic method.[50]

Unique to BPA, relative to many other forensic disciplines, is the need for contextual information (Level 3 of Dror's[5] model, Figure 37.1) to perform many of the tasks required, and the unavoidability of contextual information when attending a scene or examining crime scene photographs. Furthermore, BP analysts perform many different tasks throughout an examination, from locating blood within a scene, observing and characterizing stains and patterns, and reconstructing possible events. Therefore, the relevance and need for contextual information vary depending on what task the analyst is performing.

Osborne, Taylor, and Zajac[23] conducted a qualitative study to assess BP analysts' desire to use contextual information during a pattern classification task. Participants (n = 15) were practicing BP analysts with advanced training and court testimony experience. They were presented with photographs from two homicide scenes and asked to "think aloud" as they gave a working hypothesis for possible mechanistic cause(s) of the pattern and why they would include or exclude possible mechanisms. Then, if they believed it would help with their analysis, they could request items of contextual information. Before viewing the information, they stated why they believed it would assist their decision-making. Figure 37.2 is a visual representation of the types of information that analysts requested when asked to classify bloodstain patterns and *why* they requested that information.

Using thematic analysis, Osborne and colleagues then examined how participants incorporated the requested information into their analysis. There were four main ways: (1) support existing hypotheses, (2) create new hypotheses, (3) exclude classifications, and (4) reconstruct events in the scene.[23]

Once analysts identify the types of information that are task-relevant and those that are task-irrelevant and what purpose the information serves, the next step is to develop and employ a CIM method.

Peer Review/Independent Checking

The most appropriate type of peer review for bias minimization is when the reviewer does not know the original analyst's opinion and does not know the case circumstances. This type of review

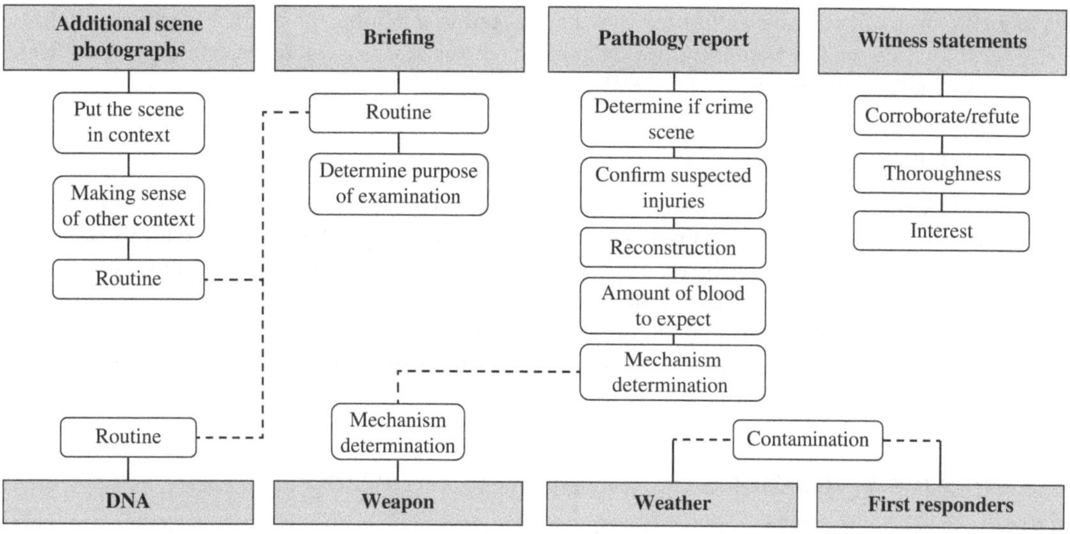

Figure 37.2 Visual representation of themes as a function of contextual information. Themes identified across multiple context items are connected with a dashed line. (This figure originally appeared in Osborne et al.[23] and is reproduced with permission.)

is different from a traditional technical review in which the reviewer has the original analyst's notes and interpretations. Osborne and Taylor[48] present an example of how this can be achieved for BPA performed in a laboratory setting. They describe a trial protocol for managing contextual information in the review process. For each item examined in the laboratory, two reporting analysts will be involved: a case manager and an independent checker. A laboratory technician (referred to as a senior technician at ESR) can prepare the materials for record taking. Each of the protocol steps from Osborne and Taylor[48] are listed below:

1. Case manager (CM) assigned to the case.
2. CM assigns an independent checker (IC). IC is informed that information regarding this case should be avoided where possible.
3. Senior technician (ST) or CM draws a diagram of the item. ST screens and samples for blood, identifying areas of staining and recording the results of any tests performed. This diagram is replicated before any bloodstain pattern interpretations are made. The original diagram is passed to the CM and the copy is put aside for the IC (or vice versa).
4. CM carries out BPA on the item(s) as per standard procedures, thoroughly documents all interpretations, and provides observation-based conclusions.
5. CM's interpretations are omitted from any material that is to be passed to the IC.
6. All case information is also omitted from material to be passed onto the IC.
7. IC conducts BPA on the item(s). IC thoroughly documents all interpretations on the diagram provided and provides observation-based conclusions.
8. CM compares IC's interpretations with his/her interpretations.
9. If any inconsistencies between CM's and IC's interpretations arise, the standard laboratory procedure to resolve inconsistencies is followed.
10. Technical review completed by IC or additional scientist after context-managed interpretations are made.

Participants' feedback about the trial was that it was not arduous to their existing processes and could be implemented with little additional time or cost.[48] Participants considered it a worthwhile procedure and the participating laboratory has expanded it to include other forensic disciplines.

While this protocol shows promise for BPA conducted in a laboratory setting, it is unlikely to be feasible at a crime scene where it is impractical to have a second analyst re-examine an entire scene with no contextual information.

Context Manager

CIM for BPA at scenes may be possible by applying the context manager model. The context manager model allows for a nominated person (the context manager) to have access to all the information (both task-relevant and task-irrelevant), but they only pass on task-relevant information to the analyst at the time that the analyst must perform their task.[46] A laboratory or sole practitioner's ability to implement this method will depend on several factors, including the number of available practitioners, resources, time, and type of scene examination. This method is also practical for laboratory-based BPA.

Alternative Hypothesis Formulation and Testing

Theories developed early in an investigation can influence how crime scene investigators interpret crime scene evidence.[51] Exposure to contextual information or early theory development may influence the interpretation and the use of information encountered later in the analysis (bias cascade effect), and may increase the overall effect of the bias as more task-irrelevant information is incorporated (bias snowball effect).[52] One way to avoid these biases is to develop and test multiple alternative and competing hypotheses.

When presenting an opinion, if an analyst uses language such as "consistent with" or "supports the theory" without stating multiple potential theories, a fact finder may infer that there is only one possible explanation. These statements without further explanation can be misleading. Although it is not always practical to test all possible theories, analysts should explicitly report that there may be other untested scenarios that the patterns are also consistent with or would support.

Statements such as "most likely to" must come with an explanation of how the analyst has tested alternative hypotheses to reach an opinion about likelihood. That is, an analyst cannot imply a "most likely scenario" if they have only tested a single scenario. Furthermore, it should be clear what other information the analyst has considered when formulating the hypothesis to test. For example, if the analyst is formulating hypotheses based on a witness statement, they must make it transparent that they have done so.

SUMMARY

All scientists should know the limitations of their science and their ability to apply that science. These limitations should be made clear to the fact finder. Furthermore, if a bloodstain pattern analyst relies on assumptions (e.g., that a pathology report is correct) to inform their opinion, this should be stated in the case notes and report. That way, if any assumptions are incorrect, the analyst has a clear and transparent way of showing the potential uncertainty in their opinion.

Bias and its many manifestations are not just a bloodstain pattern analyst issue or a forensic scientist issue, but a human issue. There are no one-size-fits-all approaches to minimizing bias, nor is there a simple one-time fix. However, by considering the issues raised in this chapter, BPA analysts will better understand how to adjust their decision-making processes and CIM strategies to serve the justice system best. Ultimately, the community should strive for reduced bias, increased reliability, and safer justice outcomes.

Key Take-Away Messages

- Bias occurs as a function of being human.
- Awareness is the first step, but not enough on its own.
- The few studies that examine bias in BPA suggest that it does exist and could negatively impact the interpretation process. More research is needed to understand the most appropriate and safe use of contextual information for the various tasks that BPA analysts engage in.
- There are ways to mitigate bias without overhauling the whole system.
- Opinions about BPA evidence should include caveats as to their subjective nature.

DEDICATION

I dedicate this chapter to Dr. Michael Taylor and acknowledge his invaluable contribution to the BPA community's understanding of the potential for bias in BPA. His thoughtful and wise words continue to influence the work I do, and I will be forever grateful for him.

Note

* The term "error rate" is specific to the context of these studies and does not suppose or generalize to an error rate for BPA as a discipline.

References

1. Nickerson, R. S. "Confirmation Bias: A Ubiquitous Phenomenon in Many Guises." *Review of General Psychology* 2 (1998): 175–220.
2. Organization of Scientific Area Committees for Forensic Science. "OSAC Preferred Terms," 2020. https://www.nist.gov/system/files/documents/2020/04/07/OSACPreferredTerms_April2020.pdf.
3. Dror, I. E. and S. A. Cole. "The Vision in Blind Justice: Expert Perception, Judgement, and Visual Cognition in Forensic Pattern Recognition." *Psychonomic Bulletin & Review* 17 (2010): 161–67. https://doi.org/10.3758/PBR.17.2.161.
4. Dror, I. E. "The Paradox of Human Expertise: Why Experts Can Get It Wrong." In *The Paradoxical Brain*, edited by N. Kapur and A. Pascual-Leone, 177–88. Cambridge: Cambridge University Press, 2011.
5. Dror, I. E. "Cognitive and Human Factors in Expert Decision Making: Six Fallacies and the Eight Sources of Bias." *Analytical Chemistry* 92, no. 12 (2020): 7998–8004. https://doi.org/10.1021/acs.analchem.0c00704
6. Dror, I. E. "A Hierarchy of Expert Performance." *Journal of Applied Research in Memory and Cognition* 5, no. 2 (2016): 121–27. https://doi.org/10.1016/j.jarmac.2016.03.001.
7. Cooper, G. S. and V. Meterko. "Cognitive Bias Research in Forensic Science: A Systematic Review.". *Forensic Science International* 297 (Apr 2019): 35–46. https://doi.org/10.1016/j.forsciint.2019.01.016.
8. Dror, I. E., A. E Peron, S-L. Hind, and D. Charlton. "When Emotions Get the Better of Us: The Effect of Contextual Top-Down Processing on Matching Fingerprints." *Applied Cognitive Psychology* 19, no. 6 (2005): 799–809. https://doi.org/10.1002/acp.1130.
9. Fraser-Mackenzie, P. A. F., I. E. Dror, and K. Wertheim. "Cognitive and Contextual Influences in Determination of Latent Fingerprint Suitability for Identification Judgments." *Science & Justice* 53, no. 2 (6//2013): 144–53. https://doi.org/http://dx.doi.org/10.1016/j.scijus.2012.12.002.
10. Langenburg, G. C Champod, and P. Wertheim. "Testing for Potential Contextual Bias Effects During the Verification Stage of the Ace-V Methodology When Conducting Fingerprint Comparisons." *Journal of Forensic Sciences* 54, no. 3 (2009): 571–82. http://dx.doi.org/10.1111/j.1556-4029.2009.01025.x.

11. Dror, I. E. and D. Charlton. "Why Experts Make Errors." *Journal of Forensic Identification* 56 (2006): 600–16.
12. Dror, I. E. and R. Rosenthal. "Meta-analytically Quantifying the Reliability and Biasability of Forensic Experts." *Journal of Forensic Sciences* 53, no. 4 (2008): 900–03. https://doi.org/doi:10.1111/j.1556-4029.2008.00762.x.
13. Stevenage, S. V. and A. Bennett. "A Biased Opinion: Demonstration of Cognitive Bias on a Fingerprint Matching Task through Knowledge of DNA Test Results." *Forensic Science International* 276 (2017): 93–106. https://doi.org/10.1016/j.forsciint.2017.04.009.
14. Osborne, N. K. P., S. Woods, J. Kieser, and R. Zajac. "Does Contextual Information Bias Bitemark Comparisons?" *Science & Justice* 54, no. 4 (2014): 267–73. https://doi.org/http://dx.doi.org/10.1016/j.scijus.2013.12.005.
15. Page, M., J. Taylor, and M. Blenkin. "Context Effects and Observer Bias—Implications for Forensic Odontology." *Journal of Forensic Sciences* 57, no. 1 (2012): 108–12.
16. Kerstholt, J. H., R. Paashuis, and M. Sjerps. "Shoe Print Examinations: Effects of Expectation, Complexity and Experience." *Forensic Science International* 165 (2007): 30–34. https://doi.org/10.1016/j.forsciint.2006.02.039.
17. Kerstholt, J. H., A. Eikelboom, T. Dijkman, R. D. Stoel, R. Hermsen, and B. van Leuven. "Does Suggestive Information Cause a Confirmation Bias in Bullet Comparisons?" *Forensic Science International* 198 (2010): 138–42. https://www.sciencedirect.com/science/article/abs/pii/S0379073810000599?via%3Dihub.
18. Nakhaeizadeh, S., I. Hanson, and N. Dozzi. "The Power of Contextual Effects in Forensic Anthropology: A Study of Biasability in the Visual Interpretations of Trauma Analysis on Skeletal Remains." *Journal of Forensic Sciences* 59, no. 5 (2014): 1177–83. https://doi.org/10.1111/1556-4029.12473.
19. Nakhaeizadeh, S., I. E. Dror, and R. M. Morgan. "Cognitive Bias in Forensic Anthropology: Visual Assessment of Skeletal Remains Is Susceptible to Confirmation Bias." *Science & Justice* 54, no. 3 (2014): 208–14.
20. Dror, I. E., and G. Hampikian. "Subjectivity and Bias in Forensic DNA Mixture Interpretation." *Science & Justice* 51 (2011): 204–08. https://doi.org/10.1016/j.scijus.2011.08.004.
21. Taylor, M. C., T. L. Laber, P. E. Kish, G. Owens, and N. K. P. Osborne. "The Reliability of Pattern Classification in Bloodstain Pattern Analysis, Part 1: Bloodstain Patterns on Rigid Nonabsorbent Surfaces." *Journal of Forensic Sciences* 61, no. 4 (2016): 922–7. https://doi.org/10.1111/1556-4029.13091.
22. Taylor, M. C., T. L. Laber, P. E. Kish, G. Owens, and N. K. P. Osborne. "The Reliability of Pattern Classification in Bloodstain Pattern Analysis, Part 2: Bloodstain Patterns on Fabric Surfaces." *Journal of Forensic Sciences* 61, no. 6 (2016): 1461–66. https://doi.org/10.1111/1556-4029.13191.
23. Osborne, N. K. P., M. C. Taylor, and R. Zajac. "Exploring the Role of Contextual Information in Bloodstain Pattern Analysis: A Qualitative Approach." *Forensic Science International* 260 (2016): 1–8. https://doi.org/10.1016/j.forsciint.2015.12.039.
24. Osborne, N. K. P., M. C. Taylor, M. Healey, and R. Zajac. "Bloodstain Pattern Classification: Accuracy, Effect of Contextual Information and the Role of Analyst Characteristics." *Science & Justice* 56, no. 2 (2016): 123–28. https://doi.org/10.1016/j.scijus.2015.12.005.
25. Scott, S. G. and R. A. Bruce. "Decision-Making Style: The Development and Assessment of a New Measure." *Educational and Psychological Measurement* 55, no. 5 (1995): 818–31. https://doi.org/10.1177/0013164495055005017.
26. Andrews, S. and R. Bond. "Lexical Expertise and Reading Skill: Bottom-up and Top-Down Processing of Lexical Ambiguity.". *Reading and Writing* 22 (2009): 687–711. https://doi.org/10.1007/s11145-008-9137-7.
27. Chaiken, S. "Heuristic Versus Systematic Information and the Use of Source Versus Message Cues in Persuasion.". *Journal of Personality and Social Psychology* 39 (1980): 752–66. https://doi.org/10.1037/0022-3514.39.5.752.
28. Taylor, M. C., and N. K. P. Osborne. "Letter to the Editor a Contribution to Contextual Information Management in Bloodstain Pattern Analysis: Preliminary Idea for a Two Step Method of Analysis." *Journal of Forensic Sciences* 63, no. 1 (2018): 341–41. https://doi.org/10.1111/1556-4029.13705.
29. Slack, D. P. "Trauma and Coping Mechanisms Exhibited by Forensic Science Practitioners: A Literature Review." *Forensic Science International: Synergy* 2 (2020): 310–16. https://doi.org/10.1016/j.fsisyn.2020.10.001.

30. Waugh, J. R. *Exposure to Traumatic Death Events and Traumatic Event-Related Stress in Crime Scene Investigators: A Multiple Regression Analysis* [ProQuest Dissertations & Theses]. Ann Arbor, MI: Capella University, 2013.
31. Rips, L. J. "Circular Reasoning." *Cognitive Science* 26, no. 6 (2002): 767–95. https://doi.org/10.1207/s15516709cog2606_3.
32. Office of the Inspector General. *A Review of the FBI's Handling of the Brandon Mayfield Case.* Washington: US Department of Justice, 2006.
33. Arthur, R. M., S. L. Cockerton, K. G. de Bruin, and M. C. Taylor. "A Novel, Element-Based Approach for the Objective Classification of Bloodstain Patterns." *Forensic Science International* 257 (Dec 2015): 220–28. https://doi.org/10.1016/j.forsciint.2015.08.028.
34. Taylor, M. C., T. L. Laber, B. Epstein, D. Zamzow, and D. Baldwin. "The Effect of Firearm Muzzle Gases on the Backspatter of Blood." *International Journal of Legal Medicine* 125, no. 5 (2011): 617–28. https://doi.org/10.1007/s00414-010-0462-4.
35. Attinger, D., Y. Liu, R. Faflak, Y. Rao, B. A. Struttman, K. De Brabanter, P. M. Comiskey, and A. L. Yarin. "A Data Set of Bloodstain Patterns for Teaching and Research in Bloodstain Pattern Analysis: Gunshot Backspatters.". *Data Brief* 22 (2019): 269–78. https://doi.org/10.1016/j.dib.2018.11.075.
36. Rossi, C., L. D. Herold, T. Bevel, L. McCauley, and S. Guadarrama. "Cranial Backspatter Pattern Production Utilizing Human Cadavers." *Journal of Forensic Sciences* 63, no. 5 (2018): 1526–32. https://doi.org/10.1111/1556-4029.13713.
37. Karger, B., R. Nüsse, G. Schroeder, S. Wüstenbecker, and B. Brinkmann. "Backspatter from Experimental Close-Range Shots to the Head. I. Macrobackspatter." *International Journal of Legal Medicine* 109, no. 2 (1996): 66–74. https://doi.org/10.1007/bf01355519.
38. Lazarjan, M., P. Geoghegan, M. C. Taylor, and M. Jermy. "Visualisation of the Air Ejected from the Temporary Cavity in Brain and Tissue Simulants During Gunshot Wounding." *Forensic Science International* 246 (2014). https://doi.org/10.1016/j.forsciint.2014.11.005.
39. Lazarjan, M., P. Geoghegan, M. Jermy, and M. C. Taylor. "Experimental Investigation of the Mechanical Properties of Brain Simulants Used for Cranial Gunshot Simulation." *Forensic Science International* 239C (2014): 73–78. https://doi.org/10.1016/j.forsciint.2014.03.022.
40. Murrie, D. C., M. T. Boccaccini, L. A. Guarnera, and K. A. Rufino. "Are Forensic Experts Biased by the Side That Retained Them?". *Psychological Science* 24, no. 10 (2013): 1889–97. https://doi.org/10.1177/0956797613481812.
41. Krane, Dan E., S. Ford, J. R. Gilder, K. Inman, A. Jamieson, R. Koppl, and I. L. Kornfield, *et al.* "Sequential Unmasking: A Means of Minimizing Observer Effects in Forensic DNA Interpretation." *Journal of Forensic Sciences* 53, no. 4 (2008): 1006–07. https://doi.org/10.1111/j.1556-4029.2008.00787.x.
42. Cole, S. A. "Implementing Counter-Measures Against Confirmation Bias in Forensic Science." *Journal of Applied Research in Memory and Cognition* 2, no. 1 (2013): 61–62. https://doi.org/10.1016/j.jarmac.2013.01.011.
43. Mattijssen, E. J. A. T., W. Kerkhoff, C. E. H. Berger, I. E. Dror, and R. D. Stoel. "Implementing Context Information Management in Forensic Casework: Minimizing Contextual Bias in Firearms Examination." *Science & Justice* 56, no. 2 (2016): 113–22. https://doi.org/10.1016/j.scijus.2015.11.004.
44. Mattijssen, E. J.A.T., R. D. Stoel, and W. Kerkhoff. "Minimizing Contextual Bias in Forensic Firearms Examinations." In *Wiley Encyclopedia of Forensic Science*, 1–7, 2015.
45. Dror, I. E., W. C. Thompson, C. A. Meissner, I. Kornfield, D. Krane, M. Saks, and M. Risinger. "Letter to the Editor- Context Management Toolbox: A Linear Sequential Unmasking (LSU) Approach for Minimizing Cognitive Bias in Forensic Decision Making." *Journal of Forensic Sciences* 60, no. 4 (2015): 1111–2. https://doi.org/10.1111/1556-4029.12805.
46. Found, B. and J. Ganas. "The Management of Domain Irrelevant Context Information in Forensic Handwriting Examination Casework." *Science & Justice* 53, no. 2 (2013): 154–58. https://doi.org/http://dx.doi.org/10.1016/j.scijus.2012.10.004.
47. Ulery, B. T., R. A. Hicklin, J. Buscaglia, and M. A. Roberts. "Accuracy and Reliability of Forensic Latent Fingerprint Decisions." *PNAS* (2011). https://www.pnas.org/doi/full/10.1073/pnas.1018707108?doi=10.1073%2Fpnas.1018707108.
48. Osborne, N. K. P. and M. C. Taylor. "Contextual Information Management: An Example of Independent-Checking in the Review of Laboratory-Based Bloodstain Pattern Analysis." *Science & Justice* 58, no. 3 (2018): 226–31. https://doi.org/10.1016/j.scijus.2018.01.001.

49. Almazrouei, M., I. Dror, and R. Morgan. "The Forensic Disclosure Model: What Should be Disclosed to, and by, Forensic Experts?". *International Journal of Law Crime and Justice* 59 (05/16 2019). https://doi.org/10.1016/j.ijlcj.2019.05.003.
50. National Commission on Forensic Science - Human Factors Subcommittee. *Ensuring That Forensic Analysis Is Based Upon Task-Relevant Information*, 2015. Page 2.
51. van den Eeden, C. A, C. J. de Poot, and P. J. van Koppen. "Forensic Expectations: Investigating a Crime Scene with Prior Information." *Science & Justice* 56, no. 6 (2016): 475–81. https://doi.org/10.1016/j.scijus.2016.08.003.
52. Dror, I. E., R. M. Morgan, C. Rando, and S. Nakhaeizadeh. "Letter to the Editor—The Bias Snowball and the Bias Cascade Effects: Two Distinct Biases That May Impact Forensic Decision Making." *Journal of Forensic Sciences* 62, no. 3 (2017): 832–33. https://doi.org/10.1111/1556-4029.13496.

CHAPTER 38

LEGAL CONSIDERATIONS FOR BLOODSTAIN PATTERN ANALYSIS EVIDENCE AND EXPERT TESTIMONY

Jonathan W. Hak

INTRODUCTION

Bloodstains at a crime scene that are analyzed and interpreted by competent, qualified experts can provide valuable insight into the dynamics and reconstruction of the events that led to the bloodletting, which can in turn assist the trier of fact in determining what happened. Bloodstain pattern analysis (BPA) evidence has been received in courts in the United States and Canada amid little fanfare and judicial resistance. Increasingly however, many forensic sciences have faced strong criticism for their lack of proven reliability and standards for the methodology employed and for the qualifications of those who employ it.[1] Rather than relying on favorable judicial rulings of the past to create the palette for the future, the utilization of methodology that is sound, testable, proven, and verifiable is essential to the continued use of BPA evidence in criminal investigations and prosecutions.

This chapter is intended to provide information for the BPA expert from a legal perspective in an effort to ensure that quality work achieves judicial receptivity. Part A focuses on important general principles applicable to forensic experts and testimony. The foundational topic in Section 1 addresses the tests used by the court for determining whether an individual should be granted the designation of an expert witness. An overview of the process used in court to make that assessment is then discussed in Section 2. Since the trial judge is charged with the responsibility of ensuring that only valid and reliable expert evidence is admitted at trial, Section 3 discusses the various judicial approaches involved in making that assessment. Finally, in Sections 4 and 5, commentary on expert report content and the importance of peer review will be explored. Part B focuses on BPA evidence specifically beginning with Section 6 which explores threshold legal challenges to the validity and reliability of BPA evidence as well as legal challenges to various aspects of BPA evidence generally and the experts who present it in court. The importance of visualizing complex forensic evidence in an effort to educate the trier of fact will be introduced in Section 7 along with suggestions for how to achieve that pedagogical objective. Finally, Section 8 makes recommendations for the effective presentation of BPA evidence in court. Throughout this chapter, the focus will be on the law of the United States and Canada.

DOI: 10.4324/9781003163695-38

LEGAL AND PROCEDURAL CONSIDERATIONS FOR EXPERT WITNESSES

What Is an Expert Witness?

An expert witness is someone with specialized knowledge in a particular area of expertise who applies that knowledge in a judicial setting. Practically, what sets experts apart from lay witnesses is that while both types of witness can provide the court with factual data, only the expert witness is permitted to evaluate the data and render an opinion as to what it means.[2] Expert witnesses assist the trier of fact in drawing inferences in areas where they have relevant knowledge and experience beyond that of a lay person.[3] Opinions and conclusions presented by expert witnesses are restricted to the subject matter of the expert's stated field of expertise. The parameters of expert witness testimony in U.S. federal prosecutions are set out in Federal Rule of Evidence 702 (amended in 2023) as follows:

> **Testimony by Expert Witnesses**
>
> A witness who is qualified as an expert by knowledge, skill, experience, training, or education may testify in the form of an opinion or otherwise if the proponent demonstrates to the court that it is more likely than not that:
>
> a. the expert's scientific, technical, or other specialized knowledge will help the trier of fact to understand the evidence or to determine a fact in issue;
> b. the testimony is based on sufficient facts or data;
> c. the testimony is the product of reliable principles and methods; and
> d. the expert's opinion reflects a reliable application of the principles and methods to the facts of the case.

Lay witness testimony is covered by Rule 701 as follows:

> **Opinion Testimony by Lay Witnesses**
>
> If a witness is not testifying as an expert, testimony in the form of an opinion is limited to one that is:
>
> a. rationally based on the witness's perception;
> b. helpful to clearly understanding the witness's testimony or to determining a fact in issue; and
> c. not based on scientific, technical, or other specialized knowledge within the scope of Rule 702.

It is therefore the expert's scientific, technical, or other specialized knowledge that sets the expert witness apart from the lay witness and justifies a broader opinion repertoire on the witness stand. Provisions similar to FRE 701 and 702 are found in state codes of evidence and govern prosecutions at the state level. There remains a further overriding test that is used to assess whether expert evidence will be admissible. Even if the evidence is admissible via FRE 702, it must also withstand scrutiny under FRE 403:

> The court may exclude relevant evidence if its probative value is substantially outweighed by a danger of one or more of the following: unfair prejudice, confusing the issues, misleading the jury, undue delay, wasting time, or needlessly presenting cumulative evidence.

This overriding test applies to all evidence and is frequently argued in the context of expert evidence that otherwise passes admissibility tests.

In Canada, the admissibility of expert witness testimony is governed by case law rather than codified rules. Admissibility is contingent upon establishing that the proposed expert evidence is relevant, necessary to assist the trier of fact, not subject to an exclusionary rule, and that the expert is properly qualified.[4] Proposed expert evidence that meets these mandatory requirements must then undergo a further assessment of probative value versus prejudicial effect, taking into account concerns of undue usage of time not commensurate with the value of the evidence and the likelihood of misleading the trier of fact.[5] This weight-based analysis will be discussed in further detail in Section 6. These additional steps are similar to those addressed by FRE 403 and equivalent state provisions.

In the seminal 2015 case of *White Burgess Langille Inman v. Abbott and Haliburton Co.*, the Supreme Court of Canada noted a jurisprudential trend in Canada towards tightening admissibility requirements and enhancing the trial judge's gatekeeping role.[6] *White Burgess* also emphasized the importance of expert objectivity, independence, and impartiality.[7] Significantly, in Canada, an expert's lack of independence and impartiality impacts the admissibility of the expert evidence, not just the weight attached to it.[8] This is a significant change in the law in Canada regarding the admissibility of expert evidence and serves as a powerful reminder that experts owe a duty to the court to provide fair, objective, and impartial evidence. In both the United States and Canada, expert witnesses are not advocates for the party who calls them to testify, but rather their sole responsibility is to assist the court.

To achieve the judicial designation of expert witness, the expert must collectively be shown to have acquired specialized knowledge through targeted study and experience in respect of the matters in question that is beyond that of a lay person.[9] Should a judge admit expert witness testimony, the trier of fact[10] is responsible for assessing the validity and reliability of the evidence and assigning the appropriate weight to it. This weighing exercise is essential, especially when the expert evidence faces opposition and when competing expert evidence is presented.

The Qualification Process for Expert Witnesses

When seeking to be qualified as an expert witness, the responsibility of the attorney leading the evidence and the proposed expert is substantial. The ability to satisfy the court that the expert is worthy of an expert witness designation is dependent upon four things:

- The ability of the expert to effectively communicate the substantive evidence in the courtroom. A brilliant expert who is a poor communicator is of rather limited value to the trier of fact.
- The knowledge and skill of the attorney leading and defending the evidence.
- The quality of the expert evidence.
- The credentials and suitability of the expert witness.

Before expert evidence may be presented at trial, the judge must first determine whether the proposed expert is sufficiently qualified through knowledge, skill, training, experience, or education to be deemed an expert. This will be determined in a *voir dire*, which is a trial within a trial to decide specific issues. In the qualification *voir dire*, the attorney leading the evidence must first state the specific area of expertise in which the expert is being tendered. This must be discussed by the attorney and the expert in advance of trial as they must both be satisfied that the stated field of expertise accurately encompasses the evidence to be presented. This is an important decision as it establishes the parameters for the testimony and alerts opposing counsel and the court about the nature of the proposed evidence.[11] When leading BPA evidence in murder prosecutions, qualifying the expert as an expert in "bloodstain pattern analysis" gives counsel and the expert the widest latitude. Some experts, attorneys, and judges prefer a more detailed description, hence there is a need for advanced discussion on this topic.

During the qualification *voir dire*, once the proposed field of expertise has been stated and the expert's *curriculum vitae* has been filed as an exhibit, questioning by the attorney leading the evidence will commence. The subject matter of the questioning is focused on qualifications, not the work the expert has done for the case. Topics covered include the following:

- An explanation of the field of expertise.
- The current professional positions held by the witness and relevant prior positions.
- Post-secondary education (university, college, technical schools).
- Specialized education, training, and practical experience.
- Instruction or presentations given by the expert in their field of expertise.
- Publications authored (or co-authored) by the expert.
- Relevant certifications and memberships in professional organizations.
- An overview of prior case work (this takes on added significance if the expert has not testified before).
- Previous occasions when the expert has been designated as an expert witness and gave opinion evidence in court.
- Peer review.
- Steps undertaken by the expert to remain current in their field of expertise.

The extent of questioning by opposing counsel and the court is dependent upon whether counsel takes issue with the expert being qualified. Even if there is no opposition, the tendering attorney should still undertake a full examination on qualifications as that will assist the trier of fact in deciding how much weight to attach to the evidence.

Most areas of expertise, including BPA, do not have judicially or legislatively imposed strict minimum qualifications. Each expert is considered on their own merits. The test is not whether the expert is the best, but rather whether the expert has sufficient relevant knowledge, skill, education, training, and experience to establish a level of knowledge superior to that of the trier of fact. Membership in applicable organizations is generally an asset as it shows commitment to professionalism.[12]

The qualification process must be undertaken each time an expert is tendered as an expert witness, as qualification by one judge in one case does not bind other judges in future cases. The ruling made by the judge as to the area of expertise in which the expert is qualified sets the topical parameters for what the expert is permitted to discuss during testimony.[13] It is improper for an expert witness to provide testimony outside the authorized area of expertise and the failure to abide by those limitations is likely to result in those portions of testimony being excluded at trial or on appeal.

Threshold Challenges to the Science Being Presented

Not only can experts be challenged regarding their professional qualifications, but the substantive evidence itself can also be challenged on the basis that it is not scientifically valid or reliable. In both scenarios, the role of the trial judge is to act as gatekeeper to ensure that only properly qualified experts give testimony on matters that are sufficiently scientifically valid and reliable to warrant admission. In the United States, the dominant test that was used by courts for most of the twentieth century was the test set out in *Frye v. United States*,[14] which hinged admission on whether the proposed scientific evidence has gained general acceptance in the relevant scientific community (the *Frye* test).[15] The legal landscape changed significantly in 1993 when the United States Supreme Court rendered its decision in *Daubert v. Merrell Dow Pharmaceuticals, Inc.*,[16] as well as its two subsequent decisions in *Gen. Elec. Co. v. Joiner*[17] and *Kumho Tire Co. v. Carmichael*,[18] collectively referred to as the *Daubert* trilogy. The test set out in *Daubert* applies in federal courts and in most state courts, while the remaining states follow *Frye* or have their own modified test.[19]

Departing from the *Frye* general acceptance approach, the *Daubert* court said that the Federal Rules of Evidence were paramount and that trial judges are required to examine the principles and scientific methodology underlying the tendered scientific evidence, rather than determining whether the conclusions are generally accepted in the relevant scientific community.[20] The Court noted that Rule 702 requires trial judges to ensure that "any and all scientific testimony or evidence admitted is not only relevant, but reliable."[21] Furthermore, in order to qualify as scientific knowledge, the inference or assertion must be derived by the scientific method and must be supported by appropriate validation, establishing a standard of evidential reliability.[22] Finally, it must be established that the trier of fact needs expert assistance. The Court set out a non-exhaustive list of factors a trial judge could consider in reviewing proffered evidence:[23]

- Whether the theory or technique can be (and has been) tested.
- Whether the theory or technique has been subjected to peer review and publication.
- The known or potential error rate of the scientific technique and the existence and maintenance of standards controlling the technique's operation.
- General acceptance in the relevant scientific community.

The Court noted that the focus must be on principles and methodology rather than on the conclusions generated. This view was qualified somewhat in *Joiner* when the Court ruled that a trial judge can disallow expert evidence when there is too great an analytical gap between the data and the opinion proffered by the expert. Trial judges are not required to admit opinion evidence which is connected to existing data only by the assertion of the expert.[24] Thus, expanding upon *Daubert, Joiner* permits a trial judge to disallow an expert's opinion if the expert's conclusion is not reliably based on accepted methodology.

The Court revisited *Daubert* a second time in *Kumho* when it concluded that *Daubert* applies to the testimony of engineers and other experts who are not scientists. The Court ruled that the trial judge's gatekeeping role applied not only to testimony based on scientific knowledge but also to testimony founded upon technical or other specialized knowledge, recognizing that it would be very difficult for trial judges to distinguish between scientific knowledge and technical or other specialized knowledge as there is no clear line that divides them.[25] The Court confirmed its opinion in *Joiner* that trial judges are permitted to assess the reliability of an expert's conclusions notwithstanding that they may be based on accepted methodology.[26] Furthermore, trial judges have broad discretion in applying *Daubert* and their findings should only be overturned on appeal if they have abused their discretion.[27]

The Court's decision in *Kumho,* while intellectually logical in its extension of the applicability of *Daubert,* is difficult to apply in criminal prosecutions as many experts called to testify are not scientists and their opinions, which are based upon training and experience, may be reliable but not in keeping with *Daubert* criteria. Interestingly, some state and federal courts have declined to require adherence to *Daubert* when reliability is dependent upon knowledge and experience of the expert rather than methodology and theory.[28] Rule 702 was amended in 2000 in response to *Daubert* and cases which applied it, including *Kumho,* to affirm the trial judge's role as gatekeeper and to set out standards for evaluating the reliability and helpfulness of all types of expert testimony.[29] Application of the *Daubert* trilogy and subsequent cases has been criticized by attorneys and academics for not following the *Daubert* test more rigorously. This area of the law is far from settled or consistently applied.[30]

The Supreme Court of Canada considered the role of trial judges as gatekeepers when deciding on the admissibility of novel scientific evidence in *R. v. Mohan.*[31] The Court stated that "... expert evidence which advances a novel scientific theory or technique is subjected to special scrutiny to determine whether it meets a basic threshold of reliability and whether it is essential in the sense that the trier of fact will be unable to come to a satisfactory conclusion without the assistance of the expert."[32] Inferentially, the Court rejected the *Frye* test, preferring instead the reliable foundation approach set out in *Daubert.*[33] In *R. v. J.-L.J.,*[34] the Court noted that while *Daubert* must be read in light of the Federal Rules of Evidence, the factors that it set out for evaluating the soundness of novel science are nonetheless helpful and worthy of consideration. Therefore, in Canada, the approach taken when assessing the admissibility of novel scientific evidence largely mirrors the *Daubert* approach.

Challenges to the validity and reliability of expert evidence being presented are significant and an adverse ruling can have a ripple effect across the country. Should an expert find that a hearing is being held on this topic, it is recommended that additional expert witnesses be considered to bolster the reliability of the methodology or techniques being presented.

Expert Reports

The expert report is the culmination of the expert's work, aside from testifying in court. It is the final written product of the expert and serves a variety of purposes, including the following:

- It documents the work, methodology, and analysis undertaken by the expert and all opinions drawn therefrom.
- It forms the basis for direct and cross-examination.
- It provides opposing experts with the full details of the expert's work so that it can be evaluated for soundness.
- It forms the basis of court mandated discovery.
- It assists the expert when testifying in court once the court grants the expert permission to consult the report.

There is no universally standardized format for expert reports and their appearance and content varies depending upon the expert, the agency or private entity for whom the expert works, and the area of expertise. Jurisdictional rules and procedure may also place additional requirements on report content, such as including a fee schedule and expert CV. The focus of this section is on the substantive content of the expert report. The structure and content of an expert report should reflect a logical and linear progression. A complete expert report should address the topics discussed in following subsections.

Case and Expert Identification

The report should have a cover page that delineates the report as an expert report and should include the name of the expert, contact information, the expert's position and employer, case name and file number, and the date the report was finalized.

Introduction

The expert should state when they were first consulted, by whom, and what they were asked to do. The expert should also indicate what information was provided to the expert and who provided it. Information provided may include a narrative of the incident, witness statements, police reports and notes, expert reports, photographs and video, forensic reports, etc. The expert should not accept nor seek out information that is not required in order to undertake the requested forensic analysis. Providing this contextual information is necessary in order to ascertain potential expert bias. All parties are entitled to know what background information the expert was provided as this may impact the objectivity of any proffered opinion.

Scene, Exhibit, and Other Examinations

Depending on the area of expertise involved, experts may attend crime scenes and other locations to conduct their analyses, and may examine exhibits or other physical objects *in situ* or at their laboratory. Scenes, exhibits, and physical objects should be fully documented and recorded via digital photographs or video as appropriate. Still images should form part of the report.

Experiments and Further Examinations

Experts sometimes find it necessary or advisable to conduct experiments or to revisit scenes or attend other locations. All such exploratory work should be fully documented both in writing and in digital photographs or video.

Examination and Analysis of Scenes, Exhibits, and Other Objects

Having described the context for the expert's work and all of the data obtained, this section should provide details of the complete examination and analysis of scenes, exhibits, and other objects. This section is typically lengthy and is usually the most detailed part of an expert report as it should set out the analytical methodology utilized by the expert. The examination and analysis should be fully documented and supplemented with photographs, diagrams, and charts as appropriate. Technical data can be included in the body of the report in the form of footnotes or appendices.

Results Achieved, Opinions Formed, and Conclusions Reached

In this section, the expert should clearly and succinctly state the conclusions and opinions that have been reached in the case. Conclusions and opinions must be full, fair, and frank, and any qualifications to them must be listed. All parties are entitled to expect that an expert witness will testify in accordance with the report. It follows that presenting new or different opinions on the witness stand for the first time will be regarded with skepticism. If an expert forms further opinions following the completion of the expert report as a result of reviewing further data or conducting additional analysis, an amended or supplemental report should be issued. Disposition of exhibits should be documented for chain of custody purposes.

Miscellaneous Considerations

The primary audience for an expert report is attorneys, police officers, and other experts. The report should be written in a manner that is readable, intelligible, and communicative. Footnotes are appropriate when further explanation of report content is needed beyond what is presented in the body of the report. Images, diagrams, and charts should be included where appropriate, either in the body of the report or in appendices. The use of a glossary is advisable to explain the meaning of technical terms endemic to the area of expertise and referred to the report. A well drafted report will often become the blueprint for direct and cross-examination and therefore of considerable benefit to the expert and the attorney. Finally, proofreading is essential as errors in a report reflect poorly on the drafter.

There is wisdom in not marking the expert report as an exhibit in a trial by jury. This issue was explored in the Canadian case of *R. v. Copeland*,[35] where the prosecution sought to have the BPA expert's report tendered as an exhibit at trial in addition to his testimony. The defense opposed the application. The Court disallowed entry of the expert report as an exhibit for the following reasons:

- It is not the practice of the court to provide jurors with transcripts and summaries of certain witnesses and not others. Filing the expert report would have the effect of unfairly emphasizing the expert's evidence over other evidence, giving the jury the evidence twice in effect.
- The expert report would reflect the direct examination but not the cross-examination and may therefore provide an unbalanced view to the jury.
- The jury is left to speculate about any content of the report that was not specifically addressed in testimony.
- The admission of a lengthy report may distract the jury.

The Court found that while the report would be of assistance to the jury, the negative effects of admitting it would outweigh any advantages. The expert's glossary was admitted, though not the report. Counsel can emphasize relevant parts of the expert evidence in their closing addresses. Though the approach on this issue varies among attorneys and differs depending upon jurisdictional preferences, there is merit in not filing the expert report as an exhibit for the jury for the sound reasons noted in this case so as to avoid trial unfairness and to avoid creating an unnecessary ground of appeal.

Peer Review

Peer review is an important component of expert witness work, where the expert's goal should be to produce high-quality reports and sound, defensible opinions. Peer review is an important step in the finalization of an expert report. Though not a specific legal requirement, once an expert has completed the report, especially one in which the expert has formed an opinion, it should be given to another qualified expert for peer review.[36] Peer review serves a number of important purposes, including:

- An independent and objective review of the expert's objectives, methodology, analysis, and conclusions.
- An assessment of whether additional examination, testing, or analysis should be undertaken.
- Commentary as to the soundness of any opinions formed.
- Suggestions on report structure and grammatical issues.

Peer review should ideally be conducted by an expert from another agency or organization so as to minimize the concerns of reviewer bias. Peer review is a significant responsibility requiring the reviewer to thoroughly assess the report and document the following:

- Is the report written in an organized, linear fashion with proper headings?
- Is the report understandable to the nonexpert?
- Have the appropriate images, diagrams, charts, etc. been included?
- Did the expert use the correct methodology?
- Has the data been appropriately analyzed?
- If applicable, is the math correct?
- Should more work be undertaken? Further analysis? Practical testing?
- Are the opinions or conclusions reached by the expert reasonable, justifiable, and defensible?
- Are the appendices, if any, appropriate?
- Are there grammatical errors?

Feedback from the peer reviewer should be documented, detailed, and meaningful. Once the expert receives the peer review, the expert must evaluate the recommendations and incorporate those deemed applicable and acknowledge the existence of the peer review in the report. Note that the expert must have sound reasons for choosing not to incorporate any review recommendations as this is valid ground for cross-examination. Peer reviewers can be called to testify by either side in the litigation and therefore conflict between the peer review and the final report should be avoided when possible.

BPA-SPECIFIC LAW AND PROCEDURE

Daubert/Frye and Related Challenges to BPA Evidence and Experts

United States

Over the past several decades, BPA evidence has been referred to by experts, counsel, and the courts as blood-flight analysis, blood splatter, blood spatter, and bloodstain pattern analysis. As BPA is the most accurate descriptor of this area of applied science and is the term used by the International Association for Identification (IAI), the Scientific Working Group on Bloodstain Pattern Analysis (SWGSTAIN), and the International Association of Bloodstain Pattern Analysts, that is the descriptor used in this chapter.

BPA evidence has faced sustained threshold admissibility challenges in the United States since the 1980s. These challenges have been grounded upon *Frye*, *Daubert*, FRE 702 (expert evidence),

FRE 403 (probative value versus prejudicial effect), as well as challenges under state-specific admissibility case law and rules of evidence. Challenges predicated on BPA and its underlying sciences being unreliable or invalid, or not generally accepted in the relevant scientific community, or arguments that the trier of fact is sufficiently able to interpret bloodstain evidence on their own have been resolutely rejected across America for decades. Specifically, BPA evidence has been routinely found to be admissible following a Rule 702 analysis, a detailed examination pursuant to *Frye* and *Daubert*, or on the basis that it has gained such widespread acceptance that the court can take judicial notice of it without holding a *Frye* or *Daubert* hearing.[37] Cases finding that BPA evidence does not pass threshold admissibility are rare indeed and easily distinguishable.[38]

Counsel have also argued that proposed experts lack the necessary qualifications to be deemed an expert witness and that experts use unreliable methodology to underpin their opinions. These latter challenges bear further commentary. As noted in Section 2, there are no legally imposed minimum educational, training, and experiential standards which must be met in order for BPA experts to be qualified as expert witnesses. Even though BPA is borne of biology, physics, and math, the requirements for formal education in those areas of science are rather lacking.[39] Both the IAI[40] and SWGSTAIN[41] publish training recommendations, but they are not particularly robust. Given the criticisms levied against low standards for qualification and the subjective nature of BPA in the National Academy of Sciences (NAS) report,[42] these training recommendations should garner some concern, though that has not been reflected in case law, which has set a rather low bar for entry as a BPA expert witness. Accordingly, individuals who have been tendered before the courts for either the prosecution or the defense or in other proceedings have ranged from people who have taken one BPA course with minimal practical experience to those with extensive training and fifty years of experience. Qualifications can be based on training and experience rather than formal educational background.[43] Further, there is no requirement that an expert be certified, licensed, or published in order to provide expert testimony.[44] This demonstrates that the assessment of qualifications requires a holistic approach.

Reflective of the relatively low bar for acceptable expert qualifications is *U.S. v. Mustafa*,[45] wherein the trial judge permitted the prosecution to present an expert in the field of "blood-flight analysis" in the prosecution of a member of the U.S. Army for murder. The expert had taken a five-day seminar on the topic, had not published, and had only worked on one prior case. The purpose of the expert evidence was to reconstruct the series of events leading to the murder. The expert's theory became the prosecution's theory at trial. On appeal, the convicted appellant challenged the admissibility of the expert evidence and the Court of Military Appeals undertook a Rule 702 analysis. The Court found that blood-flight analysis is "grounded in establish laws of physics and common sense."[46] The Court further found that the evidence would assist the trier of fact to determine facts in issue. As to qualifications, the expert had sufficient professional training and experience to be permitted to testify as to the bloodstain evidence and his theory of how they were caused. The Court upheld the ruling of the trial judge though the concurring appellate judge was critical of the expert espousing theories, preferring instead that experts state opinions and conclusions and whether the evidence supports either.[47] *Mustafa* is reflective of the seemingly relatively low bar for admission as a BPA expert though later cases have expected marginally more from proposed experts.

Decisions by trial judges as to expert qualifications are entitled to deference and will only be reversed on appeal upon a showing of clear error by the trial judge.[48] For example, in *State v. Halake*,[49] neither the prosecutor nor the "expert" witness considered the officer to be an expert in BPA, but he was nonetheless qualified as an expert by the trial judge. On appeal, it was determined that there was an insufficient basis upon which to designate the witness as an expert and the appellate court ruled that the trial judge had erred accordingly. These types of rulings are rare as counsel rarely tender witnesses as experts without there being a reasonable basis for it.

Most areas of forensic science have clearly defined occupational parameters for who is permitted to express opinions. For example, firearms experts testify about firearms, DNA experts testify about DNA, etc. Unusually, BPA experts often have other areas of professional expertise. Examples of experts who have given BPA evidence but have other occupations include crime lab directors,[50] crime scene investigators and analysts,[51] crime scene reconstructionists,[52] pathologists,[53] medical examiners,[54] serologists,[55] police investigators,[56] criminalists, chemists,[57] forensic scientists,[58] forensic consultants,[59] and DNA analysts.[60] Diluting the pool of who may provide expert BPA evidence in this manner certainly does not help to address concerns raised by the NAS report regarding expert qualifications.

Challenges premised upon FRE 403 (and state equivalents or common law tests) focus on the often-graphic nature of BPA evidence. Admissibility under these tests requires a showing that the probative value of the evidence, meaning the ability of the evidence to prove the existence or nonexistence of a fact, outweighs its prejudicial effect, referring to the tendency of the evidence to be used improperly by the trier of fact or to otherwise operate unfairly against the defendant. In *State v. Johnson*,[61] BPA evidence was admitted at trial and part of the expert's evidence included 46 color photos depicting bloodstain evidence and the victims' bodies covered with blood. On appeal, the convicted appellant argued that the evidence should not have been permitted, alleging that the expert testimony was merely a vehicle for admitting gruesome photos in an attempt to inflame the jury and increase the likelihood of a death penalty. On final appeal to the New Jersey Supreme Court, the Court found that the limited probative value of the BPA evidence warranted a careful assessment of its prejudicial effect. The prosecution outlined the legitimate purposes for leading the evidence, including depictions of what must have occurred during the murders and to rebut anticipated defense evidence that more than one assailant was involved. The appellant argued that the medical examiner had already testified as to the injuries sustained and cause of death, and that using BPA to dissect event dynamics proved neither identity nor intent. The Court found that the evidence had limited probative value and that the day-long presentation of gruesome photos and analysis placed too much focus on the condition of the victims' bodies rather than on the appellant's guilt. Accordingly, its prejudicial effect was too great and should not have been allowed. The Court directed that upon retrial the BPA evidence should be excluded absent a proper showing of probative value.[62]

Unreliable methodology employed by the expert has also been the subject of judicial commentary. In these cases, it is not the applied science of BPA that has been the subject of judicial approbation but rather the expert's chosen methodology. For example, in *Crawford v. County of Dauphin*,[63] the Court found most of the evidence proposed to be presented by the BPA expert to be in accordance with *Daubert* criteria but prohibited the expert from testifying regarding his demonstrative of medium blunt force trauma blood "spatter" overlaid onto palm prints on the basis that his methodology lacked sufficient indicia of reliability. This finding was based on the lack of calibration of the "blood spatter" device, lack of adequate controls to ensure reliable results, and an overall lack of adherence to the actual facts of the case. This ruling was an indictment of the expert's methodology, not BPA in general. Similarly, in *State v. Corbett*,[64] the defense challenged the admissibility of BPA evidence at trial on the basis that the expert failed to follow reliable principles and methods when he offered a BPA opinion utilizing staining that had not been proven to be blood, contrary to the expert's own published and peer-reviewed treatise on the subject. Even though he testified that stains should be subjected to presumptive, confirmatory, and DNA testing before a BPA analysis is undertaken, he failed to follow that sound methodology. Nor did he follow his own recommended best practice of viewing the person wearing the bloodstained clothing. Contrary to the ruling of trial judge, the appellate court conducted a Rule 702 and *Daubert* analysis and found that the expert's opinions were "based upon insufficient facts and data, and accordingly, could not have been the product of reliable principles and methods applied reliably to the facts of this case."[65] The Court found that admission of the BPA evidence was significantly prejudicial to the appellant and that this admission of unreliable expert evidence required a new trial.[66] On appeal to the North Carolina Supreme Court, the Court affirmed that the unreliable BPA evidence should not have been admitted and that a new trial was required.[67]

Trial judges have considerable latitude when assessing whether a proposed expert should be permitted to testify in an expert capacity. In a case where there are opposing BPA experts, the fact that one expert is more experienced and more credentialed than the other does not engage an admissibility ruling. Rather, these are assessments of weight to be made by the trier of fact.[68] BPA is an area of forensic science where opposing experts are common and divergences of opinion as to scene interpretation and reconstruction of the events leading to the bloodletting can be significant. For example, in some cases BPA experts have been criticized for not attending crime scenes and instead basing their opinions on photographs. In reality, defense experts are rarely retained while crime scenes still have evidence *in situ* and courts have been accepting of that situation, stating that opinions can be based in part on photographs.[69]

A further consideration is how far the BPA expert should go in offering opinion evidence. While evidence on the ultimate issue is not prohibited in Canada and most jurisdictions in the United States, BPA experts should be cautious in assessing criminal responsibility as those are matters of law, not science. The Court of Criminal Appeals of Oklahoma, in *Romano v. State*,[70] ruled that it was improper for the BPA expert to offer an opinion as to whether the person wearing blood-stained clothing was a passive observer to the stabbing. The Court found the opinion to be an impermissible prejudicial personal opinion. The Court stated:[71]

> It is one thing to say a defendant is in close proximity to a violent attack and quite another to state definitely a defendant participated in the attack. When this is done, the expert's opinion is effectivelytransformed from circumstantial to direct evidence. Because Bevel's opinion overstepped the proper bounds of blood spatter evidence his answer constitutes a personal opinion of Appellant's guilt. Bevel's personal opinion does not assist the jury in concluding Appellant stabbed decedent.

The Court found the evidence more prejudicial than probative. Even though it was the prosecutor's question that led to the expert's answer, a more prudent course of action would have been to decline providing such an answer.

Though the NAS report may still engender a renewed attack on the validity and reliability of BPA and the experts who provide testimony in court, that has not been the experience thus far based on reported case law. Courtroom-based challenges will nonetheless continue regarding the qualifications of expert witnesses and the reliability of the BPA methodology employed by them.

Canada

BPA evidence has been successfully led at trial in criminal prosecutions across Canada with reported case law going back to the 1990s.[72] At the appellate level, BPA expert evidence has been frequently referred to with approval by the court as a valuable component in the forensic fact-finding process.[73] Canadian courts are increasingly becoming aware of the impact of unreliable expert evidence.[74] Despite that, the validity and reliability of BPA evidence as an applied science and its application to crime scene evaluation and interpretation has not been a live issue in the cited trial and appellate decisions, although in some cases the reliability of the opinion evidence itself was raised as an issue, albeit will little effect. The comparative lack of *Daubert* type challenges to BPA evidence in Canada is reflective of a different legal culture when compared to the United States. Forensic and other expert witnesses face substantive challenges on the basis of expert qualifications, methodology, and opinions when deemed appropriate by opposing counsel, but experience shows that the underlying science is less likely to be challenged. There have certainly been threshold challenges to the validity of proposed expert evidence in various fields of expertise, but they tend to be the exception rather than the rule.

The most common challenges observed relate to the methodology utilized by the expert, the interpretation of the bloodstains, and the expert's qualifications. For example, in *R. v. Teske*,[75] the defense challenged the reliability of the expert's evidence, arguing that his methodology was flawed, that he was not able to support his opinions, and that his evidence was not sufficiently independent. The defense did not argue that BPA is a novel or invalid science yet urged the trial judge to follow the Supreme Court's approach in *R. v. J.-L.J.*[76] in determining whether the expert evidence was properly admissible. Accordingly, the evidence of the expert was fully presented in a *voir dire*. The defense also expressed concern that the expert used computer software as part of his methodology, but the trial judge was satisfied from the evidence presented that the expert undertook the appropriate measurements and utilized the software correctly, noting the expert's evidence that approximately the same result could be achieved without using the computer program but that the software allowed for faster and more accurate calculations. Following a detailed presentation of the expert evidence and thorough direct and cross-examination, the trial judge found the evidence to be reliable and worthy of admission. The judge found the expert to be well qualified in the field of BPA and stated that the fact that he was trained in a law enforcement environment and that his evidence favored the prosecution theory did not mean that his evidence lacked independence. Furthermore, all of the evidence was capable of independent verification. The expert evidence was thereafter presented at trial where it was robustly challenged and the defense called their own BPA expert who agreed with some of the findings but challenged others and presented differing conclusions.[77] As with all cases, the trier of fact's role is to evaluate the evidence and determine what evidence, if any, to accept. Having been ruled admissible, BPA evidence was fairly put before the court for evaluation and for an assessment of weight when deciding the facts of the case.

Commonly, meritless challenges to BPA evidence are made in the hope that the trial judge will exclude powerful, probative evidence. This was evident in *R. v. Berry*,[78] where the prosecution applied to present expert BPA evidence during the trial of the defendant for high-profile child murders and the defense opposed the prosecution's application. The expert gave extensive evidence about the applied science of BPA and its role in interpreting the physical evidence and circumstances that gave rise to the bloodletting. The expert was a certified BPA specialist with the Royal Canadian Mounted Police and this case was the first one she attended independently (without a mentor) though she had attended approximately 20 prior scenes for the purpose of BPA. The prosecution argued that the expert's evidence was necessary as it would be very difficult for the lay person to make informed factual decisions about the homicide scene without expert assistance. Oddly, the defense argued that BPA is a matter of common sense and that no expertise is required. The defense further argued that if allowed to testify, the expert should only be allowed to describe what is observable in the photographs, not any inferences drawn therefrom. The Court disagreed and found the evidence to be necessary as it would assist the trier of fact in understanding the scene evidence. The defense also argued that the expert was not sufficiently qualified to present expert evidence, noting that at the time she attended the scene, she had not yet been certified and had only attended 20 previous scenes and never on her own. The Court found her to be sufficiently qualified and ruled that any questions regarding experience were questions of weight rather than admissibility.

Qualifications at the trial level were also challenged in *R. v. Luciano*,[79] where the prosecution sought to qualify a BPA expert as an expert witness. Following a qualification *voir dire* in which the expert's qualifications were examined in detail and the court ruled that they merited an expert witness designation, the Court also noted that BPA "is not junk science."[80] This is not a case where the applied science of BPA was challenged and therefore the junk science comment is *obiter* and of limited precedential value. In the expert witness world, these types of largely baseless challenges are common as there is little to be lost by defense in challenging admissibility even though such challenges are rarely successful.

An assessment of expert qualifications occurred at the appellate level in *R. v. Hartling*,[81] in which the Ontario Court of Appeal heard an appeal from conviction for murder wherein the prosecution relied in part on BPA evidence. On appeal, the appellant sought to present fresh evidence by calling a BPA expert whose evidence would allegedly undermine the prosecution's BPA expert evidence given at trial.[82] The Court of Appeal considered whether the proposed expert was qualified to provide such evidence should the evidence be allowed on appeal. The Court noted that the expert had not worked as a BPA expert since 1998 (the trial was held in 2014) and had taken only two related courses in 1994 and 1997. The proposed expert stated that he does not get paid for his work and effectively considered it to be a hobby as a result. He was unfamiliar with a leading, relevant 2015 publication and his evidence reflected a bias in favor of the defense, rather than the independent, objective analysis expected of an expert. For these reasons, the proposed evidence was ruled inadmissible by the Court of Appeal.[83]

A similar appellate fresh evidence application was made in *R. v. Wu*,[84] where the British Columbia Court of Appeal considered a defense application to call a BPA expert as fresh evidence on appeal to counter BPA expert evidence led by the prosecution at trial. The appellant alleged that portions of the trial BPA expert's evidence were unreliable. At trial the prosecution's BPA expert began her testimony by explaining BPA, the science grounding it, and some of the types of bloodstain patterns she would be referring to in her scene examination. She then described a series of bloodletting events, documented a variety of bloodstain patterns, and opined as to how some of the victim's injuries were sustained. Neither her qualifications nor evidence were challenged at trial. The proposed fresh evidence consisted of an expert report written by a BPA expert post-conviction who criticized some of the expert's evidence. The Court ruled that the decision to not challenge the prosecution expert at trial and to not call an opposing expert was a tactical decision. Furthermore, the Court was satisfied that even if the criticisms of the proposed expert had been taken into account, it would not have affected the resultant conviction.[85] The application was therefore dismissed.[86]

One final decision worthy of note is *R. v. Cote*,[87] where the Ontario Court of Appeal ruled that the trial judge did not err in admitting photographs as part of the BPA expert's testimony. The expert had positioned a model wearing the deceased's bloodstained shirt in what the expert opined were the possible anatomical positions the deceased would have been in when stabbed and produced those photographs for the jury. Both the trial judge and the Court of Appeal ruled that the photographs were not speculative and were based on experiments undertaken by the expert and thus admissible as demonstrative evidence. This appellate endorsement of the use of demonstrative evidence to illustrate expert opinions is meritorious as it recognizes the value of visualizing opinion evidence, which will be discussed further in the next section.

Visualizing Expert Evidence

The responsibility of counsel and the expert witness in the courtroom is significant as they must teach complex content to the court in such a manner that allows the court to gain a sufficient understanding of the evidence in order to properly assess the case. When experts testify, they take on a pedagogical role as they present scientific or other specialized evidence to the trier of fact. It is therefore essential that in conjunction with the attorney leading the evidence, experts consider how to present the evidence in the most effective manner because depending on the complexity of the material, the learning curve can be vertiginous. While expert testimony must contain words, experts should ensure that their testimony is supplemented with visual evidence. Since there could be no BPA evidence without visualizing the bloodstain evidence, it follows that images are an essential component of BPA evidence.

Images are comprehended differently than text, with visual information being digested more quickly and globally along with a heightened, though not necessarily justified, sense of understanding. They are remembered better than text and lend themselves to explaining complex concepts to the court in a more concise and memorable manner.[88] The more complex the material, the more images and other visual evidence can aid in comprehension. Even mathematical data can be more effectively conveyed and comprehended if it is presented in graphical form rather than just numbers and equations. How information is presented, interpreted, and understood is dependent upon what information has been selected, to whom it is being shown, and the purposes for showing it.[89] Experts and attorneys must therefore consider how to weave visual evidence into the case narrative in a manner that makes the telling of the story more complete, more impactful, and that does justice to the evidence.

Thorough pretrial preparation will allow the expert and counsel to have command of complex evidence but the learning curve for the court must be considered. Since each party only gets one opportunity to convey its evidence to the court, it is essential that the presentation be didactically effective. It must appear, to observers and participants alike, to be seamless, surgical, informative, and efficient. When presenting complex scientific evidence, there is merit in beginning with an introductory visual presentation designed to teach the court about the science generally before focusing on specific case facts. Effective multimedia presentations convey complexity with greater efficiency than words alone and may assist counsel and experts to convey scientific, technical, or abstract information to the court.[90] When the viewer invests time and effort in an attempt to interpret and understand complex visual evidence, the viewer may believe more strongly in their interpretation because of the effort expended. An image that one must be taught to see and comprehend may achieve heightened credence as a result.[91] An expert witness who teaches complex material effectively can induce that lightbulb moment when the epistemic competence of the viewer is improved. Criminal prosecutions often involve complex scientific evidence that must be presented in such a way as to educate the court to ensure full comprehension and an understanding of the probative value of the evidence. Visual depiction is an essential component of that pedagogic exercise.

Accurate, detailed depictions of crime scenes, areas of interest, and objects provide counsel and the court with data necessary to more fulsomely comprehend available evidence and to understand what occurred.[92] Scene measurements, including the location of objects and features within a scene, are central to a proper scene reconstruction, especially given that scenes are transient and ephemeral, and that what may seem unimportant at the outset could take on great significance at trial.[93] While photographs and video are common methods of documenting a scene, computers can also be used to incorporate data points to create 3D objects and scenes in a digital visually appealing form.[94] Computer-based 3D modelling is particularly helpful when vertical dimensions of geographic, scene-based, or other features are important. There is support for the proposition that 3D modelling can be effective in adding clarity to expert testimony and for increasing viewer comprehension.[95]

Two-dimensional depictions of scenes limit the ability of the viewer to accurately assess spatial relationships of the overall scene and features and objects located within it.[96] They are also less suitable for reconstructing scenes and events using computer-generated animations or virtual reality walkthroughs. Three-dimensional laser scanning allows investigators to capture the entire geometry of a scene, including objects and other relevant aspects that may not have been noted when the evidence was gathered, thus ensuring the longevity and preservation of the scene for a subsequent comprehensive examination.[97] Crime scenes can be documented three-dimensionally in addition to other conventional methods.[98] Terrestrial laser scanning devices can quickly scan large areas, buildings, rooms, and vehicles, generating point clouds with millions of points with accuracy ranges up to 1 mm.[99] The efficiency that terrestrial laser scanning affords in documenting a scene saves investigators valuable on-site time and records data that may not initially appear relevant but may take on significance later. Multiple scanning technologies can be used to accurately measure outdoor and indoor scenes as well as vehicles and other objects. Combining different tiers of scanning technology provides a varied perspectival view of an event, maximizing the data that can be obtained from it.[100]

Counsel and the expert must determine in advance of trial whether visual evidence is being tendered for substantive purposes to establish facts or as demonstrative evidence. The epistemic and legal difference between substantive evidence and demonstrative evidence is considerable. Visual evidence that is marked as a full trial exhibit can be used by the trier of fact to make factual determinations, in contrast to demonstrative evidence which cannot be so used. Demonstrative evidence is evidence addressed directly to the senses without the intervention of testimony.[101] It includes all nonverbal evidence that is not tendered as real evidence.[102] Significantly, it possesses no independent probative value and takes the form of an object or visual depiction that is used to explain, illustrate, or assist in the comprehension of other admissible evidence in a more effective manner.[103] The viewer may find it more compelling than the underlying data used to create the demonstrative exhibit, especially when assessing scientific evidence.[104] Demonstrative evidence is typically secondary in nature, used for the derivative purpose of illustration only. A useful definition is that demonstrative visual evidence is evidence that is designed to illustrate *viva voce* and other forms of evidence by way of a visual recreation.[105] By way of example, images of bloodstains are real evidence whereas diagrams, charts, 3D models, and computer animations are generally demonstrative in nature. Both types of evidence have merit and it is important that the evidential purpose of visual components be determined before trial. Counsel who expect to prove a fact through demonstrative evidence are bound to be disappointed as the law does not permit that, while experts who use demonstrative evidence as a didactic tool will find favor in the increased comprehension of the trier of fact.

Recommendations for the Effective Presentation of BPA Evidence in Court

The purpose of this section is to make principled recommendations that are intended to guide BPA experts and counsel in the successful presentation and defense of BPA evidence in court. These recommendations are drawn from this chapter's content, case law, academic articles, and practical experience.

Recommendation 1: Qualifications of the BPA expert

BPA experts should strive to attain a high level of professional competence with particular attention to formal and practical training. IAI certification requirements should not be regarded as the zenith for training but rather the minimum standard. When judges assess whether a proposed expert is suitably qualified and when the trier of fact decides how much weight to place on an expert's testimony, robust qualifications are an essential consideration. Those qualifications should amply reflect specialized knowledge, skill, training, experience, and education.

Empirical research indicates that there is a strong relationship between experience and accuracy in the evaluation and interpretation of BPA evidence.[106] Experience can produce specialized knowledge which heightens the ability to recognize bloodstain patterns thus establishing the proposition that accurate pattern recognition requires specialized knowledge and experience.[107] However, experience alone is not enough. One of the clear challenges regarding BPA evidence and the qualifications of experts who present it is the fact that much of it is based on experience, making it less amenable to independent verification. Experts must strive to use proven, established methodology that is objectively verifiable in order to establish reliability. That level of expertise is borne collectively of robust formal education, targeted training, and experience.

Recommendation 2: The need for dedicated BPA experts

BPA and BPA expert testimony should only be undertaken by dedicated, highly trained BPA experts. Even though pathologists, medical examiners, serologists, DNA experts, etc. work with blood, that does not qualify them as experts in BPA. Allowing experts from other disciplines to provide BPA evidence dilutes the overall competence that should be expected of BPA experts and serves to lower the bar for admission.

Recommendation 3: Informative expert *curriculum vitaes* (CV)

Since experts will be assessed for current expertise by the court and the trier of fact based on past education, training, experience, and other accomplishments, it is essential that all of these attributes be fully documented in an informative CV. A CV is a constant work in progress and should fairly communicate to the reader what qualifications the expert brings to the case in question. Accordingly, BPA experts should ensure that they have a robust and informative CV.

Recommendation 4: Experts are required to be current

Experts must strive to be at the forefront of their area of expertise when undertaking BPA and providing courtroom testimony. Counsel and the court are entitled to the best evidence available and accordingly, experts should be fully conversant with the latest scientific research, practices, accepted methodologies, and should have a general understanding of any relevant legal rulings regarding BPA evidence.

Recommendation 5: Tread carefully in *Daubert, Frye,* and related challenges

When BPA and its underlying sciences are being challenged in court, counsel and the expert must give careful consideration to presenting the strongest possible foundational evidence to establish the scientific validity and reliability of BPA. It may be necessary to present additional expert witness testimony beyond that of the case expert to accomplish this task. Adverse rulings can be avoided with proper preparation and expert evidence presentation.

Recommendation 6: Expert reports

Expert reports must be comprehensive and fully describe what the expert was asked to do, all of the information provided to the expert before and during the expert's involvement in the case, scene and evidence description, detailed methodology, and the expert's opinions and conclusions. The expert report must fully reflect what the expert's courtroom testimony will be as the witness stand is not the place to deliver new and undisclosed content and opinions.

Recommendation 7: Peer review

All expert reports in which an opinion has been formed should be peer reviewed by another qualified BPA expert. Peer review should be undertaken in a meaningful way and fully documented for the expert's use and potential future testimonial obligations of the peer reviewer. Peer reviewers should have no involvement with the investigation in order to maintain objectivity. The expert should carefully consider the advice provided by the peer reviewer and incorporate all applicable recommendations, acknowledging and giving credit to the peer reviewer.

Recommendation 8: Preparing an informative visual courtroom presentation

Experts have an important pedagogical role in the courtroom. Careful consideration must be given to the effective creation and presentation of visual evidence as part of the expert's testimony. This typically includes relevant overall scene photographs, detailed images of bloodstains, measurements, diagrams, charts, etc. This information can be presented via individual exhibits or through PowerPoint™ or other similar cumulative formats. More advanced methods include 3D imagery and modelling, which focus on measured data without drawing upon graphic imagery. In order to avoid the exclusion of evidence on the basis of undue prejudice, scene images should be restricted to only those that are specifically needed to present the BPA evidence.

Finally, a brief word about presentation strategy when video and digital still images are used in court. The use of hard copy (printed) digital images and LCD projectors and screens to show video and digital still images in court are inappropriate methods of presenting visual evidence. When digital images are printed on paper, they lose fine detail that would otherwise be viewable on a high-quality computer monitor or HD presentation screen. By presenting them electronically rather than in print, portions of the image can be enlarged for more detailed examination in court.[108] Further, with annotation software, a witness can visibly mark an image shown on the witness's monitor so as to point out areas or items of relevance, such markings being visible on all courtroom monitors and capable of being printed for exhibit purposes. Other platforms such as SMART Board™ and ELMO Visual Presenter™ fulfill a similar function. Projecting images through an LCD projector onto a screen guarantees loss of detail and image resolution as the image travels through dust particles in the air and must then contend with micro-contours that are part of the screen. Additional impediments include the quality of the bulb and lens in the projector, the lighting in the courtroom, and the location of the screen in relation to the fact finders. The LCD projection approach to the presentation of evidence does a tremendous disservice to visual evidence.

Recommendation 9: Be a teacher

It is not the role of the expert to solve the case but rather to assist the trier of fact in understanding the evidence so that they can make findings of fact with confidence. Truth discovered is more powerful than truth told. By educating the trier of fact on the applied science of BPA and walking them through the methodology employed in analyzing the case evidence, the trier of fact is more likely to accept the expert evidence and apply it intelligently when deciding facts and criminal liability. An informative, didactic presentation combining testimony and visual evidence is a must for the effective BPA expert witness.

Notes

1. See, for example, National Research Council, *Strengthening Forensic Science in the United States: A Path Forward,* The National Academies Press, Washington, DC, 2009. Available at https://doi.org/10.17226/12589.
2. Feder, Harold A. and Max M. Houck, *Succeeding as an Expert Witness,* CRC Press, Boca Raton, 2008, pp. 1–5. Note that there is some scope under the lay opinion exception to the opinion evidence rule for lay witnesses to provide opinion evidence but that is limited to topics of general knowledge.
3. *R. v. Lavallee,* [1990] 1 S.C.R. 852 (SCC), Watt, David, *Watt's Manual of Criminal Evidence,* Thomson Carswell, Toronto, 2007, p. 364; Shelton, Donald E., *Forensic Science Evidence,* LFB Scholarly Publishing, El Paso, 2012, p. 1.
4. *White Burgess Langille Inman v. Abbott and Haliburton Co. [White Burgess],* 2015 SCC 23 (SCC); *R. v. Mohan,* [1994] 2 S.C.R. 9 (SCC).
5. *White Burgess,* at paras 23–24; *R. v. Mohan,* at 21.
6. *White Burgess,* at para. 20.
7. *White Burgess,* at paras 2, 32.
8. *White Burgess,* at para. 45.
9. *R. v. Mohan,* [1994] 2 S.C.R. 9 (SCC); *R. v. Lavallee,* [1990] 1 S.C.R. 852 (SCC).
10. "Trier of fact" refers to the people who are responsible for deciding the proven facts of a case. When the trial is heard by a jury, the jury is the trier of fact. When the trial is heard by judge alone, the judge is the trier of fact.
11. *R. v. Marquard,* [1993] 4 S.C.R. 223 (SCC). It is then up to opposing counsel to object if opinions are offered outside the stated area of expertise.
12. BPA experts may seek membership in the American Academy of Forensic Sciences, the International Association for Identification, and the International Association of Bloodstain Pattern Analysts. The IAI offers certification for bloodstain pattern analysts.
13. Houck, Max M. and Jay A. Siegel, *Fundamentals of Forensic Science,* Elsevier Academic Press, Amsterdam, 2006, p. 651.
14. *Frye v. United States,* 293 F. 1013 (D.C. Cir. 1923). This case dealt with the precursor to the polygraph and held that is had not gained general acceptance in the relevant scientific community. The inadmissibility of the polygraph continues today.
15. At 1014.
16. *Daubert v. Merrell Dow Pharmaceuticals, Inc.,* 509 U.S. 579 (1993).
17. *Gen. Elec. Co. v. Joiner,* 522 U.S. 136 (1997).
18. *Kumho Tire Co. v. Carmichael,* 526 U.S. 137 (1999).
19. For a helpful chart showing the test followed in each state, see Shelton, Donald E, *Forensic Science Evidence,* LFB Scholarly Publishing, El Paso, 2012, pp. 13–16.
20. The *Frye* test is subsumed among the *Daubert* criteria but is only one of many listed factors to consider.
21. At 589.
22. At 590.
23. At 593–594.

24. Joiner, supra, at 146.
25. At 141.
26. At 152–153.
27. At 158.
28. A discussion of this divergence is beyond the scope of this chapter. For more on this subject, see e.g. Shelton, Donald E, *Forensic Science Evidence*, LFB Scholarly Publishing, El Paso, 2012, pp. 18–19.
29. Federal Rule of Evidence 702, Committee Notes on Rules – 2000 Amendment, available at https://www.law.cornell.edu/rules/fre/rule_702 (accessed 15 April 2021). The commentary provides valuable insight as to the interpretation of *Daubert*.
30. "*Daubert* and its progeny have engendered confusion and controversy." National Research Council, *Strengthening Forensic Science in the United States: A Path Forward*, The National Academies Press, Washington, DC, 2009. Available at https://doi.org/10.17226/12589, at 103.
31. *R. v. Mohan*, [1994] 2 S.C.R. 9 (SCC).
32. *R. v. Mohan*, at 25.
33. The Court did not specifically refer to *Frye* or *Daubert* but in *R. v. J.-L.J.*, the Court confirmed this inferential approach.
34. *R. v. J.-L.J.*, [2000] 2 S.C.R. 600, at 615-616 (SCC).
35. *R. v. Copeland*, 2018 ONSC 3648 (Ont. S.C.J.).
36. Note that the United States Supreme Court (*Daubert*) and the Supreme Court of Canada (*J.-L.J.*) stated that peer review is an important factor in determining the validity and reliability of expert evidence.
37. *O'Donnell v. Yezzo*, 2023 WL 3791548 (U.S.D.C., N.D. Ohio, 2023); *State v. Brown*, 347 So.3d 745 (La, 2022); *Preston v. State*, 2018 WL 3447713 (Tex. App. Austin, 2018); *Bratt v. Genovese*, 2017 WL 6344449 (M.D. Fla., 2017); *Schmidt v. State*, 902 N.W.2d 590 (Iowa App., 2017); *People v. Lyons*, 2017 WL 2267163 (Ill. App. 1 Dist., 2017); *State v. Sabatini*, 2015 WL 10034280 (N.J. Super. A.D., 2016); *U.S. v. Carroll*, 2012 WL 13081293 (D.N.M., 2012); *State v. Floren*, 165 Wash. App. 1013 (Wash. App. Div. 1, 2011); *Commonwealth v. Powell*, 877 N.E.2d 589 (Mass. 2007); *People v. Hoyos*, 162 P.3d 528 (Calif. 2007); *People v. Evans*, 859 N.E.2d 642, 650-651 (Ill. App. 4th Dist., 2006); *State v. Fry*, 126 P.3d 516 (N.M. 2005); *Jones v. State*, 918 So.2d 1220 (Miss. 2005); *Holmes v. State*, 135 S.W.3d 178, 190-195 (Tex. App. Waco, 2004); *Smith v. Commonwealth*, 576 S.E.2d 465 (Va. 2003); *Franklin v. State*, 2003 WL 1563797, 6 (Tex. App. Houston [1 Dist.], 2003); *State v. Downing*, 791 A.2d 649, 654-655 (Conn. App. Ct. 2002); *People v. Whitaker*, 289 A.D.2d 84 (N.Y. App., 2001); *State v Roberts*, 14 P.3d 713, 740-741 (Wash. 2000); *Fox v. Ward*, 200 F.3d 1286, 1297 (10th Cir. 2000); *People v. Barnes*, 267 A.D.2d 1020 (N.Y. App., 1999); *State v. Biros*, 678 N.E.2d 891 (Ohio 1997); *State v. Goode*, 461 S.E.2d 631 (N.C. 1995); *Romano v. State*, 909 P.2d 92, 111-112 (Okl. Cr., 1995); *People v. Haywood*, 530 N.W.2d 497, 500 (Mich. App, 1995); *People v. Clark*, 857 P.2d 1099, 1142 (Calif. 1993); *James v. State*, 613 N.E.2d 15, 22 (Ind. 1993); *State v. Rodgers*, 812 P.2d 1208, 1210 (Idaho 1991); *U.S. v. Phillip*, 948 F.2d 241, 249 (6th Cir. 1991); *State v. Moore*, 458 N.W.2d 90, 96 (Minn. 1990); *Robinson v. State*, 574 So.2d 910, 918 (Ala. Crim. App., 1990); *State v. Mix*, 781 P.2d 751, 758 (Mont. 1989); *Commonwealth v. Mendes*, 547 N.E.2d 35 (Mass. 1989); *People v. Murray*, 537 N.Y.S.2d 399 (N.Y. App. Div., 1989); *State v. Deel*, 1986 WL 11203 (Ohio Ct. App., 1986); *State v. Knox*, 459 N.E.2d 1077, 1080 (Ill. App. 3rd Dist., 1984); *Farris v. State*, 670 P.2d 319, 328-329 (Okl. Cr., 1983); *State v. Melson*, 638 S.W.2d 342, 363 (Tenn. 1982); *State v. Hall*, 297 N.W.2d 80, 85 (Iowa 1980).
38. *State v. Owens*, 508 N.E.2d 1088, 1094 (Ill. App. 3rd Dist., 1987) Note that in *People v. Evans*, 859 N.E.2d 642, 650-651 (Ill. App. 4th Dist., 2006) the Court, referring to *Owens*, said "This court reversed the conviction, not because we found the blood-spatter analysis principle was not generally accepted in the scientific community, but because of a foundation issue. We found the State had presented insufficient evidence of the expert's qualifications, knowledge, training, or experience." *Owens* is therefore not a pronouncement on the reliability of BPA evidence.
39. Shelton, Donald E., *Forensic Science Evidence*, LFB Scholarly Publishing, El Paso, 2012, p. 151.
40. The IAI Certification Program Operations Manual lists a broad range of competencies required for certification (Section 8.1), but the prerequisites listed in Section 8.9 are rather sparse. Applicants must have at least 60 higher education semester credits, though there is no requirement as to what kind of courses or programs from which they should emanate. The training requirement is 240 hours, only 100 of which need to be specific to BPA. See https://www.theiai.org/bloodstain_pattern.php (accessed 29 April 2021).

41. SWGSTAIN requires a bachelor's degree in a field of study related to BPA, an associate degree and two years of job-related experience, or a high school diploma and four years of job-related experience. Job-related experience includes being a crime scene technician, criminalist, or police investigator. BPA specific training objectives are listed but not how many hours of training or what type of training is required to achieve those objectives. A continuing education requirement is eight hours annual BPA related training. See https://archives.fbi.gov/archives/about-us/lab/forensic-science-communications/fsc/jan2008/standards/2008_01_standards01.htm (accessed 29 April 2021).
42. National Research Council, *Strengthening Forensic Science in the United States: A Path Forward*, The National Academies Press, Washington, DC, 2009. Available at https://doi.org/10.17226/12589, at 178–179.
43. *Bratt v. Genovese*, 2017 WL 6344449 (M.D. Fla., 2017); *Correll v. Secretary Dept. of Corr.*, 932 F. Supp. 2d 1257, 1295 (M.D. Fla., 2013).
44. *Rasmussen v. City of New York*, 2011 WL 744522 (E.D.N.Y., 2011).
45. *U.S. v. Mustafa*, 22 M.J. 165 (C.M.A., 1986).
46. *U.S. v. Mustafa*, at 168.
47. Cert. denied 107 S.Ct. 444 (1986).
48. This is a uniform legal standard at both the federal and state level. See e.g. *State v. Begley*, 956 S.W.2d 471, 475 (Tenn. 1997); *Anderson v. State*, 863 So.2d 169, 179 (Fla. 2003).
49. *State v. Halake*, 102 S.W.3d 661 (Tenn. Crim. App., 2001).
50. *People v. Evans*, 859 N.E.2d 642 (Ill. App. 4th Dist., 2006); *Johnson v. State*, 2018 WL 3359559 (Md. App., 2018).
51. *Jones v. State*, 918 So.2d 1220 (Miss. 2005).
52. *People v. Lyons*, 2017 WL 2267163 (Ill. App. 1 Dist., 2017); *Kirby v. City of East Wenatchee*, 2013 WL 1497343 (E.D. Wash., 2013); *Rasmussen v. City of New York*, 2011 WL 744522 (E.D.N.Y., 2011).
53. *State v. Dreiling*, 54 P.3d 475 (Kan. 2002); *Commonwealth v. Stallworth*, 781 A.2d 110 (Pa. 2001).
54. *Wines v. Commonwealth*, 2009 WL 1830805 (Ky. 2009).
55. *Bratt v. Genovese*, 2017 WL 6344449 (M.D. Fla., 2017).
56. *Crum v. State*, 2019 WL 6335434 (Tex. App. Texarkana, 2019); *Preston v. State*, 2018 WL 3447713 (Tex. App. Austin, 2018); *State v. Langston*, 2017 WL 1968827 (Tenn. Crim. App., 2017); *U.S. v. Carroll*, 2012 WL 13081293 (D.N.M., 2012); *Holmes v. State*, 135 S.W.3d 178 (Tex. Crim App., 2004); *Franklin v. State*, 2003 WL 1563797 (Tex. App. Houston [1 Dist.], 2003); *U.S. v. Mustafa*, 22 M.J. 165 (C.M.A. 1986).
57. *McCambridge v. Hall*, 303 F.3d 24 (1st Cir. 2002).
58. *Creach v. Spokane County*, 2013 WL 12177099 (E.D. Wash., 2013); *Jones v. State*, 918 So.2d 1220 (Miss. 2005); *State v. Biros*, 678 N.E.2d 891 (Ohio, 1997).
59. *Johnson v. State*, 2018 WL 3359559 (Md. App., 2018).
60. *Bratt v. Genovese*, 2017 WL 6344449 (M.D. Fla., 2017).
61. *State v. Johnson*, 576 A.2d 834 (N.J. 1990).
62. *State v. Johnson*, at 852-853.
63. *Crawford v. County of Dauphin*, 1006 WL 898171 (M.D. Pa., 2006).
64. *State v. Corbett*, 839 S.E.2d 361 (N.C. App., 2020).
65. *State v. Corbett*, at 398.
66. *State v. Corbett*, at 412.
67. *State v. Corbett*, 855 S.E.2d 228 (N.C. 2021).
68. *State v. Langston*, 2017 WL 1968827, 9–12 (Tenn. Crim. App., 2017). Many courts have applied this procedure. *Langston* is just one example of this approach.
69. *Bratt v. Genovese*, 2017 WL 6344449 (M.D. Fla, 2017); *Durst v. Rapelje*, 483 Fed. Appx. 36, 48 (6th Cir. 2012); *Harrington v. Richter*, 562 U.S. 86, 96 (2011).
70. *Romano v. State*, 909 P.2d 92 (Okl. Cr., 1995).
71. *Romano v. State*, at 109–111.
72. See for example this selection of cases from a broad array of Canadian criminal cases relying upon BPA evidence: *R. v. Saddleback*, 2022 ABQB 187 (Alta. Q.B.); *R. v. Lu*, 2021 ONSC 4920 (Ont. S.C.J.); *R. v. Daley*, 2021 ONSC 5352 (Ont. S.C.J.);*R. v. Shearer*, 2020 BCSC 116 (B.C.S.C.); *R. v. Poorman*, 2020 BCSC 1420 (B.C.S.C.); *R. v. Montsion*, 2020 ONCJ 464 (Ont. C.J.); *R. v. Spezzano*, 2020 CarswellQue 14316 (Que. S.C.); *R. v. Zhao*, 2020 BCSC 1552 (B.C.S.C.); *R. v.*

Bellevue, 2019 ONCJ 964 (Ont. C.J.); *R. v. Wolff*, 2018 SKQB 220 (Sask. Q.B.); *R. v. Sheepway*, 2018 YKSC 4 (Y.T.S.C.); *R. v. Chief*, 2018 YKTC 36 (Y.T.T.C.); *R. v. Garnier*, 2018 NSSC 196 (N.S.S.C.); *R. v. Salomonie*, 2016 NUCJ 10 (N.C.J.); *R. v. Oland*, 2015 NBQB 243 (N.B.Q.B.); *R. v. Haevischer*, 2014 BCSC 1863 (B.C.S.C.); *R. v. Despres*, 2008 NBQB 99 (N.B.Q.B.); *R. v. Lampe*, 2007 NLTD 116 (Nfld. and Lab. S.C.T.D.).

73. See; for example, this selection of cases from a broad array of appellate cases that consider BPA evidence: *R. v. Hartling*, 2020 ONCA 243 (Ont. CA); *R. v. Salomonie*, 2020 NUCA 1 (N.C.A.); *R. v. Barton*, 2019 SCC 33 (SCC); *R. v. Durant*, 2019 ONCA 74 (Ont. CA); *R. v. Cote*, 2018 ONCA 870 (Ont. CA); *R. v. Rodgerson*, 2015 SCC 38 (SCC); *R. v. Steinhauer*, 2015 ABCA 3 (Alta. CA); *R. v. Florence*, 2014 BCCA 288 (B.C.C.A.); *R. v. Flores*, 2011 ONCA 155 (Ont. CA); *R. v. Turcotte*, 2008 BCCA 56 (B.C.C.A.); *R. v. Cousins*, 2004 NLCA 14 (Nfld. and Lab. CA); *R. v. Guiboche*, 2004 MBCA 16 (Man. CA); *R. v. Muchikekwanape*, 2002 MBCA 78 (Man. CA); *R. v. Eatman*, 1999 CarswellNB 532 (N.B.C.A.), noting that the evidence of a BPA expert, like all other experts, must be assessed for weight by the jury (at para. 15); *R. v. O'Grady*, 1999 BCCA 189 (B.C.C.A.).
74. Chin, Jason M., Jan Tomiska, and Chen Li, "Drawing the Line between Lay and Expert Opinion Evidence", *McGill Law Journal*, 63 (1), 2017,pp. 89–132, 94. Invalid forensic science has been found to be present in approximately 60% of wrongful conviction cases that included forensic scientific evidence.
75. *R. v. Teske*, 2001 CarswellOnt 1768 (Ont. S.C.J.).
76. See Section 3 of this chapter.
77. *R. Teske*, 2001 CarswellOnt 1723 (Ont. S.C.J.).
78. *R. v. Berry*, 2019 BCSC 327 (B.C.S.C.).
79. *R. v. Luciano*, 2004 CarswellOnt 4615 (Ont. S.C.J.).
80. *R. v. Luciano*, at para. 30.
81. *R. v. Hartling*, 2020 ONCA 243 (Ont. CA).
82. Fresh evidence is evidence that existed at the time of trial but for various reasons could not be put before the trial court. New evidence is evidence that only became available subsequent to the trial.
83. *R. v. Hartling*, at paras. 30–45.
84. *R. v. Wu*, 2020 BCCA 128 (B.C.C.A.).
85. *R. v. Wu*, at paras 38–63.
86. Interestingly, the proposed expert in *Wu* was the same person who was rejected as lacking proper expert qualifications in *Hartling.* Even though *Hartling* was decided one month before *Wu*, it appears that the issue of qualifications of the expert to provide the proposed expert evidence was not raised before the Court of Appeal.
87. *R. v. Cote*, 2018 ONCA 870 (Ont. CA), at paras 41–45.
88. Porter, E. G., "Taking Images Seriously", *Columbia Law Review*, 114, 2014, pp. 1687–1782, at 1752.
89. Schofield, D. and K. Fowle, "Technology Corner – Visualizing Forensic Data: Evidence (Part 1)", *Journal of Digital Forensics, Security and Law*, 8 (1), 2013, pp. 73–90, at 76.
90. Porter, E. G., "Taking Images Seriously", *Columbia Law Review*, 114,2014, pp. 1687–1782, at 1694.
91. Mnookin, J. L., "Semi-Legibility and Visual Evidence: An Initial Exploration", *Law, Culture and the Humanities*, 10 (1), 2014, pp. 43–65, at 64–65.
92. Agosto, Eros, Andrea Ajmar, Piero Boccardo, Fabio Giulio Tonolo, and Andrea Lingua, "Crime Scene Reconstruction Using a Fully Geomatic Approach", *Sensors*, 8,2008, pp. 6280–6302, at 6281.
93. Sheppard, K., J. P. Cassella, and S. Fieldhouse, "A Comparative Study of Photogrammetric Methods Using Panoramic Photography in a Forensic Context", *Forensic Science International*, 273, 2017, pp. 29–38, at 29–30.
94. Schofield, D., "Animating Evidence: Computer Game Technology in the Courtroom", *Journal of Information Law and Technology*, 1, 2009, pp. 1–21.
95. In mock jury trials, jurors were better able to understand technical anatomical and medical language used by an expert witness when evaluating cause of death in a mock fatality when they were presented with 3D digital models (88%) and 3D-printed replicas (94%) of the victim's damaged cranium, rather than photographs alone (79%). Errickson, D., H. Fawcett, T. J. U. Thompson, and A. Campbell, "The Effect of Different Imaging Techniques for the Visualization of Evidence in Court on Jury Comprehension", *International Journal of Legal Medicine, 2019*, pp. 1–5; Baier,

Waltraub, Jason M. Warnett, Mark Payne, and Mark A. Williams, "Introducing 3D Printed Models as Demonstrative Evidence at Criminal Trials", *Journal of Forensic Sciences*, 63 (4), 2018, pp. 1298–1302, at 1302.

96. Urbanová, Petra, Mikolás Jurda, Tomás Vojtísek, and Jan Krajsa, "Using Drone-Mounted Cameras for On-Site Body Documentation: 3D Mapping and Active Survey", *Forensic Science International*, 281, 2017, pp. 52–62, at 53, 60.
97. Forensic Technology Center of Excellence, *Landscape Study on 3D Crime Scene Scanning Devices (with 2018 Update)*, available online at https://forensiccoe.org/private/5dd6ad2d0ffeb (accessed 17 November 2020), at 10 of 2016 Study.
98. Sieberth, Till, Akos Dobay, Raffael Affolter, and Lars C. Ebert, "Applying Virtual Reality in Forensics: A Virtual Scene Walkthrough", *Forensic Science, Medicine and Pathology*, 15, 2018, pp. 41–47, at 41.
99. Ibid, at 41.
100. Baier, Waltraub, Michael J. Donnelly, Mark Payne, and Mark A. Williams, "A Holistic Multi-Scale Approach to Using 3D Scanning Technology in Accident Reconstruction", *Journal of Forensic Sciences*, 65, 2020, pp. 1774–1778, at 1776.
101. Black, H. C., *Black's Law Dictionary*. 5th ed., West Publishing, Minnesota, 1979.
102. Santee, D. S., "More Than Words: Rethinking the Role of Modern Demonstrative Evidence", *Santa Clara Law Review*, 52 (1), 2012, pp. 105–144, at 111. Real evidence is evidence furnished by things themselves, on view or inspection, as distinguished from a description of them by a witness. Black, H. C., *Black's Law Dictionary*. 5th ed. West Publishing, Minnesota, 1979.
103. Green, S., "50 Shades of Prejudicial: Reexamining Demonstrative Evidence Through State v. Jones", *University of Toledo Law Review*, 45 (2), 2014, pp. 319–346, at 325; Gardner, H., "Explanations and Illustrations: Demonstrative Evidence in the Criminal Courtroom", *Criminal Law Quarterly*, 38 (4), 1996, pp. 425–446, at 445.
104. Jones, A. M. and M. B. Kovera, "A Demonstrative Helps Opposing Expert Testimony Sensitize Jurors to the Validity of Scientific Evidence", *Journal of Forensic Psychology Practice*, 15 (5), 2015, pp. 401–422.
105. Sainato, V. A., "Evidentiary Presentations and Forensic Technologies in the Courtroom, The Director's Cut", *Journal of the Institute of Justice and International Studies*, 9, 2009, pp. 38–52, at 39; Mnookin, J., "The Image of Truth: Photographic Evidence and the Power of Analogy", *Yale Journal of Law and the Humanities*, 10 (1), 1998, pp. 1–74, at 67–70.
106. Bettison, Alexandra, M. N. Krosch, J. Chaseling, and K. Wright, "Bloodstain Pattern Analysis: Does Experience Equate to Expertise?", *Journal of Forensic Science*, 00, 2021, pp. 1–13.
107. Ibid, at 9.
108. Counsel may wish to control the presentation of images in court so that they can focus on specific portions of an image, thereby enhancing the impact of the image. Marcus, E., "The New Razzle Dazzle: Questioning the Propriety of High-tech Audiovisual Displays in Closing Argument", *Vermont Law Review*, 30 (2), 2006, pp. 361–392, at 382; Lederer, F. I., "Wired: What We've Learned About Courtroom Technology", *Criminal Justice*, 24 (4), 2010, pp. 18–25.

CHAPTER 39

PERSONAL AND PROFESSIONAL ETHICS IN FORENSIC SCIENCE

Max M. Houck

INTRODUCTION

Ethical dilemmas confronting forensic professionals are far reaching and prevalent in today's criminal justice system. Inherent within the criminal justice system is the power to make discretionary decisions that impacts the offenders, victims, society, as well as the forensic professional.

CULTURE AND CONTEXT

Individuals are not completely free in their selection of values and behavior. They are at the mercy of the traditions in which they are brought up, that is, culture. Prior to the Enlightenment, western cultures had no clear notion of the origins of behavior and thought differences in people. Some behaviors were thought to be from one's essential personality, which was established and fixed at birth. A close association was assumed between biology and behavior. But the nature or nurture issue is more complicated than that simple relationship; even for those behaviors for which there is a known genetic component, there is always also a learned, or environmental, component. For example, a male born into a family in China but raised in suburban Chicago is going to grow up speaking English, eating fast food, dressing in Western clothing, and cheering for the local sports teams; he is not going to exhibit some compulsive, uncontrollable appetite for fermented eggs, have an inherent dexterity with chopsticks, or have an innate fluency with Mandarin.

Ethical behavior is not acquired naturally: it must be learned or taught. Learning about proper behavior only through personal experience is inefficient and painful for the learner and others. Learning how to make ethical decisions is necessary in order to avoid the pain of unethical conduct, especially in professional situations. Manners and etiquette are precursors to morals: etiquette tells how people should interact with others in social relations and morals express ethical obligations towards others in behavior. Professional ethics involve not only the daily interactions with others but discipline-specific behaviors that may have outsized effects, especially for those in public service.

Morals are good conduct; they constitute permissible behavior, the rules that prescribe proper action, and the principles of right and wrong. Ethics, on the other hand, is the discipline and study of morality, that is, the study and analysis of what constitutes good conduct. Social questions that include any controversy over the "right" thing to do are called ethical issues. Situations in which it is difficult to make a decision, either because the right course of action is not clear or the right course of action carries some negative consequences, are called ethical dilemmas.

 DOI: 10.4324/9781003163695-39

But what about laws? Do laws not prescribe appropriate behavior, like prohibitions against stealing and killing? Moral behavior requires more than what the law requires: a law may not exist for a particular ethical situation. Ethics is central to criminal justice because morality is what helps to distinguish between right and wrong. Laws reflect and reinforce the morals and ethics of a community but do not create them. It is important to differentiate the government's moral authority to enforce the law from the immorality of the crime itself. Laws provide only the baseline or boundaries of civil behavior. Therefore, a person of good character is one who engages consistently in moral conduct, regardless of what the law demands. This is also true of a forensic organization's procedures and quality processes: it does no good to merely parrot, "I was only following the protocols," if it results in unethical behavior.

VALUES AND FACTS

Values are judgments of worth about attitudes, statements, and behaviors. Value judgments can be verified only through reason. A value judgment is any judgment that expresses whether something is "good" or "bad." Factual judgments, however, can be verified based on provable evidence; they can be verified empirically through observations. For example, saying a particular model of a car gets 35 miles per gallon is a factual judgment but saying the car is economical is a value judgment. Stating that an actor is 58 years old is factual, whereas offering that they are talented is a value judgment. Same-sex marriage being legal is factual; saying it is morally wrong is a value judgment. Remember, a statement of preference (e.g., "I like pizza with anchovies") is a statement about the speaker's values, not the thing; the person is stating their likes or dislikes, not the factual value of something.

People often confuse value judgments with factual judgments, claiming one set of beliefs, whereas they actually endorse the opposite. It is important to clarify which is being offered. Just because moral claims are sometimes offered as fact doesn't mean that they really are factual. When dealing with morality, our moral obligations tend to be what we consider to be of greater importance than other things we ought to do; this is known as the Is–Ought problem.[1] For example, a person might feel that they morally *ought* to give half of their money to charity, but it *is* not wrong if they do not. That same person may also feel that it is morally wrong to steal from a charity and feel obligated not to do that. It is difficult or impossible to say with any certainty that because something is some way (a fact) that it ought to be that way (a value), thus the Is–Ought problem. Generally, it is not obvious how one can shift from descriptive statements (how the world is) to prescriptive ones (how we feel it ought to be). Cultural and institutional facts about what is right can still vary by society; without an objective moral goal, an "ought" is difficult to establish. The greater challenge of ethical systems remains to define the essence and origins of the good and to what extent it should be pursued.

Because of this, some feel that all values, including moral ones, are merely matters of opinion and preference ("I like anchovies; don't 'yuck' my 'yum'"), relative to the person and their culture. Moral relativism, sometimes called situational ethics, is the belief that morals can be different, but none are better than another; therefore, there are no universal moral standards. Relativism can be confused with tolerance. Tolerance accepts that there are moral principles, but people should not have the views of others imposed on them. Relativism sees nothing wrong with imposing views on others because there are no general principles (so nothing can be wrong). Ethical relativism attempts to justify the way people behave, rather than focusing on how people ought to behave, which is the real subject matter of ethics. But moral relativism has an unappealing consequence: if all value judgments are subjective, then it is possible to justify any action, including the worst one can imagine.

THREE MAIN ETHICAL SCHOOLS IN CRIMINAL JUSTICE

Three main schools of thought predominate in the ethics of criminal justice systems: formalism, utilitarianism, and value ethics. Each of these and their implications will be discussed in turn; they all inform how ethical behavior is evaluated and determined.

Formalism

No good deed goes unpunished, as the cynical adage says, but it is true that sometimes well-intentioned actions produce bad outcomes. While at University, Immanuel Kant (1724–1804) came across David Hume's theory of emotivism,[2] which alleged that you can determine if a person is a "good" person if they act morally. For Hume, all actions were moral, not divinely intended, because we act as to how we feel. For Hume, feelings and emotions were the main impetus to do things, so good people did what gave them a good feeling. After studying Hume, Kant was having none of this argument. Kant went back to the original question of all ethicists: is a person good and is an action good? Knowing that people may do things for many reasons, Kant decided to base his ethical theory by examining the second part of the question. Is an action good? Kant's position is that, as rational agents, people are bound by moral requirements and that rational people would necessarily comply with them (because the moral requirements are good in and of themselves). Thus, putting aside what people *actually* do, what should be considered universally good? For Kant, the fundamental philosophical issues of morality must be addressed before all else, that is, without drawing on observations of human beings and their behavior.

Kant's system of ethics goes by a variety of names, including Kantian ethics, formalism, or deontological ethics (from the Greek for "duty"); we will use formalism in this chapter. In formalism, the morality of an action is determined by whether it conforms to or violates a moral principle: the potential consequences of the decision are not relevant in formalism. Intent is everything. Our knowledge and understanding of the empirical world can only be appreciated within the limits of our perceptual and cognitive powers. Humans have limited understanding of the world and, therefore, cannot see all the potential outcomes of any one particular action. Thus, intent is all that matters in determining whether an action is good or not.

Kant distinguished between imperatives and duties. A principle that commands an action is called an imperative. Most imperatives are hypothetical imperatives, that is, they are commands that hold only if certain conditions are met. If one wants to be a successful shopkeeper, then they should develop a reputation for honesty. If a relationship is to be beneficial, then trust should be established. If a public servant wants to be successful, then they should be humble. Hypothetical imperatives are conditioned on desires and the intended consequences of subsequent actions. Therefore, hypothetical imperatives cannot serve as the principles that determine the intentions and goals of an unconditionally goodwill because the conditions (the "ifs") could change. Duty is different. Duty connotes a person's moral obligation; it is what a person ought to do, regardless of whether it is convenient or popular or results in an unforeseen outcome. Duties must always be followed; thus, it is a categorical (not hypothetical) imperative. Categorical imperatives are principles that are intrinsically valid: they are good in and of themselves. They must be obeyed in all situations and circumstances if our behavior is to observe the moral law. The categorical imperative can only be based on something that is an "end in itself," that is, an end that is not a means to some other need, desire, or purpose. "I will lie when it gets me out of trouble," breaks the categorical imperative "do not lie." Duty has nothing to do with potential consequences. Decisions should be made based on duty, not what might happen. This is the core of Kant's philosophy: a categorical imperative is an unconditional obligation.

Kant's idea for the superiority of the categorical imperative because it is a universal law that is a moral duty that stands on its own, requires no further justification. After deciding on a possible categorical imperative to follow, the next question is whether it would be possible for everyone to follow that rule. If it is possible to will that everyone act according to that rule, then the action under consideration is morally permissible. If it is not possible for everyone to act according to that rule, the action is morally impermissible. Lying to get out of trouble is thus immoral because it is not possible to force everyone to lie to get out of trouble; some people will tell the truth anyway. For something to be a categorical imperative, it is not enough that it would be undesirable for everyone to act according to that rule, it must be impossible. In this situation, reasonable people accept the rules for themselves whether they are giving or receiving the action. The mark of immorality in formalism is that one makes an exception for oneself.

The third imperative in formalism is the Practical Imperative, where one acts in such a way that they treat humanity (yourself or another) always the same–as an end and never simply as a means to an end. Someone would befriend another because they genuinely enjoy their company, not because the other is rich and generous with money. But, likewise, killing someone to save the life of another would make a bad universal rule (violating the categorical imperative) and it uses another person as a means to an end (violating the practical imperative). Individuals are to be treated as ends in themselves and not as means to some other ends. For Kant, if all rational people were united through common, objective universal laws that applied to everyone, that would be a "kingdom of ends" where everyone was treated equally for themselves and not for some other reason.

Kant's formalism has been criticized for not being flexible, as may be obvious by now, and is echoed in the classic Latin phrase, *Fiat justitia ruat caelum* ("Let justice be done, even if the world dies"). This sounds rather drastic to modern ears. Kant's philosophy does not allow for exceptions. It also does not distinguish duties toward others in family and love relationships from duties to all other people; family does not come first, humans do. Kant's ethics do have value, however, in certain ways. Considering formalism helps uncover the difficulties of putting morality on a firm foundation. Its real value may lie not in asking if formalism would ever work but in what it reveals about morality and ethics when it does not.

Utilitarianism

In the comics, Bruce Wayne's parents were killed during a robbery; he decides to devote his life to fighting criminals as the hero Batman. In becoming Batman, Wayne took up a very Kantian position: he doesn't kill. By comparison, his archnemesis, The Joker, is insane and has no rules, killing freely with abandon (Figure 39.1). To keep The Joker from killing an untold number of innocents, should Batman break his one rule and kill The Joker? Keep this question in mind over the course of this next section.

In his classic work, *Leviathan* (originally published in 1605), Thomas Hobbes famously said that in a "state of nature," human life would be "solitary, poor, nasty, brutish and short." He meant that in the absence of political order and law, everyone would have unlimited natural freedoms, including the "right to all things" and thus the freedom to plunder, rape, and murder; there would be an endless "war of all against all."[3] The state of nature was apolitical in the sense that there were no governments and each individual retained all of their natural rights. But a state of nature is unstable, where individuals would be under a constant threat of physical harm and no constructive goals could be pursued. In order to avoid this horrible situation, people, seeing the benefits that could be gained, decided to relinquish some of their rights to a central sovereign authority while retaining other rights. This took the form of a "social contract." In agreement for relinquishing certain rights, individuals would receive protection from physical harm, security for their possessions, and the ability to interact and cooperate with other humans in a stable environment. According to Hobbes, any power exercised by the sovereign authority cannot be resisted, because the protector's

Figure 39.1 Should Batman break his one rule and kill The Joker? Think how much good would result from that. Patrick Collins via Unsplash.

sovereign power derives from individuals' surrendering their own sovereign power for protection. The individuals are thereby the authors of all decisions made by the authority. There is no doctrine of separation of powers in Hobbes's discussion, as there is in many modern governments. According to Hobbes, the single sovereign power must control civil, military, judicial, and religious powers, even the language people used.

John Locke (1632–1704) had read Hobbes. Locke believed that human nature is characterized by reason and tolerance; that human nature allowed people to be selfish, much like Hobbes did. However, Locke did not believe that humans are born with some ideas and concepts, and that these things are innate. John Locke argued that different kinds of experiences will produce differences in behavior. Everything people know they gain through experience. And, importantly, if all minds are fundamentally the same at birth, then all people are equal in their potential. Locke assumed people established a civil society to resolve conflicts in a civil way with help from government in a state of society but not in an authoritarian (or arbitrary) way, like Hobbes advocated, rather a nonarbitrary Rule of Law we all agree upon, collectively. Locke advocated governmental separation of powers and believed that revolution is not only a right but an obligation in some circumstances. These ideas would come to have profound influence on the Declaration of Independence and the Constitution of the United States. Ideas like these that become a prevalent part of the culture do so because they serve a useful purpose for a significant segment of society. The growing mercantile class in the late seventeenth century sought to challenge the economic prerogatives of the English King. The Crown stipulated who could do business with whom; one merchant was approved to sell tea, while other one was not. Merchants wanted to do business with whoever could provide goods and services most cheaply, regardless of the country of origin. Similar demands for free trade played a strong role in the French and American revolutions. Locke provided a basis for a capitalist social order based on free trade and (limited) representative democracy.

No ruler could claim absolute power over all elements of a citizen's life, *a la* Hobbes. A government which failed to adequately protect the rights and interests of its citizens or a government which attempted to overstep its authority would be failing to perform the task for which it was created. The citizens would be entitled to revolt and replace the existing government. The only hitch: this only applies to *arbitrary* decisions of the government. The French and American revolutions had terrified the aristocrats and ruling classes of Europe, who (correctly) recognized the subversive potential of Enlightenment beliefs in freedom, equality, and progress. Locke thought of the government as a body of *legitimate* consent. Governments were instituted by the citizens and rulers who had an obligation to be responsive to the needs and desires of these citizens. How, then, to decide what was best for those governed?

Jeremy Bentham (1748–1832) equated the morality of an act with the amount of happiness it produces: "it is the greatest happiness of the greatest number that is the measure of right and wrong."[4] Ethical questions are answered based on the amount and quality of good that results from an action. The morality of an act is determined, therefore, by the consequences it brings, compared with other alternative actions. In this view, ethical decisions result in the greater quantity and quality of good or happiness, whereas unethical decisions result in pain or unhappiness. According to the central principle of utility, actions are right in proportion as they tend to promote happiness, and wrong as they tend to produce the reverse of happiness (pain). Bentham even created a "felicific calculus," classifying 12 pains and 14 pleasures against which to test the "happiness factor" of an act, determining its utility. Therefore, this branch of ethics is called utilitarianism. It is not important to distinguish personal happiness from social happiness according to utilitarianism: the total amount of happiness is how pleasure is to be judged. The motivation is not important in utilitarianism. Contrary to formalism, it is the outcome that matters.

John Stuart Mill (1806–1873), born two years after Kant died, was one of Jeremy Bentham's students. Mill also focused on utility but felt that Bentham had gotten the idea very wrong. Bentham considered only *quantity* of pleasure, but Mill considered both *quantity and quality* of pleasure. Mill said, "Quantity of pleasure being equal, pushpin is as good as poetry" (Pushpin was a simple child's game of the sixteenth through the nineteenth century; think tiddlywinks). That is, Bentham's utilitarianism said that opera was equivalent to checkers if it brought the same amount of pleasure. Bentham, an early animal rights supporter, made no distinction between the pleasures experienced by beasts and those experienced by humans; thus, Bentham's utilitarianism was criticized for being a philosophy "worthy of only swine." Mill acknowledged this issue, and to sidestep the criticism, he considered both quantity and quality pleasure. For Mill, "higher pleasures" are more valuable than lower pleasures, because of their "intrinsic superiority." Mill's theory bows to human nature and it makes pleasure even more difficult to calculate, as we now have to consider unquantifiable quality of pleasure, as well as the quantity. Is chess inherently worth more than checkers? Is a Broadway play better than *The Simpsons*? Does it produce a better form of happiness? To simplify this difference, if happiness is a warm puppy, then Bentham would ask, how many puppies do we have, how warm is each one, how much happiness does each one bring? Mill, on the other hand, would ask, are they *cute* puppies, are they clean, are they thoroughbreds, are the puppies themselves happy, what colors are the puppies, are they housebroken, are they yippy, and do I have to adopt all of them?

Given the quantity and quality issue, how does one determine which is the greatest pleasure or pain? Mill thought there were two causes to an unsatisfactory life: selfishness and lack of mental cultivation. Selfishness is caring for nobody but oneself, which leads to unhappiness because it lacks both public and private affections that contribute greatly to happiness. A person with a cultivated mind is interested in everything, such as nature, art, poetry, history, and the future. Lack of mental cultivation leads to indifference to all these things and ultimately to unhappiness.

Mill believed that general consensus of those with experience was the best indicator. The experience of those (all or most) who give a decided preference determines hierarchy of pleasures, that is, their quality. Mill's utilitarianism requires a person to be a strictly impartial and disinterested spectator in assessing his or her own happiness versus that of others.

Utilitarianism has been criticized for being not practical or timely in weighing the consequences of one's actions prior to engaging in the conduct. Who would take the time to consider all the possible outcomes before taking an action? Also, people will weigh the consequences of their actions in a self-serving way, almost always ending up doing things in their own self-interest ("Only snobs go to plays; I'm watching *The Bachelor*"). In utilitarianism, as long as the outcome results in "happiness," it is acceptable to use any means to obtain it: the ends justify the means. Thus, one could justify the torture or killing of hundreds if it made thousands happy. Yet, whether selfishly or not, people do weigh some aspects of their acts and the acts of others based on pleasure and punishment.

Going back to the question that opened this section, according to Kant, Batman's choice to never kill is a categorical imperative for him, despite it not being universally true for everyone. Batman feels that killing The Joker, while preventing future deaths, would make him no better than his homicidal nemesis. A utilitarian, however, would say, while killing is bad, killing The Joker is a different matter because it would prevent him from killing and harming an untold number of victims, producing a lot of happiness. The question then remains, by not killing The Joker (in most stories, Batman locks him in Gotham's mental institution, Arkham Asylum), is Batman somehow responsible for any future deaths The Joker commits? And, by understanding what the outcome of his killing The Joker would be, is not Batman thinking in utilitarian terms? The comic book philosophy literature is more extensive than might be imagined; most superheroes are Kantian, standing for truth and justice and so forth, with some exceptions and much interesting discussion.[5]

Virtue Ethics

Virtue is one of the most revered words in all languages and generally means the disposition to make right choices. The right path to follow in seeking virtue has been the source of much debate over the centuries. Stoicism was a philosophy of serenity, tranquility, and impassiveness to suffering. Epictetus (ca. 50–138) was the leading stoic. To Epictetus, all external events are beyond our control; we should accept calmly and dispassionately whatever happens. However, individuals are responsible for their own actions, which they can examine and control through rigorous self-discipline: "Externals are not in my power, choice is." Socrates (470–399 B.C.) saw knowledge (wisdom) and virtue as synonymous. Plato (428–348 B.C.) became a student of Socrates at age 20 and was disillusioned with the corruption in Greek politics, highlighted when his mentor Socrates was put to death in 399 B.C. by the government. His book, *The Republic,* sets forth his views on ethics, describing a plan for an ideal city where few laws are needed because of the highly developed moral character of its inhabitants. Aristotle (428–348 B.C.) enrolled in Plato's Academy at age 17 and was a lifelong student of Plato. Aristotle wrote more than 400 works on a broad array of subjects, including astronomy, biology, logic, politics, physics, and ethics; the breadth of his knowledge was remarkable. In the *Nicomachean Ethics,* he provided the first systematic study of ethics in the history of the Western world, asking how ought people live their lives and are there things that are good in themselves?

Aristotle decided that there were good, rather than just useful, things as long as they are pursued for their own sake. Aristotle saw all human activities aimed at achieving some good end or result. Central to this idea is whether certain of these goods are more desirable than others. Aristotle was interested in which goods constituted the highest good, which he defined as being desirable for itself, not desirable for the sake of some other good, and all other goods are desirable for the sake of that thing. Aristotle thought that people did not strive to live well for the sake of some further goal; rather, living well (Greek, *eudaimonia*) is the highest end, and all other goals, like health, wealth, and other such things, are sought because they promote living well but not because they are what well-being consists of. Living well is the final good, the ultimate end: it is not feeling happy for a moment, rather, it is a life lived through virtuous action. Aristotle's hierarchy of goods, then, was:

- Real goods: food, shelter, health, wealth, pleasure, knowledge, and liberty, friends, and civil peace.
- Apparent goods: items that ought to be desired regardless if we really do, like deserts, good music, and fine wine.
- Ultimate good: *Eudamonia*, living well, a balanced virtuous life.

A person without friends and family, one who is powerless and weak in civil life, who is hungry and in poor health will simply not be able to find many chances to be virtuous and will be challenged to accomplish anything of great merit while they remain so. Misfortune is a temporary hindrance to happiness: "the man who is truly good and wise will bear with dignity whatever fortune sends, and will always make the best of his circumstances." Aristotle's real goods are similar in many ways to Maslow's Hierarchy of Needs (Figure 39.2) that shows that human motivation is similarly situated with the works of Aristotle.[6]

Virtue develops as a result of habit. It does not occur naturally, through reasoning, or by instruction, but by doing. Aristotle's more even-handed approach is one of the reasons why it became the most prominent theory of moral virtue. Aristotle recognized the importance of pleasure, courage, and temperament, but he places them in the context of all other goods and virtues and how they must be balanced. Moral virtue is a mean, an average, a balance between two vices involving excess on the one hand and deficiency on the other. With virtuous conduct, it is clear, except in cases of acts bad in and of themselves, virtue seeks the mean, based on the facts of the situation. Moral virtue implies that our actions are voluntary and the products of our choices. As the philosopher Mortimer Adler has said, moral virtue is the "process of conquering one's childish tendencies toward indulgence in immediate gratification." Studies of both children and adults have found that when they were praised for their character, rather than merely for good actions, they began to define themselves differently.

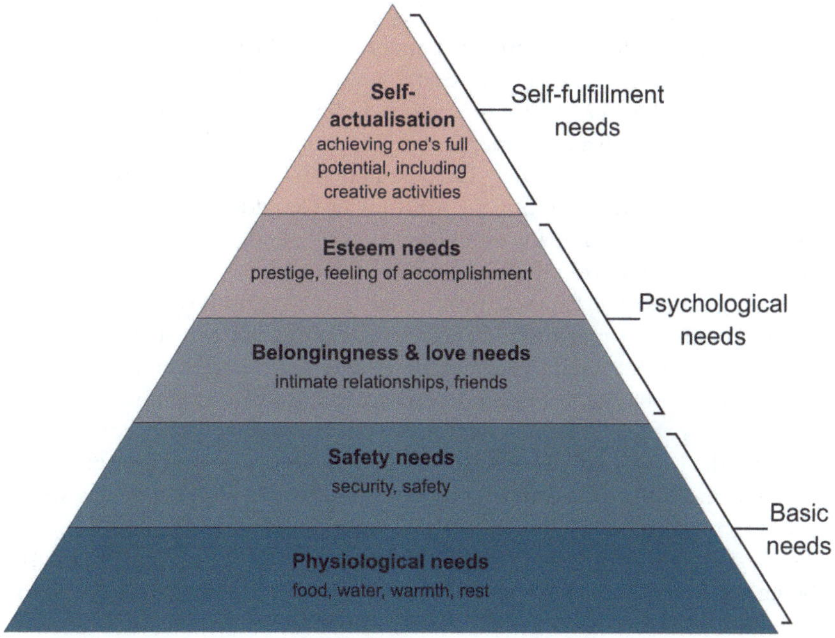

Figure 39.2 Maslow's Hierarchy of Needs, represented as a pyramid with the more basic needs at the Bottom. Creative Commons.

WHY PEOPLE MAKE POOR ETHICAL CHOICES

Personal Factors

An individual's personal situation can create the conditions for them to make less-than-ethical choices. Much like in fraud (criminal deception for personal or financial gain), three particular factors influence a person to act wrongly: pressure, opportunity, and rationalization.[7] The person may be under financial, political, or emotional pressure that leads them to act unprofessionally. Without opportunity, however, the pressure would not be enough for the person to take unethical action. Even normally ethical people are not always able to resist taking advantage of a situation. Lax oversight of report reviews, drug standards without proper access controls, leaving case files or evidence unguarded, and other openings can tempt even the most professional employee. Finally, those who commit unethical acts come up with ways to justify their behavior to themselves. For example, an analyst who alters his notes or skews the wording in a report or testimony in favor of the prosecution may do so because, although the evidence is weak, they feel the defendant is guilty.

External Factors

Most public forensic organizations are administered from within a law enforcement organization, like a police agency or prosecutor's office. This positioning immediately creates pressures on the scientist, as the realities of policing are in nearly direct conflict to those of science.[8] Both professions, however, must exhibit actual or perceived integrity. Nevertheless, both the forensic organization and its parent organization need to establish appropriate ethical cultures. An organization's cultural environment can create opportunities or pressure to make unethical choices. Pressure to achieve unrealistic objectives, such as quotas or overtime, may cause employees to cut corners or make choices that compromise ethical decision making. Those who cannot or feel like they won't have a chance of achieving a target may skirt quality checkpoints or falsify bench notes or lie about their status. Employees who feel they are not being rewarded with promotions or recognized for their work may begin acting in ethically questionable ways, working to get back at their employer, fellow employees, or get what they feel they are owed. An employee who did not get a promotion but feels they should have, for example, may feel it is appropriate to lie on their timesheet or cheat on travel expense reports. Additionally, if that person begins to complain about perceived unfairness, that attitude can spread through the organization and employees may decide to work together and act unethically against the company as a group.

Many organizations do not make ethics part of the daily activities and discussion; in these organizations, ethics only comes up after some incident or crisis. Without the consistent reinforcement of ethical behavior, employees may drift in their attitudes and start to veer towards poor choices. This does not mean managers should browbeat employees at every turn about what they should or should not do. But by making ethics an open, acceptable discussion–instead of blaming and punishing–employees are more likely to embrace and maintain a professional mindset. In one insightful example, the behavioral economist Dan Ariely ran an experiment using an honor code at MIT in 2007. He and his team asked a few hundred undergraduates to take a simple math test but did not give them enough time to complete all the problems. At the end, they asked them to grade their own tests and tell the researchers how well they had done; for every question that was reported as being correct, the students would get $1. After they were done, they were to put their tests into a shredder ... which did not really shred, so the researchers could see how much cheating had gone on. It turns out that many cheated. Ariely and his team then had a second group of students follow the same procedure but only after they first signed the MIT honor code. Merely signing the honor code *before* taking the test eliminated cheating.[9] Reminders, like signing an honor code, act as primers that unconsciously alter the way people make choices. And the reminders can be simple and passive. For example, an office provided coffee and tea for its employees but they were expected to offset the cost by putting money into an "honesty box" with suggested prices posted nearby. Each week, a new image would be placed above the price list, typically something innocuous, like flowers, but some weeks it would be a picture of a pair of eyes looking at the employee. On average, employees contributed three times as much during weeks when the eyes were posted.[10] Without priming reminders and open discussions about ethics, employees may not learn the difference between ethical and unethical behavior.

Employees who do not point out or speak against unethical conduct have a misplaced loyalty, either to the organization ("We can do no wrong.") or to their manager ("Let's not get Jenn in trouble."). Likewise, leadership is responsible for setting the ethical tone in any organization. If the leaders and managers do not set examples for what is ethical behavior, it sends the message that that kind of behavior is acceptable, and sends it to the entire organization and perhaps outside it.

FRAMEWORK FOR MAKING ETHICAL DECISIONS

As discussed, morals and ethics are not acquired naturally; they must be taught, whether it is at home or from outside sources, like education. Learning about ethics only through personal or professional experience is inefficient and painful. Being taught proper methods to make ethical decisions helps to avoid the pain of unethical conduct. Morals, either personal or professional, express ethical obligations toward others through behavior. Decisions that lead to unethical behaviors can be avoided by recognizing some of the more common fallacies in ethical thinking.

Fallacies in Ethical Thinking

A common fallacy in ethical thinking is "mine is better," as in "My ______ is (better, smarter, more correct, etc.) than your ______." As children, we do this all the time. As adults, we avoid it but the effects linger and it poses an obstacle to open-mindedness. We mistakenly assume our perspective is correct and others' is wrong. Getting yourself or others to articulate their objection can help get beyond this roadblock.

Related to this selfish perspective is the tendency for people to place an undue emphasis on internal characteristics of someone (their character or intention), rather than on external factors in explaining another person's behavior in a given situation. This is called fundamental attribution error. When interpreting one's own behavior, however, external factors are more easily recognized and are taken into account. For example, if a person sees someone running a redlight, they might think, "Look at that jerk! He's in such a rush, he could have killed someone!" If the same person runs a redlight themselves, they would instead think, "Wow! I didn't see that light change; I didn't have a chance to stop!" Fundamental attribution error can lead to misperception of the intent and actions of others.

If we use one set of criteria for judging ourselves and another for others, that is called a double standard. People may selectively consider or twist evidence to serve their self-interests. Setting aside guiding principles, people may rationalize arguments to justify their actions or decisions. Double standards are especially common in situations where a choice was made (they don't want to be wrong) or a close relationship is involved (assuming the best/worst of someone).

If a person argues that what they've done, although wrong, is still acceptable because others are either doing it or worse things, they have fallen into the ethical fallacy called *tu quoque*, Latin for "You also." It is completely irrelevant whether others are guilty of acting unethically: that person still committed the (unethical) act they are arguing against. Mothers who scold their children by saying, "Because your friend Bobby jumped off the swing set doesn't mean it's ok for *you* to do it," are arguing against *tu quoque*. This fallacy is related to the slippery slope, where the perception is that allowing one action will necessitate and lead to a further extreme and undesirable consequence. "If we allow ______ to happen, then [an even worse action] will occur." Slippery slopes are fallacious because people do not establish that the undesirable consequences *must* occur, or are causal, given the action they argue against.

The last (as far as this chapter goes) fallacy in ethical decision making is called moral prudentialism. Being prudent means to act wisely when pursuing one's own interests, like wearing seatbelts, tying their shoes, and similar acts. The error of moral prudentialism occurs when someone argues in moral favor of some activities because those behaviors benefit an individual or group, that is, the action is considered moral because it is prudent for them. If a person says, "I have a right to happiness just like anyone else, and if finding happiness means I have to have a good career, and if having a good career means I have to lie on this application form, then there cannot be anything wrong with that because it results in my happiness." The person has forsaken their duty to honesty for their personal or professional gain.

An Approach to Ethical Questions

How, then, to approach ethical questions? One way is to start with a search for universal principles, like Kant did. What behavior would be expected or desired from *any employee*? What outcome is to be avoided? Next, it helps to list the relevant facts, separating the irrelevant details and personal preferences from the central issues. After that, identify the precise moral question to be answered; list and think about the moral principles that might be used to support the positions that could be taken. Go back to the ideas of Kant, utilitarianism, and Aristotle: is a universal rule being sought or is the organization just making sure that the end, and the means to that end, are ethical. After open discussion or thought, a decision can be made, that is, define the morally permissible course of conduct. That decision can be justified using positive reasons, ethical principles, and examples; anticipate and address contrary views with an open mind and welcoming sense of learning more about the ethical aspects of the situation.

FORENSIC EXAMPLES

Sadly, there is no lack of examples of unethical behavior by forensic professionals. A complete listing of "forensic failures" is beyond the scope of this chapter (and very depressing) but a few significant examples will be discussed in light of this chapter's materials in a general taxonomy of the more common faults. Fuller treatments of ethical failures in forensic organizations are available and those interested are encouraged to read and study them.[11]

Misrepresentation of Education and Credentials

Despite the ease of internet searches, people still inflate or fabricate their educational and professional credentials. This includes saying they have degrees or training they do not have, claiming the wrong degrees or the wrong year, or misrepresenting their qualifications in some other way. For example, Robert Stites, a bloodstain analyst, told a jury he was pursuing his master's and doctoral degrees; he was not enrolled at any institution and was not taking any classes at the time. Stites also claimed he had been accepted as an expert for testimony three times when, in fact, he had not. Stites had not even completed a basic 40-hour course on bloodstain analysis. Sadly, he faced no consequences for his perjury.[12] How do employees get away with this? Employing agencies' human resources departments may not check the sources or references of applicants; after hiring, testimony transcripts may not be reviewed for quality assurance checks.

Dishonest or Falsified Laboratory Analysis

Issuing a report on analyses not actually completed is called "dry-labbing." For example, an analyst receives 100 packets of white powder from a drug seizure and is supposed to test half. He analyzes the first packet and gets the result of heroin and stops. He then photocopies or fabricates the data to make it look like he analyzed the remaining 49 packets but reports out he analyzed all 50 and they all contain heroin. In another version, samples could be mixed so that they match the intended results. Dry-labbing is a serious concern and stems from the analyst's laziness or incompetence about their duties. As a type of fraud, it can have enormous repercussions throughout a criminal justice system. The extraordinary cases of Annie Dookhan and Sonia Faruk in Massachusetts drug analysis laboratories resulted in over 40,000 drug convictions being dismissed by the courts, 190,000 cases reviewed, and millions of dollars in reparations being paid to defendants, in addition to the millions of dollars of cost to the state criminal justice system to address the scandal. Not unexpectedly, Dookhan also claimed to have a degree she did not have. Weak internal controls and lax quality processes allowed the two to deceive co-workers and stakeholders. Complaints to management went unheeded, indicating weak internal controls and little oversight.[13]

Incompetence

Forensic analysts are knowledge workers, being experienced in and attaining expertise with specific types of materials, methods, and equipment. Knowledge, education, and competency are paramount to the job. Forensic organizations must allow employees to continually learn and improve their knowledge and skills if both are to flourish. Some organizations, however, limp along with untrained personnel and uneducated supervisors. One severe example of this was the St. Paul, MN, Police Department Crime Laboratory. Through the work of two defense attorneys, it was discovered that the analysts doing the drug analysis were not qualified for that work, they did not have written protocols for their analyses, and did not conduct routine maintenance on the instruments. Their supervisor had more training as a fingerprint examiner than as a drug chemist; requests for training were always rejected. The laboratory director was a police sergeant with no background in science whatsoever. In addition, one-third of all fingerprint cases were mistakenly classified as unidentifiable and destroyed them. Outside consultants were hired to correct the issues and revise the laboratory at significant expense to the city.[14]

Interpretation that Exceeds the Data or Is Misleading

Perhaps the best worst example of interpreting evidence beyond the data or one's capability is that of Michael West, a dentist from Mississippi. Through the mid-1990s, West became a near-celebrity, after claiming to have developed techniques that only he could perform (as a quick reminder, reproducibility is a hallmark of science).[15] West boasted that his techniques could both identify bite marks on human skin and then identify the biter to the exclusion of all other humans on the planet. Notably, no other medical specialists could see these marks. West's analyses and testimony was instrumental in convicting numerous people in Mississippi, Louisiana, and at least eight other states. Flush with his "success," West expanded his expertise to other forensic methods, some of which he claimed to have invented. West testified as an expert in trace metals, trauma and wound patterns, gunshot residue, shooting reconstruction, crime scene, blood spatter, as well as fingernail scratches, liquid splash patterns, and video enhancement. In one case, West even testified about how lesbian couples solve arguments. Obviously, beyond bite marks (and even then, West once testified that he had identified someone who had bitten into a bologna sandwich), West held no qualifications in any of those disciplines, professional or otherwise. West's story is not only one of testifying beyond one's capabilities but also of pseudoscience and the problem of what constitutes forensic expertise.[16]

Testimony

It is important for forensic professionals to remember who in a courtroom is under oath to tell the truth: only them. Testimony is a difficult process to provide expert scientific information: the expert witness is communicating difficult, technical, and sometimes complex analytical processes and outcomes to a roomful of people who are ostensibly *not* experts in that topic (otherwise, why call the expert?) but they can only do so by answering the questions of attorneys assigned the job of arguing for or against the proposition that the defendant is guilty. This is a veritable minefield of misunderstandings, misguidance, and misstatements in communication. A quick example, if the witness is asked, "Do you know what time it is?," answering, "It is 12:53 pm," is incorrect; it was a yes or no question. Innocently answering with "It is 12:53 pm" leads to all sorts of follow-up questions:

- How do you know that's the time?
- Is your watch accurate? How do you know?
- Was it serviced recently? Do you have any receipts proving that?
- When was the battery last changed?
- And so on...

And being under oath to "tell the truth" has its own philosophical and ethical difficulties:

> ...the usual courtroom maxim to "tell the truth, the whole truth, and nothing but the truth" is not so easy to apply in practicality. In any given situation, what does the whole truth include? In case, the whole truth includes all the possible alternatives for a given situation, what should a forensic expert witness do when an important question is not asked by the prosecutor? Does the obligation to tell the whole truth mean that all possible, all probable, all reasonably probable, all highly probable, or only the most probable alternatives must be given in response to a question?[17]

Consider the following hypothetical exchange during testimony:

Attorney:	Do the questioned and known samples match?
Expert:	"Match" is not an accurate way to state my conclusions. The questioned and known samples did give the same qualitative, quantitative, and instrumental results in all tested traits.
Attorney:	So, does that mean they matched?
Expert:	...Uh...
Attorney:	Your honor, please direct the witness to answer the question.
Expert:	...Yes...

And now the expert is on the record as having said the two samples "match," a term they rightly objected to. Testimony requires experts to constantly be on guard for possible ethical traps; reviewing and discussing all testimony transcripts is a good idea to help hone this important component of a forensic professional's job.

Influenced by Non-scientific Considerations

Attorneys have a job: represent their client's legal interests, be it the state or the defendant. They do this by constructing an argument for their client; to get this argument before the court and into the record, they call witnesses to make statements supporting their position (attorneys are prohibited from testifying themselves). Some of these witnesses are experts. The attorneys, especially prosecutors (because they have the burden of the narrative), need to get a series of statements in a certain order to build the argument to convince the jury to their side. Attorneys, in an attempt to get the statements they need before the jury, may influence or pressure witnesses to phrase things a certain way or to not use certain words. In extreme examples, they may try to pressure or influence expert witnesses through personal or political intimidation or threats.

POTENTIAL SOLUTIONS

So what to do? How can organizations take steps to reduce or mitigate the chance of employees behaving inappropriately? First and foremost, drive out fear of retribution for calling out bad behavior. Deming made this clear regarding quality (Point # 8: Drive out fear, so that everyone may work effectively for the company) but it applies as well to ethics.[18]

An excellent example of this is the story related about an enlisted seaman who discovered that he had misplaced a tool during a combat exercise. The danger was the tool could be sucked into a jet engine during the exercise but admitting his mistake would shut down the exercise involving hundreds of military personnel and lots of expensive military equipment, as well as bring possible punishment to him. The sailor nevertheless did the right thing; reported his error, and the exercise was stopped at considerable expense. The sailor was not punished, however; rather, he was commended by his commanding officer in a formal ceremony acknowledging his bravery for acting properly.[19] If the military can do that, why not smaller organizations? By making it safe for employees to point out potential lapses in ethical behavior, organizations make it less likely for the lapses to become significant or severe.

Training employees to recognize the severity of outcomes from misconduct can also help. Most employees may not see the second- or third-order events that a single unethical action can have. Using specific examples linking the unethical behavior to the damage it causes helps the employees realize the implications of poor ethical choices. The benefits achieved by those who act unethically are usually short-term gains that are either quickly exhausted, must remain secret, or are not easily shared, and they result in pain or penalty when the conduct becomes known. The implications for the organization, however, can be magnified and extend well beyond the walls of the workplace. Managers, as visible and vital examples, should evaluate the ethical consequences of their decisions; employees will see the hypocrisy right away and any further attempts by the manager to set an example will be damaged or futile.

Organizations should develop and enforce a code of conduct that clearly states what constitutes acceptable and inappropriate behavior. The code should have consequences. The code should emphasize positive behaviors, rather than listing a litany of offenses. While ethical behavior should be its own reward (as Aristotle would remind us), specific actions that avert significant negative outcomes should be praised and that praise should be public (like the previous sailor example). Praising in public (and punishing in private) is an old management saying but it is true: making the community aware of what good behavior is tends to elicit better behavior from others.

CLOSING THOUGHTS

The modern ethicist, Michael Sandel, argues that society must return to a notion of civility, that is, citizens concerned about not only themselves but their fellow citizens:

> If a just society requires a strong sense of community, it must find a way to cultivate in citizens a concern for the whole, a dedication to the common good. It can't be indifferent to the attitudes and dispositions, the "habits of the heart," that citizens bring to public life.[20]

Most forensic professionals are public employees and even those employed by private firms still ultimately serve the public interest and safety. Forensic professionals have an outsized duty to the public to conduct themselves and their work ethically and with integrity. Suppressing what Adler called our childish desires and doing what is right for the good of society makes public service just that: a service to the public. As Sandel later notes,

> A more robust public engagement with our moral disagreements could provide a stronger, not a weaker, basis for mutual respect. ...There is no guarantee that public deliberation about hard moral questions will lead in any given situation to agreement–or even to appreciation for the

moral and religious views of others. ...A politics of moral engagement is not only a more inspiring ideal than a politics of avoidance. It is also a more promising basis for a just society.[21]

As keepers and wardens of science for the pursuit of justice, forensic professionals should also seek moral engagement personally but must do so professionally.

Notes

1. Hume, D., *A Treatise of Human Nature*, John Noon, London, 1739.
2. Wilson, Eric Entrican and Lara Denis, "Kant and Hume on Morality", *The Stanford Encyclopedia of Philosophy*, (Summer 2018 Edition), Edward N. Zalta (ed.), URL = <https://plato.stanford.edu/archives/sum2018/entries/kant-hume-morality/>.
3. Hobbes, Thomas, *Leviathan*, Duke University Press, 2007.
4. Rees, J, "Bentham, Jeremy-Comment on the Commentaries and a Fragment on Government", edited by Burns, J. and Hart, H., 1979, pp. 339–321.
5. For example, Captain America is Kantian while Iron Man is resolutely utilitarian and Spider Man definitively a proponent of virtue ethics; see White, Mark. Captain America: Civil War – conflicted heroes and a clash of philosophies, *The Guardian*, 21 Apr 2016.
6. Maslow, Abraham Harold, "A Theory of Human Motivation", *Psychological Review* 50 (4), 1943, p. 370.
7. Cressy, Donald R, *A Study in the Social Psychology of Embezzlement*, Free Press, 1953.
8. Turvey, Brent E, *Forensic Fraud: Evaluating Law Enforcement and Forensic Science Cultures in the Context of Examiner Misconduct*, Elsevier, 2013, Chapter 6.
9. Ariely, Dan and Simon Jones, *Predictably Irrational*, Harper, New York, 2008.
10. Kahneman, Daniel, *Thinking, Fast and Slow*, Macmillan, 2011.
11. Turvey (2011); Bowen, Robin T., *Ethics and the Practice of Forensic Science*, CRC Press, 2018; Downs, J. C. Upshaw, and Anjali Ranadive Swienton, eds., *Ethics in Forensic Science*, Academic Press, 2012; Brooks, Justin, *Wrongful Convictions: Cases and Materials*, Vandeplas Publishing, 2011.
12. Zambroski, James, January 18th, 2006–Day 8: Blood Spatter and Lies. Wave 3 News, January 20th, 2006. Accessed at https://www.wave3.com/story/4388523/january-18th-2006-day-8-blood-spatter-and-lies/
13. http://badchemistry.legacy.wbur.org/
14. Baran, Madeleine, Troubled St. Paul crime lab problems even worse than first thought, probe reveals. MPR News, February 14, 2013. Accessed at: https://www.mprnews.org/story/2013/02/14/troubled-st-paul-crime-lab-problems-even-worse-than-first-thought-probe-reveals
15. Feibleman, James Kern, "Scientific method", *The Hague*: Martinus Nijhoff, 1972.
16. Balko, Radley and Tucker Carrington, *The Cadaver King and the Country Dentist: A True Story of Injustice in the American South*, Hachette, UK, 2018.
17. Yadav, Praveen Kumar, "Ethical Issues across Different Fields of Forensic Science", *Egyptian Journal of Forensic Sciences*, 7 (1), 2017, pp. 1–6. Page 1.
18. Deming, W. Edwards, *Out of the Crisis*, MIT press, 2018.
19. Landau, Martin and Donald Chisholm, "The Arrogance of Optimism: Notes on Failure-Avoidance Management", *Journal of Contingencies and Crisis Management*, 3 (2), 1995, pp. 67–80.
20. Sandel, Michael J., *Justice: What's the Right Thing to Do?*, Macmillan, 2010, pp. 263–264.
21. Sandel, 2010, pp. 268–269.

Further Reading

Benforado, Adam. *Unfair: The New Science of Criminal Injustice*. New York: Broadway Books, 2015.
Blackburn, Simon. *Ethics: A Very Short Introduction*. Vol. 80. Oxford: Oxford University Press, 2003.
de Lazari-Radek, Katarzyna, and Peter Singer. *Utilitarianism: A Very Short Introduction*. Oxford: Oxford University Press, 2017.
Dunn, John. *Locke: a Very Short Introduction*. Oxford: Oxford University Press, 2003.
Scruton, Roger. *Kant: A Very Short Introduction*. Vol. 50. Oxford: Oxford University Press, 2001.
Simon, Dan. *In Doubt: The Psychology of the Criminal Justice Process*. Harvard University Press, 2012.

APPENDIX A

Visual Reference Appendix[1]

Bluestar® Forensic images:

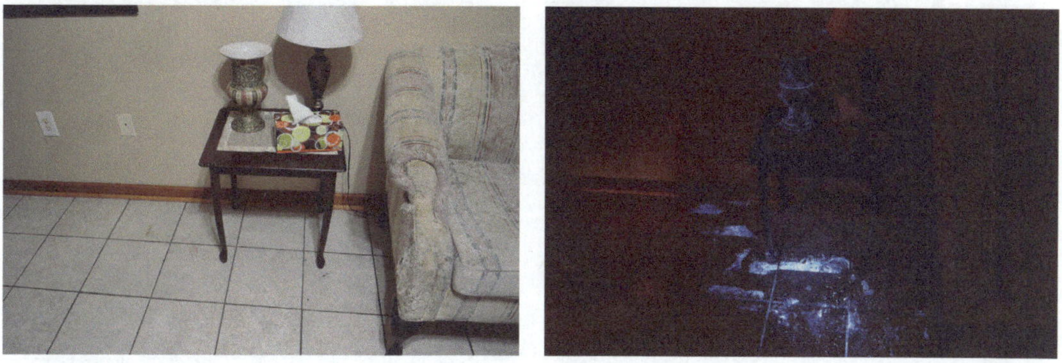

Figure A.1 (a and b) Before and after images of a table sprayed with BlueStar® Forensic blood searching reagent. (Courtesy of John Paolucci, C.S.I. Experts, Inc., New York.)

Figure A.2 (a and b) Before and after images of a shelf unit sprayed with BlueStar® Forensic blood searching reagent. (Courtesy of John Paolucci, C.S.I. Experts, Inc., New York.)

Figure A.3 (a and b) Before and after images of a wall sprayed with BlueStar® Forensic blood searching reagent. (Courtesy of John Paolucci, C.S.I. Experts, Inc., New York.)

Figure A.4 (a and b) Before and after images of a chair sprayed with BlueStar® Forensic blood searching reagent. (Courtesy of John Paolucci, C.S.I. Experts, Inc., New York.)

Figure A.5 (a and b) Before and after images of a hallway with ceramic floor tiles sprayed with BlueStar® Forensic blood searching reagent. (Courtesy of John Paolucci, C.S.I. Experts, Inc., New York.)

Figure A.6 (a and b) Before and after images of a linen closet sprayed with BlueStar® Forensic blood searching reagent. (Courtesy of John Paolucci, C.S.I. Experts, Inc., New York.)

Figure A.7 (a and b) Before and after images of a sink and cabinet sprayed with BlueStar® Forensic blood searching reagent. (Courtesy of John Paolucci, C.S.I. Experts, Inc., New York.)

Figure A.8 (a and b) Before and after images of a countertop and cabinet sprayed with BlueStar® Forensic blood searching reagent. (Courtesy of John Paolucci, C.S.I. Experts, Inc., New York.)

Cast-off pattern: A bloodstain pattern resulting from blood drops released from an object due to its motion.

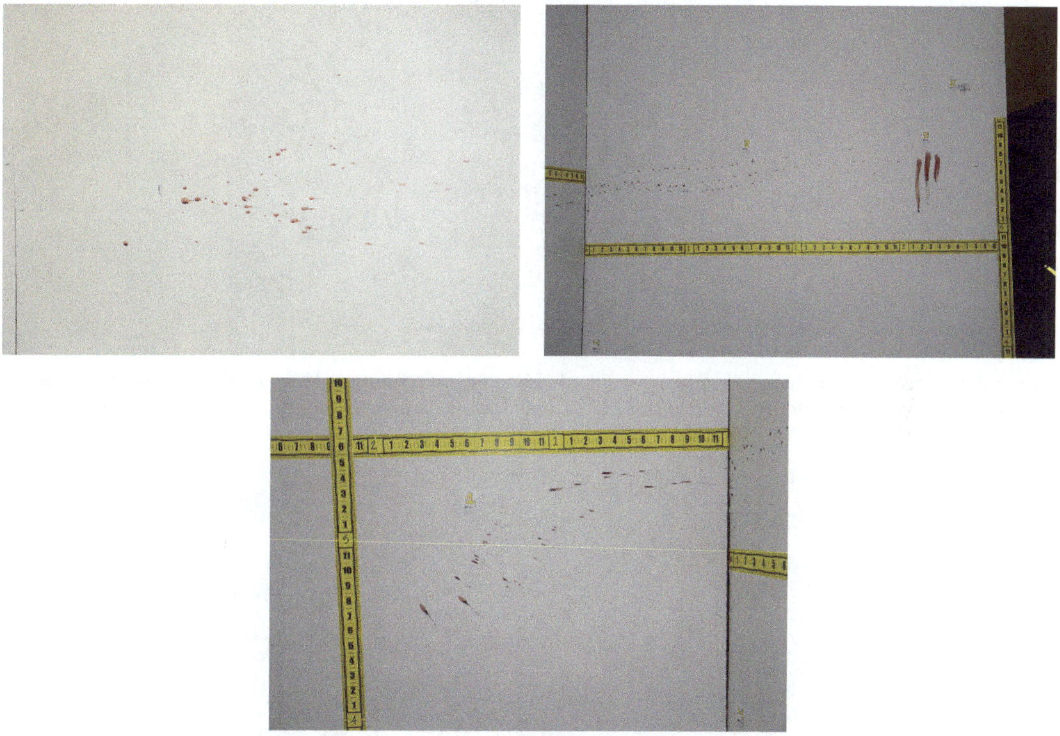

Figure A.9 (a, b, and c) Cast-off patterns. Courtesy of Jeremy Morris, Johnson County Sheriff's Office Criminalistics Laboratory, Olathe, Kansas.

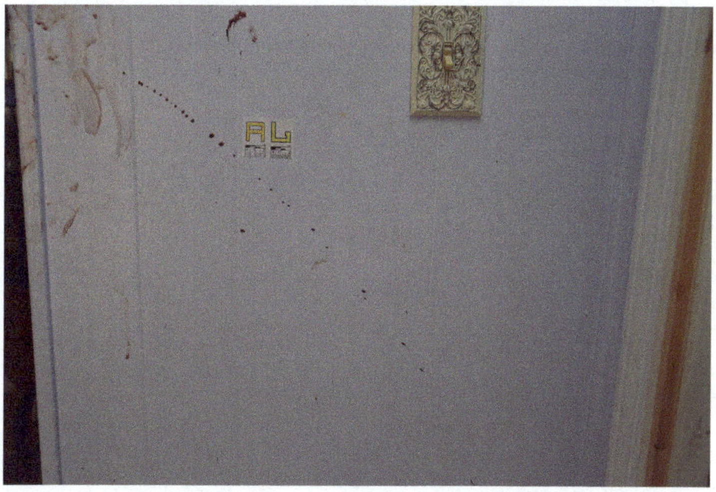

Figure A.10 Cast-off pattern on a vertical surface. Courtesy of Jeremy Morris, Johnson County Sheriff's Office Criminalistics Laboratory, Olathe, Kansas.

Complex patterns: Bloodstain patterns that exhibit multiple activities and influences.

Figure A.11 Large volume blood droplets transitioning into flow accompanied by spatter stains on a vertical surface distributed around a doorknob. Courtesy of Jeremy Morris, Johnson County Sheriff's Office Criminalistics Laboratory, Olathe, Kansas.

Figure A.12 Transfer, drip stains, flow, swipes, wipes, and spatter stains can be seen in this complex bloodstain pattern. Courtesy of Jeremy Morris, Johnson County Sheriff's Office Criminalistics Laboratory, Olathe, Kansas.

Figure A.13 The flow patterns on the 2X4 board were caused and altered by the swing motion and the impact into the blood source. Courtesy of Jeremy Morris, Johnson County Sheriff's Office Criminalistics Laboratory, Olathe, Kansas.

Figure A.14 A combination of swipes and wipes. It is not unusual to have bloodstain patterns that exhibit a combination of swipes with wipes. Courtesy of Jeremy Morris, Johnson County Sheriff's Office Criminalistics Laboratory, Olathe, Kansas.

Drip patterns: A bloodstain pattern resulting from a liquid that dripped into another liquid, at least one of which was blood.

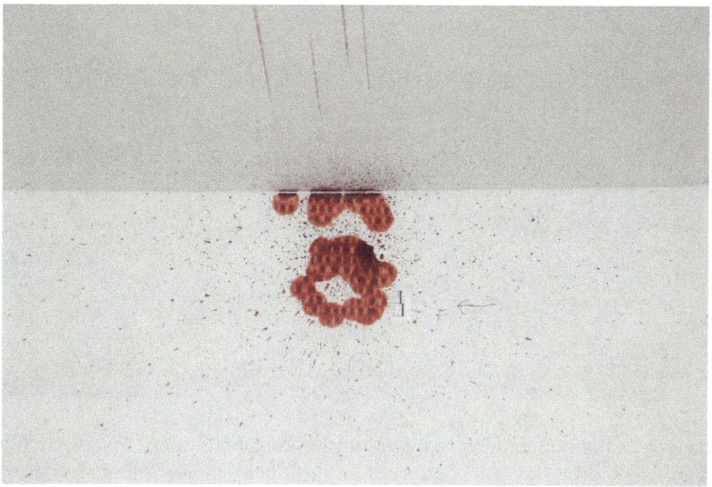

Figure A.15 Drip pattern on a horizontal surface with spatter stains deposited on the adjacent vertical surface. Courtesy of Jeremy Morris, Johnson County Sheriff's Office Criminalistics Laboratory, Olathe, Kansas.

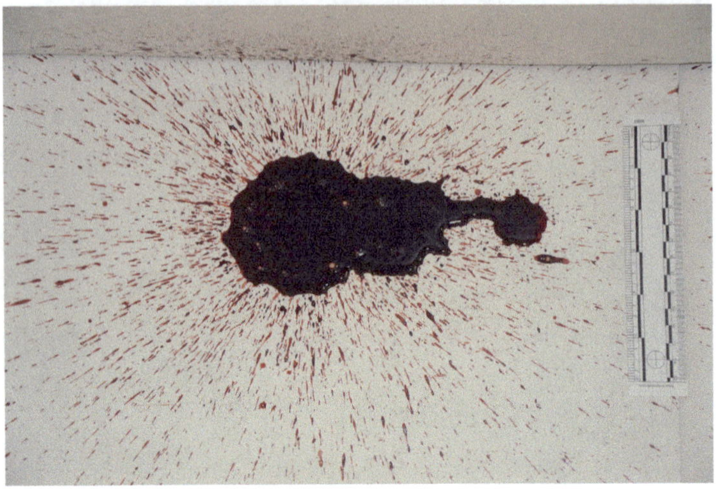

Figure A.16 Drip pattern caused by blood dripping into a pool of blood. Courtesy of Jeremy Morris, Johnson County Sheriff's Office Criminalistics Laboratory, Olathe, Kansas.

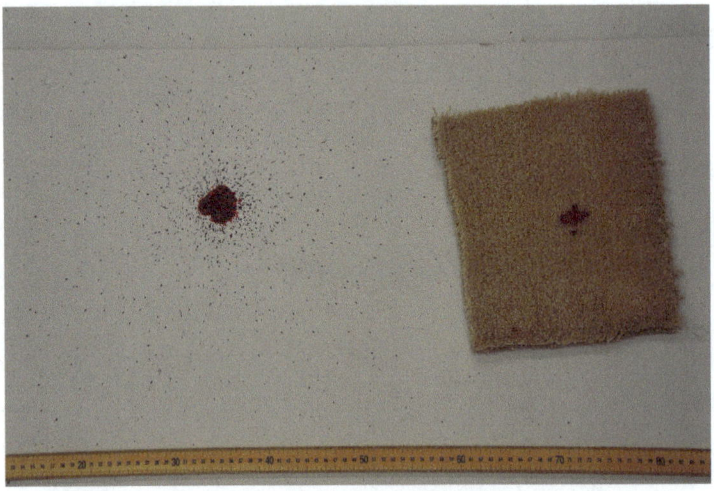

Figure A.17 Comparison of the appearance of a drip pattern on a hard nonporous surface to a drip pattern on carpet. Courtesy of Jeremy Morris, Johnson County Sheriff's Office Criminalistics Laboratory, Olathe, Kansas.

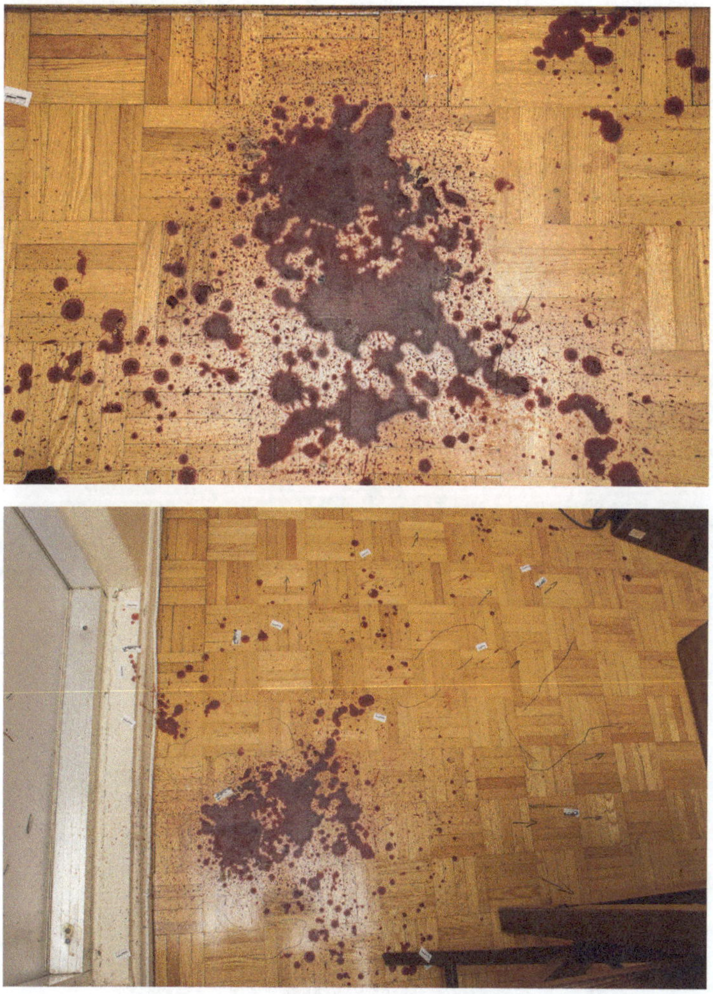

Figure A.18 (a and b) Drip pattern on parquet floor. Courtesy of Det. Tonya Hackenbrook, Peel Regional Police, Ontario, Canada.

Drip stains: A bloodstain resulting from a falling drop that formed due to gravity.

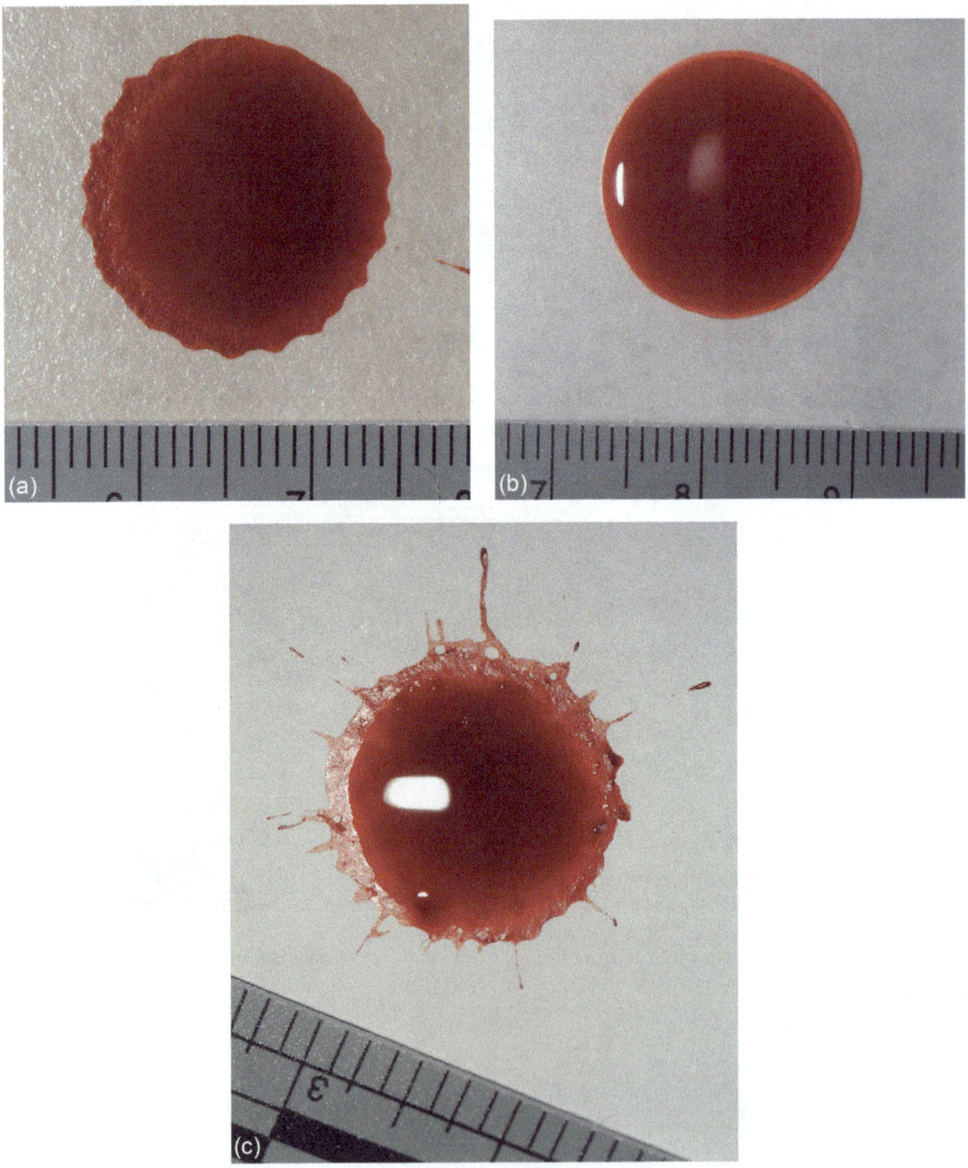

Figure A.19 (a, b, and c) Visual comparison of the edge characteristics of drip stains falling the same distance onto three different substrates. Figures: a has slightly scalloped edges, b has smooth edges, and c has spiney edges. The characteristics of the substrate and the distance the droplet falls to impact the surface affect the diameter and edge characteristics of the resulting bloodstain. Courtesy of Jeremy Morris, Johnson County Sheriff's Office Criminalistics Laboratory, Olathe, Kansas.

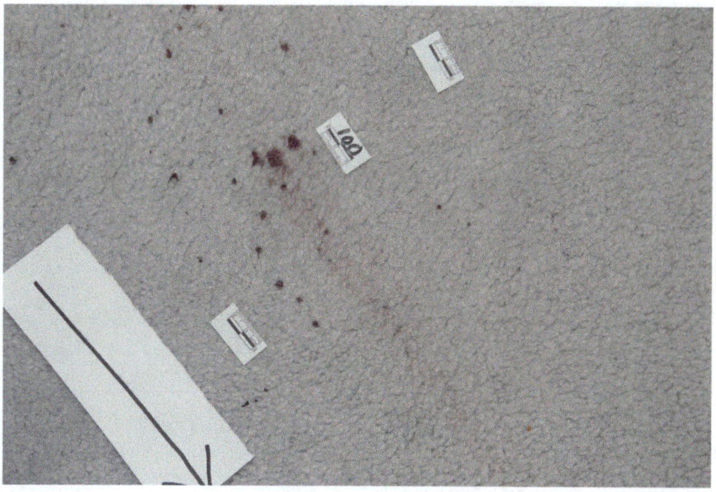

Figure A.20 Drip stains on carpet with wipe alteration of several bloodstains. Courtesy of Det. Tonya Hackenbrook, Peel Regional Police, Ontario, Canada.

Drip trails: A bloodstain pattern resulting from the movement of a source of drip stains between two points.

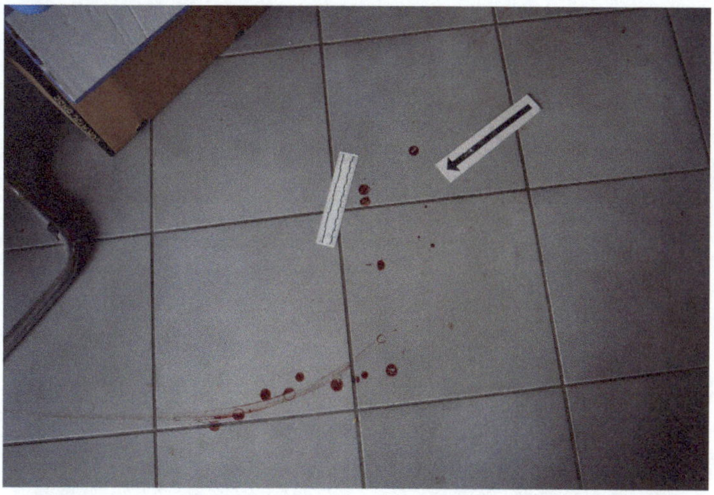

Figure A.21 Portion of a drip trail with bloodstains altered by a wipe motion. Courtesy of Gabriele Rotter, Italian National Police, Regional Forensic Science Bureau of Calabria, Ovaro, Italy.

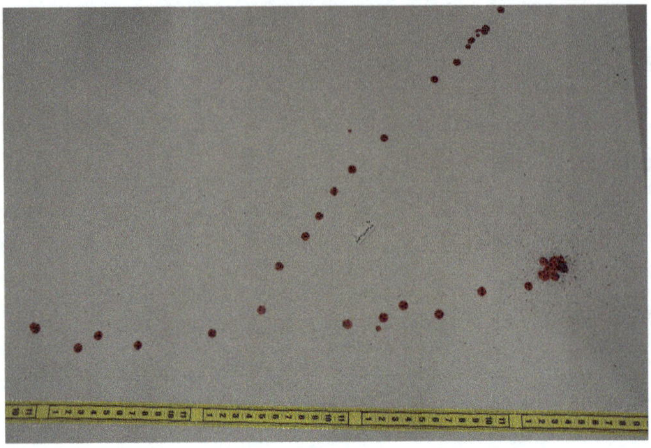

Figure A.22 Drip trails courtesy of Jeremy Morris, Johnson County Sheriff's Office Criminalistics Laboratory, Olathe, Kansas.

Expiration patterns: A bloodstain pattern resulting from blood forced by airflow out of the nose, mouth, or a wound.

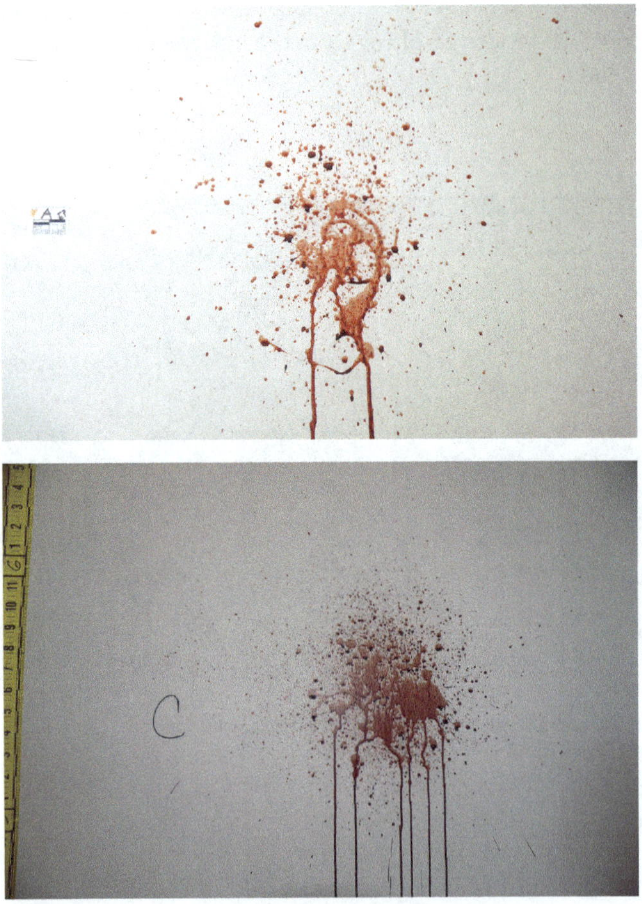

Figure A.23 (a and b) Expiration patterns on a vertical surface. Courtesy of Jeremy Morris, Johnson County Sheriff's Office Criminalistics Laboratory, Olathe, Kansas.

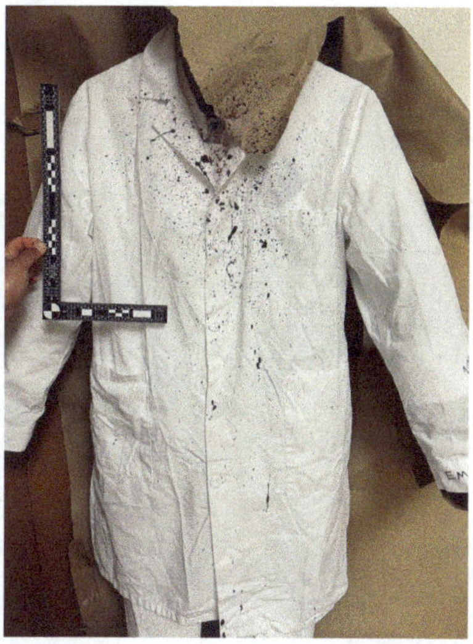

Figure A.24 Expiration pattern on the front of a white lab coat. Courtesy of Susan Rinehart (retired), Los Angeles Police Department, Forensic Science Division, Los Angeles, California.

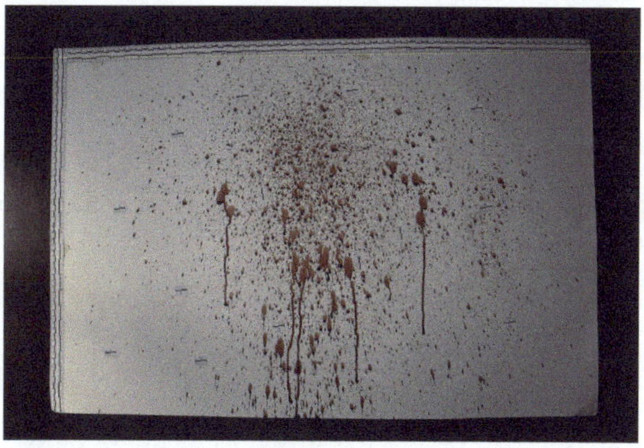

Figure A.25 A large volume of blood expelled from the mouth onto a vertical board. Courtesy of Toby Wolson, Noslow Forensic Consultations, Miami, FL.

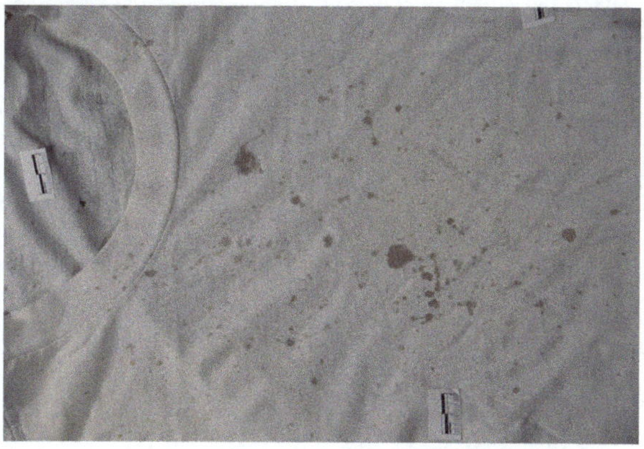

Figure A.26 Blood expelled from the mouth onto a cotton T-shirt. Courtesy of Toby Wolson, Noslow Forensic Consultations, Miami, FL.

Flow: A bloodstain resulting from the movement of a volume of blood on a surface due to gravity or movement of the target.

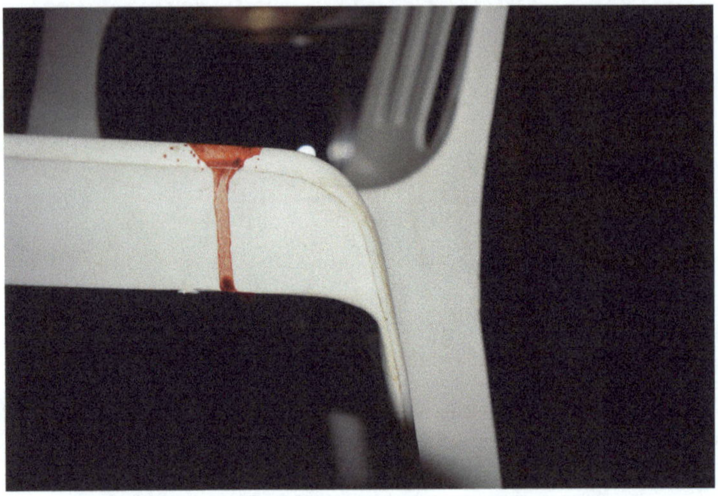

Figure A.27 Flow of blood down the side of a chair. Courtesy of Gabriele Rotter, Italian National Police, Regional Forensic Science Bureau of Calabria, Ovaro, Italy.

Forward spatter patterns: A bloodstain pattern resulting from blood drops which can be produced when a projectile creates an exit wound.

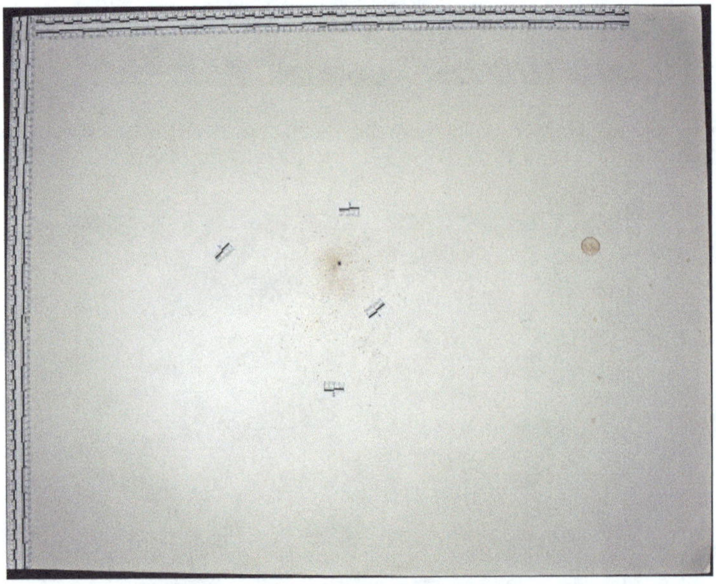

Figure A.28 Forward spatter pattern produced by shooting a blood saturated sponge positioned 8 inches out from a target board using a 22-caliber handgun firing 22-caliber LR rounds. The projectile exits the gun muzzle traveling 900 ft/s. Courtesy of Toby Wolson, Noslow Forensic Consultations, Miami, FL.

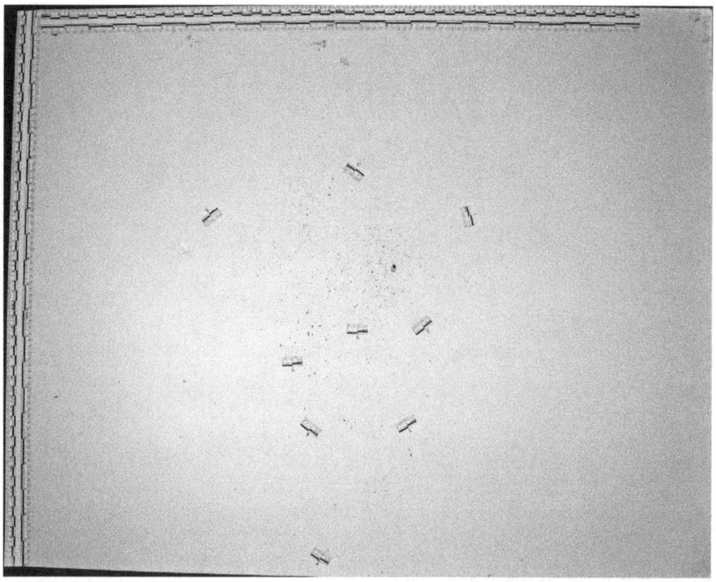

Figure A.29 Forward spatter pattern produced by shooting a blood saturated sponge positioned 16 inches out from a target board using a 22-caliber handgun firing 22-caliber LR rounds. The projectile exits the gun muzzle traveling 900 ft/s. Courtesy of Toby Wolson, Noslow Forensic Consultations, Miami, FL.

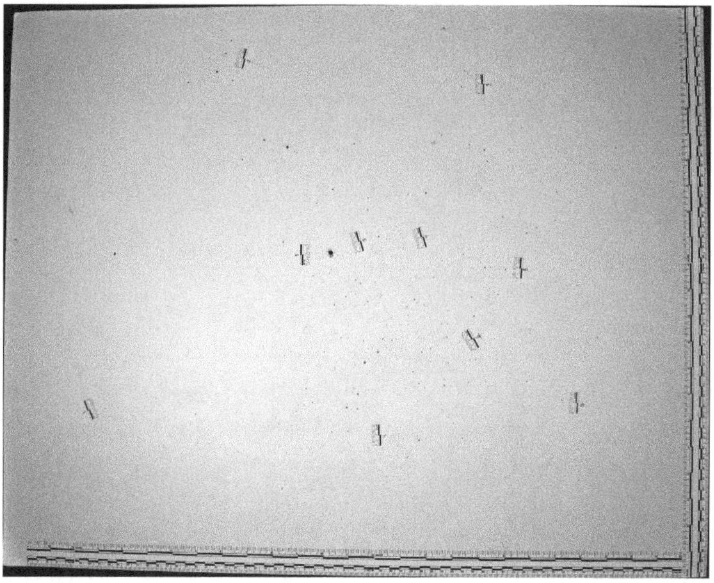

Figure A.30 Forward spatter pattern produced by shooting a blood saturated sponge positioned 32 inches out from a target board using a 22-caliber handgun firing 22-caliber LR rounds. The projectile exits the gun muzzle traveling 900 ft/s. Courtesy of Toby Wolson, Noslow Forensic Consultations, Miami, FL.

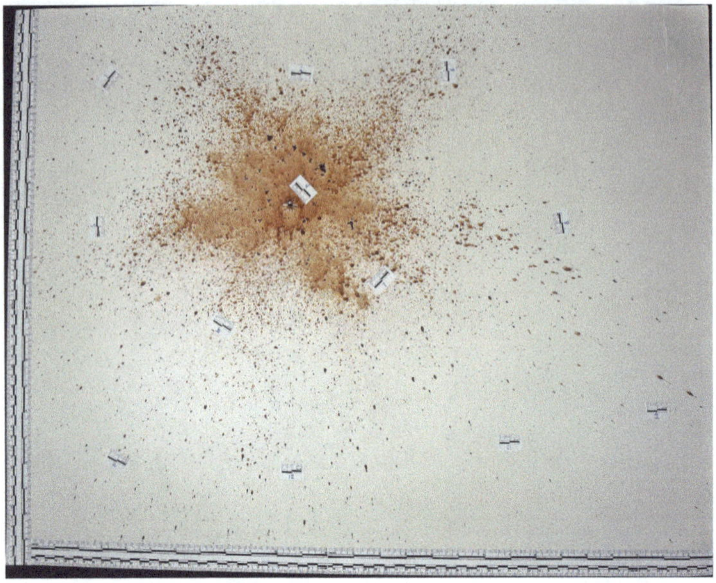

Figure A.31 Forward spatter pattern produced by shooting a blood saturated sponge positioned 8 inches out from a target board using a 45-caliber handgun firing 45-caliber 230 grain rounds. The projectile exits the gun muzzle traveling 900 ft/s. Courtesy of Toby Wolson, Noslow Forensic Consultations, Miami, FL.

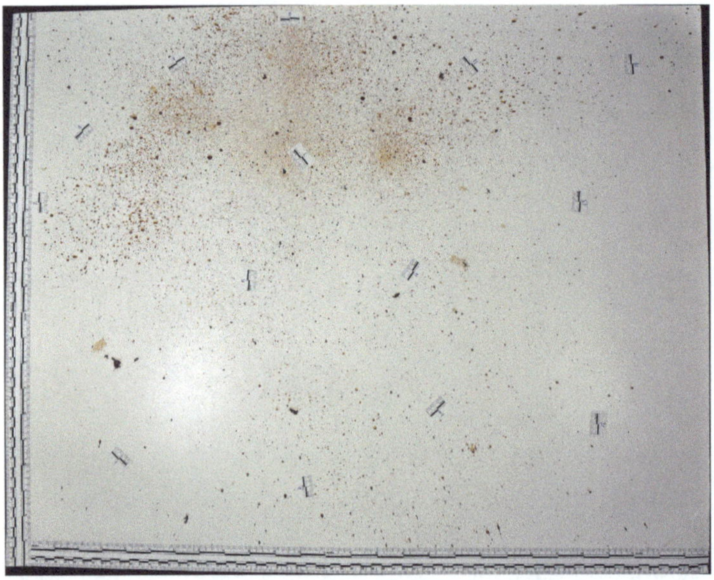

Figure A.32 Forward spatter pattern produced by shooting a blood saturated sponge positioned 16 inches out from a target board using a 45-caliber handgun firing 45-caliber 230 grain rounds. The projectile exits the gun muzzle traveling 900 ft/s. Courtesy of Toby Wolson, Noslow Forensic Consultations, Miami, FL.

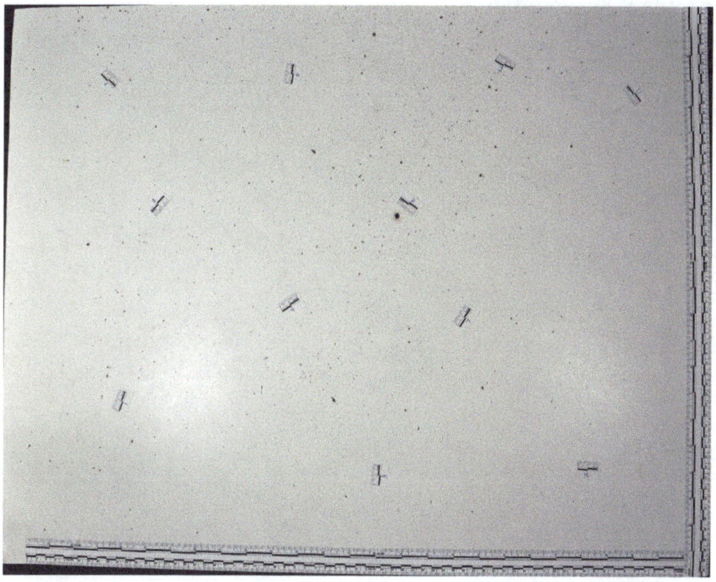

Figure A.33 Forward spatter pattern produced by shooting a blood saturated sponge positioned 32 inches out from a target board using a 45-caliber handgun firing 45-caliber 230 grain rounds. The projectile exits the gun muzzle traveling 900 ft/s. Courtesy of Toby Wolson, Noslow Forensic Consultations, Miami, FL.

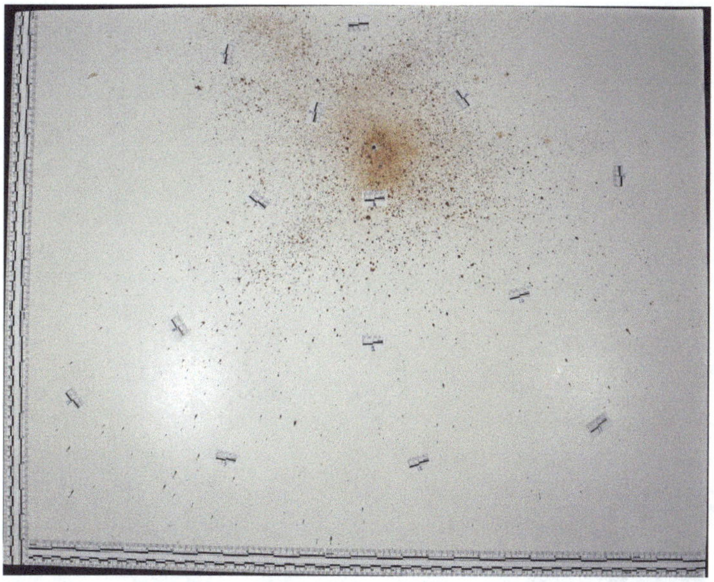

Figure A.34 Forward spatter pattern produced by shooting a blood saturated sponge positioned 8 inches out from a target board using a rifle firing 762 mm × 39 mm rounds. The projectile exits the gun muzzle traveling 2300 ft/s. Courtesy of Toby Wolson, Noslow Forensic Consultations, Miami, FL.

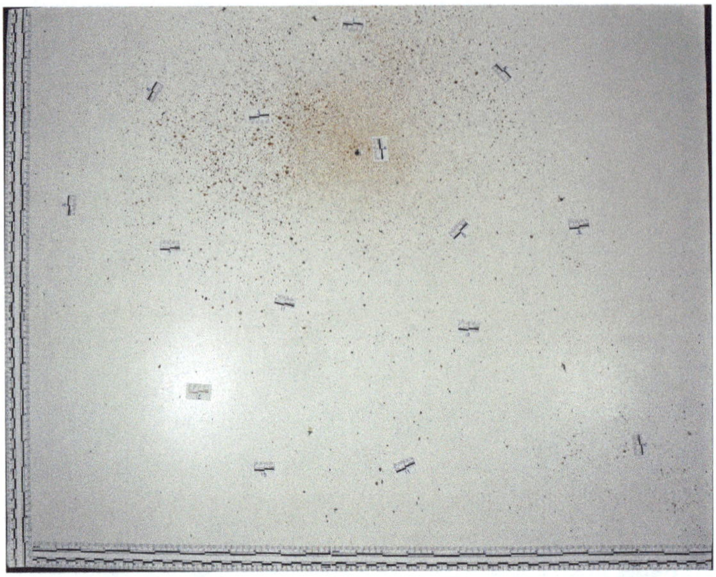

Figure A.35 Forward spatter pattern produced by shooting a blood saturated sponge positioned 16 inches out from a target board using a rifle firing 762 mm x 39 mm rounds. The projectile exits the gun muzzle traveling 2300 ft/s. Courtesy of Toby Wolson, Noslow Forensic Consultations, Miami, FL.

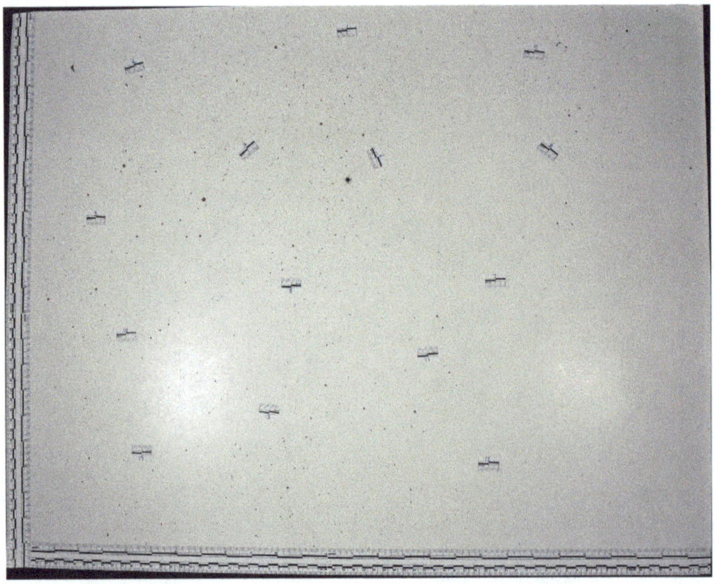

Figure A.36 Forward spatter pattern produced by shooting a blood saturated sponge positioned 32 inches out from a target board using a rifle firing 762 mm x 39 mm rounds. The projectile exits the gun muzzle traveling 2300 ft/sec. Courtesy of Toby Wolson, Noslow Forensic Consultations, Miami, FL.

Figure A.37 Forward spatter pattern produced by shooting a blood saturated sponge positioned 8 inches out from a target board using a rifle firing .233 caliber rounds. The projectile exits the gun muzzle traveling 3200 ft/s. Courtesy of Toby Wolson, Noslow Forensic Consultations, Miami, FL.

Figure A.38 Forward spatter pattern produced by shooting a blood saturated sponge positioned 16 inches out from a target board using a rifle firing .233 caliber rounds. The projectile exits the gun muzzle traveling 3,200 ft/s. Courtesy of Toby Wolson, Noslow Forensic Consultations, Miami, FL.

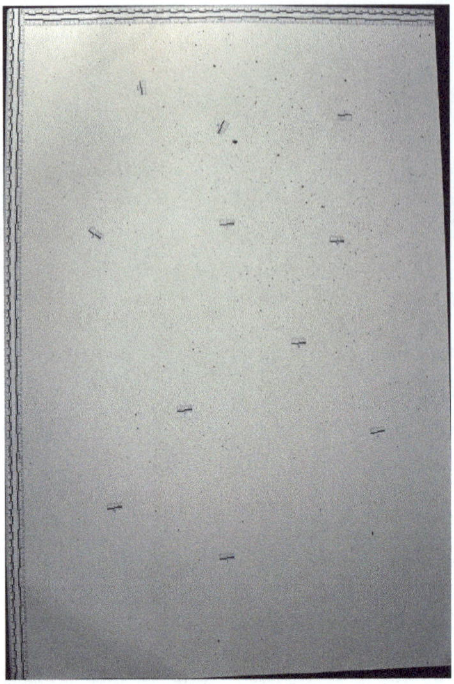

Figure A.39 Forward spatter pattern produced by shooting a blood saturated sponge positioned 32 inches out from a target board using a rifle firing .233 caliber rounds. The projectile exits the gun muzzle traveling 3,200 ft/s. Courtesy of Toby Wolson, Noslow Forensic Consultations, Miami, FL.

Figure A.40 Forward spatter pattern produced by shooting a blood saturated sponge with a .75-ounce slug traveling 1600 ft/s fired from a 20-gauge shotgun. Courtesy of Toby Wolson, Noslow Forensic Consultations, Miami, FL.

Impact patterns: A bloodstain pattern resulting from an object striking liquid blood.

Figure A.41 Impact pattern resulting from the single hit of a blood saturated sponge by a fist. The sponge was positioned 6 inches away from the vertical board at the time it was hit. Courtesy of Toby Wolson, Noslow Forensic Consultations, Miami, FL.

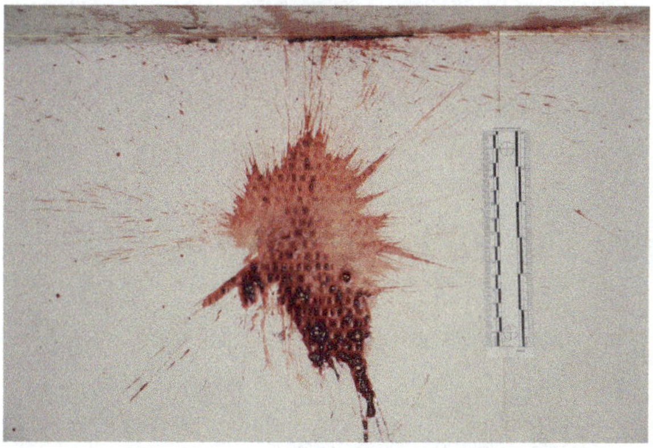

Figure A.42 Impact pattern on a horizontal surface caused by a foot stomp into a pool of blood. Courtesy of Jeremy Morris, Johnson County Sheriff's Office Criminalistics Laboratory, Olathe, Kansas.

Figure A.43 Impact spatter resulting from blunt force trauma, hitting of the victim's head more than ten times with a hammer. Courtesy of Kim Cheon-Hwoe, Seoul Metropolitan Police, South Korea.

Projected patterns: A bloodstain pattern resulting from the ejection of blood under hydraulic pressure, typically from a breach in the circulatory system.

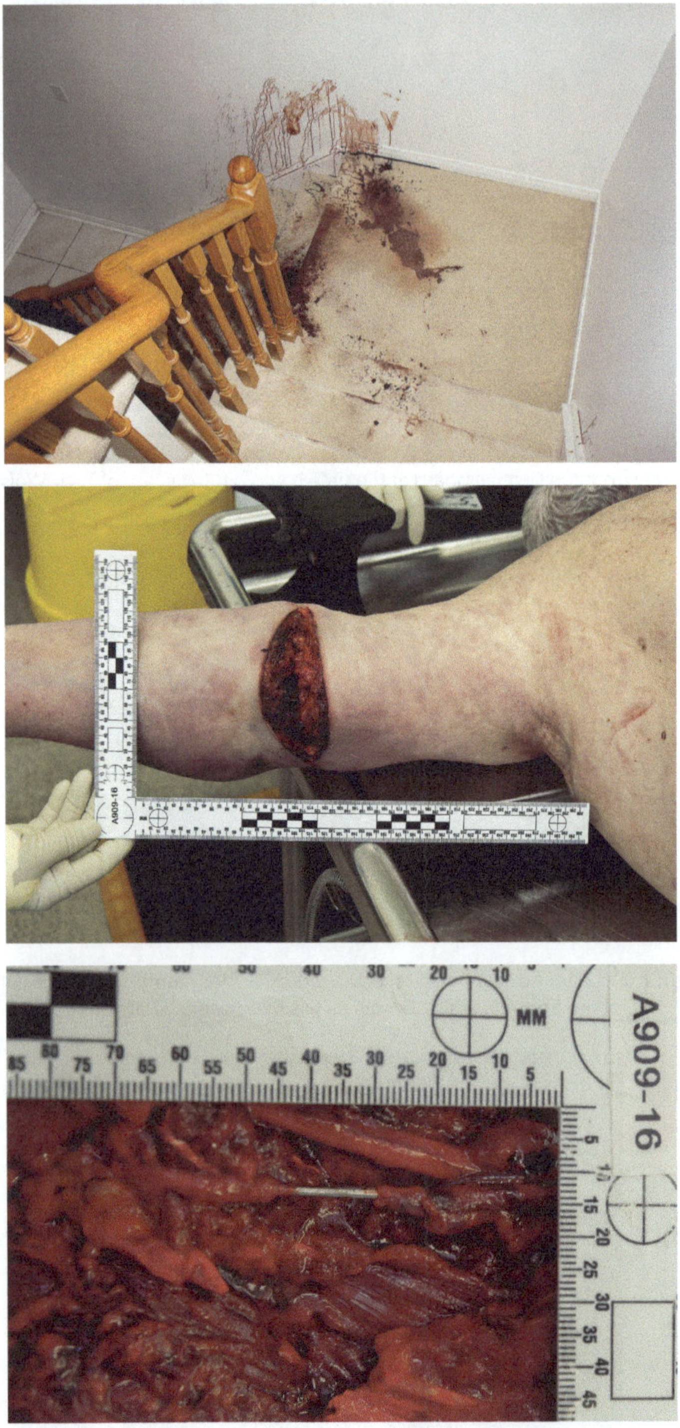

Figure A.44 (a, b, and c) Project pattern on a wall and images of the bloodletting injury. Courtesy of Det. Tonya Hackenbrook, Peel Regional Police, Ontario, Canada.

Saturation stains: A bloodstain resulting from the accumulation of liquid blood in an absorbent material.

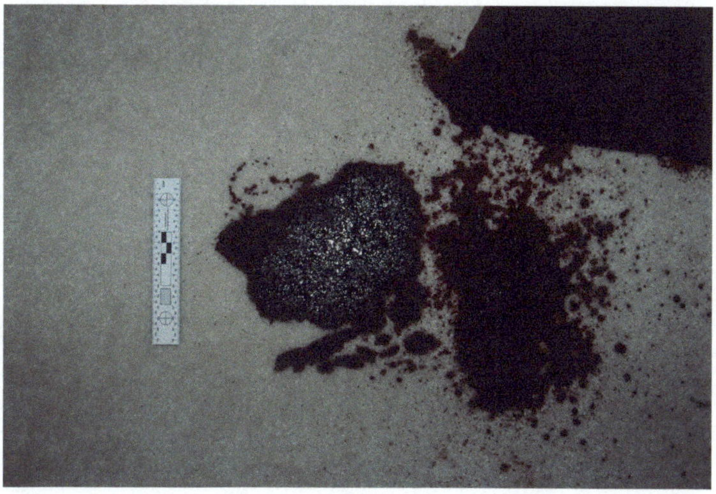

Figure A.45 A saturation stain on carpet. Courtesy of Jeremy Morris, Johnson County Sheriff's Office Criminalistics Laboratory, Olathe, Kansas.

Splash patterns: A bloodstain pattern created from a large volume of liquid blood falling onto a surface.

Figure A.46 A 5 ml of blood falling 36 inches onto a horizontal target. Courtesy of Toby Wolson, Noslow Forensic Consultations, Miami, FL.

Swipes: A bloodstain resulting from the transfer of blood from a blood-bearing surface onto another surface, with characteristics that indicate relative motion between the two surfaces.

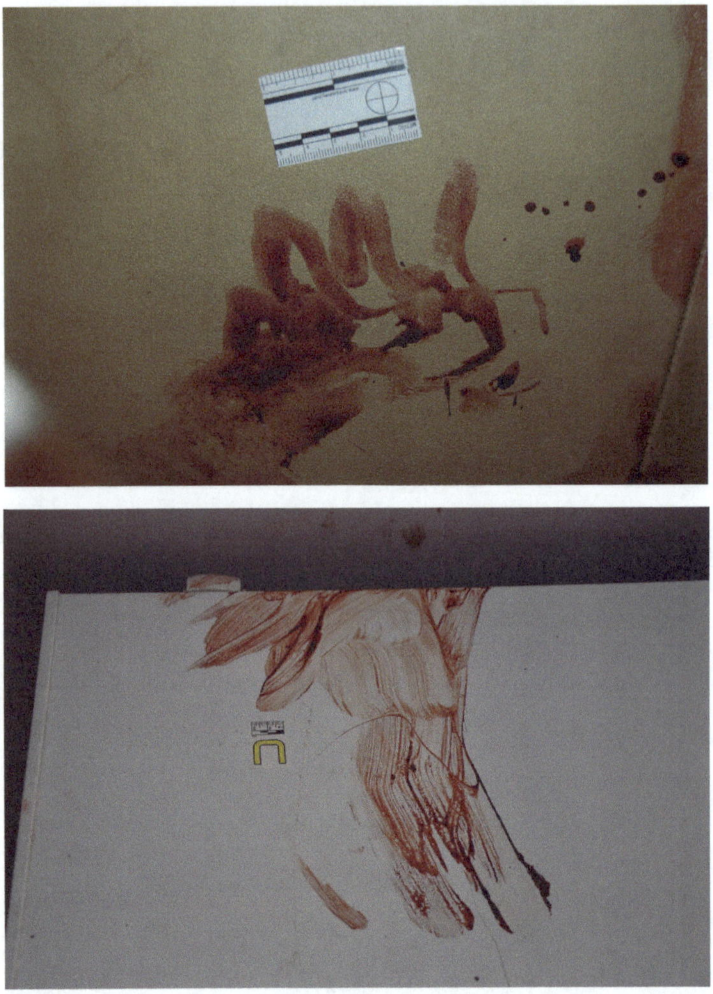

Figure A.47 (a and b) Swipe stains on two different substrates. Courtesy of Jeremy Morris, Johnson County Sheriff's Office Criminalistics Laboratory, Olathe, Kansas.

Transfer stains: A bloodstain resulting from contact between a blood-bearing surface and another surface.

Figure A.48 Transfer stain possibly from a blood-coated hand onto a fabric substrate. Courtesy of Jeremy Morris, Johnson County Sheriff's Office Criminalistics Laboratory, Olathe, Kansas.

Figure A.49 Transfer stain on concrete. Courtesy of Jeremy Morris, Johnson County Sheriff's Office Criminalistics Laboratory, Olathe, Kansas.

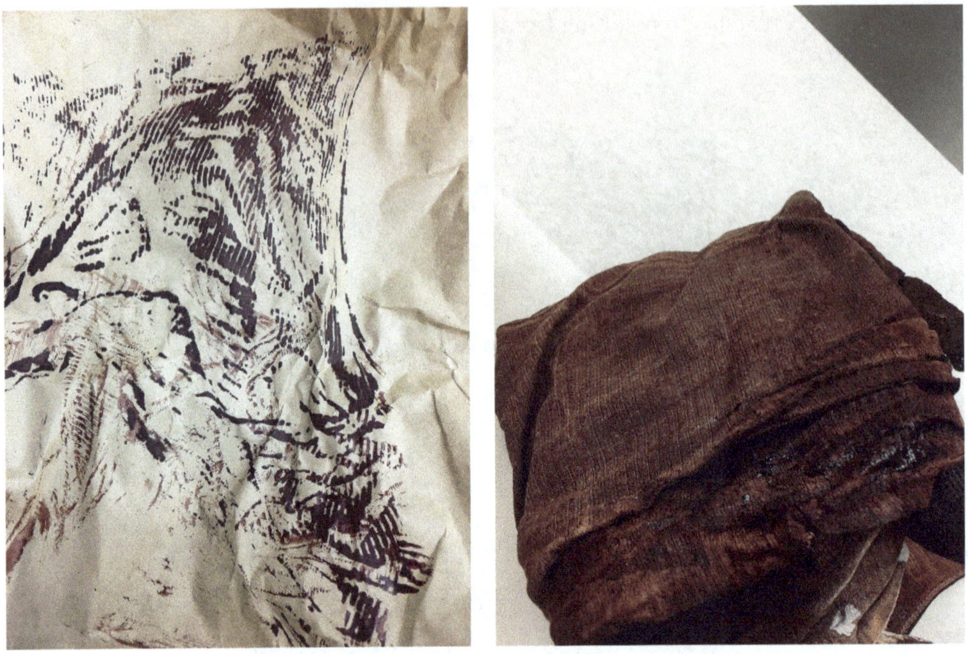

Figure A.50 (a and b) Blood transferred onto the butcher block paper used to wrap a blood saturated fabric. Courtesy of Susan Rinehart (retired), Los Angeles Police Department, Forensic Science Division, Los Angeles, California.

Note

1. ASB Technical Report 033, 1st Ed., Terms and Definitions in Bloodstain Pattern Analysis, 2017.

APPENDIX B

Forensic Resources for Bloodstain Pattern Analysis (BPA)

American Academy of Forensic Sciences (AAFS)
www.aafs.org

AAFS Academy Standards Board (ASB)
www.aafs.org/academy-standards-board

AAFS ASB Published Bloodstain Pattern Analysis Standards, Guidelines, and Technical Reports
www.aafs.org/search/standards?_page=1&keywords=&_limit=7&consensus_body=429&status_standard=4

AAFS Forensic Science Education Programs Accreditation Commission (FEPAC)
www.aafs.org/FEPAC

AAFS Journal of Forensic Sciences
www.aafs.org/journal-forensic-sciences

AAFS Reference Library
www.aafs.org/search/reference-library

Association for Crime Scene Reconstruction (ACSR)
www.acsr.org

Canadian Society of Forensic Science (CSFS)
www.csfs.ca

CSFS: BPA Discipline
https://www.csfs.ca/what-we-do/disciplines-sections/bloodstain-pattern-analysis/

MFRC High Speed Digital Video Analysis of Bloodstain Pattern Formation from Common Bloodletting Mechanisms
https://alvideo.ameslab.gov/archive/bpa-videos/

International Association of Bloodstain Pattern Analysts (IABPA)
www.iabpa.org

IABPA Journal of Bloodstain Pattern Analysis
https://www.iabpa.org/journal_of_bloodstain_pattern.php

International Association for Identification (IAI)
www.theiai.org

IAI Bloodstain Pattern Analysis Certification
www.theiai.org/bloodstain_pattern.php

IAI Journal of Forensic Identification: Article abstracts
www.theiai.org/jfi_abstracts.php

Organization of Scientific Area Committees (OSAC)
https://www.nist.gov/organization-scientific-area-committees-forensic-science

OSAC Registry
https://www.nist.gov/organization-scientific-area-committees-forensic-science/osac-registry

OSAC Bloodstain Pattern Analysis Subcommittee BPA Bibliography
https://www.nist.gov/organization-scientific-area-committees-forensic-science/bloodstain-pattern-analysis-subcommittee

Rocky Mountain Association of Bloodstain Pattern Analysts (RMABPA)
www.rmabpa.org

INDEX

Note: Page numerals in *italics* refer to figures, and those in **bold** to tables.

A

B

C

D

G

I

J

K

L

M

N

Q

R

S

T

X

Y

Z